Teaching Music
through Performance
in Band
Volume 7

Also available from GIA Publications, Inc.

MT
125
.T43

Teaching Music through Performance in Band

Volume 7

Larry R. Blocher
Eugene Migliaro Corporon
Ray Cramer
Tim Lautzenheiser
Edward S. Lisk
Richard Miles

Compiled and Edited by Richard Miles

GIA Publications, Inc.
Chicago

For a complete searchable index of works covered in the Teaching Music Series, as well as audio clips of more than 900 pieces, visit the website TeachingMusic.org.

Teaching Music through Performance in Band, Volume 7
Larry R. Blocher, Eugene Migliaro Corporon, Ray Cramer
Tim Lautzenheiser, Edward S. Lisk, and Richard Miles
Compiled and edited by Richard Miles
www.teachingmusic.org

GIA Publications, Inc.
7404 S Mason Ave
Chicago IL 60638
www.giamusic.com

G-7436
ISBN: 978-1-57999-741-0

Table of Contents

PART II: The Band Conductor as Music Teacher
Teacher Resource Guides 153

Appendixes

Indexes

ACKNOWLEDGMENTS

The following research associates are gratefully acknowledged for outstanding scholarly contributions to the "Teacher Resource Guides":

Amy Acklin
PhD Student/Music Education
The Florida State University • Tallahassee, Florida

Robert J. Ambrose
Director of Wind Studies and Ensembles
Associate Director, School of Music
Georgia State University • Atlanta, Georgia

Tamey Anglley
Doctoral Conducting Associate
Texas Tech University • Lubbock, Texas

Carolyn Barber
Director of Bands
University of Nebraska-Lincoln • Lincoln, Nebraska

James Batcheller
Central Michigan University • Mount Pleasant, Michigan

Eugene F. Bechen
Chair, Department of Music
Associate Professor of Music
Director of Bands
St. Ambrose University • Davenport, Iowa

Dennis Beck
Director of Bands
Unionville High School • Markham, Ontario, Canada

Robert Belser
Conductor and Director of Bands
University of Wyoming • Laramie, Wyoming

William Berz
Professor of Music
Mason Gross School of the Arts
Rutgers, The State University of New Jersey • New Brunswick, New Jersey

Carter Biggers
Director of Bands
Seagraves ISD • Seagraves, Texas

Erin Bodnar
Masters Conducting Associate
University of North Texas • Denton, Texas

Scott Boerma
Associate Director of Bands
Director of Michigan Marching and Athletic Bands
Donald R. Shepherd Associate Professor of Conducting
University of Michigan • Ann Arbor, Michigan

David Martin Booth
Director of Bands and Percussion Studies
Wright State University • Dayton, Ohio

C. Kevin Bowen
Director of Bands
Wake Forest University • Winston-Salem, North Carolina

Gordon R. Brock
Chair/Director of Bands
University of North Florida • Jacksonville, Florida

Andrea E. Brown
Director of Athletic Bands
Assistant Director of Bands
Austin Peay State University • Clarksville, Tennessee

John C. Carmichael
Director of Bands/Associate Professor of Music
School of Music
University of South Florida • Tampa, Florida

William S. Carson
Director of Bands, Professor of Music
Coe College • Cedar Rapids, Iowa

Katye N. Clogg
Masters Conducting Associate
Indiana University of Pennsylvania • Indiana, Pennsylvania

Susan D. Creasap
Associate Director of Bands
Morehead State University • Morehead, Kentucky

Craig Dabelstein
Coordinator of Bands, Brisbane Girls Grammar School
Director, Queensland Wind Orchestra
Queensland, Australia

DuWayne Dale
Director of Bands and Orchestra
Grant County Schools • Dry Ridge, Kentucky

Paul G. Davis
Assistant Professor of Music
Conductor of Wind Ensembles
Kennesaw State University • Kennesaw, Georgia

Joan deAlbuquerque
Associate Director of Bands
Bob Cole Conservatory of Music
California State University, Long Beach • Long Beach, California

Wayne F. Dorothy
Director of Bands and Professor of Music
Hardin-Simmons University • Abilene, Texas

Philip B. Edelman
Band Director
Goddard High School • Goddard, Kansas

Jeffrey Emge
The University of Texas at Tyler • Tyler, Texas

Karen Fannin
Director of Bands
Hendrix College • Conway, Arkansas

Dennis W. Fisher
Professor, Conducting and Ensembles
University of North Texas • Denton, Texas

Gregg Gausline
Associate Director of Bands
The University of Georgia • Athens, Georgia

Bradley J. Genevro
Director of Bands
Messiah College • Grantham, Pennsylvania

Kevin M. Geraldi
Associate Director of Bands
The University of North Carolina at Greensboro • Greensboro, North Carolina

Richard A. Greenwood
Professor of Music and Conducting
University of Central Florida • Orlando, Florida

Edward C. Harris
Director of Bands
San Jose State University • San Jose, California

Timothy Harris
Director of Instrumental Studies
Chabot College • Hayward, California

Christopher P. Heidenreich
Assistant Professor of Music Education and Associate Director of Bands
Youngstown State University • Youngstown, Ohio

Glen J. Hemberger
Southeastern Louisiana University • Hammond, Louisiana

Brad Hendry
Director of Bands
Sedro Wooley High School • Sedro Wooley, Washington

Jim Henigin
Doctoral Music Education Teaching Assistant
West Virginia University • Morgantown, West Virginia

Leslie W. Hicken
Director of Bands
Furman University • Greenville, South Carolina

Lt. Col. Timothy J. Holtan
Commander
The U.S. Military Academy Band • West Point, New York

Shelley M. Jagow
Professor of Music
Wright State University • Dayton, Ohio

Brant Karrick
Director of Bands
Associate Professor of Music
Northern Kentucky University • Highland Heights, Kentucky

Thomas Keck
Associate Director of Bands
University of Miami • Miami, Florida

Jennifer Kitelinger
Doctoral Conducting Associate
University of North Texas • Denton, Texas

Shannon Kitelinger
Doctoral Conducting Associate
University of North Texas • Denton, Texas

Carl A. Kling
Director of Bands and Orchestra
Assistant Professor of Music
Department of Music
Northwest Missouri State University • Maryville, Missouri

Amy M. Knopps
Doctoral Conducting Associate
The University of Georgia • Athens, Georgia

Kenneth Kohlenberg
Director of Bands, Professor of Music
Sinclair Community College • Dayton, Ohio

Barry E. Kopetz
Professor of Conducting, Director of Bands
Conservatory of Music
Capital University • Bexley, Ohio

Gina M. Lenox
Masters Conducting Associate
University of North Texas • Denton, Texas

Jesse Leyva
Henderson State University • Arkadelphia, Arkansas

Andrew Mast
Director of Bands
Lawrence University Conservatory of Music • Appleton, Wisconsin

Wendy McCallum
Instrumental Music Education Specialist
Brandon University • Brandon, Manitoba, Canada

Matthew McCutchen
Florida State University • Tallahassee, Florida

Donald J. McKinney
Doctoral Graduate Student Instructor
University of Michigan School of Music • Ann Arbor, Michigan

Justin J. Mertz
Assistant Director of Bands
Director, Syracuse University Marching Band
Syracuse University • Syracuse, New York

Robert Meunier
Director of Bands
Professor of Music
Drake University • Des Moines, Iowa

Stephen Meyer
Associate Director of Bands
Harrison High School • Kennesaw, Georgia

Richard Miller
Director of Bands
Hershey High School • Hershey, Pennsylvania

Christopher Morehouse
Director of Bands
Southern Illinois University Carbondale • Carbondale, Illinois

Bruce Moss
Director of Bands
Bowling Green State University • Bowling Green, Ohio

Ryan T. Nelson
Northwestern University • Evanston, Illinois

Albert Nguyen
Assistant Director of Bands
The University of Memphis • Memphis, Tennessee

Chad Nicholson
Director of Instrumental Studies
Indiana University-Purdue University Fort Wayne • Fort Wayne, Indiana

Craig Paré
School of Music
DePauw University • Greencastle, Indiana

Dawn A. Perry
Director of Bands
Wingate University • Wingate, North Carolina

Stephen Peterson
Director of Bands
Ithaca College • Ithaca, New York

Chester B. Phillips
Doctoral Conducting Associate
Hugh Hodgson School of Music
The University of Georgia • Athens, Georgia

Nikk Pilato
Assistant Director of Bands
The University of Georgia • Athens, Georgia

James Popejoy
Director of Bands
University of North Dakota • Grand Forks, North Dakota

Edwin Powell
Pacific Lutheran University • Tacoma, Washington

Kyle Prescott
Director of Bands
Florida Atlantic University • Boca Raton, Florida

Jeffrey Renshaw
Conductor
University of Connecticut • Storrs, Connecticut

Colleen Richardson
Assistant Professor of Music Education and Music Performance Studies
Wind Ensemble Director
University of Western Ontario • London, Ontario, Canada

David D. Robinson
University of Missouri • Columbia, Missouri

Angela Schroeder
Director of Bands
University of Alberta • Edmonton, Alberta, Canada

Robert M Schwartz
Director of Bands
Center Area School District • Monaca, Pennsylvania

Gary Schallert
Associate Professor of Music, Director of Bands
Western Kentucky University • Bowling Green, Kentucky

Mary K. Schneider
Director of Bands
Eastern Michigan University • Ypsilanti, Michigan

Rodney C. Schueller
Director of Bands
Texas State University • San Marcos, Texas

Kenneth Singleton
Director of Bands
University of Northern Colorado • Greeley, Colorado

Frederick Speck
Director of Bands
Head, Division of Conducting and Ensembles
University of Louisville • Louisville, Kentucky

Gary A. Speck
Professor of Conducting
Director of Concert Bands
Miami University • Oxford, Ohio

Mark Spede
Clemson University • Clemson, South Carolina

Robert Spittal
Spokane, Washington

Scott A. Stewart
Emory University • Atlanta, Georgia

Thomas Stone
Centenary College • Hackettstown, New Jersey

Douglas Stotter
University of Texas Arlington • Arlington, Texas

William Stowman,
Chair, Director of Instrumental Studies
Messiah College • Grantham, Pennsylvania

Robert C. Taylor
Director of Bands
University of Puget Sound • Tacoma, Washington

Emily Threinen
Director of Bands
Shenandoah Conservatory • Winchester, Virginia

Andrew Trachsel
Interim Director of Bands
Ohio University • Athens, Ohio

Frank C. Tracz
Director of Bands
Kansas State University • Manhattan, Kansas

Jacob Wallace
Doctoral Conducting Associate
The University of Georgia • Athens, Georgia

Mark Whitlock
Director of Bands
University of Minnesota Duluth • Duluth, Minnesota

Nicholas Enrico Williams
Assistant Director of Wind Studies
University of North Texas • Denton, Texas

Jason Worzbyt
Associate Professor of Bassoon
Associate Director of Bands
Indiana University of Pennsylvania • Indiana, Pennsylvania

Bruce Yurko
Composer
New Jersey

Christian Zembower
Director of Bands
East Tennessee State University • Johnson City, Tennessee

PART I

THE TEACHING
OF MUSIC

CHAPTER 1

FOCUS

Larry R. Blocher

I can't understand why people are frightened of new ideas. I'm frightened of the old ones.
—John Cage

Who said so, and who are they anyway?
—Ellen Langer

Focusing Properly

Presbyopia. While the word itself looks impressive (and even sounds impressive, although I have found it somewhat difficult to work into everyday conversation) I had never really thought about using it in a musical context until now. Presbyopia—at least according to folks who are paid to know these things—appears to be a rather formal name for an age-related change in the eyes—another "midlife opportunity." Basically, this change for me began with a "progressively diminished ability to focus"—blurred vision up close. The change was correctable by adjusting the lenses in my glasses.

Now these are not just ordinary lenses. These lenses have a variety of fancy names, including progressive, segmented, varifocal, graduated, and blended. For those of you who have experienced or who will experience the joy of this condition (that may be nintey million of you by 2014—gotta love the internet for useless facts) they come complete with a fancy price tag.

The lenses appear to be working. I am now able to *focus properly*. However, while the lenses are, indeed, blended, there are three distinct areas of focus in each lens. If I look through the top part of the lenses, things at a distance are now in focus. For example, in rehearsal I can once again see the percussion section from the podium (although I try not to look back there too often). If I look through the middle section of the lenses, the rest of the band "sharpens up" a bit. Finally, if I look through the bottom portion of the lenses, I not only can see the score but also the "stuff" in the score (amazing, really, what I have been missing here, and now I can no longer blame my glasses).

Anyway, the payoff for reading the fascinating eye-change account above is this: for the lenses in my glasses to really function as intended—to really

improve my overall vision, to really allow me to focus properly—I need to be aware of and understand the function of each lens area, *and* I must apply this information—look in the right place—as I look through the lenses. If I choose to look through one area of the lenses exclusively or even two areas and neglect the third, I am not able to see as clearly as intended. Similarly, when a band director considers the music "out there" for curricular selection, it seems important to look through all three parts of our blended "lenses"—the teacher/conductor lens, the composer lens, and publisher lens—to make clear, informed, intelligent music choices.

In previous chapters of the *Teaching Music* series, we have looked through the teacher/conductor lens. In Volume VI of the band series we looked through the composer lens while "doing" band composition. We left that last chapter with the goal of looking through the lens of band music publishing. This chapter in Volume VII looks through that lens.

The Publishing Lens

It seems important to agree at the outset that there are many ways to look through the band-music-publishing lens. Obviously a complete understanding of the band-music-publishing world is well beyond the scope of this chapter. Generally, the methodology chosen for any research effort is driven by the purpose of the research: what do you want to find out? Since the primary purpose of this chapter is to find out "what is," I decided to ask folks who "live" in the band-publishing world some questions about what life is like in that world. As I planned the project, I made important decisions about the design of the project *a priori* (an impressive sounding term):

1. I decided to talk with people actively involved in the band-music-publishing world at the time of this writing.

2. I decided to talk with people actively involved in publishing band music that involved music education.

3. I decided to get the perspectives of both a publisher and a composer writing for a publisher.

Based on these design criteria, I decided to talk with two composers: one working as a publisher *and* a composer within that company; and, one working as a composer *for* a publisher. The purpose of the conversations (and the resulting information that follows) was to describe views through the band publisher/publishing lens described earlier from a specialized perspective. At this point it would be traditional to suggest that generalizations be made with caution. Truth is not established. That was and is not the point.

The Conversations

Robert W. Smith is Director of Product Development for C. L. Barnhouse and an exclusive composer for Barnhouse and Walking Frog Records (see www.barnhouse.com). Ralph Ford publishes exclusively for Belwin, a division of Alfred Publishing (formerly Warner Brothers Publishing—see www.alfred.com). The results of our conversations, conducted separately, follow.

Part I: Robert W. Smith, Publisher and Composer

Publishing Band Music

Publishing is a business, and with that said, publishers are not in business to donate their time and their products, or to lose money. Like any other business, they have to make a reasonable return on their efforts. If not, the business will fail. Music educators cannot afford for publishers who publish materials for our classrooms to have their businesses fail. What that does is shift the responsibility to the consumer, not the publisher. *Publishers publish what consumers buy.* (Italics added for emphasis). And so, when somebody says "Hey, why did you guys publish that?" the answer is, "Because people buy it."

Different publishers have different philosophical approaches. Some publish strictly from a commercial perspective. Their objective is to maximize profit. In my particular case, and one of the reasons I'm with the publisher I'm with, is that for C. L. Barnhouse, the music is very important. Barnhouse is not necessarily interested in publishing whatever the latest popular style happens to be just to maximize profit. Barnhouse honors the tradition of the band, the tradition of the ensemble, and the educational validity of its products. With a philosophical approach that is musically based, Barnhouse tries to maximize their business and profit within those parameters. No matter what, publishing band music must return a reasonable profit.

Publishing—actually print materials—is not a good business. It's a steady business. It's a business where just about what you project is what you return. There are very few highs, if any, and there are often some extreme lows (the economy, for example, right now). If schools don't have the budgets, then they are not going to be buying all of the new music. They are going to be playing out of their libraries. So a publisher has to be resilient enough in terms of fiscal responsibility to be able to weather the storm.

But also, too, there isn't a time when a school will say "Hey, we've got a lot of extra money so we're gonna buy $10,000 worth of new music this year." Rarely, if ever does this happen unless folks are starting a new school and have to build a band library. The publishing business is stable, but it's not feast or famine. It's eat or starve. Feast means there's a windfall. There are no windfalls.

The Composers

As I share with my students, I believe any good musician can write a good piece. But I'm not sure they can write ten good pieces or a hundred good pieces. So there are different approaches when filling a publisher's catalog. A metaphorical approach might be to ask the question, "Do you want a glass of water or do you want the well?" If we find a well, or if we find some prospect who has the potential to become a well, then we will invest time, money, and energy working with this writer.

Part of my job as Director of Product Development at Barnhouse is to work with younger writers—young music professionals—much as I do at the university. Actually mentoring them. "Great musical thought here, but what can we do...let's really look at the impact here..." I give them some direction from a mentor's perspective on how to maximize this musical thought and take away reasons for people not to want to play their music.

It is expensive for Barnhouse to allocate hours of my time to work with a particular writer. But if we find someone who shows great potential, we are willing to make an investment. "Let's take two or three pieces and let's get them out there. Let's put money behind them. Let's get the Washington Winds to record them, etc., etc."

We do have a group of core writers. These are the people who are the metaphoric wells. We know that what they are going to give us is going to have musical and educational validity. Now musical validity is a matter of personal taste. Sometimes I have difficulty with people who think, "If I don't like it, it must not be good." I have difficulty with that. As I share with my students, you don't have the right to say, "That's not music," because as soon as you do, you give up the right to say, "this is." So as long as it's a valid form— an honest form of human expression through the thoughtful blending of sound and silence—it's music. Whether people are going to accept it or not is another question.

So we have a group of core writers who are educationally valid. Educational validity means that the music must provide certain elements that are going to fit in some kind of curricular sequence. In our industry we have a framework called grade levels. Grade levels 1–6 might be the most consistent. You don't write a Grade 3 piece with a Grade 6 flute part and a Grade 2 tuba part. We know our writers are going to be able to fit within this established curricular framework in order to maximize the opportunity for acceptance and performance in the educational world.

Production

I have lived in a corporate world where writers must produce a certain amount by a particular date. I'm not sure, personally, that's the best way to run a business. Around September 1 we start our planning for the next year. What we do first is go to our core writers and say, "Okay, Jim, what are you thinking about for this year?" Then we sit down with Jim—we actually visit him—and have a planning meeting with Jim. He may say, "I'm thinking about this," or, "I've got this commission," or "I've got this idea about this." Or, you know, he may say, "I've got a medical issue with my family and I'm not quite sure…" We are able to take these things into consideration, and on an annual basis, program for Jim because we want his selections to be great hits for him. We don't want to wear him out. Life has ebbs and flows. Stuff happens.

After we have our core writers taken care of, and we know we are going to produce X amount of things with them, we go to the next—I'll call it tier of writers. What do I mean by tier? That could be writers who have written one or two things for us before. We will check to see what they have submitted to us or what they've got. These are people we have established relationships with. After we fill those folks in, if we have a few slots left—those would be what we call our "need" kind of charts—we go to our unsolicited commissions. We don't know who the writers are, but "I like this," or "I think there's a possibility here." We fill in those last couple of spots.

From the unsolicited category we may find somebody with some promise that we could move up into that next tier. Our goal would be to find somebody that we could count on from year to year. We hopefully would build a relationship with that person that will allow him to be with us for a lifetime.

We do have some corporate folks who don't understand the creative process. There was a time, earlier in my career, where I said, "Guys, I've now lapped myself. I've turned in charts before the ones I wrote last year are in print. Something's wrong." There are all kinds of examples of how corporate mindsets affect the creative process. Barnhouse has a decidedly different approach with the human and artistic elements being the philosophical parameters we choose to work within.

Band Music as the Curriculum

I don't believe band directors in general think in curricular terms. I think that is a sad reality. I'm on a soapbox every time I go out. Band directors, by their programming, are curriculum designers. I think the method books provide a curricular framework for the first year, possibly two years. After that, I think the band directors find themselves in difficult situations caused, in part, by the realties of performance pressures. It's no longer about educating the individual child. It's all about "Does the band sound good"?" and "Have we fulfilled our service mission?" If the band sounds good, then everybody's happy.

I think it's very important for there to be a K-12 scope and sequence. Once we get into the upper part of middle school and into high school, the learning must continue based on concepts that have been introduced earlier in a student's education. Our goal is to broaden these concepts in every grade level and with every step. So we have to choose music that is going to allow this to happen. The great challenge, of course, in the high school band is that you generally have four grade levels represented: 9–12. But you know what? The concepts of tone are the same. The concepts of phrasing are the same. The concepts of harmony are the same. Rhythm—rhythmic interaction—it's all the same. So can't we choose music that is going to allow us to teach these concepts as we are rehearsing? Can't we speak at different "levels" to different people and different sections within the same rehearsal?

Critical thinking skills are incredibly important. Daily teaching objectives are incredibly important. We are being required to turn them in. I think the reality is we are making them up along the way.

Thinking as an Educator

As a composer on the podium, I think like a composer and a conductor. But as a composer/conductor on the podium, I also have to think like an educator. One of the sad realities in our world is that we don't value the educator, and that concerns me. I have this saying, "I don't think Shakespeare would have had a problem with Dr. Seuss. You have to go through Seuss to get to Shakespeare."

Sometimes I'm writing music for music's sake, so I'm not thinking about education at all. When I have that hat on, I don't care if I don't use the oboe for sixty-four bars. That's okay. The music is written for pros and it's about the artistic statement.

In the education world, I can't have the oboe rest for sixty-four bars. That's a whole day of rehearsal. The oboe students can't warm up and then sit there for an entire class period and not play. If I'm doing a Grade 6 kind of thing, it's more about the artistic statement. But even in the Grade 5 world, it's still educational. So I look at the elements I have to work with. These are my raw materials. This is what the students know at this level. Here are the scales, the harmonic awareness, and the rhythmic interactions that students are comfortable with. Here are the things they need to know. I gather my raw materials.

Once these things are set, I try to be as artistic as possible with the materials that are in front of me. Instead of starting with an artistic statement and going, "Here it is, but wait a minute, there will be kids playing this, so how can I water it down," I choose to look at the raw materials first and work to be creative from there.

been working on this other thing. I know I owe you one in a particular slot with these parameters, but I had this commission here, so I have an extra one in this slot." Basically the way the slots work is, I may have one extremely easy piece—what they call very beginning band—two slots in the beginning band series, and two slots in the young band series. I look at young band more as limited instrumentation than limited ability. I may have two slots in the concert band line—Grade 3, sometimes 2+ to 3+—and then an assignment in the symphonic band area.

Writing within Set Parameters

Within each one of these series there are set parameters. These parameters include things like ranges, rhythms, time signatures, and key signatures. By the time you get to the concert band level, pretty much everything is dictated by the needs of the music. I try to push the envelope a little bit, especially in arrangements, because I remember sitting in intermediate band. When I was in intermediate band, the first *Star Wars* music came out. One arrangement based on the main theme was just terrible. Basically it had the melody—kind of—and it was just so watered down. My band director got another arrangement of it and the music was still accessible—maybe a little high end for the level—but we rose to the occasion. "Hey, this actually sounds like the music from the movie." So when I write, I give directors escape hatches. I give them alternate rhythms and the original rhythms. If something is just going to be over the students' heads, then I will dilute it just a little bit.

With arrangements, I try to preserve the original intent of the composition. Now if it's pop music, that's different. When you are dealing with pop music that doesn't lend itself to instrumental writing, I tell my beginning arranging students to remove the quote "artist," remove the lyrics, and remove the cool sounds that you can't imitate with wind and percussion instruments. If there is anything left, it should make a pretty good arrangement. If there is nothing left, you can go ahead and write it and the people who like the tune will probably buy it, but it probably won't have a wider appeal than that.

When you remove those elements, you basically have bass, rhythm and this "Morse code." At least it sounds like Morse code, because there are maybe two or three notes in the melody—if you want to call it that. I'm not putting the music down, because millions of people can't be wrong, so I try to "preserve" it. I have found if I take a really well known pop tune and try to insert my own little thing in it, it can be an amazing failure.

With my original music for concert band, I want to write music of substance even if it's for beginning band. I really want that clarinet line that can't go above the break to move to the next note in an interesting, horizontal fashion, not just because "I have this melody and I'm stacking vertical things underneath it." I make sure things have a horizontal flow to them. I want every part to be fun to play. With the very beginning students—I learned this by talking with band directors—I make sure everyone gets the melody at some point. I try to look at all this music as being used as teaching tools. I have to sit down and figure everything out in my head (not every little detail, because that would kill inspiration). But I've got the form in my head. I've got the sequence in my head. All of the big questions are answered before I start writing anything. I have to have some anchors—a foundation—to use as a basis; a jumping off point.

When I'm writing at the younger levels, I try to put myself in the mind of the kid sitting there. "Would I like this tune enough that I would bug my band director to play it everyday?" I want to provide music that is interesting, contrasting, motivating, educationally sound, and fun. I hope it will inspire students to play.

Band Music Publishing

Publishers don't sell music. Publishers sell paper. The more paper they sell, the stronger their bottom line is. They are a business. They are in business to make money. They are in business to provide a service, and they want to provide a quality product. The quality control I work with at Alfred/Belwin is very rigorous. I believe that publishers are interested in publishing good music. They are concerned about the fact that they have to make money.

The marketplace has changed quite a bit, even in the ten years I've been doing things. There are a lot of self-publishers and a lot of small publishers. I want to align myself with a publishing company that has great marketing, because if no one knows it's there, it doesn't matter. Word of mouth doesn't work that well. Distribution is even more important. If I wasn't with a company that had the marketing and the distribution that was with Warner and now is with Alfred/Belwin, I wouldn't be receiving ASCAP royalties from Iceland, Norway, the Netherlands, Belgium, etc. 'Even the emails I get just out of the blue are interesting. "I just wanted to tell you how much my kids enjoyed playing your music." What I like to hear is that the music is giving the teachers things to use to reinforce concepts and that the students want to play it.

I can speak with confidence that the writers I associate with and that I know—my colleagues at Belwin that I've been together with for a long time—work really, really hard to make sure they are not just throwing ink on the page to see what sticks. They take it very seriously.

Commissions

When I take a commission, I talk to the commissioning party about several things, including:

- The strengths and weaknesses of the ensemble
- The kinds of music they like to play with the ensemble
- The direction they would like to go with the commission—
  any information that might help shape the music

I rarely start a commission with the idea of publishing it (although I may use the publisher's template, just in case). For example, in the case of *Suite: Sea to Sky*, I didn't even think about publishing it for a long time. It was supposed to be a nine-to-ten-minute suite in three movements, much like *Royal Canadian Sketches*. However, *Sea to Sky* turned into a twenty-one-minute, four-movement work. I completed the first movement, *March: The Lion's Gate*, and it ended up being about 2 1/2 minutes long.

After I completed the second movement, *Shannon Falls*,—it felt complete to me—I sent it to the commissioning party (I sent each movement to the gentleman who commissioned it as I completed it). He played it with his ensemble for a couple of weeks and then he called me. He said the piece was so "beautiful and captured the image of the giant waterfall that was the inspiration for the movement so well"—those were his words—that it seemed to end too soon. So I went back and re-evaluated the movement and added material that really was "missing." This is a great example of the collaborative nature of the commissioning process at its best.

Interestingly, during the time I was adding material to the second movement of the suite, I was working on a conducting project with another composer. When I listen to the *Shannon Falls* movement today, I can hear the influences of that composer on this movement. I'm influenced by what I listen to and what I'm working on at the time.

The Composer/Conductor Connection

I rarely program my own music because I don't want to be accused of self-promotion. I'm not saying it is wrong to do. Every composer/conductor has to make a personal decision here. My music is supposed to be played by other people. There is too much great music for me to say—"Okay, we need to play a Ralph Ford piece." As a composer and as a conductor, I want to learn the great music; how to conduct it and how to teach it. As I do that, as I break it apart, I see the mastery of technique. I can share this with the students in my ensemble during rehearsal.

I think we have fallen into such a trap with very high quality wind ensembles being institutionalized. In other words, they are protected and it doesn't matter what people think. "You can get out there and just set everything on fire and call it a piece. People are sitting there scratching their heads—the ten people that will go (eight of them won't come back) because there is nothing they can grab on to musically or emotionally." I'm trying to find a balance. What we do is education, entertainment, art, sequence, pacing. It's all of these.

Critics

I keep selected articles on my laptop and pull them up every once in a while just to make sure I'm not naming a piece after a subdivision. I am starting to hear things that are similar in my original music. I personally make a very concerted effort to develop a wide catalog so that I'm not competing with myself and that what I'm doing balances with what my colleagues are doing.

If I have a very successful Grade 2 overture one year, I won't write a Grade 2 overture the next year. I make an effort not to write just another piece. "Well, all we hear is that the woodwinds are flourishing parts, everything's an ostinato, and you've got all those percussionists playing all the time." Okay— great. So I wrote *Romanza*. When it was first released it sold two copies. The only percussion part was a triangle ding and a cymbal roll. I wrote it as a ballad for band. *I hear people complaining, but I see what they are buying.* (Italics added for emphasis). When it was re-released four years later, it did a little better. It was played at the Midwest last year. It was re-recorded. Maybe the recording had something to do with it. I do think the demo product that directors listen to can be a determining factor.

That brings up a whole other issue. I write a Grade 1 or 2 piece, and I hear it played by professional musicians and I go, "Wow, listen to that. Listen to how good I am." And then I go someplace where it is being played by the students it was written for and I go "Wow, listen to how good I am." I'm back to reality.

I'm still looking for my voice as a composer. My goal is to write one piece of music of substance that has legs that will be played fifty or even a hundred years from now. I'm searching for that. That means every effort I make, whether it's for my publisher, or a commission, or my own personal musical exploration, it's a chance to search for that voice and that piece that will touch people on multiple levels.

Thinking about the Third Part of the Blended Lens

As previously stated, the primary purpose of this chapter is to provide a look inside band music publishing from a publisher/publishing viewpoint. It seems important to restate that this is an initial "look" based on a limited sample. To use a phrase from earlier in the chapter, it is a "jumping off point." I chose to take the jump in an attempt to better understand this viewpoint.

If you were to ask me what I do for a living, I would tell you I am a band director—a music teacher first and foremost. While my current title might reflect something different, and while it would be a stretch to call what I do during a portion of most days musical—think about your own day so far—I am a band director. I teach music. Because I have lived in this band director/music teacher world for a while now, I know what band directors "do"—according to me.

Because I am a band director, I am interested in band music. Because composers sometimes write band music, and because music publishers sometimes publish it, it seems important to consider what composers and publishers of band music do. Band directors are "related" to composers and to publishers, at least through a common interest in music. For those same composers and publishers working in the music education area, this relationship "deepens" through a common interest in music education and music students.

From our brief conversations as documented in Parts I and II of this chapter, several points "emerge" as we work to understand the band music publisher/publishing part of the lens better:

1. Band music publishing is a business

2. Band music publishers publish what consumers buy

3. Composers writing for band music publishers write within parameters designed to "fit" student abilities

4. Both band composers and band publishers are interested in quality

5. Band composers and band music publishers are interested in the music education of students

Initial data analyses suggest (I love that phrase) that teacher/conductors (band directors), composers, and publishers may, indeed, be looking at the music, music education, and music students through different parts of the same lenses. *The challenge for all of us is to continue to work together so that we can focus our efforts most effectively.*

A View from the Other Side of the Music Stand

At this writing, the National Band Association has just undertaken a project designed to sample the opinions of music students at the secondary education level regarding activities and post-secondary plans. Soliciting the views of students who sit on the other side of the music stand each day may be important.

In Volume V of the *Teaching Music through Performance in Band* series, we reported preliminary results of a longitudinal project focused on the career choices of middle and high school students participating in honor bands across the country. One of the questions included in the study asked students to list what they liked most about their band directors in their home schools. The results below are based on data analyses of more than 1000 middle and high school responses. The top ten responses follow:

1. Is fun
2. Has strong musical talent
3. Believes in students
4. Is energetic
5. Gets into the music
6. Is skilled in music teaching
7. Is cool
8. Is patient
9. Is funny (sense of humor)
10. Includes everyone

While the sample is small and generalizations should be made with care, the results suggest that students are able to recognize "strong musical talent" and "skilled music teaching" at a relatively young age. This is both exciting and challenging. The view from the other side of the music stand—the music student "view"—offers a new set of lenses for study (and brings this whole "lens thing" to a conclusion—thankfully—at least for now).

CHAPTER 2

Imagination and Creativity: A Prelude to Musical Expression

Edward S. Lisk

Free form expression is a beautiful melody…
A gateway into the art of musical expression!
The result of an individual's inner romance
With the flow and beauty of sound.…
Sharing with the listener
The sounds of musical thought and feeling!

While attending small ensemble concerts, Midwest Clinic, and other events during the past several years, many professional performers (trios, quartets, etc.) have begun to frequently include free-form improvisation in various styles and moods. They have received overwhelming audience response by improvising different musical styles that project a variety of emotions. Most interesting are audience responses such as "Wow, they don't have any music; it's wonderful to hear how well trained they are to be able to improvise in this manner." Such words give the impression that this is musical magic that an everyday musician (student or adult) is incapable of producing. The reason for this "musical magic" and response is the fact that our conventional musical upbringing (lessons, ensembles, classes, etc.) did not include playing music without notation.

This response is intriguing to me. In my early years at Syracuse University, my friends and I would sit in the lounge and freely improvise two-part inventions, or, if there were three or four of us, we would improvise trios and quartets. Other music students were amazed, and some believed we had memorized all the Bach two-part inventions. We didn't say a word, and simply let them believe that we had committed all this music to memory.

When I began teaching, free-form expression (improvisation) was a part of my lesson program. My high school instrumental students engaged in this experience as a regular part of their musical training in the early '1970s through 1991. I believe this practice, embedded in a lesson program, is critical in the development of musical phrases. Frequently students would demonstrate their musical creations to parents who attended our parent workshops. The parents were amazed at the beautiful melodies their sons and daughters created spontaneously. These student musicians became comfortable with free-form expression and were eager to share their songs without any type of inhibition.

It was in 1991, at the International Trombone Association convention, when my high school trombone section (quartet) performed in recital at the Eastman School of Music. Their last composition was based on free-form expression. As the selection developed with the four young trombonists complimenting each other's creations, the selection became highly energized and finished with multi-phonics, which then "brought the house down" with applause and a standing ovation. They shared their musical freedom of expression, which was a regular part of their school instrumental lesson program.

During the past twenty years, I introduced "free-form expression" to countless band directors attending my graduate sessions and workshops. Their responses were similar to all who didn't believe they were capable of playing without music notation. Many resisted and were afraid to take the risk for fear of making mistakes. I encouraged them to "jump over the boundaries of notation" and discover the beauty that lies beyond the printed note. When they took the "risk," they were totally surprised at how they could create beautiful melodies.

Through my professional playing and teaching experiences, I have come to firmly believe artistic expression is found outside these self-imposed boundaries. Not until we are willing to take the risk and go outside such restrictions are we able to experience the truth and integrity of musical expression. What I found most surprising was that so many directors never engaged in such expressive techniques in their study and training.

Looking back at our past study and practice to become musicians, we were always focused on analytical precision and dared not take any liberties if not notated. I often refer to this as a "paint by number" exercise, as we cannot go outside the lines or boundaries established by music notation. Throughout my teaching I continue to encourage students and directors to take the "risk" and go outside the borders, as this is where artistic beauty and expression are found.

It should be understood that I am in no way discouraging the use of music notation. By exercising musical expression without notation, we compliment and enhance our performance when reading music notation. It is a side of musical training that is too often neglected. I have heard of too many band programs that are simply missing the mark when it comes to interpretation and musical expression.

Discover Musical Imagination

With this chapter, I introduce a procedure to eliminate fears of playing music without notation, which, as stated earlier, I refer to as free-form expression. Yes, it is being able to improvise on your instrument. To eliminate fears (both student and teacher), I replace the word "improvisation" with "the phrase, free-form expression."

The term *improvisation* can be uncomfortable for some teachers because of its association with jazz. Unfortunately, many believe improvisation is only for those with sufficient training or experience in jazz. Hopefully the suggestions found in this chapter will remove some of those mysteries and free-form expression will become a regular part of your music program.

The advantages of free-form improvisation provide a gateway into discovering the art of musical expression.

> A beautiful melody has 'feeling'
> …a beautiful melody is the result of an individual's
> inner romance with the flow of sound
> …sharing with the listener the sounds of musical thought.

I share the following quotation by notable teacher Eloise Ristad from her publication, *A Soprano on Her Head:* "When we withhold the fullness of our capabilities, we diminish those capabilities. When we explore beyond where we feel safe and secure, we discover abilities beyond our expectations." She further states,

> I use improvisation for many reasons. It can spark rich ideas for composition, for it gives us a more intimate sense of raw materials of sound. It provides an astonishing physical and emotional release, and helps develop the kind of spontaneity that can transform the way we play Bach or Mozart or Bartok. It creates a more direct personal relationship with an instrument that can melt square-shouldered bravado into keen-eared listening.

Her words elevate the importance of such a musical experience.

The beginning experiences of young musicians are best described as being consumed with the signs and symbols of music notation. From day one, their eyes are keenly focused upon that huge circle called a whole note, followed by the little black block indicating a rest. As they play each note, they dare not take their eyes off the page for fear of mistakes.

As years pass, young musicians continue to turn the pages of method books, experiencing the complexities of notation while expanding their performance vocabulary. Young instrumentalists very seldom, if at all (only with scales), venture out to discover musical sounds other than what is written. In my travels as a clinician, I often ask a student or director to play a simple, beautiful lullaby. The response is always the same; the student is shocked to think I would request someone to play a song without music.

Free-form expression/improvisation and the removal of music notation open an avenue of imagination into an individual's expressive center. We become free to listen to what we are playing while making musical decisions supporting the melodic line and its development. The significant changes in performance are because the mind is no longer consumed with a visual response to notation, but rather only listening to the flow of notes being played. Free-form expression is truly a prelude to phrasing, imagination, and musical creativity.

This may be one of the most important musical experiences for students: the opportunity for expressing themselves freely (at their level of develop- ment) without the barriers of notation or teacher-imposed expectations. It is a part of instrumental teaching that is most often neglected in the training of musicians. Usually, improvisation, when introduced, often enters the instru- mental program by way of the "jazz/blues approach.

Engaging in free-form expression produces significant improvements in phrasing and musical performance, facilitating and encouraging memorization of solo literature. Every musician and teacher at one time or another has memorized solos and other literature. Once a selection is committed to memory, the music flows freely. A good experiment is to have a student play any four measures of a solo and then repeat without the notation. The huge difference in musical flow is noticed immediately. The student responds to the musical sounds instead of being consumed in reading music. The same is true when conducting. Remove the score, and the director immediately conducts the music she is hearing instead of responding to notation in the score. I often say to directors, "Conduct and shape the music you are hearing; do not conduct the notes on the printed page." What a difference!

Notable scholar, musician, and conductor, David Whitwell writes in his essay, *On Memorization:*

> No composer can possibly notate how they really feel, because we have a notation system in which there is not a single symbol of feel- ing! We speak of interpretation of music because the musician is con- sequently forced to try to discern what the composer meant and not what he wrote. The dullest of all performances are those by musicians who play what is on the paper. Memorization *[I include free-form expression in this powerful statement David makes]* is an important means of discovering what a composer really had in mind, because it allows the musician to free himself from the visual data-form. Music is for the ear, not the eye! Once the eye is eliminated, the ear comes into play...this is the key, to *hear* what a composer wrote rather than to *see* what he wrote [emphasis added].

Memorization is the difference between performing a solo with the mind and ears totally focused on the flow and expressive qualities of music versus the eyes and fingers being consumed with a note-to-note response and other technicalities of notation. The mental connection made with the fine detail of musical phrases and listening is far more discriminating than the visual or sight response to notation.

Introducing Free-Form Expression

When introducing free-form expression, the teacher should not place any emphasis on key or scale knowledge. I make this statement because some of the suggested techniques (not jazz) written since the introduction of the National Standards actually stifle the naturalness of individual creativity by placing demands that redirect thinking away from the musical melody being created.

Within a short period of this outlined approach, your students will naturally experience success when playing free-form *melodies* and will discover the need for scale knowledge and chord qualities to expand their improvisational possibilities. This highly personal and emotive understanding expands musical meaning and value for the student musician.

I share with you several reasons for including this process as an important part of instrumental study.

Free-form expression:

1. Uncovers one's natural musical intelligence as defined by Howard Gardner in his *Theory of Multiple Intelligences*. Everyone is capable of making and appreciating music in some form. We are born into this world with the music aptitude of our mother. She sings the nursery rhymes, and we feel the pulse of her heartbeat. Music surrounds us as infants and throughout our entire life.

2. Provides an opportunity to release an individual's imagination and creativity through the sound of the musical instrument. Students are absorbed with the musical sounds they are creating. This simple approach enhances imagination without fears of being incorrect.

3. Develops the capacity to play melodic lines without being overly consumed with note values, rhythm patterns, key signatures, or any other notated indicators. By removing the limitations and restrictions of notation and bringing into focus melodic content, the often-stifled mind previously consumed with reading notes is transformed.

When I am conducting my own music, I think it's very important for students to understand the creative intent first. So I give them a sense of the whole; I give them a sense of the background; I introduce related materials, even cross-curricular materials.

When I am conducting someone else's music, I do the same thing. This is something any good music teacher could do. It is part of my score study. We call it score study, but it has to go beyond that. If the students understand the artistic intent, then it becomes a piece of music. If not, it's just an etude or an exercise. And exercises get old. If the artistic and expressive qualities are known, no matter how simple or how difficult it is, it's always fresh.

Critics

When you are writing a book, there is a formula. The book is divided into chapters. The chapters are divided into paragraphs. There's a form to each chapter, right down to each sentence. There is a form. You have to listen inside to see what is being said. Now if it's just a series of random words and thoughts the book doesn't make any sense. Nobody is going to read it. There has to be some kind of structure. I'll take a good musical idea and I'll generally do a curricular sequence of three to teach specific concepts. Then I'm done. I stop. If I wrote another one just like it, guess what, I could sell multiple thousands of copies. But I will not do it just to sell copies.

Part II: Ralph Ford, Composer

Writing for Publishers

I started publishing in 1998. My first two years were spent writing marching band arrangements just to get my feet wet. The main tests for me at the time were, would I accept an assignment in a positive way? could I write within the parameters of a particular series? and most importantly, could I make a deadline? It started with two assignments, then six assignments. My writing for concert band began when a writer for the company I was working for left the company. Suddenly there was a void that they could have taken time to fill. But because of my past experiences, and with encouragement from the company, I was offered the opportunity to enter into a five-year agreement. At that point we set the number of assignments.

As a contract writer, I write in many genres: marching band, jazz ensemble, orchestra, and concert band. As a concert band writer, I'm assigned X number of slots. Generally speaking, it's two in each series. However, that is negotiable. If I get myself into a situation where I don't think I'll be able to provide the company with quality material in a timely fashion, I may say to George, "I've

4. Enables students to become sensitive to a natural form of expression through the contour of a melodic line, creating a sense of belonging and ownership to the melody being produced.

5. Allows students to become sensitive to the feeling of resolution; moving a pitch or a series of notes within a phrase from tension to resolution or point of repose, and feeling the energy and direction of their artistic thoughts.

6. Provides a mind/body connection with the 'soul' of the individual through the sound of an instrument (thinking and decision-making). This departure from 'contrived' musical expression or meaningless notes affects the means to exercise and enhance intimate connections with melodic lines.

7. Provides opportunities to develop and apply interpretation and stylistic performance, allowing the student to go beyond the written symbols of music notation and faithfully experience the composer's musical intentions.

8. Removes the inhibitions of being incorrect or the fear of risk with musical decisions. Free-form expression will always be correct unless the teacher imposes some form of restriction or expectation. These original musical statements are a result of and are supported by the knowledge and skill experience of the individual.

The important point to remember when presenting free-form improvisation is that everything the student plays is correct! Naturally feeling insecure at the beginning stages of playing a melody without music notation, students frequently react with statements such as "I can't do this without music."

The first attempt usually begins with a line of rapid notes, and the melody becomes *busy* because of their nervousness in search of correctness. This is a natural reaction. It is very important not to make any corrections, but instead encourage experimenting with a line of notes. Such timidity is due to limited learning and performance opportunities. All prior performance experiences were musically notated with specific instructions on what to do via notation or teacher design for expression.

By removing some of these natural barriers and inhibitions, the student is free to drift in any melodic direction with any duration of notes or rhythm. The first experiences should be done in a small group or individual lesson setting and not in a full ensemble rehearsal. You will find students hesitate to take the *risk*, as they have been conditioned to only respond to notation. Believe in and support their natural musical intelligence. This will guide them into a meaningful melody, building confidence in their very own creation.

The fewer notes played, the more freedom they have to listen and become involved with the *feeling* of pitch and note direction. Encourage long, flowing melodies in a comfortable playing range to develop melodic coherency. The beauty and interest of the musical line will blossom as the student plays a longer free-form melodic phrase. *Natural musical intelligence comes to life with cohesive thought and expression by removing the barricades, which conceal the beauty of musical expression found in every person.* To release this newfound splendor requires a perceptive teacher who realizes and feels the power and depth of musical meaning.

Instructional Sequence

Utilizing the teaching sequence outlined below will successfully guide students in their first attempts with their own free-form melodies.

1. Ask the student to play a slow melody like a lullaby or a beautiful ballad.
   - Do not indicate key, tempo, or any type of musical descriptor.
   - As the student plays, you will begin to hear her musical decisions, which are top priority.

2. Encourage the student to freely start on any comfortable pitch and 'create' a melody (lullaby/ballad), experimenting with different notes and rhythms.

3. Encourage the student to play slowly while listening to the notes moving in different directions to form musical statements.

4. Be observant of the length (seconds and minutes) of the student's performance, indicating the following musical results:
   - Significant improvement in the melodic line.
   - Focused and directed listening to melody and sound.
   - Development of meaningful and/or musical patterns releasing the student's natural musical intelligence.
   - Growth in key and tonality competence as the student experiments with accidentals.
   - As confidence develops with listening, natural resolution of note patterns occurs.

5. As the student becomes comfortable playing simple melodies (usually after three to five practice sessions), suggest playing a melody that will reflect the following styles. Begin with the examples below for each style. Note that key and time signatures have not been included. This allows more freedom for the student to focus on melody.

A beautiful lullaby or ballad

In a waltz style

Fleeting, rapidly-moving notes with excitement

In the style of a march

A somber, sad melody

A happy, spirited melody

FIGURE 1.

This musical environment activates critical thinking and listening skills supporting the highest levels of engagement. Spontaneous musical decisions shape melody and provide a meaningful experience for the student. Patience is important; musical development is too often hampered by impatience from either the student or teacher.

The performance quality established through free-form expression/ improvisation makes a noticeable difference in a student's musicality. The freedom and flow of a melody line are unrestricted, as the *whole* of melody is perceived. The visual response to notation no longer hampers the mind with the technical demand of reading.

Introducing Modes

Once your students become comfortable playing free-form melodies, the next step is to introduce the various modes of a major scale. A mode is simply changing the starting note with each scale degree of a major scale and proceeding upward for one octave, as illustrated below. This is not difficult for the student as long as there is no complex theoretical information associated with modes at this time.

Theory information is presented after they have played and heard the modes. This is the same natural learning process we applied when we learned to speak, read, and write. The process begins with simply asking the student to play the C major scale. Follow this with having the student play the C major scale from D to D (the second scale degree), E to E (the third degree), F to F (the fourth degree), etc. until they have played the C major scale from B to B (the seventh degree).

This scale exercise (Figure 2) should be played in all keys for skill and listening development.

As the students play extended scales, identify the modes they are playing, (Ionian, Dorian, etc.). Play the C major scale from the second scale degree (D–E–F–G–A–B–C–D) and note that F and C were natural and not sharped as in the D major scale. Do the same with the fourth scale degree (of the major key; in C major, F–G–A–B–C–D–E–F) and note that the B was natural because there was no B-flat in the C major scale (B is not flatted, as it is in the F major scale). This scale is referred to as the Lydian mode.

The next logical step is to play the C major scale beginning on the fifth scale degree (G–A–B–C–D–E–F–G); note that there is no F-sharp in the C major scale (F is not sharped, as it is in the G major scale). This scale is referred to as the Mixolydian mode. This simple approach "opens the door" to further improvisation based on chord progressions.

The second step in developing mode awareness is to identify the appropriate chord progressions for each scale mode. Figure 3 illustrates this exercise, which should be done in all major scales.

FIGURE 2.

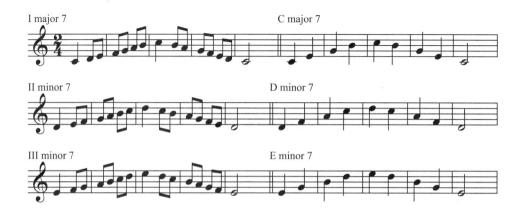

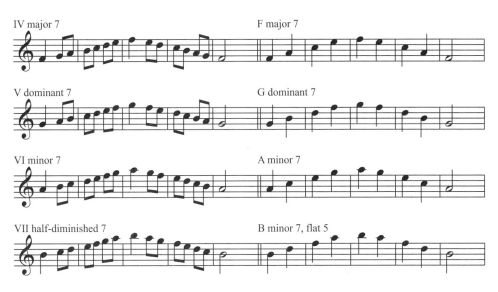

FIGURE 3.

At this stage of musical development in free-form expression/improvisation, your students are ready to move into playing melodies based on simple chord progressions such as I–IV–V⁷–I and I–IIm⁷–V⁷–I. The teaching sequence will be as follows:

1. Play a I chord on the piano.
   - Inform the student to play the scale from tonic to tonic, or the Ionian mode. These are the notes they will use when freely creating a melody based on the I Chord.

2. Play a IV chord on the piano.
   - Inform the student to play the scale from the fourth scale degree, one octave in the scale key, or the Lydian mode. These are the notes they will use when freely creating melody moving from the I to IV chord.

3. Play a V⁷ chord on the piano.
   - Inform the student to play the scale from the fifth degree in the scale key, one octave, or the Mixolydian mode. These are the notes they will use when freely creating a melody moving between the I, IV, and V⁷ chord.

4. Play the chord progression I–IV–V⁷–I and allow the student to freely play (no tempo or pulse) within each chord and create a melody based on the chords.

This instructional approach is not difficult, as chord understanding and skills are based on all scales (the Grand Master Scale as found in my earlier writings). With such scale knowledge coupled with chords, students will progress rapidly. In addition, students are ready to move into more advanced and altered chord progressions. They are able to understand and apply meaningful improvisational melodies.

• • •

I have attempted to express the most difficult tasks for a musician in defining artistic considerations for shaping a musical mind. It was my intent to share my thoughts, perceptions, and concepts that may possibly release you and your 'students' musical imagination as you enter into the vague, untouchable world of expressive communication. In closing, I must repeat an earlier statement: free-form expression is truly a prelude to phrasing, imagination, and musical creativity.

I share with you the following words...

It is the "I" that holds the answer...
It is the "I" that cannot be copied, imitated, or contrived...
The "I" is found in the Intangible, Intrinsic, Inherent, and the Innate.
The "I" words are connected through musical "I"magination...
A musical imagination that speaks through the beauty of sound...
...moving in and out of silence!

Bibliography

Blum, David. *Casals and the Art of Interpretation*. Berkeley, CA: University of California Press, Ltd., 1977.

Copland, Aaron. *Music and Imagination*. Cambridge, MA: Harvard University Press, 1980.

Lisk, Edward S. *Beyond the Page: The Natural Laws of Musical Expression*. Vol. 4, in *Teaching Music through Performance in Band*, edited by Richard Miles, 29–43. Chicago, IL: GIA Publications, Inc., 2002.

—. *The Creative Director: Intangibles of Musical Performance*. Galesville, MD: Meredith Music Publications, 2000.

Nachmanovitch, Stephen. *Free Play: Improvisation in Life and Art*. New York, NY: Jeremy P. Tarcher/Putnam, 1991.

Ristad, Eloise. *A Soprano on Her Head: Right-side-up Reflections on Life and Other Performances*. Boulder, CO: Real People Press, 1982.

CHAPTER 3

"Rehearsing" and "Teaching"

Richard Miles

Many conductors demonstrate outstanding rehearsal technique from a technical and expressive perspective, often the primary focus for those who prepare exclusively for performances with their groups. When conductors emphasize only "technical and expressive" aspects, fine performances may result; however, it is possible that performers may know very little about the music that was prepared and perfected.

The purpose of this chapter and the entire *Teaching Music through Performance* series is to encourage all conductors (school, university, community, amateur, and professional) to develop more comprehensive approaches for preparing their groups for performances with understanding and to *teach about the music*. In volume 1, chapter 2 of *Teaching Music through Performance in Band*, Ray Cramer states:

> We need to capitalize on every aspect of music to bring the "whole package" into our performance experiences, which will enhance the students involvement and musical fulfillment. Correct notes are obviously important as are attacks, releases, good balance, blend, careful intonation, clarity in texture, and articulation style. But these are all stepping stones to generating musical electricity and excitement. To accomplish this, we must, as teachers and conductors, give our students *more* than the basic musical stepping stones. They need our musical heart and soul, which can only be communicated by sharing everything we have compiled about the period, style, composer, and structure of the composition. In other words, involve the students totally, teach them *about the music, through the music* we choose. Ours is an awesome responsibility,...our energy and enthusiasm for the task must infect those over whom we have been put in charge.[1]

Two chapters in the series provide the basis of this chapter on "Rehearsing" and "Teaching"—Volume 1, "Curricular Models Based on Literature Selection" and Volume 4, "Strategies for Teaching Music in the Rehearsal." This chapter provides a more in-depth look at creative ways to teach and develop musicianship, and provides an outline and curriculum guide to help develop a sequential process and varied approach in the presentation of core and historical repertoire, musical elements, form and structure of music, technique development, and listening. In addition, information is provided to help the conductor understand the minimal technical requirements for performing the various graded levels of music.

Part I: Rehearsing

Rehearsing is the developmental process of preparing for performance, and involves the making, doing, and creating of music. Most conductors are knowledgeable with this area, and use techniques for warm-up and incorporate unique approaches to practicing music. In rehearsal, it is important to set priorities, use creative strategies, and maximize the available time. *Scheduling and Teaching Music* addresses many of these ideas and strategies, and readers are encouraged to review the text.[2]

Rehearsal ideas are presented in the *Teaching Music through Performance in Band* series and include several very important concepts. Readers should note the exceptional contributions of Edward Lisk (see volume 2, chapter 2—"The Rehearsal, Mastery of Music Fundamentals," 12–28)." Volume 3, chapter 2 (15–27) features a special section on rhythm—"Silence and the Space of Time." In volume 4, chapter 3 (29–44), he presents "Beyond The Page, Natural Laws of Musical Expression." Ideas focus on "Discovering Our Emotional Center," "Speaking Rhythm Patterns," and "Natural Laws of Expression." Volume 5, chapter 2 features a focus on "The Mysterious World of In-Tune Playing. In this text (volume 7), Lisk presents a more in-depth presentation on expressive musicianship, focusing more on "Imagination and Creativity: A Prelude to Musical Expression." The reader will also want to explore the text *The Creative Director: Alternative Rehearsal Techniques*, published by Meredith Music Publications and distributed by Hal Leonard. Lisk presents a thorough sequence of steps that help develop appropriate technique, band sound, intonation, and expression.

Rehearsal Priorities

Establishing rehearsal priorities and developing effective teaching strategies is important. In volume 4, chapter 5—"Strategies for Teaching Music in the Rehearsal" (65–95), planning steps for teaching and rehearsing are outlined, and additional aspects are covered to help with the creation of a curriculum;

the development of units of study, lesson plans, rehearsal outlines; and incorporating resources that enhance instruction and learning.

In *Instrumental Music Pedagogy*, Daniel L. Kohut provides a suggested list of priorities of where to start when addressing the fix-it areas while rehearsing the music. Often, young and inexperienced conductors start at the bottom of the priority list and first address dynamics and balance when the group is actually playing wrong notes and rhythms. The Kohut list that follows serves as a model for rehearsal focus and is especially recommended for young and developing conductors. Address the major areas first (the top of the priority list), and as improvement occurs, move on down the list.

Rehearsal Priorities

1. Rhythmic accuracy
2. Correct notes, key changes
3. Tone quality and intonation
4. Bowing and articulation
5. Precision, including rhythmic interpretation
6. Melodic phrasing and expression
7. Dynamic contrast
8. Tonal balance and blend[3]

Rehearsal Method

Recommended is the use of the Basic Rehearsal Method as addressed by Joseph Labuta in his text, *Basic Conducting Techniques* (fifth edition). He encourages the conductor to use an A, B-A approach.

First, **A: Synthesis**: sample the area to be rehearsed (read through and listen for errors). The next stage is, **B: Analysis**: correct errors by demonstrating, explaining, drilling, and evaluating. The third stage is then to repeat the first stage: **A: Synthesis**: play through the piece or section again and listen for corrections. The rehearsal procedure is repeated as needed: **B—fix-it stage, A—check and confirm stage**, etc.[4] This method is endorsed by both Kohut and Labuta, and serves as a useful procedure, especially for young and developing conductors.

Rehearsal Emphasis and Timeline

In volume 1 of *Teaching Music through Performance in Band*, Eugene Corporon presents a model of the long-range focus on preparing for performance. In his chapter, "The Quantum Conductor," he recommends rehearsing from the macro to the micro (from the beginning through the middle part of the preparation period) and then from the micro to the macro (from the middle to the final stage).

For example, in week one of a seven-week preparation timeline, first start by reading the work and analyzing what needs attention. The process continues by sampling and rehearsing smaller units, taking apart the music in weeks

two and three. In weeks four and five, rehearse in the micro (middle) stage with very specific smaller units being rehearsed. The next stage (micro to macro) starts to rebuild the music. Starting with week six through week seven, the music is rehearsed in larger units, and by the end of the process the entire work is played for continuity. (See "Planning, Pacing, and Evaluating"[5] [18–23] for further in-depth review of rehearsal techniques.)

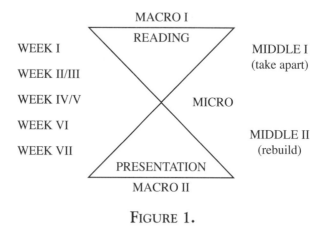

FIGURE 1.

Part II: Teaching

To many music educators, there is a distinct difference in the approach to "rehearsing" only and "rehearsing and teaching." The conductor who focuses totally on the methodology to achieve the performance—e.g., technique development, drill, repetition, special exercises, and other methods of preparation—is again encouraged to explore additional aspects of preparation for performance. Continue to use the traditional rehearsal procedures as addressed and enhance those procedures, but also "teach" the musicians about the music as the music is being prepared. Musicians who are informed about the music will potentially develop a deeper level of musicianship, appreciation, and understanding, and a listening emphasis will help encourage life-long enjoyment.

Developing a Long-Range Plan—the Curriculum

The next area is perhaps the most important aspect in this chapter, as it outlines a sequential and cyclic plan to teach music based on performing selected core and historical literature and focusing on specific content areas to emphasize over an extended period. Content areas can be presented in numerous ways, including recommended one- to two-minute segments interjected during rehearsals. (See volume 1, chapter 5—"Units of the Teacher Resource Guide" [33–39] for further ideas and suggestions.)

Content areas are presented in the following four-year curriculum design, and additional areas can be added or not presented as needed or desired. Adjustment of the areas to be presented on a yearly basis are necessary in programs that do not cycle every four years (e.g., three-year high school programs or two-year middle school programs). Consider the assessment aspects as well.

Content Areas

1. Concert repertoire
   (core and historical)
2. Musical elements (melody,
   harmony, rhythm, timbre)
3. Form and structure
4. Technique development
5. Listening

Concert Repertoire	Musical Elements	Form & Structure	Technique Development	Listening
HISTORICAL Medieval/ Renaissance/Baroque Concert One: One work from the recommended list	*M* *E* *L* *O* *D* *Y*	*O* *R* *G* *A* *N* *I* *Z* *I* *N* *G*	*O* *U* *T* *L* *I* *N* *E* *D*	*A* *P* *P* *R* *E* *C* *I* *A* *T* *I* *O*
CORE Concert Two: One Grade 2-6 Level work from this series				
HISTORICAL Medieval/ Renaissance/Baroque Concert Three: One work from the recommended list		*F* *O* *R* *C* *E* *S*	*M* *A* *S* *T* *E* *R* *Y*	*N* & ***Understanding***
CORE Concert Four: One Grade 2-6 Level work from this series	Presented Element with special FOCUS for the entire year	Presented Concepts for all music	Presented and mastered Technique Requirements for the *Grade 2-6 Level*	**More than just "HEARING" Music** Presented opportunities for Listening

FIGURE 2. Year 1, Grades 2–6

Concert Repertoire	Musical Elements	Form & Structure	Technique Development	Listening
HISTORICAL **Classical &** **Romantic** Concert One: One work from the recommended list	H A R M O N Y	O R G A N I Z I N G F O R C E S	O U T L I N E D M A S T E R Y	A P P R E C I A T I O N & *Understanding* More than just "HEARING" Music
CORE Concert Two: One Grade 2-6 Level work from this series				
HISTORICAL **Classical &** **Romantic** Concert Three: One work from the recommended list				
CORE Concert Four: One Grade 2-6 Level work from this series	Presented Element with special FOCUS for the entire year	Presented Concepts for all music	Presented and mastered Technique Requirements for the *Grade 2-6 Level*	Presented opportunities for Listening

FIGURE 3. Year 2, Grades 2–6

Concert Repertoire	Musical Elements	Form & Structure	Technique Development	Listening
HISTORICAL **Contemporary** **Part 1** Concert One: One work from the recommended list	R H Y T H M	O R G A N I Z I N G F O R C E S	O U T L I N E D M A S T E R Y	A P P R E C I A T I O N & *Understanding* More than just "HEARING" Music
CORE Concert Two: One Grade 2-6 Level work from this series				
HISTORICAL **Contemporary** **Part 1** Concert Three: One work from the recommended list				
CORE Concert Four: One Grade 2-6 Level work from this series	Presented Element with special FOCUS for the entire year	Presented Concepts for all music	Presented and mastered Technique Requirements for the *Grade 2-6 Level*	Presented opportunities for Listening

FIGURE 4. Year 3, Grades 2–6

Concert Repertoire	Musical Elements	Form & Structure	Technique Development	Listening
HISTORICAL **Contemporary** **Part 2** Concert One: One work from the recommended list	**T I M B R E**	O R G A N I Z I N G F O R C E S	O U T L I N E D M A S T E R Y	A P P R E C I A T I O N & *Understanding*
CORE Concert Two: One Grade 2-6 Level work from this series				
HISTORICAL **Contemporary** **Part 2** Concert Three: One work from the recommended list				
CORE Concert Four: One Grade 2-6 Level work from this series	Presented Element with special FOCUS for the entire year	Presented Concepts for all music	Presented and mastered Technique Requirements for the *Grade 2-6 Level*	**More than just "HEARING" Music** Presented opportunities for Listening

FIGURE 5. Year 4, Grades 2–6

Teaching with Concert Repertoire

In the first content area, Concert Repertoire, the design is based on presenting four yearly concerts. One curricular work (core or historical) is selected for special teaching and emphasis for each concert. For the four concerts, two of the works should be from core repertoire for the appropriate graded level of the ensemble and two from a historical perspective with a different period focus that would vary each year. Thus every year, musicians should perform at least two core works and two historical selections from each major style period. Over the course of four years, musicians will be exposed to a minimum of eight core works and eight historical selections that represent the stylistic aspects of most all historic periods in the development of music.

In the Core Repertoire category, any of the works presented in the series are appropriate to consider. (See Appendix B) for representative listings of core and historical repertoire by grade level and year of the curriculum sequence.)

Teaching Musical Elements

The second content area in the curriculum design addresses the Music Element that should receive focus and attention for the entire year. For example, in year one of the four-year cycle, Melody is the element addressed. The conductor should constantly bring attention to different aspects of melodic construction, deviation, or variation elements, and/or the significance from a creative or expressive aspect. Again, concentrate on the selected repertoire or include all works in the presentation.

Melody (Strategies for Teaching)

Melody or theme includes information concerning the use of tonality, scales, motives, sequence, phrases, diatonic structure and melodic design, chromatic melody, serial melody, or themes.[6] *Provide musical examples* and how to possibly play expressively, etc.

Concepts to Address

1. Themes	7. Phrases
2. Motives	8. Chromaticism
3. Modality	9. Serial
4. Tonality	10. Expression
5. Scales	11. Interpretation
6. Sequence	

Rhythm (Strategies for Teaching)

The Rhythm content area addresses beat and meter, along with the possible use of polymeter, uneven and changing meters, and non-meters.[7] Again, *provide examples* from the music, how to count, teach, and develop rhythmic independence, etc.

Concepts to Address

1. Simple time	7. Polymeter
2. Compound time	8. How to Count
3. Meter	9. Patterns
4. Uneven meter	10. Syncopation
5. Changing meter	11. Rests
6. Non-meter	

The following sources are recommended for help with teaching the mastery of rhythm fundamentals:

Creasap, Susan. *Ralph Hale Reading Slides for Concert Band.* Morehead, KY: 1993.

Moore, Stephen, *Rhythm Rulz*, CD-Rom (Volumes I & II), DVD (Software), Fort Collins, CO: Beyond The Notes, Inc., 2005.
Fussell, Raymond C. *Exercises for Ensemble Drill.* Paul A. Schmitt Music Co., 1967 (40–42).

The following pages present basic, fundamental rhythms from the Raymond Fussell text, *Exercises for Ensemble Drill* (Paul A. Schmitt Music Co., 1967, 40–42).[8] Conductors have many options for using this source, including the selection of specific rhythms for mastery from these pages and coordinating rhythm study with the music being rehearsed.

FIGURE 6.

FIGURE 7.

* Quarter rest found in foreign editions.

FIGURE 8.

Harmony (Strategies for Teaching)

The presentation of the Harmony content area may include information concerning tonality and chord construction, cadences, dissonance and consonance, and harmonic progression. Other relevant harmonic techniques are addressed as necessary, such as the use of polytonality and serial harmony. The treatment of the voice movement or texture is addressed and identified as being monophonic, homophonic, or polyphonic.[9] Consider *providing examples* of harmonic movement, chords—even an explanation of chordal construction in a very elementary form, etc.

Concepts to Address

1. Chord construction	8. Polyphony
2. Cadences	9. Tonality
3. Dissonance	10. Bitonality
4. Consonance	11. Atonality
5. Harmonic progression	12. Serial harmony
6. Monophony	13. Set construction
7. Homophony	

Timbre (Strategies for Teaching)

The focus of this content area is on the tone color of the composition and how different instruments may be used and orchestrated (woodwind, brass, percussion choirs, soloists, special instruments, etc.). This area could present aspects of characteristic tone production, blend, balance, and other appropriate fundamentals as well. Consider *providing examples* and instructional ideas and strategies.

Concepts to Address

1. Tone color	7. Special instruments
2. Orchestration	8. Variety and combination
3. Use of woodwinds	9. Characteristic tone production
4. Use of brass	10. Blend
5. Use of percussion	11. Balance
6. Soloists	

Teaching Form and Structure

The third content area addresses Form and Structure. Address the varied organizing forces used in the creation process of each work being prepared during rehearsal.

Through the study and analysis of music structure (the tonal center) and design (the melodic intent), we may better understand the musical essence the

composer intends to be expressed through the creative process of composing. So why bother and be concerned with sharing the teaching information regarding these elements?

As presented in volume 3, chapter 4 of *Teaching Music through Performance in Band* (42–80), academic accountability is enhanced in the performing ensemble when *comprehensive musicianship* concepts are presented. Therefore, "a greater musical literacy, accountability, and alignment with current educational direction can be achieved....[10] Through the process of *comprehensive musicianship* development, we become better *musicians* and we become more capable of relating to what composers intend for performers to project in and with their music. At the same time, we most likely will experience a deeper *response* to the innate expressive qualities of music."[11]

Consider providing a special handout and/or outline regarding the organizing forces listed below. In daily rehearsal, rather than name the rehearsal letter or measure as a point of reference, refer to the starting locations with reference to the structure section (e.g., "Please start at the third variation," "At the Coda please," "Begin at the Recapitulation," etc.).

Concepts to Address in Music Being Preared for Performance

1. Organizing forces for expression
    a. Melodic function
    b. Harmonic function
2. One-part form
3. Two-part or binary
4. Ternary
5. Rondo
6. Arch
7. Theme & Variation
8. Sonata
9. Ostinato forms
    a. Passacaglia
    b. Chaconne
10. Free forms
    a. Symphonic Poem
    b. Toccata
    c. Prelude
11. Multiple forms
    a. Suite
    b. Symphony
    c. Concerto

Teaching Technique Development

The fourth content area presents the basic and minimal Technique development fundamentals required to perform music in a particular graded level. One way to increase the ability of the ensemble and to move forward to the next difficulty level is to develop a series of exercises to incorporate into rehearsal (e.g., a Grade 2-level group moving to the Grade 3 level must master the minimum requirements for Grade 3, etc.).

Concepts to Address

1. Meter	7. Ornaments
2. Key signatures	8. Scoring
3. Tempo	9. Musical substance
4. Note and rest values	10. Length
5. Dynamics	11. Range
6. Articulation	

The following section is an outline of the basic technique requirements for performance of Grade 2–6 levels of music difficulty. The listing is not intended to be all-inclusive, but serves as a guide. Review each selection to be performed and note the needed fundamentals to perform each work and to make certain that all musicians are taught the needed skills to successfully perform the selection.

Cynthia Hutton is credited for the information that follows. Hutton completed a Graduate Research Project in the Doctor of Musical Arts program at the University of Colorado, Boulder under the direction of Allan McMurray June 15, 2000. She studied the classification and grading requirements of sixteen music publishers. Those findings were compiled and presented as a Lecture Demonstration Document (TMUS 8269) and also published in *BANDWORLD* magazine in 2000. The following chart is reprinted for your review with permission from the author and *BANDWORLD*.

The purpose of the *BANDWORLD* Grading Music Chart as presented by Hutton:

1. It reflects what the students can be expected to achieve at a given grade level.
2. It serves as a guideline for the composers to follow when composing for a particular grade level.
3. It serves as a guideline for band directors to make their own decision regarding the suitability of the work for their band (32).[12]

For additional technique development, Gerald Prescott and Lawrence Chidester present a recommended outline of articulation and technique development in the 1938 classic *Getting Results with School Bands*. The reproduction in figure 10 is used with permission as an example of articulation development to coordinate with the different demands of graded levels.[13]

Grade	1	2	3	4	5
Meter	Simple: 2/4 3/4 4/4 c, very minimal meter change	Add: 6/8 minimal use of 5/4 6/4 simple ¢ easy duple time meter changes	Add: 9/8 12/8 3/2 4/2 6/2 7/4 easy meter change in compound and duple time	Add: 3/8 5/8 7/8 8/8 11/8 10/2 9/2 asymmetrical meter changes	All meters, frequent and complex changes
Key Signature	B♭, E♭, F -relative minor and modes, minimal accidentals	B♭, E♭, A♭ - relative minor and modes, simple chromatic alterations and key changes	up to 5 flats*, incl. C increased use of chromatic alterations and key changes	up to 6 flats* & 2 sharps limited polytonalities, increased dissonance	Any key-within reason, frequent chromatic alterations Expanded use of polytonalities
Tempo (beats per minute)	Andante-Moderato 72-120 simple ritard. minimal changes	Andante-Allegro 60-132 ritard., accel.	Largo-Allegro 56-144 rit, accel, rall, allarg, molto rit	Largo-Presto 40-168 all tempo descriptors*	Largo-Prestissimo 40-208 frequent tempo changes
Note/Rest Value	♩ at grade 1.5	Add: easy 16th note groupings	Add: easy groupings of 6/8: very minimal use	All values in duple All values in compound More use of asymmetrical groupings	More complex use of duple and compound
Rhythm	Basic duple rhythms Dotted rhythms and simple ties at 1+. 2-part independence	Basic rhythms in duple, very simple compound, simple eighth-note syncopation, up to 3-part independence	more use of compound rhythm more use of syncopation up to 4-part independence	All rhythms except complex compound or complex 16th syncopation up to 5-part independence	Add complex subdivision and syncopation, frequent changes, multiple part independence
Dynamics	p to f, short	pp to ff simple fp; 4 bar phrases	pp to ff longer, some subito changes, cross dynamics, more use of fp	ppp to fff long more complex subito changes, cross dynamics	All dynamics, emphasis on complexity, cross, subito long
Articulation	Basic attack and release (TAH-DAH), slur & accent, minimal use of staccato	Add: tenuto, staccato, legato 2 articulations simultaneously	Add: marcato, sfz, sffz 3 articulations simultaneously	Increased style demands: secco, leggiero, pesante, portato, flutter tongue 4 articulations simultaneously	Frequent changes, multiple tonguing, multiple articulations simultaneously
Ornaments	None	Simple trills and single grace notes	Trills with entry or exit grace notes; double or triple grace note figures	Any length of grace note figures, trills, turns, mordents. Notate turns and mordents.	Add: increased complexity with frequent use
Scoring	Reduced instrumentation. Limited section exposure. Part distribution by like families or like registers. Voicing changes at phrase points	Reduced instrumentation. Limited solos for: fl, cl, tpt, a.sax. Section division and independence. More exposed percussion. Solos cross-cued. Begins use of contemporary notation.	Expands instrumentation. Limited solos ob/hn/bar. Part division within sections, more independence. Solos cross-cued. More exposed percussion, includes piano	Full range of instrumentation. Exposed parts for any instrument. Increased variety of timbre combinations. More use of the piano as instrumental color	Multiple solos, transparent textures, independent counterpoint. More exposure of E♭ clarinet, eng. hn. and other auxiliary instruments.
Musical Substance	Emphasis on fundamental concepts. Clever use of basic elements.	Continued emphasis on developing reading and performance skills. Content varies in style & requires expressive response in performance	Adds new musical concepts, requires recognition of form, style and composer intent through performance interpretation. Musical meaning not immediately obvious.	Adds more complex musical challenges, requires a constant aural awareness and alertness to the musical architecture and meaning	Demands an understanding of a wide range of styles, requires alertness to form, creative originality, emotional content & contrast, and provokes intellectual satisfaction. Frequent changes in both sound and silence

Interdependent

Length	1-3 minutes	2-5 minutes	2-8 minutes	2-20 minutes	Any Length
Considerations	Avoid awkward leaps, tutti scoring from beginning to end and clarinets crossing the break	Well placed rest for endurance. Includes clever counter lines. Keep players in their best range. Avoid frequent changes.	*minimal use of C, D♭ increased use of tempo fluctuation. Avoid extreme ranges for players.	*increased use of rubato and sudden changes, minimal use of 6 flats *baritone saxophone with low A key	Content is both musically and technically demanding, frequent changes
Percussion Usage	timpani optional, no pitch changes. No snare drum rolls, single flams ok, sus. cym. rolls ok., rhythms may be one level more advanced than wind parts	2 timpani, allow time for simple pitch changes, Simple rolls on snare drum, rolls on tambourine, triangle, bass drum ok	4 timpani, two hand mallets, more exotic effects, coin scrapes, brushes	4 hand mallets, more exotic effects, bowed vibraphone or crotales, multiple mallet parts	All techniques, within reason
Flute	(range notation)	2.5 (range notation)	(range notation)	(range notation)	(range notation)
Oboe	(range notation)	(range notation)	(range notation)	(range notation)	(range notation)
Bassoon	(range notation)	2.5 (range notation)	(range notation)	(range notation)	(range notation)
Clarinet	1.5 (range notation)	2.5 (range notation)	(range notation)	(range notation)	(range notation)
Alto Clarinet / Bass Clarinet	B.S. (range notation)	B.S. (range notation)	B.S. (range notation)	B.S. (range notation)	B.S. (range notation)
Alto, Tenor Baritone Sax	B.S. (range notation)	(range notation)	3.5 (range notation)	B.S. (range notation)	(range notation)
Trumpet	(range notation)	2.5 (range notation)	(range notation)	4.5 (range notation)	(range notation)

		2.5	3.5		
Horn	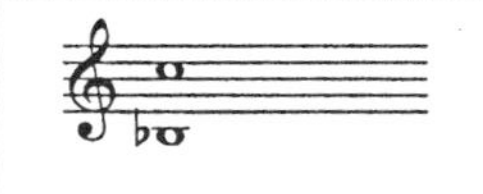	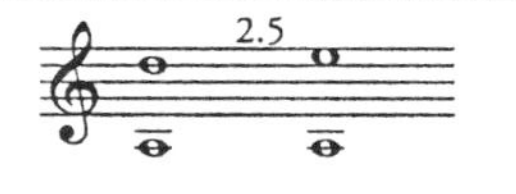	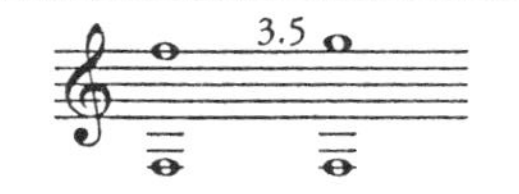	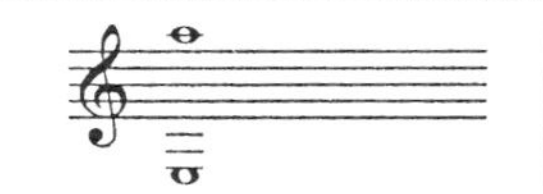	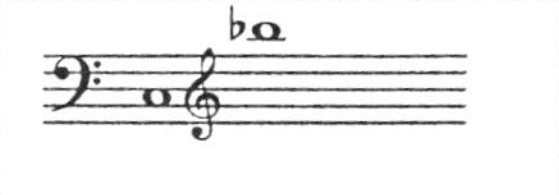
Trombone/Baritone	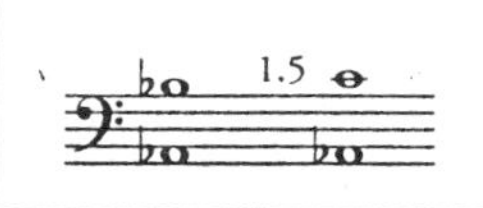 1.5	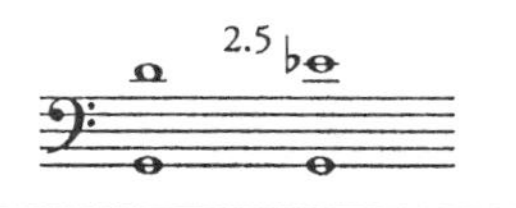 2.5	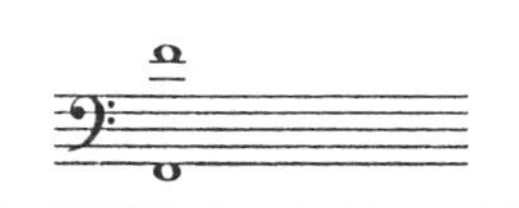 3.5		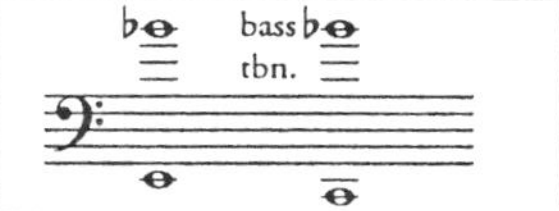 bass tbn.
Tuba		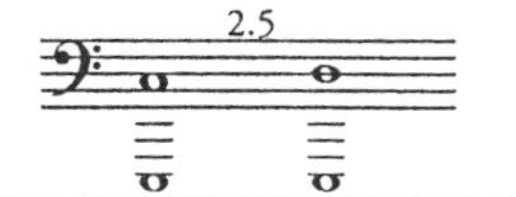 2.5	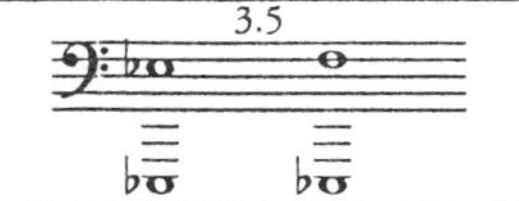 3.5	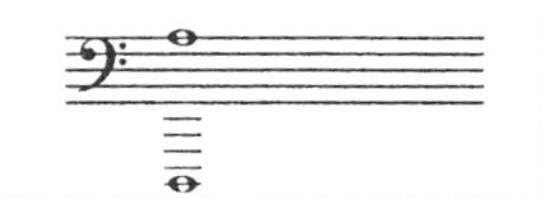	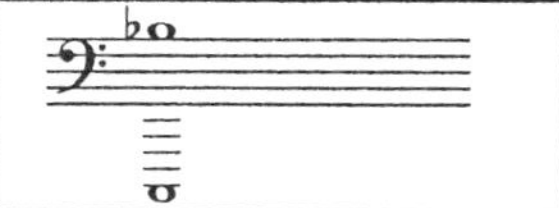
Percussion Instruments	snare drum, bass drum, sus. cymbal, crash cymbal, finger cymbal, bells, xylophone, 2 timpani (26",29"), triangle, woodblock, tambourine, claves, maracas, cowbell, sleigh bells, temple blocks	Add: tom-toms, timbales, gong, tam-tam, chimes, guiro, castanets, shaker, rachet, vibraslap, mark tree, wind chimes, flexatone	Add: piano, vibraphone, 2 timpani (23",32"), conga, tenor drum, whip, marimba, lion's roar, cabasa	Add: crotales, harp, celesta (synthesizer), variety of sizes: membranes, cymbals, trian-gles, woodblocks, tam-tams for special effects	All percussion instruments, including wide range of special effects

Chart input & layout–Angel McDonald ©Moonworks 2001

FIGURE 9.

Suggested Articulations, Phrasings and Rhythms

FIGURE 10.

Teaching Enjoyment and Understanding through "Listening"

The fifth content area presents the need for each and every ensemble to experience "listening" to music. The purpose of this emphasis is to stress the importance of developing appreciation and understanding of music by listening to varied sounds, ensembles, and interpretations of the music being performed. There is more than just "hearing" the music. Often groups achieve exceptional levels of performance and develop no appreciation or understanding of what they performed. The emphasis on listening can assist in helping create lifelong consumers of music as well as performers. All too often, by not teaching the listening and appreciation aspects of the music we rehearse and perform, we are in danger of creating a population of artistic performers with little or no desire to consume or enjoy other performances.

The National Standards for Arts Education strongly endorses the listening process in music. "Because music is an integral part of human history, the ability to listen with understanding is essential if students are to gain a broad cultural and historical perspective. The adult life of every student is enriched by the skills, knowledge, and habits acquired in the study of music."[14]

As stated by Aaron Copland in *What to Listen For In Music*:

If you want to understand music better, you can do nothing more important than to listen to it. Nothing can possibly take the place of listening to music...

Music begins with a composer; passes through the medium of an interpreter; and ends with you, the listener. Everything in music may be said, in the final analysis, to be directed by you—the listener. Therefore, to listen intelligently, you must clearly understand not only your own role but also that of composer and interpreter and what each one contributes to the sum total of a musical experience (15, 158).[15]

Teaching how to become a good listener is very important in the process of developing musicianship. Craig Wright in *Listening to Music* says:

Listening to music is an art, and like all the arts it requires preparation and discipline. Part of the preparation involves learning what to listen for and what to expect in music. For this, we must have some knowledge of how music works. How do melodies unfold? How do musical phrases work together to mark the progress of a piece? How does a composer get from one section to the next, and how does he or she signal that the conclusion is near?[16]

In volume 2, chapter 5 of *Teaching Music through Performance in Band*—"Whole Brain Listening"—Eugene Corporon provides an extensive discussion regarding the role of critical and analytical "listening" in rehearsal and performance (69–90). Readers are encouraged to review his in-depth presentation.

> A basic premise of this book is *the more you know about the music, the greater your achievement and enjoyment will be.* While there are a number of important issues which go into successful musicing, none is more central or crucial than listening. The ability to *hear what is so* is key to learning and teaching a composition. As the person in charge, we are responsible for creating, molding, and shaping the listener's perceptions of the work of art.
>
> There is no doubt that our decision making influences what our performers and audiences *hear.* We must be able to help others hear what we hear and catch sight of our imagined vision. In other words, what is heard in the mind's ear and seen in the mind's eye must be transmitted in order to guide the listening and seeing of others.
>
> Before we can teach people how to play the piece, we have to teach them how to hear the music. Webster's dictionary defines the word "listen" as "to make a conscientious effort to hear." "Hear" is defined as "to become aware of, to notice, to pay attention to, to learn about." The goal is to help people *hear* what they are *listening* to (72).[17]

Find opportunities to actively engage in critical, analytical, and appreciative "listening" experiences in rehearsal. Consider listening to recorded excerpts played before and following rehearsals. Listen to performances of varied interpretations during rehearsal and/or consider playing recordings of a similar performance style. Also, consider listening to references with correct style or appropriate balance for the historical period, etc. Appreciation and understanding through "listening" should become primary instructional goals to accompany the performance process.

Assessment

Review the suggestions on assessment as presented by Larry Blocher in "The Assessment of Student Learning in Band" in *Teaching Music through Performance in Band*, volume 1 (27–29). He states:

> Selecting an appropriate assessment procedure to determine the musical "it" that students learned during the rehearsal and performance process, and deciding how to use this information, involve informed decision-making by band directors. Informed decision-making about assessment in a performance setting forces band directors to ask "what is it that I want my students to learn and remember from the rehearsal

and performance experience in band?" When the band rehearsal and performance are viewed as an opportunity for teaching the skills and knowledge required for musical performance and musical understanding, any number of assessment strategies may be appropriate.[18]

Conclusion

In closing, "Rehearsing" and "Teaching"—both aspects presented together may lead to more performer involvement and musical fulfillment. In volume 1 of *Teaching Music through Performance in Band*, Tim Lautzenheiser presents the essential element of a successful band. It is "The Teacher, The Conductor, The Director, The Leader." He states:

> The integration of substantive content and sensitive context is the key to success for any exemplary educator. In the field of music it is an absolute necessity. Bringing the data to the students is only one step in the growth process; presenting it in a fashion they understand and appreciate is equally challenging.

> The *art of music* combined with the *art of teaching* creates a forum of opportunity for every aspiring musician. It is necessary to bring both of these components to the rehearsal room if we expect to achieve our professional goals of *teaching music through performance in band.*[19]

> Components for teacher success can be measured, taught, learned, and, generally, blended into every rehearsal. There is no mystery. What has been labeled as charisma is merely an execution of various behavioral patterns carefully timed to focus young performers in a purposeful direction. The art of teaching, much like the art of music, is based on the strategic use of personality characteristics every educator can master.

> The great conductors are passionately devoted to their art form. They love the music, they love their students, and they are driven to share this passion with everyone. We authors tip our hats in thankful admiration and appreciation to exemplary models of teaching expertise. Outstanding mentors continue to set the standards for the profession as they passionately develop the leaders of tomorrow by *Teaching Music through Perfomance in Band* today.[20]

Recommended Sources

The following can help guide the reader in a more in-depth and informed perspective of the many ideas presented in this chapter.

Ensemble Musicianship Development and Rehearsal Sources

Erickson, Frank. *The Artistry of Fundamentals for Band*. Van Nuys, CA: Alfred Publishing Co., 1992.

Fussell, Raymond C. *Exercises for Ensemble Drill*. Minneapolis, MN: Paul A. Schmitt Music Company, 1967.

Hovey, Nilo. *TIPPS for Band*. Van Nuys, CA: Alfred Publishing Co. (Belwin Mills), 1959.

Kohut, Daniel L. *Instrumental Music Pedagogy*. Englewood Cliffs, NJ: Prentice-Hall, Inc., 1973.

Lake, Mayhew, arr. *Sixteen Chorales by J.S. Bach*. Milwaukee, WI: Hal Leonard/G. Schirmer, 1938.

Moore, Stephen, *Rhythm Rulz*. CD-ROM (volumes 1 and 2), DVD (software). Fort Collins, CO: Beyond The Notes, Inc., 2005.

Ployhar, James D. *I Recommend*. Van Nuys, CA: Alfred Publishing Co. (Byron Douglas/Belwin Mills), 1972.

Ployhar, James D. and George B. Zepp. *Tone and Technique through Chorales and Etudes*. Miami, FL: Belwin Mills, 1985.

Smith, Claude T. *Symphonic Warm-Ups for Band*, Milwaukee, WI: Hal Leonard Corporation (for Jenson Publications), 1982.

Williams, Richard and Jeff King. *Foundations for Superior Performance*. San Diego, CA: Neil A. Kjos Music Company, 1997.

Special Instructional Resources and Teaching Texts

Camphouse, Mark, ed. *Composers on Composing for Band, Volume 1*. Chicago, IL: GIA Publications, 2002.

_____. *Composers on Composing for Band, Volume 2*. Chicago, IL: GIA Publications, 2004.

_____. *Composers on Composing for Band, Volume 3*. Chicago, IL: GIA Publications, 2007.

Casey, Joseph L. *Teaching Techniques and Insights for Instrumental Music Educators*. Revised Edition. Chicago, IL: GIA Publications, 1993.

Cooper, Lynn G. *Teaching Band & Orchestra*. Chicago, IL: GIA Publications, 2004.

Ericksen, Connie M. *Band Director's Curriculum Resource (Ready-to-Use Lessons & Worksheets for Teaching Music Theory)*. West Nyack, NY: Parker Publishing Company, 1998.

Fieldstein, Sandy, ed. *A Practical Guide for Recruitment and Retention* (with CD). Music Achievement Council, 2006.

Fraedrich, Eileen. *The Art of Elementary Band Directing*. Ft. Lauderdale, FL: Meredith Music Publications, 1997.

Garofalo, Robert J. *Blueprint for Band—A Guide to Teaching Comprehensive Musicianship through School Band Performance*. Ft. Lauderdale, FL: Meredith Music Publications, 1983.

_____. *Guides to Band Masterworks, Volume 1*. Ft. Lauderdale, FL: Meredith Music Publications, 1992.

_____. *Instructional Designs for Middle/Junior High School Band—Guides to Band Masterworks, Volume 2*. Ft. Lauderdale, FL: Meredith Music Publications, 1995.

_____. *Rehearsal Handbook for Band and Orchestra Students*. Ft. Lauderdale, FL: Meredith Music Publications, 1983.

Hutton, Cynthia. "BANDWORLD Grading Chart Revision." Lecture Demonstration Document TMUS 8269, Unpublished Document, University of Colorado College of Music, 2000.

_____. "BANDWORLD Grading Chart Revision." Ashland, OR: BAND-WORLD, 2000.

Labuta, Joseph A. *Basic Conducting Techniques*, 5th ed. Upper Saddle River, NJ: Prentice Hall, 2004.

_____. *Teaching Musicianship in the High School Band*, rev. ed. Ft. Lauderdale, FL: Meredith Music Publications, 1997.

Lisk, Edward S. *The Creative Director: Alternative Rehearsal Techniques*, 3rd ed. Ft. Lauderdale, FL: Meredith Music Publications, 1991.

McBeth, W. Francis. *Effective Performance of Band Music*. San Antonio, TX: Southern Music Company, 1972.

Miles, Richard B. and Larry R. Blocher. *Scheduling and Teaching Music*. Chicago, IL: GIA Publications, 1999.

Miles, Richard, ed. *Teaching Music through Performance in Band* (a series of ten band texts and accompanying CD recordings). Chicago, IL: GIA Publications, 1997–2008.

Miller, William. *Band Director Secrets of Success*. N. Alan Clark, ed. Lakeland, FL: Aiton Publishing, 1997.

Nowak, Jerry and Henry Nowak. *The Art of Expressive Playing*. New York, NY: Carl Fischer, 2004.

Pegram, Wayne F. *Practical Guidelines for Developing the High School Band*. West Nyack, NY: Parker Publishing Company, Inc., 1973.

Prescott, Gerald R. and Lawrence W. Chidester. *Getting Results with School Bands*. Minneapolis MN: Paul A. Schmitt Music Co., 1938.

Rapp, Willis M. *The Wind Band Masterworks of Holst, Vaughan Williams, & Grainger*. Ft. Lauderdale, FL: Meredith Music Publications, 2005.

Salzman, Timothy, ed. *A Composer's Insight: Thoughts, Analysis and Commentary on Contemporary Masterpieces for Wind Band, Volume 1*. Ft. Lauderdale, FL: Meredith Music Publications, 2003.

_____. *A Composer's Insight: Thoughts, Analysis and Commentary on Contemporary Masterpieces for Wind Band, Volume 2*. Ft. Lauderdale, FL: Meredith Music Publications, 2004.

_____. *A Composer's Insight: Thoughts, Analysis and Commentary on Contemporary Masterpieces for Wind Band, Volume 3*. Ft. Lauderdale, FL: Meredith Music Publications, 2006.

_____. *A Composer's Insight: Thoughts, Analysis and Commentary on Contemporary Masterpieces for Wind Band, Volume 4*. Galesville, MD: Meredith Music Publications/Hal Leonard, 2008.

Stycos, Roland, *Listening Guides for Band Musicians*. Portland, ME: J. Weston Walch Publisher, 1991.

Music in the Middle/Junior High School. Albany, NY: The University of the State of New York/The State Education Department/Bureau of Curriculum Department, 1988.

VanderCook, H. A. *Expression in Music*. Milwaukee, WI: Hal Leonard Corporation (Rubank) Revised Edition, 1942.

Williamson, John E., comp. and Ken Neidig, ed. *Rehearsing the Band*. Cloudcroft, NM: Neidig Services, 1998.

Wise, Philip C. *So…You're the New Band Director: Now, What?* Oskalossa, IA: C. L. Barnhouse Company, 1996.

Inspirational Teaching and Leadership Development Sources

Lautzenheiser, Tim. *Everyday Wisdom for Inspired Teaching*. Chicago, IL: GIA Publications, 2005.

_____. *Music Advocacy and Student Leadership (Key of Every Successful Music Program)*. Chicago, IL: GIA Publications, 2005.

_____. *The Art of Successful Teaching: A Blend of Content & Context*. Chicago, IL: GIA Publications, 1992.

_____. *The Joy of Inspired Teaching*. Chicago, IL: GIA Publications, 1993.

Web Resources

Wisconsin Comprehensive Musicianship through Performance Project. Includes CMP teaching plans.
http://www.wmea.com/CMP/publications/insight/25years.html

Teaching Music through Performance. GIA Publications. Includes recordings and instructional resources. http://www.teachingmusic.org/

The Wind Repertory Project by Nikk Pilato. Includes instructional resources and information on literature for winds. http://www.windrep.org/

NBA Selective Music List, 2008. The National Band Association. Includes a very large graded listing of works for band. http://www.nationalbandassociation.org/

SmartMusic: Educational Software for Music Teachers and Students. A commercial site that offers individual instrument parts for the band music, and
options for students to perform with the pre-recorded band music:

http://www.smartmusic.com/

Endnotes

1 Ray Cramer, "What Materials Are You Going to Use to Teach 'About Music'
   'Through Music' While 'Performing Music?'" Teaching Music through Performance
   in Band, Volume 1 (Chicago, IL: GIA Publications, 1997), 9–10.
2 Richard Miles and Larry Blocher, Scheduling and Teaching Music (Chicago, IL: GIA
   Publications, 1999).
3 Daniel L. Kohut, Instrumental Music Pedagogy (Englewood Cliffs, NJ: Prentice-Hall,
   Inc., 1973), 226.
4 Joseph A. Labuta, Basic Conducting Techniques, 5th ed. (Upper Saddle River, NJ:
   Prentice Hall, 2004), 92–94.
5 Eugene Corporon, "The Quantam Conductor." Teaching Music through Performance
   in Band, Volume 1 (Chicago, IL: GIA Publications, 1997), 18–23.
6 Richard Miles, ed. Teaching Music through Performance in Band, Volume 1
   (Chicago, IL: GIA Publications, 1997), 36.
7 Ibid.
8 Raymond C. Fussell, Exercises for Ensemble Drill (Minneapolis, MN: Paul A.
   Schmitt Music Company, 1967), 40–42.
9 Miles, 36.
10 Richard Miles, ed. Teaching Music through Performance in Band, Volume 3
   (Chicago, IL: GIA Publications, 2000), 42–43.
11 Ibid, 68.
12 Cynthia Hutton, "BANDWORLD Grading Chart Revision." Lecture Demonstration
   Document TMUS 8269 (Boulder, CO: Unpublished Document University of
   Colorado, 2000), 32.
   _____. "BANDWORLD Grading Chart Revision." Ashland, OR:
   BANDWORLD, 2000.
13 Gerald R. Prescott and Lawrence W. Chidester, Getting Results with School Bands
   (Minneapolis, MN: Paul A. Schmitt Music Company, 1938), 77.
14 National Standards for Arts Education, (Reston, VA: Music Educators National
   Conference, 1994), 59.
15 Aaron Copland, What to Listen for in Music, rev. ed. (New York, NY: The
   American Library, 1957), 15, 158.
16 Craig Wright, Listening to Music, Third Edition (Toronto, ON, Canada: Wadsworth,
   a Division of Thomson Learning, 2000), 1–2.
17 Eugene Corporon, "Whole Brain Listening." Teaching Music through Performance
   in Band, Volume 2 (Chicago, IL: GIA Publications, 1997), 72.
18 Larry Blocher, "The Assessment of Student Learning in Band." Teaching Music
   through Performance in Band, Volume 1 (Chicago, IL: GIA Publications, 1997), 30.
19 Tim Lautzenheiser, "The Essential Element to a Successful Band: The Teacher • The
   Conductor • The Director • The Leader." Teaching Music through Performance in
   Band, Volume 1 (Chicago, IL: GIA Publications, 1997) 57.
20 Ibid, 66.Exercises for Ensemble Drill

CHAPTER 4

The Cornerstones for Program Success

Tim Lautzenheiser

Author's note

We all know there is no guaranteed "instant success" formula in the field of music education. Everyone has to go through a pathway of self-discovery, and it is often not an easy journey. Our colleges and universities continue to prepare some of the finest aspiring young artists, many of whom have indicated they want to commit their lives to the world of band, choir, or orchestra education. While some of these candidates do become lifetime members of the music world, far too many leave the teaching ranks after a very short tenure.

Why? After many personal interviews (with some of many of these one- or two-year veterans), it is apparent their choice to seek a new career had little to do with their love of music, but rather with their perceived sense of ineffectiveness in dealing with the overwhelming ""responsibilities off the podium.

In most cases, the beginning educator felt well prepared to embrace the rigors of "teaching music," and, in fact, pointed to this aspect of the teaching schedule as *the best part of the school day*. However, dealing with *all else* was simply more than they could bear...and, sadly, the passion for teaching music became secondary to vocational survival.

We have discovered there are many who have profited from a close association with a seasoned teacher who assumes the role of a mentor, guide, coach, trusted listener, loyal friend, etc. With this option at hand, the new teacher has a reliable source of information offering a tried-and-proven set of possible answers to a myriad of questions. Those who have been to the well have much valid advice to bring to the forum, and in many cases it has been the saving factor.

Please read the following thoughts knowing the data is derived from "observing" many of the finest master teachers in the profession. By no means

will a bird's eye view of five select cornerstone success-components shift the course of anyone's teaching habits, but it can alert the reader to the opportunities possible in every musical teaching and learning environment.

By definition, a *cornerstone is*:

- something that is essential, indispensable, or basic
- the chief foundation on which something is constructed or developed

Introduction

Why do we teach music? It is one the first philosophical inquiries serving as an introductory question for every music education student, and it is also one we all must revisit time and time again. Countless books, essays, and research documents have been devoted to this important query, and, perhaps, our challenge is to recognize the collective value of all these important contributions. Through this process we then develop and create our own sense of purpose.

Simply put:

> We are educating students in the realm of music literacy so they can connect to and tap the unlimited potential of their creative minds. Our educational goal is to teach the mastery of musical skills, so our students can access quality music and experience the joy of an ever-evolving sense of aesthetic expression.

There are certainly many spinoff benefits garnered by students involved in music learning and music making. By being in a first-class music program, they develop better organizational abilities, learn the value of teamwork, have the opportunity to test their leadership talents, and embellish many life skills that will serve them in every aspect of their personal and professional journey. These are *all* positive by-products generated via the music ensemble experience, However, they do not constitute the fundamental *why* of our efforts and energies.

We teach music because it is, unto itself, a standalone academic subject. Music touches a part of our psyche that helps us regulate our lives. Music helps us understand and express our moods and attitudes. Music helps us reorganize our thoughts and feelings while keeping us on track. Music allows us to respond appropriately in social structures that are often confusing and complex. Participation in music avails the musician of the infinite journey of creative expression, connecting to a language understood, communicated, and appreciated by all humankind around the globe. *Music for the sake of music*.

What role does the director, conductor, teacher, and/or mentor play in bringing this philosophical blueprint to fruition? Why do some programs thrive while others struggle to survive? Isn't it a combination of the message and the messenger? We all know the immeasurable value of the message; let us begin to investigate the key elements of the successful messenger. What have these master teachers (messengers) discovered, and what can we learn from studying and replicating their templates of success?

Observation

After four decades of working with some of the finest music programs in the world, it has become obvious there are marked likenesses that serve as part of the predictable framework of the successful band, choir, or orchestra program, and much of it is directly linked to directors and their approach to the art of teaching music. Above all, these people are dedicated students of musical growth; never arriving, always seeking, searching, and learning.

The following pages of this text reveal five off-the-podium cornerstone teaching areas that are found in many, perhaps most, of the outstanding music educators. While they all have a unique style, the following "cornerstones" are predictably evident in all.

Cornerstone 1: Continuing Education

I began my education at a very early age—in fact, right after I left college.
—Winston Churchill, 1874–1965

With modern technology and the ongoing exchange of breakthrough data, the educational process (school) is not something we do, but it is something we *continue to do* throughout our lives; it is never-ending, and is gaining momentum at warp speed.

Veteran educators are clearly aware "that the more we know, the more we know we don't know." Therefore it is necessary to constantly seek out the latest trends, techniques, discoveries, improvements, and educational bene-fits. It can be both exhilarating and exhausting, but it is a condition that is here to stay.

It is so easy and tempting to ignore the latest contributions, from the newest literature to technological breakthroughs. 'It is far easier to "do it the way we've always done it"—to not complicate the agenda with all this "new stuff" that really has not stood the test of time (often a convenient ratio-nalization)—than it is to venture into the realm of the unknown. It is also much safer, but how can our students grow unless we grow? Shouldn't we be the role models of and for ongoing self-improvement?

Times are changing. Unlike days gone by, the teacher is no longer in a position of being THE all-knowing expert. Our students in many instances are more technological savvy than we are.

The Winston Churchill quote above is a wonderful bit of wisdom: we must heed the message within. "The completion of college requisites and the celebration of our graduation merely provides the gateway to the commencement—the commencing, beginning, or start—of our real education." Today's master teachers are also today's master students as they embrace the responsibilities of their awareness.

Cornerstone 2: The Value of Time

The one equalizing factor in this world is *time*. We all have twenty-four hours in the day—no more, no less. We can't bank it or save it, we either spend it or lose it. It's not a matter of "trying to get more time," but rather "managing the time" we have. What are the secrets to effective and efficient time management?

Make "Teacher-Only" Responsibilities a Prioirty

We often confuse "busy" with "productive." All too often we are busy, but we are not necessarily productive. It is easy to get caught in escape activities and, in turn, lose valuable time. It's important to focus on "teacher-only" tasks and develop a team of volunteers to take on other aspects of the work agenda.

Stuffing music folders, setting up chairs and stands, taking attendance, etc., can be accomplished by a select group of student leaders and/or officers. It is beneficial to take the time to teach someone else the "right way" to prepare music folders and the rehearsal room for the upcoming class. The rewards are twofold: students embrace more ownership of the ensemble's success, and the conductor/director is now free to spend his time learning the musical score along with other "teacher-only" duties (areas where the educator's expertise is wanted and needed).

All of this is so apparent, and yet from time to time, most of us find ourselves living in a sense of urgency because we do not have enough *time*. Why does this dilemma exist in the first place? The world of psychology suggests we subconsciously avoid more difficult responsibilities because:

1. *Doing less-challenging duties helps us avoid the disappointment we experience in unknown territory*. In other words, it is more comfortable and less taxing to stuff music folders and organize music stands than it is to analyze the thematic material of a new composition. We are not as likely to fail or feel as inadequate; it's an attempt to feed our sense of accomplishment, but the impact is short-lived. Avoidance is a human

condition; it is not that we do not know what to do, rather, we simply do not want to do it; in turn we look for opportunities that will divert our focus and still keep us busy.

2. *If we complete all the work there is to do, we might become dispensable;* we will not be needed. Therefore we must ensure we have a long list of responsibilities yet to accomplish. Subconsciously we really fear completion might jeopardize our perception of existence. Of course the irony is, the moment we finish one project, two new ones appear instantly. Every master teacher knows that the more we do, the more there is to do.

A review of these two conditions suggests we are effected by our own choices. If so, then we have the wherewithal to shift our emphasis and dedicate our time, effort, and energy to "teacher-only" obligations and duties so we can have a greater impact on our programs.

Acclaimed author and time-management consultant Stephen R. Covey offers several suggestions we can easily tailor to our teaching situations. The following checklist is an adaptation designed to accommodate the music educator in supporting a healthy program.

1. *What needs to be done right now?* What has to be accomplished immediately to meet a deadline and avoid a crisis situation?

2. *Does the task require personal attention or can it be assigned?* If it can be delegated to a responsible person, do so and move ahead to the next responsibility on the list.

3. *Is the energy being used within a personal sphere of influence to produce a positive result?* Beware of spinning your wheels; don't waste time if you don't sense forward motion.

4. *Is there an alternative way to create better results?* Avoid the "we've always done it this way" pattern of thinking.

5. *Does it feed the mission of excellence?* If not, do not do it.

No, this prioritizing template will not solve every problem, but it will clear up much of the confusion that prevents us from making logical choices concerning the investment of our time. It is also brings with it a tone of honesty so we are not tempted to fall into the all-too-familiar trap of *we don't have enough time.*

Avoid Communication Bottlnecks

In any ensemble class or rehearsal we must measure quantum time. If there are fifty people in the room and someone asks a question, the amount of time needed to respond (to complete the conversation) must be multiplied by fifty. For example: Two minutes devoted to a verbal exchange concerning a misprint in the second clarinet part is really one hundred minutes of used time. (Two minutes multiplied by fifty people equals one hundred minutes of "product potential.") This is not to say the problem should be ignored, but if it can be resolved outside the priceless ensemble time, it will be to everyone's advantage.

Establish a Culture of Excellence

From the moment young musicians walk into the room until the end of rehearsal, there should be a detailed plan for the most advantageous use of time. It is important to create, maintain, and support an attitude of positive learning through the establishment of a safe, challenging, and encouraging environment that reflects and respects the integrity of the musical art form. Unfortunately much time can be squandered because the expectation of excellence has not been properly explained (and reinforced) for the members of the organization. It is imperative we link self-discipline and group maturity to culture of the learning climate. (This is not to thwart the social aspect of the ensemble experience; however, rehearsal time *is* for rehearsal; 'use the time accordingly.)

Conerstone 3: Emphasizing the Why

The good teacher tells.
The excellent teacher explains and demonstrates.
The master teacher inspires.
—William Arthur Ward

Ward's words ring true in every aspect of our educational community; and perhaps they are most vivid in the world of music education. If we analyze the wisdom of his quote, we can apply it to our daily teaching habits and help us create a healthy atmosphere supporting the entire spectrum of music learning, music making, and music listening.

The Good Teacher Tells: The What

The very essence of educational process is "passing information from one source or mind (the teacher) to another source or mind (the student)." This represents the *what* in the curriculum. From "What year did Columbus land on the shores of America" to "What is wrong with the intonation in the low brass section," we are all trained to bring to our classrooms and rehearsals rooms a library of evolving valuable data (the *what*) to expand and improve the lives of our students. Even as we continue our own education via workshops, graduate school, seminars, conventions clinics, etc., we add to our own informational library. We know more *what*.

However, if all we do is *tell* our students this important data without holding them accountable for integrating it into their lives, we may be nothing more than yet another source of facts and figures. The overriding question is, "Is the material communicated in a way our students will realize it has a positive impact in relation to their well-being"? Rather, is it relevant to their lives, and does it have a lasting effect? Most certainly the *what* is a crucial foundation block, but we certainly cannot stop at this point in the process.

The Excellent Teacher Explains and Demonstrates: The How

This area of music education is one of the most exciting, since our discipline begs for explanation and demonstration. Successful music teachers know ""that hands-on learning processes are required for high-level achievement. We simply do not instruct *what* to do, but we show our students *how* to do it. We are participants as we sing, play, or explain by performing a phrase on a chosen instrument. Not only do we address the *how* of each vital skill, we *demonstrate* the tone we are seeking, the needed style, and the musical picture we are trying to paint. The class or rehearsal requires so much more than simply "telling students *what* to do"; it is a matter of discovering countless ways to *explain* the various avenues of efficiently and effectively reaching the given goal.

The Master Teacher Inspires: The Why

To inspire: to establish a creative atmosphere where the students are "in the spirit" of the moment and can express themselves in a way they far exceeds the *doing*, but begins to connect with the *feeling*. This is the *why* of learning. It is taking the *what*, combining it with the *how*, and venturing into a new realm of *why*. Master educators know when young musicians connect with *why*, they are making music; it is then that the motivation to strive for a higher level of proficiency takes on a whole new meaning. It triggers the intrinsic desire of the learner, and this opens the floodgates of expression for a lifetime.

As music educators we have a direct line to the inner emotions of our students. Much of the school day is "impressionistic" (i.e., learning the information and replicating it on a test). But music is "expressionistic." All members of the class or ensemble has the opportunity to bring their emotions to musical portrait; all have a unique value and play a key role in the creative process; all contribute their *spirit* to the musical community.

Unquestionably, any master teacher will use a combination of both intrinsic and extrinsic motivation techniques to bring student musicians to a higher level of technical proficiency, but—when all is said and done—the dominant motivation will come from the performers. It is their collective contribution that fuels the journey of musical excellence. The key to tapping the unlimited resource of human potential lies in the understanding of *why* we are being asked to do *what* we are being asked to do, and knowing *how* to accomplish the given task.

For Our Students

We must carefully explain the *why* so students can be empowered to contribute with the understanding of the personal and group benefits that will come from their invested efforts.

For Our Professional Welfare

We must take the time to step back and constantly look at the *why* of our thoughts and actions. Boredom, frustration, and burnout are the result of becoming disconnected with our reasons *why* we chose to be directors and conductors in the first place.

For Our Parents and Boosters

Do these great supporters *really* understand the lasting impression of music learning? Are they cognizant of the compelling data highlighting the extended benefits of music study? There is more to this than joining the band, buying an instrument, and attending concerts; far more. We have to make available to them *why* music is such a crucial aspect of the positive growth and development of every child.

For the Health of the Program

Let us be reminded we are privileged to be a part of an educational system that supports music education…and we get to teach it! Chosen musical standards determine how our students approach all situations they face, and when they understand *why* we set bar so high, they will also see the importance it plays in every facet of their lives.

What is about presenting information; *how* requires explanation and demonstration; *why* is the gateway to inspiration.

Cornerstone 4: Music for All: Sharing the Good News

How many people are aware of the following?

> Music learning activates various areas of the brain and synchronizes the mind for learning at a fast pace while stretching the memory to a higher level of retention. Music enhances cognitive learning and facilitates growth in many areas of mind development. As we learn more about the integration of emotional intelligence and cognitive learning patterns, it is ever apparent the study of music has a direct relationship to the measured success of the individual/student via reasoning, creative thinking, decision-making, and problem solving.

How many people should be aware of this information? We must bring this to the attention of everyone.

Like it or not, politics and education often go hand in hand. Since the school culture represents our most valuable natural commodity (children), it has a high priority on every political agenda. Veteren teachers know there is always a new and improved academic blueprint linked to every candidate's platform. From Back to the Basics to No Child Left Behind, each administration offers a new conceptual perspective certain to raise the level of learning for all students. The seasoned professional is often leery (and weary) of the latest slick phrase designed to attract the public's attention. In the ongoing commentary taking place in faculty lounges throughout our country there is an opportunity for us as music educators to establish a strong foothold highlighting the importance of music and arts education as it relates to positive development of the whole child.

Since administrators are being measured and evaluated on how well students score on various tests, school curriculums are being designed so every aspect of the learning process can be assessed in some fashion. While we can test, measure, and assess certain skills required for musical achievement, we are at a disadvantage when compared to a subject that is strictly cognitive in nature (i.e., math, history, English, etc.). If we are to justify the existence of music as part of the daily schedule, then we may have to expand our approach to include music advocacy. This is not to suggest we sidestep the obvious— music for the sake of music—but rather to expand the awareness of decision-makers: parents, administrators, colleagues, board of education members, community leaders, and (most importantly) the students themselves.

Since most of us were not trained to be music advocates, it is tempting to simply turn our backs on the ongoing discussions that will ultimately impact our music programs, our school culture, and society's future. If we do so, the fate of music programs is in the hands of those who are making decisions without a complete understanding that the value of music reaches far beyond the holiday concert or the spring festival. While these showcase performances are

certainly a vital aspect of every musical organization, this is only the tip of the iceberg when we stand back and view the impact music learning brings to the entire educational forum.

The following information is compelling, and it needs to be given to those who are responsible for creating curricular mandates.

- Every child has the propensity to be a music-maker. Modern-day technology has allowed brain researchers to determine that music and art is part of our neurobiological system.

- All learning is enhanced via the development of musical mind-maps. Ongoing studies demonstrate the transfer of intellect from music to other areas of academic achievement.

- Music learning continues to be the most efficient and effective pathway to the development of important life skills, including problem solving, creativity, decision-making, and reasoning.

- The development of emotional intelligence is one of the strongest outcomes of music study. It prepares the student in the areas of social skills, self-discipline, time management, and aesthetic appreciation. Simply put, it teaches one how to be a sensitive and cooperative individual.

- Studying music develops thinking that encourages the exploration of the unknown, develops social harmony, requires alternative thinking habits, encourages multiple perspectives, and helps diminish survival prejudices. Successful music-making requires an emphasis on cooperation rather than competition.

In our efforts to avoid any contamination of our philosophical foundation, we may be prone to sidestep the indirect benefits of music study. However if we truly believe music is central to all learning, it is imperative that we not only embrace the latest data, but we tout it to those who will determine every facet of the school day from the hourly schedule to faculty assignments.

As stated, we are trained to be music teachers, not music advocates. While many colleges and universities are integrating music advocacy as a key component of various requisite classes, it is still foreign territory to most. However, if we, as music educators, are not the outspoken proponents for music education, who will be?

Cornerstone 5: The Master Teacher's Top Ten (or Everyday Wisdom for Being an Exemplary Role Model)

Pilots have a mandatory checklist they must go through before they are allowed to take off. It is designed to protect their lives and the lives of their passengers. Even the most seasoned flyers are required to walk through each of these requisites before leaving the ground. Perhaps it would be equally as effective if we, as music educators, had a similar checklist, a series of reminders to protect the lives of our musical passengers.

Know the Value of Personal Energy

Music is energy supported by aural motion. Whether it is the energy the teacher exudes from the podium, or the energy required to sustain a rigorous class schedule, meet performance demands, or take care of organizational obligations, the time-on-task for a music teacher is never-ending. We must face the fact the music teacher sets the pace for all students who are part of our ensembles and classes.

Express Appreciation

In every situation we are either appreciating or depreciating our environment, the given climate, and the atmosphere around us. When we appreciate a student, colleague, administrator, or parent, we lift ourselves as well as the recipient of the acknowledgement. In turn when we depreciate those around us with sarcasm or cynicism, we simultaneously chip away at our own self-confidence. Successful educators are quick to recognize and support individual and group growth, while also focusing on areas where improvement is wanted and needed. Musical success is an ever-changing combination of positive reinforcement (appreciation) strategically mixed with the never-ending quest for excellence.

Exemplify Optimism

Every student wants to be a member of a quality organization. Successful teachers always find victories throughout the process of learning. Since music is a language of expression, it affords the learner to feel as well as think. To be discouraging (removing the courage) may push the student away from the goal, whereas encouragement (creating the presence of courage) will oftentimes serve as the needed momentum for the student to embrace the challenges at hand. We certainly want avoid false praise (a shallow and dangerous tool), but we must always strive to establish an optimistic approach to tackling curricular objectives.

Avoid the Game of Comparison

We live in a competitive society, and—like it or not—we have auditions for chair placements, elections for officers, tryouts for solos, etc. Despite these built-in traditions, successful educators focus on intrinsic motivation (the opportunity to learn and to make great music) rather than extrinsic motivation (the chance to score higher than the neighboring school at a festival). If the goal is to reach a high level of musical performance, then the emphasis is on the process rather than the product. If the process is supported by the theme of quality music making, the product or outcome will reflect the investment.

Put People First

Taken directly from Stephen Covey's bestseller, *Seven Habits for Highly Successful People,* "Choose to understand before being understood." Each day we have budding young artists in front of us with one burning question in their inquisitive minds: "What will we do in music class or rehearsal today?" These special students chose to be in music because they want to play or sing; they want to express. When they sense we are confident about their abilities (as well as our own) and that we care for them as fellow musicians, the possibilities are limited only by the imagination.

Be Willing to Fail

This paradoxical concept is one of the masked secrets of successful people. We know failure is part of the pathway to outstanding achievement. Growth, in any aspect of life, requires risk-taking; one must enter the realm of the unknown and be willing to be disappointed while refusing to turn back until there is a sense of satisfaction that only comes from attaining a new understanding and a greater awareness of the possibilities at hand. To be in a state of creativity we must relinquish control and overcome fear. In essence, we must persevere in our ongoing climb to a new summit of quality regardless of the number of times we stumble and fall. Persistence is our most important companion in this quest.

Think Creatively

We live in a fast-paced society; our students are programmed to move quickly; therefore we must open our minds to new ways of thinking and being. If we do not, we are doomed to: remain the same: status quo, predictable, boring, simply going through the motions, stale. Rich rewards go to those who stand back and see the bigger picture, seek new opportunities, and look for ways to create artistic and emotional beauty within the learning environment. We must put meaning into everything by interpreting the present so it serves as a guide the future. This determines whether we flourish or flounder. Creative thinking can be the turning point in bringing new life to our programs.

Maintain a Healthy Sense of Humor

Unfortunately, many have linked "sense of humor" with "lack of substance." In the communication world, humor is the shortest distance between two people. Let's not confuse humor with flippancy, silliness or mere entertainment; humor is the way the human psyche creates emotional release. One of the traits of superior teaching is the ability to efficiently and effectively connect with students, and there are certainly times when a hearty laugh or an amusing tale will serve as the best teaching tool. And, above all, we must be able to laugh at ourselves. Teachers are humans, and humans make mistakes, so we must be willing to join in the laughter when we stub our toes. Then we can take a deep breath and get back to work. Humor is a lubricant of the mind and soul; keep smiling, and everything will run much smoother.

Demonstrate Professionalism

Self-improvement is ongoing, and true professionals are always striving yet never arriving, but continued growth is evident, and it is mirrored in and by ensemble members. Role modeling is arguably still one of the most effective forms of teaching. That being the case, we have much to offer through our dress, language, demeanor, and every aspect of our chosen behavior. Here is the opportunity to allow all contributing members of the group to witness the commitment and dedication we expect from them; it is the chance to "walk the talk," and do it with a sense of class and dignity.

Enjoy Teaching Music

Certainly everything on the daily to-do list is not always pleasurable or fun; much of it can be mundane and utilitarian. However, it seems like a small price to pay to have the opportunity to introduce a student to the priceless treasure of music. They cannot duplicate this knowing in any other facet of the educational community. There is no substitute for music; music itself is the reason to master the skills of music making. What greater gift could we possibly bring to young, impressionable minds? Music teachers do make a difference.

Conclusion

Cornerstone: a basic foundation block needed to support the framework of a structure or an ideology.

No doubt there are many key cornerstones supporting the successful music educator. Each of the five chosen for this essay has the wherewithal to be a separate study within itself; volumes could be devoted to a detailed exploration of any and/or all of these concepts. Hopefully the given ideas will initiate further thought, reading, and thinking, and—most importantly—some creative inclusion of these ideas.

In review:

Cornerstone 1: Continuing Education

We know the mind is not limited in its capacity to learn, and the more we bring to our knowing and knowledge, the more we can offer our students. Great teachers have a voracious appetite to continue along their own educational expedition.

Cornerstone 2: The Value of Time

The Declaration of Independence states: "We hold these truth to be self-evident, that all men are created equal...." Certainly one of the equalizing factors is time. It is not a question of, "Do we have enough time?" but rather, "What do we do with the time we have?"

Conerstone 3: Emphasizing the *Why*

Unless we truly can grasp the *why* of *what* we are doing, we may simply be "going through the motions." When we challenge our pedagogical lesson plans to clearly explain the *why*, the outcome of our teaching efforts is dramatically increased.

Cornerstone 4: Music for All: Sharing the Good News

Every human being is "wired to make music." The vast majority of music makers learned the language of music by being involved in a school music program. As we develop the language of musical understanding, we are also creating an archetype of mind capacity for other areas of curricular success. Music makes the difference.

Cornerstone 5: The Master Teacher's Top Ten
(or Everyday Wisdom for Being an Exemplary Role Model)

Everyday wisdoms suggests "a simple, easily understood" menu of ideas, and that is precisely what the fifth cornerstone offers. Wisdom is based on the knowledge of doing what is true or right coupled with good judgment as to the chosen action. The described top ten will serve as a dependable checklist for future success.

In the words of Albert Schweitzer:

I don't know what your destiny will be but one thing I do know, the only ones among you who will be truly happy are those who have sought and found how to serve.

Strike up the Band...

CHAPTER 5

Historical Highlights of the Wind Band: A Heritage and Lineage

Part 2: The French Revolution to the Present

Eugene Migliaro Corporon

This chapter is a continuation of "Historical Highlights of the Wind Band: A Heritage and Lineage Part One: Antiquity to Classical," published in Volume VI that outlines the development of the wind band as a highly artistic and valued performance medium. The goal is not to present a complete history, but rather to focus on some of the historical highlights of wind band development. The material included in these two chapters is information that I hope will become a part of the general knowledge base of the students in my class entitled "The History and Philosophy of the Wind Band." The purpose of the course is to provide an overview of the development of the medium and its repertoire from ancient times to the present and to create an appreciation for the unique contributions that the discipline has made to the art and history of music.

The presentation of the information has been divided into two chapters to accommodate the two-semester structure of my class. The first chapter explores ancient history through the Classical era. The second chapter begins with the French Revolution and works forward to the present. The breadth of this topic is staggering, so by necessity I have had to limit the investigation to what I consider to be the most pivotal moments in time. Admittedly this makes the work very subjective and personal. I encourage all who share an interest in this topic, and wish to delve further into historical accounts for greater detail to consult the resources listed at the end of this chapter in "Read More About It." It is my sincere hope that these chapters will cultivate a respect for the medium and provide an introduction to the time-honored history of the wind band. In the words of the great jazz composer and arranger Quincy Jones, "If you know where you've come from, it's easier to get where you are going."

Nineteenth Century

In his book, *A Concise History of the Wind Band* (St. Louis: Shattinger Music, 1985), David Whitwell outlines three distinct periods of development in the nineteenth century. He offers the following division of dates: the First Period (Political Revolution, 1789–1830), from the French Revolution through the end of the Napoleonic wars, during which an entirely new concept of band is revealed, primarily driven by function rather than aesthetics; the Second Period (Industrial Revolution, 1830–1855), which is full of extraordinary developments in old and new wind instrument types and sees a huge growth in both the size and instrumentation of bands; and the Third Period (Artistic Revolution, 1855–1900), a time that has come to be known as the Golden Age of Bands because of the virtuosity and popularity of wind bands and their expanded growth throughout Europe and the United States.

Political Revolution, 1789–1830 (First Period)

Most authors on the history of wind music agree that the French Revolution gave birth to the modern band. To be more specific, many cite the year 1789 as the beginning of the era. This is the year that the forty-five-member National Guard Band was founded in Paris by Bernard Sarette (1765–1858). Sarette is, without a doubt, one of the most important figures in the history of the modern band. In its first year of existence the group almost doubled in size, registering seventy members by 1790. The ensemble had a long and distinguished history, making it possible for other groups in France and throughout Europe to flourish.

While Sarette can be credited with the administrative direction and success of the band, it was Francois Joseph Gossec (1734–1829) who was responsible for the tremendous musical growth of the organization. His able assistant was Charles Simon Catel (1773–1830). Both of these gentlemen composed for the band and they enlisted the assistance of other composers such as Luigi Cherubini (1760–1842) and Etienne Mehul (1763–1817), who made major contributions to the repertoire. The four of them are often credited with writing some of the first music of serious artistic merit for the modern band. H. G. Farmer, a leading English scholar of military music, offers the following insight regarding the period:

> What contributed most to France's pre-eminence in military music was the need for it. Secondly, it had composers of the mettle of Gossec, Catel, Mehul and Cherubini in command. Thirdly, the band of the National Guard was composed of the greatest virtuosi in Europe.

This group proved to be a very valuable political tool and was acknowledged early on as an effective means of delivering the new government's message to the people. The most notable achievements of this ensemble were: increasing the size of the military band; establishing the clarinet as the main melodic vehicle for the group; the introduction of doubling parts (sometimes many times over); and the politicization of music. Sarette was indeed an extraordinary leader and a true visionary, and his story is integral to the success of the modern band.

Bands in Paris introduced new ideas that set the nineteenth-century wind band on a very different path from its eighteenth-century ancestor, the Harmonie. Harmoniemusik in the courts was declining in the early 1800s, while large military bands were growing and thriving throughout Europe. While previous Harmonie and military groups had between eight and fourteen players, the new ensembles were made up of a minimum of forty-five musicians. Whitwell points out that the increase in size was due more to function than aesthetics. The fact that many of the most important performances during this first period were for massive audiences in the open air necessitated expanding the group so that it could have maximum impact.

Along with size came a richer and more diverse instrumentation. The clarinet emerged as the fundamental melodic vehicle. Oboes and bassoons continued to be integral to the instrumentation, but they were no longer the dominant timbre, as they had been in the Baroque. A logical outcome of expansion was the doubling of parts. This was especially true for the clarinet section. These instrumentalists served a role in the band comparable to that of the violins in an orchestra.

The Garde Republicaine Band of Paris began its life as a civic organization made up of "citizens of the state." This varied greatly from the "aristocratic" wind bands or Harmonie of the eighteenth century. It is important to recall that Les Grande Hautbois (the oboe/bassoon band of Louis the XIV) had provided an aural coat of arms for the King of France for 150 years. It has been suggested that moving away from that sound to one dominated by clarinets in the woodwinds could be construed as a symbolic move away from the monarchy in the direction of the citizens.

The power of the band to politicize music cannot be underestimated. The band became an essential part of the various festivals that played an important role in uniting the citizens and promoting new ideas of freedom in France. The band's ability to ignite and incite the masses did not go unnoticed. Richard Franko Goldman offers the following in his book, *The Wind Band* (Boston: Allyn and Bacon, 1961):

> It was the French Revolution with its great emphasis on popularization and democratization, even of the arts, that produced (in 1789) the Band of the National Guard and the forward movement of band music from that time on.

The National Guard Band played a number of important festivals, memorials, and celebrations. The forces for major events could have included both singers and instrumentalists, and might have numbered in the thousands. They had a tremendous impact on the emotional fervor of the citizens in attendance and were able to communicate the political ideas of the new government to the masses. Because the political success of these events went well beyond the expectations of those in charge, they became highly valued.

An equally important contribution of Sarette and his band was the development of educational institutions. The education of musicians became a necessary part of sustaining the ensemble and its mission. Early support for the band was tied to their festival participation. As this work was not steady or predictable, Sarette called for the establishment of a conservatory or "military music academy" to train musicians for the military. This would also give his professional musicians in the band a source of permanent employment. The Chronique de Paris issued this strong statement of support for Sarette's idea:

> The music of the National Guard deserves to be distinguished by the influence it has had over the Revolution. We would refuse to see what is obvious if we contested this influence and we wouldn't know the consequence of this powerful art if we had not believed that the sums of money for its progress were well used. If we weren't certain of the fact, we would just notice the impressive words of La Fayette who repeated several times that "he owed more to the music of the National Guard than he did to its bayonets."

Sarette was successful in building a consensus for his idea, and on June 8, 1792 the General Council in Paris prepared the order for the creation of a free music school of the Parisian National Guard. This institution was the predecessor of the National Conservatory of Music.

It is interesting that the Paris National Guard Band can be thought of as both a civic and military institution. Sarette remained fluid with this and the history of the ensemble shows its involvement in both camps. By 1793 Sarette had decided that the band's future would be more secure with the French National Government rather than as a civic institution attached to the city of Paris. In order to dramatize his position to create a National Institute of Music, he made a decision to take the entire band into the convention hall on November 8, 1793 to perform. The performance achieved the expected result and the National Institute of Music was established later that year. Sarette's fervor for this new alignment of support can be felt in this excerpt from a public speech that he gave some time after November 8 but prior to the acceptance of his proposal:

Everyone knows the effects of music and the power over the spirit…Instruction is very necessary because not all music prompts the result we expect for the festivals and battles, and further, all instruments must not be used indifferently. The composers discuss their works in the Institute, and they adopt or reject the different characters, which can be given to their compositions according to the expected result. In the same Institute we train the students for performance in our festivals. Others are trained who must be sent to the departments for their festivals or to the armies to entertain the warlike spirit in the garrison and in battle.

Because the public spectacles must be guided in order to excite and keep the republican spirit in the souls of the spectators, music has an important role, and education will help us to place well-trained musicians in these various public festivals…

Because the national holidays can only be held in the open air, stringed instruments cannot be used. The quality of their sound does not allow them to be heard. We must then prefer the wind instruments only, over which the atmosphere does not have the same influence; their volume of sound is eight times greater than the volume of stringed instruments.

Music of Note: New Wine in Old Bottles

While there are many fine works connected to this period (a discography can be found in "Hear More About It" at the end of this chapter), I would like to discuss one piece of particular interest, the *Commemoration Symphony* of 1815 by Anton Reicha (1770–1836). This composition is worthy of special attention because it creates a bridge between the old eighteenth-century Harmonie traditions and the new wind band of the nineteenth century. David Whitwell, editor and publisher of the piece, believes that "This is truly one of the most remarkable large-scale compositions in the history of the wind band."

The bands of the French Revolution grew to massive sizes between 1789 and 1800 to support the plethora of festivals and ceremonies. However, things changed as Napoleon waged war throughout Europe. War was expensive, and he needed to finance his campaigns. Accordingly, Napoleon only permitted larger military bands if the officers assumed responsibility for the expenses. This was a long-standing tradition in the military prior to the revolution. Because the emperor believed in the practicality and effectiveness of trumpet signals for troop movement, he continued to supply financial support to the Trumpet School at Versailles, even when finances were over-extended. The school flourished between 1805 and 1811, educating as many as 600 trumpet players for military duty. In an attempt to conserve money, Napoleon issued an ordinance in 1807 that restricted the official size of infantry bands to nine players. For anyone who had been present at the great festivals of the early days of the revolution, this was clearly a regression.

It was during this frugal period of limited instrumentation that Anton Reicha wrote his *Commemoration Symphony*. To abide by Napoleon's edict, Reicha choose to compose his work for three small bands rather than one large one. Each of the groups had a piccolo, two oboes, two clarinets in C, two horns, two bassoons, two trumpets, and a string bass or contrabassoon. This instrumentation follows the Harmoniemusick tradition of adding a piccolo and trumpets to the standard octet to form band instrumentation typical of the military. With a little bit of creative problem-solving, Reicha was able to generate a band of thirty-six players (plus six army drums and four small field guns) while still conforming to Napoleon's edict.

The work is antiphonal (not unlike that of Gabrieli) and calls for the three bands to be separated on the stage. One group serves as the concertino while the other two provide the tutti or full organ stop. The three-movement work lasts twenty-three minutes and is innovative both musically and conceptually. There is a lengthy forward provided by the composer that details performance requirements and specifications. The inclusion of these details was unusual for its day. The use of field gun shots in the middle movement is also not typical. Reicha offers the following:

> This work is composed to commemorate: 1st, the memory of great exploits; 2nd, the death of heroes and great men; 3rd, to celebrate any important future event… The place selected for the performance must be large and open (uncovered) and the orchestra must be a distance of 50 steps from the audience…It is imperative to use the exact number of instruments mentioned in the score, otherwise the work would not sound as effectively…The musicians must not be too close to each other, so that the sound gets more widely spread.

What is perhaps most interesting here is that this work straddles two periods. It clearly relies on the Harmoniemusik traditions of the eighteenth century while expanding the size and instrumentation of what will come to be known as the modern band by the end of the nineteenth century.

Industrial Revolution, 1830–1855 (Second Period)

The nineteenth century evolved as the most intense and diverse period of wind instrument development and experimentation since the Renaissance. In many ways it was even more adventurous. It rivaled the proliferation of wind instrument types of the Renaissance.

There were many innovations in this period, but none more important than the introduction of the valve to brass instruments. The solution for making brass instruments other than the trombone fully chromatic was finally at hand. There were many people working on the problem, but the ones most often credited with finding an answer are Charles Clagget (Dublin), Heinrich Stölzel (Berlin), and Friedrich Blühmel (Berlin). All worked to discover or solidify the idea of a system that could make it possible for a variety of brass instruments to be fully chromatic.

Another earth-shattering development was the invention of the tuba. Bands and orchestras alike had struggled for centuries to find a proper bass instrument for the wind section. A number of possibilities were explored, including the serpent, ophicleide, and bass horn. All other prototypes were abruptly put aside when Wilhelm Wieprecht (1802–1872) patented the tuba in Berlin in 1835.

There were many important developments in the woodwind family during this time. The work of Theobald Boehm (1794–1881) was most significant for the flute, but led to additional applications to all of the woodwinds. Boehm's initial improvements between 1831 and 1846 had to do with key placement and mechanisms. After that time he turned his attention to the bore of the flute, developing the cylindrical design which replaced the conical flute that had dominated the instrument for 150 years.

The clarinet (invented in 1690 by John Denner) began the nineteenth century with only six keys. By the end of the century, some models had as many as nineteen keys. Frenchmen Hayacinthe Klosé (1808–1880) is credited with applying the Boehm ring system to the clarinet in 1843.

The newest instruments on the scene in the nineteenth century were those of Adolphe Sax (1814–1894). His contributions were many, and included the development of the bass clarinet into the instrument we know today. Sax is also credited with inventing the contra-bass clarinet, which along with the contrabassoon and double bass anchors the bottom of the woodwind section. He also made modifications and improvements to the valve.

Of course Sax's most acknowledged accomplishment is the invention of the saxophone. This family of instruments, which includes the sopranino, soprano, alto, tenor, baritone, and bass saxophone, has become an integral and indispensable component of wind music performance. Sax was also responsible for inventing the Saxhorn family of brass instruments that contributed one permanent member to today's instrumentation, the euphoni-

um. Additionally, he standardized the keys of E-flat and B-flat, which helped to create a sonorous sound. Sax, not unlike Grainger, advocated and revived the Renaissance concept of complete, homogeneous families, or consorts of instruments.

Sax, a Belgium native, moved from Brussels to Paris in 1842. He was seen as a threat by the traditionalists of Paris led by Michele Carafa (1787–1872). An opera composer, Carafa was born in Naples and studied in Paris with Cherubini. He served as Professor of Counterpoint at the Paris Conservatory as well as the Director of the Gymnase de Musique Militaire, where most musicians of the Army were trained. His adversaries worked to discredit Sax, and might have successfully run him out of the city were it not for two very important allies, General de Rumigny and Hector Berlioz.

In 1845, a commission in Paris was charged to study the conditions and effectiveness of French military music. They investigated many issues, including the size and instrumentation of bands as well as the concept of doubling parts to expand the instrumentation. One of the most important events of the century occurred as a result of the commission's work. It was decided that a live field test should be held on April 22, 1845 to determine the best instrument designs as well as the most effective instrumentation. This grand experiment was held on the Champ de Mars, where the Eiffel Tower (built between 1887 and 1889) now stands. Two groups representing opposite schools of thought were invited to participate. Carafa represented the traditionalists and status quo, while Sax represented the futurists with his newly-designed instruments. This event was undoubtedly one of the first documented "Battle of the Bands" in music history. There was a great deal at stake both artistically and commercially, for whomever won would surely have the opportunity to fill many new instrument orders. The commission's decision favored Sax, but because of political issues it took nine years (until 1854) for any recommendations to be implemented.

It was during this period that the Musique de la Garde republicaine was founded in 1848 by Georges Paulus (1816–1898). This was a major event in band history. The group, conceived as a true wind orchestra, initially had fifty-four musicians and included ten clarinets. Today they have 113 members and twenty-four clarinets. In 1993 the group changed its name to the Orchestre de la Garde republicaine. This ensemble patterns itself after the modern orchestra, performing primarily transcriptions. Clarinets replace the string section, Clarinet 1 for Violin 1 and Clarinet 2 for Violin 2. Saxophones, saxhorns, euphoniums, and two double basses are used to replace the low strings.

In addition to this body of string substitutes, there is the normal solo section of woodwinds and brass that would be found in a typical orchestra. The substitution instruments literally become the string section, sitting where the strings would normally be placed. The solo wind section sits in its traditional position. The substitute instruments often play directly from string parts and take great pride in not needing transposed or adapted parts. The organization is made up of some of the finest players in France and performs at the highest level of professional standards. This is also a model that is used by the Royal Symphonic Band of the Belgian Guides, another of the world's great wind orchestras.

The Musique de la Garde republicaine toured the United States in 1872. This was their first performance abroad. It was because of this tour that the French gained an impeccable reputation for virtuosity and musicianship that was modeled for subsequent years in America. The group made one more tour of America in 1953, playing seventy-one concerts. Once again their performances were heralded as spectacular, and their influence was pervasive. The Orchestre de la Garde republicaine has had a 160-year history of excellence, and is one of several professional European ensembles that continue to make music at the highest-level, set standards in Europe, and influence wind bands throughout the world.

Hector Berlioz is responsible for creating a most valuable resource during these years. His work had a great deal to do with the development and clarification of instrumentation during this period. Berlioz's *Treatise on Orchestration* (*Grand Traite d'instrumentation et orchestraition modernes*), published in 1843, remains one of the most important resources on the topic. This book served as a major reference, providing technical and practical information on the instruments of the orchestra, with special emphasis on the winds. Berlioz's music and writings led conductor Felix Weingartner to aptly refer to him as "the creator of the modern orchestra."

The timeline of instrumental development given in figure 1 is based on the document prepared by Kenneth Berger and found in "The Band in the United States—A Preliminary Review of Band Research and Research Needs" (Band Associates, 1961, 33). Additional events have been added to highlight the great number of improvements and modifications that were made from the Baroque period through the nineteenth century. Although these are but a few of the developments, the list does reveal a basic timeline and give insight to the tremendous flurry of creative activity among instrument manufacturers during the nineteenth century.

Berlioz frequently commented on bands and band music during the period. David Whitwell has compiled a wonderful reference entitled *Berlioz on Bands* (Northridge: WINDS, 1992) that chronicles Berlioz's involvement and interest in the medium.

Another important figure of the nineteenth century, Nicolai Rimsky-Korsakoff (1844–1908), had an avid interest in bands and made lasting and significant contributions to the field of orchestration. Rimsky-Korsakoff was appointed Inspector of Russian Naval Bands in 1873, a post he held for over ten years. His book, *Principles of Orchestration*, (Edition Russe de Musique, 1922) is still an essential read on the topic.

YEAR	DEVELOPMENT
1467	Tieffenbruker builds a true Violin
1542–1610	Gasparo de Sala establishes the form of the Violin
1608	Monteverdi writes *Orfeo* (orchestra established)
1644–1737	Birth and death dates of Stradivarius
1677	A key is finally added to the Flute
1690	First Clarinet by Denner appears
1770	Bassett horn appears
1793	Bass clarinet appears in early form
1808	Woodwind key-ring is patented
1810	Ivan Mueller brings out a thirteen-key clarinet Keyed bugle appears
1815	Piston valve invented
1818	Valve patented by Heinrich Stölzel and Freiderich Blühmel
1823	Rollers for the clarinet appear German silver used for keys
1825	Cornet à piston appears in France
1830	First three-valve brasses appear Uhlman's Vienna twin-piston valve appears
1832	Horizontal rod axles appear on woodwinds Boehm cylindrical wooden flute Rad-Maschine rotary valve by Joseph Riedl
1835	Tuba patented by Wieprecht and Moritz Prussia Berliner-pumpen valve appears
1838	Multiple-action keys appear
1839	Perinet's improved piston valve appears
1840	Key-rings used more widely Saxophone invented
1843	Saxhorns invented Klose and Buffett improve the clarinet (Boehm system adapted)

FIGURE 1.

The writings of Berlioz and Rimsky-Korsakoff helped to chronicle and codify wind instrument development in the nineteenth century. These two texts, along with the more recent work of Kent Kennan and Donald Grantham in their book *The Techniques of Orchestration* (Upper Saddle River, NJ: Prentice Hall, 1952), are invaluable resources for investigating the history and art of modern orchestration. I would be remiss if I did not also mention two other wonderful resources, entitled *The History of Orchestration* by Adam Carse (New York, NY: Dover Publications, Inc., 1964) and *The History of Musical Instruments* by Curt Sachs (New York, NY: W.W. Norton & Company, Inc., 1940).

Music of Note: Sound Principals

One of the earliest pieces of interest from this period after the Anton Reicha's *Commemoration Symphony* in 1815 is the *Partita for Band* (1825) by Franz Krommer. Readers of the first chapter in this series will recall that Krommer was one of the preeminent composers of Harmoniemusik. In fact, he is often cited along with Haydn and Mozart as being the last of the three most important composers of the genre. Although called a *Partita*, the work demonstrates a move away from the Harmoniemusik tradition and might more aptly be referred to as a *Symphonie*. It really is a new style of music with a new instrumentation and reflects the changing times.

As mentioned earlier, Reicha's *Commemoration Symphony* looked back with its instrumentation and forward with its sonics. It is important to note that Reicha taught Hector Berlioz. It is no coincidence that Berlioz's *Symphonie Funebre et Triumphal* of 1840 shares much in common with the earlier work of his teacher, Reicha.

The Berlioz *Symphonie* was commissioned for a ceremony involving the transference of the remains of the heroes of the Revolution of 1830 to a newly constructed monument in the Place de la Bastille. Berlioz claims to have used two hundred musicians for the event, which included a procession through the streets of Paris. Richard Wagner (1813–1883) had this to say in *Mein Leben* (Munich, 1963, 228) regarding the premiere:

> It was, however, the latest work of this wonderful master, his *Trauersymphonie fur die Opfer der Julirevolution*, composed for massed military band during the summer of 1840 (July 28) for the anniversary of the obsequies of the July heros, and conducted by him under the column of the Place de la Bastille, which had at last thoroughly convinced me of the greatness and enterprise of this incomparable artist. It is a fact that at that time I felt almost like a little school boy by the side of Berlioz.

Wagner would later make an important contribution to the repertoire, his *Trauermusik on themes of "Euranthe" by Carl Maria von Weber* (1844). In this case, the piece was for a Dresden candlelit evening processional that involved bringing the body of his teacher, von Weber, back home to Germany.

A final dedicatory work that should be mentioned here is the *Funeral March* (1866) of Edvard Grieg (1843–1907). He composed it on the death of his best friend, Rikard Nordrak, who wrote the Norwegian National Anthem. Grieg conducted his *Funeral March* throughout Europe, and it was played for Grieg's own funeral. In addition to Reicha, Krommer, Berlioz, Wagner, and Grieg, many nineteenth-century composers contributed to the advancement of the genre. A more complete list may be found in the appendix.

Musical Revolution, 1855–1900 (Third Period)

Two of the most important personalities of the Golden Age of Bands are Wilhelm Wieprecht (1802–1872) of Prussia and Andreas Leonhardt (1800–1866) of Austria. Each of these men had tremendous impact on the development of wind bands in their respective countries.

Wilhelm Wieprecht was perhaps the most influential military musician of the nineteenth century. He was highly respected by musicians and critics alike. A gifted conductor, arranger, and administrator, he did a great deal to elevate Prussian ensembles to their position of leadership in Europe and the world. Wieprecht was born in 1802 into a family of musicians. He studied clarinet, trombone and violin. Wieprecht set out to make his way in the world in 1821 at the age of nineteen. He ended up in Berlin in 1824 as a chamber musician in the court, and it was here that he heard a Prussian military band play the *Overture to Figaro* by Mozart—an event that had a life-altering effect. Wieprecht describes this moment:

> When I heard in Berlin for the first time an infantry band in its full instrumentation, I was seized by an emotion I have never been able to explain to myself. Was it the rhythm, the melody, the harmony, or other elements which affected me so deeply? As I then followed this band on their march to the watch parade, and there heard them play the Overture to Mozart's *Figaro* in a closed circle, there came into my heart the firm decision that I would dedicate myself from now on to military music. (*Whitwell Nineteenth-Century Wind Band*, 32)

Wieprecht succeeded Georg Abraham Schneider (1770–1839) as head of Prussian military bands in 1838. He hoped to make the position a regular commissioned rank. He was successful due in part to a "monster concert" that he organized in Berlin for a state visit of Kaiser Nicholaus of Russia.

The King of Prussia asked Wieprecht to organize a great musical event for the visit. Wieprecht seized the opportunity to combine sixteen cavalry bands that totaled more than a thousand winds and two hundred percussionists. The program was typical of the day, and included marches and opera transcriptions as well as the "Hallelujah Chorus" from Handel's *Messiah.* The concert was a smashing success, and did much to make Wieprecht one of Berlin's most notable citizens. Wieprecht's influence on the nineteenth-century wind band is well documented. Suffice it to say that he was truly a major icon in the development of wind music, and deserves a great deal of credit for establishing the ensemble as a serious artistic medium.

Another of the influential men of the nineteenth century was Andreas Leonhardt, who was the central figure in Austrian military music. At the end of the eighteenth century, a typical Austrian infantry band consisted primarily of the traditional Harmoniemusik instrumentation. After 1840, the Austrian bands began to be acknowledged throughout Europe as being very virtuosic and capable of great music making. Whitwell believes that this was because Austria turned to established civilian musicians for its military bandleaders, a tradition that is followed in some European countries even today.

Leonhardt was appointed "Armeekapellmeister," a newly created position that gave Austria a focused direction for their military bands comparable to that of Prussia and France. He was responsible for reorganizing and standardizing Austrian army music in 1851. He worked to elevate the status of the conductor, and fought to enlarge the bands, establishing the size of a basic infantry band at forty-eight men, with an additional twelve apprentices allowed during peacetime. More players could be added, but, as it was in other countries, the expense of any extra players was to be born by the officers of the regiment.

Leonhardt, like Wieprecht, saw the value of organizing and presenting "monster concerts." The first of these extravaganzas took place in 1853. Leonhardt combined thirty-seven of his bands to form an ensemble of 1200 woodwinds and brass with 300 percussionists. The event, which took place in Olmutz, was a performance for the Tsar of Russia and the Emperor Franz Joseph of Austria. Events such as these did a great deal to solidify the importance of bands in the cultures of their countries.

One of the most significant events of the century that served as a testimony to the Golden Age of bands in Europe was the World Band Competition of 1867 held in Paris. Whitwell offers the following in his book, *A Concise History of the Wind Band*: "At no time during the nineteenth century did military bands so capture the attention of the general public as they did on July 21, 1867 when ten bands, representing nine countries, met in Paris for the purpose of artistic competition." In his book, *The Wind Band* (Boston: Allyn and Bacon, Inc., 1961), Goldman offers: "Perhaps the greatest band contest of all time took place in Paris in 1867. Bands from France, Austria, Prussia, Belgium, Spain, Russia, Holland, Baden and Bavaria took part, each playing a required piece (Weber's *Oberon Overture*) and one piece of its own choice."

Band	Conductor	Chosen Work	Composer
Grenadier Regiment Band of Baden	Burg	*Finale of the Loreley*	Mendelssohn
First Engineer Corps Band of Spain	Maimo	*Fantasy on Spanish Melodies*	Gevaert
Second Guard Regiment of Foot and Second Guard Regiment of Berlin (combined)	Wieprecht	*Fantasy on The Prophet*	Meyerbeer
Seventy-third Regiment Band of Austria	Zimmerman	*Overture to William Tell*	Rossini
Band of the Guides and Grenadier Regiment of Belgium (combined)	Dender	*Fantasie on Themes from William Tell*	Rossini
First Infantry Regiment Band of Bavaria	Siebenkas	*Introduction and Bridal Chorus from "Lohengrin"*	Wagner
Chasseurs and Grenadiers Band of the Netherlands (combined)	Dunkler	*Fantasie on Themes from "Faust"*	Gounod
Garde Republicaine Band of France	Paulus	*The Bridal Chorus from "Lohengrin"*	Wagner
Band of the Mounted Guards of Russia	Dorffeld	*Overture to "Life of the Tsar"*	Glinka
Guides of the Imperial French Guards of France (musicians from the theaters of Paris assembled for this performance only)	Cressonois	*Fantasie on "The Carnival of Venice"*	Arban

FIGURE 2.

The event, organized by Georges Kastner, offered a first-prize gold medal along with a cash prize of 5,000 FR. It was held during an international exhibition that helped to assure an audience. A twenty-man jury, which included Kastner and composers Ambrose Thomas, Felicien David, and Leo Delibes, along with music critics Hans von Bulow and Eduard Hanslick, adjudicated the event. Thirty thousand people turned out to hear the competition concerts. The order of appearance, along with the name of the conductor and chosen work of each band is given in figure 2.

According to official accounts, the Prussians led by Wieprecht were the clear winners, having received twenty votes in the original balloting, followed by eighteen for the French Garde Republicaine Band and seventeen for the Austrians. However, a second ballot was taken for some reason (perhaps political), and Wieprecht describes what happened next:

> ...but then the bourgeoisie intervened and the jury left and returned a second time, having decided not to give one 5000 FR prize, but three 2500 FR prizes. General Mellinet had me step forward, announced the results and asked me if I was satisfied with it... that the Austrians and French be given a share in the laurels. I said yes, naturally, and everyone was happy about it. Especially to me was given, along with the 2500 FR, which I gave to my band, a large gold medal (taken from A. Kalkbrenner, *Wilhelm Wieprecht, Berlin 1882*, 58).

The paper Allegemeine Militair-Zeitung reported that members of all ten bands were received and acknowledged by the French Emperor Napoleon III:

> The Emperor Napoleon (III) was prevented from appearing at the competition, due to a death at court. However, he had already the day before, at 6:30 in the evening, had all the musicians introduced to him and the Empress in the Tuileries Gardens. He was very personable, had every band play their national anthem and a march, and had the individual bands march past him. Additionally, on the 30th all the musicians are invited to Versailles for a great (post competition) festival banquet.

The competition was proof positive of the impact that German military music had throughout Europe. All the participating conductors were German except those from France and Spain. One last observation gives a glimpse of the overall enthusiasm the public demonstrated for this event. The visiting Prussian Band, conducted by Wieprecht, gave a farewell concert in the Tuileries Gardens following the competition. Reports of the time state that 200,000 Parisians (one fifth of the inhabitants of the city) tried to attend this concert. Witnesses claim, "people climbed onto the backs of chairs and onto the backs of their neighbors trying to see the band." The World Band Competition gives testimony to the achievements, significance, and artistry of the bands of the nineteenth century. David Whitwell's assertion found below seems very accurate by all accounts:

> Never during modern history has there been a century when the prestige of the military was so high as it was during the nineteenth century… It was the last century in which war could be a grand adventure… This close connection between the military and society in general during the century extends, of course, to military bands. Consequently, one can not speak of nineteenth century court music without speaking of musicians in military uniforms, and the same can be said for church and civic affairs.

British Bands, 1820–1900

In the early nineteenth century, the officers of the regiment, rather than the government, financially supported English military music. While Prussia, Austria, France, and other European countries went through a period of new instrument development and refinement from 1820–1845, the British did not. David Whitwell feels this was because "…they lacked a strong personality, like Wieprecht in Prussia, Leonhardt in Austria, or Sax in France, to influence the thinking of the military as a whole." Apparently, a central policy regarding instrumentation did not develop until the advent of the band journals in England. In the early stages of development the instrumentation of each band was left to the individual bandmaster.

It is noteworthy that no British band participated in the World Band Competition of 1867. The Royal Artillery Band was invited, but the British government would not grant them permission to go. The development of a unified concept had just not occurred yet and that fact seemed to keep the English from being competitive. Finally, an initiative to unify the bands was undertaken in 1857. That led to a military music class being offered at Kneller Hall. James Smyth, leader of the Royal Artillery Band, and Henry Schallehn, a former leader of the Seventeenth Lancers Band, established the class. The class began training British bandmasters and was officially recognized in 1875. By 1887 the class had become The Royal Military School of Music. To this day this prestigious music school is known simply as Kneller Hall.

During this period, one of the most important contributions of the British was the development and dispersal of the band journal. Up until about 1850, very little band music was available in print. The conductors or musicians of each group arranged most of the music specifically for the individual bands. Mid-century, that changed drastically, due to the work of Carl Boose. He was a German bandmaster who spent his life in Darmstadt before migrating to England. Not surprisingly, even the British turned to the Germans for leadership in the band world. The instrumentation that he advocated in his journal followed the Prussian-German model, and this accounts for the British being influenced more by the Prussians than the Austrians or the French.

Starting in 1846, the firm known as Boosey and Company began to issue *Boose's Journal*, edited by Carl Boose, bandmaster of the Scots Guards. The journal met with great success, and other publishers were quick to follow Boose's lead. The band music journals did a great deal to standardize and unify British instrumentation while supplying music that was well arranged. Through their colonization, the English had placed armies, and therefore bands, all over the world. The journals provided an invaluable resource for all ensembles, especially those in remote locations. Another important publication that had similar significant impact was the *Chappell Army Journal* that followed later in the century. Schott is also credited with contributions in this field. A typical band journal from 1856 would include overtures by Mendelssohn and Wagner as well as symphonies by Mozart, Beethoven, and Mendelssohn.

American Bands, 1738–1900

As one might expect, early American bands followed European and specifically English models. According to Richard Franko Goldman in his book, *The Wind Band*, the earliest American bandmaster was Josiah Flagg (1738–1794) of Boston. Flagg published his *Collection of the Best Psalm Tunes in 1764*, which was engraved by Paul Revere. He organized numerous concerts, and in 1771 one of those concerts featured vocal and instrumental music "accompanied by French Horns, Hautboys, etc.," played by the 64th Regiment Band. Flagg formed his own band in 1773, which played performances in Boston's Faneail Hall.

There are two important early American bands of significance that merit mention here. The first was the Massachusetts Band formed in Boston in 1783. It changed its name in 1820 to the Boston Brigade Band. This band, which will be discussed later in this chapter, eventually became known as Gilmore's Band when Patrick Gilmore assumed leadership of the group.

The second ensemble is the United States Marine Band in Washington DC, which celebrated its 210th anniversary in 2008. The band, which is America's oldest musical institution, was officially organized in 1798. By the end of 1800, the group consisted of two oboes, two clarinets, two horns, one bassoon, and a drum. The influence of Harmoniemusik is apparent in this instrumentation. The Marine Band has been referred to as the "Presidents Own" since it was founded. President John F. Kennedy offered the following regarding the band: "The Marine Band is the only force that cannot be

transferred from the Washington area without my express permission and, let it be hereby announced that we, the Marine Band and I, intend to hold the White House against all odds."

According to Goldman, the instrumentation and size of the group grew slowly. Many civilian bands demonstrated greater proficiency than the Marine Band in its early years. In 1861 they were authorized a membership of thirty musicians. By 1899, they finally achieved an instrumentation of sixty musicians. Although the band continued to grow in size and artistry, it is generally accepted that the Marine Band made its greatest progress under the leadership of John Philip Sousa from 1880 to 1892.

Just as they did in Europe, brass bands developed in popularity in the United States. Brass-band musicians served on both sides during the Civil War. Clearly, brass and percussion instruments proved to be more practical outside; however, occasionally a few woodwind instruments, primarily piccolo and clarinet, would be added to the ensemble.

The Civil War bands were mostly brass bands using keyed bugles and over-the-shoulder saxhorns. The over-the-shoulder design allowed soldiers marching behind the band to hear the music. Following the war, many musicians returned home and began the town bands that owe their heritage to the brass bands of the Civil War. One of the most famous of these was the Danbury, Connecticut Band led by George Ives, father of Charles Ives. Charles drew on his experiences with his father's band for source material in many of his compositions, among other things.

The oldest civilian concert band still performing in the United States today was formed in Allentown, Pennsylvania in 1828. The first fully professional band of its time was the Independent Band of New York founded in 1825. Thomas Dodworth and his son Allen, both of whom were British, were members of this band.

The Dodworths, including another son, Harvey, were very active and effective musicians. They were highly influential in New York City. Because of the prestige and influence of the Dodworths and the practicality of learning a brass instrument, most early American bands adopted a brass band instrumentation. Thomas Dodworth, the father, led the City Brass Band. Eventually that band divided into two groups, one of which was led by Allen, the son, and was known as the National Brass Band. The Dodworths were involved in other aspects of music, including a music store, publishing company, and a school of music, which trained fifty bandmasters and 500 musicians for service in the Civil War.

According to Goldman, "the credit for reversing the trend to all-brass bands belongs to two New York Bandmasters, Kroll and Reitsel." In 1853 they reorganized the New York Seventh Regiment Band as a mixed woodwind, brass, and percussion ensemble. It is assumed that this influenced the

Dodworth family, who adopted a similar instrumentation and changed the name of their National Brass Band to the Dodworth Band. The Dodworths dominated the New York band scene following the war until Patrick Gilmore arrived in 1873.

Patrick Sarsfield Gilmore (1829–1892) is often referred to as the man who changed band history in America. He was born in County Galway, Ireland on December 25, 1829. He immigrated to America by way of Canada in 1848 at the age of nineteen. He was an exceptional cornet virtuoso, and has been credited with establishing the superiority of the cornet over the keyed bugle. His reputation was secured when he outplayed the famous keyed bugle virtuoso Ned Kendall in a heralded head-to-head competition. Gilmore led the Boston Brass Band from 1852 to around 1855, when he assumed the leadership of the Salem Brass Band.

Gilmore became leader of the Boston Brigade Band in 1859. It was at this time that the band changed its name to Gilmore's Band. He became the artistic and administrative director, assuming complete responsibility. In fact this was a precondition he required before accepting the job. The original group had thirty-two players. This ensemble was absolutely a business venture for Gilmore: it was fully professional. Like his contemporaries in Europe, he organized a number of spectacular festivals or "monster concerts." This series of successful events included: the Grand National Band of 1864; the National Peace Jubilee of 1869; and the World Peace Jubilee of 1872. They were well received and famously popular. These concerts turned him into a celebrity.

Gilmore was one of the greatest promoters of all time. Even though he was criticized from time to time for being a "showman," he did much to popularize good music and outstanding performance. Many feel that Gilmore was to the American band what Theodore Thomas (1835–1905), the first renowned American orchestra conductor and founder of the Chicago Symphony, was to the American orchestra. The World Peace Jubilee featured many bands and orchestras from Europe. This contact with the great musical organizations of the world made a lasting impression on their counterparts in America. Groups that appeared are given in figure 3.

According to Richard Franko Goldman, the chorus for the Jubilee consisted of 20,000 voices, the band numbered 2000 and the orchestra almost 1000—numbers that would impress even Bernard Sarette and his French Revolution colleagues. The event gave American bandmasters and musicians a chance to compare their accomplishments to those of other, more famous ensembles from abroad. Undoubtedly, the European groups provided a model and set standards for the future in America.

Most agree that Gilmore did his best work after he accepted the leadership of the Twenty-Second Regiment Band of New York in 1873. Under his direction, the band became known, once again, as Gilmore's Band. His group was

made up of the finest virtuosi and well-known soloists of the day, including cornetists Arbukle and Levy as well as trombonist Innes.

ORGANIZATION	CONDUCTOR
The Band of the Grenadier Guards	Daniel Godfrey
The Orchestra of Johann Strauss	Johann Strauss
Kaiser Franz Grenadier Regiment Band	Heinrich Saro
National Band of Dublin	Edwin Clements
Garde Republicaine Band	Georges Paulus
United States Marine Band	Herman Fries
New York Ninth Regiment Band	D. L. Downing

FIGURE 3.

Gilmore's Band toured the United States and Canada several times. He took the group to Europe in 1878, where they were lauded as being the equal of any in the world at the time. They skillfully performed transcriptions of standard orchestral repertoire as well as marches and special arrangements. His concepts of instrumentation and programming became the standard until 1920, when Edwin Franko Goldman introduced a new approach.

There is unanimity of opinion that John Philip Sousa (1854–1932) was not only the March King, but also one of the most famous conductors who ever lived. In his book, *Bands of America* (New York: Doubleday & Co., 1957), H. W. Schwartz reminds us that the period from 1880 to 1925 was the most prosperous era for the professional touring band. The Sousa Band was perhaps the most popular musical organization of the time. Thanks to the contributions of the Europeans and people like Gilmore, the band had developed into a musical organization that was quite capable of serious artistic expression and spectacular entertainment.

Sousa was born on November 6, 1854 in Washington DC. Although his principal instrument was the violin, he learned to play trombone, E-flat alto horn, and cornet. Sousa's father was a member of the Marine Band. In 1868, at the age of fourteen, Sousa enlisted as an apprentice to the Marine Band and served almost seven years. Sousa was offered an opportunity to become the fourteenth conductor of the Marine Band in 1880, and is credited with a complete reorganization of the group. Sousa toured widely and established an outstanding reputation. The success of these tours surely impacted the approach he would take with his professional band in later years.

Sousa left the Marine Band in 1892 in order to assemble his own concert band. The first performance of his new group was in Plainfield, New Jersey on September 26, 1892. This was just two days after the death of Patrick Gilmore. Many who heard that performance felt the torch had been passed.

Sousa felt strongly that the mission of the band was to entertain and not to educate. He often said that his purpose was to give the public what it wanted. Another cornerstone of his philosophy was that he modeled the instrumentation of his group after the English; he believed that bands in England had "nearly a correct band instrumentation." According to Goldman, "Sousa's Band, like all other great bands, was not middle heavy, nor was it large."

Sousa learned from the best, following the repertoire and programming concepts of the Gilmore Band. Of course he added his own marches, as well as the compositions of others. Every program included no less than six marches. He regularly featured singers (The Ladies in White) and instrumental soloists who enjoyed a star-like status with his public, including cornet virtuosos Herbert L. Clarke and Frank Simon as well as trombonist virtuosos J. J. Perfetto and Simone Mantia.

The band also presented operettas and songs. Sousa's compositional style was influenced by composers such as Offenbach, along with Gilbert and Sullivan. Sousa penned at least 136 marches. The first was *The Review* written in 1873 and the last two were *The Northern Pines* and *Kansas Wildcats*, both done in 1931. Sousa played standard repertoire and transcriptions of established composers and, in addition, he sought out and performed original music for band. He presented his programs in rapid fire, keeping the audience engaged and entertained. Sousa was highly respected and admired as a conductor and administrator, and many emulated his style in both the professional and educational world.

Sousa was a tireless advocate for increasing the artistry and musicianship of conductors in the profession. He showed interest in original compositions for band and championed composers such as Percy Grainger (1882–1961). Sousa is credited with being one of the first people in music to understand that touring could have a tremendous impact on the reputation of a group and conductor. He took his marvelous band of renowned virtuosos all over the world and built a fan base that would be the envy of any popular music group today. There is no doubt that the wind band world was advanced and enhanced through the genius and artistry of John Philip Sousa.

A number of fine ensemble leaders and soloists flourished during this period of professional proliferation. Among them were: Monsieur Antoine Jullien, Victor Herbert, Alessandro Liberati, Thomas Preston Brooke, Giuseppi Creatore, Patrick Conway, Frederick Innes, Arthur Pryor, Herbert L. Clarke, Frank Simon, and many others too numerous to mention here. This was truly the Golden Era of the American professional band. All captured the attention of their audiences at a time when there was no radio, television, recordings, or movies. Inspiring and exciting live music appeared in your town. The only way to hear music was to attend, and this created a

concert-going public. In short, there was very little competition for the public's attention, and bands filled the entertainment void in grand style.

Twentieth-Century Chamber Winds: European Roots

It is widely acknowledged that there was a continuous lineage of professional wind ensembles that served court and civic functions from the late Middle Ages to the end of the Classic period. Modern repertoire orchestras developed out of private opera orchestras. As they did, wind players in these groups organized chamber concerts featuring primarily wind music. This tradition is clearly linked to the Harmoniemusik of the eighteenth century and lives on today in groups such as the Netherlands Wind Ensemble, the Detroit Chamber Winds, the Collegium Musicum Pragense, the London Wind Soloists and the Orpheus Chamber Orchestra.

One of the most important early examples of this type of ensemble was "La Société de Musique de Chambre pour Instruments à Vent," founded in 1879 by flutist Paul Taffanel (1844–1908). This organization played a number of concerts in Paris and did much to commission and promote wind chamber music. Because its founder was a flutist, it also had a great deal to do with the flute becoming an integral member of the Harmoniemusik ensemble. The original group fell by the wayside but was reorganized in 1895 by oboist Georges Longy (1868–1930) and Professor of Clarinet at the Paris Conservatory, Prosper Mimart (1859–1928). Longy had probably first heard the ensemble when he was a student. His teacher, Gillet, was one of the original members. Numerous works were composed and arranged for this ensemble, the most famous of which was the *Petite Symphonie* (1885) by Gounod.

Additionally, in 1895 a similar ensemble was founded in Paris by another flutist, Georges Barrère (1876–1944). He called the group "La Société Moderne Pour Instruments à Vent." They commissioned a number of works, including *Divertissement, Op.* 6 (1914) for piano and winds by Roussel and *Lied et Scherzo, Op.* 54 (1910) by Schmitt. Both of these groups were interested in performing new works for winds in addition to playing standard classic and romantic works from the chamber winds repertoire.

As fate would have it, both Longy and Barrère came to America to make their musical fortunes. Longy came to become Principal Oboe with the Boson Symphony and Barrère came to become Principal Flute of the New York Symphony Orchestra.

Georges Longy founded the Longy Club of Boston in 1900 five years before Barrère established his organization in New York. They were active for seventeen years. It was modeled after the well known "La Société de Musique de Chambre pour Instruments à Vent" of Paris. The ensemble that Longy had reformed in Paris had been transplanted to America. It is known that two members of the Longy Club of Boston were children of members of the original Paris ensemble, clarinetist Grisez and oboist Sautet.

Shortly after his arrival in 1905 Barrère formed the New York Symphony Quintet. He received a note from Camille Saint-Saens praising his newly formed group. It read:

Dear Mr. George Barrère,

> *In continuing the work of La Société Moderne d'instruments à Vent, in New York, which you founded so successfully in Paris, you will contribute to the art in America, by introducing many interesting works too little known there, to the American public.*

> *My best wishes are with you. I have no doubt your enterprise will be crowned with success.*

Most devotedly,
Camille Saint-Saens

The original quintet was expanded to an ensemble of eleven winds in 1911 and given the name "The Barrère Ensemble." The group included two flutes, two oboes, two clarinets, two bassoons, two horns, and a trumpet. Early performances included the *Octet in F* by Haydn and the *Octet, Op. 103* by Beethoven.

David Whitwell's research indicates that the Longy Club became a respected part of Boston musical life by its sixth season and the Barrère Ensemble in New York enjoyed a similar reputation. The two groups flourished and solidified the importance of wind chamber music in American musical life at the dawn of the twentieth century. The chamber winds repertoire is rich and extensive thanks to these early pioneers who had no way of knowing how important the music they commissioned, promoted, and performed would become to today's contemporary wind band.

Twentieth-Century Orchestral Winds: No Strings Attached

One of the most important European events of the early twentieth century was named after the small German town where it was held. The Donaueschingen Music Festival was started in 1921 and was sponsored by Prince Max Egon Furst von Furstenberg. The intention was to feature chamber works of young composers from Germany and Austria. Paul Hindemith was sought out to direct the festival and chair the music selection committee. Hindemith made a decision to take the festival in a slightly different direction in 1925 by highlighting musical genres that would benefit from additional

repertoire. The first to be featured was a capppella choral music. The next year, 1926, Hindemith and his committee turned their attention to music for military band. Hindemith's expressed intent was to upgrade the quality of the literature available for performance amateurs and for military wind bands. Four composers were commissioned to write pieces for the festival. A list of works is given in figure 4.

WORK	COMPOSER
Konzertmusik fur Blasorchester, Op. 41	Paul Hindemith (1895–1963)
Drei lustige Marche, Op. 44	Ernst Krenek (1900–1991)
Kleine Sernade fur Militarorchester	Ernst Pepping (1901–1981)
Spiel fur Blasorchester	Ernst Toch (1887–1964)

FIGURE 4.

This event was prophetic indeed, for the specified instrumentation of the compositions revealed a philosophy that would later become a central tenant of wind ensemble philosophy. Other works of this nature are given in figure 5.

WORK	COMPOSER
Symphonies of Wind Instruments	Igor Stravinsky (1882–1971)
Concerto for 23 Winds	Walter Hartley (b. 1927)
Hill Song No. 2	Percy Grainger (1882–1961)
Concertino for Piano	Karel Husa (b. 1921)
Mass No. 2 in e minor	Anton Bruckner (1824–1896)
Le Bal de Beatrice d'Este	Reynaldo Hahn (1875–1947)

FIGURE 5.

Twentieth-Century Symphonic Winds: A New Repertoire

Many credit Edwin Franko Goldman (1878–1956) with creating an entirely new kind of concert band in the 1920s. H. W. Schwartz writes:

> A new kind of concert band has taken their [i.e., the old "business bands"] place, and the man who best typifies this new kind of band and marks this transition is Dr. Goldman. The Goldman Band survived the automobile, the phonograph, the movies and the radio, powerful forces that crushed the famous bands of yesteryear. For three decades it has stood as America's foremost symbol of what a modern concert band

should be...Although the Goldman Band is a local band, through radio it has been shared with the nation. Furthermore the personal influence of the great conductor of the Goldman Band has spread from coast to coast. For many years he championed various movements of which the aim was to raise the standards of musical performance by the concert band. He battled for original compositions, written by eminent composers, expressly for band performance. He advocated improvements in the instrumentation of the concert band and in more adequate publication of band music.

Goldman studied with Antonin Dvorak at the National Conservatory and was one of a select number of students of Jules Levy, the famous cornetist. Goldman played in the New York Metropolitan Opera Orchestra under such conductors as Mahler and Toscanini. His off-season with the Opera was spent playing in and conducting bands. He founded the Goldman Band in 1911. Goldman began a series of summer concerts in 1918 "on the Green" of Columbia University financed by subscription. In 1924 members of the Guggenheim family began to support the concerts. These concerts continued for years and did a great deal to advance the band as a serious performance medium and legitimize the repertoire. The following excerpt from an article written in 1948 by Henry Cowell provides additional perspective:

> This is no slight achievement, but Dr. Goldman has made an even more significant contribution to music as a result of his determination to improve the quality of music available to the symphonic band, and his interest in keeping the Goldman Band in active touch with the living music of the day. That it is now possible to offer a program of fine art music of great variety and interest, all written expressly for the band by famous living composers is very largely due to the efforts, influence and persuasiveness of Dr. Goldman. No mean composer of lively marches himself, in the Sousa tradition; Dr. Goldman began many years ago to urge the best-known composers of Europe and America to contribute to the repertory of good music for band by writing with wind instruments in mind. His success in this undertaking has made it unnecessary for bandmasters to depend any longer on the artistically deplorable arrangements, for winds, of music conceived for strings.

Goldman worked tirelessly to create an original repertoire and develop professional ensembles capable of great musicing. He instituted the first American competition for a new serious work for band in 1920. In his book *The Wind Band*, Goldman's son Richard writes: "His greatest contribution lies unquestionably in the area of band repertoire." By 1942 Goldman was able to present a complete program of concert works composed specifically for the group. According to his son: "On July 21 of that year the Goldman Band gave

what was probably the first such concert in the history of band music." The program included:

Part I

Christmas March .... .Edwin Franko Goldman
Spring Overture ....Leo Sowerby
Canto Yoruba ....Pedro Sanjuan
Rhapsody, Jericho ....Morton Gould
A Legend ....Paul Creston

Part II

Newsreel ....William Schuman
First Suite in E-flat ....Gustav Holst
Festive Occasion ....Henry Cowell
A Curtain Raiser ....Richard Franko Goldman
Lost Lady Found ....Percy Grainger
English Folksong Suite ....Ralph Vaughan Williams

To honor Goldman's seventieth birthday, the League of Composers presented a historic concert in Carnegie Hall on January 3, 1948. Percy Grainger and Walter Hendl conducted the band. The performance celebrated the accomplishments of Goldman's ongoing commitment to the medium and its repertoire. The program for that performance was:

Toccata Marziale ....Ralph Vaughan Williams
Suite Française ....Darius Milhaud
Theme and Variations, Op. 43a ....Arnold Schoenberg
The Power of Rome and the Christian Heart ....Percy Grainger
Shoonthree ....Henry Cowell
Canto Yoruba ....Pedro Sanjuan
La Marche sur la Bastille ....Arthur Honegger
Prelude ....Albert Roussel
Le Palais Royal ....Georges Auric
Symphony No. 19 ....Nicholas Miaskovsky
    (first performance in America)

I have listed these programs because I feel that they were revolutionary in nature and give great insight to the vision that Goldman had for the medium. The 1948 program illustrated how far we had come and announced a new era for wind music. It set the stage for the explosion of original repertoire that was to follow. Goldman can surely be credited with rescuing the band from a purely functional or entertainment-oriented fate. He set the wind band on a clear path and revealed to all what was possible. He so enlightened the profession that we still rely on his accomplishments to illuminate the way ahead.

Goldman and other band conductors understood the importance of the radio when it came to reaching a greater audience across the United States. In 1924 there were 2.5 million radio sets in America. By 1934 the number had grown to more than 14 million. Each radio was played an average of four and a half hours a day. Bands were frequently heard on radio broadcasts during these years. The United States Marine Band had a weekly series of broadcasts that began on June 7, 1922.

According to Richard Hansen in his book *The American Wind Band: A Cultural History* (Chicago: GIA Publications, 2005), one of the most important contributors in this area was Frank Simon. Simon was the former assistant principal cornetist in the Sousa Band. He initiated two programs for radio broadcast on Cincinnati's WLW and WSAJ in 1925. In 1926 Henry Fillmore formed his band and began broadcasting over WLW as well. By 1928 Goldman's Band was broadcasting twice a week over NBC, reaching 150 million listeners. Frank Simon also made weekly broadcasts with his Armco Company Band on Sunday's beginning in 1929. Even Sousa, who hated electronic recordings, conducted his band on broadcasts from New York between 1929 and 1932. A modern-day version of these early broadcasts occurred in 1981 when National Public Radio broadcast a series of thirteen one-hour wind band/ensemble concert programs entitled "Windworks," hosted by Fred Calland with commentary by Frederick Fennell. The "Windworks" program was chosen to be the United States entry for the Prix Italia that year.

On March 6, 1932 Sousa died unexpectedly in Pennsylvania after a rehearsal with the Ringgold Band of Reading. His death foreshadowed the end of an era. Only the Goldman Band, Frank Simon's Armco Company Band, the Philco Company Band led by Herbert Johnston, and the Long Beach Municipal Band led by Herbert L. Clarke maintained professional and semi-professional activities beyond Sousa's death. As professional groups began to fade, the band found a new home in the academic environment of public education. It would not take long for bands to thrive in these surroundings. Standards of performance reached a professional level in many universities throughout the country as music education took hold in America.

Music Education: Bands Find a Home

The presence of music in the public schools can be credited to the work of Lowell Mason (1792–1872). His inclusion of singing classes in the curriculum of Boston grammar schools in 1838 was the beginning of public music education in America. Thanks to the pioneers of the nineteenth century, America continues to lead the way in performance-based public school music education.

According to Richard Franko Goldman "...the first fruitful efforts to organize an instrumental program in a school system were those of Will

Earhart in Richmond, Indiana around 1900." At about this same time, Albert Austin Harding (1880–1958) began his work at the University of Illinois. Harding must be considered one of the earliest and most important figures in the college band movement. Another benchmark event occurred in 1918 when Joseph E. Maddy (1891–1966) was made supervisor of instrumental music in the schools of Rochester, New York.

Choirs and orchestras received the primary emphasis in the early stages of public school music education. The band lagged behind at first but soon caught up. A notable early school band program was that of A. P. McAllister's in Joillet, Illinois. Bands grew rapidly, and by 1932 over a thousand school bands were taking part in national contests.

In addition to the outstanding work of these early music education advocates, national professional associations and other educational institutions began to appear. Their expressed purpose was to elevate music education and uplift the profession at large. Groups of this nature continue to flourish. A short chronology of some of these organizations is found in figure 6.

YEAR	ORGANIZATION
1907	Music Supervisors National Conference Music Educators National Conference
1926	National School Band Association
1928	National Music Camp at Interlochen Founded by Joseph Maddy
1930	American Bandmasters Association Founded by Edwin Franko Goldman
1938	College Band Directors National Association Began as a committee within MENC Founded by William D. Revelli
1946	Midwest Clinic An International Band and Orchestra Conference
1953	American School Band Directors Association
1960	National Band Association
1969	Women Band Directors International
1970–1977	National Wind Ensemble Conference
1977	Association of Concert Bands
1981	World Association for Symphonic Bands and Ensembles Founded by Frank Battisti Supported by William Johnson and Timothy Reynish

FIGURE 6.

The opening paragraph of the College Band Directors National Association (CBDNA) Declaration of Principles eloquently states the group's purpose, which is shared by many of these organizations. It reads: "We affirm our faith and our devotion to the College Band, which, as a serious and distinctive medium of musical expression, may be of vital service and importance to its members, its institution and its art." In addition to believing in the band as a "serious and distinctive medium," the World Association for Symphonic Bands and Ensembles (WASBE) Statement of Purpose goes on to say: "We are completely dedicated to enhancing the quality of the wind band throughout the world and exposing its members to new worlds of repertoire, musical culture, people and places."

These organizations and many others (including numerous state organizations) have done much to advance the cause of wind bands in America and throughout the world. The profession is well organized and offers numerous opportunities for growth to anyone seeking to expand their musical abilities and knowledge. All are dedicated to the idea of "Teaching Music through Performance in Band."

Bands in the Schools: Separate but Equal

School bands were initially formed to lend support at athletic events and bolster school spirit. They provided students who were not drawn to choir or orchestra another avenue for pursuing their musical interests. It was the functional and social aspect of band that brought it into public education. Many early groups had incomplete instrumentation, poor instruction, unsatisfactory instruments, and low quality music. Similar to what went on at the end of the Civil War, bands began to improve following World War I. This was due primarily to the veterans returning home who had received training in the service bands. They assumed teaching positions and began to influence the quality of music education for band students.

It wasn't until 1912 that accreditation was proposed for music classes in secondary schools. Band was included in that proposal, but was not a high priority. By 1923, Edgar B. Gordon, in an address to music supervisors at a sectional meeting of the MSNC in Cleveland, acknowledged how far the band had come:

> The high school band is no longer an incidental school enterprise prompted largely by the volunteer services of a high school teacher who happens to have had some band experience, but rather an undertaking which is assigned to a definite place in the school schedule with a daily class period under a trained instructor and with credit allowed for satisfactory work done.

This acceptance was key to the transformation that bands would undergo as they moved from the professional world to the educational curriculum. The stage was set for the educational expansion that followed.

Raising the Standards: National Contests

The advent of concert band contests is credited with raising the standards of school bands in America. The first national event was the School Band Contest of America, held in Chicago in 1923 and sponsored by band instrument manufacturers. The contests were judged by luminaries of the day, including Sousa, Harding, Goldman, Simon, and others. The impact of these contests was dramatic. In fact Joseph Maddy claimed, "The radical changes in instrument manufacturing, band publications, and improved performance standards which occurred would have taken one hundred years had it not been for the contest movement," According to Stephen Rhodes, "Over the next decade and beyond it helped bring stability to school band programs that had struggled in the past, while raising the standards of performance and literature in America's school bands." Reputations were made as a result of these contests.

Founding Fathers: Orchestral Template

Albert Austin Harding (1880–1958) was asked to direct the University of Illinois band while still a senior in the College of Engineering. After two years in this position, Harding was named Director of Bands in 1907. He held that position until his retirement in 1948. This appointment made the University of Illinois the first university to establish a band department under the leadership of a Director of Bands. Harding expanded the band's involvement in military ceremonies and athletic events and additionally began to place greater emphasis on the concert band. He was a close friend of John Philip Sousa. Sousa left half of his library to the Unversity of Illinois (the other half was donated to the United States Marine Band). Harding served as president of the American Bandmasters Association in 1937.

University and college bands in the late 1940s and early 1950s were modeled after the University of Illinois Concert Band. They performed a repertoire of transcriptions, marches, and a small number of original compositions. As early as 1919, A. A. Harding was inviting school band directors to rehearsals of the University of Illinois Concert Band to help improve their rehearsal techniques and increase their knowledge of the repertoire. Harding made many transcriptions of large, late-nineteenth-century orchestral works, including compositions by César Frank, Serge Prokofiev, Maurice Ravel, Richard Strauss, and many others. Harding's band had a very complete instrumentation of over 100 players, perhaps emulating the size of a modern-day orchestra. Goldman offers the following regarding this important ensemble: "In every phase of university band activity—marching, concertizing, repertoire and, not the least important, organization and management—Dr. Harding's Illinois Band became a model for others."

Mark Hindsley (1905–1999), Harding's assistant and successor at Illinois, was one of the most important band directors of this period. Hindsley began playing the cornet at age ten. He also played the double bass. He did his undergraduate work in chemistry, but also received a Master of Arts Degree in Music in 1927 from the University of Indiana. While at Indiana he was the director of the university band. Hindsley became Assistant Director of Bands at the University of Illinois in 1934. He had played first cornet for Harding in the College Band at the National Music Camp at Interlochen in the summer, and had studied various band techniques with him while there.

World War II interrupted his work at Illinois, but he was able to return in 1946. He was elected president of the College Band Directors National Association that same year. Later he also served as president of the American Bandmasters Association. Hindsley was appointed acting Director of Bands at the University of Illinois in 1948 and became Director of Bands in 1950. He retired in 1970. Mark Hindsley was one of the most admired conductors in the wind band profession, and his legacy lives on in perpetuity. Hindsley was a prolific arranger and author who strongly believed in keeping the concert band large. He offered this definition of a band in an article:

> I use the term concert band to describe a concert-playing organization, to distinguish it from the marching band or other related groups constituted primarily for out-of-doors non-concert performances.... Some have found it to their liking to further describe the concert-playing band as a "symphonic" band, a "symphony of winds," etc.... In the wind field, the term "wind ensemble" has come into some recent popularity.... To be sure, all musical groups are ensembles, but, excluding the bona-fide chamber music, most wind ensembles today are bands in tuxes or tails [instead of uniforms?]...cutting the size of such heroic musical instruments as the full symphony orchestra and concert band is a cheap way to secure clarity, and then only at the sacrifice of the noblest and grandest of musical sounds.

William D. Revelli (1902–1994) began his teaching career in Hobart, Indiana. While there he developed an award-winning program of national acclaim. Revelli won five National Championships in a row before becoming Director of Bands at the University of Michigan in 1935. Frank Battisti in his book *The Winds of Change* (Galesville, MD: Meredith, 2002), states: "Revelli became the most influential band director on the national scene and a symbol for excellence and perfection in band performance." He founded the College

Band Directors National Association in 1941. Revelli believed an organization was needed to provide leadership in the nation and to address the direct concerns of the college band director. He was the organization's first president, serving at a difficult time during the war years from 1941 through 1945.

Under Revelli's guidance, The University of Michigan band program influenced thousands of students and produced hundreds of band directors. Revelli played the violin, and this influenced and informed his programming. The Michigan Symphony Band was famous for its performances of transcriptions of orchestral literature. These were a substantial part of the band's repertoire at the time; however, Revelli premiered and programmed many new compositions as well. There were many success during his tenure, but none more significant than the tour that the Symphony Band took to the Soviet Union, Romania, Egypt, Greece, and five other near east countries over fifteen weeks in 1961. His goal was to have his band sound like a symphony orchestra, something they did quite often. Revelli's groups achieved incredible results, and his influence was irrefutable.

The Wind Ensemble and Wind Symphony: Another Revolution

There were two pivotal events in the 1950s that permanently changed the philosophy and affected the repertoire of the wind band. The founding of the Eastman Wind Ensemble in 1952 by *Frederick Fennell* (1914–2004), and the establishment of the American Wind Symphony in 1957 by *Robert Austin Boudreau* (b. 1927).

In its first few years, the Eastman group was known as the Eastman Symphonic Wind Ensemble, a title that was insisted upon by Howard Hanson, director of the Eastman School of Music. Hanson and Mercury records apparently felt that this title would help to elevate the image of the organization. Fennell preferred simply to call the group the Eastman Wind Ensemble and eventually the name was simplified. From the outset, the group was focused on high-quality music. Fennell discussed the first concert in an article found in *The American Music Teacher* dated March 1953.

> This evening of music began with a *Ricercare* for wind instruments by Adrian Willaert (1480–1562) and ended ten compositions later with the *Symphonies of Wind Instruments* by Igor Stravinsky…the wonderful effect this concert had upon the discriminating audience and the press is a pleasure to recall, as is the reaction of the players which was positive, articulate and enthusiastic in the extreme. The direct result of this evening of original music for wind instruments was the establishment in the Fall of 1952 of the Eastman Wind Ensemble.

Perhaps the most obvious difference between Fennell's group and the status quo was the reduced instrumentation. He initiated a "one-on-a-part concept" except for some flute and clarinet doublings. The group was much leaner than the typical concert band of the day. Frank Battisti has excerpted Fennell's comments found in the April 1987 issue of *The Instrumentalist*, where he discusses the concepts that led him to this new instrumentation:

> ...the [instrumentation followed the] basic format of the British military band...increasing it to allow for triples among the reeds required for Stravinsky's *Symphonies*, each player would be the soloist his private teacher always taught him to be...I could hear how clean this sound was going to be...we would sit in the straight rows of orchestral seating...I wanted a carefully-balanced instrumentation capable of performing styles from the 16th century and moderate-sized chamber music to Paul Hindemith's new Symphony in B-flat.

Richard Hansen in his book *The American Wind Band: A Cultural History* gives this perspective:

> Fennell selected a fifty-two-piece ensemble as his core ensemble from which to perform a "fixed" symphonic wind ensemble repertoire. He then drew players from this ensemble in order to perform music of various wind and percussion media. This was a courageous step for Fennell, who had modeled the Eastman Symphonic Band after A. A. Harding's Symphony Band from the University of Illinois. This caused much confusion and argument within the profession, which persists today. However, the music Fennell and the Eastman Wind Ensemble performed and the artistry with which they performed it have never been questioned.

Fennell realized that this new genre would require new works. He made it his personal crusade to interest and entice significant composers to write for the group. It was in this spirit that he sent out over 400 letters to composers around the world, calling for them to contribute to the repertoire. Additionally he planned from the outset to produce quality recordings. Fennell met with Mercury Records producer David Hall in April 1952 to plan production of the first LP.

All of the works that Fennnell suggested could be found on a piece of paper he carried in his wallet in the event that an opportunity to record wind music might arise. Fennell was adamant that the first recording should not duplicate previously recorded material. The list, which was made up of all original American compositions, is given in figure 7.

Work	Year	Composer
Divertimento	1950	Vincent Persichetti
Ballad	1946	Morton Gould
George Washington Bridge	1950	William Schuman
Suite of Old American Dances	1949	Robert Russell Bennett
Commando March	1943	Samuel Barber

FIGURE 7.

The history of this most unique musical organization has been well documented in *The Wind Ensemble and its Repertoire* (Rochester, New York: University of Rochester Press, 1994) by Donald Hunsberger and Frank Cipolla. Additionally, Fennell himself wrote eloquently about the ensemble and the concept in a letter to Francis McBeth that was later published as a pamphlet entitled *The Wind Ensemble* (Arkadelphia, Arkansas: Delta Publications, 1988). McBeth's observations (quoted below) can also be found in this publication.

> When Frederick Fennell created the wind ensemble and chose the name, he performed one of the most ingenious acts of the 20th century. Fennell saw into the future. He saw a coming repertory for the winds. He was well aware that the name band was a four-letter word to many, many serious musicians. He wanted to present serious wind literature to audiences, but realized that the term band was an albatross around the neck of "serious intent" to many people because of the past. Every wind conductor in the United States is indebted to Frederick Fennell, more than any other man, for improving our status with the "serious music" community. What he did was a stroke of genius. History will be very kind to Fred.

One of the biggest misconceptions of this decision is that Fennell was advocating the wind ensemble replace the symphony band. Fennell speaks directly to this issue in a letter to Wayman Walker, Director of Bands at the University of Northern Colorado dated February 10, 1958:

> …since the first word was uttered on the Wind Ensemble, it has been my unmistakable and consistent practice to state that the Wind Ensemble was no substitute for anything but an adjunct to existing groups and a direction in *new* music toward which those who wished may turn their musical vision… The Eastman School of Music still has its 120 player Symphony Band and I continue to be its conductor…

Some considered this bold move a threat to the American concert band, when in reality I am convinced that it saved the concert band from obscurity by reinventing itself and embracing a broader repertoire. The advent of the wind ensemble as a concept (I prefer this over the word "movement") made it possible for the art form to expand and move forward, gaining greater acceptance and importance throughout the century.

Following his tenure at Eastman, Fennell conducted in various situations throughout the world. He joined the faculty at the University of Miami in Florida as the conductor of the Orchestra and Wind Ensemble, and had a distinguished career at that institution. Incredibly, at the age of seventy, Fennell began a second career outside of academia. He became the conductor of the Tokyo Kosei Wind Orchestra, Japan's most respected professional wind band, a position he held from 1984 to 1996. Following that Fennell served as their Conductor Laureate from 1996 to 2004, the year of his death. Once again he demonstrated an unbridled burst of energy and creativity, giving full seasons of concerts while recording and touring extensively. He released over ninety recordings with Kosei that have become mainstays in the discographies and collections of all who admire wind music.

It is impossible to discuss the 1950s without examining the founding of the American Wind Symphony (The American Waterways Wind Orchestra) by Robert Austin Boudreau in 1957. Unlike Fennell's instrumentation, which was based on the British band model, the instrumentation of Boudreau's group relied on a double orchestra wind section plus percussion. The saxophone and euphonium were excluded from this instrumentation and have remained so throughout the years.

Originally the Wind Symphony was made up of six flutes, two piccolos, six oboes, two English horns, six clarinets, two bass clarinets, six bassoons, two contrabassoons, six horns, six trumpets, six trombones (including bass trombone), two tubas, percussion, harp, keyboards, and string bass. It is important to note that while occasionally certain pieces could call for six separate parts per instrument, not all of the music did. Much of this music is playable by smaller forces than those listed above. Boudreau never relinquished his advocacy for this instrumentation. He has this to say about the founding of the group in Pittsburgh:

> I was able, through some persistence, to convince a lot of people to donate facilities and labor to help us move ahead. We decided the word "no" would never get us there. Eventually, Henry J. Heinz II agreed to co-sponsor the wind orchestra, along with support from Duquesne University. The first concerts were played on a makeshift stage made from "derelict coal barges" on the banks of the Allegheny River.

The American Wind Symphony commissioning project may be the largest single source of original, twentieth-century wind literature. Richard Hansen states that, "During a fifty-year time frame, Boudreau has commissioned a mammoth body of music from an array of international composers. C. F. Peters published 159 of them from 1957 to 1991."

There has been a great deal of speculation about why this collection of interesting works has not been programmed with greater frequency. Perhaps it has something to do with the fact that the instrumentation excludes saxophones and euphoniums, the two most important solo wind instruments of the past 120 years. The standard instrumentation of the modern wind symphony has embraced these instruments, and they have become an integral part of most groups. Boudreau's commissioning project was chronicled in *The American Wind Symphony Commissioning Project: A Descriptive Catalog of Published Editions, 1957–1991* (New York: Greenwood Press, 1991), by Jeffrey Renshaw.

A unique feature of Boudreau's ensemble was their manner of presenting concerts. Affectionately called the Barge Band by many of its alumni, they have traveled the American and European waterways, performing concerts along riverbanks to thousands of enthusiastic listeners. The membership of the ensemble comes from a talent pool of students from music schools across the country and the world. Boudreau envisioned a multimedia concert that would involve a combination of artistic disciplines including music, dance, drama, and art. His concept was innovative and engaging. His ideas were very different from those of other conductors, but those ideas proved to be very successful.

Boudreau offered concerts that were original in content, thought provoking, and artistically vivid. The outdoor nature of the concerts, which put a new twist on the old "concert in the park" model, necessitated coming up with a barge that would make it possible to amplify the performances. This vessel, called the Point Counterpoint II served as a floating arts center with displays of contemporary sculpture, paintings, and crafts. The barge itself morphed into a modern sculpture, placing the musicians in a somewhat non-traditional seating arrangement. This yielded a performance venue that was as creative as their presentations. Their stated purpose was "To bring the arts to people where they live," and they were extremely accomplished at doing that.

Robert Austin Boudreau was very entrepreneurial in forming and sustaining this ensemble. He set out to assemble an orchestra made specifically of winds and percussion, present entertaining, quality concerts in audience-friendly venues, commission repertory on an unequaled scale from a world wide group of composers, provide performing opportunities for young musicians, and spread musical culture and goodwill.

He was an incredible success, and his staying power has been impressive. This ensemble and Boudreau's accomplishment must be considered one of the defining moments in the history of wind music.

The Next Generation: Concepts Converge

There are five more prominent university wind band conductors who deserve mention in the scheme of things. Frank Battisti (b. 1931), Harry Begian (b. 1921), Donald Hunsberger (b. 1931), John Paynter (1928–1996), and H. Robert Reynolds (b. 1934). They represent a twentieth-century generation of conductors who guided and contributed to the development of the wind band during their primary careers and continue to do so in retirement. As a group, they did a great deal to unify the medium and clarify its purpose. Their work as conductors, teachers, authors, editors, arrangers, lecturers, and recording artists is superlative.

The cumulative impact of these five icons of the profession is staggering. They are collectively responsible for hundreds if not thousands of the most successful teachers, conductors, and performers in the profession. Their incomparable productivity is of the highest quality and their legacy reaches deeply into the medium. As time passes, the impact of their many contributions will be more measurable; however, at this point in time their accomplishments can only be viewed as overwhelming.

Frank L. Battisti is Conductor Emeritus of the New England Conservatory Wind Ensemble. He was the founder of that ensemble and conducted it for thirty years. The ensemble is considered to be one of the premiere ensembles of its kind in the world. Battisti and his ensemble appeared at numerous conferences, and have recorded on the Centaur, Albany, and Golden Crest labels. He began his career at Ithaca High School in Ithaca, New York. He was Director of Bands there from 1955 until 1967.

Battisti has demonstrated a passion for commissions, and has premiered numerous works by world-renowned composers. He is a past president of the College Band Directors National Association and is also a member of the American Bandmasters Association. Battisti founded the World Association of Symphonic Bands and Ensembles as well as many other organizations. He was a visiting fellow at Clare Hall, Cambridge University, England in 1986 and 1993. Battisti is the recipient of numerous honors and awards.

Harry Begian was Director of Bands at the University of Illinois from 1970 until his retirement in 1984. He came to prominence as the Director of Bands at Cass Technical High School in Detroit, Michigan, where he developed one of the finest high school bands in the country. His first college position was at Wayne State University, a position he held for three years. Following that he spent three years as Director of Bands at Michigan State University before joining the faculty at the University of Illinois.

Begian studied trumpet with Leonard Smith, conductor of the Detroit Concert Band, and flute with Larry Teal (flute professor at the University of Michigan). He received his masters degree from Wayne State University in Detroit and earned his doctorate degree at the University of Michigan in Ann Arbor. Begian appeared as a guest conductor, adjudicator, clinician, and lecturer throughout the United States and Canada. He was a charter member of the American School Band Directors Association and is past president of the American Bandmasters Association and the College Band Directors National Association. He has received numerous awards throughout his career. He has more than sixty LP recordings of concert performances with the University of Illinois Symphonic Band. After just one year of retirement, Begian returned to the podium as conductor of the Purdue University Symphonic Band from 1985–1987. In February of 1994, he was enshrined in the Hall of Fame of Distinguished Band Conductors.

Donald Hunsberger is Conductor Emeritus of the Eastman Wind Ensemble. He served as its music director from 1965 to 2002. The Eastman Wind Ensemble continued its development as an international performance model under his leadership. His numerous recordings can be heard on Sony Classics, CBS Masterworks, Mercury Records, DGG Records, Phillips, and Decca, among others. The ensemble took six tours of Japan and Taiwan between 1990 and 2000 under his direction.

Hunsberger performed over 100 premiere performances while conductor of the ensemble. He is well known for his arrangements as well as his musico-logical writings. He is a past president of the College Band Directors National Association and has served as a board member on the boards of the World Association of Symphonic Bands and Ensembles and the Conductor's Guild. Hunsberger has also created and conducted performances of orchestral accom-paniments to over eighteen silent films with fifty orchestras, including the National, San Francisco, Houston, Vancouver, Utah, Rochester, and Calgary Philharmonic orchestras, among others.

John Paynter graduated from Northwestern University in 1950 with a bachelor of music degree and went on to receive a master's degree in theory and composition in 1951. Paynter served as Acting Director of Bands, covering for Glenn Cliffe Bainum, while working on his masters, and was appointed Assistant Director of Bands in 1951 upon completion of his degree. When Bainum retired in 1953, Paynter was appointed Director of Bands, becoming only the second person to hold that position in Northwestern history. Paynter greatly admired Bainum and often acknowledged his influ-ence. He offered the following: "Simply said, Mr. Bainum was my idol, my mentor, and my conscience."

Paynter was fiercely supportive of the community band movement in America, and in 1956 he was central in establishing the Northshore Concert Band. He went on to help facilitate community groups worldwide. Paynter's

record of service to the profession is astonishing. He served as President of the College Band Directors National Association, the World Association for Symphonic Bands and Ensembles, the American Bandmasters Association, and the Big Ten Band Directors Association.

He also directed the Midwest Band and Orchestra Clinic for decades, impacting the careers of tens of thousands of music educators from around the world. He was co-founder and Honorary Life President of the National Band Association, and became a tireless advocate for quality music education. Paynter spent his life making sure others could grow professionally and personally. His musicianship was impeccable, and under his leadership the Northwestern Symphonic Wind Ensemble became one of the most musically important ensembles of its kind in the world.

H. Robert Reynolds is Director of Bands Emeritus of the University of Michigan and is currently Principal Conductor of the Wind Ensemble at the Thornton School of Music at the University of Southern California. His appointment followed his retirement, after twenty-six years, from the School of Music of the University of Michigan. For the past twenty-five years he has also been the conductor of The Detroit Chamber Winds and Strings, which is made up primarily of members from the Detroit Symphony.

Reynolds began his career in the public school of Onstead, Michigan. He has conducted recordings for Koch International, Pro Arte, Caprice, and Deutsche Grammophon records, and has conducted all over the world in many of the major concert halls. Reynolds has premiered works and won the praise of many of the world's most noted composers. He is a past president of the College Band Directors National Association and has received the highest national awards from Phi Mu Alpha, Kappa Kappa Psi, the National Band Association, and many others. He currently serves on the Awards Panel for the American Society of Composers, Authors and Publishers (ASCAP).

Programs of Note: Advancing the Cause

From the 1930s on, many of the university band programs attained a level of excellence comparable to the most stringent professional standards. It is always dangerous to name programs and people for fear of leaving someone out; however, it is important to acknowledge the contributions of some of the programs that emerged as leaders in higher education to provide a perspective. Apologies are offered in advance to omissions from this list, as it is not meant to be exhaustive. Figure 8 lists but a few of the institutions where important contributions were made and those involved:

INSTITUTION	LEADER(S)
Arizona State University	Richard Strange
Baylor University	Donald I. Moore
	Richard Floyd
Bowling Green State University	Mark Kelly
California State University Northridge	David Whitwell
Cincinnati College-Conservatory of Music	Frank Simon
	Robert Hornyak
Drake University	Don Marcouiller
Eastman School of Music	Frederick Fennell
	Donald Hunsberger
Florida State University	James Croft
Indiana University	Frederick Ebbs
	Ray Cramer
Ithaca College	Walter Beeler
Luther College	Weston Noble
Michigan State University	Leonard Falcone
	Harry Begian
	Kenneth Bloomquist
	John Whitwell
New England Conservatory of Music	Frank Battisti
Northwestern University	Glenn Cliffe Bainum
	John Paynter
Oklahoma City University	James Neilson
Purdue University	Al G. Wright
Royal Northern College England	Timothy Reynish
The Ohio State University	Donald McGinnis
University of Arkansas	Elden Janzen
University of Calgary	Vondis Miller
University of California at Los Angeles	Clarence Sawhill
University of Colorado	Hugh McMillen
University of Houston	Eddie Green

INSTITUTION	LEADER(S)
University of Illinois	A. A. Harding
	Mark Hindsley
	Harry Begian
	James Keene
University of Iowa	Frederick Ebbs
	Frank Piersol
	Myron Welch
University of Kansas	Russell Wiley
	Kenneth Bloomquist
	Robert Foster
University of Michigan	Nicholas Falcone
	William D. Revelli
	H. Robert Reynolds
University of Minnesota	Frank Bencriscutto
University of North Texas	Maurice McAdow
	Robert Winslow
University of Northern Colorado	Wayman Walker
University of Southern California	William Schaeffer
University of Tennessee	W. J. Julian
University of Texas	Bernard Fitzgerald
University of Wisconsin	Raymond Dvorak
	H. Robert Reynolds
University of Wisconsin Milwaukee	Thomas Dvorak
West Texas State University	Gary Garner
West Virginia University	Don Wilcox

FIGURE 8.

Looking Ahead: Where Are We Going?

There is, of course, a great deal of history to follow from 1970 to the present. It is not within the scope of this chapter to recount what has expertly been told by Battisti in his book *The Winds of Change*, Hansen in his book *The American Wind Band: A Cultural History*, and Donald Hunsberger and Frank Cipolla in their book *The Wind Ensemble and its Repertoire*. All of these authors have done a remarkable job of chronicling the development of the wind band since 1952.

In my opinion, the real story of the past fifty-six years centers on repertoire development, programming philosophy, and commitment to building an ongoing relationship with the artistic composers of our time. The path established by the visionaries who preceded us has become clearer and well defined. There is no doubt that the wind band is being taken seriously in the twenty-first century. We have fully acknowledged that our future cannot be found in the orchestra's past and that our purpose goes way beyond entertaining the masses.

We have continued to encourage composers to partner with us and advance the art. The repertoire has been broadened and deepened thanks to our many allies in the composition world. There is no group of instrumentalists more active in commissioning new music than the wind band. Future success lies in our ability to continue to interest significant composers to write for the medium. Most who do find it to be a positive and uplifting experience. This quote by Pulitzer-Prize-winning composer John Corigliano (b. 1938) from the forward to *A Composer's Insight, Volume III: Thoughts, Analysis and Commentary on Contemporary Masterpieces for Wind Band*, edited by Timothy Salzman (Galesvile, MD: Meredith Music Publications, 2006) gives testimony to the progress that has been made:

> In my experience, the skills of the player (in the wind band) are surprisingly comparable to that of the orchestral professional; but, unlike the symphony, the culture of these organizations encourages a delight in new repertory, new notations, and new techniques. Rehearsal time allows for real learning, not just reading; and the conductors of today's bands are always teachers first. The audience looks forward to a new piece, and the form lives on a healthy balance of old and new—just like orchestral music used to, albeit back in the day of the horse and carriage. Is it any wonder, then, that all my composer-colleagues are happily writing for concert band, and enjoying extraordinary artistic fulfillment? The only remaining question is, what took us so long?

Our forbearers realized early on that they had a responsibility to bring original wind band music into the world. The quality of wind music performance continues to be sustained at a very high level. Numerous academic, civic, military, and professional ensembles around the globe maintain the highest standards of performance. Creativity and open-mindedness is key to continuing our musical growth. It has always been about imagination and the music. We are responsible for the future of our art. Our performances must remain artistically viable and musically convincing. Our passion for the discipline has got to be expressed in our work. Composers need to be able to trust us with their hearts and souls. Quality and significant work will secure our future, but only if we are vigilant and keep asking for music from the composers we respect and admire. Almost every great work we value as an aesthetic model was the result of a request. More often than not, someone within the profession shares the responsibility for the genesis of a new piece.

It is clear that the history of the wind band must continue to be explored and explained. Additional research and writing is critical. The profession has to take an active role in encouraging, and maybe even commissioning, analytical studies that will contribute to the documentation of our history. Just as we have sought out composers to write our music, we must seek out musicologists to write our story.

When one discusses the value of the wind band medium, invariably the conversation turns to the state of the repertoire. There are countless pieces being added to the literature by a multitude of composers. I use the term literature to refer to the entire body of music that is rapidly being created. The challenge is to determine which works are worthy of becoming an integral part of the repertoire.

In today's wind band, modernity has yielded a concept of "flexible instrumentation," where the group can be as big or as small as the composer wants it to be. The size and instrumentation is expandable and contractible. Rather than being driven by an arbitrary number, the forces assigned are determined by the artistic needs of the composition. At this point in time there continues to be three primary "tributaries of contribution" that flow into the repertoire pool. Today's wind conductors draw upon these three genres of music to create interesting and varied programs. I have listed each area in figure 9 with a sample piece.

Genre	Work	Composer
Chamber Winds	*Gran Partita k.361 (k. 370a)*	Mozart
Orchestral Winds	*Symphonies of Wind Instruments*	Stravinsky
Symphonic Winds	*Symphony in B-flat*	Hindemith

FIGURE 9.

What began as a perceived movement in 1952 with the Eastman Wind Ensemble under the leadership of Frederick Fennell became a philosophy of programming dictated by the composer's wishes and preferences and guided by the innovative genius of Fennell. I am not sure that Frederick Fennell invented the Wind Ensemble as much as discovered it. The concept was really created by composers throughout music history writing exclusively for winds and percussion in a variety of sizes, forms, and settings.

It was a crucial step for the medium when we decided to embrace all three of the tributaries listed above. It opened hundreds of years of repertoire that was for the most part languishing in a sort of "unclaimed zone." The true genius of what Frederick Fennell and others who followed did, in addition to

providing the concept of "flexible instrumentation," was to assume responsibility for the performance of these works. Fennell's insight showed that very interesting programs could be created using new and old music that demanded a variety of instruments and forces. Embracing this broader definition of what a wind band could be resulted in much more intriguing and diversified programs. This in turn highlighted the fact that wind bands have been an integral part of music history as long as there has been music history.

Elevating pieces from the literature into the repertoire requires repeated quality performances that give all a chance to fully evaluate the artistry, value, and significance of a work. Often, repeated performances are difficult to sustain; however, repeated hearings are ever more possible because of the number of recordings available. The robust dedication to chronicling the present through wind recordings is truly unique in music history. Early recording projects, like those of the Marine Band in 1890 were prophetic. They recorded more than sixty pieces on wax cylinders for the Columbia Phonograph Company that were among the most popular recordings of the time.

Recording allows new works to become immediately available to thousands of listening enthusiasts, sometimes just hours after their premiere. It is not unusual for a new composition to appear on multiple discs within a year of its first performance. This allows everyone to revisit a work as often as they like. I believe that this is a valid way of moving a piece along at an incredible speed, and accounts for the quicker rate of acceptance or rejection of a work. It is becoming more and more evident that the recording and distribution of a new work is an essential component in its success and does help to supplant the need for repeated concert performances in order to evaluate its significance.

Recording is an effective way of disseminating valuable information. It allows us to expand the repertoire at an ever-increasing rate of speed. In my opinion, this is a positive thing: the faster the better. Each recording that is produced is offered to the profession at large as examples of music that ought to be accepted into the repertoire. In a sense a recording serves as a "nomination ballot." Not all pieces are or should be recognized as worthy by the profession at large; however, recordings provide a wonderful forum for discussion and comparison while stimulating critical thinking.

Wind bands have developed a symbiotic relationship with recording that can serve their purpose very well. It is a wondrous technology that allows one the ability to stay in constant contact with the growth patterns of the profession and medium. It is somewhat ironic that the very technology that John Philip Sousa saw as a potential threat to the band's future may end up being one of its greatest allies in perpetuating the art.

Codetta: Empowering Allies

I close by sharing some words of encouragement and support from three of the most respected composers in America. Norman Dello Joio (1913–2008) contributed a number of valued pieces throughout his life. An enthusiastic supporter of the medium, he offered the following:

> It seems but yesterday that at the persuasion and urging of Paul Bryan of Duke University, I wrote my first work for band the *Variants on a Mediaeval Tune*. I am ever thankful to him for opening for me [the] examination of new areas of sound. Happily for me these sounds entered the heart of many of you, and looking back, I now am aware of how significant a role handling wind instruments played in my creative life. As a result I joined you all in giving allegiance to a great art form, Music for Band.

No composer in history has contributed more to the wind repertoire than Vincent Persichetti. (1915–1987). His artistry, vision, and support did more to advance the cause of wind music in America and around the world than any other composer in the twentieth century. Persichetti's words found below encapsulate the progress bands have made:

> I'd been composing in a log cabin school house in El Dorado, Kansas, during the summer of 1949: working with some lovely woodwind figures, accentuated by choirs of aggressive brasses and percussion beating. I soon realized the strings weren't going to enter, and my *Divertimento* began to take shape. Many people call this ensemble BAND. I know that composers are often frightened away by the sound of the word "band" because of certain qualities long associated with this medium—rusty trumpets, consumptive flutes, wheezy oboes, disintegrating clarinets, fumbling yet amiable baton wavers, and gum-coated park benches! If you couple these conditions with transfigurations and disfigurations of works originally conceived for orchestra, you create a sound experience that's as nearly excruciating as a sick string quartet playing a dilettante's arrangement of a 19th century piano sonata.

> When composers think of the band as a huge, supple ensemble of winds and percussion, the obnoxious fat will drain off, and creative ideas will flourish. There are many excellent bands in this country, which play as well as the fine orchestras. My *Parable for Band*, a compendium of musical colorings demanding virtuoso technique and flexible shaping of phrases, has had countless first-rate performances. Every musician is asked to play meaningfully and skillfully, even the

second bassoonist and second alto saxophonist—and they do!

And finally, Arnold Schoenberg (1874–1951), who changed the aural land-scape of music forever. Schoenberg discusses the genesis of his *Theme and Variations*, Op. 43a, which was premiered by the Goldman Band in 1945, in the excerpt from his correspondence found below:

> My dear friend, the late Carl Engel, then president of the G. Schirmer, Inc., had asked me frequently to write a piece for wind band. He complained that the great number of such bands had an important influence on the development of love for music in America, but unfor-tunately there are only a small number of good original compositions available, while for the most of their playing they are limited to arrangements. A considerable part of these arrangements reveals a poor or at least a low taste; and besides they are not even well orches-trated... It is one of those works that one writes in order to enjoy one's own virtuosity and, in addition, to give a group of amateurs—in this case, wind bands—something better to play. I can assure you—and I think I can prove it—that as far as technique is concerned it is a mas-terpiece; and I know it is inspired. Not only because I cannot write even ten measures without inspiration, but I really wrote the piece with great pleasure.

Consider what a positive situation we enjoy at this moment in music history. Each year that passes provides a greater amount of quality music to keep alive. If the last sixty-five years is any indication, we can look forward to a future filled with incredible works of art from the world's best composers that demand to be sustained. We are responsible for the character and excellence of the music that will be created and performed. It has become completely certain that the substance and value of our work influences who our allies will be. Our charge is to *preserve* the music of the past, *promote* the music of the present, and *encourage* the music of the future.

Read More About It

Battisti, Frank. *The Winds of Change*. Galesville, MD: Meredith Music Publications, 2002.

Berlioz, Hector. *Grand Traité d'instrumention et d'orchestration modernes*. Edited and revised by Joseph Bennett. Translated by Mary Cowden Clarke. London: Novello, Ewer and Company, 1882.

Bierly, Paul E. *John Philip Sousa, American Phenomenon*. Westerville, Ohio: Integrity Press, 1973.

Carse, Adam. *The History of Orchestration*. New York: Dover Publications, Inc., 1964.

Cipolla, Frank, and Donald Hunsberger. *The Wind Ensemble and Its Repertoire: Essays on the Fortieth Anniversary of the Eastman Wind Ensemble*. Rochester, NY: University of Rochester Press, 1994.

Fennell, Frederick. *Time and the Winds*. Hunterville, NC: Northland Music Publishers, 1954.

Fennell, Frederick. *The Wind Ensemble*. Arkadelphia, AK: Delta Publications, 1988.

Goldman, Richard Franko. *The Concert Band*. New York: Ferris Printing Company, 1946.

Goldman, Richard Franko. *The Wind Band, its Literature and Technique*. Boston: Allyn and Bacon, 1961.

Hansen, Richard. *The American Wind Band: A Cultural History*. Chicago: GIA Publications, 2005.

Kennan, Kent, and Donald Grantham. *The Techniques of Orchestration*. Upper Saddle River, NJ: Prentice-Hall, 2002.

Renshaw, Jeffrey H. *The American Wind Symphony Commissioning Project: A Descriptive Catalog of Published Editions, 1957–1991*. New York: Greenwood Press, 1991.

Rimsky-Korsakov, Nicolai. *Principles of Orchestration*. Edited by Maximilian Steinberg. New York: Dover Publications, 1964.

Sachs, Curt. *The History of Musical Instruments*. New York: W. W. Norton & Company, Inc., 1940.

Salzman, Timothy, ed. *A Composer's Insight: Thoughts, Analysis and Commentary on Contemporary Masterpieces for Wind Band*. Volume Three. Galesville, MD: Meredith Music Publications, 2002.

Schwartz, H. W. *Bands of America*. Garden City, NY: Doubleday & Company, Inc., 1957.

Whitwell, David. *Berlioz on Bands: A Compilation of Berlioz's Writings on Bands and Wind Instruments*. Northridge, CA: Winds, 1992.

Whitwell, David. *A Concise History of the Wind Band*. Saint Louis, MO: Shattinger's Music Company, 1985.

Whitwell, David. *The History and Literature of the Wind Band and Wind Ensemble*. 11 Vols. Northridge, CA: Winds, 1982–1990.

Whitwell, David. *The Longy Club: A Professional Wind Ensemble in Boston (1900–1917)*. Northridge, CA: Winds, 1988.

Hear More About It

TITLE	COMPOSER	ALBUM TITLE	ENSEMBLE	CONDUCTOR	COMPANY	NUMBER	PUBLISHER
Adagio and Rondo	Carl Maria von Weber (1786–1826)	Carl Maria von Weber: Music for Winds	Music for a Sunday Afternoon	Jean-Claude Malgoire	CBS Records Masterworks	M 39011	Musica Rara
Apollo March	Anton Bruckner (1824–1896)/ arr. Tom C. Rhodes	Water Music	Kosei Wind Orchestra	Kazuyoshi Akiyama	Kosei Publishing	KOCD-3072	Southern Music Company
Chant Funeraire, Op. 117	Gabriel Faure (1845–1924)	Teaching Music through Performance in Band: Volume 6, Grades 4–5	North Texas Wind Symphony	Eugene Migliaro Corporon	GIA	CD 684	Hal Leonard Corporation
Commemoration Symphony	Anton Reicha (1770–1831)/ ed. David Whitwell	Memorials	University of Cincinatti-College of Music Wind Symphony	Eugene Migliaro Corporon	Klavier	KCD 11042	Winds
Concertino for Oboe	Carl Maria von Weber (1786–1826)	Carl Maria von Weber: Music for Winds	Music for a Sunday Afternoon	Jean-Claude Malgoire	CBS Records Masterworks	M 39011	Musica Rara
Concerto for Clarinet	Nicolai Rimsky-Korsakov (1844–1908)	Your Seat	Tokyo Kosei Wind Orchestra	Frederick Fennell	Kosei Publishing	KOCD-4001	Edwin F. Kalmus and Co.
Concerto for Trombone	Nicolai Rimsky-Korsakov (1844–1908)/ arr. Otto Zurmühle	Windpower	Kosei Wind Orchestra	Chikara Imamura	BIS	CD-848	Molenaar
Dance of the Jesters	Peter Tchaikovsky (1840–1893)	Teaching Music through Performance in Band: Volume 2, Grades 4–5	North Texas Wind Symphony	Eugene Migliaro Corporon	GIA	CD 551	Curnow Music/Hal Leonard
Dionysiaques, Op. 62, No. 1	Florent Schmitt (1870–1958)	Songs and Dances	University of Cincinatti-College of Music Wind Symphony	Eugene Migliaro Corporon	Klavier	K-11066	Theodore Presser Company (Rental)

TITLE	COMPOSER	ALBUM TITLE	ENSEMBLE	CONDUCTOR	COMPANY	NUMBER	PUBLISHER
Florentiner Op. 214	Julius Fucik (1872–1916)/arr. Mahew L. Lake/ed. Frederick Fennell	Teaching Music through Performing Marches	North Texas Wind Symphony	Eugene Migliaro Corporon	GIA	CD 563	Carl Fischer, LLC
Four Chorales for Popular Festivals	Charles Koechlin (1867–1950)	Hector Berlioz	Musique des Gardiensde la Paix	Désiré Dondeyne	Calliope	CAL 9859	
Funeral March (in memory of Rikard Nordraak)	Edvard Grieg (1843–1907)/trans. Eriksen/ed. Fennell	Trittico	Dallas Wind Symphony	Frederick Fennell	Reference Recordings	RR-52CD	Ludwig-Masters Publications
Grande Symphonie Funèbre et Triomphale	Hector Berlioz (1803–1869)	Berlioz	The Wallace Collection	John Wallace	Nimbus Records	NI 5175	Ludwig-Masters Publications
Huldigungsmarsch (Homage March)	Richard Wagner (1813–1883)/ed. William Schaefer	Romantic Sensibilities	Wisconsin Wind Orchestra	Lawrence Dale Harper	Mark Recording Service, Inc.	2483-MCD	Shawnee Press, Inc.
March	Carl Maria von Weber (1786–1826)	Marsche and Blasmusik	Blaser des Rundfunk-Sinfonie-Orchestrers Berlin	Hans-Peter Kirchberg/Sebastian Weigle	Capriccio	10 499	
Marcia Funebre	Giuseppe Filippa (1836–1905)	Romantic Sensibilities	Wisconsin Wind Orchestra	Lawrence Dale Harper	Mark Recording Service, Inc.	2483-MCD	
Military March in F	Peter Tchaikovsky (1840–1893)	The World of the Military Band	The Band of the Grenadier Guards	Peter Parkes	Decca Records	452938	
Notturno Op. 34	Louis Spohr (1784–1859)	Harmonie Und Janitscharenmusik	Octophoros	Paul Dombrecht	Accent	ACC8860 D	Tetra/Continuo Music Group
Occident et Orient Op. 25	Camille Saint-Saens (1835–1921)	Marine Band Showcase Vol. 2	United States Marine Band	John Bourgeois	GIA		Maecenas Music/Masters Music
Ouverture fur Harmoniemusic, Op. 24	Felix Mendelssohn (1809–1847)/arr. John Boyd	Romantic Sensibilities	Wisconsin Wind Orchestra	Lawrence Dale Harper	Mark Recording Service, Inc.	2483-MCD	Ludwig-Masters Publications

TITLE	COMPOSER	ALBUM TITLE	ENSEMBLE	CONDUCTOR	COMPANY	NUMBER	PUBLISHER
Partita for Band (Symphony)	Franz Krommer (1759–1831)		Cincinatti Symphony Band	Robert Hornyak	Corporon Private Collection		
Radetzky March	Johann Strauss (1804–1849)/ arr. Reed	Sound Off!	United States Marine Band	John Bourgeois	United States Marine Band		C. L. Barnhouse, Inc.
Requiem for Louis XVI	Charles Bochsa (1789–1856)				Corporon Collection		
Scherzo for Band "Fanfare for the Italian Crown"	Gioacchino Rossini (1792–1868)	Teaching Music through Performance in Band: Volume 5, Grades 4–5	North Texas Wind Symphony	Eugene Migliaro Corporon	GIA	CD 638	Hal Leonard Corporation (Out of Print)
Siegessinfonie "Wellington's Victory of 1813"	Ludwig van Beethoven (1770–1827)	Harmonie Und Janitscharenmusik	Octophoros	Paul Dombrecht	Accent	ACC 8860 D manuscript	
Symphony in B flat	Paul Fauchet (1881–1937)/ arr. Gillette and Campbell-Watson	Bells for Stowkowski	Showa Wind Symphony	Eugene Migliaro Corporon	CAFUA	CARUA 0049	M. Whitmark & Sons
Tema con Variazioni	Carl Maria von Weber (1786–1826)	Carl Maria von Weber: Music for Winds	Music for a Sunday Afternoon	Jean-Claude Malgoire	CBS Records Masterworks	M 39011	Musica Rara
The "Lads of Wamphray"	Percy Grainger (1882–1961)	Teaching Music through Performance in Band: Volume 2, Grades 4–5	North Texas Wind Symphony	Eugene Migliaro Corporon	GIA	CD 551	Carl Fischer, LLC
The Battle of Leipzig	Václav Vincenc Masek (1755–1831)				Corporon Collection		Corporon Collection
The Warriors	Percy Grainger (1882–1961)	Convergence	North Texas Wind Symphony	Eugene Migliaro Corporon	Klavier	K-11110	Theodore Presser Company (Rental)

TITLE	COMPOSER	ALBUM TITLE	ENSEMBLE	CONDUCTOR	COMPANY	NUMBER	PUBLISHER
Trauermusic nach Themen aus "Euryanthe"	Richard Wagner (1813–1883)/ arr. Votta & Boyd	Romantic Sensibilities	Wisconsin Wind Orchestra	Lawrence Dale Harper	Mark Recording Service, Inc.	2483-MCD	Ludwig-Masters Publications
Two Marches for the Sultan Abdul Medjid I	Gaetano Donizetti (1797–1848)/ed. Townsend	Marsche and Blasmusik	Blaser des Rundfunk-Sinfonie-Orchestrers Berlin	Hans-Peter Kirchberg/ Sebastian Weigle	Capriccio	10 499	Theodore Presser Company
Two Marches for the Sultan Abdul Medjid II	Gioacchino Rossini (1792–1868)/ed. Townsend	Sound Off!	United States Marine Band	John Bourgeois	United States Marine Band		
Variations for Oboe	Nicolai Rimsky-Korsakov (1844–1908)	Russian Concert Band Music	Stockholm Concert Band	Gennady Rozhdestvensky	Chandos	CHAN 9444	McGinnis & Marx Music Publishing

See More About It

Fisher, Dennis, ed. Fennell, Hindsley, and Revelli. *History of the School Band Movement: As Told by Those Who Were There*. Digital video disc DVD-794. GIA Publications, Inc., 2008.
Fisher, Dennis, ed. Fennell, Hindsley, and Revelli. *Master Conductors: A Legacy of Wisdom*. Digital video disc DVD-708. GIA Publications, Inc, 2007.
Fisher, Dennis, ed. Fennell, Hindsley, and Revelli. *Master Conductors: The Art of the March*. Digital video disc DVD-755. GIA Publications, Inc., 2008.
Gabriel, Arnald and Tim Lautzenheiser. *Master Conductors: Col. Arnald D. Gabriel*. Digital video disc DVD-726. GIA Publications, Inc., 2006.

CHAPTER 6

Exploring the Japanese Band Culture

A Personal Journey from Delong to Tokyo

Ray Cramer

So long as the human spirit thrives on this planet, music in some living form will accompany and sustain it and give it expressive meaning.

—Aaron Copland

Introduction

After reading the title of this chapter, you must be thinking, "Where in the heck is Delong?" That would be a good question, as few people in this world have heard of Delong, unless of course you lived in Knoxville, Abington, or even Maquon, Illinois. I wouldn't bet on many in those towns having heard of Delong, either.

If you care to google Delong, Illinois, you will be amazed (I was) that it actually comes up. It is in Knox County (home of the Lincoln/Douglas debate) and the map of Delong shows three north-south streets and two east-west streets. The railroad track that shows on the map has not been in existence since the 1930s. However, that happens to be the town closest to where I grew up. Notice I said *closest* to where I grew up.

My father used to tell people we lived at "Eleventh and Plum—eleven miles plum out in the country." Delong was a very nice, small (very small) rural town. I'm not sure "town" would be the correct description, either, but it did have a grocery store, gas station, post office, hardware store, soda fountain, drug store, and clothing store—all in the same thirty-by-fifty-foot building. The owners were way ahead of their time (a.k.a. strip mall), but in Delong, it was just the general store.

The town did have a two-room schoolhouse, with one room housing grades 1 through 3 and the other 4 through 6. There was one church, the Delong Congregational Church, which housed one of the five existing pianos in town and a very large garage in which Sam Cline housed his fertilizer business. On Thursday night, Sam would park all of his fertilizer trucks

outside, sweep the floor (if he had time), hang up a big white sheet, set-up folding chairs, and show movies with an admission price of twenty-five cents for adults and ten cents for children under twelve. This only took place in warmer weather, as the garage was not heated.

One of the small houses in town contained the local telephone switchboard. Every residence in the community had crank telephones hanging on a wall of their home. When someone wanted to call you, the switchboard operator would plug into your party line and dial—no, crank your number. Ours was two shorts and three longs. There were few secrets in the community, for everyone on your line knew your ring and would often listen in just to catch up on the latest gossip in the community. Delong probably had a population of ninety when I was growing up, including family pets.

I did not live in town, but grew up on a farm one mile from town (and I use the word loosely in Delong's case). It was just close enough that when you earned twenty-five cents for some odd job or mowing a yard, you could bike to the general store and buy a pop and a bag of salty peanuts for fifteen cents and still have a dime left over for the piggy bank, which in my case, was an old sock I kept in my dresser drawer.

There was no piano in our house, nor a record player or TV, but I did listen faithfully to my favorite radio programs, where I heard my first classical music (even though I didn't know it at the time) on shows like *The Lone Ranger* and *Sergeant Preston of the Yukon*. Other than the radio there was no other music in our home.

Occasionally I would hear my older sisters hum or sing some popular music they knew, but that certainly did not inspire me to pursue a music profession. That inspiration actually did not begin until sometime during my sixth-grade year in our local two-room school.

A music teacher from the city (population 1,672) visited our class carrying several different wind instruments that I had never seen or heard. After a short demonstration of these instruments, he asked the students which instrument they would like to play. The most popular choices were the trumpet, clarinet, saxophone, flute, and of course, percussion.

No one had chosen trombone, and I thought it was the most interesting one of all because it looked cool, and he played these really neat glissandos during the demonstration. (I had no idea what a glissando was, but it sounded like it would be fun to play.) As I surveyed the situation, no one else had picked the trombone, so right away I thought to myself, "That would make me the first chair player!"

This same logic served me well when I decided to go out for football. Everyone wanted to play one of the skill positions because of the honor and visibility; no one wanted to play center or linebacker, so as a result I was always a starter from then until I graduated.

I convinced my parents I *really* wanted to play the trombone, so my father finally agreed and sold a couple of hogs so we could by a Pan American trombone. I was so happy, and from the very first lesson I could play glissandos like a pro. My parents tired of this very quickly and my dad deemed that the best practice area for me would be the in barn. Better for my parents, but egg and milk production dropped off dramatically in the next few weeks.

As the weeks progressed, I found out there was an expectation to *practice* in order to learn real notes and rhythms. The glissandos became increasingly less fun, and the practice time was cutting into my fishing, football, baseball, bike-riding, and in general, having fun time. So, like so many disillusioned young musicians at that age, I quit. This did not sit well with my parents, especially my dad, because it cost him two hogs, and the trombone was not sturdy enough to patch a hole in the fence.

Had it not been for a new music teacher who moved into our school district, I would have missed out on the most fantastic career one could imagine. Somehow this new teacher, Mr. Zimmerman, found my name on a list and saw I had not signed up for junior high instrumental music. Mr. Zimmerman just showed up at our farm (at Eleventh and Plum) one afternoon, questioning why I had not signed up for band. I told him it was quite simple: "I was a terrible player, did not enjoy playing the trombone, didn't like to practice, and the only thing I did learn to do fairly well was play glissandos."

He proceeded to get his own trombone out of the car and played some of the most beautiful sounds I had ever heard that did not involve a glissando. Even my father smiled and thought it had potential as a musical instrument rather than using it as farm equipment, like a water pump for the horse tank. He asked me to get out my trombone (I was hoping it was still in my closet and that my dad had not flattened it out to patch a hole in the grain bin) and proceeded to give me a lesson right then and there.

Within thirty minutes I was playing better than I had ever sounded before without playing a single glissando. Mr. Zimmerman convinced me I was a natural, blessed with a great embouchure, a nice, focused sound, and that I would really enjoy the experience of playing in his band. He also offered to give me lessons each week, at no cost (can you believe that?) if my parents would just bring me to town (not Delong, but the city of population 1,672) once a week for a lesson.

I had no idea at this young age where this new perception of music making would take me. Never underestimate *your* power to motivate and inspire young people. Mr. Zimmerman, and others along the way, did just that, and it changed my life and propelled me into the great profession of teaching and a life-long joy of conducting bands.

I have been blessed with the opportunity to have experiences in our profession at every level. I spent my first seven years teaching in public school instrumental music programs ranging from my first job, where the high school enrollment was 53 students (in the whole school, only 16 in band) to a program with an enrollment of 3,600 students in three grades at my last public school job at Parma Senior High School, just outside of Cleveland.

At Parma Senior High School, every student in the top band of ninety players and most of the second band, also studied privately with top professional musicians in the Cleveland area, including members of the Cleveland Orchestra. Those seven years involved four different schools before I accepted a position as the Assistant Director of Bands at Indiana University. Little did I know I would spend the next thirty-six years of my life (the last twenty-four as Director of Bands) at this fantastic institution, teaching and conducting in one of the nation's great schools of music, the Jacobs School of Music. This position presented to me the great pleasure of working with some of the most talented young musicians in the country and without question, a world-renowned faculty.

Japan, the Land of the Rising Sun and Lots of Outstanding Bands

My first time to experience the country of Japan and to hear Japanese bands was in 1984 when the IU Symphonic Band was invited to perform at the joint ABA/JBA convention in Tokyo. I was in my second year as the Director of Bands, and taking a trip like this was a challenge, a thrill, and frightening, all at the same time. During our sixteen-day tour, the band performed seven concerts in cities around Japan, providing the opportunity to hear several outstanding Japanese bands in the various locations. At the ABA/JBA convention, we were able to hear the Kosei Wind Ensemble (the group's name at that time) under the direction of their newly-appointed music director and conductor, Frederick Fennell.

On the same program we heard two of the top military bands from Japan along with two outstanding high school bands. Needless to say, they were impressive performances, and opened our eyes to the performance level of Japanese bands ranging from school to professional bands.

After our arrival in Tokyo, our first rehearsal took place at the Musashino Academy of Music. This was the largest music school in Japan, with approximately 4,000 music majors in the program. Of the 4,000, there were 2,000 piano majors. Can you imagine that? There was no way of knowing then that six years later I would be invited to conduct their top wind ensemble for a semester, thus beginning a professional relationship that has now extended to eighteen years.

These experiences have given me the opportunity to enjoy extended tenures with two major institutions in two different cultures. These two universities have provided a framework in which I could continue to grow professionally, participate, experience, and investigate the impact each culture has had on the other. I will relate more about the Musashino Academy of Music and its influences on the Japanese band culture later in this chapter.

Historical Foundations

In 1853, United States Navy Admiral Perry broke the policy of no foreign contact with Japan when he sailed into Tokyo Bay with a fleet of nine ships. On board this fleet was a small military band that performed the first band music in Japan. There is no record of the instrumentation of that band, but we can assume it mirrored the accepted size and instrumentation found in other U. S. military bands of the period.

The Meiji Period began in 1868, and there were English and French bands stationed in Yokohama that performed on a regular basis. It wasn't until 1871 that the first Japanese Navy Band was formed, comprised of thirty-six instrumentalists. Much like the French model of the time, the band was woodwind-dominated. One year later the first Japanese Army Band was established with a French Bandmaster as the teacher/conductor. Throughout the remainder of the nineteenth century, Japanese bands continued to grow and were mainly influenced by foreign teachers and conductors.

A retired Japanese army bandmaster led the first Japanese high school band, organized in 1903 in Kyoto. The first band association was formed in 1934, and the following year saw the first local band contest established in Nagoya and Tokyo. In 1939 the All-Japan Band Association was formed, resulting in the first All-Japan Band Contest held in Osaka. This major contest continued for three years, but it was discontinued in 1943 due to World War II. This contest did not resume again until 1956. After World War II, Japan adopted the American Educational System of 6–3–3.

The 6–3 system was compulsory, but the last three years of high school were not because of the need for a larger work force following the war. Almost all of the schools were co-educational, except for some technical high schools, traditional all-girl high schools, and a few private schools. Band activities resumed very slowly.

It is common knowledge that the person most influential in helping re-ignite the Japanese band movement after the war was Toshio Akiyama. However, being the humble person that he is, he asked me to acknowledge others he felt deserve equal notice. Here is Toshio's list of additional movers and shakers in this rebuilding effort.

Pioneer and Leading Band Directors in Japan 1950~1960

1. Kansai Area (Osaka)
   Ichitaro Tujii (1910–1986), Director of Osaka City Concert Band
     (professional)
   Kiyoshi Yano (1902–1973), Director of Tenri HS Band
   Takeshi Tokutsu (1917–1982), Director of Imazu JH Band
   Masamori Matsudaira (1925–2008), Director of Kureha Elementary
   School Band
   Takeo Suzuki (1923–2005) Director of Hankyu Department Store
   Band (Pioneer of Marching Band, especially Stage Show)

2. Chubu Area (Nagoya)
   Terumi Jinno (1899–1987), Director of Toho HS Band
   Susumu Yamamoto (1907–1989), Director of Gamagori Junior
     HS Band

3. Kanto Area (Tokyo)
   Masato Yamamoto (1916–1986), Director of Tokyo University
     of Fine Arts Symphonic Band
   Yoshio Hiroka (1898–1988), Director of Ochanomizu JH Band
     (author of an individual instrumental method)
   Tetsuya Hiroka (1930–), Director of Kanto Gakuen HS Marching
     Band (pioneer of marching band in Japan, son of Yoshio)
   Tomoaki Mito (1901–1987), President of Music Publishing
     Company, author and conductor
   Toshio Akiyama (1929–), Band Director, Sakuragi JH, Omiya Tech
     HS; in 1958, he founded the Sony Concert Band

4. Influential American Band Directors
   George Howard, Director of USAF Band, visited Japan in 1956
     leading the first foreign band to perform in Japan after the war
   Paul Yoder, encouraged Japanese directors to establish the Japanese
     Band Directors Association
   Clarence Sawhill, Director of Bands at ULCA, who gave the
     very first band clinics in Japan following the war

5. Later influences from 1960 to the present
   Francis McBeth, with his book Effective Performance of Band Music
   Fred Fennell, Conductor of Tokyo Kosei Wind Orchestra (1984)
   Alfred Reed, Visiting Professor at Senzoku School of Music
   All visiting professors at Musashino Academy of Music

Harold Walters was a visiting clinician for Rubank Publishing Company presenting new teaching materials and methods for young musicians. Paul Yoder, American composer, conductor, and educator, was a frequent visitor and became a very popular and often-performed composer in the country. In 1951 Akiyama started the Sakuragi Junior High School Band in Omiya City, Saitama Prefecture with twenty-five members. Toshio shared that they used all second-hand instruments (that was all they could find and afford) except for drums.

Within a short time the band became one of the premier young bands in the country. Following his outstanding work with his junior high band he directed the Omiya Technical HS band to a lofty national status. In 1958 Akiyama founded the Sony Concert Band and was the conductor of that outstanding corporation band for the next forty-two years.

To get a better understanding of American bands, Akiyama became the first Japanese band director to visit the United States in 1963 to observe band activities and to study at the Eastman School of Music. Following that year he invited many American band directors to Japan and introduced new band music and method books to Japanese directors. American bands became the model for Japanese bands in size, tonal production, and literature performed. It seems, however, in recent years Japanese bands have become a model for bands around the world as they exhibit their outstanding performance standards.

The Japanese Educational System

Japan is a relatively small country in terms of land area—about the size of California—but with a population of 127,433,494, according to a 2007 census. School education is under the supervision of the national government. The Ministry of Education has total control for hiring teachers and decisions on curriculum offerings. There are approximately 24,000 elementary schools, 10,000 junior high schools and 5,000 high schools in the country. As mentioned earlier, the present system adopted (for the most part) after World War II remains largely intact today. As opposed to the philosophy after the war, when high school was optional, today over ninety-five percent of junior high school graduates enter high school.

Music in the Schools

Classes begin daily at 8:30 AM and continue in almost every school until 3:30 or 4:00 PM. Saturday mornings are also utilized for the purpose of academic classes, except on the second and fourth Saturdays of the month. The school term is much different than in American schools. In Japan, the academic year is divided into three terms, with the first beginning in April, the second in

September and the third in January, with summer vacation falling between July 20 and August 31.

Generally speaking, there are two elementary music classes a week with the classroom teacher in charge. During these classes the focus is on rhythm instruments, singing, and the use of recorder-type instruments to learn note reading. They also listen to many recordings to instill sensitivity to music. I have listened to some elementary classes sing, and I am very impressed with their ability to sing in tune, producing a very pleasing sound.

Fifth- and sixth-grade students who wish to learn a wind or percussion instrument do this exclusively after school hours in what is a club activity. Many of these instrumental classes are taught by what Akiyama calls a "hobby teacher"—a person interested in band and who is willing to take on this assignment, but not necessarily musically trained to teach.

Junior high music classes continue with the same schedule, with music classes meeting twice a week. These classes provide the same basic emphasis as the elementary classes, but include a music laboratory system with multiple keyboards for advanced study in music theory, technical training, and even composition.

For those students who continue with their instrumental music training, the schedule is much more intense, with daily rehearsals, especially if the band wishes to compete in various contests. Once a student reaches high school, music courses are no longer offered. Due to intense testing in order to get into better universities, many students choose a more academic course of study. Unfortunately, much the same occurs in the United States.

Band Activities

Concert band offerings in the schools, regardless if they are public or private, take place almost exclusively after the school day, continuing as a club activity. As such, it is important to note that almost all clubs require students to pay a fee to participate.

The monthly fee for participation in band clubs normally runs in the neighborhood of 2,000 Yen ($20 USD). These funds go toward the purchase of new music, instrument repair, some travel costs, and administrative expenditures.

Teachers who have a keen desire to see these ensembles flourish direct these organizations, including orchestras and choirs. According to information supplied by Toshio Akiyama, there are approximately 1,000 elementary concert bands in Japan, ranging is size from forty to sixty members.

Junior High School concert bands probably comprise the largest segment of band activity in Japan. There are about 7,000 bands at this level, with probably half being strongly competitive, which requires students to be present for rehearsal at least two hours every day after school, including Saturday and Sunday. Some bands rehearse even longer periods of time, especially if they desire to reach the coveted position of inclusion in the All-Japan Band Contest held each October and November in Tokyo.

High school concert bands number around 3,800, and are organized in much the same manner as junior high ensembles. The main reason there are not more high school bands is, once again, related to the pressure students feel for academic excellence. This results in fewer ensembles and with fewer upperclassmen taking part. By the time students reach their senior year they are focusing on the all-important college entrance exams and do not have the time to participate in these activities.

Another thing I have noticed during the past fifteen years in my visits to Japan is the fewer number of boys participating in bands. Just as in America, athletics, other club activities, and the need to work part-time jobs to earn extra money in particular leads boys away from band participation. For those bands that wish to seriously compete in the All-Japan Band Contest, the time demand for rehearsal is even more extreme than for junior high ensembles. For the high school ensembles that make the final contest, rehearsal require-ments can be over thirty hours a week, all of which occur after school and on Saturday and Sunday. I will share more about the specifics of this incredible contest later in the chapter.

The performance capability of Japanese bands has increased dramatically in the past twenty-five years. There are many contributing factors to this but here are a few perspectives.

- Education of the directors has improved significantly with school of music training
- A great enthusiasm for bands and band literature
- The popularity and significance of the contest system
- The influence of visiting American conductors, clinicians, and com-posers
- Developing better tonal and pitch concepts based on American trends
- Greater understanding and support from schools and parents
- Improved instrumentation and a better focus on tonal concepts, bal-ance, and blend
- More emphasis on performing quality original compositions for wind band
- The increase of beautiful concert venues throughout the country

Contest

The All-Japan Band Contest is one of the most fascinating events I have ever witnessed. The process and intense competition that permeates the atmosphere of this contest season dominates the thoughts and efforts of students and directors alike. Literally every director in the country takes interest in the event, and many attend even if their own ensembles are not involved. Without question, this competitive atmosphere has contributed more significantly to raising the performance standard of Japanese bands than any other individual factor. School bands rehearse intensely for months leading up to the contest season. In my own estimation, perhaps too many hours are focused on the two pieces they will perform. The contest is not just for junior and senior high school bands. There are five categories in which bands may participate.

- Junior high school
- Senior high school
- College or university
- Industrial or corporation
- Community

I am not sure of the total number of bands participating in 2006, as I only attended the senior high contest day. However, for the three-day event, I am sure there were nearly ninety bands selected from Japan's ten districts, with all of the above categories represented. The junior- and senior-high contests are held separately, with the other three categories occurring on a separate day; they change from city to city each year. Over 10,000 bands begin the process with the first prefecture-level contest (like American state-level events) held in August. District-level contest is held in September, with the final contest taking place in October and November in Tokyo, held in the largest concert hall in Japan—Fumonkan Hall—which seats approximately 5,500.

The junior- and senior-high contest is held on two consecutive days with twenty-eight bands each day. These fifty-six bands represent the top winners in each of the districts. Some districts have more than one representative because of the population of that district. Competing bands must limit the size of the ensemble to fifty members.

Each year the Japan Band Association commissions five Japanese composers to write a required composition for the contest. These compositions vary in difficulty, representing junior high to university level. However, any group, in any category may select any of the five pieces to play for their required selec-tion. It is not unusual for a junior high ensemble to perform the more advanced selections. The performance time of these commissioned numbers is between three to five minutes.

The ensemble then performs a showcase number of their own choosing in the remaining time. Since total performance time allowed is only twelve minutes, the audience is instructed to applaud only following the final number as the band is leaving the stage in order not to take any performance time away from the band. Each ensemble has a fifteen-minute stage time, but that includes time to enter and exit. If a competing band goes over their time limit even by one second, the band is excluded from the evaluation.

Bands compete for a Gold, Silver, or Copper rating. The adjudication panel is comprised of nine people representing every level of teaching and conducting as well as specialists in winds, brass, and percussion. During the three days of the contest there will be twenty-seven different adjudicators, nine for each day.

There is no recording of adjudicators made, and scores are not provided to adjudicators. Adjudicators watch and listen only. Following a performance, they write very brief comments, and indicate their rating on a form provided by the All-Japan Band Directors Association.

When the morning or afternoon session is finished (fourteen bands in each session), scoring sheets are collected by an officer of the AJBA so that all adjudicator scores may be calculated. Then the Board of Directors of the AJBA discuss where the lines will be drawn to establish Gold, Silver, and Copper ratings. Following this procedure, the President of the AJBA will show adjudicators this result to get their agreement. There are rarely any changes made by adjudicators. A public awards ceremony then takes place announcing the final results to the audience and all fourteen bands. You have never heard such loud cheers when the Gold medal winners are announced.

Another astounding fact of this event is the size of the audience. I mentioned earlier the concert hall seats 5,500. There is standing room only. After the morning session, the hall is cleared and another 5,500 attend the afternoon session. Tickets for each session are $20. Many people purchase tickets for both sessions. It would seemingly unnerve the young people participating, but they seem to take it all in stride, always exhibiting great poise and professionalism.

I have discussed the contest in detail, as is deserving of this huge event, but I would like to share one last observation involving the stage change between bands. Every band has its own particular set-up and uses their own percussion equipment. As a band is leaving the stage, every person has a piece of equipment assigned to them to take offstage while the next band enters, carrying, pushing, or pulling their own equipment.

At the same time bands are leaving and entering, a stage crew is re-adjusting chairs for the next group. They allow forty-five seconds between bands, and the amazing thing is that they stay within this time frame. The entire event is truly mind-boggling.

Each year several American directors travel to Tokyo in order to visit schools and attend the two-day junior- and senior-high contest. Their response mirrors what I have said many times: "You have to see it and hear it to believe it!"

Directors have asked me if there is any opportunity for those students who wish to participate in some form of solo and ensemble contest. The short answer is, "Yes!" There are many options for this kind of contest, depending on the location of the school district. Otaki, Director of Bands at Saitama-Sakae High School, shared the following information:

> There are a lot of ensemble contests held nationally each year. In Saitama prefecture, we are allowed to enter two ensemble groups from each school. There are try-outs prior to the contests in order to choose those two entries. So, most students experience ensemble performance. There are numerous contests named "for Jr. and Sr. High School Students" organized by different associations and companies (such as AJBC, each instrumental association, instrument and music shops, and Shobi Music College and Toho Music College) and we let students know about them as we receive announcements.

Rehearsal Technique/Procedure

Before launching into rehearsal techniques, it might be interesting to know a little bit about the general instrumentation of these competitive ensembles. In the past few years I have seen a general trend to smaller ensembles at both the high school and university level. Some instrumental departments with large numbers of students in the total program will generally use a larger ensemble for their regular concerts. As I mentioned earlier, bands that compete in the All-Japan Band Contest have a fifty-member limit for their performance. It might be interesting to see a typical fifty-member instrumentation, with minor alterations, depending on personnel and literature being performed:

1	Piccolo	4	Saxophones (2–1–1)
4	Flutes (2–2)	5	Horns
2	Oboes (one doubling EH as needed)	6	Trumpets
2	Bassoons	4	Trombones
9	B-flat clarinets (1 doubles on E-flat as needed)	2	Euphoniums
		2	Tubas
2	Bass clarinets (1 doubles on contrabass clarinet as needed)	2	Double basses
		5	Percussion

This instrumentation has the capacity to play with power, depth, and richness of sound, and yet the ability to be wonderfully transparent and light.

For the top fifty-six junior and senior high school bands reaching the final contest, there is a rehearsal style and procedure employed in order to achieve their goal. I most certainly have not observed all of these schools, but I have visited several that do make the finals to witness firsthand what happens in the course of a rehearsal.

Keep in mind that most of these ensembles rehearse daily, including week-ends, for a lengthy period of time. A typical weekly schedule for these top bands is to meet daily after school (4:00 PM) for four hours, six hours on Saturday, and four hours on Sunday afternoon. I can hear your question burning through the page right now: "How do they get students to commit and adhere to such a schedule? I could never get my students to agree to such a demanding rehearsal schedule."

I hear you, and agree that it would be difficult to get most American students to see the benefits of such a demanding schedule. This is where you must understand the cultural differences between the two countries. Japanese tradition, going back century upon century, relishes the concept of group identity. There is a sense of commitment, pride, and confidence that comes from group activities. As such, the time commitment is not as important as the *result* of the time spent together in any type of ensemble experience. (I firmly believe this previous statement should be a fact in *any* rehearsal, even if it only lasts an hour!) If at the end of a four-hour rehearsal the students feel *rewarded* by seeing *improvement* in their performance level, then the time is justified.

My wife and I often take early morning walks or bikes rides in our Tokyo neighborhood and observe business, fire station, office workers or police station personnel doing group exercises together in the parking lot before beginning their daily responsibilities. The exercise is important, but the real thrust is pulling together thoughts and focus for the work that is ahead, knowing the group is beginning on the same page.

Looking specifically at these lengthy rehearsals: There is a procedural routine, carefully outlined rehearsal objectives, and a breakdown of specified times of when various parts of the rehearsal will take place. I can assure you that in most of the top programs, there will be some personnel change from one musical selection to another. If you do not adhere to the schedule, students will either be early or late for their segment of the rehearsal.

Rehearsal begins with students standing and bowing to the director as a group asking to be taught. The director responds with, *"Yoi rehearsal ni si ma shou"* (Let's have a good rehearsal). The director then makes specific announcements, focusing on rehearsal goals.

The director launches into the warm-up and tuning segment. In the rehearsals I have attended, this portion is extremely important, and a significant amount of time is devoted to these fundamentals. In almost every situation, this portion of the rehearsal is not conducted by the director, but rather by the concertmaster, a band officer, or other designated student leader.

During this warm-up, the leader carefully monitors the pitch and tone production of each individual and section. Sometimes a listening device is used, but more often than not students rely on careful listening and matching pitches to their section leader. As the process proceeds, when a new section is to begin the tuning process, the section leader must match pitch with the previous section leader. The most commonly used technique is to begin with the lowest voices in the ensemble and work to the top, each time checking the pitch level with the lower voice.

After the designated leader feels the individual pitch level has been attained, they proceed to full ensemble warm-ups. This usually involves unison and chorale exercises. Also as part of this warm-up process the group does some solfege and chorale singing, and I mean belt-it-out singing. The singing of Japanese band students would make most symphonic choirs proud. There is strong belief that if you can't sing it in tune, you can't play it in tune. I know many outstanding American programs that employ the same philosophy.

The materials used for these warm-ups are both manuscript and some of the most commonly-published materials one would find in American band rooms. This warm-up period will last up to one hour or more. The ensemble will then take a short break and begin the pre-set rehearsal order. The director now takes the podium and initiates the rehearsal of the specific segments to rehearse.

In every rehearsal room I have visited, an electric piano stands next to the director's podium. If the director detects a pitch problem she turns to the keyboard and asks the students to refocus the chord, or listen to the melody as it fits into the chord structure, or if a partial of the chord is out of tune, have those with just that part of the chord play with the keyboard to attain the proper pitch.

For example, if the third of the chord is out of tune, the director will play the root and fifth and have students play the third until it fits properly with the root and fifth. The emphasis is on individual listening.

In some American band rooms, I have observed all members of the band with their own listening device attached to their instrument to monitor their own pitch level. This can work well and is practical in a shorter rehearsal time frame, but when the device is removed, do students listen more carefully than before? While electronic pitch devices are quick and practical, I would much rather see students rely on their ears to make pitch adjustment. Don't forget, the only pitch adjustment device in the Eastman rehearsal hall when Fennell was the conductor was a sign in the front of the room that just said, **LISTEN.** This is a little subtler than the sign I saw in an American high school band hall that read, **TUNE IT OR DIE!** That would be seriously stressful!

The other aspect of these long rehearsals that impresses me is student attentiveness and concentration level. I have sat in on several of these long rehearsals, and have conducted a few of that length as well. The conductor never has to say a thing about talking during rehearsal. Golden silence. Again, this is a cultural thing, but I have always been tremendously impressed by the ability of the Japanese bands to sit still without any talking for such long periods of time. And to top it off, they stand at the end of the rehearsal, bow to the conductor and say "thank you" for teaching them. With that many hours of focused rehearsal in a week's time, it is no wonder that these top bands achieve such a high performance standard.

There are some negative aspects to this type of rehearsal. In some schools students and directors rely too much on rote teaching, which leads to a more mechanical performance and poor sight-reading skills. Students taught this way also do not learn to read well, so more individual practice time is required to learn a new piece of music.

Not so much today, but some early directors used pretty severe discipline in order to achieve satisfactory results. But, was that not the case in the United States as well a few generations ago? I am happy to share that this practice is not very common any longer in Japan or in the United States. Just

as in the States, when students are subjected to extra, long hours of out-of-school rehearsals, there is a burn-out that takes place, to the point where students do not wish to participate in any kind of ensemble after high school. This is one of the reasons why most of the music schools in Japan have witnessed a decline in enrollment in the past few years.

The other two reasons for a drop in enrollment at most universities is a declining national population and the economy. Once instrumental students attain a certain proficiency level through club activity and wish to improve, they begin private lessons with an approved teacher. Most high-attaining school programs have a list of recommended teachers that has been assembled by the director.

There is another philosophy that is effectively utilized by some directors, involving older students teaching the younger students in the program. Otaki who conducts the Saitama-Sakae high school band (one of the outstanding programs in the country, I believe), utilizes this system to great success. Following is what he explained to me about this system.

> When the new students start the band, they form groups of a couple of new students for one older student. This is called Senpai-Kohai method. *Senpai* are the older students, and younger are called *kohai*. Senpai teaches kohai every little thing, not only about the instrument and performance technique but also band club rules, principles and everyday life in high school. So, Senpai looks after kohai and his behavior. Learning communication skills through the band is very important. It influences everyday life in high school.

When I asked Otaki how he goes about choosing leaders in this system, this is what he shared.

> We select a leader by elections. Each student has numerous sides to them, and the students themselves know each other better than I or other teachers do. That is why students elect their own leader, and the quality of that selection determines their seriousness in choosing as well as the band club's future.

On the surface this seems dangerous, as one would assume that personalities and personal feelings could cause friction between students. Here is where cultural differences come into play again. It is the *respect* factor that is such a deeply ingrained concept in the country. You see it at every level, in every kind of relationship or personal transaction. It can be observed daily, as people meet for the first time, in the manner and depth of the bow.

While handshakes are taking place more and more due to foreign influences, the bow in Japanese society is still most important. For example, if a younger person meets an older person, then the bow must be lower. Music students from elementary to professional level refer to their teachers and ensemble conductors as *sensei*. This is an honorific expression showing the highest level of respect, regardless of the profession. So younger students respond well to the leadership of older music students and appreciate the time and energy they share so they might improve.

This is so excellent to observe. Directors examine leaders carefully to make sure they have the personality, skill, and desire to make a difference in younger students' lives. Where I see this form of instruction taking place, I see a program that is progressive, focused, and musically savvy. Students exhibit a fantastic attitude and have a deep respect for each other and the overall program.

The history of current Japanese bands is relatively short, beginning only in the mid-1950s. This methodology and pedagogy of rehearsal technique goes back to the time when many bands were led by teachers who were not formally trained as musicians in a university or school of music, but who directed the band because they were interested and available to spend the time. However, without the proper training, they relied on repetitive techniques. Today, more and more of the outstanding young conductors are well trained. Many have visited and studied in America, and learned that achieving musical excellence can occur without lengthy and repetitive rehearsals. I am delighted to see this style of preparation taking place more and more.

College, University, and Schools of Music

Colleges and universities are numerous in Japan, and while I do not have an exact number, I can assure you there are well over a thousand. This does not include the many private institutions or music schools also present in Japan. However, within the college and university systems, there are probably only 350 that include band programs.

Once again, the stress on academics is so strong in most of these institutions that there is not time for these extra musical organizations. The institutions that do have band programs are generally not considered as having the top ensembles at the university level. However, the All-Japan Band Contest does provide a category where these bands can compete if they desire. This goal provides these better university bands an outlet and a goal for high achievement.

In addition to college and universities, there are over a hundred schools of music of varying sizes in the country. Probably half of these schools offer some type of music education course of study. This in itself is having a positive impact on the training of future band directors. It is generally agreed among Japanese directors that there are eleven or twelve top schools of music in Japan with outstanding symphonic bands and wind ensembles. Seven of these top schools of music reside within the city of Tokyo.

At one time or another I have heard the bands from these institutions, and can attest to the high quality of their music making. The size of these bands and the kind of literature performed has changed pretty dramatically in the past ten to fifteen years. While most of these schools now embrace the wind ensemble concept, a few still make use of the concert band format popular in the United States from 1950 to the mid-1980s, with groups of 90–130 members or more, depending on the school.

The literature of choice in most of these bands was transcriptions of famous orchestral works. At the All-Japan Band Contest, transcriptions are still a fairly common choice for the showcase selection, even with the fifty-member limit.

In the past few years, schools of music that have traditionally had very large symphonic bands are now changing to wind ensembles and inviting guest conductors to help them achieve satisfactory results with wind ensemble literature selection and performance practice.

One school of music that adopted the wind ensemble concept early on is the Musashino Academia of Musicae. This large and very fine school of music in Tokyo began the wind ensemble concept in 1954, only two years after the Eastman Wind Ensemble was formed.

The Musashino Academia of Musicae

Naoaki Fukui founded the Musashino Academy of Music in 1929 with a focus on promoting western classical music in Japan. World harmony through music has always been a principal goal of the school. Guest teachers, conductors, and performers from all parts of the world have played a significant role in creating the international flavor and awareness of the school.

Musashino Academia has three campuses: the Iruma campus for freshmen, sophomores, the new music environment management class, and students studying for a doctorate; the Ekoda campus for juniors, seniors, the virtuoso class, and graduates studying for a master's degree; and the Parnassos Tama campus, which focuses primarily on child and adult training.

In keeping with its international philosophy and with facilities and a curriculum comparable to the world's finest music schools and conservatories, Musashino has one of the finest collections of original music manuscripts and a major instrument museum. The collection of world instruments consists of some 5,000 pieces. There is also a collection of Japanese instruments, both folk and traditional.

Membership in the Musashino wind ensemble is selected every year from the best junior and senior wind and percussion students, and usually rehearses twice a week in two-hour sessions. Since its inception, the ensemble has given great thought to the content of its programs, accepting ideas and advice both from within Japan and internationally.

The main focus of the ensemble's study has been American wind ensembles, well known for its high-level programs, the richness of compositions by American composers, and conductors. The school feels a great sense of honor and gratitude for the opportunity to perform in 1995 and 2006 at the Midwest Clinic.

The Musashino wind ensemble has recorded fourteen CDs under the Sony label. In keeping with their philosophy, there have been nine American guest conductors, and one each from Czechoslovakia and Bulgaria since 1971. Most of the American conductors have been there multiple times. Working with these outstanding young people is a rich and rewarding experience. A guest conductor spends an entire semester with the ensemble, which allows for a wonderful bond to take place between the conductor and students.

Like most ensembles within Japanese schools of music, performance standards are very high and expectation for outstanding performances is assumed. Lending to the aesthetic satisfaction in these performances is the concert halls in which most of these ensembles perform. While major cities in America may boast of one or two great concert halls, Tokyo probably has ten or twelve major concert venues that are beautiful and acoustically exquisite, and most concerts are sold out. (This last statement was a big surprise to me since, most university concerts in the United States struggle to assemble a modest audience at best.) Not only are the concert halls filled to capacity, but ensembles need to be prepared to play at least three or four encores.

Another fact about concerts in Japan is the huge number of young students who attend these programs. I love looking out in the audience and see the age range in attendance. The Japanese people love bands, and they love to hear new music. During the summer, when most of the junior and senior high bands are diligently preparing their contest music, it is appropriate to include on the program one or two of the required numbers. Just before these numbers are performed, young musicians in the audience will pull their music out of their backpack so they can follow their part while the music is being performed. You can tell by their smiles if you played the music to their satisfaction. In my conclusion I will include some observations and additional comments from a few of the other American guest conductors.

The Midwest Clinic and the International Connection

The Midwest Clinic (an international band and orchestra convention) has long promoted ensembles and clinicians from other countries. This outreach only helps to strengthen music education, performance standards, and music industry and philosophical collaboration around the world.

Not only is every American state represented at the convention, but also there are additionally over forty different countries in attendance each year. This is very pleasing to the Midwest Clinic, which plans to continue the importance of this collaboration for the foreseeable future. With travel costs continuing to spiral upward everyday, the Clinic truly hopes it can continue to attract outstanding ensembles from around the world.

Until 1991, the country that had performed the most concerts at the Midwest Clinic was Canada, having presented groups on five different occasions dating back to the first performance in 1952. There have been fifteen different countries featured in performances in the last seventeen years. Since 2000, Japanese bands have regularly been featured at the convention. These groups represent almost every category of wind ensemble in Japan, specifically, professional, corporation, university, and high school groups.

A few years ago the Midwest Clinic offered an invitation to a Japanese elementary band to perform, but the community determined they would not be able to raise the necessary finances to make the trip to Chicago. I know there are many outstanding elementary bands that would love to perform at this international convention. We hope it will take place in the future.

The first Japanese band to perform at the Midwest Clinic was the Fukuoka Technical University High School Concert Band under the direction of Takayoshi Suzuki in 1987. Many American directors know the conductor as Tad. He has been on the faculty at the University of Nevada in Las Vegas for several years. I well remember his performance at Midwest. Sitting as close to the front as I could get (a practice that goes all the way back to my first Midwest Clinic in 1960), the thrill I got from the fantastic sound, musical expression, and flawless technique still resonates in my musical memory. That performance was the talk of the convention, and even today many directors, including myself, remember with clarity the impact it had on the audience. Midwest attendees from that performance on have fallen in love with Japanese bands.

Following that first performance, there have now been ten other presentations by Japanese bands, including the Ensemble Liberte Wind Orchestra that will perform in December 2008.

I believe the first Japanese band director to attend the Midwest Clinic was Toshio Akiyama. I do not know the year he first attended, but I do know he has not missed a clinic since. This happens to many people. Over the years, Toshio single-handedly encouraged other directors to attend the Midwest

Clinic. He recognized from the beginning what directors could learn by attending performances, clinics, and the exhibits. For several years now, the number of directors from Japan registering at Midwest Clinic far surpasses that of any other foreign country. However, in the past two or three years, it has been encouraging and rewarding to see groups of directors attending for the first time from China and Russia. It is the Midwest Clinic's goal to continue the pursuit of attracting international attendees and performing ensembles from around the globe.

Other Japanese Band Activity

I have, as accurately as possible, shared information related to bands ranging from elementary through the university level. Thus far I have mainly focused on the top ensembles, exploring their activities, methodology, and philosophies. However, there are thousands of bands which, for one reason or another, choose to not compete at the All-Japan Contest level. Among these non-competitive bands there are still many outstanding ensembles that wish to focus on student development through performance in band to encourage participation at some level of music throughout their lives. In the following paragraphs you will see the impact this is having by the number of community bands that now function in Japan.

There are many superior military bands in Japan, representing the Army, Navy, and Air Force. There are thirty in all within the country, but the Army (Japan Ground Self Defense Band) claims the majority with nineteen groups. As in the United States, these bands provide a wonderful source of musical fulfillment and security for student musicians who graduate from one of the universities or schools of music and wish to pursue a professional playing career. I have heard several of these ensembles in concert, and their performances have been highly rewarding, both musically and technically.

Corporation bands in Japan have been an integral part of band activity for many years. I was informed that, twenty-five years ago, there were nearly 300 corporation bands throughout the country. Recently, the difficult Japanese economy has caused many corporations to discontinue their bands due to financial concerns. I understand this scenario, but feel bad for the musicians, as they had a tremendous sense of pride and commitment to these ensembles. Even with the economy forcing the termination of many of these groups, there still is a significant number of corporation bands in the country—nearly 100.

These groups rehearse weekly and present formal concerts three or four times a year in beautiful concert venues. For example, the Yamaha Symphonic Band (which performed at the Midwest Clinic in 2005) rehearses twice a week for two hours. Membership consists entirely of musicians who work daily in the Yamaha plant in Hamamatsu. Devoting two hours twice a week for

rehearsal is quite a commitment after putting in a full day's work. If you heard their concert in Chicago, then you will understand that the members feel the time is well spent in order to achieve the performance level they enjoy.

Company and corporation bands are prevalent in Japan, but the number of community bands is staggering, and keeps growing each year. Nearly 1,800 of these bands are active in Japan. This is exciting and encouraging, for it gives the impression that musicians understand and realize that participation in a music group helps reduce stress levels (and believe me they need this) and helps provide a more fulfilling life. Playing in an organization like a community band can change one's perspective on life. One Japanese statistic that makes me very sad is the incredibly high suicide rate. The old saying, "music soothes the savage beast" must contain significance for the thousands of people who participate in community bands.

There are also a large number of police and fire department that function throughout the country. These groups perform *many* concerts throughout the year and present clinics and concerts in schools throughout their prefecture.

There are five professional bands in Japan: the Tokyo Wind Orchestra, Osaka City Symphonic Band, Tokyo Symphonic Band, Siena Wind Orchestra, and the Philharmonic Winds Osakan. Only the Tokyo Kosei Wind Orchestra and Osaka Symphonic Band offer full-time employment for musicians. While the other groups pay their members, it is only on a concert-to-concert basis and not full-time employment.

If you have kept track of the numbers presented in this chapter, you can easily ascertain that band activity at every level is exceedingly popular. Once again, Toshio Akiyama told me last summer there are probably close to 14,250 active bands in Japan. Is band important and popular in Japan? A rhetorical question, I believe!

Literature

I briefly commented earlier that many of the top bands at the university and high school levels perform transcriptions on a pretty regular basis. These transcriptions are standards that have been popular in the United States as well, the Mark Hindsley transcriptions being the most-often performed.

A problem occurs at the All-Japan Band Contest, as ensembles have ten minutes or less to perform a showcase number. So directors make major cuts in the music or hire a composer or arranger to make alterations in order to fit the time allowed. More often than not, directors of the top ensembles commission special arrangements of either classic orchestral repertoire or to alter original major works for wind band to fit their time limitations.

At the first All-Japan Band Contest I attended in 1990, there were few original works for band performed as a showcase selection. Most bands performed transcriptions. When I attended the contest in 2006, I was delighted to see that over half of the showcase numbers were major, original works for band. However, the problem of length remains. So these original works often require selective cuts to stay within the time limit.

One particular work stands out, as it was a major work that I knew was nearly thirty-five minutes in length. The band played the major themes very skillfully knit together into one satisfying ten-minute work. It was very cleverly done and did not leave me musically unsatisfied. The composer might not have thought it was so great, but it received a flawless performance and was enthusiastically received by the 5,500 in attendance. I think any composer would like to have his compositions so beautifully performed and received by so many people at one hearing. I am sure it prompted many directors to buy the music, and their performances would likely be of the entire work.

More and more conductors from America guest-conduct in Japan each year. These conductors are very knowledgeable of the best compositions being written and performed by the top American wind ensembles. They are bringing these fine works to Japan and its wind ensembles, and their regular conductors and audiences are eagerly adopting these new compositions. That being said, I need to unequivocally state I have been impressed by the quality and quantity of band music being written by outstanding Japanese composers.

During my first trip to Japan (now nearly twenty-five years ago), I had the opportunity to hear many bands in concert. I was surprised then to discover very few original works by Japanese composers. Those that I did hear were not of the musical depth that one would hear today. Now there are many outstanding Japanese composers writing exceedingly fine works for wind band. These excellent works are being performed regularly around the world.

In the spring of 2007 I had the opportunity to guest-conduct in a program called Kyo-en. Kyo-en is sponsored by Brain Music Company and features eight different bands. Every number on the afternoon and evening program is a world premier written by a Japanese composer. Some compositions are highly demanding, requiring the most mature and proficient ensemble. Other works are geared for younger ensembles, but still quality pieces for the less-proficient band.

I was very impressed by the quality, creativity, and depth of these compositions. Wind band literature written by Japanese composers is growing by leaps and bounds, as the cliché goes. I would like to have added a representative list of composers at this point in the chapter, but out of fear of forgetting (and upsetting) someone, I defer to your desire to check publisher websites to find many of these outstanding compositions. To keep up with this growing demand and to find a means for distribution, there is an expanding list of music publishers in Japan. Toshio supplied me with a list of thirteen

publishers now in operation. That represents quite a shift from twenty-five years ago.

Musashino Academia of Musicae Reprise

Musashino Academia of Musicae is a very unique school. The enrollment numbers have dropped, as is true for most institutions of higher learning in Japan due to the economic downturn and population decline. The school still remains the largest in Japan, and is faithful to the founding principal of exposing their students to guest teachers, conductors, and performers from Europe, America, and within its own country. This focus plays a significant role in creating the international flavor and awareness of the Academia of Musicae.

As I mentioned in the introduction, my journey to Tokyo came out of the proverbial blue. Late one night in the summer of 1990 I received a call from Robert Bergt, chair of the music department at Valparaiso University. I had known Robert for a few years, as we would see each other at various professional meetings. At the time, he was the full-time orchestra director at Musashino, having taken a long-term leave of absence from Valparaiso. In keeping with the school's policy of inviting conductors from America, President Fukui asked him to contact me to see if I would be interested in conducting their wind ensemble in the coming fall.

I had known of this ensemble and heard recordings (LPs at the time) and knew the group was very fine. After discussing this with my wife Molly, and, of course, Dean Webb of the IU School of Music, I decided to take a leave without pay (I had just taken my first sabbatical the previous spring, so without pay was the only way), as this might possibly be my only opportunity to experience a new culture and wind ensemble experience. That late night call was the beginning of a long and rewarding relationship. It has become a second home for us, as we have developed so many close friendships there over the years.

The fact is, we have been able to tour with the wind ensemble throughout Japan and have probably seen more parts of the country than most students in the band or their parents. It is an association I hope will continue for several more years. I harbor a deep love and respect for the administration, faculty, staff, and students—especially the students, for they are extremely bright, diligent, cooperative, friendly, and a joy to conduct. Here are a few brief comments and impressions from other American guest conductors who have worked at Musashino in recent years.

Ken Bloomquist, Director of Bands Emeritus, Michigan State University

It is imperative that we as teachers and conductors create an atmosphere in which the educational process can flourish. My first rehearsal with the Musashino Wind Ensemble was very exciting. I gave the downbeat to what I considered to be a difficult concert opening selection. To my amazement they performed the piece virtually note-perfect. Following rehearsal I went back to my residence and told my wife, "I've got a problem!" I reiterated the rehearsal experience and wondered out loud what in the world I was gong to do for the next three months. Remembering my maxim of creating an atmosphere where the educational process can flourish carried me throughout, and in the process I was able to elevate my expectations to another level. The joy of rehearsing every detail and nuance and never losing the interest and dedication of the performers, most of whom were junior and senior college students, was a dream come true.

We must always pursue perfection. This sounds like an impossible goal and the arrogant raving of a conductor who is ignoring reality. But the work ethic displayed by the Musashino Wind Ensemble is all-encompassing. It is realized out of accomplishing the impossible, a love of making music, satisfying inner needs to learn, and pleasing parents, conductors, teachers, audience, and self. Plain hard work satisfies the old adage that "practice makes perfect!"

Russell Coleman, Director of Bands Emeritus, University of Central Missouri

Before my first trip to Tokyo, I had heard several Japanese bands perform in the United States. I was very impressed with their excellent intonation and technique, but disappointed in their rigid performances and a general lack of musical expression. It was my goal to see if I couldn't improve that with the wind ensemble. It was a very pleasant surprise to learn that when you encouraged and *freed* them to express themselves musically, they played with just as much heart as any group I have ever heard! It was a joy to turn them loose and listen to their wonderful musicianship. In pondering this pleasant occurrence I reached the following conclusions:

1. Japanese culture is very rigid in allowing people to show or express any emotion.
2. People tend to avoid drawing attention to themselves.
3. They grow up in a very structured environment.
4. It is not proper to show emotion.
5. Younger musicians, however, have a desire to put their hearts into the music.

In my subsequent trips as their guest conductor, the ensemble often brought me near to tears as I heard what wonderful music they made as they put their hearts into their performances.

Richard Hansen, Director of Bands, St. Cloud State University

It is rare in today's society that we experience *profound silence*. Surrounded by and steeped in all sorts of electric gadgets and conveniences, and driven into our hectic lifestyles with "noisy wheels," we rarely experience profound silence. We suffer as much or more from noise pollution as we do air pollution. As a boy growing up in Iowa, I sometimes experienced special moments of pure silence in the country. Recently, the only time I have experienced this in America is on treks to northern Minnesota boundary waters. It seems oddly strange then, that the place I have known the phenomenon of profound silence most frequently is in the bustling city of Tokyo, for, as with New York, Tokyo never sleeps. Nonetheless, as I walk through the narrow, little, winding paths into the neighborhoods, I have on numerous occasions known the air to be completely devoid of sound. It is like taking a breath of fresh air.

Directly related to profound silence in Japanese daily life is the extraordinary ability of Japanese musicians to listen (*kiite*). Profound silence has a tremendous impact upon musicians' ability to produce beautiful sounds. Sounds coming out of silence are not only a matter of the physics of sound, but the *feelings* of serenity inside players caused by the calm of silences. This elevates musicians' skills to match teachers, conductors' articulations and singing, and student section leaders. Recorded and live sound models and matching cultivate extraordinary playing skills in Japanese wind band musicians. Musicians tend to grow from student leadership models in Japan most powerfully and accurately. Their listening and matching skills are so keen, that when "model" professional recordings are flawed, students will match even the flaws! The conductor must be *very* careful to sing and articulate accurate models, because what you give is what you will very precisely get!

The influence Musashino Academy of Music has had on Japanese band culture is clear, and perhaps best stated by Naotaka Fukui, President of the school. He precisely states,

I have no doubt that our connection with guest conductors has helped to create what is known as the "Musashino Sound," a sound much admired for its dynamic range and beauty, and a sound seen as a target level by all concerned with wind ensemble work in Japan.

One of the facts I find so exciting is that, of the wind and percussion students in the school, almost seventy-five percent are in the music education curriculum. Each year at the All-Japan Band Contest there are bands whose directors are Musashino Alumni. This speaks well for their education and for the future of music education in Japan.

Hands Across the Sea: a Conclusion

My brother Eddie was stationed in Japan in the early 1950s, and I remember the fascinating stories he shared about his experiences. He brought home exotic gifts, silk kimonos for my sisters, exquisite fans and silk scarves for my mother, and a miniature samurai sword for me, which I loved showing to my grade school buddies. Today I would be arrested for taking this to school— even in Delong. I do not recall what my father received, but I do know he was happy to have his son back in Delong. Oh yes, the journey (sorry, I got wrapped up in nostalgia there for a moment).

In the first program I conducted at Musashino, it seemed obvious that a march I should and needed to play was the great Sousa march, *Hands across the Sea*, thinking it would be politically correct and appropriate. The band performed it with a spirit and bravura that would make the Marine Band proud. The audience responded enthusiastically, making me smile, thinking how smart a move this was. It wasn't until subsequent visits that I realized Japanese audiences *love* American marches, and they are *always a hit!*)

Hands across the Sea portrays the image that collaborative ideas and concepts go both ways. The interpersonal relationship of extended friendship and camaraderie, and enjoying the exhilaration that comes in making exciting and memorable music together are experiences I could not have anticipated growing up in Delong (while playing nasty glissandos on my Pan American trombone). Having the opportunity to spend nearly three months with the students and live in a real Japanese neighborhood, attending a local Japanese Baptist Church (very rare in Japan), shopping and eating at small mom-and-pop stores and restaurants, and buying vegetables on the street where you watch the farmer pick the vegetables, gives one a much more complete picture of what daily life is like in Japan.

Because of the length of the residency, the Musashino engagement offers these kinds of non-musical experiences that contribute tremendously to understanding the culture and how that impacts the musical heart and face of

the students. Many guest conductors who visit Japan are generally there for a relatively short time, live in hotels, eat out every meal and have little chance to interact with students and faculty outside of rehearsal. I know the students receive a wonderful musical experience, but the guest does not have the opportunity to feel the culture.

Over my teaching career, one of the tenets of my ensemble experience has been to learn students' names as quickly as possible. I feel this establishes a positive atmosphere and an important relationship with students that helps solidify communication through the music. American names are easy, but I did worry the first time about learning Japanese names quickly. Students in Japan are rarely called by name in class and almost never in a rehearsal situation. However, with my philosophy in this regard, I determined to do my best to learn their names so I could call them by name in rehearsal and around school or even on the street in Ekoda. Once I knew the wind ensemble set-up and the names of students in the set-up, I diligently set about memorizing names before the first rehearsal. At that rehearsal I endeavored to put faces with names. During the second rehearsal I went around the ensemble and called every student by name; they were flabbergasted—they always are. (I'm not sure there is a Japanese translation for *flabbergasted,* and if there is, it might take five minutes to speak.) I follow this format each time I return to the school.

Communicating in rehearsal was another story, for I found out very quickly that even though Japanese students have had several years of English study, none of it embodies verbal communication or conversational skills. Working with an interpreter (which was not an option anyway) takes forever.

You might ask the group to "Please start at number forty-two, and could you play a little softer?" I can say that in three seconds (or less if I am pressed for time), but an interpreter might take a full minute to say the same thing. So I would resort to what most people do when trying to communicate in some other language than their own: I spoke much louder and slower, "Please...start...at...number...forty...two," then raised my arms in preparation for the downbeat. Horns quickly came to playing position, I gave the downbeat and only one person played a very tentative note! So I thought, "Okay, they don't understand, 'Please start at number forty-two.'" That's when I came to the realization that, if I was to have a rehearsal that moved with quickness and pacing, I was going to have to learn how to say "Please start at number forty-two" in Japanese.

I began to make a list of rehearsal phrases I used with my IU wind ensemble and asked for help translating these into Japanese. Like student names, I started to memorize phrases that I knew would be useful in every rehearsal. I did learn very quickly how to say numbers, where to tell the group to start, how many measures before or after, or to play the pick-up, and many other rehearsal necessities. The students are very patient and understanding, and I believe appreciate the fact that I try to communicate in their native tongue. I also have made some embarrassing blunders I will not go into here, but if you want to hear a couple, you will have to—well, never mind.

The Japanese band movement has developed and grown expansively through interaction with American, European, and Japanese conductors, composers, and performing artists. Japanese directors desire to continue our association to delve even deeper into the concepts of sound, literature, and conducting technique. A major goal of mine during each visit to Musashino is to help mold tonal concepts into the sounds I have in my head through the many years of conducting the IU wind ensemble. The exposure of Japanese bands to American conductors and audiences at the Midwest Clinic and other association meetings around the United States has helped to elevate performance expectations. Our methods and procedures may be very different due to educational and cultural differences, but the musical glue that binds us together is the intense power and magnetism in music performance.

Before my final paragraphs, I want to take this opportunity to express my thanks and gratitude to Toshio Akiyama for providing me with the numbers and factoids I used throughout this chapter. They came from two sources: the first from a paper he assembled for the seventh WASBE conference held in Hamamatsu in 1995; the second from an email he sent me following a personal meeting we had this summer in Tokyo, where I asked him several questions pertaining to specific facts about Japan band activity. No director in Japan has a better understanding and knowledge of the Japanese band movement than Toshio.

Akiyama has been a vital part of Japanese band expansion for nearly sixty years. If you go with Toshio anywhere, you had better be prepared to run, for he can move through a congested train station faster than anyone half his age—no, make that two-thirds his age—especially if they have two bad knees. Fortunately, I was tall enough that I could keep track of his full head of white hair among the throng of all-black hair. Thank you, Toshio, for everything you have done in the past and for the impact I know you will continue to have on the band movement in Japan. The respect you have among directors is well deserved. Thank you!

I truly hope you have found this chapter to be informative, interesting, and insightful, and that it has provided a clearer picture of the Japanese band culture and Japanese life in general. For me, a farm boy who grew up at Eleventh and Plum (near Delong), whose musical experience began by letting things slide (sorry about that, but you should hear me play Lassus Trombone),

this has been a growing, thrilling, rewarding, and humbling but always joyful experience finding new ways to communicate the magnificence embodied in music-making, regardless of the culture.

Many American directors have the belief that Japanese musicians and ensembles play with fantastic technique but little emotion or expression. As Russ Coleman expressed in his brief comments, this is just not the case. These young people feel deeply and express themselves in many ways that should be visible as well as audible to audiences. I love watching Japanese ensembles perform, the way they move with phrases and accents. This is natural for them. They have grown up feeling the music in this manner. Their movements match the musical character and style.

Karada de Ongaku o hyogen shite (Move with the Music). They know this phrase well and respond to the music, not just the notes.

Ongaku wa kokoro kara dete kuru mono desu (Music comes from the heart!) I have witnessed emotion, tears on stage during a performance responding to a beautiful phrase, backstage hugs and laughter, and congratulating one another on a job well done, just as with our American students.

The title of this book series, *Teaching Music through Performance in Band,* could not be more significant or meaningful than the subject of this chapter. As directors and music educators, we must always make it our goal and mission, regardless of age level or culture, to teach and inspire students to explore the richness of music and help them to fully experience the joy in making music together.

What I have discovered during my forty-seven years in this profession is that if we, the teachers and conductors, are *passionate* about what we do, are *committed* to the music we are conducting, are *compassionate* people and *respect* the people in front of us, our jobs will be incredibly rewarding.

Music can name the unnamable and communicate the unknowable.
—Leonard Bernstein

This can happen in Delong or Tokyo. Well, probably not Delong, as the two-room school and the general store are now family dwellings, and three of the five pianos no longer exist. However, there might be some young farm boy just waiting to discover the joy of playing glissandos.

With Masashino students, I use the phrase "play with heart" more than any other. Our bodies are made up of many different elements and a large percentage of water, but the heart can be one hundred percent musical. *Always play with heart and you will never be musically unfulfilled!*

In Delong we said goodbye with the phrase, "See you later." In Japan they say, *"Sayonara."* When in Japan, I teach students as many cultural collaborations as possible, and ask them to combine the American and Japanese phrases for "goodbye," so I end by saying, *"Sayo-later."*

PART II

THE BAND CONDUCTOR AS MUSIC TEACHER

Teacher Resource Guides

Grade Two

Teacher Resource Guide

Apache Lullaby

Michael Colgrass
(b. 1932)

Unit 1: Composer

American composer Michael Colgrass began his musical career in Chicago as a jazz drummer, leading his own jazz group by the age of twelve. He studied percussion and composition at the University of Illinois, graduating in 1954, where his studies included training with Darius Milhaud at the Aspen Festival and Lukas Foss at Tanglewood. From 1956–1967 he spent time freelancing in New York City with the New York Philharmonic, Dizzy Gillespie, the American Ballet Theatre, and the Metropolitan Opera; and performing drum set with the original *West Side Story* orchestra and the Columbia Recording Orchestra's *Stravinsky Conducts Stravinsky* series, as well as numerous other ballet, opera, and jazz ensembles. In 1967, Colgrass gave up playing to devote himself to acting, theatre directing, fencing, voice, modern dance, and composition. In addition, he spent time in Europe on a Rockefeller Grant studying clown training and Grotowski Physical Training.

Colgrass received a Pulitzer Prize in 1978 for *Music for Déjà Vu*, a concerto for four percussionists and orchestra which was commissioned by the New York Philharmonic. In the course of his career, he has been awarded two Guggenheim Fellowships, a Rockefeller Grant, an Emmy Award, and First Prize in the Barlow and Sudler International Wind Ensemble Competitions for his composition for winds and percussion entitled *Winds of Nagual*.

He remains an active clinician in "performing excellence," a combination of physical training, dance and Neuro-Linguistic Programming designed to assist participants in the techniques of performance. In 2004, he authored an article that appeared in the *Music Educators Journal* in which he explains his system of teaching music creativity to demonstrate to children how to write and perform new music of their own. His style represents a variety of musical idioms derived from his work as freelance percussionist and from his study of serialistic, jazz, and tonal techniques.[1]

Unit 2: Composition

Apache Lullaby was intended for beginning Grade 1 band and is Colgrass' first attempt at music for this stage of player; however, by the composer's admission, it may be more suitable for a Grade 2 ensemble. Several factors merit this higher consideration, including a duration of almost five minutes, transparency of parts, emotional content, and the independence of parts.

As is typical of the composer's style, the origin of the work and its setting are intricately wound together to give the work a double significance. In his program notes, Colgrass indicates that his melody is based on the singing he heard by an Apache Indian mother to her young child. Because of his desire to depict the "quality of the supernatural," he altered the melody from the pentatonic form into a modal mode, which to him suggested a "feeling of timelessness."[2]

In addition, Colgrass uses what he describes as a dark tone and, along with a variance to the melody, combines to convey the elements that he feels exemplify the native Indian philosophy. With his compositional technique, he seeks to infuse an ominous ingredient to the work, one that he hopes conveyed the Indian beliefs of contact with the spirits.

Unit 3: Historical Perspective

Apache Lullaby was composed for the Longmeadow Commission Work Project, the ambition of which was to have a work written specifically for the Williams Middle School Concert Band of Longmeadow Public Schools in Massachusetts. The project was to involve the commissioning of Michael Colgrass and to have him appear in a period of residency in the school district. The goals established by the educators involved included having personal contact with the composer, preparing and performing his music, and allowing the students involved to participate in the creation of a new work for wind band.

Colgrass's use of an original Apache melody for the theme allows the music educator many teaching possibilities regarding the historical perspective of the work. Students could study and begin to gain an appreciation for the culture of Apache Indians. Utilizing other selections to create an entire concert program based on American Indian themes and ideas could allow an entire unit of study done in conjunction with other disciplines across the curriculum.

Unit 4: Technical Considerations

Michael Colgrass has designed all the technical considerations of this work for beginning band. In terms of range, all the wind instruments fall within the one-octave range of the concert B-flat scale. To achieve the modal implications, several notes out of the scale are used in the alto saxophone, clarinet and flute parts; however, the repeating patterns can be removed from context to create practice exercises for students.

Colgrass has designated all the divided parts with the colors of red, yellow, and blue instead of the usual numbers of 1–2–3. The composer hopes his system will avoid the characterization and stigma attached to ranking young and impressionable instrumentalists. Each divided part demonstrates similar range and technical demands so that the director must use higher-achieving performers on each colored part.

Some performers are required to play at half- or whole-step intervals between like instruments, a skill that will need to be reinforced by the educator. The instrumentation is standard for wind band, and all specialty instruments are doubled in common instruments. The trombones are asked to use cup mutes.

The final measure is indicated as open and allows the flutes, clarinets, and saxophones to enter freely on a given five-note motive. The conductor controls the length of the measure and can indicate when the players begin. Colgrass suggests the measure might last fifteen to twenty seconds.

Unit 5: Stylistic Considerations

The style of the selection is primarily a legato style typical of a chorale. Extensive slurs throughout demonstrate the length of phrase and the shape of melodic lines. Legato lines are used to demonstrate to young performers the connection between the same notes. The only accents in the work are found in the low brass in a tutti section at m. 90. Marked *Boldly* by the composer and the only tutti section of the work, the performers must articulate more force-fully than at any other time in the work.

Unit 6: Musical Elements

MELODY:
Colgrass states that the melody is primarily pentatonic with later alterations to a modal form that he creates. After the initial rendition, the melody is fragmented throughout until a section indicated by *Boldly*. His alterations of the melody make excellent teaching episodes for students in which they can discover how the modifications alter the tone and bring a darker tone to the work.

HARMONY:

The work stays in concert B-flat; however, altered tones and non-harmonic tones add continued interest to the composition despite the simplicity of key. As Colgrass has demonstrated in other works for young band, the mood and emotional content are the result of the creativity of the composer. Simple harmony is masked with interesting colors and effects that generate interest for the listener as well as the performer through use of non-harmonic tones.

RHYTHM:

The rhythmic contents come from the opening melody in the form of fragments that are manipulated throughout the work. The rhythm of the wind and percussion parts are limited to quarters, eighths, and dotted quarters, which are to be expected in a Grade 1 selection. The most difficult part for young performers might be the layering created in like instruments in which the independent counting of the performer is crucial to the accuracy of the effect created. The educator should consider isolating such passages with the individual players so that students will have a chance to practice the part separately before putting the passages together. The percussion parts provide characteristic repeating rhythmical passages in the opening sections.

TIMBRE:

Timbre is one of the most important elements of this work, as it provides a dark color, suggests the changing mood, and gives Colgrass the ability to create variations on the lullaby. Most of *Apache Lullaby* is characterized by the layering of parts in which one part or instrument begins a motive and sustains the pitch, while another part or instrument continues the idea. Color is further added to the variations by the sustaining of half- and whole-step pitches which add to the intensity of the phrase.

One of the most interesting sounds that Colgrass employs is the addition of four graduated steel bars, three to five feet in length, at the climax of the work. While Colgrass admits the bars have no symbolic meaning, he feels the sound is crucial to the dramatic moment at the height of the work, a sound he describes as "raw and clanging." The composer suggests hanging the bars and striking them with a hammer. In the first performance, holes were drilled in the bars, which were hung from a freestanding chalkboard. During the first performance with the composer, the students charged with playing the bars used earplugs because of the volume of sound requested by Colgrass. Gong, bass drum, tom-tom, and timpani provide the other percussion colors.

Unit 7: Form and Structure

The form of *Apache Lullaby* as outlined by the composer is to use the lullaby theme as the basis for a set of variations. Colgrass uses the addition of modal elements to convey the ideas that he finds important to native Indian philosophy.

Section	Measure	Event and Scoring
Introduction	1–10	The flutes layer fragments of the lullaby
Theme	11–27	Flutes carry the theme in its most complete form, with similar layering found in beginning
Variation	28–89	The second episodic section uses small and fragmented motivic ideas from the opening lullaby colored by sustained tones in woodwind and muted trombones
Variation	90–120	The third section is marked by a bold tutti band rendition of the lullaby theme
Variation	121–160	During the fourth section, the lullaby theme is bent into a modal form; fragments of the original lullaby that occur in various orchestrations throughout the ensemble characterize this section
Closure	161	Gradually the work fades into an open measure in which Colgrass indicates the notes to be played but allows the performer to determine the speed and timing

The form of this work could be used by the music educator to help students work towards a greater understanding of the technique used by Colgrass. The original folk tune could be used to understand how the composer created variations and the manner in which he alters the melody to create the darker tone.

Unit 8: Suggested Listening

Bulla, Stephen. *On the Hawkeye Patrol*, Kentucky: Curnow Publications, 2006.

Colgrass, Michael:

The Beethoven Machine, New York: Carl Fischer, 2003. Found in *Teaching Music through Performance in Band, Volume 6*.

Old Churches, St. Paul, MN: American Composers Forum, 2002. Found in *Teaching Music through Performance in Band, Volume 4*.

Daugherty, Michael. *Alligator Alley*. St. Paul, MN: American Composers Forum, 2003. Found in *Teaching Music through Performance in Band, Volume 5*.

Kirby, Rick. *Garden of the Gods*. New Glarus, WI: Daehn Publications.

Sweeney, Michael. *Legends in the Mist*. Milwaukee, WI: MusicWorks, 1996.

Unit 9: Additional References and Resources

Anthology of North American and Eskimo Music. Michael Asch, producer. Folkways Records and Service Corp. 1973. http://www.smithsonianglobalsound.org/containerdetail.aspx?itemid=922

Cassaro, James P. "Colgrass, Michael." In *Grove Music Online*. L. Macy, ed. http://www.grovemusic.com

"Colgrass, Michael (Charles)." In *Baker's Biographical Dictionary of Musicians*. N. Slominsky and L. Kuhn, eds. New York: Schirmer Books, 2001.

News: American Composers Forum through *BandQuest*. http://www.bandquest.org/who/Longmeadow.shtml

The author wishes to thank the composer Michael Colgrass for his willingness to correspond on information in this article. In addition, Daniel Albert, music teacher in the Longmeadow, Massachusetts Public Schools, and Christopher Nelson-Unczur, band director at Herberg Middle School in Pittsfield, Massachusetts, both contributed information regarding the first performance of *Apache Lullaby*.

Contributed by:

Christopher P. Heidenreich
Assistant Professor of Music Education and
Associate Director of Bands
Youngstown State University
Youngstown, Ohio

---

1 James P. Cassaro, "Colgrass, Michael," *Grove Music Online*, L. Macy, ed., http://grovemusic.com

2 Michael Colgrass, Program notes for *Apache Lullaby* (New York: Colgrass Music, 2003).

Teacher Resource Guide

April

Aaron Perrine
(b. 1979)

Unit 1: Composer

Aaron Perrine was born in McGregor, Minnesota and earned his bachelor's degree in music education and trombone performance from the University of Minnesota, Morris in 2002. As an undergraduate, he received two Minnesota Music Educators Association Collegiate Composition Awards, the Edna Murphy Morrison Music Award, and the Chancellor's Award.

After moving to Minneapolis in 2002, Perrine started a masters degree in music education at the University of Minnesota; studies included jazz arranging with Dean Sorenson and composition with Judith Zaimont. He completed the degree in 2006. While still working towards this degree, Perrine began teaching instrumental music to grades seven through twelve at Humboldt High School, St. Paul in 2004. He currently teaches at Brooklyn Center High School, Brooklyn Center, Minnesota.

Along with his teaching responsibilities, Perrine maintains a busy composing schedule, having already completed commissions for Farmington Middle School, Richfield Middle School, Oakton Community College, and Central High School, St. Paul. His works are published by C. Alan Publications. *Fever Flash* and *Inner Sanctum*, written for younger bands, and *Shimmer*, intended for more advanced ensembles, are due for publication in the fall of 2008.[1]

Unit 2: Composition

April was a finalist in the 2006 Frank Ticheli Composition Contest, sponsored by Manhattan Beach Publishing. Commissioned by the Farmington Middle School East 2005–2006 Seventh Grade Concert Band in Farmington, Minnesota, *April* was the second piece that director Joshua Pauly commissioned Perrine to write; the first piece was entitled *Move*.

Inspiration for the title *April* came from Perrine's realization that the students would be practicing the piece throughout the month of April, and his initial musical experiments with harmony and melody reminded him of spring. He wanted to create a less typical and more mature-sounding work that focused on lyricism, phrasing, tone, and interesting harmonies:[2]

> My goal was to write a piece of music that was lyrical and expressive, yet accessible for young bands. *April* is a musical depiction of the efflorescence of spring.[3]

Unit 3: Historical Perspective

Many composers, including such musical icons as George Gershwin, Leonard Bernstein, and Igor Stravinsky have found inspiration in the jazz idiom. Sometimes the jazz reference is blatant, as in Bernstein's *Prelude, Fugue, and Riffs*, written for jazz band instrumentation, but often the influence is less overt.

Perrine subtly reflects his jazz training through harmonic language. *April* is saturated with extended chords, suspensions, and added seconds (fourths, ninths). There are also a few brief references to the Lydian mode. All of these harmonic devices are commonly found within the jazz idiom.

Another allusion to the jazz idiom is found in Perrine's opening melodic ostinato, or what he calls "the groove"[4] established by the piano and mallet percussion parts. Similar to a jazz rhythm section, this groove propels the music forward, adds harmonic interest, and provides a foundation for melodic material. Perrine suggests listening to two jazz compositions for some insight into his style:

> The very best listening piece that comes to mind is Maria Schneider's *Hang Gliding*. The rhythm section establishes the groove, while a lyrical melody floats above it.... Another jazz piece that could be used is Herbie Hancock's *Maiden Voyage*.[5]

Unit 4: Technical Considerations

April includes an obbligato piano part that should be easily playable by a band member with some piano training. The bells and marimba highlight the piano part, while the timpani provide the heartbeat or pulse. Three more percussion players are required to cover the snare drum, bass drum, suspended cymbal, and wind chimes parts. Therefore, in addition to the pianist, six percussionists are required.

Instrument ranges are narrow and comfortable for this grade level: G4–C6 for flute, A3–D5 for clarinet 1, A3–C5 for clarinet 2, and C4–D5 for trumpet 1. Clarinet 2 crosses the break twice, but in both instances, clarinet 1 doubles the part. The clarinet and trumpets are two-part divisi, but all of the other parts only require one player. The oboe, bassoon, and tuba parts are doubled by other instruments within the ensemble and can be omitted should reduced instrumentation be necessary.

The piece is in simple duple time (4/4) and at a constant tempo (quarter note = 130) throughout. The key signature is E-flat major, but students will benefit from learning the D-flat and G-flat Lydian modes, as there are brief excursions to these tonal centers.

Unit 5: Stylistic Considerations

Suspensions (4–3, 9–8) and added seconds (ninths, fourths) are a salient feature of this composition. Therefore, performers must be encouraged to emphasize dissonance instead of backing away from unfamiliar sounds. This piece also relies heavily on dynamic nuance, and care must be taken to maintain balance within the dynamic swells, especially when extended harmonies are involved. Other pieces for wind ensemble that demonstrate similar harmonic characteristics within a lyrical context are Reynold's arrangement of Lauridsen's *O Magnum Mysterium*, and *Lux Aurumque* or *October* by Eric Whitacre. These pieces would provide valuable aural examples for students.

Unit 6: Musical Elements

MELODY:
The melody uses the key signature of concert E-flat major, with a few D-flats occurring during transitions, but it rarely concludes or rests on E-flat. Phrasing is in regular two-, four-, or eight-measure phrases, and the opening melody repeats frequently within both the A and B sections of the ABA'B' form.

Perrine's melodies are inspired by and grow out of his harmonic choices:

> In my writing, melody is often derived from harmony and *April* is no exception. The opening melodic statement in the two solo clarinets (figure 1) is taken from the piano voicing in m. 1 (figure 2), where the third and fourth are voiced together and "rub" against each other. This 4–3 suspension is found many other places in the piece.[6]

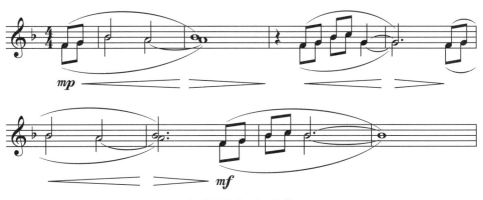

FIGURE 1. Mm. 4–12, melody performed by clarinet duet

FIGURE 2. Mm. 1–2, piano

HARMONY:

Although *April* features extended harmonies (sevenths, ninths, elevenths, and thirteenths) or added seconds (ninths, fourths), harmonies are approached in such a manner as to make them manageable for level two players. For example, the horns play the sharp eleventh found in the G-flat$^{\text{maj}13,\,\#11}$ chord at m. 15. This sounds like a difficult note for young horn players to pitch, but the note is in a comfortable range and approached by step. Also, the pitch was modeled by the flutes four measures earlier.

Perrine offers another example of how he approached writing more mature harmonies for less advanced students:

> Another example of a sophisticated sound that is easy to play occurs in m. 9. The melody simply repeats itself, while the harmony changes below it, leaving a D-flat Lydian sound that is easy to perform (figures 3 and 4).[7]

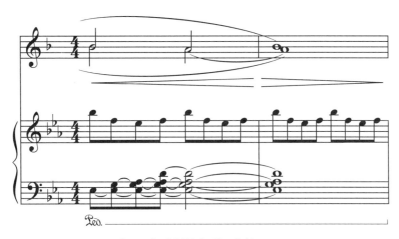

FIGURE 3. Mm. 5–6, clarinet melody and piano accompaniment

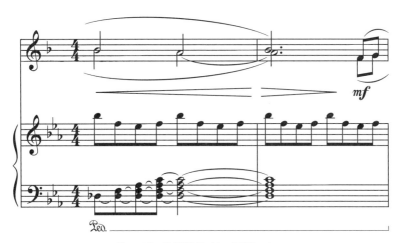

FIGURE 4. Mm. 9–10, clarinet melody and piano accompaniment

RHYTHM:

The piece opens with a two-measure melodic ostinato performed by the piano and percussion. This figure provides the forward momentum for the A sections. In the B sections, the ostinato disappears and responsibility for the rhythmic drive transfers to the snare and bass drum.

The rhythmic writing is straightforward, but Perrine repeatedly uses two very similar syncopated figures (figures 5 and 6). It will be necessary to point out and rehearse each pattern separately to ensure proper execution.

FIGURE 5. Mm. 22, 26, 34, 64, 68, and 76.

FIGURE 6. Mm. 28, 30, 36, 70, 72, and 78.

TIMBRE:

April is in ABA'B' form, and the texture is vastly different between the A and B sections. The A sections are more transparent. While the opening melodic phrase repeats, interest is maintained through harmonic variation and the addition of instruments. Within the B sections, the texture is much thicker and the accompaniment is more active. Therefore, the B sections will undoubtedly get too loud. Students must be reminded to get softer after the initial attack of any dotted half or whole note. This dynamic adjustment will allow the moving lines, in either the melody or the accompaniment, to be heard.

Unit 7: Form and Structure

SECTION	MEASURE	EVENT AND SCORING
A	1–4	Introduction; piano and percussion ostinato; E-flat$^{\text{maj7 (add 9, 11)}}$
	5–8	Melody performed by a clarinet duet (solo clarinets 1 and 2)
	9–12	Melody repeats; more instruments join the melodic texture; suspended cymbal enters; arrival of D-flat$^{\text{maj13, #11}}$ (D-flat Lydian mode)
	13–18	Melodic extension; arrival of G-flat$^{\text{maj13, #11}}$ and the loudest point of the A section at m. 15; snare and bass drum take over responsibility for rhythmic drive from the piano, timpani, and mallet percussion
B	19–26	Melody played by trumpet 1, alto saxophone, and tenor saxophone; E-flat major finally established; new accompanying melody by flute, oboe, clarinet 1, bells and piano; ostinato by marimba; syncopation in low brass and low reeds; thicker texture; four-measure phrases

SECTION	MEASURE	EVENT AND SCORING
	27–34	Melody continues in the same instruments until m. 31, where the texture thins dramatically, leaving clarinets and oboes to finish the melodic idea
	35–42	Begins like m. 27; melody diverts at the end of m. 37, where the texture abruptly thins and the battery percussion drops out
	43–44	Ostinato from m. 9 returns and builds into A'; all other instruments fade-out; D-flat^{maj13}
A'	45–48	Return of the introduction and E-flat^{maj7} (add 9, 11)
	49–52	Melody returns; thicker orchestration; wave effect created by note oscillations in the flute, oboe, clarinet, and horn; at the end of m. 51, flute and oboe echo a melodic fragment; bassoon, bass clarinet, baritone saxophone, and euphonium play descending connecting material reminiscent of m. 40
	53–56	Melodic extension; harmony reverts to D-flat$^{maj13, \#11}$ (D-flat Lydian mode)
	57–60	Similar to mm. 15–18; arrival of G-flat$^{maj13, \#11}$; battery percussion returns
B'	61–86	Repeats mm. 19–44 with slight changes in orchestration (phrase structure: 4-4-8-10)
Codetta	87–91	Returns to opening texture (piano, mallet percussion, and timpani) with the addition of wind chimes and suspended cymbal; D-flat^{maj7} (add 9, 13)
	91	Major seventh (E-flat and D), a final reference to E-flat major

Unit 8: Suggested Listening

Hancock, Herbie. *Maiden Voyage*.
Lauridsen, Morten. Arr. Robert Reynolds. *O Magnum Mysterium*.
Schneider, Maria. *Hang Gliding*.
Whitacre, Eric:
    Lux Aurumque
    October

Unit 9: Additional References and Resources

Lauridsen, Morten. Robert Reynolds, arr. *O Magnum Mysterium*. Songs of Peer, Ltd., 2003.

Perrine, Aaron. *April*. C. Alan Publications, 2008.

Richardson, Colleen. Interviews with Aaron Perrine. May 23 and 25, 2008.

Whitacre, Eric. *Lux Aurumque*. Eric Whitacre & Carpe Ranam Productions, 2005.

_____. *October*. Eric Whitacre & Carpe Ranam Productions, 2000.

Websites:

Aaron Perrine. www.aaronperrine.com/

NPR Basic Jazz Recording Library. www.npr.org

Maria Schneider. www.mariaschneider.com

Contributed by:

Colleen Richardson
Assistant Professor of Music Education and Music Performance Studies
Wind Ensemble Director
University of Western Ontario
London, Ontario, Canada

---

1 Aaron Perrine, telephone interview, May 23, 2008.
2 Ibid.
3 Email from Aaron Perrine, May 25, 2008.
4 Aaron Perrine, telephone interview, May 23, 2008.
5 Email from Aaron Perrine, May 25, 2008.
6 Ibid.
7 Ibid.

Teacher Resource Guide

As Winds Dance

Samuel R. Hazo
(b. 1966)

Unit 1: Composer

Samuel R. Hazo is a native of Pittsburgh, Pennsylvania, where he attended college and began his teaching career. He received his bachelors and masters degrees from Duquesne University, where he was awarded Duquesne's Outstanding Graduate in Music Education and has served on its University Board of Governors. He has taught music in both primary and secondary school settings, including posts as a high school and collegiate band director. His accomplishments as a music educator have been acknowledged by the Southwestern Pennsylvania Teacher's Excellence Foundation by being named a "Teacher of Distinction" on two separate occasions.

His distinguished career as a composer and arranger has included commissioning projects for all levels of wind bands from middle school honor bands to the top collegiate ensembles in the nation. He has also written original scores for television, radio, and the stage. Prominent ensembles such as the Tokyo Kosei Wind Orchestra, the Birmingham Symphonic Winds (UK), and the Klavier Wind Project recordings conducted by Eugene Migliaro Corporon have performed his compositions.

Hazo's works have appeared on numerous National Conferences and Symposia, including the Music Educators National Conference, Midwest Band and Orchestra Clinic, World Association for Symphonic Bands and Ensembles Convention, National Honor Band of America, National Band Association/Texas Bandmasters Association Convention, and the College Band Directors National Association Convention. He was the first composer in history to be awarded both prizes for the composition contests (William D.

Revelli in 2003 and Merrill Jones in 2001) sponsored by the National Band Association.

Hazo resides in his hometown of Pittsburgh, Pennsylvania with his wife and two children. He is a clinician for the Hal Leonard Corporation and is sponsored by Sibelius Music Software.

Unit 2: Composition

As Winds Dance was commissioned by Stephen Kraus, director of bands at the McKnight and Peebles School in the North Allegheny School District in Pittsburgh, Pennsylvania. The piece was conceived as a teaching tool to help students learn the concept of syncopation. The composer writes in his notes from the published score by Boosey & Hawkes:

> I can still hear my college sight-singing professor, Dr. Louis Munkachy, telling us, in his thick Hungarian accent, "Repetition is the mother of knowledge." For every bit of truth this statement holds, it is equally true that repetition is the natural enemy of the eleven- to thirteen-year-old. Their motto more resembles: I did it great once; therefore, greatness must flow from me. So, in trying to compose a piece that painlessly introduced middle level students to syncopation, I knew that repetition had to be present, but disguised so as not to look like something instructive. Moreover, the students would need to perceive (on their own) that the musical needs of the piece dictated how many times a syncopated pattern would recur. I believe that balance exists in "As Winds Dance."

The composer successfully disguises the repetition of the syncopated figure by frequently changing orchestration to keep the music engaging. He also uses chord choices (major and minor sevenths and ninths, and one chord made up of every note in the C whole tone scale) that are not often heard in music written for young bands.

Unit 3: Historical Perspective

Over the past several years, Hazo has contributed a wealth of music to wind band repertoire. A sampling of his compositional output will reveal a substantial influence from his work in writing for film, radio, and television. His harmonic language is inflected by the usage of traditional tonal harmonies colored by jazz chord extensions. He writes tuneful melodies and his works are tied together with an infectious rhythmic drive.

Listening to the following pieces will give one a good sense of Hazo's compositional style:

Exultate
In Heaven's Air
Perthshire Majesty
Novo Lenio
Ride
Sevens
Sky is Waiting
Solas Ane

Unit 4: Technical Considerations

The technical challenges for this piece are focused around familiarity with B-flat and E-flat major. The melodic content of the piece is basically stepwise motion and small interval movement of no more than a fifth.

The pedagogical focus of this piece is to teach syncopation in a way so that students internalize the feel of the rhythmic pulse. The tempo (quarter note = 146) ensures that the pulse will move along and not become stagnant. The composer mixes the feel of the downbeat pulse with the syncopation accent in a repeatable two-bar phrase that ties the entire composition together. A similar rhythmic motive is introduced halfway through the piece to provide context and contrast in learning this difficult musical concept.

The phrasal structure of the piece lays out in four-bar increments. However, the syncopation is written in such a way that the barline is obscured somewhat, which forces students to carry the phrase across to the next measure. Furthermore, the accents on weak beats also tend to make the barline indistinct and shift the feel of the meter.

The orchestration of the piece is constructed in such a way so that everyone in the ensemble has an opportunity to play the main theme of the piece at least once during the course of the composition. This reinforces the pedagogical purpose of the piece, which is to internalize the feel of a syncopated rhythmic figure.

The percussion parts are written for timpani, snare drum, crash cymbals, and glockenspiel. The composer suggests that more than one snare drummer can be used within the section, knowing that most middle school band classes will have an abundance of percussionists on hand.

Unit 5: Stylistic Considerations

The dance-like nature of the piece is derived from the interplay of the brisk tempo, strong sense of syncopation and pulse, and the proper placements of accents. The teaching of these accents should be first approached from the standpoint of stressed and unstressed quarter notes. If not careful, students will tend to use too much tongue on accented notes, producing a harsh attack that will negatively affect tone quality. Emphasis should be placed on clarity of attack, using a "tee" consonant supported by a free-flowing reservoir of air.

The snare drum can be used successfully to demonstrate the different sound of an accented note by asking the percussionist to play straight quarter notes, alternately loud and soft. This will demonstrate that an accent can be derived by playing unaccented notes more softly.

This piece is also a good tool for teaching dynamic contrasts. There are ample opportunities to rehearse *piano*-to-*forte* crescendos and also several subito dynamic changes. In addition, the coda of the piece presents a balance problem between the melodic line in the clarinets and trumpets versus the rest of the ensemble sustaining block chords. Some effort will need to be made here to readjust the dynamics of the sustained chords so that the melodic content can be heard clearly.

Unit 6: Musical Elements

MELODY:
The melodic content is diatonic by nature and moves stepwise within the keys of B-flat and E-flat major. There are two instances where a melodic fragment moves downward by a fifth and upwards by a fourth.

HARMONY:
The composer makes use of traditional tertian harmonies with the addition of seventh and ninth extensions to add a jazz inflection to the color of the piece. Tonality is structured around the key centers of B-flat and E-flat major. An interesting sonority is built on all the notes of a C whole tone scale in two cadence points in the score. The composer at times substitutes suspended seventh chords in place of an expected dominant seventh at cadence points.

RHYTHM:
The basic feel of this piece is derived from two syncopated rhythmic figures, one of which is used extensively as an ostinato and melodic figure. The meter is 3/4 for the entire piece, with the tempo remaining constant at quarter note = 146. The rhythmic content consists of various combinations of half notes, quarter notes and rests, and eighth notes and rests. Accents on weak beats plus the syncopated figures tend to shift the feel of where barlines should land.

TIMBRE:
The composer uses tutti block scoring to state the initial appearance of the ostinato rhythmic pattern. Subsequently, he layers a countermelody on top of the melodic ostinato to thicken the texture. The percussion section is used to accentuate the underlying rhythmic ostinato during sustained chords in the winds.

Toward the end of the piece as he settles into E-flat major, the composer combines the main rhythmic melodic idea with the countermelody plus block woodwind chords to create the dense texture for the climax of the piece.

Unit 7: Form and Structure

SECTION	MEASURE	EVENT AND SCORING
Introduction	1–8	Percussion presents rhythmic motif 1; woodwinds play falling dominant to tonic interval that defines key center of B-flat major
A	9–16	Theme A (based on rhythmic motif 1) is presented by entire ensemble harmonized in the key of B-flat major
A	17–24	Countermelody (theme A') is performed by saxes, horns, trumpets, and bells on top of theme A
B	25–28	Theme B is presented by flutes, clarinets, trumpets, horns, and alto sax built on E-flat^{maj7} chord
B	29–34	Rhythmic motif 2 is presented by the full ensemble and snare in unison rhythm
A	35–42	Return of rhythmic motif 1 in B-flat major; bells anchor motif in open fifth (B-flat to F); soprano and alto voices perform countermelody (theme A') on top of motif
B	43–54	Snare changes rhythmic background to triplets; punch chords based on E-flat^{maj9} played by tutti; chord progression suggests theme B; cadential progression takes us back to B-flat major
A	55–62	Return of rhythmic motif 1 and theme A; unison rhythm in low reeds and low brass, plus clarinets and trumpets
A	63–70	Full ensemble states theme A; cadence prepares modulation to E-flat major (ii-V^7-I)
A	71–78	Theme a presented in low woodwinds, low brass, and glock; countermelody (theme A') performed in trumpet and horn
Closing	79–86	Rhythmic motif 1 stated in snare and glock; dominant to tonic melodic interval repeated in clarinets and trumpets
Coda	87–93	Woodwinds sustain E-flat major; brass chord is added on top of rhythmic motif 1 that is performed in percussion

Unit 8: Suggested Listening

Barnes, James. *Yorkshire Ballad*.
Erickson, Frank. *Rhythm of the Winds*.
Grundman, Clare. *Kentucky 1800*.
McBeth, W. Francis. *Canto*.
Nelhybel, Vaclav. *Ritual*.
Ticheli, Frank. *Portrait of a Clown*.
Williams, J. Clifton. *Variation Overture*.

Unit 9: Additional References and Resources

Hazo, Samuel R. *As Winds Dance*. London, GB: Boosey & Hawkes, Inc.,
    2003.
_____. http://www.samuelrhazo.com
Lisk, Edward S. *The Creative Director: Alternative Rehearsal Techniques*.
    Oswego, NY: Lisk Publishing, 1987.
McBeth, W. Francis. *Effective Performance of Band Music*. San Antonio, TX:
    Southern Music Company, 1972.
National Band Association. *Selective Music List for Bands*.
    http://www.nationalbandassociation.org/
Rush, Scott. *Habits of a Successful Band Director*. Fort Wayne, IN: Focus on
    Excellence, 2003.
Trachsel, Andrew. "In Heaven's Air." *Teaching Music through Performance in
    Band, Volume 5*. Richard Miles, ed. Chicago: GIA Publications, Inc.,
    2004.
Wakefield, Williams. "Exultate." *Teaching Music through Performance in Band,
    Volume 5*. Richard Miles, ed. Chicago: GIA Publications, Inc., 2004.

Contributed by:

Leslie W. Hicken
Director of Bands
Furman University
Greenville, South Carolina

Teacher Resource Guide

AspenSong

Walter Cummings
(b. 1953)

Unit 1: Composer

Walter Cummings has taught band for fourteen years at the college, high school, and middle school levels in Mississippi, New Hampshire, and Colorado, and is owner of Grand Mesa Music. His compositions for school band are rapidly gaining wide acceptance, and have been performed throughout the United States, Canada, and Australia by a variety of school, clinic, and community bands. Cummings is currently a freelance composer and low brass performer, and teaches low brass at Mesa State College. Playing positions held by Cummings include tubaist with the Grand Junction Symphony and Mesa State College Faculty Brass Quintet.

Walter Cummings received his bachelor of music education and master of music degrees from the University of Southern Mississippi, the master of music education degree from the University of Colorado, and the doctor of arts degree in Conducting from the University of Northern Colorado.

Composition prizes won by Cummings include the Colorado Music Educators Association Band Composition Contest, as well as six ASCAP Awards for Excellence in Serious Music Composition.

Unit 2: Composition

The composer writes:

> *AspenSong* was inspired by a hike I took in Colorado's White River National Forest in the fall of 1999. The aspen trees were at the height of their golden glory under a perfect blue sky. Gentle breezes caressed the yellow leaves, causing them to shimmer and quake (hence the nickname "quaking aspen").

The White River National Forest encompasses nearly 2.3 million acres of land and has peaks of over 14,000 feet, resulting in panoramic views of the abundant aspen trees.

This single-movement work is ninety-four measures in length and lasts approximately five and a half minutes. Thematic and accompaniment materials are presented in varying voices, and are scored in varying combinations. Doublings are used when logical, but some independence will be required. Repetition is used to make the piece cohesive, while new timbres and textures abound to allow the music to remain organic.

Unit 3: Historical Perspective

Nature and one's place in it has been an inspiration for musical compositions throughout history, from Vivaldi's *The Four Seasons* and Beethoven's *Symphony No. 6*. Wind music has contributed similar works as well, including Grainger's *Walking Tune* and Whitacre's *Cloudburst*. Many wind works with themes, if not titles, inspired by nature are available in today's market.

Unit 4: Technical Considerations

AspenSong is scored for full band including, flute 1–2, oboe, bassoon, clarinet 1–3, bass clarinet, alto saxophone 1–2, tenor saxophone, baritone saxophone, trumpet 1–3, horn in F, trombone 1–2, euphonium (treble and bass clef), tuba, and percussion. Percussion parts will require five players, including two mallet parts for bells and marimba (which can, if necessary, be performed by one player). Percussion parts 1–2 will require two performers each.

The work begins loosely centered on C minor, weaves ambiguously in and out of varying tonalities, and ends in E-flat major. While there are no key changes, accidentals abound throughout. Ranges required for performance are above those of a second-year player (i.e., alto saxophone 1 to C6; trumpet 1 to G5), thus making the piece more suited to a middle school ensemble. Rhythmic constraints are minimal, with dotted-quarter-and-eighth-note rhythms being the most difficult. There are many passages consisting entirely of eighth notes, so internalization of pulse and subdivision are essential. The conductor should reinforce eighth-note subdivision on a regular basis. All three clarinet parts go over the break.

Unit 5: Stylistic Considerations

Legato articulations abound in this work. Careful attention must be given to the many dynamic contrasts in the piece. Generally, dynamic changes are parallel across the ensemble; however there are several instances of contrary dynamics that will require rehearsal. Dynamics ranges are from *mp* to *ff*. Most of the accompaniment is linear, which will offer young musicians a new approach to accompaniment techniques than is offered by most compositions. There are several opportunities for quasi-soli sectional playing, which will require some level of independence in each section. Tempo is consistently *andante*, with the exception of a brief twelve-measure *più mosso* section.

Unit 6: Musical Elements

MELODY:

With the exception of sections B and C of the piece, all melodic lines are at least doubled. Sections B and C, while short, have a great deal of soli melodic writing. The main melody (see figure 1) appears in the minor mode at first, but appears in the major mode in fragmentation near the end of the piece. Alterations of the melody and its fragments appear often in the work. Contrapuntal techniques appear often.

Copyright © 2000 Grand Mesa Music Publishers

FIGURE 1. Main theme, tenor saxophone

HARMONY:

Many of the harmonies in this work are either implied or embedded in the linear accompaniments and are mainly diatonic.

The linear nature of many of the harmonies will allow for in-depth discussion of accompaniment techniques and an analysis of implied harmony. In addition students could be encouraged to compose their own linear accompaniments to short melodies.

RHYTHM:

Common time is used for the entire piece. While rhythmic demands of performers are minimal, several layers of rhythmic activity occur at the same time, and will require some isolation and rehearsal. Strict eighth-note accompaniments appear throughout, and will require some measure of rehearsal to ensure consistency (see figure 2).

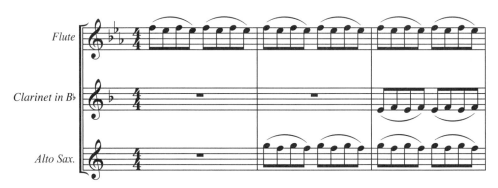

FIGURE 2. Eighth-note accompaniment

TIMBRE:

AspenSong contains many timbre shifts and uses full-ensemble as well as soli and sectional orchestration. Shifting timbres will allow for in-depth discussions of tone production, blend, and balance. In addition, there are several opportunities for soloistic playing and each section shares melodic and accompaniment material.

Unit 7: Form and Structure

SECTION	MEASURE	EVENT AND SCORING
Introduction	1–6	Percussion begins introduction; woodwinds and muted trumpet begin eighth-note accompaniment
A	7–12	Low brass and low woodwinds present main melody with eighth-note accompaniment by clarinet, flute, alto saxophone, and bells
	13–18	Extension of melody by high brass, flute, and oboe; melodic accompaniment by low brass and low woodwinds while eighth-note accompaniment continues in clarinet and alto saxophone
B	19–30	Quasi-canonic transitional material beginning with soloistic work with increasing orchestration
C	31–49	Contrapuntal development of main theme and its fragments; increased fragmentation at m. 44
	50–72	*Più mosso*; contrapuntal development continues in numerous voices

Section	Measure	Event and Scoring
A'	73–85	Full-ensemble statement of theme and accompaniment
Coda	86–94	Final statements of theme and its fragments

Unit 8: Suggested Listening

Copland, Aaron. *Down A Country Lane*.
Cummings, Walter:
    Crescent Moon Floats in Blue-Pink Sky
    Song for the Winter Moon
Grainger, Percy Aldridge:
    Australian Up-Country Tune
    Walking Tune
Holsinger, David. *On A Hymnsong of Phillip Bliss*.
Nelson, Ron. *Aspen Jubilee*.
Work, Julian. *Autumn Walk*.

Unit 9: Additional References and Resources

Henigin, Jim. Email to Walter Cummings.
Recording available from the publisher.
Grand Mesa Music Publishers: www.grandmesamusic.com

Contributed by:

Jim Henigin
Doctoral Music Education Teaching Assistant
West Virginia University
Morgantown, West Virginia

Teacher Resource Guide

Be Thou My Vision
Larry Clark
(b. 1963)

Unit 1: Composer

Larry Clark is vice president for Carl Fischer Music in New York, where he serves as editor-in-chief and coordinates all of Carl Fischer's publishing in all genres of music. Prior to this appointment he served as an instrumental music editor for Warner Brothers Publications in Miami. His diverse background includes serving as the director of bands at Syracuse University and considerable public school teaching in the state of Florida.

Larry is well known as a composer and arranger of music for band and orchestra. His works have been performed internationally and appear on numerous contest/festival performance required music lists. He is an ASCAP award-winning composer, has over 200 publications in print, and is in demand to write commissions for bands and orchestras across the country. Rhythmic vigor and spirit, colorful scoring, and playability at every performance level characterize his music.

Larry's music has been influenced by variety of composers and teachers. He credits his father, a long-time band director in Florida, for teaching him the joy of music. Robert W. Smith influenced him early in his writing career, and his decision to pursue composition and arranging was influenced further by John Hillard, composition professor at James Madison University. Larry considers himself to be a product of the school band movement. His works are highly influenced by the standard band repertoire of composers such as Holst, Grainger, Schuman, and Persichetti.

Larry is in demand as a clinician and guest conductor around the country. He also is co-author with Sandy Feldstein of the innovative new band method

The Yamaha Advantage. He holds a bachelors degree in music education from Florida State University and masters degrees in conducting and composition from James Madison University in Virginia.[1]

Unit 2: Composition

From the composer's program notes:

> *Be Thou My Vision* was commissioned by the Burns Middle School Band in Brandon, Florida under the direction of Kevin Lewis. It was premiered in May of 2006 with the composer conducting.
>
> This has always been one of my favorite hymns, and when I was asked to write a piece based on a standard hymn I was quick to take the opportunity to compose a set of variations on this poignant melody. This famous hymn is based on the Irish folksong "Slane" and originates from around AD 400 at the time of St. Patrick. Taking this into account, I tried to incorporate some aspects of Irish music into the fabric of this piece.
>
> The piece begins with a composed fanfare based on open intervals to give it the sound of ancient modal music. This is followed by an original melody for piccolo solo over drones in the lower voices. This melody is used to set the mood and used later to add variety to the piece. The hymn tune then follows in a full chorale section by the brass, then woodwinds, then brass again. The piccolo theme returns to connect the piece into the variations of the hymn tune that follows. The first variation of the hymn tune is my salute to the famous band composer Percy Grainger. This section has aspects reminiscent of his style of writing. This is followed by an abrupt change in tempo and key in a darker setting of the hymn with shifting tonalities throughout the presentation of the hymn tune. The opening fanfare returns in the woodwinds and leads to the next variation, which is in the style of an Irish jig. The use of the bodhrán, which can be substituted by a tom-tom, sets the mood for this lilting 6/8 section. The piccolo and horns state the tune with harmonic punctuations by the brass. An abrupt change in tempo in the percussion sets up the climactic presentation of the hymn tune in the brass with the Irish jig figures continuing in the woodwinds. This leads to a return of the fanfare material to close out the composition in dramatic fashion.[2]
>
> The 181-measure work is five minutes, thirteen seconds long.

Unit 3: Historical Perspective

The words to this hymn come from the Irish monastic tradition. Some scholars argue that they may date from 700 CE. It is an example of a *lorica* or breastplate—almost a sort of incantation to be recited for protection arming oneself for spiritual or physical battle.

The text is set to the hymn tune "Slane." This tune is of Irish folk origin. It is named for a hill about ten miles from Tara hill in County Meath. It is on Slane Hill (around AD 433), according to an account in the *Confessions of St. Patrick*, that the Irish saint defied the command of the pagan High King Loigaire by lighting the paschal candle on Easter Eve. St. Patrick's act was done in defiance of the king's edict that no fire could be ignited before the royal fire was lit by the king's hand on Tara hill. The royal fire was kindled to celebrate the pagan spring festival and symbolized the return of light and change of season following the darkness of winter. Loigaire was so impressed by Patrick's devotion that, despite his defiance (or perhaps because of it), he let him continue his missionary work. The rest is history.[3]

The words for the hymn are as follows:

Be Thou my Vision, O Lord of my heart;
Naught be all else to me, save that Thou art.
Thou my best Thought, by day or by night,
Waking or sleeping, Thy presence my light.

Be Thou my Wisdom, and Thou my true Word;
I ever with Thee and Thou with me, Lord;
Thou my great Father, I Thy true son;
Thou in me dwelling, and I with Thee one.

Be Thou my battle Shield, Sword for the fight;
Be Thou my Dignity, Thou my Delight;
Thou my soul's Shelter, Thou my high Tower:
Raise Thou me heavenward, O Power of my power.

Riches I heed not, nor man's empty praise,
Thou mine Inheritance, now and always:
Thou and Thou only, first in my heart,
High King of Heaven, my Treasure Thou art.

High King of Heaven, my victory won,
May I reach Heaven's joys, O bright Heaven's Sun!
Heart of my own heart, whatever befall,
Still be my Vision, O Ruler of all.[4]

Unit 4: Technical Considerations

The key centers of E-flat and F are used in the work. The fastest rhythmic duration is a sixteenth note, and the piece contains several dotted-eighth-and-sixteenth-note figures in the two key centers. Understanding of one-to-the-bar concepts, performing a fast 6/8 time in two, and stylistic demands presented throughout the work will be of importance in addressing the technical demands of the work. Presentation of precise definitions of the articulations presented in each section or variation in the work will serve to be very beneficial to the performer. Reinforcement of the styles in the work with representative listening activities will also serve to develop the students' understanding of how the Grainger and jig portions of the work should be performed. The work is scored as follows: flute 1 (piccolo), flute 2; oboe; clarinet 1–3; alto clarinet; bass clarinet; bassoon; alto saxophone 1–2; tenor saxophone; baritone saxophone; trumpet 1–3; horn 1–2; trombone 1–2; baritone TC; baritone BC; tuba; mallet percussion (chimes, bells, xylophone); timpani; percussion 1 (snare drum, bass drum); and percussion 2 (crash cymbals, bodhrán or tom-tom, triangle, suspended cymbal).

Unit 5: Stylistic Considerations

The dynamic range of the piece is from *piano* to *fortissimo*. Many expressive opportunities exist in the piece and care should be taken to deliver the appropriate shape of the hymn tune phrases in the work. Much effort should be placed on performing the lines in a cantabile manner—performing in a melodious and graceful style, full of expression. Discussion and analysis of the hymn, reinforced with a wide variety of representative listening examples, will be very beneficial to students performing this work. Careful analysis of the suggested listening examples will help students to better understand the stylistic and compositional influences on the work from Percy Grainger and Robert W. Smith.

Unit 6: Musical Elements

MELODY:
The tonality of the work begins in E-flat major and changes to F major. The piece is diatonic in nature. Rehearsal and reinforcement of these scales, both on an individual and group level, will help students to develop a tonal concept of the piece. Directors will also find it beneficial to analyze and identify instruments with primary melodic roles in rehearsal and have students mark their music accordingly. Identification of instruments responsible for secondary melodic lines within each presentation of the main theme will also prove to be helpful. Constant discussion of balance demands between the melodic lines and supporting material will also be valuable, so

that the listener is able to identify the melody throughout the piece, especially in the thicker textures of the work.

HARMONY:

Harmonies are generally triadic and diatonic in nature and reflect the influences of Grainger and Smith. The piece provides a wealth of harmonic material to analyze and listen to, as students can compare the harmonies and textures in Grainger's "The Lost Lady Found" (from *Lincolnshire Posy*) to the harmonies and textures in the piece. The piece also provides an excellent opportunity to learn about and explore theme and variations concepts. Discussion and analysis of the differences between the hymn tune and the variations in the work will serve as an invaluable teaching strategy. These concepts should also be reinforced by studying and analyzing theme and variations in Grainger's *Lincolnshire Posy*. Use of classroom activities that involve students creating and presenting their own theme and variations would also serve as an important learning opportunity.

RHYTHM:

The fastest rhythmic duration is a sixteenth note, and the piece contains dotted-eighth-and-sixteenth-note figures. The work contains the following meters: 3/4, 4/4, 6/8, and 5/4. Opportunities exist for students to develop their skills with one-to-the-bar concepts. Understanding of cut-time concepts in a fast 6/8 tempo in the jig portion are also important to success in performance of the work. A variety of tempos and tempo changes in the work will also be of concern for a successful ensemble performance.

TIMBRE:

Clark's skill as a composer and arranger are evident in the work, as he offers many sounds reminiscent of many quality wind works of the past. A variety of timbres are created through various instrument combinations and groupings. Creation of timbres consistent with the likes of Grainger, Smith, etc., are presented here with clarity. Clark does an excellent job of effectively exploring the textural and timbral opportunities available for wind bands playing at this level. Exposing students to the bodhrán, other traditional Irish instruments, and "trad" music in general would greatly heighten the learning experience provided in presenting this piece.

Unit 7: Form and Structure

MEASURE	EVENT AND SCORING
1–9	Tutti fanfare based on open intervals
10–17	Original melody presented by way of a piccolo solo over drones in lower woodwinds and brass

MEASURE	EVENT AND SCORING
18–33	Hymn tune appears in brass choir, in legato, chorale-like texture; response from woodwind choir followed by brass response
34–40	Original piccolo melody presented again in flute and clarinet sections
41–48	Developmental, transition based on two-measure, legato, melodic fragments to connect the piece to the variations of the hymn tune that follows
49–64	Variation 1: Grainger-esque presentation of hymn tune in clarinet section
65–80	Variation continues in similar stylistic and rhythmic fashion with hymn tune presented in clarinets, alto saxophones, and horns. Brass and percussion emphasize accents presented in hymn tune
81–96	Variation continues with full woodwind choir presenting the hymn tune in a lyric, textural tribute to Percy Grainger; hymn tune doubled by bells
97–114	Abrupt change in tempo and key center begins transition to second variation; legato phrases presented by the brass choir are followed by a response from the woodwind choir, which is then followed by a response from the brass choir
115–119	Opening fanfare presented in woodwind choir to finish transition to second variation
120–139	Variation 2: Following a four-measure bodhrán (or tom-tom) solo in 6/8 time, the hymn tune is presented as an Irish jig; piccolo and horns state the tune with harmonic punctuations by the brass
140–166	Abrupt change in tempo set up by a three-measure drum break; the jig continues in the upper woodwinds and percussion at a faster pace than before in a new key center; a rhythmically augmented version of the hymn tune is presented by the alto saxophones, trumpets, and horns, with the rest of the woodwinds and brass providing thick, full, chordal accompaniment

MEASURE	EVENT AND SCORING
167–174	Hymn tune presented in full tutti texture with minimal percussion
175–181	Opening fanfare returns to conclude the work in a dramatic fashion

Unit 8: Suggested Listening

Clark, Larry:
  Allegiance
  Pantomime
  Seven Springs
  Twist of Fate

Grainger, Percy:
  Children's March
  Colonial Song
  Country Gardens
  Lincolnshire Posy
    (movement 6, "The Lost Lady Found")
Smith, Robert W.:
  The Ascension
  Ireland: Of Legend and Lore

Unit 9: Additional References and Resources

Clark, Larry. Email correspondence with the composer. May, 2008.

Miles, Richard, ed. *Teaching Music through Performance in Band, Volume 1.*
    Chicago: GIA Publications, Inc., 1997.

Websites:
    Larry Clark. http://www.larryclarkmusic.com
    Carl Fischer. http://www.carlfischer.com
    Cyberhymnal. http://www.cyberhymnal.org
    A-team. http://ateam.blogware.com/blog

Contributed by:

Eugene F. Bechen
Chair, Department of Music
Associate Professor of Music
Director of Bands
St. Ambrose University
Davenport, Iowa

---

1 From Larry Clark's personal website, http://www.larryclarkmusic.com
2 Larry Clark, program notes from score.
3 http://ateam.blogware.com
4 www.cyberhymnal.org

Teacher Resource Guide

Childgrove

Frederick Speck
(b. 1955)

Unit 1: Composer

Frederick Speck, director of bands and professor of music at the University of Louisville, conducts the Wind Symphony and New Music Ensemble, and teaches conducting and composition. His music has been performed by such ensembles as the Louisville Orchestra, the Denver Symphony, and Speculum Musicae, and recorded by such artists as Richard Stoltzman. Twice the recipient of the University of Louisville President's Award for Outstanding Scholarship, Research, and Creative Activity, his work has also been recognized the through fellowships and commissions from such organizations as the Barlow Endowment, the National Endowment for the Arts, the Indiana Arts Commission, and the Pennsylvania Council for the Arts. He holds BM and MM degrees from Bowling Green State University and the DMA degree from the University of Maryland. Speck's other band works include *Dance Toccata, Fantasia on a Southern Hymn Tune*, and *Kizuna*.

Unit 2: Composition

Childgrove is an original band work commissioned by the Beaumont Middle School Symphonic Band of Lexington, Kentucky, Teresa J. Elliot and Ashley P. Burris, conductors, to commemorate their performance at the 2005 Midwest International Band and Orchestra Clinic in Chicago, Illinois. The composer states in the score:

Childgrove first came into print as one of the tunes in the collection Playford's *Dancing Master*. These editions were published beginning in the mid-seventeenth century by John Playford (1623–1686) and later, his son, Henry Playford (c. 1657–1701). The "band" of that day would have included the sounds that ranged from pipes and tabors, to lutes, viols, and dulcimers. This symphonic band setting retains an element of the spirit of the past, while drawing on the rhythmic energy and instrumental color of the present.

Childgrove, composed in 2005, is seventy-one measures long and approximately three minutes in length.

Unit 3: Historical Perspective

Instructions and music for English Country Dance first appeared in publisher John Playford's *The English Dancing Master* (1651). A form of folk dance, English Country Dance (ECD) was first popular with the landed gentry, as well as the aristocracy, in England and eventually France. The music featured melodies from folk tunes, popular ballads, and stage music that were tuneful and enjoyable to hear as well as sing. The dance steps were simple and easily learned. The composer writes about the sources that influenced his setting of *Childgrove*:

> Originally, when these dances were performed, the simple melody was repeated, each time acquiring varied ornamentation from the melody player, while the accompanying players either added other decorations or maintained the pulse for the dances. Similarly, in this version of *Childgrove*, the scoring moves from an initially direct statement of the tune through varied repetitions and ornamentations. Near the end, all the musicians join in a rich texture that is comprised of a counterpoint of various elements of the dance.

English Country Dance, in its varied forms of contra dance and square dance, remains popular today throughout the United States, where clubs and dance societies host events and offer instruction at all levels of mastery.

Unit 4: Technical Considerations

Childgrove is written for full band, including piccolo (solo parts and some doubling of flute 1), flute 1–2, oboe, B-flat clarinet 1–3, B-flat bass clarinet, bassoon, alto saxophone 1–2, tenor saxophone, baritone saxophone, trumpet 1–3 (all three need cup mutes—or parts played "in stand"; straight mute needed for solo trumpet 1), horn 1–2, trombone 1–3 (straight mute needed for solo trombone 1), euphonium, tuba, timpani, snare drum, medium suspended cymbal, tenor drum, bass drum, tambourine, bells, vibraphone, and marimba (timpanist plus seven percussionists needed).

The piccolo has solo passages independent of the flutes, although both parts are of similar difficulty. Second parts are of lesser difficulty throughout the score. The oboe and bassoon scores contain one part each and are doubled elsewhere to favor ensembles with few or no double reeds. The alto saxophones consistently function separately from the horns, with the first alto saxophone often scored in tandem with trumpet 1 or the upper woodwinds. Brass high ranges extend to G5 (one instance) in trumpet 1, C5 in horn 1, C4 in trombone 1–2, and F4 in the euphonium part.

The concert key signature of four flats defines both F Aeolian and B-flat Dorian. Students may become familiar with the sounds of these modes through the use of scale exercises that teach them to identify both pitches as the tonic. The melody itself is quite agreeably mastered owing to its comfortable range and largely stepwise construction. Additionally, with the playable range of the tune, as well as its primarily stepwise motion, the teacher could prepare a unison version of the tune for all students to play. This exercise would help students hear the modes in a melodic context, and as a listening exercise, assist students in learning how to adjust and balance to the presence of any three phrases of the tune. Unison rehearsal of the melody may also be used to define the style of articulation and note length.

Percussionists must be challenged to produce quality sounds on each instrument, particularly with the variety of timbres that are evident throughout the work. For example, smooth, even rolls on snare and tenor drums, full tone and well-centered pitch on timpani, and mallets that allow the keyboard instruments to sound with clarity but without surface clicks from the bars. The section's sense of time must be solid and confident, since it often works independently from other sections in the band. The tempo of the work, quarter note = 98, is a challenging pulse to maintain without rushing or slowing down. The percussion, in addition to maintaining the dance tempo, must also establish the mood and energy level of the piece.

Unit 5: Stylistic Considerations

Performance goals for *Childgrove* should include three important characteristics: 1) consistent, unwavering timekeeping; 2) a lifted articulation in separated notes that remains centered in tone quality; and 3) always balancing to the melodic line. The original tune *Childgrove* was created to accompany dancing, which by necessity needs to follow the rhythm and movement of the human body in motion. Any ensemble that accompanies dancing, from traditional drum and pipe, to ballet orchestras, to rock and roll bands, understands that it must first be solid and secure in keeping a tempo that helps the body move with coordination and ease. All concert ensembles, as one of their primary goals, address the challenges of playing together in time, but imagine having to accompany movement. A valuable lesson can be learned (an effective rehearsal technique for both players and conductor) by performing this music as an accompaniment to live dancing.

The articulation of Baroque performance includes a lifted or detached style that is neither short nor clipped in tone. Taking full breaths must be a core technique for all wind instruments, even in this style. The difference is that, in a lifted style, the notes should be detached from one another by stopping the air with little or no tongue (a "tah" articulation, rather than "tut" or "taht"). Practicing this articulation as part of a regular warm-up routine will help the entire ensemble achieve uniform initiations and releases.

The basics of a homophonic texture require that the melody be consistently present, no matter what the dynamic or scoring. The composer presents the melodic phrases through a wonderful variety of instrumental combinations (for example, the B phrase in mm. 16–19 alternates between solo flute and muted trumpet, and tutti flute and piccolo). One creative way to allow students to aurally identify these presentations of the melody could be, following the exercise of having all students play all three phrases of the melody (see Unit 4, paragraph 3), to have it played from the beginning without any accompaniment. Point out the students how the melody is passed from one section or combination of instruments to another. As stated in the score, this variety in scoring achieves one of the composer's important goals for this work:

> Although the pre-existing tune is used as a melodic source, the musical attribute of creating textural variation is still prominent in the work. This is of great appeal to me as a composer regardless of the surface attributes of the style, or the difficulty level of the work.

Unit 6: Musical Elements

MELODY:

The tune *Childgrove* can be divided into three phrases: A, B, and C. Each four-bar phrase is repeated to create the following pattern: AA BB CC. Two primary key areas, B-flat Dorian and F Aeolian (natural minor), make up the melodic segments. The key signature (for C instruments) throughout is four flats (two flats for B-flat instruments, three flats for horn in F, one flat for E-flat instruments). The Dorian mode is the scale formed by playing D–E–F–G–A–B–C–D (all white keys on the piano). The Aeolian mode is the natural minor mode, identified by playing A–B–C–D–E–F–G–A.

Dorian mode: B-flat–C–D-flat–E-flat–F–G–A-flat–B-flat
Aeolian mode: F–G–A-flat–B-flat–C–D-flat–E-flat–F

Scale exercises will help acclimate students to each mode, as well as to the aural sensations of playing in the Dorian and Aeolian. Another suggestion would be to have half of the ensemble intone the tonic and dominant notes (B-flat and F for Dorian, and F and C in Aeolian) while the other half of the ensemble plays through scale exercises in each mode. Each segment of the melody (as is typical of the style of modal tunes) centers around the tonic and dominant scale degrees, so students will easily hear and identify them. Articulation is simple, featuring regular groupings of two slurred eighths and two tongued eighths. Sixteenth notes are present in each of the three phrases, but are stepwise in motion and are slurred or tongued in groups of two.

HARMONY:

The harmonic structure confirms the use of both Dorian and Aeolian modes with consistent dominant to tonic movement at cadences that precede the presentation of the tune. For example, the opening of the work emphasizes B-flat Dorian through a strong tonic to dominant introduction (mm. 1–7), with occasional G-flats to add harmonic motion to the dominant F. Even with the variety of rhythmic motion evident in all voices, the texture is primarily homophonic, with the tune featured above a simple, unobtrusive harmonic foundation. A polyphonic texture is apparent, though, whenever two segments or phrases of the tune are juxtaposed. For example, the A phrase of the tune is reiterated starting in m. 24 in the clarinets, while the B phrase enters four beats later in flute 1. This texture forms an interesting counterpoint to the harmonic foundation that supports both phrases of the tune.

RHYTHM:

The rhythms used in the melody reflect those of the original tune. Accompaniment rhythms, though, are consistent with the repetitive long-short-short or short-short-long patterns used in folk or country dance music. In fact, it is through the range of rhythmic motives in differing proportions that the composer provides interest and variety underneath the presentations of the tune (which basically remains the same rhythmically throughout the work). For example, groupings of halves and quarters become quarters and eighths, which become eighths and sixteenths as the music moves forward.

Another rhythmic aspect of the piece, which is appropriate for this grade level, is the composer's setting of the tune above simpler rhythmic versions that complement the rhythm of the tune. Clarinets 1–2, for instance, present the A phrase of the tune in m. 24, while clarinet 3 highlights the same phrase with a less complex line that provides both melodic and harmonic support. Similarly, while piccolo, flute 1, and clarinet 1 present the B phrase of the tune in m. 53, flute 2, clarinet 2, and clarinet 3 present a simpler version of the tune's rhythmic outline.

TIMBRE:

As with many works for younger ensembles with an expanded percussion section (this work is scored for timpani and seven percussion parts), *Childgrove* relies on a wide variety of instruments that are available to the middle school band. These include snare drum, medium suspended cymbal, tenor drum, bass drum, tambourine, bells, vibraphone, and marimba (lowest required note is B-flat 3). The composer specifically suggests the types of mallets that should be used for the keyboard instruments (acrylic mallets for bells, hard yarn mallets for vibraphone, and medium hard yarn mallets for marimba). In addition to the traditional sounds that are created on the non-pitched percussion instruments, a unique type of "stick click" is specified by the composer in the score to imitate similar sounds in a variation of folk dance, the Morris Dance:

> Stick clicks with drum sticks or dowel rods. If dowel rods, 3/8" diameter by 6-1/2" long (may also be performed on snare drum rim at *mp* dynamic). Three sticks are needed per player. Two are held in a "V" in the LH between the thumb, index, and middle fingers, with the third held in the RH. Rolls are played in the small of the "V" between the sticks. Additional players may be used on stick click section if desired.

The dynamic range of the work extends from soft playing at *p* and *mp* to louder dynamics of *mf* and *f* (*ff* is reserved for only the final note of the piece). A good deal of the work is focused on the moderate range of *mp* to *mf*, so *f* passages, as well as subtle diminuendos to *p*, are striking in their contrast to the predominant medium dynamics. These contrasts are not only accomplished through the use of the entire ensemble, but also through scoring for smaller groupings, such as flute, oboe, and clarinet, or saxophone and trumpet.

With the active rhythms and corresponding lifted articulation needed for clarity, it will be important to help students continue to achieve a full, core tone through staccato or detached passages of notes. For example, with the eighths and sixteenths prominent in the ensemble from mm. 49–57, avoiding a "tut" type of articulation in favor of a "tah" style of tone or tonguing will allow the crisp articulation to still have a round, centered quality to it. Likewise, longer half- and quarter-valued notes in the accompaniment (e.g. mm. 8–15) require full breaths and consistently moving air, even at the *piano* dynamic level. This will not only all the students to blend, but to also control the sharpness in pitch.

Unit 7: Form and Structure

SECTION	MEASURE	EVENT AND SCORING
Introduction	1–7	Establishment of key of B-flat Dorian
A	8–15	First presentation of A portion of tune (AA)
B	16–23	B portion of tune (BB)

Section	Measure	Event and Scoring
A	24–32	A portion of tune presented again, but now with C phrase of theme superimposed above it (AA CC)
Development	33–40	Brief section that exploits an inverted fragment of the A phrase of the tune
A'	41–48	Return of A portion of the tune, with varied scoring (AA)
B'	49–56	Return of B portion of the tune, with new textures in scoring, as well as new rhythmic pulsation underneath (BB)
C	57–65	B and C portions of the tune presented superimposed above each other (BB CC)
Coda	66–71	Return of rhythmic and harmonic elements of the Introduction

Unit 8: Suggested Listening

Clark, Larry. *Contradanse*.
The English Country Dance Collection. http://www.cds-boston.org/ecdc/
Margolis, Bob:
    Royal Coronation Dances
    Soldiers' Procession
    Sword Dance
Terpsichore. *Postcards*. Cincinnati Wind Symphony. Eugene Migliaro
    Corporon, conductor. Klavier 11058. 1993.

Unit 9: Additional References and Resources

Country Dance and Song Society. Haydenville, Massachusetts.
    http://www.cdss.org/sales/english_dance.html
"English Country Dance." Wikipedia.
    http://en.wikipedia.org/wiki/English_Country_Dance
Ian Russell: "England; Traditional Music; Music and Dance." *Grove Music
    Online*. L. Macy, ed. http://www.grovemusic.com
Sharp, Cecil J. *The English Country Dance, Volume 4*. London: Novello,
    1900s. Graded series containing the description of the dances together
    with the tunes.

Contributed by:

Craig Paré
School of Music
DePauw University
Greencastle, Indiana

Teacher Resource Guide

Colors of a New Day

Aaron Meacham
(b. 1987)

Unit 1: Composer

Aaron Meacham was born in 1987 in Louisville, Kentucky. When he was five, his family moved to the small town of Madison, Indiana, where Aaron started learning piano and guitar. As a high school freshman, Aaron became quite interested in composition. He began lessons with band director and composer/arranger William Spencer-Pierce, who helped nurture and encourage Aaron's growing interest in composition.

Aaron is currently pursuing a bachelor of science degree in mechanical engineering and a bachelor of arts degree in music at the University of Kentucky. He has studied composition under William Spencer-Pierce and Joseph Baber and is a euphonium student of Skip Gray. In addition, Aaron is a member of the University of Kentucky Wind Ensemble, Tuba-Euphonium Ensemble, Wildcat Marching Band, and Kappa Kappa Psi National Honorary Band Service Fraternity. Over the past few years Aaron has written and arranged pieces for piano, woodwind quintet, brass ensemble, and concert band. Currently, Aaron has plans to attend graduate school and study either music theory or musical or architectural acoustics.

Unit 2: Composition

Originally written for piano, *Colors of a New Day* was arranged for concert band at the request of band director Scott Maack in 2005, and was premiered by his Madison Consolidated High School Concert Band in Madison, Indiana in the same year.

The work was a second-round finalist in the state-wide Project XL (Excel) arts competition in Indiana and was also a finalist in the first Frank Ticheli Composition Contest in 2006.

The composer comments in the score on his piece:

> I wanted to write very lyrical melodies that set well within the ranges of most high school instrumentalists. I also intended it to be somewhat easy. The accompaniment provides both harmonic structure for the melody and complementary countermelodic material. I tried to bring interest to the piece by utilizing contrasting "chamber" ensembles, as the piece is really based on just one original melody. For example, in the first seventeen measures, the melody is played by the clarinets and accompanied by the low brass and reeds. The next repetition is presented by a woodwind ensemble, with a more playful accompaniment.

Colors of a New Day is indeed a lyrical work, is to be played at seventy-six beats per minute, and runs slightly over three minutes in duration. The conventional tonality supports folk-like melodic material that students will enjoy and audiences will remember. The four soundings of the melody contrast nicely and the third presentation uses a solo trumpet in a comfortable middle range. The piece is a challenging Grade 2 for a couple of reasons. First, the material requires expressive and well-supported playing to do justice to the music, particularly with a Gaelic-styled ornamentation that appropriately flavors the work. Second, there are eighth-note arpeggios for vibraphone and marimba that are more advanced than most Grade 2 musicians will face. They mostly double the woodwinds but the parts occasionally function independently.

Unit 3: Historical Perspective

Colors of a New Day is the composer's first work for concert band and is expected to be published in the near future. He has a few other works for wind band, as of yet, unpublished.

Unit 4: Technical Considerations

This Grade 2 work would be best played by a well-instrumented ensemble. Double reeds are occasionally exposed and independent from the other woodwinds, but the piece could still be successfully performed without either. The pre-publication instrumentation is:

Flute	no *divisi*, ranges mostly in the staff to D above the staff
Oboe	no *divisi*, nothing exposed, often mirrors flute range to D above the staff, but does not sustain that higher range

Clarinet	three parts, all reach above the break, first to D above the staff, first and second have legato arpeggiation across the break
Bass clarinet	often doubles tenor sax, mostly harmonic support with some moving eighths and arpeggiation, ranges to G on the top of the staff
Bassoon	no divisi, mostly harmonic support with some moving eighths and arpeggiation, ranges to F above middle C
Alto saxophone	no divisi, some eighth-note arpeggiation, sixteenth-note scale passages, range to B above the staff
Tenor saxophone	often doubles bass clarinet, mostly harmonic support with some moving eighths and arpeggiation, ranges to B-flat above the staff
Baritone saxophone	mostly doubles tuba, ranges from one A below the staff (easily changed to in staff) to G on top of the staff
Trumpet	two parts, some lyrical unison but must play independently as well, range does not reach above the staff
Horn	two parts, strong countermelodic content in unison and harmony, one short sixteenth-note scale passage in an easy range, ranges mostly within the C octave but first briefly extends to top-line F
Trombone	two parts, safe range mostly in the C octave with some notes extending to bottom-line G
Euphonium	mostly harmonic support, safe range extends to D above middle C
Tuba	sustained writing with some optional divisi, safe ten-note range from A-flat to C
Timpani	minimal playing, only eight measures of sustained rolls on three pitches near the end
Bells	minimal playing, only eight melodic measures near the end, some two-mallet work
Vibraphone	eighth-note arpeggiation is likely taken from the original piano version, difficulty is more likely Grade 3
Marimba	eighth-note arpeggiation is likely taken from the original piano version, difficulty is more likely Grade 3
Suspended cymbal	three rolls near the end

The piece is a flowing, melodic work that provides a great vehicle for training the basics of blend, balance, and intonation. The melodies demand thoughtful phrasing and a beautiful tone quality. The meter is an expressive 3/4 and the verse endings are either slowed by ritard or in the case of the first verse, slowed by augmenting time with a 4/4 measure. There are exacting rhythmical challenges requiring differentiation between a two-eighth-note pattern and a sixteenth-and-dotted-eighth-note pattern in the melody. One four-note flourish of thirty-second notes in the melodic woodwinds is idiomatic and also is within a phrase-ending ritard.

A brief eight-measure departure from the tonal center of F major to D-flat major is also an appropriate hurdle for young musicians. The tonal shift is accomplished only through accidentals and offers an opportunity to introduce the sense of the richness of D-flat major. All challenges are attainable and are excellent teaching tools.

Unit 5: Stylistic Considerations

Colors of a New Day is similar to an English or Canadian folksong, and requires thorough attention to playing through and completely finishing phrases. This lyrical style of music should be core repertoire for every band program, and young musicians would be well-served to work on a piece of music like this every day.

A wide range of dynamic expression is also required in this piece, which will focus musicians on control at the extremes of the dynamic range. The melody will be easily balanced with the countermelody, and the harmonic support will not easily obscure either of the moving parts. The brief shift to D-flat major will rekindle interest for both musicians and listeners, and is handled very smoothly by the composer.

The expressiveness of the piece will allow a conductor plenty of latitude in shaping the work to his or her artistic tastes, as well as appropriately challenging the ensemble to sensitively handle releases and attacks.

Unit 6: Musical Elements

MELODY:
The simple, tonal melody is presented four times, and there is no development. The first sounding is by unison clarinets, the second by flute, oboe, and alto saxophone, and builds to a tutti finish. The third verse is thinly scored with solo trumpet, and the final begins with alto saxophones and trumpets, and again crescendos to a large and dramatic finish. The key centers of F and D-flat major offer few technical challenges, allowing musicians to focus on producing a rich, beautiful, collective sound.

If the appropriate instruments have not yet begun working on vibrato, this work is a good vehicle for teaching it, particularly if the ensemble has a couple of competent demonstrators. The trumpet solo in particular will benefit from the warmth of a controlled vibrato.

The benefits of daily warm-ups that include chorale playing will be evident in the execution of this work.

HARMONY:

Strong countermelodic material is present from the first measure and is a strong feature of the piece. The horn section often figures prominently in the countermelodies, giving the players necessary and hopefully welcome exposure. The horns play both with and without support from other sections, and as such, must be secure in playing independently.

An interesting piano-like arpeggiation occurs in the upper woodwinds and the mallet percussion. This accompaniment must be heard but may not overshadow the melodic material.

Low brass and woodwinds function predominantly in supporting harmonic roles and should not have difficulties with the comfortable tonalities of the work. One measure of success will rely on the bass instruments' ability to tune the D-flat tonal center.

Each of the four presentations of the melody reach satisfying conclusions with traditional cadences.

RHYTHM:

Rhythms are predictable and interesting. Similar gestures may appear on down-beats as pairs of quarter-, eighth-, or sixteenth-note rhythms, which provide a nice twist to the predictable melodic form. These contrasting rhythms will require careful attention from students who may be rote learners. It will be critical to correctly read and interpret the figures.

Brief sixteenth- and thirty-second-note gestures should be easily learned, as they lie well under the fingers.

TIMBRE:

Clarinets and trumpets are the two sections that have soli opportunities. The woodwind choir has a brief opportunity alone and the remainder of the work is more densely scored. The tonal colors change frequently, forcing students to listen across the ensemble. Blending the mallet moving lines with the wood-winds will be an excellent opportunity for both groups to listen beyond their own sections.

Unit 7: Form and Structure

The form of *Colors of a New Day* is strophic and is without either an intro-duction or coda. The work presents four complete verses with a brief tonal shift in the first half of the final verse. The work finishes in the original key.

SECTION	MEASURE	EVENT AND SCORING
Verse 1	1–17	Melody presentation by unison clarinet section in F major with a strong counter-melody in horns; harmonic support in low reeds and brass
Verse 2	18–22	Melody moves to flute, oboe, and alto saxophone; only woodwinds provide harmonic support
	23–33	Tutti ensemble supports mid-point and final *fortes* of the verse; key vibraphone eighth-note arpeggiation makes a first appearance
Verse 3	34–41	Trumpet solo with light woodwind and marimba eighth-note arpeggiation as accompaniment
	42–45	Woodwinds contrast by taking the melody for only four measures; tutti accompaniment
	46–50	Solo trumpet joins upper woodwinds on melody; accompaniment is more transparent to effectively execute a long decrescendo to a *piano* dynamic
Verse 4	51–58	Tonal shift to D-flat major; melody presented by tutti trumpets, alto and tenor saxophones; upper woodwinds and bells introduce a brief canonic treatment of the melody as a call-and-response
	59–67	Returns to F major in a tutti finish; culminates in a *molto ritardando* with a crescendo to *fortissimo*, the greatest dynamic of the work; slows beyond the dynamic peak and decrescendos to a final *mezzo forte*

Unit 8: Suggested Listening

Grainger, Percy:
    The Sussex Mummers' Christmas Carol
    Ye Banks and Braes O' Bonnie Doon
Holst, Gustav:
    Suite No. 1 in E-flat
    Suite No. 2 in F
Ralph Vaughan Williams. *English Folk Song Suite.*

Contributed by:

Lt. Col. Timothy J. Holtan
Commander
The U. S. Military Academy Band
West Point, New York

Teacher Resource Guide

Echoes from a Russian Cathedral

Piotr Ilyich Tchaikovsky
(1840–1893)
transcribed by Kenneth Singleton
(b. 1947)

Unit 1: Composer

Piotr Ilyich Tchaikovsky is one of the most beloved composers of the Romantic era. His beautiful melodies, often reflecting a distinctively Russian flavor, are matched by the passion and power of his orchestral writing. He is best known today for his six symphonies (mainly the last three), three ballets (*Swan Lake*, *Sleeping Beauty*, and *The Nutcracker*), concertos (especially the *First Piano Concerto* and the *Violin Concerto*), and various orchestral works (*Fantasy-Overture Romeo and Juliet*, *1812 Overture*, *Capriccio Italian*, and *Marche Slav*). Several of his operas are still performed, as are many of his chamber music works, songs for voice and piano, and piano pieces.

Tchaikovsky was an extremely sensitive child, and following the death of his mother in 1854, began to actively compose music and play the piano. He was graduated from the St. Petersburg School of Jurisprudence in 1859, but quickly found that life in the legal profession was not to his liking. In 1861 he began studies at the Russian Musical Society, and when the Society became the St. Petersburg Conservatory the following year, Tchaikovsky became a composition pupil of Anton Rubenstein. His student works were well received and, upon graduation from the Moscow Conservatory in 1866, Tchaikovsky joined the faculty as a teacher of harmony. His first major success was the *Fantasy-Overture Romeo and Juliet*, completed in 1869 (and later revised).

Many successes followed, including the premiere of his *First Piano Concerto* in Boston in 1875.

In 1876 Tchaikovsky received a commission from Nadeshda von Meck, a wealthy widow and supporter of the arts. More commissions followed, plus regular monetary allowances. Even though the two never met face-to-face, for the next fourteen years Mme. von Meck provided Tchaikovsky with financial, artistic, and moral support.

In the final two decades of his life Tchaikovsky and his music were in great demand, and he toured most of the major cultural centers of Europe and the United States. Shortly after the premiere of his *Sixth Symphony* in St. Petersburg, Tchaikovsky died of either cholera or arsenic poisoning. To this day historians debate whether or not Tchaikovsky committed suicide.

Unit 2: Composition(s)

Throughout his life Tchaikovsky concentrated the majority of his energies toward the creation of orchestral music and operas. However, he did compose choral music, beginning with several celebratory pieces written between 1863–1875. As he approached the age of forty, Tchaikovsky's Russian Orthodox religious faith became increasingly important to him. This is reflected in a 1878 letter to Mme. von Meck:

> There is nothing like entering an ancient church on a Saturday, standing in the semi-darkness with the scent of incense wafting through the air, lost in deep contemplation to find an answer to those perennial questions: wherefore, when, whither and why?

The year 1878 was a most productive one for Tchaikovsky. He completed the opera *Eugene Onegin*, the *Fourth Symphony*, and the *Violin Concerto*. Between May and July of that year he created his best-known sacred work, a monumental setting of the *Liturgy of St. John Chrysostom*, op. 41. The *Liturgy* was premiered in the church at the University of Kiev in 1879, and later performed in Moscow. Tchaikovsky's publisher, Jurgenson, published the *Liturgy* in 1878, but the clergy of the Imperial Chapel were upset that a sacred work was performed in the same public venue as secular music, and they were able to halt publication and confiscate the existing copies. Jurgenson sued, eventually won, and the work was finally published in 1881.

St. John Chrysostom (c. AD 347–407) was named Archbishop in the Greek Orthodox Church in Constantinople in 398. He quickly gained a reputation for the eloquence of his speech—in fact his name in Greek Russian means "Golden Mouth." Because of his outspoken criticism of many powerful and influential people, John was eventually exiled. After his death his body was returned to Constantinople, and he eventually achieved sainthood. The *Liturgy of St. John Chrysostom* is central to Russian Orthodox worship in much the same way as the mass in Roman Catholicism.

The *Liturgy* consists of prayers, psalms, and hymns, some chanted by individuals or small groups, others sung by choir or congregation. Every aspect of the *Liturgy* is sung—nothing is spoken. Instruments are not allowed in Russian Orthodox services. Tchaikovsky's setting of the *Liturgy* is written for mixed chorus, usually in four parts but occasionally splitting into eight. Not including the chants, there are fifteen separate musical numbers in the *Liturgy*, totaling around seventy minutes of music. The portion of the *Liturgy* used in the present band transcription is the ninth number, titled *After the Creed—The Grace of Peace*. This is the celebratory music that follows the singing of the Creed.

Legend was originally composed as one of *Sixteen Children's Songs* for voice and piano (1883), and was arranged by the composer for four-part mixed choir in 1889. The text is by Alexey Plescheyev. *Legend* is not a liturgical work, but may be considered a spiritual song, similar to folk music but inspired by religious subjects. The choral version was included in the *Oxford Book of Carols* in 1928, in an English translation titled *The Crown of Roses*.

These two works are transposed down a whole step for the present band transcription *Echoes from a Russian Cathedral*. Otherwise the musical materials are as Tchaikovsky wrote them, and the pieces can be performed separately or together as a set. The repeat of mm. 91–104 is not indicated by Tchaikovsky, and the director may choose to observe or ignore it.

Echoes from a Russian Cathedral was commissioned in 2004 by the Mountain View High School Concert Band (Loveland, Colorado) and their director, Peter Toews.

Unit 3: Historical Perspective

When Prince Vladimir was baptized in 988, Christianity became the state religion of Russia. Since Christianity was brought to Russia through Greek missionaries, the Greek Orthodox Church became the model for the new Russian Orthodox Church. The Greek church, centered in Byzantium, also provided the early model in the area of music. The music was entirely vocal and based on monophonic chant. During the reign of Ivan the Terrible (1533–1584), the Russian church gained power and developed schools of highly trained singers who consistently demanded more challenging music. Eventually, western polyphony found its way into Russian church music, and by the eighteenth century, composers were being imported from western Europe.

The first Russian-born church composer of importance was Dmitry Bortnyansky (1751–1825), who studied with esteemed Italian import Baldassare Galuppi (1706–1785). Inspired by the "Russian Five" (Mily Balakirev, Nicolai Rimsky-Korsakov, Modeste Moussorgsky, Alexander Borodin, and César Cui), the 1860s saw a resurgence in Russian church music, based on historical models (the original chant melodies and modal harmonies) as well as rising nationalism. Many of these orchestral composers used the old chants and hymns in their orchestral works. Rimsky-Korsakov's *Russian Easter Overture* and the opening of Tchaikovsky's *1812 Overture* immediately come to mind. It was in this environment that Tchaikovsky created his *Liturgy*, which inspired Sergei Rachmaninoff (1873–1943) to create his own masterful setting of the same text in 1910. Twentieth-century masters of Russian church music include Alexander Kastalsky (1856–1926), Alexander Grechaninov (1864–1956), and Pavel Tschesnokov (1877–1944).

Unit 4: Technical Considerations

In transcribing two of Tchaikovsky's miniature choral masterpieces for wind band, every effort has been made to retain the clarity and aesthetic values of the original versions. However, band and chorus are distinctly different media, and some differences between the originals and the transcriptions are more obvious than others.

1. The choral versions have words, which automatically imbue the works with meaning and help clarify the form.
2. The choral versions have more immediacy, since singers do not have instruments between them and their audience. Plus, choruses frequently sing from memory.
3. Because of the instrumental ranges in bands, octaves are frequently added in the transcription (mainly upper octaves in the soprano voice [see mm. 1–8] and lower octaves in the bass voice [see mm. 9–16]).
4. Most of the instrumental parts stay within the range of an octave (except when transposed an octave higher or lower), and it is most important that all players maintain a consistency of tone throughout these ranges and at all dynamic levels, taking special care that the tone quality does not become distorted, especially m. 89 to the end.
5. As stated earlier, all Russian church music is performed by voices only—no instruments. Further, percussion parts in this transcription are entirely supportive in nature, and should never bring attention to themselves. That being said, the percussion can add quite a bit of interest to the sound, such as deep bass drum rolls in mm. 10, 14, 26, and 30; brilliant chimes in mm. 33 and 37; and atmospheric suspended cymbal in m. 79. Some or all of the percussion parts may be omitted at the conductor's discretion.
6. In the present band transcription, most of the tempi and dynamics are Tchaikovsky's own. Some articulations are added to facilitate a choral-like performance. The breath marks correspond to Tchaikovsky's text punctuations, and must be observed, even if an actual breath is not taken. "NB" is short for "no breath."

7. Since this transcription is designed for younger bands, the oboe, bassoon, and horn parts are not essential.

8. These works may be performed as a set or separately, and are highly recommended to mature bands as well as younger ensembles.

9. If played by a large band, it may be most effective to play mm. 1–88 slower than marked, but only if the phrases can be sustained with quality sound and intonation.

Unit 5: Stylistic Considerations

Since there are no instruments in Russian Orthodox services, it is essential that the band play in an emotional choral style—with purity of tone and smooth connection of notes (unless indicated otherwise).

It is important that the four-part writing is balanced, while keeping in mind that Russian choral music almost always emphasizes lower voices more than upper ones. Indeed, much Russian choral music was written entirely for men's voices. Prior to 1880, even mixed (SATB) choral works, such as those in this transcription, were likely intended to be sung by boys on upper parts and men on lower parts. Boys' voices do not usually project as strongly as the voices of mature women, so the men will naturally tend to dominate the sound and balance. Therefore a band balance that favors the lower instruments is preferred. At the same time, it is essential that the instruments within each of the four separate parts are well blended and balanced. For example, at m. 33 the tune is in the tenor voice and is marked *forte*. There will be a tendency for the saxophone sound to dominate, whereas a preferable timbre is a blend between horn and trombone, with saxophones adding weight.

Some balance issues may be solved by redistribution of parts, either within the section or between sections. For instance, if there is the usual proliferation of flutes, some of them may be added to the oboe part. Should there be an abundance of trombones, one or more can be added to the euphonium part, if that will help the balance.

Tenuto dashes imply a firm beginning of the note (but not an accent) then sustain, with perhaps a miniscule space before the next note. Accented notes (mm. 89, 93, 94) should not be overplayed. Staccato notes (mm. 91, 92) should be separated, but not played short.

Unit 6: Musical Elements

MELODY:

Legend was originally written as a voice-and-piano song, and later transcribed (by the composer) for mixed chorus. It is essentially a spiritual song, which in this case has elements of folksong as well as church music. For example, the opening tune (mm. 1–8) has a distinctive Russian folk music flavor. The second half of the phrase (mm. 9–16) sounds more like a liturgical chant. The full sixteen-measure phrase (or verse) appears (with modification) three times. The final nineteen bars is essentially a homophonic hymn, based on a rising—then descending—melodic line.

The Grace of Peace is, for the first twenty-one bars, a beautifully-shaped homophonic hymn, with instrumentation shifts in the band corresponding to the phrases of text in the original. The final allegro (beginning m. 89) opens with declamatory chords, and is immediately followed by two measures of imitative polyphony—the only polyphony in either of these works. What follows is additional declamatory (mm. 93–94) and hymn-like writing (starting in m. 95).

In both *Legend* and *The Grace of Peace* the majority of the melodic writing consists of repeated pitches, stepwise motion, or skips of a third. The most noticeable wide melodic interval is the descending fifth in *Legend* (see mm. 1–4, etc.). There are wider skips in the accompanying voices (see mm. 17–24).

HARMONY:

Legend is cast in D minor (mm. 1–8) and D Dorian (mm. 9–16). The key of D minor is implied because of the raised leading tone (C-sharp) in m. 3. There is no raised leading tone in mm. 9–16, making the phrase D Dorian. The next phrase (mm. 17–24) is also in minor (the sixth and seventh scale steps are now raised), but the harmonization has been changed. The first chord in m. 17 is G minor (first inversion), and the opening chord in m. 21 is Gm^7. (In mm. 1 and 5 they were both D minor chords.)

The harmonic complexity in mm. 17–24 must be carefully balanced and tuned for this second statement of the theme to sound appreciably different from the first, especially since the music in mm. 25–32 is identical to that in mm. 9–16. The third statement of the main theme (in the tenor voice, starting m. 33, in D minor) is accompanied by the soprano, alto, and bass voices, playing a motif clearly derived from the theme in mm. 9–16. The harmonies here are essentially the same as in mm. 1–8. The final measures of this section (mm. 41–48) are a fragmented version of mm. 1–8, again in D Dorian.

The closing section (beginning m. 49) has a surprising F-sharp^{dim7} chord (mm. 53 and 61), followed in m. 55 by a diminished ninth chord that is resolved, then immediately followed by a V^7 chord. The work ends quietly in D minor. Because most of the harmony found in *Legend* is quite simple and straightforward, it is essential that the few surprises be carefully balanced and tuned.

The Grace of Peace begins in F major, shifting to B-flat major at m. 89. The harmonies are simple, except for secondary dominant chords in mm. 69 and 81. There are also secondary dominant chords in mm. 97–99, which briefly create the illusion of a modulation to F major. The piece ends gloriously in B-flat major.

RHYTHM:

Neither *Legend* nor *The Grace of Peace* present any significant rhythmic issues. Pulse is quite another matter. Although most of this music sounds better when not played in strict time, accomplished rubato playing always makes reference to the pulse. When playing rubato, the players are usually either increasing or decreasing the pace, but the essential pulse must always be clear. In rehearsing the band it may be best to maintain strict time with a metronome until the players are totally comfortable with the pulse, then gradually wean them away from it. Another technique might be playing in a rubato style with the metronome on, occasionally relaxing into the steady pulse, then intentionally moving away from it.

TIMBRE:

Converting choral music (which is most often homogeneous) to wind band music (which tends to be heterogeneous) presents a number of issues. Hopefully, many of these have been resolved by the transcriber. Nonetheless, it will always be left to the band director to ultimately determine issues of balance, blend and timbre. For instance, when should brass players sound like brasses and when should they blend with the woodwinds? Should flutists play with vibrato, or should they generally use a straight tone? Is it likely that saxophonists can blend with any instrument if they are using metal mouthpieces? What hardness of reed will give clarinets the biggest and warmest sound? Some issues are easy to address, and for others the band director may need help. One source is a knowledgeable clinician (in this case, perhaps a choral director with expertise in Russian music). Another source is a supply of excellent recordings of the works or genres that are to be performed (see Unit 8 for suggestions). It is essential that both students and director study these recordings in depth.

Unit 7: Form and Structure

Legend:

The text, corresponding measures, and musical motifs in *Legend* are as follows:

MEASURE	MOTIF	TEXT (ENGLISH TRANSLATION)
1–8	A	When Christ was a child he had a garden, and there he grew many roses
9–16	B	Three times a day he watered them, for he planned to someday weave himself a wreath

MEASURE	MOTIF	TEXT (ENGLISH TRANSLATION)
17–24	A'	When the roses were in full bloom, he summoned the neighborhood children
25–32	B	They each plucked a rose, until the garden was bare
33–40	A''	"How will you weave yourself a wreath?" they asked. "Your garden has no more roses."
41–48	B'	"You have forgotten that I have been left the thorns," Christ said
49–56	C	And from the thorns they made him a prickly wreath
57–67	C'	And instead of roses, drops of blood adorned his head

The Grace of Peace:

In a church performance, a phrase of chant, sung by a solo voice, precedes the first phrase of text and music, with additional chants sung between each ensuing phrase of text and music. These chant segments are not used in this transcription, nor in many performances and recordings of the complete *Liturgy*.

The text and corresponding measures in *The Grace of Peace* are as follows:

MEASURE	TEXT (ENGLISH TRANSLATION)
68–72	The grace of peace! A sacrifice of praise!
73–75	And with your spirit.
76–78	We lift them up unto the Lord!
78–88	It is fitting and right to bow down to the Father, and the Son, and the Holy Spirit: the Trinity, one in essence and undivided.
89–91	Holy! Holy! Holy! Lord of Sabaoth!
91–95	Heaven and earth are full of Thy glory!
95–97	Hosanna in the highest!
97–100	Blessed is He who comes in the name of the Lord!
100–105	Hosanna in the highest!

In the original, there follows a double Amen (four measures), which is not used in many performances or recordings, nor in this transcription.

Thematically, mm. 79–88 is a continuous homophonic version of the three separate phrases comprising mm. 68–78. Similarly, mm. 100–105 is an extended version of mm. 95–97.

Unit 8: Suggested Listening

The following recordings are highly recommended to both instructor and students.

Ancient Echoes. Music by Bortnyansky, Grechaninov, Tschesnokov, Tchaikovsky, and others. Chorovaya Akademia, Alexander Sedov, conductor. BMG, 09026–68055–2. A great introduction to Russian sacred choral music, sung by a wonderful Russian men's chorus.

Images of Christ. Music by Tchaikovsky, Rachmaninoff, Palestrina, Bruckner, Barber, Stravinsky, Byrd, and others. The Cambridge Singers, John Rutter, conductor. Collegium Records, COLCD124. A wide variety of sacred music, including the English version of Tchaikovsky's *Legend (The Crown of Roses)*, all sung by an outstanding English choir.

Russian Church Music. Music by Bortnyansky, Grechaninov, Tschesnokov, Kastalsky, Stravinsky, and others. Slavyanka, Paul Andrews, conductor. Harmonia Mundi, 907098. A fine selection of music and great performances by an American men's chorus specializing in Russian music; includes Tschesnokov's *Salvation is Created*, Stravinsky's *Our Father*, and the traditional O *Lord, Save Thy People*, used by Tchaikovsky in *1812 Overture*.

Tchaikovsky, P. I.:

Liturgy of St. John Chrysostom. USSR Ministry of Culture Chamber Choir, Valeri Polyansky, conductor. BMG Melodiya, 74321–25186–2. Includes all fifteen numbers in the Liturgy (does not include chant segments). A highly refined performance by a fabulous male/female choir.

Liturgy of St. John Chrysostom. Bulgarian A Capella Choir, Georgi Robev, conductor. EMI, 7243 5 68661 2. 2-CD set. An impassioned, complete male/female chorus performance. Includes all fifteen numbers in the Liturgy, plus the chant segments. Also includes six liturgical hymns.

Liturgy of St. John Chrysostom. Moscow Choral Academy Boys and Men's Choir, Victor Popov, conductor. Le Chant du Monde, RUS 288096. Impassioned singing by a legendary Russian chorus. Liturgy does not include chant segments. Includes eleven of the fifteen numbers in the Liturgy, plus four choruses, including *Legend*.

Unit 9: Additional References and Resources

Brown, David. *Tchaikovsky: The Early Years (1840–1874)*. New York: W. W. Norton & Company, 1978.

_____. *Tchaikovsky: The Crisis Years (1874–1878)*. New York: W. W. Norton & Company, 1982.

_____. *Tchaikovsky: The Years of Wandering (1878–1885)*. New York: W. W. Norton & Company, 1986.

_____. *Tchaikovsky: The Final Years (1885–1893)*. New York: W. W. Norton & Company, 1992. An excellent four-volume study of his life and work.

Garden, Edward. *Tchaikovsky*. London: J. M. Dent & Sons Ltd., 1973. A concise overview of Tchaikovsky and his music.

Mihailovic, Alexandar, ed. *Tchaikovsky and his Contemporaries (a Centennial Celebration)*. Westport, CT: Greenwood Press, 1999. Scholarly proceedings from a conference at Hofstra University commemorating Tchaikovsky's death. Includes chapters on the choral music.

Mountfield, David. *Great Composers: Tchaikovsky*. Secaucus, NJ: Hamlyn Publishing Group Limited, 1990. A good introduction for younger readers, numerous illustrations, many in color.

Rachmaninoff, Sergei. Kenneth Singleton, arr. *Published Band Transcriptions of Russian Orthodox Choral Music: Russian Liturgy*. Grand Junction, CO: Grand Mesa Music, 1999. Includes five sections from Rachmaninoff's setting of *The Liturgy of St. John Chrysostom*.

Tchaikovsky, P. I. Kenneth Singleton, transc. *Hymn to the Saints*. Grand Junction, CO: Grand Mesa Music, 2006. A concise, thirty-two-bar masterpiece.

Tschesnokov, Pavel. Bruce Houseknecht, arr. *Salvation in Created*. Park Ridge, IL: Neil A. Kjos, 1957. A classic band transcription of a Russian choral standard. See *Teaching Music through Performance in Band, Volume 4*.

Tschesnokov, Pavel. Jay Gilbert, arr. *Two Chorales*. San Antonio, TX: Southern Music Company, 1995. An excellent scoring of two lesser-known works.

Contributed by:

Kenneth Singleton
Director of Bands
University of Northern Colorado
Greeley, Colorado

Teacher Resource Guide

Four Breton Dances
Timothy Broege
(b. 1947)

Unit 1: Composer

Born November 6, 1947, Timothy Broege was a piano and theory student of Helen Antonides while growing up in his hometown of Belmar, New Jersey. He received his higher education from Northwestern University, where he received his bachelor of music degree with highest honors in 1969. While at Northwestern, Broege studied composition with M. William Karlins, Alan Stout, and Anthony Donato, as well as piano with Francis Larimer and harpsichord with Dorothy Lane. Since that time he has held various positions in music from public school music teacher in Chicago and Manasquan, New Jersey, to his current position of organist and director of music at First Presbyterian Church in Belmar (a position he has held since 1972) and organist and director of music at the historic Elberon Memorial Church in Elberon, New Jersey. Groups such as the Meadows Wind Ensemble and the U. S. Military Academy Band have performed his music throughout the world. His composition talents are in constant demand from ensembles that range from middle school bands to professional performers. The list of his works is quite considerable. Other notable works for wind band are *Sinfonia VI: The Four Elements*, *America Verses*, and *Theme and Variations*.

Unit 2: Composition

In the far west of France, you will find the Brittany, or Breton, region of this fascinating country. The Breton language is of Celtic descent with close relations to Welsh, Cornish, Manx, Scottish, and Irish Gaelic. The traditional dances of this region vary by their geographical region. There are three types of dances found in Brittany: the oldest, commonly danced in lines and/or circles, such as the *gavotte* and *an dro*; newer dances from the seventeenth and eighteenth centuries, such as the *jabadao* and *bal*; and third, the most recent introduction of couples dances of the nineteenth and twentieth centuries such as the *polka*, *mazurka*, and *schottisches*. It is from the oldest variety that Broege takes his inspiration for this work. Four tunes have been woven together to create this simple yet fascinating new work for band: "An Dro," "Gavotte du Bas-Leon," "Dans loup," and "Dans mout." Each of the first three are heard individually in succession while the fourth is super-imposed on the first two.

Unit 3: Historical Perspective

Commissioned by director of instrumental music Mike Kamuf for the Baker Middle School Band of Damascus, Maryland, *Four Breton Dances* was completed in December of 2006. Although a new piece for band, it incorporates elements of music that predate the existence of the United States. The four dance tunes date as early as the late Renaissance period of music. One characteristic of the Renaissance that can be found in this composition is the use of modal harmony with the slight transition to tonal harmony (prevalent in the late Renaissance). The instrumentation for both of the melodic lines (clarinet—descendent of the reed pipe), the harmonic drone (reminiscent of the bagpipe) and the clever use of percussion (tambourine and tom-tom) is also historically associated with the Renaissance. Breton dances were well known for their use of dance leaders who would sing the song that accompanied a certain dance, the dancers then repeating the melody sung to them. This is known as *call-and-response*.

Unit 4: Technical Considerations

Technical considerations for this piece are not extreme. Where tonal centers are concerned, a teacher of young students might shy away from a piece in a minor mode or in any mode, for that matter. However, while this work is very modal in nature, the key signatures themselves are very common and usually learned in the first year of organized instruction. Students must be familiar with the keys of F (D Aeolian), E-flat (C Aeolian), and B-flat (G harmonic minor). Accidental use is limited to the harmonic minor sections of the work.

Rhythmically, there are a few concerns. Students must be familiar with different eighth-and-sixteenth-note combinations as well as the dotted eighth note, syncopation, and quarter notes tied across the bar. The use of hemiola is evident in the 3/4 sections, in which the composer has placed the first two dance tunes (in duple meter) in 3/4. The range is accessible by most students after their first year of instruction, but it is perhaps a bit more rhythmically advanced than most first-year students.

Unit 5: Stylistic Considerations

As the title suggests, the music should be played with a dance-like quality. There should be light separation of all notes not slurred, especially those with staccato articulations. Beats 1 and 3 of the duple meter sections should receive the most emphasis, lending to the feel of the dance. In the 3/4 sections, all melodic lines should lead to beat 1 of each measure. This will add a certain lilt to the piece.

While the first two sections are slow in tempo, they should not feel labored. Always keep things playful and light. Instruments that present the drone should not overpower those of the melody. Players of these parts should play as if their parts are heard from a distance. Most melodic themes are four measures in length. The first two measures of each theme should be considered the call of the dance leader while the last two measures represent the response of the dancers themselves.

Unit 6: Musical Elements

MELODY:

All melodic lines in *Four Breton Dances* are modal in nature. This may be frightening at first to the young band student or the beginning band director, but this is a great opportunity to expose students to something other than the typical B-flat major key signature and tonality. All melodies are very conjunct, with the largest interval leap being a fifth. This should make the learning and teaching of the melodic lines go easier.

As mentioned before, try to have each melodic line go to beats 1 and 3 in the 4/4 sections and to beat 1 in 3/4. This will give the students target points for learning the melody.

Since the melodic lines are limited to few instruments at a time, write out each melody in a unison line for the full band and pass it out to the students with the piece. When you begin to teach the melodic line, instead of having students sitting idly by while you work with a small portion of the band, every student will be engaged and learning more about the work in the process. Work slowly at first to establish rhythmic precision and then gradually increase to the desired performance tempo.

HARMONY:

Harmonically, this piece is quite simple. The most prevalent harmonic structure is the use of the drone. It can be found in variation throughout the "An dro" and "Dans loup." There is a simple i-V-i-V progression supporting the "Gavote du Bas-Leon," and "Dans mout" has no harmonic structure since it is a unison line.

RHYTHM:

As has been stated before, this is a piece of different dance tunes. Hence, the rhythmic stability comes from a classic formula: strong beats 1 and 3, weak beats 2 and 4. This should be maintained throughout the 4/4 sections. Once into the 3/4 sections, you will find that the previously stated duple meter "An Dro" and "Gavote du Bas-Leon" have now been restated in 3/4 time. This produces an effect known as hemiola (an effect found in many Renaissance pieces).

TIMBRE:

Renaissance dance music tended to have a very reedy sound, probably because these instruments were most accessible to the general population. The composer has devoted the majority of melodic lines to the flute, clarinet (descendent of the reed pipe), and muted trumpet, which is often substituted for the oboe in many works. The composer's use of percussion is also critical to the overall sound of the piece. You want to use a small tom-tom that has a high pitch but not too high. This will allow the music to feel light and dance-like. Also try to use a tambourine with a fairly bright jingle.

Unit 7: Form and Structure

SECTION	MEASURE	EVENT AND SCORING
Intro	1–4	Percussion
"An Dro"	5–20	Theme A (mm. 5–8): two-measure call-and-response (C&R)
		Theme B (mm. 9–12): two-measure C&R
		Repeat A and B (mm. 13–20)
"Gavote du Bas Leon"	21–44	Theme C (mm. 21–24)
		Theme D (mm. 25–32): four-measure C&R
		Repeat C and D (mm. 33–44)
"Dans loup"	45–63	Theme E (mm. 45–48)
		Theme F (mm. 49–53)
		Repeat E and F (mm. 54–63)
Extension	64–70	Low brass/reeds
"An Dro"	71–86	3/4 hemiola; flute, clarinet, trumpet have scalar accompaniment
"Das mout"	87–98	Mixed meter
"Gavote du Bas Leon"	99–114	Same as "An Dro"
"Das mout"	115–128	Mixed meter

Unit 8: Suggested Listening

Aumont, Michel. *Clarinettes Armorigenes (An Naer)*.
     www.cdroots.com/annaer-301.html

Margolis, Bob. *Soldier's Procession and Sword Dance. Teaching Music through Performance in Band, Volume 1*. Eugene Corporon, conductor, North Texas Wind Symphony. GIA Publications, CD-418.

Unit 9: Additional References and Resources

www.timothybroege.com
www.geocities.com/Vienna/1160/Brittany.html

Contributed by:

Carter Biggers
Director of Bands
Seagraves ISD
Seagraves, Texas

Teacher Resource Guide

Jessie's Well

Ralph Hultgren
(b. 1953)

Unit 1: Composer

Ralph Hultgren was born in Box Hill, Victoria, Australia, and now resides in Newmarket, Queensland. Hultgren is currently head of pre-tertiary studies at the Queensland Conservatorium, Griffith University, where he also directs the Wind Symphony program and lectures in conducting and instrumental pedagogy. He began his professional music career as a trumpet player in 1970, and has since performed with the Central Band of the Royal Australian Air Force, the Melbourne Symphony Orchestra, the Australian Brass Choir, and has worked as a freelance musician for the theatre, opera, cabaret, and recording studios.

From 1979–1990, Hultgren was composer/arranger in residence for the Queensland Department of Education's Instrumental Music Program. During this time he produced 185 works for that department. His works have been performed widely within Australia as well as internationally. Hultgren has been nominated for the prestigious Sammy and Penguin Awards for his television soundtracks, and has twice won the coveted Yamaha Composer of the Year Award for his symphonic band works. In 1998 he became the recipient of the Citation of Excellence, the Australian Band and Orchestra Directors' Association's highest honor.

Unit 2: Composition

Jessie's Well is a single-movement work, approximately five minutes in length. It is scored for traditional wind band (minus piccolo) with modest percussion writing for timpani, cymbals, and bass drum. The two bassoon parts are not cross-cued, so conductors will need to rescore these if not present in their ensemble.

In the words of the composer:

> *Jessie's Well* is a simple story that comes from the pure heart of a young child, immersed in her love for her daddy and overjoyed at the peace he has found. The melody is Jessie's story, incomplete at times, like the simple wandering of a child. It is Jessie wandering, singing and not finishing the song, as a child often does. The melody drifts in and out but comes back to be completed, like it had never been the intention to leave it incomplete.

Unit 3: Historical Perspective

Jessie's Well was composed in 2004 and is a lyrical work written mostly in a chamber music style. The piece was commissioned by a friend of the composer, involving a deeply personal story; therefore, Hultgren does not indicate the specific commissioning conductor or ensemble. The work is similar in design to the music of Frank Ticheli and Timothy Mahr. Ralph Hultgren, like David Stanhope and Brian Hogg, among many others, continues the legacy of Australian wind band composers in the tradition of Percy Grainger.

Unit 4: Technical Considerations

Range, key, and rhythmic demands all stay within the expected parameters of this difficulty level. The piece is centered in F major with modal derivations that maintain the same key signature. The flute part includes one G6. The clarinet parts extend from F-sharp 3 to D6, with the third part encompassing the entire staff. The first trumpet part continues to G5. There are four horn parts, but the third and fourth parts are cross-cued throughout, most frequently to trombones. The piece is set in 3/4 time, with tempo ranging from 66 to 80 beats per minute. The lyrical demands of the piece provide a significant challenge to student musicians, as does the thin texture that underpins the majority of the work. This music is approachable at a level where students should engage it musically, not just technically.

Unit 5: Stylistic Considerations

Jessie's Well has a conversational quality about it, as fragments of the melody are frequently passed from one instrument to another. It is important for musicians to listen within the ensemble to imitate the style of the performer before them. The orchestration is transparent for much of the work, so confident soloists are needed on flute, oboe, clarinet, trumpet, and horn. A legato playing style must be used by all ensemble members with unaccented articulations throughout the work, especially in tutti *forte* passages.

Dynamics are used regularly and effectively to bring forth the melodic line. Students must be aware of their volume within the ensemble, particularly when shaping a diminuendo at the end of a phrase. Furthermore, the few *fortissimo* dynamic levels that exist must not be overplayed. This is a sensitive work that must be performed with relative dynamics throughout. The conductor should also find enjoyment by incorporating rubato as necessary to give the melody ebb and flow.

Unit 6: Musical Elements

MELODY:

The principal melody is sixteen measures long. Though it is an original melody, it is folk-like in nature with its cantabile character. The melody exhibits a consistent phrase length and a gentle arch in design, rising to the octave at midpoint and returning home at the end of the phrase. The composer uses the Mixolydian scale for most of the melodic material, with occasional movement to the Dorian scale for an unsettled, melancholy feel. Teachers would be well served to use this piece as an opportunity to teach scalar alteration through the use of modes.

HARMONY:

The harmony of *Jessie's Well* is mostly diatonic with subtle and chromaticism. The harmony is both relevant and approachable by the listener and performer, and serves to produce affective communication.

RHYTHM:

The rhythms in this piece are uncomplicated, overwhelmingly consisting of half, quarter, and eighth notes. Within each setting of the primary melody, there exists a three-measure segment that includes a triplet in one measure, an eighth and two sixteenths in the next, and duple eighth notes in the third measure.

Students must be careful to clearly differentiate between the triplet and the eighth-and-two-sixteenth-notes combination. This can be addressed during the rehearsal warm-up by alternating the rhythms within scalar passages. Overall, pulse should be more of a concern to the conductor and ensemble than rhythm. If not careful, it is likely that tempo will rush in this piece.

FIGURE 1. Mm. 67–74

TIMBRE:

Timbre is one of the most interesting elements of this composition. Hultgren very effectively combines instrumental colors and uses choirs within the band to enhance the mood of the piece. Furthermore, the frequent use of thinly scored combinations creates intimate, chamber music-like episodes. Also, the tessitura of the selected instruments frequently mimics the contour of the melody.

Unit 7: Form and Structure

Overall, this work is in strophic song form with an introduction and coda. The two versions of the "song" presented in mm. 60–93 represent the full essence of the work, with previous and following sections alluding to, yet not completely presenting, the narrative.

SECTION	MEASURE	EVENT AND SCORING
Introduction	1–4	Solo flute and clarinet establish F as tonic and suggest the Mixolydian scale
	5–12	Tutti ensemble layers in with motivic elements and growing dynamics to the peak of this phrase
	13–17	Full, open scoring that withdraws to a bitonal A-flat/D-flat chord; tempo slows
A	18–25	Trumpet solo introduces first half of principal theme at a faster tempo; clarinet solo and horns add countermelody and harmony
	26–32	Incomplete statement of second half of melody in woodwind choir; horizontal interweaving of melodic lines intensifies the character, then recedes away; sparse brass harmonic support

SECTION	MEASURE	EVENT AND SCORING
	33–35	Motivic extension in woodwinds
B	36–46	Contrapuntal setting of first half of principal theme in trumpet 1, counter-melody in trombones, harmony in remainder of brass choir; ensemble grows to phrasal climax on beat 2 of measure 44
	47–53	Second half of melody stated by bassoon with countermelody in bass clarinet and horn; very thin texture
	54–59	Transitional chromatic phrase derived from introductory material; energy grows through rapid addition of instruments and dynamic shaping
C	60–67	Brass introduces first full statement of principal melody in F major
	68–75	Full ensemble continuation of heroic second half of principal melody
D	76–83	Trumpet and alto saxophone state first half of principal melody; countermelody in upper woodwinds and horns
	84–94	Second half of melody includes flute, oboe, and clarinet as well; added tenor harmonic part for more depth; energy builds through m. 88, then tapers away
Coda	95–103	Thin texture motivic unwinding; tempo slows, dynamics decrease; closure on sustained F major chord

Unit 8: Suggested Listening

Hultgren, Ralph:
    Bright Sunlit Morning
    Bushdance
    Masada
    Moto Perpetuo
Whirr, Whirr, Whirr!!!
Grainger, Percy:
    Australian Up-Country Tune
    Irish Tune from County Derry
    Sussex Mummer's Christmas Carol
    Ye Banks and Braes o' Bonnie Doon

Mahr, Timothy:
   Everyday Hero
   Sol Solator
Ticheli, Frank:
   American Elegy
   Sanctuary

Unit 9: Additional References and Resources

Ellerby, Martin. "Chocolate, Vanilla, and Strawberry: The Music of Ralph Hultgren." *Winds* (Spring 2005): 16–19.

Lourens, Alan. "With Trumpets Sounding." In *Teaching Music through Performance in Band, Volume 2.* Richard Miles, ed. Chicago: GIA Publications, Inc., 1998: 199–201.

Websites:
"About Ralph Hultgren."
   http://www.brolgamusic.com/composers/about/ralphhultgren.htm
"Ralph Hultgren."
   http://www.kjos.com/detail.php?division=1&table=author&auth_id=573
"Ralph Hultgren."
   http://www.bandworld.org/MagOnline/MagOnline.aspx?f=NOVOS&p=BWpgNOVOS13

Contributed by:

Thomas Keck
Associate Director of Bands
University of Miami
Miami, Florida

Teacher Resource Guide

Katsista
Iroquois Campfire

Michael Grady
(b. 1966)

Unit 1: Composer

Composer and teacher Michael Grady was born into a musical family on July 12, 1965, in Bradford, Pennsylvania. While pursuing his undergraduate and graduate degrees at Indiana University of Pennsylvania, Grady studied composition with James Staples and Daniel Perlongo, and euphonium with Gary Bird. Grady has also studied with composer Quincy Hilliard at the Villanova University Summer Music Studies. An Orff-certified instructor, Grady teaches elementary band and general music at School Street Elementary in the Bradford, Pennsylvania school district where he grew up and where he has worked for the past twelve years.

In addition to numerous pieces composed for his students in Bradford, and several commissions for Pennsylvania ensembles, Grady has had some of his euphonium music published by the International Tuba and Euphonium Association. Grady's *Soliloquy for Unaccompanied Euphonium* has served as one of the competition pieces for the prestigious Leonard Falcone Euphonium Contest. His *Concerto for Euphonium and Piano* won the 1988 Eastern United States Columbia Pictures/MTNA Composition Contest. Lloyd Bone, in his *Guide to the Euphonium Repertoire*, states: "The Euphonium Source Book calls the concerto both 'powerful' and 'gorgeous,' and recommends it 'highly.'"[1]

Grady has had several compositions for young band published by Northeastern Music and by Kjos, and *Katsista* was a finalist in the first Frank Ticheli Composition Contest in 2007.

Unit 2: Composition

Grady's composition *Katsista* gets its title from the Iroquois word for fire—in particular the ritual fire that represented the seat of power in the Iroquois nation. Grady explains that the inspiration for the piece came while he was spending time with his wife and twin sons sitting around the fire. He remembered stories of the Iroquois Midwinter Festival, and the ritual of extinguishing and rekindling the ceremonial fires. This colorful celebration, which includes expressive chants, feather dances, and drum dances, was a natural inspiration for a piece of music for young band. Grady says that Iroquois music is "characterized by plaintive melodies and frequent use of flutes."[2] He also lists a number of percussion instruments used in Iroquois music, including "rawhide and wooden water drums, rattles, and ankle bells."[3] As a result, flute and percussion predominate.

Grady points out that the melody of *Katsista* is his own, but suggests that it does parallel Native American song construction in its "simplicity, inflection and quiet beginning."[4] The steady use of percussion reflects the ceremonial dance aspect of the midwinter ceremony.

Unit 3: Historical Perspective

Grady's *Katsista* offers an opportunity for teachers to discuss, with respect, Native American culture. In particular, this composition invites teachers to discuss the peaceful coexistence of the six Iroquois Nations (Oneida, Onondaga, Seneca, Cayuga, Mohawk, and Tuscarora) of upstate New York, and their tribal traditions and customs. The Midwinter Festival depicts the interrelationship between destruction and renewal, and the extinguishing and rekindling of the household fires represents this dichotomy and parallels the rebirth of the sun in midwinter.

Unit 4: Technical Considerations

Katsista: Iroquois Campfire is considered a Grade 2 piece by the publisher, Neil A. Kjos, and is set in the comfortable key of G minor. The technical demands of Grady's composition are minimal. *Katsista* remains entirely diatonic except for occasional A-flats used to form A-flat major and F minor chords. Several of the instruments have no accidentals whatsoever.

The parts for most of the instruments rest comfortably in the primary octave (give or take a step) of the basic range. The first cornet range, for example, barely exceeds a single octave, from C4 to D5. Trombones and baritones remain in the most comfortable range of the instruments, from A2 to B-flat 3, mostly in unison with each other and with baritone saxophone. The tuba parallels these instruments an octave lower with only a few exceptions, throughout the piece.

The bassoon part is one of the most difficult, requiring the player to reach as low as D2, as well as having several passages that feature both G3 and A-flat 3, notes that can prove challenging for half-hole technique and intonation.

The clarinet 2, alto clarinet, and bass clarinet parts do not go over the break. The first clarinet part has one of the widest ranges, playing both above and below the break (top note G5, low note C4), and the part does cross the break in both directions in a slurred passage of half notes. The bass clarinet part does play its lowest note several times, but other than that, instrument ranges are not extreme.

The percussion parts, as might be expected, are some of the most unusual for a piece at this level. While they are not technically or rhythmically challenging, the simple fact that eight players are required sets this piece apart. What this means is that some bands, with a plethora of percussionists, will find this work to provide more of a challenge than compositions with fewer percussion parts, while other smaller bands may shy away from the piece because of the percussion requirements. While the full character of the piece can not be achieved without covering all the parts, *Katsista* can still be performed effectively by groups with fewer than eight percussionists. Most of the instruments required should already be readily available in middle schools, and the marimba part may alternatively be played on xylophone. In other words, *Katsista* is accessible to bands with minimal percussion resources (in the way of both players and equipment) as well as groups with extensive resources.

The rhythmic nature of the piece consists exclusively of notes at eighth-note speed or slower, so *Katsista* should not pose too much of a technical challenge for any of the players. The meter is 4/4 throughout, at a steady tempo of quarter note = 106, with a *ritardando al fine* for the last seven measures.

Unit 5: Stylistic Considerations

Katsista opens with four measures of rather delicate percussion, which can be made more effective by careful attention to the cross accents between instruments. The timpani sets the tonality by using an open fifth on G and D. Then, to represent the gentle flickering of a new flame, the winds begin on a unison D with staggered entrances. This gradual enhancing of the richness of the tone, and the seamless steady growth is an effective portrayal of the rebirth of a fire from embers, and allows the teacher to emphasize careful balance and dynamics. Students will need assistance making unobtrusive entrances.

Because *Katsista* is meant to portray the ceremonial dances of Iroquois celebrants, the piece maintains a steady tempo throughout, with the exception of the ritardando in the final seven measures, so tempo modifications are not an issue with this composition. Perhaps more important is the opportunity to be strict with young musicians about maintaining a flawlessly steady tempo.

Just like a fire that gradually grows and does not have any sudden, extreme changes, the dynamic element in *Katsista* remains rather consistent and does not change drastically at any point in the music. The steadiness of *Katsista* has a calming effect that is rare in music for young bands.

Unit 6: Musical Elements

MELODY:

The melodic material in *Katsista* is quite simple. A three-note rising pattern, presented both in its original form and inverted, forms the basis of a simple, almost pentatonic-sounding melody. Fragments from the melody are used for interludes, contrasting material, and transition material before the melody returns in its original form.

HARMONY:

The harmonic language of *Katsista* is both straightforward and elegant. The use of open fifths and pedal points emphasize the aboriginal nature of the music. Minor chords predominate, along with some major chords and only a few chords with sevenths.

RHYTHM:

The basic rhythmic patterns consist of eighth, quarter, and half notes. There are no syncopations, no sixteenth notes, and dotted quarters appear only in one eight-measure section, and only in five of the instruments. Despite the simplicity of the rhythmic character of *Katsista*, the rhythms combine with the pitch choices to form a recognizable and memorable melody. Probably the most important rhythmic device is the use of cross-accents in the percussion parts.

TIMBRE:

The prominence of percussion and flutes represent the Iroquois instrumentation of the Midwinter Festival.

Katsista is well balanced enough so that most ensembles will be able to bring out the important parts with very little instruction from the conductor. There are a few call-and-response aspects that will require some attention from the conductor, and balance within the percussion section may also require attention. The piece is attractive to both audience and performers, and also gives several good teaching opportunities for the conductor.

Unit 7: Form and Structure

Although the form of *Katsista* is not regular, the balanced use of familiar and contrasting materials keeps the piece organized and effective. Often compositions that create their own form seem to ramble without direction, but Grady uses motivic relationships to avoid that pitfall in *Katsista*. Familiar material does return, but subtly varied from the preceding presentation—with slight changes in rhythm or orchestration, with the addition of a counter-melody, or set in a different pitch center—just enough variety to maintain interest without failing to be cohesive.

SECTION	MEASURE	EVENT AND SCORING
Introduction	1–4	Percussion introduction with cross accents, open fifth G and D in timpani establishes the key
	5–8	Winds enter with D-natural pedal and occasional rising fourths up to the tonic
	9–12	Clarinets and saxophones begin to harmonize, setting up the tonality; the fourths separate into a rising third and a whole step
A	13–21	Rising third and whole step of introductory materials are manipulated and extended to form a melody of eight measures with a one-measure extension
	22–29	Melody is repeated, with slight changes in instrumentation, accompaniment, and harmonization
Interlude	30–37	The interlude is based on the melodic material—primarily the first three notes in augmentation—and remains simple so that the percussion parts can easily be heard
A'	38–45	A variation on the melodic material, this time at the subdominant level, resolving back to the tonic
Extension	46–51	A fragment of the melody extends the tonic harmony
Transition	52–59	Contrast is provided by a new rhythmic idea (dotted-quarter-and-eighth); this new material is introduced in a four-measure descending sequence that repeats with some changes in instrumentation

SECTION	MEASURE	EVENT AND SCORING
A"	60–67	Another variation of the melody, pitting the original rhythms against an augmented adaptation of the original material
A'''	68–75	A similar presentation of the melodic material, this time at the subdominant level and reaching a climactic two-measure quarter-note descent (*ff* and accented) before returning to two measures of material reminiscent of the introduction and a diminuendo
Final A	76–84	The coda starts out like the original melody, then distills to the rising fourths and thirds of the introduction before resolving to an open fifth for the final measure; the composer indicates a *ritardando al fine* for the last seven measures of *Katsista*; although Grady does not request a diminuendo after the *mezzo forte* of m. 77, it is only natural for the sound to decay as it slows and becomes less complex, and a delicate *decrescendo al niente* or *morendo* might be an appropriate interpretive decision on the part of the conductor

Unit 8: Suggested Listening

Chattaway, Jay. *Mazama*.
Grady, Michael:
    The Foggy Dew
    Perseus and the Sea Monster
    Walking with Pride
Grainger, Percy Aldridge. *Spoon River*.
Hilliard, Quincy. *Ghost Dance*.
Sweeney, Michael. *Ancient Voices*.

Unit 9: Additional References and Resources

Grady, Michael. Conductor's score for *Katsista: Iroquois Campfire*. San Diego, California: Kjos Music Press, 2007.
———. Personal correspondence with the composer. May, 2008.
Hale, Horatio. *The Iroquois Book of Rites*. Whitefish, Montana: Kessinger Publishing, 2004.
Katsista: Iroquois Campfire. Neil A. Kjos Music Company.

Kurath, Gertrude Prokosch. "Iroquois Midwinter Medicine Rites." In *International Folk Music Journal 3* (1951): 96–100.

Websites:
http://www.kjos.com/detail.php?division=1&prod_id=WB369&table
=product
http://www.manhattanbeachmusiconline.com/frank_ticheli/html/
contest.html
http://www.nemusicpub.com/music/catalog.cfm
http://www.sacred-texts.com/nam/iro/index.htm
http://www.wampumchronicles.com/hiddenhistory.htm
http://www.wind-brass.com/shop/wind/w00765.html

Contributed by:

William S. Carson
Director of Bands, Professor of Music
Coe College
Cedar Rapids, Iowa

---

1 Lloyd Bone, *Guide to Euphonium Repertoire: The Euphonium Source Book* (Bloomington, Indiana: Indiana University Press, 2007), 42.

2 Michael Grady, conductor's score for *Katsista: Iroquois Campfire* (San Diego, California: Kjos Music Press, 2007), 2.

3 Ibid.

4 Ibid.

Teacher Resource Guide

A Little Tango Music

Adam Gorb
(b. 1958)

Unit 1: Composer

English composer Adam Gorb was born in 1958 in Cardiff and started composing at age ten. At age fifteen, he wrote a set of piano pieces, *A Pianist's Alphabet*, of which selections were performed on BBC Radio 3. He studied music at Cambridge University from 1977 to 1980, where his principal teachers included Hugh Wood and Robin Holloway. Upon graduation, he divided his time between composition and working as a musician in the theatre. In 1987, he began private studies with Paul Patterson and then enrolled at the Royal Academy of Music in 1991, where he studied composition and earned a master of music degree with highest honors, including the Principal's Prize in 1993. Gorb has taught at the London College of Music and Media, the Junior Academy of the Royal Academy of Music, and is presently head of the School of Composition and Contemporary Music at the Royal Northern College of Music in Manchester.

Gorb is a prolific composer, and his oeuvre includes works for orchestra, wind ensemble, choir, chamber ensembles, and instrumental solos. In particular, his works for wind band have earned him worldwide acclaim, with several works being regarded as standard repertoire. In 1994, he won the U. S. Walter Beeler Prize for his work *Metropolis*. Since then, his steady output of exceptional works for wind band has developed into one of the most important wind ensemble catalogues by a contemporary composer. His major works for wind band include, but are not limited to, *Metropolis*, *Awayday*, *Yiddish Dances*, *Dances from Crete*, *French Dances Revisited*, and *Adrenaline City*.

Unit 2: Composition

A *Little Tango Music* was written in 2007 and is published by G & M Brand. Notes provided in the score by the composer state, "This is a short sequence of melodies inspired by the curvaceous, melancholic and dangerous dance from Argentina that is the tango. The three brief movements can be played in any order, or separately."[1]

A *Little Tango Music* was composed with younger players in mind, but is certainly worthy of performance by ensembles at more advanced levels. Though technical demands are moderate, the work embodies a wealth of educational and musical merit, compositional craft, and creativity. "This miniature suite of three movements attempts to show in a trio of snapshots the varied moods and colors of the tango."[2] Beautiful melodies partnered with infectious, syncopated rhythms are combined to create a delightful and refreshing work for less-experienced players.

When asked to comment on the inspiration for the work, Gorb responded, "I've always been greatly inspired by the tango in all its guises, ranging from the "Habanera" in Bizet's *Carmen*, through its more mysterious deployment in the music of Debussy and Ravel, and a more satirical approach adopted by Stravinsky and Kurt Weill, and perhaps most vividly conveyed in the seductively violent music of Astor Piazzolla.[3]

During preparations for rehearsals, conductors should note that the score lacks adequate rehearsal numbers, especially in the second and third sections. To maximize rehearsal time, conductors should take time to write measure numbers in the score and all parts. In addition, crescendo and decrescendo markings are sparse throughout.

Performance time is approximately four minutes and twenty seconds.

Unit 3: Historical Perspective

The origins of the tango and its music evolved in Argentina in the late nineteenth century. The dance form derives from the Spanish *habanera*, the Uruguayan *milonga* and *candombe,* as well as numerous cultural influences present in the working class neighborhoods in and around Buenos Aries, which were occupied with thousands of European immigrants. As a musical genre, its development parallels that of the dance with roots spanning the globe.

In the early years of the twentieth century, the bandoneon, an instrument similar to the accordion, was introduced to Buenos Aries from Germany. It became one of the primary instruments of the *orquesta tipica* or tango orchestra, which traditionally includes two violins, two bandoneons, piano and double bass, although other instruments such as guitar, flute, and clarinet are often incorporated, as well as vocalists. Over the past century, composers have written tangos for solo instruments to ensembles of varying sizes, including large symphony orchestras.

Around 1910, musicians and dancers from Buenos Aries began traveling and performing throughout Europe, beginning in Paris and then later to Berlin, London, and other major cities throughout Europe. By 1913, the tango craze reached New York City. As the dance and musical style became more popular, it crossed socio-economic boundaries from its roots in the slums in Buenos Aries, where it was considered a street dance or form of entertainment found only in salons and brothels, to middle- and upper-class societies throughout Europe and the United States. After gaining in popularity overseas, the dance was re-exported back to Argentina, where it was embraced by the upper class.

Perhaps the most influential person associated with the tango as a musical form is Argentinean musician and composer, Astor Piazzolla (born Mar del Plata, Argentina in 1911; died Buenos Aries, 1992), who wrote more than 200 individual tangos, as well as chamber and orchestral works. He was regarded as a virtuoso bandoneon player and is also known for his orquesta tipicas, Quintet Tango Nuevo and Sexteto Tango Nuevo.

Some popular tangos include: *Tango*, Op. 65, No. 2 by Isaac Albeniz, *Blue Tango* by Leroy Anderson, *Tango Jalousie* by Jacob Gade, *Adios Nonino* and *Libertango* by Astor Piazzolla, and *Tango* by Igor Stravinsky.

Unit 4: Technical Considerations

A Little Tango Music is scored in a standard concert band configuration: flute 1–2, oboe, bassoon, B-flat clarinet 1–3, B-flat bass clarinet, alto saxophone 1–2, tenor saxophone, baritone saxophone, trumpet 1–2, horn in F 1–2, trombone 1–2, euphonium, tuba, percussion 1–2. Keys of B-flat and F major and G and F minor are used, so ensembles will need to be familiar with those scales. Brass ranges are moderate throughout, with trumpet 1 going to a G above the staff and trombone ascending to E-flat above the staff. Flute 1 range requires players capable of producing F6 and G6 comfortably.

The composer's choice of meter in the first movement will require players to read and comprehend rhythms notated in 2/4 but played in four, with the eighth note receiving the primary pulse. Rhythms involving thirty-second notes are used, but look more difficult than they are to perform.

All sections will be required to articulate sixteenth notes cleanly at MM 116. Additionally, sixteenth-note triplets in the second theme of the last movement will require facility from flute, oboe, clarinet 1–2 and alto saxophone. The syncopated rhythmic figure and tie over the barline in mm. 107–108, resulting in a hemiola, will require careful counting.

Transparent textures and scoring in places will require confident playing from all sections.

Unit 5: Stylistic Considerations

Perhaps the greatest challenge in performing *A Little Tango Music* for younger bands will be achieving correct style. The music is mature and sophisticated, and will require careful attention to detail with regard to articulations, weight and length of notes, phrasing, and balance.

The first movement should be conducted in four, with the eighth note receiving the primary pulse. The traditional tango-type rhythm employed in the accompanying voices must never be too heavy, regardless of the indicated dynamic. Remember, this is music to dance to; thus the players must associate their approach to articulation as being "light on their feet." Tango musicians often add a *subtle* emphasis of weight and length to the last note of each measure of the rhythmic ostinato in order to lead to the downbeat.

There will be some tendency for younger players to rush the staccato eighth notes and allow the tempo to gradually increase. In m. 9, the clarinets introduce a rhythmic motif that is present in the first and third movements. There will be some tendency to rush through these figures; especially the notes on count 2. A slight emphasis (weight and length) can be given to the first of the two slurred notes (counts 3 and 4), with the second note shortened slightly to achieve separation.

The second movement is written in 4/4 with the tempo marked at MM 152. Conductors of younger bands may need to rehearse at first in four, but should eventually conduct in two. This movement flows better in two and should be felt in two in order to achieve the correct style. It is suggested that both conductor and players listen to the "Tango-Ballade," from Kurt Weill's *Threepenny Opera Suite* to assist in the understanding of the appropriate performance style for the movement.

A traditional Cuban habanera-type rhythmic ostinato is used throughout the movement and serves as the "engine." Care must be taken to avoid accenting or placing any emphasis on the second note within the pattern. In addition, players will tend to rush the last two quarter notes in each measure of the ostinato. At all times, this habanera rhythm must have a light staccato articulation and never be overbearing to the melody. The dotted-eighth-and-sixteenth-note rhythms occurring in mm. 51–54 and 74–75 should have a subtle swing feel. This tango must feel delicate, graceful, and flowing.

The last movement begins with a bold Spanish pasodoble-like melody in the low brass and low woodwinds. Players will want to let loose here, but must play with a controlled sound and not play louder than they can articulate cleanly—especially on the sixteenth notes in m. 4.

The first theme is presented in m. 82 with the clarinets. The second note of the syncopated figure in this melody is marked staccato, but is not in mm. 86–87 and mm. 90–95. Attention must given to ensure that the quarter notes that are not marked staccato are played longer. Conductors may choose to lengthen the last two quarter notes in m. 92 in the alto and tenor saxophone parts and the quarter note on count 3 in m. 95 for clarinets. Playing them as marked can make the ensemble sound immature.

The traditional tango rhythm ostinato is altered in m. 97 with the addition of a slur from the last note of each measure to the downbeat of the next. Care must be taken to ensure that players note the subtle differences in articulations with this rhythm throughout the movement and play them as marked.

Unit 6: Musical Elements

MELODY:

All of the melodies in *A Little Tango Music* allow conductors and players the opportunity to form their own interpretations with regard to phrasing and expressive playing. They are beautiful, lyrical, simple, yet sophisticated, and perhaps most importantly, memorable.

The score unfortunately, is rather vague with regard to crescendo and decrescendo markings. There are only three crescendos and five decrescendos indicated in the entire score; however, dynamic markings are specified.

In most instances, expression markings indicating the contour of the melodic line are absent throughout the work, but conductors should certainly communicate their desire for phrase direction and shape to the ensemble. In the first theme, comprised of two eight-bar phrases (mm. 3–18), consider a crescendo through the dotted quarter in m. 4, then a decrescendo until the dotted quarter in m. 6, where players should be instructed to crescendo again and push through without a breath to achieve eight-bar phrasing. Staggered breathing may be necessary for younger players in order to achieve this phrasing. Certainly conductors will want to add a subtle crescendo to the rhythmic motif first presented in m. 9, and also with the tenuto eighth notes in m. 14.

The second theme, in m. 36, is comprised of a series of sequences and is structured in an eight-bar phrase. Because of the rests interspersed throughout the melody, younger players may tend to think of this in two-bar segments. Players should crescendo and intensify each sequence, relaxing on the last two bars of the eight-bar phrase to provide a contour to the entire line. The melody at m. 36 may be performed by a soloist or all the first trumpets. Conductors could also substitute other instruments here if desired. Possible substitutions include solo oboe, clarinet, or euphonium.

The third theme in the last movement, beginning in m. 82, is also derived from a series of sequences. Younger players will tend to shorten the note value of the half notes at the end of the first two measures and should be instructed to eliminate any space between the half note and the downbeat. As with the sequences in the melody of the second movement, players will need to crescendo during each sequence to provide direction and contour. Conductors may wish to instruct clarinets to avoid the tendency to play the quarter notes in mm. 86–87 too short. The five-measure countermelody voiced for first flute and oboe beginning in m. 90 must be played in one breath.

The second theme (B theme) of the final movement, appearing first in m. 101, consists of repetitions of a short melodic motif to comprise the melody. A subtle crescendo and decrescendo with the peak on count 3 will provide charm and grace to this eloquent tune. A crescendo here will also aid the musicians in accurately executing the sixteenth-note triplets. Younger players will tend to rush through the triplet figures. The countermelody in clarinet 3 in m. 105 is marked *piano*, and may get lost in the balance with the rhythmic accompaniment, as does the trumpet countermelody in mm. 109–113.

HARMONY:
The harmonic vocabulary of the work is very straightforward, with tonalities focused in B-flat and F major, and G and F minor. Scales, arpeggios, chorales, and etudes in these keys will help prepare students for rehearsing and performing the work.

RHYTHM:
As with any music associated with dance, the rhythmic component in *A Little Tango Music* is extremely important. Primary rhythmic concerns pertain to the composer's choice of meter in the first and second movements. The first movement is written in 2/4 with eighth-note = 92. This movement must be conducted and felt in four so as to feel the music as a dancer would; step equals beat. Since the meter is 2/4, reading the note groupings of two beats per bar and the use of thirty-second notes will be a challenge for less-experienced players.

Fortunately, this same rhythmic motif is also incorporated in the third movement, but notated in 4/4, which will be much easier for younger musicians to count and comprehend. Conductors should present the rhythm from the third movement first, and then have the students compare both rhythms notated in the two meters.

The second movement is in 4/4 with quarter-note = 152, but it could be taken in two, with the half note = 76. Syncopated rhythms (m. 37) and dotted-eighth-and-sixteenth-note figures (m. 51) notated in 4/4 but performed in two will require the players to fully understand counting and performing sixteenth-note-based rhythms in cut time. Care must be taken to avoid the tendency to accent the second note of the syncopated rhythmic figures that appear throughout the piece. In addition, players may also have a tendency to rush the last two staccato quarter notes of the habanera rhythm.

TIMBRE:
The work is scored in comfortable keys and instrumental ranges that will enable bands to achieve a warm and characteristic ensemble sound. Contrasting colors are achieved through major and minor tonality and variations in scoring and texture. Additional colors are created through the inclusion of various percussion instruments. Choose castanets over woodblock in the last movement to achieve an authentic sound for the genre.

Unit 7: Form and Structure

A *Little Tango Music* is comprised of three brief sections or movements that may be performed alone or in combination with the other movements. The first movement consists of a sixteen-measure melody comprised of two eight-bar phrases that are presented twice (AA').

The second movement begins *attacca*, though conductors could certainly opt for a brief pause between movements, especially if doing so will facilitate the meter and tempo change with younger players. The melody for this movement is also comprised of two eight-measure phrases which are repeated (BB'). The second movement segues into the third movement without pause.

If conductors choose to alter the order of the movements or to conclude with the second movement, the ensemble should end on count 3 of m. 75 and replace the quarter-note anacrusis on count 4 with a quarter rest. The last movement begins with a bold introduction, reminiscent of a break strain from a Spanish pasodoble. It consists of an introduction, then AA'BB' and coda, resulting in binary form.

SECTION	MEASURE	EVENT AND SCORING
Movement 1		
Introduction	1–2	Unison statement of traditional tango rhythm; G minor tonality
Theme A, phrase 1	3–10	Melody stated in unison in alto and tenor saxophones over tango rhythm accompaniment; rhythmic motif/counter-melody introduced with clarinets and woodblock beginning in m. 9
Theme A, phrase 1	11–19	Half cadence in m. 19 has an element of surprise when the phrase ends on a major seventh (C-sharp) on the dominant chord
Theme A', phrase 1	20–27	Harmonized theme is restated in upper woodwinds and trumpets; rhythmic and harmonic accompaniment becomes more active

SECTION	MEASURE	EVENT AND SCORING
Theme A', phrase 2	28–35	High point of movement occurs on down-beat of m. 30, with diminuendo to end
Movement 2 Theme B, phrase 1	36–51	Theme is stated in trumpet 1 over tradi-tional habanera-type rhythm in clarinets and bassoon; B-flat major tonality
Theme B, phrase 2	44–51	Flutes and oboe in octaves
Extension	51–54	The swing motif is reminiscent of Kurt Weill's *Threepenny Opera Suite* and 1920s Berlin Cabaret
Theme B, phrase 1	55–70	Theme is presented for a second time in trombone and tenor saxophone, with flutes and clarinet 1 playing a canon-type countermelody offset by one measure
Theme B, phrase 2	63–70	Clarinet, alto saxophone, and tenor saxophone in octaves with canon-type countermelody remaining in flutes and oboe
Codetta	71–75	Two-measure motif taken from the main theme is stated in trumpet and trombone over sparse rhythmic and harmonic accompaniment
Movement 3 Introduction	76–81	Introduction theme is boldly stated in octaves through low brass and low wood-winds over unifying rhythmic motif from the first movement; F minor tonality
Theme C	82–89	Syncopated melody is presented in clarinets over traditional tango rhythm from the first movement
		Rhythmic motif/countermelody from the first movement reintroduced in flutes, saxophones, and trumpets

Section	Measure	Event and Scoring
Theme C	90–96	Melody is restated in saxophones and continued by clarinets against a flowing countermelody voiced for flute 1 and oboe
Interlude	97–98	Bold, *fortissimo* statement of traditional tango rhythm in brass and low woodwinds serves as an interlude and modulation to parallel major
	99–100	Interlude continues; F major tonality
Theme D	101–108	Melody is stated softly in octaves through the clarinets over continuing tango rhythm accompaniment
Theme D	109–115	Theme is restated with alto saxophone 1 in canon with flute and clarinet; counter-melody is presented in trumpet 1
Extension	116–119	Extension in 2/4 and 3/4 meter is similar to hemiola in mm. 107–108
Theme D Fragment	120–123	Fragment of theme D, voiced for oboe and alto saxophone, serves as a link to the coda
Coda	124–128	Abrupt modulation back to F minor and recapitulation of introduction theme

Unit 8: Suggested Listening

Albeniz, Isaac, arr. L. Baril. *Tango*, Op. 65, No. 2. *Let's Dance*. Angèle Dubeau & La Pieta. Analekta FL23125. 1999.

Anderson, Leroy. "Blue Tango." *Leroy Anderson—Orchestra Music, Volume 1*. BBC Concert Orchestra. Leonard Slatkin, conductor. Naxos 8.559313. 2008.

Bizet, Georges. "Habanera" from *Carmen*. *Carmen*. Philharmonia Orchestra, David Perry, conductor. Chandos Chan3091–92. 2002.

Gandolfi, Michael. *Vientos y Tangos*. *Poetics*. North Texas Wind Symphony. Eugene Migliaro Corporon, conductor. Klavier KCD-11153. 2005.

Gade, Jacob. *Jalouise, Tango in Blue*. Barcelona Symphony Orchestra and Catalonia National Orchestra. Jose Serebrier, conductor. BIS BIS-CD-1175. 2005.

Gorb, Adam:
A *Little Tango Music*. www.calanpublications.com/mp3/tango-full.mp3
Yiddish Dances. *Dances with Winds*. Royal Northern College of Music Wind Orchestra. Clark   Rundell, conductor. Chandos Chan10284. 2004.

Piazzolla, Astor:
   Escualo (Shark). *Piazzolla Volume 2*. Intime Quintet. Alba ABCD119.
   1994.
   Libertango. *Soul of the Tango: The Music of Astor Piazzolla*. Yo Yo Ma.
   Sony SK63122. 1997.
Stravinsky, Igor. *Tango*. *Tango in Blue*. Barcelona Symphony Orchestra and
   Catalonia National Orchestra. Jose Serebrier, conductor. BIS BIS-CD-
   1175. 2005.
Weill, Kurt. "Tango-Ballade" from *Threepenny Opera Suite*. *Kurka: The Good
   Soldier Schweik*. The Atlantic Sinfonietta. Andrew Schenck, conductor.
   Koch 6644. 1991.

Unit 9: Additional References and Resources

Gorb, Adam. *A Little Tango Music*. Wingrave, Buckinghamshire, England:
   G. & M. Publications Ltd., 2007.

Websites:
   www.adamgorb.co.uk/biography.htm
   www.c-alanpublications.com/
   www.timreynish.com/gorb.htm
   www.youtube.com/watch?v=RUAPf_ccobc
   www.totaltango.com/acatalog/tango_brief_intro_91.html
   www.history-of-tango.com/tango-dance.html
   www.grovemusic.com

Contributed by:

Gary Schallert
Associate Professor of Music, Director of Bands
Western Kentucky University
Bowling Green, Kentucky

---

1 Adam Gorb, program notes for A Little Tango Music.
2 Email correspondence with the composer, May, 2008.
3 Ibid.

Teacher Resource Guide

Lullaby for Noah

Joseph Turrin
(b. 1947)

Unit 1: Composer

Joseph Turrin is on the composition faculty of the Hartt School of Music in West Hartford, Connecticut and Montclair State University in Montclair, New Jersey. His career has afforded him the titles of composer, orchestrator, conductor, pianist, and teacher.

He studied composition at the Eastman School of Music and Manhattan School of Music. As a composer, Turrin has written many compositions for the New York Philharmonic, including music for the brass section, various solo and chamber works, and a piece for winds and percussion. His *Illuminations for Solo Trombone and Wind Symphony*, written for Joseph Alessi and the University of New Mexico Wind Symphony, was awarded first prize in the 2004 National Band Association William D. Revelli Memorial Composition Contest.

In addition to being a composer, Turrin has also conducted the Pittsburgh, Baltimore, New Orleans, Detroit, and the New Jersey Symphonies. As a pianist, he has performed on many recordings and appeared as the orchestral pianist for the New Jersey Symphony. He has worked as a composer and orchestrator for many films, as well as writing for musical theatre. He also did the orchestrations for the 1992 Olympic Fanfare for the summer Olympic ceremonies in Barcelona, Spain.

In 2002, Turrin wrote *Hemispheres*, commissioned by Kurt Masur for Masur's final concert with the New York Philharmonic Orchestra. Regarding Turrin's music, Masur has said, "I have always liked composers who are reflecting on the musical sound of their country. Joseph Turrin does it in a very convincing way. I have taken great delight from getting to know his scores, which I have conducted in New York, in Europe, and in Asia."[i]

Unit 2: Composition

Notes from the composer as given in the score:

> *Lullaby for Noah* was composed for Noah Donald Koffman-Adsit and commissioned by Glen Adsit and the Hartt School Wind Ensemble. When Glen asked me to compose a lullaby for his son, Noah, I was completely taken with the idea. I wanted to write a piece that was simple and eloquent. As I composed this piece, I thought of that wonderful main theme of Elmer Bernstein's score for the film, *To Kill a Mockingbird*—how provocative and song-like—beautifully shaped and filled with a quiet melancholy. There is also a touch of melancholy in this lullaby and perhaps a longing for the innocence that once was our basic nature.
>
> When I approach a child, he inspires in me two sentiments; tenderness for what he is, and respect for what he may become.
> —Louis Pasteur

Lullaby for Noah was published in 2008 by C. Allan Publications.

Unit 3: Historical Perspective

As a contemporary composer, Joseph Turrin is still in the process of making his place in history. His diverse talents have given him many opportunities for acknowledgement and he has been the recipient of numerous rewards and commissions.

The Oxford Dictionary of Music defines lullaby as a "cradlesong, usually in triple rhythm." Lullabies have a largely vocal heritage, but instrumental lullabies have been written for many years. Often, in the Romantic era, these types of pieces were labeled with the French word *berceuse* (Chopin's *Berceuse*, Op. 57) or the German *wiegenlied* (Brahms's *Wiegenlied: Guten Abend, gute Nacht*, Op. 49, No. 4.)

The lullaby has been used in contemporary music as well. Within the wind band genre, many young band pieces have been named after lullabies. Some of these are also venues for exploring multiculturalism and the varying beliefs about the lullaby within differing cultural contexts.

Unit 4: Technical Considerations

Lullaby for Noah provides the band ensemble the opportunity for lyrical playing. The orchestration is written with full wind ensemble divisions, including five trumpet parts. Tone color is an important part of lyrical pieces, especially this piece. Therefore, a full ensemble is necessary to provide the many layers of sounds written.

Marked in 3/4 time, the piece does have four bars of 4/4 and four occasions of one or two measures of 5/4.

A piccolo solo is prominent in the beginning and end of the piece. A flute soloist responds to both piccolo solos. Both solos require musical maturity from the performer.

While the harp part is always doubled by other instruments, the part should be covered. The composer does state that "if harp is not available, the part may be played on piano."

The contrabass part is covered by the tuba. There is minimal percussion writing, only requiring two players: one for timpani (two pitches), the other for triangle and suspended cymbal.

Some of the ranges are challenging for young band players: flute 1 (A6), first oboe (D6), bassoon (E4), trumpet 1 (B5), and horn 1 (F-sharp 5). The range of the upper woodwinds and trumpet 1 are only used at climatic points and not for very long.

All instrument sections must be capable of independent playing; even clarinets 2–3 have divisi parts in the middle of the piece. Accurate intonation is also needed for the close harmonies. Trumpets 1–3, as well as all trombones, require cup mutes.

Unit 5: Stylistic Considerations

Marked *Gently Flowing, quarter note = 94*, this pieces does have some marked areas for slight relaxing and pushing of tempos. The composer makes a note for the conductors to "keep the tempo flowing at all times. Entrances should be gentle and played sensitively giving special care to intonation and phrasing."

As the title implies, this is great piece for working on warm sounds and legato style. The dynamics range from *pianissimo* to *forte*. There are many opportunities within the tone clusters for players to work on tuning and performing close intervals without losing sensitivity.

Unit 6: Musical Elements

MELODY:

This piece has very poignant melodies. Whoever has the melody, a soloist or small groups of players, should use these opportunities to create a sensitive performance. Most melodies have a strong sense of leading to certain repeated notes.

HARMONY:

Lullaby for Noah uses many diatonic clusters. Written in the key of C major, there are never any accidentals. However there are many chords made with seconds. The harmony is also reminiscent of the pandiatonicism in Copland's music.

The opening measures introduce an ostinato that repeats a major seventh moving to a half step. This underlying harmony is the accompaniment for piccolo and flute solos. Other cluster chords make up the additional ostinati in other accompaniment sections. Though he uses many seconds, Turrin still creates a feel of C major throughout. However, it is not until the last two measures of the piece that a C major chord occurs without added seconds.

RHYTHM:

For the most part, this music is not excessively rhythmically challenging. The piccolo player and the solo flute both have a few melodic quintuplets. All other parts have very basic rhythms, with the most complex being dotted quarter notes and some moving eighth-note lines starting off of the beat.

TIMBRE:

For the tone of this piece, the ensemble must be able to find the "touch of melancholy (and)… a longing for the innocence that once was our basic nature" Turrin refers to in the program notes. Soloists, solo lines, and small groups within the piece must all be able to find a dark, warm, sound and maintain that richness, even when playing non-triadic chords.

With the harmony clusters, the balance of instruments is imperative so that no one instrument is dominating the sound.

Unit 7: Form and Structure

SECTION	MEASURE	EVENT AND SCORING
A	1–14	Opening clarinet and harp ostinato, piccolo solo
A	15–19	Flute solo, with low reed accompaniment
A	19–25	Transition to B section with chords in woodwinds; then piccolo, bass clarinet, and tenor saxophone share a short melody

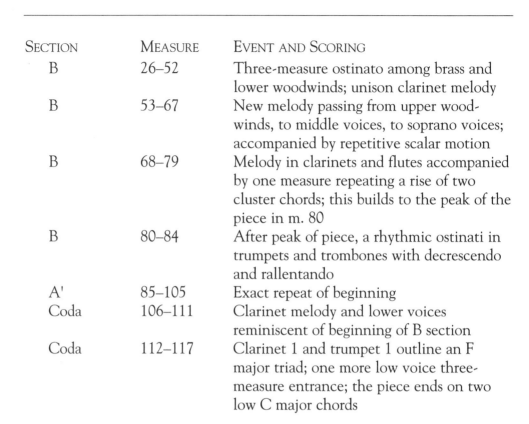

SECTION	MEASURE	EVENT AND SCORING
B	26–52	Three-measure ostinato among brass and lower woodwinds; unison clarinet melody
B	53–67	New melody passing from upper woodwinds, to middle voices, to soprano voices; accompanied by repetitive scalar motion
B	68–79	Melody in clarinets and flutes accompanied by one measure repeating a rise of two cluster chords; this builds to the peak of the piece in m. 80
B	80–84	After peak of piece, a rhythmic ostinati in trumpets and trombones with decrescendo and rallentando
A'	85–105	Exact repeat of beginning
Coda	106–111	Clarinet melody and lower voices reminiscent of beginning of B section
Coda	112–117	Clarinet 1 and trumpet 1 outline an F major triad; one more low voice three-measure entrance; the piece ends on two low C major chords

Unit 8: Suggested Listening

Turrin, Joseph:
> *Hemispheres*
> *Serenade Romantic*
> *Two Sketches*

Other examples of the lullaby in band literature:
> Anderson, Leroy. *Trumpeter's Lullaby.*
> Bassett, Leslie. *Lullaby for Kirsten.*
> Brisman, Heskel. *Uganda Lullaby.*
> Bulla, Stephen. *An Irish Lullaby.*
> Colgrass Michael. *Apache Lullaby.*
> McGinty, Anne. *Chippewa Lullaby.*
> Swearingen, James. *A Child's Lullaby.*

Unit 9: Additional References and Resources

Hansen, Richard K. *The American Wind Band: A Cultural History.* Chicago: GIA Publications, 2005.

Kennedy, Michael. *The Oxford Dictionary of Music.* Second ed., revised. Oxford University Press, 2006.

http://www.josephturrin.com

Contributed by:

Katye N. Clogg
Masters Conducting Associate
Indiana University of Pennsylvania
Indiana, Pennsylvania

---

1 http://www.josephturrin.com/

Teacher Resource Guide

Music for the King's Delight
A Suite from Centuries Past

Pierre La Plante
(b. 1943)

Unit 1: Composer

A native of Milwaukee, Wisconsin, Pierre La Plante attended The University of Wisconsin at Madison, earning a bachelor of music degree in 1967 and a master of music degree in 1972. A lifelong resident of Wisconsin, he grew up in Sturgeon Bay, and began his teaching career in 1967 in Blanchardville, Wisconsin, where he eventually returned to conclude his teaching career with the Pecatonia Area Schools District in 2001. His teaching included experience at the elementary, high school, and college levels, in classroom, instrumental, and vocal music. A composer of both band and choral music, several of his over two dozen band works have appeared on various state contest lists. Though retired from his career as a music educator, he is still active as a bassoonist with various community groups and continues to compose.

Unit 2: Composition

Music for the King's Delight is a single-movement, through-composed work which is based on four pieces spanning three centuries. The first section is entitled *Mr. Purcell's Riggadoon,* and the melody comes from Henry Purcell's "A Choice Collection of Lessons for the Harpsichord or Spinnet." This was an early primer for keyboard instruments. The second section of the piece is entitled, Music from the Theatre. In this case, the melody is "Over the Hills and Far Away" from *The Beggar's Opera* by John Gay. The very expressive third section of the piece is "Squire Wood's Lamentation on the Refusal of His

Halfpence." The source this time is a composition for Irish harp by the seventeenth-century Irish composer Turlough O'Carolan. Finally, "Lazy Pirate's Jig No. 1" is the basis of the fourth section. The original melody was composed by contemporary English composer Michael Raven.

Music for the King's Delight is performed without breaks between the various sections. A performance of the piece will take approximately six minutes and forty seconds. La Plante states in the score that all of the melodies "are meant to delight both king and commoner alike," and this piece will require a musically mature and accomplished ensemble in order to meet the challenges of this charming composition.

Unit 3: Historical Perspective

Henry Purcell lived from 1659 to 1695. A rigaudon (also spelled rigadoon) is a dance of French origin from the seventeenth century, which was popular in the courts of both French and English rulers through the eighteenth century. Characterized by regular eight-measure phrases and a duple meter, La Plante's band treatment of the dance form retains the style, elegance, and simplicity of the original melody. *The Beggar's Opera* has been an important influence on English comic opera and stage musicals since it was first performed in 1728. "Over the Hills and Far Away" is but one of the sixty-nine songs that comprise English poet and dramatist John Gay's (1685–1732) satirical ballad opera. German composer Johann Pepusch supplied the overture and instrumental arrangements to accompany Gay's popular melodies.

Turlough O'Carolan (1670–1738) wrote hundreds of pieces during his lifetime. Blinded by smallpox at the age of eighteen, he traveled throughout Ireland as an itinerant harpist, composing songs for various patrons. The Irish harp O'Carolan would have used had no pedals; it was tuned to either a modal or diatonic scale, and La Plante has chosen the key of A-flat major, in keeping with the diatonic melody of "Squire Wood's Lamentation on the Refusal of His Halfpence." A jig is a folk dance popularized in Ireland, commonly written in 6/8. The name is derived from the French word *gigue*, or from *giga*, which is an Italian short piece from the Middle Ages. "Lazy Pirate's Jig No. 1" is composed in traditional style, and provides an exciting finish to the suite.

Unit 4: Technical Considerations

There are both musical and technical challenges for young players in this composition. The piece uses the key of B-flat major and 2/2 as the meter for the first two sections of the piece. For the slow, expressive third section, the composer shifts to the key of A-flat major and 4/4 meter. To conclude the piece, the key signature moves to F major and then returns to B-flat major, using 6/8 meter. Solid technique and familiarity with the compound meter is essential in the final jig to convincingly suggest the dance origins of this section, especially at the marked tempo of a dotted quarter note = 112–118.

Clear and precise articulations are required of all of the wind players. There is also contrasting, lyrical, and sostenuto playing required in "Squire Wood's Lamentation on the Refusal of His Halfpence." The first flute part reaches to A-flat 6, with a concluding B-flat 6, but these are marked ad libitum, and so the lower octave may be played instead. An optional solo flute may play the first phrase of this section of the piece. All of the clarinet parts cross the break, with clarinet 1 ranging up to a C above the staff. Clarinet 1 also includes several divisi sections that will require the section to be split.

There is a short oboe solo that is cued in the alto saxophone part, and the bassoon line is also occasionally cued for the tenor saxophone. The highest note in trumpet 1 is an ad libitum B-flat above the staff, but there are also A naturals above the staff with which the players must contend. Trumpet 2 also ranges up to an A above the staff in a divisi section, though trumpet 3 does not venture above the staff.

Both trombone 1 and euphonium are required to play up to a G natural above the staff. Tuba and bass clarinet are provided with a short ossia section in the last portion of the piece in order to accommodate limited technical ability at the fast 6/8 tempo.

The piece will require five percussionists, using timpani, xylophone, bells, vibraphone, chimes, standard drums, and small percussion instruments. The limited chimes part can be substituted with a "ship's bell," as the composer notes in the score. The vibraphone part requires that the player be able to handle three mallets.

Unit 5: Stylistic Considerations

Music for the King's Delight presents the band with excellent opportunities to experience settings of music that derive from the late Baroque period. Of the four sections of the piece, three can be said to be dance-like in character, and one is very much a song. As a result, the band will need to focus on precise, rhythmic interpretations that emphasize clarity of attacks and releases, and consistency in pulse and time-keeping.

Special attention will need to go into the preparation of the percussion parts. The use of tambourine, drums with the snares turned off, sleigh bells, and rhythms played with sticks on the shell of the bass drum can add a Baroque flavor to the appropriate songs if performed tastefully.

The lyricism and more-exposed scoring of the third section of the piece, "Squire Wood's Lamentation…" will allow the band to emphasize sostenuto articulations and the shaping of phrases through dynamics and projection of the air stream. The opening rigaudon is a stately dance in 2/2, marked at a half note = 80–84.

Stylistically, the alternating eight-measure phrases suggest the Baroque treatment of dynamics; the brass choir is marked *f*, while the answering woodwinds are *p*. The final, and loudest statement of the theme occurs when the full band finally plays together, mimicking the Baroque concept of terraced dynamics.

The second section of the piece continues in simple duple meter at a slightly slower tempo, suggesting an even more dignified dance. The staccato articulations in the low brass and woodwinds reinforce the rhythmic nature of this section. A *poco ritard* sets up the last statement of the dance theme, which is softer and features more exposed writing. This approach prepares the players for the 4/4 meter of the third section, the song "Squire Wood's Lamentation...."

Marked *semplice e molto espressivo*, this sections opens with an optional flute solo at the tempo of a quarter note = 68–78. Aside from four measures requiring a tutti *f* dynamic at the climax of this song, the dynamics in this song are no louder than *mf*.

A plaintive quality is suggested by the subtitle of the song and through the open scoring, requiring a great deal of control and restraint from all of the wind instruments.

Lastly, as in the first two sections of the piece, the percussion instruments provide a rhythmic framework for the duration of the final section of the composition, the jig. Special attention will need to be given to the marked articulations. Accents are used extensively in order to propel the rhythmic figures forward. In this dance, all members of the band eventually take part. Therefore, low brass and woodwind instruments will need to be precise in articulation in order to maintain the very marcato style established by the upper instruments and the percussion.

If possible, the band should listen to recordings of Baroque dance music as well as a quality performance of this piece (see Unit 8 for suggestions).

Unit 6: Musical Elements

MELODY:

Given the origins of each of the songs used, the piece is quite melodically driven. The writing often employs the use of antecedent and consequent phrases, giving the opportunity to discuss this concept with the band. Another teaching opportunity lies in how various instruments are used to accompany and support the many melody lines. The regular use of eight-measure phrases can lead to a lesson on how to create shape in each phrase through the use of crescendo and decrescendo, an important lesson for percussion instruments as well.

HARMONY:

La Plante has used comfortable keys for the band in this composition. Harmonies are triadic in nature and remain diatonic through to the end. There is an excellent use of a deceptive cadence just before the last section of the piece, which can lead to a teaching unit on the various kinds of cadences and how they are used.

RHYTHM:

With dance-like origins for most of this composition, the band will need to establish a very strong rhythmic character throughout. The use of 2/2 meter in the first two sections of the piece and 6/8 meter for the concluding jig offer an opportunity to focus on the importance of counting and of feeling subdivisions in these meters.

Although the rhythmic ideas used in the piece are quite straightforward, the facility required to perform at the marked tempo may cause counting issues in the 6/8 jig. Having a portion of the band clap steady dotted quarter notes with percussion playing a steady background of eighth notes will help in rehearsing various sections of the band through the conclusion of the piece.

TIMBRE:

Because of the frequent use of homophonic texture in the first half of the piece, the brass and woodwind choirs will need to be adept at supporting and accompanying melodic material with full, mature tone quality. Just as importantly, the polyphonic writing of the concluding jig will afford ample opportunity to work on the concepts of balance and blend with the band. The percussion section in this composition is treated as an equal partner in creating variety and character in the overall timbre, and so will benefit from time devoted to sectional rehearsal and idiomatic use of the many instruments employed.

Unit 7: Form and Structure

SECTION	MEASURE	EVENT AND SCORING
Introduction	1–2	Percussion establishes duple meter
Section A	3–11	Brass first states the rigaudon melody; B-flat major
	11–19	Woodwinds and xylophone state the same melody, marked *p*
	19–27	Brass section, marked *forte*, states the consequent, contrasting phrase of the melody
	27–35	Woodwinds now repeat the consequent phrase at *mp*

Section	Measure	Event and Scoring
	35–43	Woodwinds, now marked *f*, restate the antecedent phrase of the rigaudon melody
	43–51	Tutti winds and full percussion again state the antecedent phrase of the rigaudon melody; countermelody in the horns and alto saxophones
Bridge	51–53	Bass drum rhythmic pattern; no change in meter or key signature
Section B	53–69	Woodwinds, horns, and tuba state the lyrical eighth-note melody of section B; joined by trumpet, sleigh bells, and euphonium at m. 61
	69–77	New melodic material in trumpets; low brass enter a measure later in a canon-like consequent phrase
	77–85	Lyrical treatment of section B melody scored against staccato quarter notes in the remaining winds and all percussion
	85–93	Upper woodwinds state consequent phrase of theme; trumpet 1 echoes this two measures later; *poco ritard* and decrescendo lead into *a tempo* at m. 93
	93–101	Restatement of the lyrical melody of m. 53, passing between flute 1, solo oboe and soli clarinets; ritard and diminuendo to a deceptive cadence and fermata
Section C	102–111	Key is A-flat major and meter becomes 4/4; optional flute solo of melody with clarinets accompanying at m. 107
	111–119	Melody restated by all flutes, joined by clarinet 1 and piccolo, accompanied by woodwinds and horns
	119–125	Second melody stated in clarinet 1 and alto saxophone 1
	125–133	Final melody of section C in woodwinds and trumpet 1; tutti climax at m. 129; deceptive cadence in m. 132
Section D	133–143	Flutes and bassoons state jig theme in F major, 6/8 meter
	143–167	Woodwinds and brass alternate statements of jig theme and consequent phrases at contrasting dynamic levels

Section	Measure	Event and Scoring
	167–183	New key of B-flat major; trombones state the jig theme at *f* accompanied by brass section; tuba and bass clarinet then also state the theme accompanied by flute ostinato
	183–191	Shortened consequent phrase in the horns, euphonium, and trombones, followed by a tutti bridge to m. 191
	191–203	Theme restated in trumpet 1, flutes, and clarinet 1
	203–219	Theme is fragmented and manipulated harmonically by various instruments; a gradual diminuendo to set up the return of the jig theme
	219–229	Final, *p* statement of jig by flutes and oboes is augmented by a four-measure codetta

Unit 8: Suggested Listening

La Plante, Pierre:
> *American Riversongs*
> *English Country Settings*
> *In the Forest of the King*

Gay, John. *The Beggar's Opera.*

Stuart, Hugh M. *Three Ayres from Gloucester.*

Nelson, Ron. *Courtly Airs and Dances.*

Meyer, Richard. *The Ayres of Agincourt.*

Unit 9: Additional References and Resources

Apel, Willi, ed. *Harvard Dictionary of Music.* Second ed. Cambridge, MA: The Belknap Press of Harvard University Press, 1970.

Best, Nicholas. *The Kings and Queens of England.* London: Weidenfeld & Nicolson Ltd., Orion Publishing Group, 1995.

Camphouse, Mark, ed. *Composers on Composing for Band, Volume 2.* Chicago: GIA Publications, Inc., 2004.

Grout, Donald Jay. *A History of Western Music.* New York: W. W. Norton & Co., Inc., 1973.

Miles, Richard, ed. *Teaching Music through Performance in Band, Volume 1.* Chicago: GIA Publications, Inc. 1997.

_____. *Teaching Music through Performance in Band, Volume 4.* Chicago: GIA Publications, Inc. 2002.

Rehrig, William H. *The Heritage Encyclopedia of Band Music.* Paul E. Bierley, ed. Westerfield, Ohio: Integrity Press, 1991.

Sadie, Stanley, ed. *The New Grove Dictionary of Music and Musicians.* 1995 ed. London, England: Macmillan Publishers Limited, 1995.

Williamson, John E. *Rehearsing the Band.* Kenneth L. Neidig, ed. Cloudcroft, New Mexico: Neidig Services, 1998.

http://www.jwpepper.com/catalog/

Contributed by:

Dennis Beck
Director of Bands
Unionville High School
Markham, Ontario, Canada

Teacher Resource Guide

Poème

Todd Stalter
(b. 1966)

Unit 1: Composer

Todd Stalter serves as director of bands at Eureka High School in Eureka, Illinois and chair of the Fine Arts Department for Community Unit School District 140. At Eureka he oversees all aspects of the high school band program and teaches general music grades K-4 along with fifth and sixth grade brass and percussion lessons and technique classes.

Stalter's concert bands have consistently earned superior ratings at Illinois High School Association contests, and his marching bands have won the Illinois Class 1-A state championship seven times, from 2000 through 2006. He is also active as a church musician, serving as principal trumpet and arranger for the Grace Brass at Grace Presbyterian Church in Peoria, Illinois.

Recent compositions by Stalter have been performed at the Midwest Band and Orchestra Clinic, the Illinois Music Educator's All-State festival, the Blue Lake Fine Arts Camp, the Music for All Summer Symposium, the University of Illinois Summer Youth Music Camp, and by the Emory University Wind Ensemble, the Prairie Wind Ensemble of Peoria, Illinois, and abroad in Great Britain, Japan, Germany, and Australia.

Todd Stalter received his bachelor of music education (cum laude) and master of music in Trumpet Performance from Illinois State University, where he studied trumpet with Richard Lehman and James Buckner, and conducting with Stephen K. Steele. He has served as a conducting assistant for Robert W. Smith, Gary Green, Larry Gookin, and Marguerite Wilder at the Music for All Summer Symposium.

256

Unit 2: Composition

Poème was composed in the spring of 2006 as a gift to Freddy Martin, director of bands at the Westminster School in Atlanta, Georgia, in gratitude for Martin's emotional and inspiring 2005 Midwest International Band and Orchestra Clinic performance of *As the Robin to the* Meadow (another of Stalter's compositions), and was premiered by the Atlanta Youth Wind Symphony in May 2006. The piece is approximately two minutes, forty seconds in duration, is at the Grade 2 level of performance, and is published by Alfred Publishing Company as part of its Young Symphonic Band Series.

Unit 3: Historical Perspective

Todd Stalter's eleven published compositions for the modern concert band focus on the developing musician, and range in difficulty from Grade 1 to 3. Stalter recently described *Poème* as music "written from the heart to the heart," and noted that "one of the things that inspires me to write music for that Grade 2 to 2.5 area is that young musicians *can* communicate musically, if they're given the opportunity to do so with a piece that 'says something'."[1]

Unit 4: Technical Considerations

The scoring for *Poème* is designed for young bands with limited instrumentation: flute, oboe, bassoon, clarinet 1–2, alto clarinet, bass clarinet, alto saxophone 1–2, tenor saxophone, baritone saxophone, trumpet 1–2, horn, trombone 1–2, euphonium, euphonium TC, and tuba.

Also available for download from www.alfred.com/worldparts are "world parts" for trombone 1–2 in B-flat treble clef, trombone 1–2 in B-flat bass clef, B-flat euphonium in bass clef, B-flat tuba in treble and bass clefs, and E-flat tuba in bass and treble clefs. Percussion scoring is for the following instruments: bells, suspended cymbal, bass drum, crash cymbals, and timpani. All parts may be covered by a minimum of four players.

Ranges for each instrument cover the comfortable playing range for second-year players. Flutes must be able to maintain an F6 at soft and loud dynamics. Clarinet 1 players must be able to easily cross the break and play G5; clarinet 2 players do not have to cross the break, but must be able to play low F. Brass ranges generally remain within the staff, but trumpet 1 must be able to play G5, and trombone 1 must be able to play the F above the staff.

Key signature remains constant in the key of concert C minor, and there are relatively few, but common accidentals in all parts. Meter remains a constant 4/4 throughout the thirty-eight measures, and tempo is a gentle *adagio* throughout the work. Dynamics cover the range from *pianissimo* to *fortissimo*, including the use of crescendo and decrescendo marks.

Unit 5: Stylistic Considerations

The prevailing style of *Poème* is a gentle, flowing legato that builds to an emotional peak before returning to a calm, peaceful ending. All parts make use of long phrases, encouraging young students to develop the phrase and support long musical lines. When developing the phrase, care should be taken to teach students the concepts of "playing through the barlines" (without added emphasis on the downbeat), and allowing consecutive notes in a phrase to "touch each other" so there is a feeling of constant forward motion, with no breaks between consecutive notes.

Unit 6: Musical Elements

MELODY:

The melodies used in *Poème* consist of lyrical lines composed of stepwise and intervallic motion, usually in four-measure phrases. For the majority of the piece, upper voices in woodwinds and brass carry the melodies, but the climactic section in the middle of the piece allows some of the mid-voice instruments (bassoon, tenor saxophone, and euphonium) to present melodic material. Melodies are generally diatonic, with a few accidentals present to create dissonance against the underlying harmonies.

HARMONY:

The key signature for the entire composition is three flats at concert pitch, indicating C minor tonality at the beginning of the piece. Tonal center also explores the keys of F major and A-flat major before coming to rest in G major. Harmony underlying the melodies is created both by the use of contrapuntal lines as well as chordal scoring. Dissonances that quickly resolve are created by the use of passing accidentals in the melodic lines.

RHYTHM:

The rhythmic structure of *Poème* is consistent with the skills expected of second-year players. All players must be able to divide the beat accurately to play pairs of eighth notes evenly, and players of the melodic lines must also be able to execute the dotted-quarter-and-eighth-note rhythm accurately. Because of the *adagio* tempo in combination with the legato style, teachers will want to caution players about the tendency of slurred eighth notes to compress (reaching the second eighth note early). Two suggestions to correct this problem are:

1. Rehearse all slurred passages with a quick legato tongue to coordinate finger movement with tongue movement. Then return to the written slurs while maintaining the accurate movement of the fingers.
2. Rehearse the eighth-note passages by stretching the first eighth note of all pairs, in order to give it a feeling of extra length.

TIMBRE:

Poème primarily uses a warm, rich scoring that is derived from excellent combinations of instruments in counterpoint as well as clear chordal scoring beneath simple melodic lines. The climactic section in the middle of the piece provides a contrasting moment of bright energy to the serenity of the beginning and ending sections.

Unit 7: Form and Structure

SECTION	MEASURE	EVENT AND SCORING
Section 1		
Phrase 1	1–8	First statement of melody (three-part clarinet counterpoint, Oboe, bassoon, and horn doublings; C minor)
Phrase 2	9–12	Second statement of melody (harmonized woodwinds accompanied by chordal low brass; independent bell part; C minor)
Phrase 3	13–16	Trumpet solo over pedal C
Section 2		
Phrase 4	17–24	Rising melodic line through the ensemble; transition toward F major; building intensity to climax
Phrase 5	25–28	Full ensemble climax; timpani solo; F major
Section 3		
Phrase 6	29–33	Full ensemble scoring; upper voice melody with chordal accompaniment in mid and low voices; cadence in A-flat major
Phrase 7	34–38	Full ensemble cadence in G major; trumpet and clarinet melody over chord; bell solo

Unit 8: Suggested Listening

Barnes, James. *Yorkshire Ballad.*
McMichael, Catherine. *Pax.*
Spittal, Robert. *Pacem—A Hymn for Peace.*
Stalter, Todd:
    As the Robin to the Meadow
    Castles and Dragons
    Clouds that Sail in Heaven
    Lightning!
    Sketches on a Kentucky Hymn Tune
    Then I Saw the Lucent Sky

Stuart, Hugh. *A Hymn for Band*.
Ticheli, Frank. *A Shaker Gift Song*.

Unit 9: Additional References and Resources

Alfred Publishing Co., Inc., Van Nuys, CA, 91410.

Websites:
    Todd Stalter bio. http://alfred.com/img/authors/stalter.html
    Poème recording.
http://www.alfred.com/alfredweb/front/ProductDetail.aspx?itemnum=
    %20%20%20%20%2026825&pubnum=0

Contributed by:

C. Kevin Bowen
Director of Bands
Wake Forest University
Winston-Salem, North Carolina

---

1   Todd Stalter, email message to author, April, 2008.

Teacher Resource Guide

Radio Flyer

John Gibson
(b. 1946)

Unit 1: Composer

John Wesley Gibson was born in Amarillo, Texas on February 28, 1946. He earned composition degrees from Texas Tech University and the University of North Texas, and has held teaching positions in the Amarillo public schools, at the University of North Texas, the University of Arizona, McMurry University, and Southern Methodist University. Gibson is equally comfortable composing for concert band, orchestra, chorus, percussion ensemble, and musical theatre. His eclectic and accessible style is consistently colored by his personal experiences.

Gibson has completed commissions for the symphony orchestras of Amarillo, Tucson, and Lubbock, Texas as well as the orchestras at McMurry, St. Thomas, and Texas Tech Universities. He is the resident composer for the internationally-acclaimed Dallas Wind Symphony, and is currently working on a piece about Ellis Island that was commissioned by the Air Force Band of Liberty. His most widely-performed works for band include *California Suite, Horizon, Spirit Sleeping, Resting in the Peace of His Hands, American Anthem,* and *Children of Pearl Harbor.* In addition to his busy composition schedule, Gibson serves as the Director of Creative Services in the Office of Development at Southern Methodist University.

Unit 2: Composition

Radio Flyer stems from Gibson's childhood memories of riding through his neighborhood in a little red wagon. His goal for the piece was to portray the magical experiences of discovery and exploration that children can have in a wagon, on a bike, or simply by exploring on foot. The work is divided into seven scenes, each of which depicts either a real place in Amarillo where Gibson grew up or a vivid memory from his youth.

The piece opens in the spirit of Edvard Grieg with flutes announcing the arrival of a lazy summer "Morning." The tempo is quarter note = 72 and the music requires controlled legato tonguing from all winds. A short call-and-response between upper woodwinds and orchestral bells leads to a rousing full-ensemble (minus trumpets) fanfare in m. 8. The image portrayed is that of a young boy awakening groggily before excitedly leaping out of bed in a rush to join his friends for a day of adventure.

In m. 11 the tempo suddenly increases to quarter note = c. 128 as the "Wagon" theme is introduced for the first time (see Unit 6, figure 1). A driving ostinato in flutes, oboes, clarinets, and jingle bell stick propels the music forward as saxophones and brass instruments represent the children dashing through the streets. Here Gibson uses syncopated block chords, heavy accents, changing key signatures (B-flat, D-flat, E-flat), meter changes (4/4, 3/4, 2/4), and rapidly shifting dynamics to convey a sense of action, daring, and fun.

The tempo slows back to quarter note = 72 in m. 45 as the children and their wagon approach "The Old Church." Here the piece takes on a noticeably reverent tone as flutes, oboes, and clarinets take the melodic lead with a line that hints at modality and is clearly derived from ancient religious liturgical music. Meanwhile, saxophones, low winds, and low brass intermittently enter with short, simple phrases reminiscent of Gregorian chant that further enhance the sacred ambiance of the music.

In m. 69 Gibson leaps "Back in the Flyer" and tears off down the road again. This short recapitulation (ten measures) leads directly into "The Foundry." A foundry is a factory that produces metal castings, and appropriately, the music becomes much more machine-like, repetitive, and abrasive. To depict the tedious monotony often associated with factories, Gibson uses five simple, short (one- to three-measure) motifs and layers them on top of each other.

Percussionists add to the industrial color by providing such metallic sounds as anvil or brake drum, non-ringing tubular chimes, and suspended cymbal bell played with a brass mallet. This section will undoubtedly be many young players' introduction to the concept of minimalism.

One of Gibson's favorite childhood memories is of feeding the ducks at "The Cemetery Pond," which is the next stop in the neighborhood. In m. 101

the tempo slows to quarter note = 60 as the music becomes a leisurely, flowing chorale. The lyrical melodic line is played by trumpets, flutes, clarinets, orchestral bells, bassoons, and bass clarinets, giving the impression of a lazy afternoon watching ducks glide across the water.

The final leg of the journey, "Heading Home," begins in m. 121 as the children in the wagon make a mad dash home for dinner. The tempo races to quarter note = 128 as saxophones, brass, and percussion return to the persistent syncopated block chords while upper woodwinds play a running eighth-note line that portrays the wagon turning corners and zigzagging through neighbors' yards in a frantic attempt to beat the clock. The piece ends with an augmented statement of the wagon theme signifying a safe and exciting ending to the journey.

Unit 3: Historical Perspective

Radio Flyer was commissioned in 2005 by Kimberly Tucker and the DeSoto West Junior High School Wind Symphony, and premiered at their Spring Concert that same year. Gibson worked with the band prior to the performance and explained to them how the piece was a representation of his childhood memories from growing up in the 1950s—his neighborhood with the park, church, factory, and cemetery, and of exploring the area with his own radio flyer. The piece is designed to convey images from a safer time in America's history when children were free to roam, explore, play, and discover without fear of society's ills.

Unit 4: Technical Considerations

This piece offers a number of technical challenges for young bands. It moves freely between B-flat, D-flat, and E-flat major, and between 2/4, 3/4, and 4/4 meters. A successful performance of *Radio Flyer* will be obtained by ensembles that are capable of playing a variety of articulations (slurs, accents, staccatos, tenutos, tenuto accents, etc.), performing different dynamic levels (*piano* to *fortissimo* with several subito changes and many rapid crescendos and decrescendos), and of handling different tempos (from MM 60 to 128).

The ranges are all appropriate for strong middle-school or junior-high ensembles, with flutes never exceeding F6, clarinets C6, trumpets F5, and other instruments in equally feasible tessitura. Instrumentation is fairly standard for a young band, the exceptions being that the score does include two parts for oboes, bassoons, and alto saxophones, and three parts for trombones. Five percussionists are needed to cover all parts which include timpani, suspended cymbal, crash cymbals, jingle bell stick, snare drum, bass drum, gong, ratchet, anvil, tubular chimes, and orchestral bells. The percussion parts are not terribly difficult, but all are important to an accurate depiction of the work. Gibson notes, "Radio Flyer does have some challenging spots, keys, etc., but I believe it is better to challenge kids than to let them off the hook with music that requires little thought, and has little association with their real lives."[1]

Unit 5: Stylistic Considerations

Unlike many pieces written for young bands in which the sole intention appears to be teaching one or two musical concepts, *Radio Flyer* requires ensembles to explore a variety of stylistic challenges. As the musical journey progresses the players encounter different styles; smooth and reverent while visiting the church, fast and fun while riding in the flyer, mechanical and rigid at the foundry, and fluid and charming at the cemetery pond. This piece offers myriad opportunities to work on clarity of attacks and releases, and provides young players the chance to learn to shape short phrases without being overly concerned with running out of air.

Unit 6: Musical Elements

MELODY:

Six of the seven "scenes" in *Radio Flyer are* melodically driven ("Foundry," the minimalist section, is the exception). The tunes are all simple, singable, and sit comfortably in each instrument's tessitura. This provides students the comfort of being able to concentrate on musicality rather than being overly concerned with conquering complicated technical passages. The one melodic motif that permeates throughout the piece is the "Wagon" theme, which first appears in trumpets in m. 12, appears in several forms throughout the work, and is heard for the final time in an augmented version in the piece's penultimate measure.

FIGURE 1. Wagon motif

HARMONY:

Harmonically the piece is fairly simple and straighforward. The music is primarily based in major keys throughout, with the exception of "The Old Church," which is in G minor. The harmonic language is almost entirely tertiary with much use of open fifths. This is not to say that the piece is devoid of interesting harmonic moments. In the "Foundry" section, low winds and low brass establish an ostinato that is actually a tritone played fifteen times, ending in a jarring tone cluster in m. 95.

RHYTHM:

The piece uses whole notes, dotted half notes, half notes, dotted quarter notes, quarter notes, eighth notes, and simple sixteenth-note rhythms. There are a few places in the score where the rhythms will cause difficulty for young players. In mm. 15, 37, and 121 low winds and brass play syncopated block chords in the pattern below.

FIGURE 2. Block syncopated chords

The other rhythmically tricky spot begins in m. 84, when clarinets have an eight-note recurring pattern that is offset by one and a half beats every measure.

FIGURE 3. Clarinet offset pattern

TIMBRE:

There are numerous thematic components in the piece that make it particularly interesting. The percussion writing uses several interesting colors, such as ratchets, anvils, and dampened tubular bells that are rarely heard in young band music. While there are no solos in the work, Gibson does not shy away from exploring thin textures that composers often avoid due to the intonation issues that arise when the full ensemble is not playing.

Of particular interest are the cascades from high tessitura instruments to low that serve as transitional material between several of the sections, the chant-like chords in the church, and the hammering repetitiveness in the "Foundry" section. Each of these clever programmatic devices will be enjoyed and appreciated by players and audience alike.

Unit 7: Form and Structure

The piece is written in a quasi-rondo style.

Section	Measure	Event and Scoring
"Morning"	1	Soft opening in woodwinds; full band fanfare
"Radio Flyer"	11	Tempo increases; upper woodwinds play an ostinato over brass and saxophone block syncopated chords
"The Old Church "	45	Tempo slows; chant-like
"Back to the Flyer"	69	Recapitulation of m. 22
"The Foundry"	80	Repetitive and minimalistic
"The Cemetery Pond"	101	Chorale in which melody is passed among several instruments
"Heading Home"	121	Energetic finale; block chords return

Unit 8: Suggested Listening

Dello Joio, Norman. *Scenes from the Louvre*.
Gibson, John:
    Resting in the Peace of His Hands
    Spirit Sleeping
Grieg, Edvard. "Morning Mood" from *Peer Gynt Suite*.
Mussorgsky, Modest. *Pictures at an Exhibition*.
Spaniola, Joseph. *ESCAPADE*.

Unit 9: Additional References and Resources

Battisti, Frank L. *The Winds of Change: The Evolution of the Contemporary Wind Band/Ensemble and its Conductor*. Galesville, MD: Meredith Music Publications, 2002.
Dvorak, Thomas L., Cynthia Crump Taggart, and Peter Schmaltz. *Best Music for Your Band*. Bob Margolis, ed. Brooklyn: Manhattan Beach Music, 1986.
Kreines, Joseph. *Music for Concert Band*. Tampa: Florida Music Service, 1989.
Whaley, Garwood, ed. *The Music Director's Cookbook: Creative Recipes for a Successful Program*. Galesville, MD: Meredith Music Publications, 2005.

CONTRIBUTED BY:

Matthew McCutchen
Florida State University
Tallahassee, Florida

---

1 John Gibson, correspondence with the author, June 29, 2008.

Teacher Resource Guide

Scenes from Terezin
2005

Jack Stamp
(b. 1954)

Unit 1: Composer

Jack Stamp is professor of music and director of band studies at Indiana University of Pennsylvania (IUP). A percussionist, Stamp received his DMA in conducting from Michigan State University, where he studied with Eugene Corporon.

Stamp's primary composition teachers have been Robert Washburn and Fisher Tull. Recent studies include work with noted American composers David Diamond, Joan Tower, and Richard Danielpour.

Stamp has received the Orpheus Award, was named a Distinguished Alumnus of Indiana University of Pennsylvania, received the Citation of Excellence from the Pennsylvania Music Educators Association and has been inducted into the American Bandmasters Association.[1]

Unit 2: Composition

Scenes from Terezin was written in fulfillment of a commission by Kimberly Sisson-Conklin and the J. T. Lambert Intermediate School seventh- and eighth-grade bands, East Stroudsburg, Pennsylvania, and was completed in 2005. In his program notes, Stamp indicates that the premise for the commission came from a collection of "poems and drawings by children from the Terezin Concentration Camp from 1942–1944"[2] that were provided by Conklin.

The work consists of four movements, each movement based on the text of one of the poems. The composer strongly urges performers to obtain and read the relevant poems prior to the performance of each movement. Each of the four movements is based on and contains a simple seven-note melody that is haunting and chant-like.

Reflecting the subject matter, the work is generally somber and thoughtful throughout. The composer indicates that the work is "intended to bring young musicians closer to the horror of the Holocaust."[3]

The work is written in a freely tonal twentieth-century style. Because each of the movements is based on an individual text, the character of each movement is unique within the work. The recurring seven-note Terezin theme provides continuity throughout the work. Each of the movements is less than two minutes long; the total performance time without pauses is approximately six minutes and forty-five seconds.

The work features individual instrument choirs as well as full-ensemble playing, and there are moments of both great power and delicacy in the composition. Movement 3 prominently features percussion in a musical setting that is reminiscent of Husa's *Music for Prague, 1968*. Overall, the work recalls *Music for Prague*, and would serve as an excellent introduction to that work.

Variation of the recurring Terezin theme is a constant within the work. Specifically, this theme is frequently stated in diminution and a syncopated augmentation based on a three eighth-note grouping, in the style of a hemiola.

Unit 3: Historical Perspective

Scenes from Terezin is based on one of the darkest episodes in human history: the Holocaust, in which over six million Jews were killed in the span of a few years. This is a period in history often taught in grades seven through nine, which is analogous to the difficulty level of the work. Because this theme runs through many academic subjects, significant opportunities exist for cross-curricular teaching.

Terezin was a concentration camp, and literature on concentration camps and the Holocaust in general is abundant. Additionally, historical context can be gained through commonly-read works of literature from this period, examples of which include *The Diary of a Young Girl*[4] by Anne Frank and *Night*[5] by Elie Wiesel.

The extent to which historical perspective is brought to this work is up to the individual teacher; however, the composer has made it clear that the significance of this perspective is crucial to the effective performance of the work. Should the teacher wish, connections could be made to similar situations in other parts of the world, including Bosnia, Serbia, Tibet, and many countries in Africa, providing students with a broader context for the material.

Unit 4: Technical Considerations

Scenes from Terezin is written well within the technical demand range for a work of this grade level. All instruments stay within their developmentally appropriate ranges and there are no rapid scalar or arpeggiated passages in the work. Meter changes are frequent; however, are all quarter-note-based meters. Only one movement (4) contains a significant tempo change. The range of articulations includes slurs, accents, and staccato markings, and these are employed in an idiomatically consistent manner. There is sufficient doubling to ensure that most bands will be able to perform the work. Competent horns in F and percussion are integral and necessary.

Percussion is independently scored throughout, requiring bells, chimes, vibraphone, bass drum, tom-toms, snare drum, triangle, suspended cymbal (scraped), finger cymbals, claves, sleigh bells, woodblock, tambourine, and timpani. The various metallic accessory instruments are critical parts of the orchestration. The timpanist must be able to tune between movements, the snare drummer needs to have command of rolls and flams, and the keyboard percussionists must have good tempo control in repeated patterns.

All players will be challenged by the rhythmic and counting demands of the work. *Scenes from Terezin* is filled with 3:2 syncopations across barlines. Imitative entrances that require careful and attentive entrances are frequent. The work is written in such a way that these challenges are reasonably consistent.

There are no key signatures in the work; all notes are written with accidentals. It will be necessary to make sure students are familiar with less-common enharmonic notes, such as F-flat and C-flat. In most cases, the tonality stays constant within each phrase. The general tonal centers of the work are fairly standard; however, the D-flat and G major scales will need to be mastered.

Balance and blend within individual sections and the ensemble as a whole are challenging at times. This is especially true as the harmonic texture becomes more complex. There are many instances of extended tertian chords that will need to be balanced carefully to be effective; the teacher will need to make these instances clear to students. Balance will also need to be carefully monitored in the contrapuntal sections of the work, and students will need to listen for subsequent entrances of melodies so that they can adjust their volume within the texture.

Unit 5: Stylistic Considerations

This work is written in the twentieth-century style, rhythmically, harmonically, and texturally. Tutti sections demand confident playing from all ensemble members. Wind players will need to be aware of their relationship to the percussion section, as these parts often work in tandem within the texture. In those sections where wind players and percussionists have similarly articulated passages, performers will need to listen carefully to match each other with appropriate style.

The work contains some very dissonant sections, and students will need to learn how to function within that dissonance. This is an aspect of twentieth-century music that often goes unattended in performance and rehearsal, but it is important to the style of this piece. Listening to good recordings of similar works will be of use here, as it will provide a library of sounds into which the students can tap (see Unit 8 for suggestions).

Unit 6: Musical Elements

MELODY:

Many of the melodies in *Scenes from Terezin* are based on the seven-note Terezin theme, given in figure 1.

FIGURE 1. Terezin theme

Because this theme is prevalent in the work, students should learn to recognize it, both within their own parts and in the parts of their peers. The melody is often varied in the work, and students will have to be good "musical detectives" to track down all of its occurrences.

Large intervallic leaps are avoided in the work, so playing the melodies with good horizontal intonation should be achievable. The Terezin theme occurs in many keys, and students will need to have the facility to perform it without hesitation. The director may want to have students learn it in a variety of keys, perhaps using the circle of fourths or fifths as a guide. Further, the students will need to have considerable command of enharmonic equivalents in order to perform this work.

HARMONY:

The prevalence of dissonance and polytonality in this work will make harmonic understanding a challenge. The director will want to carefully analyze the various chord and cluster structures and design exercises to create a comfort level for students within this language. Here again, listening to recordings is key to gaining understanding.

Effective performance will be enhanced if students know what the next section is going to sound like before they play it. If they can audiate approaching tonal changes, they can predict and perform them with greater accuracy. Many sections in this work rely on imitation and layering to create harmony horizontally. Students must know and be comfortable with their individual lines to maximize this technique.

RHYTHM:

While the Terezin theme is rhythmically simple, its treatment within the work is not. Many instances of hemiola and other syncopation are present. The director may want to investigate various alternative conducting devices to assist performers in executing the work. For example: in areas where the entire ensemble performs identical hemiolas, the director may want to explore conducting the music rather than the meter.

In imitative polyphonic sections, students will need to perform lines with precise and consistent rhythm to ensure a solid performance. There are many spots in this work where the director may wish to teach rhythm on a single note, or through the use of chanting, clapping, or similar techniques.

TIMBRE:

Jack Stamp is a careful orchestrator and uses instrumental combinations to create very specific effects. In movement 2, the woodwind layering is complimented by the almost exclusive use of metallic sounds in the percussion section. Timpani are the only membranophones present, and this correlates with a specific timbre in the low woodwinds. Percussionists must choose sticks and mallets carefully, and their approach to their instrument should be musical and thoughtful. The composer carefully considers color in the fugal section of movement 3, as is evidenced by his assignment of subject entrances.

There are no external timbral effects in the work; no mutes or extended instrumental techniques appear. Within the ensemble, performers who are grouped together should understand their role and strive to create a consistent sound within and between sections. Because the nature of the work is often dark and somber, opportunities for teaching students contrast in tone color from bright to dark appear in abundance. Along with instrument-specific techniques to create this contrast, the director may want to try rehearsing different sections of the work in both bright and dark manners so that students better perceive the contrast.

Unit 7: Form and Structure

SECTION	MEASURE	EVENT AND SCORING
Movement 1: "An Evening in Terezin," 33 measures		
Theme 1	1–5	Terezin theme stated in horns, with percussion interjections and low brass countermelody
Theme 1a	6–10	Theme repeated and extended
Transition	11–16	Transitional material; motivic development of Terezin theme
Theme 1b	17–23	Terezin theme stated in upper winds; low brass restates countermelody in syncopated augmentation

SECTION	MEASURE	EVENT AND SCORING
Theme 1c	24–28	Terezin theme stated in ensemble tutti; low brass repeats this in syncopated augmentation
Codetta	29–33	Thematic elements transformed by progressive shortening of motive

Movement 2: "Home," 19 measures

Introduction	1–6	Layered, dreamlike introduction; layering (*klangfarbenmelodie*) results in a tone clusters that imply D-flat tonic
Theme 1	7–12	Simple, lyrical melody in D-flat, played by woodwinds and euphonium
Theme 2	13–14	Terezin theme; full ensemble; harmonized in D-flat
Codetta	15–19	Return to the layering of the introduction

Movement 3: "I am a Jew," 44 measures
(NB: mm. 1–14 and 38–44 scored for percussion alone.)

Theme 1	1–7	Terezin theme stated alone and in canon by pitched percussion, with non-pitched percussive interjections; D-flat tonality
Transition	8–11	Introduction of overlapping ostinato (motor figure) in keyboard percussion
Theme 1a	12–14	Terezin theme stated in diminution; expansion of non-pitched percussion interjections
Fugue	15–23	Terezin theme treated fugally in three-measure segments, starting on C, with each successive entrance up a perfect fifth
Theme 1b	24–26	Final, tutti statement of Terezin theme; conclusion of fugue
Development	27–37	Development of Terezin theme in alternating sections of diminution and augmentation; various tonal centers
Coda	38–44	Percussion alone; recalls introduction

Movement 4: "Birdsong," 46 measures

Introduction	1–6	Free interpretation of Terezin theme; homorhythmic statement in brass and saxophone
Transition	7–12	Tempo change; establishment of syncopated ostinato in D minor

Section	Measure	Event and Scoring
Theme 1	13–25	Light, allegro theme in upper woodwinds; based on Terezin theme; restated in canon; D minor
Theme 1a	26–34	Allegro theme restated, adding brass and percussion interjections; B minor
Theme 2	35–41	Tutti statement of Terezin theme in 3:2 rhythmic scheme; low winds accompany in augmentation; G major
Coda	41–46	Fragments of thematic material developed; driving to end in C major (C^{maj7})

Unit 8: Suggested Listening

Adams, John. *On the Transmigration of Souls*. New York Philharmonic. Lorin Maazel, conductor. Nonesuch B0002JNLNM. 2004.

Husa, Karel. *Music for Prague, 1968. Recollections*. North Texas Wind Symphony. Eugene Migliaro Corporon, conductor. Klavier 11124. 2002.

Stamp, Jack. *Past the Equinox, the Music of Jack Stamp*. Various conductors and ensembles. Klavier B000003JVS. 2005.

Unit 9: Additional references and resources

Volavková, Hana. *I Never Saw Another Butterfly: Children's Drawings and Poems from Terezín Concentration Camp, 1942–1944*. New York: McGraw-Hill, 1964.

Frank, A., O. Frank, and M. Pressler. *The Diary of A Young Girl: The Definitive Edition*. New York: Bantam, 1997.

Wiesel, E. *Night, with Connections*. New York: Holt, Rinehart, and Winston, 1999.

Contributed by:

Richard Miller
Director of Bands
Hershey High School
Hershey, Pennsylvania

---

1 "Jack Stamp," http://www.kjos.com/ detail.php?table= author&auth_id=1152

2 Jack Stamp, unpublished program notes for Scenes from Terezin, provided by the composer (2005).

3 Ibid.

4 A. Frank, O. Frank, and M. Pressler, *The Diary of A Young Girl: The Definitive Edition*. (New York: Bantam, 1997).

5 E. Wiesel, *Night, with Connections*. (New York: Holt, Rinehart, and Winston, 1999).

Teacher Resource Guide

Tribute

Travis J. Cross
(b. 1977)

Unit 1: Composer

Travis J. Cross was recently appointed to the music faculty at Virginia Polytechnic Institute and State University. An assistant professor of music, he will conduct the University Symphonic Wind Ensemble and teach courses in conducting. He is currently completing his doctoral coursework at Northwestern University in Evanston, Illinois, where he studies with Mallory Thompson. He previously earned the bachelor of music degree cum laude in Vocal and Instrumental Music Education from St. Olaf College in Northfield, Minnesota, and the master of music degree in conducting from Northwestern University.

Cross taught for four years at Edina (Minnesota) High School, where he conducted two concert bands and oversaw the marching band program. In 2004, he was selected to participate in the inaugural Young Conductor/ Mentor Project sponsored by the National Band Association. That same year he received the Distinguished Young Band Director Award from the American School Band Directors Association of Minnesota. From 2001–2003, Cross served a two-year term as a recent graduate on the St. Olaf College Board of Regents. In 2006, he was named a Jacob K. Javits Fellow by the United States Department of Education.

A graduate of Ankeny (Iowa) High School, Cross served as staff arranger for the Ankeny Marching Hawks from 1995–2002, during which time the band earned top honors at contests in Iowa, South Dakota, and Wisconsin. In 1996, he was named Collegiate Composer of the Year by the Minnesota Music Educators Association. His original works and arrangements for band, choir, and orchestra have been performed by college, high school, and civic ensembles across the United States, Canada, United Kingdom, and Singapore and are published by Boosey & Hawkes, Daehn Publications, and Theodore Music.[1]

Cross's composition teachers have included Peter Hamlin and Timothy Mahr. He has participated in workshops and master classes with many of the leading teachers of wind band conducting and is frequently in demand as a guest conductor and adjudicator.[2]

Unit 2: Composition

Tribute was commissioned by the Southwest Iowa Bandmasters Association and premiered by their eleventh-and-twelfth-grade honor band on January 16, 2006, with the composer conducting. The piece begins with two statements of the main theme, presented first with relatively straightforward accompaniment and then with a descant in the upper woodwinds. A contrasting section features a lilting eighth-note motive that moves throughout the ensemble, leading to the climactic return of the main theme. A brief coda reprises both of the primary melodic ideas in alternating trumpet solos and brings the piece to a close.[3]

Tribute is a lyrical, single-movement work and is approximately four minutes and thirty seconds in length. It is published by Boosey & Hawkes as part of the Windependence series and is listed at the Advanced Apprentice Level (repertoire for less experienced instrumentalists who possess limited technical proficiency).

Unit 3: Historical Perspective

Tribute is one of Cross's eleven works for symphonic wind ensemble listed to date on the Theodore Music website (http://www.theodoremusic.com/). As an active composer, he continues to write for the wind band medium and has many upcoming commissions. His transcription for symphonic wind ensemble of Ralph Manuel's *Alleluia* is published by Daehn Publications and his *Be Thou My Vision* is published by Boosey & Hawkes also as part of the Windependence series.

Unit 4: Technical Considerations

Tribute is scored for full band, with parts for horn 1–2 and trombone 1–2, and includes four percussion parts plus timpani. Percussion 1 includes bass drum, triangle, and crash cymbals, and requires two percussionists as written. Percussion 2 is written for suspended cymbal, played with mallets and by scraping a coin across the cymbal. Percussion 3 includes orchestra bells played with soft plastic mallets. As Cross describes, "Soft plastic mallets should be used on the orchestra bells, not hard plastic or brass. The part is intended not as melodic reinforcement, but rather to add a little bit of shimmer to the upper woodwind timbre. This is especially important in m. 67, where the bells, triangle, and suspended cymbal scrape gently color the last note of the piece."[4] Percussion 4 includes vibraphone. The timpani part requires re-tuning after the modulation.

Cross has provided cues in mm. 64–67 for the horn 1 melody in the alto saxophone part and in m. 67 for an important oboe melody in the trumpet 1 part. Cross also gives suggestions for the performance of this work with only one bassoonist. He writes, "In mm. 21–24, the bassoon parts essentially double the tuba and euphonium. In mm. 54–57, the bassoon parts essentially double the tenor and baritone saxophones. If only one bassoonist is available, the player should cover whichever part is more necessary to the ensemble. An acceptable alternative in the aforementioned measures would be for the bassoonist to play the second part note on beat 1 and the first part note on beats 2 through 4."[5]

Tribute uses the key signatures of C major in mm. 1–28, and A-flat major in mm. 29–end. There are only two accidentals used in the piece: a chromatic passing tone (concert C-sharp) in the bass clarinet, baritone saxophone, euphonium, and tuba parts in m. 13; and a B-flat in the same parts with bassoon added in m. 28.

Simple duple meter of 4/4 is used throughout the piece. Students must be comfortable with the rhythmic values of whole, half, quarter, and eighth notes and rests, as well as reading eighth and quarter notes tied across the barline. All parts except bass clarinet, baritone saxophone, trombone 1, euphonium, tuba, percussion 1–2, and timpani will encounter a quarter-note triplet as well.

Range considerations: F6 for flute 1, B5 for clarinet 1. A majority of the trumpet and horn parts lie within the staff. C6 for trumpet 1 (although Cross has provided an alternative part for three measures, lowering the overall highest note to A5), D5 for trumpet 2, A-flat 5 for horn 1 (Cross has provided an alternative part for three measures, lowering the overall highest note to F5), and F4 for trombone and euphonium. Clarinets 1–2 are asked to play over the break, but clarinet 3 stays below the break for the entire piece. The battery percussion parts do not present any specific problems. Mallet percussion parts often double the melodic lines; the vibraphone part includes playing two-note (thirds), scalar passages.

Unit 5: Stylistic Considerations

To achieve the appropriate feeling and pacing of the piece, students must strive to perform legato phrases and to perform all articulation and dynamic markings as notated. Cross notates all articulations clearly, including: slurs, tenutos, and accents. Dynamic markings range from *piano* to *fortissimo* in all parts. Students must be able to control crescendos and diminuendos, and must be able to produce an *mfz*. As Cross describes, "The *mfz* marking represents a firm but unaccented weight, pressing into the dissonance and then relaxing slightly as the note sustains. The intended sound should be stressed more than a simple tenuto, but not nearly as accented as an *sfz* marking would imply."[6]

Cross has indicated a beginning tempo of quarter note = ca. 60–66, and at m. 13 (*più mosso*), a quarter note = ca. 66–72, with a rallentando into mm. 50 and 54. These slight tempo deviations do not present any major concerns. Cross also gives an interpretive suggestion for the coda: "Although no breath marks are written at the end of mm. 59, 65, and 66, short luftpauses may be added at the discretion of the conductor."[7]

One of the most difficult aspects of the performance will concern balance between the melody and accompaniment. A chordal accompaniment is often found in the low brass, along with bassoons, bass clarinet, and tenor and baritone saxophones. It is imperative that the accompaniment provides support, yet not overpower the melodic lines. These performers must also strive for long phrases, trying not to breathe after every whole note. Suggesting places to breathe, and more importantly, teaching students how to correctly mark breath marks in their parts, is important.

Unit 6: Musical Elements

MELODY:
Cross has indicated two main themes used during the piece. The main theme, beginning at mm. 1, 13, and 46, encompasses a major ninth with frequent leaps. The main theme is often reserved for the upper woodwinds, trumpet 1, and horn 1. Therefore, it would be ideal to have students transpose the melody for their instrument so that everyone can take part in analyzing and performing it. To maintain the character of the piece, it is imperative that students play all notes, whether notated with a slur or not, in a legato fashion.

The second melody, beginning at m. 29, consists of a rising eighth-note motive. Cross has clearly indicated slur marks over every two notes; students need to be careful not to clip the second eighth note. Having students mark the second eighth note with a small tenuto may help their performance of this motive.

HARMONY:
Cross has chosen to work within a relatively simple harmonic context, using diatonic chords with few alterations, but to great effect. There are multiple opportunities to define and discuss nonharmonic, or nonchord tones, including passing tones, suspensions, ritardations, anticipations, appogiaturas, and escape tones.

There are many moments of harmonic interest, but three of the most striking occur at mm. 13, 28–29, and 41–42. At m. 13 the bass line (bass clarinet, baritone saxophone, euphonium, and tuba) provides motion using the chromatic passing tone, C–C-sharp–D. The modulation to A-flat major at m. 29 is approached using a flat seventh scale degree in the original key of C major (V^4_2 /vi in A-flat) resolving to I in A-flat. In m. 41, Cross uses a deceptive cadence (V^7–vi) for a poignant moment before the restatement of the main theme.

RHYTHM:

The piece remains in 4/4 throughout, with the eighth note the smallest rhythmic value. The main challenge is to perform rhythms comprised of ties across the barline and syncopations. Developing a clear and consistent system of counting and marking parts will be helpful for students to negotiate these measures. Students should also be advised to crescendo across the barline to take advantage of nonharmonic tones and the tension and release presented by their use.

Cross does write a quarter-note triplet at the end of the second, four-measure phrase in the A and A' sections. Preceded by either a half note or two quarter notes, students can easily subdivide the beat into triplets to anticipate the necessary grouping. Ensembles also will enjoy working out the quarter-note triplet against moving quarter notes as well.

TIMBRE:

Although the tone color does not change substantially throughout the piece, Cross has carefully orchestrated the melodic material and attention should be given to balance the melody when two or more instruments are being doubled. For example, at the beginning, Cross has written clarinet 1 and horn 1 in unison, allowing the horn color to predominate with support by the clarinet. With the anacrusis to m. 5, the clarinet and horn sound in octaves, the clarinet now easily being heard above the horn. The solo oboe 1 enters on the anacrusis to m. 9, in unison with the clarinet, and then the horn regains the melody, played once again in unison with the clarinet on the anacrusis to m. 11. Within a short twelve-measure phrase, the melody color has progressed from horn to clarinet to oboe, and then returning back to horn.

Unit 7: Form and Structure

SECTION	MEASURE	EVENT AND SCORING
A	1–12	Andante main theme; C major; abb'
	1–4	a: Unison melody in clarinet 1 and horn 1; harmonic motion I to I^6_4
	5–8	b: Melody at the octave in clarinet 1 and horn 1; harmonic motion IV (with suspensions) to V (G–C–D)
	9–12	b': Unison melody oboe 1 and clarinet 1, then horn 1 and clarinet 1; harmonic motion IV to V (with 4–3 suspension)

SECTION	MEASURE	EVENT AND SCORING
A'	13–26	*Più mosso* main theme; C major; abb″
	13–16	a: Unison melody clarinet 2–3, alto saxophone 1–2, and trumpet 1–2, then clarinet 2, alto saxophone 1, and trumpet 1; introduction of descant in upper woodwinds and bells; countermelody in horn 1–2 and euphonium
	17–20	b: Unison melody clarinet 2, alto saxophone 1, and trumpet 1; continued descant in upper woodwinds and bells; continued countermelody
	21–26	b″: Solo trumpet 1 with low brass accompaniment (mm. 23–24 melodic extension, with added flute and bells)
Transition	27–28	Introduction of "lilting eighth-note motive"[8] in flutes, oboes, clarinet 1, and vibraphone; then adding piccolo, alto saxophones, horns, and bells; harmonic motion to A-flat major using m. 28, beat 4 pivot chord, V_2^4/vi to I
B	29–45	Contrasting section; A-flat major
	29–32	c: Unison melody in oboe 1 and clarinet 1; moving line in horn 1; chordal accompaniment
	33–35	d: Melody adds oboe 2, clarinet 2–3, trumpet 1–2, and vibraphone; whole-note harmonic rhythm IV–V(7)–I with main theme reminiscence in tenor saxophone and horns
	36–39	c': Unison melody in flute 1, oboe 1, and clarinet 1; lilting eighth-note motive passed between alto saxophone 1, trumpet 1, clarinets 2–3, bassoons, and tenor saxophone
	40–42	d': Melody in clarinet 1 and trumpet 1 (augmented motive, quarter notes, in flutes and oboes); whole-note harmonic rhythm IV–V7–vi, deceptive cadence
	43–45	Motive passed between trumpets and alto and tenor saxophones, horns, and vibraphone; harmonic motion vi–[Vmaj7/IV]–IV–V7

SECTION	MEASURE	EVENT AND SCORING
A″	46–59	Main theme; A-flat major; ab
	46–49	a: Melody at the octave in clarinet 1, then 2, and trumpet 1; descant in upper woodwinds and bells; m. 49 beginning of quarter-note countermelody in alto saxophones, horns, and vibraphone; rallentando
	50–53	Maestoso b‴: Unison melody in piccolo (sounds at the octave), flutes, oboes, clarinet 1, and trumpet 1; rallentando
	54–59	Andante b″: Solo flute 1 and oboe 1 with woodwind and percussion accompaniment (mm. 56–57 melodic extension, with added clarinet 1–2 and alto saxophone 1)
Coda	60–67	A-flat major
	60–63	Main theme reminiscence and lilting eighth-note motive passed between solo trumpet 1 and solo trumpet 2
	64–67	Final main theme reminiscence in horn 1 with final lilting eighth-note motive in solo oboe 1

Unit 8: Suggested Listening

Selections:
   Barnes, James. *Yorkshire Ballad*.
   Daehn, Larry. *As Summer Was Just Beginning*.
   Erickson, Frank. *Air for Band*.
Recordings:
   Holsinger, David. *On a Hymnsong of Philip Bliss*.
   Teaching Music through Performance in Band, Volume 1, Grades 2 and 3.
   North Texas Wind Symphony. Eugene Corporon, conductor. GIA
   Publications CD-418.
Cross, Travis J. *Be Thou My Vision. Dreams and Visions*. St. Olaf Band.
   Timothy Mahr, conductor. St. Olaf Records WCD 30102.
Ticheli, Frank. *Amazing Grace. Teaching Music through Performance in Band,
   Volume 1, Grade 4*. North Texas Wind Symphony. Eugene Migliaro
   Corporon, conductor. Keystone Wind Ensemble. Jack Stamp, conductor.
   GIA Publications CD-490.
Whitacre, Eric. *October. Teaching Music through Performance in Band, Volume
   5, Grade 4*. North Texas Wind Symphony. Eugene Migliaro Corporon,
   conductor. Keystone Wind Ensemble. Jack Stamp, conductor. GIA
   Publications CD-638.

Unit 9: Additional References and Resources

Cross, Travis J. *Tribute*. New York: Boosey & Hawkes, 2007.
Theodore Music. http://www.theodoremusic.com

Contributed by:

Christopher Morehouse
Director of Bands
Southern Illinois University Carbondale
Carbondale, Illinois

---

1 "Travis J. Cross," http://www.theodoremusic.com
2 Travis J. Cross, score notes for *Tribute* (New York: Boosey & Hawkes, 2007).
3 Ibid.
4 Ibid.
5 Ibid.
6 Ibid.
7 Ibid.
8 Ibid.

Teacher Resource Guide

Variations on a Sailing Song
Carl Strommen
(b. 1940)

Unit 1: Composer

Carl Strommen is a major composer and arranger of instrumental and vocal music, recognized as one of the most-often performed composers of educational music in the United States. A graduate of the City College of New York, Strommen was the director of bands at the Mamaroneck Public Schools, Mamaroneck, New York for many years. He studied composition with Stephan Wolpe and arranging with Rayburn Wright and Manny Album. He is a member of the faculty at the CW Post campus of Long Island University, where he teaches orchestration and arranging. Recognized by ASCAP as a consistent writer in the Standard Awards category, Strommen is also active as a clinician, lecturer, and guest conductor. His music for band is published by Carl Fisher, Belwin (Warner Brothers), and Alfred Music.

Unit 2: Composition

Variations on a Sailing Song was written in 2006 and published by Carl Fisher. The piece is a vigorous, lively sea chantey that should be played with gusto and enthusiasm. The work is cast in seven variations based on the familiar melody *What Shall We Do With The Drunken Sailor*. The variations are set throughout the ensemble so that everyone will play the theme at one point, and each variation is in a contrasting style that make the work very colorful. *Variations on a Sailing Song* uses traditional tonalities and straightforward rhythms that are common for music written in for middle school bands. The work is considered to be a Grade 2 and falls within the technical considerations of that level. It lasts roughly two minutes and twenty seconds.

Unit 3: Historical Perspective

Variations on a Sailing Song is based on the popular sea chantey *What Shall We Do With The Drunken Sailor*, also known as *Sailor's Holiday*. It is known as a work song, and was often sung when raising a sail or raising the anchor, which is the reference for "up she rises" in the song's chorus. Such songs were the only ones allowed in the Royal Navy. Only two or three verses were sung, but often verses were added until the task was completed. Many versions of the song have been used throughout the world, including versions for chorus, band, and orchestra.

Unit 4: Technical Considerations

The technical considerations for the work are moderate for music of the Grade 2 level. The piece is written in G minor, so students should be familiar with the concert E-flat major and G minor scale. There are several dotted-eighth-and-sixteenth-note rhythms and some eighth-and-two-sixteenth-note figures for the ensemble, as well as rapid sixteenth-note passages for flutes, clarinet 1, alto saxophones and xylophone. The sixteenth-note passages are derived from the G minor scale, and so should not present too much of a problem. Two of the variations are entirely comprised of percussion instruments. Strong mallet players as well as a strong timpanist will be needed to cover melodic lines and solos. While the solos are only for one measure, they are important to the overall layout of the percussion variations. In m. 46 there is a chromatic bass line in all of the low brass and low reeds that will need to be reinforced. In the same variations, the woodwinds and the first trumpets have a call-and-response. Balance is extremely important in this section so that each all of the voices are heard. Most of the work is in 4/4, with a few meter changes in the first variation, but none that will pose any problems to players. The standard symphonic band instrumentation is appropriate for middle-level ensembles. There are also two one-measure solos for the timpani.

Unit 5: Stylistic Considerations

Several style changes occur throughout this short, two-minute work. The opening starts out vigorously, with aggressive rhythms that will need to be played with clean articulation. As the second variation begins at m. 17, the style becomes lyrical. Students will need to be cautious not to play the same articulated style that the low brass and low reeds are playing underneath the upper voices.

The percussion variation (variation 4) is set up in the style of a hocket. The battery and mallet percussion have rhythms that are connected to make up the melody that has been heard throughout the piece. The fifth variation is a call-and-response among the upper woodwinds and trumpet 1 against the lower voices. The melody is augmented and played under a chromatic bass line. Eight measures later, the call-and-response incorporates legato style with articulated rhythms.

The percussion variation occurs again and is not as melodic this time. Chimes have the melody toward the end of the variation. The seventh variation acts as a coda to the piece, starting out with a lyrical tutti presentation, and then transforms to the opening five measures, ending the piece the same way it started.

Unit 6: Musical Elements

MELODY:

Variations on a Sailing Song is based on the familiar song *What Shall We Do With The Drunken Sailor*. The use of theme and variations has been a major part in music of the twentieth century, and large amount of wind literature uses theme and variations as its form. Such works include William Schuman's *Chester*, Arnold Schoenberg's *Theme and Variations*, and Charles Ives's *Variations on America*. The first presentation of the theme is at m. 6, stated in the woodwinds. The phrases feature a combination of articulated and legato elements. Detail to contrasting articulations is the key to a successful performance of this piece.

HARMONY:

The use of the G minor scale is used throughout the work. The harmonies are diatonic and should not pose any problems to young musicians. It would be in the musicians' best interest to be fluent with the G minor scale and G minor triad with various articulations and styles. In the fifth variation, striving for balance in the call-and-response section will require a bit of attention. Each of the voices are important to hear when the piece approaches m. 50.

RHYTHM:

The dotted-eighth-and-sixteenth-note rhythm that is played by most of the ensemble is used throughout the piece. Working on the rhythm and finding an articulation that makes the introduction sound lively and majestic will require a bit of work from the ensemble. It is very easy for the rhythms to sound fatigued.

The eighth-and-two-sixteenth-notes pattern found in m. 6 is used throughout the seven variations as well. The same sort of attention to detail as in the opening measures needs to be given to this rhythm. Augmented variations on the rhythms that occur in the first variation are also executed through out the piece. They are often legato and should not slow the tempo down.

TIMBRE:

The timbre of this work often relies on the groups of instrument families and their abilities to play together. The composer does an excellent job of orchestrating the variations of woodwinds, brass, and percussion families with appropriate groupings. The percussion variations give the piece a different tone color, using the battery and mallet instruments to perform the melody and rhythms heard throughout the work. Through this technique, the composer encourages a characteristic tone quality and careful listening from the ensemble.

Unit 7: Form and Structure

SECTION	MEASURE	EVENT AND SCORING
Introduction	1–5	Moderato tempo; use of dotted-eighth-and-sixteenth-note rhythms throughout the ensemble
Variation 1	6–16	Presentation of the "What Shall We Do with the Drunken Sailor" theme
Variation 2	17–28	Augmented/legato statement
Variation 3	29–37	Back to the same style of the first variation
Variation 4	38–45	First percussion statement, presented in the style of a hocket
Variation 5	46–57	Augmented/lyrical statement, presented in a call-and-response setting
Variation 6	58–67	Second percussion statement
Variation 7	68–77	Similar to the coda
Coda		

Unit 8: Suggested Listening

Broege, Timothy. *Theme and Variations*.
Chance, John Barnes. *Variations on a Korean Folk Song*.
Ives, Charles. *Variations on America*.
Schoenberg, Arnold. *Theme and Variations for Band*, Op. 43a.
Schuman, William. *Chester*.
Shaw, Robert and Alice Parker. *What Shall We Do with the Drunken Sailor* (choral version).
Strommen, Carl:
　Afton Variations
　Cumberland Cross
　Storm Mountain Jubilee
　To A Distant Place
　Variations on a Sailing Song (orchestra version)

Unit 9: Additional References and Resources

Carl Fisher Music, New York, NY. www.carlfischer.com
Miles, Richard, ed. *Teaching Music through Performance in Band, Volume 4.*
    Chicago: GIA Publications, Inc., 2002, pp. 154–158.
Strommen, Carl. Score and parts. New York: Carl Fisher Music (YPS54F),
    2006.

Contributed by:

Robert M Schwartz
Director of Bands
Center Area School District
Monaca, Pennsylvania

Teacher Resource Guide

Whirlwind

Jodie Blackshaw
(b. 1971)

Unit 1: Composer

Australian composer Jodie Blackshaw has worked in schools from outback
Australia to inner city Sydney, teaching music to students of all ages and
conducting a variety of concert bands. Through her teaching, conducting, and
composing, Blackshaw has ardently searched for a new approach to young
band. She is passionate about music education, and desires that her music
not just be another piece, but an educational and spiritual journey for both
students and director.

Blackshaw studied composition with Larry Sitsky at the Australian
National University Canberra School of Music, earning a bachelor of music
in composition in 1992. She describes her studies with Sitsky, who stressed the
importance of finding one's own voice and direction, as a process of self-
discovery.[1] In 2001, she completed her Graduate Diploma in Education,
concentrating her skills on conducting and classroom teaching. During this
time, Blackshaw discovered the Orff-Schulwerk approach to music education,
which impacted her compositional style.

Currently, Blackshaw composes, works with bands on her music, and
teaches clarinet and saxophone. In 2005, Blackshaw submitted two of her
works in the First Frank Ticheli International Composition Contest.
Whirlwind received first prize in the Beginning Band category, and
Terpsichorean Dances took second place in the Young Band division.
Manhattan Beach Music publishes *Whirlwind,* and *Terpsichorean Dances* is
scheduled for publication. Blackshaw's current projects include a work for
young band and two pieces for more advanced players.[2]

Unit 2: Composition

Blackshaw composed *Whirlwind* in 2005, and Hill Country Middle School (Austin, Texas) presented the premiere at the Midwest Band and Orchestra Conference in 2006. *Whirlwind* is a one-movement work and is six and a half minutes long. This piece works effectively for both small and large bands.

The inspiration for *Whirlwind* comes from an Aboriginal story that describes how the brolga, an Australian crane, came into existence.[3] In one version of this tale, a skilled dancer named Brolga is dancing alone and is swept off her feet by an evil spirit, Waiwera, who is disguised as a whirlwind. When Brolga's tribe discovers she is missing, they search for her, following the trail of the whirlwind. When the tribe discovers Brolga and Waiwera, Waiwera realizes he is no match for the armed tribe. Instead of relinquishing Brolga, Waiwera turns her into a bird so that no one can have her.[4]

The genesis of *Whirlwind* was influenced by Blackshaw's study of Orff-Schulwerk, an approach to music education that emphasizes the development of listening skills and musical independence.[5] In this method, students learn rhythm through speech and movement, sing songs, and play in ensembles with Orff instruments. At the beginning, students learn aurally without the aid of notation; the intent is to stimulate students' creativity and musicality as well as foster careful listening in activities in which a student is participating.[6]

Whirlwind is constructed around a melody of four pitches: A–C–D–E. In Aeolian mode, (A minor) this set of pitches is versatile because it lacks the half step, much like Orff's La-centered scale (A–C–D–E–G–A).[7] Notable in Blackshaw's music is her writing for homemade instruments. In *Whirlwind*, four percussionists are asked to play the whirly: a length of corrugated irrigation hose that is spun around the head to create a singing sound. Blackshaw also writes parts for each student on either water-glass chimes or homemade rattles. The composer provides conductors with detailed information on where to acquire and how to create each of these instruments.

Unit 3: Historical Perspective

Whirlwind begins and ends with aleatoric sections which portray a storm. Aleatoric music is mostly a phenomenon of the late twentieth century, however there are precursors in Medieval music as well as earlier in the twentieth century in the music of Charles Ives.[8] Blackshaw labels the aleatoric sections in *Whirlwind* "Soundscapes," inviting students to create their acoustical environment within set parameters, all specifically described in the program notes inside the score. Blackshaw believes that if students are involved in the creation of a piece, they will take more ownership. Although Blackshaw achieves a distinctive and original sound in *Whirlwind*, her application of aleatoric writing in this piece is similar in concept, length, and notation to the aleatoric writing in the young band works by Michael Colgrass: *Apache Lullaby*, *Gotta Make Noise*, and *Old Churches*.

Unit 4: Technical Considerations

Blackshaw chooses the key of A minor for educational reasons; because many beginner band works are in F major, B-flat major, or E-flat major, she thought it important to teach a key that is found less often in the beginning band repertoire.[9] The ranges of all instruments fall within their middle to lower registers. Rhythms consist of quarter and eighth notes as well as dotted half notes tied to half notes. Most of the wind writing is slurred.

Blackshaw writes for a variety of textures in *Whirlwind*. Her solo writing is flexible, in that she writes the first solo (letter B) in all parts and leaves it up to the conductor to decide the instrumentation. This solo, consisting of four short phrases, may be played by one player or divided into two or four parts.[10] Toward the end of the piece (letter H), Blackshaw writes another solo with echo. She scores these solos for clarinet and trumpet, but different instrumentation may be used if desired.[11]

Whirlwind requires six percussionists. Blackshaw creates layered percussion ostinati in two-bar patterns to support the melody, similar to basic accompaniment patterns used in Orff-Schulwerk.[12] In the percussion soli, Blackshaw writes fragments of the melody in each part, requiring students to listen and create one continuous line. The bass drum player is asked to execute long, quiet rolls. Blackshaw specifies mallet choices and gives direction for techniques such as playing a suspended cymbal in the center of the timpani.

Blackshaw includes information entitled "Know Your Stuff" online at the Manhattan Beach Music website (http://whirlwind.manhattanbeachmusic.com/html/know_your_stuff.html). There is a page for each instrument, including a conductor score and structure diagram. This guide, available for download, contains material to teach students the four pitches required, including fingering charts. It also introduces concepts such as perfect fourths and fifths, stepwise music, and music that contains a mixture of steps and leaps. Once students are able to play the material in "Know Your Stuff," they will easily be able to play the melody in *Whirlwind*.[13]

Unit 5: Stylistic Considerations

Because Blackshaw believes young band music should possess a strong educational focus, she asks the following question about her compositions: "What do I want students to achieve by playing this piece?" In *Whirlwind*, Blackshaw's goals for students are to engage in careful listening, become aware of intonation, and work to develop self-expression.[14]

The aleatoric nature of this work allows for a wide variety of interpretations. In the Soundscape sections in free time, the composer calls for the melody to be played "like a whirlwind: slowly, getting faster, then slowly again."[15] In the Soundscape at letter C, entrances of the last phrase of the melody are staggered and cued by the conductor. Each player is invited to interpret this phrase in their own individual way: fast, slow, fast then slow, slow then fast, etc., thus creating the effect of a whirlwind starting to form. This is not a metered section; it is a layering of the last phrase of the melody in a semi-random form. Students should sustain the last note using staggered breathing techniques until two measures after letter D.[16]

Blackshaw encourages students to explore other possibilities within the framework of the piece. For example, when working with an honor band in the IMPACT (Instrumental Music Program Australian Capital Territory) program in Canberra, Australia in May 2008, Blackshaw encouraged the soloist at letter B to experiment with the melody, keeping the same four pitches, but changing the order; the only parameter was that the rhythm and the last note could not change.[17]

Unit 6: Musical Elements

MELODY:
While technique is not difficult, this piece does require smooth, gentle, and expressive playing. To help teach this concept, Blackshaw created text to fit with the melody and to tell a story. Repetition of the words matches the repetition of pitches:

> Whirlwind round brolga girl in the day
> Whirlwind round brolga girl run away
> Whirlwind round brolga girl run away danger here
> Rush precious brolga girl, don't stay[18]

In her pedagogical approach, Blackshaw first teaches the piece aurally and then provides students with the sheet music. When working with a group for an extended period of time, Blackshaw teaches using a variety of Orff-Schulwerk activities, including work with movement, non-melodic percussion, and activities such as creating rounds and ostinati. To internalize the sections of *Whirlwind* constructed in two- and four-part rounds, the composer recommends that students form groups and sing the melody in canon with rubato to experiment with different interpretations, match style, and to listen to the counterpoint between voices.[19]

HARMONY:
Most of *Whirlwind* is polyphonic, with the exception of the solo at letter B, which is monophonic. Polyphonic writing in *Whirlwind* is measured at one- or two-measure intervals with entrances at the beginning of the measure; in the free time sections, there is no prescribed duration between entrances. Homophonic writing is not present in this work.

To provide a foundation to listen for good intonation, Blackshaw writes a part for drone that sustains a pedal tone A. The composer recommends the drone be played on an electronic keyboard, cello, or string bass, or to use an indigenous Australian sound, a didgeridoo pitched in A. In addition to the drone, Blackshaw creates bordurs for glockenspiel and timpani. These rhythmic patterns using the pitches A and E establish the interval of a perfect fifth, providing students a focal point for which to listen. In Orff-Schulwerk, pedal tones and bordurs are often used to provide a foundation for matching pitch; these function in a similar fashion in *Whirlwind*.[20]

RHYTHM:

The same melody is employed throughout *Whirlwind* in both the free time sections and in 3/4 time. In the free time Soundscape portions, the composer overlaps the entrances of the melody and players are asked to play with rubato; in the two- and four-part round sections at letters E and G, a steady pulse persists. As stated above, Blackshaw engages students with text to help teach the melody and internalize the rhythm.

TIMBRE:

Blackshaw is fascinated by timbre and tone color.[21] In her works she explores different types of sounds for band, and her writing encourages students to focus on listening while they play. In several parts of the piece, players have the opportunity to work on tone without the concern of typical balance problems. During two of the Soundscape sections, ensemble members play homemade instruments, allowing them to focus exclusively on musicality and expression without concern for technique. Overlapping entrances in the Soundscapes, at the discretion of the conductor, allow for flexibility; entrances can be different each time, providing different models for which to listen.

Unit 7: Form and Structure

The composer has provided a chart of the structure of *Whirlwind* online as part of the "Know Your Stuff" material.[22]

SECTION	MEASURE	EVENT AND SCORING
A	1	Free time; Soundscape Four percussionists play whirlies; wind players play homemade rattles and water glass chimes
B	2	Free time; solo (theme) with whirlies
C	3	Free time; Soundscape Last phrase of theme is played in staggered entrances accompanied by whirlies

SECTION	MEASURE	EVENT AND SCORING
D	4–23	*Andante con moto;* 3/4 meter Percussion solo and ostinato established with traditional instruments
E	24–43	Two-part round (theme) Percussion ostinato
F	44–55	Percussion soli Composite rhythm of percussion soli at D is fragmented and split between percussion instruments
G	56–92	Four-part round (theme) Percussion ostinato with whirlies
H	93	Solo (theme) with echo Whirly and percussion accompaniment
1	94	Free time; Soundscape Like A, percussionists play whirlies and wind players play water-glass chimes and homemade rattles

Unit 8: Suggested Listening

Blackshaw, Jodie:

    Terpsichorean Dances. The First Frank Ticheli Composition Contest. University of North Texas Symphonic Band. Dennis Fisher, conductor. Mark Recordings 7290-MCD.

    Whirlwind. The First Frank Ticheli Composition Contest. University of North Texas Symphonic Band. Dennis Fisher, conductor. Mark Recordings 7290-MCD.

    Whirlwind. Midwest Clinic 2006. Hill Country Middle School. Cheryl Floyd, conductor. Mark Recordings 6776-MCD (CD).

    Whirlwind. Midwest Clinic 200., Hill Country Middle School. Cheryl Floyd, conductor. Mark Recordings 6776-MCD (DVD).

Colgrass, Michael:

    Apache Lullaby
    Gotta Make Noise
    Old Churches

Sitsky, Larry:

    Armenia
    Fall of the House of Usher
    Flute Sonatas 1–2–3
    The Golem
    Violin Concerto No. 2 "Gurdjieff"

Unit 9: Additional References and Resources

Fannin, Karen. Interview with Jodie Blackshaw. May 12, 2008.

Frazee, Jane. *Discovering Orff: A Curriculum for Music Teachers*. New York: Schott, 1987.

Kinder, Keith. "Presenting the First Prize Winner Jodie Blackshaw for *Whirlwind*." *MBM Times* 2(2007): 36–38.

Randel, Don Michael, ed. *The New Harvard Dictionary of Music*. Cambridge, MA: The Belknap Press of Harvard University Press, 1986.

Warner, Brigitte. *Orff-Schulwerk: Applications for the Classroom*. Englewood Cliffs, NJ: Prentice Hall, 1991.

Websites:

Manhattan Beach Music. http://www.manhattanbeachmusic.com
Aboriginal brolga story.
http://www.dreamtime.auz.net/default.asp?PageID=54

Contributed by:

Karen Fannin
Director of Bands
Hendrix College
Conway, Arkansas

---

1 Jodie Blackshaw, telephone conversation with author. May 12, 2008.

2 Blackshaw, telephone conversation.

3 Ibid.

4 For more information, go to http://www.dreamtime.auz.net/default.asp?PageID=54

5 Jane Frazee. *Discovering Orff: A Curriculum for Music Teachers*
(New York: Schott, 1987)

6 Ibid., 14–25.

7 Ibid., 36.

8 Don Michael Randel, ed. *The New Harvard Dictionary of Music* (Cambridge, MA: The Belknap Press of Harvard University Press, 1986), 28–29.

9 Blackshaw, program notes for *Whirlwind*.

10 Blackshaw, telephone conversation.

11 Ibid.

12 Frazee, 33.

13 Blackshaw, email to the author, May 29, 2008.

14 Blackshaw, telephone conversation.

15 *Whirlwind* score, 2.

16 Blackshaw, e-mail to the author.

17 Blackshaw, telephone conversation.

18 Ibid.

19 Ibid.

20 Frazee, 38–43.

21 Blackshaw. Telephone conversation.

22 http://www.manhattanbeach.com

Grade Three

Teacher Resource Guide

Ambrosian Hymn Variants

Donald H. White
(b. 1921)

Unit 1: Composer

Donald Howard White was born on February 28, 1921 in Narberth, Pennsylvania. He attended Temple University, where he earned a BS degree in music education and then went on to complete both the MM and the PhD degrees from the Eastman School of Music. White did post-doctoral work in composition at the Philadelphia Conservatory of Music. His principal teachers include Howard Hanson, Bernard Rogers, and Vincent Persichetti.

White's compositional output includes works for band, orchestra, chamber ensembles, and solo works. White is a trumpet player and has written successful solo works for trumpet, trombone, and euphonium. His *Tetra Ergon for Bass Trombone and Piano* (1973) and *Lyric Suite for Euphonium and Piano* (1970) remain classic works for these solo instruments. The composer created a wind ensemble accompaniment for the *Lyric Suite* shortly after its premiere.

White joined the faculty of DePauw University in 1947 and became the director of the School of Music in 1974, a position he held until 1978, when he requested a return to full-time teaching. In 1977 White conducted the premiere of his *From the Navajo Children* with the Eastman Wind Ensemble and chorus. White remained at DePauw until 1981 when he accepted a position at Central Washington University as professor of theory and composition. He retired from Central Washington University in 1990 and was granted *Professor Emeritus* status. He resides in Colorado Springs, Colorado.

Unit 2: Composition

When Donald White submitted his newest composition to his publisher in 1974, its title was *Aeterna Christi munera*, however the publishers changed the title to *Ambrosian Hymn Variants*, and so it remains today. "Aeterna Christi munera" (The Eternal Gifts of Christ the King) is an Ambrosian hymn found in the *Historical Anthology of Music* (HAM); its simple lines create an ideal subject for this theme and variations. The work is well suited for high school and university bands with its modal-like melody and challenging harmonic structure. Because the rehearsal numbers are oddly spaced it would improve the efficiency of rehearsals if all players and the conductor numbered their measures. Published by Ludwig Music for full symphonic band, the work is six minutes in duration.

Unit 3: Historical Perspective

Composers often choose hymns or folksongs as thematic material for variations. The hymn theme in *Ambrosian Hymn Variants* dates to ancient times. The origin of the Ambrosian chant is attributed to St. Ambrose (AD 340–397), Bishop of Milan, but no conclusive evidence has been found that unequivocally supports this claim. "Aeterna Christi munera, The Eternal Gifts of Christ the King," has been traced to the ninth century, when it appeared in the *Musica enchiriadis*. Although the melodies in this source are indeed ancient, musicologists continue to question whether or not St. Ambrose penned "Aeterna Christi munera."

St. Ambrose composed at least fourteen hymns, most in the Iambic dimeter form (in ancient times, combinations of short and long syllables in triple meter; modern poetry uses combinations of weak and strong syllables). A line of verse is divided into feet, a foot being one "set" of the short/long combination of syllables/notes, not necessarily a measure as noted in the following examples. Each is a sample of two feet in 3/4:[1]

Iamb   q | h   q | h   (short/long, short/long)

Trochee | hq | hq   (long/short, long/short)

"Aeterna Christi munera" evokes the triple meter by virtue of its syllabic orientation:

Ae-ter-na Chri-sti mu - ne - ra   et mar - tyr-um vic - to - ri - as

FIGURE 1. Aeterna Christi munera, ninth c.

Figure 2 is a reconstructed version showing the long and short pulses of the Iambic meter.[2]

Ae - ter - na   Chri - sti   mu - ne - ra   et   mar - tyr - um   vic - to - ri - as

FIGURE 2. Aeterna Christi munera, as reconstructed

White's theme employs the hymn as found in the *Historical Anthology of Music*.

Unit 4: Technical Considerations

Ambrosian Hymn Variants is scored for full symphonic band. The percussion parts include timpani, tubular bells, gong, suspended cymbal, triangle, snare drum, tenor drum, and cymbals. Trumpets, cornets, and trombones will need straight mutes.

The instrument ranges are indicative of writing in the 1970s. While flute and clarinet ranges extend into the upper regions of the instruments' capabilities, saxophone and horn ranges are quite conservative. So while the flute range extends to C7 and clarinet 1 to A6, alto saxophones only play to G-sharp 4. The horn range is extremely conservative by today's standards, extending only from C4 to F-sharp 5. Trumpets and cornets are not required to exceed G5, with trumpet 1 extending to a modest A5. All low brass parts are within a comfortable range.

Ambrosian Hymn Variants incorporates a wide range of dynamics (*piano—fortissimo*) and the articulations include a light staccato, accents, and marcato accents. Preparation for the performance of this work might include daily scale studies using a variety of articulations at various dynamic levels. Special care should be taken to develop a light staccato. Students will need a focused air stream and proper tonguing techniques to execute the melodic material of variation 1. Consider using an amplified metronome to practice the following tonguing exercise. Once students can cleanly articulate the exercise at the slower tempo, begin to vary the tempo, articulation, and dynamic level. Play the pattern through on one note then go up by steps, half steps, or around the circle of fifths.

The hymn tune theme and variation 2 are slow, sustained sections that will expose the band's tone and balance. The extended phrases will challenge developing high school bands and advanced middle school ensembles. Use chorales and breathing exercises to improve air support and tonal control. Because good intonation is a bi-product of a well-defined embouchure and proper breath support, students should be encouraged to consistently practice to maintain a characteristic tone. The harmonic structure of this composition includes a rich vocabulary of chords that will only be in tune with careful attention to tone, intonation, and balance.

All trills begin on the written pitch and trill upward. Students should note that accidentals within the trill notation define the upper note. If the trill is over a B but includes a sharp sign (*tr#~*), the student will alternate rapidly from B to C-sharp.

Snare and tenor drum players will need to perform flams at a fast tempo in 6/8. The driving snare line in variation 3 requires a steady pattern of eighth notes with intermittent flams and marcato accents.

FIGURE 3. Tonguing Exercise

Unit 5: Stylistic Considerations

The composer uses simple but concise terminology to convey the style of the various sections of this work. The initial statement of the hymn is marked "Slowly," and the term *maestoso* indicates the nature of the thematic material. The absence of articulation markings allows the conductor to establish the legato character of the ancient hymn. Play examples of Gregorian chant to help students understand the ethereal quality of the music. Use a "dah" articulation to create a seamless flow and maintain phrase lengths as indicated by the music. Most phrases are four or five measures in duration, however the final seven measures of the theme should be played in one breath.

Variation 1 is moderato in tempo and staccato in style with lilting eighth- and sixteenth-note rhythms. Use a light articulation and adequate space between notes to achieve the lively dance-like quality. This is especially necessary at the *forte* segment of the variation, where heavy tonguing will bog down the tune and the tempo.

Teaching tip: Create warm-up exercises that teach students to put space between notes. This can be achieved with simple conducting exercises at various dynamic levels. Set a metronome at sixty and have students play a series of pitches in a legato style. Use scales, a simple melody, or write out the theme of this variation for the full band. Continue to repeat the passage, but have students put more space between notes on each subsequent repetition of the pattern. Maintain a slower tempo so that students can hear the difference. As students become more aware and concise in their articulation of the staccato, increase the tempo and transfer to the music.

Variaion 2 is a hymn. Use legato style and a "dah" articulation. The phrasing is four measures, six measures, five measures, and eight measures. Develop the capacity to play long phrases through simple breathing exercises.

Teaching tip: Breathing exercises are only as effective as the manner in which they are executed. For fun, have students lie on the floor and put their music folders on their tummies. Set the metronome at sixty and ask them to exhale all their air and then do the following:

1. Breathe in for four to eight counts (depends on the maturity of the group).
2. Hold the breath for four to eight counts.
3. Exhale for four to eight counts.
4. Hold the breath for four to eight counts.
5. Repeat the pattern three times.

As students gain control, increase the number of counts of inhale and exhale.

Variation 3 is marked *Fast*. This driving and powerful variant in 6/8 gets much of its character from the snare drum line with its practically non-stop eighth notes. Short marcato brass entrances punctuate throughout the segment while woodwind trills also create intensity. The ensemble must maintain the fast tempo (dotted quarter note = 144) while being rhythmically precise and harmonically balanced. The combinations of slurs, staccato and marcato notes, and accents will challenge students to develop a vocabulary of articulations.

Teaching tip: Use warm-up time to develop a vocabulary of articulations. Start in simple 4/4 and have the band play a scale (the scale of the week or day will do just fine). Play four quarter notes to each pitch and ask students to use the articulation they see in the conductor's pattern. Not only will this develop articulations within the band, it will encourage students to look up and to interpret what they see into sound.

Unit 6: Musical Elements

MELODY:

A quick comparison of the ninth-century version of the hymn (figure 1) and White's theme (figure 3) establishes the composer's commitment to the character of the early setting. Although the keys are identical, the composer indicates that choice of key had more to do with ranges of band instruments than an attempt to remain true to the original hymn.[3] The multiple meters convey the flow of the hymn's text.

FIGURE 4. *Ambrosian Hymn Variants*, theme

Variation 1 is an immediate contrast to the hymn theme. The soft dynamic level coupled with staccato eighth notes give this variation a lighter, more joyful quality. Pay attention to the articulation and the clarity of the rhythms. The contrapuntal nature of this variation requires accuracy of rhythm and a steady pulse.

FIGURE 5. Variation 1 (segment), mm. 23–33

Variation 2 conveys a religious, meditative quality. Use legato tonguing throughout this variation. Have students sing their parts to improve intonation. Numerous accidentals appear in this segment, as there is no key signature.

HARMONY:

The intonation challenge of *Ambrosian Hymn Variants* lies in the harmonic and contrapuntal aspects of the work. The composer uses a colorful vocabulary of harmonies throughout the composition. Figure 5 is representative of the chordal structure of the music. Notice the combinations of consonance and dissonance throughout this figure. Numerous seconds and clusters evoke a sense of pain and release as they resolve from dissonant to consonant tonalities.

FIGURE 6. Variation 2 (segment), mm. 113–122

Tuning approaches will vary depending on the nature of the chord. For an interesting and illuminating discussion on the tuning and balance of twentieth century band music, see W. Francis McBeth's *Effective Performance of Band Music*.

RHYTHM:

Ambrosian Hymn Variants is rhythmically straightforward. The most demanding rhythmic component is found in variation 3, where the composer includes duplets within the 6/8 meter. Students will be challenged to divide beats into triplets and duplets. The tonguing exercise (figure 3) will help prepare students for the shift from duple to triple.

Teaching tip: Have students count aloud: "1–2–3" for the triplet and "1–and" for the duple. Use a metronome and ask the students to count patterns: 1–2–3–1-and; 1–2–3–1–2–3–1-and; etc. Have students pat their feet in time with the metronome to help internalize the pulse. Once the band is speaking accurate rhythms, use the same exercise but have students play a pitch varying the triplet with the duplet.

TIMBRE:

The timbre of ancient hymns evokes an ethereal quality with their simplistic melodic lines and rhythms. Characteristic tone is an essential component in the interpretation of all music, but is especially appropriate for this work. The alternation of woodwind and brass choirs is an integral part of the form and timbre. Strive for a pure tone with limited use of vibrato in the flutes and saxophones. In the tutti sections it is important to balance and blend woodwinds and brass so the woodwind color is maintained within the ensemble's sound. The percussion is always in a supportive role and must never overpower the winds. Consider developing woodwind and brass choirs for solo and ensemble festival to enhance students' understanding of the tonal quality of these unique ensembles.

Unit 7: Form and Structure

Ambrosian Hymn Variants is a theme and variations. The initial hymn theme is presented and followed by three variations: *Moderato* in 2/4, *Slowly* in multiple meters, and *Fast* in 6/8.

SECTION	MEASURE	EVENT AND SCORING
Introduction	1–3	Slowly; tubular bells
Theme	3–23	Multiple meters: 3/4, 4/4, 2/4 combinations to enhance early hymn free meter; initial statement in cornets with horn and trombone accompaniment; woodwind choir enters in the fifth measure of the hymn tune; brass choir response followed by full band
Variation 1	23–113	Moderato; 2/4 meter in a light staccato style; initial statement in piccolo and flutes; clarinets enter in a brief canon, providing contrapuntal interest; interplay of brass and woodwind sections; interspersed cornet, horn, trombone, and tuba solos
Variation 2	113–137	Slowly; brass choir with woodwind choir response; full band to the end of the variation

SECTION	MEASURE	EVENT AND SCORING
Variation 3	137-end	Fast; 6/8 meter with first real involvement of percussion; snare drum drives throughout variation with eighth-note pattern punctuated by flams and marcato accents; winds add melodic material and strong punctuated rhythms; marcato brass entrances answered by trills in woodwinds; winds use duplet rhythms within the 6/8 meter
	155–172	Driving woodwind melody with low brass punctuated response
	172–181	Muted cornets with percussion
	188–204	full band in unison rhythm, duplets and triplets; snare drum in 6/8 continues
	204–218	Fragments of melodic material are passed from brass to woodwinds
	218–230	Cornets, trumpets, horns, and baritones in almost unison rhythm drive thematic material with woodwind punctuations
	230–242	Continuous eighth notes are maintained until the final two bars, where duplets bring this variation to its end
	242–278	Marcato; trombones provide the underlying hymn tune while the rest of the band continues patterns of eighth notes in both triplets and duplets
	278–298	Full band plays harmonized hymn tune

Unit 8: Suggested Listening

Dello Joio, Norman. *Variants on a Medieval Tune*.
Tull, Fisher. *Sketches on a Tudor Psalm*.
White, Donald H.:
    Concertino for Timpani, Winds, and Percussion. 1976.
    Dichotomy. 1966.
    For the Navajo Children. For chorus and wind ensemble. Unpublished. 1978.
    Introduction and Allegro. 1968.
    Lyric Suite for Euphonium and Piano. 1974.
    Miniature Set for Band. 1964.
    Patterns. 1977.

Unit 9: Additional References and Resources

Apel, Willi. *Harvard Dictionary of Music.* Second ed. Cambridge, MA: The Belknap Press, 1970.

Creasap, Susan. Interview with Donald White. June 1, 2008.

Davison, Archibald T. and Willi Apel, eds. *Historical Anthology of Music.* Cambridge, MA: Harvard University Press, 1950.

Gookin, Larry. Email correspondence, May 29–30, 2008.

McBeth, W. Francis. *Effective Performance of Band Music.* San Antonio, TX: Southern Music Company, 1972.

Smith, Norman and Albert Stoutamire. *Band Music Notes.* Lake Charles, LA: Program Note Press, 1989.

White, Donald H. *Ambrosian Hymn Variants.* Cleveland, OH: Ludwig Music, 1974.

_____. *Miniature Set for Band.* North Dakota State University. Wayne Dorothy, conductor. MP3 file available at http://www.hsutx.edu/academics/music/concertbandmusic.html

Contributed by:

Susan D. Creasap
Associate Director of Bands
Morehead State University
Morehead, Kentucky

---

1 Willi Apel, *Harvard Dictionary of Music,* 2nd ed. (Cambridge, MA: The Belknap Press of Harvard University Press, 1970), 32.

2 Apel, 32.

3 Donald White, interview with author, June 1, 2008.

Teacher Resource Guide

America Verses

Timothy Broege
(b. 1947)

Unit 1: Composer

Timothy Broege was born in Belmar, New Jersey, on November 6, 1947. As a child he studied both piano and theory. While earning his bachelor of music degree at Northwestern University, he studied composition, piano, and harpsichord. Broege taught in the public schools of Chicago from 1969 to 1971, and then taught elementary music in Manasquan, New Jersey, until 1980. From 1985 to 1995 he taught both piano and recorder at the Monmouth Conservatory of Music. Broege currently serves as organist and director of music at First Presbyterian Church in Belmar, positions he has held since 1972, and organist and director of music at Elberon Memorial Church in Elberon, New Jersey.

Broege has nearly 150 works published for large ensembles, chamber ensembles, solo instruments, voices, keyboards, guitar, recorders, and school bands. He appears frequently as a guest composer/conductor and clinician, and received the 1994 Edwin Franko Goldman Award from the American School Band Directors Association for his works for school bands.

Besides his compositional and church music activities, Broege is an active recitalist on harpsichord and recorder. He also enjoys jazz composition and performance, serving as the pianist with The John Gronert Jazz Trio since 2006.

Unit 2: Composition

America Verses was composed in 1997 at the suggestion of publisher/composer Bob Margolis, who was interested in publishing a school band piece based on a well-known tune. The work consists of a set of four variations, or "verses," on the tune known by the English as "God Save the Queen" and in the United States as "America," or "My Country, 'Tis of Thee." It is a single-movement composition of 117 measures and is approximately five and a half minutes in length.

America Verses was published by Manhattan Beach Music in 1998 and was premiered by the Small College Intercollegiate Band at the thirtieth National Convention of College Band Directors' National Association in Austin, Texas in February, 1999. The piece was selected to be a part of this concert of new and recent pieces intended for less-advanced middle and high school groups.

Unit 3: Historical Perspectives

Written in 1997, *America Verses* is not a piece of celebratory patriotism. With its thoughtful first and last verses, the listener is led to reflect and consider the complex history of this country. It must be noted that the composition reflects the ambivalence of a "pre-9/11" America—a period of relative peace, economic prosperity, and a weakened sense of patriotism and nationalism, all of which changed following the terrorist attacks of September 11, 2001.

Broege included the following note with the published score:

> The history of America is complex, to say the least, and the joys and sorrows of American life are equally complex. There has been much to celebrate and much to lament; much to be proud of and much to regret... If the composer loves his country—which he does—that love is conditioned by an awareness of how much remains to be done before America is transformed into an enlightened, creative, and just society. It is for the listener to determine the message of the work, to decide whether the music ends on a note of despair, or in a mood of hushed optimism.

Unit 4: Technical Considerations

This piece provides the opportunity for students to work on many styles of articulation at several dynamic levels.

In the slow and sustained phrases of verses 1 and 4, students should strive to move their fingers quickly on note changes despite the slower tempo in order for the ensemble to play together. Students will need to understand the concept of staggered breathing for the long, sustained phrases to be performed correctly. An awareness of phrase lengths and avoiding "unison" breaths will be necessary to achieve the desired balance and blend. The long note values and phrases of verses 1 and 4 create opportunities to work on tone quality through the appropriate use of air and embouchure formation.

Most of the wind parts incorporate staccato markings as well as slurring in verses 2 and 3. The staccato quarter notes should be light without harsh artic- ulations. The syncopated ragtime melody should have space and bounce, but not choppy nor with too harsh of articulation. Students should be monitored for understanding and correct interpretation of articulation markings. Consider vocally modeling articulations with student imitation to improve understanding and performance.

The dynamic range of the piece is *pianissimo* through *fortissimo*. The com- poser gives much attention to the area of dynamic indication. Every desired dynamic change is clearly notated in each part. All wind parts include the use of independent section dynamics as well as *subito piano* and *fortissimo*. Crescendos and decrescendos are clearly defined, and must be executed smoothly with proper support in order to maintain the intended balance and blend.

Because the melodic material of the piece is a well-known tune, it is important that the performers are aware of who should be in the spotlight at all times. Because the verses are variations, performers might need guidance as to what is melodic material, especially during transitional phrases. Performers will also need to understand who has the countermelody and its role in the balance between the melodic material and the accompaniment.

Unit 5: Stylistic Considerations

In the manner of most any variation set, *America Verses* presents different stylistic elements with each section.

Verse 1 is marked *Slowly, always sustained, with reverence*. Careful atten- tion will need to be made in order to clearly hear the melody in the horns over the countermelody. A trumpet is to double the horns if necessary. Crescendos and decrescendos of the countermelody must be even and balanced.

FIGURE 1. Verse 1, horns

FIGURE 2. Verse 1, countermelody

The tempo of verse 2 is slightly faster. The accompaniment seems to be in the style of Schumann's *Chester*. However, it will be important to keep performers from rushing. The melody should always be played legato, while the accompanying ensemble chords are played in a light, gentle staccato style.

FIGURE 3. Verse 2, saxes

Verse 3 is marked *Tempo di Rag, gently, not fast,* and the composer indicates that this should continue the pulse of verse 2. The clarinet melody should be semi-legato, while the accompaniment is relaxed and light. The "Grand Cakewalk" at m. 74 should be slightly slower and grandioso—the loudest and most joyful section of the work. Uniform ensemble articulation style will be of utmost importance to proper musical expression of verses 2 and 3.

FIGURE 4. Verse 3 ragtime melody, clarinets

The tempo of verse 4 is marked *Broadly, with resignation,* and the phrases should be slow and sustained, building to a climax at m. 105. From this point on the piece returns to its quiet thoughtfulness. The last measures should be performed as softly and slowly as possible.

FIGURE 5. Verse 4

Unit 6: Musical Elements

MELODY:
The melodic material for *America Verses* is the hymn tune "America," or "My Country, 'Tis of Thee." The tune is characterized by ascending motion that continues until it reaches its highest point near the end.

The melody is more easily recognizable in verses 1 and 4, and most of verse 2. Verse 3, or ragtime, is the least straightforward, but still follows the ascending melodic movement of the "America" tune.

HARMONY:

The harmonic structure of the piece is relatively simple. The composition's tonal outline consists of two half steps separated by a perfect fifth:

Verse 1:   E-flat minor
Verse 2:   D minor (alternating with a minor)
Verse 3:   B-flat major
Verse 4:   A minor

The descending half-step motion of the opening and closing sustained timpani pitches represent the work's harmonic outline. This is also presented in the descending line of the final pitches of the chimes. The descending harmonic scheme is in contrast with the ascending motion of the "America" tune heard in each verse.

Students are not presented with a key signature, only accidentals. The harmonic structure of this piece presents a "learning moment" to expose less-advanced musicians to possibly unfamiliar keys.

RHYTHM:

Each verse presents a different rhythmic variation to go along with the harmonic change. Though the original "America" tune is in 3/4, the time signature is not used in this work.

Verse 1 is presented more traditionally, with dotted quarter notes and eighth notes, though it is in 4/4. The composer uses a rest on beat 1 of the measure and elongates the final note of each phrase by a beat to present the melody and countermelody in 4/4.

Verse 2 is presented with a more syncopated feel in 2/2. There is one measure of quarter notes in 3/2 (m. 43). It will be important for performers to keep the eighth notes of the countermelody even in order to maximize the musical effect of the syncopation. Performers will need to have an understanding of the use of tied notes in syncopation.

FIGURE 6. Verse 2 countermelody, "Land where my fathers died" phrase

Verse 3 continues in 2/2 as the ragtime melody is introduced. Again, maintaining even eighth notes through subdivision will help with ensemble timing and musical expression during the syncopation of the verse.

The half-note pulse of verse 4 should be similar to the quarter-note pulse of verse 1. The verse is almost entirely in 4/2, with one measure of quarter notes in 3/2 (m. 104). Performers will gain experience reading breves and dotted whole notes in this verse.

Besides the different tempos of each of the four verses, there are several tempo changes indicated by the composer—usually during transitional material. All are notated in English terms.

TIMBRE:

Because of the slow, sustained writing of the first and last variations, the timbre of *America Verses* is dependent on the balance and blend of all of the voices at the lower end of the dynamic spectrum. The piece can serve as an opportunity to listen for the moving line and adjust accordingly to create the appropriate timbres.

The timbre of verse 2 is dependent on the balance of the accompaniment. Uniform note length will need to be established for the staccato chords.

Verse 3 provides the greatest timbral change as the key moves to B-flat major. The higher tessitura of the orchestration provides a timbral difference for this ragtime verse, as well.

The percussion parts (timpani, percussion 1 [mallets and chimes], percussion 2 [snare and bass drums], percussion 3 [gong, triangle, woodblock, cymbals, tambourine, and suspended cymbals]) add timbral color in several phrases of the piece. The composer makes special mention of the importance of the chimes, timpani, and string bass notes at the end of the piece. The chimes should be off-stage or at a distance, if at all possible. If no string bass is available, the final timpani roll may need to be played more loudly.

Unit 7: Form and Structure

SECTION	MEASURE	EVENT AND SCORING
Verse 1		E-flat minor; slow and sustained
	1–4	Countermelody derived from "America" tune presented in parallel chords
	5–18	Melody presented in the horns (optional doubling by trumpet)
	19–20	Transition
Verse 2		D minor/A minor; *più mosso*
	21–30	Countermelody derived from "Land where my fathers died" phrase is presented in flutes, oboes, and clarinets
		Melody reply is presented in alto and tenor saxophones
		Low brass and reeds accompaniment (a la Schumann's *Chester*); D minor
	31–38	Syncopated melodic derivation presented in woodwinds; A minor
	39–43	*Chester* accompaniment returns under woodwind melody; D minor

SECTION	MEASURE	EVENT AND SCORING
	44–48	Syncopated melodic derivation returns to end verse; A minor
	49	Transition
Verse 3		B-flat major; playful
	50–57	Introductory material
	58–65	Ragtime melody presented by clarinets
	66–73	Countermelody added by bassoons, tenor saxophones, and euphoniums
	74–83	The "Grand Cakewalk" (slightly slower, *grandioso*, happiest moment of piece)
	84–91	Transition material
	92–93	Verse 4 countermelody introduced in flutes, oboes, and clarinets
Verse 4		A minor; somber reflection
	94–95	Introductory harmonic establishment
	96–109	Piccolo, oboe, bells, and muted trumpet present melody in parallel tenths; countermelody presented in flutes, clarinets and trumpets
	110–117	Coda; prayerfully Chimes offstage Last string bass/timpani notes fade to *niente*

Unit 8: Suggested Listening

Broege, Timothy:
> *Jody*
> *Sinfonia XVI: Transcendental Vienna*
> *Theme and Variations*
> *Three Pieces for American Band Set No. 2*
> *Train Heading West and Other Outdoor Scenes*

Copland, Aaron. *A Lincoln Portrait.*
Gershwin, George. *Porgy and Bess.*
Ives, Charles. *Variations on "America."*
Schumann, William. *New England Triptych.*

Unit 9: Additional References and Resources

Broege, Timothy. *America Verses.* Brooklyn: Manhattan Beach Music, 1998.
Broege, Timothy. "*America Verses.*" Email to Andrea Brown. May 27, 2008.
Miles, Richard, ed. *Teaching Music through Performance in Band, Volumes 1–6.* Chicago: GIA Publications, 1997, 1998, 2000, 2002, 2005, 2007.

Websites:
www.manhattanbeachmusic.com/html/america_verses.html
www.timothybroege.com
www.wind.windrep.org/Timothy_Broege

Contributed by:

Andrea E. Brown
Director of Athletic Bands
Assistant Director of Bands
Austin Peay State University
Clarksville, Tennessee

Teacher Resource Guide

...and the antelope play
John Alan Carnahan
(b. 1955)

Unit 1: Composer

Born and raised in Pennsylvania, John Carnahan now resides in Southern California. He is the conductor of the Wind Symphony and Director of the Bob Cole Conservatory of Music at California State University, Long Beach, where he has been a professor of music since 1988. Prior to his appointment at Long Beach, Carnahan served as assistant director of bands at the University of Texas, Arlington, where he taught music education courses and conducted the marching and symphonic bands. Before his years in Arlington, he was director of bands at Clovis High School in Clovis, California. John Carnahan received his bachelor of music degree from Duquesne University in Pittsburgh, Pennsylvania, and a master of education degree from the University of San Francisco.

In addition to his university duties, Carnahan is active nationally as a guest conductor, adjudicator, lecturer, and composer and arranger. He has conducted ensembles at the California Music Educators Association Convention, the Texas Music Educators Association Conference, the College Band Directors National Association Southwestern and Western Division Conferences and internationally in Europe, Japan, and Korea. He has presented numerous clinics and performance demonstrations for statewide and regional music education organizations and conferences. His innovative and thought-provoking sessions on ensemble rehearsal techniques and the art of conducting are always very well received. His commissioned pieces have received many performances and his arrangements have been heard throughout the United States.

Unit 2: Composition

...and the antelope play is the winner of the 2007 College Band Directors National Association Young Band Composition Contest and is published by Manhattan Beach Music. It is a tone poem for winds and percussion. The piece is one movement, eight and a half minutes in length. As stated in the program notes:

> This tone poem represents a geographical and historical account of the transformation of the Antelope Valley in the high desert of California. The work portrays aspects of cultural change from ancient times through the displacement of the Native American culture, to modern times. *...and the antelope play* is a programmatic piece with through-composed sections. Each section is entitled relative to the story: "...first there was wind"; "...morning light"; "...behold the valley"; "...and the antelope play"; "...the plight of the valley"; "...the spirit remains"; "...and the antelope?"; "...the valley home."

> Thematic material for the piece is based solely on melodic fragments and word association from the well-known song of the west, "Home on the Range." Although well hidden, one may find the themes by word association more readily than by melodic association. The ellipsis points preceding the title are for the three missing words of the song, "Where the deer..."[1]

> Below are the words to the song, "Home on the Range":

> Oh, give me a home where the buffalo roam,
> Where the deer and the antelope play;
> Where seldom is heard a discouraging word,
> And the skies are not cloudy all day.
> Home, home on the range,

Unit 3: Historical Perspective

The Antelope Valley is in the southwest corner of the Mojave Desert spanning seventy-five miles (approximately sixty miles northeast of Los Angeles). It is named after the pronghorn antelope that used to roam the valley in large numbers. Spanish settlers came to the valley in 1769, driving out the antelope. In recent years, the pronghorn antelope has been reintroduced into the valley and is growing, but in small numbers.

The Antelope Valley was inhabited by several American Indian groups of Shoshonean ancestry, including the Serrano, Kitanemuk, Kawaiisu, and Tataviam from about BC 1000 to AD 1800. Many groups either lived here or traveled through here to trade. This valley was an ideal place because of the many rivers and easy accessibility from all directions. Most of the groups were destroyed by the arrival of the Spanish settlers. They conquered the groups and used many of them for manual labor.

This information is significant, because this work portrays aspects of cultural change from the American Indian to the Spanish invasion and ends with sounds from the flute and air through the horns indicating that the spirit of those American Indian groups remains even today in the Antelope Valley.

Unit 4: Technical Considerations

The range of instruments is normal for a Grade 3 piece. Trumpet 1 goes up to a G5 as well as horn 1. The highest note for piccolo and flutes is an F6, and for trombone 1, it is an F4. Clarinet 1 goes up to a C-sharp 6; tubas go down to an A-flat 1. It is possible for this piece to be performed with only two horns, one on the horn 1–2 part and one on the part for horn 3–4. The parts where the four horns split are doubled in the alto saxophones or clarinets.

There is a short trombone smear from position six-to-one-to-six, and one measure where trumpets use plungers. Although there are only three percussion parts, each part requires two players. With the timpani part, a total of seven percussionists are required to play the following instruments: timpani, snare drum, bass drum, suspended cymbal, triangle, slapstick, temple blocks, crash cymbals, wooden wind chimes, bells, and xylophone.

Unit 5: Stylistic Considerations

In the beginning of the work, air blown through horn should be constant and at different speeds. Carnahan writes, "*ad lib. **pp**–**ff***." Snare drum with brushes signifies the sound of tumbleweeds blowing across the valley and should begin slowly, get faster, and end slowly. Carnahan writes how many seconds should be used for each effect. This is approximate and should be at the discretion of the conductor.

In the solo recorder part, the directions say "slowly flat." This can be accomplished by the player dropping the jaw and slowly stopping air flow. When the instruction to "slide" is given, the player should put the fingers of the right hand down together slowly until they reach the low C, for an effect of a slide downward. The solo recorder should rest two to three seconds between breath marks.

Many directions are written in the score. For instance, in the section titled "...the plight of the valley," the composer specifically asks for a very wide Mariachi vibrato in the trumpets to imitate the sound of Spanish trumpets, indicating that the Spaniards had come to the valley.

For an effective ending, winds should begin moving air through the horn softly, gradually getting louder, and then disappearing softly at the end. The air should be guided by the last triangle sound in the final measure of the work. Also, no vibrato should be used in the flute solo.

There are various tempos in this work. Pay special attention to the accelerando in mm. 31–36 in order to arrive at the marking of 158 in m. 37. A slower tempo will lose the forward momentum of this section.

Articulations are clearly marked throughout the work and should be followed exactly as written.

UNIT 6: MUSICAL ELEMENTS

MELODY:

Carnahan quotes parts of "Home on the Range" throughout this piece. The first time we can find a quote is in the word association of "and the skies" beginning in the upper woodwinds in M. 3:

FIGURE 1. Mm. 3–4, "And the skies," flute

There is augmentation of the melody in trombones and euphonium in mm. 8–10. This quotes the words "Oh, give me a home":

FIGURE 2. Mm. 8–10, "Oh, give me a home," tenor trombone

The only time this same motive is clearly heard is at the end of the work, mm. 144–145, in clarinets and saxophones:

FIGURE 3. Mm. 144–145, "Oh, give me a home," clarinet in B-flat

The triplet eighth notes throughout this work quotes "and the antelope play." We hear the portion of "and the antelope" in the triplets beginning in m. 32 in the trumpets followed by clarinets:

FIGURE 4. M. 32, "And the antelope play," cornet

There are other quotations as well, including "home on the range" in the quarter-note triplets in the flutes beginning in m. 56:

FIGURE 5. M. 56, "Home on the range," flute

The quotation of "where the deer" is heard beginning in the alto saxophones in m. 31:

FIGURE 6. M. 31, "Where the deer," alto saxophone

Almost all of the material used in the melody of this work is taken from fragments of the song "Home on the Range."

HARMONY:
The key centers in this piece include the major keys of C, B-flat, and F. Chordal construction is voiced very well, with chord roots in the bass and not many thirds in the chords. This makes it easier to tune the chords.

RHYTHM:
This piece is a very good teaching tool of various notes with triplets. Included in this work are triplet sixteenths, triplet eighths, triplet quarters, and triplet half notes. Figure 7 gives a warm-up suggestion:

FIGURE 7. Warm-up suggestion

Timbre:
There is a large solo for recorder, which is preferred, but can be substituted with flute. There is also a solo part in trumpet 1, flute 1, and piccolo. Except for a few soli parts in trumpets and trombones, almost all woodwind and brass parts are doubled throughout.

Unit 7: Form and Structure

The form is in a loose ABA structure. Since there are titles for various sections, the work is analyzed below by those titles.

Section	Measure	Event and Scoring
"…first there was wind"	1	Wind through horns; percussion sounds of the valley
"…the spiritworld"	2	Solo recorder over the wind through horns
"…morning light"	3–12	Sounds of the morning light in upper woodwinds
"…behold the valley"	13–30	Melody in clarinets and horns with flutes and oboes added in
Transition	31–36	Mixed motives in woodwinds and high brass (see Unit 6)
"…and the antelope play"	37–78	Sounds of antelope playing emphasized in low woodwinds, tuba, and temple blocks; melody in trumpets and clarinets
"…the plight of the valley"	79–94	Sounds of the Spanish Calvary in trumpets
"…the spirit remains"	95–102	Solo piccolo accompanied by percussion with quotation of "…and the skies" in the bells
"…and the antelope?"	103–120	Augmented melody from mm. 37–78 (…and the antelope play) in flutes, clarinets, and solo trumpet
"…the valley home"	120–143	Earlier melodies and motives from mm. 13–30 and mm. 31–36 (…behold the valley)

SECTION	MEASURE	EVENT AND SCORING
Coda	144–160	Melody in clarinets and alto saxophones ending with solo flute over wind through horns and solo triangle, all fading to silence

Unit 8: Suggested Listening

Blackshaw, Jodie. *Whirlwind.*
Gillingham, David. *Council Oak.*
Hanson, Howard. *Chorale and Alleluia.*
Jenkins, Joseph Wilcox. *American Overture for Band.*

Unit 9: Additional References and Resources

...and the antelope play. Score. Manhattan Beach Music.

Websites:
    The Antelope Valley Indian Museum.
        http://www.avim.parks.ca.gov/index.shtml
    The Antelope Valley California Poppy Reserve.
        http://www.parks.ca.gov/default.asp?page_id=627
    The Antelope Valley. http://en.wikipedia.org/wiki/Antelope_Valley

For more information, contact the composer at jcarnaha@csulb.edu

Contributed by:

Joan deAlbuquerque
Associate Director of Bands
Bob Cole Conservatory of Music
California State University, Long Beach
Long Beach, California

---

1 *...and the antelope play,* score (Manhattan Beach Music).

Teacher Resource Guide

Antiphon
Fisher Tull
(1934–1994)

Unit 1: Composer

Fisher Aubrey Tull entered into composing and arranging as an undergraduate trumpet student at North Texas State Teacher's College in Denton, Texas in the 1950s. During his time there, he created over 100 arrangements for dance bands and radio productions, and was the first staff arranger for the North Texas lab bands. He subsequently returned to North Texas to complete masters and doctoral degrees in music theory, trumpet performance, and composition. His primary composition teacher was Samuel Adler.

Tull served on the faculty of Sam Houston State University in Huntsville, Texas from 1957 until his death in 1994, at which time he held the rank of Distinguished Professor of Music. He served as department chair from 1965 to 1982, and was named a Piper Professor, an award recognizing superior university teaching in the state of Texas, in 1984. Tull had a long and productive career as a composer, and a substantial portion of his output is for wind band, including such major works as *Sketches on a Tudor Psalm*, *Passing Fantasy*, and the winner of the 1970 Ostwald award, *Toccata*.

Unit 2: Composition

Antiphon was composed for the 1971 Tri-State Music Festival Honor Band held in Enid, Oklahoma. The work is dedicated to the honor band and the festival director, Milburn Carey.

The title refers to a hymn sung in alternate parts by two groups of singers. The word is derived from the Greek *anti*, meaning opposite, and *phone*, meaning sound. The composer uses brass and woodwind sections in responsive fashion throughout the work, creating form and growth through the interplay of these timbral blocks.

The scoring is for symphonic band, including four horn parts, three cornet, and two trumpet parts, and substantial percussion writing, requiring four players in addition to a timpanist. A celesta part is included for two measures only, and is doubled in muted trumpet and vibraphone.

Unit 3: Historical Perspective

Completed in 1970, *Antiphon* was composed within a few years of Fisher Tull's award-winning *Toccata* and his widely performed *Sketches on a Tudor Psalm*. These works are each twice the length of *Antiphon*, and require greater technical facility from performers.

A seventeenth-century antecedent for *Antiphon* is found in the antiphonal instrumental music of Giovanni Gabrieli. *Antiphon* employs sectional scoring, motivic construction, and imitative counterpoint similar to Gabrieli's works. The quartal, bitonal and non-functional harmonic language of Tull set *Antiphon* apart as a Modern work, albeit with the textural and structural characteristics of seventeenth-century instrumental music.

Unit 4: Technical Considerations

Antiphon requires a modest set of technical skills for performance. Brass and woodwind players are required to perform tenuto, staccato, and accent articulations, frequently within the same motive. Clarity and specificity of these articulations are vital to an effective performance.

Facility with key centers throughout the circle of fifths is requisite for performance. While the primary motivic materials of *Antiphon* are presented in the keys of B-flat and G major and G minor, a continuous movement through tonal centers throughout the work generates extended sections in the keys B minor, E major, and C-flat minor. Sixteenth notes are presented in the woodwinds for only one beat of scalar pitches under a slur, and in the brasses for one beat of repeated pitches well within single-tonguing tempo.

Antiphon is primarily in 3/4 meter with several moments where 4/4 is briefly used to allow for motivic expansion or to delineate changes in the form. A single borrowed rhythm is found in a quarter-note triplet played by all woodwinds in m. 55. While the timpanist must perform a pitch change on one drum within fourteen beats, this is the most challenging element of the percussion score.

Unit 5: Stylistic Considerations

As a work that uses a formal structure from the 1harmonic language of the seventeenth and twentieth centuries, *Antiphon* is a neoclassic selection. The block scoring requires particular attention to balance between antiphonal elements, particularly when brasses and woodwinds are scored in responsive fashion.

A bold, declamatory style is the dominant voice of *Antiphon*, and is interrupted only during the contrasting imitative section between mm. 33 and 60. Care must be taken to allow for accents to sound full and deliberate without sounding percussive or piercing. The bitonality and non-functional tertian harmonic language require specific attention to balance within the scored block structures. As an element of rehearsal, individual players may need to sound assigned pitches linearly in order to be certain that each pitch is contributing to the vertical chord.

The indicated tempos of quarter note = 112 for the outer sections and quarter note = ca. 88 for the middle section provide for only a portion of the musical contrast, and should be adhered to. The confident, decisive affect of the outer sections cannot be conveyed at faster tempos, while the imitated subject of the middle section loses identity and momentum if performed too slowly.

Unit 6: Musical Elements

MELODY:

Antiphon is a motivic work without extended themes. The primary declamatory motives are presented individually in the first forty-eight measures, including the introduction and repeated section between mm. 10 and 33. The middle section is imitative in four voices, with the subject consisting of a three-note ascending motive and a four-note descending one. The fourth entrance is treated with both rhythmic displacement and diminution, creating tension and propelling the work into the final declamatory section. In this final section, the motives of the first forty-eight measures are augmented, contracted, and combined to create variety and growth. This motivic manipulation establishes trajectory and momentum.

Players unfamiliar with this type of construction may find it useful to perform each of the motives individually outside of context, perhaps by extracting the ideas from the work for rehearsal, in unison, as an exercise. This may be particularly helpful in identifying motives that begin on beats other than one, a device employed frequently as the work comes to conclusion.

HARMONY:

The harmonic language of *Antiphon* is modern, including quartal harmony, bitonality, and non-functional tertian techniques. The introduction of *Antiphon* begins with a diagonal event, a staggered entrance of the brasses over four beats, arpeggiating a quartal structure with B-flat as a foundation. This figure is presented again at m. 20 over a D-flat in the tuba, and with less space between the entrances.

Antiphon also employs tertian harmonies, although in a non-functional manner. The section in C-flat beginning at m. 23 is prepared with a progression of D-flat major followed by G-flat major, but the progression is then interrupted with an extended C minor chord. Another example is found in the transition from the middle section into the final section, where a key area in G minor abruptly changes mode to G major, and then moves to E major without preparation at m. 60.

Immediately following this transition is an example of bitonal harmony. At m. 60 the repeated motive of the trumpets, cornets and horns in E major is set against a similar motive in C Mixolydian found in the bass voices entering at m. 61. As the motives continue to be layered in the final moments of the work, the bitonality becomes more pervasive. In the last measures of the work, trumpets and cornets move through C-flat and A-flat major, punctuating a sustained D major from the low brass and woodwinds. The work then resolves with a final crescendoing D major chord from all voices.

RHYTHM:
The motivic construction of *Antiphon* leads to the placement of dotted-quarter-and-eighth-note figures beginning on various portion of the measure. These musical ideas, aurally familiar but visually unique, require particular attention to accurate counting of rests, and secure performance of sustained notes tied over barlines.

TIMBRE:
The block scoring nature of *Antiphon* requires very little soloistic independence, although the comparatively thin texture of the imitative section beginning at m. 33 may be somewhat startling. Woodwind and brass sections are treated as distinct scoring blocks throughout the majority of the work. The percussion section serves to emphasize the identifying rhythmic character of each motive from either block, and performs independently from m. 70 through 73 to prepare the final dramatic end to *Antiphon*.

Woodwinds and brasses are finally scored simultaneously, with intertwining and juxtaposed motivic figures, from m. 74 to the end of the work, and arrive at the only rhythmic tutti in the final climactic measure.

Unit 7: Form and Structure

SECTION	MEASURE	EVENT AND SCORING
Introduction	1	Diagonal entrance of all brass
A (declamatory)	2–3	Motive a; trumpets, cornets
	4	Introductory material
	5	Motive b fragment; tutti
	6	Motive c, brass
	7	Motive d; horns
	8	Motive c; clarinets, saxes
	9	Motive e; horns
	10	Motive c; woodwinds
	11	Motive d; cornets
	12–13	Motive e; saxophones, trombones, tuba
	14	Motive f; tuba, euphonium
	15–17	Motive a expanded; saxophones, cornets, tuba
	18	Motive c; flutes, oboes, vibraphone
	19	Motive e; clarinets, low woodwinds, saxophones
	20	Introductory material
	21 -22	Motive b; brass
	23	Motives a and e; woodwinds
	26–29	Motives c and e; horns and woodwinds Repeat back to m. 10
B (imitative)	33	First voice (motives g and h); woodwinds
	34	Second voice
	35	Third voice (one beat early)
	38	Fourth voice (one beat delayed)
	39–42	Motive i; trumpets, celesta, vibraphone
	43–47	Four-voice imitative section; brass
Transition	50–51	Motive i; trumpets, oboes, flutes
	52	Motive f; cornets
	53–54	Motive i (varied); woodwinds
	55–59	Motive f (varied); trombones, cornets, woodwinds
A' (declamatory)	60	Motive d; cornets, trumpets, trombones
	61–63	Motive f; tubas, euphoniums
	64	Motive c; horns
	65	Motive f; trombones, tubas
	66–67	Motive c (fragmented); brass
	68–70	Motive f (fragmented); trombones, cornets, woodwinds

SECTION	MEASURE	EVENT AND SCORING
	71–73	Transition; percussion soli
	74–76	Transition; cascading tutti
	77	Motive f; low brass, low woodwinds
	78–85	Ostinato; timpani
	80–86	Motives c, d, and e (fragmented); clarinets, saxophones
	87	Motive c; woodwinds
	88–89	Motive d; brass
	89–90	Motive D; woodwinds
Coda	90–93	Inversion of introductory figure; brass
	94	Final chord; tutti

Unit 8: Suggested Listening

Gabrieli, Giovanni. *Symphoniae Sacrae*.
Stravinsky, Igor. *Symphonies of Wind Instruments*.
Tull, Fisher:
　　Liturgical Symphony
　　Nonet

Unit 9: Additional References and Resources

Arnold, Dennis. "Giovanni Gabrieli." In *Oxford Studies of Composers, No. 12*. London: Oxford University Press, 1974.
Kenton, Egon. *Life and Work of Giovanni Gabrieli*. Neuhausen-Stuttgart: American Institute of Musicology, 1967.

Contributed by:

Kyle Prescott
Director of Bands
Florida Atlantic University
Boca Raton, Florida

Teacher Resource Guide

Blackwater

Fergal Carroll
(b. 1969)

Unit 1: Composer

Fergal Carroll is well known as a music educator abd composer, and is active as a guest conductor throughout his native Ireland. Born in Tipperary in 1969, he began his musical training on trumpet and piano, and later studied composition with Eric Sweeney at the Waterford Institute of Technology. He received the master of arts in composition from the Royal Northern College of Music in Manchester, England, where he studied with Anthony Gilbert and Adam Gorb. Carroll has been commissioned by ensembles throughout the United Kingdom, writing mostly works for wind band, but also for orchestras, choral ensembles, and chamber ensembles.

His composition style leans toward mostly lyrical works in the Grade 3 to 4 difficulty level, focused on the needs of school ensembles, but his opus is of such quality musical creations that they are performed by ensembles throughout the band world. Among Carroll's other notable works for wind symphony are *Winter Dances* (2002), *Song of Lir* (2004), *Silverwinds* (2006), and *Tipperary Rhapsody* (2008).

Unit 2: Composition

Blackwater was written in 2005 on a commission from Timothy Reynish, who also conducted the premiere on March 1, 2006, leading the Ithaca College Wind Ensemble. Carroll designed the single movement work for bands at the Grade 3 to 3-1/2 difficulty level, and its duration is about six minutes. The compositional style is lyrical and dance-like, and could also be considered somewhat nationalistic, since its inspiration is from the River *Blackwater*, the largest river in southwest Ireland which flows through the counties of Waterford and Cork before emptying into the Celtic sea at Youghal. An old Irish tune, "Cape Clear," is the source for the main theme, written over an original ground, which then becomes the contrasting B material of *Blackwater* in a dance-like section in 5/4 meter.

The themes are mostly diatonic, with easy rhythmic (and infrequent ostinato) background in mostly the mid and low voices, and with interspersed arpeggiated lines in the accompanying woodwinds. In comparison with other wind band works of this level, *Blackwater* is quite "Grundman-esque" in that every instrument has an important, musically satisfying part for a majority of the work, and the doublings of lines are constantly changing in pairings for interesting color aggregations (and insuring that all lines are covered for bands with incomplete instrumentation). It is an excellent work from which to teach lyrical playing, foreground to background balance, fronts and backs of notes and lines, and of course, listening.

Unit 3: Historical Perspective

Fergal Carroll is a young composer with a background as a school band music conductor and educator, and his music is purposeful toward the improvement and development of young musicians. *Blackwater* among a growing list of quality European band music written as not just good teaching music, but fine performance literature, and its folk music character is, as earlier noted, similar to the school band music output of Clare Grundman. Conductors who choose the teaching/performing repertoire of composers such as Robert Sheldon and Steven Reineke will find *Blackwater* and other works by Carroll to be quite suitable and balancing in their teaching. Written in 2005, *Blackwater* fits in with the neo-Romantic style of much band education literature, and its folk-like character makes it pleasing to audiences.

Unit 4: Technical Considerations

Blackwater's technical demands are mainly in the realm of the components of lyrical playing. The rhythmic challenges will be easy for bands that have success on most music at the Grade 3 to 3-1/2 level. The rhythmic motive in the main theme is a measure-to-measure alteration of quarter notes in 3/4 with the implied 6/8 of a dotted quarter followed by a quarter (or tied eighths) plus an eighth note. The tempo is quarter note = 158, and the quickest notes are constant eighths for a maximum of four measures, plus infrequent sixteenth-note diatonic tetrachords employed as anacruses.

Instrumentation should pose few problems for Grade 3-level bands. Bands that do not have any or sufficient oboes, bassoons, or an E-flat sopranino clarinet will find these lines to always be doubled. A full horn section of four is needed: most of the horn lines are creatively doubled, except for mm. 151–163 and mm. 216–219. This is also an excellent work for the horn section, satisfying musically, and full of techniques to teach invaluable components at this level, including *a2* playing and full section harmonies within easily accessible ranges.

There are no parts published for English horn, contra-alto or contrabass clarinet, soprano saxophone, or double bass. Percussion includes timpani (three required) plus four percussion parts, which could be assigned for a section of more than five players, but there is ample time within each of the four percussion parts for comfortable and secure changing of instruments. The mallet parts in the percussion 3 part (glockenspiel, xylophone, and chimes) are medium-easy in level.

Ranges are well within the capabilities of most bands at this difficulty level. Notable are the highest oboe 1 note, D6, which begins an arpeggiated line, and the sopranino clarinet, approached diatonically, with a written C-sharp above the staff. Trumpet 1 extends to a written G just above the staff throughout, and ends on an A one ledger line above the staff. Horn 1 extends only up to a written top-line F.

Tonally, *Blackwater* is centered in G and D minor, with a hint of F major relating to the latter. Warm-up scales and arpeggios in those easy keys could be considered as a way of focusing students' ears in preparation for rehearsal. The harmonic structure infrequently deviates from basic triadic progressions, and those variances occur as intervals of seconds in woodwind descant pedals or pyramidic tone stacking in the brass. Isolation of those sections (opening material in woodwinds, the A-to-B transition material in mm. 134–137, transitional mm. 225–229, and closing material in mm. 253–258) for intonation and security would be good focal points in rehearsing.

Unit 5 Stylistic Considerations

The primary teaching focus of this work is in the aspects of the musical line. Insistence (and persistence) of accurate and appropriate fronts and ends of notes, both as individual players and in ensemble, could easily be successfully taught and that success assimilated for use with other literature. Dynamics and articulation indications are sparse, providing an excellent opportunity for the conductor to teach "reading into the music" the unwritten dynamics needed by good players to shape musical lines, and unwritten articulations to bring out the composer's implied style. The style of the melodic lines and harmonic accompaniments to those lines will not be unfamiliar or difficult for the players, so the teaching focus can be on developing greater musicality.

Unit 6: Musical Elements

MELODY:

The melodies of the two similar themes are mostly diatonic, and are range-wise and ear-wise quite accessible to bands playing at this level, even in the sightreading stage. As common in folk or folk-like music, sequential sub-phrases are compositional elements, and this is an easy work in which to make players aware of and reactive to this technique. Collaborative lines are mostly diatonic with some common arpeggiation in the upper woodwind parts.

HARMONY:

The straightforward harmonic structure within G and D minor will not be difficult for performers. The melodic implication of the related major key (yet resolving in minor) which is common to folk music can be a characteristic listening component to employ while teaching *Blackwater*. The work is mostly homophonic (and that characteristic of folk-influenced music can be brought out in the teaching) with episodes of polyphonic writing in the opening material.

RHYTHM:

As noted Unit 4, the rhythmic demands are minimal and less-than-normal Grade 3 to 3-1/2 rubrics, yielding to higher lyrical playing and listening demands. The general meter is 3/4 with logical 4/4 phrase extensions. The B section of *Blackwater* is a light 5/4 dance-like section with the same rhythms employed in the 3/4 section, making this an ideal teaching tool for bands less comfortable with 5/4 meter, and that meter maintains a three-plus-two pattern throughout. The use of sixteenth notes at a tempo of quarter note = 158 is minimal and limited to only the high- and mid-voiced instruments.

TIMBRE:

The tone colors Carroll uses in *Blackwater* are perhaps one of the primary attractions of this work. There are relatively few tutti sections employed, saved mostly for hallmark moments within formal sections, for transitions, and for the closing material. The composer constantly changes instrumental pairings to bring to the ear a wide palette of musical colors. The percussion scoring is never dominating or ostinato in use and is quite tastefully balanced with the winds throughout. His scoring provides opportune teaching moments for matching tone, balance, and tuning with other instruments with a line.

Unit 7: Form and Structure

The musical form of *Blackwater* is A-B-A (ternary) with binary periods within the sections. It begins with a slow (quarter note = ca. 68) fifteen-bar introduction, and closes with a two-part coda. This straightforward and easily heard architecture can provide the conductor with the opportunity to teach recognition of formal segments and relationships using higher level musical language with young players. For example, once the section has been identified, and appropriate to the learning level in subsequent rehearsals, the conductor may say "Let's begin at the first A section" (key change, m. 16), or "Today, we are going to work on the B section" (mm. 137–186). Other large sections are: return of A (m. 192) with introductory material from mm. 186–191, and the coda (m. 237), identified because of the new material in the woodwinds. An interesting conclusion to using *Blackwater* as a teaching/listening tool would be to ask students to identify the ending tonality—whether the work ends in G major or minor, there is no third of the chord present.

Unit 8: Suggested listening

Blackwater is a wonderful, lyrical yet dance-like work based on an Irish folk tune, and discriminative listening can either be focused on works of similar, lyrical folk-based style, or ethnically in an Irish/Celtic genre. For the former, any of the many versions of folksongs by Percy Grainger would be suitable. These works also provide the opportunity to teach the binary form of folk dances, the form of "Cape Clear," compared with the strophic form of many vocal folksongs.

Similarly, lyrical and dance-based folk music in band arrangement form can be heard in the recorded works of Clare Grundman, such as in any one of his four *American Folk Rhapsodies*, or his *Irish Rhapsody*. For the latter, Celtic music in a band setting in a different timbre than *Blackwater* can be heard in Robert W. Smith's *Ireland: of Legend and Lore*, or in Elliot del Borgo's *Gaelic Rhapsody*. There is also a plethora of original folk music that can be accessed online by students for supplemental study via a search for "Irish folk music."

Unit 9: Additional References and Resources

In addition to the information provided in the score to *Blackwater*,
  additional updated data, including other works by Fergal Carroll may be
  found at: http://www.cmc.ie/composers/composer.cfm?composerID=158
Online access to a recording of *Blackwater*, along with many other works by
  the publisher, may be found at: http://www.maecenasmusic.co.uk/
A good site to begin researching folk music of Ireland may be found at:
  http:// www.contemplator.com/ireland/

Contributed by:

Robert Belser
Conductor and Director of Bands
University of Wyoming
Laramie, Wyoming

Teacher Resource Guide

Colorado Peaks

Dana Wilson
(b. 1946)

Unit 1: Composer

American composer, jazz pianist, conductor, and teacher Dana Wilson continues to leave his mark on wind band music that began with his receipt of the 1987 Sudler International Wind Band Composition Prize and the ABA/Ostwald Prize in 1988 for his work, *Piece of Mind*. Wilson holds a doctorate from the Eastman School of Music and serves as Charles A. Dana Professor of Music at the School of Music at Ithaca College.

Wilson's compositions have been performed throughout the world, with commissions from such diverse organizations as the American Composers Forum, Chicago Chamber Musicians, Detroit Chamber Winds and Strings, and Southeastern College Band Directors Consortium, as well as performances by top artists such as hornist Gail Williams, clarinetist Larry Combs, trumpeters James Thompson and Rex Richardson, and oboist David Weiss. Among his many works for wind band are *Colorado Peaks* (2005), *Concerto for Horn and Wind Ensemble* (1997), *Dance of the New World* (1992), *Day Dreams* (2006), *Evolution* (1999), *Kah!* (1999), *Piece of Mind* (1987), *Sang!* (1994), *Shakata: Singing the World into Existence* (1989), *Shortcut Home* (1998), *To set the darkness echoing* (2005), and *Vortex* (1999).

Unit 2: Composition

Written in 2005, *Colorado Peaks* was commissioned by the St. Vrain Valley Honor Band near Denver, Colorado. Written for large concert band, the piece has recurring thematic material throughout but does not adhere to a set formal structure, just as the peaks of the Rocky Mountains are bound by no set pattern. The work, filled with gentle syncopation, simple chromaticism, and timbral variety, is essentially based on two ideas: a crisp quarter-note pulse representative of hiking and the broad reach of the distant mountains first presented in the horns. There is also a tranquil section intended to be introspective, indicative of all such hiking journeys as metaphors for, and ultimately about, inward growth. The piece is approximately five minutes and thirty seconds in duration. Regarding *Colorado Peaks*, the composer states:

> Because the piece was commissioned by an ensemble in Colorado, I wanted the piece to make some reference to the awe-inspiring Colorado Rockies. The work is not, however, a depiction of their majesty. Instead it suggests a person's relation to them via a rugged and persistent climb.[1]

Unit 3: Historical Perspective

With over fifty mountain peaks reaching above 14,000 feet and over 500 that exceed a 13,000-foot elevation, Colorado is home to the highest peaks in the Rocky Mountains and is the only state that lies entirely above an elevation of 1,000 meters (3,281 feet). Since the gold rush of the nineteenth century, Colorado and the Rocky Mountains have been a fixed icon of the grandeur and splendor of the American spirit. In 1876, Colorado became the thirty-eighth state in the United States of America and still is one of the fastest-growing states in the union today. No doubt people are drawn to the state by its beautiful scenery and rugged mountains. The peaks of Colorado have been source material and inspiration for music, art, literature, and film for years, and will likely continue to be the muse of artists yet to come. For wind band music alone, composers such as Douglas Akey, Brian Balmages, Kristin Kuster, David Maslanka, Ron Nelson, Joseph Schwantner, Robert W. Smith, and James Swearingen have found inspiration in the Rocky Mountains and its peaks.

Unit 4: Technical Considerations

The technical demands of *Colorado Peaks* are well within the expected parameters of the Grade 3 difficulty level. About the demands of the work Dana Wilson states, "The piece is designed to be accessible technically to a band of moderate ability. The instrumental ranges are modest, the rhythms are rather simple and repetitive, and there are few passages requiring extended concentration."[2]

The parts and score to *Colorado Peaks* are free of key signature and use accidentals throughout to accommodate its shifting tonal centers. The piece is not written in a set key, but does remain grounded in specific tonal areas for most of each phrase. Shifts in tonal center along with frequent use of the melodic and intervallic half-step require that performers have mastery of the chromatic language. Performers should not mistake the chromatic nature of the piece as free of tonality, but rather look for and embrace the mixed-modal sounds created through the composer's jazz influence.

The tempo for most of the piece is quarter-note = 126, with a brief tranquil interlude at quarter-note = 96. The sixteenth note is the smallest division of the beat and is most often used as melodic embellishment rather than in extreme virtuosity. One exception is mm. 135–146, where flute, oboe, and clarinet have constant sixteenth-note chromatic figures. This passage presents a great opportunity to reinforce the chromatic scale within the context of a piece of music.

Clarinets are just above the break throughout mm. 135–146, leaving performers free of the idiosyncrasies of the throat tones. Other than fast-moving melodic passages, brass players are sometimes asked to play repeated sixteenth notes, a great opportunity for reinforcing double-tonguing in the context of music. There are five separate percussion parts: timpani and percussion 1–4. The percussion parts require simple melodic skill on keyboard instruments and accurate rhythmic control to the sixteenth-note subdivision on all other parts. Other rhythmic considerations include frequent use of syncopation, ostinato, hemiola, and asymmetrical patterns.

Ranges for the piece are conservative with few exceptions. Trumpets are rarely asked to play above the staff, but do go up to A5 (where C4 is middle C) with an optional B-flat 5 to C6 in the last four measures. Horns rarely play above the staff, but do play up to A5 a few times. Clarinets have moderate ranges, and clarinet 1 is seldom asked to play up to C6 and D6.

Unit 5: Stylistic Considerations

Articulation and ensemble clarity are the keys to a stylistic performance of *Colorado Peaks*. There are a wide variety of written articulations in the piece that provide stylistic contrast throughout. To bring out the subtlety of the piece, performers must create a difference between the accent, tenuto-staccato, accented-staccato, and staccato articulations. One methodology of creating clear articulations within an ensemble is to consider the length of notes in percentage where a full-length tenuto note is 100%, a tenuto-staccato note is 75%, and a *staccato* note is 50%. These percentages create three distinct articulations: notes that touch, notes that are long yet lifted, and notes that are light and lifted (tenuto, tenuto-staccato, and staccato). Once mastery of note length is achieved, performers should only add weight to the accent to create articulations such as the accented-staccato and the accent. Other irregular articulations and stylistic considerations within the piece are the fall and the trombone glissando.

The key to ensemble clarity in *Colorado Peaks* is matching articulation style and prioritizing multiple layers sounding simultaneously. As the melodic material of the piece shifts and layers are added on top of one another, the conductor and performers must consciously prioritize which element of the music the audience should perceive as most important. A successful performance of *Colorado Peaks* will have vivid and clear colors where each voice is easily distinguishable. To think of the piece as a work of art, the clarity of color should be that of the highest quality digital photography as opposed to the painting *Water Lilies* by Claude Monet, with its blended and muted colors that run together.

Unit 6: Musical Elements

MELODY:
After establishing a steady pulse-like feel similar to hiking in the mountains, the horn introduces theme A, a lyrical and elongated melody portraying the broad reach of distant mountains. There are two main thematic ideas in the piece: theme A, found at m. 16 (expansive descending melody filled with consonant skips and chromatic neighboring tones) and theme B, first heard at m. 41 in the saxophones (playful melody with passages of repeated eighth and sixteenth notes). Each melodic theme undergoes change and development throughout the work until the final presentation of theme A in augmentation at the end of the piece.

HARMONY:
Much of the piece is built on a single pulse-like repeated tone in the bass voice. A perfect example is the repeated B-flat in trombone and bassoon at the beginning. These repeated notes give different sections of the piece a tonal center that act as a harmonic home base. The repeated tones usually ascend and descend with each melodic change, and thus give the piece a harmonic architecture similar to the contour of a mountain. In addition to changing tonal areas, the piece contains frequent use of controlled dissonances of major and minor seconds. Performers must be comfortable with hearing and performing these intervals in tune.

RHYTHM:
The rhythms in *Colorado Peaks* are straightforward and aided by a metronomic pulse throughout. Simple syncopations and melodic quarter-note triplets provide the greatest rhythmic complexity to individual performers. For the ensemble, the greatest rhythmic demand is the precise combination of different layers that create a composite rhythm of heightened complexity. The piece sounds far more intricate and difficult than it is for any one performer.

TIMBRE:

The characteristic sound of this piece is born from the mixture of instruments woven together. The uniqueness of instrument combinations provides the audience and performers a colorful timbre pallet. Dana Wilson points out "that virtually all the instrumental families are featured at some point, benefiting the performers and providing constant timbral variety"[3] to the piece. He goes on to state that there are "frequently shifting textures, such that musicians play much of the piece but the thickness of the full band only emerges at key dramatic moments."[4] Even at its most densely-scored moments, there is not one instance in the piece in which every part plays at the same time. Percussion plays a key role in providing a variety of colors to the piece. From a timpani solo paired with a trumpet fanfare to a vibraphone duet with flute in the interlude, the percussion offers unique sounds through the composer's scoring and the performer's implement selection.

Unit 7: Form and Structure

SECTION	MEASURE	EVENT AND SCORING
Introduction	1–15	Tonal centers: B-flat, C; hiking quarter-note pulse in trombone and bassoon with syncopated interjections from saxophones
Theme A	15–40	Tonal centers: C, D, G, D; horn, oboe, and clarinet 1 introduction of theme A followed by trumpet, then a long, chromatic descending variation by upper woodwinds with a partial canon in trombone and bassoon
Theme B	41–55	Tonal centers: D, G, F, E-flat, D-flat, B-flat, E-flat, D-flat, B-flat; saxophone introduction of theme B (a lively melody with repeated tones and sixteenth-note figures); followed by clarinet, then flute, alto saxophone, and clarinet
Transition	56–61	Tonal center: B-flat; transition back to theme A using material similar to the introduction
Theme A	62–66	Tonal center: B-flat; powerful statement of theme A by oboe and upper tessitura in trombone and euphonium

SECTION	MEASURE	EVENT AND SCORING
Interlude	67–84	Tonal centers: G, B-flat, D-flat, C; a reflective and tranquil section with manipulations and fragments of themse A and B; sensitive percussion writing for vibraphone and timpani, along with a lyrical flute solo
Transition	85–92	Tonal centers: D-flat, G, D; steady quarter-note pulse starts again as if a hiking journey is resuming
Theme B	93–120	Tonal centers: D, E, F-sharp, G, D, E, F-sharp, A, D; Development of theme B first introduced by alto and tenor saxophones; development continues through clarinet and alto saxophone exchange, horn with upper woodwind flourishes, trombone with glissandos, alto saxophone, and a thick ensemble conclusion of theme B
Theme A fanfare	121–134	Tonal centers: B-flat, D; timpani introduces a martial style, followed by trumpet duet of theme A in a regal fanfare style; later joined by trombone
Theme A	135–142	Tonal center: A; theme A presented in augmentation by low voices with chromatic sixteenth notes in upper woodwinds
Coda	143–150	Tonal center: final cadence in B-flat; acceleration to the final cadence with syncopation, building intensity, and dense scoring

UNIT 8: SUGGESTED LISTENING

Kuster, Kristin. *Lost Gulch Lookout*. Recording title not available at time of publishing. The University of Georgia Wind Ensemble. John P. Lynch, conductor. Naxos. 2008.

Schwantner, Joseph:

...and the Mountains Rising Nowhere. Composer's Collection: Joseph Schwantner. University of North Texas Wind Symphony. Eugene Migliaro Corporon, conductor. GIA Publications, Inc. CD-657. 2006.

...and the Mountains Rising Nowhere. Live in Osaka. Eastman Wind
Ensemble. Donald Hunsberger, conductor. Sony Records SK47198.
1992.

Wilson, Dana:

Dance of the New World. Wildflowers. University of North Texas Wind
Symphony. Eugene Migliaro Corporon, conductor. Klavier 11079.
1996.

Kah!. Angels and Demons. Drake University Wind Symphony. Robert
Meunier, conductor. Mark Records 3814-MCD 2001.
Piece of Mind. Tokyo Kosei Wind Orchestra. Frederick Fennell, con-
ductor. Kosei Publishing Company KOCD 3569. 1992.

Shakata: Singing the World into Existence. Vortex: Music of Dana Wilson.
Ithaca College Wind Ensemble. Stephen Peterson, conductor. Mark
Records 4327-MCD. 2003.

Shortcut Home. Teaching Music through Performance in Band, Volume 5,
Grades 4 and 5. University of North Texas Wind Symphony. Eugene
Migliaro Corporon, conductor. GIA Publications CD-638. 2005.

Vortex. Time Pieces. University of North Texas Wind Symphony. Eugene
Migliaro Corporon, conductor. Klavier Records 11122. 2001.

Vortex. Vortex: Music of Dana Wilson. Ithaca College Wind Ensemble.
Stephen Peterson, conductor. Mark Records 4327-MCD. 2003.

Unit 9: Additional References and Resources

Ferrari, Lois. "Two Symphonic Wind Ensemble Compositions of Dana
Wilson: *Piece of Mind* and *Shakata: Singing the World into Existence.*"
Doctoral diss., Eastman School of Music, 1995.

Hemberger, Glen J. "Shortcut Home." In *Teaching Music through Performance
in Band, Volume 4.* Richard Miles, ed. Chicago: GIA Publications, Inc.,
2004.

_____. "Piece of Mind." In *Teaching Music through Performance in Band,
Volume 1.* Richard Miles, ed. Chicago: GIA Publications, Inc., 1997.

Wilson, Dana. *Colorado Peaks.* Unpublished, 2005.

Website:
http://www.ithaca.edu/wilson/

Contributed by:

Chester B. Phillips
Doctoral Conducting Associate
Hugh Hodgson School of Music
The University of Georgia
Athens, Georgia

1 Dana Wilson, program notes from *Colorado Peaks* (2005).
2 Dana Wilson, letter from the composer, April 25, 2008.
3 Ibid.
4 Ibid.

Teacher Resource Guide

Dedicatory Overture
James Clifton Williams
(1930–1976)

Unit 1: Composer

James Clifton Williams, known as Jim to his friends, was born in Traskwood, Arkansas on March 26, 1923. He began his musical study in the seventh grade on an old mellophone purchased by his father. In 1936 he moved to Little Rock, Arkansas, where he played in the band and orchestra at Westside Junior High School. He also began experimenting with composition at this time, producing his first work for full orchestra, *Manassas Overture*. While performing in the band and orchestra at Little Rock High School under the direction of L. Bruce Jones, he composed *First Symphony* for orchestra and *Processional* for band, along with many now-forgotten works.

After graduating from high school, James enlisted in the Army Air Corps and was assigned to the 307th Air Force Band in Louisiana. While there he played horn and trombone, and served as drum major. He was later transferred to Ellington Field in Houston, Texas, where he composed *Peace* for the Houston Symphony Orchestra.

In 1945 James enrolled at Louisiana State University, studying composition and horn. He graduated in 1947, married Maxine Friar Bardwell, and moved to Rochester, New Yori and continued his studies at the Eastman School of Music with Bernard Rogers, Howard Hanson, and Arkady Yegudkin. He received the MM in 1948 and entered the doctoral program at the Eastman School of Music, but elected to withdraw from the program when he was offered a faculty position at the University of Texas in Austin.

While at the University of Texas (1949–1966), Williams continued to compose significant repertoire for a variety of ensembles and won the Texas

Composer's Contest with *Legend* for orchestra in 1950. After receiving this honor Williams decided that he needed a more distinguished-sounding name and began calling himself Clifton Williams. Williams received his first national recognition in 1956–57, when he won back-to-back Ostwald Awards for composition from the American Bandmasters Association with *Fanfare and Allegro* and *Symphonic Suite*, both of which have been included in previous volumes of *Teaching Music through Performance in Band*. While at the University of Texas, Williams mentored many student composers, including W. Francis McBeth and John Barnes Chance.

In 1966 Williams became chair of the theory and composition department at the University of Miami. He served there until his death from cancer on February 12, 1976.

Unit 2: Composition

Dedicatory Overture was commissioned in 1963 by the Epsilon Upsilon Chapter of Phi Mu Alpha Sinfonia for the dedication of the new music building at the University of Evansville in Indiana. It is a single movement work, of moderate difficulty, with contrasting sections, about eight minutes in length. It is one of Williams's thirty-one published band works and is among those most frequently performed. The middle hymn-like section of the work is based on the university's alma mater, known today as the "Hymn to Evansville" or the "University Hymn." It was composed in 1926 by Mary Ellen McClure, a Class of 1925 graduate, with words by McClure and Evaline Tureck. The song was the second-place winner in a school music contest, but was much more popular than the first-place winner, and became the school song by default.

Dedicatory Overture is preceded by *The Sinfonians* (1960), *Variation Overture* (1961), *Castle Gap*, and *Trilogy* (1962) and followed by *Air Force Band of the West* and *March Lamar* (1964), *Border Festival, The Ramparts*, and *The Strategic Air Command* (1965).

Unit 3: Historical Perspective

In the early 1960s a significant number of fine composers contributed compositions that remain frequently performed by school bands and are recognized as outstanding repertoire. Some of these works include:

The Leaves are Falling	Warren Benson
Incantation and Dance	John Barnes Chance
Variations on a Korean Folk Song	John Barnes Chance
Emblems	Aaron Copland
Sinfonietta for Concert Band	Ingolf Dahl
Scenes from the Louvre	Norman Dello Joio
Variants on a Mediaeval Tune	Norman Dello Joio
Third Suite	Robert E. Jager

Night Soliloquy	Kent Kennan
Elegy for a Young American	Ronald Lo Presti
Liturgical Music for Band	Martin Mailman
Chant and Jubilo	W. Francis McBeth
Prelude and Fugue	Vaclav Nelhybel
Trittico	Vaclav Nelhybel
Bagatelles for Band	Vincent Persichetti

Clifton Williams considered the band to be virgin territory with an enormous audience and set about working to elevate the quality and status of the band and its repertoire.

Colonel Arnold D. Gabriel states: "The many works of Clifton Williams represent a significant contribution to music for wind and percussion ensembles and the symphonic band repertoire. Mr. Williams's greatest contribution in the band world was not a specific piece of music but rather the great quantity of his music that set the standard for other composers."[1]

Unit 4: Technical Considerations

Dedicatory Overture is published with a transposed full score by Hal Leonard Publishing. The condensed score is now out of print. Tonal centers are shown with accidentals rather than key signatures in both score and parts. The composition uses an extended instrumentation that includes parts for English horn, two oboes, two bassoons, E-flat soprano, contra-alto, and contrabass clarinets, a split euphonium part, and string bass. The work is, however, playable by ensembles without full instrumentation, as the instruments that are typically problematic are doubled in parts more commonly found. There are four horn parts, with the third and forth in unison except for about a dozen notes. There is a brief, four-measure horn solo, doubled in the English horn. Trumpets and trombones require straight mutes. Percussion instruments include bells, tympani, snare drum, bass drum, crash cymbals, and suspended cymbal.

Ranges are not problematic for medium-level ensembles. Exceptions may include trumpet 1 (written A and B above the staff), trombone 1 and euphonium (A above the staff), trombone 3 (E-flat above the staff), and tuba (top-line A).

Time signatures include 4/4, 2/2, 3/2, and 7/4 (written as alternating measures of 4/4 and 3/4). There are frequent tempo changes (twelve) with tempos varying from quarter note = 80 to 112. The work is not rhythmically difficult, though there are syncopated entrances and several places that reverse the traditional emphasis in a 4/4 measure (1**23**4 rather than **1**2**3**4).

While the work is tonal, there are sections and chords borrowed from other key and tonal centers. This tendency toward bitonality sometimes provides surprising and interesting harmonies and chord progressions.

Unit 5: Stylistic Considerations

The composition calls for separated as well as lyrical styles. The style markings in the score include four articulations: staccatissimo ('), accent (>), staccato (.), and tenuto (–), as well as the terms *quasi hymn, poco animando, Cantabile,* and *Maestoso.* There is a fair amount of ambiguity in the intended style of some sections which leads to a variety of interpretive possibilities. For example, the opening Moderato measures can be interpreted as legato with breath marks or as fanfare-like with a more separated style (recommended). Similarly, repeated accented half notes may be interpreted as connected or slightly separated. These same concerns apply again from rehearsal letters F to I. It is important to remember that once an interpretation has been chosen, similar figures should be played in a similar style whenever they appear, regardless of instrumentation. The addition of more style markings such as those given above as well as legato and marcato would be helpful to the ensemble.

The middle section of the composition, from rehearsal letters D to E, is the above-mentioned "University Hymn." It is unusual in that it is built on three-measure phrases. Again, Williams's intent is ambiguous. We do not know if he intends the phrases to elide without breaks, make use of rhythmic breaths (on beat 4 or the *and* of beat 4), add time for breaths, or let the winds breathe while the timpani rolls through to beat 1. It may be helpful to consider the words of the original hymn:

> School of our fathers, known of old,
> Our Alma Mater we revere,
> We give thee loyalty untold,
> We love thee more and more each year;
> And when sweet memories of thee return
> Of lessons learned of friendships made,
> Thy spirit in our heart doth burn;
> We face the future unafraid.

Williams uses the original hymn but modifies the end of each phrase by adding suspensions (rehearsal letter D: mm. 3, 9, 12, 21, and 24), passing tones (rehearsal letter D: mm. 6 and 18), and a crescendo (rehearsal letter D: m. 21). Since this section is marked *Andante, quasi-hymn,* how the hymn would be sung should be a consideration in determining a musical interpretation. Remaining portions of the work provide adequate stylistic information.

Unit 6: Musical Elements

Aside from tone and intonation, balance and style are the two most important musical elements impacting the performance of *Dedicatory Overture*.

BALANCE:
Careful attention should be paid to the teaching and application of McBeth-style pyramidal balance throughout the work. Balance between contrasting melody, ostinato patterns, and counterpoint must allow all parts to be heard and none covered. Careful attention to balancing the many dissonances (major and minor seconds) in the work will appropriately thicken the sound of the ensemble. Be careful that both notes of these intervals are heard equally. The concept of matching the presence of the notes accounts for more than just loudness. With the exception of the hymn, the melodies are full of thirds, fourths, fifths, and sevenths. It is critical that students match the presence of the higher and lower notes in the larger intervals.

In the hymn, the moving notes must be heard against the held notes. Williams uses ample part doubling throughout the work. Even so, careful attention should be afforded the relative timbres of the different instruments. Students should be well aware of the other instruments with which they play and know which timbre should be dominant in any passage.

STYLE:
Refer to the comments in Unit 5: Stylistic Considerations. It is imperative that students match style and inflection, that high and low voices, woodwinds and brass, play the same things in precisely the same ways.

Unit 7: Form and Structure

SECTION	MEASURE	EVENT AND SCORING
A	1–19	Introduction; fanfare theme in trumpet, trombone and euphonium, with percussion interludes and tutti chords; D minor and B-flat major; alternating tempi (*Moderato, più mosso*)
B	20–39	Fanfare theme; G minor and C major; motivic counterpoint; transition using fanfare theme fragments; ritard
D	40–63	Hymn; full band in three-measure phrases; F major; alternating tempi (*Andante, poco animando, a tempo*)
E	64–75	Transition based on hymn in four-measure phrases; first woodwinds, then full band

SECTION	MEASURE	EVENT AND SCORING
F, G	76–99	2/2; percussion introduction; theme 2 based on intervals in fanfare theme; fugal entrances on tonic (B-flat), then on dominant (F)
G	100–107	Motivic development material based on intervals from counterpoint at rehearsal letter B
H	108–117	Theme 2; F major; woodwind ostinato
	118–125	Motivic development material based on intervals from counterpoint at rehearsal letter B
I	126–143	Fanfare theme; augmented in upper woodwinds (G minor) with motivic development material as accompaniment
J, K	144–165	Transition using motivic development material. In D-flat, then in E-flat, then G; *molto rallentando* to *Adagio* in 3/2
L	166–175	*Allegretto* in 7/4; transparent scoring; G-major melody in upper voices over C pedal in bass voices
M, N	176–196	*Maestoso;* fanfare theme in F minor over D-flat pedal with percussion interjections; woodwind chords; *rallentando* and cadences in F major

Unit 8: Suggested Listening

Giannini, Vittorio. *Dedication Overture*.
McBeth, W. Francis:
    Chant and Jubilo
    Divergents
Williams, James Clifton:
    Caccia and Chorale
    Fanfare and Allegro
    The Sinfonians
    Symphonic Suite

Unit 9: Additional References and Resources

Daniel, Joe R. "The Band Works of James Clifton Williams." PhD diss., University of Southern Mississippi, 1981.

Kerr, Stephen P. "A Brief Biography of James Clifton Williams." *Journal of Band Research* 34 (Fall, 1998): 25–37.

Kopetz, Barry. "Clifton Williams' *Dedicatory Overture*." *The Instrumentalist* 46 (January 1992): 24–37.

Lisk, Edward S. *Intangibles of Musical Performance*. Fort Lauderdale, FL: Meredith Music Publications, 1996.

McBeth, W. Francis. *Effective Performance of Band Music*. San Antonio, TX: Southern Music, 1972.

Smith, Norman E. *Program Notes for Band*. Chicago: GIA Publications, 2000.

VanderCook, H. A. *Expression in Music*. Miami: Rubank, 1942.

Wojcik, John. "Classic Works by Clifton Williams, from *Arioso* to *The Ramparts*." *The Instrumentalist* 55 (November 2000): 32–36.

_____. "Music for Wind Band by James Clifton Williams: an Annotated List." DMA diss., University of Kansas, 1993.

Contributed by:

Wayne F. Dorothy
Director of Bands and Professor of Music
Hardin-Simmons University
Abilene, Texas

---

1 Kerr, Stephen P. "A Brief Biography of James Clifton Williams." *Journal of Band Research* 34 (Fall 1998): 25–37.

Teacher Resource Guide

Different Voices

Rick Kirby
(b. 1945)

Unit 1: Composer

Rick Kirby was born in Boston, Massachusetts and was educated in the New England area. After arriving in Wisconsin in 1974 he taught in several high schools and universities, finally heading the distinguished band program at Waukesha West High School. He retired from public school teaching in 2001 to pursue a full-time career as a composer and arranger.

Kirby has arranged or composed for many marching bands, including groups from Wisconsin, Illinois, Kansas, Ohio, Arizona, and California. He is presently the staff arranger for the award-winning Sound of Sun Prairie Marching Band and the past Wisconsin State Champion Waukesha West High School Marching Band. Kirby has also been involved in many commissioning projects, including writing compositions for concert bands, jazz ensembles, choirs, and other instrumental ensembles.

In the spring of 2004 Kirby assumed leadership of the Waukesha Area Symphonic Band and is the director of the Carroll University Jazz Ensemble. He is also the associate conductor of the Youth Wind Orchestra of Wisconsin.

Rick Kirby is the 2002 recipient of the Wisconsin Music Educators Association's Distinguished Service Award. This award is given to a music educator for lifelong meritorious service, excellence, and dedication to music education in Wisconsin.

Unit 2: Composition

Different Voices was commissioned by the Central Middle School Band in Waukesha, Wisconsin. It is scored for modern American wind band and is published by Boosey and Hawkes as part of the Windependence Repertoire Essentials Series. The difficulty as assigned by the publisher is listed as Apprentice Level—Advanced. The work is constructed in three movements titled: "The Spoken (Dialogues)," "Whispers," and "The Voices of Song." Approximate length of the work is nine minutes twenty seconds.

The composer provides the following program note in the score:

> Each movement of this composition represents several of the different manners in which the human voice produces sound and becomes a vehicle of communication—therefore the title *Different Voices*. Except for the whispering in the second movement, the piece does not attempt to simulate the actual sound of the human voice but rather attempts to depict the spirit by which that sound is produced. The first movement entitled "The Spoken (Dialogues)," portrays a dialogue between several groups represented by the different sections of the band. The second movement, "Whispers," begins very quietly, swells to a climactic level and concludes with the peacefulness of the beginning. "Voices of Song," the final movement, is simply a joyous celebration of the ability of the world's oldest musical instrument, the human voice, to sing.

Unit 3: Historical Perspective

Ideas for discussion with students could largely center on the source material for the work: *The human voice as a means of expression*. Students could investigate the history of the voice in song, possibly tracing the development of the human voice in art and worship from early Greece through the Medieval period, to the rise of Renaissance choral music, art song, etc.

In what ways does modern culture celebrate the human voice as a means of artistic expression? Does the hit TV show *American Idol* say anything about the power of the human voice in our society?

In what ways does the composer represent the human voice in this work? Be sure to point out the obvious: The dialogue between sections in movement 1. The contemporary technique used in movement 2 with the "whispering whispers," the beautiful singing melody in movement 2 and the joyful and triumphant choral motif in the beginning of movement 3. But it might be more interesting to ask the students what *they* hear. Students might find interactions or metaphors within the music that the composer did not intend. It is always amazing to hear what students come up with when asked to generate relationships between abstract sound and the world around them.

Unit 4: Technical Considerations

This work is a much-welcomed addition to the young band repertoire. Historically, music for young band has offered challenges that fit students' needs but lack artistic merit. *Different Voices* offers band directors well-needed challenges for their students, but within the framework of an artistic and meaningful experience.

It is scored for a typical young band with single oboe, bassoon, horn, and alto sax parts. It also only requires two trombone parts and a full but basic percussion set-up. An element of interest in this piece is the integral piano part. The piano needs are not extreme, but require a confident and musically sensitive player. There is an extended clarinet solo. Trumpet 1 goes up to an A above the staff. This high trumpet part could be edited down an octave if necessary, because that voice is doubled in flute and clarinet.

Rhythmically this piece is well within the reach of good young bands. There is a section in movement 1 that uses an alternation between 5/8 and 7/8 meters.

What gives this piece its artistic flavor is the harmonic language employed by the composer. More than any other element in the work, this will challenge the young band for which it is intended. The chords used will require the director to isolate several passages to insure that students are on the correct partials in the brass.

Unit 5: Stylistic Considerations

I. The Spoken (Dialogues)

Careful attention to articulation is the overriding skill needed for mastery in this movement. The opening trumpet fanfare and subsequent iterations of this idea need to be marcato and separated. The contrast between this section and the smooth, flowing, melodic ideas of the *Vivo* should be well highlighted. Achieving a true soft dynamic in the trumpets with proper lightness and separation at m. 15 will be a challenge. Careful attention to articulation and the differences between markings at m. 40 are crucial to achieving the dancing or lilting effect. In addition to articulation, this movement has dynamic contrast as an element of stylistic concern. Achieving true contrast is always difficult. The decrescendo in the final twelve bars from *ff* to *ppp* is a great exercise in long-term, controlled dynamic change.

II. Whispers

This movement will challenge students to play with good waltz style while maintaining a smooth legato texture. Achieving a Satie-influenced dance feel will require students to place appropriate weight on downbeats without interrupting the natural flow of the lyrical line.

III. The Voices of Song

As with movement 1, articulation plays a crucial role in achieving an authentic performance. Bands will tend to not play with enough separation on the fanfare motives at the beginning of the movement, as well as the more rustic melodic material introduced at m. 26. Achieving a correct balance between melody and accompaniment will give students much to think about in this movement. Solid homophonic texture allows directors to discuss balance and educate students about the proper dynamic editing that all good bands know how to do.

Unit 6: Musical Elements

MELODY:

The first movement begins with the following melodic idea in the trumpets:

FIGURE 1. Trumpet in B-flat

This idea is repeated by trombone 1. It is developed later in the movement.

In contrast to this fanfare idea, we are then presented with the following legato passage in the clarinets, horns and piano:

FIGURE 2. Clarinet 1 in B-flat

The following melody is introduced after the beautiful piano soliloquy at the beginning of movement 2:

FIGURE 3. Clarinet 1 in B-flat

This melody is subsequently restated by woodwind choir.

The third and final movement contains joyous fanfare motives at the beginning followed by the more folk-like, or rustic melody in the trumpet and piccolo:

FIGURE 4. Trumpet 1 in B-flat

HARMONY:
Different Voices declares its harmonic language very early. We know right away that this is not your usual piece for young band. After the fanfare figures in mm. 1–4 in movement 1, we get a taste of the true harmonic flavor that is to be used throughout the rest of the work. Mm. 5–6 reveal how ninth chords and tritones will be used throughout the rest of the piece. The use of these tones, as well as modal mixture throughout, give the listener a unique experience when compared to most music written for young band.

RHYTHM:
As stated earlier in Unit 5, rhythm is not one of the more challenging aspects of this piece. But the following passage represents a sequence of events in movement 1 that could be used to teach mixed meter in 5/8 and 7/8:

FIGURE 5. Piccolo

TIMBRE:

Study of movement 1 yields the most opportunities to teach tone color and texture. Listen to how the composer creates a dialogue between brass and woodwinds at the beginning. The combination of clarinet, horn, and piano at m. 9 creates a much different timbre compared with the previous dichotomy of brass versus woodwinds. The interplay in the dance/chatter motive at m. 40 again provides a stark contrast between brass and woodwinds. These two sound groups are combined at m. 60 to create an exciting climax to the movement.

Unit 7: Form and Structure

SECTION	MEASURE	EVENT AND SCORING
I. "The Spoken (Dialogues)"		
A	1–14	Brass fanfare followed by woodwind response; trumpet ambiguity leads to next section
B	15–40	Trumpet ostinato with mixed lyrical melody; flowing melodic statement in brass from mm. 32–40
C	40–89	Chatter/dance motive is traded between woodwinds and brass; repeat of melodic statement from m. 32 occurs in m. 56; chatter slowly dies away to nothing
II. "Whispers"		
Intro	1–12	"Whispering whispers" technique in mm. 1–2; piano soliloquy in mm. 3–12
A	12–48	Clarinet solo with piano accompaniment mm. 17–25; melody repeated in flutes, oboe, and clarinets; secondary melody presented by flutes, oboes, and trumpets
B	49–64	New melody introduced fully scored in trumpets, horns, flutes, oboe, and clarinets
Coda	65–87	Return of introductory material and new melody in clarinet reminiscent of melodic ideas from the movement
III. "The Voices of Song"		
A	1–21	Joyous fanfare motives in brass with driving percussion and low brass accompaniment
B	22–44	Homophonic texture with rustic/folk melody in piccolo and muted trumpet

SECTION	MEASURE	EVENT AND SCORING
C	45–66	Tutti choral motives followed by a return of fanfare rhythmic texture to conclusion

Unit 8: Suggested Listening

Satie, Erik. *3 Gymnopedies*. 1888.

Unit 9: Additional References and Resources

Kirby, Rick:
> *The Water Is Wide*. Daehn Publications.
> *Tales of a Minstrel Boy*. Daehn Publications.
> *Garden of the Gods*. Daehn Publications.
> *Suncrest—A Concert March*. Daehn Publications.

Contributed by:

Christopher Bianco
Director of Bands
Western Washington University
Bellingham, Washington

Assisted by:

Brad Hendry
Director of Bands
Sedro Wooley High School
Sedro Wooley, Washington

Teacher Resource Guide

DreamCircus

Rob Deemer
(b. 1970)

Unit 1: Composer

Rob Deemer, born in DeKalb, Illinois, is currently serving as chair of the composition department and assistant professor of composition at the State University of New York at Fredonia. He holds the doctor of musical arts degree in composition from the University of Texas, the master of music in composition and a performer's certificate in conducting from Northern Illinois University, as well as an Advanced Certificate in Scoring for Film and Television from the University of Southern California. His teachers have included Dan Welcher, Donald Grantham, Jan Bach, and Timothy Blickhan. He has participated in individual master classes or workshops with John Corigliano, William Bolcom, George Crumb, Elmer Bernstein, David Raksin, Jerry Goldsmith, Melinda Wagner, Christopher Theofinidis, and Christopher Young.

Such ensembles as the Chicago Trombone Quartet, the Millar Brass Ensemble, the Tosca String Quartet, the MacArthur String Quartet, the Austin Civic Orchestra, the Kishwaukee Symphony, the University of Texas Symphony Orchestra and New Music Ensemble, the Northern Illinois University Wind Ensemble, and the Roosevelt University Wind Ensemble and New Century Ensemble have performed his works. In addition to his work in concert music, Deemer has extensive experience as a composer for film, theatre, and dance, with over thirty films and documentaries to his credit. As a conductor of concert works, Deemer has led the Northern Illinois University Philharmonic and Wind Ensemble, the Rock Valley College Orchestra, and most recently served as Assistant Director of the University of Texas New

Music Ensemble. Frequently conducting contemporary music, he has recently given world premiere performances of works by Per Bloland, David Wolff, and Anthony Burgess, as well as conducting works by Melinda Wagner, Christopher Theofanidis, David Froom, and Carter Pann.

Unit 2: Composition

DreamCircus was composed in 2000 on a commission from the University Band at the University of Northern Illinois, Lawrence Stoffel, conductor. The work is programmatic, representing "…a musical rendition of a child's dreams…"[1] The two primary kinds of music in the piece may then be related to the title: the slower, more expressive music can be seen to represent the dreamer falling into and out of sleep, while the faster, march-like music reflects the child's experiences, perceptions, and memories a of circus and the kind of music one might hear there. *DreamCircus* was a finalist in the first Frank Ticheli Composition Contest sponsored by Manhattan Beach Music, and is approximately four minutes and forty-five seconds in duration. The work is published by C. Alan Publications, Inc.

Unit 3: Historical Perspective

The composer's note given above is a critical piece of information when placing *DreamCircus* in a historical and stylistic context. The connection to circus music is strengthened by the use of a quotation from the circus march *Entry of the Gladiators* (also known as *Thunder and Blazes*) by Julius Fucik in the second section of the work. The quotation is not literal, much in the way our memories are not completely reliable on awakening, or, in the words of the composer, "…it's obviously an obscured quotation in the Ives tradition…"[2] These primary associations, circus music, marches, and Charles Ives, suggest many possible avenues of exploration for the conductor/teacher and her students.

Unit 4: Technical Considerations

In the author's opinion, *DreamCircus* is a Grade 3 work; with only a few exceptions the ranges, rhythms, meters, and technical demands lie well within this classification. The two main key centers of the work are F and B-flat major. These are not difficult keys, although the B sections in B-flat can be highly chromatic at times. Four time signatures are employed, all duple meters: 2/4, 3/4, 4/4, and 5/4. The meters change enough to keep the music from being predictable, but should not present any problems.

    The upper woodwinds (piccolo, flutes, oboes, and B-flat clarinets) carry almost all of the technically difficult music, which is evenly divided between disjunct and chromatic passagework. There are brief, but very exposed, solos for flute, oboe, clarinet, and horn in the A sections of the piece. Oboe in particular has three short solos, something not often seen in Grade 3 works.

Among the brass, only trumpet 1 has music that exceeds Grade 3 difficulty, and this is limited to a very brief passage in mm. 43–48.

As much of the work is in the style of a march, albeit a "wacky" one (the composer's direction in the score at m. 19), many instruments assume their traditional roles in that genre: tubas, bassoons, bass clarinet, and baritone saxophone often play downbeats; horns, occasionally joined by alto and tenor saxophones, play upbeats; euphonium, sometimes in conjunction with tenor saxophone or trombone, plays a line which could be described as a countermelody. Over two dozen percussion instruments are called for in the score, some of which are for a very specific effect, such as a police whistle, duck call, antique car horn, alarm clock, siren whistle, and "dog's squeaky toy"; most of these devices further reinforce the connection to the circus.

Unit 5: Stylistic Considerations

As mentioned previously, there are two primary moods in *DreamCircus*, and the music reflects these in a number of ways, especially in regard to form, tempo, and articulation. Conductors wishing to challenge their ensemble expressively will be gratified by the A music, while the B sections present the challenges of articulation and tonal control at higher dynamic levels. *DreamCircus* should not present insurmountable difficulties in the individual parts, but rather in the Ivesian spirit of the piece, which manifests itself in collage and will require some explanation and demonstration for ensembles not accustomed to this kind of musical dialectic.

Unit 6: Musical Elements

MELODY:
The A music in *DreamCircus* is overwhelmingly diatonic, while the B music is both more disjunct (B1) and chromatic (B2). Because the piece is cast in familiar keys, the only specialized technique required is a firm grasp of the chromatic scale, which most ensembles work on in a systematic way.

HARMONY:
As with the melodic writing, the A music is also very diatonic. Even though the music is layered, the effect is one of calm, perhaps even serenity, because the music unfolds gently over a tonic pedal. The B section is more linear, and the harmonies resemble those of a march, which is what this section depicts. The most frequent accidental—besides the chromaticism present—is the raised fourth scale degree, which is quite common in tonal music.

RHYTHM:
Rhythms fall easily under the Grade 3 umbrella with two possible exceptions: (1) sixteenth-note triplets appear once in mm. 18, 30, and 40; and (2) the "Scotch snap" (a sixteenth note followed by a dotted eighth note) appears in

the trumpet 1 passage mentioned previously (mm. 43–45). There are occasional meter changes in *DreamCircus*, in the author's view, mostly to avoid square and predictable phrasing, but this should not be difficult, even for young ensembles.

TIMBRE:

DreamCircus does not rely on a preponderance of tutti scoring, and this is deliberate on the part of the composer to introduce younger players to different textures.[3] Indeed, the work is scored creatively for less experienced players; the most exposed solos are not technically difficult, the difficult music is given to the most agile instruments, instrument groups change with thematic material in the B section, and percussionists are integrally involved. In all, the orchestration is both original and admirable.

Unit 7: Form and Structure

DreamCircus has two main sections which both return, in very abbreviated form, at the end of the piece; thus the form of the overall work is ABA'B'. The phrase structure, while easy to discern, is not predictable. More than once the symmetry of phrases is disturbed when Deemer extends the consequent phrase, thus performers and listeners are kept somewhat off balance.

SECTION	MEASURE	EVENT AND SCORING	
A	1–3	Theme A1	Horn, clarinet, flute solos
	4–13	A1: 4 + (4 + 2)	Developed in canon with layered diatonic harmony
	14–18	A1	Oboe solo; accompanied by clarinet and flute
B	19–22	Introduction to "Wacky March"; alternation of 3/4 and 4/4 create interest and forward motion through metric tension	
	23–32	B1: 4 + (4 + 2)	B1 in clarinets
	33–42	B1: 4 + (4 + 2)	B1 repeated in upper woodwinds; prominent countermelody in tenor saxophone, trombone, and euphonium
	43–55	Quote from *Entry of the Gladiators* appears (B2), and is juxtaposed with B1: (5 + 4) + 4	
	56–64	Motive from B1 developed: (4 + 4)	
	64–74	B2 augmented appears alone, then with B1: 4 + (4 + 3)	

Section	Measure	Event and Scoring
	75–86	B1 in close canon: (4 + 4) + 4
	87–95	B1 augmented in solo oboe, taken over by woodwinds: (5 + 4)
A'	96–104	A1 returns in canon: (5 + 4)
	105–107	Flute, clarinet, glockenspiel, and crotales present head motive of A1 in canon
B'	108–111	Codetta: augmented version of B2 returns; *ritardando al fine* until the dreamer is awakened by an alarm clock in the final measure

Unit 8: Suggested Listening

DreamCircus has been recorded as part of a two-disc set of "Winners and Finalists from the first Frank Ticheli Composition Contest" on the Mark label. The citation is given below in Unit 9. The composer's website, also given below, has descriptions and sound files of his other compositions, and these are of great value in becoming familiar with his work. In addition, several other works for band, in this author's view, are closely allied to *DreamCircus* in spirit and intent; some of these pieces could even be programmed on the same concert:

> Broege, Timothy. Several works, but most relevant might be *Three Pieces for American Band, Set No. 2*, in which original music is cast in borrowed stylistic contexts as varied as Jazz and Renaissance music, then juxtaposed, as in *DreamCircus*. This might lead to an exploration of originality and how composers rely, consciously or not, on their influences in the compositional process.
>
> Ives, Charles. *Country Band March*. A dizzying collage employing over a dozen march and patriotic tunes. The association here is the march form, and how Ives assaults the listener with familiar music, often in a way that is intended to be comic, or experienced in a less-than-perfect way.
>
> Tubb, Monte. *Intermezzo*. A work about a young dancer dreaming that alternates hazy, impressionistic music with darker, more ominous music. Among the connections to *DreamCircus* is the exploration of dream states and the sense of the unreal found in them.

Unit 9: Additional References and Resources

http://www.robdeemer.com
http://www.manhattanbeachmusic.com

Contributed by:

Gary A. Speck
Professor of Conducting
Director of Concert Bands
Miami University
Oxford, OH

1 Liner notes from Mark Masters Recording, 7290-MCD.
2 Email correspondence between Rob Deemer and Gary Speck, May 27, 2008.
3 Ibid.

Teacher Resource Guide

Ferne Weite
ein Landschaftsbild

Rolf Rudin
(b. 1961)

Unit 1: Composer

Rolf Rudin was born in the Bavarian metropolis of Frankfurt am Main, Germany, on December 9, 1961. His composition teachers have included Hans Ulrich Engelmann at the Frankfurt Academy of Music and Bertold Hummel at the Bavarian State Conservatory of Music, Würzburd. He was awarded a study scholarship by the German Students' Foundation and, in 1990–1991, studied for half a year at the Cité Internationale des Arts, Paris on a scholarship from the Bavarian Ministry of Culture. Upon graduation from the Frankfurt Academy in composition (1991) and conducting (1992), Rudin served on the music theory faculty there from 1993 to 2001. He has since made his home with his wife Brigitte in nearby Erlensee, from which he operates his publishing firm, Edition Flor. Rudin is widely sought as a guest composer, lecturer, and conductor throughout Europe and around the world. Recent engagements include lectures on German music theory pedagogy at the Eastman School of Music in 2006. His many works for chamber ensemble, choir, orchestra, and wind band have been recorded and performed live for broadcasts in Germany, Austria, Switzerland, the Netherlands, Italy, Australia, Ireland, and the United States.

Unit 2: Composition

Ferne Weite was completed in 2005 on a commission from the Vorspessart Band Association. Vorspessart, the northernmost area in the Aschaffenburg district at the gates of the Rhine-Main region, is among the most densely-wooded territories in Germany. The full title of the work, *Far Distance: A*

Landscape View (or Portrait), suggests a pastoral depiction of scenes from the composer's own experience. Like Rudin's earlier work, *Der Traum des Oenghus*, the piece is highly romantic in its thematic interplay and contrast, and in its variety of texture. A simple source motive is developed across two large sections, slow then fast, in the manner of a French overture, with contemporary rhythmic and harmonic structures and a cyclical return to opening materials at the climax of the work. The single movement is performed in about eight minutes.

Unit 3: Historical Perspective

This work comes as part of an established wave of European music for wind band that began to make its way to American bands and conductors in the 1980s. The Vorspessart Band Association, founded by a dozen wind orchestras in 1953, now boasts over forty member ensembles comprised of nearly 2,000 musicians. Commissions for new art music for band from consortia in the United States and abroad have yielded a new repertoire of increasing breadth and depth of quality.

The romantic nature of the piece parallels that of recent programmatic works by Jan Van der Roost, Donald Grantham, and David Gillingham. Rudin's evocation of pastoral images is similar in approach to recent efforts by David Maslanka and Frank Ticheli. The development of a complete, multi-faceted, formal structure from a single motivic germ dates to the earliest masterworks for wind band, including the *Suite in E-flat* of Gustav Holst.

Unit 4: Technical Considerations

Scoring is crafted toward effective performance by a fairly small ensemble of as few as twenty-one winds and four percussion. The minimum forces required without additional rescoring are two flutes, three B-flat clarinets, two alto saxophones, one tenor saxophone, three trumpets, two cornets or flügelhorns, two horns, two trombones, two baritones, two tubas, three percussion, and timpani. Additional parts for oboe, E-flat clarinet, bass clarinet, bassoon, baritone saxophone, and third parts for horn and trombone are scored in order to give the full band ample opportunity to perform the work well. A fourth percussionist provides ease in transitions between instruments. No exotic or non-standard instruments are required for the percussion battery, though the list is varied. Wind parts are entirely idiomatic, requiring no extended ranges or techniques.

Although titles, instrument names, and stylistic indications on the parts are in German, the conductor's score provides an adequate, though not complete, lexicon for effective instruction across cultural lines.

Unit 5: Stylistic Considerations

Fullness of tone and connectedness of line are of primary importance to the performance of this piece. Variations of registration, texture, and articulation require that players consider different approaches to tone color as their role and their line change contextually. Blend of color and line must be maintained at all times within individual sections so that balance may be achieved among instrument groups toward an effective and clearly discernable ensemble interpretation.

Unit 6: Musical Elements

MELODY:

The melodic elements of the work are developed from the head motive of the primary theme, introduced in mm. 1–2:

FIGURE 1. Mm. 1–2

The scoring of the figure and the antiphonal interplay it bears to the accompaniment allow for players to develop a sense of playing across the barline and phrasing completely to the release point. The first alteration of the motive comes in the third phrase of the theme, where it is inverted (mm. 5–6):

FIGURE 2. Mm. 5–6

The contrasting articulations of the two versions may be used to encourage students to develop a legato sound that matches the fullness and duration of tone when slurring.

The syncopated nature of the Allegro section of the work is characterized by the alteration of the head motive to establish theme A in mm. 66–69:

FIGURE 3. Mm. 66–69

A more lyric B theme, first presented in mm. 98–105, is derived from an inversion of head motive A, recalling the consequent phrase of the original theme from the beginning of the work:

FIGURE 4. Mm. 98–105

In nearly all cases, players are required to be aware of accompaniment and contrapuntal secondary figures in order to develop a sense of transparency, allowing lines to flow and parts to interact with one another. There are a number of chromatically altered passages to master, though the majority of melodic, sequenced, and arpeggiated figures are diatonic to E-flat major and C minor.

HARMONY:
Rudin generates harmonic interest throughout the work by framing melodic themes and motives with a number of related progressions. In many cases, players are challenged to balance and tune progressions of somewhat distantly related chords. The economy of materials used is such that players are afforded opportunities to develop an aural sense of more and more complex structures. The plagal inflection that accompanies the opening statement of the primary theme, E-flat major–G-flat major–A-flat major–E-flat major, returns in various forms throughout the piece. Intensity builds through mm. 122–131 as the composer expands the original progression and extends its tertian harmony:

E-flat–G-flat–A–E^{13}–F^{13}

The *dolce* presentation of theme B in mm. 244–257 is given a sense of subtle urgency by an elegant progression through the circle of fifths, first of alternating dominant and half-diminished seventh functions, and then of seventh chords diatonic to the home key:

$A^{ø7}$–D^7–$G^{ø7}$–C^7–$F^{ø7}$–B-flat^7–E-flat (home)–A-flat^{maj7}–$D^{ø7}$–Gm^7–Cm^7–Fm^7–B-flat^7

The gradually increasing drive that characterizes the work's coda begins in m. 274 with ascending, stepwise root movement over a B-flat pedal:

E-flat(I♮)–Fm–Gm⁷–A-flat–B-flat–C-flat–D-flat–E-flat–
F-flat–G-flat–A-flat–B-flat–C-flat–D-flat–E-flat–Fm–E-flat

The transition that follows in mm. 264–287 features a rapid-fire, beat-by-beat reiteration of the progression from mm. 252–257, leading to a return to the home key once again. Players are given the opportunity to develop an aural sense of that progression in the *dolce* setting and may then be prepared to perform the coda more effectively. Likewise, the return of the opening plagal inflection in mm. 313–316 gives added perspective to that progression as well.

RHYTHM:
The rhythmic ostinato that underpins the thematic material in the second large division of the piece grows out of and is reinforced by the hemiola pattern introduced at m. 62. The interdependence of rhythmic elements is such that all players will benefit from exercises in which they become familiar with one another's parts. With respect to the passage beginning at m. 66, brasses could be given the low brass melody while woodwinds and percussion play the hemiola rhythm, following which parts could be exchanged. The hemiola could alternately be performed over repeated eighth notes, as in the tambourine part, and as isolated accents, as in the bongo part.

TIMBRE:
Colors are combined in several ways that serve to enhance variations in texture. Players will need to be keenly sensitive to their role in any given passage in order that they may effectively interpret overlapping figures. During the *Grandioso* passage beginning at m. 222, for example, the marcato presentation of theme A by the reeds must remain dark and fully connected in order to provide adequate contrast to the accented and somewhat separated statement of the primary theme material in the upper woodwinds.

Unit 7: Form and Structure

SECTION	MEASURE	EVENT AND SCORING
Moderato		
1	1–8	Primary theme is developed from the source motive in m. 1; clarinet melody is inverted for the second half of the theme; antiphonal accompaniment in saxes, horns, and low brass; E-flat major
	9–16	Primary theme repeats in flutes, now without inversion; simple chordal accompaniment in clarinets and low winds frames countermelody in horn and cornet

SECTION	MEASURE	EVENT AND SCORING
	17–24	Motivic development of primary theme; source motive is extended rhythmically as texture thickens gradually; C minor
	25–28	Transitional return to E-flat major as rhythmic extension of source motive is isolated and sequenced
2	29–37	Reiteration of source motive in E-flat (m. 28) leads to renewed motivic development, first between solo trumpet, solo horn, and tutti clarinets, beginning in C minor; progression toward E-flat major amid increased dynamics and registration
	38–44	Truncated primary theme, fully orchestrated, in E-flat major
	45–52	First half of theme in original form in upper woodwinds in counterpoint with rhythmic augmentation of theme in horns and cornets over B-flat pedal; second half of theme begins in trumpets and trombones, the first pitch of each phrase anticipated and sustained, and concludes in saxes and horns; texture thins and dynamics fade toward a return to E-flat major
Codetta	53–61	Primary theme, augmented, in solo glockenspiel against upper woodwind countermelody; cadential extension in mm. 60–61 resolves in elision with arrival of new tempo
Allegro		
Introduction/ Transition	62–65	3/4 hemiola in woodwinds and percussion sets up syncopated nature of ensuing passages; E-flat major
1	66–81	Syncopated theme A in low winds recalls source motive and primary theme material from mm. 1–8; second half of theme extended through shifting meters; cadential extension underpinned by syncopated germ that will serve as a rhythmic ostinato through much of the remainder of the work

SECTION	MEASURE	EVENT AND SCORING
	82–97	Theme A in trumpets, joined by alto saxes in m. 90
	98–113	Sequential, *leggiero* theme B overlapping in flutes recalls inversion of the source motive in mm. 5–8; clarinet and bassoon ostinato frames by hemiola in tambourine; theme is augmented in solo glockenspiel; A-flat major
	114–121	First half of theme A in low brass and saxes; C minor
Transition	122–127	Theme A head motive sequenced through E-flat major, G-flat major, A major
	128–131	Tutti syncopated ostinato rhythm over hemiola in percussion; extended tertian harmony: E^{13}–F^{13}
	132–141	Sequential, ascending bell tone figures above B-flat pedals in bass voices and F pedal trills in upper woodwinds
2	142–149	Theme B in solo glockenspiel over very light accompaniment in reeds and suspended cymbal; hemiola in triangle; E-flat major
	150–165	Development of theme A head motive; fragment migrates through the ensemble as the harmonic center moves from C minor out to C major (m. 162) and back to E-flat major
	166–171	Extension of motivic development as hemiola presence expands in woodwinds and percussion
	172–179	Orchestration thins to hemiola ostinato surrounding head motive A in augmentation in solo trumpet and glockenspiel
3	180–195	Theme A returns, beginning in low reeds, horns, and euphonium; E-flat major
	196–211	Theme B extended and sequenced Harmonic center shifts through inflections toward G minor and B-flat major, returning to E-flat major
	212–221	Head motive A sequenced as tempo slows and dynamics increase

SECTION	MEASURE	EVENT AND SCORING
4	222–243	*Grandioso.* Theme A in upper reeds as upper woodwinds recall primary theme from beginning of work; cadential extension reduced to rhythmic ostinato on B-flat pedal
	244–257	*Dolce* theme B harmonized by elegant progression through circle of fifths; syncopation and hemiola figures increase intensity as dynamics and orchestration expand and tempo slows
	258–265	"Hymnisch" 4/4 return of primary theme material from beginning of work; E-flat major
	266–273	*Più mosso*; fanfare sequence of original source motive; dynamics, orchestration, and registration increase toward cadential elision with arrival of coda
Coda	274–283	*Più allegro*; 3/4 rhythmic ostinato returns as B-flat pedal; harmonic root movement ascends by step as harmonic rhythm and dynamics increase
	284–293	Rapid-fire, beat-by-beat reiteration of the harmonic progression from mm. 252–257; head motive A sequenced, seemingly toward a return to E-flat
	294–301	*Molto allegro*; deceptive cadence punctuates return of tutti rhythmic ostinato figure over percussion hemiola; extended tertian harmony broadens to B-flat[13] (m. 301)
	302–321	Paring away of harmonic layers to *piano* ostinato on E-flat pedal against original harmonic progression from m. 2 (mm. 313–317)
	322–336	Ostinato fills out to sequence of head motive A toward an emphatic final statement; E-flat major

Unit 8: Suggested Listening

Gillingham, David R.:
Cantus Leatus
A Light unto the Darkness
Waking Angels
Grantham, Donald:
Don't You See?
Southern Harmony
Holst, Gustav. *First Suite in E-flat for Military Band*, Op. 28.
Maslanka, David:
Symphony No. 2
Tears
Rudin, Rolf:
Autumnal Song (Herbstgesang): Homage to Robert Schumann
(for orchestra)
Patera, after Alfred Kubin (for chamber ensemble)
Choreographie (for orchestra)
Der Traum des Oenghus (for band)
Ticheli, Frank:
Amazing Grace
Shennandoah
Van der Roost, Jan:
Canterbury Chorale
Puszta

Unit 9: Additional References and Resources

Lisk, Edward S. *The Creative Director: Intangibles of Musical Performance*. Ft. Lauderdale, FL: Meredih Music, 2000.
Noble, Weston. *Creating the Special World: A Series of Lectures*. Chicago: GIA Publications, 2007.
Porter, Darwin. *Frommer's Germany 2008*. New York: Frommer's Press, 2007.
Thurmond, James Morgan. *Note Grouping: A Method for Achieving Expression and Style in Musical Performance*. Ft. Lauderdale, FL: Meredith Music, 2000.

For more information on the Vorspessart Band Association, go to http://www.blasmusikverband-vorspessart.de

Contributed by:

James Batcheller
Central Michigan University
Mount Pleasant, Michigan

Teacher Resource Guide

Latin Folk Song Trilogy

William Himes
(b. 1949)

Unit 1: Composer

A native of Chicago, Illinois, and born to Salvation Army officer parents, William Himes attended the University of Michigan, where he earned bachelor and master of music degrees in music education and performance. He taught instrumental music for five years in the public schools of Flint, Michigan and was also an adjunct professor at the University of Michigan-Flint, where he taught the low brass studio. Additionally, he served as bandmaster of the Flint Citadel Band of the Salvation Army during his time in Flint, Michigan.

Himes has served as the music director of the Salvation Army's Central Territory since 1977. His role as music director encompasses eleven of the Midwestern states of the United States. He is also conductor of the Chicago Staff Band, which is an internationally recognized ensemble that has had successful performance tours of Panama, Mexico, Chile, Canada, Singapore, the Philippines, Hong Kong, England, and Australia. The band's tour of England in 1987 included performances in the Royal Albert Hall and Buckingham Palace, during which the band and Himes were able to meet Her Majesty Queen Elizabeth. On July 2, 2000 at the International Millennial Congress in Atlanta, Georgia, General John Gowans awarded the honor of "Order of the Founder" to Bandmaster William Himes for "giving exemplary service and leadership under the baton of the Chief Musician with an over-whelming desire to win souls." The Salvation Army's highest honor, the "Order of the Founder" is bestowed to a person who is considered to reflect the qualities and character of the organization's founder.

In high demand as a conductor, composer, lecturer, clinician, and euphonium soloist, Himes has appeared in these roles throughout the United States, Canada, Australia, New Zealand, Sweden, Denmark, Norway, and the United Kingdom. Well known for his compositions and arrangements, Himes has more than 100 publications with numerous manuscripts awaiting publication. These compositions are frequently aired on international broadcasts and recordings.

Unit 2: Composition

Written as a three-movement suite, *Latin Folk Song Trilogy* is based on the music of Latin America. Published by Curnow Music Press in 2000, the work is listed as a Grade 3 in difficulty and, in the preface of the score, is included in a list of 25 other pieces by Curnow Press as part of its National Heritage Series. The pieces listed showcase early music and folksongs of the United States, Europe, Asia, and Latin America.

The three movements, titled "El Tortillero (The Tortilla Vendor)," "Huainito," and "Riqui Ran," are presented in a contemporary setting for wind band while adhering closely to the original presentation from the countries in Latin America to which the folksongs are related. Himes states in the score that "although these three South American folksongs differ completely from one another, they share one common characteristic, tunefulness."

Latin Folk Song Trilogy is approximately eight minutes in length. The work is scored for flute (with piccolo), oboe, clarinet (3), E-flat alto clarinet, B-flat bass clarinet, bassoon, alto saxophone (2), tenor saxophone, baritone saxophone, trumpet (3), horn (2), trombone (3), euphonium, tuba, and double bass. Percussion scoring includes timpani (3), bells and xylophone for mallet percussion, and tambourine, snare drum, shaker (or maracas), and bongos (percussion 1), and triangle, claves, castanets, guiro, crash cymbals, maracas, suspended cymbal, and bass drum (percussion 2).

Unit 3: Historical Perspective

The use of folksongs in compositions has been a major influential source of material for composers throughout history in many genres of music. Folklore represents the feelings and history of a nation, but it is sometimes difficult to understand different traditions, the costumes, the population, and even more difficult with food or language. But, music has always been regarded as a universal language, expressed and understood by most people of the world in an easier way. Thus folksongs help the listener, performer, or conductor to understand the music of a different nation or country. Composers who have written works containing folksongs, of their own country or others, have included these works for band among many others in every musical genre:

Appalachian Spring	Aaron Copland
Southern Harmony	Donald Grantham
Kentucky Harmony	Donald Grantham
Second Suite in F	Gustav Holst
William Byrd Suite	Gordon Jacob
Suite Francaise	Darius Milhaud
La Fiesta Mexicana	H. Owen Reed
Capriccio Italien	P. I. Tchaikovsky
Capriccio Espagnol	P. I. Tchaikovsky
Cajun Folk Songs	Frank Ticheli
Cajun Folk Songs II	Frank Ticheli
Shenandoah	Frank Ticheli
Shaker Gift Songs	Frank Ticheli
English Folksong Suite	Ralph Vaughan Williams
Sea Songs	Ralph Vaughan Williams
Laboring Songs	Dan Welcher
Zion	Dan Welcher

In *Latin Folk Song Trilogy*, movement 1, "El Tortillero (The Tortilla Vendor)," is a song from Chile, South America. The country of Chile has a rich tradition of folkloric music, with profound roots in Spanish tradition, and also with Argentine and Mexican influences.

In the program notes to the score, Himes states that the folksong recounts a bittersweet tale of unrequited love. The tortilla street peddler sings a hopeful, cheerful melody in attracting a fair maiden who is stolen his heart. But much to his disappointment, the romance is not to be, which causes the vendor to sing his chorus:

Now with deep sadness, my wares I cry for them.
Who'll buy my good tostadas? Tortillas! Buy them!

"El Tortillero" is considered to be a part of the Chilean folksong type called a *tonada*. A tonada is a more general style of composition where strict metric rules are not needed as much as other types of folksongs. Most tonadas have accompaniment of guitar, piano, or both, but other instruments are not excluded. It is stated that tonadas survive as part of the purest Chilean folk-lore, and not by the creation of the great Chilean musicians.

Movement 2, "Huainito," is a brief, sad love song of Argentine origin which expresses the story of a broken heart. The term, *huainito*, is a general term for lament. No other information on this folksong from Argentina, South America can be found.

"Riqui Ran," movement 3 of *Latin Folk Song Trilogy*, is a children's song from Puerto Rico. Program notes from the score state that the song dwells on typical childhood food fantasies that include bread, candy, and honey. Sources state that during Puerto Rico's colonial years, a series of musical traditions evolved that were based on the folk songs and romantic ballads of eighteenth- and nineteenth-century Spain. Much of this folk music is part of the heritage of the *jíbaro*, which is a Puerto Rican peasant, with origins in the Andalusian region of Spain, and eventually this music became intermixed with the music that was either imported or native to Latin America.

Unit 4: Technical Considerations

The three movements of *Latin Folk Song Trilogy* present many challenges for performers of younger, public school bands and lower-level high school and college ensembles. As Himes states in the program notes of the score, the three South American folk songs share the common characteristic of tuneful-ness. Therefore, attention must not only be given to the balance and projection of the specific melody, but also to its lyricism and vitality.

Movement 1: "El Tortillero (The Tortilla Vendor)"

Written in 3/4 meter and 137 measures in length, the primary importance of the movement is to achieve a lively character relative to the folksong. The prescribed tempo of *Waltz*, dotted half note = 60, is a concern in having the performers effectively maintain this tempo throughout the piece, performing a feel of one macro beat per bar. This waltz feel must stay *leggiero* while also continuing to drive to maintain the lively character of the music. With the movement in a one-beat-per-bar waltz pulse, the concern of slowing and dragging the tempo is great.

Performers must have a technical, thorough understanding of the B-flat and E-flat major key centers and scales, with hints of Lydian and Dorian modes during these key center sections. The use of accidentals is limited to the established harmonic progressions in those key center areas of the work.

Primary note lengths and rhythms of the work are quarter, dotted half, and eighth notes (usually paired eighths). Stated right from the beginning in m. 5–8, the rhythm of half note, two quarter notes tied across the bar, half note provide a duple hemiola effect that may challenge performers' time-keeping skills to a degree. Supporting this duple hemiola rhythm is the driving rhythm of two eighth notes, single eighth, two eighth notes, which should help the previously-mentioned rhythm with proper time-keeping.

Good preparatory work on these rhythms will help proper proficiency and performance of these patterns in preventing rushing or dragging, especially the latter. The conductor could help this hemiola effect by conducting to or with this rhythmic pattern for musical phrasing. Although problems with this may occur with the underlying rhythm of three single eighth notes per measure that will still be in a one-per-bar feel. Performers must be able to concentrate and play these respective rhythms against each other within the melodic or rhythmic parts of the work. This rhythmic hemiola effect is stated again later in the movement.

Himes states that the rhythmic motif of quarter rest, two pairs of eighth notes, single eighth note, stated in the first four measures, always needs to lead to beat 1 with a feeling of crescendo. Although stated more heavily with an accented flourish in the introduction, this motif must then lighten up once the first theme begins at m. 17, but without losing the implied crescendo. Performers must be able to effectively change texture from driving, lively rhythms to lighter, more lyrical phrases to detached, petite characteristic playing.

Instrumental ranges in woodwinds and brass are moderate and should be easily accessible for proficient performers. Main concerns include several very exposed sections (sometimes only two different instruments or parts are playing after a full ensemble section) that will challenge the confidence of players and sections, and unison lines or phrases across several instrumental sections of the ensemble where intonation tendencies may need to be addressed.

Movement 2: "Lament—Huainito"
Written in 6/8 and marked eighth note = 92, this movement is the shortest in length with forty-seven measures, and is a complete reversal in mood and tempo from movement 1.

With the prescribed tempo of *Doloroso*, which means mournful, grieving (Persichetti used this musical term often), Himes states that performers must maintain an unhurried sense of tempo, allowing lots of time and opportunity for expression, and rubato at certain spots in the movement would be even better. Conductor and performer must think and perform in the eighth-note pulse. The whole movement is written in C minor.

Note lengths and rhythms throughout the movement are centered around the dotted quarter note, the offbeat quarter note (with an eighth-note rest preceding it), the triple pairing of eighth notes, and some sixteenths.

The first eight measures begin with a four-measure call-and-response section by brass and woodwinds, respectively. This four-measure phrase has a mixture of dotted quarter notes (to provide foundation) against the offbeat quarter note with the melody of sixteenths and single eighth notes above this. The biggest concern with this introductory phrase or section is not to rush the eighth-note rest in the melody and in the parts with offbeat quarter notes. If performers are not relaxed and expressive, the phrase will sound constricted and tense. And performers must always keep the underlying eighth-note pulse subdivision in order for the tempo to be maintained.

Instrumental range is very moderate and should be no problem at all for performers. Finger dexterity and proficiency is a must to effectively perform the sixteenth-note melodic passages smoothly and musically.

Movement 3: "Riqui Ran"

This folksong and movement is presented in 2/4 meter, is 101 measures in length, and is written in the keys of B-flat and F major. The tempo is prescribed as a lively *Allegro festivo* with a quarter note = 108.

As observed in the relationship of movement 1 to movement 2, the contrasting mood and character from movement 2 to movement 3 is very apparent. The movement begins with the percussion section stating a rhythmic ostinato that continues throughout the majority of the movement. This ostinato will be of great help to the winds in maintaining the proper tempo during the movement. Alternating rhythms of dotted-eighth-and-sixteenth note followed by a single eighth and paired eighths occur in low brass and horns, serving as another underlying rhythm in the movement.

The main concern with this motivic rhythm is making sure it doesn't become heavy and begin to drag the tempo, or that the parts entering on beat 2 do not enter late and begin dragging the tempo. The melody is a combination of mostly eighth notes with occasional quarter notes that is exchanged between the higher brasses and woodwinds, treated as distinctive and contrasting voices. This call-and-response echo effect is effective as long as the instrumental sections enter in time and maintain the lively tempo and nature of the folksong and movement.

The texture changes in the middle section of the movement, but tempo remains *l'istesso* or constant. Because the texture changes to legato and becomes more sonorous (see Unit 5) in this middle section, maintaining the proper, constant tempo may be problematic unless addressed.

The first section is reprised beginning at m. 72. The tempo marking for this returning section is faster with the prescribed tempo (*Allegro vivo*) of quarter note = 120. Care must be taken in making certain that this section is more lively and exciting while making sure it is not too fast for the proficiency of the performers to play it correctly and cleanly.

Continued excitement is then established for the upcoming accelerando which occurs at m. 88 (*Vivace*, quarter note = 132). Again, cohesion is the utmost necessity with clarity of rhythms, balance of melody against accompaniment, and voicings while also establishing an exciting conclusion to the movement and whole work.

The last unison rhythm of single eighth note, two eighth-note rests, two sixteenths, and a single eighth can be problematic. Performers may have a tendency to either 1) want to rush the eighth rests to play the two sixteenths; 2) crush the sixteenth rhythm by rushing the tempo and rhythm; and/or 3) crush the sixteenth rhythm by not tonguing cleanly and clearly. Attention to these possibilities is tantamount.

Instrumental ranges are again in the moderate range and should be no problem for proficient performers. Accurate and appropriate dynamic changes need to be addressed for ensemble balance and contrasting moods established by the composer.

Unit 5: Stylistic Considerations

The three movements of *Latin Folk Song Trilogy* include distinctive stylistic elements. Preserving the spirit, energy, and mood of the original Latin melodies and folksongs must be the focus of rehearsals. As Himes states, attention must not only be given to the balance and projection of the specific melody, but also to its lyricism and vitality. The musical and emotional elements of the music of each movement will be achieved if proper tone quality, phrasing, articulation, expression, and dynamic contrasts are adhered to by performers.

Movement 1: "El Tortillero (The Tortilla Vendor)"

Himes states that the rhythmic motif of quarter rest, two pairs of eighth notes, single eighth note, stated in the first four measures, always needs to lead to beat 1 with a feeling of crescendo. Although stated move heavily with an accented flourish in the introduction, this motif must then lighten up once the first theme begins at m. 17, but without losing the implied crescendo. Throughout the movement, performers must be able to effectively change texture from driving, lively rhythms to lighter, more lyrical phrases to detached, petite stylistic playing.

The tempo of the movement is a faster, one-beat-per-bar, waltz feel or pulse (dotted half note = 60). Because of this tempo, the stylistic qualities throughout the movement needs to remain *leggiero*. Because of the driving pulse from measure to measure in continuing to maintain tempo, performers may tend to begin playing too heavily, which will eliminate the lighter, waltz qualities of the music and folksong with which the movement is associated. The opening dynamics are *forte* with some rhythmic accents, and younger performers will tend to relate *forte* playing to playing in a heavier musical style.

Attention must be given to the staccato quarter note at the beginning of each phrase of the main theme (first stated at m. 17). Separation must happen in order to remain true to the stylistic character of the folksong melody. This rhythm of staccato quarter note, half note tied to another half note continues into the melody of the second major section starting at m. 49. The underlying countermelody also contains this stylistic rhythm.

A *secco* staccato style of playing must happen with the single eighth notes in the ensemble accompaniment during the movement. Secco means "dry." A secco staccato style of playing relates to the length, quality, and separation of a single note to other successive single notes. Younger performers will tend to associate playing a single eighth note as just staccato and clip off the note in terms of separation and note length. Instructing performers about *secco* staccato (a combination of both staccato and tenuto style markings) will help them play the notes and rhythms in a style more characteristic of the Latin folksong mood and energy. This underlying accompaniment happens in the introduction in the low woodwinds and brass, and also in later sections of the movement, particularly at mm. 69, 108, and after m. 130 at the close of the movement.

Movement 2: "Lament—Huainito"
Marked *Doloroso* at the beginning of the movement and then *con calore* at m. 17, this movement is a complete contrast to movement 1. The overall stylistic qualities must be sonorous and legato, without a hint of accent or staccato playing. As the tempo markings state, the mood and character of the performing must be grievous or mournful (*doloroso*), yet with warmth (*con calore*). These musical markings are not as well known to younger performers (Persichetti uses these terms more often), and thus they may not understand when observing these terms for the first time. Careful instruction will assist them in being able to promote the proper mood and character needed for this Latin folksong of lament.

The sixteenth-and-eighth-note melody (or obbligato melody motif) that occurs throughout the movement will present challenges of proper stylistic playing for performers. The single eighth note at the end of each rhythm of the melody motif must not be clipped and played with a staccato marking. Performers need to be aware that this single eighth note must have some length to it to preserve and present the proper character and style of the music. Younger performers will tend to dismiss this last note (thus, clipping it) in attempts to continue on to the next successive rhythm or melodic grouping of notes. As stated in Unit 4, a sense of unhurriedness and relaxation must be present in the performers' playing.

Because of the qualities of the underlying offbeat eighth-rest-and-quarter-note rhythm throughout the movement, performers playing this rhythm will tend to want to play the quarter notes with some accent. This style of playing is completely opposite of the stylistic character and mood associated with this movement. Performers must be instructed that a legato attack is needed (rounded tongue) and that the dynamic of *piano* is paramount for proper presentation and balance.

Movement 3: "Riqui Ran"
Stylistically, this movement presents the fewest challenges to the performer in comparison to movements 1 and 2. The dotted-eighth-and-sixteenth-note rhythm at the beginning of the movement (occurring again at later stages in the movement) must be stylistically played with some slight separation between the dotted eighth and the sixteenth note for rhythmic clarity. The

pairs of eighth-note rhythms present throughout the movement must also be played equally in terms of stylistic attack, with both eighth notes having a slight length of duration. They should not be played staccato, and the second eighth note should not be played short or clipped.

With rhythmic, faster music, performers will tend to think vertically from note to note or rhythmic grouping to rhythmic grouping. In the first section of this movement, performers must play more linearly and think of phrasing to ensure more musicality.

Starting at m. 48 with section B (see Unit 7), a total change of style and mood occurs. This chorale section changes to a cantabile, legato style of playing. Although the style changes, tempo remains constant, thus performers must make certain that by playing longer, sostenuto note lengths, the lively character of the movement continues.

At m. 64, the mood and character begins to transition back to that of the earlier section. The underlying pulse of single eighth notes in the lower woodwinds and brass must again be played with a secco staccato style of note length. And this note length (with single eighth notes) remains this same secco staccato once the earlier section returns at m. 72.

Once the tempo begins to accelerate toward the end of the movement, stylistic qualities and character will challenge younger performers tending to associate faster tempi with heavy, pesante playing. Care must still be taken that the pairs of eighth notes be equally played (length) and the second eighth note is not played shorter or clipped. Again, having performers think linearly will also help the flow and folksong stylistic character of the movement.

UNIT 6: MUSICAL ELEMENTS

Latin Folk Song Trilogy includes many teaching opportunities and challenges regarding each of the four main musical elements. The composition is important for the qualities and characteristics that Himes includes from each of the three Latin folksongs in this contemporary setting for wind band.

MELODY:
  Teaching concept:
    Use of older, existing melodies and folksongs in a new composition

  Strategies:
    Review history of older melodies and folksongs and the culture related to them
    Explain transcription of melodies and folksongs for other uses in music composition
    Discuss techniques of orchestration and composition by the composer during rehearsals

Discuss the subject of the probability of teaching these older melodies and folksongs by rote and the passing down of them over time from generation to generation

Teaching concept:
Use of pentatonic, diatonic, chromatic, and modal melodies and motives

Strategies:
Explain differences between the various melodies used in compositions
Teach these melodies in several keys related to those used in this composition
Explain the use of melodic and/or rhythmic motives contained through-out the composition (e.g. motives used as rhythmic accompaniment, use of call-and response echo effect between voices and groups in the ensemble)

Teaching concept:
Use of phrasing and form in music

Strategies:
Discuss use of phrasing and melodic contour and direction
Discuss the varied forms used by the composer for each movement (binary form and its variances: double binary form, rounded binary form, and two-part form)
Visually show and represent the form through prepared diagrams

HARMONY:
Teaching concept:
Reharmonization

Strategies:
Discuss the many types of modes as compared to major and minor scales and those modes used occasionally in each movement (Lydian and Dorian)
Discuss the use of chromaticism for harmonic color and variety
Discuss use of seventh chords and polychords (movement 3) and their purposes

Teaching concept:
Consonance versus dissonance

Strategies:
Use examples during warm-up exercises of passing tones, chromaticism, suspensions, appoggiaturas, and other non-harmonic tones in creating dissonance

Compare these examples to specific places in the composition

Encourage and support musical confidence when dissonance occurs in specific places in the music or a particular part of the instrumental section for harmonic color

RHYTHM:

Teaching concept:
Use of underlying subdivision in varied time signatures

Strategies:
Explain the differences between the time signatures used in this composition (3/4, 6/8, 2/4) and how accurately playing each is achieved through internal thinking and counting of subdivisions

Explain the relationship of tempo to eighth-note subdivision with rushing and/or dragging of tempo

Explain changing meters from quarter-note and eighth-note meters and how the eighth note does not change (if tempo stays the same), or how the eighth note can represent the role of quarter note if the tempo is slower and the eighth note represents the pulse (movement 2)

Teaching concept:
Use of hemiola

Strategies:
Discuss how using hemiola can help assist time-keeping skills from one performer or section to another

Discuss the difference between duple and triple meter and the comparison of eighth-note subdivisions

Use examples during warm-up exercises of several sections playing rhythms in duple meter while the other sections play rhythms in triple meter

Discuss the use of musical phrasing and rhythmic grouping in relation to syncopation, where the weaker beat from measure to measure becomes the stronger beat (in movement 1)

Discuss how conducting overall rhythmic groupings instead of the underlying quarter-note beat enhances the musical effect and phrasing of the rhythmic structure (movement 1).

Teaching concept:
Use of ostinato

Strategies:
Explain how the compositional technique of ostinato rhythms helps the rhythmic flow of the music

Show various examples of ostinato used in the composition and how
these support and add to the melodic content of the original folksong

Explain how various rhythmic groupings of ostinati ("playing with
time") develop the compositional technique of hemiola (duple
against triple)

TIMBRE:
Teaching concept:
Orchestration

Strategies:
Discuss the apparent compositional challenges in transcribing vocal to
instrumental music

Encourage, support, and develop listening skills for intonation improvement in relation to the written orchestration

Develop performer awareness to the pairing or combination of
instruments in this composition

Use of characteristics of woodwind, brass, and percussion ensembles
within the wind band to explain how each, separately and combined,
creates colorful orchestration

Teaching concept:
Melodic tessitura

Strategies:
Discuss how high and/or low tessitura influences intonation with specific
notes, chords, and even solo and soli sections

Plan for and include the required and appropriate registers in ensemble
warm-up exercises

Explain the difference between conjunct and disjunct melodies and
accompaniment, show examples, and explain the problems with each
in relation to register and intonation

Teaching concept:
Tone color with key and tonal center relationships

Strategies:
Discuss how different keys and tonal centers affect the tone color
characteristics of ensemble sound

Explain how parts of a triad and/or extended chords affect the darkness
or brightness of chordal harmonies and ensemble sound

Discuss how different styles and articulations in music will promote
and/or affect the tone color of an ensemble

Use exercises of keys and modes contained in the composition to clarify
and promote listening to the tone color of each performer within the
ensemble

Unit 7: Form and Structure

Section	Measure	Event and Scoring
Movement 1: Double binary form		
Introduction	1–16	Rhythmic motives introduced; tonic to dominant and chromatic eighths in low woodwinds and brass; B-flat major established with hints of Lydian (raised fourth) mode
A	17–48	
a	17–32	Theme introduced; eighth-note rhythmic motive accompaniment; B-flat major with some Lydian mode traits
a^1	33–48	Theme restated; full ensemble accompaniment; texture thicker; melodic countermelody in high woodwinds; material sounds in F major (V), with some Dorian mode traits
B	49–82	
a	49–64	Thicker texture continues with rhythmic motive in middle voices; obbligato in flute and oboe and countermelody in low woodwinds and brass; B-flat major with hints of Lydian mode; section is repeated fully
b/Interlude	65–82	Material from introduction is stated verbatim; modulatory and chromatic (mm. 65–78); E-flat major established at m. 79
A^1	83–99	
a	83–98	Thematic material and accompaniment restated from opening section A with some development; E-flat major
a^1	83–99	Section is repeated fully
B^1	100–123	
a	100–115	Thematic material from section B restated in high woodwinds; accompaniment material different in low brass and woodwinds; eighth-note rhythmic motive present in trumpets; E-flat major with hints of Lydian and Dorian mode
a^1	100–111	Section repeated

SECTION	MEASURE	EVENT AND SCORING
Transition	116–123	Second ending of subsection; alternating quarter notes in melodic and accompaniment parts predominate; E-flat major
Coda	124–137	
a	124–129	Thinner texture; melody in flute and clarinet from section B (mm. 57 and/or 108)
b	130–137	Material similar to introduction is stated; rhythmic motive present; divergent chromaticism in ending four measures

Movement 2: Two-part form

Introduction	1–8	Conjunct, four-measure melody motive in sixteenth notes; dotted-quarter- or quarter-note accompaniment underneath (stated first in brass, then repeated verbatim in woodwinds); C minor tonality
A	9–23	
a	9–16	Four-measure antecedent-consequent phrasing; conjunct, eighth-note melody in trumpets and horns; dotted-quarter- or quarter-note accompaniment sparse in low woodwinds and brass
b	17–23	Full ensemble scoring with sustained melody in flute, clarinet 1, and trumpet; eighth-and-sixteenth-note countermelody in middle voices with offbeat quarter-note accompaniment
Transition	24–27	Restatement of material from introduction (in woodwinds); C minor tonality continues
A¹	28–42	
a	28–35	Material from section A restated but rescored slightly (melody in clarinets and saxes); flute obbligato from introduction; sparse accompaniment
b	36–42	Restatement of material from mm. 17–23

SECTION	MEASURE	EVENT AND SCORING
Codetta	43–47	Sixteenth-and-eighth-note melody motive in flute and oboe with sparse dotted-quarter- and offbeat-quarter-note accompaniment (stated first in woodwinds, then repeated by brass); ending chord is C major (picardy third)

Movement 3: Rounded binary form

Introduction	1–8	Percussion alone in opening four measures, answered by brass on alternating rhythms of dotted-eighth-and-sixteenth notes and two eighth notes (mm. 5–8); B-flat major
A	9–47	
a	9–20	Melody in trumpets on conjunct eighth-and-quarter-note rhythms with accompaniment of dotted-eighth-and-sixteenth-notes and two eighth notes in middle and low brass; percussion continues with rhythmic ostinato with high wood-winds occasionally on eighth-note motives
b	21–29	Continuation of melodic and rhythmic material with material from introduction restated in last four measures
a¹	30–39	Melody in trumpets (developed slightly) with alternating eighth-note accompaniment in middle voices
b¹	40–47	Continuation of melodic and accompaniment material; tonality modulates to F major (dominant key)
B	48–71	
a	48–63	Texture changes to quarter and half note chorale melody and accompaniment; conjunct melody in alto sax and horns; percussion rests; F major tonality
b	64–71	Texture changes to be more like earlier section A (foreshadowing) with conjunct quarter-note melody (horn, trombone, trumpet) with single eighth-note accompaniment in low woodwinds and brass; percussion enters with subsection ending in fermatas to cadence back to A again

Section	Measure	Event and Scoring
A¹	72–93	
a	72–87	Restatement of melodic and accompaniment material, but developed slightly; percussion ostinato reappears; B-flat major tonality
a¹	88–93	Alternating eighth-note rhythms across the ensemble; tempo accelerates to *Vivace*
Coda	94–101	Uses material from introduction to conclude the movement and work in full ensemble scoring

Unit 8: Suggested Listening

Gandolfi, Michael. *Vientos y Tangos*.
Ginastera, Alberto. *Dances from Estancia*.
Himes, William:
   Amazing Grace (arr.)
   Cause for Celebration
   Creed
   Doxology
   Jericho (arr.)
   Kenya Contrasts
   Life Dances
   Ulterior Overture
Reed, H. Owen. *La Fiesta Mexicana*.
Stamp, Jack. *Bandancing*, movement 2: "Tango."
Tchaikovsky, Piotr Ilyich. *Capriccio Espanol*
Williams, Clifton. *Symphonic Dance No. 3:* "Fiesta"

Unit 9: Additional References and Resources

Abel, Willi. *Harvard Dictionary of Music*. Second ed. Cambridge, MA: Belknap Press of Harvard University Press, 1972.
Camphouse, Mark, ed. *Composers on Composing for Band, Volumes 1, 2, and 3.* Chicago: GIA Publications, 2002, 2004, 2007.
Hansen, Richard K. *The American Wind Band: A Cultural History*. Chicago: GIA Publications, 2005.
Himes, William. Score program notes to *Latin Folk Song Trilogy*. Wilmore, KY: Curnow Music Press, 2000.
Rehrig, William H. *The Heritage Encyclopedia of Band Music*. Paul E. Bierley, ed. Westerville, OH: Integrity Press, 1991.
Sadie, Stanley, ed. *Norton Grove Concise Encyclopedia of Music*. New York: W. W. Norton & Company, 1988.

Smith, Norman E. *Program Notes for Band*. Chicago: GIA Publications, 2002.

Websites:
Central Territory Order of the Founder Recipients. http://www.usc.salvation-army.org.htm
Chilean Traditional Music Page. Musica chilena: archivos MIDI y textos/Chilean music.
  http://www.geocities.com/Vienna/Strasse/1791/chile.htm
Feature Interview: Bill Himes, O. F.
  http://www.abc.au/sundaynights/stories/s1675035.htm
Music of Puerto Rico.
  http://www.musicofpuertorico.com/index.php/genre/folk.htm

Contributed by:

Christian Zembower
Director of Bands
East Tennessee State University
Johnson City, Tennessee

Teacher Resource Guide

Lock Lomond

Frank Ticheli
(b. 1958)

Unit 1: Composer

Ticheli received his doctoral and masters degrees in composition from The University of Michigan. He joined the faculty of the University of Southern California's Thornton School of Music in 1991, where he is professor of composition. From 1991 to 1998, Ticheli was composer-in-residence of the Pacific Symphony, and he still enjoys a close working relationship with that orchestra and their music director, Carl St. Clair.

Ticheli is well known for his works for concert band, many of which have become standards in the repertoire. In addition to composing, he has appeared as guest conductor of his music at Carnegie Hall, at many American universities and music festivals, and in cities throughout the world, including Schladming, Austria, at the Mid-Europe Music Festival; London and Manchester, England, with the Meadows Wind Ensemble; Singapore, with the Singapore Armed Forces Central Band; and numerous cities in Japan, with the Bands of America National Honor Band.

Frank Ticheli is the winner of the 2006 NBA/William D. Revelli Memorial Band Composition Contest for his *Symphony No. 2*. Other awards for his music include the Charles Ives and the Goddard Lieberson Awards, both from the American Academy of Arts and Letters, the Walter Beeler Memorial Prize, and First Prize awards in the Texas Sesquicentennial Orchestral Composition Competition, Britten-on-the-Bay Choral Composition Contest, and Virginia CBDNA Symposium for New Band Music.

Unit 2: Composition

Ticheli states in the score:

> In my setting, I have tried to preserve the folksong's simple charm, while also suggesting a sense of hope, and the resilience of the human spirit. The final statement combines the Scottish tune with the well-known Irish folksong, "Danny Boy." It was by happy accident that I discovered how well these two beloved songs share each other's company, and I hope their intermingling suggests a spirit of human harmony.

> Loch Lomond was commissioned by Nigel Durno, for the Stewarton Academy Senior Wind Ensemble of East Ayrshire, Scotland, with funds provided by the Scottish Arts Council. The premiere performance was given on June 18, 2002 by the Stewarton Academy Senior Wind Ensemble at Royal Concert Hall in Glasgow, Scotland.

Unit 3: Historical Perspective

At the time in Scottish history when "Loch Lomond" was a new song, the United Kingdom (which united Scotland, England, and Wales) had already been formed. But the Highland Scots wanted a Scottish, not an English King to rule. Led by their Bonnie Prince Charlie (Prince Charles Edward Stuart) they attempted unsuccessfully to depose Britain's King George II. An army of 7,000 Highlanders were defeated on April 16, 1746 at the famous *Battle of Culloden Moor*.

It is this same battle that indirectly gives rise to this beautiful song. After the battle, many Scottish soldiers were imprisoned within England's Carlisle Castle near the border of Scotland. "Loch Lomond" tells the story of two Scottish soldiers who were so imprisoned. One of them was to be executed, while the other was to be set free. According to Celtic legend, if someone dies in a foreign land, his spirit will travel to his homeland by "the low road,"— the route for the souls of the dead. In the song, the spirit of the dead soldier shall arrive first, while the living soldier will take the "high road" over the mountains, to arrive afterwards.

The song is from the point of view of the soldier who will be executed: When he sings, "ye'll tak' the high road and I'll tak' the low road," in effect he is saying that you will return alive, and I will return in spirit. He remembers his happy past, "By yon bonnie banks...where me and my true love were ever wont to gae [accustomed to go]" and sadly accepts his death: "the broken heart it ken nae [knows no] second Spring again."

The original folksong uses a six-note scale; the seventh scale degree is absent from the melody. The lyric intertwines the sadness of the soldier's plight with images of Loch Lomond's stunning natural beauty.

LOCH LOMOND

By yon bonnie banks,
And by yon bonnie braes,
Where the sun shines bright, on Loch Lomond
Where me and my true love
Were ever wont to gae
On the bonnie, bonnie banks of Loch Lomond.

Chorus
Oh! ye'll tak' the high road and
I'll tak' the low road,
An' I'll be in Scotland afore ye',
But me and my true love will never meet again
On the bonnie, bonnie banks of Loch Lomond.

'Twas then that we parted,
In yon shady glen,
On the steep, steep side of Ben Lomond
Where in purple hue
The Highland hills we view,
And the moon coming out in the gloaming.

(Chorus)

The wee birdies sing
And the wild flowers spring,
And in sunshine the waters are sleeping.
But the broken heart it kens
Nae second Spring again,
Tho' the waeful may cease frae their greeting.

(Chorus)

Some words in the Scots language:

ben	mount (mountain)
bonnie	beautiful
braes	slopes (hillsides)
frae	from
gae	go
glen	valley
gloaming	twilight (dusk)
kens	knows
nae	no

waeful	woeful
wee	tiny
wont	accustomed
yon	yonder

Unit 4: Technical Considerations

Loch Lomond is scored for full band: flute 1/piccolo, flute 2, oboe 1–2, clarinet 1–3, bass clarinet, E-flat contrabass clarinet, bassoon 1–2, alto saxophone 1–2, tenor saxophone, baritone saxophone, trumpet 1–3, horn 1–2, trombone 1–3, euphonium BC and TC, tuba, timpani, and percussion 1–2.

The work centers around the keys of B-flat and E-flat major. The work is in simple time (4/4) with rhythmic considerations including sixteenth notes, dotted-note values, grace notes, ritardandos, a tempo, and fermatas.

Unit 5: Stylistic Considerations

Stylistically, always keep in mind that the melody is folk music in nature. Folk music by definition is oral in tradition, and is often performed in a relatively simple style. The concept of folk music is difficult to define precisely, and the lines between it and other types of music such as art, popular, religious, and tribal music are blurred. Ticheli states in the score that performers should play throughout in a "connected, legato style, and try not to fall into the temptation of dragging below the tempo markings. The music should flow, not float."

Unit 6: Musical Elements

MELODY:
In mm. 39–46, strive to maintain equal balance between the melody (trumpets 1–2) and the countermelody (clarinets 1–2, alto saxophone 1, joined by clarinet 3 in m. 43). In mm. 57–65, the sustained notes should remain well in the background, like a very quiet string orchestra. The piccolo and clarinet solos should sound easily in the foreground without being forced. Beginning in m. 89, the countermelody drops out, leaving only the two main melodies. Again, strive to maintain roughly equal balance between them, allowing neither melody to overpower the other.

In mm. 81–89, there are three main ideas sounding in counterpoint with one another: 1) the "Loch Lomond" melody (clarinet 1, trumpet 1, euphonium, supported by clarinet 2–3 and trumpet 2–3); 2) the countermelody (piccolo, flute, oboe); and 3) the "Danny Boy" melody (alto saxophone and horn). The two melodies should sound in the foreground, and in roughly equal balance, whereas the countermelody may sound in the middle ground. Although all other players are supportive in nature, they should nonetheless play with a full, rich sound.

HARMONY:

The harmonic language of the work is traditional tonal harmony, often with chord extensions. The opening of the work in centered around B-flat major and modulates to E-flat major in m. 39, where it remains until the development section (mm. 66–81). Ticheli returns to B-flat major in mm. 82, and remains there until the end of the work. Please pay special attention to the harmonies, as this is what dictates where the ensemble and individuals should breathe.

RHYTHM:

The meter is simple 4/4 with the smallest subdivision being sixteenth notes, presented in the upper-woodwinds. While the melody contains some sixteenth notes, most of the rhythm is simple, composed of eighth, quarter, and half notes. Tempos are clearly marked and include ritardandos, a tempos, and fermatas.

TIMBRE:

Timbral clarity is particularly challenging where layers of voices require careful balance to hear all musical lines. In mm. 98–99, bring out those notes with tenuto markings (clarinet 2 and horn 1 in m. 98; horn 2 and euphonium in m. 99), and allow them to linger a bit.

Unit 7: Form and Structure

SECTION	MEASURE	EVENT AND SCORING
Introduction	1–11	B-flat
First statement	12–27	B-flat
Canonic interlude	28–38	B-flat, modulating
Second statement, with countermelody	39–57	E-flat
Solo clarinet and piccolo in parallel twelfths	58–66	E-flat over D-flat
Development (main melody plus countermelody)	66–81	E-flat, A-flat, F, D-flat
Final statement with its countermelody, and entrance of "Danny Boy" as a second countermelody	82—end	B-flat

Unit 8: Suggested Listening

Grainger, Percy:
  Colonial Song
  "Irish Tune" from *County Derry*
  Ye Banks and Braes O' Boonie Doon
Ticheli, Frank:
  Amazing Grace
  Ave Maria/Schubert
  Cajun Folk Songs
  Sanctuary
  Shennandoah

Unit 9: Additional References

Ticheli, Frank. *Lock Lomond.* Brooklyn, NY: Manhattan Beach Music, 2002.
Randel, Don Michael. *The New Harvard Dictionary of Music.* Cambridge,
  MA: Harvard University Press, 1996.

Websites:
  Frank Ticheli. www.frankticheli.com
  Manhattan Beach Music. www.manhattanbeachmusic.com

Contributed by:

Timothy Harris
Director of Instrumental Studies
Chabot College
Hayward, California

Teacher Resource Guide

Mayflower Overture

Ron Nelson
(b. 1929)

Unit 1: Composer

Ronald J. Nelson was born in Joliet, Illinois on December 14, 1929. He earned all composition degrees from the Eastman School of Music, including a bachelor of music (1952), a master of music (1953), and the doctor of musical arts (1956). While at Eastman, he studied with Bernard Rogers and Howard Hanson.

In 1954 he studied at the École Normale de Musique and, in 1955, at the Paris Conservatory on a Fulbright Fellowship. Nelson began his compositional study in France with Arthur Honegger, but due to Honegger's subsequent illness, Nelson finished his work with Tony Aubin. Upon Nelson's return to the United States, he spent a year finishing his doctorate at Eastman before accepting a position as assistant professor on the faculty of Brown University, later attaining the rank of associate professor (1960) and full professor (1968). He served as chairman of the music department from 1963–1973, and in 1991 was awarded the Acuff Chair of Excellence in the Creative Arts, becoming the first musician to hold the chair. Nelson retired from Brown University in 1993 and currently resides in Scottsdale, Arizona.

Nelson has received numerous commissions, including those from the National Symphony Orchestra, Rochester Philharmonic, the United States Air Force Band and Chorus, Rhode Island Philharmonic, Aspen Music Festival, Brevard Music Center, Musashino Wind Ensemble, and countless colleges and universities. He has also received grants and awards from The Rockefeller Foundation, the Howard Foundation, ASCAP, and several from the National Endowment for the Arts. In 1993, his *Passacaglia (Homage on*

B-A-C-H) made history by winning all three major wind band composition awards: the National Band Association Composition Contest, the American Bandmasters Association Ostwald Award, and the Sudler International Wind Band Composition Award. Some of his notable works for wind band include *Rocky Point Holiday*, *Medieval Suite*, and *Aspen Jubilee*, among others.

Unit 2: Composition

Mayflower Overture, an original tone poem for band composed in 1958, is dedicated to Frederick Fennell and the Eastman Wind Ensemble. The piece is Ron Nelson's first significant work for band and the only one by the composer scored in the classic style of band composition with large sections of wind instruments. Nelson was never satisfied with the work and nearly withdrew it, later producing a revised version in 1997 after years of altering the piece during conducting engagements. It was written at the suggestion of Walter Rodby (1917–2005), an internationally acclaimed composer, arranger, and educator. His connection to Nelson was established during Rodby's time as music (vocal) director at Joliet Township High School and Joliet Junior College. Additionally, the piece was written to commemorate the arrival in 1957 of *Mayflower II*, a replica of the original ship that reenacted the original voyage.

The work aims to depict the epic journey of the Pilgrims to the new world and is presented in three sections. The first, "Departure," gives the listener the impression of being at Plymouth for the launch of the *Mayflower*. The second section is "Storm," a powerful portrayal of the violent thunderstorms encountered during the voyage. The third and final section, called "Arrival in the New World," depicts the first sight of land in November of 1620. As the final section unfolds, the joy and exuberance of being free in a new land is presented both with reverence and great optimism. The themes for the overture are three Pilgrim hymns taken from the *Ainsworth Psalter* (1612): Psalm 3 (in major and minor), Psalm 136 (or Psalm 84, one that has the same melody) and Psalm 100 ("Old Hundredth").

Mayflower Overture is a Grade 3 composition approximately six minutes and forty seconds in length and is published by Boosey & Hawkes.

Unit 3: Historical Perspective

Up until the time of the maiden voyage to America, the *Mayflower* was a cargo ship used mostly for the transport of wine and other goods to various countries in Europe. The ship was approximately 100 feet in length and twenty-five feet in width.

The Pilgrims began their original voyage with both the *Mayflower* and the *Speedwell*, but the *Speedwell* supposedly encountered severe leaking problems and both ships returned to England. It was later revealed the crew of the *Speedwell* sabotaged the vessel to get out of their sailing contract. The

Mayflower subsequently set sail alone for America, complete with approximately 100 passengers and a crew of thirty members. The sixty-six day voyage to America was difficult and frequently stormy. Passengers often found courage and peace in singing during difficult times during the voyage, especially when storms forced them under decks.

From a compositional standpoint, a conductor unfamiliar with the piece would likely be surprised to discover this work was originally composed in 1958, as it possesses a more contemporary sound when performed by a wind ensemble. Despite the fact Nelson had the "Revelli band" sound as a model when composing the work, both large symphonic bands as well as smaller wind ensembles can perform the piece.

Unit 4: Technical Considerations

The instrumentation called for in this piece is standard by contemporary expectations. The list on the cover of the score erroneously lists a fourth tenor trombone, but only three tenor parts as well as bass trombone are written in the score. Other than the required thunder sheets, percussion instrumentation is standard.

From the opening of the work until its conclusion, Nelson masterfully disguises tonal centers through the use of creative modulations and chromaticism. The work does not remain in one key center for long, as the opening moves from D to G major and eventually settles in C major just before the start of the chromatic second section, one that features alterations between C major and minor. As the second section concludes, the piece is firmly in F major with solo statements of Psalm 136 (or 84). The final section begins in F major, but quickly moves to B-flat to set up the aleatoric material in the woodwinds. The familiar psalm "Old Hundredth" is presented in E-flat before finishing in A-flat major, also the key of the final "Alleluia."

The technical demands of the work are slightly more challenging than one would encounter in most typical Grade 3 pieces. The meters presented in the work include 2/4, 4/4, and 6/4, with varying tempos. The rhythmic content does not pose a challenge in regard to technique or facility, as the most difficult rhythms are aleatoric sixteenth notes in the woodwinds and an overall scheme that uses mostly eighth notes and eighth-note triplets in the other families. The ranges for wind instruments are, for the most part, playable by high school players. The clarinet writing does fall in line with other works of the era in regard to a higher tessitura. The trombone and euphonium do have a written B-flat 1 that is sustained, while trumpet 1 writing maintains a relatively high tessitura.

The woodwinds, clarinets in particular, have many written trills. This was an initial concern on the part of the publisher, who desired to change the trills to eighth notes. Nelson strongly disagreed, and states in the score that whole-

or half-step trills are acceptable and players may execute an easier trill near the given pitches should difficulties be encountered. Trills also appear in the horn parts.

One of Nelson's compositional attributes is the use of aleatoric elements. Mm. 106–117 feature the woodwinds creating a glittering texture through the use of improvised and randomly repeated melodic patterns. Each player is to improvise to the extent of their given abilities and should not attempt to play with other players. Percussion instrumentation calls for the use of thunder sheets, an absolute necessity in order to accurately portray the storm.

Unit 5: Stylistic Considerations

Perhaps one of the most appealing elements of this work is the incorporation of a great variety of style, from its scoring to the mood each section creates.

The work features an array of articulation markings, including slurs, tenutos, accents, mezzo staccatos, and marcatos. Despite their differences in sound, each should be executed with great sostenuto. Lyrical presentations of the psalms abound and must be presented in a strong vocal/singing style. The composer has clearly indicated his desires in regard to dynamics and phrasing. There are several moments when players are called on to execute crescendos and decrescendos, both short and long in duration. The key to attaining the best results is proper balance through listening and matching energy within sections and families of instruments, as well as controlling the sound and pitch center at the extremes of each dynamic marking.

As noted earlier, when Nelson composed this work, the standard for band sonority was that of the University of Michigan Symphony Band, conducted by William D. Revelli. Although elements of that concept of sound are present in this score, a more contemporary approach to ensemble timbre is certainly acceptable and gives the work a more contemporary flavor.

A few conductors recommend doubling the timpani with bass drum and using two sets of chimes during the final three measures. This will give greater strength to the timpani part while reinforcing the church bell effect in the chimes. Although the last note is marked marcato, this note must have body, which is usually best produced by adding a tenuto to the marked articulation. It is further recommended this be done with the single eighth note in m. 132.

Unit 6: Musical Elements

MELODY:

Nelson uses three psalm tunes in the course of the work which, by their nature, lend themselves well to developing instrumentalists due to their largely stepwise motion. Nelson does alter the melodies on occasion, and transitional sections do include chromaticism. Figure 1 shows copies of the psalms as they appear in the *Ainsworth Psalter*.

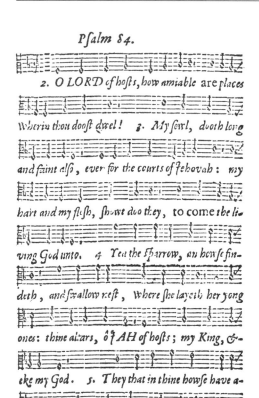

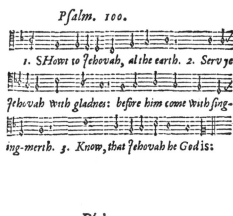

FIGURE 1. Facsimilies from the *Ainsworth Psalter*

HARMONY:

The harmonies presented in *Mayflower Overture* are mature and advanced for a Grade 3 work, and are not drastically different than one would find in more difficult pieces by this composer. Therefore, a firm, functional knowledge of basic harmonies and sonorities (unisons, thirds, fourths, fifths, sixths, and octaves) should be established prior to programming the piece. "Old Hundredth" is presented in octaves, and Psalm 3 is presented in canon. As stated above, the work has several graceful modulations through the use of secondary dominants and common chords.

RHYTHM:

The rhythmic content of the work is straightforward and does not exceed the boundaries of a Grade 3 work. The only exception is the woodwind aleatoric section, which uses randomly repeated patterns.

TIMBRE:

Nelson's orchestration typically calls on the forces of the full ensemble, regardless of the mood being created by the music. Even in its more rhythmic and driving sections, there is an underlying feeling of lyricism, or music that is vocal or choral in nature. The challenge for the conductor is properly balancing the accompaniment against melody and countermelody, especially in sections with louder dynamic markings.

Unit 7: Form and Structure

SECTION	MEASURE	EVENT AND SCORING
Section 1: "Departure"	1–22	Full ensemble opening; melody in low brass and reeds with trumpet rhythmic support; woodwind fragments of Psalm 84
	23–26	Brass presents Psalm 100 in augmentation
	27–41	Psalm 3 in C major
Transition	42–46	Psalm 84 in accented eighth notes; chromatic transition
Section 2: "Storm"	47–74	Psalm 3 presented in C minor with canonic imitation in low voices; woodwinds accompany with trills
Transition: "Calm after Storm"	75–92	Psalm 3 in C major in woodwinds; horn solo with countermelody
Closing section	93–98	Woodwind soloists present Psalm 84
Section 3: "Arrival in the New World"	99–105	Low brass and reeds state same melody as opening (variation on Psalm 100)
Chant	106–117	Brasses present Psalm 100 in unison (E-flat major); woodwinds with aleatoric material
	118–131	Psalm 100 and variation of Psalm 84 sound simultaneously
Alleluia	132–end	Powerful full ensemble variation of Psalm 100 closes the work

Unit 8: Suggested Listening

Nelson, Ron:
> *Medieval Suite*
> *Morning Alleluias for the Winter Solstice*

Zdechlik, John. *Chorale and Shaker Dance.*

Unit 9: Additional References and Resources

Ainsworth, Henry, Lorraine Inserra, and H. Wiley Hitchcock. *The Music of Henry Ainsworth's Psalter* (Amsterdam, 1612). Brooklyn, NY: Institute for Studies in American Music, Dept. of Music, Brooklyn College of the City University of New York, 1981.

Ron Nelson. The Keystone Wind Ensemble. Jack Stamp, conductor. Klavier K11168.

Websites:
  http://en.wikipedia.org/wiki/Mayflower
  http://www.rootsweb.ancestry.com/~mosmd/
  http://ronnelson.info/

Contributed by:

Rodney C. Schueller
Director of Bands
Texas State University
San Marcos, Texas

Teacher Resource Guide

Postcard from Singapore
Suite of Singaporean Folk Songs

Philip Sparke
(b. 1951)

Unit 1: Composer

Philip Sparke gained much of his early recognition as a composer by writing music for brass band. It was in this realm where he first enjoyed great success and was asked to provide test pieces for a number of important brass band championships. Familiarity with his music led a number of wind band associations to commission him to write for concert band. This was rather natural for Sparke, since he had studied trumpet and composition as well as played in the wind orchestra at the Royal College of Music.

A number of his earlier wind band compositions won awards, and his growing reputation led to an association with the band movement in Japan. That relationship produced a commission (*Celebration*) from the Tokyo Kosei Wind Orchestra, which eventually released a recording of Sparke's music. The worldwide distribution of the recording led to more commissions and a greatly enhanced presence in the United States.

In 1996, the U. S. Air Force Band commissioned and recorded *Dance Movements*, which won the Sudler Prize for Wind Band Composition in 1997. Philip Sparke is very active internationally as a conductor and adjudicator, and controls his own publishing company, Anglo Music Press. In addition to his musical activities, Sparke is reputed to enjoy photography, good food, and fine wine.

Unit 2: Composition

According to the program notes provided with the score, *Postcard from Singapore* was commissioned by M.A.S.T. Music, Singapore, for a concert featuring Sparke's music to be given by the Singapore Armed Forces Central Band. He was the guest conductor for the premiere, which took place on July 23, 2003. There are three movements based on traditional folk songs which are popular with children in Singapore. Movement 1 is built around the beloved folksong "Gelang Sipaku Gelang," which is associated with the Geylang area and addresses community spirit and living together in harmony. Movement 2 uses a folksong from Tanjung Katong, an area on the southeastern coast of Singapore. The song, which is popular with children's choirs, is "Di-Tanjung Katong." Movement 3 is a setting of two melodies: "Lenggang Kangkung," which tells of the graceful swaying of watercress in the rice paddy fields, and "Munnaeru Vaalibaa," with which Sparke cleverly combines with the first melody to produce an interesting polyphonic texture.

Unit 3: Historical Perspective

The musical culture of Malaysia has been influenced by several foreign elements, most especially Hindu culture from India, Islamic culture from Arab countries, and later on, the Western world, primarily England. By the turn of the twenthieth century, the British had introduced Western musical instruments such as trumpet, saxophone, clarinet, and piano, as well as various Western musical styles. The evolution of Malaysian music may be compared with the development of musical culture in America. This parallel is based on the contention that Malaysia is a developing nation in the process of creating its own unique and instantly recognizable musical identity which blends elements from its various component cultures, much the same as America did through the eighteenth century.

It is not possible to ascertain the exact composition dates of the traditional folksongs quoted in *Postcard from Singapore*, but it is relatively easy to find examples of traditional and non-traditional performances of those folksongs on various websites. The score does not require the use of any traditional Malaysian instruments except temple blocks.

Unit 4: Technical Considerations

There are no major technical difficulties in this score, but there are polyrhythmic figures and some range issues that indicate a level of medium-easy to medium-difficult. In movement 1, which is in common time and at an allegro tempo, quarter-note triplets occur with great frequency. To complicate matters, they often follow a dotted-quarter-and-eighth-note figure, requiring a precise shift of internalized division by players for accurate rhythmic performance.

Movement 2 is less technically demanding but requires more musical sensitivity and some secure soloists, particularly oboe, which is not cross-cued.

Movement 3 journeys through at least five key centers and contains more syncopation and polyphonic texture than its two predecessors. Lightness and clarity of staccato articulation is especially important to achieve in the final movement of *Postcard from Singapore*. The instrumentation is fairly typical for this difficulty level. Only two horns are required, but doubling each would enhance the harmonic color. There is a part for E-flat clarinet that is doubled throughout by other upper woodwinds, and a part for alto clarinet which is treated in the same manner. Inclusion of the E-flat clarinet might help achieve a bit of a more indigenous quality in terms of timbre (see Unit 6, under Timbre).

Unit 5: Stylistic Considerations

As indicated above, light staccato is an absolute necessity for a successful rendering of portions of *Postcard from Singapore*. Equally important is the use of a well-defined legato articulation style, particularly in movement 2. Sparke is quite clear about his stylistic intentions through the use of a variety of markings, including the use of accents, accents over staccatos, *forte-pianos*, and tenuto over staccato. The use of a lift or a tongue-stop staccato at the end of slurs that precede staccato notes must be taught.

Careful execution of the ample dynamic indications provided will greatly enhance the variety and contrast possible in this composition. The absence of the same will render this work deadly dull. As a general caveat, remember to begin crescendos softer and decrescendos louder. The use of the term *espressivo* indicates that Sparke is allowing for players, especially soloists, to provide shape and inflection in certain places without his micromanagement of dynamics. Listening to examples of the folksongs performed in more traditional Malaysian instrumental settings might affect interpretation. It would certainly shed a different light on the current setting being examined in this guide.

Unit 6: Musical Elements

MELODY:
The melodies in *Postcard from Singapore*, although based on traditional folksongs, sound surprisingly western. They are clearly diatonic and, in their original form, are generally structured in phrases of regular length. One may actually hear fragments of familiar music in certain portions of the songs. The movement 1 melody ("Gelang Sipaku Gelang") may remind somewhat older, American conductors of the theme from "Leave it to Beaver," while the second half of the melody in movement 2 ("Di-Tanjung Katong") sounds quite like the protestant hymn, "What a Friend We Have in Jesus." Although

it may not be appropriate to make such comparisons, in the absence of a definitive origin of the folksongs, there is the possibility of some cultural borrowing. Since the Malaysian words are easily available for each song, having the band learn to sing them would have not only cultural value, but would positively affect phrasing, articulation and intonation. It should be noted that when Sparke uses fragments of a folksong as a basis for expository composition, the phrase lengths are not necessarily symmetrical.

HARMONY:

As with the melodies, the harmony used in this setting is generally common practice in nature and European in origin. The basic structures are relatively simple and triadic, but often colored with a rather generous sprinkling of sixths, sevenths, and other non-triadic tones. Of greatest interest is Sparke's use of modulation to create variety and harmonic movement. It would be beneficial to analyze the use of accidentals in this work to discover whether or not the composer is simply providing a non-chord tone or if he is moving through a modulatory passage.

RHYTHM:

The quarter-note triplet found in movement 1 will necessitate a careful explanation of how this borrowed rhythm functions in a polyrhythmic setting. Begin by drawing two eighth-note triplets on a black (or white) board. Make sure the triplet mark is at the stem end of the note. Use a counting system to identify the parts of the beat (which is being divided in a compound division—three parts). I prefer *one-te-tah* for a triplet that occurs against one beat. Therefore, two beats of eighth-note triplets would be *one-te-tah, two-te-tah.*

Next, tie the eighth-note triplets into pairs. Beneath each pair write a quarter note (there will be three). That is the structure of a quarter-note triplet. To feel it correctly, have students count the eighth-note triplets, eventually accenting the beginning of each tie: *ONE-te-TAH, two-TE-tah.* Next, have the accent cover the end of the tie without saying the softer syllable. The final result will be a very even *one-tah-te,* three quarter notes placed against two.

Regarding the syncopations found in movements 2 and 3, it would be beneficial to explain the emphasized quality of the offbeat notes in the melody to secure a somewhat weighted performance of those pitches.

TIMBRE:

If one were to listen to the more traditional performances of these folksongs, a general impression of the timbre might be that the music is rather bright and edgy. This could affect the interpretation of *Postcard from Singapore* if one were to strive for a more traditional rendering. The fact that this composition is presented in a traditional wind band setting would seem to indicate that the composer's intention was for it to be performed with a concern for conventional methods for achieving a balanced and blended palette of western wind instrument colors. In other words, attention must be paid to octave doublings of the melody to achieve sufficient lower pitch projection, and chord structures will require the same scrutiny. In general, Sparke does a very nice job of treating the melodic material coloristically by presenting full statements or segments in various instrumental combinations. A less-common but effective doubling used in this work is the pairing of alto saxophone with trumpet at the unison level, which Sparke seems to prefer over doubling horn with alto saxophone.

Unit 7: Form and Structure

SECTION	MEASURE	EVENT AND SCORING
Movement 1: "Gelang Sipaku Gelang," 4/4, *Allegro*, quarter note = 138, ca. 2:45		
Introduction	1–5	Fanfare-like opening in F major
Transition	6–7	Accompaniment only
Extension of introduction	8–12	First folksong material used with a phrase elongation; in tenor voice
	13–16	Repeat of that material doubled by bass voice
	17–21	Original material that builds to the first climax of the movement
Transition	22–23	Accompaniment only with even-note syncopation; temple blocks added; diminuendo
A	24–36	First full statement of original folksong; in soprano voices; *mezzo forte*
A	37–48	Second full statement of folksong in soprano voices (*forte*) with a counter-melodic figure derived from the folksong entering imitatively one measure later (m. 38)
Transition	49–51	Extension of folksong ending; modulation to D minor
Development (B)	52–58	Fragmentation of melodic motive from folksong; timbral movement
	59	Modulation to B-flat major
	60–71	Brass statement of first half of folksong

SECTION	MEASURE	EVENT AND SCORING
	64–71	Incomplete woodwind statement of second half of folksong with a transition and modulation back to F major
A	72–82	Powerful restatement of folksong in trumpet and alto saxophone with two derivative, countermelodic elements, one in upper woodwinds, the other in tenor voices
Coda	83–89	Return to fanfare figure from the beginning with a final quarter-note triplet tag in tenor voices; *fortissimo*

Movement 2: "Di-Tanjung Katong," 4/4, *Andante,* quarter note = 68, ca. 3:00

Introduction	1–4	Clarinet solo; E-flat major; *piano* dynamic
A	5–8	Oboe solo introduces first phrase of folksong
	9–12	Oboe plays second phrase; obbligato in flute and imitative figure in alto saxophone
B	13–20	Trumpet solo melody ("What a Friend") passed to alto sax; melodic doubling increases, leading to a *forte-piano*
	21	Modulation to F major
A	22–25	First phrase of folksong in upper voices with an imitative accompaniment derived from the melody; *forte*
	26–29	Second phrase continues in alto sax and trumpet; derivative figure continues in clarinets and flutes, providing a delicate sixteenth-note staccato texture; diminuendo into m. 30
	30–37	Section B of melody with flowing accompaniment
	38	Extension of section B of folksong
Closing passage	39–42	Mirror of introduction but in F major

Movement 3: "Lenggang Kangkung" and "Munnaeru Vaalibaa," 2/4, *Allegro vivo,* quarter note = 138, ca. 3:20

Introduction	1–16	Introductory material derived from "Lenggang" melody (1) fragments over a B-flat pedal in the bass voice
	16–19	Accompaniment vamp and decrescendo

SECTION	MEASURE	EVENT AND SCORING
A	20–27	Melody 1 (section a) begins with only percussion accompaniment; basic style is detached
	28–34	Second half of melody 1 (section b) stated in alto sax, clarinet 2–3, and oboe
	35–42	Melody 1 occurs again, this time in trumpet with brass accompaniment; E-flat major; undulating clarinet sixteenth-note figure underscores melody
	43–51	Section B of melody 1 in upper woodwinds with an exact canonic statement in low voices at a one-measure following distance
	52	Abrupt modulation to the key of F major
	53–60	Section A of melody 1
	61–68	Section B of melody 1 stated in glock with clarinets providing running, scale-like accompaniment
	71–78	Abrupt modulation to A-flat major; section A of melody 1 in clarinet and sax, *piano*
	79–87	Back to F major; section b of melody; dissonant figures in accompaniment (minor seconds)
	88–89	Crescendo to climax of section A
	90–98	B-flat major; section a of melody 1; generally homophonic texture; *forte*
	98–105	G major; section b of melody 1; imitation at a one-beat following distance for a three-level polyphonic texture
	106	3/4 measure that transitions abruptly back into B-flat major and common time
B	107–114	4/4 time; second folksong (melody 2); a-a-b-a form; accompaniment fragments based on melody 1; B-flat major; style is more legato
	115–118	Section B of melody 2; *mezzo forte*
	119–122	Last section A phrase in complete melody 2; quick modulation to C major
	123–139	Second complete statement of melody 2
A	140–147	Return to 2/4 time and melody 1; section A

Section	Measure	Event and Scoring
	148–157	Saxes and oboe perform section b of melody 1 in major sevenths, perhaps referring to a Malaysian musical idiosyncrasy
Transition	158–161	Return to E-flat major and both melodies
A + B	162–177	Melody 1 in upper woodwinds; melody 2 in trumpets, saxes, and euphonium; *forte*; E-flat pedal in bass
	178–185	Melody 1, section B and melody 2, section B in counterpoint
	186–193	Section A of melody 1 extended over section A of melody 2 to allow a complete statement of the final section A of melody 2
Coda	194–201	Crescendo to *forte*

Total time: ca. 9:05

Unit 8: Suggested Listening

Bartók, Béla. Arranged by Yo Goto. *Jocuri Poporale Romanesti.*
Davis, Albert Oliver. *Three Airs from Gloucester.*
Erickson, Frank. *Norwegian Folk Song Suite.*
Jacob, Gordon. *An Original Suite.*
Jager, Robert. *Three Chinese Miniatures.*
Mashima, Toshio. *Les trois notes du Japon.*
Stevens, Halsey. *Ukrainian Folksongs.*

Unit 9: Additional References and Resources

Gritton, P. *Folksongs from the Far East.* London: Faber, 1991.
Knowlton, M. and M. J. Sachner. *Children of the World: Malaysia.* Milwaukee, WI: Gareth Stevens Publishing, 1987.
Lyons, K. and Martin Loh. *Malaysian Children's Favorite Stories.* Boston, MA: Tuttle, 2004.
Smith, Norman E. *Program Notes for Band.* Chicago: GIA Publications, Inc., 2002.
Sparke, Philip. *Between the Two Rivers: Music by Philip Sparke.* Deutsche Blaserphilharmonie. Walter Ratzek, conductor. Milwaukee, WI: Anglo Music Press c/o Hal Leonard Music, 2004.

Websites:

Abdullah, Mohd Hassan. *Idiosyncratic Aspects of Malaysian Music: The Roles of the Kompang in   Malay Society.* University Pendidikan Sultan Idris, Malaysia: http://portal.unesco.org/
culture/es/files/21753/10891249663abdullah.pdf/abdullah.pdf
Malaysian Music. http://www.cyloong.com/Multicultural/SEA.html
Philip Sparke. http://www.philipsparke.com

Contributed by:

John C. Carmichael
Director of Bands/Associate Professor of Music
School of Music
University of South Florida
Tampa, Florida

Teacher Resource Guide

Song for Lyndsay

Andrew Boysen, Jr.
(b. 1968)

Unit 1: Composer

Andrew Boysen, Jr. is currently an associate professor of music at the University of New Hampshire, where he teaches beginning and advanced conducting, composition, and conducts the Wind Symphony. Earning his bachelor of music degree from the University of Iowa in 1991, he went on to complete a master of music in wind conducting from Northwestern University in 1993 and a doctor of musical arts in wind conducting at the Eastman School of Music. Boysen is an active guest conductor and clinician appearing with high school, university, and festival ensembles all over the United States and Great Britain.

Composing since age nine, he has written works for concert band, symphony orchestra, brass choir, brass quintet, horn choir, and piano. His works have been performed all over the United States. Boysen has received commissions from the Herbert Hoover Presidential Library, the Iowa All-State Band, the Rhode Island All-State Band, the Massachusetts Instrumental and Choral Conductors Association, the Nebraska Bandmasters Association, and various high school and university bands. His awards and accolades include winning the International Horn Society Composition Contest in 2000, the University of Iowa Composition Prize in 1991, and the Claude T. Smith Memorial Band Composition Contest in 1991 for *I Am* and again in 1994 for *Ovations*.

Unit 2: Composition

Song for Lyndsay was commissioned by Jack Stamp at Indiana University of Pennsylvania. It is an expansion on a short and unnamed piano piece that Boysen wrote for his wife, Lyndsay, in 2005. The wind piece is larger in length and scope than the source material; in the score, Boysen describes it as "a very personal work…more than anything else a simple love song dedicated to Lyndsay and what she has meant in my life." The piano piece is used as a starting point, and the material in the winds is either based on or a direct quotation of it. Lyrical in nature and just over five minutes long, the challenge in performing *Song for Lyndsay* lies in phrasing, rubato, and the use of many dissonance-to-consonance resolutions through suspension and retardation. Solo horn and solo flute are prominent throughout; this scoring is deliberately and symbolically used because Boysen plays the horn and his wife the plays the flute.

Unit 3: Historical Perspective

The piano piece was composed in the spring of 2005 and the wind piece followed shortly thereafter. It is among the latest in a long line of pieces that are either about or dedicated to the composer's spouse. The arrangement of Stephen Foster's *Jeanie* is another example of this in the wind literature. Also common is the practice of basing a wind piece on a piano work while preserving the piano timbre by adding it to the texture, as exemplified in Percy Grainger's *Children's March*. The harmonic language is tonal and functional, though there is extensive use of added notes and sonorities for color.

Unit 4: Technical Considerations

The instrumentation used in *Song for Lyndsay* is that of a standard concert band with added piano, which is prominently featured as it frequently plays passages from the original source piece. Ranges in the piece are relatively typical for a work of this level, but the conductor should note that the flute must play a high B-flat and the horn must play an A above the staff.

The work includes a diverse array of percussion instruments with extensive use of mallets: triangle, marimba, orchestra bells, chimes, vibraphone, timpani, bowed crotales, suspended cymbal, tam-tam, and wind chimes are called for.

Solo horn and solo flute are present throughout many passages and are essential, as the texture is extremely thin in these instances, often only horn and piano. Trumpets and trombones are asked to play with straight mutes in m. 27. Students are often asked to play in choirs, sometimes thinly scored.

Rhythms in the piece are mostly based on quarter-, eighth-, and dotted-quarter-note figures. There are three instances of sixteenth-note figures and one triplet. Metrically, the piece often changes from 4/4 to 3/4 to 2/4 and back to 4/4; there is one 5/4 bar during a heavy ritard in m. 87, leading to the major climax. The tonal center mainly moves between C minor and E-flat major.

Unit 5: Stylistic Considerations

Song for Lyndsay makes heavy use of ritard and a tempo. The tempos through-out the piece are slow, with heavy rubato at the ends of phrases and just before climaxes and impacts. Boysen notates many ritards and asks that ensembles "make enough of them." The approach to the main climax of the piece at m. 88 features a ritard all the way down to eighth note = 63; conductors will want to conduct a subdivided beat for at least part of m. 87.

Dynamically, the piece demands that players play very softly; they must often execute a decrescendo over several phrases to *niente*. The piece requires the ensemble to play at a tutti *fff* at m. 88. Most articulations in the work are of the legato or tenuto variety; the few accents that exist in the winds are accompanied by legato markings.

Unit 6: Musical Elements

MELODY:
Much of the melodic material is based on the intervallic progression of a downward major second followed by a downard minor third (concert C to B-flat to G) when the tonal center is C minor. This is eventually altered to a downward minor second followed by a downward major third when the tonal center shifts to E-flat major (concert E-flat to D to B-flat). The melody often is scored in the piano as a direct quotation of the source material. Boysen creates new melodies and countermelodies to the piano theme and scores them predominantly in solo flute and solo horn. By the end of the piece the melody is scored in traditional fashion in the upper winds and upper brass.

HARMONY:
The tonal center of the piece begins in C minor and modulates to E-flat major. Boysen makes heavy use of 4–3 suspensions on dominant chords and 2–3 retardations on major or minor tonic chords. He often adds sixths for color; this happens most often during the introduction in Gm^7 chords. These tech-niques create the aforementioned dissonance-to-consonance resolutions effectively. Students will need to listen for the resulting close intervals that are created, as the harmonic motion of the piece depends heavily on tension and release.

RHYTHM:
There are few, if any, rhythmic challenges in this piece. Ensembles should be aware of the often-changing time signature; Boysen uses this as a device to extend phrases. The conductor must reinforce the concept of subdivision

during the instances of *molto ritard* in order to keep the group together. Legato articulations and sensitivity to releases when phrases are tied across barlines are essential.

TIMBRE:
Song for Lyndsay is at times a piece for solo piano with wind accompaniment, a piece for horn and flute duet, and a straight-ahead concert band piece. In the latter instances, Boysen makes use of woodwind and brass choirs, saving tutti passages for the climactic moments in the piece.

Unit 7: Form and Structure

SECTION	MEASURE	EVENT AND SCORING
Introduction	1–10	Foreshadowing of theme B in solo horn with piano accompaniment; piano plays Gm⁷ chords with an added sixth
A	11–14	Main melody from source piece presented in C minor in piano
	15–26	Second melody from source piece in woodwind choir with piano accompaniment
	27–34	Main melody from original piano piece in brass choir; trumpets and trombones are muted; C minor tonality remains
B	35–42	Melody from introduction in solo flute with piano and clarinet accompaniment
Transition	43–49	New melody in upper winds; texture gradually thickens to add brass; harmony prepares to cadence in E-flat major
	50–57	First climax and denouement in E-flat major; tutti
B'	58–67	Theme B melody in solo horn with solo flute countermelody; accompaniment in winds and piano
	68–75	Tutti crescendo and ritard building to second climax
A'	76–85	Second climax in m. 76; sempre *ff*; tutti; main melodies from section A return, now in E-flat major
	86–87	*Molto crescendo* and *molto ritard* through the end of the 5/4 bar (m. 87); build to major climax and modulation

SECTION	MEASURE	EVENT AND SCORING
Coda	88–94	Major climax in C minor in m. 88 with a 2–1 suspension; dynamic softens and texture gradually thins to upper winds only
	95–101	Solo flute and solo horn drive cadence to final key of E-flat major and decrescendo to *niente*; piano ends piece with theme A' and arpeggiated E-flat major chord to end the piece very softly

Unit 8: Suggested Listening

Boysen Jr., Andrew:
　I Am
　Ovations
Foster, Stephen. Arranged by John Kinyon. *Jeanie*.
Grainger, Percy. *Children's March*.

Unit 9: Additional References and Resources

Garofalo, Robert J. *Instructional Designs for Middle/Junior High School Band*. Fort Lauderdale, FL: Meredith Music Publications, 1995.
Kreines, Joseph. *Music for Concert Band*. Tampa, FL: Florida Music Service, 1989.
Mertz, Justin J. Interview with Andrew Boysen, Jr. May, 2008.
Randel, Don Michael, ed. *The New Harvard Dictionary of Music*. Cambridge, MA: Harvard University Press, 1996.

Contributed by:

Justin J. Mertz
Assistant Director of Bands
Director, Syracuse University Marching Band
Syracuse University
Syracuse, New York

Teacher Resource Guide

Spirals of Light

Sean O'Loughlin
(b. 1972)

Unit 1: Composer

Sean O'Loughlin is a native of Syracuse, New York. His diverse musical background includes orchestrating for television and film. Equally at home working with Blue Man Group, Natalie Merchant with the Boston Pops Orchestra, or a district honor band, O'Loughlin's prodigious output is innovative and extensive. Commissions from the Boston Pops Orchestra, the Hollywood Bowl Orchestra, and the Los Angeles Philharmonic enhance his impressive credentials. He has served in a conducting capacity with numerous major orchestras as well.

Born in 1972, he has at a young age become active in composing for both band and orchestra. His music is vibrant and energetic, and his work with venues such as the Los Angeles Philharmonic Youth Concert Series serve to enhance and give a unique angle to his growing body of literature for educational publications through Carl Fischer. He earned degrees at Syracuse University and New England Conservatory, and was also a composition fellow at the Henry Mancini Institute.

Unit 2: Composition

Spirals of Light is a work that is festive in nature. It was written for the North Carolina 2006 All-District Band (grades nine and ten) as a commission from the South Central District Bandmasters Association.

Published in 2007 by Carl Fischer Music, this work, structured loosely in ABA form, offers excellent training tools for the growing ensemble. Within the brief four-minute composition, opportunities for solo winds, mallet percussion, and the teaching of subdivision of rhythms abound. There is interest for both player and listener. Two main ideas are incorporated. The first is a fanfare-like statement; the second, an Irish folk-like melody, is presented in a brisk 6/8 feel and, in the middle section of the work, within a 4/4 context incorporating a variety of melodic shapes. The work is suitable for young band concert programming and festivals. It can readily serve as a celebratory opener or a work within the body of a program.

Unit 3: Historical Perspective

The work was freely composed with a specific North Carolina honor band in mind, and served this purpose well. Additionally, if fits in to a wide body of literature at the Grade 3 level that is suitable for training ensembles. Particularly significant training elements that can be incorporated in teaching this work include the areas of wind and percussion colors and balances, and rhythmic and ensemble clarity.

Unit 4: Technical Considerations

As a medium-level work, *Spirals of Light* is laced with level-appropriate technical demands, including ranges and rhythms. Independent solos in flute, alto saxophone, and horn are musically challenging yet accessible for a young player. The percussion scoring is suitable and active with mallet work.

Clarity of articulation and rhythmic demands provide challenge. The allegro sections require accurate subdivision of rhythms and a clean, accurate ensemble metric feel. The metric transfer of the steady eighth note from the 6/8 section into the 4/4 feel of section B is a modulation of pulse not often seen in this level of music, and it is woven into the work in a seamless way. There is appropriate balance between chamber-like and tutti scoring, each within a context that does not lose the interest of performer or listener.

There is ample opportunity for slow and lyrical, as well as allegro and highly rhythmic playing. Both textures fit the educational and musical goals for musicians at this level of proficiency.

Unit 5: Stylistic Considerations

The majority of the work is rhythmic, even when moving out of the 6/8 feel into the middle 4/4 section. Lyrical work in the 4/4 section is more often than not accompanied in a way that will require careful attention to articulation and rhythmic subdivision.

The melodic ideas require appropriate breath control and support. The work is moderate to fast in tempo, utilizing tempos of dotted quarter note = 100–108, and quarter note = 66–84.

Unit 6: Musical Elements

MELODY:

The main melodic treatment is that of an Irish-like folk melody, first presented in the alto saxophones at m. 32. This melody is treated in various ways and in different musical contexts throughout the work. There is also a fanfare theme that is predominant and drawn on often for both melodic and rhythmic textures. It is first heard in the introduction at m. 14.

HARMONY:

The overall casting of the work is in E-flat, but the composer frequently includes some subtle dissonance to add flavor and intensity to the voicing. While clearly tonal, the conductor must take care in teaching appropriate blend of voices and balance of the brass and woodwind families, both as separate entities and as combined forces. Opportunities are frequent for tuning open intervals, both in homophonic melodic treatment and in the accompaniment settings.

RHYTHM:

An even eighth note with a frequent syncopated feel will provide the greatest rhythmic challenge for most young ensembles. An appropriate lilt is necessary for the Irish-like melody, and the fanfare idea must be steady, balanced, and driven. In the first transition to 4/4 at m. 84, and throughout most of the middle section, the intensity does not subside. Later, at m. 130, as the composer prepares for the return of the 6/8 meter, there is a more relaxed flow that could even call for subtle rubato and an interpretive shaping of the phrase.

As in much music conceived for young players, an early understanding of internalizing the pulse through appropriate subdivision will have educational and musical benefits as players mature. The piece provides for much opportunity in this regard, in both syncopated and less-energetic types of rhythms.

TIMBRE:

The work highlights the woodwind, brass, and percussion families, sometimes independently, and frequently in various combinations. Ample chamber-like sections are also scored. The tutti sections suggest careful balance and listening to accommodate the melodic voices. The sonorities provide an interest for the listener, and are not out of the ordinary for tuning, balance, and blend.

Unit 7: Form and Structure

SECTION	MEASURE	EVENT AND SCORING
Section A		
Introduction	1–13	Spirited, oscillating woodwinds with brass punctuation; a hint of melodic material presented in flute and mallet
Fanfare theme	14–27	Begins with punctuated syncopation in trumpet and horn in four-bar segments; adds trombone and ultimately full ensemble; interval of descending fourth is recurring and prominent
Bridge	28–31	Timpani solo in the style of the fanfare theme; low, sustained winds accompanying at the interval of a fifth
Theme	32–39	Irish lilt presented in alto saxophone; delicate, low tom-tom accompaniment with sporadic additional color in percussion; the fifth interval, E-flat to B-flat, provides a drone accompaniment
Theme	40–47	Horn joins saxophone on melodic line; interspersed pedal E-flat in low winds; chordal punctuation in upper woodwinds
Bridge	48–57	Melodic, oscillating fragments presented in flute 1, oboe, clarinet 1, mallet; contrasting line moving in parallel rhythm in other woodwinds; brass and percussion punctuate this idea, building to a return of the theme via a dominant chord
Theme	58–65	Theme stated in trumpet and horn; tutti accompaniment
Transition	66–83	Interchange of rhythmic tutti sections and percussion; rhythmic feel of fanfare theme evident; tutti sections incorporate ideas fragmented from melodic textures, particularly the descending fourth from the fanfare statement and the descending, diatonic scale pattern
Section B		
Introduction	84–85	Clarinet and vibe, softly in quarter- and eighth-note fashion

Section	Measure	Event and Scoring
Development	86–96	Solos in alto saxophone, horn, and flute incorporate main theme, but with a more plaintive, 4/4 rhythmic feel; the fifth interval (E-flat to B-flat) with an added concert F continues in the rhythmic accompaniment (trumpet, clarinet, and mallet)
	97–130	Still in 4/4 context, elongated thematic material appears; alternating lyrical and fanfare ideas; combinations of woodwind and brass families appear independently between tutti ensemble sections; a pair of 3/4 measures (mm. 126–127) provide anticipation for a crescendo into the upcoming transition
Transition	130–135	A lush section; slower, with tutti flowing lines and rich, inner motion
Section A Introduction	136–140	Tutti chord with horn and alto saxophone calls at the interval of a fifth
Theme	141–149	Melody in alto and tenor saxophone and upper woodwinds; full band accompanies with rhythmic punctuation
Theme	150–168	Augmentation of theme treated canonically, coupled with steady, oscillating eighth notes slurred in upper woodwinds; build to high point incorporates material derived from fanfare theme
Bridge	169–170	Accented rhythmic woodwind fragments with mallet and triangle in the style of the fanfare theme
Theme	171–178	Horn and trumpet perform opening theme with tutti, although slightly varied, accompaniment as previously stated; melody is harmonized in a parallel rhythm
Bridge	179–181	Rhythmic motive from fanfare with woodwind flourishes
Coda	182–200	Begins with fanfare material from opening introduction, mainly heard in brass; builds to tutti ensemble with exciting woodwind flourishes and syncopated punctuations in brass and percussion, bringing the work to a dramatic close

Unit 8: Suggested Listening

Applebaum, Stan. *Irish Suite*.
Boysen, Andrew. *Kirkpatrick Fanfare*.
Erickson, Frank. *Irish Folk Song Suite*.

Unit 9: Additional References and Resources

Email from composer. June 5, 2008
Miles, Richard, ed. *Teaching Music through Performance in Band, Volume 6.*
    Chicago: GIA Publications, 2007.
http://www.grayslacks.com

Contributed by:

Bruce Moss
Director of Bands
Bowling Green State University
Bowling Green, Ohio

Teacher Resource Guide

Symphony No. 4
Movement 1: Fast
Movement 2: Smooth and Flowing
Movement 3: Scherzo and Trio
Movement 4: Fast

Andrew Boysen, Jr.
(b. 1968)

Unit 1: Composer

Andrew Boysen, Jr. is assistant professor of music at the University of New Hampshire, where his responsibilities include conducting the UNH Wind Symphony and teaching courses in conducting, composition, and orchestration. Prior to his appointment there, he served in a similar capacity at Indiana State University. Before beginning his collegiate teaching career, Boysen served as band director for Cary-Grove High School in Illinois, and simultaneously served as conductor of the Deerfield Community Concert Band. A prolific composer for wind band, Boysen has composed over forty-five works for concert band.

Unit 2: Composition

Written in 2004, *Symphony No. 4*, for winds and percussion is a four-movement work of approximately fourteen minutes total duration, published by Kjos Music Company. Listed by the publisher as a Grade 3-1/2 level work, the composition is intended for performance by young band, and to serve as an approachable "first symphony performance experience" for young musicians.

The work employs the four movements traditionally associated with the historical Classical symphony, complete with the conventions and forms typical for each movement. In order to ensure performance practicality for younger players, however, each movement is considerably abbreviated from what one would normally expect in a traditional symphony. The composer's intent as stated in the score is for the piece to "provide teaching opportunities through the ability [of school band directors] to discuss each movement and draw comparisons to the forms and traditions expressed in other symphonies.? As Boysen's symphony is harmonically based on the octatonic scale and uses tetrachords derived from it, there are many factors for educators to teach, share, and discuss with their students. In addition to the forms of the traditional symphony, the work is also an example of a cyclical form, where the materials of movement 1 are strongly reiterated in the final movement in order to strongly and decisively bring the symphony to a unified and dramatic conclusion.

Unit 3: Historical Perspective

The creation of *Symphony No. 4* is the result of a commissioning project initiated by Chip De Stefano and the McCracken Middle School Bands located in Skokie, Illinois. The objective and intent of the composition is best described in the composer's own words, taken from the score's performance notes:

> I wanted to write a piece that would be exciting and fun for his [Chip De Stefano's] students to play, but would also treat the middle school ensemble as a viable medium for artistic expression. In other words, I wanted to compose a piece that was as serious and musical as I would write for a college ensemble, while still recognizing the necessary technical limitations of the age. For some time, I had been considering writing a symphony for younger students, and this seemed like the perfect opportunity.

Unit 4: Technical Considerations

Movement 1

There are very few technically-related difficulties with respect to rhythm, range, or facility that present themselves within movement 1. The opening two measures are non-metered, cued events of fifteen seconds duration each, which allow for most performers to vocalize. Not until the third measure does the music proceed in a metered, brisk 4/4 tempo (quarter note = 168).

In all, movement 1's melodic material is comprised of two themes, each based on a four-note subset derived from an octatonic scalar structure (C–D-flat–G–E). These two themes and the ideas derived from them are the basis of all subsequent thematic and motivic units employed throughout the remainder of the symphony.

The particular melodic intervals which characterize the four-note motivic fragments in the movement's primary theme are set within an octatonic milieu. This melodic material may initially present a challenge to young players in terms of the harmonic and aural perception required for its performance. However, because of the repetitive nature of the melodic themes throughout, these likely will become quickly familiar to young students, and present no particular difficulty for them once they have cleared the initial hurdles of learning the piece.

Movement 2

Unlike the music performed in movement 1, movement 2 begins with significantly more exposed music, thus students will be required to play with greater individual confidence. The thematic and rhythmic materials used throughout the movement present no substantive technical demands. There are essentially no high- or low-range technical demands of concern, with one exception: In the phrase that comprises mm. 25–32, trumpet 1 must begin on a written A4 above the staff and then ascend to a high C6. The requirement to play in this high range may be difficult for some younger trumpeters. However, this phrase also constitutes the movement's musical climax, and is the only phrase within the movement where full-textured tutti scoring occurs. Supported by this full ensemble texture, trumpet 1 is instructed to play these high range notes at a *fortissimo* dynamic level, thus making the performance of this phrase more likely to achieve than if it were written at a softer dynamic.

Another overall technical consideration is the demand for players to perform with longer sustained phrases. Younger musicians may need to master ample breath intake in order to securely perform several longer, slurred passages in this movement.

A final technical challenge may involve the percussion section. Within the movement's slow, sustained phrases, the timing of the required punctuations from the percussion section may not be immediately obvious to young players. They will need to dependably count longer sections of rests, and then confidently perform such figures precisely at the correct moments. Further, the percussion writing, scored for five individual performers, never occurs in unison. Rather, the parts are quite independent of one another, thus each percussionist must concentrate faithfully and consistently in order to accurately count rests and effectively perform individual passages with security and confidence.

Movement 3

The first and most obvious technical consideration in this movement is that of rhythm. As with traditional symphonies, this movement is cast as a scherzo and trio, written in 6/8. Further, Boysen takes advantage of the opportunity to contrast compound metric beat divisions of two against alternative beat divisions of three, thus creating the effect of rhythmic *hemiola*. Independence of counting, therefore, will be a key challenge and a necessary requirement for all performers.

Further, in mm. 19–25, Boysen has woodwinds continuing in 6/8 compound time while simultaneously casting brass and percussion in 2/4. Thus for eight measures the ensemble performs in metric counterpoint, amounting to three against two within each beat division. This rhythmically-oriented challenge is reminiscent of the full ensemble challenge found in the final movement of Holst's *Second Suite in F*. In terms of demands related to instrumental range, the movement presents no significant difficulties.

Movement 4

As in movement 3, the technical demands of the final movement are more of an ensemble than individual challenge. The first three measures amount to timed, non-metered events, where individual woodwinds and three percussionists perform independent cells of notes. Each cell has its own rhythmic, as well as pitch class identity.

In the fourth measure a brisk 4/4 (quarter note = 152) is established. Here the brass section plays rhythmically in unison against the woodwind and percussion cells. While the brasses can easily follow the conductor and perform the straightforward unison rhythms of mm. 4–15, woodwinds and percussion must keep track of each measure while maintaining the ongoing performance of their motivic cells at a pace consistent with the movement's opening three measures. Thus during mm. 4–15 these cell materials must be heard as music seemingly independent of the conducted tempo. Therefore, while learning the piece initially, these twelve measures may prove to be significantly challenging, as the passage calls on woodwinds and percussion to think independently, and yet keep track of the actual conducted tempo, amounting to a kind of musical multi-tasking challenge.

The percussion vamp, characterized by a repeated, dotted, rhythmic motive, and scored for timpani and tom-toms, must be stable. Young players must be sufficiently skilled in order to accurately play these repetitive, dotted, rhythms while faithfully maintaining the movement's overall quick-paced tempo.

Beginning at m. 34 all woodwind and brass performers become vocalists, singing unison pitches. In order to initially begin these vocalizations with pitch accuracy, students must be able to audiate (pre-hear) their starting pitches in advance of having to actually sing them, amounting to their ability to evince a fundamental grasp of relative pitch.

The movement presents few demands in terms of instrumental ranges. However, for six brief measures, (mm. 90–95), trumpet 1 must ascend from a written G5 to a B-flat 5. Finally, during the coda (m. 134) all woodwinds are called on to perform independent cell motives as in the movement's beginning. Here, however, they must confidently and decisively arrive together at m. 145 to perform boldly in full unison with the brass in order to bring the movement to a secure and musically dramatic conclusion.

Unit 5: Stylistic Considerations

Movement 1, *Fast*, requires confident rhythmic playing with special attention to uniformity of articulation.

Movement 2, *Smooth and Flowing*, calls for lyrical and sensitive playing for its more elegant melodic phrases while calling on individuals and sections to play confidently, soloistically, and uniformly in mostly exposed passages.

In movement 3, *Scherzo and Trio*, demands uniformity of articulation and an assertive, yet more agile approach to the style.

Finally, movement 4, *Fast*, essentially combines the elements of style and articulation called for in all previous movements.

Unit 6: Musical Elements

MELODY:
The principal melody of movement 1, based on four tones from the octatonic scale (C–D-flat–E–G), is first heard in the non-metered event that begins the symphony, scored for orchestra bells. In the second event (m. 2) the four notes are reiterated and layered by vocalizations from wind players. This primary theme is then very prominently stated and expanded by clarinets and alto saxophones in mm. 7–13, and then even more assertively restated by piccolo, flutes, oboes, clarinets, and trumpets in mm. 16–25.

The movement's second theme, based merely on four tones (D-C-sharp–D–B) occurs in mm. 28–25, first rendered by horns and euphoniums, and then answered canonically by oboes, then flutes, respectively. Melodic materials and fragments during the development section (mm. 49–71) are based on the movement's primary theme and its accompaniment. The primary theme appears boldly in augmentation, stated by *fortissimo* trumpets and trombones in mm. 62–71. The recapitulation section (mm. 72–101) uses the primary theme (mm. 76–82) as well as the canonic and layered secondary theme material (mm. 85–101).

Movement 2 is a chaconne, with the ground stated in mm. 1–8 by horns, low woodwinds, and low brass. This eight-measure ground is reiterated six times throughout the movement. The melody, an expanded version derived from the secondary theme of movement 1, begins with flute in m. 9 and is eventually joined by clarinets and alto saxophones. A semi-augmented version of this theme is given by piccolo, flutes, clarinet 1, alto saxophones, and trumpets, and constitutes the climax of the movement (mm. 25–32).

In movement 3, *Scherzo and Trio*, clarinets present an eight-measure melody (mm. 11–18) based on the expanded version of the original secondary theme. This melody is strongly reiterated by the full woodwind section in mm. 19–26. At m. 40, a horn soloist presents a compound-metered version of the symphony's primary theme. The solo horn is eventually fortified by solo first trumpet in mm. 48–55.

Movement 4, *Fast*, inverts the themes as they were originally presented during movement 1. In this final movement the primary theme is based on the original secondary theme, and movement 4's secondary theme is based on the original primary theme.

The primary theme of movement 4 is boldly stated by piccolo, flutes, oboes, clarinets, and trumpets at m. 20. It is then layered canonically by two subsequent groups: low woodwinds and low brass, beginning m. 20, beat 3; and alto saxophones, horns, and first trombones, beginning in m. 22. These staggered, canonic entrances continue throughout mm. 20–31.

Vocalizations akin to the non-metered event originally heard in movement 1 occur across mm. 32–50, based on the pitches C and D-flat. During this vocally *sostenuto* section, melodic interjections from orchestra bells and vibraphone occur repetitively, based on movement 1's original octatonic pitch subset of C–D-flat–G–E.

The secondary theme of movement 4 (the primary theme from movement 1) is clearly and lyrically stated as a solo alto saxophone solo in mm. 53–62. Immediately following, the entire wind section vocalizes this same theme in mm. 63–72.

The development section's melodic materials begin with trombones and euphoniums (mm. 73–76) presenting melodic variations of the the primary theme of movement 4. These melodic gestures continue with flutes and clarinets (mm. 77–80), but also demonstrate derivation from the original flute melody of movement 2. The melodic gestures continue with trumpets (mm. 80–85), saxophones (mm. 84–89), oboes and clarinets (mm. 87–89), and piccolo and flutes (mm. 88–80). A nearly tutti statement of the melodic gesture appears as a partially augmented version across mm. 88–96. A final reiteration of the augmented version is stated by trombone 1 in mm. 98–105.

With the recapitulation section, the primary theme of movement 4 appears in canonic fashion (mm. 106–117), duplicating the staggered, canonic group entrances of the melodic material, just as in mm. 21–31. Across mm. 122–133 the movement's secondary theme (the primary theme of movement 1) is clearly and concisely stated by piccolo, flutes, clarinets, trumpets, and xylophone. A final restatement of this theme appears in augmentation, forcefully played at a bold *fortississimo* dynamic by the entire wind section, bringing the symphony to its dramatic conclusion (mm. 145–151).

HARMONY:

Although set in a largely octatonic milieu, the symphony is essentially tonal throughout. In movement 1, *Fast*, all eight tones of the octatonic scale are woven into the harmonic fabric. The key center begins and remains essentially in C during the introduction and throughout the statement of the primary theme (mm. 1–13). During the transition (mm.14–25), the key center shifts from C to G by means of ascending chromatic shifts within the accompanying voices. The harmonic underpinnings remain centered in G during the statement of the secondary theme (mm. 26–48).

The development section, based on the primary theme and its accompaniment, is centered on both G and E-flat (mm. 49–71). During the recapitulation section (mm. 72–101) and coda (mm. 102–106) the key center remains fixed on C.

Movement 2, *Smooth and Flowing*, is centered on E-flat and continuously employs two alternating tetrachords throughout. The two tetrachords are each subsets of the full octatonic scale: the first is comprised of the pitches E-flat–E–G–B-flat, and the second, D-flat–C–A–G-flat. Note that the two tetrachords are inversions of one another.

Movement 3, *Scherzo and Trio*, juxtaposes two major chords based on the octatonic scale (C and G-flat major) during section A. The key center throughout the entire movement remains essentially in C.

Movement 4, *Fast*, uses essentially the same harmonic language as movement 1, retaining the octatonic milieu of previous movements. Like movement 1, the introduction and first section of the exposition (mm. 1–31) are centered in C. As the exposition continues, the transition (mm. 32–50) shifts the harmonic center from C to D-flat. The statement of the secondary theme (mm. 51–72) remains in D-flat and continues there throughout the development section (mm. 73–105). The symphony's primary key center of C returns with the recapitulation section (mm. 106–133), and remains the harmonic center throughout the coda (mm. 134–151).

RHYTHM:

Marked to be performed at a lively 4/4 tempo (quarter note = 168), movement 1 employs only the simplest of rhythmic motives and devices, reserved largely to the repetitive usage of quarter and eighth notes throughout. The dotted quarter note is occasionally used as a motivically-oriented device that distinctively characterizes the symphony's primary theme.

Movement 2, written in 3/4 meter at a smooth and moderately fast tempo (quarter note = 120), poses few rhythmic difficulties in its overall use of simple rhythmic devices. Occasional motivic interjections, such as those played by trumpet 1 (mm. 17–18) and trombone 1 (mm. 19–20) should not be overly challenging for first-chair players and, if necessary, could be treated as solos as an effective alternative to interjections played by an entire section.

Movement 3, written in compound 6/8 meter, is to be performed at a lively tempo (dotted quarter note = 126). Due to the movement's compound nature, the challenge level for the entire ensemble, rhythmically speaking, will likely be somewhat greater than the symphony's other movements. Nevertheless, the rhythms found throughout movement 3 are quite accessible for average high school musicians. A distinctive rhythmic feature is in the way the composer takes liberal advantage in his use of hemiola, juxtaposing the metric perception of the piece being in two against an alternative perception of the music being in three. This phenomenon occurs in the first eight measures and continues throughout the remainder of the movement. Another rhythmic feature is immediately observable in mm. 19–26, where woodwinds continue in 6/8 compound meter while brass and percussion are in 2/4.

Movement 4 reiterates the rhythmic and motivic language first heard in movement 1, but takes advantage of such devices as augmentation and expanded canonic layering. Movement 4 also provides the entire woodwind section, along with three percussionists, with individual rhythmic/motivic cells that are randomly repeated during the opening three measures, (non-metered events), and then continued across the conducted, fast-metered opening section (mm. 4–15).

TIMBRE:
Disparate and contrasting timbres are abundant throughout movement 1 beginning with the scintillating percussion sounds (orchestra bells, vibra-phone, tam-tam, chimes) in mm. 1–2 (non-metered events, fifteen seconds each). Special effects, such as the timbres created by bowed vibraphone and by striking the bowl of the timpani with mallets, are also employed. As another very distinctive special effect, the entire wind section is called on to vocalize (on "Ah" vowels, rather than specific text) during m. 2 (a non-metered, fifteen-second event).

The presentation of the primary theme is set in a straightforward tutti texture for full band. The secondary theme, however, clearly demonstrates con-trasts of wind instrument colors through its use of staggered, canonic layering while being accompanied by free, random, pitch class cells performed by clarinets, bassoons, and low saxophones. Further, the five percussion players, whose parts are independent of one another, filter a variety of timbrel sounds throughout, including the use of suspended cymbal rolls, wind chimes, tom-toms being played with the hands, and scraping the tam-tam. Throughout movement 1 distinctive textural changes are clearly evident throughout, contrasting tutti scoring with sections of more exposed individual performance.

Movement 2 contrasts very articulated motivic injections from individual soloists within a very ethereal and sustained backdrop. An example is where a solo clarinetist is called on to punch through such motivic language randomly throughout the initial eight measures while a low, soft, and mysterious ground is sustained by low clarinets, horn, trombone, euphonium, and tuba. A soft, sustained tam-tam stroke adds to the mysterious milieu.

As the ground continues, the texture grows thicker and more layered, beginning with a flute solo in mm. 9–23, which is joined by clarinets. At m. 25 the ground is played by nearly the entire ensemble at a *fortissimo* dynamic while horns and euphoniums punch through the texture with the motivic injections formerly played by solo clarinet. The movement then tapers down again in texture and ends as quietly and mysteriously as it began.

Movement 3 comes alive with the beginning of section A, eight measures chock-full of rhythmic, articulate energy and strong, full sonorities played simultaneously by the full ensemble. Section B immediately brings contrast in mm. 11–18, where the theme, based on the secondary theme from movement 1 is played by unison clarinets in the low, chalumeau register at a subtle *mezzo forte*. The theme is then immediately reiterated by the entire woodwind section in unison at a lively and resilient *forte*.

Great timbrel and textural contrasts are immediately apparent with section C (m. 36). Here a rhythmic pedal point on G-flat is played by flutes and vibraphone, leaving the texture otherwise empty of sound. This leads to a horn solo in mm. 40–59 with occasional injections by muted trumpet, muted trombone, tambourine, wind chimes, orchestra bells, chimes, and splash cymbal. After the *da capo*, the movement concludes with a highly energized coda section replete with full ensemble sonorities.

Movement 4 recaptures the ethereal essence of movement 1, with randomized pitch cells played freely by all woodwinds and three of the five percussionists. At m. 5 the entire brass section strongly and forcefully proclaims unison motivic fragments against and in contrast to the continuing, randomized, woodwind pitch cells.

Beginning at m. 16 timpani and tom-toms join in presenting a bombastic and repetitive vamp characterized by dotted rhythms. Soon afterward the canonic layering of themes (as heard in movement 1) occurs against the bombastic percussion underpinnings (mm. 20–31).

During the transition (mm. 32–50), the "Ah" vowel vocalizations return, performed by the entire wind section against the ongoing percussive vamp along with injections of the original primary four-note theme performed by orchestra bells and vibraphone. The bombastic percussion vamp becomes a kind of dialogue between bongos and the timpani/tom-tom combination.

At m. 51 the vocalizations meld into a completely and continuously sustained sonic fiber, while muted trumpet and sandblock work in tandem to provide a more subtle vamp rhythm in contrast to the previous bombastic version. Interspersed injections of color from the marimba, and eventually the guiro, bring the exposition to a conclusion.

The development section (mm. 73–105) features contrasting wind colors, beginning with low brass then followed by flute and clarinet, trumpets, alto saxophone, and oboe and clarinet. These voices build and thicken the texture until a dramatic, full-ensemble peak occurs in mm. 90–95 as the bombastic percussion vamp returns.

The recapitulation (mm. 106–133) features staggered canonic entrances once again, now in a thicker texture, more recurrent and closely overlapping one another than in any section previously heard in the symphony. The recapitulation builds into the coda (mm. 134–151), where the woodwind random cells are constrasted against the bombastic percussion vamp rhythms and strong, unison brass utterances. A strong, dramatic, unison statement of the primary theme by the entire wind section brings the symphony to a powerful conclusion.

Unit 7: Form and Structure

SECTION	MEASURE	EVENT AND SCORING
Movement 1: *Fast*, sonata form		
Intro	1–2	Key center: C
		Principal melody
Exposition		
Theme 1	3–13	Key center: C
		Principal melody reiterated
Theme 1	14–25	Key center: C–G (with transition)
Theme 2	26–48	Key center: C–G
Development	49–71	Key centers: G and E-flat
		Materials based on theme 1 and its accompaniment
Recapitulation		
Theme 1	72–82	Key center: C
		The inversion of the theme 1 material appears as countermelody
Theme 2	83–101	Key center: C
Coda	102–106	Key center: C
		Based on accompaniment materials first heard with theme 1
Movement 2: *Smooth and Flowing*, chaconne form		
Intro	1–8	Begins with three non-metered events, containing independent cells of notes for each separate woodwind part, intended to be randomly repeated; each cell contains its own rhythm
Melody	9–16	Melody begins with flute

SECTION	MEASURE	EVENT AND SCORING
Building of orchestration	17–24	Texture thickens and builds
Climax	25–32	The movement reaches its musical apex
Receding melody	33–40	Melody recedes
Coda	41–48	

Movement 3: *Scherzo and Trio,* traditional scherzo and trio form

A	1–8	Key center: C
B	9–26	Key center: C
A	27–35	Key center: C
C	36–59	
A	1–8	Key center: C
B	9–26	Key center: C
A	60–74	Key center: C

Movement 4: *Fast,* sonata form

Intro	1–15	Key center: C
Exposition		
Theme 1	16–31	Key center: C
		Based on theme 2 from movement 1
Transition	32–50	Key ceners: C, D-flat; employs subset C–D-flat–G–E
Theme 2	51–72	Key center: D-flat
		Based on theme 1, movement 1
Development	73–105	Key center: D-flat
		Materials based on theme 1, but also recalls melody from movement 2
Recapitulation		
Theme 1	106–117	Key center: C
Theme 2	118–133	Key center: C
Coda	134–151	Key center: C

UNIT 8: SUGGESTED LISTENING

Benson, Warren: *The Solitary Dancer.*
Boysen, Jr., Andrew:
   I Am
   Kirkpatrick Fanfare
Higdon, Jennifer. *Rhythm Stand.*

Holst, Gustav: *Second Suite in F*, Op. 28, No.2, movement 4: "Fantasia on the 'Dargason.'"

Unit 9: Additional References and Resources

Boysen, Jr., Andrew. *Symphony No. 4 for Winds and Percussion*. Composer's score liner notes San Diego, CA: Neil A. Kjos Music Company, 2006.

Contributed by:

David Martin Booth
Director of Bands and Percussion Studies
Wright State University
Dayton, Ohio

Teacher Resource Guide

Thanksgiving Anthem
William Billings
(1746–1800)

arranged by Walter Hartley
(b. 1927)

Unit 1: Composer

William Billings was a leading composer of early American music and is widely considered today as the father of American choral music. His career began as a tanner, as he lacked any formal training in music and composition. He learned compositional techniques through studying the choral works of English composers such as William Tans'ur, Aaron Williams, John Arnold, and Uriah Davenport. In his lifetime Billings composed over 340 works, most of which were sacred choral pieces intended for singing schools and churches, including fifty-two anthems, fifty-one fuging tunes, and four canons, but no instrumental music or solo songs.

Many of his hymns and anthems were compiled into six collections titled *The New-England Psalm-Singer* (1770), *The Singing Master's Assistant* (1778), *Music in Miniature* (1779), *The Psalm-Singer's Amusement* (1781), *The Suffolk Harmony* (1786), and *The Continental Harmony* (1794). His first collection, *The New-England Psalm-Singer*, was the first to dedicate its contents to a single American composer. This achievement is nothing short of amazing, considering his handicaps; biographers describe that he was blind in one eye, had a short leg and a withered arm, all the while horribly addicted to tobacco.

In concert band literature, examples of William Billings's music can be heard through William Schuman's *New England Triptych*, a composition originally set for orchestra in 1956, which includes "Be Glad Then America," "When Jesus Wept," and "Chester." "Chester" is considered Billing's best-known work and was adopted by the Continental Army during the American Revolution, making it an unofficial national hymn. Schuman later revised and lengthened the piece in 1956 and re-titled it into the popular work *Chester Overture for Band.*

Walter S. Hartley, a native of Washington, DC, began composing at age five and became seriously dedicated to it at sixteen. He studied composition at the Eastman School of Music, where he earned all of his college degrees, including a PhD in composition in 1953. While at Eastman, some of his teachers included: Burrill Phillips, Thomas Canning, Herbert Elwell, Bernard Rogers, Howard Hanson, and Dante Fiorillo.

Hartley is also professor emeritus of music at Fredonia State University in Fredonia, New York. Currently, he functions as an unofficial composer-in-residence at the University of North Carolina at Charlotte, where he has lived since 2004. Hartley has composed several recent works, including *Suite No. 3 for Saxophone Quartet.* In addition to composing and at teaching at the collegiate level, Hartley also taught piano, theory, and composition at the National Music Camp, now Interlochen Arts Camp, from 1956 to 1964.

Hartley's list of acknowledged works is now over 200, dating from 1949 through 2008, and most of these are published. He is a member of the American Society for Composers, Authors and Publishers (ASCAP), from which he has received an annual award for achievement in serious music since 1962. Many ensembles, including the National Symphony Orchestra, Oklahoma City Symphony, Eastman-Rochester Orchestra, and the Eastman Wind Ensemble, have performed Hartley's music. The Koussevitzky Foundation commissioned his *Chamber Symphony* of 1954, his *Concert Overture* for orchestra received a prize from the National Symphony Orchestra in 1955, and his *Sinfonia No. 3* for brass choir won for him the 1964 Conn Award. Since that time he has received many commissions, from college and high school musical organizations to United States service bands, and his selections have been included on many recordings. He and the former Sandra Mount were married on June 17, 1960, and have two daughters and five grandchildren.

Unit 2: Composition

As stated in the preface of the score:

> Thanksgiving Anthem is a transcription for concert band of William Billings's choral anthem "O Praise the Lord of Heaven," first published by this early Boston composer/singing master in this 1794 collection *The Continental Harmony.* Walter Hartley completed his transcription (one of many instrumental settings, mostly for winds, that he has made

of choral works by Billings and other early American composers) on Christmas Day, 1999.

Interestingly, this composition is also listed under the titles *Thanksgiving Hymn* and *Thanksgiving Hymn [Anthem Psalm XLVII: for Thanksgiving]*; however, it is officially published as *Thanksgiving Anthem*. The composition was published in 2002 by Masters Music Publications, Inc. The duration of the piece is approximately four minutes.

Unit 3: Historical Perspective

When the pilgrims and puritans left England in 1620 to pursue religious freedom in America, they emigrated from a country that had a highly developed musical culture. Although these musical traditions remained with them, most of which were directly tied to the church service, their plans for music education of the young was measured against the basic necessity for survival in the rural colonies. Soon each generation was less musically inclined than the one before it.

By the eighteenth century, music was mostly transmitted orally, as few knew how to read music, and because of the lack of any training, performance levels were very poor. Since singing was at the heart of the religious service, church officials became growingly irritated at this low level and decided to remedy the situation through the concept of singing schools.

Around 1720, ministers began to compile hymn tunes into manuals in an effort to train people to sing through reading music. Many of the manuals included English hymns and anthems in addition to German chorales, but by the time of the Revolutionary War in 1776, many of these published manuals also included original American hymn tunes. As stated earlier, William Billings's first collection, *The New-England Psalm-Singer* (1770), was the first to dedicate its contents to a single American composer. With his six compilations, he was identified as one of the most successful compilers and composers of these manuals for the singing school movement.

His 1794 collection, *The Continental Harmony*, included "O Praise the Lord of Heaven: An Anthem for Thanksgiving." This piece was based on Psalm 148 and is the basis of Hartley's material for this arrangement. Billings and Wentworth Dillon, fourth Earl of Roscommon, modified the text as follows for the collection:

O praise the Lord of heaven: praise him in the height, praise him
   in the death.
O praise the Lord of heaven: praise him all ye angels, praise Jehovah.
Praise him, sun and moon and blazing comets.
Praise the Lord.

Let them praise the name of the Lord:
For he spake the word and they were made;
He commanded and they were created.
Admire, adore.

Ye dragons whose contagious breath,
People the dark abodes of death,
Change your dire hissings into heavenly songs,
And praise your maker with your forkéd tongues.
O praise the Lord of heaven.

Fire, hail and snow, wind and storms,
Beasts and cattle, creeping insects, flying fowl,
Kings and princes, men and angels,
Praise the Lord.

Jew and gentile, male and female, bond and free,
Earth and heaven, land and water,
Praise the Lord.

Young men and maids, old men and babes,
Praise the Lord.

Join creation, preservation and redemption: join in one.
No exemption nor dissension,
One invention and intention, reigns through the whole,
To praise the Lord, praise the Lord.

Hallelujah, hallelujah, praise the Lord.
Hallelujah, hallelujah, praise the Lord.

Harley's other instrumental settings of William Billings's choral works include *Easter Anthem* (1994), *Rose of Sharon* (1996), movement 2 of *Angel Band Suite "Africa"* (1999), and *New England Christmas Music* (2003).

Unit 4: Technical Considerations

Basic considerations of *Thanksgiving Anthem* include the following: instrumentation and instrument ranges are comparable with most Grade 3 literature and do not explore any extremities. Percussion parts, however, are minimal, including only timpani and snare drum. Time signatures included are 2/4, 3/4, and common time. Tempo markings include *Andante* (quarter note = 80) and *Più mosso* (quarter note = 120). Tempo adjustments include one ritardando at the final cadence.

Dynamic range extends from *piano* to *fortissimo*. The composition is primarily in the key of F major with only brief moments of D minor. Writing exhibits a brass and woodwind choir format in addition to single-instrument choirs, mixed instrumental pairings and full ensemble at the concluding cadence. There are no instrumental solos included in this arrangement.

Other considerations include dovetailing and elision of phrases around the ensemble as well as quick transitions into subsequent phrases and meter changes. The ensemble must be confident in their entrances, as the melodic material is isolated and sequenced around the ensemble. The most demanding technical passages of the work include the trumpet 1 sixteenth-note passage in mm. 49–56 in addition to the final section, mm. 92–104 (end) for the full ensemble that could prove to be challenging for young players at tempo.

Unit 5: Stylistic Considerations

Before and throughout the rehearsal process it will be beneficial to the conductor and the ensemble to listen to vocal examples of the work in addition to exploring the text. This will provide invaluable insight for specific phrasing, articulation, and overall concept of the composition that will have to be translated to an instrumental setting. To help students internalize this concept, have students sing the anthem (or portions of it, considering the difficulty of some vocal passages). Because this anthem centers on the concept of praise, the style should be confident and articulate with moments of legato and smooth texture. Special attention must be paid to the prevailing melodic line to adequately balance it against the intertwining texture of counterpoint and elided phrases.

Unit 6: Musical Elements

MELODY:
In *Thanksgiving Anthem*, melodic elements are tonal, primarily stepwise, and rooted in F major. There are two excerpts the conductor can isolate to help the ensemble understand the anthem and hymn style of this arrangement in order to achieve the stylistic items surrounding the melodic line as outlined in Unit 5.

First, the opening phrase, "O praise the Lord of heaven" is announced at a *forte* dynamic and must be played with great confidence and energy. The energy must be matched between the choirs, and through isolating this phrase the ensemble can quickly understand the distinctive style they need to play with for the majority of the work. Contrasting this, the *piano* statement of the phrase, "change your dire hissings into heavenly songs, and praise your maker with your forkéd tongues" can be used to emphasize the cantabile style of traditional hymn tunes. There are few of these *piano* melodic statements, but they offer moments of repose and purity to the composition.

HARMONY:

Harmonic elements of this work stay within the tonal center of F major with only two moments of D minor that help accentuate the meaning of the text. Writing is primarily triadic or in octave movement throughout the separated instrument groupings and full ensemble. Cadence points are present throughout the composition to help outline the sentence structure of the text and conclusions of ideas. It is important for students to understand these points of arrival in the music, and subsequently the harmonic progression leading up to the arrival point, as well. It will also be beneficial for the conductor to isolate these cadence points so that they will be performed with the correct balance, dynamic, and intonation.

RHYTHM:

Rhythmic elements in *Thanksgiving Anthem* range from typical hymn-like rhythmic structures of whole, half, and quarter notes, to passages of sixteenth-note virtuosity. As outlined in Unit 4, the most demanding technical passages of the work include the trumpet 1 sixteenth-note passage in mm. 49–56 and the final section, mm. 92–104 (end). Both of these passages are to be performed at quarter note = 120, and it is advisable not to play beyond Hartley's suggestion to ensure a quality performance. Keep in mind this was originally a choral work, so these sixteenth notes should mimic the smooth succession of pitches in the voice. Another passage to isolate is mm. 20–21, where some students may need assistance in understanding the rhythmic combination in m. 21, beat 3.

It is important for the ensemble to understand the idea of dovetailing throughout mm. 28–36. Here the phrase first begins in the saxophone choir, horn 1–2, and euphonium; with the first portion of the phrase, then in m. 29, beat 3, trumpet, trombone, and tuba take over to continue the rest of the phrase. These two groups must work together to perform a seamless, unified phrase. This is also evident throughout mm. 65–82, where melodic material is bounced around the ensemble and again must be unified to form the collective statement.

Furthermore, at m. 37 there is a quick transition to not only a new phrase, but also a new tempo, meter, and rhythmic structure. This transition will be challenging for the ensemble, and it would be beneficial to isolate this passage. Another difficult transition is moving into m. 49, where again there is a change in meter and rhythmic structure, especially in the trumpet part, as previously indicated.

The final section is virtuosic in nature because it is the final celebration and states the phrase, "Hallelujah, hallelujah, praise the Lord." It is an effective, exciting climax, contributing to the transcription of originality and spirit of Billings's composition.

TIMBRE:

To achieve the appropriate timbre for this piece, the conductor and ensemble should listen to a choral recording of the work (see Unit 8). This will immediately give reference to the appropriate style for the anthem and to the prevailing melodic line so balance can be achieved throughout the composition. A number of tonal colors can be explored through the brass and woodwind choral settings, in addition to the single instrument choirs and the mixed instrumental pairings Hartley orchestrates.

Unit 7: Form and Structure

MEASURE	EVENT AND SCORING
1–3	Brass choir and timpani statement of the opening phrase "O praise the Lord of heaven"; key of F major is established as the tonal center; meter is 3/4, and the tempo is *Andante*, quarter note = 80
4–6	Woodwind choir and snare drum echo of opening phrase "O praise the Lord of heaven"
6–9	Elision of text "praise him in the height, praise him in the death"; phrase begins with euphonium and tuba in octaves, then moves to horn in unison and finishes with flute, oboe, and clarinet 1 in octaves
10–12	Restatement of opening phrase, "O praise the Lord of heaven" in trumpet and trombone 1–2
12–20	Elision of text from opening phrase to "praise him all ye angels, praise Jehovah"; "Praise him all ye angels" sub-phrase first begins in upper woodwinds, euphonium, tuba, and timpani in thirds before dovetailing to unison horns in m. 13, trumpet 1 in m. 14, and flute and oboe in octaves in mm. 15–16; final portion of the phrase, "praise Jehovah" is voiced on an F major triad in flute, oboe, horn, trumpet, euphonium, tuba, timpani, and snare drum in mm. 17–18; a saxophone choir statement echoes before eliding with the next phrase and section
20–22	Meter changes to common time in m. 20; clarinet 2–3, bass clarinet, and bassoon state the next phrase, "praise him sun and moon and blazing comets" in octaves above the saxophone choir
22–27	Elision of text to "Praise the Lord"; this phrase first begins in trumpet and trombone 1–2 before moving to flute and clarinet 1–2; the two groups pass the phrase back and forth twice before euphonium and tuba enter in m. 26; in m. 23 meter changes to 3/4, and for the first time in the piece, the dynamic changes to *piano*)the composition has been voiced at *forte* up until this point)

MEASURE	EVENT AND SCORING
28–36	Meter changes to common time in m. 28; saxophone choir, horn 1–2 and euphonium begin in octaves with the first portion of the next phrase, "Let them praise the name of the Lord"; in m. 29, beat 3, trumpet, trombone, and tuba take over the rest of the phrase, "for he spake the word and they were made; he commanded and they were created; admire, adore"; from mm. 31–33, saxophone choir, horn 1–2, and euphonium briefly interject in addition to adding to the cadential texture from mm. 35–37; flute, oboe, clarinet, and snare drum also join the F major cadential texture in mm. 35–36
37–40	Tempo changes to *Più mosso*, quarter note = 120, in m. 37; meter changes to 2/4 in m. 38; clarinet and saxophone choir begin the next phrase in m. 37, "Ye dragons whose contagious breath, people the dark abodes of death"; this is voiced at a *fortissimo* dynamic, and cadences in D minor on "abodes of death" in m. 40
41–60	Meter changes to common time in m. 41; tonal center shifts back to F major; flute, oboe, clarinet choir, bassoon, horn 1–2, trumpet 1, euphonium, tuba, and timpani, voiced at a *piano* dynamic, state the beginning of the next phrase, "Change your dire hissings into heavenly songs, and praise…"; in mm. 47–48 the orchestration minimizes to trumpet, trombone 1–2, and timpani on the later half of the phrase, "your maker with your forkéd tongues"; meter changes to 2/4 in m. 49; there is also a four-and-a-half-measure crescendo from *piano* to *forte* in mm. 49–53; euphonium and tuba add to the orchestration in mm. 50–56; together the phrase builds to another cadence in D minor on "tongues"; a woodwind choir, voiced primarily at *fortissimo*, reaffirms F major, echoes and cadences on the last portion of the phrase, "and praise your maker with your forkéd tongues"
61–64	The original tempo and meter returns in m. 61 with a restatement of the opening phrase, "O praise the Lord of heaven"; it is voiced at a *fortissimo* dynamic and is also modified from the original statement in mm. 1–3

MEASURE	EVENT AND SCORING
65–82	In mm. 65–67 the melodic material moves to a clarinet and saxophone choir along with horn 1–2 in octaves on the phrase, "Fire, hail and snow, wind and storms"; melodic line moves briefly to upper woodwinds on "beasts and cattle" in m. 68 before moving to another group, voiced at a *piano* dynamic: horns, euphonium, and tuba on "creeping insects, flying fowl" throughout mm. 69–70; this segmented trend continues throughout the rest of the phrase, mm. 71–82 bouncing to various clusters around the ensemble; in mm. 71–73 trumpet and trombone 1 state, "Kings and princes, men and angels, praise the Lord"; in m. 74 flute and oboe state, "Jews and gentile"; saxophone choir continues with, "male and female" in m. 75; flute and oboe come back with "bond and free" in m. 76; trombone and euphonium state, "earth and heaven" in m. 77 before passing the melody to a clarinet choir which continues, "land and water, praise the Lord" in mm. 78–79; saxophones and horn 1–2 state "young men and maids" in m. 80 before moving to the end of this segmentation section with an F Major cadence in horns, trumpets, euphonium, and tuba on "old men and babes, praise the Lord"
83–91	In m. 83 tempo changes to *Più mosso,* quarter note = 120; this section hints toward the virtuosic ending of the composition; a moving eighth-note line begins at a *piano* dynamic before cresendoing into a *fortissimo* dynamic in m. 88; the eight notes are voiced as a woodwind choir along with horns 1–2; the phrase accompanying the eighth notes includes, "Join creation, preservation and redemption: join in one; no exemption nor dissension, one invention and intention, reigns through the whole"; in m. 88 the orchestration moves to a nearly full ensemble minus the saxophone choir to state at a *fortissimo* dynamic, "to praise the Lord, praise the Lord"
92–106	This last section of the composition exhibits the most virtuosic melodic material of the entire piece and is the only section that is repeated; the entire section is dedicated to one phrase: "Hallelujah, hallelujah, praise the Lord"; ending cadence confirms the tonal center that has been present throughout almost the entire piece, F major

Unit 8: Suggested Listening

Billings, William:
> *Early American Choral Music, Volume 1: His Majestie's Clerkes*. Paul
> Hiller, conductor. Hmf Classical Exp. 2001.
> Arranged by Walter Hartley. *Thanksgiving Hymn. Music in the Air*. The
> Eastern Wind Symphony. William Silvester, conductor.
> Klavier,11132. 2002.

Hartley, Walter. *Angel Band. Teaching Music through Performance in Band,
Volume 4*. North Texas Wind Symphony. Eugene Migliaro Corporon,
conductor. GIA Publications CD-552. 2003.

Schuman, William:
> *Chester. American Dreams*. Cincinnati Wind Symphony. Eugene
> Corporon, conductor. Klavier 11048. 1992.

Unit 9: Additional References and Resources

"William Billings." In *Grove Music Online*.
> http://www.grovemusic.com.proxy-remote.galib.uga.
> edu:2048/shared/views/article.html?section=music.03082.

Miles, Richard, ed. "Chester." In *Teaching Music through Performance in Band,
Volume 2*. Chicago: GIA Publications, 1998.

_____. "Angel Band." In *Teaching Music through Performance in Band,
Volume 4*. Chicago: GIA Publications, 2003.

*New England Triptych: 1. Be Glad Then, America; 2. When Jesus Wept; 3.
Chester*. Interview with William Schuman. *William Schuman*. The
Keystone Wind Ensemble. Jack Stamp, conductor. Klavier 11155. 2005.

Websites:
> The Music of William Billings.
> > http://www.amaranthpublishing.com/billings.htm
> Walter S. Hartley. "Biographical Introduction."
> > http://www.walterhartley.com

Contributed by:

Amy M. Knopps
Doctoral Conducting Associate
The University of Georgia
Athens, Georgia

Teacher Resource Guide

Voices of the Sky
Samuel R. Hazo
(b. 1966)

Unit 1: Composer

Samuel R. Hazo was born in 1966. He currently resides in Pittsburgh, Pennsylvania with his wife and children. In 2003, he became the first composer in history to be awarded the winner of both composition contests sponsored by the National Band Association. He has composed for the professional, university, and public school levels, in addition to writing original scores for television, radio and the stage. His original symphonic compositions include performances with actors Brooke Shields, James Earl Jones, David Conrad, and Richard Kiley. He has also written symphonic arrangements for three-time Grammy Award-winning singer/songwriter Lucinda Williams.

Hazo's compositions have been performed and recorded worldwide, including performances by the Tokyo Kosei Wind Orchestra (national tour), the Birmingham Symphonic Winds (UK), and the Klavier Wind Project's recordings with Eugene Migliaro Corporon. Additionally, his music is included in the series *Teaching Music through Performance in Band*. Hazo's works have been premiered and performed at the Music Educators' National Conference, Midwest Band and Orchestra Clinic, World Association for Symphonic Bands and Ensembles Convention, National Honor Band of America, National Band Association/TBA Convention, and College Band Directors' National Association Convention, and also aired in full-length programs on National Public Radio. He has served as composer-in-residence at Craig Kirchhoff's University of Minnesota Conducting Symposium and has also lectured on music and music education at universities and high schools internationally. In 2004, Hazo's compositions were listed in a published national survey of the Top Twenty Compositions of All Time for wind band.

Hazo has been a music teacher at every educational grade level from kindergarten through college, including tenure as a high school and university director. He was twice named Teacher of Distinction by the Southwestern Pennsylvania Teachers' Excellence Foundation. He received his bachelor's and master's degrees from Duquesne University, where he served on the Board of Governors and was awarded as Duquesne's Outstanding Graduate in Music Education. Hazo serves as a guest conductor and is a clinician for Hal Leonard Corporation. He is also sponsored by Sibelius Music Software. Recordings of his compositions appear on Klavier Records and Mark Records.[1]

Unit 2: Composition

Voices of the Sky was commissioned in the summer of 2003 by Cynthia L. Houston, conductor of the Murchison International Baccalaureate School Band in Austin, Texas. Murchison is a member of the Austin Independent School District.

The composer states in the score:

Consider that we will never see the same sky twice in our lives. Therefore, each day the sky must express itself in a new way. Additionally, its colors and moods are of such a range that they reach the extremes of our comprehension. The sky holds the brightest and darkest things we will ever see. It possesses every color in the spectrum. It can be stagnant or move with swift motion. Its personality can change in an instant or remain the same all day. An overcast sky can make us feel closed in and a clear sky creates in us the feeling that we're infinitely expansive. The morning sky gradually breathes life into us, and at sunset, the sky slowly paints all of its colors to the edge of its canvas, and then off. All day it hides its stars like secrets that can only be told in the dark. Translating the many qualities of the sky into musical moods was one of the main objectives of this piece. Please read further, as the dedication addresses the other objective (see below).

He also adds the following information regarding the Murchison International Baccalaureate program:

...the curriculum has a component called "Homo Faber," meaning "man the maker." The commissioning of *Voices of the Sky* served as an opportunity for me to work with Murchison's students in this wonderful educational arena that encourages creativity, imagination and, most importantly, artistic expression.

On February 14, 2004, the composer penned the following dedication for the work while flying "somewhere over Kansas":

It is with tremendous honor and immeasurable gratitude that *Voices of the Sky* is dedicated to Paula Crider, Professor Emeritus at The University of Texas at Austin, as well as my dearest and most admired friend. As unequivocally special as Paula Crider is to the world, she is dearly significant to both Cindy Houston and to me.

Admired by all who meet her, she is the perfect combination of compassionate teacher, impeccable conductor, consummate musician, well-rounded intellectual and mother hen; fulfilling all of those roles with absolute grace. Moreover, those fortunate enough to know her appreciate that she will remain the truest of friends through the best and worst of times. She holds absolutely sacred her role as an educator, and she has no tolerance for those layered with fraudulence or arrogance. Just yesterday, as I congratulated her on her recent and most deserved honor as the 2004 Texas Bandmaster of the Year, she completely played it down; further embodying the derivation of her name, as the translation of Paula is "one who is humble." When Cindy Houston called me in the summer of 2003 to commission this piece, and she told me that it would be dedicated to Paula, I was overjoyed at the opportunity.

Unit 3: Historical Perspective

Inspired by the tribute to Paula Crider, Hazo uses both the interpretation of imagery and the interpretation of analogy as catalyst for the work. A verse by nineteenth-century poet R. L. Sharp was read to Crider as a child, and she in turn has shared it with thousands of students over the years in the Texas Longhorn Band and in other situations. The poem reads:

> Isn't it strange that princes and kings
> And clowns that caper in sawdust rings,
> And common people like you and me
> Are builders of eternity?
>
> Each is given a box of tools,
> A shapeless mass and a book of rules.
> And each must make, ere life is flown,
> A stumbling block or a stepping stone.

Published in 2005, *Voices of the Sky* was inspired by both nineteenth-century prose and the modern-day spirit of a talented educator. As a result, the piece is characterized by an ancient-sounding melody set with modern-day harmony and orchestration which provides for sense of hopeful reminiscence. A faster section provides contrast within the same harmonic scheme.

Unit 4: Technical Considerations

Generally, *Voices of the Sky* is an opportunity to work on a well-connected legato style with the ensemble. The majority of the piece is dedicated to long lines and lush harmony. The composer indicates in the score that the piece is to be played "beautifully, with all notes connected."

There are opportunities for solo trumpet, as well as some chamber music playing for the woodwind sections. The tutti writing allows for focus on balance, blend, and intonation. A faster middle section will challenge the ensemble to develop likeness of articulation style and to work on the juxtaposition of consecutive dotted quarter notes (as in 6/8) against the three even quarter notes of 3/4 meter. The meter throughout is quarter-based, but shifts constantly between 4/4, 3/4, and 2/4.

An additional technical consideration is related to some passage work for woodwinds. In particular, grace notes and *gruppettos* in melodic passages regularly occur in woodwind parts. Given the concert key of A-flat major, these passages will require attention to guarantee accuracy.

The work remains in A-flat throughout. Hazo's orchestration provides variety of color and depth, and lends itself well to the teaching of these concepts. The physical demands of the work are outweighed by the intellectual challenges of style, balance, phrasing, and shape. Even in the faster passages, the writing is very characteristic and appropriate for the intended level. Beyond the focus on lyrical playing, the primary area of concentration is likely to be achieving clarity in the faster section, marked quarter note = 160.

Unit 5: Stylistic Considerations

Voices of the Sky presents excellent opportunities for work on lyrical playing and the shaping of beautiful lines. The folk-like tune must be treated in a legato style, connected, linear, and with great shape. Care should be taken so that articulation should not disrupt the flow of the melodic content. A clear, marked style of articulation can and should be more present in the faster section of the work. The dotted-quarter rhythms in this section could be treated with a more lifted style in order to provide contrast with the initial melodic material.

This composition uses a wide dynamic range in all parts, and therefore opportunities to work on ensemble sound in both soft and loud passages. Woodwind parts present more technical challenges than brass parts, but both offer equal opportunity for expressive playing in a variety of dynamic ranges and with contrasting articulation patterns. Percussion parts add color and are generally supportive in nature, with no obscure or difficult issues to be confronted.

Unit 6: Musical Elements

MELODY:

The central element of this composition is the melody. Folk-like and pentatonic in nature, the tune itself serves as a wonderful melodic study for all instruments. It is diatonic, has a few smaller leaps, and has wonderful shape. Teaching this tune by ear to the entire ensemble would be an excellent ear-training study. It would also raise awareness for the tune, thereby enhancing balance issues as the ensemble works on the piece. In addition, teaching other melodies of this nature (pentatonic, shaped notes, etc.) constitute an opportunity to discuss a variety of historic origins for melodies in music.

HARMONY:

This piece has a very interesting harmonic vocabulary. Diatonic in nature, Hazo's use of dissonance and extended chords provides a very full, fresh sound. The first forty-nine measures of the work reveal no surprises and should prove quite accessible for students. After the faster section beginning at m. 50, the work transitions back to the initial melodic/harmonic material. It is at this juncture (m. 84) that the use of dissonance and harmonic extension becomes more prevalent. Again, all are rooted in the overall diatonic scheme and should require no introduction of special or advanced analysis for clarification. Hazo's excellent orchestration takes full advantage of the lush, dark harmonies created by his chord choices.

RHYTHM:

Special focus during the preparation of this work will be in two areas: mixed meter and the juxtaposition of consecutive dotted quarter notes (as in 6/8) against the three even quarter notes of 3/4 meter. Beyond these major considerations, the rhythmic elements of the work are appropriate for the level of the composition. A few sixteenth-note passages and the aforementioned grace-note patterns constitute the other rhythmic challenges in the work.

Development of exercises to emphasize the similarities between 6/8 and 3/4 would be helpful, and could be done both with and without instruments. Rehearsing the faster music on a single concert pitch will highlight challenges and allow the ensemble to use appropriate articulation to bring clarity to the rhythm.

TIMBRE:

After the strength of the melody in this work, the colors derived through orchestration are the next most obvious attribute. Hazo's orchestration will maximize balance and blend in any ensemble. Achieved primarily through his treatment of woodwind and brass choirs, the full ensemble sections should provide opportunities to address balanced, blended, tutti playing. Use of metallic percussion sounds (vibes, wind chimes, and suspended cymbal) enhance the score a great deal.

Focus for preparation of the woodwinds parts should be on intonation. Lines written in octaves exist throughout and will provide a challenge for young players. Woodwind parts also feature some moments of chamber music, where more soloistic playing should be encouraged and developed. Tutti sections for woodwinds will prove to make up the majority of the work here.

Focus for brass players will be in the area of blend. Dark, resonant sounds must be encouraged. Sounds in the upper brass (trumpets and horns) that blend with one another should be cultivated through listening and proper physical techniques. Preparation for this type of piece should involve a very relaxed approach to the instrument in which the sound of the breath (dark and open) is as important as the sound of the horn. A full, relaxed breath will lead to a full, relaxed tone. Likewise, brass players should be encouraged to play with very open syllables such as "oh" or "oo." Especially in regard to articulation, the syllables "doh" or "doo" will yield more appropriate results than "ah/tah" or "ee/tee." Singing passages in the brass section is always a viable means of achieving this end. Awareness of breathing can be equally effective.

Unit 7: Form and Structure

Formal considerations for this piece are relatively easy. The overall form of the work is ABA, or slow-fast-slow. The piece opens with slow introductory music and a reserved, legato presentation of melodic ideas. The exposition of the entire theme is stated first in solo trumpet. After tutti treatment of the tune, there is a faster developmental section followed by a return to the main thematic material.

MEASURE	EVENT AND SCORING
1	Fermata; wind chimes
2–11	Introduction; entrance of thematic elements
12–19	Exposition of theme A in trumpet, then woodwinds
20–49	Theme A; statements of primary melodic material continue
50–83	Section B ; driving; quarter note = 160; 6/8 feel in 3/4
84–86	Tempo I; transition; subito arrival; quarter note = 54
87–98	Return of theme A; tutti statements
99–102	Statement of theme A in woodwinds; chamber setting
103–108	Statement of theme by solo trumpet
109-end	Ending; chords to closing cadence

Unit 8 Suggested Listening

Daehn, Larry. *As Summer Was Just Beginning*
Hazo, Samuel:
    Blessings
    In Heaven's Air
Grainger, Percy. *Ye Banks and Braes O Bonnie Doon*.
Wallace, Tom (arranger). *Jesus, Jesus, Rest Your Head*.

Unit 9 Additional References and Resources

Hazo, Samuel. *Voices of the Sky*. Score. Hal Leonard Corporation.
www.samuelhazo.com

Contributed by:

William Stowman, Chair
Director of Instrumental Studies
Messiah College
Grantham, Pennsylvania

---

1 Taken from the composer's personal website, www.samuelhazo.com

Teacher Resource Guide

Were You There?

Thomas Stone
(b. 1957)

Unit 1: Composer

Thomas Stone is a native of Oshkosh, Wisconsin. He received his bachelor's degree in music from Lawrence University, where he studied composition with Steven Stucky, and his master of music degree from DePaul University in 1983. He has extensive experience as a conductor and teacher in both private and public schools in Wisconsin, Illinois, and Florida. He earned a doctor of musical arts degree in wind conducting at the University of Cincinnati College-Conservatory of Music, where he was a student of Eugene Migliaro Corporon. His many published works for band and chamber ensembles have been performed by many of the world's leading organizations, including the Cincinnati Wind Symphony, the University of North Texas Wind Symphony, the Dallas Wind Symphony, the Longy Club of Boston, and the United States Marine Band. He is a pioneer in PDF music publishing and founded Maestro and Fox Music in 2007 (www.maestroandfox.com), where he serves as proprietor and editor-in-chief.

Stone has provided CD liner notes for Klavier Records and GIA Publications that pertain to recordings by the Cincinnati Wind Symphony, the University of North Texas Wind Symphony, the Keystone Winds, and the U. S. Air Force Band. He is currently conductor of the wind ensemble and professor of music at Centenary College in Shreveport, Louisiana. In addition to teaching conducting, orchestration, and courses in music education and music technology, Stone conducts the Centenary Summer Band, a professional ensemble funded by corporate sponsors and the American Federation of

Musicians. He is listed in *Who's Who Among America's Teachers*, and *Who's Who In America*. He is married to soprano Jennifer Dowd.

Unit 2: Composition

Were You There? was composed as part of a larger commission for the New Trier High School Wind Ensemble of Winnetka, Illinois, and conductor John Thomson. Also created as part of the same commission were *Primoridial Lights* (Maestro and Fox Music) and *Ancient Visions* (Daehn Publications).

Unit 3: Historical Perspective

The American spiritual finds its roots in music created extemporaneously by African-American slaves at camp meetings and other gatherings during the early nineteenth century. Three types of spirituals are identifiable as distinct forms of the genre: 1) slow and expressive; 2) fast, rhythmic, and syncopated; and 3) responsorial. Spirituals were Christian songs sung by the American slaves in the hope that God might favor them in light of their bondage and suffering. Often there were hidden meanings in the words that expressed hope that freedom from servitude might soon be achieved. Spirituals were first published in the 1867 volume *Slave Songs of the United States* by William Francis Allen, Charles Pickard Ware, and Lucy McKim Garrison.

Unit 4: Technical Considerations

Although *Were You There?* is written with no key signature, the piece is tonal and each statement of the melody is assigned a definite key center with accidentals inserted into the music as needed. Keys that appear in this setting are the major keys of B-flat, G, E, and F. Thomas Stone writes:

> I've always been fascinated by Spirituals. Good ones have a way of stirring the deepest emotion in all who are receptive to their raw expressive force. And *Were You There?* is perhaps the most compelling of all Spirituals. Often I've wondered why there aren't dozens of band arrangements of this hymn tune. When I set out to work out my own setting, its difficulty became abundantly clear. Range! Singers object to the vertical dimension of the *Star Spangled Banner*, and *Were You There?* is almost as rangy; one octave and a perfect fourth! The pinnacle note of the melody, high "do," delivers the KO punch.

The expansive dimension of the melody requires mature players to perform the solo lines for horn (high F) and trumpet (high A). The opening horn solo is cued for solo alto saxophone, for which the high G should be no obstacle. Trumpet 1 ascends to high B above the staff, but only once (m. 38).

The brass quartet thematic statement at m. 27 requires two trumpet and two trombone players who are comfortable performing solo lines. The great preponderance of accompanimental parts throughout the work are conceived linearly, and thus require a mature level of musical independence to render. Quarter-note triplet figures at the climax, mm. 47–48 will demand considerable rhythmic skill as well.

Unit 5: Stylistic Considerations

Performers must remember that in attempting *Were You There?*, they are recreating vocal music through instrumental performance. Listening to or singing the spiritual tune will deepen their understanding of the song, but it may also be helpful to the conductor in choosing the proper tempo (not too slow). If, in singing the song at a chosen tempo, the words seem ponderous or unsingable, the tempo is too slow.

The opening introductory section of *Were You There?* is marked *Freely* with quarter note = 60. The conductor should think of mm. 1–8 as an introduction; slightly improvisatory and gestural in nature, recalling the responsorial form of the spiritual as depicted by the conversation between solo horn and woodwind choir. The reediness of the below-the-staff clarinet and bass clarinet parts should be elicited. The *ten.* (tenuto) indication could be interpreted as a brief phrasal fermata or "pause/stretch on this note." The thematic statement in the brass at m. 9 is marked *More motion* at quarter note = 72–76. A sense of flow is important throughout the remainder of the work, or at least until the final, culminating thematic statement at m. 41. It is essential, therefore, that at m. 9, a not-too-slow tempo is assumed so as not to burden the music with plodding weightiness.

Grace notes in the flute and oboe should not be over-played. Place them just before the note and leading to the note that follows, but not too early and not too heavy in style.

Unit 6: Musical Elements

Spirituals are predominantly pentatonic. "Amazing Grace" is strictly so; *Were You There?* is mostly pentatonic. One pitch in the pickup to the final phrase violates this language. It is, nonetheless, a truism that the pentatonic language of the spiritual dictates that the chromatic (colorful) interval, the half step, is absent to a large degree from this genre.

Composers dealing in modes and scales lacking the half-step know such music will pall quickly to the ear unless chromaticism is available to create tension, color, and interest. Thus, whole tone and pentatonic scales are most intelligently used in passing within larger works, serving only as brief oases of relief rather than as the basis for any large-scale composition. Those who created and sang spirituals must have realized intuitively, subconsciously, that the absence of the half step created a dilemma for the ear, and that half steps needed to be inserted into the melody to create and sustain interest. Thus grace notes, or blue notes arose over time as part of the spiritual idiom.

Grace notes are used in several of the statements of the melody in *Were You There?* Several of the piece's thematic iterations are abbreviated statements. The three-fold repetition of the word "tremble" is avoided until the final two declarations of the tune. These truncations save the expressive force of this phrasal extension for the most powerful moment in the work and avoid its becoming tedious by overuse. The following are words commonly used to sing the spiritual *Were You There?*:

Were you there when they crucified my Lord?
Were you there when they crucified my Lord?
Oh! Sometimes it causes me to tremble, tremble, tremble.
Were you there when they crucified my Lord?

Were you there when they nailed Him to the tree?
Were you there when they nailed Him to the tree?
Oh! Sometimes it causes me to tremble, tremble, tremble.
Were you there when they nailed Him to the tree?

Were you there when they laid Him in the tomb?
Were you there when they laid Him in the tomb?
Oh! Sometimes it causes me to tremble, tremble, tremble.
Were you there when they laid Him in the tomb?

Unit 7: Form and Structure

SECTION	MEASURE	EVENT AND SCORING
Introduction B-flat major	1–8	Theme announced in solo horn with responsorial accompaniment in woodwinds
Statement 1 G major	9–16	Trumpet soloist accompanied by linear quarter-note motion in low brass
Statement 2 E major	18–26	Theme in flutes and oboes with counter-subject in solo horn; accompanied by linear quarters in clarinets and saxes; bass clarinet and bassoon play melodic bass line
Statement 3 F major	27–36	Brass quartet plays theme and harmonization reminiscent of brass band; flutes play thematic derivative as countersubject; bass clarinet and bassoons play melodic bass line

SECTION	MEASURE	EVENT AND SCORING
Transition	37–40	Transition accumulates instrumentation and builds dynamically to m. 41
Statement 4		
F major	41–50	Culminating tutti thematic statement
Coda		
B-flat major	51–57	Reed choir recalls final phrase of theme; flutes, trombones, and horn extend final phrase
	58	derivative conclusion featuring trumpet, oboe, flutes, and bells

Unit 8: Suggested Listening

Gillis, Don. "Spiritual" from *Symphony 5-1/2*.
Gillingham, David. *Spiritual Dances*.
Gould, Morton:
    Ballad for Band
    Spirituals for String Orchestra
Holsinger, David. *On An American Spiritual*.
Norman, Jessye:
    Spirituals in Concert. Deutsche Grammophon.
    Spirituals. Phillips.
Reed, H. Owen. *Spiritual*.
Stone, Thomas:
    Primordial Lights
    Shadows of Eternity
Zaninelli, Luigi. *Five American Gospel Songs*.

Unit 9: References and Resources

Anderson, Iain. "Reworking Images of a Southern Past: The Commemoration of Slave Music After the Civil War." *Studies in Popular Culture* 19 (1996).
Epstein, Dena J. *Sinful Tunes and Spirituals: Black Folk Music to the Civil War*. Urbana and Chicago: University of Illinois Press, 1977, 2003.
Fisher, Miles Mark. *Negro Slave Songs in the United States*. 1953 reissue. New York: Russell and Russell, 1968.
Krehbiel, Henry Edward. *Afro-American Folksongs*. Reprinted. Baltimore, MD: Clearfield, 1993. Da Capo Press, 2000.
Lovell, Jr., John. *Black Song: The Forge and the Flame—The Story of How the Afro-American Spiritual Was Hammered Out*. New York: Macmillan, 1972.

Radano, Ronald Michael. "Denoting Differences: The Writing of the Slave Spirituals." *Critical Inquiry* 22 (1996).

Sadie, Stanley, Ed. *New Grove Dictionary of Music and Musicians*. London: Macmillan, 1980.

Slonimsky, Nicholas, ed. *Baker's Biographical Dictionary of Musicians*. Eighth ed., rev. New York: Schirmer Books, 1991.

Smith, Norman, and Albert Stoutamire. *Band Music Notes*. Rev. ed. San Diego, CA: Neil A. Kjos, Jr., Publisher, 1979.

Southern, Eileen. *The Music of Black Americans: A History*. Third ed. New York: W. W. Norton, 1997.

Stone, Thomas. "Morton Gould-Champion of the Band." *BD Guide* 9 (January/February 1995): 2–5.

Stowe, David. *How Sweet the Sound: Music in the Spiritual Lives of Americans*. Cambridge, MA: Harvard University Press, 2004.

Contributed by:

Thomas Stone
Centenary College

Grade Four

Teacher Resource Guide

Aue!

Christopher John Marshall
(b. 1956)

Unit 1: Composer

French-born composer Christopher Marshall has spent the majority of his
adult life in the New Zealand capitol of Auckland. He received his early music
education in New South Wales, Australia, later earning a master of music with
honors from Auckland University. Marshall was a Mozart Fellow in
Composition at the University of Otago in Dunedin, New Zealand, and later
received a Fulbright Award as composer-in-residence at the Eastman School
of Music. Since 1996, he has been composer-in-residence at the University of
Central Florida in Orlando. Despite his extensive musical education and
background, he considers himself largely self-taught as a composer, one whose
strong influences have included the music of John Adams, John Corigliano,
Arvo Pärt, and John Tavener.

Unit 2: Composition

Aue! (pronounced ow-WAY) was commissioned by a consortium of over
sixty individuals and organizations from around the globe, representing such
countries as Australia, Canada, Finland, Japan, Norway, Scotland, the United
Kingdom, and the United States. The work was premiered on April 7, 2001
by the Chetham (UK) Wind Orchestra at the Royal Northern College
of Music in Manchester as part of the British Association of Symphonic
Bands and Wind Ensembles (BASBWE) Conference. The seven-minute,
332-measure work is a through-composed tone poem, and is Marshall's first
venture into composing for the wind band medium. Following its initial

publication, Maecenas published a revised second edition incorporating errata and scoring modifications. Marshall has since published three additional works for band: *L'homme arme: Variations for Wind Ensemble*, *Okaoka*, and *Resonance*. *Aue!* is a musically original, substantive, and rewarding piece that is worthy of its inclusion in the repertoire.

Unit 3: Historical Perspective

Christopher Marshall is a frequent world traveler, gathering experiences from diverse musical cultures, styles, and sounds. From his curiosity was spawned a fascination with Maori, a New Zealand war chant considered particularly powerful and intense. The Maori is most frequently characterized by its loud chanting, flailing of arms, and stomping of feet. Marshall's interest in diverse Polynesian music led to three years of residing at Vaia'ata in Savai'i, a village located in Western Samoa. Marshall writes in the score of his time in Samoa that, "often in the evenings you could hear sounds from the villages carried on the sea breeze—songs, dances, bells, drums—all filtered and transformed by the mists of the rain forest." It is from those sounds that *Aue!* was inspired.

Those who program the work can easily incorporate a brief lesson on the Samoa, a country whose history of division and war includes outside ownership by Germany and the United States before its eventual independence from New Zealand in 1962. Located halfway between Hawaii and New Zealand in the Polynesian South Pacific, the nine-island chain is noted for its popular dances, songs, and diverse musical culture.

Aue! is not strictly programmatic, as there is no specific story line or single element that takes the listener on a predefined journey. Instead, the work centers on Samoan songs as experienced by the composer, and treated with tonalities and textures less-commonly infused in band literature. *Aue!* presents the Samoan tune *Faleula E*, or "People of Faleula," a chant from the Mau movement advocating independence from New Zealand, and a predominant rhythm on tin and log drums that accompanies the Sasa, or slap dance, a popular dance in which rows of performers dance in rapid, synchronized movements in time to the drums. The history of these songs and dances, and the historical development of the Samoan islands provide a great deal for the musician to consider when exploring a historical perspective.

Unit 4: Technical Considerations

There is an element of freedom in the scoring of *Aue!* which allows ensembles that lack a complete instrumentation to experience the work. Clarinet 4 is offered in the absence of oboe 2; soprano saxophone and extensive cross-cueing assist or replace E-flat clarinet; euphonium 2 covers in the absence of bassoon 2; horn 2–3 cues are in saxophone, trombone, and bassoon as needed.

The piece can be performed with as few as two horns, covering parts 1 and 4. Percussion requirements outside of the standard cymbals, bells, chimes, bass drum, timpani, and triangle include high and low log drums, tin drum, and whistle. If a tin drum is not available, the composer suggests an inverted biscuit tin (literally) on the snare drum with the snares off. *Aue!* can be performed with four percussionists.

The piece does not present an extreme level of technical difficulty, but does require an ensemble adept at counting (both rhythms and measures of rest), and one familiar with triplet figures. The transparency of the scoring creates challenges in balance, and strict attention must be paid to dynamics to ensure each note of the long sustained chords, many rising only from *pianissimo* to *mezzo piano* levels, are heard.

The piece is essentially written in two alternating tempi: quarter note = 96, and quarter note = 144, a fifty percent increase in pulse. There are measures in 2/4, 3/4, 4/4, and 5/4, although these are not presented in rapid succession and should cause little difficulty in execution. It is important to maintain the noted tempos throughout, as the feel of the work should remain smooth and free flowing. Ranges for instruments are reasonable and accessible. Brass parts are frequently muted, with horns requiring a traditional mute, trumpets a small cloth or bag, trombones a small towel, and euphonium and tuba a larger cloth.

Unit 5: Stylistic Considerations

Aue! affords the opportunity to explore a variety of contemporary sounds and tone colors while addressing an array of highly rhythmic figures and ideas. There are four primary chords that rise and fall, as if swells of the Samoan tide:

E⁷	E–G-sharp–B–D
F-sharp m⁷	F-sharp–A–C-sharp–E
D^maj7	D–F-sharp–A–B
Caug⁷	C–E–G-sharp–B

The chords should be well balanced and even in their path, never rising to a level that might overshadow the thematic material. Frequently it is found that one set of chords gives way to another, with arrival peaks occurring at differing moments. Much of the work centers on timbre and color, from the fabric muting of the brasses to the stereo-like effect of the high and low log drums located on opposite sides of the stage. There is an Ivesian quality of layering that requires command of dynamic shading, and a clear knowledge of musical role is necessary to determine whether a given part is of primary or secondary importance. A rehearsal challenge may be the unpredictability of thematic material intersecting with the nearly always-present chord shifts.

Unit 6: Musical Elements

MELODY:

The melodic elements of *Aue!* are relatively short fragments, generally no longer than eight measures in length. Extracting these figures from the musical score and providing excerpts for all the musicians to explore can assist in maintaining group focus on the overall scope of the piece. This is especially important for members of the horn section, whose four-note chord is presented with only a slight change in note length for most of the first 272 measures of the piece. Having an ensemble listen to recordings of Samoan songs or view videos of native dances can provide an opportunity to understand the importance of song and dance in a less familiar culture.

HARMONY:

The linking of sections and melodies is achieved through the use of four essential seventh chords that constantly shift, but ultimately unify the piece. Spending rehearsal time familiarizing the ensemble with these chords, including their horizontal outlining in the vibraphone, can help provide better insight into the structure of the piece.

RHYTHM:

The essence of the songs found in *Aue!* are light and bright, and performance of the rhythms should reflect this style. There is use of triple against duple, longer sustained melodies concurrent with faster and more highly rhythmic figures, and an ever-increasing textural variety achieved through layering. As new or changing voices are added to existing rhythms, attention must be paid to unifying note lengths as well as to articulations matching across the ensemble.

TIMBRE:

There is no shortage of intriguing and less-frequently-used section and ensemble colors in *Aue!* The four unifying chords are generally assigned to differing voices to achieve noticeable shifts in timbre, with horn remaining an unwavering constant on the E^7. The unusual use of cloth-muted brass successfully achieves the effect of softening the sound in a considerably different manner than with traditional cup or straight mutes. The use of log drums provides a distinctively unique quality to the piece and is an important element in the work.

Unit 7: Form and Structure

SECTION	MEASURE	EVENT AND SCORING
1	1–11	Introduction; first statement of seventh chords; 2/4; quarter note = 96
2	12–33	Vibraphone triplets; oboe thematic figure A

Section	Measure	Event and Scoring
3	34–42	E-flat clarinet and flute thematic figure B (Samoan song)
4	43–58	Alto saxophone and conch shell thematic figure C; vibraphone re-enters
5	59–72	Cloth muted trumpets thematic figure D; flute "chirps"; 3/4 and 2/4; quarter note = 144
6	73–84	Vibraphone re-enters; oboe thematic variant on figure A; 2/4; quarter note = 96
7	85–98	Augmented figure B in trumpet; 3/4; quarter note = 144
8	99–116	Alto saxophone and conch shell figure C; percussion expanded
9	117–136	Clarinet variation of figure D (Samoan song); greater frequency of chords
10	137–145	Oboe thematic figure on A; 3/4 and 2/4; quarter note = 144
11	146–156	Flute, oboe, and bassoon thematic figure E; *forte*
12	157–170	Percussion use expanded; unmuted low brass thematic figure F (m. 168); 2/4; quarter note = 96
13	171–210	Alto saxophone, conch shell figure C; increased rhythmic activity
14	211–237	Triplet outlines of seventh chords in clarinet and bassoon; piccolo and flute figure D; unmuted tuba statement of thematic figure G (m. 216)
15	238–281	Alto and tenor saxophone figure D; low brass syncopated figure F; 3/4 and 2/4; quarter note = 144; increased texture and layering of sound
16	282–321	Chords eliminated; fragments of all thematic figures layered; *ff*
17	322–332	Figure D (Samoan song); 5/4 and 4/4; quarter note = 168

Unit 8: Suggested Listening

Adams, John:
> Common Tones in Simple Time
> Harmonielehre

Corigliano, John:
> Gazebo Dances
> Symphony No. 1

Ives, Charles. Variations on "America."

Pärt, Arvo. Fratres.

Villa-Lobos, Heitor:
> Amazonas
> Uirapuru

Unit 9: Additional References and Resources

Boyd, John. Reflections. Philharmonic a Vent Wind Orchestra. Klavier CD 11166. 2006.

Heron, Mark. Aue! by Christopher Marshall: A Guide to Rehearsal and Performance. Unpublished paper. wasbe.com/en/resources/aue.pdf

Marshall, Christopher John. Aue! for Wind Orchestra. Boca Raton, FL: Maecenas Music MC0061. Distributed by Masters Music Publications.
_____. Composer website. vaiaata.com/composer.html

Contributed by:

Glen J. Hemberger
Southeastern Louisiana University
Hammond, Louisiana

Teacher Resource Guide

Cyprian Suite
Carol Barnett
(b. 1949)

Unit 1: Composer

Composer and flutist Carol Barnett is a graduate of the University of Minnesota, where she studied with Dominick Argento, Paul Fetler, and Bernhard Weiser. She is a charter member of the American Composers Forum and has served on its board. Among the ensembles which have performed her works are the Women's Philharmonic, Saint Paul Chamber Orchestra, Minnesota Orchestra, Westminster Abbey Choir, Ankor Children's Choir of Jerusalem, Israel, Nebraska Children's Chorus, the Gregg Smith Singers, and the Harvard Glee Club. In 1991 she was a fellow at the Camargo Foundation in Cassis, France, and in 1999 she was awarded a travel grant from the Inter-University Research Committee on Cyprus. Composer-in-residence with the Dale Warland Singers from 1992 to 2001, she is currently a studio artist and instructor at Augsburg College in Minneapolis.

Unit 2: Composition

Cyprian Suite is one of several works composed by Carol Barnett following her trip to Cyprus in 1999. As stated in the program note in the score, "Each of the four movements is based on a Cypriot folksong."

Movement 1, "Servikos," is an instrumental dance in Serbian style. Three minutes in length, this lovely movement is presented in eight-measure phrases. Simple counterpoint provides interest and two-part imitation is used as a compositional technique. The low reeds are provided interesting and challenging parts requiring excellent unison playing in tandem with the upper woodwinds. The composer also uses the layering of entrances in order to achieve dynamic increases as well as sound mass intensification. A thinly-scored coda gracefully concludes the movement.

Movement 2, "Aya Marnia," presents a stark contrast to the rhythmic vitality of movement 1. Four minutes in length, it is a beautiful lullaby. A rising four-note line serves as an ostinato and supports this enchanting melody.

Movement 3, "Exomológhisis," perhaps contains the most interesting subject matter of the folksongs on which the suite is based. The lyrics to the song reveal the concerns of a man who is confessing his sins to a priest. Three minutes in length, the theme is presented in two unevenly proportioned phrases supported by a one-measure rhythmic ostinato.

Movement 4, "Agapisá Tin," is a challenging movement scored primarily in 7/8 meter. The theme is presented unadorned and supported by nothing more than a perfect fifth pedal point. An extensive percussion ostinato occurs just before letter D prior to the layering of various wind colors. Thematic material is presented in variation before the final return to the original G tonal center and dramatic conclusion.

Important commonalities to note regarding the four movements are that each begins with a brief introduction, ostinati are used extensively in each movement, the folksongs are presented simply and unadorned following a brief introduction, and there is a quasi-developmental or variation section in each movement. A full performance of *Cyprian Suite* takes approximately four-teen minutes. The difficulty of the work lies in its changing meters and thinly-scored sections for low reeds and low brass. All musicians must be confident in their ability to accurately subdivide the beat in order for an effective performance to occur.

Unit 3: Historical Perspective

The folk music of Cyprus is quite similar to that of Greece and Turkey. It includes a variety of dances such as the sousta, syrtos, zeimbekikos, tatsia, and the kartsilamos suites. The traditional music of Cyprus has a modal quality and is most commonly based on one of the *makams*. (The makam is a system of melody types which provides a set of rules one uses in order to compose.) Not of equal temperament, each makam uses a specific set of intervals (*cinsler*) and melodic development (*seyir*). The concepts used are loosely related to the concept of modes in Western music. Makams are comprised of a tetrachord plus a pentachord and include three important tones: 1) the *durak* (tonic), 2) the *güçl* (dominant), and 3), the *yeden* (leading tone).

Cypriot songs are many and varied, though among the most common types are the *fones*. These are traditional tunes which provide models for the creation of songs. Different verses are adapted to them, and this represents an extension of the Greek practice. The most common structures of fones are the AA and AB forms. The folk music of Cyprus was originally handed down by oral tradition, hence many older Cypriots knew one of the fones and would use them to sing for particular occasions.

Concerning rhythm, Cypriot songs use many of the rhythms of Greek tradition. These include 7/8 (3 + 2 + 2), 5/8 (3 + 2), and 9/8 (3 + 2 + 2 + 2), as well as other various compound rhythms. Standard meters are also used in Cypriot songs as well.

Few works have been written for modern wind band utilizing Cypriot folksongs, and part of the reason may be the complexity of the metric subdivision required for their performance and the use of unusual modal scales. Works for comparison include *Aegean Festival Overture* by Andreas Makris and *Greek Dances* by Nikos Skalkottas. Both pieces are superb, though the musical maturity required for their inclusion on concerts precludes performance by many ensembles. They require superb technique, great breadth of expression, and subtle musical nuance. While similar musical characteristics are required to perform *Cyprian Suite*, the piece is written in a manner that is within the grasp of many fine high school and university ensembles. While musical maturity is required, Barnett's piece is less technically challenging than the works by Makris and Skalkottas.

Each movement of the suite requires fluent unison precision by all instruments. Articulation markings have been carefully added to assist in achieving uniform style, and excellent intonation will be required within the unison sections. Percussion parts are thoughtfully composed and complement the wind textures. Specifically, mallet parts are commonly in unison with upper woodwinds and must be appropriately balanced.

While the orchestration of *Cyprian Suite* is of a mildly contemporary character, the harmonic material is premised on the unique, specific modality of the fundamental scale within each movement. This modal quality is quite striking, and the composer has not attempted to westernize the accompaniment material. Rather, each movement sounds fresh and creative to the listener, due in part to the composer's careful choice of melodic materials and her ability to maintain textural clarity. Musical lines are often exposed, and this creates wonderful opportunities for the ensemble to perform with nuanced dynamic contrast and musical sensitivity.

Unit 4: Technical Considerations

The technical considerations required to perform *Cyprian Suite* are different for each movement. Movement 1 is in a G modal tonal center and the scale required is similar to that of the harmonic minor, though the frequent accidentals present some performance challenges. It would be prudent of the conductor to include this scale as part of the daily warm-up.

467

FIGURE 1. Movement 1, scales

Evenness of the sixteenth-note subdivision is essential for uniform execution of the many lines, particularly when voices enter on the second subdivision. There are several passages that will require good tongue and finger coordination. Removing slurs for rehearsal and slowing the tempo will assist in improving accuracy in these passages.

Within the thinly-scored sections, achieving proper balance will be important. Two-part imitative sections will require reduced volumes in order to achieve clarity of line. Ostinato passages will need to be insistent and not lose their character the longer they are repeated within the texture. The isolated 3/8 measures that appear near the end of the movement, while not difficult, will require special attention to ensure an evenness of subdivision.

Movement 2 requires a slow, supported ostinato and a focused pedal point. The tonal center is D modal and the melodic line begins on the lowered seventh of the scale. Slow-moving counterpoint prevails in this gorgeous movement, and uniformity of pitch as the pedal point alternates between instruments is essential.

Long phrases are the norm, and with the tempo at dotted quarter note = 50, this will require excellent breath control. A tonal center shift to F-sharp minor at letter C presents some challenges, and parallel triads must be carefully tuned. Small vestiges of the whole-tone scale appear within the melody, and the fragmentation of the melodic line among numerous voices must be rehearsed in a way that allows the linear nature of the music to come through. The coda is a series of parallel chords, and each chord must be balanced as the music approaches its conclusion within the original D tonal center.

Movement 3 places responsibility for the repetitive accuracy of the ostinato on many performers. The melody is an F modal tonal center and appears in its entirety in the unison statement in the trombone section. The meters are 2/4 and 3/4 throughout.

Challenges include balancing tone clusters (based on the scale) and maintaining transparency of line in the developmental section. Stretto is used, giving the music a sense of polytonality, and the tubas have a challenging part requiring periodic, wide intervallic skips. Tonal shifts to distant keys occur prior to returning to the home key. The interval of the seventh is important within this movement, and augmentation of the melodic line is used.

FIGURE 2. Movement 3, scales

Movement 4 requires the ensemble to be fluent in 7/8 meter, subdivided as 3 + 2 + 2. The tonal center is G modal (resembling G natural minor); the melody is originally stated by tenor and baritone saxophone, then moves to tuba. It is dance-like in character.

There is an extensive ostinato passage for the percussion section that requires layering of individual colors beginning four measures before letter D. This ostinato is later transferred to the clarinets and is split between the three parts. The challenge is to maintain the balance of the ostinato during tonal shifts and against the percussion ostinato. Fragmentation of the melodic line is used freely and creatively within the texture, and balancing triads and diminished seventh chords is an important area requiring attention. Also important will be developing a sense of linear continuity (the melodic fragments) within the full ensemble.

Unit 5: Stylistic Considerations

Movement 1: "Servikos"

"Servikos" must be performed in the spirit of the Serbian dance. Melody should range in style from lighthearted at the beginning to frenzied much later in the movement. Careful attention to consistency in the execution of the ostinato will pay a dividend in the quality of performance. The varied orchestration of each section will dictate the balance required, and light staccato will be necessary during the portions that are thinly orchestrated.

FIGURE 3. Here: Movement 1: "Servikos"

Movement 2: "Aya Marina"

Aya Marina requires a simple, lyrical approach in order to achieve the childlike quality of the lullaby. Excellent breath control and consistent phrasing will be required of clarinets in the opening presentation and throughout the movement. Shaping the contour of the melody will also be part of the musical challenge. This should also be addressed when the tonal center shifts to F-sharp minor. The ability to make music during the development section will be a challenge, specifically as the melodic fragments are shaped in accordance with their natural design and connected to the entering lines that follow.

FIGURE 4. Movement 2: "Aya Marina," lullaby

Movement 3: "Exomológhisis"

"Exomológhisis" should be performed with a touch of sarcasm due to the nature of the text (not included with the score but available via the internet). As such, adherence to a consistent style of articulation should be emphasized as the trombone section states the entire theme in unison. The half step of C to D-flat will require special attention within the context of the melodic line as its pitch accuracy is critical.

The ostinato pattern supporting the movement will require long-term stylistic consistency without dropping in intensity. As the composer presents the thematic material in a section of stretto at letter C, maintaining excellent balance between the various voices will be of primary concern. Whereas there are so many unison lines, emphasis on both the style of the melody and intonation will be a constant concern.

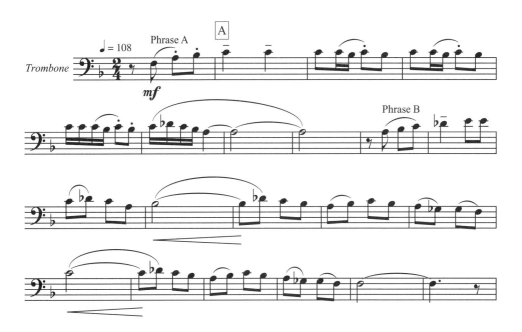

FIGURE 5. Movement 3: "Exomológhisis"

Movement 4: "Agapisá Tin"

The energetic character of the folksong "Agapisá Tin" provides inspiration for the dance-like character of the final movement. Modal in concept, the movement gradually builds in momentum. The 7/8 meter that prevails is not difficult to manage, though the extended slurs in the opening presentation can lead to heaviness in its execution. Maintaining proper tempo without over-accentuation on the short beats should assist in avoiding this pitfall.

The lengthy, exposed percussion ostinato should be faithfully subdivided to ensure excellent entrances from the saxophone section and the upper woodwinds at letter G and beyond. Close adherence to like-instrument sectional balance issues will allow for clearly articulated passages in the woodwinds. The final presentation of the thematic material should have an increase in tension and energy, not losing sight of the merits of maintaining proper balance as the musical frenzy builds to a dramatic conclusion.

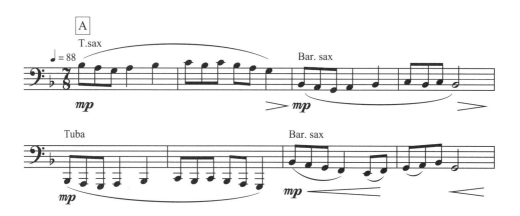

FIGURE 6. Movement 4: "Agapisá Tin"

Unit 6: Musical Elements

MELODY:

As these melodies are based on Cypriot folksongs, the character and tonality of all four movements are based on the unique scales used as the tonal basis for each movement. Movement 1 is a lively melody in a G modal tonal center. The use of both the natural and raised fourth gives the melody its unique flavor. The natural shape of the melody provides an ample clue as to the contour the conductor might use in performance. The third phrase of the structure provides opportunity for unusual musicianship due in part to its scalar nature.

FIGURE 7. Movement 1: "Servikos," mm. 57–63

"Aya Marina" is a quaint, plaintive theme in a D modal tonal center. Part of its quality derives from the supporting two-measure ostinato and also the use of the lowered seventh of the scale. This lack of a leading tone tendency is a common characteristic of Cypriot folksongs, and its use is partly responsible for giving the music its modal character. Simple in conception, "Aya Marina" contains many interpretive possibilities. Its range is a modest major sixth in expanse and its soothing quality is fully supported by the designation of lullaby.

"Exomológhisis" (confession) is an energetic theme in the modal tonal center of F. The scale on which it is based uses a minor second and a minor sixth. The phrase structure of the melody is AB, and portion A is but eight bars in length while portion B is twelve. Fragments of the melody are reused during the development section.

"Agapisá Tin" is a delightful theme couched in a G modal tonal center and in 7/8 meter, subdivided as 3 + 2 + 2. Structured in AABB form, portion A is but a sixth in expanse. Section B is primarily in the subdominant and a fifth in range. The careful use of staccato in the first phrase and tenuto in the second differentiates the character of the two phrases, and the rhythm of the first phrase heavily influences the development section later in the movement.

HARMONY:

Harmonies have been creatively conceived using the modal scale unique to each folksong as the starting point. In movement 1, the G modal tonal center is established using a dominant-to-tonic root movement and through open fifths as a pedal point. Points of dissonance are created by simultaneously sounding both C and C-sharp over the tonic (letter D) for extended periods of time. Use of the tritone and the half step creates moments of tension and release.

The melody in movement 2 has a tonal center of D and is also presented over a perfect fifth used as a pedal point. Clarinets engage in simple counterpoint in the initial thematic presentation. Traditional harmony is used at letter C, with the appearance of parallel minor triads and minor seventh chords appearing at letter E. The ending of the movement contains a stunning progression of minor triads and seventh and ninth chords, all supported by ascending parallel fifths in the bass voices.

The melody in movement 3 is in an F modal tonal center and moves primarily by steps. The composer harmonically supports the theme with triads and chord clusters that are derived from the thematic material (F–G-flat–B-flat–C). Harmonic material is also derived from motives scored in parallel sixths, fifths, and thirds. The tonal center shifts to E, though the influence of the original tonal center (F) is clearly intended to be prominent. Other harmonic devices used are pedal points and thematic movement in major triads.

Movement 4 begins with a descending minor third (B-flat–A–G) to establish the G modal tonal center, though the rising minor third of E natural to G in mm. 4–6 also represents an important harmonic feature of the movement. The theme is supported by a perfect fifth used as a pedal point. Diminished triads are foreshadowed at m. 50 in the timpani and marimba ostinato, and diminished seventh chords and extended harmonies appear throughout the section beginning at letter G. Pedal points appear periodically in upper voices, and thematic material is scored in parallel sixths (letter J). Fragments of melodic material are used in modulatory sections (see mm. 108–112), and the decidedly modal character concludes with a strong G minor triad in the final measure.

RHYTHM:

The pulse is firmly established in each of the four movements, and this is achieved in a variety of ways. Snare and high tom-tom establish the beat in movement 1. Clarinets establish the dotted-quarter-note pulse in movement 2 through the scale pattern D–E–F–G. Movement 3 begins with an ostinato in clarinet and tambourine comprised of a pattern made up of a dotted-eighth- and-sixteenth note figure followed by two eighth notes. The 7/8 meter of movement 4 is established through the subdivision of the melodic line in the pattern of 3 + 2 + 2.

Changing meters are used in each of the movements. The first movement is in 2/4 meter and shifts to 3/8 sparingly. This shift interrupts the melodic line only near the very end of the movement. Movement 2 moves freely between 6/8 and 9/8 meters in an easily flowing manner, with 6/8 being the primary meter. Movement 3 is in 2/4 and 3/4 meters and is the most rigid movement of the suite. Movement 4 opens with a mournful 4/4 introduction followed by entrance of the melody in 7/8. This second meter permeates the remainder of the movement, with several brief excursions into 6/8, 2/4, 3/4, and 4/4 meters.

Each of the folksongs used in the suite are very different in style, and provide excellent material for the teaching and reinforcing of metric subdivision. Movement 1 will require students to move from 2/4 to 3/8 with the sixteenth note being prominent. Creating an exercise such as the one given in figure 8 and using it during the warm-up will be helpful.

FIGURE 8. Movement 1, rhythm exercises

Movement 2 presents no pressing difficulties, due to the slow character of the lullaby. The rhythm of the melody in movement 3 requires multiple ensemble entrances on the "and" of beat 1. The other challenge is the isolated ostinato pattern within the development section (mm. 90–94).

Movement 4 presents several different challenges for the ensemble. The 7/8 meter is always subdivided as 3 + 2 + 2, hence working on this pattern during the warm-up will be important. The interactive ostinato in the upper woodwinds at letter G will require attention. Rehearsing the two parts independently will solve the issues of subdivision necessary for this passage to sound as one line.

TIMBRE:

One of the unique strengths of the *Cyprian Suite* is the manner in which Carol Barnett uses tone color. Pure instrument colors are often used and combined creatively with a variety of percussion colors. Such combinations lead to a clarity of sound that is most attractive. This clarity comes at a cost, however; each musician must play all lines with confidence and precision, including members of the low reeds and low brass. Full ensemble passages must retain their clarity, and contrast is achieved through periodic passages of woodwind and brass choirs.

Clarity is most difficult to achieve in the contrapuntal sections of the piece. During such passages, it is fruitful to rehearse each entrance separately, grouping instruments playing like parts. This allows work on uniform articulation, intonation, and proper blend and balance simultaneously. For example, the tone colors in movement 2, letter C are stunning, but difficult to perform musically. Spending adequate time on blending the various voices carrying similar parts is most important and allows the conductor more latitude in shaping the direction of the melodic material.

Percussion colors are carefully selected and thoughtfully orchestrated within each movement of the suite. The section ostinato in movement 4, beginning at m. 34, is layered very musically in its entrances, and the pairings of percussion and woodwind colors at letter G present unusual opportunities for exceptional color highlighting. Reducing the dynamic level in the woodwinds during rehearsal will assist in bringing out the essential timbres within the percussion section. This same concept may be applied within the tutti passages of the full ensemble as well.

Unit 7: Form and Structure

There is a wonderful, unifying aspect to the four movements of the *Cyprian Suite*. On the largest possible scale, the movements are arranged tonally as follows:

Movement	1	2	3	4
Tonality	G	D	F	G

The key relationships are musically satisfying to the ear, and the movements connect in a natural manner. On a smaller scale, while widely differing in character, the movements are structurally very sound in their organization. Each begins with a brief introduction followed by the initial statement of the folksong. This presentation tends to be simple and straightforward. However, the form of each folksong varies in both length and structure, as follows:

Movement	Theme	Phrase length
1	aabbaaccdd	five eight-measure phrases (each eight-measure phrase is a pair of two four-measure phrases)
2	aab	5 + 4 + 5
3	ab	8 + 12
4	aabb	8 + 8 + 8 + 8

SECTION	MEASURE		EVENT AND SCORING
Movement 1			
Introduction	1–8		Introduction based on the rhythm of thematic material
Theme	9–95		
Letter A	9–16	a	Unison clarinet presentation
Letter B	17–24	a	Upper woodwinds and trumpet; pedal point in perfect fifths
Letter C	25–32	b	Clarinet unison over D pedal point
Letter D	33–40	b	Unison in upper woodwinds, bass clarinet, bassoon, alto sax, tenor sax; ostinato in brass and percussion
Letter E	41–48	a	Theme in trumpet 1; syncopation using half steps; uses percussion rhythm from the introduction
Letter F	49–56	a	Theme presented in two-part imitation
Letter G	57–63	c	Theme in oboe and clarinet 1; phrase elided to next phrase, making it a seven-measure phrase
Letter H	64–71	c	Theme in woodwinds and glockenspiel

Section	Measure		Event and Scoring
Letter I	72–79	d	Four-bar idea sounding repeatedly; ostinato continues; layers of colors added every four measures
Letter J	80–87	d	Four-bar idea continues with piccolo, flute, and oboe over previous material; low brass assumes ostinato
Letter K	88–95	e	Melody in oboe and clarinet 1
Letter L	96–103	e	Variant of "e" repeated with 3/8 bar replacing the phrase ending; alto sax, bass clarinet, and bassoon assume melody
Letter M	104–111	e	Tutti statement in two-part imitation; all woodwinds engaged in melody; all brass on the ostinato
Letter N	112–119	e	Tutti statement in three-part imitation; final measure in 6/8 to accommodate lengthened phrase
Coda			
Letter O	120–126	a	Clarinet states modified phrase "a" with select notes deleted
Letter P	127–134	a	Bass clarinet and marimba state abbreviated theme; D pedal point in flute, V-I cadence on the offbeats of the final measure with addition of C-sharp for tension
Movement 2			
Introduction	1–4		Ascending four-note ostinato over D pedal point
Theme (first time)			
Letter A	5–19	aab	(5 + 4 + 5) without extensions; theme in clarinet 1; counterpoint added in clarinet 2; melody begins on the seventh of the scale

SECTION	MEASURE	EVENT AND SCORING
Theme (second time)		
Letter B	20–39	Ostinato continues played down a second; tonic to dominant progression in bass voices and timpani; melody is delayed by one count; two-part imitation begins at m. 29
Development		
Letter C	40–51	Tonal center shift to F-sharp; fragments of "a" portion of theme used; parallel minor triads used beginning at m. 44
Letter D	52–59	Tonal center shift to B minor; parallel triads continue
Letter E	60–67	Appearance of scale passage in baritone sax and euphonium
Letter F	68–75	Bass clarinet and tenor sax contain whole-tone influence; parallel fifths over A-flat pedal point
Letter G	76–87	Phrase "b" over parallel fifths; augmentation of melodic line
Coda		
Letter H	88–99	Return of introduction and theme in D tonal center; "a" phrase is up a fourth; the second "a" is elided to previous phrase and up a third
Letter I	100–107	Fragments of "a" over ascending ostinato; parallel sixths, sevenths, and fourths used
Letter J	108–115	Woodwinds descending on a series of primarily minor chords; bass voices moving in ascending parallel fifths; upper woodwinds voices converge on a unison D to close the movement
Movement 3		
Introduction	1–4	Rhythmic ostinato in clarinet and tambourine

SECTION	MEASURE	EVENT AND SCORING
Theme (first time)		
Letter A	4–30	Theme presented in unison trombone; rhythmic ostinato joined by flute at m. 13; scale passage at m. 24 in piccolo, flute, oboe, and glock
Theme (second time)		
Letter B	31–52	Melody presented in bass voices; answer to melody in upper woodwinds (m. 35) using thematic fragment; "b" portion B of melody supported by chord cluster at m. 39; half-step answer in upper woodwinds in parallel thirds (m. 45); two-octave scale passage concludes (mm. 49–52)
	53–56	Tonal center shift down a half step to E-natural
Development		
Letter C	57–74	Appearance of "a" in stretto over tonal center A; major seventh (E over F) influence on harmony; tuba line transitions to new tonal center (mm. 73–74)
	75–103	Partial statements of "b"; trombone plays theme in parallel major triads (m. 79); appearance of new rhythmic motive based on original ostinato (m. 78)
Theme (third time)		
Letter D	104–124	Return of ostinato a major third higher than the original
Theme (fourth time)		Presented half step lower and shortened
Letter E	125–136	Theme in D tonal center over E ostinato; serves as transition; "b" portion is partially presented and augmented, slowing the rhythmic motion (m. 133)

SECTION	MEASURE		EVENT AND SCORING
Theme (fifth time)			
Letter F	137–144		Theme returns to original F tonal center, supported only by ostinato in the snare drum; scale returns in parallel fifths connecting "a" and "b" material (mm. 142–143)
	145–156		Harmonic cluster returns (minus the note F) in support of "b" melodic material; "b" is augmented creating a sense of slowing; extension used in mm. 154–156 using alternating half steps
	157–166		Final portion of "b" phrase stated in augmentation; chord cluster sustained for four measures (mm. 162–165) prior to cadence on perfect fifth
Movement 4			
Introduction	1–9		Descending minor third (B-flat–A–G) outlines G modal tonal center; rising G-minor arpeggio in clarinet 3; descending scale on G in mm. 7–9; E to G in mm. 4–6 is harmonically important
Theme (first time)	10–37	(aabb)	
Letter A	10–17	a	First phrase split between tenor/baritone sax and tuba; perfect fifth used as pedal point
Letter B	18–25	a	Repetition of first phrase in upper woodwinds
Letter C (first time)	19–33	b	Third phrase harmonized with E-flat over C, implying the subdominant of G
Letter C (second time)	19–37	b	Repetition of third phrase, adding alto sax and brass

SECTION	MEASURE	EVENT AND SCORING
Development and Variation	34–45	Ostinato section in percussion emphasizing temple blocks and high woodblock; colors layered
Letter E	46–53	Timpani added, emphasizing minor third from the introduction; marimba layered at m. 46, providing diminished triad quality
Letter F	54–60	Ostinato continues
Letter G	61–69	Saxophone section plays two-part melody, emphasizing diminished seventh; clarinet section assumes ostinato
Letter H	70–83	Two-bar melody moves up a third; G pedal point continues; in m. 76 alto sax and horn add a G scale, outlining the rising seventh and emphasizing the tritone
Letter I	84–93	Descending minor third motive reappears; woodwind and percussion ostinato continues
Letter J	94–112	Return of theme scored in sixths, supported by series of half-diminished seventh chords; final five bars (mm. 108–112) serve as transition to return of the full ensemble
Letter K	113–120 b	Tutti appearance of third phrase of theme; return of G tonal center to reinforce approach of the piece's conclusion
Letter L	121–133 b	Fourth phrase scored in thirds; melody is varied slightly and extension added; brief tom-tom transition (mm. 131–133)

Section	Measure	Event and Scoring
Return of theme		
Letter M	134–146	Modified return of "a" portion of theme; thinly orchestrated using trombone to begin melody; metric changes accommodate the modified theme; scoring suggests a recall of the first presentation at m. 10
Letter N	147–154 b	Third phrase harmonized; scale added in low reeds and brass
Letter O	155–164 b	Fourth phrase harmonized; small variation and extension added to emphasize the conclusion on a G-minor triad

Unit 8: Suggested Listening

Allen, Fred J. *Bosnian Folk Songs*.
Cesarini, Franco:
    Bulgarian Dances, Op. 35
    Greek Folk Song Suite
Chobanian, Loris. *Armenian Dances*.
Gorb, Adam. *Yiddish Dances*.
van Lynschooten, Henk. *Suite on Greek Love Songs*.
Makris, Andreas. Arranged by ajor Albert Bader. *Aegean Festival Overture*.
Stevens, Halsey. Arranged by Wm. E. Schaefer. *Ukrainian Folksongs*.
Ticheli, Frank. *Cajun Folk Songs*.
Turina, Joaquin. Arranged by John Krance. *Five Miniatures*.
Woolfenden, Guy. *Illyrian Dances*.

Unit 9: Additional References and Resources

Barnett, Carol. *Cyprian Suite*.New York: Boosey & Hawkes Music Publishers.
Chistodoulou, Menelaos N. and Konstantinos D. Ioannidis. *Kypriaka démodé asmata*. Cyprus Research Centre, 1986.
Miles, Richard, ed. *Teaching Music through Performance in Band, Volumes 1–6*. Chicago: GIA Publications, 1997, 1998, 2000, 2002, 2005, and 2007.
Rehrig, William H. *The Heritage Encyclopedia of Band Music: Composers and Their Music*. Paul E. Bierley, ed. Westerville, OH: Integrity Press, 1991.
Tompolis, Sozoy. *Kypriakoi Rythmoi Kai Melodies*. Leukosia: Cyprus, 1966.
West, M. L. *Ancient Greek Music*. New York: Oxford University Press, 1992.

Websites:

Cyprus Music on Kypros. http://www.kypros.org/Real/Music.html
Michalis Tterlikkas "Mousa" Music Troupe.
http://mousalyra.com.cy/english/diskografia_kypaia_foni1.htm
Music of Cyrpus. http://www.ucy.ac.cy/~ethno/article2.htm

Contributed by:

Barry E. Kopetz
Professor of Conducting, Director of Bands
Conservatory of Music
Capital University
Bexley, Ohio

Teacher Resource Guide

Dream Journey
Op. 98

James Barnes
(b. 1949)

Unit 1: Composer

James Barnes is the division director for music theory and composition at the University of Kansas, where he teaches music composition, orchestration, arranging, and wind band history and repertoire courses. Beginning in 1975, he served as KU's staff arranger, assistant, and later, associate director of bands for twenty-seven years. Immediately prior to his tenure on the faculty at his alma mater, Barnes earned both his bachelor's and master's degree. His principal composition teachers included John Pozdro and Allen Irving McHose.

Barnes's numerous publications for concert band and orchestra are performed worldwide at such venues as Tanglewood, Boston Symphony Hall, Lincoln Center, Carnegie Hall, the Kennedy Center in Washington, DC, Tchaikovsky Hall in Moscow, and the Tokyo Metropolitan Concert Hall. Since 1984 his music has been exclusively published by Southern Music Company, San Antonio, Texas.

Barnes twice received the American Bandmasters Association Ostwald Award for outstanding contemporary wind band music. He has been the recipient of numerous ASCAP Awards, the Kappa Kappa Psi Distinguished Service to Music Medal, and the Bohumil Makovsky Award for Outstanding College Band Conductors, among other significant honors and grants. The Tokyo Kosei Wind Orchestra has recorded three compact discs of his music, and Southern Music Company has released three albums of his compositions.

Barnes has traveled extensively as a guest composer, conductor, and lecturer throughout the United States, Europe, Australia, Taiwan, and

Singapore. He has guest conducted in Japan more than thirty-five times. He is a member of the American Society of Composers, Authors and Publishers (ASCAP), the American Bandmasters Association, and numerous other professional organizations and societies.

Unit 2: Composition

Dream Journey was commissioned by the Austin, Texas Independent School District for the twenty-fifth anniversary of their All-City Honor Band. Subtitled "A Tone Poem for Symphonic Band," this single-movement work is listed by the composer as Grade 5 with a running time of eight and one half minutes. It was premiered in February of 1997 with the composer conducting.

Barnes described the inspiration for *Dream Journey* in the score: "[It] was inspired by a real dream of mine, where I thought I was riding in an extremely fast train (maybe a *Shinkansen*—a bullet train) through time, past brilliant lights and colors, at the speed of sound."

Unit 3: Historical Perspective

Grove Music Online defines the symphonic poem (Ger. *symphonische Dichtung*) as an orchestral form in which a poem or program provides a narrative or illustrative basis. The origins of the form can be found in Beethoven's overtures, and its evolution traced through the works of Berlioz, Mendelssohn, Liszt, Dvořák, Tchaikovsky, and Dukas, reaching an apex in the works of Richard Strauss. According to Hugh MacDonald, the form "satisfied three of the principal aspirations of the nineteenth century: to relate music to the world outside, to integrate multi-movement forms (often by welding them into a single movement) and to elevate instrumental program music to a level higher than that of opera, the genre previously regarded as the highest mode of musical expression."[1]

When asked if *Dream Journey* was his first deliberate foray into to the genre, Barnes replied, "Several of my works are programmatic by nature. Try my *Trail of Tears*. How about *Lonely Beach*, which is a tone poem about D-Day that I wrote for the Army Band? Also, there's *Legend*, which is a tone poem about the phoenix bird. My *Wild Blue Yonder*, which I just wrote for the Air Force Band, is a tone poem about what it must feel like to fly a fighter plane." He went on to note that his third, fourth, and fifth symphonies are also programmatic.

Unit 4: Technical Considerations

The instrumentation of *Dream Journey* is prodigious, and was designed to take full advantage of the resources made available to the composer by the circumstances of the commission. The composer also revealed, "To get the sorts of tone clusters and effects that I needed, I required a large group." The score calls for a minimum of seventy-one players, including an expanded saxophone section (SAATB), English horn, double bass, and piano, plus divisi euphonium and tuba parts (requiring at least two and four players respectively).

Similarly, each of the three flute parts call for a minimum of two players, with all doubling on piccolo if possible. Each of the three B-flat clarinet parts calls for at least four players, and each of the four trumpet and four horn parts requires at least two players. Although the percussion section is also quite large, the composer does not call for any particularly unusual instruments (with the possible exception of the need for five timpani).

The sheer bulk of the instrumentation is reminiscent of Gunther Schuller's massive *In Praise of Winds* (1981). However, Barnes has taken pains to cross-cue critical solo lines in at least two other voices (e.g., the prominent bassoon solo is cued in both baritone saxophone and euphonium). Therefore, the work is playable by ensembles of more modest proportions, but the depth of color and ultimate sonic impact would suffer.

The score itself is a photograph of the composer's manuscript, which created some challenges for the publisher. The original employed many different sizes of paper. The discrepancies resulted in the blank spaces found throughout the published score (pages 4, 7–14, 18, 32–36, 51–52). Fortunately, these sections are driven by a highly predictable ostinato and layering effect which will enable the conductor to negotiate the frequent page turns with relative ease.

Unit 5: Stylistic Considerations

Barnes describes *Dream Journey* as his "second leap" into minimalist techniques, the first being the end of *Legend*.

According to Grove Music Online, minimalism is "a term borrowed from the visual arts to describe a style of composition characterized by an intentionally simplified rhythmic, melodic and harmonic vocabulary."[2] Keith Potter further asserts, "The Americans La Monte Young, Terry Riley, Steve Reich and [Philip] Glass, all born within eighteen months of each other in 1935–7, are widely considered pioneers in the evolution of musical minimalism."[3]

Dream Journey is essentially a composition exercise. Like Ravel's *Bolero*, the composer has chosen a small amount of material to manipulate using various techniques over an extended period of time. However, unlike Ravel, Barnes uses multiple ostinatos to represent the basic octatonic material, and *Dream Journey* is approximately half the duration of *Bolero*.

The introduction of *Dream Journey* into the *Allegro Vivo* also bears more than passing resemblance to John Barnes Chance's *Incantation and Dance* in its contour and coloration. While Barnes was aware of the similarity as he wrote it, the allusion was nothing more than a useful device to get the work off the ground.

Unit 6: Musical Elements

MELODY:

One hallmark of many minimalist compositions is a deliberate de-emphasis of melody. Barnes's *Dream Journey* reflects this aspect of the style in that it is primarily a celebration of texture with a single melodic idea recurring for relatively brief spans of time.

HARMONY:

The initial melodic resting tone is A, gradually moving to C at its completion. The arrival at C is destabilized shortly thereafter with the addition of F-sharp. Frequent juxtaposition of these pitches creates tension throughout the work.

The principal melody is constructed using a so-called "Model A" version (van den Toorn) of the octatonic scale. "If any work affected *Dream Journey*, it was my Third Symphony, because both employ extensive use of octatonic scales." Octatonicism pervades the composition primarily in the construction of the numerous ostinato patterns as well as the tone clusters used to punctuate the form. In all, there are six rhythm and/or pitch ostinatos that serve as the frame for the composition.

FIGURE 1. Six ostinato patterns

Each pattern is derived from a corresponding octatonic scale. For example, Ostinato 1 is built from a B-flat, "Model B" (van den Toorn) scale.

RHYTHM:

When asked about his choice of meters (2/2 and 3/2), Barnes wrote in the score, "'White notes' give the music more resonance and flow." This concept is illustrated through the two principal rhythmic motives of the work.

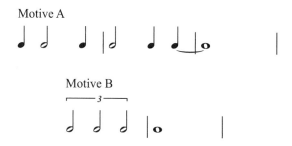

FIGURE 2. Principle rhythmic motives

The eye is drawn through the bars more readily, and players' instinct to supply more air in longer note values is exploited. Barnes described a purely practical reason as well: "I just thought *alla breve* would best fit what I wanted to hear, and I also thought that the simpler notation wouldn't scare the kids half to death when they first read it. We only had two days to put this together at the premiere."

TIMBRE:

Two sections of *Dream Journey* call for improvisation on the part of performers: mm. 271–292 and mm. 391–417. This screening material in the woodwinds over the broad melody in the brass creates an effect reminiscent of movement 1 of Hindemith's *Symphony in B-flat*. According to the composer, "This was just the easiest way to get the effect I wanted there. That's the only time I use 'box notation': when it's easier for the band to make it up than if I wrote it out."

The texture of *Dream Journey* relies heavily on layering. The additive nature of most sections demands a well-balanced ensemble with strength of tone on all parts to support the pyramid and cascade effects. In this work, Barnes's approach to scoring hearkens back to the wind band classics of the 1950s and 1960s (by Vincent Persichetti, William Schuman, Clifton Williams, etc.). The woodwind, brass, and percussion teams tend to be "blocked" rather than blended, and instrumental roles are predictable (with the possible exception of the extended bassoon solo).

Unit 7: Form and Structure

SECTION	MEASURE	EVENT AND SCORING
Introduction Ω^4	1–10	Emergence of motive A (percussion)
	11–43	Principal melody (bassoon)
	19–34	Tone clusters provide atmosphere
A	44–83	Motive A provides foundation for layering of repetitive gestures; additive, every eight bars after m. 52
	84–110	"Train" gestures added (Doppler effect tone clusters in woodwinds and brass); motive A continues
B	110–121	Ostinato 1 provides foundation for layering (four-bar segments); motive A returns m. 114
	122–138	Ostinato 2 introduced (piano) under elongated tone cluster Doppler gestures; motive A continues
Transition	139–144	Ostinato activity ceases; rhythmic clusters in woodwinds recall railroad crossing signals; emergence of motive B outside of melodic context
C	145–170	Ostinato 3 provides foundation for layering of repetitive gestures (additive)
	157–170	Low brass Doppler gestures
Transition	171–178	Ascending gestures evolved from ostinato 3
	179–182	Descending scales
D	183–208	Ostinato 4 provides foundation for layering of repetitive gestures (additive); change of meta-metric grouping to three (groups of three, six, or nine measures in lieu of two, four, or eight)
Summary	209–220	Use of motive A with rhythmically manipulated (augmented or diminished) "split" scales; return to metric groupings to two, four, and eight bars
	221–228	Material evolved from ostinato 2 with tone cluster (low brass)
	229–238	Return of motive A and material related to section B (mm. 44–83)

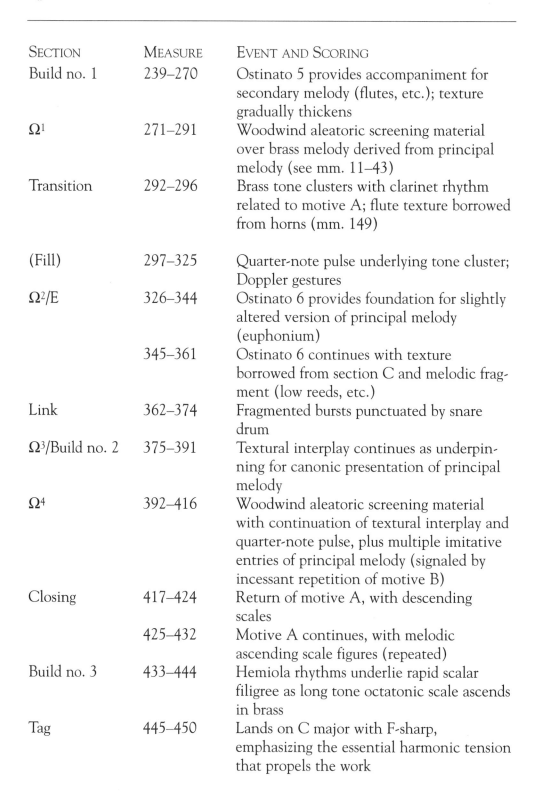

SECTION	MEASURE	EVENT AND SCORING
Build no. 1	239–270	Ostinato 5 provides accompaniment for secondary melody (flutes, etc.); texture gradually thickens
Ω^1	271–291	Woodwind aleatoric screening material over brass melody derived from principal melody (see mm. 11–43)
Transition	292–296	Brass tone clusters with clarinet rhythm related to motive A; flute texture borrowed from horns (mm. 149)
(Fill)	297–325	Quarter-note pulse underlying tone cluster; Doppler gestures
Ω^2/E	326–344	Ostinato 6 provides foundation for slightly altered version of principal melody (euphonium)
	345–361	Ostinato 6 continues with texture borrowed from section C and melodic fragment (low reeds, etc.)
Link	362–374	Fragmented bursts punctuated by snare drum
Ω^3/Build no. 2	375–391	Textural interplay continues as underpinning for canonic presentation of principal melody
Ω^4	392–416	Woodwind aleatoric screening material with continuation of textural interplay and quarter-note pulse, plus multiple imitative entries of principal melody (signaled by incessant repetition of motive B)
Closing	417–424	Return of motive A, with descending scales
	425–432	Motive A continues, with melodic ascending scale figures (repeated)
Build no. 3	433–444	Hemiola rhythms underlie rapid scalar filigree as long tone octatonic scale ascends in brass
Tag	445–450	Lands on C major with F-sharp, emphasizing the essential harmonic tension that propels the work

Unit 8: Suggested Listening

Adams, John. *Short Ride in a Fast Machine*.
Chance, John Barnes. *Incantation and Dance*.
Hindemith, Paul. *Symphony in B-flat*.
Ravel, Maurice. *Bolero*.
Reich, Steve. *Drumming*.
Riley, Terry. *In C*.
Schuller, Gunther. *In Praise of Winds*.
Schuman, William. *George Washington Bridge*.
Strauss, Richard. *Don Juan, Ein Heldenleben*.
Whitacre, Eric. *Ghost Train*.
Williams, J. Clifton. *Fanfare and Allegro*.

Unit 9: Additional References and Resources

Camphouse, Mark, ed. *Composers on Composing for Band*. Chicago: GIA
    Publications, 2002.
MacDonald, Hugh: "Symphonic Poem." In *Grove Music Online*. L. Macy, ed.
    http://www.grovemusic.com
Miles, Richard, ed. *Teaching Music through Performance in Band, Volumes 1,
    2, 3, and 6*. Chicago: GIA Publications.
Potter, Keith: "Minimalism." In *Grove Music Online*. L. Macy, ed.
    http://www.grovemusic.com

Contributed by:

Carolyn Barber
Director of Bands
University of Nebraska-Lincoln
Lincoln, Nebraska

---

1 Hugh MacDonald, "Symphonic Poem," Grove Music Online, L. Macy, ed.,
    http://www.grovemusic.com
2 Keith Potter, "Minimalism," Grove Music Online, L. Macy, ed., http://www.grovemu-
    sic.com
3 Ibid.
4 The omega symbol is used rather than an ordinary letter to express the unusual nature
    of the initial bassoon material. Because the composer is using minimalist—especially
    layering—techniques, the bassoon material really isn't "A" (or B, or C, etc.) in a
    formal sense. The form derives from texture rather than melody (again, stemming
    from the minimalism). The omega melody is a distinct entity that is not necessarily
    structural, hence the non-roman alphabetic character.

Teacher Resource Guide

El Camino Real
A Latin Fantasy

Alfred Reed
(1921–2005)

Unit 1: Composer

Alfred Reed was born in New York on January 25, 1921 to Austrian parents who appreciated good music and encouraged Alfred in his music studies. He began studying trumpet in high school, but by seventeen he had started composition lessons with Paul Yartin, who instilled in Reed the importance of studying the music of J. S. Bach before being seduced by modern composing techniques.[1] From 1938 to 1942 he worked as staff composer and assistant conductor for the Radio Workshop in New York. While in the military he served as associate conductor of the 529th U. S. Air Force Band, and on his discharge he enrolled in the Julliard School, where he studied with Vittorio Giannini. It was Giannini who told Reed that he could not imagine any music surviving that did not combine "Italian melody and German symphonic craftsmanship"[2]: a lesson obviously well learned. In 1948 he became the staff composer and arranger for NBC and later also worked for ABC.

In 1953 Reed became the conductor of the Baylor University Symphony Orchestra, where he completed bachelor's (1955) and master's (1956) degrees. In 1955 he became an editor at Hansen Publications and began his study of composing for young bands. He then joined wind ensemble advocates Frederick Fennell, Clifton Williams, and John Kinyon on the staff at the University of Miami. He initially taught theory, composition, music marketing, and music education (1966–1993), and succeeded Frederick Fennell as conductor of the wind ensemble (1980–1987). Reed enjoyed a collaboration with the Tokyo Kosei Wind Orchestra from 1981 and became a major figure in the Japanese band movement. Alfred Reed is regarded as one of the most popular composers for wind ensemble thanks to compositions such as *A Festival Prelude* (1962), *Russian Christmas Music* (1968), *Armenian Dances* (1974), *Praise Jerusalem!* (1988), and his series of transcriptions of music by J. S. Bach.

Unit 2: Composition

El Camino Real: A Latin Fantasy is dedicated "to the men and women of the United States Air Force Reserve, especially the musicians of the Band of the Air Force Reserve, Lt. Col. Ray E. Toler, Commander and Conductor." The work was composed during the end of 1984 and completed in early 1985. It was premiered on April 15, 1985 in Sarasota, Florida, by the 581st Air Force Band, conducted by Lt. Col. Ray E. Toler.

El Camino Real is Spanish for "the Royal Road," a term used to describe any road under the jurisdiction of the Spanish crown. Today, El Camino Real usually refers to the 600-mile California Mission Trail that stretches from Mission San Diego de Alcalá in San Diego to Mission San Francisco Solano in Sonoma.

The composition is based on two Spanish flamenco guitar chord progressions, the jota and the fandango, and follows a traditional three-part construction of fast-slow-fast. Like most of Reed's compositions, this work is written in a melodic, post-Romantic style. *El Camino Real* is ten minutes long and of Grade 4 standard.

Unit 3: Historical Perspective

Reed was conductor of the wind ensemble at the University of Miami when he composed *El Camino Real* (1985). This weekly contact with the wind ensemble explains the high level of detail in his score, particularly with regard to instrumentation and timbre.

The term *fantasy* (or fantasia) has been applied to different styles of music since the 1600s, but generally means a composition with an improvisational character and where the form is of secondary importance. Many composers have used the fantasia, including Bach, Sweelinck, Chopin, and Schumann but Reed's use of the fantasy is probably more akin to Tchaikovsky's fantasy overtures *Hamlet*, Op. 67, *Romeo and Juliet*, and *The Tempest*, Op. 18.

El Camino Real was not Reed's first foray into Latin American music having, already based his *Second Suite for Band* on this style. He follows other composers (both orchestral and wind ensemble) who have used Spanish and Latin American music as the stylistic and melodic basis for new compositions: Chabrier (*Espana*, 1883), Rimsky-Korsakov (*Capriccio espagnol*, Op. 34, 1887), H. Owen Reed (*La Fiesta Mexicana*, 1954), and Clifton Williams (*Symphonic Dance No. 3 'Fiesta'*, 1967).

Unit 4: Technical Considerations

Confident oboe and baritone soloists are necessary for the short solos: they are not technically difficult but are extremely exposed. A good mallet percussion player is essential to perform the four-mallet vibraphone and marimba parts as well as the xylophone part.

A crisp and rapid articulation is needed from all players, with many passages requiring staccato and marcato articulations at a speed of quarter note = 132–160.

The highest note for trumpet is a written C6, and for cornet, B5. Trumpet 1 needs to be able to sustain B5 for four measures at *fortissimo*. Trumpet players require cup and straight mutes; cornet players require straight mutes. The highest note for horn is a written G5, and horn players also need mutes.

Playing on the second half of each beat can prove challenging for the trombones and horns (mm. 7–25, 89–106, 248–279, 25–42, and 230–248). Rehearse them with the bass line and percussion and ensure the bass part does not drag. Have the horns and trombones fill in their rests with notes and play all six eighth notes in the measure, then have them accent the second half of each beat. When they are confident with this have them slowly drop the added notes and feel the rests in their place.

The challenge with the slow section is not the meter changes, but to have the band follow closely so the conductor can subtly tease out the tenutos at the end of each measure—too short, and they will not produce the melancholia required, too long, and each measure will sound like an 8/8 measure.

Disregard the score's metronome markings and choose tempi that are suitable for the ensemble and performance venue. The initial *Allegro brillante* is marked quarter note = c. 132 (and two measures later, quarter note = 144). Consider this a minimum tempo for an exciting performance. On the two recordings listed in Unit 8, Reed himself conducts the *Allegro brillante* sections at quarter note = 160.

The metronome markings in the middle section can cause confusion. M. 135 is marked eighth note = c. 92, and m. 151 is marked at a slower tempo of eighth note = c. 88. Reed conducts those two sections at eighth note = 80 and eighth note = 100 respectively: the opposite of what is marked on the score. Similarly, m. 165 is marked *meno mosso*, but is taken by Reed at eighth note = 110—faster than the previous section. (The *meno mosso* section does give the feeling of less movement, as it is played with a feel of two beats per measure in contrast to the previous sections with three beats per measure.)

The ensemble can practice scales in the key areas of D natural minor, D Phrygian (D–E-flat–F–G–A–B-flat–C–D) and G Phrygian (G–A-flat–B-flat–C–D–E-flat–F–G). In mm. 91–104 and 234–247, Reed uses a scale comprising the bottom tetrachord of a major scale and the upper tetrachord of a natural minor scale: at m. 91 in the key of D (D–E–F-sharp–G–A–B-flat–C–D) and at m. 234 in the key of G (G–A–B–C–D–E-flat–F–G), but as the melodic material is scalic anyway (the "melodizing of harmony"[3]), it is easier to rehearse the scalic passages slowly and in context.

Unit 5: Stylistic Considerations

El Camino Real is based on two traditional Spanish dance forms: the jota and the fandango. The outer sections are based on the jota, a lively dance from northern Spain. It is in triple time (often 3/8) and usually accompanied by a guitarist, singer, and castanets. Reed has composed his version in 3/4 and included the castanets, but simulated the effect of rhythmic guitar strumming with an offbeat rhythm in the trombones (mm. 7–24) and horns (mm. 25–42). It is important to maintain an unrelenting and exciting feel to the outlying sections to retain the rhythmic momentum of the fiery Spanish dance.

The middle slow section is based on the fandango. A traditional fandango can be in simple triple or compound duple time, and again, is generally accompanied by guitar and castanets. In this section, Reed has simulated the guitar by using another stringed instrument: the harp. He has varied the traditional fandango considerably, in meter, tempo, and harmony, but it still retains the sensuous feel of the original dance. Achieving long, flowing lines is the most important part of realizing the languorous feel.

Unit 6: Musical Elements

MELODY:
The melody of the outer sections is based on two scales: natural minor and Phrygian mode. The melody starts in D natural minor (mm. 9–42) and then moves to D Phrygian (m. 43) and G Phrygian (m. 59). Measure 75 reverts to D Phrygian for the transition back to the first theme. Reed now raises the third to produce a scale comprising the bottom tetrachord of a major scale with the upper tetrachord of a natural minor scale (mm. 91–104 and 234–247). Reed uses the technique of "the melodizing of harmony," whereby the notes of the melody outline the harmony and give the impression of multiple voices in a single melodic line.

The melody of the fandango section starts in A natural minor (mm. 135–150) and then moves to A major (mm. 153–156) and C major (mm. 157–160). The melody of the 6/8 section is presented in F major in a flowing and stepwise style.

HARMONY:
The chords of the opening jota section change infrequently and initially are in D minor. It is not until m. 59 that the tonality changes to G before moving to D major (m. 75) for the transition back to the main theme. The

return of the opening material (m. 198) begins in D minor before moving to G major (mm. 230–279).

The fandango section is based on the Andalusian cadence (i–VII–VI–V, or Am–G–F–E). Reed manipulates the progression by delaying the introduction of each chord: at m. 135 he gives an Am followed by a G before reverting to Am. In the next measure he extends the cadence Am–G–F. It is not until m. 138 that we hear an E chord, and then only briefly. Reed uses enough of the Andalusian cadence to give the music its Spanish sound, but he teases it out and makes the listener wait for the full cadence and a clear presentation of the E chord (m. 150).

RHYTHM:

Mm. 3–6 use the unconventional meter of 4/4 + 3/4: alternating meter changes each measure. The slow middle section (mm. 135–164) has many meter changes. Conducting every eighth note of this section makes the meter changes easier and makes it more possible to conduct the many tenutos and small tempo changes with subtlety.

TIMBRE:

Alfred Reed was a master of orchestration, and he expressed specific views on timbre and instrumentation from the start of his composing career. By 1985 Reed was adapting scores to suit the two varieties of bands: the one-player-per-part wind ensemble and the much larger concert band or wind orchestra. At several places in the score for *El Camino Real*, Reed gives suggestions on how to adapt the instrumentation to suit either of these two ensembles.

Reed's opinion of orchestration and timbre is best stated in his words.

> The scoring of this work embraces the modern conception of the integrated symphonic band, with fully balanced instrumentation and the separation of the brass into three distinct tone color groups: the horns, the trumpet-trombone group and the cornet-baritone-tuba group. The woodwind writing is centered around the balanced clarinet choir as the basic woodwind color in the band, and the section balances and doublings are conceived as carefully as in symphonic orchestras.[4]

There is no mention in the program notes to *El Camino Real* of these views, but these ideals, as expressed in many of his scores composed before and after *El Camino Real*, should apply to this score.

To reproduce faithfully the timbre of Reed's writing it is important to strive for perfect instrumentation: Reed believed a fully balanced clarinet choir, including E-flat, alto, bass, and especially contrabass clarinets to be the backbone of the modern concert band (the equivalent of the string section of an orchestra)[5]. It is also important to have the cornet parts played on real cornets and not trumpets. Rarely do trumpets and cornets play the same material, so getting the instrumentation right in this instance is an important aspect of realizing the work correctly. The string bass, harp, vibraphone, and marimba are also essential for performance.

Unit 7: Form and Structure

SECTION	MEASURE	EVENT AND SCORING
A: "Jota"		
Introduction	1–8	Woodwind sixteenth notes; D Phrygian
Theme 1	9–24	Melody in horns, alto saxophones, and English horn accompanied by tuba, trombones, snare drum; D natural minor
Theme 1	25–42	Melody in clarinets; countermelody in cornets (straight mute), English horn, and oboes followed by trumpets (mm. 35–40); accompaniment in tuba, horns, castanets, snare drum; tenor line in bassoons, bass clarinet, and tenor saxophone
Theme 2	43–58	Trumpets; D Phrygian
Theme 2	59–74	Melody in clarinets, oboes, English horn, and tenor saxophone; G Phrygian
Transition	75–90	D Phrygian
Theme 1	91–104	Melody in woodwinds and horns; accompaniment in basses and trombones; D major
Transition	105–128	Timpani solo
B: "Fandango"		
Introduction	129–134	Oboe solo; A natural minor
Theme 3	135–151	Oboe solo then joined by flutes, E-flat clarinet, clarinet 1, and alto saxophone; accompanied by harp and vibraphone; A minor
Theme 3	152–156	Melody in oboes, English horn, E-flat clarinet, and alto and tenor saxophone; countermelody in bassoons, alto clarinet, and baritone; A major
Theme 3	157–160	Melody in flutes, clarinets, alto saxophones, and horns; countermelody in bassoons, alto clarinet, tenor saxophone, and baritone; C major
Transition	161–164	Woodwinds

Section	Measure	Event and Scoring
Theme 4	165–172	6/8; melody in marimba, E-flat clarinet, clarinet 1, cornet 1, and tenor saxophone; accompanied by marimba and harp; F major
	173–179	Melody in English horn, alto saxophone 1, horns, and marimba
Theme 4	180–185	Melody in marimba, oboe 1, E-flat clarinet, clarinet 1, and cornet 1; countermelody in bassoon 1, alto clarinet, tenor saxophone, baritone, bass clarinet, baritone saxophone, and trombone 1
Transition	186–191	Baritone solo
Transition	192–197	Horns (based on theme 3)
A: "Jota"		
Transition	198–201	Percussion, timpani solo; D natural minor
	202–209	Melody in clarinets; countermelody in flutes and oboes
	210–225	Melody in horns; countermelody in clarinets, flutes, oboes, and alto saxophone
	226–233	Fanfare figure in trumpets; transition to G major
Theme 1	234–247	Melody in trumpets and trombones
Theme 4	248–267	Melody in woodwinds (this time in 3/4); accompaniment in basses, trombones, snare drum, and castanets; countermelody in bassoons, horns, and alto saxophone
	268–279	Melody in saxophones and horns
Coda	280–283	D Phrygian
	284–305	Based on theme 1; G Phrygian

Unit 8: Suggested Listening

Chabrier, Emmanue. *Espana*. 1883.

Reed, Alfred:

> *El Camino Real. Salutations!* Tokyo Kosei Wind Orchestra. Alfred Reed, conductor. KOCD- 3009. 1989.

> *El Camino Real. Alfred Reed Live! Volume 1: Armenian Dances*. Senzoku Gakuen Symphonic   Wind Orchestra. Alfred Reed, conductor. Klavier K11103. 1998.

> *Second Suite for Band:*"Latino-Mexicana." 1980.

Reed, H. Owen. *La Fiesta Mexicana*. 1954.

Rimsky-Korsakov, Nikolai. *Capriccio Espagnol,* Op. 34. 1887.
Williams, Clifton. *Symphonic Dance No. 3: "Fiesta."* 1967.

Unit 9: Additional References and Resources

DeCarbo, Nicholas. "Alfred Reed—Composer Of Our Time," *The Instrumentalist* 40, no. 3 (1985): 20–24.

Jordan, Douglas M. *Alfred Reed: A Bio-Bibliography.* Westport, CT: Greenwood Press, 1999.

Moss, Lee. "Composer Alfred Reed's Thoughts On Creativity." *The Instrumentalist* 32, no. 8 (1978): 34–35.

Reed, Alfred. Program notes for *A Festival Prelude.* Edward B. Marks Music Company, 1962.

_____. Program notes for *El Camino Real.* Edward B. Marks Music Company, 1986.

_____. "How a Composer Works." *The Instrumentalist* 44, no. 11 (1990): 48.

_____. "Some Thoughts On Band Instrumentation." *The Instrumentalist* 45, no. 2 (1990): 12.

_____. *The Balanced Clarinet Choir.* Kenosha, Wisconsin: G. Leblanc Corporation, 1955.

_____. "The Composer and the College Band." *Music Educators Journal* 48, no. 1 (1961): 51–53. http://www.jstor.org/stable/3389717

_____. "The Instrumentation of the Band." *Music Educators Journal* 49, no. 1 (1962):56–61. http://www.jstor.org/stable/3389765

_____. "The String Bass in a Wind Group." *The American String Teacher* 38 (1988): 66–69.

Rehrig, William H. *The Heritage Encyclopedia of Band Music.* Paul E. Bierley, ed. Westerville, OH: Integrity Press, 1991.

Smith, Norman and Albert Stoutamire. *Band Music Notes.* Lake Charles, LA: Program Note Press, 1989.

Stagg, David. "A Comprehensive Performance Project in Band Conducting with a Catalogue of Original Works for Wind Ensemble or Concert Band by Alfred Reed from 1953 to 1983 with Performance Comments on Selected Works." DMA diss., University of Iowa, 1985.

Waltman, David. "Alfred Reed." In *A Composer's Insight: Thoughts, Analysis and Commentary on Contemporary Masterpieces for Wind Band.* Timothy Salzman, ed. Galesville, MD: Meredith Music Publications, 2003, 119–130.

Contributed by:

Craig Dabelstein
Coordinator of Bands, Brisbane Girls Grammar School
Director, Queensland Wind Orchestra
Queensland, Australia

1 Douglas M. Jordan, Alfred Reed: A Bio-Bibliography (Westport, CT: Greenwood Press, 1999), 11.
2 Ibid, 19.
3 Alfred Reed, Program notes for El Camino Real (Edward B. Marks Music Company, 1986).
4 Alfred Reed, Program notes for A Festival Prelude (Edward B. Marks Music Company, 1962).
5 Alfred Reed, The Balanced Clarinet Choir (Kenosha, WI: G. Leblanc Corporation, 1955), 3.

Teacher Resource Guide

Incidental Suite
Claude T. Smith
(1932–1987)

Unit 1: Composer

Claude Thomas Smith was born in Monroe City, Missouri on March 14, 1932. Smith received his undergraduate education from Central Methodist College in Fayette, Missouri and the University of Kansas. Upon graduating, Smith spent time as an instrumental music educator in the public schools of Nebraska and Missouri. Throughout his time as a public school teacher, Smith had several pieces published by Wingert-Jones Publications, which included *Honor Guard* and *Citation*. In addition to these pieces, Smith also created a band method book titled *Symphonic Warm-ups for Band* that is still used by music educators today.

After teaching in the public schools until 1976, he accepted a faculty position at Southwest Missouri State University in Springfield, Missouri. He was responsible for teaching composition, theory, and horn, and also conducted the University Symphony. Smith won many awards as a composer, including the National Band Association Award from the Academy of Wind and Percussion Arts, the Distinguished Service to Music Award from Kappa Kappa Psi, and multiple ASCAP Composer's Awards. Throughout his life Smith created a large body of works that included 110 pieces for band, twelve orchestral selections and fifteen choral works. Smith met with an untimely death on December 13, 1987.

Unit 2: Composition

Incidental Suite is a three-movement piece composed in 1966 and published by Wingert-Jones Publications. The composition is written for traditional wind band instrumentation, including traditional percussion parts. The movements are "Tarantella," "Nocturne," and "Rondo."

The performance time for *Incidental Suite* is approximately ten minutes. This composition, like many of Smith's works, is very user-friendly; that is to say, it is composed in a way to keep all instrumentalists of the ensemble engaged and interested in rehearsal and performance. All sections of the ensemble have opportunities to carry the melodic line through the composition. *Incidental* Suite also highlights great tutti ensemble playing while still providing opportunities for soloists. The piece is on several state music lists.

Unit 3: Historical Perspective

Incidental Suite was composed at a time where there was continued and significant growth in wind band repertoire. In addition to this piece, Smith also composed several additional compositions that lent themselves to being successful teaching tools in the public schools. These pieces included *Emperata Overture* and *God of Our Fathers* as well as many others.

Harmonically, Smith composed *Incidental Suite* using very traditional, triadic harmony. His departure from this nineteenth-century tradition is in the rhythmic writing, which shows signs of influence from Stravinsky and his contemporaries. This twentieth-century concept is apparent in many of Smith's compositions. This piece is extremely rhythmic in nature, especially in the "Tarantella" and "Rondo" movements. His use of 7/8, 9/8, and 6/8 meters in addition to quarter-note triplets provides a rhythmic density and texture that was very progressive for the time.

Unit 4: Technical Considerations

Movement 1: "Tarantella"

Movement 1 provides mostly rhythmic considerations. The tempo marking is *Allegro vivo*. Brass and woodwind scoring is in the middle register, yielding no significant problems. With the key of this movement centering on D minor, key signature and related accidentals are also not a major concern.

Smith uses orchestration techniques that require several different voices to assist with presentation of the melodic line. The melody is not presented in any one particular instrument, but instead is interwoven among several instruments, with no one particular instrument carrying the entire line. This requires the ensemble to stay rhythmically engaged throughout the entire movement. There are several solo measures at the end of the movement in bassoon, bass clarinet, oboe, clarinet, and flute. All of these solo lines are cross-cued throughout the ensemble. Trumpets and trombones will need cup mutes to perform the last eight bars of the movement.

Movement 2: "Nocturne"

Movement 2 is *Andante*, and not nearly as rhythmically challenging as movement 1. It opens with several solos that include bassoon, oboe, flute, horn, and an extended alto saxophone solo. The end of the movement contains an extended flute and clarinet duet and ends with an extended flute solo. Each of these extended solos is no more that two phrases in length. The key is again centered on D minor. The challenges in this movement are balance and shaping of phrase. Musicians need to be aware of who is carrying the melodic lines to ensure they are audible.

Movement 3: "Rondo"

Movement 3 is much like movement 1 in its rhythmic construction. The tempo marking is *Allegro moderato*. Rhythmic energy in this movement is created by employing a combination of multiple meters, including 6/8, 7/8, and 4/4. In addition there are several places where triplets are performed over duple meters. These places will create clarity issues throughout the ensemble. Instrument rangees are normal, excepting the above-the-staff B-natural for trumpet 1 a few places in the movement.

Unit 5: Stylistic Considerations

In movements 1 and 3, style is created mostly by note length, articulation, accents, and balance. *Incidental Suite* reaches its fullest potential in movements 1 and 3 when the ensemble is very clear and cohesive with articulation and note lengths. In addition to achieving rhythmic clarity, the ensemble must also be very aware of balance between the independent parts of the composition to ensure all parts are audible.

Movement 2, legato and andante in nature, will require musicians to use an entirely different set of skills to perform it well. While staying observant to balance between soloist and accompaniment, each ensemble member must remember to shape phrases much the same way soloists do at the beginning of the movement. Due to balance concerns, many times there is no shape, or limited shape, to the accompaniment parts that support the main melodic material, and the overall musical presentation does not reach its fullest potential.

Unit 6: Musical Elements

MELODY:
The melodic material in *Incidental Suite* is very traditional in key center and presentation. The melody and countermelodic material in movement 1 need to be balanced well so each can be heard. Although there is much rhythmic

activity in this movement, the melodic material needs to be played with precise articulation and note lengths. Each instrument that carries the melody needs to work toward smooth transitions of that melody when the orchestration shifts to another voice.

The melody of movement 2 differs in style from movements 1 and 3. Solo instruments are used extensively for presentation of melodic material. The ensemble needs to closely listen to the melody and how it is presented initially in able to present it in the appropriate style.

Movement 3 has very similar makeup to movement 1. Attention to balance, articulation, and note lengths will allow the melodic line to be presented in the appropriate style.

HARMONY:
The harmony that Smith uses in all three movements is triadic in nature and centers on D minor. The dissonances he uses are presented in ways that resolve themselves to the tonic key of each movement. These traditional harmonies are sometimes framed by twentieth century compositional techniques.

RHYTHM:
Movements 1 and 3 of *Incidental Suite* are very similar with regard to rhythmic intensity and use of meter. This rhythmic energy is set in two very distinct ways. The first uses tutti writing. The composer sets melodic materials in actively rhythmic lines and then uses other voices to accentuate certain parts of that line. The second is his use of orchestration to present melodic material. Smith uses different voices to construct the melodic line without any individual instrument carrying the entire melody. These compositional techniques are used extensively in movements 1 and 3. Movement 2 is comprised of basic rhythmic writing except for short bursts of rhythm that occur in a few isolated spots.

TIMBRE:
Incidental Suite is composed with a traditional wind band orchestration. The timbre created throughout the three movements is very characteristic of pieces composed in the 1960s. Smith uses diverse groupings of woodwind and brass instruments to create contrast with regard to density of timbre. This creates very interesting sound combinations for the listener.

Unit 7: Form and Structure

Incidental Suite has a very traditional sound. The suite has three movements (fast-slow-fast) to create the structure usually associated with this terminology.

SECTION	MEASURE	EVENT AND SCORING
Movement 1: "Tarantella"		
Introduction	1–8	Use of hocket in presenting melodic materials from movement 1 between brass and woodwinds
Theme A	9–22	Melody in flute and clarinet with low brass and low woodwind accompaniment
Theme A'	23–30	Theme A in upper woodwinds with a countermelodic line in baritone and bassoon
Theme B	31–53	Melodic materials in hocket between upper woodwinds and brass
Theme A'	54–65	Melody and countermelody with full orchestration
Fugue on theme A	66–85	Used in woodwind parts on theme A materials
Theme B	86–108	Melodic materials in hocket between upper woodwinds and brass
Theme A'	109–120	Full orchestration of melodic and countermelodic materials
Theme A'	121–130	Same melodic and countermelodic materials stated with reduced orchestration and soft dynamic
Coda	131–end	Based on theme A material
Movement 2: "Nocturne"		
Introduction	1–4	Theme A in solo bassoon and solo oboe
Extension	5–11	Theme A melodic material set in 2/4
Extension	12–15	3/4 introduction of theme A
Theme A	16–23	Melodic lines in solo alto saxophone with clarinet accompaniment
Theme A'	24–31	Melody in alto saxophone; countermelody in solo flute with clarinet accompaniment
Theme B	32–49	Theme B melodic material in upper brass and woodwinds
Theme C	50–58	Woodwind statement of theme C melodic material with brass and percussion accompaniment

SECTION	MEASURE	EVENT AND SCORING
Theme A'	59–66	Melody in upper woodwind; countermelody in middle voices
Variation on extension	67–75	Flute and clarinet duet on extension material
Theme B	76–93	Same instrumentation as last statement of theme B
Theme C	94–102	Same instrumentation as last statement of theme C
Theme A	103–110	Full orchestration of theme A
Theme A	111–116	Theme A in flute solo with brass accompaniment
Coda	117–end	Solo alto saxophone and clarinet with brass

Movement 3: "Rondo"

SECTION	MEASURE	EVENT AND SCORING
Introduction	1–4	Percussion section presents melodic materials
Theme A	5–13	D. S.; melodic material in oboe, clarinet, and trumpet with full tutti
Theme B	14–27	Coda; Theme B material in hocket between sections of the entire ensemble
Theme A	28–35	Same presentation as m. 5–13
Theme C	36–47	Theme C material in full tutti
Transition	48–55	D. S. al coda; Transitional material back to theme A with full orchestration
Coda	56–end	Full orchestration presenting variations on themes from movement

Unit 8: Suggested Listening

Smith, Claude T.:
   Choral Prelude
   Danse Folatre
   Emperata Overture
   Eternal Father Strong to Save
   Flight
   God of Our Fathers
   Variation on a Hymn by Louis Bourgeois

Unit 9: Additional References and Resources

Jones, Mary Louise. "Claude Thomas Smith: American Composer, Conductor, and Music Educator." DMA diss., University of Missouri-Kansas City Conservatory, 1992.

Miles, Richard, ed. *Teaching Music through Performance in Band, Volume 5*. Chicago: GIA Publications, Inc., 2004. 432–437.

Sadie, Stanley. *The New Grove Dictionary of Music and Musicians, Volume 7*. Second ed. New York: Macmillan Publishers Ltd., 2001.

Slonimsky, Nicolas, Laura Kuhn, and Dennis McIntire. *Baker's Biographical Dictionary of Musicians, Volume 2*. New York: Schirmer Books, 2001.

Contributed by:

Bradley J. Genevro
Director of Bands
Messiah College
Grantham, Pennsylvania

Teacher Resource Guide

Introit for Band

Fisher Tull
(1934–1994)

Unit 1: Composer

Fisher Tull was born September 24, 1934 in Waco, Texas and died in Huntsville, Texas on August 23, 1994. He received all of his degrees (bachelor of music in education, master of music in trumpet performance and music theory, and doctor of philosophy in composition) from the University of North Texas. In 1957 he joined the faculty of Sam Houston State University and served as the chair of the music department from 1965 to 1982.

Fisher Tull has received awards in composition from the Texas Composers Guild, American Society of Composers, Authors and Publishers (ASCAP), the Friends of Harvey Gaul, Artists Advisory Council of the Chicago Symphony Orchestra, Willamette Arts Festival, National Flute Association, and the Arthur Fraser Memorial. In addition to these awards he was granted the Distinguished Men of Music medal by Kappa Kappa Psi, the national honorary band fraternity, and the Orpheus Award by Phi Mu Alpha Sinfonia. He was held in wide esteem as conductor and clinician of his music, and traveled extensively in those roles. He was an elected member of the American Bandmasters Association.

Unit 2: Composition

Introit is based on the sixteenth-century hymn melody "Rendez à Dieu," or "Return to God." About eight minutes in length, the piece uses techniques from different periods in music history as variations (there are three variations and a coda). Opening the piece is a homorhythmic, chorale presentation of the hymn in woodwind and brass choirs. Tull then creates a five-part fugue exclusively featuring the percussion section. He fragments the theme throughout the ensemble in the third section, and in the fourth section, he presents the theme in augmentation underneath ostinato figures in the woodwind section. As a coda, Tull uses block chords throughout the ensemble, imitating the sounds of bells. The difficulty level of this piece is approximately Grade 4.

Unit 3: Historical Perspective

The hymn on which *Introit* is based, "Rendez à Dieu," has been used in many different pieces of music throughout history. It was originally written by the French composer Louis Bourgeois as part of the Psalm settings for which he became famous. This particular hymn tune was probably first published in his *Calvinist Psalter,* which includes adaptations of popular chansons and old Latin hymns as well as original melodies for the new, metrical, French translations by Clément Marot and Théodore de Bèze.

Unit 4: Technical Considerations

There are many meter changes throughout the beginning of the piece, where the hymn is presented in a chorale fashion. The quarter note is constant throughout fluctuations between 4/4 and 3/2 meters.

In the second section of the piece, featuring the percussion section, the tempo changes to *Allegro* and percussionists are asked to play fairly difficult passages crisply and with marked accents, as well as with sudden, drastic, dynamic changes. This section alternates between 3/4 and 4/4 meters.

In the third section, where the theme is fragmented, Tull is very explicit in his desire for the articulation of each note, as each note has a marking (slur, accent, staccato, legato, etc.). Trumpet 1 must be able to alternatively double tongue in this fragmented section. This section does not have any meter changes.

In the fifth section, where the ostinato is in flutes and clarinets, it is important that the tempo stays constant and that the half- and whole-note melody (in augmentation) is heard underneath it. This will be especially challenging in mm. 117–123, as it is only the low reeds (bass clarinet, bassoons, and baritone saxophone) that have the tune underneath the ostinato. The conductor must also give the half-note lines appropriate shape throughout this section, as there are no dynamic or stylistic indicators.

In the bridge between the end of this augmentation section and the resurgence of the hymn-like playing from mm. 138–145, it is important that the accented lines, especially in the brass, do not become to lugubrious, and instead give the music an overall direction and drive with plenty of space between the notes.

The coda section, imitating bells, contains plenty of dynamic challenges, such as *sforzando-piano,* which must be controlled exceedingly well for a convincing performance. The final chords of the piece pit alto saxophones against each other in a major second dissonance. The saxophonists must work hard to keep this interval wide enough, and not compress it into a minor second, which will be the tendency.

Unit 5: Stylistic Considerations

The biggest challenges throughout this piece are the sections where the composer has imitated chorale style, such as the beginning. The conductor must feel free to use accelerando and ritardando at will, as appropriate to phrasing. For a convincing musical performance, the melody (generally in the soprano lines) must always be apparent, but the middle voices cannot be lost.

In Variation 1, the percussion feature, notes must be crisp and played without any rubato, with specific deference paid to dynamic contrasts, which serve as both an anchor-point when entrances occur in the fugue, and as an interest-builder.

Throughout the rest of the piece, it is imperative that the ensemble follows Tull's dynamic and stylistic markings. The accents must always include space, and the tenuto markings in this piece are generally best approached by adding a little bit of an accent to the front of each note. One of the great things about playing Tull's music is that there is very little guesswork in playing style due to the plethora of articulation markings used.

Unit 6: Musical Considerations

MELODY:
Everything in this piece emanates from the original hymn tune in the beginning of the work, given in Figure 1. When encountered in the chorale setting, the conductor must make musical decisions as to how to shape phrases, and add appropriate dynamics, tempo fluctuations, etc.

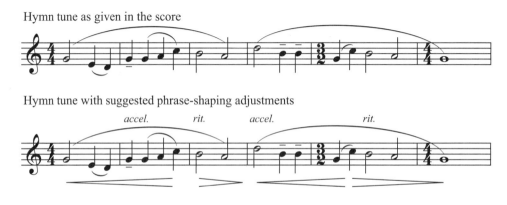

FIGURE 1. Suggested phrase-shaping adjustments

HARMONY:

There are no examples of dodecaphonic tendencies or non-traditional harmonies in this piece. There are no key signatures; rather Tull has chosen to write accidentals into the parts. The score is transposed. The piece opens in G major, and stays there throughout the entire opening section, and although there are moments of B-flat major, A minor, and G minor, each phrase always ends in G major. There is a judicious use of deceptive cadence in this opening section.

The second section does not contain any harmonic elements. The fragmented section is the most harmonically challenging because of the frequent use of unisons and octaves, giving players little chance to ground themselves harmonically.

The augmented section is set up by a woodwind ostinato which does not function harmonically. The next recapitulation of the hymn-like theme is in m. 145, and the harmonic language is very similar to the beginning. At m. 161, there are clashing dissonances which are supposed to produce bell-like sounds. The piece ends on a climactic C major chord with the ninth present in the alto saxophone.

RHYTHM:

This piece features rhythm in an interesting way by using the percussion section in the fugue. The rhythms must be crisp, and exactly subdivided. It may be helpful to have percussionists practice this section by playing together all the rhythms that they have in order to develop a section idea of how it is supposed to sound before dividing into parts in the actual fugue. Another example of the rhythmic difficulties in this piece are in the woodwind ostinato over the augmentation section. Starting in m. 115, Tull creates an ostinato that includes triplet quarter notes, eighth notes grouped in threes, quarter notes, and quarter notes off the beat. Figure 2 gives the rhythmic representation of the ostinato.

TIMBRE:

For a convincing performance of this piece, students and conductor must know what type of sound they are looking for before instrument there is put to mouth. The first section must be chorale-like in sound and texture, with timbre differences emanating from the use of different choirs (woodwind and brass). The second section must be dry and driving. In the fragmented section, brass must use a *characteristic* brass sound, but must avoid sounding "blatty." In the augmentation section, the low winds must combine to create a timbre of their own, encompassing the low brass and low reed sound, and must be forceful enough to cut through the ostinato parts above. Blend and balance are paramount, especially in the chorale sections of the piece.

FIGURE 2. Variation 3: ostinato rhythms, mm. 115–117

Unit 7: Form and Structure

SECTION	MEASURE	EVENT AND SCORING
Chorale section		
Introduction	1–2	Horns and percussion set the somber mood for the beginning of the piece
Woodwind statement 1	3–8	Woodwind choirand baritone present first statement of the theme; horn 1–2 interjects in mm. 5 and 8; chimes are also present in this section
Woodwind statement 2	9–14	Same instrumentation and events
Brass Statement	15–20	Brass section presents the hymn tune assisted by bass clarinet and chimes.
Woodwind statement 3	21–25	Same orchestration as before; passing tones added in inner parts of the chorale; horn 3–4 join in m. 24
Brass statement 2	26–30	Same orchestration as brass Statement 1 with bassoon added in m. 29
Woodwind fragment	31–32	Woodwind choir presents a fragment of the theme

SECTION	MEASURE	EVENT AND SCORING
Brass fragment	33	Brass choir presents a fragment of the theme
Woodwind coda	34–36	Woodwind choir finishes the chorale section with the ending of the chorale

Percussion section (variation 1)

Introduction	37–41	Percussion is homorhythmic, losing volume with stepped dynamics
Fugue	42–63	Five-part percussion fugue; entrances every five measures
Bridge	64–70	Staggered brass entrances in octaves while percussion is homorhythmic again

Fragmented section (variation 2)

Section 1	71–76	Brass section fragments the theme above percussion; careful attention must be paid to articulations here; woodwinds enter one beat before mm. 76 and climax on m. 76, then immediately decrescendo
Section 2	77–88	Tom-toms and snare drum solo for two measures before trumpet, horn, tenor saxophone, and bassoon enter in m. 78; trumpet 1–2 play constant sixteenth notes underneath the rhythmic interplay and fragmentation; horn and woodwinds; dynamics build again until m. 88, when there is a decrescendo
Bridge	88–89	Descending line in bass clarinet, baritone saxophone, and trombone 3 take the listener to the next section and continue throughout it
Section 3	90–95	Brass and woodwind sections present material opposite each other in each measure; the section should get louder and more intense at each statement until the diminuendo at the end of m. 94
Section 4	96–103	Clarinets, bassoons, and alto saxophones start a building process by groups, as in earlier sections of this variation; oboes, bass clarinet, and lower saxophones enter in m. 99; horn 1 and flutes enter in m. 103 and lead to the climax at m. 104

513

SECTION	MEASURE	EVENT AND SCORING
Section 5	104–108	Tutti scoring in layers; brass, saxophones, bassoons, and bass clarinets present thematic material; piccolo, flutes, oboes, and clarinets emphasize previous two measures of this section
Section 6	109–114	Theme is now *piano* and presented in upper woodwinds with periodic interjections by trumpets, trombones, and percussion; horns, trombones, and euphonium finish the section beginning in m. 113

Augmented section (variation 3)

Introduction	115–116	Rhythmic ostinato is established in flutes, clarinets, and chimes
Section 1	117–122	Thematic material is presented underneath the ostinato by bass clarinet, bassoons, and baritone saxophone
Brass interruptions	123–129	Interruptive outbursts by brass cascading from trumpet to baritone; the *sforzando* hit on bat three of m. 128 must be clear and non-brassy
Ostinato re-established	130–131	Another ostinato is established in woodwind parts
Section 2	132–137	Tubas, baritones, bassoons, and bass clarinets have thematic material, as in the first section of this variation
Bridge	138–144	Interruptions spread from the brass throughout the ensemble, cascading and growing into the final section

Coda

Hymn section	145–156	The entire ensemble recapitulates the opening material, now in a triumphant manner; diminuendo into m. 152 for the final statement of theme with smaller voicing
Bell section	157-End	The ending of the piece should sound like the pealing of church bells, with *sforzando-piano* spots exceedingly well controlled; the fermatas in mm. 168–169 should have small breaks between them; should crescendo to the end

Unit 8: Suggested Listening

Merriman, Thomas. *Theme and Variations for Brass Ensemble*.
Tull, Fisher:
    Fanfare for Band and Antiphonal Brass
    Saga of the Clouds
    Sketches on a Tudor Psalm
    Variations on an Advent Hymn

Unit 9: Additional References and Resources

Kreines, Joseph. *Music for Concert Band*. Tampa, FL: Florida Music Service, 1989.
Smith, Norman. *Program Notes for Band*. Chicago: GIA Publications, 2000.
Fryer, C. A. "An Annotated Bibliography of Selected Chamber Music for Saxophone, Winds and Percussion with Analyses of *Danses Exotiques* by Jean Françaix and *Nonet* by Fisher Tull." DMA diss., University of North Texas, 2003.

Contributed by:

Frank C. Tracz
Director of Bands
Kansas State University
Manhattan, Kansas

Philip B. Edelman
Band Director
Goddard High School
Goddard, Kansas

Teacher Resource Guide

Kingfishers Catch Fire
John Mackey
(b. 1973)

Unit 1: Composer

Born in New Philadelphia, Ohio in 1973, John Mackey has written for ballet, modern dance, theater, and concert music. Mackey received musical training from the Cleveland Institute of Music and The Juilliard School, studying composition with Donald Erb and John Corigliano. His music has been performed by notable ensembles such as the Brooklyn Philharmonic, the Dallas Symphony, and many of the leading university band programs. Mackey regularly receives commissions from dance companies, including Parsons and Alvin Ailey. He is the recipient of numerous awards, including seven ASCAP Concert Music Awards, and two Morton Gould Young Composer Awards. His frequently performed *Redline Tango* (2003) for wind ensemble won the Walter Beeler Memorial Composition Prize and the American Band Association Ostwald Award. Other significant wind ensemble works include *Sasparilla* (2005), *Turbine* (2006), *Strange Humors* (2006), *Concerto for Soprano Sax and Wind Ensemble* (2007), and *Turning* (2007).

Unit 2: Composition

Kingfishers Catch Fire was commissioned by a consortium of Japanese wind ensembles organized by Mamoru Nakata. The Japan Wind Ensemble Conductors Conference 2007 Special Band performed the world premier of this work in Kurashiki, Japan on March 17, 2007. The composer writes:

A "kingfisher" is a bird with beautiful, brilliantly colored feathers that look in sunlight as if they are on fire. Kingfishers are extremely shy birds and are rarely seen, but when they are seen, they are undeniably beautiful. The first movement, "Following falls and falls of rain," is suspended in tone, but with hope, depicting the kingfisher slowly emerging from its nest in the early morning stillness, just after a heavy rain storm. The second movement, "Kingfishers catch fire," imagines the bird flying out into the sunlight. The work ends with a reference to (and a bit of a pun on) Stravinsky's "Firebird."

Kingfishers Catch Fire is approximately twelve minutes in duration. The instrumentation includes: three flutes (one doubling on piccolo), pairs of oboes and bassoons, contrabassoon, E-flat clarinet, four B-flat clarinets, bass and contrabass clarinet, soprano, alto, tenor, and baritone saxophone, four trumpets in C (plus additional antiphonal trumpets), two flugelhorns, four horns in F, three tenor trombones, bass trombone, euphonium, tuba, double bass, piano, and percussion (marked for timpani and six players, including bowed vibes and bowed crotales).

Unit 3: Historical Perspective

With the success of *Redline Tango*, Mackey quickly became a sought-after composer with numerous commissions and recordings from prominent school music programs. Drawing on his experience writing music for dance choreography, his music employs fast and driving rhythms. Phillips' dissertation (see Unit 9) discusses many of the compositional features of Mackey's music, including his use of ostinati, polyrhythms, cross-rhythms, composite meter, and shifting accent patterns. *Kingfishers Catch Fire* is a refreshing new addition to wind band repertoire, demonstrating beautiful lyricism and sonorous chorale sections in movement 1 and pulsating and energetic rhythms in movement 2.

Unit 4: Technical Considerations

The scoring in movement 1 resembles that of chamber music, with small groupings of instruments and highlighted soloists, including clarinet, offstage trumpet, and bassoon. The slow tempo (quarter note = 52) paired with the thin scoring requires special attention to breath support, intonation, and phrasing.

Movement 2 requires proficient technical facility from the ensemble, both in the execution of rapid passages and clarity of articulation. The intricacies of the layered rhythmic patterns and driving tempo require the ensemble's constant attention to the pulse, style, and balance of the work. Range considerations include the high tessitura of the trumpet, horn, and euphonium, with sounding pitches C6, F5, and B-flat 4, respectively. This movement also requires the special effects of bowed crotales and bowed vibraphone.

Unit 5: Stylistic Considerations

Movement 1 suggests the journey of a kingfisher bird as it leaves the comforts of its nest and acclimates itself to the environment after a rainstorm. There is a sense of mystery and timidity in the slow unfolding of the musical lines. This requires attention to nuance from the performers in the rise and fall of the music. Legato tonguing and beautiful tone production should be maintained throughout, a challenge, given the soft dynamics, slow tempo, and transparent orchestration.

The style in movement 2 is in stark contrast to movement 1, with fast and driving ostinati and a soaring, chorale-like melody. Clarity of articulation and careful placement of accents is key to balancing the multiple rhythmic layers and maintaining a steady pulse. Attention to balance is especially critical during statements of the main theme, where the melody should have a strong presence in the midst of the complex and multi-layered texture.

Unit 6: Musical Elements

MELODY:

The melodic material in movement 1 is comprised of small motivic gestures, elongated solo lines, and brass chorales. Characteristic of Mackey's compositional style, the impetus of the music is not melodically driven; rather, melodic material emerges from the overall sound and texture palette. Recurring motives include the echo figures of A to G sharp and E to F sharp, (first presented in the opening clarinet solo). In addition, the dangling leading tone figure in the offstage trumpet solo and the rising stepwise gestures of the brass chorale are woven throughout the movement.

It is no coincidence that the first pitch of movement 2 begins with an A, bringing resolution to the long-awaited leading-tone suspension of movement 1. The opening two-measure rhythmic and melodic ostinato in the B-flat clarinet serves as a foundation of developmental material throughout movement 2. While the melodic construction of the ostinato is centered on F major, the leap of a major seventh highlights the dominant key of C major. This initial interaction of tonic and dominant foreshadows the constant interplay between the two keys.

Recurring melodic patterns are given in figures 1–3.

FIGURE 1. Mm. 1–2, opening clarinet ostinato

FIGURE 2. Mm. 21–28, shifting accent pattern in bassoon

FIGURE 3. M. 172, low brass ostinato

HARMONY:

The harmonies in movement 1 are drawn from various pitch clusters and scales, emphasizing D and A major and minor. As often found in Mackey's writing, the harmony does not conform to the traditional rules of chord progressions and voice leading. For example, the root movement in movement 1 emphasizes pitches D, A, and E, but the supporting chords include a variety of sound clusters, seventh chords, and extended harmonies that are not necessarily connected to these chord roots. The most salient harmonic development in this movement is the beautiful writing of suspensions and dovetailing in the minor setting of the brass chorales.

The harmonic structure of movement 2 is organized into two categories: harmonies implied from the linear voice leading of ostinati and/or melodic fragments, and lush chordal accompaniments that support the main theme. Keys of F, C, and B-flat major seamlessly interact through pivot chords and tonicization. The skeletal harmonic frame for the main theme chord progression includes a B-flat major seventh, C major, and F major seventh chord. The inner voice leadings include 4–3 and 2–1 suspensions, creating a fabric of lush and complex colors. The most climactic of these suspensions accompanies the soaring melodic leap of a minor seventh, orchestrated over a descending scale pattern from E-flat-D–C–B-flat. The final six measures of the work references Stravinsky's *Firebird* with a sustained F in the upper voices and succession of chords in the lower voices.

RHYTHM:

The rhythm in movement 1 is free flowing, yet with a sense of momentum. Recurring rhythms include the metered flute trills and a pulsated quarter-and-half-note motive in the brass chorale. The technique of augmentation is used in the development of the rising five-note figure as well as the off stage trumpet solo.

Marked at quarter note = 164–172, the rhythmic material in movement 2 is a complex web of driving ostinatos and accumulated layers that move quickly through mixed meters of 2/4, 3/4, 4/4, and 5/4. While the initial ostinato is in strict duple meter, the layering of melodic fragments distorts the security of pulse, introducing syncopated lines with shifting accent patterns. Hemiolas result from the culmination of polyrhythms and accent patterns, heard most notably in the triple-based melodic theme against the duple-based ostinatos.

TIMBRE:

Creating new and interesting timbres for wind ensemble is arguably one of Mackey's greatest strengths as a composer. The timbres of movement 1 parallel its programmatic underpinnings with a sound palate that slowly emerges from rising flugelhorn lines to a clarinet solo that is hesitant, yet curious in character. The texture oscillates between thin, soloistic scoring and rich brass chorales. Adding to the mysterious nature of the work is the emphasis of non-traditional instruments, such as the contrabass clarinet, soprano saxophone, and bowed vibraphone and crotales.

The timbre of movement 2 is brilliant and vibrant, heightened by the high tessitura of the horn, trumpet, and euphonium. Mackey's concept of "thick and thin" scoring is demonstrated with solo ostinatos, accumulating layers and rich chordal sections. Massive sound blocks and antiphonal trumpets strengthen the final statement of the main theme.

Unit 7: Form and Structure

MEASURE	EVENT AND SCORING
Movement 1: "Following falls and falls of rain"	
1–4	Unfolding of D minor pitch collection
5–16	B-flat clarinet solo; focus on A–G-sharp and E–F-sharp motive; thin orchestration
17–29	D–E–F-sharp–G-sharp–A cluster in flutes; offstage trumpet solo with dangling leading-tone figure; brass chorale set in D minor; solo fragments in A major
30–37	Brass chorale transposed to A minor juxtaposed against solo fragments in the parallel major
38–48	Development of D minor brass chorale; cadence on E major seventh chord with unresolved 4–3 suspension

MEASURE	EVENT AND SCORING
49–54	Bassoon solo derived from clarinet solo in m. 5; return of D cluster in flute trills
55–61	Return of brass chorale in A minor
62–69	Ascending A minor figure in clarinet; transposition and augmentation of trumpet melody in m. 3; return of D cluster in flutes; ends with solo trumpet (augmentation of dangling leading-tone suspension figure); leading tone amplified by bowed vibraphone and crotales

Movement 2: "Kingfishers catch fire"
Opening

1–20	Introduction of ostinato in B-flat clarinet; C–F–E motive in flute; melodic fragments in flute, oboe, and saxophone
A	Increased layering; meter changes; syncopated lines and accent shifting; B–flat–A–B–flat–C motive introduced in low voices in m. 28
B	First appearance of E-flat in piano and low voices; descending cadential line from E-flat to B-flat from mm. 49–52
C	Return of opening ostinato; augmentation of B–flat–A–B–flat–C motive in low brass; fragment of main theme in mm. 63–66
D	First full statement of main theme in oboe, soprano saxophone, trumpet, trombone, euphonium, and glockenspiel; chordal suspensions in brass accompaniment
E	Continuation of main theme; cadence on C pedal tone leads the pitch center back to F major
F	Return of opening ostinato in 5/4 meter; reduced instrumentation; thin scoring provides contrast to previous build of energy; new lyrical melody in brass in m. 118
G	Increased layering of lines, return of previous motives, antiphonal trumpets- m. 135
H	B–flat–A–B–flat–C ostinato set in low voices leads to augmentation of main theme set in quarter notes; ritardando leads into m. 158
I-J	Tempo change: quarter note = 60; full choral setting of main theme; antiphonal trumpets; absence of rhythmic ostinatosand melodic layering
K	A tempo; culmination and return of various melodic layers and ostinatos; call-and-response in antiphonal trumpets; *ritardando* leads into m. 188

MEASURE	EVENT AND SCORING
L	Final six measures; reference to *Firebird*; cadential extension leading to F major; sustained concert F in upper voices; block seventh and ninth chords in low voices; overlapping ascending scales in antiphonal trumpets

Unit 8: Suggested Listening

Mackey, John:
> *Concerto for Soprano Sax and Wind Ensemble*
> *Turning Turbine*
> *Sasparilla*
> *Strange Humors*

Redline Tango. Wind Band Classics. University of Kansas Wind Ensemble. John P. Lynch, conductor.

Unit 9: Additional References and Resources

Phillips, R. "John Mackey: The Composer, His Compositional Style and a Conductor's Analysis of *Redline Tango* and *Turbine*." Unpublished doctoral thesis, Louisiana State University.

For more information on John Mackey, visit composer's website at http://www.ostimusic.com/

Contributed by:

Amy Acklin
PhD Student/Music Education
The Florida State University
Tallahassee, Florida

Teacher Resource Guide

Lachrymae

Yo Goto
(b. 1958)

Unit 1: Composer

Yo Goto received his bachelor of music education degree from Yamagata University, Japan, after which he studied composition with Shin-ichiro Ikebe at the Tokyo College of Music. In 2001, Goto moved to Texas to study composition with Cindy McTee at the University of North Texas, where he completed his master of music degree in composition as well as a master of music education degree.

Yo Goto's works have been performed at numerous conventions such as WASBE, CBDNA, TBA, FMA, and the Midwest Clinic, and have been chosen as test pieces for the All-Japan Band Contest. His compositions for winds include *Lux Aeterna, Impromptu, Quadrille for Band, A Poetry of Breeze, A Prelude to the Shining Day, WINGS,* and *Dancing in Air.* Goto has also composed works for percussion ensemble, solo timpani, solo vibraphone, and solo harp.

As a distinguished educator and researcher in the field of wind music, Yo Goto is frequently in demand as a lecturer on the topics of selecting music for school band programs and the educational goals of band teaching. In 2000, Goto received the Academy Award from the Academic Society of Japan for Winds and Bands.

Unit 2: Composition

Lachrymae was commissioned by the Executive Committee for Twenty-first-Century Wind Music in Japan. The piece is a requiem for victims of political and religious conflicts throughout the world. The people mourned in this piece include not only the victims of September 11, 2001, but all innocent people killed by "righteous" forces throughout history. The composer states that *Lachrymae* is a protest against political violence.

There are elements in the piece which create a feeling of conflict, such as the dissonances, the machine-gun-sounding fanfares of trumpets and horns, and the snare and field drum parts. A sharp contrast is the serene melody of the chorale sections, which is a quotation from a pavanne of John Dowland (1563–1626). The juxtaposition of a Renaissance tune and the twentieth-century compositional technique of indeterminacy creates an auditory distance between past and present. This is one example of how musical simultaneity is explored in *Lachrymae*. The composer writes: "it is important that composers organize musical time from multidimensional viewpoints to provide new experiences of time for the audience."[1]

Unit 3: Historical Perspective

The composition borrows the melody from the dirge "Lachrimae Antiquae," a pavanne of John Dowland (1563–1626). John Dowland, a lutenist and composer in England, wrote "Lachrimae Antiquae" as the first pavanne in a set of consort music titled *Lachrimae or Seven Teares* in 1604. "Lachrimae Antiquae" is an example of standard late-Elizabethan five-part dance music scoring with a single soprano part, three parts, and a bass voice.

Lachrymae incorporates four important compositional techniques from the twentieth century: the use of quotation, controlled indeterminacy, polyrhythmic structure, and simultaneous juxtaposition of different musics all contribute to the musical simultaneity found in *Lachrymae*. Although borrowing musical materials in composition is not a new technique, quotations of Middle Ages and Renaissance music have been used in recent music as isolated elements from "the outside world" which clash with the prevalent style rather than correspond with it.[2] This clash, which is found in *Lachrymae* between Dowland's pavanne melody and the modern, dissonant fanfares, creates an auditory distance between past and present.

The controlled indeterminacy, which has been developed by composers such as Witold Lutoslawski and Joseph Schwanter, is created in *Lachrymae* by freely repeated events and spatial notation. The composer juxtaposes measured rhythms and indeterminate rhythms to create a polyrhythmic structure. As well, the piano solo beginning in m. 99 is to be played in an independent tempo, creating a polymetrical effect. Similar to the music of Charles Ives, Goto positions different musics concurrently, such as the fanfares of the trumpets and the pavanne melody. The overall effect of the layering of separate musics is the possibility of multiple directions; the music often ends up in unexpected places.[3]

Unit 4: Technical Considerations

The main technical consideration is the interpretation and performance of the spatial notation. There are two different ways the composer notates the spatial notations which indicate the tempo. 1/X denotes one conductor beat per bar. The length of the bar is indicated in seconds. 2/M, 3/M, 4/M, etc. denote two, three, and four conductor's beats per bar, with M referring to a metronome setting. For both notations, rhythmic notation is proportional. If a musical gesture or event occurs immediately following a solid or dotted line, it should begin on the conductor's beat. Those events occurring between dotted lines should be determined by performers and should not be synchronized.

The fanfare figures require oboes, trumpets, and horns to double or triple tongue. All clarinets, including bass clarinet, have thirty-second-note ascending and descending patterns at quarter note = 80. The patterns are alternating whole and half steps. The difficulty for performers in this passage at mm. 37–44 is not only to keep the thirty-second notes even, but also to enter independently on different subdivisions of the beat.

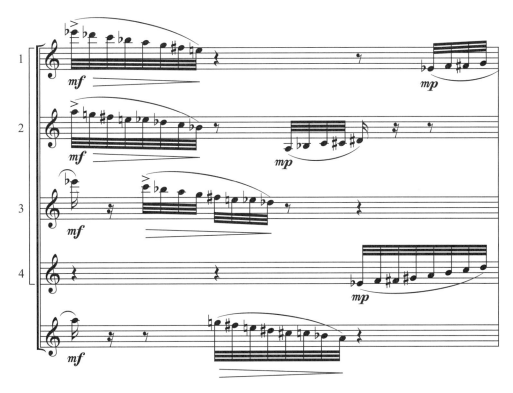

Copyright © 2007 Bravo Music, Inc.

FIGURE 1. M. 42, thirty-second notes, clarinets

Instrumentation requirements include: piccolo, two flutes, two oboes, English horn, bassoon, four B-flat clarinets, B-flat bass clarinet, E-flat alto saxophone, B-flat tenor saxophone, E-flat baritone saxophone, two B-flat trumpets, two horns, two trombones, euphonium, tuba, double bass, and piano. The four percussion parts require only one player per part. Percussion 1: vibraphone, snare drum, field drum (offstage), suspended cymbal, sizzle cymbal, and bell tree. Percussion 2: glockenspiel and four tom-toms, tam-tam. Percussion 3: crotales, marimba, and bass drum. Percussion 4: tubular bells and xylophone. Percussion and piano play a crucial role in the piece.

Unit 5: Stylistic Considerations

Lachrymae requires the conductor and performers to understand the spatial notation used. The indeterminate rhythms should not be synchronized. The chorale sections require performers to understand the simplistic, sostenuto style of the dirge melody, which often contrasts with the indeterminate rhythms surrounding it. As musical simultaneity is the main focus of *Lachrymae*, performers must be aware of and balance the contrasting musical ideas or events that occur simultaneously yet should not be synchronized. For example, in mm. 70–79, the pavanne melody is found in measured rhythms in the brass while woodwinds and percussion have indeterminate rhythms.

The articulation demands require performers to go from aggressive accents to sostenuto, legato sections. The dynamics also require a wide range of expressiveness, from *ppp* to *fff*. Performers need to have control over dynamic contrast in order to create both short diminuendos and long diminuendos to *niente*.

Unit 6: Musical Elements

MELODY:
Melody is borrowed from the dirge "Lachrimae Antiquae," a pavanne of John Dowland (1563–1626) from *Lachrimae or Seven Tears*. It can be heard in the double reed chorale which transitions into a saxophone and clarinet chorale. Later it is heard in a brass chorale while flutes play indeterminate rhythms above. The final quote of the dirge melody occurs in the piano in its own tempo.

HARMONY:
The harmonic language of *Lachrymae* contrasts tonality and atonality. The open fifth of A and E, which is often sustained in the lower voices, is an example of tonality. The chorale sections of the dirge melody also contain traditional harmonies. In the atonal sections, the harmony is based on a fundamental mode or scale which alternately sets notes whole and half steps apart, for example, F–G–A-flat–B-flat–B–C-sharp–D–E.

RHYTHM:
Both spatial and traditional notations are used. Rhythmic independence is important, as measured and indeterminate rhythms are often juxtaposed and there are many occurrences of overlapping rhythmic figures.

TIMBRE:
Choirs of instruments playing the pavanne melody are often juxtaposed with voices which are playing indeterminate rhythms—for example, the double reed choir and brass fanfare interjections at m. 56. The choirs should be thought of as consorts of instruments, reminiscent of the Renaissance period from which the pavanne melody is taken. Percussion timbres are very important and include crotales, tubular bells, sizzle cymbal, and bell tree. An offstage field drum at the end creates a new timbre. As well, the piano melody near the end of the piece creates a new timbral effect not found in any other section of the piece.

An important shift in timbre occurs at mm. 62–64 between the double reed choir and saxophone/clarinet choir. As the double reeds fade away, we are left with a new timbre from the saxophones and clarinets.

Unit 7: Form and Structure

SECTION	MEASURE	EVENT AND SCORING
A	1–9	Percussion in spatial notation; m. 4, woodwinds with sustained pitches; mm. 6 and 8, woodwinds with indeterminate rhythms; m. 9, trumpet and snare drum crescendo
B	10–20	Brass fanfare; woodwind flourishes, alternating half and whole steps
C	21–30	Horn melody; sustained bass open fifth (A and E); improvised tubular bells; oboe and saxophone interjections in mm. 25–26
Transition	31–36	Bassoon, bass clarinet, and euphonium ascending in half and whole steps figure; m. 36, dissonant oboe interjections
D	37–43	Clarinets have thirty-second-note ascending patterns over tuba, string bass, and bassoons; m. 41, addition of flute and oboe fanfare interjections
E	44–55	Tuba (string bass) and euphonium d woodwinds, and percussion in spatial notation; m. 51, trombones, bass clarinet, and baritone saxophone added to bass melody

SECTION	MEASURE	EVENT AND SCORING
F	56–62	Oboe, English horn, and bassoon have traditional notation pavanne melody in C minor versus spatial notation in mm. 56–57; m. 58, interruption of pavanne melody
	62–69	Saxophone and clarinet choir take over pavanne melody in A minor
	69–79	Brass in traditional notation with pavanne melody in A minor; woodwinds, percussion, and piano in spatial notation; clarinets in ascending patterns; m. 79, sizzle cymbal only
C/B/F	80–94	Sustained open fifth (A and E) in low brass, bass clarinet, and double bass; horn melody from section C; m. 82, addition of trumpet fanfare and woodwind flourishes from section B; m. 86, addition of double reed choir from section F
A^1	95–98	Percussion in spatial notation (continues until the end)
I	99–105	Piano solo of pavanne in independent tempo; sustained pitches reminiscent of horn melody in brass and woodwinds; m. 100, oboe and flute interjections; m. 103, offstage trumpet fanfare and field drum
J	106–107	Sustained open fifth (A and E) in double bass; m. 107, final flute flourishes

Unit 8: Suggested Listening

Dowland, John. *Lachrimae* or *Seven Tears*.

Finish Line. Showa Wind Symphony. Eugene Migliaro Corporon, conductor.
    Digital disc. CARFUA Records, Inc. 2008.

Goto, Yo.
    Calls from the Heavens Above
    Lachrymae
    Lux Aeterna

Ives, Charles:
    The Unanswered Question
    Country Band March

Kyo-en XI. Kawagoe Sohwa Wind Ensemble. Masato Sato, conductor.
    Digital disc. BRAIN Co., Ltd. 2008.

Shooting Stars. Showa Wind Symphony. Eugene Migliaro Corporon, conductor. Digital disc. CARFUA Records, Inc. 2004.

Teaching Music through Performance in Band, Volume 5 Grade 4. North Texas Wind Symphony. Eugene Migliaro Corporon, conductor. GIA Publications CD-638.

Unit 9: Additional References and Resources

Goto, Yo. *Lachrymae*. Deerfield, FL: Bravo Music Inc., 2007.

_____. "Voci Lontani for Flute, Trumpet, Percussion, Piano, and String Quartet: Critical Essay and Score." MM diss., University of North Texas, 2004. In *Dissertations and Theses @ University of North Texas* database. Publication no. AAT 1424438.

Griffiths, Paul. "Aleatory." In *Grove Music Online*. L. Macy, ed. http://www.grovemusic.com

Holman, Peter and Paul O'dette. "John Dowland." In *Grove Music Online*. L. Macy, ed. http://www.grovemusic.com

Trachsel, Andrew. "Lux Aeterna." In *Teaching Music through Performance in Band, Volume 5*. Richard Miles, ed. Chicago: GIA Publications, 2004.

Contributed by:

Erin Bodnar
Masters Conducting Associate
University of North Texas
Denton, Texas

---

1 Y. Goto, "Voci Lontani for flute, trumpet, percussion, piano and string quartet: Critical essay and score," (MM diss., University of North Texas, 2004. In *Dissertations & Theses @ University of North Texas* database), 24.

2 Y. Goto, 22.

3 Y. Goto, 4–5.

Teacher Resource Guide

Lament (for a Fallen Friend)
Robert Spittal
(b. 1963)

Unit 1: Composer

Robert Spittal was born in Cleveland, Ohio in 1963. Musicians have described his music as inventive, witty, and full of musicality. His music frequently combines sophisticated artistic forms and techniques with a non-patronizing sensitivity toward audience accessibility. This duality—the musician's concern for aesthetic sophistication and artistic integrity, and for communicating openly and directly to a listener—has been developing since Spittal's teens, when he was both a classical flutist studying at the Cleveland Institute of Music Preparatory School, and a freelance saxophonist playing in jazz and rhythm-and-blues bands. His interest in wind music led him to study conducting with Craig Kirchhoff, Michael Haithcock, and Eugene Corporon, and he received the doctor of musical arts degree in conducting from the Cincinnati College-Conservatory of Music in 1995.

Unit 2: Composition

The composer writes,

> *Lament* is an elegy—a reflection on a life taken before its rightful time. The work is intended to evoke the many conflicted feelings we experience when mourning and remembering a fallen friend, from the reflective and sorrowful, to the hopeful and inspirational. Amidst the reverent music, sudden dynamic gestures and surprising harmonic twists occur, representing the passionate feelings of anger and frustration we feel when faced with the absurdity of life ended too soon. The

characteristic phrasing and harmonies of nineteenth-century American hymns, and the stirring rhythms of the Civil War funeral march, provide a poignant, constructive and metaphorical framework for *Lament*. While a period piece, the hymn tune and other materials are entirely original, and not based on any particular piece of music.

Unit 3: Historical Perspective

The composer describes *Lament* as a historical period piece that draws on the Civil War funeral march and nineteenth-century sacred harmonies as inspiration. However, the composer uses these influences mainly as a metaphorical framework for the elegiac intent of the music. The greater meaning of the work is not to be found in the piece's stylistic connections to the past, but in the expressionistic devices used to convey the array of emotions experienced while grieving the loss of a friend. These devices include sudden and often syncopated percussive outbursts, rapid, and prolonged dynamic shaping, and conflicts between duple and triple rhythms.

Unit 4: Technical Considerations

The central key of the work is A-flat major, which is firmly established in m. 14. Chromaticism is prevalent, and there are frequent modulations within phrases to the closely-related keys of C minor and E-flat major. Mastery of these scales is required.

The most serious technical challenges to the performers are rhythmic. Performers are required to execute, with clarity and a variety of articulation, challenging thirty-second-note, sixteenth-note, and dotted-note figures within the slow, expressive pace of the pulse (usually quarter note = c. 56). To achieve an effective performance, students and conductor will be required to subdivide challenging, often syncopated rhythmic patterns with great precision.

Instrumental ranges are not extreme, but both trumpet 1–2 are required to play B-flat above the staff. Solos are brief, but require expressive playing. There are solos for flute, snare drum, trumpet, oboe, piccolo, and alto saxophone. Marimba and/or vibraphone, bells, and chimes play important roles in the performance of the work. There are a few examples of asymmetric meter (5/4), but in the context of the slow tempo, students previously unexposed to them should not have much difficulty.

Unit 5: Stylistic Considerations

Lament requires musically sensitive playing from each member of the ensemble. Attention must be paid to the pacing of the music so that the shorter phrases of the work do not interfere or distract from the larger phrase shapes. The conductor is encouraged to be deliberate and attentive to all stylistic markings, such as rubato, maestoso, and *dolce*, and to always encourage an expressive, cantabile style. Points of dramatic emphasis and repose need to be approached with great care. For example, the music in mm. 5–6 presents a particularly difficult challenge if there is not enough ritard in the repose. The ritardando should be *immediate* and *molto*, with the tempo in m. 6 no more than a powerful quarter note = 40.

Articulation markings are very detailed in the score, and time should be taken to review the significant variety of symbols of articulation and their substantial impact on the expression of the music.

Unit 6: Musical Elements

MELODY:

All of the melodic material in *Lament* is based on a hymn tune composed in a nineteenth-century style by Robert Spittal. A single, complete statement of the hymn tune (in AABA form) structures the work from m. 14 to the end. The melodies in the A sections of the hymn tune (mm. 14–32 and m. 36 to the end) should be performed in a deliberate, but always cantabile style. The melody of section B (mm. 32–35), which serves as a bridge to the final, climactic statement of section A, is more motivic than songful, but the melody should remain expressively lyrical throughout.

Mm. 1–13 is a freely rubato introduction that sets the stage for the eventual entrance of the hymn tune in m. 14. The melodies here are based on motives drawn from the first measure of the hymn tune at m. 14. For example, the additive triad in mm. 1–3 foreshadows the opening triadic motif at m. 14. The lyrical eighth-note lines in mm. 3–4, the descending figures in mm. 7–9, the *dolce* figures in 11–12, and the sixteenth-note figures in m. 13 are all based on the descending eighth notes in the first measure of the hymn tune.

HARMONY:

Harmony is one of the strongest "period" elements in the piece. Conventional hymn-like, four-part harmonic progressions are presented in a homophonic texture. The chord progressions are laced with chromaticism, reminiscent of the nineteenth-century American hymn style. Harmonic tension and release are important expressive elements in the music, and chromatic dissonances should be brought to the fore, especially in the louder music. A prime example of this occurs in m. 35, where the already significant tension of the dominant chord is enhanced with a chromatic, dissonant, trombone glissando.

RHYTHM:

The prevailing meter is common time, but 5/4 occurs in mm. 3–5 and m. 35. The slow tempo of the music makes the execution of these meter changes relatively simple. However, the greater rhythmic challenge is in the variety of rapid, subdivided rhythmic figures, as well as the frequent placement of strong accents between beats, such as in mm. 20, 22, 28, 37, and 40.

TIMBRE:

Lament provides many opportunities for students to explore the element of timbre as an expressive device. The scoring ranges from whisper-soft to epic, and often shifts from one to the other in just a few measures, or even a few beats. The composer intends to evoke a variety of emotions and feelings through the music, and musicians should take great care to project these evocations not only with dynamic contrast and varieties of articulation, but also by carefully considering the palette of colors presented in the music.

Unit 7: Form and Structure

SECTION	MEASURE	EVENT AND SCORING
Introduction	1–6	Whisper-soft mallets on E-flat (V) lead to plaintive wind entrances outlining a triad motif from the hymn tune, and harmonic "sighs" in mm. 4–5; quiet music gives way to full, powerful chords in m. 6
	7–9	Quiet, flowing lines based on the descending motif of the hymn tune scored sequentially in woodwinds, horns, euphonium, and basses
	10–13	Music cadences in E-flat major (V); funeral march style introduced by snare; descending motif continues to be developed additively; D-flat added to E-flat major harmony in m. 12 indicates modulation to A-flat major; music builds toward cadence point at m. 14
A	14–23	Hymn tune introduced by tutti band in funeral march style; tune interrupted by bell tree and aggressive snare drum solo, which rapidly decays *a niente*; hymn tune returns in flutes and woodwinds, and scoring quickly builds to a climactic tutti accent in m. 20; melody handed to low brass and woodwinds in m. 20, then is quietly transferred through the ensemble in mm. 21–23; m. 21 introduces triple subdivision for the first time

SECTION	MEASURE	EVENT AND SCORING
A	24–31	Maestoso brass and upper woodwinds begin second statement of section A; m. 26, quiet woodwinds build toward tutti chord at m. 28, followed by a bold statement by brass and woodwinds in m. 28; chromatic swell in mm. 29–30 recedes into the bridge (section B)
B	32–35	E-flat pedal supports flowing, additive counterpoint in woodwinds; tension builds through the phrase, and is enhanced in m. 35 with *molto ritard* crescendo, extension of the meter (5/4), and gradually more chromatic dissonance; bridge climaxes at the return of section A at m. 36
A	36–41	Climactic, final statement of section A, more chromatic and powerful than before; in m. 41, maestoso style gives way to *molto ritard* and diminuendo, and a quiet fermata in M. 41 on a V/ii chord sets the stage for a reflective closing
	42–47	Final two bars of the hymn tune are developed into a reflective, quiet closing phrase, in which the melodic material is handed about quietly among winds; deceptive cadence in m. 44 extends the closing music; a final resolution in A-flat major occurs in m. 45, and clarinets, marimba, and vibraphone diminuendo *a niente* in the final breath of the piece

Unit 8: Suggested Listening

Spittal, Robert:
   Consort for Ten Winds
   Pacem—A Hymn for Peace
   Prelude and Scherzo

Unit 9: Additional References and Resources

Miles, Richard, ed. *Teaching Music through Performance in Band, Volume 6.*
   Chicago: GIA Publications, Inc., 2007.

Website:
   Robert Spittal. www.robertspittal.com

Contributed by:

Robert Spittal
Spokane, Washington

Teacher Resource Guide

Metroplex
Three Postcards from Manhattan

Robert Sheldon
(b. 1954)

Unit 1: Composer

Robert Sheldon, born February 3, 1954, is currently concert band editor for Alfred Publishing Company. He also serves as conductor of the Prairie Wind Ensemble in residence at Illinois Central College, and teaches composition at Bradley University. His compositions, recognized primarily for their educational value, have had a significant impact on the body of repertoire for school bands of varying levels. These works provide appropriate technical, lyrical, and harmonic challenges for developing musicians, and are appealing to audiences of school band programs.

Sheldon is internationally recognized as a composer, conductor, and clinician. He has been honored by the American School Band Directors Association with the *Volkwein Award* for composition and the *Stanbury Award* for teaching excellence. He has also been a twenty-time recipient of the Standard Award given annually by the American Society of Composers, Authors, and Publishers for his concert band compositions. In 1990, the International Assembly of Phi Beta Mu honored him as the International Outstanding Bandmaster of the year. Sheldon has been the topic of articles published in *The Instrumentalist, Teaching Music,* and *School Band and Orchestra Magazine.* Additionally, he is one of eleven American band composers featured in *Composers on Composing Music for Band* (GIA).

Sheldon received a bachelor of music in music education from the University of Miami and the master of fine arts in instrumental conducting from the University of Florida. His teaching experience includes work in both

Florida and Illinois public schools, and he has served on the faculty at Florida State University.

Unit 2: Composition

Metroplex: Three Postcards from Manhattan, composed in 2005, is listed as opus 110 in Sheldon's catalogue. It is published by Alfred Publishing Company, which grades the work at 4.5 (medium-difficult). It is 122 measures long, with a duration of approximately four minutes and twenty-five seconds. The work, commissioned by the Normal Community West High School Band of Normal, Illinois and its director, Lisa Preston, was premiered on March 19, 2005 at Carnegie Hall with the composer conducting.

Program notes, provided by the composer and included in the score, read as follows:

> A musical portrait of Manhattan's cityscape, *Metroplex* opens with a vision of the New York skyline, tall buildings and concrete canyons. This leads to an urban jazz scene in one of Harlem's clubs. Finally, the music takes us on a wild taxi ride through the heavy traffic of this incredible city. The skyline is seen once more as we leave Manhattan, hopefully to return again soon.[1]

Additional notes, provided by the composer for this article, are as follows:

> Since this piece was to be premiered in Carnegie Hall (and it has apparently been performed there many times since) I wanted it to be a musical souvenir for the band that commissioned the piece, and consequently opted to present three pictures of the city that the band members might recognize as part of their "Big Apple" experience. Since this was to be a relatively brief piece, I decided that "postcard-size" segments were appropriate!

> The first postcard represents the initial impression of the city, looking up at the enormous skyscrapers represented by powerful blocks of chords and shifting harmonies. I can recall my first time there and peering up at the sky, feeling a sense of dizzying height as the clouds flew by above the tops of the buildings; this can be heard in the rising eighth-note patterns that create small tone clusters rising higher and higher. Musical vertigo perhaps...

> This ends with an English horn solo (cued in saxophone) that acts as a transition to a jazz/blues inspired postcard representing the entertainment venues in the city. Harp, vibes, and string bass (all cross-cued for other instruments) provide a colorful accompaniment to an alto sax solo that leads to a screaming big-band moment before winding down

and recalling the opening English horn statement that brings this post-card to a close.

The tempo immediately bursts into a frantic and fast-paced taxi ride through the streets of Manhattan. The mix of meters and references to traffic sounds and car horns are intertwined with jazz-influenced pas-sages driving toward the closing section, during which time Manhattan can be seen in the distance (from the New Jersy side of the Lincoln Tunnel exit ramp), but all the while still in very heavy traffic. The energetic and noisy finale includes lots of percussion that accompanies a previously heard motive in the brass, followed by a trombone section smear that leads to a rapid-fire and jazz-inspired ending.[2]

Unit 3: Historical Perspective

The compositional practice of creating images through music dates to the early twentieth-century Impressionistic era of music history, and is often associated with composers Claude Debussy and Maurice Ravel, due to their use of programmatic content. The use of jazz influences in classical music also dates to that time, with early examples found in the works of Darius Milhaud and Igor Stravinsky.

In this contemporary work, Sheldon draws together a number of sources in order to paint his picture of New York City. His music is reflective of that of other composers who have created images of this city, including William Schuman's use of bitonality, rising scale lines, and long-note chord structures in *George Washington Bridge*, and the multi-faceted use of jazz found in Leonard Bernstein's *West Side Story*. Other contemporary band composers who have also found inspiration in metropolitan settings include, among others, John Harbison in *Three City Blocks*, Martin Ellerby in *Paris Sketches*, Scott Boerma in *Cityscape*, and Mark Camphouse in *Three London Miniatures*.

Unit 4: Technical Considerations

Metroplex provides a variety of technical challenges for performer and con-ductor alike. As one might suspect from the publisher's grading of the work, it contains rapid modal and chromatic scale passages performed in sixteenth notes at quarter note = 160; the use of thirty-second-note scale runs in the upper woodwinds at quarter note = 80; syncopated figures that combine six-teenth notes with eighth notes, and/or tied eighth-and-sixteenth-note combinations performed at quarter note = 160; mixed meters, including the use of 3/4, 4/4, 5/4, 6/8, and 7/8 time signatures; and, rapid single-tonguing of repeated eighth notes at quarter note = 160.

The piece also requires a mallet percussionist who can perform four-mal-let passages with appropriate vibraphone pedaling technique; rapid octave double stops with accented and unaccented notes performed on xylophone; and the execution of three-mallet technique on rapidly changing chords, also performed on xylophone. The multi-mallet voicing positions present some awkward challenges to the performer.

There are no particular range issues in *Metroplex*. Conductors should, however, be sure to consider that the trumpet 1 range does include C6. This pitch is to be performed with either a vibrant, lead jazz trumpet presence, or with a clear, symphonic tone, dependent on the musical situation.

The work features typical band instrumentation with the inclusion of harp, English horn, and string bass. These instruments are usually doubled or cued in other parts, although the harp glissandi, which provide an important coloration to the piece, are not present elsewhere. Likewise, the string bass part offers an essential color for the jazzy, second "postcard" of the work. However, these considerations should not deter bands with less-complete instrumentation from performing *Metroplex*.

Piccolo doubles flute at the octave when appropriate. Flute divides into two parts, while oboe, bassoon, alto clarinet, and bass clarinet parts do not divide. The clarinet section is divided into three parts, and the saxophone section is comprised of the standard alto 1, alto 2, tenor, and baritone parts. The brass section instrumentation is standard with the exception of calling for two F-horn parts. Divisi aprts are not present in either tuba or euphonium. The score calls for six percussionists, but the parts can be covered by five players, with all mallet parts being performed by one player, as there is ample time provided for switching between vibraphone and xylophone. Percussion 1 calls for wind chimes. This is really a mark tree part, as determined by the explicit glissandi directional marks found beginning in m. 7.

The publisher provides additional parts for bands worldwide that feature different instrumentation than that of the typical bands found in the United States. These are available for downloading from the publisher's website (www.alfred.com/worldparts).

Unit 5: Stylistic Considerations

Robert Sheldon employs four basic styles within this work. The opening fanfare and similar sections rely on full-length, symphonic sounds that feature both brilliance and warmth. Performers should take great care to produce good sounds using wind without overuse of the tongue.

The second, lyrical style, found beginning in m. 7, should be performed *molto legato*, with little interruption from the tongue when it is used to delineate slur markings. According to the composer, this section "should have a lifting feeling, like looking up at clouds and then you get a little dizzy."[3]

The third stylistic consideration is found in the bluesy section beginning in m. 30. In order to achieve the desired jazz feel of this section, performers should be taught to apply a consistent triplet subdivision, as notated. A comparison can be made between this section and Oliver Nelson's scoring of *Stolen Moments* for jazz ensemble. In general, the groove can be characterized as laid back, with all figures being performed on the back-side of the beat.

Both alto saxophone and trumpet are featured as soloists during this section of the piece. Players should be encouraged to employ a jazz-style vibrato, and to seek freedom from notational constraints. The conductor may choose to have both of these soloists stand up during their solos in order to create a jazz-like ambiance.[4]

All performers should be taught to use proper jazz articulations, including the use of "du," "dah," and "daht," rather than syllables beginning with a "t" consonant, in order to make this section sound idiomatically correct. They should also be taught appropriate ghosting techniques in order to bring out the differences between accented and unaccented notes within this section. The marcato accents found in mm. 45–46 should be taught as "daht" syllables, and should end with a "t" consonant in order to achieve the appropriate length and separation. These notes should not be clipped by using a "dit" articulation.

Questions may arise about the duple and quadruple subdivisions of the beat employed at various times during the jazz section. Due to the care exercised with the rhythmic notation throughout this section, it is evident that the composer desires the existence of these cross-rhythmic relationships.

The fourth stylistic consideration occurs beginning in m. 57 and continues throughout the remainder of the piece. The groove of this section should be on the front side of the beat in order to create an intense rhythmic drive. Attention should be paid to the buoyancy of this section, particularly to the lightness of the underlying tongued, rhythmic ostinatos, and to the accented versus unaccented notes contained within these figures. While this section is thickly scored, it is important to maintain both appropriate style and balance in order to produce the desired buoyancy and forward momentum of this quasi-double-time groove section. Care should be exercised with the percussion throughout this section to ensure that these sounds reflect the overall buoyant nature of the music and do not become overbearing.

Throughout the work, attention should be given to the trombone glissandi, as they occur, in order to ensure that the ending pitches are heard and are performed accurately.[5]

Unit 6: Musical Elements

MELODY:

The melodic construction of *Metroplex* is based on traditional language, primarily diatonic, modal, and chromatic scale motions. Theme 1 is found in mm. 1–6. It provides material that is recycled and transitioned into different key centers throughout various sections of the piece. A secondary melodic motion is found beginning in mm. 9–11. It is modal, featuring a rising motion of clustered pitches. The third melody is freely composed as a part of the jazz section, and is reflective of jazz ballad writing. A fourth melodic motif, found beginning in m. 61, is constructed of descending pitches belonging to B-flat major. A freely composed section follows, which, along with the fourth motif and the fanfare melody, is recycled, leading to the end of the piece.

HARMONY:

Sheldon employs a variety of harmonic techniques in this predominantly polyphonic piece. These include the use of bitonality, chord clusters, poly-modality, pedal tones, jazz chord structures, and traditional harmonic motion. The work transitions from section to section without the use of traditional cadence technique. The opening key signature of E-flat major has little bearing on the key center of the work, as the piece flows freely through brief tonicizations during the opening fanfare section. These tonicizations are often far-removed from the original key signature. The key signature does, however, have an impact on the F Dorian harmony of the jazz postcard. The key change to B-flat major found in m. 61 does depict the final key center of the piece.

RHYTHM:

Two types of rhythmic intricacies present within the piece will need careful attention. The first is encountered during the jazz section beginning in m. 30, and requires accurate subdivision of the triplet rhythms, particularly regarding the placement of last eighth-note triplet figures found on beats 1 and 3 in the accompaniment parts.

The second rhythmic intricacy can be found beginning in m. 71 as the ensemble works toward accurate sixteenth-note subdivisions of both the syncopated figures, and of the rhythmic interplay between these figures and the running sixteenth-note figures that are found in the flutes, clarinets and saxophones. Difficulties may be encountered in mm. 82–87 with the sixteenth note overlapping, if these figures are not accurately subdivided.

Difficulties may also be encountered during the 7/8 measures of the piece, beginning in m. 61, due to the asymmetrical nature of the rhythmic patterns. The 7/8 measures fall into groupings of two, and should be divided into conducting patterns of either 2 + 2 + 3 or 3 + 2 + 2. Care should also be exercised so that the ensemble uses eighth-note subdivisions when transitioning between 7/8 and 3/4 meters so that an accurate pulse may be discerned, and so the piece will maintain forward momentum.

TIMBRE:

During postcard 1, fanfare chords should be balanced according to their bitonal structure, from the bottom to the top, in order to achieve a sonic richness that demonstrates both breadth and depth of tone quality. Particular care should be taken with the trumpet parts in both mm. 23 and 25 so that the concert G major chords are heard, as the scoring is dense at these moments.[6] Percussion sounds should feature more tone than impact in order to achieve the Copland-like sonorities called for during these sections.

Beginning in m. 7, attention should be paid to the balance between the underlying, repeated eighth-note figures, the sustained low voice pedal tones, and the rising melodic figures found in piccolo, flute, oboe and clarinet, with clarinet treated as the dominant line in order to achieve the desired rising linear motion. Percussion should enhance these effects by using appropriate mallet choices that add to the overall color of the piece. Care should be exercised with the mark tree sounds so that they do not become a prominent feature of the scoring. Likewise, the suspended cymbal should support, not dominate the sound structure, as the majority of the crescendo should be saved for the transition to the fanfare's return found in m. 12.

During postcard 2, add a two-measure crescendo/diminuendo to the chords found in the clarinets, harp, and vibraphone in mm. 30–37 to enhance their rising and falling motions.[7] These figures should support the melodic motion throughout the jazz section.

Mm. 43–46 should be treated as a dirty blues shout section with trumpets and trombones dominating the balance. According to Kenneth Kohlenberg, Director of Bands at Sinclair College in Dayton, Ohio, who observed Robert Sheldon rehearsing *Metroplex*, the composer desires that trumpets and trombones play with bells up during these measures, and that percussion plays a prominent role as well.[8]

During postcard 3, careful consideration should be given to the balance between syncopated rhythmic figures, bass line, and melodic figures scored for alto and tenor saxophone and clarinets found in mm. 71–79 and similar sections. Likewise, attention should be given to interplay between all lines in mm. 82–87 in order to achieve the appropriate balance and rhythmic intricacy of this passage. Trumpet 1 may be allowed to release last on the final note of the piece, as is often the case with big band performances in jazz style.[9]

The interjections of bass drum and whip found in m. 83 and the percussion ensemble tutti found in mm. 116–117 must be sufficiently full yet balanced with the wind section. The snare drummer should be encouraged to lead the ensemble in mm. 96–107 by performing with great energy rather than overplaying the dynamic level. In order to achieve an idiomatic sound, the hi-hat part should be performed using the shoulder rather than the tip of the stick, and cymbals should be allowed to splash together slightly when performing the open hi-hat sounds found in mm. 108–115.

Unit 7: Form and Structure

Metroplex is divided into three sections that depict the three postcards mentioned in the title of the work. Postcard 1 is the fanfare section, postcard 2 features jazz writing, and postcard 3 is the frenetic cab ride that combines newly-composed materials with music from the earlier fanfare melody.

SECTION	MEASURE	EVENT AND SCORING
Postcard 1	1–29	Section 1, featuring two melodic ideas: fanfare music and rising melodic figures
	1–6	Opening fanfare featuring brass and percussion; woodwind interjection in mm. 5–6 Momentary arrival in D major/C major in m. 6
	7–8	Transitional material composed over C major pedal; two rhythmic and melodic ostinatos present
	9–11	Rising melody in flutes, clarinets, and piccolo composed over C major pedal
	12–15	Fanfare return with arrival in C major at m. 15
	16	Transitional material encapsulated
	17–21	Fanfare melody in legato style followed by rising lines now in horns and trumpets
	22–26	Fanfare returns; arrival in D major in m. 26
	26–29	Transition to postcard 2 provided by English horn solo featuring chromatic melody; harmonic motion from D major to C major
Postcard 2	30–56	Jazz section
	30–42	Individual instrument solos featuring alto saxophone (mm. 34–37) and trumpet (mm. 38–41); featured chord progression: Fm^9–Gm^7/C–Fm^9–B-flat^{maj7}/C
	43–46	Ensemble shout section featuring trumpet, trombone, and percussion sections
	47–49	Alto saxophone solo
	50	English horn solo reminiscent of earlier melodic figure
	51–56	End of jazz section with cadence figure using cluster chord pyramid in m. 56

SECTION	MEASURE	EVENT AND SCORING
Postcard 3	57–122	Cab ride section using newly-composed materials and fanfare melodic ideas; use of driving rhythms and mixed meter at quarter note = 160
	57–60	Transition and introduction of section
	61–70	Newly-composed melodic material passed from alto saxophones and trumpet 2–3 (mm. 61–62) to low reeds, euphonium, and tuba (mm. 63–64), then to flutes, trumpet 1, and clarinet 1 (mm. 65–67); leading to sixteenth-note runs in upper woodwinds (mm. 68–69)
	71–87	Quasi-double-time groove section featuring underlying syncopations with sixteenth-note melodic figures in upper woodwinds
	88–95	Repeat of mm. 61–67 with new transition in m. 95
	96–107	Combination of fanfare melody in augmentation with the fast woodwind obbligato lines of the cab ride section
	108–115	Exact repeat of mm. 72–79 elided with held brass chord; trumpets begin repeat of earlier material in m. 109
	116–122	Closing materials leading to octave B-flats

Unit 8: Suggested Listening

Bernstein, Leonard. *West Side Story.*
Copland, Aaron. *Fanfare for the Common Man.*
Nelson, Oliver. *Stolen Moments.*
Schuman, William. *George Washington Bridge.*

Unit 9: Additional References and Resources

Camphouse, Mark, ed. *Composers on Composing for Band.* Chicago: GIA
  Publications, Inc., 2002.

Recordings:
  Images: The Music Of Robert Sheldon. The Washington Winds.
  Infinite Horizons. The Washington Winds.
  Teaching Music through Performance in Band, *Volumes 3 and 5.* North
    Texas Wind Symphony.

Websites:
www.robertsheldonmusic.com
www.alfred.com

Contributed by:

Robert Meunier
Director of Bands
Professor of Music
Drake University
Des Moines, Iowa

Teacher Resource Guide

Missouri Shindig

H. Owen Reed
(b. 1910)

Unit 1: Composer

Herbert Owen Reed was born in 1910 in Odessa, Missouri, a small town near Kansas City. He began his musical training early in life playing trumpet in the town band and studying piano with Odessa's leading musician, Mrs. Felts. Reed enrolled at the University of Missouri in 1929 but transferred to Louisiana State University in 1933. There he received his bachelor of music (1934) and his master of music (1936) degrees, both in music composition, as well a bachelor of arts in French (1937). At LSU, Reed studied composition with Helen Gunderson, whom he credits with influencing him to enroll in the doctoral program at the Eastman School in 1937. There his principal teachers were Howard Hanson and Bernard Rogers. (In later years, he studied composition with Bohuslav Martinu in 1942 at Tanglewood, and with Roy Harris in Colorado Springs in 1947.)

Following graduation from Eastman in 1939, he joined the music faculty at Michigan State University, where he taught until his retirement in 1976. During his long career at MSU, he had a strong commitment to teaching and had well over 100 private composition students. Some of his more recognized students include David Maslanka, Adolphus Hailstork, William Penn, and David Gillingham, whom he taught following his retirement. He also wrote some ten theory books and workbooks, several of which have become widely-adopted texts.

He has received many awards, including a Guggenheim Fellowship, a Huntington Hartford Foundation Resident Fellowship, a Helene Wurlitzer Foundation Resident Fellowship, the George Romney and Greater Michigan

Foundation Citation for Distinguished Contributions in the Arts, and the Neil A. Kjos Memorial Award. In 1994, the American Bandmasters Association—along with President Bill Clinton—presented Reed with the Edwin Franco Goldman Memorial Citation.

His compositions are very stylistically eclectic. Much of his earlier music (composed prior to 1958) is in a neo-Romantic style, perhaps due to the influence of his teacher Howard Hanson. His most popular composition, *La Fiesta Mexicana,* belongs to this period, as does *Missouri Shindig.* Beginning in 1959, his music took a very different direction, becoming very complex, often featuring very advanced serial techniques. His very emotional work for band, *For the Unfortunate,* is an example. He returned to a more conservative approach in his latter works, although his palette continued to expand within this general style, employing many techniques, such as minimalism.

Unit 2: Composition

Missouri Shindig was composed in 1951 and was Reed's third composition for concert band. *Spiritual* (1947) and *La Fiesta Mexicana* (1949) were his earlier works. The Baylor Golden Wave Band, conducted by Donald Moore, premiered *Missouri Shindig* on April 6, 1952. Reed conducted an early performance of the Michigan State Band on May 28, 1952.

It is inspired both musically and programmatically by an old square dance tune, "Give the Fiddler a Dram"(see figure 1), a favorite of Reed's father, who played country fiddle. The tune is not unlike many folk tunes, in that the melody, harmony, and form are relatively simple, yet it possesses considerable charm. Perhaps the most unusual aspect of the tune is the form. It is split into three related phrases. The first and third are eight measures long and are both repeated. The middle phrase, however, is only six measures in length and is not repeated.

Reed also used this same fiddle tune in his folk-opera, *Michigan Dream* (1955), as well as *The Touch of the Earth* (1971), a suite for band based on themes from the opera.

Missouri Shindig is somewhat programmatic in nature, providing a glimpse into Reed's impression of a Missouri hoedown. There is also a play on the title of the fiddle tune: giving the fiddler a dram—a serving of an adult beverage that one might consume at such a grand occasion. In a note in the score, Reed summarizes the plot.

> As it opens there is a gradual development of the excitement as the party gets into full swing. The square dancers reflect the various moods of the fiddlers as they first become exhilarated, next clownish, then sentimental. The party is momentarily interrupted as the tune "How Dry I Am" is heard in the distance; however it is soon in full swing again and the dancing is resumed.

The work shows Reed's love of theatrical elements, something that is found in almost all of his compositions. Here, the highlight of the middle section features an offstage duet featuring a cornet and trombone playing "How Dry I Am," a fitting pairing with giving the fiddler a dram!

Missouri Shindig is approximately six minutes in duration and is fittingly dedicated to Reed's parents.

Figure 1. "Give the Fiddler a Dram"

Unit 3: Historical Perspective

Compositions and arrangements based on folk music have strong roots in the concert band tradition in the United States. For example, there are many engaging compositions by Clare Grundman in this genre; Frank Ticheli has continued the tradition as well.

On first impression, one might think that *Missouri Shindig* is a simple setting of this square dance tune. While the general inspiration is the fiddle tune, the composition goes well beyond a basic setting, as it employs many developmental techniques and introduces original material as well. It is hardly a straightforward arrangement, but is a composition in its own right.

Unit 4: Technical Considerations

For a work of this overall difficulty level, basic technique might be a bit challenging for some ensembles. While not fiendishly difficult, there are a great many technical flourishes, found especially in the woodwinds, cornets, trombone 1, and baritone horn.

There are a number of important solos requiring a fair number of mature players. The longest is for clarinet (mm. 126–136 and 142–144), which begins the portrayal of the clownish elements. The sentimental role is given to a solo cornet (mm. 151–160). There are also important lines for piccolo, flute, trombone, and tuba, as well as brief, offstage solos for cornet 2 and trombone 2.

Rhythm might present a challenge for some ensembles. Many players are not as comfortable with cut-time as they should be. This might be especially problematic, given the pronounced emphasis on syncopation.

Unit 5: Stylistic Considerations

Missouri Shindig is a work of considerable optimism and good-hearted fun. The work needs to be performed with enthusiasm and joy. Maintenance of tempo is one of the most important ways to generate and keep this positive energy.

A note in the score indicates that "*Missouri Shindig* may be proceeded by the playing of 'Give the Fiddler a Dram,' performed by either a solo fiddler or fiddler and guitarist (or chording pianist) dressed in bib overalls and straw hat." Given Reed's preference for things theatrical, this country flair is certainly encouraged.

Unit 6: Musical Elements

MELODY:
As has been noted, the basic melody is "Give the Fiddler a Dram" (see figure 1). However, what could be a fairly straightforward presentation is anything but. Even in the first statement, Reed alters the tune. Most commonly, he interrupts it, often with the angular motive presented in the introduction (see figure 2).

FIGURE 2. Mm. 3–7, introductory motive

Because of these many interruptions, as well as Reed's approach to orchestration where the line is passed between instruments, the melody rarely has a continuous quality. The sense of line might be lost and appear choppy if performers do not connect these motives as they are passed between instruments. Only in this way can the phrase be preserved.

HARMONY:
The harmony of the original fiddle tune is basic, with largely tonic and dominant harmonies (see figure 1). In *Missouri Shindig*, Reed takes this relatively simple piece and adds considerable harmonic spice. In addition to shifting key centers at various points, Reed also introduces more subtle twists—too many to note here. One very brief example is an E-minor triad in m. 8 in what is largely a section in E-flat major. At a parallel event (m. 19), this triad in C minor is followed by one in F major. These quick sonorities bring considerable charm and tonal variety to this simple tune.

Beginning at m. 45, Reed takes a different tack. Here the melody is in C major. However, the accompaniment is rooted in B-flat, although without a third most of the time. This bi-tonal approach is yet another approach giving interest to "Fiddler."

Quartal and quintal harmony is found in much of Reed's music, and is used in *Missouri Shindig*. A very clear example is heard in the introductory motive in mm. 3–7 (see figure 2). Quartal/quintal (intervals of fifth-fourth-fifth) chords move to triads, here with no fifth; this is a central feature of the motive. Other quintal structures can be found as well, the cornet parts at mm. 46–47 and 52–53, and horn parts at mm. 49–50 and 55–56, for example. The intervals noted above starting in m. 45 are another. These sonorities are striking, given the generally tertian nature of the piece.

RHYTHM:
As stated above, syncopation is a strong feature. The introduction motive in mm. 3–7 (see figure 2) is one very obvious example, and it plays a central role. The use of this strongly syncopated figure brings considerable contrast to the very regular rhythmic structure of the fiddle tune.

Reed is quite fond of rhythmically "misplacing" figures so that metrical emphasis becomes displaced. In some works such as *Renascence*, he uses brackets to show how particular passages should be phrased. His approach in *Missouri Shindig* is not as complex and is fairly straightforward. One good example is found at letter F, where the clarinet soloist plays the "Fiddler" melody in a "slightly corny" fashion. The solo is delayed after each two-measure motive (effects of an adult beverage?), with the result that the metrical emphasis is shifted by a beat. What was originally the downbeat now becomes the downbeat. The process continues with the melody alternating between the "correct" and "incorrect" metrical positions.

TIMBRE:
Reed is well known as a master orchestrator, and his use of interesting wind colors gives *Missouri Shindig* considerable charm.

While the piece was composed with a traditional concert band in mind, the full ensemble is not usually employed. Essentially, the entire group plays only in the final section. At most other times Reed chooses to use rather thin scoring, resulting in very different textures.

The frequent use of soloists also generates considerable contrast in terms of texture and color. One of the more interesting examples is the piccolo and tuba duet in mm. 137–141 during the midst of the "slightly corny" section.

Unit 7: Form and Structure

The larger form of the piece does not directly follow any of the traditional conventions, largely because of its programmatic orientation. The work is conveying an impression of a Missouri hoedown where the revelers partake of a bit too much adult beverage.

However, it might be viewed as an episodic (ABA) form with a rather extended introduction. (The introduction and section 1 could be combined and considered to be one larger structure.) With this loose ABA structure, section 1 (A) is a presentation of the tune, "Give the Fiddler a Dram." Section 2 (B) portrays the various moods described by Reed: first exhilarated, then clownish, and finally sentimental. Following a quote of "How Dry I Am," the music comes to a complete stop. Section 3 (A) returns "Give the Fiddler a Dram" to the fore. At first, the presentation is very straightforward; then the overall energy is increased with considerable structural fragmentation and development.

Section	Measure	Event and Scoring
Introduction	1–44	
	1–26	Alternation of motives from "Give the Fiddler a Dram" (see figure 1) and introductory motive (see figure 2)
	27–44	Sustained chords followed by "Fiddler" and introductory motive
Section 1	45–120	"Give the Fiddler a Dram"
	45–56	Phrase 1 of "Fiddler" with one-measure interjections
	57–60	Transition using material from introduction
	61–66	Phrase 2 of "Fiddler" with melody alternating between cornets and clarinets; tutti at end
	67–76	Phrase 3 of "Fiddler"
	76–85	Transition
	86–93	Phrase 1 of "Fiddler" complete without interruptions; introductory motive in accompaniment
	94–100	Phrase 2 of "Fiddler" with one-measure interruption at end
	101–113	Phrase 3 of "Fiddler" extended and developed in middle
	112–120	Closing
Section 2	121–170	"Overindulging"
	121–126	Introduction
	127–147	"Clownish" phrases 1 and 2 of "Fiddler" (clarinet solo) in two-measure units that are interrupted and metrically displaced
	148–160	"Sentimental" four-measure introduction, then phrase 2 of "Fiddler" (cornet solo)
	161–170	"How Dry I Am" versus "Fiddler"(offstage versus onstage); then closing
Section 3	171–210	Recapitulation and development of Section 1
	171–178	Straightforward presentation of phrase 1 of "Fiddler"
	179–202	Starting with phrase 2 material, development of various motives from "Fiddler" and "How Dry I Am"
	203–210	Coda

Unit 8: Suggested Listening

Adams, John. *Gnarly Buttons* (second movement).

Bennett, Robert Russell. *Suite of Old American Dances.*

Copland, Aaron:
   Appalachian Spring
   The Red Pony
   Rodeo

Gillis, Don. *Shindig* (ballet). 1949.

Gould, Morton. *Inventions.*

Reed, H. Owen:
   "Give the Fiddler a Dram." *American Images.* Janey Choi, violin. Mark
      Masters 4238-MCD. 2002.
   Missouri Shindig. American Images. Rutgers Wind Ensemble. William
      Berz,   conductor. Mark Masters 4238-MCD. 2002.
   Missouri Shindig. The Composer's Voice: H. Owen Reed. The Keystone
      Wind Ensemble. Jack Stamp, conductor. Klavier K11147. 2004.

Unit 9: Additional References and Resources

Berz William. "An Annotated Bibliography of Materials Written about H.
   Owen Reed." *WASBE Journal* 13 (2006): 83–99.

_____. "An Overview of H. Owen Reed's Music for Wind Ensemble."
   Journal of Band Research, 40, no. 1 (Fall, 2004): 1–21.

_____. "Another 'Lord Of The Rings': Two Works by H. Owen Reed."
   WASBE Journal 11 (2004): 74–88.

_____. "H. Owen Reed," in *A Composers Insight, Volume 2.* T. Salzman,
   ed. Galesville, MD: Meredith, (2003): 152–170.

_____. "Three Early Works For Band By H. Owen Reed." *WASBE Journal*
   10 (2003): 95–105. This article includes discussion on *Spiritual, Missouri
   Shindig,* and *Renascence.*

Contributed by:

William Berz
Professor of Music
Mason Gross School of the Arts
Rutgers, The State University of New Jersey
New Brunswick, New Jersey

Teacher Resource Guide

Noisy Wheels of Joy

Eric Whitacre
(b. 1970)

Unit 1: Composer

An accomplished composer, conductor, and lecturer, Eric Whitacre is one of the bright stars in contemporary concert band music. Regularly commissioned and published, Whitacre has received numerous composition awards as well as a Grammy nomination. The American Record Guide named his first recording, *The Music of Eric Whitacre*, one of the top ten classical albums in 1997. His twenty-eight published works have sold well over 100,000 copies worldwide. Whitacre received his master of music in composition from The Juilliard School, where he studied composition with Pulitzer Prize-winner John Corigliano.

Unit 2: Composition

Conceived as a raucous *opera-buffa*-style overture, *Noisy Wheels of Joy* was commissioned by the Band Composers Masterworks Consortium and premiered at the 2001 American Bandmasters Association Convention by the University of Nevada, Las Vegas Wind Symphony, conducted by Tad Suzuki. The work is dedicated with deepest gratitude to Jim Cochran. The composer includes the following in the score:

> *Noisy Wheels of Joy* is just pure, simple fun, written in the tradition of the great comic operatic overtures, and was designed to start the program with a bang. The structure is quite formal, but the three themes (love, adventure, and *buffa*) get thrown around the wind symphony with wild abandon.

Unit 3: Historical Perspective

Comic opera first developed in eighteenth-century Italy as *opera buffa*, which was an alternative to opera seria. It quickly made its way to France, where it became *opera comique* and eventually the French operetta. Both the Italian and French forms were major artistic exports to other parts of Europe. The *singspiel* developed in Vienna and spread throughout Austria and Germany. As in the French *opera comique*, the *singspiel* was an opera which included spoken dialogue. Many countries developed their own styles of comic opera, incorporating the Italian and French models along with their own musical traditions.

Unit 4: Technical Considerations

Keys of E, C, and A major and C minor are the primary tonalities, with brief episodes of D, G, and E-flat major. Rhythms are straightforward and the meter is primarily 4/4 with a few changes to 2/4 and 3/4. Short and witty solos are written for bassoon, trumpet, and piano. There is an extended clarinet solo which will require a strong soloist.

Unit 5: Stylistic Considerations

Noisy Wheels of Joy begins with a brief introduction which is slow and serious in character. The indicated tempo is quarter note = 60. This introduction also includes tempo gradations of *accelerando, con moto*, and *ritardando*. The mood quickly changes to the primary adventure and *buffo* character, with short solos from bassoon and clarinet. The body of the work then commences with a metronome marking of quarter note = 165. This work requires great precision as ostinato figures are used throughout. There are also wonderful moments of heavy, light, and lyrical character.

Unit 6: Musical Elements

Light in character, several solos are presented in clarinet, bassoon, and piano. Wonderful colors are explored with the effective use of English horn, soprano saxophone, harp, and celeste. Special effects are employed which enhance the overall impression of the work, such as flutter-tonguing, stopped horn, and glissandi. Whitacre's composition offers excellent balance of thin and tutti scoring.

MELODY:
All melodies in this work are diatonic. Familiarity with the scales of C, E-flat, G, D, and E major and G minor is highly recommended. Daily studies of these scales will create a more accurate execution of the melodic material. Exercises developed using the chromatic scale will also be of assistance at the conclusion of the piece.

HARMONY:
The potential of beautiful sonority is presented at the beginning and in mm. 49 and 104. Develop exercises focusing on the interval of a perfect fifth and major and minor triads. Sharing general knowledge of just intonation with the ensemble will be extremely helpful in tuning major and minor thirds.

RHYTHM:
Precision is of utmost importance while performing this work. Underlying rhythms are often present and will be a challenge to the performers. Split the ensemble in half, with one half playing eighth notes of a specific key. While this group keeps a steady pulse, have the other half of the ensemble perform different scale patterns. This will be especially helpful without a conductor or by having students close their eyes.

TIMBRE:
Because of the staccato nature of much of the harmony, this piece may become extremely bright and harsh. While the composer desires portions of this piece to be bright, other areas will need to be balanced for appropriate sonority. Take sections with repeated eighth notes, slow the tempo, and have the eighth notes performed in sustained style to allow the ensemble to internalize the tonality. Throughout the entire rehearsal process continue to promote a relaxed and open tone quality, as tension may increase due to challenging ranges and enduring articulation.

Unit 7: Form and Structure

SECTION	MEASURE	TONALITY
Introduction	1–16	E major
A	17–54	C major
B	55–103	C minor
A	105–118	E-flat major

Unit 8: Suggested Listening

Bizet, Georges. *Carmen.*
Mozart, Wolfgang Amadeus:
    Don Giovanni
    The Marriage of Figaro
Rossini, Gioacchino:
    The Barber of Seville
    William Tell
Strauss II, Johann. *Die Fledermaus.*
von Suppe, Franz:
    Light Cavalry
    Poet and Peasant

Whitacre, Eric:
  Cloudburst
  Equus
  Lux Aurumque
  October
  Paradise Lost
  Sleep

Unit 9: Additional References and Resources

Grout, Donald J. *A Short History of Opera*. Third edition. New York: Columbia University Press, 1988.

Grout, Donald J. and Claude V. Palisca. *A History of Western Music*. Fifth edition. New York: W. W. Norton, 1996.

Kreines, Joseph. *Music for Concert Band*. Tampa, FL: Florida Music Service, 1989.

Randel, Don Michael. *The New Harvard Dictionary of Music*. Fourth Edition. Cambridge, MA: Belknap Press, 2003.

Whitacre, Eric. *Noisy Wheels of Joy* Score. Milwaukee, WI: Hal Leonard Corporation, 2001.

Contributed by:

Gregg Gausline
Associate Director of Bands
The University of Georgia
Athens, Georgia

Teacher Resource Guide

Raag Mala

Michael Colgrass
(b. 1932)

Unit 1: Composer

Michael Colgrass is arguably one of the most important figures in modern American music. His career as a composer spans more than fifty years, during which he has distinguished himself with a singular musical voice. His awards include First Prize in the Barlow and Sudler International Wind Ensemble Competitions, an Emmy Award for the PBS documentary *Soundings: The Music of Michael Colgrass*, and the 1978 Pulitzer Prize in Music for his ground-breaking work *Déjà Vu*.

In addition to composing, Colgrass is a published author and a certified trainer of neuro-linguistic programming. Recently he has focused much of his energy on the training of young musicians, this commitment being evidenced in his output of five works for young band since 2000.

Colgrass was born on April 22, 1932 in Chicago, Illinois and grew up in Brookfield, a suburb located sixteen miles to its southwest. The composer's proximity to a major metropolitan area afforded him many professional opportunities during his formative years.

> I formed and ran my own band during elementary school, playing for school and professional events and dances. In high school I had a jazz band and played all kinds of gigs. I also went into Chicago and sat in with good jazz musicians.[1]

Following high school, Colgrass enrolled at the University of Illinois to pursue a percussion performance degree under Paul Price. Though enormously talented, he was, by his own admission, not a diligent student, his studies hindered by constant evening work in jazz bands.

> I was not very good at [theory] because I hated to do it, and I didn't do it! …I remember one time a theory teacher said "Michael, I'm going to give you a D because I think you really tried." Fact is, I hadn't tried![2]

Colgrass's introduction to composing came quite unexpectedly.

> [Paul] Price invited me to a percussion ensemble concert in last ditch attempt to get me to be a serious classical music student. After the concert he asked me what I thought of it. I arrogantly told him I admired the students' playing but that I thought the music was "terrible." These were works by Varese, Harrison, Cage, Cowell… He took a long look at me and said quietly, "If you don't like what you heard, why don't you try your hand at it." I was thunderstruck by his suggestion because I thought you had to be dead to write music. He showed me some scores and I immediately dived into my first piece, "Three Brothers" for nine percussionists…I've been writing ever since.[3]

Colgrass completed his coursework at the University of Illinois in 1954. Following a two-year stint as timpanist in the Seventh Army Symphony Orchestra in Stuttgart, Germany, he moved to New York City, where he worked as a freelance musician and composer. In 1966 he married Ulla Damgaard Rasmussen, whom he had met in Denmark. Following the birth of their son Neal in 1970, they moved to Toronto where they remain.

Colgrass has written twelve works for wind band. His "adult" pieces are *Winds of Nagual* (1985), the wind band arrangement of *Déjà Vu* (1987), *Arctic Dreams* (1991), *Urban Requiem* (1995), *Dream Dancer* (2001), *Bali* (2005), and *Raag Mala* (2006). In addition he has written five works for "young" wind band. These include *Old Churches* (2000), *Apache Lullaby* (2003), *The Beethoven Machine* (2003), *Got to Make Noise* (2003), and *Mysterious Village* (2007).

Unit 2: Composition

Raag Mala was commissioned by James Smart and the Southern Utah University Wind Symphony. Begun in late 2004 and finished early in 2005, it was given its premiere on April 19, 2006 by the commissioning ensemble and conductor. Written in a single continuous movement, the 333-measure work is approximately thirteen minutes in length.

Colgrass subtitled the piece "Music of India through Western ears," explaining,

I don't attempt to replicate Indian music in this piece... Nor do I intend to create a hybrid of East-West musical styles... Instead my aim is to filter Indian music through my Western musical experience and cast it in a new way.[4]

Regarding the genesis of the work, the composer writes,

Raag Mala was inspired by the many concerts of Indian classical music I have heard over the years. A music society called "Raag-Mala"–meaning a garland of ragas—brings the best classical musicians and singers to Toronto every year. I have often left these concerts singing the ragas I had heard and embellishing on them from my own imagination. *Raag Mala* is the result of those musings.[5]

The instrumentation calls for forty-three players: six flutes (two double on piccolo), two oboes, six clarinets, bass clarinet, E-flat contra-alto clarinet, two bassoons, alto, tenor, and baritone saxophones, six trumpets, four horns, three trombones, one euphonium, one tuba, synthesizer, piano, and five percussionists. Each part is vitally important and there are no cues to be found in the music. While the score does call for one player per part, doubling of the euphonium and tuba parts is acceptable as long as appropriate balance is maintained.[6]

Unit 3: Historical Perspective

Indian classical music, like Western music, is based on a twelve-note scale. The series of five or more notes on which a melody is founded is called a *raga*. The *raga* determines the manner in which the melody is built and specifies the ascending and descending movement of the scale. In describing *ragas*, scholar Piero Scaruffi, in an online article titled "Indian Classical Music," states,

The goal of the *raga* is to create a trancey state, to broadcast a mood of ecstasy. The main difference with western classical music is that the Indian *ragas* are not "composed" by a composer, but were created via a lengthy evolutionary process over the centuries... Many *ragas* share the same scale, and many *ragas* share the same melodic theme. There are thousands of *ragas*, but six are considered fundamental.[7]

Rhythmic structure in the music is determined by patterns called *talas*. These can be thought of as similar to meter in Western music.

There exist two distinct styles of Indian classical music: *Hindustanic* music, found in northern India and its surrounding regions, and *Carnatic* music, from the south. According to one source,

The *Hindustani* style developed after India was invaded by the Moguls in the thirteenth century… [Meanwhile] the indigenous music of India continued uninterrupted and became the *Carnatic* style, dominant in the areas never conquered by the Moguls.[8]

The influence of Indian classical music on Western music can be seen most readily in jazz. Such diverse artists as John Coltrane, Chick Corea, and George Brooks have incorporated, to a greater or lesser degree, elements of Indian music in their own compositions. The influence in Western classical music has been much less pronounced, though it is interesting to note that Colgrass's penultimate work for wind band, *Bali*, draws its musical inspiration directly from the Hindu island of the same name.

Unit 4: Technical Considerations

The first two-thirds of *Raag Mala* consists of extended solos for flute 1, clarinet, alto saxophone, and trombone. While the range of each part is modest, the soloists are asked to play with great rhythmic freedom and must be able to shade pitches in quarter- and eighth-step intervals. Careful and frequent listening to authentic Indian classical music will assist soloists in performing in the appropriate style.[9] Also, soloists may wish to practice by singing their part, moving to the instrument only after they feel comfortable singing in the proper style, with pitch shadings.

The ensemble parts do present some challenges, but do not approach the difficulty of the four solo parts. In the program notes that accompany the score, Colgrass states that the ensemble parts were intended for a Grade 4 ensemble.

Trumpet 1, horn, and all three trombones must be able to flutter-tongue very well. Flutes, clarinets, and trumpets are required to execute difficult repeated tremolos. At one point, horns must play tightly stacked non-diatonic chords while stopped.

The music is rhythmically complex. Frequently beats are subdivided into dissimilar pulse groupings. All musicians must be able to accurately feel and execute quintuplets, as this rhythm appears not only in individual parts, but also in tutti passages.

Given the complexity of the music, the written ranges are quite modest. Aside from a *pianissimo* D-sharp 6 in trumpet 2 and a *pianissimo* tremolo between D-sharp 6 and C6 in trumpet 1, none of the wind parts should be out of the range of the advanced high school musician.

The piece requires five percussionists, but the parts are written in score form without specifying part assignments. The following assignments are suggested:

Player 1   glockenspiel, bongos, and bass drum (m. 93 only)
Player 2   crash cymbals, chimes, tenor drum, field drum,
           and vibraphone (except mm. 221–226)
Player 3   crotales, marimba, and three cymbals
Player 4   timpani and bass drum (except m. 93)
Player 5   tam tam, timbales, and vibraphone (mm. 221–226 only)

Unit 5: Stylistic Considerations

Rhythm and pulse play a very important role in *Raag Mala*. Throughout the piece, Colgrass mimics Indian music by creating rhythmic and metric freedom. This is evidenced not only by the thirty-one written tempo adjustments in the score and frequent meter changes, but also by the composer's indication in the program notes that soloists are to play with great freedom. Colgrass asks that soloists use the printed rhythms, and even to some degree the pitches, only as a guide, stating,

> East Indian music is free in tempo. It is often sung and the singer takes many liberties with the pulse, especially when embellishing a pitch. Also, they will slide very subtly with their voice, going into and out of a pitch an eighth-tone or quarter-tone flat or sharp for expressiveness. I encourage this kind of playing in these solo parts.[10]

Articulations in the ensemble parts are meticulously marked. Frequently, slurred phrases end with an accent. These should be performed with breath and not tongue. Also, brass must be able to legato-tongue in the last third of the piece.

The dynamic range of the music is quite wide, with the softest marking **ppp** and the loudest **fff**. Rapid dynamic changes occur throughout the score (see figures 1–2).

FIGURE 1. M. 131, bassoon 1

FIGURE 2. Mm. 102–104, trombones

Unit 6: Musical Elements

MELODY:

Colgrass uses only original melodies in *Raag Mala*, though he acknowledges the influence of Indian music on these ideas. His use of the natural and raised fourth, sixth, and seventh scale degrees give the melodies their characteristic Indian sound. Three motives, drawn from the clarinet, flute, and trombone solos, form the melodic material for the piece (see figures 3–5).

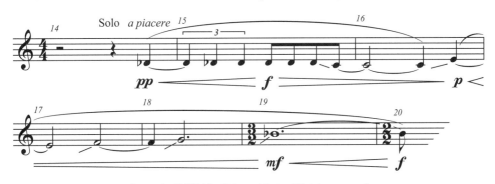

FIGURE 3. Mm. 14–20, melodic motive 1, clarinet 1
(notated in concert pitch)

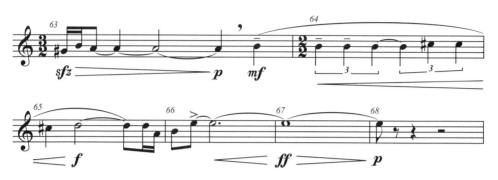

FIGURE 4. Mm. 63–68, melodic motive 2, flute 1

FIGURE 5. Mm. 144–145, melodic motive 3, trombone 1

HARMONY:

The harmonic language of *Raag Mala* ranges from contemporary and highly dissonant to traditional. Extended harmonies, particularly the major seventh chord, appear frequently. Traditional major and minor tonality is often obscured by the alternation or simultaneous use of both the lowered and natural third scale degree. By contrast, several sections use only an open fifth drone as accompaniment.

At times, the tonality shifts unexpectedly from ambiguous to clear. As seen in figure 6, mallet percussion and flutes play gestures with no real harmonic centering. This is followed by three successive open fifths rooted on C, A-flat, and E. As these opening gestures subside, the synthesizer enters with arpeggios on the pitches C and G, tonicizing C clearly.

RHYTHM:

Rhythmic motion in *Raag Mala* encompasses a wide range. Sections of relative rhythmic stasis are contrasted with moments of frenetic motion. Rhythmic activity tends to intensify at moments of climax or during responses in call-and-response sections. For musical impact, Colgrass frequently uses tutti unison rhythms to create tremendous blocks of sound. Also, the quarter-note triplet rhythm is pervasive throughout the entire work.

Perhaps the most salient rhythmic feature of *Raag Mala* is the composer's use of overlapping musical gestures with dissimilar rhythms. One such example is given in figure 7.

FIGURE 6. Mm. 1–6, score in C

FIGURE 7. M. 86, mallet percussion

TIMBRE:

Colgrass possesses a unique ability to create fresh and interesting colors with wind band. It is this skill that, to a large extent, makes *Raag Mala* such a compelling composition. Colgrass accomplishes this in several ways. First and perhaps most strikingly is the orchestrational restraint he shows. With the full forces of the modern wind band available, he frequently uses only a few instruments at a time, giving the music an intimate, chamber-like texture. The first wind tutti occurs at m. 255, nearly ten minutes into the work. At no time do all winds and percussion play simultaneously. As is typical with many of his works for wind band, Colgrass uses double reeds very sparingly. Oboe 2 plays in only seventeen of the 333 measures, and bassoon 2 plays only slightly more often.

Secondly, in a style almost reminiscent of Persichetti, Colgrass frequently makes use of shifting choirs of sounds. One such example can be found in mm. 208–221, where the instrumentation in the wind parts is as follows:

Measure(s)	Instrumentation
208–210	Brass
211	Upper woodwinds
212–214	Brass
215	Upper woodwinds
216–217	Brass
218–219/2	Low reeds
219/3–220	Brass
221	Upper woodwinds

Third, Colgrass's inclusion of a synthesizer part with organ setting creates a mysterious tapestry on which much of the music is painted. The intentional scoring of this part for synthesizer rather than organ underscores the composer's wish that the instrument never overpower the ensemble.

Finally, Colgrass draws attention to color by overlapping instruments with dissimilar rhythms and melodic material (see figure 8). By doing so, he is able to blur the rhythmic, melodic, and harmonic landscape, drawing the listener's ear instead to tone color.

FIGURE 8. mm. 239–242, score in C

One of the most unique timbral sections of the work occurs in mm. 301–319 (see figure 9). Scored for flutes, clarinets, trumpets, and alto saxophone, nine of these instruments play a nineteen-measure melody in parallel motion. The remaining woodwinds each ornament one of the melodic lines with tremolos. The resulting sound may be one of the most unique non-aleatoric colors ever created with wind instruments.

FIGURE 9. Mm. 301–306, flutes only

Unit 7: Form and Structure

SECTION	MEASURE	EVENT AND SCORING
Section 1		
Introduction	1–14	Opens with pointillistic gestures in mallet percussion and flutes; after a series of three open fifths rooted on C, A-flat, and E respectively, synthesizer enters, outlining perfect and augmented fifths rooted on C; in m. 8 a melodic gesture appears in piano and brass, evolving slowly over six /measures
Clarinet solo/ melodic motive 1	15–62	C major; long, unevenly-phrased clarinet melody, first six measures of which form melodic motive 1; modest range that stays mostly on the staff; points of rest in the melody are filled with responses by the ensemble

SECTION	MEASURE	EVENT AND SCORING
Flute solo/ melodic motive 2	63–101	A major; section begins with an open fifth rooted on A; drone in synthesizer moves to vibraphone; four measures of the solo form melodic motive 2; compared to clarinet solo there is more rhythmic motion in both solo and accompaniment parts with faster-moving call-and-response; intensity created in last four bars when all six flutes play fast-moving passages
Transition to alto saxophone solo	102–104	Three-bar transition in brass; first appearance of melodic motive 3; rapid dynamic changes
Alto saxophone solo	105–143	A major continues; accompaniment is more melodic than before; intensity is created through three tempo increases toward end of solo
Trombone solo/ melodic motive 3	144–203	E major; first two measures form melodic motive 3; solo is very free rhythmically, with the most tempo changes of any of the solos; in last ten measures, soloist is joined by two other trombones, much of it flutter-tongued, to create a very thick tapestry
Section 2 Transition to first tutti	204–207	G major; use of melodic motive 3
First tutti	208–230	G major; melodic material derived from melodic motive 2; calls primarily in brass, responses in woodwinds and percussion; section closes with a statement of melodic motive 3
Fantasia	231–243	D major; short fragments that increasingly overlap; accompaniment in synthesizer, cymbals, and timpani
Second tutti	244–254	Fast-moving wind clusters answered by short percussion bursts
Chorale	255–270	C major; tutti winds for first time; theme based on melodic motive 1

SECTION	MEASURE	EVENT AND SCORING
Piano interlude	271–300	F minor; based on melodic motive 2 but with lowered third; piano takes on role of melody and drone accompaniment; four short statements interspersed with ensemble interjections
Tremolo section	301–319	Based on melodic motive 2; scored for flutes, clarinets, alto saxophone, and trumpets, half playing melody, half ornamenting with tremolos; *pp* dynamic throughout
Closing	320–333	F major; melodic motive 3 in vibraphone with crotales and chimes accompanying; recollection of pointillistic trumpets from the beginning; piece closes mysteriously on Fm$^{\#5,\,maj7}$ chord

Unit 8: Suggested Listening

Colgrass, Michael:

  Bali. Teaching Music through Performance in Band, Volume 6, Grade 4. The University of North Texas Wind Symphony. Eugene Migliaro Corporon, conductor. GIA Publications, CD-684. 2007.

  Raag Mala. The Georgia State University Symphonic Wind Ensemble. Robert J. Ambrose, conductor. 2007. Available from the author or the composer.

Messaien, Olivier. *Oiseaux Exotiques*.

Various artists. www.musicindiaonline.com

Unit 9: Additional References and Resources

Ambrose, Robert Joseph. Email correspondences with Michael Colgrass. May 15, 2008.

Colgrass, Michael. *Raag Mala*. New York: Colgrass Music, 2006.

Mathes, James. "Analysis: *Winds of Nagual* by Michael Colgrass." Journal of Band Research 23, no. 1 (Fall, 1987).

Neal, Alicia. "Traveling of the Mind: An Interview with Michael Colgrass and an Analysis of *Raag Mala*." DM diss., Northwestern University, 2007.

Contributed by:

Robert J. Ambrose
Director of Wind Studies and Ensembles
Associate Director, School of Music
Georgia State University
Atlanta, Georgia

1 Michael Colgrass, email to the author, May 15, 2008.
2 Alicia Neal, "Traveling of the Mind: An Interview with Michael Colgrass and an Analysis of *Raag Mala* (DM diss., Northwestern University, 2007), Appendix B, 39.
3 Michael Colgrass, "Michael Colgrass Online," http://michaelcolgrass.com
4 Michael Colgrass, *Raag Mala* (New York: Colgrass Music, 2006), i.
5 Ibid.
6 During the recording session for *Raag Mala* by the Georgia State University Symphonic Wind Ensemble, Colgrass, who was present, approved of the ensemble's use of doubled euphonium and tuba.
7 Piero Scaruffi, "Indian Classical Music," http://www.scaruffi.com/history/indian.html
8 Cosmopolis online, "Indian Classical Music," http://www.cosmopolis.ch/english/music/64/indian_classical_music.htm
9 The website www.musicindiaonline.com is an extraordinary resource for recordings of Indian music, all of which can be streamed.
10 Colgrass, *Raag Mala*, ii.

Teacher Resource Guide

Rejouissance
Fantasia on Ein' feste Burg

James Curnow
(b. 1943)

Unit 1: Composer

James Curnow was born in Port Huron, Michigan in 1943 and raised in Royal Oak, Michigan. He lives in Nicholasville, Kentucky where he is president, composer, and educational consultant for Curnow Music Press, Inc. of Lexington, Kentucky. He also serves as composer-in-residence on the faculty of Asbury College in Wilmore, Kentucky, and as editor of all music publications for The Salvation Army in Atlanta, Georgia.

Curnow received his formal training at Wayne State University in Detroit, Michigan and at Michigan State University, where he was a euphonium student of Leonard Falcone and a conducting student of Harry Begian. He studied composition and arranging with F. Maxwell Wood, James Gibb, Jere Hutchinson, and Irwin Fischer.

James Curnow has taught instrumental music in the public schools and at the college and university levels. He is a member of several professional organizations, including the American Bandmasters Association, College Band Directors National Association, World Association of Symphonic Bands and Wind Ensembles, and the American Society of Composers, Authors and Publishers (ASCAP). In 1980 he received the National Band Association's Citation of Excellence. He was chosen Composer of the Year in 1997 by the Kentucky Music Teachers Association and the National Music Teachers Association. He has been the recipient of annual ASCAP standard awards since 1979.

As a conductor, composer, and clinician, Curnow has traveled throughout the United States, Canada, Australia, Japan, and Europe, where his music has received wide acclaim. He has won several awards for band compositions, including the ASBDA/Volkwein Composition Award in 1977 (for *Symphonic Triptych*) and 1979 (for *Collage for Band*), the ABA/Ostwald Award in 1980 (for *Mutanza*) and 1984 (for *Symphonic Variants for Euphonium and Band*), the 1985 Sixth International Competition of Original Compositions for Band (for *Australian Variants Suite*), and the 1994 Coup de Vents Composition Competition of Le Havre, France (for *Lochinvar*).

Curnow has been commissioned to write over 200 works for concert band, brass band, orchestra, choir, and various vocal and instrumental ensembles. His published works now number well over 400. His most recent commissions include the Tokyo Symphony Orchestra, the U. S. Army Band, the Atlanta Committee for the Olympic Games, 1996, and the Kentucky Music Teachers Association/National Music Teachers Association in 1997.

Unit 2: Composition

Rejouissance was commissioned by the St. Joseph, Michigan Municipal Band in 1987. It is written "in honor of, and lovingly dedicated to John E. N. Howard to celebrate forty years as Conductor, 1948–1987."

The work is based on the Martin Luther chorale, "Ein' feste Burg" (A Mighty Fortress Is Our God). The character of the composition is intended to capture the essence of the French word "rejouissance," meaning enjoyment or to make happy. Curnow relays in the score's notes to the director that "…in music of the seventeenth and eighteenth centuries, the term was used to denote a short composition of a lively or playful nature, which brings enjoyment to the listener."

Unit 3: Historical Perspective

"Ein' feste Burg" was composed by Martin Luther in 1529 and inspired by Psalm 46. The first of the psalm's eleven verses are:

1. God is our refuge and strength, an ever-present help in trouble.
2. Therefore we will not fear, though the earth give way and the mountains fall into the heart of the sea,
3. though its waters roar and foam and the mountains quake with their surging.

It has become one of the most recognized of Martin Luther's chorales, and has been used as a source for compositions of many composers, beginning with Johann Sebastian Bach. In his corpus of musical compositions, Bach used twenty of Martin Luther's chorales as material. Twice he incorporated "Ein' feste Burg," once in his *Chorale Prelude for Organ* (BWV 720) in 1719, and then in his *Cantata for the Feast of the Reformation* (BWV 80) in 1724. Of Bach's 279 cantatas, BWV 80 is arguably the most famous.

The chorale is also the basis for the final movement of Mendelssohn's *Symphony No. 5* ("Reformation"), as well as Wagner's *Kaisermarsch*. It is heard in Meyerbeer's opera *The Huguenots*, and used as material for concert overtures by Joachim Raff and Otto Nicolai.

Unit 4: Technical Considerations

Rhythmic and tonal demands make this work engaging and rewarding for performers. The mastery of various key centers will be important as the fantasia evolves harmonically. While centered on E-flat, performers will also encounter moments of D-flat, C, G-flat, A-flat, F-flat, and C-flat. Hearing, anticipating, and tuning the changing key centers will be a worthy challenge. There are some double flats to navigate that are easily taught.

Many of the technical demands are scalar. There are brief passages in the woodwinds where focused study of the sixteenth-note patterns will quickly create a strong result.

Range demands are modest; flutes have a brief encounter with B-flat 6, oboe to C5, bassoon to E-flat 4, clarinet to D5, trumpet 1 briefly to C5, trombone 1 briefly to G4, and the remaining instruments within comfortable ranges.

There are a number of brief oboe solos, and one English horn passage. These are cued in saxophone parts.

Percussion parts are engaging. Three written percussion parts employ triangles, suspended cymbal with various effects required, snare drum, crash cymbals, scraped cymbal, tambourine, and mark tree. Two keyboard percussion parts are scored comfortably for two players (though more may be used) and employ bells, vibraphone, xylophone, and chimes. Specific instructions for a variety of mallet choices and vibraphone effects help to enhance the various timbre effects of the fantasia.

Unit 5: Stylistic Considerations

This work requires command of a wide spectrum of stylistic performance. The fantasia incorporates the strength of the chorale, bold fanfares, percussive textures, brilliant flourishes, and intricate contrapuntal moments. Woodwinds have moments of effervescent sixteenth-note passages that set a light texture, then must carry a fully-harmonized melodic passage for woodwind choir. Brasses are required to execute bold melodic statements, pulsating rhythmic passages, and then gently sustain the tonal center beneath delicate woodwind melodies.

Unit 6: Musical Elements

MELODY:

Being a fantasia, the melodic content is comprised of the development of a number of melodic motives. Some are used only once in a particular section of the fantasia; others are used transitionally. Three motives recur during the work, and one (motive A) is the melodic thread that weaves through the piece. The melodic material is generally scalar in character, with intervals of more than a fourth rare.

The motives are based on melodic fragments from the chorale, "Ein' feste Burg." Some have their origin from the final phrase of the chorale, utilizing the descending diatonic passage that begins the phrase.

FIGURE 1. Chorale excerpt 1

Others are based on an ascending interval, which begins the third phrase of the Chorale.

FIGURE 2. Chorale excerpt 2

For this study, eight melodic motives have been identified.

FIGURE 3. Motive A

FIGURE 4. Motive B

575

FIGURE 5. Motive C

FIGURE 6. Motive D

FIGURE 7. Motive E

FIGURE 8. Motive F

FIGURE 9. Motive G

FIGURE 10. Motive H

HARMONY:

The harmonic structure is mostly traditional triadic harmony. There are brief moments of bitonal harmony, such as in m. 67, where B-flat minor is super-imposed over C-flat. Pedal points are used at various times in the fantasia to

keep the tonality grounded underneath modulatory passages (mm. 29–34 and 41–58).

RHYTHM:
Standard time signatures of 4/4, 3/4, and 2/4 are used rather seamlessly to create subtle shifts in rhythmic feel. Rhythmic patterns in the work are engaging to the listener. Once performers master the techniques of the basic eighth-and-sixteenth-note patterns found at mm. 25 and 82 and the eighth-note triplet patterns found at m. 90, the piece will become quite secure. Basic dotted rhythm figures and syncopations are found throughout.

TIMBRE:
The fantasia nature of the work demands creating a wide palette of color. There are brilliant woodwind flourishes in sections 1, 5, and 6 that set a background for bold brass melodies. There are moments of pulsating rhythmic figures for low brass in section 2, and upper woodwinds in section 4. Section 3 features fluid contrapuntal writing that engages the full ensemble. Moments abound throughout the work for brief but intricate solo work. Perhaps the highlight of the piece is the setting of the chorale, which begins with solo trumpet, then unison brass melody against fluid woodwind passages, followed by full brass choir contrasted with woodwind choir, and then building to a peak incorporating the full ensemble. Balancing the many textures of the fantasia will result in a rewarding performance.

Unit 7: Form and Structure

As noted in the score, this composition is written as a fantasia, "a composition in which 'free flight of fancy' prevails over contemporary conventions of form or style." Though it is through-composed, there are three identifiable sections to the fantasia which lead to the full statement of chorale, followed by a brief closing section which returns the opening material.

SECTION	MEASURE	EVENT AND SCORING
1a	1–24	*Allegro giocoso*; E-flat; introductory material by full ensemble; initial presentation of motives A and B in various brass and woodwind combinations
2a	25–42	D-flat and B-flat major and B-flat minor; sustained chords in lower winds underneath motive C presented in solo voices by oboe and flute, then harmonized in single reeds, flutes, and trumpets; motive D then presented in solo horn, euphonium, and tuba

SECTION	MEASURE	EVENT AND SCORING
2b	43–57	A-flat; foreshadowing of chorale in upper woodwinds, answered by motive E in solo horn and trumpet; transitional chorale phrase to F-flat stated in brass, answered by solo oboe and flute
2c	58–67	*Meno mosso* (quarter note = 76); transitional section incorporating a descending diatonic passage underneath chorale fragments stated by horns and saxes; motive E stated in solo flute, then in augmentation, first by trumpets, then clarinets and flutes; arrives at a fermata on a B-flat minor chord in upper woodwinds over C-flat chord in remaining ensemble
3a	68–74	*Andante moderato e espressivo* (quarter note = 72); E-flat; a contrasting slow section that returns to E-flat, characterized by warm, sustained chords in the low voices, pulsating eighth-note figures in clarinets and horns, with the introduction of motive G in solo English horn (cued in alto saxophone) and answered by solo clarinet
3b	75–81	*Poco agitato;* E-flat; beginning of a transitional section that will again move to C-flat through the sustained low-voice chords; pulsating eighth-note passages become diatonic and complement the addition of motive H sounded in trumpets, alto saxophones, clarinets, oboes, and flutes; an accelerando and syncopated rhythms transition to the next section of the fantasia
4a	82–94	*Tempo primo* (quarter note = 132); E-flat; return to tempo is signaled by a percussive sixteenth-and-eighth-note pattern in keyboard percussion, flutes, oboes, and clarinets; this texture continues as motive B returns at m. 84, first in the brass, then in woodwinds; the percussive pattern gives way to an arpeggiated triplet pattern at m. 92 as trumpets and horns signal a return of motive A

SECTION	MEASURE	EVENT AND SCORING
4b	95–106	C minor; ascending sixteenth-note scale flourishes in double reeds and clarinet 1 and percussive eighth notes toning C's in flutes, clarinets, and keyboard percussion set a background texture for a new melodic episode, motive H, stated first by trumpet 1, then harmonized to the third in trumpet 2, and then in three-part tertian harmony in trumpet 3; motive H cadences to a sustained C minor chord at m. 103, where motive E returns, stated first in lower reeds and euphonium, then in horns and alto saxophone, then in trumpets
4c	107–118	A return of the percussive sixteenth-and-eighth-note pattern found at m. 82, now heard in upper woodwinds and trumpets, signals the beginning of this transitional section; a strong and simple melodic motive heard in low brass, horns, saxophones, and low reeds modulates the section to B-flat at m. 110; a sounding of motive A at m. 113 in low brass and low woodwinds leads to a descending scalar passage heard first in low voices, then trumpets, horns, and saxophones, then in upper woodwinds; this leads to a full statement of the chorale, "Ein' feste Burg."
5 (chorale)	119–143	*Andante moderato e maestoso* (quarter note = 76); B-flat; a simple flowing quarter-note harmony is set in the single reeds, and the first phrase of the chorale is stated by solo trumpet at m. 122; a brief fanfare in trombones and trumpets leads to the second phrase of the chorale, stated in unison trumpets and trombones, now heard on top of flowing eighth-note figures in upper woodwinds; the third phrase of the chorale is carried by horns and trombone 1 beginning at m. 132, embellished by a brief trumpet fanfare figure and arpeggiated flourishes in flute, oboe, clarinet, and alto saxophone; the final phrase of the chorale

| 6 | 144–154 | is presented, first in a soft woodwind choir, then answered slightly stronger by brass choir, and then gloriously finished with full ensemble while horns, euphonium, tenor sax, and alto clarinet support with an ascending eighth-note scalar passage; the section ends with a dramatic caesura |
| | | *Tempo primo* (quarter note = 126–132); B-flat and E-flat; this closing section is comprised of two parts: the first is a return of the original setting of the opening material, with the same sixteenth-note flourish figure in woodwinds and a final statement of motive A made by trumpets; this statement modulates in m. 149 to a return to E-flat in m. 150 (*Grandioso*), where a final bold sounding of the final phrase of "Ein' feste Burg" is heard in the brass before the dramatic ending cadence from the full ensemble |

Unit 8: Suggested Listening

Bach, Johann Sebastian:

> *Cantata for the Feast of the Reformation*, BWV 80. *J. S. Bach: Cantatas, Volume 22*. Amsterdam Baroque Orchestra and Choir. Ton Koopman, conductor. Challenge Classics. B000GYI59I.

> *Chorale Prelude on "Ein' feste Burg" for Organ*, BWV 720. *Bach Organ Works, Volume 16*. Gerhard Weinberger, Organ. CPO Label CPO777135.

> Transcribed by Leopold Stokowski. *Chorale "Ein' feste Burg ist unser Gott,"* movement 8, BWV 80. *Bach-Stokowski*. Leopold Stokowski Orchestra. Leopold Stokowski, conductor. EMI. EMI663852.

Curnow, James. *Rejouissance*. Concordia University Wind Symphony. Richard Fischer, conductor. Mark Masters 3077-MCD.

Luther, Martin. *Musik der Reformation: Ein' feste Burg is unser Gott*. Dresden Kreuzchor, Capella Fidicinia Leipzig. Hans Gruss and Ulrich Shicha, conductors. Berlin Classics B0000035ST.

Mendelssohn, Felix Bartoldy. *Symphony No. 5 in D Major*, Op. 107. *Mendelssohn Symphony No. 4 and 5*. John Gardiner, conductor. Vienna Philharmonic Orchestra. Deutsche Grammophone DGG2894591562.

Nicolai, Otto. *Sacred Festival Overture: "Ein' feste Burg ist unser Gott."* Cologne Rundfunkorchester. Michail Jurowski, conductor. Cappricio.

Raff, Joachim. *Overture: "Ein' feste Burg ist unser Gott."* Slovak State Philharmonic Orchestra. Urs Schneider, conductor. Marco Polo K233455.

Wagner, Richard. *Kaisermarsch, WWV 104. Muzik in Luzern.* Luzern Symphonic Wind Band. Franz Schaffner, conductor. Gall GLL855.

Unit 9: Additional References and Resources

Durr, Alfred and Richard D. P. Jones. *The Cantatas of J. S. Bach: With Their Librettos in English-German Parallel Text.* New York: Oxford University Press, 2005.

Freytag, Gustav and Henry E. Heinemann. *Martin Luther.* Whitefish, MT: Kessinger Publishing Company 2007.

Sadie, Stanley, ed. John Tyrell, exec ed. *The New Grove Dictionary of Music and Musicians.* Second ed. London: MacMillan, 2001. 309–387.

Websites:

James Curnow. http://curnowmusicpress.com

J. S. Bach. http://jsbach.org

_____. http://www.classicalarchives.com/bach.html

University of Maryland libraries.

http://www.lib.umd.edu/PAL/SCPA/ABA/Ostwald/curnow.html

Contributed by:

Paul G. Davis
Assistant Professor of Music
Conductor of Wind Ensembles
Kennesaw State University
Kennesaw, Georgia

Teacher Resource Guide

Rikudim
Four Israeli Dances for Band

Jan Van der Roost
(b. 1956)

Unit 1: Composer

Jan Van der Roost was born in Duffel, Belgium, on March 1, 1956. He studied trombone, music history, and music education at the Lemmensinstituut in Leuven (Lovain). Van der Roost went on to study and qualify in conducting and composition at the Royal Conservatory of Ghent and Antwerp in 1979. He currently teaches composition at the Lemmensinstituut in Leuven (Belgium), is special guest professor at the Shobi Institute of Music in Tokyo, guest professor at the Nagoya University of Art (Japan), and visiting professor at Senzoku Gakuen in Kawasaki (Japan).

Van der Roost is a versatile and accomplished composer who has written over fifty works for wind, brass, and fanfare band. He has also written works for chamber orchestra, symphony orchestra, choir, and chamber ensembles. Van der Roost is in demand as an adjudicator, lecturer, clinician, and guest conductor. His musical activities have brought him to more than thirty-five different countries on four continents. Jan Van der Roost's international following is reflected in the origins of his commissions, coming from such countries as Belgium, Holland, ?Switzerland, Italy, the US, Japan, Spain, France, Singapore, Austria, Canada, Norway, Germany, Finland, Luxembourg, and Hungary.

Unit 2: Composition

Composed in 1986 and inspired by Jewish dances, *Rikudim* is a four-movement suite that is approximately nine minutes in duration. Van der Roost did not draw on authentic folk melodies as source material for *Rikudim*, but rather composed the piece in the style of Israeli folk dances. These four idiomatic movements capture the both melancholy and optimistically festive characteristics of Jewish dance music.

Unit 3: Historical Perspective

Rikudim draws it's title from the Hebrew word *rikud*, which means "dance." This root is coupled with the plural ending "-im" to translate the title to "dances." Originally, Israeli folk dances were introduced as way to create a new culture in an old-new land. This was achieved by combining elements from other dance cultures with the music and themes of modern Israel. Most of these dances were created as a way of celebrating the spirit of the new country.

Some have drawn comparisons of Israeli folk dancing to American country-western line dancing, as they have both a fixed and repeating choreography or set of steps that go with a specific piece of music. The origin of the movements themselves is quite diverse, with roots in the Romanian *horo*, Arab *dabke*, traditional Yemenite life cycle celebrations, and the dancing and klezmer music of Eastern European Jews.

Unit 4: Technical Considerations

Rikudim is a technically-challenging piece suited best for a secure and proficient high-school-level ensemble. In general, the piece is very repetitive in nature and contains both *da capo al fine* and *da capo al coda* directions. Van der Roost layers many of these sections "1st time only" or "2nd time only" to give each section a sense of melodic growth. Students must be skilled in correctly following the road map of each movement, especially when abrupt tempo changes occur.

Reflecting the dance nature of the title, the tempos in *Rikudim* are usually fast, ranging from quarter note = 76 to eighth note = 184. Further challenging performers are the varied simple and compound meters in each movement: 2/4, 4/8, 5/8, and 7/8. Low woodwind and brass performers must have strong rhythmic consistency in executing the many ostinatos that are the foundation of the dance-like pulse. Individual rhythmic skill is demanding for the melodic lines in the upper woodwinds and brass, with dotted rhythms, grace notes, and asymmetrical phrases throughout the work. Both melodic and accompaniment lines contain many syncopated figures that require a strong sense of group pulse.

Ranges are appropriate for an average high school band and do not extend into extreme levels. There are, however, many large intervallic leaps in the upper woodwinds, bassoons, and euphoniums. Piccolo and flute must have the ability to rapidly double-tongue, as several sections contain sixteenth-note passages that are too fast to single-tongue. Clarinets and alto saxophones perform many of the same technically-challenging lines as well, but with slurred articulation. The English horn, labeled "alto flute" in the score, as well as the E-flat clarinet, are very important in regard to ensemble timbre and orchestration. Cues for English horn are provided in the alto saxophone part, and bassoon is often cued in the tenor saxophone as well. Brass players are often asked to perform with straight mutes, and tambourine is important from a rhythmic and timbre standpoint.

They keys of C major and minor, G minor, and E-flat and B-flat major are employed throughout *Rikudim*. Of these tonal centers, C minor is the most frequently-used key, and is presented in several forms: natural minor, harmonic minor, and double-harmonic minor (harmonic minor with a raised fourth scale degree). Double-harmonic minor is very common in Jewish folk melodies, where the scale pattern is referred to as *Mi Shebarach*. This scale is eastern European in origin, and is heard in gypsy and klezmer music. Another scale pattern of great importance in klezmer music, *Ahava Rabboh*, is employed in movement 2, where the fifth mode of G harmonic minor is used.

Unit 5: Stylistic Considerations

Precise execution of the various indicated tempos in *Rikudim* is essential for the correct dance style to be communicated. Within each movement the piece changes tempos several times; sometimes subtle and predictable, while other times, immediate and spontaneous. The ensemble must be confident and secure to execute seamless transitions and to give the feeling of both melancholy and spur-of-the-moment celebration.

During slower passages, bass lines are articulated in a tenuto manner and melodic lines are played full value. This is especially true for longer note values. As the tempo accelerates it is imperative that articulation evolves to a light and separated style. Contrast must be exaggerated within individual parts that contain staccato, marcato, and accented articulations. This holds true when different instruments have varied articulations simultaneously, resulting in the communication of both song and dance stylistic layers.

In order to achieve the correct ensemble timbre, it is especially important that upper woodwinds, upper brass, and percussion parts are prominent. These instruments frequently have the melodic material, and are chief in expressing the various moods (sweetness, pain, folly). Furthermore, English horn and E-flat clarinet, central to authentic sound and style, should be prominent and balanced appropriately.

Unit 6: Musical Elements

MELODY:

Understanding the various keys and modes used in Jewish folk music are crucial in performing the melodies of *Rikudim*. In particular, it is imperative that students understand the Mi Shebarach and Ahava Rabboh modes. The Mi Shebarach mode of C harmonic minor, with its raised fourth scale degree, shapes melodic material in movements 1 and 4 . In movement 2, melodies are based on the fifth mode of the G harmonic minor, or G Ahava Rabboh. The first, fourth, and fifth modes of the harmonic minor scale evoke the provocative sound of the traditional Jewish klezmer dance music. Rehearsal plans that identify the similarities and differences of each intervallic pattern will help improve melodic facility, expression, and intonation.

HARMONY:

In traditional klezmer music, harmony is especially secondary to melody. Since *klezmorim* (klezmer performers) often had to perform for long events, it was difficult to keep the instruments in tune, especially the many-stringed *cymbalom*. Therefore, the harmony is dominated by simple open fifths and tertian chords. Another fundamental characteristic of traditional Jewish music is the alternation between a minor key and its relative major (and vice-versa). Warm-up instruction focusing on the harmonic relationship between E-flat major and C minor is recommended and would be particularly applicable to movement 3 of *Rikudim*. This would also allow for opportunities to address intonation tendencies within each key, and how they change depending on the mode employed.

RHYTHM:

A secure and consistent pulse is the heart of *Rikudim's* spirited, dance-like feel. Because the tempo changes with such frequency, it is important that there is consistency in instruction to build confidence in performers. Refer frequently to a metronome to check rhythmic integrity.

Rikudim contains down-beatand after-beat relationships similar to a march, yet at a much faster tempo. If performers are aware of listening responsibilities and how parts are rhythmically integrated, there is a much better chance of group tempo remaining reliable and constant. Singing these accompaniment rhythms with and without a metronome is a rehearsal technique that would prove beneficial in this area.

An advantageous follow-up to this could also be applied to mixed-meter sections. In movement 2, 5/8 meter is used, and in movement 3, 7/8 meter. Understanding the eighth-note groupings within each, as well as the relationship between melody and accompaniment, will lead to ensemble rhythmic precision.

TIMBRE:

Special focus on balance will ensure the projection of proper group sound. During the slower and moderate tempo passages, a dark, exotic, and mysterious ensemble timbre should be communicated. The distinct sound of the English horn and bassoon should be prominent. Muted brass is often employed to achieve a similar type of timbre. These performers should be reminded about intonation tendencies that go with muted brass. During the more frequent faster sections, the ensemble should have a light, agile, and excited sound. The balance should emphasize the tonic and dominant scale degrees, while the third scale degree should be secondary and focus on intonation.

Unit 7: Form and Structure

SECTION	MEASURE	EVENT AND SCORING
Movement 1		
Introduction	1–8	*Andante moderato* (quarter note = 76); 2/4; eight-measure repeated phrase with alternation between C major and minor; melody in upper woodwinds
	9–16	Variation of original melody of first four measures; melody in upper woodwinds, muted trumpets, and trombones; continued alteration of C major and minor; repeated eight-bar phrase
	17–26	*Poco meno mosso* (eighth note = 112); scoring thins to highlight melodic content in upper woodwinds; tonal center shifts to C double-harmonic minor or C Mi Shebarach; last two measures repeat
Bridge	27–32	Flute solo; light woodwind scoring continues; lyric articulations; *poco ritardando*; fermata in m. 32 with *Da Capo al Fine* (m. 16)
Movement 2		
	1–10	*Allegretto con eleganza* (quarter note = 168); 5/8 meter; eight-bar repeated phrase; countermelody in upper woodwinds and glockenspiel begins on repeat; C minor alternated with use of C major; fermata in m. 10 to set up new tempo and tonal center

SECTION	MEASURE	EVENT AND SCORING
	11–27	*Allegro con moto* (quarter note = 152); key center changes to C major, with a few inflections of C minor; brass enters with runs in woodwinds; four sub-phrases of four-bar material; fermata in m. 27 (similar to m. 10) to set up return to *Da Capo al Coda*
Coda	28–38	*Poco meno mosso* (quarter note = 112); G Ahava Rabboh mode used in upper woodwind melody; repeated eight-bar phrase; legato melody contrasted by staccato and accented accompaniment in brass; ascending chromatic runs in ending section typical of klezmer music
Movement 3		
	1–9	*Andante con dolcezza* (eighth note = 184); melody in upper woodwinds and trumpets; repeated eight-bar phrase with two four-bar sub-phrases; E-flat major tonal center
	10–19	*Poco con delore*; two five-bar phrases with melody in upper woodwinds; alternation between C minor and E-flat major (characteristic of klezmer music); 5/8; no percussion scoring
Bridge	20–31	Alternating woodwind and brass phrases; shifting tonal centers of G minor that lead back to the original key of E-flat major and original meter of 7/8; *Da Capo al Coda* at m. 31
Coda	32–36	Scoring thins; dynamics are marked *morendo* to final fermata at m. 36; two-bar fragment of melody ends movement
Movement 4 Introduction	1–4	*Con moto e follemento* (quarter note = 138+); return of alternating C major and minor key center; fast trills in woodwinds and marcato accents in accompaniment

SECTION	MEASURE	EVENT AND SCORING
	5–21	Two repeating eight-bar phrases; fast, sixteenth-note passages in woodwinds answered by bold, syncopated rhythms in brass and percussion; C minor and E-flat major key centers intertwine
	22–30	*Poco meno mosso* (quarter note = 108); exotic timbre featured in oboe, English horn, and bassoon solos; C Mi Shebarach mode from movement 1 returns; *D. S. al Coda*
Coda	31–44	*Con fuoco e forza;* **ff** dynamics; fast ascending runs in woodwinds; syncopated and full rhythms in brass and percussion; tonal center returns to beginning key of C minor

Unit 8: Suggested Listening

Van der Roost, Jan:

> *Puszta. Teaching Music through Performancein Band, Volume 4*, Grade 4. The University of North Texas Wind Symphony. Eugene Migliaro Corporon, conductor, GIA Publications CD-603.

> *Rikudim. The Wind Music of Jan Van der Roost, Volume 2*. The Royal Military Band of the Netherlands. DHR 10.005.

Unit 9: Additional References and Resources

Berk, Fred. *100 Israeli Folk Dances: Choreographed in Israel and Available on Records Recorded in America*. New York: Israel Folk Dance Dept. of the American Zionist Youth Foundation, 1978.

Morris, Henry. *Balkan and Israeli Folk Dances*. London: Ardmore & Beechwood, 1966.

Websites:
> http://www.janvanderroost.com
> http://www.israelidance.com/
> http://www.nuc.berkeley.edu/students/scott/musproj/klez.html

Contributed by:

Jesse Leyva
Henderson State University
Arkadelphia, Arkansas

Teacher Resource Guide

Shadow Rituals

Michael Markowski
(b. 1986)

Unit 1: Composer

Michael Markowski was only nineteen years old when he penned his award-winning composition for wind band, titled *Shadow Rituals*. Born in 1986 in Mesa, Arizona, Markowski is currently pursuing a degree in film and media production from Arizona State University. In addition to his studies in music business and law, and recording engineering, Markowski studies music composition with Karl Schindler.

Michael had the opportunity to compose *Malediction* (2004), an orchestral work commissioned by Maestro Robert Moody and the Phoenix Symphony Orchestra, which was premiered in January 2005. In addition to commissions, Michael also has practice in scoring music to independent films and theatre. He has written and filmed several short movie musicals, two of which include *Hobos in Space* and *Conan: The Musical* (http://www.conanmusical.com/). Other works for band include *Turkey in the Straw* (2007), *Ngoma* (2006), *joyRIDE* (2005), and *Blue Ambience* (2003). All are categorized as Grade 4 works with the exception of *joyRIDE*, which is listed as Grade 5. Michael has also composed choral and chamber works, and continues to explore new compositions for wind band. Markowski currently resides in Tempe, Arizona.

Unit 2: Composition

Markowski's *Shadow Rituals*, composed in 2005, was unanimously selected as the winner of Category 2–Young Band of the Frank Ticheli Composition Contest, sponsored by Manhattan Beach Music. *Shadow Rituals* was one of over 100 contest entries that arrived at the judge's panel. It is classified as a Grade 4 work, and the title *Shadow Rituals* is denoted by the composer in the score notes as a "dark and mystical dance—a reflection of something primitive or ancient." The work received its world premiere performance under the baton of Matthew Luttrell with the Arizona State University Wind Symphony. The work continues to be an admired work for programming with select honor bands and high schools across the country.

Shadow Rituals is described by Keith Kinder as "a dazzling display of rhythmic energy, attractive melody and colorful scoring..."[1] Upon a first listen of the work, it is difficult to ignore the pervasive rhythmic drive and energy as a unifying foundational premise. However, on further listening, the melodic ingenuity of such a young composer quickly surfaces. The work essentially employs two themes from beginning to end, along with a brief third theme that is actually constructed of intervals from the first theme. Both primary themes are altered by means of canonic imitation, retrograde, augmentation, and counterpoint. A steady, bright tempo of quarter note = 186 is maintained as a constant from the downbeat to the final note. Contrasts in tempo are not necessary for this composition that showcases its craft with imaginative melodic and rhythmic alterations.

Unit 3: Historical Perspective

Shadow Rituals is dedicated to Frank Ticheli and written specifically for the Frank Ticheli Composition Contest, in which Manhattan Beach Music awarded composer Michael Markowski first place in 2006. In the composer's words from the score: "I can remember sitting in my junior high school band reading through my first Frank Ticheli piece; I remember it because I found his style so unlike the other arrangements and 'standards' that we performed. Now, several years later, I realize the remarkable inspiration Ticheli's music has made on my own writing and growth as a musician." Obviously impacted by the compositions of Frank Ticheli, Markowski was able to weave a fine hybrid of his own original ingenuity with Ticheli's stylistic influence. *Shadow Rituals* received its premiere performance on February 14, 2006 in Tempe, Arizona under the baton of Matthew Luttrell and the players of the Arizona State University Wind Symphony.

Unit 4: Technical Considerations

Rhythmic combinations present challenges both to players and conductor, who must determine appropriate conducting groupings. It is necessary for players to maintain a steady tempo and subdivide with accuracy to perform the many syncopations and shifting meters with clarity.

The range of the work is amenable to each instrument, with the highest note in trumpet notated as concert A (above staff). The clarinet writing is

most active in the chalumeau register and rarely leaves the comfort of the staff until near the end, where a concert E-flat (above staff) is required.

The tonal center is primarily E-flat major, with prominent use of the intervals of minor second, minor third, perfect fifth, minor sixth, and major seventh. In m. 138 clarinets and saxophones are required to scoop and flutes are required to flutter. Beginning at m. 94, there are brief, seven-measure canonic solos for euphonium, bassoon, alto saxophone, and clarinet. Attention to articulation and balance are important to performing the varying texture and orchestration of melodic and rhythmic motifs.

Unit 5: Stylistic Considerations

Shadow Rituals is a mystical dance intended to assume a dark character in order to replicate something primal or ancient. A primitive musical temperament is displayed in a rhythmic and energetic fashion that engages both performers and listeners throughout. Careful placement of all dynamics, tempos, and articulations leave little room for taking any liberty with such precise indications of the composer's intentions. It is important that all musical details are strictly adhered to in order to preserve the energy and creative qualities of the piece. Care must be taken to stress the placed accents at various dynamic markings in addition to performing staccatos with a light, yet dry separation.

Unit 6: Musical Elements

MELODY:

For the most part, melodic units are structured around the tonality of E-flat Phrygian, with intervallic motifs being integral to the persistent energy and driving melodic unit. There is a pervasive use of intervals in both primary themes: minor second, minor third, and perfect fifth.

The melody of theme A is first presented by clarinet in a ten-measure phrase structure (4 + 6). The intervals of a perfect fifth, minor third, and minor second are most prevalent in the construction of this melody, with a major seventh used at the end of both statements of the motif. The style of theme A is presented with precise articulation of accent and staccato. This melody is somewhat disjunct from beginning to end, but is compacted into short melodic units that continue to provide continuity. Near the middle of the piece, beginning at m. 82, the melody is augmented by full instrumentation in tiered fashion in reverse score order. The composer cleverly takes theme A and augments the melody while also presenting it in partial canon from brass through woodwinds.

FIGURE 1. Mm. 5–14, theme A, clarinets

Horns first present the eight-measure melody of theme B beginning at m. 45. The intervals of perfect fifth and minor second construct the unit to this syncopated melody. Similar stylistic considerations of theme A are also applied to theme B where accents and staccato are still present. However, extra care must be taken to slightly exaggerate the accents to clearly define their presence on beat 3 and the second half of beat 4 in 4/4 meter and the second half of beat 2 in 3/4 meter. Failure to do so may result in only a slight difference of stylistic weight between the actual written accents and the organic strong downbeats. Keep the staccatos quite detached and dry in order to maintain the appropriate amount of space before each accent and/or syncopation.

FIGURE 2. Mm. 45–53, theme B, horns

HARMONY:

Tonality centers around E-flat, which is clearly established in the opening of the work with a sustained E-flat unison in tuba and timpani. Although the opening theme may originally sound as if written in E-flat major when it begins with the interval of perfect fifth, the ear quickly shifts to Phrygian mode when the minor sixth and minor seventh intervals are used at the apex of the first two motifs. By m. 26 there is a moment when the ear may feel more grounded in the key of C-flat major, but this is fleeting, as the work continues to come back to E-flat. An exception to the returning root of E-flat is at the end of the work, when there is a shift to A-flat Aeolian.

RHYTHM:

The rhythmic component is the primary catalyst of this piece, which is immediately apparent in the introduction by percussion. The conductor must decide on the most appropriate conducting pattern for the piece, which predominately *feels* to be in 5/4 meter, but actually frequently rotates between 5/4, 4/4, and 3/4 meter. An assessment must be made in order to determine the best grouping of rhythms for conducting patterns. The difficulty surfaces when there are different grouping of rhythmic patterns simultaneously between the melody and countermelody or accompaniment lines.

One suggestion is to conduct the 5/4 meter in a five-pattern grouped in quarter notes as 3 + 2 or as a four-pattern grouped in eighth notes as 3 + 3 + 2 + 2 (two dotted quarters followed by two quarters).

Another suggestion is to conduct the 5/4 meter in a three-pattern grouped in eighth notes as 3 + 3 + 4 (two dotted quarters and a half). And yet a further suggestion may be to conduct the 5/4 meter in a four-pattern grouped in quarter notes as 1 + 1 + 1 + 2 (three quarters and a half). Regardless of which method you choose to conduct the patterns, it is imperative that the tempo remains constant in order to correctly capture and sustain the driving rhythmic energy that engages both performer and listener.

The rhythm is augmented beginning at m. 82, and it is possible to conduct in a larger subdivision in an effort to portray a moment of rhythmic calming. The section indicates a 5/4 meter with a possible conducting pattern of two with a half-time feel grouped as either 3 + 2 or 2 + 3, and continuing the half-time feel in the 4/4 meter with a pattern of two (half notes) and the 3/4 meter with a pattern of one (dotted half).

Despite which pattern groupings a conductor chooses, there is potential for the tempo to slow on the syncopations and tied notes. Avoid this rhythmic inaccuracy by placing appropriate space and detachment on the staccato, and releasing sound *on* the tied eighth-note rather than *after* it.

TIMBRE:

Shadow Rituals is a tremendous work that exhibits the innate character of the entire wind band. Scoring is often grouped by woodwind versus brass choir, and then uniting the two at key bridges. There are also many sections where the texture is thick, employing all choirs with contrapuntal and occasionally tutti affect. The instrumental coloring is especially affective at m. 82, where the timbre evolves in unfolding layers from low brass to high woodwinds.

The employment of clarinet timbre in the chalumeau register is effective in maintaining the underlying strength and intensity of the rhythm. Only as the piece evolves and moves closer to the ending do clarinets play more in the clarion register. Although rhythmic units continue to drive the work, there are brief moments of thicker chordal structure. Rehearse these sections with fine attention to balance and detail of dynamic shading. Failure to do so may result in overbalancing by the recurring rhythmic units.

Unit 7: Form and Structure

SECTION	MEASURE	EVENT AND SCORING
Introduction	1–4	Percussion sets rhythmic motif in 5/4 meter; E-flat tonal center established by tuba and timpani
Theme A	5–14	Clarinets present theme A (figure 1) in the antecedent phrase, with tenor saxophone joining the texture in the consequent phrase at m. 9; intervallic content primarily includes perfect fifth, minor second, and minor third; alto saxophones and low reeds set the accompaniment line while punctuating the 5/4 meter
Theme A[1]	14–25	Theme presented by piccolo, flutes, and glockenspiel; accompaniment line in remainder of woodwinds include canonic fragments of theme A (minor third intervals); clarinets, low reeds, and horns; at m. 18 a motif based on theme B, not yet presented in full, is first suggested by clarinets, low reeds, and horns; ascending stepwise line sets accompaniment in low brass

SECTION	MEASURE	EVENT AND SCORING
Theme A	26–35	Theme A returns with antecedent phrase in clarinets coupled with accompaniment line in remainder of woodwinds performing canonic fragments of theme A (minor second intervals); flutes join the consequent phrase beginning at m. 30, together with ascending stepwise accompaniment line in trumpets and horns; E-flat tonal center continues to be outlined by low brass and timpani
Bridge	36–44	Introductory material to theme B is revealed by piccolo, alto saxophone 1, trumpet 1, and glockenspiel at m. 36, and by trombones at m. 41
Theme B	45–52	Full statement of theme B (figure 2) presented by horns; flutes, oboes, and clarinets join the antecedent phrase at m. 49; remaining accompaniment parts continue to punctuate the changing meter as well as reinforce E-flat as the tonal center
Theme A²	53- 62	Theme A in augmentation in low reeds and low brass; joined in original time at m. 57 by piccolo, trumpets, and glockenspiel; rapid ascending line in accompaniment by woodwinds and horns
Theme A³	63–70	Theme A fragment presented in canon throughout woodwinds; accompaniment line in trumpets and horns include fragments of theme A (minor third intervals); new tonal center of C minor established by low reeds, low brass, and timpani, with a return to E-flat by the end of the phrase
Theme B¹	71–81	Theme B in flutes, oboe, and clarinets accompanied by countermelody of a theme A fragment in alto saxophones and trumpets; remaining lines punctuate changing meter and maintain E-flat as tonal center

SECTION	MEASURE	EVENT AND SCORING
Theme A[4]	82–93	Melody of theme A is presented in counterpoint in chorale fashion by brass choir, followed by woodwind choir; counterpoint material juxtaposes 5/4 meter in 3 + 2 against 2 + 3; the same metric juxtaposition exists in the percussion choir
Theme A[5]	94–115	This section may be viewed as new material, and thus termed as theme C; however, it uses similar intervallic content and direction from theme A (perfect fifth, minor second, and minor third); the melodic four-measure fragment of theme A is presented in both original and retrograde form by solo euphonium; original and retrograde form then continues in canon presented by solos in bassoon, alto saxophone, clarinet, then by flutes, oboes, and trumpet 3, then trumpet 2, then trumpet 1; minor third and minor second interval relation is reinforced by accompaniment in low reeds and trombones, and again by clarinets and alto saxophones
Theme B[2]	116–138	Woodwinds perform theme B fragment in counterpoint with theme A fragment; remaining lines punctuate changing meter and maintain E-flat as tonal center; beginning at m. 128 brass states the same theme B fragment in canon with woodwinds
Theme A[6]	139–151	The full antecedent phrase of theme A is presented by saxophone choir while accompanied by the sustained root of each phrase in low brass and timpani; the consequent phrase in woodwinds is actually made up of the theme B motif, accompanied by a countermelody fragment of theme A in trumpets and horns

SECTION	MEASURE	EVENT AND SCORING
Theme A	152–171	The original theme returns in its entirety in trumpets and is slightly rhythmically altered in order to fit the parameters of 3/4 (sounds like 12/8) versus the original 5/4 meter; at the same time, the theme is juxtaposed with itself as it is presented in augmentation by woodwinds and horns; the result is somewhat of a restrained feeling; tonal center begins in E-flat Phrygian and modulates through various keys before arriving at D-flat
Coda	172–179	A woodwind flourish is contrasted with brass chords; the woodwind flourish is constructed of the perfect fifth and minor third intervals of theme A, while brass chords are constructed of the perfect fifth and minor second intervals of theme A
	180–182	Woodwinds present fragment of theme A melody accompanied by sustained A-flat chord in brass; tonal center of A-flat Aeolian
	183–186	Tension increases with thicker texture and increased dynamics; tutti presentation of first two measures of theme B, and concluding with perfect fifth to minor third interval that has been so prevalent throughout the structure of the work

Unit 8: Suggested Listening

Adams, John. *Short Ride in a Fast Machine.*
Bernstein, Leonard. *Profanation from Jeremiah.*
Markowski, Michael:
    JoyRIDE
    Malediction (for symphony orchestra)
Ticheli, Frank:
    Cajun Folk Songs
    Nitro
    Vesuvius

Unit 9: Additional References and Resources

Kinder, Keith. "Presenting the First Prize Winner: Michael Markowski for
    Shadow Rituals." MBM *Times*, 2: 33.

Websites:
    Michael Markowski. www.michaelmarkowski.com
    Manhattan Beach Music. www.manhattanbeachmusic.com
    Shadow Rituals. http://shadowrituals.com/

Contributed by:

Shelley M. Jagow
Professor of Music
Wright State University
Dayton, Ohio

---

1 K. Kinder, "Presenting the First Prize Winner: Michael Markowski for *Shadow Rituals*."
MBM Times (issue 2), 33.

Teacher Resource Guide

They Hung Their Harps in the Willows

W. Francis McBeth
(b. 1933)

Unit 1: Composer

W. Francis McBeth is a widely published composer, clinician, and educator with significant musical contributions to the orchestral, band, choral, and chamber genres. McBeth studied at Hardin-Simmons University, the University of Texas, and the Eastman School of Music. He has worked extensively with ensembles throughout the United States and has performed in Germany, France, Italy, England, Scotland, and Iceland. He taught at Ouachita Baptist University from 1957–1996, where he was the Trustees' Distinguished University Professor and resident composer.

McBeth has been recognized with the Presley Award at Hardin-Simmons University, the ASBDA Edwin Franko Goldman Award, and the prestigious Howard Hanson Prize from the Eastman School of Music. In 1975, McBeth was appointed Composer Laureate of the State of Arkansas. He is a member and past president of the American Bandmasters Association and has served as a contributing editor to *The Instrumentalist* magazine. *Masque, Kaddish, Through Countless Halls of Air,* and *Of Sailors and Whales* represent but a few of McBeth's many notable compositions for wind band.

Unit 2: Composition

They Hung Their Harps in the Willows was commissioned by the Plano East Senior High Band in Plano, Texas, and it was premiered on February 16, 1989, with McBeth conducting. The piece was written in memory of Claude T. Smith. The work's title is derived from Psalm 137:

By the rivers of Babylon,
there they sat down and wept.
Upon the willows in the midst
of it, we hung our harps.

According to McBeth, there are no programmatic connections with Psalm 137; rather, the quote provides a general guiding concept for the composition.[1] *They Hung Their Harps in the Willows* is a dramatic musical work that explores dynamic extremes and abrupt textural shifts while maintaining an economical approach to melodic materials.

They Hung Their Harps in the Willows is eight minutes and twenty-five seconds in duration, and is classified by the publisher as a Grade 4 piece. While technical demands are not excessive, the skills needed to control timbre and pitch while effecting extreme dynamic changes suggest a need for fairly experienced performers. This through-composed piece is unified by a primary melodic motive that is supported by a secondary theme. The two musical ideas occur with independence at the outset and ultimately combine in support of a fervent climax. The unrestrained formal design and aggressive dynamic manipulations suggest a Romantic interpretation of phrasing; the work bears close relation to pieces from the tone poem genre. Students have many opportunities for expression, and this piece requires a strong commitment to the composer's instructions to yield an impactful performance.

Unit 3: Historical Perspective

Although *They Hung Their Harps in the Willows* may not follow Psalm 137 literally, an examination of the event depicted in this quote may reinforce the composer's expressive intentions. This biblical reference evokes the anguish displayed by Israelites after the Babylonian conquest of Jerusalem. The Israelites refusal to sing songs of praise is reinforced by the physical act of hanging their harps in trees.[2] The full psalm ends with a description of violent acts against the Babylonians.

To connect listeners with the emotional underpinnings of the psalm, McBeth maintains the structure of the primary motive while altering dynamics, articulations, textures, and tempos. For example, dynamic shifts from *p* to *ff* can occur over half-note, quarter-note, or even eighth-note durations. The indication of *sffzp* occurs multiple times, further reinforcing aggressive dynamic manipulation. The composer harkens to a non-Western tonal environment, with harmonic abstractions that accompany a melody suggesting minor and Phrygian modes. A traditional harmonic resolution to a major triad is reserved exclusively for the end of the piece.

Along with dynamic developments, McBeth underscores the intensity of the biblical reference with textural shifts. Sparse, chamber-like textures generally escalate to include the full ensemble. These climactic moments shift abruptly, repeating the process multiple times. As textures and dynamics increase, articulations become more accented and rhythmic values become shorter. The composer thereby integrates a variety of musical elements to enhance dramatic impact.

Unit 4: Technical Considerations

When preparing this work, one of the foremost considerations for most student ensembles is transparency or timbral clarity. The primary theme is based on the leap of a minor sixth, and this musical gesture occurs in a variety of dynamic areas and ranges. The performers' clarity of tone can be disrupted by the numerous accents and *sffzp* indications that articulate these minor-sixth leaps. Younger players may interpret these markings with a heavy tongue and pinched embouchure, especially when they occur in the upper register. Conductors must be ever-attentive to tone quality to prevent musical "noise" from detracting from a pure sound.

Rhythmic activity is conservative. In a few instances, melodic and accompaniment parts operate with rhythmic independence (for example, a hemiola begins in m. 79, supporting an ostinato in the upper woodwinds). A more common disruption to musical motion is the stretching of melodies over barlines. This technique destabilizes predicted phrasal lengths; as a result, the conductor should encourage players to maintain melodic flow regardless of the placement of barlines. In these situations, students must continue to subdivide and internally count tied notes to maintain metronomic security.

Accents generally occur when the dynamic level is *f* or louder. In these sections, young players tend to clip or otherwise shorten note lengths, especially when they follow slurred passages. To enhance the tone quality, students should infer accent markings to include length and weight (as with a full bow). This emphasis will improve melodic flow and decrease the likelihood of rushing in these areas.

Unit 5: Stylistic Considerations

To successfully lead listeners through this dramatic work, performers must exercise musical restraint and sensitivity. An overzealous approach to loud dynamics will diffuse the points of climactic arrival. The ensemble must understand the overall direction of the piece and adjust individual dynamic levels to enhance large-scale musical development. For example, a tutti indication of *ff* does not imply the same dynamic for every player. Select a core group from the ensemble that produces the appropriate color for a given sonority and have the rest of the ensemble play "into" that sound. Otherwise, those instruments with a naturally higher tessitura can quickly overwhelm the overall balance.

Slurred, duple patterns occur frequently in this work. Generally, these are ascending eighth notes, but they are augmented into quarter-note patterns in the latter portion of the piece. Weight and length should be given to the first of the two notes, followed by a de-emphasis of the second note. Some conductors "lift" the second eighth note in these areas, while others choose to connect the patterns with no break whatsoever. Conductors should determine the appropriate style and strive for a consistent application throughout the ensemble.

McBeth lists several points in the score notes, describing an inadequate dynamic effectiveness by many ensembles. Many of these events coincide with considerable dynamic changes over short rhythmic durations. The composer singles out areas where a soft dynamic must be observed to allow for a clear transmission of the melody. When asked about the need for these written notes in the score, McBeth responded, "Too many bands play *mezzo forte* all of the time because they cannot play soft and directors won't let them play loud!"[3] There is little doubt that McBeth places a high priority on the proper execution of dynamics in this composition.

Unit 6: Musical Elements

Melody:

They Hung Their Harps in the Willows provides students opportunities to develop an aural familiarity with minor and Phrygian modes. Further, melodic fluctuations in dynamics help younger players explore phrasal shaping in novel ways. Conductors can develop activities that improve student success in these areas while simultaneously increasing individual control over sound and timbre.

One method of increasing facility and building accuracy in melodic leaps is to take the following basic exercise inspired by Emory Remington's standard brass warm-up activity, except it should ascend in the key of A minor (see figure 1).

FIGURE 1.

Repeat this exercise in E Phrygian mode. Relate both scales to the key of C major as a means of connecting them to other modal scale patterns (see figure 2).

FIGURE 2.

With both patterns comfortably in place, isolate the leaps of a third, fifth, and sixth. Encourage players to increase air in the lower note to promote a clean articulation of the upper note. Often, students de-emphasize the lower note and overblow the upper note, yielding inaccurate partials (see figure 3).

FIGURE 3. A minor

In the primary motive of *They Hung Their Harps in the Willows*, the sixth scale degree generally resolves to the fifth. Have a part of the class vocally sustain the sixth scale degree while the rest of the ensemble plays the exercise. Allow the singers to resolve to the fifth with the ensemble. This melodic tendency should be reinforced by players when they perform the composition, as well. Consider an increase in volume on the sixth scale degree followed by a slight decrease in volume when arriving at the fifth scale degree to engage listeners with the melodic line.

To develop controlled dynamic shaping, select a pitch that is comfortable for the ensemble, such as F concert. Starting with whole notes at a slow tempo (around quarter note = 68), have players practice shaping from *pp* to *ff* and back to *pp*. Be aware that many young ensembles diminuendo too soon without sustaining the upper dynamic (see figures 4a-b).

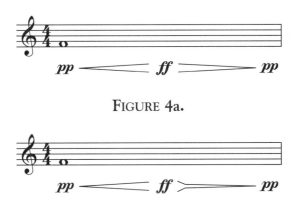

FIGURE 4a.

FIGURE 4b. Avoid this shape

When the ensemble can perform the proper dynamic shape while maintaining appropriate balance and blend, move to half notes, quarter notes, and eighth notes (see figures 5a-c).

FIGURE 5a.

FIGURE 5b.

FIGURE 5c.

Finally, to prepare for the melodic style found in this piece, add ties to the eighth-note pattern (see figure 6).

FIGURE 6.

Develop a variety of exercises based on these concepts to reinforce key areas and articulations found throughout the work.

HARMONY:

A recurring theme in this composition features a unison melodic line accompanied by thick, tonally abstracted sonorities (for example, mm. 1–5, 16–19, and 117–119). These harmonic structures can be dissected into triadic derivations, but the sonic impact is simply a collection of pitches in whole- or half-step intervals. To improve clarity and intonation, conductors can isolate these sonorities and provide aural anchors for students.

In m. 2, the accompaniment sonority consists of the pitches E–F–G-flat–A–B-flat–C–D-flat. To illustrate embedded triadic harmonies, isolate the G-flat major seventh chord (G-flat–B-flat–D-flat–F). Next, have them play the F major 'seventh chord (F–A–C–E). These two harmonies contain all of the pitches in the overall chord. Have one play, then the other, then both at once, and challenge students to selectively listen for the independent chords while playing the complete sonority.

Another approach is to draw the whole- and half-step relationships from the sonority. For example, have students with E and F play together, then those with F and G-flat, B-flat and C, and so on. The most common issue in these types of intervals is the tendency for players to adjust pitch up if they are playing the bottom note or down if they are playing the top note. The resulting interval can resemble a unison with poor intonation. Encourage students to understand where they fall within the intervallic relationships and adjust pitch away from the opposing note to open the interval. This often improves harmonic clarity.

RHYTHM:

When more than one rhythmic concept is presented simultaneously, conductors can adapt individual parts in rehearsal to promote an ensemble-wide understanding of the compositional impact. For example, mm. 78–86 feature three distinct rhythmic schemes that must work in conjunction to support the climax. Upper woodwinds with ostinatos will tend to crush the sixteenth notes. Players of middle voices with a broad melody must demonstrate confidence while executing rhythms across barlines; additionally, they must allow the hemiola of the lower voices to be clearly audible. Try adapting each part to reflect key rhythmic elements of the other parts (see figures 7a-b). The more familiar students are with the overall rhythmic structure, the better they can integrate the parts into a complete presentation.

FIGURE 7a. Upper woodwind ostinato adapted with hemiola

FIGURE 7b. Brass melody adapted with ostinato rhythm

TIMBRE:

Characteristic tone color should be maintained throughout the aggressive dynamic ranges of this piece. A beautiful sound is the first priority, then expanding the volume of that sound to both the softest and loudest volumes will assure a mature musical presentation. There are several activities that can direct students' focus to their quality of sound. For example, at rehearsal letter I, most of the ensemble has accents or *sffzp* followed by crescendos and dynamic indications of *ff*. Consider removing all elements except pitch and rhythm. While maintaining a *mezzo forte* dynamic at a much slower tempo (such as quarter note = 72), ask students to perform lines with all attention on sound, blend, and balance. Next, have them perform the same section at the softest possible dynamic, still very slowly. With subsequent repetitions, increase tempo and ask students to add articulations and expressive markings within a soft dynamic environment. The overall concept of controlling sound and listening more actively should be reinforced.

Next, ask students to perform this section at the written dynamic with all expressive markings, but do not allow them to use the tongue. All accents and *sffzp* markings must be enacted with air. A slower tempo is suggested at first. Young players can become overly dependent on the tongue to perform articulations at louder dynamics. This activity, if revisited periodically, reminds students that without proper air support, the tone will be uncharacteristic and out of tune despite the tonguing style. When re-introducing the tongue, instruct students to only use enough articulation to start the note. Good air support should be retained as the primary energy behind accents and *sforzandos*.

Unit 7: Form and Structure

SECTION	MEASURE	EVENT AND SCORING
Introduction	1–6	Bell-like call-and-response; low brass dynamic swell with abstracted harmonic structure
Theme 1	7–10	A minor or E Phrygian suggested; clarinet melody; sparse accompaniment
Theme 1 extended	10–15	Delayed harmonic resolution; flute and clarinet
Introduction developed	16–22	Resolution to A minor; full ensemble with dynamic swells
Theme 1 developed	23–33	Key center manipulated; sparse, chamber-like texture

SECTION	MEASURE	EVENT AND SCORING
Theme 1 developed	34–42	D minor; thicker texture; aggressive dynamic shaping
Theme 2 introduced	43–51	G minor; horns and clarinets build to tutti climax
Themes 1–2 integrated	52–86	Culminates in C minor; thin texture; contrapuntal; builds to full ensemble and loud dynamic
Transition	87–99	C minor scale segments; *fff* percussion
Theme 2 augmented	100–105	Arrival at brief C major triad; tutti
Theme 1 developed	106–110	Shift back to C minor; horn *ff* melody
Themes 1–2 developed	111–119	C minor; introductory gesture returns; *fff* fermata
Theme 1 closing	120–129	Introductory gesture with triadic accompaniment and soft fermatas; C major triad concludes the piece

Unit 8: Suggested Listening

McBeth, W. Francis:
  Kaddish
  Masque
Smith, Claude T. *God of Our Fathers*.
Thompson, Virgil. *A Solemn Music*.

Unit 9: Additional References and Resources

Camphouse, Mark. *Composers on Composing for Band*. Chicago: GIA Publications, Inc., 2002.

Hamlin, Hannibal. "Psalm Culture in the English Renaissance: Readings of Psalm 137 by Shakespeare, Spenser, Milton, and Others." *Renaissance Quarterly* 55, no. 1. (2002): 224–257.

McBeth, W. Francis. *Effective Performance of Band Music*. San Antonio, TX: Southern Music Company, 1972.

McBeth, W. Francis. Telephone interview. May 1, 2008.

Salzman, Timothy, ed. *A Composer's Insight: Thoughts, Analysis, and Commentary on Contemporary Masterpieces for Wind Band, Volume 2*. Galesville, MD: Meredith Music, 2003.

Contributed by:

Chad Nicholson
Director of Instrumental Studies
Indiana University-Purdue University Fort Wayne
Fort Wayne, Indiana

---

1 W. Francis McBeth, telephone Interview, May 1, 2008.
2 Hannibal Hamlin, "Psalm Culture in the English Renaissance: Readings of Psalm 137 by Shakespeare, Spenser, Milton, and Others," *Renaissance Quarterly* 55/1 (2002):226.
3 W. Francis McBeth, telephone Interview, May 1, 2008.

Teacher Resource Guide

Three Dances of Enchantment

Luigi Zaninelli
(b. 1932)

Unit 1: Composer

Performers and audiences around the world know the music of Luigi Zaninelli as work that excites the senses and stimulates the mind. Following high school, Gian-Carlo Menotti brought him to the Curtis Institute of Music. At age nineteen, the Curtis Institute sent him to Italy to study composition with the legendary Rosario Scalero (teacher of Samuel Barber and Menotti).

Upon graduation, Zaninelli was appointed to the faculty of the Curtis Institute. In 1964, he returned to Rome to compose film music for RCA Italiana. During that period, Zaninelli became conductor/arranger for Metropolitan Opera soprano Anna Moffo.

During his career, Zaninelli has served as composer-in-residence at the University of Calgary and the Banff School of Fine Arts. Since 1973, he has been the composer-in-residence at The University of Southern Mississippi.

Among his numerous honors are a Steinway Prize, ASCAP Awards since 1964, and Outstanding Achievement Award, Province of Alberta. In 1991, he became the first three-time winner of the Mississippi Institute of Arts and Letters Music Award.

With more than 300 published works to his credit, Zaninelli has been commissioned to compose for all mediums, including opera, ballet, chamber music, orchestra, band, chorus, and solo songs. He also has composed several movie and television scores, including the PBS documentaries *The Islander*, *Passover*, and *The Last Confederates*. His one-act opera, *Mr. Sebastian*, was premiered in 1995, followed by the first performance of his first full-length opera, *Snow White*, in March 1996.

Zaninelli recently premiered his tribute to George Washington in Constitution Hall, Washington, DC. He was commissioned by the Mount Vernon Ladies' Association to create a work commemorating the 200th anniversary of the death of George Washington, a year-long commemoration throughout 1999. The result, *A Crown, a Mansion, and a Throne,* was performed by Colonel Lowell Graham and the United States Air Force Symphonic Wind Ensemble and sung by soprano Daisy Johnson.

Unit 2: Composition

Three Dances of Enchantment was completed in July of 2006 and dedicated to James F. Keene, conductor of the University of Illinois Wind Symphony. The composer provides the following notes in the score.

> *Three Dances of Enchantment* is a suite of three dances inspired by personal experiences in my life which, through the years, continue to resonate in my memory.
>
> I. "The Via Veneto" [foxtrot] is a musical reminiscence of those "dolce vita" days I spent on one of Rome's most fashionable streets. Here, as a young film composer, I watched and learned, with great fascination, about the world of Italian film-making.
>
> II. "She Walks through the Fair" [waltz] is a haunting, bittersweet melody which I discovered on my visit to Ireland. Dedicated to Kylie Charra Keene.
>
> III. "The Feast of Saint Rocco" [tarantella] is a joyous Italian-American celebration dedicated to Saint Rocco held every summer in my hometown of Raritan, New Jersey. It was here, in my father's arms at the age of five, that I first experienced the vibrant, bold tartness of an Italian band. It was loud and so wonderful!

Unit 3: Historical Perspective

The use of dance music or dance-themed compositions has been a major part of the wind bands history. Susato's collection of *Dances from the Danserye* (1551) is but one of the most recognized early examples of this tradition. Zaninelli continues this tradition with the current work. Here he pays tribute to the origins, mostly through style and programmatic note, to three dance styles.

Movement 1, "The Via Veneto," is cast as a foxtrot—an American social dance in 4/4. Introduced in 1913, it became a genre encompassing many patterns of steps. It borrowed freely from extant dance types and engendered new variants. Dance-band musicians applied the name to thousands of popular tunes in 4/4 in moderate tempo with a two-beat or walking bass lines. The Via Veneto in Rome is one of those quaint peaceful roads famous for strolling and its open-air cafes like the Café Bussi and Café Rosati. In the 1960s, the film *La Dolce Vita* put the Via Veneto in the limelight of society life and the paparazzi. It is this image that Zaninelli is portraying from his young film-composing days.

Movement 2, "She Walks through the Fair," is a setting of an Irish folk waltz. The waltz is the most long-lived and continuously-favored among ballroom dances, in part because of its ability to adapt to new styles of dancing, music, and changing social conditions. Beginning as a daring, even risqué, intrusion from the lower classes into the polite world, it evolved into a symbol of grace, sophistication, and elegance. This sweet, melancholy song is set in a call-and-response style and is dedicated to Kylie Charra Keene. The text follows:

My young love said to me, "My mother won't mind
And my father won't slight you for your lack of kind."
And she stepped away from me and this she did say
"It will not be long, love, till our wedding day."

As she stepped away from me and she moved through the fair
And fondly I watched her move here and move there
And then she turned homeward with one star awake
Like the swan in the evening moves over the lake.

The people were saying, no two e'er were wed
But one had a sorrow that was never said
And I smiled as she passed with her goods and her gear
And that was the last I saw of my dear.

Last night she came to me, my dead love came in,
So softly she came that her feet made no din
As she laid her hand on me and this she did say:
It will not be long, love, 'til our wedding day.[1]

Movement 3, "The Feast of Saint Rocco," is a traditional tarantella—a folk dance of southern Italy that takes its name from the town of Taranto (not, as is often said, from the tarantula or from the dance to cure its bite). It is in a rapid, accelerating 6/8 with shifts between major and minor. The tarantella was taken up by various composers of the nineteenth century, often as a piece with continuous eighth notes and of some technical difficulty. "The Feast of Saint Rocco" celebrates this patron saint as the protector against the plague and all contagious diseases. Celebrated on August 16, Zaninelli's depiction of the feast is a rollicking tarantella reminiscent of the raucous town bands that would be playing at such a festive, open-air celebration.

Unit 4: Technical Considerations

This three-movement work is very representative of the technical needs usually requested by the composer. The instrumentation is as follows: piccolo, flute 1–2, oboe 1–2, English horn, solo clarinet 1–2, clarinet 1–3, bass clarinet, contra-alto clarinet, alto saxophone 1–2, tenor saxophone, baritone saxophone, trumpet 1–3, horn 1–4, trombone 1–3, bass trombone, euphonium, tuba, timpani, snare drum, bass drum, triangle, tambourine, suspended cymbal, tam-tam, crash cymbals, xylophone, orchestra bells, vibraphone, and marimba. An optional string bass part is included.

With the lighter textures of the first two movements, the string bass is more of a needed timbre rather than an optional part. The marimba part is actually published as a part for marimba, optional harp, and optional electric piano. The marimba and harp parts are scored for different effects, and the overall presentation of movement 1 is enhanced by the exchange of these sounds. The harp part in movement 2 (a necessary part) is written in a manner that can be played effectively on electric piano if harp is not available.

Movement 1 presents several solo opportunities: muted trombone, piccolo, clarinet, and alto saxophone. There is a jaunty alto saxophone duet at m. 38 as well. The meter is in common time with a tempo marking of half note = 80–85. This movement contains a fair amount of chromatic alterations and shifts from major to minor modes within phrases. Also, careful attention to the metric shifting of the downbeat in the accompaniment poses performance challenges (e.g., mm. 13–17).

Movement 2 features a piccolo solo in combination with lightly scored melodic percussion and harp throughout. The tempo is moderate (quarter note = 85), with allowances for rubato and stretching of the time. The 3/4 meter is only interrupted by the composer's choice to metrically lengthen the cadence points during the more fully-scored sections of the movement.

Movement 3 is very straightforward in 6/8 meter. Rapid, light articulation is demanded of all members of the ensemble, but double-tonguing technique is not required. Once again major/minor mode shifting is present, requiring careful attention to chromatic alterations in the pitch content. At mm. 11 and 82, trumpets, horns, and trombones are required to flutter-tongue.

Unit 5: Stylistic Considerations

Movement 1. The foxtrot must maintain a light, crisp character. A steady tempo in performance will heighten the slightly off-balance effect of the movement due to the composer's frequent use of syncopated passages in the upper woodwinds (mm. 17–18) and the use of the opening material as ornamentation throughout the movement. Solo lines must be projected without being forced, so keeping the accompaniment balanced so that the melodic percussion is in good balance with wind parts is a must. This two-step lightness is crucial to successful performance of the movement.

Movement 2. This moderate waltz must be performed in a very sustained manner. The piccolo solos should have a music box quality, while the more fully-scored sections of the movement should have a warm, lush quality without any edge to louder dynamic levels.

Movement 3. While the composer mentions his recollection of the wonderfully loud town bands in his depiction of this music, there must be an energetic lilt and bounce that keeps this movement tumbling forward with excitement rather than a harsh, percussive drive. The only *fortissimo* dynamic marking is in the final measure of the movement. Therefore keeping the articulation light is of the utmost importance in providing for a clean, transparent performance of the work. It is the exchange of melodic fragments and the kaleidoscopic orchestrational colors that add to the frenzied excitement of the movement.

Unit 6: Musical Elements

Movement 1, "The Via Veneto."

MELODY:

The melodic content of this movement primarily consists of chromatic ascent centered on E rising to B and then settling back down to E through a descending fourth. Accompaniment fragments contain the melodic interplay of half versus whole steps throughout the movement and are used to give an uneasy or unstable feel to the direction of the melodic lines.

HARMONY:

This movement is ultimately centered tonally in G major; however, the internal harmony for the first phrase is an Em^7–D-sharp m/E, with E serving as a pedal point. This creates the effect of a mode shift in every bar and plays on the melodic use of chromatic alteration. This use of harmonic neighbor tones adds to the "wormy" effect of the music.

RHYTHM:

This movement uses basic rhythmic motives with additions of syncopation at cadence points for added excitement and an almost stumbling musical effect, as well as shifting the accompaniment pattern to sound as if the downbeat is offset by half a count.

TIMBRE:

The use of piercing and nasal solo colors (saxophone, muted trombone, and clarinet) with a light accompaniment texture creates a light, hazy or misty sound to the music. Frequent orchestration changes between high and low groups of instruments are held together by sinewy solo lines.

Movement 2, "She Walks through the Fair."

MELODY:
The melodic content of the waltz is a simple stepwise tune rising from D to A with a lowered-seventh scale degree. The melody is very slightly altered to add varied harmonic color as the movement progresses.

HARMONY:
Tonal centers are D, F, and G major.

RHYTHM:
Very simple use of rhythm in this movement is in keeping with the folksong origins of the work. The only rhythmic deviation from the basic 3/4 meter occurs when the composer metrically stretches cadence points with 5/4 measures, giving these phrases an improvised quality.

TIMBRE:
Use of solo piccolo, harp, bells, and vibraphone creates a very light timbre, as if the music were part of a dream or memory (ethereal, or otherworldly). The more fully-scored sections are warm and inviting, due to scoring in the most comfortable registers of the chosen instruments.

Movement 3, "The Feast of Saint Rocco."

MELODY:
Like movement 1, there is a playfulness of chromatics in the melodies of the tarantella. The main theme starts on E with a rise of a major third, ultimately landing on E-flat. The effect is reminiscent of the traditional tendency of the tarantella to shift frequently between major and minor modes.

HARMONY:
A and E minor are the predominate tonal areas.

RHYTHM:
The traditional tarantella rhythm (see figure 1) is used predominantly. This movement also presents itself as driving and relentless because of the persistence of the rhythmic motives.

FIGURE 1. Traditional tarantella rhythm

T IMBRE:

This movement is the most fully-scored of the three, setting it apart by having a thicker, darker timbre. Frequent exchanges between high- and low-tessitura sound groups helps to keep the frantic nature of the movement alive and well.

Unit 7: Form and Structure

SECTION	MEASURE	EVENT AND SCORING

Movement 1: "The Via Veneto"

Section	Measure	Event and Scoring
Introduction	1–4	Woodwinds
A	5–22	Muted trombone solo and clarinet obbligato (second time)
B	23–37	Flute and alto saxophone melodic element
C	38–51	Alto saxophone soli with syncopated melody
A'	52–67	Flute and clarinet soli
A"	68–85	Piccolo, flute, alto saxophone, and euphonium soli
C'	38–51	D. S.; alto saxophone soli with syncopated melody and piccolo obbligato
A'	52–67	D. S.; flute and clarinet soli
A"	68–81	D. S.; piccolo, flute, alto saxophone, and euphonium soli
Coda	86–100	Reprise of introduction; piccolo and tuba soli at m. 97

Movement 2: "She Walks Through the Fair"

Section	Measure	Event and Scoring
Call 1	1–8	Piccolo solo with harp and percussion; D major
Response A	9–23	Flute and alto saxophone melodic lines; horns have melodic line at m. 21; D major
Call 2	24–31	Piccolo solo with harp and percussion; D to F major
Response B	32–46	Trumpets and horns share melodic lines; F major
Call 3	47–50	Piccolo solo, truncated; to G major
Response C	51–66	Melodic lines for flute, oboe, clarinet and horn, and euphonium, trumpet, and full ensemble; G major
Call 1'	67–77	Piccolo solo with harp and percussion with final cadence; G major

SECTION	MEASURE	EVENT AND SCORING
Movement 3: "The Feast of San Rocco"		
Introduction	1–11	
A	12–29	Trumpet and horn melodic element
B	30–45	Flute, oboe, and clarinet melodic element
C	46–61	Solo piccolo and clarinet
D	62–82	Woodwind and trumpet fanfare with *molto ritard* at m. 81
A	83–100	Repeat of mm. 12–29
B'	101–120	Repeat of mm. 30–45 with trumpet and countermelody
D/A	121–140	False start of material from section D followed by section A with extension
Coda	141–146	Trumpet melodic element
Coda	147–160	D' material; horn rips; *molto ritard* and *a tempo* for final bar; D to F major
Response B	32–46	Trumpets and horns share melodic lines; F major
Call 3	47–50	Piccolo solo, truncated; to G major
Response C	51–66	Melodic lines for flute, oboe, clarinet and horn, and euphonium, trumpet, and full ensemble; G major
Call 1'	67–77	Piccolo solo with harp and percussion; G major

Unit 8: Suggested Listening

Corigliano, John. *Gazebo Dances*.
Hearshen, Ira. *Divertimento*.
Wolfenden, Guy. *French Impressions*.
Zaninelli, Luigi:
    Danzetta
    Jubilate
    Lagan Love (Irish Folk Song)
    Tarantella
    The Magic Ballroom
        I. Theresa's Two-Step
        II. Pamela's Waltz
        III. Tango Della Rosa

Unit 9: Additional References and Resources

Randell, Don Michael, ed. *The New Harvard Dictionary of Music.* Cambridge, MA: Belknap Press of Harvard University Press, 1986.

Sadie, Stanley, ed. *The New Grove Dictionary of Music and Musicians.* London: Macmillan, 1980.

Zaninelli, Luigi. Program note for *Three Dances of Enchantment.* Greensboro, NC: C. Alan Publications, 2007.

Contributed by:

Carl A. Kling
Director of Bands and Orchestra
Assistant Professor of Music
Department of Music
Northwest Missouri State University
Maryville, Missouri

---

1   www.ireland-information.com

Teacher Resource Guide

To set the darkness echoing

Dana Wilson
(b. 1946)

Unit 1: Composer

Dana Wilson's musical training, performance experience as a jazz and rock pianist, and life interests combine to form his unique compositional voice—the juxtaposition of American vernacular styles, non-Western cultural practices, and contemporary concert music. He is a notable and extremely prolific composer for the wind ensemble medium. Wilson's first composition for winds, *Piece of Mind* (1987), was awarded the prestigious Sudler International Composition Prize and American Bandmasters Association Ostwald Award and has been recorded and performed by numerous university and professional ensembles. Since 1987 he has contributed over twenty new works to the wind band repertoire designed for ensembles at all levels of experience. These include (among others): *Shakata: Singing the World into Existence* (1989), *Winds on the Steppes* (1991), *Dance of the New World* (1992), *Sang!* (1994), *Shortcut Home* (1998), *Vortex* (1999), *...the harder they fall* (2004), *Colorado Peaks* (2005), and *Day Dreams* (2006).

The works of Dana Wilson have been commissioned and performed by such diverse ensembles as the Chicago Chamber Musicians, Detroit Chamber Winds and Strings, Buffalo Philharmonic, Memphis Symphony, Dallas Wind Symphony, Voices of Change, Netherlands Wind Ensemble, Syracuse Symphony, and Tokyo Kosei Wind Orchestra. Solo works have been written for such renowned artists as hornist Gail Williams, clarinetist Larry Combs, trumpeters James Thompson and Rex Richardson, and oboist David Weiss. His compositions have been performed throughout the United States, Europe, Asia, and Australia, and are published by Boosey & Hawkes and Ludwig

Music Publishers. Wilson holds a doctorate from the Eastman School of Music, where he studied composition with Samuel Adler. He is currently Charles A. Dana Professor of Music at Ithaca College, a position he has held since 1978.[1]

Unit 2: Composition

Wilson often incorporates extra-musical associations in his compositions, as evidenced by the creative titles that comprise his works list. The composer believes titles are extremely important, since they offer an interpretive framework and meditative introduction to his music. In his program note, Wilson explains the genesis of this work:

> *To set the darkness echoing* was commissioned by a consortium of schools in Cobb County, Georgia, in the Atlanta area. Although this wonderful part of the country is known for its many attributes, my primary association with it is as a keystone of the Civil Rights movement, in part because it was the home of Martin Luther King, Jr. One reason that Dr. King was so successful—and the Civil Rights movement had such an impact—is that through nonviolent protest, he held a mirror up to ourselves, forcing us all to see how we—not others—were behaving. In this process, to use the words of poet, Seamus Heaney, Dr. King "set the darkness echoing," and thus, inspired profound change. It is a great lesson for all of us that in our personal and social lives, we need not be afraid to set the darkness echoing, for it is in this process that we truly learn about ourselves and come to terms with the truths in our lives.[2]

To set the darkness echoing is a single-movement work in ternary form, approximately eight minutes in duration. Performers and audience members will instantly relate to the energy and drama of this excellent concert closer or contest piece.

Unit 3: Historical Perspective

The intersection of popular and elite traditions is considered one of the most significant cultural events of the twentieth century, as this phenomenon influenced nearly every trend that followed. Many composers, both European and American, have absorbed various aspects of jazz into their compositional styles. As a composer who has embraced postmodern eclecticism, Wilson attributes many of the compositional devices present in *To set the darkness echoing* to the strong influence of jazz:

My jazz background manifests itself in several ways: melodic conception, harmonic voicings, rhythmic syncopation, and freedom. Much of my music has a groove, or at least a steady pulse. Often an entire movement stays at a consistent tempo. I employ layering techniques, rooted in African music and developed in jazz and later styles. I often employ a constant bass line. Sometimes I have to work consciously to "break out" of these.[3]

As an early member of the baby boomer generation, self-proclaimed New England progressive, and graduate of Bowdoin College with a BA in psychology, Wilson's personal identity has been shaped by his interests in the mind, societies, and relationships. It is no surprise, then, that the last line of Seamus Heaney's poem "Personal Helicon," and its conjuring of the work of Martin Luther King, Jr., provided the initial inspiration for *To set the darkness echoing*. Exploration of this poem and its relevance to the American Civil Rights movement will provide excellent context for student performers.

Personal Helicon (for Michael Longley)[4]

As a child, they could not keep me from wells
And old pumps with buckets and windlasses.
I loved the dark drop, the trapped sky, the smells
Of waterweed, fungus and dank moss.

One, in a brickyard, with a rotted board top.
I savoured the rich crash when a bucket
Plummeted down at the end of a rope.
So deep you saw no reflection in it.

A shallow one under a dry stone ditch
Fructified like any aquarium.
When you dragged out long roots from the soft mulch
A white face hovered over the bottom.

Others had echoes, gave back your own call
With a clean new music in it. And one
Was scaresome, for there, out of ferns and tall
Foxgloves, a rat slapped across my reflection.

Now, to pry into roots, to finger slime,
To stare, big-eyed Narcissus, into some spring
Is beneath all adult dignity. I rhyme
To see myself, to set the darkness echoing.

Unit 4: Technical Considerations

Wilson's masterful idiomatic writing makes this piece an appropriate choice for Grade 4 high school ensembles, as the technical challenges are relatively limited. Some performers may struggle with the extensive chromaticism, since many of the figures employ sharps and flats in close succession; however, the short and repetitious melodic patterns should be easily internalized with concentrated practice.

Wilson's orchestration is another important technical consideration. The work emphasizes bass voices, requiring strong players on bassoon, bass clarinet, and tuba (preferably two players on each instrument). There is extensive writing for percussion, requiring five players to cover: vibraphone, suspended cymbals, tambourine, tam-tam, marimba, bells, ride cymbal, bongos, chimes, triangles, tom-toms, log drum, bass drum, afushi (or cabasa), snare drum, and timpani.

There are short solos for clarinet, trombone, flute, and English horn, though the latter is also cued to alto saxophone. The brass ranges are very reasonable, despite higher tessituras at the final climax, where trombone 1 has a written A-flat, horn 1 has a written A, and trumpet 1 has a written B-natural (with the option to play the figure down an octave). The work requires four horns in order to cover the frequent four-voice chords scored for that section. Though the score calls for oboe and English horn, it is possible to cover the part with one player. There are no other divisi parts, which should allow smaller groups to perform the work without modification.

Unit 5: Stylistic Considerations

With its groove orientation, much of the energy is derived from rhythm in this work. Students will need strong subdivision skills and must be able to play independently. The abundant syncopation and vernacular articulations should be very familiar to performers, provided that they are encouraged to apply their knowledge of popular styles to the piece.

Unit 6: Musical Elements

MELODY:
Organic unity is a high priority for Wilson, and the seminal ideas for *To set the darkness echoing* are presented in the opening measures. These include: a descending minor second "moaning motive" (first presented by bowed vibraphone in m. 2); an "echo motive" (first presented by the bass drum in m. 4); a chromatic ostinato walking bass line (first presented by bassoon and bass clarinet in m. 35); and a primary theme that emphasizes the clash between the major and minor third (first presented by saxophones in m. 37). All of the melodic figures are derived from the blues (D–F–G–A-flat–A-natural–C–D) and octatonic (D–E-flat–F–G-flat–A-flat–A–B–C–D) sets, so students should

be encouraged to practice these scales. Students may also benefit from improvisation exercises that allow them to hear each of the scale degrees against a tonic major triad.

HARMONY:

Modal mixture is perhaps the most prevalent harmonic technique in Wilson's music, and is particularly evident in his frequent use of the sharp-nine chord, a dominant seventh chord quality that contains both a major and minor third, or split third. The composer attributes the constant conflict between major and minor in his music to the blues, and notes that many American composers have explored this technique. The sharp-nine chord plays a heavy role in *To set the darkness echoing*, and it can be seen most clearly in the "interlude" sections (for example, the C#9 chord in m. 54). This chord also serves as the foundation of the head motive of theme 1, which includes the major and minor third separated by an octave.

In addition to the split third, Wilson explores open sonorities in the work, as evidenced by the perfect fourth drone in m. 1 (marimba), the quintal stacking in m. 20 (vibraphone, flutes, and clarinets), and the "interruption fanfare" in m. 196 (trumpets). These sonorities either clash directly with the tritone (an important interval in the blues and octatonic sets), or offer relief from it. Tonally, the work centers around the pitch D, though Wilson provides ambiguity by also emphasizing the key of G and employing plentiful chromaticism. In an attempt to explore new relationships that define tonality, Wilson shows a strong preference for root motion by third (for example, the movement from C to E-flat to G-flat in mm. 192–194). The prevalence of root motion by the interval of a second or third is evident in the key relationships, as shown in figure 1.

FIGURE 1. Key relationships
Pitches represent key centers; numbers represent measures.
The first three read this way: M. 1, D major; m. 27, E-flat major;
m. 35, G major.

RHYTHM:

Wilson's music contains abundant syncopation derived from jazz and rock, and his mastery of these styles is evident in the use of idiomatic articulations. Rhythmic complexity is further achieved by frequent meter changes, utilizing 4/4, 3/4, 2/4, and 6/8, as well as limited use of simultaneous duple and triple subdivisions. Helpful rehearsal strategies include singing parts with a subdividing metronome and, most importantly, having the ensemble play without the conductor beating time. These strategies will help individuals develop stronger internal subdivision skills and allow the ensemble to take full responsibility for the groove.

TIMBRE:

As the title suggests, Wilson emphasizes the bass voices to achieve a certain darkness in the piece. He also deliberately uses extended ranges to create a slightly strained sound (for example, the high clarinet solo at m. 67, or the low flute melody at m. 102). By scoring these instruments in less comfortable registers, Wilson hopes to offer coloristic variety and manipulate the psychological state of the listener. Wilson's ample writing for percussion, as well as the use of special color devices, such as bends, glissandi, falls, and a variety of mutes, add to the association with jazz.

Unit 7: Form and Structure

TERNARY FORM
Introduction: A–B–A'

SECTION	MEASURE	EVENT AND SCORING
Introduction	1–34	
	1	Perfect fourth drone, A–D (marimba)
	2	Moaning motive (bowed vibraphone)
	4	Echo motive (bass drum)
	9	Moaning motive (English horn)
	11	Blues scale introduced: D–E–F–A-flat (flutes)
	14	Moaning motive (muted trombone)
	15	Moaning motive (clarinets)
	27	Theme 1 foreshadowed (flutes)
A	35–95	
	35	Theme 1 (saxophones) Ostinato 1 (bassoon and bass clarinet)
	46	Theme 1, canon (saxophones vs. timpani and tom-toms)
	54	Interlude 1 (V$^{\#9}$ chord emphasized)
	59	Theme 1, canon (saxophones, oboe, and clarinet 1 vs. flutes, and vibraphone) Ostinato 1 (bassoons and bass clarinets)

623

SECTION	MEASURE	EVENT AND SCORING
	67	Theme 2 (clarinet solo, then clarinets 1–2) Ostinato 1, inverted contour (tuba)
	80	Interlude 2 (repeat of mm. 54–58, with one-measure extension played by flute 1)
	86	Theme 1 (clarinets and saxophones); ostinato 1, original contour (bassoon, bass clarinet, euphonium, and tuba) Syncopated interjections (flutes, trumpets, and horns)
	94	Descending octatonic scale presented in its entirety: D–C–B–A–A-flat–G-flat–F–E-flat (vibraphone, sustained in winds)
B	96–180	
	96	Move to 6/8 compound meter Ostinato 2 (marimba) Octatonic fragments (clarinet)
	102	Theme 3a, octatonic (flutes)
	124	Theme 3b, octatonic (English horn)
	125	Ostinato 2 (log drum)
	126	Echo motive (bass drum)
	139	Moaning motive voiced in parallel, second-inversion minor triads
	140	Echo motive (tom-toms and horns)
	165	Echo motive (bass drum and horns)
	168	Echo motive (trumpets)
	175	Ostinato 1 presented in upper woodwinds in overlapping layers, combining duple and triple subdivisions
A'	181–231	
	181	Theme 1, canon (saxophones and clarinet 1 vs. flutes) Ostinato 1 (bassoon and bass clarinet) Echo motive (tom-toms)
	189	Theme 1 (saxophones and clarinet 1)
	192	Interlude 3 (V$^{\#9}$ chord emphasized)
	196	Fanfare interruption; move from tritone to perfect fifth (trumpets)
	201	Build to climax (ride cymbal and thematic fragments based on theme 1, ostinato 1, and interlude motives)

Section	Measure	Event and Scoring
	220	Climax (bass voices play ascending octatonic figures while treble voices play descending octatonic figures)
	230	Final cadence (moaning motive in bass voices from E-flat to D, while upper voices sustain a D-minor triad with major seventh and ninth extensions)

Unit 8: Suggested Listening

As an introduction to the tonal world of Wilson's music, students should listen to several blues recordings that emphasize the conflict between major and minor thirds, such as: "St. Louis Blues" by Bessie Smith, "I Can't Be Satisfied" by Muddy Waters, "Folsom Prison Blues" by Johnny Cash, and "I Got a Woman" by Ray Charles.

Single-movement works by Dana Wilson that share common traits with *To set the darkness echoing* include:

> *Dance of the New World*
> *Shakata: Singing the World Into Existence*
> *Shortcut Home*
> *Vortex*

Unit 9: Additional References and Resources

Emge, Jeffrey David. "Third-Stream Music for Band: An Examination of Jazz Influences in Five Selected Compositions for Winds and Percussion (Gunther Schuller, Timothy Broege, Dana Wilson, John Harbison, Donald Grantham)." Doctoral diss., University of Cincinnati, 2000.

Ferrari, Lois. "Two Symphonic Wind Ensemble Compositions of Dana Wilson: *Piece of Mind* and *Shakata: Singing the World into Existence*." Doctoral diss., Eastman School of Music, University of Rochester, 1995.

Halseth, Robert. "Teacher Resource Guide: Dance of the New World." In *Teaching Music through Performance in Band*, *Volume 2*. Richard Miles, ed. Chicago: GIA Publications, 1998. 577–583.

_____. "Teacher Resource Guide: Piece of Mind." In *Teaching Music through Performance in Band*, *Volume 1*. Richard Miles, ed. Chicago: GIA Publications, 1997. 444–449.

Hemberger, Glen. "Teacher Resource Guide: Shortcut Home." In *Teaching Music through Performance in Band*, *Volume 5*. Richard Miles, ed. Chicago: GIA Publications, 2004. 480–484.

Mailman, Matthew. "Teacher Resource Guide: Shakata, Singing the World into Existence." In *Teaching Music through Performance in Band*, *Volume 2*.

Richard Miles, ed. Chicago: GIA Publications, 1998. 627–630.

Mathes, James. "Analysis: *Piece of Mind* by Dana Wilson." *Journal of Band Research* 25, no. 2 (Spring 1990): 1–12.

Salzman, Timothy. *A Composer's Insight: Thoughts, Analysis and Commentary on Contemporary Masterpieces for Wind Band, Volume 4.* Galesville, MD: Meredith Music Publications, forthcoming.

Taylor, Robert. "The Vernacular Made Artful: An Analysis of Dana Wilson's Vortex and Dance of the New World." Doctoral diss., Northwestern University School of Music, Evanston, 2005.

Wilson, Dana. "Dana Wilson." *Composers on Composing for Band, Volume 2.* Mark Camphouse, ed. Chicago: GIA Publications, 2004. 269–293.

_____. "Guidelines for Coaching Student Composers." *Music Educators Journal*, July, 2001: 28–33.

_____. Phone interview and email correspondence with author. May, 2008.

For additional information about Dana Wilson, including current errata lists, visit the composer's website at http://www.ithaca.edu/faculty/wilson

Contributed by:

Robert C. Taylor
Director of Bands
University of Puget Sound
Tacoma, Washington

---

1 Extracted from the composer's website, http://www.ithaca.edu/faculty/wilson

2 D. Wilson, program notes for *To set the darkness echoing* (New York: Boosey & Hawkes, 2006).

3 R. Taylor, *The Vernacular Made Artful: An Analysis of Dana Wilson's Vortex and Dance of the New World* (Evanston, IL: Northwestern University School of Music, 2005), 18.

4 S. Heaney, *Death of a Naturalist* (London: Faber and Faber, 1966).

Teacher Resource Guide

Winter Dances
Fergal Carroll
(b. 1969)

Unit 1: Composer

Fergal Carroll was born in Tipperary, Ireland, where he began playing the trumpet and piano. From 1993 to 1997 he studied music at the Waterford Institute of Technology, majoring in composition with Eric Sweeney. He graduated with a first-class honors degree and was awarded the 1997 Good Shepherd Arts Award.

In 1998 he undertook an MA in composition at the Royal Northern College of Music (RNCM) in Manchester, studying with Anthony Gilbert and Adam Gorb. While in Manchester he also studied with Simon Holt and Martin Butler. He was awarded the Sellars' Award in 1999 and the Mrs. Leo Grindon Prize for composition in 2000. He has been commissioned by, among others, the Birmingham Music Service and Warrington Borough Council/North West Arts Board (UK). In September 2005 he left teaching and was commissioned as a band officer and conductor in the Irish Defense Forces. Currently, Carroll conducts the Army No. 1 Band, which is based in Cathal Brugha Barracks in Dublin, Ireland.

His music has been performed in the United Kingdom, Switzerland, New Zealand, United States, and Canada. His wind compositions include *Amphion* (1998), *Drumslade* (2001), *Winter Dances* (2002), *The Piper of Brafferton* (2004), *Song of Lir* (2004), *Juan for the Road* (2004), *Chapel Royal* (2004), *Dance of the Fir Darrig* (2005), *Blackwater* (2005) and *Silverwinds* (2006). Carroll's music is now published both by Maecenas Music and Brasswind Publications.

Unit 2: Composition

Winter Dances was commissioned by the Cultural Services Department of the Warrington Borough Council with financial support from the Regional Arts Lottery Programme for the North Cheshire Concert Band conducted by Mark Heron. The first performance was given at the BASBWE Festival of Winds, RNCM, Manchester, on March 23, 2002, and the European Premiere at The Forum, Werwik, Belgium, on May 24, 2003.

In the program notes given in the score, the composer writes,

> *Winter Dances* was commissioned to mark the opening of *The Pyramid*, Warrington's purpose built arts venue. It was written to allow performance with dancers and in order to accommodate this, each of the three movements has its distinct character. The movements are titled *November*, *December*, and *January* (as Ireland uses the Celtic calendar these are our winter months, although given our usual weather, I could probably have called a movement July or August!).

> 1. "November" begins with an unrelenting quaver (eighth) pulse in the high woodwinds, punctuated by figures from the low instruments. These become more rhythmically complex as the movement continues. Short, tuneful fragments more fully scored, try unsuccessfully to interrupt until the movement dies away.

> 2. "December" features a soprano saxophone over a slowly repeating ground bass. Against this are put fragments from *Coventry Carol*, an obvious reference to the occurrence of Christmas in this month.

> 3. "January"—the start of each New Year—is the quickest and liveliest movement. The main rhythmic motif is stated immediately before the first theme is played by horns and saxophones. This theme is taken up by the different sections of the band and, as it is developed, combines with other themes, some more rhythmically complex, in the build-up to a climactic conclusion.

Winter Dances is published by Maecenas and is approximately nine minutes in length.

Unit 3: Historical Perspective

This work was conceived to be suitable for performance with dancers, although this is not required. The premiere of *Winter Dances* included young dancers from the community around Warrington, Cheshire, which was specified in the terms of the commission. Because of this Carroll made sure the outer movements November and January were quite rhythmic and pulse-driven and December, as a contrast, more relaxed and fluid.

Unit 4: Technical Considerations

Winter Dances for concert band contains medium to medium-advanced technical demands. It uses the following instrumentation: piccolo, two flutes, two oboes (oboe 2 doubling English horn), E-flat clarinet, 3 B-flat clarinets, alto clarinet, bass clarinet, two bassoons, two E-flat alto saxophones (alto saxophone 1 doubling B-flat soprano saxophone), B-flat tenor saxophone, E-flat baritone saxophone, four horns in F, three trumpets in B-flat, three trombones, euphonium, two tubas, timpani, and three percussion. There is no cross-cuing in the entire work.

The soprano saxophone has an important solo in movement 2, but the composer supports this being written into alto saxophone 1. However, the composer did specify the soprano saxophone, so the performance might be less successful without that instrument. Less critical is the English horn, which is doubled by oboe 2. Almost all of the part could be covered by the oboe or written into alto saxophone 2 or bassoon. The alto clarinet has some essential lines, but these could be written into other woodwind voices if this instrument is not available. Though the composer specifies two tubas, there is only one part. Two would be best for balance, although it could be successfully performed with one player.

The percussion writing is very integral to *Winter Dances*. The instruments include timpani, suspended cymbal, tom-toms, mark tree, snare drum, wood-block, triangle, tam-tam, tambourine, crash cymbals, xylophone, glockenspiel, and chimes. This piece requires a competent timpanist, while percussion 1 and 3 also have prominent parts.

Technical demands include double-tonguing in the trumpet soloist part in movement 1, and English horn and soprano saxophone soloists in movement 2, which could require more advanced players. There are also balance and tuning issues between groups of soloists through movement 2 of which players should be made aware.

Rhythmically, there are many time signature shifts throughout movement 1, which include varying 7/8 meters toward the end of the piece. The first 7/8 measure is broken into 3 + 2 + 2, and the second measure is broken into 2 + 3 + 2. Less-advanced ensembles might need to focus more time on these meter changes.

Unit 5: Stylistic Considerations

Winter Dances requires the ensemble to play in numerous styles while highlighting the dance aspect of the piece. "November" features a quaver (eighth-note) pulse, which contains fast, pointed eighth notes that are played throughout the movement, adding an energy to the dance. This quaver pulse is very important to the movement and should be felt, but not cover the melodies or slow down. This movement also features a wide range of dynamics from *ff* to *pp* at the end of the movement.

"December" is mostly legato and flowing. There is some fanfare-like playing required in the brass, but balance and tuning are the biggest issues in this movement.

"January" is a quick, lively, and high-energy movement. Syncopation and staccato playing are required in this movement from all players. There is a very large range of dynamics, and some independent playing for individuals and sections. Timbres often vary drastically in this movement, from sparse and transparent to full tutti.

Unit 6: Musical Elements

MELODY:
"November" contains many fragmented melodies throughout the movement. "December" is the slow movement and features sustained and expressive melodies in the key of G minor. "January" is the fastest movement, with lots of syncopation within the melodies as well as the accompaniments.

HARMONY:
"November" uses quintal harmony throughout. "December" remains in the key of G minor, but ends on the dominant D major chord, which is the first use of this chord. "January" features basic harmonies, but uses stacked major and minor seconds to create tension along with the energy created by rhythm.

RHYTHM:
"November" features the use of syncopation and a quaver (eighth-note) pulse that creates energy. "December" uses straightforward rhythms. "January" uses very syncopated, short, and energetic rhythms to help create energy.

TEXTURE (TIMBRE):
In "November," the quaver (eighth-note) pulse is usually stated in high woodwinds, and melodies are usually in middle voices. The very end of the movement features a decrescendo that adds voices, creating an interesting timbre effect. "December" features a large amount of woodwind versus brass. Tutti concert Fs are used often, and there is lots of added color and texture, with sixteenth-note passages in high woodwinds throughout. In "January," there are often shifts between woodwinds, brass, and full tutti. There are also

some sections of sparse orchestration followed by sections of loud, full tutti writing.

Unit 7: Form and Structure

Winter Dances is in three movements. There is a pause between movement 1, but movements 2 and 3 should be attacca.

SECTION	MEASURE	EVENT AND SCORING
Movement 1: "November," quarter note = c. 140, *Quick, precise*		
A1	1–15	Introduces quaver (eighth-note) pulse in high woodwinds; motive 1 in low voices centered around concert G
B1	16–25	Quaver pulse shifts voices; theme 1 introduced in horns, based around three-note motive of B–A–E-flat, then joined by trumpets and trombones; tutti statement of three-note motive in m. 25
A2	26–35	Return of section A material, but more compressed; low brass melody added; horn melody added on top of section A material, which are both taken from theme 1
C1	36–43	Quaver pulse shifts again and is more fragmented; theme 2 introduced in trumpet, trombone, and horn
A3	44–52	Return of section A material, but with melody taken from "God Rest Ye Merry Gentlemen," stated in horn 1–2, alto saxophone 1, and alto clarinet; this melody alternates with a statement of motive 1 in low voices
C2	53–60	Return of section C material, but melody becomes more compressed; no quaver pulse; high woodwinds add color and texture
A4	61–70	Return of section A material with a new melodic fragment alternating with motive 1 in low voices
B2	71–77	Return of section B material, but with altered melody
C3	78–85	Return of section C material; interrupted by quaver pulse in m. 80; continues into m. 86, where the last return of section A material occurs

SECTION	MEASURE	EVENT AND SCORING
A5	86-end	Return of section A material for the final time; two measures of 7/8 meter occur: m. 89 is divided 3 + 2 + 2, m. 90 is separated into 2 + 3 + 2; last three measures of the movement descend in eighth notes, but adds voices that decrescendo into a quintal chord at a *pianissimo* dynamic; last sound is timpani in final measure

Movement 2: "December," quarter note = c. 72, *Elegant*

Introduction	1–3	Introduction consisting of flute and English horn solo line with glockenspiel counter-melody; high woodwinds provide accompaniment with stacked chord into a fermata in m. 3
A1	4–13	Mm. 4–5 set up key of G minor; soprano saxophone statement of theme 1 begins in m. 6 with sparse accompaniment
A2	14–22	Soprano saxophone joined by piccolo and euphonium in another statement of theme 1; accompaniment thicker in this statement of section A material; color added by sixteenth-note passages in high woodwinds
Transition 1	23–31	Transition material stated mainly in brass with arpeggiations in horn and trumpet voices; euphonium takes over a solo in mm. 25–27, which builds to an F-major chord into m. 31; woodwinds and chimes state two quarter-note concert Fs, ending the transition material
B1	32–39	Section B contains the same accompaniment figures from section A, but with theme 2 being stated in trumpet; accompaniment sparse; piccolo states an answer motive in mm. 35–36 that returns later
B2	40–48	Theme 2 stated in trombone and euphonium with similar accompaniment as the statement before; theme 1 added in piccolo, English horn, bassoon 1, and soprano saxophone at a louder dynamic than theme 2; answer motive stated again in horns in mm. 43–44

SECTION	MEASURE	EVENT AND SCORING
Transition 2	49–57	Transition material returns, but has added color with woodwind sixteenth-note passages; builds to an F major chord into m. 57, but brass state the two concert F quarter notes instead of woodwinds
Introduction	58–62	Introduction material returns, but stated in the entire woodwind section; brass interrupts with tutti concert F quarter notes taken from the end of transition material; rhythm changes to two concert F eighth notes in brass in m. 61; m. 62 extends the introduction material
B3	63–66	Section B material returns with theme 2 in alto saxophones, tenor saxophone, horns, and trumpets; answer motive stated in high woodwinds in m. 66
Codetta	67-end	Tutti statement of chords in quarter notes that builds to a D-major chord and decrescendos to a *ppp* dynamic to end the movement

Movement 3: "January," quarter note = c. 152, *With energy*

Introduction	1–8	Introduction consisting of an energetic statement of short, syncopated eighth notes broken into two measures, interrupted by timpani; energetic eighth-note statement again in m. 4 extended by clarinets, continuing into a high woodwind technical passage into the next section; sets up the key of D minor
A1	9–16	Theme 1 introduced in horns and alto saxophone with clarinet, trombone, euphonium, and tuba accompaniment
A2	17–24	Theme 1 shifts to flute 1 and clarinet 1 with woodwind and low brass accompaniment
A3	25–32	Varied statement of theme 1 in trumpet 1 with a euphonium countermelody and brass accompaniment
Transition	33–40	Transition material begins in m. 33 with moving eighth notes that shift voices and modulate to the key of B-flat into the next section

Section	Measure	Event and Scoring
B1	41–53	Theme 2 introduced in high woodwinds over a syncopated accompaniment; meters shift throughout this section between 5/4, 2/4, and 3/4
Introduction	54–64	Introduction material returns, but varies from the beginning statement with altered rhythms and added interjections in trumpets and horns; woodwinds state a technical passage in mm. 61–64 that begins with low woodwinds in eighth notes and moves higher in instrumentation and faster in rhythm into the next section; return to the key of D minor
A4	65–74	Section A returns with a two-measure introduction in clarinets; theme 1 stated in piccolo with sparse accompaniment that crescendos into the next section
A5	75–84	Theme 1 shifts to trombones with energetic eighth notes interjected in alto saxophones, horns, trumpets, and percussion
C1	85–92	Theme 3 introduced in flutes and oboes; energetic eighth-note motive from introduction in mm. 88–89 marked "loud clap" in full ensemble
C2	93–102	Clarinets join theme 3 and echo with piccolo, flutes, and oboes in mm. 97–101; syncopated horn accompaniment
B2	103–118	Theme 2 restated exactly from the section B1 at m. 41 until m. 114, where descending sixteenth-note passages are passed around the woodwind section
Introduction	119–123	Introduction material returns, but shortened
A and C1	124–131	Theme 1 stated in alto saxophone and horns; theme 3 stated in piccolo, flutes, and oboes, with full accompaniment underneath

Section	Measure	Event and Scoring
A and C2	132–146	Theme 1 shifts to alto saxophone and trumpet 1; theme 3 stated in flutes, oboes, and clarinets; mm. 143–146 are an extension: beginning with low voices, a chord is built based on the pitches B-flat–E–F, which builds up the ensemble into the last section
Codetta	147-end	Codetta section begins with section B material in mm. 147–148; introduction material returns in mm. 149–150; varied statement of theme 1 in low voices in mm. 151–152 with a syncopated descending line while the ensemble plays an *fp* chord underneath that crescendos into a tutti ensemble concert D in the final measure

Unit 8: Suggested Listening

Blackwater. Volume 3: Ithaca College. Timothy Reynish, conductor.

Symphonic Band. Timothy Reynish, conductor. Mark Custom Recording Service, Inc.

Song of Lir. Band Songs. Rutgers Wind Ensemble. William Berz, conductor: Mark Masters. 2004.

Winter Dances. Reflections. Philharmonia à Vent. John Boyd, conductor. Klavier. 2002..

Unit 9: Additional References and Resources

Heron, Mark. "*Winter Dances* by Fergal Carroll: A Guide to Rehearsal and Performance." *Winds Magazine*, July, 2006: 1–8. www.markheron.co.uk

For a complete listing of works by Fergal Carroll, consult the Irish Contemporary Music Centre's website: www.cmc.ie/composers (Biographical information used in Unit 1 of this teaching guide was adapted from this source.)

Contributed by:

Tamey Anglley
Doctoral Conducting Associate
Texas Tech University

Grade Five

Teacher Resource Guide

Cityscape

Scott Boerma
(b. 1964)

Unit 1: Composer

Scott Boerma is associate director of bands, director of Michigan Marching and Athletic Bands, and the Donald R. Shepherd associate professor of conducting at the University of Michigan. Previously he was director of bands at Eastern Michigan University. He began his career teaching music in the Michigan public schools at Lamphere and Novi High Schools. Boerma earned his MM in music education at the University of Michigan, where he studied composition with William Bolcom, and his BM in music education at Western Michigan University, where he studied composition with Ramon Zupko. He is currently working toward completion of his DMA in wind conducting at Michigan State University. Boerma has also studied composition with Anthony Iannaccone at Eastern Michigan University.

Although he did not compose concert band works for most of his years as a public school teacher, Boerma has written fifteen new pieces within the past eight years. Several of these works have been performed by the "The President's Own" Marine Band, the University of North Texas Wind Symphony, the Tokyo Kosei Wind Orchestra, the Dallas Wind Symphony, the University of Illinois Wind Symphony, and the University of Michigan Concert Band, to name a few, and they have been heard in such venues as Carnegie Hall, the Myerson Symphony Center, Hill Auditorium, and the Krannert Center for the Performing Arts. Other published works at the time of this volume's release include *Fanfare for a Golden Sky*, *Poem*, *Porta Nigra*, *Silver*, *Cauldron*, *Sesquicentennial Fanfare*, and *Bora Bora*.

Also a prolific arranger, Boerma is commissioned yearly to write for many high school and university marching bands, and drum and bugle corps throughout the United States, as well as in Japan, the United Kingdom, the Netherlands, and Thailand. From 1989–2006 he was the music arranger and head brass instructor for the Madison Scouts Drum and Bugle Corps. Most of the Big Ten University marching bands have performed Boerma's arrangements. He has also written arrangements for the Detroit Chamber Winds Brass.

Unit 2: Composition

Cityscape, a symphonic fanfare for winds and percussion, was written for and dedicated to James F. Keene and the University of Illinois Wind Symphony. The work was designed to make a bold opening statement for the ensemble's 2006 performance in New York City's Carnegie Hall. Intense, clashing harmonies and tight, vertical rhythms combine with moments of calm, yet unsettled release to depict the atmosphere within the endless canyons of metal and cement in the heart of the city.

This three-and-a-half minute work is listed as a Grade 5 in difficulty due to the flurry of notes throughout, the rhythmic independence required of the players, the intervallic and harmonic complexity, the 12/8 time signature, and its *Very Fast* (dotted quarter note = 174) tempo marking. However, the brass ranges are reasonable for this level, and the technical passages lay well on the instruments. The work has received many fine performances by high school bands as well as university and professional ensembles.

Unit 3: Historical Perspective

Cityscape is the second of three works written by Scott Boerma at the request of James Keene for the University of Illinois Wind Symphony. *Fanfare for a Golden Sky* (2000) and *Sonorities* (2008) were also intended to exploit the resources of this large, exciting ensemble. *Cityscape* was premiered at the University of Illinois on October 30, 2005 and was then performed in Carnegie Hall in New York City on February 17, 2006.

Unit 4: Technical Considerations

Thick, clashing harmonies and angular melodies with large intervallic leaps require brass players (horns in particular) to be extremely accurate with partial placement. For example, in mm. 86–90, careful attention must be given to each statement of the melodic fragments to ensure pitch accuracy.

Vibraphone and marimba parts include two brief moments that require players to demonstrate four-mallet technique. In mm. 21–22, the vibraphonist must also carefully check for note accuracy. The D-natural in the second chord is often missed because the accidental is a bit difficult to notice in the printed part. This vibraphone statement is imperative to the composition, as it demonstrates a harmonic color that binds the work together. The second passage requiring four-mallet technique occurs in mm. 80 and 82 for both vibraphone and marimba. At the end of the percussion interlude (mm. 84–85), it is imperative that the vibraphone and marimba motives are heard clearly above the ensemble and that the rhythms are played precisely together.

Accurate timpani tuning is essential throughout the work. In mm. 62–77, the timpani provides a pedal point that shifts down two half-steps during the phrases, creating harmonic movement that supports the shifting colors above. Another important descending scale occurs in mm. 123–129.

Large dynamic contrasts abound throughout, requiring musicians to be in control of their breath support, embouchures, and oral cavities in order to maintain pitch during crescendos and decrescendos. For example, brass players will have a tendency to force their pitch sharp during crescendos and flat during decrescendos. Woodwinds will often have the opposite tendencies, although flutes will tend to flatten on decrescendos as well.

Dynamics are meticulously notated. Close attention must be given to the exact beginnings and endings of dynamic changes, and students must be encouraged not to allow crescendos and decrescendos to proceed too quickly (e.g., mm. 8–9, 18–20, 35–36, 45–46, and 122–123). Also, musicians must note the exact dynamics to which decrescendos lead (e.g., mm. 29–30 and 46–47). Excitement will be generated through the distinct contrast of dynamics throughout. Maximizing the soft end of the dynamic spectrum will make louder statements resound. This is especially important when expressing *fp* and *ffp*, which are often used as a way to bring out other prominent lines that will not be heard otherwise. The use of tutti silence is also vital in mm. 40 and 135. Dynamic interplay like that seen in mm. 45–52 will bring the piece to life.

Players should avoid breathing between consecutive long tones (e.g., mm. 15–16, 116, and 133–134). Stagger breathing may be employed to carry phrases until their more logical breath points. Tones should be released directly on the eighth note to which they are tied (e.g., mm. 6, 17, 40, 42, 96, 97, 100, and 135) or on the rest that follows any non-tied note. Trills should connect to the next note or rest without breaking in between.

The conductor must look for key lines to bring out when clarifying balance. For example, the soft, yet accented whole- and half-note entrances in mm. 10–12 and 129–131 create ascending scales that must be noticed below the flurry of woodwind activity above. Also, the descending chromatic lines in alto saxophone 2 and horn 3–4 in mm. 31–33 and also in bassoon 1, alto saxophone 2, and tenor saxophone in mm. 118–120 must be heard through the thick textures.

The articulation and shape of accents throughout should be clear and precise. Separation must be given between marcato accents, especially on the duplets in mm. 55 and 136. The articulated eighth notes played by woodwinds in mm. 98–117 must be light and detached.

Players must be careful not to clip the length of dotted quarter notes to which grace notes or glissandos lead (mm. 89–90). In other words, all dotted quarter notes should be played for a full, long beat, not shortened due to the grace note "rips."

There is an optional stopped horn moment in mm. 65–66. The strength of this attack and the "buzz" that follows are the important considerations here. If players are not able to confidently attack the note precisely on beat 2, they should refrain from stopping the horns.

At several points in the composition brass is asked to play fast, slurred eighth notes (e.g., mm. 12–14, 75–77, 131–132). These passages should be approached with flowing, woodwind-like style.

Unit 5: Stylistic Considerations

Since the work is a fanfare, it must be performed with great energy and confidence. The tempo marking of "Very Fast (dotted quarter note = 174)" should not be taken lightly. Anything slower will lack momentum. Although the conductor will be tempted to conduct in two, it is important to maintain the relentless drive of the work. Passages with long, extended chords (e.g., mm. 15–22, 62–77, 102–117, and 133-end) may provide appropriate opportunities to conduct in two, but the conductor must make sure that the tempo does not relax as a result.

Unit 6: Musical Elements

MELODY:

The use of angular, chromatic lines with moderately large intervallic leaps defines the melodic nature of the work. Time spent slowly practicing melodies, identifying precise pitches throughout, will be necessary. Fragments of the melodies are intertwined, inverted, and augmented to create constant motivic interplay. Three main melodic ideas are presented throughout the piece. Figures 1a-c provide piano reductions of these from the score in concert pitch.

FIGURE 1a. Mm. 23–27, theme A with countermelody

FIGURE 1b. Mm. 29–30 and 33–34, theme A'

FIGURE 1c. Mm. 46–51, theme B

HARMONY:

Although *Cityscape* is considered tonal in nature, traditional harmonies are rare, and traditional harmonic progressions do not exist. Major chords can be found hiding in textures throughout the work, but they are surrounded by sevenths, ninths, elevenths, and thirteenths, voiced in unusual ways. Identifying and tuning the root, fifth, and third of each stacked chord, and then adding the extended notes, will aid the musicians in a more complete understanding of their role within the textures. This will lead to a higher level of intonation success. Two examples of the unifying harmonic progression are given in figures 2a-b, in piano reductions from the score in concert pitch. The tonality basis is given above each chord.

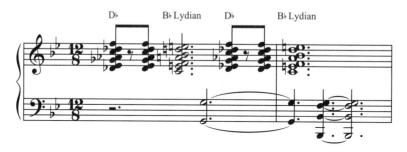

FIGURE 2a. Mm. 7–8, harmonic progression

FIGURE 2b. Mm. 133–134, harmonic progression

The work begins with a strong D-flat Lydian bias but quickly turns to a recurring B-flat Lydian influence. Harmonic progressions throughout are extremely chromatic, but the piece closes by returning to the opening D-flat Lydian-based tonality.

RHYTHM:
Rhythmic confidence and independence are essential for a successful performance of this work. Although the piece employs a 12/8 time signature throughout, the use of duple rhythms and unpredictable entrances and releases will require great attention. Note the interplay between triple and duple rhythms in figures 1a-c. In more complex areas, musicians may find it helpful to write reference beat numbers here and there in their parts, as rhythmic assumptions will surely result in missed rhythms.

TIMBRE:
As a symphonic fanfare, there are inherently many forceful tutti ensemble passages. The different sections of the band often play traditional roles:

dazzling woodwind licks and powerful brass and percussion statements. However, there are times throughout where the roles are shared or exchanged, so musicians must be willing to express each particular section appropriately. While there are no significantly unusual combinations of voices, there are several, somewhat thinly-scored passages in which individual characteristic tones are imperative for proper blend. Tutti sustained statements (e.g., mm. 15–20 and 133-end) must be given great balance, tone, and intonation attention to achieve grand, organ-like effects.

Unit 7: Form and Structure

SECTION	MEASURE	EVENT AND SCORING
Introduction	1–22	Bold statements foreshadow motives to follow and are enhanced by virtuosic eighth-note runs; main harmonic progression stated; tonality influenced by D-flat Lydian
Theme A	23–28	Main theme and countermelody introduced by horns, baritones, and trombones; tonality influenced by B-flat Lydian
Theme A'	29–36	Main theme begun again by horns but then expanded by others to include more motivic material
Transition	37–44	Fragments of themes stated by various instruments; tutti climax achieved; woodwind flourish leads into next section
Theme B	45–52	Secondary theme introduced by horns; motives from theme A are interspersed
Transition	53–61	Powerful dialogue between upper and lower voices creates tension; low and then middle voices conclude with a fade into next section
Interlude	62–77	Calmer, yet still unsettled, expression of motives by woodwinds; tonality influenced by B-flat Lydian, with an E-natural pedal point; brass then answer with same style; brass flourish into next section
Development	78–85	Percussion manipulation of motives, with chromatic woodwind interplay in background; opening tonality influenced by A-flat Lydian but quickly becomes obscure; percussion and woodwinds combine together to create an E-flat unison resolution

Section	Measure	Event and Scoring
Development	86–95	Brass fanfares of melodic fragments; no discernable tonality; woodwinds gradually add, and all crescendo toward next section
Transition	96–101	The most consonant moment of the work; brass triumphantly states open fifths in B-flat, with woodwinds providing interjections; woodwinds then establish repeated eighth-note interplay that will continue for the next two phrases
Theme A	102–114	Main theme and countermelody augmented and restated with tutti scoring; woodwinds continue repeated eighth notes above; tonality influenced by B-flat Lydian
Theme A'	115–123	Augmentation continues briefly in brass and then returns to its original form in woodwinds; tonality alludes to E-flat Lydian but ends with a D-flat Lydian bias; climax achieved before fading into next section
Transition	124–132	Motives traded from high to low voices; eighth-note flourishes reminiscent of the introduction lead to an abrupt halt; tonality shifts throughout
Coda	133–139	Bold tutti statements of main harmonic progression; tonality influenced by D-flat Lydian

Unit 8: Suggested Listening

Boerma, Scott:
  Bora Bora
  Cauldron
  Equinox
  Fanfare for a Golden Sky
  Fjords
  How Can I Keep From Singing
  Let There Be Peace
  Poem
  Porta Nigra
  Sesquicentennial Fanfare
  Silver
  Sonorities

Windjammer
Zirk (for horn and band)

Unit 9: Additional References and Resources

Boerma, Scott. *Cityscape*. New York: Boosey & Hawkes, Inc., 2007.
Miles, Richard, ed. "Teacher's Resource Guide: Poem." In *Teaching Music through Performance in Band, Volume 6.* Chicago: GIA Publications, 2007.

Websites:
Arrangers' Publishing Company. www.arrpubco.com
Boosey & Hawkes, Inc. www.boosey.com
Neil A. Kjos Music Company. www.kjos.com
Madison Music Works, LLC. www.madisonmusicworks.com

Contributed by:

Scott Boerma
Associate Director of Bands
Director of Michigan Marching and Athletic Bands
Donald R. Shepherd Associate Professor of Conducting
University of Michigan
Ann Arbor, Michigan

Teacher Resource Guide

Concertante
for Wind Instruments
Norman Dello Joio
(b. 1913)

Unit 1: Composer

Norman Dello Joio is undoubtedly one of the most prolific and successful American composers of the twentieth century. Born in New York to two church organist parents, he began piano lessons at age four and later organ lessons at age fourteen with his godfather, Pietro Yon, organist at Saint Patrick's Cathedral. In 1939 he was accepted as a scholarship student at The Juilliard School, studying composition with Bernard Wagenaar.

Following his studies at Juilliard, he began his career as an organist at St. Anne's Church in New York, but decided that he wanted to pursue his interests as a composer. Studies with Paul Hindemith soon followed in 1941 at Tanglewood and Yale University. Over the course of his career, Dello Joio has composed prolifically for almost every performing medium, including band, choir, orchestra, opera, ballet, television scores, solo piano, and concerti for several instruments. Over the course of his career, he has won almost every major award for composition in the United States, including the Pulitzer Prize in 1957 for *Meditations on Ecclesiastes*, two Guggenheim Fellowships, an Emmy Award in 1965 for *Scenes from the Louvre*, and the New York Music Critics' Award in 1948 for *Variations, Chaconne, and Finale*.

From 1959 until 1972, Dello Joio was director of the Ford Foundation's Contemporary Music Project, which placed seventy-three composers in residence in seventy-seven public schools across the United States. This highly successful project was responsible for creating a wide body of quality literature for highs school bands, choirs, and orchestras from such composers as John Barnes Chance and Martin Mailman.

As an educator, he taught at the Mannes School of Music in Sarah Lawrence College, and was Dean of the Fine and Applied Arts School of Boston University from 1972 to 1978. Upon retiring from Boston University, he moved back to Long Island, New York and has continued to accept commissions from ensembles and individuals from across the country.

Unit 2: Composition

Concertante was commissioned in 1972 by Warren Mercer and the North Hills High School Symphonic Band, located in Pittsburgh, Pennsylvania. During Mercer's tenure as director of bands from 1961 to 1992, he founded the North Hills Commissioning Project, which has produced forty works for band from such notable composers as Don Gillis, Edward Madden, Robert Jager, Jerry Bilik, Rex Mitchell, and Vaclav Nelhybel. Under Mercer's direction, the North Hills High School Symphonic Band regularly performed at such venues as the Pennsylvania Music Educators Association Conference, the Midwest Band and Orchestra Clinic, the Mideast Band Clinic, and the Kennedy Center for the Performing Arts. Additionally, they regularly performed with such artists as Arthur Fiedler, conductor of the Boston Pops Orchestra, and Tommy Newsom, lead alto saxophonist of the Tonight Show Band.

Concertante for Wind Instruments is in two movements. The composer has provided the following program note for this composition:

> The work is in two contrasting movements. The first movement, *Adagio, molto sostenuto*, in its very opening indicates the thematic material that binds the total composition. This is done by a melodic twelve-tone statement. The second section, *Allegro con brio*, is a kaleidoscopic antiphonal dance in 6/8, suggesting a saltarello.

Unit 3: Historical Perspective

Over the course of his career, Norman Dello Joio has written many works for band that have become standard pieces in the repertoire. Beginning with *Variants on a Medieval Tune* in 1963, works such as *Scenes from the Louvre*, *Fantasies on a Theme by Haydn*, and *Satiric Dances* regularly appear on high school, collegiate, and professional band programs. In 2003, Dello Joio wrote a letter to the College Band Directors National Association, expressing his thanks for the continued support for his works for band:

> I am delighted to know and to thank the National Association for its recognition of my work and its role in the wide and active world of American bands. It seems but yesterday that at the persuasion and urging of Paul Brian [sic] of Duke University, I wrote my first piece for band, the *Variants on a Medieval Tune*. I am ever thankful to him for opening for me examination of new areas of sound. Happily for me

these sounds entered the hearts of many of you, and looking back, I now am aware of how significant a role handling wind instruments played in my creative life. As a result I join you all in giving allegiance to a great art form, Music for Band. And in conclusion, may I say that I am a privileged composer to play a part in its continued development.

Unit 4: Technical Considerations

The first movement of *Concertante* presents challenges in terms of rhythm, pitch, and control at soft dynamic levels. The two primary rhythmic motives found in the first three measures must be subdivided at the sixteenth- and thirty-second-note level to insure an accurate performance. Mm. 29–34 and 48–53 use many woodwinds above the treble clef staff, where it is often challenging to accurately tune and blend with the rest of the ensemble. Finally, many of the solo and tutti entrances found within this movement are at soft dynamic levels, frequently at *p* and *pp*. In order to play these passages in tune and in tone, proper air speed and support must work together to enable these quiet entrances.

The primary challenges of movement 2 include rapid articulation, matching note lengths of the repeated eighth notes, and the wide leaps often found in several of the woodwind parts. Beginning in m. 150, the brass must be able to rapidly articulate sixteenth-note figures found in several locations. Given the printed tempo, the ability to double-tongue may be a necessity for an accurate performance.

The constant use of repeated, articulated eighth notes binds much of movement 2 together. The majority of these entrances are traded off between woodwinds and brass, creating challenges for maintaining uniform note lengths between instruments and registers. Lastly, several woodwind parts contain wide leaps that are technically very difficult given the printed tempo.

Special consideration needs to be given to alto clarinet in mm. 59–63. During this four-measure passage, alto clarinet plays many of these unison pitches one octave lower than everyone else. This passage has not been cross-cued in the score. If an alto clarinet is not available, this passage must be assigned to one or more instruments to cover it in the written octave.

Unit 5: Stylistic Considerations

Movement 1 of *Concertante* focuses on legato playing in all registers at all dynamics and ranges, particularly at the soft end of the dynamic spectrum. Additionally, care needs to be given to the length and types of releases found in the solo and ensemble passages. Since many of the sections of this work are created by silence, how an ensemble enters and comes out of silence will dictate how effective this movement is. Movement 2 requires the ensemble to play rapidly articulated pitches that are detached, lifted, and full of energy.

Unit 6: Musical Elements

Perhaps the most interesting element of this work is that Dello Joio chose to base much of the melodic material on a twelve-tone row: C–B–F-sharp–F–D–A–E–E-flat–B-flat–D-flat–A-flat–G. It was very unusual for him to write with this technique, in that he had done so on only three other occasions. Rather than imposing the strict rules of twelve-tone composition set forth by Arnold Schoenberg and Anton Webern, he incorporates twelve-tone technique within his own compositional style, much like Aaron Copland and Igor Stravinsky did later in their careers. Dello Joio's melodic and harmonic language is very tonal, utilizing tertian and modal harmony. In this work he successfully binds twelve-tone technique with his own compositional language.

Unit 7: Form and Structure

Movement 1: *Adagio, molto sostenuto*

MEASURE	EVENT AND SCORING
1–10	Introduction of primary rhythmic motives
	• mm. 1–2; horn
	• m. 3; clarinet
	Tone row presented in retrograde1–2
	• mm. 1–2; horn, notes 12–9
	• m. 4; oboe, notes 8–5
	• m. 6; flute, notes 4–1
	• m. 10; bass clarinet, bassoon, and baritone saxophone, notes 12–10
	Note 12 (G) used as tonal center in transition to m. 11
11–22	Tone row presented in prime form
	• m. 13; clarinet and alto saxophone, notes 1–4
	• m. 16; alto clarinet, bass clarinet, bassoon, tenor saxophone, and baritone saxophone, notes 5–8
	• m. 20; euphonium, notes 9–12
	Statement of tone row accompanied by:
	• C pedal point
	• shifting chords in flute, horn, trombone, and glockenspiel
	Mm. 21–22; G tonal center established by ensemble
23–28	Tone row presented in retrograde
	• mm. 23–24; cornet 1; notes 12–9
	• mm. 25–26; piccolo, flute, and oboe; notes 8–5
	• mm. 26–27; cornet 1, trumpet 1–2; notes 4–1
	Mm. 27–28; C tonal center established by ensemble

MEASURE	EVENT AND SCORING
29–35	Chromatic melody consisting primarily of minor thirds and seconds in piccolo, flute, oboe, clarinet, bass clarinet, bassoon, and horn Melody harmonized by chords derived from descending chromatic movement
36–39	Transition; thirty-second-note motive in clarinet and cornet, harmonized by bass clarinet, bassoon, trombone, euphonium, and tuba
40–45	Tone row presented in retrograde: • mm. 40–41; flute; notes 12–9 • mm. 42–43; clarinet; notes 8–5 • mm. 44–45; cornet; notes 4–1
45–54	Chromatic melody consisting primarily of minor thirds and minor seconds in woodwinds Melody harmonized by chords derived from descending chromatic movement
55–63	Tone row presented in prime form • mm. 59–61; clarinet; notes 1–8 • mm. 61–62; bass clarinet; notes 9–12 M. 63; G tonal center established by ensemble
64–73	Mm. 68–69; flute; notes 12–9 Harmonized by brass; C major chord with added D

Movement 2: *Allegro con brio*

1–30	M. 5; introduction; first appearance of theme A; constant eighth-note activity in woodwinds
31–54	Theme B stated in m. 37 by flute, oboe, and trumpet; continued in bassoon, trombone, and euphonium
55–58	Cadential extension
59–62	Transition; piccolo, flute, oboe, clarinet, and alto clarinet
63–80	Theme B stated in m. 65 by piccolo, flute, oboe, and trumpet, with different accompaniment
81–84	Cadential extension
85–94	Theme A; woodwinds and horn
95–101	Transition; false beginning of theme A
102–112	Antiphonal entrances of constant eighth notes
113–116	Transition
117–122	Development of second half of theme B accompanied by constant eighth notes
123–128	Theme A in brass (minus tuba)
129–136	Melody derived from theme B; eighth-note accompaniment in low woodwinds

MEASURE	EVENT AND SCORING
137–138	Transition
139–149	Theme A alternating between woodwind and brass consorts
150–175	Imitation of euphonium statement in m. 157
176–177	Transition derived from theme B
178–199	Melody derived from theme A
200–202	Transition; grand pause and timpani solo
203–211	Theme A
212–222	Legato theme; piccolo, flute, and trumpet; dotted-note accompaniment
223–230	Transition; chord structures similar to those found in movement 1, mm. 11–19
231–244	Tone row presented in retrograde; flute and clarinet
245–265	Tone row in prime form; cornet
266–273	Transition
274–288	Coda; rhythmic motive of theme A; establishment of C tonal center

Unit 8: Suggested Listening

Copland, Aaron. *Inscape*.
Dello Joio, Norman:
 Caccia
 Colonial Ballads
 The Dancing Sargeant
 Fantasies on a theme by Haydn
 From Every Horizon
 Satiric Dances
 Scenes from the Louvre
 Songs of Aberlard
 Variants on a Medieval Tune
Hindemith, Paul. *Symphony in B-flat*.
Schoenberg, Arnold. *Suite for Piano*, Op. 25.
Stravinsky, Igor. *In Memoriam: Dylan Thomas*.
Webern, Anton. *Symphony*, Op. 21.

Unit 9: Additional References and Resources

Dello Joio, Norman. *Concertante for Wind Instruments*. The Composers Voice: Norman Dello Joio. The Keystone Wind Ensemble. Jack Stamp, conductor. Klavier 11138. 2003.
Composer's official website. http://fp.enter.net/~debrat42/

Contributed by:

Jason Worzbyt
Associate Professor of Bassoon
Associate Director of Bands
Indiana University of Pennsylvania
Indiana, Pennsylvania

Teacher Resource Guide

Divertimento

Leonard Bernstein
(1918–1990)

arranged by Clare Grundman
(1913–1996)

Unit 1: Composer

Leonard Bernstein was a pianist, composer, conductor, author, and lecturer. He was the first American-born composer to achieve worldwide attention, and was the first American-born conductor of the New York Philharmonic Orchestra. His formal musical training included studies at Harvard, where he received the only A ever given by Fritz Reiner, and the Curtis institute of Music. His composition teachers included Walter Piston, and his conducting teachers included Serge Koussevitsky.

He achieved early fame as a conductor in 1943 while assistant to Bruno Walther, when he had to conduct a complete concert with the New York Philharmonic with only a few hour's notice when Walther became ill. This early triumph demonstrated both his proclivity for interpretation and his ability to learn scores quickly. From 1958 to 1969 he was music director of the New York Philharmonic, but afterwards maintained a close relationship with that orchestra for the rest of his life. He maintained a long friendship with American composer Aaron Copland, and was a champion of American composers, most notably Charles Ives.

As a composer, Bernstein wrote four symphonies, choral music, music theatre, and music for television and film. During his lifetime he was perhaps best known for his music to *West Side Story* (1957) and for his fifty-three television broadcasts as conductor and friendly lecturer in the *Young People's*

Concerts (1962–69). Indeed, the 1950s and 1960s were probably the peak of his career as conductor, composer, and American musical icon.

Bernstein's personal life was in many ways a reflection of his musical life. Although he married and fathered three children, his sexuality was a constant source of gossip. His flamboyant and effusive personality was mirrored in both his music and in his conducting, and by the late 1960s he was criticized as too emotive a conductor. He created controversy by embracing some radical elements of the Black Panther party and through some scandalous public behavior.

However, *Mass*, premiered in 1971 for the opening of the Kennedy Center for the Performing Arts in Washington, DC, became recognized as a major composition, as it was a summation both of much of his music and much of the music of the twentieth century. The last few decades of his life were spent promoting music education through music festivals such as Tanglewood and in frequent appearances as conductor, especially with the Israel Philharmonic Orchestra.

Unit 2: Composition

Divertimento was written in 1980 to celebrate the centennial of the Boston Symphony Orchestra, Seiji Ozawa, conductor. It is a tribute to the orchestra, a summation of Bernstein's music, and a tribute to American musical styles. The composition is in eight movements, and all but two take less than two minutes to perform. The musical material is generated from the two notes, B and C, the smallest tonal interval and a direct reference to "Boston Centennial." From this germ, both melodic and harmonic material is generated.

Movement 1, "Sennets and Tuckets," is borrowed from Shakespeare, in which the phrase was used to signify a general fanfare. This movement recalls much of the "Kyrie Eleison" from Bernstein's *Mass*. The "Waltz" (movement 2) is in a fast seven and is reminiscent of Bach's *Minuet in G*, and originally featured the string section alone. In the transcription, Grundman uses only woodwinds.

Movement 3, "Mazurka," is written only for double reeds and harp; there are no cues written for oboes, English horn, bassoons, and contrabassoon. The end of the movement directly quotes the oboe cadenza from movement 1 of Beethoven's *Symphony No. 5*. The "Samba" (movement 4) is in a fast duple meter and is reminiscent of the scoring and textures used in both the "Mambo" from *West Side Story* and in *Fancy Free*.

The "Turkey Trot" (movement 5) also quotes from *West Side Story*, in this case the ensemble number "America." "Sphinxes" (movement 6) refers to the inscrutable men of the twelve-tone serial technique (Schoenberg and Webern) and is also a sly reference to Bernstein's own use of serialism in the later portion of his life. In this movement, two twelve-tone rows are answered tonally.

Movement 7, "Blues," is written only for brass and percussion and uses tone rows to bookend solos by euphonium and trombone (tuba and trombone in the original version). This movement is reminiscent of *Prelude, Fugue, and Riffs.* The finale begins with "In Memoriam," a fughetta for three flutes and is also based on a twelve-tone row. This short prelude is a tribute to the deceased members of the BSO. The fughetta proceeds directly to the finale "March, the BSO Forever." This is an obvious pun on the Sousa March *Stars and Stripes Forever.* In the finale, material from the first movement, the "Kyrie Eleison" from *Mass,* and the *Overture to Candide,* are presented in six broad sections with three themes. The last section of the march recaps three themes simultaneously.

The scoring for band includes parts for e-flat clarinet (required), contrabassoon (not cued, but could be substituted), harp (cued, but greatly loses the effect), and six percussion parts.

With solos for virtually every instrument, extremes of ranges expected, scoring for the complete double reed section, and a wide variety of styles presented, *Divertimento* is a transcription that is very true to the original in every way, and best performed by only the most mature ensembles with complete instrumentation.

Unit 3: Historical Perspective

In and around 1980, much of the art music written was heavily influenced by Minimalism, Pop, and modern Jazz. Bernstein, however, never really changed his basic compositional style since 1971, when his *Mass* was premiered. In that composition, he explored a panoply of styles, incorporating and juxtaposing chant, pop, marching band, blues, twelve-tone, and more traditional orchestral sounds. In the *Divertimento,* he again fashions a summation of both a variety of genres and of his compositional techniques. The direct predecessor to this idea may be Luciano Berio's *Sinfonia 1968,* in which Berio presented multiple styles, themes, and genres simultaneously. The major difference between *Sinfonia 1968* and *Divertimento* is that Bernstein presents these ideas in the form of a suite. Much of *Divertimento* is dedicated to reminiscing about the composer's earlier works as well as references to other Classical compositions. In particular, references to Bernstein's *Mass, West Side Story,* and *Candide* are most obvious. The transcription for band was completed in 1984, and remains consistent to the scoring of the original. The general compositional styles in *Divertimento*—odd meters, brilliant melodic writing, occasional use of complex harmonies, and extremes of both texture and dynamics—are indicative of Bernstein's compositions.

Unit 4: Technical Considerations

The major tonal centers are C, G, A-flat, E-flat, and B-flat. Conductors should ensure that all members of the ensemble are fully proficient in these major scales throughout the entire range of their instruments. Movement 3 requires knowledge of the C minor scale. Rhythmic considerations are a significant concern, especially when coupled with the articulation and tempo requirements. Bernstein's use of syncopation creates challenges in rhythmic precision for both melodic and supporting voices, as shown in figure 1.

FIGURE 1. Movement 4, "Samba," mm. 16–18

Independence of individual parts is extreme in some movements, most notably movements 3 (double reeds and harp only) and 7 (brass and percussion only). Figure 2 illustrates independence of parts, syncopation, and difficulty in counting compound meter for the brass instruments.

FIGURE 2. Movement 7, "Blues," mm. 16–17

Independence of parts is also achieved through canonic writing in movements 1 and 8.

Of course, a primary indicator of Bernstein's compositional style is his use of asymmetric meters, particularly fives and sevens. Movement 2 is in seven and movement 8 features a section in five.

FIGURE 3. Movement 2, "Waltz," mm. 10–13

FIGURE 4. Movement 8, "March, 'The BSO Forever,'" mm. 29–32

Movements 5 and 7 feature alternating measures of four and three beats, creating a *de facto* asymmetrical meter.

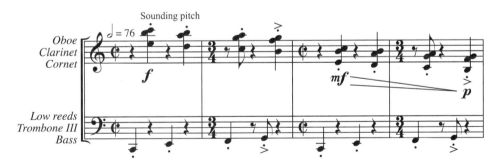

FIGURE 5. Movement 5, "Turkey Trot," mm. 1–6

General technical demands range from the mild (movements 2 and 3) to the moderate (movements 4, 5, and 7) to challenging (movements 1, 5, and 8). Trumpets and horns will find this composition especially challenging.

FIGURE 6. Movement 1, "Sennets and Tuckets," mm. 38–42

FIGURE 7. Movement 5, "Turkey Trot," mm. 65–67

FIGURE 8. Movement 8, "March, 'The BSO Forever,'" mm. 138–142

As the above figures show, many instruments also have technical demands due to range. All flutes and piccolos (two in the final movement) must play altissimo C; E-flat clarinet must play the highest G; all trombones and euphonium must perform high A; all cornets and trumpets except cornet 3 must play well above the staff; and the horns must all play high B-flat. In general, all wind instruments but the low reeds, tenor sax, baritone sax, and tuba have difficult technical demands.

Unit 5: Stylistic Considerations

Bernstein is very detailed in his use of articulation—a trait of composers like Mahler from the post-Romantics. Each movement has discrete styles of articulation. Movements 1, 4, 5, and 8 will require a very separated style of articulation. Movement 2 is the only section marked in the "classical" style (with direct allusions to Bach) and will require a light approach. The performers in movement 3 (double reeds) will use a legato approach throughout, especially in the melodic lines. Movement 7 is unique in its blending of classical and jazz styles and wide variety of dynamic and articulation markings. As this movement is very reminiscent of *Prelude, Fugue, and Riffs*, it will be appropriate to use a little more air than normal to articulate accents, staccato markings, and notes at the end of crescendos. Movement 8 will also require some knowledge of swing technique, especially the use of slight accents on the last third of the beat.

Regarding balance, movements 1 and 8 bear obvious similarities, and performers should be aware of obvious differences in potential volume between brass and woodwind choirs. Many of the soprano and alto voices, especially piccolo, flutes, oboes, clarinets, cornets, trumpets, and horns, have parts written in the upper extremes of the instrument's range. When these instruments are expected to perform in the highest part of the range, they should play softer to produce a more characteristic sound. The rest of the ensemble can then lessen volumes to match.

At all times, an idea of "pyramid balance" should govern the approach to dynamics. This approach suggests that, in any given texture, instruments with lower pitch should play slightly louder than the instruments with higher pitches. For *Divertimento*, this would be true both within sections and between sections. Movement 4 is a good example to use both to teach the pyramid theory of balance and as a warm-up before rehearsing this composition.

Movements 3 and 7 offer both the conductor and student the widest range of interpretive possibilities: in tempo, articulation, dynamic range, possible rubato, and a short cadenza. Since movement 3 is scored for double reeds and harp, and movement 7 for brass and percussion, conductors could experiment arranging these movements for the opposite family of instruments—for example, scoring movement 7 for woodwinds and percussion.

Unit 6: Musical Elements

MELODY:
Movements 1–5 and the march of movement 8 have tonal melodies. Movements 1 and 5 present melodic material primary as an arpeggio elaborated with a half step (see figure 5). Melodic chromaticism is present in every movement but movement 5. The melodic ideas for movements 5, 7, and the prelude to movement 8 come from twelve-tone serialism. These rows are easy to trace. A great idea for teaching and discussion would be to ask the class how the titles of the movements are associated to melodic arpeggiation, chromaticism, diatonic writing, and serialism.

HARMONY:

Since *Divertimento* is constructed around the germ of a half step, many of the harmonies are made more complex by the addition of a half step. This may take the form of seventh chords in its simplest form (figure 5), or may suggest exotic scales like a blues scale (figure 2). In spite of the use of half steps in both melody and harmony, most cadences are traditional. The most adventurous harmonies are in movement 7, "Blues," and are worth the time it would take to prepare a reduced score. This movement features some blues elements as well as serial technique and whole-tone influences. A great assignment for the advanced student would be to trace the use of the half step as both generator and additive in melody and harmony.

RHYTHM:

Movement 2 (figure 3) provides a typical Bernstein melody, in a fast seven. In this case, the harmonic rhythm and the melodic beaming show each measure should be counted in three beats per measure. The first beat is a compound beat. Students could mark measures as (Δ | |) to show where the compound and simple beats are.

In the case of the march (figure 4), the measures in five are counted in two beats per measure, with the second beat being the compound beat (| Δ). Trio 2 of the march hints at the type of polymeter found in the *Overture to Candide*. In m. 79 of the march, the melody is clearly in cut time, but the accompaniment is in a fast three (compare the tuba and low reeds with the horns and vibraphone). In the fast, syncopated sections of movements 1 and 8, rehearsing should be done first by counting rhythms in slow four, then by playing at a slow speed until the ensemble has internalized the syncopation.

TIMBRE:

The unison sections of movements 1, 6, and 8 can provide chances for the ensemble to match tonal colors and characteristic sounds both within each section and between sections. Movement 1, in particular, has thematic material scored for just woodwinds, just brass, and the entire ensemble. Movement 6 has two simple statements of a tone row presented by wood-winds, then brass in octaves and unisons. This provides the same opportunities for teaching blend and balance as would a warm-up chorale.

Unit 7: Form and Structure

SECTION	MEASURE	TONAL CENTER	INSTRUMENT(S)
Movement 1: "Sennets and Tuckets," ABA form			
Fanfare	1–8		
A	9–23		
	a1; 9–14	C	Woodwinds
	a2; 15–23	G, in canon	Brass

SECTION	MEASURE	TONAL CENTER	INSTRUMENT(S)
Transition	24–26		
B	27–50		
	27–32	C	
	33–38	B-flat	
	39–42	A-flat	
	43–50	E-flat implied	
A	51–68		
	a1; 51–56	C	Woodwinds
	a2; 57–68	G to C	Brass/tutti

Movement 2: "Waltz," strophic form

A1	1–18	G major	
	theme; 1–9		Flutes
	developed; B-flat 10–18	Oboe and clarinet	
A2	19–36	G major	
	theme; 19–27		Alto sax
	developed; 28–36	B-flat	Oboe and alto sax
A3 and codetta	37–47	G major	

Movement 3: "Mazurka," binary form

A	1–10	C minor	
B	11–18	C major	
A	19–28	C minor	
B	29–35	E-flat major	
Codetta	36–44	C minor	

Movement 4: "Samba," ABA form

A	1–18	E-flat	
	introduction; 1–4		
	theme; 5–15		
	transition; 16–18		
B	19–34		
	introduction; 19–21		
	false entry; 22–25		
	transition; 26–29		
	development; 30–34		
A	35–52		
	introduction; 35–38		
	theme; 40–47	E-flat	
	codetta; 48–52		

Section	Measure	Tonal Center	Instrument(s)

Movement 5: "Turkey Trot," strophic

Introduction	1–6	C major	
A1	7–18		Clarinet
A2	19–30		
	introduction; 19–22		
	theme; 23–30		Oboe
Digression	31–38	G to F by sequence	
A3	39–46		English horn, alto sax, and horn
Development	47–56	Unspecific	
A4	57–64	C major	Piccolo and oboe
Coda	65–74		

Movement 6: "Sphinxes," strophic

A1	1–5	Row 1, starting on C; cadences on F7 chord	
A2	7–11	Row 2, starting on B-flat; cadences on A-flat major	

Movement 7: "Blues," ABA form

A	1–7	C blues	Cornet
B	8–15	Unspecific	Euphonium and trombone; polychords over D bass, then over F-sharp bass
A	16–22	C blues	
Cadenza	23–24	Twelve-tone row in cornet	

Movement 8a: "In Memoriam," fughetta in three parts
Twelve-tone row; pitch classes [11, 0, 3, 1, 8, 6, 9, 7, 2, 5, 4, 10]

Movement 8b: "The BSO Forever," modified march form
Fanfare (from movement 1, m. 15)

	1–10	B-flat	
A (theme 1)			
	11–33	C, shifts by sequence	
	a1; 10–16		
	a2; 17–23		

SECTION	MEASURE	TONAL CENTER	INSTRUMENT(S)
	b; 23–28		
	a3; 29–33		
Trio 1 (theme 2)		A-flat	
	34–53		
	a1; 34–39		
	a2; 40–45		
	a3 plus theme 2; 46–53		
Coda I	54–69	A-flat	
	Theme 2 plus theme B from movement 1, simultaneously		
Concluding material	70–78	D-flat; see movement 1, mm. 43–50	
Trio 2 (theme 3)		C	
	79–86		E-flat clarinet
	a1; 79–86		
	a2; 87–93		
Coda 2	95–144; same as Coda 1 plus theme 3, simultaneously		
	a; 95–110	C major	
	b; 111–126		
	(trio 2 reprise)	A-flat major	
	a; 127–144	C major	

Unit 8: Suggested Listening

Bernstein, Leonard (related works):
    Candide (final revised version). 1989.
    Fancy Free. 1944.
    Halil. 1981.
    Mass. 1971.
    Prelude, Fugue, and Riffs. 1949.
    A Quiet Place. 1983.
    West Side Story. 1957.
The following recordings include *Divertimento:*
    1996 Commemoration. U. S. Navy Band. LCDR John R. Pastin, conductor. United States Navy. 1996.
    Bernstein. City of Birmingham Symphony Orchestra. Paavo Järvi, conductor. Virgin Classics ASIN B000F3T38W. 2006.
    Bernstein 70. Israel Philharmonic Orchestra. Leonard Bernstein, conductor. Polygram Records ASIN B00000E4BU. 1990.
    Bernstein Conducts Bernstein. Israel Philharmonic Orchestra. Leonard Bernstein, conductor. Polydor International. 1980.

Bernstein: Symphonies No. 1 and 2/Divertimento. BBC Symphony
Orchestra. Leonard Slatkin, conductor. Chandos ASIN
B00117Z6KK. 2001.

Bravo Music. Fukuoka Technical University HS Band. Takayoshi Suzuki,
conductor. Bravo Music BOCD-7128.

Leonard Bernstein. Bournemouth Symphony Orchestra, Marin Alsop,
conductor.   Naxos American ASIN B000BK53HY. 2005.

Unit 9: Additional References and Resources

Baker, Theodore. "Bernstein, Leonard." In *Baker's Biographical Dictionary of
Music and Musicians.* Sixth ed. Rev. Nicolas Slonimsky. New York:
Schirmer Books, 1984.

Bernstein, Leonard. *Findings.* New York: Simon and Schuster, 1982.

Burton, Humphrey. *Leonard Bernstein.* New York: Doubleday, 1994.

Ciucevich, David. Liner notes for *Leonard Bernstein:
Serenade–Facsimile–Divertimento.* Naxos American: ASIN B000BK53HY.
2005.

Peyser, Joan. *Bernstein: A Biography–Revised and Updated.* New York:
Billboard Books, 1998.

Contributed by:

Jeffrey Emge
The University of Texas at Tyler
Tyler, Texas

Teacher Resource Guide

Flag of Stars
Gordon Jacob
(1895–1984)

Unit 1: Composer

Gordon Jacob was born on July 5, 1895, in Upper Norwood near London. Jacob studied piano in his youth and his interest in music was encouraged by some of his older siblings. His first small compositions were performed by ensembles while attending Dulwich College (1908 to 1914), after which Jacob joined the army in World War I. In 1917 Jacob was taken prisoner by the Germans and was able to arrange and compose music for small instrumental ensembles comprised of fellow prisoners at the prison camp.

Upon returning home after the armistice was signed in 1918, Jacob first entered a school of journalism, but was then awarded a grant to study at the Royal College of Music. His composition teachers included Charles Villiers Stanford, Ralph Vaughan Williams, and Herbert Howells. Jacob graduated from the Royal College of Music and was immediately hired as a member of the faculty in 1926 and remained there until his retirement in 1966. Teaching composition and orchestration, many pupils became well-known composers including, Malcolm Arnold, Imogen Holst, Joseph Horovitz, Elizabeth Maconchy, and Bernard Stevens.

Throughout his tenure at the Royal College of Music Jacob earned many awards and honors. He authored several music texts, including, *Orchestral Technique, How to Read a Score, The Composer and His Art,* and *The Elements of Orchestration.*

Before his death on June 8, 1984, in Saffron Walden, Jacob composed over 700 pieces of music, making him one of England's most prolific composers. He knew most of the professional musicians in Great Britain during the span of

his career and composed many works, including concertos and chamber music, at the request of these celebrated performers. Jacob wrote some forty works for band, chamber winds, and brass band, including *An Original Suite*, *William Byrd Suite*, *Music for a Festival*, *Symphony AD 78*, and *Old Wine in New Bottles*.

Unit 2: Composition

Flag of Stars was commissioned by Pi Kappa Omicron Band Fraternity at the University of Louisville, Kentucky. Completed on April 17, 1954, it was published by Boosey and Hawkes in 1956. The full title on the score's first page is, *Flag of Stars, Salute to America, Symphonic Overture*. Also included in the score is Jacob's program note:

> The overture was written during the end of 1953 and the beginning of 1954 and is intended as a gesture from an inhabitant of the Old World to those of the New.

> The introductory fanfare and the slow section which follows it recalls the sacrifices made by your country in both world wars in the struggle with dark forces of destruction. The allegro is prompted by thoughts of the energy, vitality and cheerfulness of the American people—young, optimistic, and full of their faith in their destiny. The second subject in 3/4 time might perhaps suggest a sort of national song and right at the end there is a brief quotation from the "Star Spangled Banner." But apart from any extra-musical meaning the work is constructed solidly on Classical formal lines though its musical language is that of the twentieth century (but not of an extreme type).

The title takes inspiration from Walt Whitman's poem, "Thick-Sprinkled Bunting," first appearing in 1865 and published as "Flag of Stars, Thick-Sprinkled Bunting" in the 1867 edition of *Leaves of Grass*. In Jacob's preface in the printed score the composer quotes not Whitman's "Thick-Sprinkled Bunting," but instead the final stanza from another of Whitman's poems, "Song of the Redwood Tree."

> Fresh come to a new world indeed, yet long prepared,
> I see the genius of the modern, child of the real and the ideal,
> Clearing the ground for broad humanity, the true America, heir of the
>   past so grand,
> To build a grander future.

This poem was printed in *Harper's Magazine* in 1874 and then included in the 1881 edition of *Leaves of Grass*. Perhaps Jacob was thinking diplomatically when he decided to quote the more optimistic, idealizing poem, "Song of the Redwood Tree," instead of Whitman's more cynical "Thick-Sprinkled Bunting."

The work is 368 measures with a performance timing of ten minutes and forty-five seconds.

Unit 3: Historical Perspective

The first performance was on May 11, 1954, at the University of Louisville by the University of Louisville Concert Band, conducted by Ernest Lyon. *Flag of Stars* was one of several works commissioned and premiered by the musicians at the University of Louisville. It was during the middle of the twentieth century that many band conductors, including Frederick Fennell and William Revelli, encouraged and commissioned American and European composers to write new, original works for concert band.

Flag of Stars is a concert overture. Concert overtures first appeared in Europe during the Romantic era. Similar to operatic overtures, these works are one-movement compositions, most often in sonata form, with picturesque concepts often suggested by the title. Felix Mendelssohn was influential in promoting the concept of concert overtures by writing seven, including one for band in 1824. Some famous concert overtures from the period include *Jubilee Overture* by Carl Maria von Weber, which incorporates *God Save the King* at the close. Tchaikovsky's *1812 Overture* incorporates parts of the French national anthem, *La Marseillaise*, throughout. A number of works for band have incorporated the *Star Spangled Banner,* including *National Emblem* by Edwin Bagley and *Early Light* by Carolyn Bremer.

Unit 4: Technical Considerations

Overall, *Flag of Stars* is in B-flat major as indicated by the key signature. Accidentals are not used excessively, but appear throughout the work, as Jacob uses modal and minor keys and an occasional run of unusual harmonies. The opening fanfare, starting on written octaves on D in cornets and trumpets, presents potential intonation difficulties. Adding mutes at m. 27 increases the potential for problems. Conductors should address two rhythmic-related considerations. Having the continuous line of sixteenth notes at m. 31 performed smoothly by alternating players may be a challenge for some groups. Conductors should remind the waiting player to listen and breathe early in order to avoid a late entrance.

The last three sixteenth notes of the main rhythmic motive in the 5/8 measures may be difficult to perform together, as they have a potential to be rushed or crushed. A pattern of 2 + 3 shown by the conductor may help to stabilize the ensemble's rhythm, especially during the initial rehearsals, throughout the 5/8 sections.

Unit 5: Stylistic Considerations

Jacob has indicated specific tempo markings in *Flag of Stars*. The fanfare sections are marked quarter note = 80. The *Adagio* sections, first appearing at m. 15, have quarter note = 52. The *Allegro* begins in 5/8. Jacob includes the instruction that these measures should be conducted as "two beats in the bar," at quarter note = ca. 112. This makes the eighth note equal to 224. Conductors may want to observe this as they conduct the 2/8 + 3/8 pattern.

Creating an accurate performance. Notes with marcato accents (first observed in the initial fanfare section) should probably be performed with no diminuendo. Those notes with side-wedge accents (e.g., mm. 58 and 105–107) may be played with firmly-articulated fronts. The wedge staccato accents (m. 152) probably indicate firm articulation with some separation between the notes. The staccato dots (m. 169) would then indicate a lighter style of articulation with separation. The conductor should also consider the sudden changes that create contrasts in style. Brass and woodwinds beginning at m. 108 should observe the very different dynamics and articulations.

Unit 6: Musical Elements

MELODY:
The most recognizable melody in *Flag of Stars* is the quote from the "Star Spangled Banner" that appears in mm. 355–362. Written in sonata form, the first theme begins at the *Allegro* at m. 43. The shape of this first theme, with its descending fifth followed by an ascending arpeggio up an octave, is comparable to the first six notes of the "Star Spangled Banner." Jacob wrote that this first theme, in a meter of 5/8, represents "thoughts of the energy, vitality and cheerfulness of the American people." The second theme begins at m. 108 in 3/4 meter. This theme is more lyrical as Jacob called it "a sort of national song."

HARMONY:
Overall, *Flag of Stars* is in B-flat major as indicated by the key signature. Accidentals are not used excessively, but appear throughout, the work as Jacob uses modal and minor keys and an occasional run of unusual harmonies. Jacob employs common practice key relationships in his use of sonata form. Theme 1 at m. 43 is in B-flat major and theme 2, beginning at m. 108, is in the dominant, F major. The introductory fanfare section creates a sense of C minor as cornets and trumpets begin on octaves on C and introduce the A-flats in measure 3. Theme 1 makes use of the Dorian mode on B-flat with A-flats and D-flats introduced in m. 46. As theme 2 begins at m. 108, brass uses notes of the F natural minor scale. The recapitulation section finds the return of theme 1 in B-flat major at m. 235, and theme 2 in B-flat major, as expected, at m. 326.

RHYTHM:

This work is very rhythmic throughout and the most significant rhythm is the triplet. Both the opening fanfare section and the *Adagio* section of the introduction use the eighth-note triplet as a borrowed rhythm. The most prominent feature of theme 1 of the *Allegro* is the group of three sixteenth notes at the end of each of the 5/8 measures. The triplet feeling is continued through theme 2, as it is written in 3/4 meter. The feeling is heightened in the development section as mm. 158–227 use 3/8 meter.

Some players during initial rehearsals of the work may have difficulty with the rhythms used in the 5/8 sections. Problems may be alleviated if the conductor rehearses the sections slowly and indicates a clear and steady 2 + 3 pattern.

TIMBRE:

Flag of Stars uses an expanded instrumentation compared to some of the other original works for band that were composed at a similar time in the 1950s. Works by Vincent Persichetti, Morton Gould, Paul Creston, and even others by Jacob do not always include parts for English horn, contrabass clarinet, and bass saxophone.

Unit 7: Form and Structure

SECTION	MEASURE	EVENT AND SCORING
Introduction	1–14	Brass fanfare
	15–26	*Adagio* in contrapuntal texture
	27–30	Fanfare
	31–42	*Adagio* with sixteenth-note accompaniment
Exposition	43–78	Theme 1a
	79–94	Theme 1b
	95–107	Theme 1a
	108–124	Theme 2
	125–142	Theme 2 with rhythmic accompaniment
Development	142–157	Development of theme 1
	158–227	Development of theme 1 in 3/8
	228–234	*Adagio* motives from introduction
Recapitulation	235–300	Theme 1a
	301–312	Theme 1b
	313–325	Theme 1a
	326–342	Theme 2
	342–346	Theme 2 with fanfare accompaniment
	347–354	Theme 2, full scoring
Coda	355–362	"Star Spangled Banner" quotation

SECTION	MEASURE	EVENT AND SCORING
	363–368	Final flourish
		Theme 1 in flutes and clarinets
		fanfare in trumpets

Unit 8: Suggested Listening

Bagley, Edwin. *National Emblem*.
Bremer, Carolyn. *Early Light*.
Jacob, Gordon:
 Music for a Festival
 An Original Suite
 William Byrd Suite

Unit 9: Additional References and Resources

Baker, Theodore. "Gordon Jacob." In *Baker's Biographical Dictionary of Musicians*. Eighth ed. Rev. Nicolas Slonimsky. New York: Schirmer, 1992.

Rehrig, William H. *The Heritage Encyclopedia of Band Music*. Westerville, OH: Integrity Press, 1991.

Smith, Norman. *Band Music Notes*. Chicago: GIA Publications, Inc., 2000.

Trachsel, Andrew. Booklet notes for *Composers Collection: Gordon Jacob*. GIA Publications, Inc. CD-747.

Whiston, J. Alan. "Gordon Jacob: A Biographical Sketch and Analysis of Four Selected Works for Band." PhD diss., University of Oklahoma, 1987.

Whitman, Walt. *Leaves of Grass*. New York: Norton, 1973.

Websites:
 Gordon Jacob. www.gordonjacob.org
 "Overture." Encyclopedia Britannica Online. www.britannica.com

Contributed by:

Kenneth Kohlenberg
Director of Bands, Professor of Music
Sinclair Community College
Dayton, Ohio

Teacher Resource Guide

Geometric Dances
Roger Cichy
(b. 1956)

Unit 1: Composer

Roger Cichy has a diverse background as both a composer/arranger and a music educator. He holds bachelor of music and master of arts in music education degrees from the Ohio State University. As a music educator, Cichy has had a successful career as a band director at levels ranging from elementary school to college.

In 1995, he resigned his position at Iowa State University to devote full-time to composing and arranging. As a freelance composer and arranger, Cichy writes for high school and college bands, professional orchestras, and the commercial music industry. He has over 275 compositions and arrangements credited to his name.

His composition mentors include Edward Montgomery, Marshall Barnes, and Joseph Levey. Cichy has received numerous composition awards from The American Society of Composers, Authors, and Publishers for serious music. His works range from small ensemble literature to compositions and arrangements for marching and concert band and symphony orchestra. He is widely sought as a composer for commissions, and frequently appears as a composer-in-residence and guest conductor.

Unit 2: Composition

Geometric Dances was commissioned by the Indiana Bandmasters Association for the 2005 Indiana All-State High School Honor Band. It is a four-movement dance suite written with progressive meters 2/4, 5/8, 6/8, and 7/8 (adding an eighth note to the time signature from the previous movement). Cichy chose this concept to exploit various meters, and, in the case of the 5/8 and 7/8 meters, engage in variations of eight-note groupings within a beat.

Geometric Dances is Grade 4 difficulty, approximately twelve minutes in length and published by Ludwig-Masters Music Publications (Boca Raton, Florida).

Unit 3: Historical Perspective

"Suites" are defined as ordered sets of instrumental pieces or movements. Suites of dances have been popular forms for composers for centuries, collected by Renaissance composers for the actual purpose of accompanying social dance (mid-1500s–1620s), and later codified in the Baroque era (c. 1600–1750) as more abstract instrumental pastiches. Telemann, Handel, and Bach all composed numerous keyboard, solo instrument (especially flute, violin, and cello), and orchestral suites.

By the mid-1700s the dance suite was replaced by the symphony and concerto, but it continued to be a favorite of composers worldwide. Since that time, suites have taken the form of both original sets of pieces connected by a theme (*The Planets* by Holst) as well as music extracted from ballets (*The Nutcracker Suite* by Tchaikovsky), operas (*Carmen Suite* by Bizet), musicals (*Oklahoma! Symphonic Suite* by Rodgers and Hammerstein, arranged by Victor Young), and movies (*Suite from "Psycho"* by Herrmann).

There are hundreds of wind compositions in the suite category, including cornerstones of the repertoire such as Gustav Holst's *First Suite in E-flat* and *Second Suite in F* and Ralph Vaughan Williams' *Folk Song Suite*. Other notable titles in this genre include Gordon Jacob's *"William Byrd" Suite*, Percy Grainger's *Lincolnshire Posy*, Darius Milhaud's *Suite Francaise*, Robert Russell Bennett's *Suite of Old American Dances*, and Ron Nelson's *Courtly Airs and Dances*.

Some of Roger Cichy's other suites include *Galilean Moons* (1996), *Colours* (1997), *First Flights*, *Bugs* (2000), *Sounds, Sketches, and Ideas* (2002), and *New Millennium, Different World, New Beginnings* (2004).

Unit 4: Technical Considerations

Key areas in this piece are generally "band-friendly"—B-flat and E-flat major (with a Spanish Gypsy scale altering the tonality), F Mixolydian, B-flat and C major, and B-flat major. Cichy does not hesitate to add chromatic and modal inflections throughout his music, but generally sticks to singable, scalar melodies and consonant harmonies.

There is prevalent passagework for upper woodwinds, requiring drill and repetition. Brass ranges are generally conservative, but continual playing requires significant endurance.

Geometric Dances presents rhythmic challenges to the ensemble, especially the proliferation of asymmetrical meters (5/8 and 7/8) and the many rhythmic patterns. Groupings tend to be regular and repetitive, but not without a surprise shift now and then (e.g., 3 + 2 + 2 shifts to 2 + 2 + 3).

As with many of Cichy's works, a percussion section of timpanist plus five other players is required, as well as a large stable of instruments. Percussionists are required to play soloistically in a number of introductions and transitions, as well as provide rhythmic structure, tempo maintenance, and color to all movements.

Unit 5: Stylistic Considerations

Each movement of *Geometric Dances* presents an opportunity to explore a variety of performance styles, including march (movement 1), dance (movements 2 and 4), and ballad (movement 3). The brisk movements are all generally light and dance-like, but because each contains significant doublings and tutti scoring, players will need to guard against playing too heavily and loudly.

Accents should be reinforced with air rather than harsh tonguing, and the balance of melody and tune to accompaniment and rhythm should be continually observed and adjusted. Titles of the movements lead us to understand that some of the music is tongue-in-cheek, so an element of light-hearted humor should be ever-present in performers' minds.

Unit 6: Musical Elements

MELODY:
Cichy's melodies are catchy and tuneful, often employing an economy of means and frequent repetition to achieve his goal. Along with traditional diatonic scales for bases, he infuses scalar and modal systems into his dances, including a Spanish(Gypsy) scale (modified Phrygian) in "Quadratic Permutations" and a Mixolydian flavor in "Pentangular Concoctions."

HARMONY:
Harmonies tend to be consonant with significant coloring of dissonances, modality, extended tertians, and seventh chords.

RHYTHM:
Rhythm is the overriding principle of this entire piece, with an emphasis on a different meter in each movement. Asymmetrical meters tend to be grouped regularly, with occasional shifts in the orientation.

TIMBRE:
Cichy's scoring vacillates among soloistic and chamber settings, family scoring (all woodwinds, all brass, all percussion, etc.) and tutti performance.

There is a strong sense of melody above accompaniment and rhythmic under-pinning, with relatively little use of counterpoint, imitation, or superimposition.

Unit 7: Form and Structure

Geometric Dances is a four-movement work, with a configuration of march-fast-slow-fast.

I. *Quadratic Permutations*, 2/4
The opening movement is straightforward and emphasizes the subdivision of the beat to create four strong eighth notes within each bar, two beats and two offbeats, hence the reference to the quadrate. With this as the backbone for the movement, the permutations occur with the various textures that accompany the melody and the transformation of the melody through various instrumentations. Somewhat like a frantic march in character, "Quadratic Permutations" is a fast dance with an ethnic-sounding melody based on a Spanish (Gypsy) scale (F–G-flat–A–B-flat–C–D-flat–E-flat–F), although no particular ethnos was intended.

SECTION	MEASURE	EVENT AND SCORING
Introduction	1–14	F pedal (B-flat tonal center) and march snippets
A	15–32	Oboe and clarinet melody; brass downbeat/offbeat accompaniment
A	33–49	Melody in alto saxophones, horns, and muted trumpets; countermelody in upper woodwinds
B	49–54	Brass fanfare
Re-introduction	55–58	Downbeat/offbeat patterns
A	59–74	Lyrical presentation of melody in upper woodwinds; *paso doble* accompaniment in saxophones, trumpets, horns, and percussion
B	75–81	Brass fanfare returns with tuba, clarinets, and saxophones
Transition	82–89	Woodwinds, bass, and percussion march fragments and Spanish scale snippets Bell tones in chimes and horns build-up in low woodwinds and brass crescendo to key change
A	97–112	March tune in horn, trombone, and euphonium; figurations in upper woodwinds; accompaniment in low brass and percussion

SECTION	MEASURE	EVENT AND SCORING
Transition	113–117	March accompaniment and chromatic runs to final section
A	118–133	Final section; tune in saxophones, trumpets, and euphonium; tutti scoring; countermelody in upper woodwinds and mallets
Coda	134–138	Accelerando; homophonic tutti rhythm; ends B-flat major

II. *Pentatonic Concoction*, 5/8

Movement 2 relies primarily on the eighth-note grouping of 3 + 2, although the reverse (2 + 3) is used at time to create a short disruption and contrast to the first pattern. The middle section of this movement delves into a more hypnotic state of the dance and the arrhythmic melody wanders through the repeated accompaniment using the 3 + 2 pattern.

SECTION	MEASURE	EVENT AND SCORING
A	1–9	Dance tune (3 + 2 grouping) in piccolo and castanets; mm. 8–9 accompaniment set up in bassoons, saxophones, and clarinets
A	10–18	Dance tune in upper woodwinds and xylophone; mm. 17–19 horn, trumpet, and trombone punctuations
A	19–26	Dance tune in clarinets and trumpet 1; accompaniment in low woodwinds, saxophones, horns, trumpets, and tubas; brief shift to 2 + 3 and 7/8 insertion
Transition	27–31	Accompaniment based on brass punctuations
	32–35	Quiet 5/8 accompaniment in tuba, trombone, and euphonium; solo interjections from oboe 1 and trumpet 1
B	36–45	Theme 2 (3 + 2 grouping) in flute and clarinet with light low brass and percussion accompaniment
B	46–53	Theme 2 harmonized in fourths; bass clarinets and horns added; piccolo and xylophone countermelody
Extension	54–59	Continuation of dance pattern; decrescendo
	60–63	Upper woodwind punctuation, brass flourish; accompaniment pattern

677

SECTION	MEASURE	EVENT AND SCORING
A	64–69	Dance tune in piccolo, flutes, and bells; sleigh bells and light accompaniment in saxophones, horns, and clarinets
Transition	70–72	Unison descending figure in trombones (glissando), horns, and low woodwinds; punctuation fanfare figures
A	73–79	Dance tune in clarinets, alto saxophone, and trumpet 1; slight variations in melody and shift to 2 + 3 pattern
	80–81	New dance accompaniment in low brass and low woodwinds
Transition	82–89	Solo fragments in clarinet 1 and oboe 1; rhythmic buildup; woodwind flourish and crescendo
A	90–98	Dance tune in upper woodwinds, trumpet 1, and xylophone; countermelody in horns; tutti texture
Coda	99–103	Fanfare accompaniment with woodwind punctuations; oboe 1 solo fragment, final hit (F unison)

III. *Hexagonal Undulations*, 6/8

The slow movement follows a standard 6/8 meter format, utilizing mostly woodwinds and their lyrical capabilities. Somewhat waltz-like in character, "Hexagonal Undulations" makes use of the Mixolydian scale and the repeated major tonic chord followed by a minor dominant seventh chord to create the undulations.

SECTION	MEASURE	EVENT AND SCORING
A	1–8	Lyrical melody in clarinet and alto saxophone; waltz-like accompaniment in bass, bass clarinet, clarinets, and marimba
A	9–19	Lyrical melody in flutes, oboes, bells, and clarinet 1; horn, euphonium, and triangle add to offbeat; section ends in C-flat major
B	20–23	New melody in flute and marimba; sustained chords in clarinets; countermelody in English horn; broken chords in bassoons
	24–27	Trio of English horn, alto saxophone, and horn; ritardando, buildup, and fermata on G dominant seventh

SECTION	MEASURE	EVENT AND SCORING
A	28–35	C major; tutti scoring; lyrical melody in upper woodwinds, horns, trumpet 1, and bells; waltz accompaniment in ensemble
A	36–43	Lyrical melody in clarinet alto saxophone
Coda	44–48	Fragment in oboe 1, response in English horn, then flute 1; ending chord is C^{maj7}

IV. *Heptomical Infusions*, 7/8

The final movement is an assortment of several musical styles and sounds in turn whimsical, jazzy, sinister, lopsided, ritualistic, and polyrhythmic. It exploits the use of 7/8 meter and its various combinations of eighth-note groupings. Commonly found are groupings of 3 + 2 + 2 and 2 + 2 + 3, and in the middle section of this movement both are superimposed as melody and accompaniment.

SECTION	MEASURE	EVENT AND SCORING
Introduction	1–2	Percussion only opening (brushes, temple blocks, and sand blocks); 3 + 2 + 2 grouping
A	3–9	Dance tune in flute 1 and clarinet 1; downbeat accompaniment in bass clarinet and bassoon
A	10–17	Dance tune in piccolo, oboe, clarinets, alto saxophones, and xylophone; added accompaniment in low brass and percussion
B	18–24	Homophonic texture in all brass, saxophones, and bass clarinet
A	25–30	Dance tune in upper woodwinds, alto saxophones, and trumpet 1; tutti accompaniment
Transition	30–36	Fragment in piccolo, oboe, and clarinet; new accompaniment in low brass, saxophones, and bass clarinet; 3 + 2 + 2 grouping with castanets, cabasa, and shekera
C	37–44	New dance tune in oboe and clarinets; light downbeat accompaniment in saxophones, trumpets, trombones, and tubas; continued dance texture in percussion
Transition	45–48	Woodwinds alternating 3 + 2 + 2 and 2 + 2 + 3 with syncopation

Section	Measure	Event and Scoring
	49–52	Brass and timpani repeat woodwind re-establishment of accompaniment pattern
C	55–62	New dance tune in upper woodwinds and trumpet; tutti texture
	63–66	Tutti presentation of transition figure; timpani solo; transition figure from end of theme 1
A	67–73	Recapitulation of dance tune in oboe, clarinet, and alto saxophone; woodwind, horn, euphonium, and percussion background
A	74–79	Tutti texture; dance tune in upper woodwinds, alto saxophone, and trumpet; winding chromatic countermelody in bassoon, bass trombone, tuba, and bass
Coda	80–88	9/8 and 5/8 insertion; sustained cluster over percussion accompaniment; percussion-only measure; tutti texture and rhythmic ending

Unit 8: Suggested Listening

Geometric Dances. Southern Illinois University-Edwardsville Symphonic Band. John Bell, conductor. Mark Custom ASIN: B0012Y0XSC.

Other music by Roger Cichy:

> *Diversions. Bugs.* University of North Texas Symphonic Band. Dennis Fischer, conductor. Mark Custom ASIN: B00028ATVU.
>
> *North Central Winds. New Millennium, Different World, New Beginnings.* North Central Winds. Adam Brennan, conductor. Mark Custom ASIN: B0012XPMFC.
>
> *Tributes. Divertimento.* North Texas Wind Symphony. Eugene Corporon, conductor. Klavier ASIN: B000003M5Y.

Other representative suites:

> Bennett, Robert Russell. *Suite of Old American Dances.*
>
> Holst, Gustav:
>> *First Suite in E-flat*
>>
>> *Second Suite in F*
>
> Horowitz, David. *Dance Suite.*
>
> Milhaud, Darius. *Suite Francaise.*
>
> Persichetti, Vincent. *Divertimento for Band.*
>
> Susato, Tielman. *The Dansereye.*
>
> Vaughan Williams, Ralph. *Folk Song Suite.*

Unit 9: Additional References and Resources

Burkholder, J. Peter, Donald J. Grout, and Claude T. Palisca. *A History of Western Music, Volume 7*. New York: W. W. Norton, 2005.

Websites:
http://www.c-alanpublications.com/composers/cichy-roger.html
www.geocities.com/cichymusic

Contributed by:

Scott A. Stewart
Emory University
Atlanta, Georgia

Teacher Resource Guide

Kizuna

Frederick Speck
(b. 1955)

Unit 1: Composer

Frederick Speck has contributed a wide array of compositions to the field of wind band, orchestra, and chamber music. He currently serves as the director of bands and professor of music in composition at the University of Louisville, where he has twice received the President's Award for Outstanding Scholarship, Research and Creative Activity. A native of Ohio, he holds a BM and MM from Bowling Green State University and a DMA from the University of Maryland.

Speck's compositions have been performed worldwide by prominent ensembles such as the Warsaw National Philharmonic Orchestra, Denver Symphony, and Louisville Orchestra. He has received a Barlow Endowment Commission and a fellowship from the National Endowment for the Arts. Notable works include *Concerto for Clarinet and Orchestra* (1993), recorded by Richard Stoltzman, and *Dance Toccata* (2004) for wind band. Speck is an advocate for new music and recently premiered the latest Karel Husa commission for wind band entitled, *Cheetah* (2006).

Unit 2: Composition

Kizuna was commissioned by the World Association for Symphonic Bands and Ensembles (WASBE), and received its premier by the Senzoku Garden College of Music Wind Ensemble at the 2005 WASBE conference in Singapore. The composer writes in the score:

From the moment that WASBE President Dennis Johnson and I began considering a new work to celebrate the Singapore Conference, the imagery of an east/west confluence of ideas became central to the discussion. From that point, a work developed that merges eastern and western nuances in tonal languages that freely embrace one another and are at times, musically "inter-lingual." Though much of the work unfolds by revealing solo passages that allow individual personalities to be exposed, the music also develops a sense of physical strength through several notable tutti sections, the greatest of which concludes the work. This process of joining together and gaining strength is reflected by the title, *Kizuna*, a Japanese word which means a kind of mental connection between people resulting in the creation of a strong bond. It is derived from the roots "ki" which means trees and "zuna" or tsuna" which means ropes.

Kizuna is approximately ten minutes in duration. The solo demands and complexity of rhythm and phrase structure require the facility demonstrated by advanced wind ensembles.

Unit 3: Historical Perspective

Historical records suggest that music was a part of Japanese culture as early as the third century, although the preservation of styles and traditions come from the Nara Period (AD 552–794). The development of Japanese music was influenced by the Chinese T'ang dynasty (AD 618–907), Korean culture, and Buddhist religion.

While it is difficult to generalize the rich history of Japanese music, for the purpose of overview, it can be grouped into four historical periods:

1. Ancient Japanese court music known as *gagaku* (453–1185)
2. Medieval narratives and theatricals known as *noh drama* (1185–1615)
3. Edo period, during which traditional music for the koto (zither), shakuhachi (bamboo flute), and the shamisen (three-stringed lute) flourished (1615–1868)
4. Music following the Meiji restoration, which introduced Western and electronic music (1868-present)

It is important to note that while Western music has continually morphed and adopted new styles, Japanese music has strived to preserve elements from its ancient musical heritage.

Unit 4: Technical Considerations

Kizuna challenges the expressive and technical facility of all players, providing solo opportunities for each instrument. The most prominent solos are for flute, English horn, bass clarinet, saxophone, trumpet, and trombone. Extended techniques include flutter-tonguing in flute and trumpet and *jete* in the double bass (the succession of bouncing down bows).

In the brass section, it is necessary to have three mutes for trumpets (straight, cup, and harmon) and a harmon and straight mute for trombones. The percussion instrumentation is quite extensive, using three Chinese cymbals, bamboo and brass wind chimes, sandpaper blocks, a variety of suspended cymbals, mallet instruments, woodblocks, and other standard instruments.

Unit 5: Stylistic Considerations

In Japanese music, the beauty of individual tones and the experience of the performer are of utmost importance. The compact sound of chamber music is often preferred over the large sonorous sounds of a full ensemble. *Kizuna* demonstrates this through extended and intricate soli sections where rhythmic and melodic ideas intertwine between players. Unlike melodies presented in Western music, the solos in *Kizuna* are independent musical ideas, requiring each soloist to perform with full range of expression and nuance as layers accumulate.

An important style in Japanese music is *Jo-ha-kyu*, a concept that describes the story development in noh theatre. At its basic definition, it means the beginning, middle, and end. More importantly, it represents a ratio of tension and stress, starting with a peaceful opening (jo), developing with an outburst of sound (ha), and concluding with a rush of energy to the end of the idea (kyu). This idea is threaded throughout *Kizuna*, seen on a small scale in the rhythmic development of solo lines (percussion, mm. 14–16) and in a larger scale of phrase development (mm. 42–58).

Unit 6: Musical Elements

MELODY:
Three distinct ideas shape the character of the melodic lines. The opening flute and bass clarinet trio in m. 8 represents the first idea, layers of quasi-improvisational solo lines based on pentatonic scales. The chief component for these lyrical melodies is the intervals sol-ti-do. Many of the melodies begin on a lowered seventh scale degree (ti), which initially sounds as the primary tone. For instance, at first glance, the opening accompaniment and melody seem to focus around D and A, but as the flute line develops, the emphasis of solfege syllables ti-do reveals that E is the central pitch. The primary solo passages occur in mm. 1–58, 134–188, and 286–299.

The second melodic idea is the development of rising lines, presented as scales or arpeggios in either duple- or triple-based rhythms. The initial idea is presented in the vibraphone line in m. 19. Throughout *Kizuna*, this line develops within longer phrases that build toward a series of climatic arrivals as seen in mm. 47–58, 103–112, 238–245, and 250–270. The most monumental of these is in the final measures (310–320), concluding *Kizuna* with layers of brilliant and searing rising scales.

The third characteristic is the use of fanfare and bell-tone figures. At times the fanfare figures serve as an arrival point (mm. 54–57, 82–84) or as an addition to the contrapuntal texture (mm. 94–112). The bell-tone figures assist in transition sections, providing contrast in tone color and highlighting rhythmic pulsations (mm. 113–130, 199–205, and 217–245).

HARMONY:
The harmonic structure in *Kizuna* does not follow the principles of traditional Western chord progressions and triads. Rather, the harmonic language is expressed through tonal centers that are established by the voice leading of individual lines. The recurring sol-ti-do motive helps to establish the central tone, often found in the linear melodic gestures, not the accompaniment. Layers of scale tones, stacked chords of open fifths, and clusters of the sol-ti-do motive create complex yet resonant harmonic structures, even in the transparent sections.

RHYTHM:
The meter in *Kizuna* is primarily 4/4 or 2/2 with quarter note = 90 or 180. Many of the rhythms in *Kizuna* are complex, including combinations of five-, six-, and seven-note tuplets, as well as rapid thirty-second-note passages. Both solo lines and tutti sections seamlessly weave in and out of duple- and triple-based rhythms, oscillating between extended sections of tranquil melodies and driving, syncopated fanfares.

TIMBRE:
The combination of eastern and western musical influences results in myriad rich and expressive colors throughout *Kizuna*. Timbres inherent to Japanese music are highlighted in the percussion instrumentation and chamber setting of solos, creating a transparency of individual tone color. Western timbres materialize in the strong tutti sections with angular rhythms and robust blocks of sound. Particularly striking are the interwoven saxophone quartet joined by the extremes of piccolo and tuba solos (m. 49), the visceral percussion soli followed by a complete character change of tranquil cascading triplets (mm. 131–147), and the intensity of the high tessitura and driving six-note tuplets in the closing measures.

Unit 7: Form and Structure

SECTION	MEASURE	EVENT AND SCORING
Section 1	1–59	
Introduction	1–7	Double bass and percussion
	8–17	Melody set in flute; solo lines develop around sol-ti-do motive
	18–24	Rising syncopated line set in vibraphone, trumpet, clarinet, and oboe
	25–32	Rapid flourishes in trumpet and trombone
	32–38	Return of initial melody and solo passages
	39–46	Pulsating eighth-note accompaniment; minimalist-like rhythmic pattern; saxophone soli
	47–53	Increased layering of musical ideas; combination of triplet and syncopated rhythms; return of rising chromatic line
Culmination	54–59	Fanfare in low woodwinds and brass; explosive solo in Chinese cymbals
Section 2	59–133	
	59–68	Three-part round in oboe and clarinet; rhythmic accompaniment in flute; call-and-response triplet pattern in brass and percussion
	69–81	Gradual acceleration; texture thickens with added layer of rising quarter-note triplet figure; chromatic modulation
	82–85	Building tension culminates in brass fanfare
	86–101	Return of layers from m. 59; new fanfare melody in m. 94 in oboe and alto saxophone
	102–112	Brass fanfare returns; ascending scale in trumpet leads to culminating chord at the fermata
	113–133	A tempo; transition material; combination of duple and triple rhythms; blocks of sound in low woodwinds and brass help to slow down pressing energy; percussion soli m. 131
Section 3	134–245	
	134–147	Tranquil in character; cascading thirds; trading of triplet figures in accompaniment
	148–171	Trombone solo

SECTION	MEASURE	EVENT AND SCORING
	170–185	Alto saxophone duet
	176	Return of percussion accompaniment from Section 1
	205	Melodic fragment in low woodwinds, double bass and tuba; rising line in euphonium
	217	Pointed triplet fragments press energy forward
Section 4	246–285	
	246–270	Pointed, driving rhythms; rising modal lines
	271–285	Energy unwinds; English horn solo at m. 284 provides bridge into next section
Section 5	286–320	
	286–308	Recapitulation; a tempo; return of double bass and percussion from section 1; rapid solo flourishes
	309–320	Ascending pentatonic scales set in high tessitura; accelerando m. 314-end

Unit 8: Suggested Listening

Speck, Frederick:

Concerto for Clarinet and Orchestra. Richard Stoltzman and the Warsaw Philharmonic. George Manahan, conductor. MMC2078.

Dance Toccata. Commissioned Works of the Bishop Ireton Wind Ensemble, Volume 2. The Washington Winds. Garwood Whaley, conductor.

Kizuna. Beyond Horizons: New Voices for Winds. The University of Louisville Wind Ensemble at Comstock Hall. Frederick Speck, conductor. http://louisville.edu/music/ensembles/bands.html

Kizuna. WASBE 2005 Singapore Concert. Senzoku Gakuen Wind Ensemble. Dennis L. Johnson, conductor. 6039 MCD.

Night Moves. For solo cello, solo marimba, and chamber winds. *WASBE 2007 Killarney, Ireland Concert.* Frederick Speck, conductor. University of Louisville Wind Ensemble.   7214 MCD.

Unit 9: Additional References and Resources

Galliano, Luciana. *Yogaku: Japanese Music in the Twentieth Century.* Foreword by L. Berio. London: The Scarecrow Press, 2002.

Malm, William P. *Japanese Music and Musical Instruments.* Tokyo: Charles E. Tuttle Company, 1959.

_____. "Some of Japan's Musics and Musical Principles." In *Musics of Many Cultures*. Elizabeth May, ed. Berkeley: University of California Press, 1980. 48–62.

_____. *Six Hidden Views of Japanese Music*. Berkeley: University of California Press, 1986.

Hughes, David W. "Japan I, 4: Scales and Modes." In *New Grove Dictionary of Music and Musicians*.

Wade, Bonnie C. *Music in Japan: Experiencing Music, Expressing Culture*. New York: Oxford University Press, 2005.

Contributed by:

Amy Acklin
PhD Student/Music Education
The Florida State University
Tallahassee, Florida

Teacher Resource Guide

Krump

Scott McAllister
(b. 1969)

Unit 1: Composer

Scott McAllister was born in Vero Beach, Florida and completed his doctorate in composition at the Shepherd School of Music at Rice University. Also an accomplished clarinetist, McAllister has performed with major symphony orchestras, most notably the Houston Symphony. McAllister's *Black Dog,* a work for clarinet and orchestra (also available for wind ensemble) was recently recorded by world renowned clarinet virtuoso Robert Spring. This is the work by which most band directors know his music.

McAllister has received numerous commissions, performances, and awards throughout the United States, Europe, and Asia, including ASCAP, The American Composers Orchestra, The Rascher Quartet, The Leipzig Radio Orchestra, *I Musici de Montreal,* Charles Neidich, The Verdehr Trio, Jacksonville Symphony, *Da Camera,* The Ladislav Kubik Competition, The United States New Music Ensemble, The Florida Arts Council, and The Florida Bandmaster's Association. He has been featured at the Aspen, Chautauqua, and The Prague/American Institute Summer Festivals. His music is self-published and is available through his website at www.LYDMusic.com. Scott McAllister is professor of composition at Baylor University, lives in Crawford Texas, and is the proud father of two sons.

Unit 2: Composition

Krump was commissioned by a consortium of eleven universities organized by Edwin Powell, director of bands at Pacific Lutheran University. Powell became interested in McAllister's music after hearing The University of Kentucky perform *Black Dog* at the 2003 CBDNA National Conference in Minneapolis, Minnesota. Once sufficient interest was verified, McAllister and Powell entered into the contract that produced *Krump*. The following universities and their directors joined to form the consortium:

Abilene Christian University	Steven Ward
California State University at Sacramento	Robert Halseth
Eastern Washington University	Patrick Winter
Humboldt State University	Paul Cummings
Pacific Lutheran University	Edwin Powell
Southern Illinois University Carbondale	Christopher Morehouse
Southwest Minnesota State University	John Ginocchio
Texas Tech University	Sarah McKoin
University of North Texas	Eugene Migliaro Corporon
University of Tennessee	Gary Sousa
University of Texas at Tyler	Jeffery Emge

McAllister includes the following program notes with the score.

Much like breakdancing was a benchmark of inner-city culture in the 80s, a dance movement called Krumping is creating its own subculture among teens in Los Angeles neighborhoods such as Compton, South Central, and Watts. Informed equally by hip-hop, African tribal rituals, pantomime and martial arts, Krumping is a frenetic, hyper-fast-paced dancing style. Dancers gather in school grounds, parking lots, and yards to perform and "battle dance" each other; participants are typically vocal opponents of violence, thus making the Krumping scene an alternative to the gang wars that plague the areas where Krumping is popular. Theatrical face paint is also worn by the dancers, which gives Krumping its other moniker, "clowning."

Krump is an acronym for Kingdom Radically Uplifted Might Praise. It is a dance form that was pioneered by Tight Eyez (a.k.a. Ceasare Willis) and Li'l C along with a group of others, namely Big Mijo, Slayer, and Hurricane. It is an aggressive and spiritual form of dance with Christian roots. Its movements include Chest Pops, Stomps, Arm swings, Syncs, Puzzles, Bangs, and Kill-Offs. There are supposedly three levels to Krumping: Krump, Buckness, and Ampness.

This work is inspired by Krumping. Fast and fiery music is juxtaposed with free, hymn-like, ethereal slow sections, while instrumental groups and soloists in the ensemble get a chance to "Krump," emulating the energy and passion of this dance.

The inspiration for *Krump* came while McAllister was watching the David LaChapelle documentary film *Rize*. The film is a poignant look at the lives of Krumpers and Clown Dancers in South Central Los Angeles. Viewing this film is immensely helpful when preparing this work.

Krump was premiered by Pacific Lutheran University on October 14, 2007. Scott McAllister was present for the performance and much of the information included in this guide came from that interaction.

Unit 3: Historical Perspective

It is difficult to categorize McAllister's music into any one style or genre. He calls his music somewhere between "Maximalism and Minimalism," acknowledging some Minimalist tendencies while pointing out that it does not fit this category very well because there is more going on. He jokingly claims that if you had to categorize his music it would have to be "Mediumism." For *Krump*, McAllister is certainly economical with musical material, but there is great breadth in the manner and sequence in which the material is used.

One fact is certain: his compositions are heavily influenced by the music to which he listened as a young man. As a classically trained clarinetist, this means composers like Mozart and Stravinsky. As a youth in the 1970s and 1980s, it means popular bands like Led Zeppelin, Alice in Chains, and Nirvana, among many others. These influences result in highly unique-sounding concert works that infuse popular culture.

The inclusion of popular song into art music is certainly not new and goes back as long as we have written historical records. An example of this trend is evidenced by pieces like *Missa l'homme armé* by Guillaume Dufay, circa 1450. What makes McAllister's work significant is that he states unapologetically that his compositions are influenced by the popular and commercial music of the 60s through the present. This makes him one of the first Modern composers to assimilate commercial, non-jazz, or non-folk music as heard on radio, vinyl, compact disc, and MP3. McAllister explains that he does not arrange or quote music as much he likes to capture the essence of the music's energy, though you will hear quotes in some of his pieces.

As for performance practices, his works are clearly twentieth-century. Rhythms are driving and articulations are aggressive, ala Stravinsky. Yet harmonically, though at times dissonant, McAllister is surprisingly traditional, with a few unconventional twists.

Unit 4: Technical Considerations

While *Krump* is not prohibitively difficult, it does require skill from every section within the ensemble. There are extensive solo passages and tricky ensemble rhythms. The "Battle Dance" section in the middle features difficult clarinet, tuba, trumpet, and xylophone solos as well as fast-moving woodwind and brass soli sections. The composer has spoken of writing more solo and soli passages so that each conductor may custom-build the section to the strengths of their band. These additional solo passages are not yet extant as of the writing of this guide, but should be available soon. Multiple tonguing is required throughout the work and the mallet parts are involved.

Perhaps the most difficult issue with *Krump* is pitch. The chorale sections are scored in a transparent and open manner, and some extended registers are used, especially for trumpet and clarinet.

There are some points where balance is an issue. Flutes playing in the middle register often compete against brass and clarinets in the upper register, making them hard to hear. The flute soli is scored very low. It is acceptable to add alto flute to this part, but the composer does not want it taken up an octave.

The instrumentation calls for piano, harp, two vibraphones, and two bass drums. Amplifying the piano and harp is recommended. A quick note about the harp: It provides a nice color, but if not available, it may be omitted.

One of the bass drums is a kick drum. The speed and regularity of the kick drum part is such that it is suggested that either a double pedal is used or the drum be mounted on a stand and played with two hard mallets. As stated in the score, the other bass drum is to be prepared with "a thin piece of metal over the head of the drum" so it "sound(s) like large speakers in a trunk." A little experimentation will be needed in order to get the right sound. The E-flat soprano clarinet part is essential in the soli section. Tenor sax is often written divisi.

Unit 5: Stylistic Considerations

Krump is a study in contrasts. In order to make decisions on these contrasts it is important to know what the sections represent. There are essentially three major parts that appear and return. They roughly coincide with characters and events in the film *Rize*. The sections are titled "Chorale," "Slow Motion," and "Battle Dance."

The "Chorale" section represents the spiritual nature of the participants. They attend church, they pray, yet there is poignancy to their lives because they feel surrounded by violence, prejudice, drug abuse, and poverty. The "Chorale" section is gentle and reverent, and contains a progression of beautiful chords that drift through the scoring in a manner that perhaps is best described as *klangfarbenmelodie*. Entrances should be made beneath the texture and gradually crescendo to assume greater prominence in the timbre. Gentle emphasis of the many suspensions could be thought to represent poignancy and certainly adds expression. Some careful use of rubato is appropriate. These more introspective passages need to be very gentle and almost romantic in interpretation.

The "Slow Motion" section is a little faster than the "Chorale" and alludes to the incredible slow motion dance footage in the film. There is also a super slow motion section that cannot be rushed. Take great care to achieve solid blend and good intonation between trumpets and horns. This section is fluid and contains many alternations of duple and triple rhythms. The beautiful flute solo should be pure and resonant in quality. Rely on steady marimba and vibraphone players to provide the motor.

The "Battle Dance" section attempts to capture the aggressiveness of Krumping as well as the competitive nature of the activity. Its rhythms are driving and need to be cleanly articulated. There are many rhythmic dialogues between instrument groups, and articulation should be precise and unified. Careful balance of the dialogue is essential. Contained within this section is a "Solo Krump," where individual instruments play accompanied only by the two bass drums. The challenge of the "Solo Krump" is to maintain the formidable energy of the tutti sections.

The work ends quietly with a surprise. The last note should have the effect of a sudden gun shot.

Unit 6: Musical Elements

MELODY:

Krump is tonal. Melodies introduced in each section generally stay in the same key and are very tuneful.

Within the "Chorale" the melody is often developed by the way non-chord tones interact and resolve with chord tones. Orchestrational shifts supply ample timbral contrasts as well. This is why this section can perhaps be best described as *klangfarbenmelodie*. The progression is elegant and simple, centering around B-flat, E-flat, and A-flat major with an occasional C major chord thrown in. What makes it interesting is how the chords often will go to meet the "blue" note instead of the opposite, which is more traditional.

The "Slow Motion" section is more traditional, with long phrases in flute and low instruments. Again, emphasis should be placed on non-chord tones. This brings out an expressive yearning. Beginning at m. 64 there is a sudden tempo change that sends the music into to super slow motion. The melody is in triplets while mallet instruments maintain eighth notes. Rhythmic precision is critical at this point.

After a few measures of music that is reminiscent of the "Chorale," the "Battle Dance" section begins. This section is marked "Competitively," but take care that no section actually wins the battle. Good taste should be the overriding ,concern though this music is certainly aggressive. The example in figure 1 is of a theme that is heard throughout the rest of the work. This theme often occurs at the beginning or the climax of a section. Be sure to drive through the rhythm and crescendo to the last note.

FIGURE 1.

HARMONY:

As discussed previously, *Krump* is tonal, but often chords resolve to meet the "blue" note or non-chord tone. Figure 2 gives a reduction of the first thirteen measures of the "Chorale."

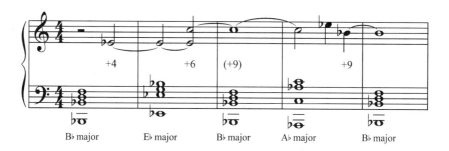

FIGURE 2.

Note how the E-flat suspension is added, and, instead of resolving downward to the third of the B-flat major chord, the chord itself shifts to E-flat major. This is played out over and over as non-chord tones shift to different non-chord tones or become voices in the chord setting up another "blue" note. The listener becomes aware that linear interest is generated by this interaction.

As the work becomes more angular, so does the harmony. There are often conflicts of seconds and fourths, but it essentially remains tonal and has few harmonic surprises. There will often be a repeated grounding pedal that supplies the listener with a very satisfying home base.

RHYTHM:

The rhythm in *Krump* is syncopated and at times difficult. Multiple polyrhythms are created by layering duple and triple figures. There are also syncopated canons that need to be balanced properly. Matching volume and articulation is the key to getting all of these to speak. The conductor may want to create rhythm exercises to help teach the ensemble to play with precision.

McAllister is quite clear that he does not want rhythmic precision to compromise the feel and energy of the passages in the solo section. They need to be uncontrolled and wild, much like the dance itself. "Let them rip, and if they are a little loose, so be it" (from the score).

TIMBRE:
The timbre of the "Chorale" section has already been covered in comments above about harmony and *klangfarbenmelodie*. The only addition is that the sound is warm and lush.

The "Slow Motion" section is scored transparently, and each voice should be clear and resonant. There is lightness to the entire section, and upper voices are often prominent, accompanied by keyboard percussion.

The "Battle Dance" section is dense and active in texture, but individual instrumental colors should still speak. Clarity is quite a bit more difficult in this section, but is nonetheless very important in order to achieve the composer's intention. Often consorts of mixed instrumental groups will play in conflict or trade lines back and forth. This results in a dialogue in which bright sounds throw themes to darker sounds. All the while the percussion, especially the bass drums, lay down a very aggressive, almost tribal rhythmic underpinning. Again, balance and articulation are the keys to getting this section to speak.

Unit 7: Form and Structure

SECTION	MEASURE	EVENT AND SCORING
"Chorale"	1–36	
"Slow Motion"	37–91	Super slow motion in mm. 64 and 80; truncated "Chorale" returns in m. 87
"Battle Dance"	92–257	Solo Krump in mm. 162–234; this is the section where McAllister plans to add solos that can be plugged in
"Chorale"	258–298	
"Battle Dance"	299–324	
"Slow Motion"	325–350	
"Battle Dance"	351–359	
Coda	360–377	It is worth noting that the coda contains a trap; six measures before the end, at m. 372, there is a sudden stop in the music that is again from the "Chorale"; after five measures of this, the piece comes to an abrupt end with a sudden *fortissimo* hit that is sure to jolt the audience out of their seats

Note that, even though there is variety in the structure of the form, once a section is learned, it is essentially the same each time it returns. This can streamline the preparation process tremendously.

Unit 8: Suggested Listening

Chameleon, Baby C, Poke. *Krump 1, The Chameleon Mix.* The Krump
  Kings. 2005.
LaChapelle, David. *Rize.* David LaChapelle Studios. 2005.
McAllister, Scott:
  "X" Concerto for Clarinet. Black Dog. Arizona State University
    Orchestra. Gary Hill, conductor. Robert Spring, clarinet soloist.
    Summit Records DCD 412. 2005.
  Black Dog: Rhapsody for Clarinet and Wind Ensemble. Black Dog. Arizona
    State University Wind Ensemble. Gary Hill, conductor. Robert
    Spring, clarinet soloist. Summit Records DCD 412. 2005.
Mozart, Wolfgang Amadeus. *Clarinet Concerto,* KV 622. Any recording.
Stravinsky, Igor. *The Rite of Spring.* Any recording.

McAllister's *"X" Concerto for Clarinet* has multiple motives from Mozart, Stravinsky, Alice in Chains, and Nirvana. It is a must-listen for understanding and appreciating the aesthetic of his music.

Unit 9: Additional References and Resources

Guerra, Gabo. "Krumping." http://www.urbandictionary.com/
McAllister, Scott. *Krump.* LYDMusic, Crawford, Texas, 2007.
Wikipedia. "Krumping." http://en.wikipedia.org/wiki/Krumping (This is the
  site from which McAllister obtained the information used to write the
  program note found in the score.)

Contributed by:

Edwin Powell
Pacific Lutheran University
Tacoma, Washington

Teacher Resource Guide

Limerick Daydreams

Nathan Daughtrey
(b. 1975)

Unit 1: Composer

Nathan Daughtrey is a native of North Carolina, where he currently resides. He received his BM in music education and his MM and DMA degrees in percussion performance from the University of North Carolina at Greensboro. He was a percussion student of Cort McClaren and studied composition with Greg Carroll. He served for three years as visiting lecturer of percussion at UNCG, where he taught applied percussion and directed a percussion ensemble.

Daughtrey has received numerous commissions from professional performers, university ensembles, and high schools for his percussion and band works. His compositions have been heard throughout the United States, Japan, Thailand, Australia, Germany, and Canada. His works are regularly performed at festivals and contests as well as concert performances. He has been honored to have compositions performed at such prestigious events as the Percussive Arts Society International Convention, the Midwest Band and Orchestra Clinic, and the International Double Reed Society Conference.

With several awards to his credit, he is the only composer to win both second- and third-place prizes in the same year in the Percussive Arts Society Composition Contest (2005).

Unit 2: Composition

Limerick Daydreams is based on the Irish reel, *Highway to Limerick*. The piece was originally written for percussion ensemble and piano and received the second-place prize in the Percussive Arts Society Composition Contest in 2005. It was subsequently rewritten and scored for full symphonic band. The band version of the piece was premiered by the University of North Texas Symphonic Band in April, 2006.

Limerick Daydreams is a fantasia that makes extensive use of thematic fragmentation and cleverly explores a wide variety of stylistic, rhythmic, and harmonic treatments. The piece is 331 measures in length with an approximate performance time of twelve minutes. It is published by C. Alan Publications, Greensboro, North Carolina.

Unit 3: Historical Perspective

Folk music has long been at the heart of both written and oral lore and legend. The historical homage within different cultures and ethnicities is what defines a people and their heritage. Irish culture is often identified, recognized, and defined by its music. Ranging from melancholy to playful and from boisterous to wistful, Irish music explores the full range of human emotion.

Highway to Limerick is among the most recognizable and familiar Irish reels. The dance style known as the reel is typically defined in eight-measure phrases and is performed by two or more couples. The music is generally in phrases of four or eight measures, in duple meter, and makes use of extensive repetition. The reel as both a music and dance style is frequently associated with the folk cultures of Ireland and Scotland. Its introduction into early American folk traditions came largely from immigrants who brought their heritage and ethnic and cultural identifications with them. The energy and appeal of the reel is both engaging and infectious, often suggesting a celebration or party atmosphere.

Unit 4: Technical Considerations

Limerick Daydreams is scored for full band with the instrumentation of piccolo, flute 1–2, oboe 1, oboe 2/English horn, bassoon 1–2, B-flat clarinet 1–3, bass clarinet, alto saxophone 1–2, saxophone, baritone saxophone, B-flat trumpet 1–3, horn 1–4, trombone 1–3, euphonium 1–2, tuba, piano, and percussion. The extensive use of percussion can be performed by as few as six players; however, more players can be used if available. The extensive list of equipment needs are timpani, tambourine, bells, crotales, xylophone, temple blocks, piccolo snare drum, vibraphone, marimba, conga drums, bongos, tom-toms, tam-tam, chimes, snare drum, wind chimes, suspended cymbal, small China cymbal, sandblocks, triangle, bell tree, bass drum, and finger cymbals.

Although the key of A minor is used and recurs throughout the piece without change, there is extensive use of shifting key centers, modality, and major/minor key relationships. Those changes are accommodated through the use of neutral-key, a notation technique that uses accidentals to define new tonal centers or key relationships. The use of different meters include duple-based meters as well as the extensive use of the compound meters of 12/8 and 9/8, along with an extended section alternating between 7/8 and 5/8. The continuity of eighth-note pulsation is essential to the piece.

Instrument ranges are extensive and take the melodic instruments of flute and trumpet to A6 and B5 respectively. Horn, trombone, and euphonium ranges are moderate, with G4 being the highest note for euphonium. Euphonium divisi exists throughout, often serving as an extension of the tuba voice.

Articulations in all voices are typical of the Irish reel and compound meter. Clarity of staccato and accents is essential to the style. The use of proportional dynamic contrasts and musical effects must be defined and adhered to in order to achieve the desired musical effects.

Rhythmic interaction within and between voices, especially with percussion voices, is paramount. Tempo consistency and rhythmic clarity are also essential. It can be helpful and instructive to use percussion instruments and sounds as a way to model and establish articulation style in the winds. Using percussion as a guide for how sound is pronounced will be very helpful in establishing articulation style and consistency in the woodwinds and brass and create a unifying timbre with percussion.

Unit 5: Stylistic considerations

Limerick Daydreams offers the opportunity to teach and refine a wide variety of contrasting styles. The opening slow section is mysterious in nature and uses a layered, chordal density. The extensive use of compound meter requires a solid command of triple and duple relationships. A brief woodwind choral in the middle of the piece allows for lyrical playing, and an extended section that alternates 7/8 and 5/8 is highly rhythmic and interactive between winds and percussion. The return of the defining reel style in compound meter accelerates and intensifies to the exciting conclusion of the piece.

Tempo extremes range from quarter note = 52 to dotted quarter note = 168. Duple treatment of the slow tempos and compound meters in the fastest ones provide the impression of an even wider tempo range. This accommodates the styles that range from mysterious to melancholy and from lively to raucous.

Unit 6: Musical Elements

MELODY:

The primary melodic theme of the *Highway to Limerick* serves as the obvious ongoing connection throughout the piece. The numerous variations of this theme in compound meter are contrasted by duple meter treatments in various key and tonal structures. It is important to identify and bring forward the melodic fragments and motives throughout.

HARMONY:

Harmonic variety and interest is created through extensive use of Dorian modality in contrast to both major and minor modes. The use of voices in parallel to the melody in intervals other than thirds and sixths creates an interesting harmonic variation. While a number of tonal centers appear, the most frequent key centers are A and F minor. There is extensive simultaneous use of duple- and triple-based layers of both arpeggiated and diatonic material. These ostinato-like figures create both a harmonic screen and motor-driven momentum. The contour and shape of these figures often overlap in ways that pull the listener's ears in interesting ways.

RHYTHM:

Compound meter serves as a recurring rhythmic structure, as is common in the reel. An extensive rhythmic section alternating 7/8 and 5/8 meters incorporates fragmentation of the theme. The obvious common link between rhythmically complex sections is the continuity of the eighth-note subdivision.

TIMBRE:

Scoring throughout the composition relies heavily on the interaction of various wind instrument combinations with the percussion. This revision for full band from the original composition, originally conceived for percussion ensemble and piano, retains much of the source material's percussion writing. Solo passages are written for piccolo, flute, oboe, English horn, clarinet, and euphonium. Although not scored as a solo instrument, piano serves an extensive role and often is used prominently. Scoring ranges from very transparent to quite dense.

Unit 7: Form and Structure

SECTION	MEASURE	EVENT AND SCORING
Introduction	1–30	Harmonic density is created by stacking notes from low to high, creating growth and expansion at a slow and legato tempo
	30–43	Extension of introduction into percussion, which establishes the compound meter feel at the primary tempo of quarter note = 132

SECTION	MEASURE	EVENT AND SCORING
A	44	Primary theme introduced in solo flute; subsequent repetitions in woodwind and brass consorts use parallel harmony and vertical rhythmic accompaniments
A	63	Duple melodic motive in low brass with compound meter accompaniment; G minor
	75	Same motive in saxophones; G minor
	82	Melodic motive in clarinet consort; C minor
Transition	93	Vertical rhythmic punctuations used to set up transition into duple-based variations
A	108	Low brass in duple meter; F minor
A	115	Metric augmentation to *alla breve* with compound meter accompaniment in flute and percussion
B	136	Lyrical treatment of melody in English horn and saxophone with countermelody in euphonium; E major; 3/4 meter
	147	Ornamentation and expansion of lyrical section B
B	162	Lyrical variation in upper woodwinds; F minor
C	173	Rhythmic variation of theme introduced in percussion; alternating 7/8 and 5/8 meter; quasi-latin feel in percussion throughout
	185	Brass scoring of melodic motive; continuation of Latin feel; vertical harmonic structure; F minor
	197	Latin style melodic treatment in solo flute with clarinet harmonic punctuations
	215	Melodic variation in euphonium, creating the impression of improvisation; accompanying harmonic punctuations in brass
D	244	Compound meter returns; energetic tempo of quarter note = 152; major key tonality established; D major to E major
	256	Second half of main theme, first in trumpets, then tutti at m. 262
	269	Primary theme returns in flutes over chorale accompaniment in low brass; C minor

Section	Measure	Event and Scoring
	278	Theme repeated in clarinets; F minor
Coda	287	Compound meter rhythmic energy over expansive chordal extensions in brass
	301	Compound meter; upper woodwind variation of melodic motive over duple meter in percussion and piano builds to a frenzy
	315	Tempo and energy increase through rhythm and chordal expansions propel to the A-major conclusion

Unit 8: Suggested Listening

Boysen, Andrew. *Kirkpatrick Fanfare*.

The Chieftains. The Best of the Chieftains. Sony. 1992.

Galway, James:
    Celtic Minstrel. RCA Victor. 1996.
    James Galway and The Chieftains in Ireland. RCA Victor. 1990.

The Green Mountain

The Highway to Dublin

Infusion. University of North Texas Symphonic Band. Dennis W. Fisher, conductor. Mark Custom Recordings MCD 6364. 2004.

The Irish Washerwoman

Unit 9: Additional References and Resources

Apel, Willi. *Harvard Dictionary of Music*. Cambridge, MA: Harvard University Press, 2000.

Daughtrey, Nathan. Correspondence with composer, 2008.

Daughtrey, Nathan. *Limerick Daydreams*. Greensboro, NC: C. Alan Publications, 2006.

Contributed by:

Dennis W. Fisher
Professor, Conducting and Ensembles
University of North Texas
Denton, Texas

Teacher Resource Guide

Mannin Veen

Haydn Wood
(1882–1959)

Unit 1: Composer

Haydn Wood was a prolific writer of both popular and serious music in the first half of the twentieth century. Born in Slaithwaite, West Yorkshire (in northern England) on March 25, 1882, Wood lived for most of his youth on the Isle of Man, a British dependency in the Irish Sea between England and Ireland. He learned to play the violin at an early age from an older brother, and at age sixteen enrolled in violin performance studies at the Royal College of Music. The success of a post-graduate performance tour led Wood to further his studies at the Brussels Conservatory.

He studied composition with Charles Stanford at the Royal College of Music and subsequently wrote a handful of serious works, including an award-winning string quartet and a now-lost symphony. He authored more than 200 popular songs for voice and piano, including "Roses of Picardy," "A Brown Bird Singing," and "Love's Garden of Roses." These songs were arguably his most profitable and best-known works.

Folksongs became prominent in his later writings. Several of his orchestral works, such as *A Manx Rhapsody* (1931), *Manx Overture* (1936), and *Mylecharane* (1946), referenced songs from his childhood home, the Isle of Man (or Mannin). His compositional output includes orchestral works, suites, marches, choral works, and solo pieces. Wood spent many of the last twenty years of his life as the director of the Performing Rights Society, a British organization of composers and publishers founded to collect royalties for the performances of its members' music. He died on March 11, 1959 in London.

Unit 2: Composition

Mannin Veen (which is Gaelic for "Dear Isle of Man") was written originally in 1933 as a work for orchestra. The band transcription was published by Hawkes and Company (now Boosey and Hawkes) in 1936.[1] Wood's only original work for band is *Merridale*, an unpublished quick-step march written for the Slaithwaite Band in 1948.[2]

This composition displays Wood's innovative use of melodic development through the fusion of the folksongs into a single piece. The first folk tune, "The Good Old Way," is a traditional Manx air written mostly in Dorian mode. The song was converted to a Methodist revival hymn in the late nineteenth century and can be found in print as early as 1896 in William Henry Gill's *Manx National Songs*. Gill gives the text of the tune as:

O Good Old Way, how sweet thou art,
May none of us from thee depart,
But may our actions always say:
"We're marching on the Good Old Way."

(chorus)
For I have a sweet hope of glory in my soul,
For I have a sweet hope of glory in my soul,
For I know I have, and I feel I have
A sweet hope of glory in my soul.

Our conflicts here, though great they be,
Shall not prevent our victory;
If we but strive and watch and pray,
Like soldiers on the Good Old Way.

(chorus)

The lively second folksong, "The Manx Fiddler," is a reel, a traditional Scottish or Gaelic dance akin to the American hoedown. In the program notes to the piece, Wood writes:

Chaloner (likely English politician James Chaloner), writing in the middle of the seventeenth century, remarked that the Manx people were "much addicted to the music of the violyne, so that there is scarce a family in the Island, but more or less can play upon it; but as they are ill composers, so are they bad players."

The third folksong is a traditional Manx ballad, included in the 1896 compilation *Manx Ballads and Music*. "Sweet Water in the Common" tells the story of a Manx custom of the gathering of a twenty-four-man jury to resolve issues of boundaries and watercourses:

There was William of the Close,
And Quilliam Glen Meay,
Walking upon the high-road,
Fright'ning all the people,
Going to Castletown,
Coming home at break of day,
Singing "sweet water in the common,
We will never lose it."

In the Long Jury there were
But three men from each parish,
To seek out the watercourse
For the chief mill at Greeba.
Part of them on the right hand,
And part on the left hand,
And they ran the watercourse,
Where it had no right to be.

The watercourse was west,
But the water ran east,
That was all on account of
The silver and the gold.
Our horses they drank of it,
And the cattle when thirsty,
And sweet water in the common,
We will never lose it.

The final tune is an old hymn, "The Harvest of the Sea," sung by fishermen as a song of thanksgiving after their safe return from fishing. Wood only uses an abbreviated version of the hymn in *Mannin Veen*. This hymn can also be found in William Henry Gill's *Manx National Songs*:

Hear us, O Lord, from Heav'n Thy dwelling place.
Like them of old in vain we toil all night.
Unless with us Thou go, Who art the Light;
For them we plough the land and plough the deep,
For them by day the golden corn we reap,
By night the silver harvest of the sea.

Thou, Lord, dost rule the raging of the sea.
When loud the storm and furious is the gale;
Strong is Thine arm, our little barques are frail;
That we may reap Contentment, Joy, and Peace;
And, when at last our earthly labours cease,
Grant us to join Thy Harvest Home above.

Unit 3: Historical Perspective

Haydn Wood was one of the most prolific composers of light concert music in Great Britain. The genre of "light music," while not clearly defined, refers to less serious music designed to be immediately pleasing to its audiences. Major British composers such as Edward Elgar, Ralph Vaughan Williams, Gustav Holst, and Gordon Jacob wrote at least some of their works in this style. Several works in the band tradition have also been written in this style, including Percy Grainger's *Shepherd's Hey* (1913), William Walton's *Façade, An Entertainment* (1922), Malcolm Arnold's *Four Scottish Dances* (1957), and Derek Bourgeois' *Serenade* (1965).

This work is also part of the nationalist movement in Great Britain in the early part of the twentieth century. Partly generated by the events surrounding the two world wars, feelings of patriotism sparked many musical works with British themes, including Vaughan Williams's "London" Symphony (1913), Holst's *Hammersmith* (1930), and Walton's *Crown Imperial* (1937). It was also during this period that many compositions, such as Holst's *Second Suite in F* (1911) and numerous works by Vaughan Williams and Grainger, began to include British folksongs as a melodic source.

Unit 4: Technical Considerations

Since only a condensed score is available for the work, an examination of individual parts is highly recommended. A lengthy list of errata for both score and parts, is included in "Interpreting Wood's *Mannin Veen*," by Barry Kopetz (see Unit 9).

Wood's scoring and instrumentation of *Mannin Veen* are the most important considerations in preparation and performance of the piece. The work demands a large section of versatile clarinet players. Wood wrote nine distinct clarinet parts, including four essential B-flat clarinet parts and a split bass clarinet part. While alto and contrabass clarinet can easily be omitted, E-flat clarinet contains several solo passages that, when covered by cues in the solo clarinet part, create breathing and endurance problems. Low woodwind sounds are also vitally important to the texture in many places. Low woodwind players must be able to produce full, resonant sounds in low registers.

Mannin Veen makes use of a variety of different tonal areas and scale patterns. The major keys of G, C, F, and B-flat are all featured prominently, while several other keys appear for shorter periods of time. Players must not only be able to perform the usual scalar patterns associated with these keys, but must also be able to play the accompanying harmonies in tune. Wood also incorporates Dorian (mm. 1–8), pentatonic (mm. 51–54) and whole-tone (mm. 291–292) passages into the piece, along with numerous chromatic l ines. These compositional devices can easily serve as an introduction to these concepts.

Breathing is another important consideration. Ensemble breaths should be notated after each of the four-measure phrases in the initial statements of "The Good Old Way" (mm. 1–16) and "Manx Fisherman's Evening Hymn" (mm. 175–190). Elsewhere in the piece, breathing concerns are resolved by the use of overlapping phrases. Clarinet players should work out staggered breathing in advance (mm. 262–278 and 295–312), keeping in mind that E-flat clarinet cues may complicate breathing matters.

Wood's dynamic markings may be misleading. Clarinet players should overplay their dynamic markings in lower registers, especially when carrying the melody. All solo cornet lines should be played one dynamic level fuller when sharing the melody with flutes (mm. 62–70, 100–104, 220–228, 247–248, 259–262, and 265–278).

While *Mannin Veen* can be a very effective conclusion to a concert, it places great physical demands on players. The piece takes approximately ten minutes to perform with the full ensemble playing together during much of that time. Since the most physically demanding segment of the piece is its final forty measures, the organ, if used, very effectively supports the band in this climactic section.

Unit 5: Stylistic Considerations

The four folksongs that are the basis for *Mannin Veen* dictate distinct style considerations for player and conductor.

Sostenuto playing is very important to "The Good Old Way," "Manx Fisherman's Evening Hymn," and "Sweet Water in the Common" sections, since these tunes are hymns and ballads. Since Wood is careful not to put repeated notes underneath a slur, it is logical to conclude that these repeated notes should also be legato. These slurs should only be separated by lightly tonguing and should not have any added weight or separation. Notes with tenuto markings should be given slightly more weight and separation. Note that repeated notes in lower instrument ranges (such as mm. 189–196) must be slightly more separated to be heard distinctly. This will ensure that the organ-like texture Wood intended will be heard even when organ is not present.

Articulations in "The Manx Fiddler" should be more separated than in other sections. Accompanying eighth-note patterns should be played with a bounce and separated, although still long enough that each individual chord can be heard. A light, crisp staccato should be used (except where Wood has indicated otherwise) to create the dance-like feel of the original folksong. The overall style of "The Manx Fiddler" should never be compromised by choosing an overly aggressive tempo or by rushing the accompanying eighth-note patterns.

Tempo control is important in other sections of *Mannin Veen* as well. There are several written tempo fluctuations throughout the piece, both quickening and slowing. Some of these (e.g., mm. 17–32) are long, gradual changes that require patience from both conductor and ensemble. None of these tempo changes should be overly dramatic, keeping with the overall intent of Wood's music. The conductor should also consider the articulation requirements of each transition, so that the resulting tempo allows players optimal opportunity for the intended style.

Unit 6: Musical Elements

MELODY:

The melodies of *Mannin Veen* are drawn from the four folksongs. Wood rarely embellishes the melodies, but instead relies on fragments of them for variation. The transformations of these melodic fragments also serve as the primary device for transitions from one folksong section to the next. These melodies also may occur in the sections of the other folksongs by either taking the style of that section or by serving as a countermelody.

HARMONY:

The harmonies used throughout *Mannin Veen* are mainly tonal, and explore numerous major and minor keys in diatonic fashion. Chromatic harmonies are used in several instances, both in internal voices as a coloristic device or in bass voices as a transitional device between two tonal areas. Pedal point is often used in bass voices throughout the piece (such as in mm. 33–36, 41–46, 97–100, and 313–316).

RHYTHM:

For a work requiring this level of technical maturity, rhythms are very simple, in accord with the folk nature of the original songs. The entire work is written in simple duple meter and exhibits predictable phrase structures throughout. While rhythmic matters are not of major concern, Wood's use of complimenting rhythms in sustained passages (such as mm. 201–204) could be particularly effective in the introduction of the concept of counterpoint.

TIMBRE:

As with all folksong arrangements, timbre is a key component of *Mannin Veen*. Various sections of the piece explore different instrumental textures from the low, rich sounds of clarinet and low voices in the first statement of "The Good Old Way" to the brighter sounds of upper woodwinds in portions of "The Manx Fiddler" and the tutti, organ-like sound of the final statement of "Manx Evening Fisherman's Hymn."

Unit 7: Form and Structure

SECTION	MEASURE	EVENT AND SCORING
"The Good Old Way"		
	1–16	Complete statement of the tune in D Dorian mode by solo clarinet and clarinet 1 with D minor harmonies in low woodwinds and low brass
	17–32	Melodic development of "The Good Old Way" theme using chromatic harmonies; tempo quickens gradually through all sixteen measures
	33–40	Melodic development continues, builds to climax with tutti forces in a four-octave tessitura at m. 37
	41–46	Variation of "The Good Old Way" theme with chromatic harmony against a C pedal point
	47–50	Slurred five-note motive from "The Good Old Way" theme is introduced in clarinet, bassoon, and euphonium as a transition into next section; accelerando begins
	51–54	Accelerando ends while transition continues in cut time; articulation changes from legato to staccato
"The Manx Fiddler"		
	55–62	Complete statement of "The Manx Fiddler" in F major by solo clarinet and clarinet 1
	63–70	Staccato treatment of "The Good Old Way" theme by cornet and upper woodwinds in D minor
	71–76	Partial restatement of "The Manx Fiddler" in F major by clarinet and flute
	77–80	Phrase extension
	81–88	Tutti statement of developmental theme based on fragments of "The Good Old Way" and "The Manx Fiddler" in D minor; developmental theme immediately restated in F major
	89–96	Solo fragments of initial theme made by flute, clarinet, and cornet in various keys

SECTION	MEASURE	EVENT AND SCORING
	97–104	Restatement of "The Manx Fiddler" by solo clarinet and clarinet 1 in C major with legato accompaniment; restatement continues in flute and solo cornet with staccato accompaniment
	105–106	Phrase extension
"Sweet Water in the Common"		
	107–122	Complete statement of "Sweet Water in the Common" by cornet 1; thin accompaniment in low woodwinds and tuba with legato articulations
	123–136	Complete statement of "Sweet Water in the Common" by solo clarinet; accompaniment is staccato
	137–140	Phrase extension
	141–152	Melodic development of both "The Manx Fiddler" and "Sweet Water in the Common" themes in low woodwinds and euphonium
	153–164	Further development of "The Manx Fiddler" and "Sweet Water in the Common" themes
	165–170	Incomplete statement of "Sweet Water in the Common" theme in G major with chromatic harmony
	171–174	Phrase extension
"Manx Fisherman's Evening Hymn"		
	175–188	Complete statement of "Manx Fisherman's Evening Hymn" by clarinets, saxophones, low woodwinds, and low brass in G major
	189–196	Phrase extension
	197–206	Variation of "Manx Fisherman's Evening Hymn" in F major by oboe soloist, then joined by clarinets, cornets, and euphoniums
	207–212	Re-transition back to "The Manx Fiddler" theme
"The Manx Fiddler"		
	213–220	Complete "The Manx Fiddler" theme in F major in solo clarinet and clarinet 1
	221–228	Staccato treatment of "The Good Old Way" theme by cornet and upper woodwinds in D minor

SECTION	MEASURE	EVENT AND SCORING
	229–236	Partial restatement of "The Manx Fiddler" in F major by clarinet and flute
	237–238	Phrase extension
	239–246	Tutti statement of developmental theme based on fragments of "The Good Old Way" and "The Manx Fiddler" in D minor; developmental theme immediately restated in G major
	247–254	Solo fragments of initial theme made by flute, cornet, clarinet, and oboe in various keys
	255–264	Restatement of "The Manx Fiddler" by solo clarinet and clarinet 1 in B-flat major with legato accompaniment; restatement continues in flute and solo cornet with staccato accompaniment
"Sweet Water in the Common"		
	265–278	Complete "Sweet Water in the Common" theme returns in B-flat major by flutes, oboes, and solo cornet; clarinet sixteenth-note pattern
	279–282	Phrase extension
	283–286	Fragments of "The Good Old Way" with tutti sustained harmonies and C pedal point in bass voices
	287–294	Melodic development of "The Good Old Way" theme
"Manx Fisherman's Evening Hymn"		
	295–308	Complete "Manx Fisherman's Evening Hymn" theme stated in tutti voices (with organ); "The Manx Fiddler" countermelody continues in clarinet
	309–312	Phrase extension
	313–324	Variation of "Manx Fisherman's Evening Hymn" theme stated in tutti voices (with organ) with prominent countermelodic line in bass clarinet, horn 1–3, trombone 1, and euphonium
	325–334	Coda based on fragments of "The Manx Fiddler" theme; builds to overall climax at m. 331

Unit 8: Suggested Listening

Grainger, Percy. *Molly on the Shore*.

Walton, Sir William. Arranged by W. J. Duthoit. *Crown Imperial*.

Wood, Haydn:

> *Mannin Veen* (version for orchestra). *Joyousness—The Music of Haydn Wood*. Light Symphony Orchestra. Haydn Wood, conductor. Guild GLCD-5121.
>
> *Mannin Veen* (version for wind band). *...nite ridin' on da riva*. Arkansas State University Wind Ensemble. Thomas J. O'Neal, conductor. Mark Custom Recordings 2610-MCD.
>
> *Mannin Veen* (version for wind band). *Music for Winds and Percussion, Volume 2*. Northern Illinois University Wind Ensemble. Stephen Squires, conductor. Music Educator's DR HSB-002.
>
> *Mannin Veen* (version for wind band). *Retrospective*. United States Marine Band. Col. Timothy W. Foley, conductor. United States Marine Band USMB-CD18.

Unit 9: Additional References and Resources

Gill, William Henry. *Manx National Songs*. London: Boosey, 1896.

Kopetz, Barry. "Interpreting Wood's *Mannin Veen*." *The Instrumentalist*, January 1994: 30–34+.

Moore, Arthur William. *Manx Ballads and Music*. Douglas, Isle of Man: G & R Johnson, 1896.

Scowcroft, Philip L. *British Light Music—A Personal Gallery of 20th-Century Composers*. London: Thames Publishing, 1997.

Smith, Norman E. *Program Notes for Band*. Chicago: GIA Publications, 2002.

Wood, Haydn. Program notes for *Mannin Veen: A Manx Tone Poem* (band version). London: Hawkes and Son, 1933.

Websites:

> Isle of Man. http://www.gov.im/ (Official governmental and informational site.)
>
> Haydn Wood. http://www.haydnwoodmusic.com/ (Unofficial biographical site operated by Wood's great-niece Marjorie Cullerne and Wood expert Gilles Gouset.)

Contributed by:

David D. Robinson
University of Missouri
Columbia, Missouri

1 Email from Majorie Cullerne, June 1, 2008.
2 Email from Gilles Gouset, June 1, 2008.

Teacher Resource Guide

Minstrels of the Kells

Dan Welcher
(b. 1948)

Unit 1: Composer

American composer and conductor Dan Welcher was born in Rochester, New York in 1948. He has composed in many genres, including opera, concerto, symphony, vocal literature, piano solos, and various kinds of chamber music. He began his musical training as a pianist and a bassoonist, earning degrees from the Eastman School of Music and the Manhattan School of Music.

In 1972, he joined the Louisville Orchestra as its principal bassoonist and taught music theory and composition at the University of Louisville. In 1978, he accepted a faculty position at The University of Texas at Austin, where he created the New Music Ensemble and served as the assistant conductor of the Austin Symphony (1980–1990). From 1990–1992, Welcher was the composer-in-residence at the Honolulu Symphony Orchestra through the Meet the Composer Orchestra Residency Program. Currently, Welcher holds the Lee Hage Jamail Regents Professorship in Composition at The University of Texas at Austin.

Welcher's works for wind ensemble and concert band include: *Arches* (1984), *The Yellowstone Fires* (1988), *Castle Creek* (1989), *Zion* (1994), Symphony No. 3, "Shaker Life" (1997), *Spumante* (1999), *Perpetual Song* (2000), *Songs Without Words* (2001), *Minstrels of the Kells* (2002), *Glacier* (2003), and *Symphony No. 4*, "American Visionary" (2005).

Unit 2: Composition

Minstrels of the Kells was commissioned by the Big Twelve Band Directors Association and is dedicated to the memory of the late James Sudduth, former director of bands at Texas Tech University. Using melodies from the repertoire of traditional Irish music, *Minstrels of the Kells* is divided into two movements, "Airs in the Mist" and "Reelin' and Jiggin'." About the piece the composer writes in the score:

> "Airs in the Mist" consists of three old melodies, with a little slip-jig added in the last of them for spice. Irish ballads always tell stories, and these three tunes are no exception. When an Irishman begins to sing a ballad, it is usually because something in the conversation has reminded him of a song. But I have chosen these three for their musical contrast, not for any extra musical storytelling. The three tunes are "Loch na gCaor," "Port na bPucai," and "Blind Mary."

> "Reelin' and Jiggin'" is completely the reverse of the first movement, in terms of spirit. Marked "Relentlessly happy," it consists of a chain of ever-brighter reels and jigs (in that order). These, unlike the airs, have no stories to tell, despite their colorful titles—they are simply good dance tunes. The dance tunes are: "Come West Along the Road," "Ger the Rigger," Gypsy Princess," "Road to Lisdoonvarna," "The Wild Irishman," and "The Humours of Ennistymon."

Movement 2 allows for the optional insertion of an Irish folk or pub band, and the piece continues its Irish influence with an extensive tin whistle soli performed by flute, oboe, and clarinet.

Unit 3: Historical Perspective

John Cody Birdwell of Texas Tech University approached Dan Welcher with the idea of writing a piece to honor the memory of former Texas Tech Director of Bands James Sudduth. The idea of using Irish melodies was suggested by Birdwell because Sudduth, like Birdwell, had an affection for all things Celtic. Welcher was then introduced to Chris Smith, who provided many Irish tunes for his consideration. He carefully went through all of the them and decided to use the lesser-known melodies for his new composition. *Minstrels of the Kells* was premiered by the Texas Tech University Symphonic Wind Ensemble under the direction of John Cody Birdwell on April 21, 2002.

Unit 4: Technical Considerations

The instrumentation of *Minstrels of the Kells* is consistent with today's large wind ensembles. However, there are a couple additions to movement 2 that need to be considered. Welcher suggests that the optional insertion of the folk or pub band between mm. 182–183 be coordinated and rehearsed so that there is a seamless transition. Ideally, there should be no break in sound from the beginning to the end of the section. In mm. 202–238, the composer calls for tin whistles in the key of G and D. These parts must be played on the suggested instruments in order to achieve the desired effect.

The playing range for most instruments are within the practical ranges of advanced players. The piece does not contain many complex rhythms. However, the ensemble, particularly woodwinds, must be in complete command of technical skills to execute the fast scalar passages and the fiddle music contained in movement 2.

Unit 5: Stylistic Considerations

One of the dangers in performing a piece that contains several different melodies strung together is that the melodies are at risk of sounding the same. To remedy this, Welcher has been very specific with metronome and style markings to assist the conductor and performer. Additionally, the lyrical music contained in movement 1 should unfold as if it were sung by an Irish folk singer. Movement 2 contains one dance tune after the other. The style should be light and effortless, as if played on a fiddle.

Unit 6: Musical Elements

MELODY:

The melodies, as stated earlier, come directly from the repertoire of traditional Irish music. They are modal in nature and contain embellishments such as pitch bending and grace note ornaments.

HARMONY:

The harmonies found in *Minstrels of the Kells* are in Welcher's contemporary language, which, at its core, is a mixture of functional harmony and modern techniques. For example, he uses polytonality and asynchronous notation along with traditional harmonies and cadences to add variety and interest to the melodies.

RHYTHM:

Rhythm is a driving force in *Minstrels of the Kells*. The jigs and reels in movement 2 are full of energy with relentless eighth notes that dance around the agogic accents. In movement 1, the interpolation of two slip-jigs gives the listener the impression of two different tempos occurring simultaneously.

TIMBRE:

Welcher creates a variety of different colors through his unique orchestration. In some sections the piece is like chamber music. In others he employs the full force of the ensemble to provide a soundscape of warm-to-bright colors.

Unit 7: Form and Structure

SECTION	MEASURE	EVENT AND SCORING
I. "Airs in the Mist"		
Introduction	1–7	Slow and solemn beginning with open-fifth whole notes in horns; short, dancing rhythms in suspended cymbal, woodblocks, timpani, and double bass forecast the music and style of movement 2
"Loch na gCaor"	8–28	Alto saxophone solo presents "Loch na gCaor" melody followed by a repeat of the melody in flute, oboe, and alto saxophone; the second statement of the melody is accompanied by oscillating triplet eighth-note figures in upper woodwinds
	29–49	Continuation of the melody is stated by piccolo, flutes, E-flat clarinet, saxophones, and trumpets; rhythmic activity in wood-wind accompaniment increases from triplet eighth-notes to sextuplets
	50–52	Oboes, clarinets, saxophones, and trumpets end "Loch na gCaor" melody with long, sustained notes in low reeds and low brass
Transition	53–58	A motivic figure is passed between clarinets, saxophones, and horns; oboe 1 imitates seagull sounds
"Port na b Púcár"	59–62	Soft, asynchronous music in piccolo, flutes, clarinets, and oboe imitates sounds of the ocean and seagulls
	63–79	Euphonium solo presents "Port na b Púcár" melody; sixteenth-note runs in upper woodwinds
	80–94	Second statement of the melody begins with solo trumpet and euphonium and later expands to include piccolo, saxophones, trumpets, and euphoniums
Transition	95–99	Motivic figures pass between trumpets and horns; soft, asynchronous music imitating the ocean and seagulls returns
"Blind Mary"	100–104	Soft, flowing introduction in clarinets, bassoon, and horns

Section	Measure	Event and Scoring
	105–126	Solo oboe, clarinet, and soprano saxophone present "Blind Mary" melody; piccolo performs the slip-jig "Hardiman the Fiddler"
	127–138	Melody continues with flute, oboe, clarinets, and alto saxophone; flute, piccolo, and piano performs "Drops of Springwater" slip-jig
	139–147	Flutes, oboes, clarinets, saxophones, and trumpets end "Blind Mary" melody; long, sustained chords in tutti accompaniment
Closing	148–157	Movement ends with restatement of "Loch na gCaor" in solo flute

II. "Reelin' and Jiggin'"
"Come West Along the Road"

	1–25	Cut time; "Come West Along the Road" melody is played by clarinet and oboes; whole-note accompaniment in bassoons and saxophones
"Ger the Rigger"	26–49	"Ger the Rigger" melody is played by piccolo, alto saxophone, and flute; open-fifth whole-note accompaniment in oboes, clarinets, and piano
	50–67	"Come West Along the Road" melody returns in upper woodwinds; horns and trombones trade whole notes back and forth
	66–72	"Ger the Rigger" melody returns in oboe 1 and muted trumpet solo; open-fifth whole-note accompaniment in low reeds and saxophones
"Gypsy Princess"	73–82	"Gypsy Princess" melody is played by piccolo and orchestra bells; "Ger the Rigger" performed in canon by oboe 1, trumpet 1, English horn, and trumpet 3
Transition	83–87	Transitions to 6/8 by through oscillating eighth notes in alto saxophone, tenor saxophone, and clarinet
"Road to Lisdoonvanna"		
	88–109	"Road to Lisdoonvanna" melody is played by oboes, English horn, and flutes; oscillating eighth notes continue in clarinet

718

SECTION	MEASURE	EVENT AND SCORING
	110–125	Melody continues in bassoons, tenor saxophone, baritone saxophone, bass clarinet, and euphonium
Transition	126–131	Staccato eighth notes in upper woodwinds and horns
"Dan O'Keefe's Slide"		
	132–141	"Dan O'Keefe's Slide" melody is played in bassoons, saxophones, and euphonium; alternating eighth-note figures between flutes, oboes, and piano (group 1) and clarinets and marimba (group 2)
	142–145	Melody continues in flutes and oboe 1
Transition	146–170	Motives drawn from "Dan O'Keefe's Slide"; full ensemble
Percussion interlude		
	171–182	Percussion soli; section can be vamped
Optional insert of pub or folk band		
"The Wild Irishman"		
	183–198	"The Wild Irishman" melody is played in alto saxophone and then soprano saxophone
"Come West Along the Road"		
	199–218	"Come West Along the Road" returns in tin whistles played by clarinet section
"Ger the Rigger"	219–234	"Ger the Rigger" returns in tin whistles played by flutes and oboes while "Come West Along the Road" continues
"The Humours of Ennystymon"		
	235–266	"The Humours of Ennystymon" melody begins in soprano saxophone and piccolo trumpet and is later joined by piccolo, flute, oboes, and clarinet 1
	267–282	Melody continues in upper woodwinds
Closing	283–289	Tutti ensemble; fast eighth-, sixteenth- and quintuplet-note scale passages

Unit 8: Suggested Listening

Arnold, Sir Malcolm. *Four Scottish Dances*. 1957.
The Chieftains. *Water from the Well*. RCA records. 2000.
Welcher, Dan:
    Zion. 1994.
    Symphony No. 3: "Shaker Life." 1997.
        I. *Laboring Songs*
        II. *Circular Marches*
    Songs Without Words. 2001.
Williams, Ralph Vaughan. *English Folk Song Suite*. 1924.

Unit 9: Additional References and Resources

McCutchan, Ann. *The Muse that Sings: Composers Speak about the Creative Process*. New York: Oxford University Press, 1999.
Porter, James. *The Traditional Music of Britain and Ireland*. New York: Garland, 1989.
Pine, Richard, ed. *Music in Ireland*. Dublin: Irish American Book Co., 1998.

Websites:
    www.danwelcher.com
    www.presser.com/welcher.html

Contributed by:

Albert Nguyen
Assistant Director of Bands
The University of Memphis
Memphis, Tennessee

Teacher Resource Guide

Partita for Wind Orchestra

Robert Linn
(1925–1999)

Unit 1: Composer

Born in San Francisco, California on August 11, 1925, Robert Linn began his study of music and the piano as a young man. By the age of sixteen he had already organized his own jazz band in addition to composing all of the group's arrangements. Following his first year at San Francisco State University, Linn transferred to the University of Southern California, where he subsequently earned both his undergraduate and master degrees.

Noted among Linn's composition teachers were Halsey Stevens, Darius Milhaud, Roger Sessions, and Ingolf Dahl. Following graduation from USC in 1951, he worked as a professional jazz pianist, arranger, and composer throughout the Los Angeles area. In 1957, Linn joined the ranks of the faculty of music at USC, where he also served as chairman of the Music Theory and Composition Department from 1973 to 1990.

Linn's broad spectrum of compositional output encompasses works for solo piano, strings, chorus, organ, orchestra, chamber winds, chamber winds and strings, symphonic winds, and film. His compositions have been published by Theodore Presser, Carl Fischer, Lawson-Gould, Shawnee Press, Columbia Music, Belwin-Mills, Avant Music, Western International, and Walt Disney Music, and several of them have been recorded on the Crystal, Orion, TrueMedia, and Golden Crest labels.

Linn's eight works for winds and percussion include concertos for flute, piano, and soprano saxophone, a concerto grosso for trumpet, horn, and trombone as well as works for large symphonic band. It is notable that his *Elevations for Wind Orchestra* was premiered during the 1964 CBDNA Conference on the same program as Aaron Copland's *Emblems*.

As a recipient of several commissions and awards, Linn's compositions have been performed on six continents and by some of the world's most prominent symphony orchestras and wind ensembles. He also served as president of the Los Angeles Chapter of the National Association for American Composers and Conductors. An ardent traveler and photographer, Linn and his wife journeyed to over 150 countries. Robert Linn passed away in Los Angeles in October 1991.

Unit 2: Composition

Commissioned in 1980 by the Baylor University Bands and the Golden Wave Club, *Partita for Wind Orchestra* is dedicated to Donald I. Moore as a tribute to his thirty years of devoted service to Baylor University. Shortly after its premiere on April 28, 1980, the score was reported as missing and was primarily forgotten. Subsequent to its mention in a 1998 conversation regarding misplaced or forgotten gems for wind band, Baylor University was contacted, only to discover that no score was extant and accuracy of the parts could not be verified. Although the composer could not produce a score, a conductor's score was eventually obtained and in April 1999 the IUP Wind Ensemble, under the direction of Jack Stamp, premiered *Partita* for the second time.

The term *partita* refers to variation or in its plural form for an entire work, *partite*. The term was used as early as 1584 in Vincenzo Balilei's collection of works for lute, which included a *Romanesca con cento parti*, with each section constituting a variation. Perhaps the term is a derivative of the French word *partie*, as in the suites from the 1690s that were occasionally called *Parthien*. However, many understand the term *partita* as a suite similar to the six "Partitas" in Bach's *Clavier-Übung* (1731).

Scholars may disagree, but in seems clear that Linn has made free use of the term to describe his tripartite work. Approximately seven minutes in length, the moderate technical challenges are somewhat increased by the large interval leaps and close harmonies.

Partita is scored for full concert band with divisi parts for flute, oboe, B-flat clarinet, bassoon, alto saxophone, trumpet, horn, and trombone. Scoring also includes a string bass part that functions separately from the tuba and low woodwind voices and is a critical component to stylistic elements of the work. The percussion section is comprised of three parts performing eleven different instruments which state melodic content and serve as section-defining devices.

Unit 3: Historical Perspective

Although the true nature of the partita form may be somewhat blurred through historical performance and compositional practice, *Partita* is replete with variations or modifications of the opening motive. The harmonic language retains studio jazz and contemporary stylistic and harmonic elements that distinguish it from earlier partita expressions from the sixteenth century.

Unit 4: Technical Considerations

The moderate technical demands in combination with the constantly shifting centricity, large, asymmetrical, intervallic motivic elements, syncopated rhythms, high tessitura for trumpet and horn, metric modulation, and limited tutti passages present a variety of rehearsal and performance challenges.

From the initial statement of the primary motive in low brass and wood-winds, it becomes apparent that all sections will need to be very secure with the intervallic asymmetry of the melodic material. Not just the mechanics of the technical demands are at play, but sensitivity to pitch and interval rela-tionships as well. The performance of motivic fragments either soloistically or with additional instrumentation will require specific attention. The sparse scoring and continual voice exchange will pose some potential challenges in maintaining the integrity of the eighth note and tempo in general.

Beginning in m. 90, a more relaxed section ensues, exposing even larger intervals in a progression of solo woodwind statements. Tuning intervals within closely stacked chord voicings will need to be isolated. A warm-up procedure that divides the ensemble into two groups that move independently through slow scalar passages will be helpful.

Players will have opportunity to tune a greater variety of intervals that can easily be addressed one at a time. Directors may also consider an ensemble exercise which progresses through both ascending and descending intervals within a major scale that focuses attention on minor seconds through octaves. Both exercises are common approaches that remain effective.

Following the return of the opening material in m. 123, the section begin-ning at m. 145 integrates a progressive layering of ostinato eighth notes and quarter-note triplet figures that may create some ensemble precision issues. With the entrance of the six graduated drums in m. 179, the work builds to a final climax that will need to be measured in intensity in order to be most effective. The increase in tutti statements and rhythmic energy will require diligence in tempo integrity. The exposed, sustained unison between alto saxophone 1 and trumpet 3 may also require some attention.

Although the percussionists are divided into three parts, they do have eleven separate instrumental voices to play that offer a variety of performance challenges. The non-idiomatic timpani part mirrors the asymmetrical melodic material, as do the mallet voices. The six-drum voice serves to drive the energy push to the climax. Its inherent rhythmic diversity from the more augmented statement in the winds will need to be heard but not overpower the ensemble texture.

M. 206 begins a two-measure tutti statement in rhythmic unison that may need to be addressed for clarity of articulation style and rhythmic precision. The codetta begins with an exposed, high-tessitura statement in flute 1 and trumpet that will require attention to pitch and execution.

Partita promises to provide ample opportunities for artistic music-making and the expression of highly-energized rhythmic elements appropriate for mature high school and college ensembles.

Unit 5: Stylistic Considerations

The character and style of the Allegro sections leave little doubt in the interpretation of the quality and amplitude of the articulation and dynamic markings. As the scoring becomes thinner, the dynamics and character change follow suit. Both A sections reinforce this trend, while the more subdued and pensive middle *espressivo* section is striking by contrast. Great care should be given to this contrast and the clarity of style that the well-marked articulations bring to the work. Readily discernable are the jazz and commercial influences that Linn experienced as a young musician and jazz pianist during the Big Band era.

That being said, it should not be construed that *Partita* is a jazz piece, but merely a composition that demonstrates such influences both harmonically and stylistically.

Linn's mentors were also instrumental in his stylistic development, and additional exploration of the works of Halsey Stevens, Darius Milhaud, Roger Sessions, and Ingolf Dahl would be instructive. Frank Ticheli followed Robert Linn at USC and one can hear the possibility of Linn's influences in Ticheli's work.

Unit 6: Musical Elements

Partita offers a musical freshness that has survived the almost thirty years since its inception. Melodic and rhythmic elements offer a diversity of technical challenges and aural contrast. Dynamic indications are clearly marked and provide sufficient guidance regarding issues of balance. Stylistic nuances, dynamic and textural contrast, unpredictable voice leading, and structural craft all contribute to a strong musical statement.

MELODY:
Whether stated assertively or thoughtfully, the inherent intervallic asymmetry and rhythmic unpredictability of the melodic material is present throughout the work. Extensive use of fragmentation, skeletonization, transposition, inversion, and rhythmic alteration are apparent in the rough sequence of variations.

FIGURE 1. Mm. 1–2, Primary motive, horns and trombones

HARMONY:

The key centricity remains quite ambivalent throughout. Linn's use of regularly shifting key centers, close harmonies, and his proclivity for inverted minor eleventh chords, give the work a sense of harmonic restlessness and jazz orientation.

FIGURE 2. Mm. 67–68, minor eleventh chord voicings, brass

RHYTHM:

Linn's subtle use of metric modulation allows for a continuous flow of forward momentum and never seems contrived or gimmicky. The pervasive syncopated rhythms and tied-note values disguise the frequent changes in meter, providing a seamless quality to the work. It will be incumbent on players and conductors to establish a secure sense of pulse and meter without sacrificing the sometimes contrary nature of the asymmetrical phrasing. The underlying eighth-note ostinato should remain a paramount fixture in the performance of this piece. Even in the slower pace and augmented rhythms of section B, the eighth-note pulse is rarely missing.

TIMBRE:

Linn's acute understanding and efficient use of the color spectrum of the wind band is striking. The judicious use of percussion colors demonstrates an understanding of their potential to contribute melodically and stylistically. Percussion instruments are never overused, but always bring clarity to the musical expression at any given point in the work. Close harmonies in the muted brass offer a taste of the studio sound without being pervasive. Linn injects the timbre of the saxophone quartet and clarinet choir as effective chamber groups within the larger instrumentation. Even in the restatement of particular motivic gestures, his scoring choices produce a slightly different variation in tone colors, thereby increasing auditory interest.

Unit 7: Form and Structure

SECTION	MEASURE	EVENT AND SCORING
Section A	1–7	Introduction of primary melodic material stated by low brass and woodwinds; by m. 3, statements exhibit immediate diminution, rhythmic manipulation, and fragmentation of motivic elements; section defining percussion resolution on downbeat of m. 8
	8–20	Continued presence of layering, rhythmic alteration, contrary motion, and exploration of triplet quarter-note figure leading to first small climactic point
	21–25	Variations of initial motive from mm. 1–2 are freely transposed and embellished with trill figures
	26–29	Transitional material offers disguised metric modulations and thinner scoring, leading to new variation at m. 30
	30–45	Horn 3–4 initiate ostinato eighth-note pattern that serves as connective tissue for isolated canonic statements of motivic fragments; trumpet bell tones reinforce primary melodic points in woodwinds and vibraphone; skeletonized version of motive stated by piccolo and flute 1
	46–66	New variation statement is characterized by saxophone quartet alternating with clarinet choir responses; scoring gradually expands to include flutes, oboes, and bassoons; m. 63 introduces brief alto saxophone solo accompanied by clarinets, quickly disintegrating to inverted pyramid of voice exchange to new variation
	67–89	Trumpets and trombones alternate legato accompanying figures with horns, characterized by minor-eleventh-chord harmonies; low woodwinds and brass provide augmented versions of motivic elements in a sostenuto style; flute 1 and oboe 1 initially begin skeletonized version of melodic material, but soon take up the

		more sostenuto style of the bass line, but in contrary motion and with simple voice leading; sax color returns at m. 83 with more agitated material; trumpet initiates transition to large *adagio* B section with gradually augmented rhythmic figures that supply a comfortable retardation of the pace
Section B	90–98	Solo flute initiates rhythmically altered version of motive, reinforcing the new *espressivo* section with subsequent entrances by solo clarinet and oboe
	99–114	Flute 1 and solo alto saxophone introduce duet accompanied by clarinets and vibraphone; duet in oboes and clarinet 1 begin gradual increase in dynamic energy and scoring; metric modulation is disguised by voice leading and tied rhythms
	115–122	Clarinet choir statement reinforces more reflective mood with F4 pedal in horn voice; flute 1 statement of gradually descending melodic fragments accompanied by muted brass, ending on A-flat major chord
Section A'	123–127	First entrance of six-graduated-drum voice reinforces presentations of motivic fragments by woodwinds and muted brass
	128–135	Flute 1 and trumpet 1 present eight-measure restatement of opening motive and tutti scoring material; simultaneous augmented versions of motive are presented by alto saxophone and trumpet 2 (version A at twice the original duration) and horns (version B at four times the original duration)
	136–178	Material from mm. 30–89 returns, freshly presented and compressed with altered scoring and further development; syncopated motive undergoes a progression of exchanges between trumpet voices, building to the initiation of an extended concluding section

SECTION	MEASURE	EVENT AND SCORING
	179–191	Reintegration of six-graduated-drum voice initiates an emphatic statement of primary motive in augmentation and in stretto-like fashion; longer note values and increased dynamic energy build tension
	192–207	Return of original motivic material rescored and compressed in length; m. 200 brings back material from mm. 13–20 transposed up a perfect fifth
Codetta	208–213	Delayed entrance of soprano brass and woodwinds by one beat increases the tension as motivic fragments begin in high tessitura and proceed in a downward pyramid progression of layering to the final climax

Unit 8: Suggested Listening

Linn, Robert:
    Concerto for Flute and Wind Orchestra. 1980.
    Elevations for Wind Orchestra. 1964.
    Overture for Symphony Orchestra. 1952.
    Partita for Wind Orchestra. 1980.
    Piano Concerto No. 1 with Wind Ensemble. 1985.
    Propagula for Wind Orchestra. 1970.
    Quartet for Saxophones. 1953.
    Seven Canons for Solo Clarinet. 1974.
Ticheli, Frank: *Wild Nights*.

Unit 9: Additional References and Resources

Battisti, Frank. *The Twentieth Century American Wind Band/Ensemble*. Fort Lauderdale, FL: Meredith Music, 1995.
Brock, Gordon R. Email interview with Jack Stamp. May 15, 2008.
_____. Email and phone interview with Virginia Linn. May, 2008.
Randel, Don Michael, ed. *The New Harvard Dictionary of Music*. Cambridge, MA: Harvard University Press, 1996.

Website:
    www.robertlinn.org/index.htm

Contributed by:

Gordon R. Brock
Chair/Director of Bands
University of North Florida
Jacksonville, Florida

Teacher Resource Guide

Passacaglia

Tim Jackson
(b. 1972)

Unit 1: Composer

Born in Preston, England, Timothy Jackson is a noted horn player, having studied at the Royal Academy of Music, Manchester University, and the Royal Northern College of Music. After five years as a member of the Orchestra of the Royal Opera House, he joined the Philharmonia Orchestra and now appears regularly as both soloist and principal horn with orchestras throughout the United Kingdom and Europe.

Jackson is currently composer-in-association with the Onyx Brass, and has received commissions from the Academy of Saint Martin in the Fields, the Halle, British Telecom, the British Horn Society, and others. His music has been recorded for CD by EMI, Chandos, Intim, Meridian, and Polygram, and broadcast on national radio in countries including Australia, Belgium, Britain, Canada, France, and Switzerland.

Jackson currently lives and works in London, where he is professor of horn at the Royal Marines School of Music.

Unit 2: Composition

The composer notes in the score that there is no specific program to this piece except that "it was originally conceived as the finale of a symphony for thirty-two horns, and it was Tim Reynish—himself a distinguished former professional horn player of course—who suggested that I rework it for symphonic winds."

In his program note contained in the score, Jackson writes:

One of the great strengths of the original line up, particularly in this movement, is the ensemble's capacity to create a really homogeneous sound, and as I considered the new version I had it in mind to exploit this feature. I hope the result is something band directors will enjoy using to work on the blending of sound and balance within the wind ensemble. It's also a sound world which particularly suits the passacaglia form, with its uninterrupted flow and development of ideas, the continuous unfolding variations and expansion of material over an ever-present, underlying motif (the motif here is heard initially on unison clarinets and bassoons underpinned by bass drum strokes). Like most passacaglia, the pulse is steady, and it begins in a rather solemn, contemplative mood. As the work progresses though the spirit is transformed, with more rapid musical figures increasingly emerging contrapuntally from the texture to bring it (I hope!) to a triumphantly positive conclusion.

Unit 3: Historical Perspective

Originally the final movement of the composer's *Symphony for 32 Horns*, *Passacaglia* was commissioned to celebrate the twenty-fifth anniversary of the British Horn Society by the eight British music conservatories. It was premiered at the Guildhall School of Music and Drama in London on October 22, 2005. This extensively reworked version for wind band was commissioned in 2006 by Hilary and Timothy Reynish in memory of their son William.

Unit 4: Technical Considerations

Passacaglia is scored for standard American band instrumentation: piccolo, flute 1–2, oboe 1–2, B-flat clarinet 1–3, bass clarinet, bassoon 1–2, alto saxophone 1–2, tenor saxophone, baritone saxophone, B-flat trumpet 1–2, horn 1–4, trombone 1–3, euphonium, and tuba. Five percussionists are required, using timpani, suspended cymbal, crash cymbals, bass drum, tubular bells, glockenspiel, and marimba. Lines are very often doubled in at least two parts, allowing for some deficiencies in instrumentation or player confidence.

There are two principal technical requirements for a successful performance of *Passacaglia*: the ability to sustain long phrases and the ability to produce a legato articulation throughout the full dynamic range of the work. The passacaglia melody is a four-measure phrase under one slur, marked *sostenuto*. At the marked tempo of *lento assai*, each player must maintain full intensity for this extended period, as well as continue to do so through several repetitions of the melody. The composer has staggered some slurs so that all players do not breathe together.

As the work progresses from *piano* to *fortissimo*, each player must maintain a connected style for both legato and accented notes. Accents cannot be allowed to interrupt the continuous flow of sound.

Other technical demands in *Passacaglia* are minimal. Ranges are not excessive, with the exception of extended lower-range demands for tuba in several places. Some rhythmic challenges, an extended chain of syncopations (mm. 65–72), triplet figures (mm. 73–80), and sixteenth- and thirty-second-note passages (mm. 81–88) may require some additional attention.

Unit 5: Stylistic Considerations

The style of *Passacaglia* is legato throughout. Long, slurred phrases are only sporadically accompanied by legato markings on quarter notes (mm. 17–18, 31–32, 39–40) and accent marks for occasional emphasis (mm. 35, 38–39). As the piece approaches its climax late in the piece (mm. 73-end), accents are used on moving parts, but these markings should not be interpreted as a shortening of note length. Accented eighth-note triplets (mm. 73–80) are followed by unmarked sixteenth notes (mm. 81–84) which lead to accented sixteenth- and thirty-second-note passages (mm. 85–88) as the piece slows to its conclusion. All notes should be played full value regardless of the articulation marked. The ability to articulate smoothly and consistently is extremely important to maintain the proper style of the *Passacaglia*.

Unit 6: Musical Elements

MELODY:

The principal melodic material is the four-measure passacaglia theme in half notes. Slur markings change from instrument to instrument in order to maintain the *sostenuto* effect. A secondary melodic line, marked *espressivo*, is used to accompany the theme in several places.

A successful performance of *Passacaglia* will require every student to recognize the theme. Consider transposing and duplicating the theme for each section and playing the theme together as a class. Explore various expressive possibilities.

The theme is presented in its half-note form for most of the work. It is presented in augmented (whole-note) form at the climax of the piece, mm. 73-end.

HARMONY:

The harmonic language of *Passacaglia* may be heard as being derived from the later part of the Romantic period. There is extensive use of chromaticism, both in the theme and its accompaniment. The predominate key area is F major, with arrivals on the tonic chord at numerous structural points throughout the work. Other key areas are briefly explored (e.g., B-flat at m. 30 and E at m. 45).

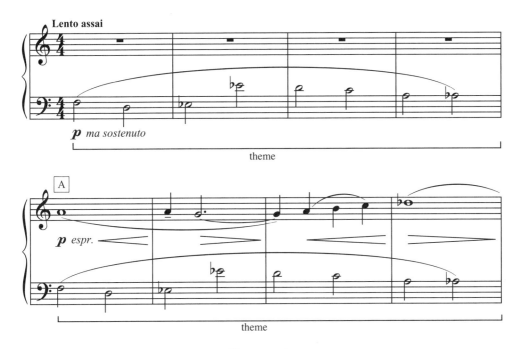

FIGURE 1.

RHYTHM:

The half-note passacaglia theme is first accompanied by quarter-note moving lines. As the work progresses to its climax, accompaniment figures move to syncopated quarter notes in m. 65 (figure 2), to eighth-note triplet figures in m. 73 (figure 3), and finally to the most complex figure in m. 85 (figure 4).

FIGURE 2. Mm. 65–68

FIGURE 3. Mm. 73–74

FIGURE 4. M. 85

These rhythmic figures are not combined until the final few measures, when syncopated quarter-, sixteenth-, thirty-second-notes, and triplets are heard together.

TIMBRE:

Extensive doubling of lines is used throughout the piece, diminishing the importance of unique instrumental colors. Blend between instruments and sections thus becomes an important teaching aspect for this work; no one instrumental color should ever predominate. As *Passacaglia* was originally conceived as a work for thirty-two players of the same instrument (horn), conductors can use this piece to address the concept of blend throughout the ensemble without sacrificing the composer's original intent. As Jackson writes in his introduction in the program notes provided in the score: "I hope the result is something band directors will enjoy using to work on the blending of sound and balance within the wind ensemble."

Unit 7: Form and Structure

A passacaglia is a set of ground-bass or ostinato variations which repeat unchanged throughout the piece, accompanied by freely varied upper lines. It is closely related to the chaconne. Timothy Jackson's *Passacaglia* conforms to this description, with the inclusion of augmented statements of the theme at the end of the work. A principal countermelody is often present.

SECTION	MEASURE	EVENT AND SCORING
Section 1	1–44	Section 1 begins with five four-measure iterations of the passacaglia theme; the first phrase states the theme alone, with ensuing phrases each adding more complexity to the accompaniment; in m. 21, the theme, having been heard up to this point in the lowest voices, is moved to upper instruments for three iterations; it returns to the lowest voices in m. 33; section 1 closes with the strongest dynamic level so far in the first tutti scoring of the work; the final phrase of this section returns to the soft dynamic of the beginning as section 2 begins

SECTION	MEASURE	EVENT AND SCORING
Section 2	45–72	Section 2 begins almost as if returning to the beginning, with the main theme and repeat of the first principal countermelody; however, the key center briefly moves to E major before returning to F major by the second phrase; the five iterations at the start of this section repeat the use of the theme and countermelody in similar fashion to that of the first five iterations at the beginning of the work; the section's final two iterations serve as a transition and intensity-building bridge to the final section
Section 3	65–90	Section 3 is characterized by the use of the passacaglia theme in augmented form; no longer a four-measure iteration in half notes, the theme is now eight measures long and notated in whole notes; each of the three iterations in this section increases in dynamic level, rhythmic activity, and rhythmic complexity

Unit 8: Suggested Listening

Bach, Johann Sebastian. *Passacaglia and Fugue in C minor*, BWV 582.
Holst, Gustav. *First Suite in E-flat*, movement 1.
Purcell, Henry. *Dido and Aeneas:* "When I am laid in earth."

Unit 9: Additional References and Resources

http://www.timreynish.com
http://www.maecenasmusic.co.uk
Silbiger, Alexander. "Passacaglia." The New Grove Dictionary of Music and
    Musicians. S. Sadie and J. Tyrrell, eds. London: Macmillan, 2001.

Contributed by:

Douglas Stotter
University of Texas Arlington
Arlington, Texas

Teacher Resource Guide

Radiant Joy

Steven Bryant
(b. 1972)

Unit 1: Composer

Steven Bryant is an active composer and conductor. He has written for wind ensemble, orchestra, electronic and electro-acoustic creations, chamber music, and music for the web. Steven's music has been performed by ensembles throughout North America, Europe, and Asia. His orchestral works *Loose Id* and *Alchemy in Silent Spaces* have both been performed by The Juilliard Symphony.

Bryant has received commissions from the Amherst Saxophone Quartet, the Indiana University Wind Ensemble, the U. S. Air Force Band of Mid-America, the Calgary Stampede Band, and the University of Nevada Las Vegas Wind Orchestra. His compositions have been recorded by Eugene Corporon and the University of North Texas Wind Symphony, Ron Hufstader and the El Paso Wind Symphony, William Berz and the Rutgers University Wind Ensemble, and Thomas Leslie and the University of Nevada Las Vegas Wind Orchestra. Steven has also created a re-composition of the Iggy Pop and the Stooges song, *Real Cool Time*, for the independent Italian record label, Snowdonia, as well as music for portions of the Virtual Space Tour at www.space.com.

Steven is a founding member of the composer-consortium BCM International: four stylistically-diverse composers from across the country dedicated to enriching the repertoire with exciting works for mediums often mired in static formulas. BCM's music has generated a following of champions around the world, several thousand fans in an active online community, and two recordings: BCM *Saves the World* (2002, Mark Custom Records) and BCM *Men of Industry* (2004, BCM Records).

736

Steven studied composition with John Corigliano at The Juilliard School, Cindy McTee at the University of North Texas and Francis McBeth at Ouachita University. He resides in Austin, Texas. For more information, you may visit his website at http://www.stevenbryant.com.

Unit 2: Composition

Radiant Joy was commissioned by Jack Stamp for the Indiana University of Pennsylvania Wind Ensemble and the first performance of the work was in October 2006. *Radiant Joy* was the first work that Steven had written in nearly two and a half years. His absence from composing was the result of a very challenging period in his personal life. Bryant had originally intended that the first composition he would write after his break would be a twelve-tone, serial work that was to be in the style of Schönberg or Webern.

After several unsatisfying attempts, Bryant discarded the plan and began to write a work that reflected the newfound joy he now had for life after his difficult times had passed on. The result is a piece that has rhythmic vitality and presents harmonic material that has the sounds of the funk, jazz, and fusion music of the 1970s and 80s.

The vibraphone plays an important role, both musically and symbolically. Besides having exposed and important solo lines, the vibraphone serves as a symbolic reflection of joy and the "good vibes" the composer wishes for the performers, the audience, and himself. In 2007, the National Band Association awarded his *Radiant Joy* the William D. Revelli Composition Award.

Unit 3: Historical Perspective

The jazz-funk style is a mostly American genre and was popular throughout the 1970s and the early 1980s. It is derived by the integration of Funk, Soul, and Rhythm and Blues, as well as styles from the jazz idiom. This resulted in the creation of a genre of music that has diverse sounds using soul, funk, and/or disco with jazz improvisation, jazz orchestrations, riffs, and sometimes soul vocals. This music is characterized by a strong back beat called "a groove." Other names that have been used for this style of music include soul-jazz and jazz-fusion.

Jazz-funk musicians absorbed the street sound of funk rhythm, which gave the genre a danceable rhythm. Jazz-funk style is usually less vocal, has challenging instrumental arrangements, and features some instrumental improvisation. At the beginning of its inception jazz-funk was looked down on by jazz hardliners. Jazz artists who began to play this music were accused of selling out to the popular disco music of the 1970s. Some established jazz musicians who began to play this style were John Coltrane, Miles Davis, and Herbie Hancock. Donald Byrd was heavily criticized when he released the album *Black Byrd* on the Blue Note label, but the LP went on to become the best-selling album by Blue Note during that era. Today these jazz artists are praised for their musicianship and are considered influential jazz musicians.

Unit 4: Technical Considerations

Radiant Joy was written for standard band instrumentation. The conductor should note that the orchestration calls for two bass clarinets, soprano saxophone, four trumpets, two euphoniums and piano. The doubling in the bass clarinet and euphonium parts should not be of great concern if there is only one musician in each of these sections. These split parts are all doubled elsewhere in the score, and this lack of instruments will not detract from the quality of the performance.

Conductors who are considering this work for performance should also note that there are several parts that will require technically-advanced players to execute the music. In particular, soprano and baritone saxophone parts have a high degree of difficulty and are very exposed. Much of the piece has soprano and baritone saxophone playing very rhythmically challenging parts in octaves. Also, the end of the work calls for an intricate duet between baritone saxophone, piano, and mallet percussion.

The score calls for six percussionists plus a pianist. Three strong mallet players are required and the pianist must also be technically accomplished. The percussion requirements include glockenspiel, vibraphone, marimba, triangle, two suspended cymbals, and two hi-hats. The other percussion parts are easier in nature and can be covered comfortably by three players. The hi-hat plays an important role in the piece, and its player must be rhythmically solid to produce the correct style required by the work.

Another feature of jazz-funk style is the importance of the instrumental arrangements. This style of writing can be intricate and difficult for performers. This is very true for *Radiant Joy*. Bryant requires every instrument to play sixteenth-note figures at some point. Note that the more demanding passages are found in woodwinds, upper trumpets, and percussion. These passages are all largely diatonic and should not influence directors to shy away from programming the work. Ranges for all instruments are basically reasonable. Of possible concern is the flute writing, which goes up to a B-flat 3 and the optional A-flat two octaves below the staff in the tuba part.

Unit 5: Stylistic Considerations

Jazz-funk style includes a departure from the swing feel of the 1940s Big Band era to a straight feel known as "the groove." Groove rhythm feel comes from a genre prevalent in artists such as James Brown. Jazz-funk also draws influences from traditional African music, Latin American rhythms, and Jamaican reggae.

Another characteristic of jazz-funk music is the use of electric piano and electric bass guitar, particularly in jazz-fusion. The use of these instruments provided a strong rhythm-section feel like that of a jazz band. Because of this it is important that the ensemble have a solid percussion section. Be sure to have mallet players and a pianist that are technically accomplished. This will ensure that parts are performed with the fluidity required of soloists and soli sections. Hi-hat plays an important role in the piece, and the hi-hat player must be rhythmically solid to produce the correct style required of the work.

Radiant Joy requires that the conductor understand the style of musicians like Herbie Hancock and Stanley Clarke, or groups like Weather Report, the Blackbyrds, or Earth, Wind and Fire. While it is true the instruments used in these bands are much different than those in the standard wind band instrumentation, the syncopation, drive, and feel of their music is required in this composition. It is imperative that the ensemble have a well-developed sense of pulse and be able to articulate the intricate technical passages with accuracy.

Unit 6: Musical Elements

A first glance, the score to *Radiant Joy* might lead the conductor to consider this work a lesser challenge for the average ensemble. To the contrary, both performers and the conductor will find the exposed solo lines, rhythmic complexity, and the jazz-funk style to be quite demanding. An understanding of the musical elements of the work will help reveal an approach to teaching and performing this work.

MELODY:
Radiant Joy is a work primarily based on the motivic development of two descending patterns: A-flat–G-flat–F and A-flat–G-natural–F. A single melody will be difficult for the listener to isolate, as the melodic material sounds much like improvised solos which ride on top of the augmented motivic patterns. Of more importance are the changes in orchestration and rhythm each time the main motive, solo, or soli line statements appear. In this case the repeated and changing textural sonorities are as important as melody.

HARMONY:
Radiant Joy is tonal and uses both major and modal harmonies. A harmonic study of this composition will reveal that the piece is primarily in E-flat major. The composition also uses the Mixolydian mode in flutes and clarinets in m. 86. Bryant prefers to not use traditional key signatures because doing so limits tonal implications and chromatic movement. Rather than listening for only melody and accompaniment, musicians should listen to how the composition expands and grows and how it moves into and through different sections. A discussion on how Bryant uses motivic development and its effect on the listener's perception of harmonic progression will help students' understanding of the composition.

RHYTHM:

Bryant's frequent use of syncopation and extended sixteenth-note passages in exposed sections are possibly the most demanding aspect of *Radiant Joy*. Due to the rhythmic complexity of the work, students must be able to understand and apply the concept of subdivision as they prepare their parts and perform with the ensemble. Because of the amount of syncopation and the contrasting exposed sixteenth-note passages that occur together, musicians must have a solid sense of time. This will ensure that the ensemble will stay together and not fall apart. All students must be secure with their rhythm so that they can understand how it relates to other rhythms happening in the piece at the same time.

TIMBRE:

Bryant's orchestration plays an important role in the development of this composition. The percussion section not only provides the rhythmic drive for *Radiant Joy*, but is also prominent in the area of melody and texture. The introduction begins with all the mallets and piano; when winds enter, they are secondary to the texture of the work.

The sound of *Radiant Joy* is never thick, and one could say that the orchestration is generally transparent. This is the case for a majority of the composition. Even at the most intense moments, the balance between winds and percussion must be controlled so that percussion can be heard. This concern becomes evident in the soli sections between saxophones and mallet instruments.

Unit 7: Form and Structure

SECTION	MEASURE	EVENT AND SCORING
Introduction	1–16	The motive first appears in vibraphone and is expanded with an interplay between glockenspiel, marimba, and piano; flutes, clarinets, and brass enter in second half of the sixteen-measure introduction
Section A	17–57	The first statement of the melodic line begins in m. 18 and is scored in soprano and baritone saxophone; in m. 30 trumpets take the melody and are later joined by woodwinds; the last statement of this melody returns to the entire saxophone section as the end of section A approaches
Development	58–85	Development of introductory material in vibraphone, with interjections of theme A in piano; tonality is centered around E-flat

SECTION	MEASURE	EVENT AND SCORING
Development	85–113	Development continues as material from the introduction is inverted; interjections of material from section A become more frequent until m. 106, where both the introduction and section A material have equal importance
Intro (restatement)	114–121	This material is taken directly from mm. 9–16
Recapitulation of section A	122–163	This section begins with section A material from mm. 17–39; the material in m. 144 is taken from m. 40, but this time trumpets join with saxophone section
Coda	164—End	A retrograde of sorts from the opening material of the work; begins with baritone saxophone and piano in a duet on section A material; vibraphone enters later with material from the introduction; the work concludes quietly with vibraphone stating the open theme

Unit 8: Suggested Listening

Bonney, James. *TranZendental Danse of Joi*: "Men of Industry."
Bryant, Steven. *Radiant Joy*. www. stevenbryant.com
Lewis, Ramsey. "Sun Goddess."
Weather Report. "Heavy Weather."
www.rhapsody.com/jazz/jazzfunk

Unit 9: Additional References and Resources

Berz, William. "Parody Suite." In *Teaching Music through Performance in Band, Volume 5*. Richard
    Miles, ed. Chicago: GIA Publications, 2004.
Bryant, Steven. "Dusk." In *Teaching Music through Performance in Band, Volume 6*. Richard Miles, ed. Chicago: GIA Publications, 2004.
Coryell, Julie and Laura Friedman. *Jazz-Rock Fusion: The People, the Music*. Hal Leonard Corp. 1978, 2000.
McCutcheon, Matthew. "Radiant Joy." Unpublished article for the *NBA Journal*. 2008.

Websites:

BCM International. www.bcminernational.com

Steven Bryant. www.stevenbryant.com

Steven Bryant's MySpace page. www.myspace.com/stevenbryant

Contributed by:

Mark Whitlock

Director of Bands

University of Minnesota Duluth

Duluth, Minnesota

Teacher Resource Guide

Selamlik

Florent Schmitt
(1870–1958)

edited by Stephen Meyer
(b. 1985)

Unit 1: Composer

Born in Lorraine, France in 1870, Florent Schmitt was a renowned French composer who studied at the Paris Conservatoire with both Massenet and Fauré. Often classified as an impressionistic composer, Schmitt was inspired by the sounds of Ravel and Debussy as well as the largely orchestrated works of Strauss and Wagner. In 1900 he succeeded in claiming the prestigious Prix de Rome with his cantata *Sémiramis*. In fact, the harmonic and rhythmic idioms of Schmitt's compositional style influenced Stravinsky's orchestration in *Le Sacre du printemps*. Stravinsky once stated that Schmitt's works are "some of the greatest masterpieces of Modern music."

While in Paris, Schmitt worked as a music critic for *Le Temps*, the city's most popular newspaper. As a critic he created considerable controversy with his thoughtless habit of shouting out criticisms, some of an anti-Semitic nature. Schmitt's ultimate allegiance towards Germany at the outbreak of World War I eventually caused Stravinsky and others to rescind their support of Schmitt's music, and his works went unheard for decades. Even so, Schmitt continued to write, earning the Legion of Honor in 1952. He later died in 1958 in northern France. Schmitt's most famous works continue to be *La Tragédie de Salomé*, a ballet scored for massive orchestra, *Dionysiaques*, scored for large wind band, and *Lied et Scherzo*, written for double woodwind quintet and solo horn.

Unit 2: Composition

Selamlik [si-lahm-lik], subtitled "Turkish Dance for Harmonie," is an original composition for wind band written in 1906, seven years before Schmitt's more notable wind band work, *Dionysiaques*. It was premiered in June 1909 by La Musique de la Garde Républicaine under the direction of Guillaume Balay. The work itself was inspired by a trip Schmitt took to Turkey in 1905, and the title refers to the portion of the Turkish home reserved for the company of men.

The new edition of this work was compiled by Stephen Meyer in 2006 from the original parts to conform to more contemporary wind band instrumentation. However, it still maintains the unique orchestration and complex compositional style of the original.

Unit 3: Historical Perspective

Written at the turn of the century, *Selamlik* was composed at a time when Maurice Ravel, Gabriel Fauré, and Camille Saint-Saëns dominated the French composition scene. Their works displayed a unique approach to orchestration with the incorporation of new modes and harmonies. Additionally, the exotic nature of Eastern European folksongs became a source of inspiration to major composers. Both Beethoven and Mozart wrote a Turkish march based on traditional melodies, and Béla Bartók based many of his compositions on folk tunes of his native Hungary.

In *Selamlik* Schmitt combines a melody that reflects Turkish music tradition in its elaborate use of modes with his distinctive detail in orchestration. Each instrument plays a key role, melodies are presented and transferred in fragments, and there is a greater focus on horizontal melody rather then vertical harmonic progression. At the time this style was revolutionary for the wind band medium, as the repertoire was mostly dominated by marches scored for military bands and *harmoniemusik* written for small chamber ensembles. Many of the techniques used in *Selamlik* were later incorporated into Schmitt's masterpiece for wind band, *Dionysiaques*, and composers such as Igor Stravinsky and Paul Hindemith found inspiration in the new colors Schmitt generated from the wind ensemble.

Unit 4: Technical Considerations

Selamlik is scored for large wind ensemble and demands great responsibility and independence among every instrument and part. Note that there are five individual clarinet parts and parts for E-flat clarinet, B-flat trumpet 1–2, C trumpet 1–2, flugelhorn 1–2 and tuba 1–3 in addition to contemporary wind ensemble instrumentation.

While the tempo of the work is only quarter note = 84, the piece requires great technical demand and precision from each instrument, as there are numerous sixteenth-note passages in all voices. Also, knowledge of chromatic and modal scales is necessary at quicker tempos, as much of the piece is built on these fundamentals. Moreover, a strong ability in articulation is vital, since all brass instruments are expected to articulate sixteenth-note triplets in both low and high tessituras.

Unit 5: Stylistic Considerations

Selamlik is a dance that should be played in a lighthearted, steady manner. All melodic figures need to bounce and move with forward motion in order to build emotion and energy, especially when they are passed among instruments. Attention to and differentiation between various articulations must be a priority as well. Conductors and performers must also be able to distinguish between accented, marcato, and staccato style markings.

Note that whenever a grace note appears in the piece, it is not the grace note but the following note that must be emphasized. This gives the work a more buoyant, uplifted, and spirited feel. Likewise, the initial tempo never changes throughout the piece, thus requiring a strong sense of pulse and ensemble awareness from all performers. Finally, to achieve the transfer of melody and building of intensity effectively, performers and the conductor must also be aware of frequent shifts in dynamic range (e.g., in m. 77, the entire spectrum of dynamics, *pianissimo* to *fortissimo*, is written in the space of four measures).

Unit 6: Musical Elements

MELODY:
There are two main thematic ideas that occur throughout the piece. Theme A is first stated in full at m. 15 in the euphonium, baritone saxophone, and bassoon. This theme can be characterized as the dance theme, with a lifted and separated style. Theme B is first heard in alto saxophone at m. 52. It contrasts to theme A in that it is very lyrical and expressive in nature. While both are seemingly simple in context, Schmitt takes fragments of each and uses them numerous times in variation. They are heard with different instrumentation, harmonies, articulations, and tonal centers. Therefore, it would be beneficial to have the entire ensemble learn each of the themes together during daily warm-up to clarify style and phrasing.

HARMONY:
Selamlik is composed with horizontal motion, not vertical, being dominant. Therefore, there is little opportunity for harmonic analysis to determine tone center. Nevertheless, in their primitive forms, both themes A and B center around F, but the key signature at both the beginning and m. 130 suggest B-flat as the tonal center. An extreme range of tessitura is scored in all

instruments; consequently, performers must be comfortable in listening and adjusting in these capacities.

RHYTHM:

The rhythms incorporated into *Selamlik* are simple and straightforward. However, rhythmic precision is critical, since fragments of the melody are passed from low to high or high to low instruments. Consider incorporating into the daily warm-up an exercise with the ensemble broken up into three different groups of instruments, ideally low, middle, and high. Have group 1 play eight sixteenth notes on a concert F, followed by groups 2 and 3 doing the same in succession. Modify this exercise by using various scales, different articulation markings, and/or rhythmic cells that appear in *Selamlik*. Ultimately this activity focuses on matching and definition of style, clarity of rhythm, and strengthening of pulse within the ensemble.

TIMBRE:

By incorporating the use of different combinations of modes and scales, *Selamlik* emanates a very dark and exotic sound. Therefore, when melodies are carried from one instrument to another, especially from low to high voices, this timbre must not change. Likewise, it is very easy in densely-scored sections for the quality to become bright and piercing instead of rich and mysterious.

Unit 7: Form and Structure

SECTION	MEASURE	EVENT AND SCORING
Introduction	1–10	F-minor tonal center; partial statement of theme A in full ensemble
Theme A	11–27	Four-bar introduction followed by first statement of theme A in baritone saxophone, bassoon, and euphonium; last two bars of theme are then repeated in tenor saxophone and bassoon at m. 23
Transition	27–33	M. 1, beat 2 of theme A is used as transitional material in euphonium and tuba; octave leap heard in opening bar of theme A is heard in reverse and passed from low to high tessitura instruments in mm. 30–33
Theme A	33–47	Theme A is heard in clarinets with C minor as tone center; flutes, bassoon, and trumpets repeat last two bars of theme A at m. 39; eighth notes that open theme A are then heard and passed for two measures; the octave leap is then added

Section	Measure	Event and Scoring
Transition	47–51	Low voices accent a chromatic scale to transition to theme B
Theme B	52–70	Theme B is first heard in saxophone family; clarinet family repeats with a new harmony at m. 56; melody is then transferred to flute and alto saxophone family at m. 60, again with new harmony; at m. 64, the rhythmic motive from the second bar of theme B is used, but with a descending scale passage; it is then heard as articulated accents in all low voices, with sixteenth-note triplets in all other voices to lead into letter E
Theme A	70–84	Restatement of opening in full ensemble; m. 76 is different and a motif made of a two-sixteenths-and-eighth-note fragment is transferred again from low to high voice instruments
Theme A	84–96	Theme A heard in E-flat clarinet and B-flat cornet with arpeggiated accompaniment in clarinets; flute repeats last two measures of theme A at m. 90; eighth-note motif from the opening measure of theme A is repeated and echoed to lead into letter G
Transition	97–110	Same transition theme heard at m. 27 is passed from low to high instruments, cycling through many keys; at m. 104, the eighth-note motif from the opening measure of theme A is passed from high to low voices, leading to the climax of the work at letter H
Theme A	110–130	Theme A is heard in high voices and euphonium; beginning at m. 118, the fifth measure of theme A is heard three times, modulating up a half-step each time; the trill heard at the end of the introduction in m. 10 is then expanded and stair-steps down the score from high to low voices, each instance a half-beat off from the next

SECTION	MEASURE	EVENT AND SCORING
Theme B	130–147	Theme B is heard with full instrumentation in a lyrical and expressive manner; trumpets play the sixteenth-note triplet motif as well; at m. 138, the first two measures of theme B are used as a canon between instruments; however, this motif changes to an accented rather than a lyrical figure as it descends down the scale; the sixteenth-note triplet motif is transferred between from low to high voices in the brass to lead into letter K
Themes A and B	148–156	Accented figure from theme B is heard at m. 147; second bar of theme A is heard at m. 148; these melodies begin to overlap one another as energy builds and sixteenth-note runs shift and stair-step up the score from low to high voices
	157–182	First two bars of theme A are heard in succession with eighth-notes being echoed in the brass; at m. 162 the second bar of theme A is heard with a different tonal center in each measure while shifting from high to low voices; at m. 169 this technique reverses and the same motif begins in low voices and transitions to higher voices while moving up the scale; at m. 175, the opening eighth-note figure is heard in a descending scale from high to low instruments
Recapitulation	183–200	Theme A is heard in low voices in a similar fashion to m. 11; the second measure of theme A is then passed from low to high instruments until a descending modal scale begins at m. 198 and gains momentum to close the work

Unit 8: Suggested Listening

Beethoven, Ludwig van. "Turkish March" *from The Ruins of Athens*.
Mozart, Wolfgang A. *Turkish March*.
Schmitt, Florent:
> *Dionysiaques*
> *La tragédie de Salomé*
> *Lied et Scherzo*
> *Psaume XLVII*
> *Semiramis*
Stravinsky, Igor:
> *La sacre du printemps*
> *Symphony of Wind Instruments*

Unit 9: Additional References and Resources

Carley, Lionel. *Frederick Delius: Music, Art, and Literature*. Aldershot: Ashgate, 1998.
Ferroud, Pierre-Octave. *Autour de Florent Schmitt*. Paris: Durand, 1927.
Hucher, Yves. *Florent Schmitt: l'homme et l'artiste, son époque et son oeuvre*. Paris: Éditions Le Bon Plaisir, 1953.
_____. *L'oeuvre de Florent Schmitt*. Paris : Durand, 1960.

Contributed by:

Stephen Meyer
Associate Director of Bands
Harrison High School
Kennesaw, Georgia

Teacher Resource Guide

Sinfonietta for Wind Ensemble

Bruce Yurko
(b. 1951)

Unit 1: Composer

Bruce Yurko received his bachelor of science in music education from Wilkes College and his master in performance from the Ithaca College School of Music. While attending Wilkes College he studied horn with Douglas Hill and corresponded with Vincent Persichetti. At Ithaca College he studied conducting with Thomas Michalik, horn with Jack Covert, and composition with Karel Husa.

From 1974 to 1981 Yurko served as director of bands at Madison High School in Madison, New Jersey and from 1981 to 2005 he was the conductor of the wind ensemble, orchestra, and chamber music program at Cherry Hill High School East in Cherry Hill, New Jersey. From 1982 to 2003 he also conducted the Cherry Hill High School West Wind Ensemble. Yurko was the conductor of the Princeton University Wind Ensemble from 2000 to 2004. In 1987 the Cherry Hill East Wind Ensemble, under Yurko's direction, toured the Soviet Union, performing concerts in Moscow, Leningrad, and Tallinn, Estonia. The school's wind ensemble and orchestra also performed in Carnegie Hall and in the Philadelphia Orchestra's Verizon Hall.

Yurko has served as guest conductor of three Regional Honor Wind Ensembles in New Jersey as well as the All-State Symphony Band and Wind Ensemble. He has also appeared as guest conductor in Maine, Delaware, New York, Pennsylvania, Virginia, Maryland, North Carolina, Georgia, and Texas.

Yurko has attended a variety of conducting workshops as a participant. He has also studied conducting with Frederick Fennell, Donald Hunsberger, H. Robert Reynolds, and Eugene Migliaro Corporon.

In 1990 the National Band Association awarded Yurko and the Cherry Hill High School East Wind Ensemble the "Citation of Excellence." He retired from Cherry Hill High School East in 2005. Yurko began a teaching position at Messiah College in September 2008.

Bruce Yurko has written over twenty works for band. His *Percussion Concerto*, commissioned by Jack Stamp and the Indiana University of Pennsylvania Wind Ensemble, has been performed by noted wind bands such as the Eastman Wind Ensemble, Donald Hunsberger, conductor, the Florida State University Wind Orchestra, James Croft, conductor, and most recently, the University of North Texas Wind Symphony, Eugene Migliaro Corporon, conductor, in a performance at the 2006 Percussion Arts Society International Conference (PASIC) convention in Austin, Texas.

Ludwig Music, Southern Music, C. Alan Publications, and Masters Publications of Kalmus Music publish Yurko's compositions.

Unit 2: Composition

Donald Magee, who worked closely with the composer on the project, and the Vernon Township High School Wind Ensemble commissioned the composition in 1999 as part of the twenty-fifth anniversary celebration of the New Jersey high school. The composer dedicated the work to James Croft, characterizing him in the notes in the score as "an amazing musician, conductor and educator."

Sinfonietta for Wind Ensemble is scored for one player per part, which fits the instrumentation of the Vernon Township High School Wind Ensemble. The full score is written and published in concert pitch. C. Alan Publications made the score and parts available to the public in 2003. Written in seven movements, the approximate performance time is twelve and a half minutes and uses the following instrumentation:

Flute 1–4
Piccolo in C
Oboe 1–2
B-flat soprano clarinet 1–6
B-flat bass clarinet
E-flat contrabass clarinet
Bassoon 1–2
E-flat alto saxophone 1–2
B-flat saxophone
E-flat baritone saxophone
B-flat trumpet 1–6
Horn 1–4
Trombone 1–3
Euphonium

Tuba

Piano

Tympani

Percussion 1 (five tom-toms and bass drum)

Percussion 2 (snare drum)

Percussion 3 (field drum, temple blocks, and vibraphone)

Percussion 4 (crash cymbals, chimes, vibraphone, temple blocks, orchestra bells, tambourine, and xylophone)

Percussion 5 (tam-tam, woodblock, and suspended cymbal)

Unit 3: Historical Perspective

The term sinfonietta was possibly first used by Swiss-German composer Joachim Raff as the title for his 1873 work, op. no. 188 in F, for ten wind instruments. Music in this form is generally more simply constructed and less emotionally complex than that found in a full symphony. Sinfonietta is also a word that describes small ensembles that range in size between chamber groups and full orchestras. There are a variety of professional and amateur ensembles using the name Sinfonietta.

Although the composer did not include titles for each of the seven movements in the score, conversations with Yurko indicate historical compositional references. Movements 1 and 7 are fanfares which originated in the Middle Ages. A chant and hymn, also with origins in the Middle Ages, are used in movement 2. Yurko considers movement 3 a danza, which dates from Cuba and Puerto Rico dances in the early nineteenth century. Movement 4 is representative of a Renaissance dance. The ballad of movement 5 began in the Medieval period as a dance and gave way to the song connotation it now holds during the fourteenth century. Movement 6 is an elegy, which was first a type of poetic meter used by the early Greeks for expressing sorrow through lyric poetry.

Unit 4: Technical Considerations

1. Students will need to become comfortable performing with one person per part.
2. The orchestration presents atypical performance and listening challenges. Examples include:
   - Movement 1 uses six independent trumpet parts.
   - Movement 2 is written for horn 1–4, trombone 1–3, euphonium, tuba, and percussion.
   - Movement 3 includes six independent B-flat clarinet parts, bass clarinet and contrabass clarinet, and percussion.
   - A double reed quartet (oboe 1–2 and bassoon 1–2) comprises the instrumentation for movement 4.

- Movement 6 is composed for saxophone quartet (alto saxophone 1–2, tenor saxophone, and baritone saxophone), percussion 1–5, piano, and tympani.
- Movement 6 consists of a flute quartet and vibraphones 1–2.
- Movement 7 is the only music composed for the full ensemble.

3. Trombone and bassoon players will need to be comfortable performing in tenor clef.
4. All brass parts require straight mutes (including tuba) in movement 7.
5. Making clear distinction between the wide ranges of dynamics, from ***ppp-fff***, should be considered.
6. Balancing the clusters of sounds (concert pitches D–E-flat–G-flat–C–B-flat–D-flat) during the fanfare of movement 1 will need close attention.
7. The percussion ensemble writing throughout will require mature percussionists for an effective performance.
8. Specific rhythmic challenges include:
   - Hemiola between trombones and woodwinds/percussion in movement 1.
   - The "rag-like" writing for saxophone quartet in movement 4.
   - The active, pointillist percussion parts found in the danza of movement 3.
   - The fanfare rhythms of movement 1.
9. Extreme tempos are found in movements 1 and 7 (quarter note = 144+) and movement 3 (quarter note = 132–152)
10. Part acquisition problems will be found in:
    - Rapid woodwind passages in movements 1–7.
    - Six independent trumpet parts in movements 1–7.
    - Trombone parts in movements 1–7.
    - Clarinet writing in movement 3.
    - Saxophone quartet in movement 4.
    - Independence of four-part flute writing in movement 4.

Unit 5: Stylistic Considerations

Stylistic considerations are relative to each of the seven movements.

Movements 1 and 7

Aggressive, pointed, detached articulation prevails. Wind instruments must match the percussive style at upper dynamic levels. Listen to Karel Husa's *Music for Prague 1968*, movement 4 for a good model.

Movement 2

The chant is forceful, legato, and cantor-like with flexibility. Listen to Gregorian chantto hear flow of sound. The hymn is in a romantic style. Listen to Franz Liszt's music for men's chorus to emulate tone and style.

Movement 3

The pace is furious. Light, detached articulation in the percussion is paired with a long, legato clarinet line.

Movement 4

The double reed quartet should emulate Renaissance dance characteristics. There is, however, some flexibility with tempo.

Movement 5

Listen to Scott Joplin rags for examples of accents, syncopation, character, and the overall jagged rhythmic style. The composer also suggests a reference to the Beatles tune "When I'm Sixty-Four."

Movement 6

The character and style is that of a waltz. Listen to waltzes by the Austrian-Hungarian, late-Romantic composer Franz Lehar for style.

Unit 6: Musical Elements

Movement 1 (see figures 1a-c)

MELODY:

The single thematic idea is an arpeggiated, ascending six-note theme, first presented rhythmically in tom-toms, then repeated harmonically with trumpets. The theme is later varied slightly harmonically, augmented, and in a descending manner, heard in trombones.

HARMONY:

The relationship of sounds is based on a tone cluster comprised of the pitches D–E-flat–G-flat–B-flat–C. These notes are arpeggiated, clustered as chords, used for effect in woodwind passages, and inverted.

RHYTHM:

The opening 2/4 meter gives way to a driving 6/8. Constant eighth notes fill each of the eighty-seven measures in this meter.

TIMBRE:

The timbre of the beginning fanfare is dictated by the full spectrum of wind ensemble colors at upper dynamic levels and homorhythmic writing. The timbre shifts to brass and percussion choirs at the end of the movement.

FIGURE 1a.

FIGURE 1b.

FIGURE 1c. Trombone 1

Movement 2 (see figures 2a-b)

MELODY:

The one-measure, descending, flexibly rhythmic chant is first heard in horn, euphonium, and tuba. After the one-measure descending line, keyboard percussion and piano continue the sixteenth-note thought in tempo. The eight-measure hymn is first heard contrapuntally, and then repeated in a chordal style.

HARMONY:

Both the chant and the hymn are centered around D minor. An occasional tritone appears which creates tension.

RHYTHM:

The pulse is flexible throughout. The chant alternates musical statements between low brass and percussion with ritardandos and a tempos. The hymn uses the flexibility heard in a typical song from the Romantic era.

TIMBRE:

The overall dark quality is preserved by the orchestration, which includes horn, euphonium, and tuba. Areas of stagnant rhythms in the chant instruments are filled delicately with keyboard percussion.

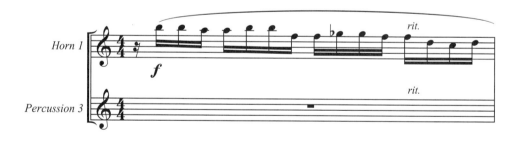

FIGURE 2a.

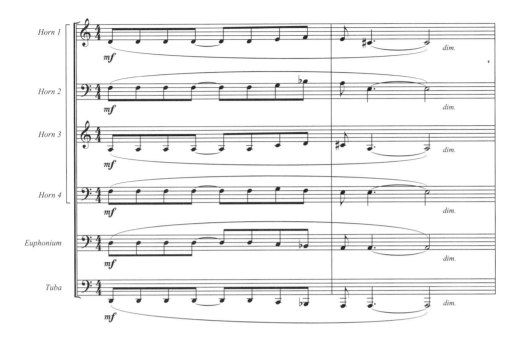

FIGURE 2b.

Movement 3 (see figures 3a-b)

MELODY:
The first eight measures of the sixteen-measure phrase are conjunct and chromatic within a small range. The last eight measures change to disjunct and span the range of a ninth.

HARMONY:
The first measures state the opening six-note theme found in movement 1 with keyboard percussion.

RHYTHM:
Meter shifts from 6/8 to 9/8 frequently. The pulse is quick and relentless. The frenetic pace of the triple feel in the clarinet melody and active percussion writing is often slowed with duple interruptions.

TIMBRE:
Clarinet choir explores the full range of the harmonic series and dynamics.

FIGURE 3a.

FIGURE 3b.

FIGURE 3b. (continued)

Movement 4 (see figure 4)

MELODY:

This tuneful melody is scalar and diatonic while using ascending and descending directions. The form is AABACAABA.

HARMONY:

Harmony is centered around B-flat major with typical cadences.

RHYTHM:

There is much rubato to be explored. The underlying pulse uses six beats per measure.

TIMBRE:

Double reed quartet (oboe 1–2 and bassoon 1–2) creates the colors of this movement. The comfortable registers ensure a pleasing overall sound.

FIGURE 4.

Movement 5 (see figure 5)

MELODY:

Three melodic ideas make up the ragtime. Each is eight measures in length. The first two include a short introduction and incorporate the range of a perfect fifth. The third melody expands the range to an augmented ninth. The melodic form is ABCBA.

HARMONY:

Sections A and B incorporate major sounds followed by flat thirds and sixths to help create the bluesy effect. Section C uses the chord progression of D–B-flat–G major.

RHYTHM:

Jagged, syncopated rhythms of early twentieth-century ragtime prevail. The meter is 2/4, with measures of 3/8 throughout that keep the feel unbalanced.

TIMBRE:

Saxophone quartet, tambourine, suspended cymbal, snare drum, bass drum, and piano create the color of the music.

FIGURE 5.

Movement 6 (see figure 6)

MELODY:

Flute 1 carries each of the two eight-measure, waltz-like melodies. The second melody is related rhythmically to the first. The cadenza is also in the first flute part.

HARMONY:

The first melody uses two basic chords, F-sharp$^{7(\flat5)}$ and B^{dim7}. The second melody is centered around E-flat minor.

RHYTHM:

The 3/4 meter combined with the tempo creates an easy-feeling waltz. There are ritardandos at the end of each phrase. An underlying arpeggiated eight-note line provides stability for the floating melody.

TIMBRE:
The flute quartet and two vibraphones provide a light yet haunting quality.

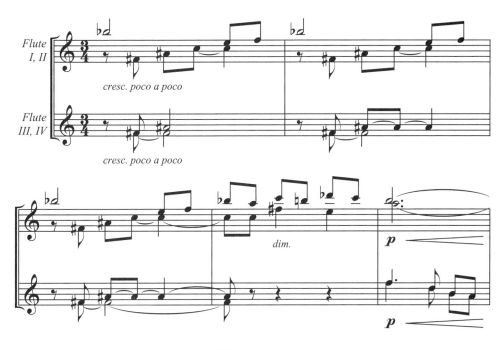

FIGURE 6.

Movement 7 (see figures 1a-c above)
MELODY:
The arpeggiated, ascending six-note theme from movement 1 returns. This theme is later varied slightly harmonically, augmented, and in a descending manner, heard in trombones. The fanfare that began the work closes movement 7.

HARMONY:
The relationship of sounds is based on a tone cluster comprised of the pitches D–E-flat–G-flat–B-flat–C. These notes are arpeggiated, clustered as chords, used for effect in woodwind passages, and inverted.

RHYTHM:
The opening 6/8 meter gives way to the final 2/4 fanfare. The constant eighth notes of the 6/8 and the sixteenth-note 2/4 fanfare exists throughout.

TIMBRE:
The opening timbre consists of alternating brass, woodwind, and percussion choirs. The timbre of the fanfare is dictated by the full spectrum of wind ensemble colors at upper dynamic levels and homorhythmic writing.

Unit 7: Form and Structure

SECTION   MEASURE   EVENT AND SCORING

Movement 1: *Con Spirito*, quarter note = 144+

	1–24	2/4	Fanfare for wind ensemble
	25–39	6/8	Percussion ensemble theme 1
	40–84		Trumpet and percussion theme 1
	84–111		Trombone theme 2 or vary theme 1 Trumpet and percussion continue

Movement 2: *Misterioso*, quarter note = 60

	112–133	4/4	Chant-like-low brass and French horn ensemble converse with percussion ensemble
	134–157		Hymn-like; horn and low brass ensemble

Movement 3: *Furioso*, quarter note = 132–152

	158–172	6/8	percussion ensemble introduction (snare drum and woodblock in canon)
	173–196		Bass clarinet theme; clarinet 1 enters in m. 190
	197–204	9/8	Full clarinet and percussion ensembles in transition
	205–222	6/8	Full clarinet ensemble statement
	223–230	9/8	Transition (clarinet and percussion)
	231–246	6/8	Clarinet ensemble statement
	247–258	9/8	Transition (clarinet and percussion)
	259–274	6/8	Clarinet ensemble statement
	275–294	9/8	Bass clarinet, clarinet 1, and percussion interplay to end

Movement 4: *Andante espressivo, rubato*, eighth note = 108

	295–303	6/8	Section A of melody (oboe 1 accompanied by oboe 2 and bassoon 1–2)
	304–307		Section B of melody
	308–315		Section C of melody (bassoon 1 melody with bassoon 2 basso, then oboe 1 with trio accompaniment)
	316–327		Melody sections A and B (double reed quartet)

SECTION	MEASURE	EVENT AND SCORING

Movement 5: *Allegro marcato*, quarter note = 126

	328–331	2/4	Introduction (saxophone quartet and percussion ensemble)
	332–347		Rag theme 1
	348–350		Transition
	351–365		Theme 2; *Allegro grazioso, rubato* (quarter note = 104)
	366–381		Bridge (piano and saxophone trio); *Allegro marcato*, quarter note = 126
	382–389		Theme 2
	390–393		Introduction
	394–409		Theme 1

Movement 6: *Tempo di valzer, molto espressivo*, quarter note = 112–116

	410–425	3/4	Unaccompanied flute quartet, theme 1
	426–435		Theme 2, flute quartet with vibraphone 1–2)
	436–442		Extension
	444–449		Theme 2; flutes and vibraphones
	450		Flute 1 cadenza
	451–466		Theme 1; flute quartet
	467–78		Theme 2; flute 1 and vibraphones

Movement 7: *Presto, marcato*, dotted quarter note = 144+

	479–500	6/8	Overlapping statements of theme 1 presented in full woodwind section and vibraphones 1–2
	513–531		Muted brass statements of motifs and augmented variants of theme 1
	532–552		Theme 1 and variants combined
	553–580	2/4	Opening fanfare music from movement 1

Unit 8: Suggested Listening

Chance, John Barnes. *Legacy of John Barnes Chance.* Illinois State University Wind Ensemble. Stephen Steel, conductor. Albany Records. 2005.

Dahl, Ingolf. *Sinfonietta.* Depaul University Wind Ensemble. Donald DeRoache, conductor. Albany. 2001.

Gregorian Chant. Performed by Benedictine Monks. Angel Records. 1993.

Janacek, Leos. *Sinfonietta,* Op. 60. London Philharmonic. Neville Mariner, conductor. London. 1997.

Joplin, Scott. *Complete Works of Scott Joplin*. Richard Zimmerman, pianist. Delta. 1993.

Poulenc, Francis. *Sinfonietta*. New London Orchestra. Ronald Corp, conductor. Helios. 1998.

Raff, Joachim. *Sinfonietta, Op. 188*. Basel Radio Symphony. Andres Joho, conductor. Tudor. 1995.

Yurko Bruce:

>   *In Memoriam: Kristina for Wind Ensemble*. University of North Texas Wind Symphony. Eugene Migliaro Corporon, conductor. GIA Publications.

>   *Night Dances for Wind Ensemble*. University of North Texas Wind Symphony. Eugene Migliaro Corporon, conductor. GIA Publications.

Unit 9: Additional References

"Bruce Yurko: In Memoriam: Kristina." In *Teaching Music through Performance in Band, Volume 2*. Richard Miles, ed. Chicago: GIA Publications, 1998.

"Bruce Yurko: Night Dances." In *Teaching Music through Performance in Band, Volume 1*. Richard Miles, ed. Chicago: GIA Publications, 1997.

"Bruce Yurko: Pastoral Nocturne." In *Teaching Music through Performance in Band, Volume 4*. Richard Miles, ed. Chicago: GIA Publications, 2002.

"Bruce Yurko: Danza No. 2." In *Teaching Music through Performance in Band, Volume 6*. Richard Miles, ed. Chicago: GIA Publications, 2007.

Tower, Ilbrook. "Bruce Yurko's *Concerto for Wind Ensemble (1973–1974), for Horn and Wind Ensemble (1975)*, and *for Trombone and Wind Ensemble (1977)*." Ann Arbor, MI: UMI Company, 1995.

Contributed by:

Richard A. Greenwood
Professor of Music and Conducting
University of Central Florida
Orlando, Florida

Bruce Yurko
Composer
New Jersey

Teacher Resource Guide

Strange Humors

John Mackey
(b. 1973)

Unit 1: Composer

John Mackey, born October 1, 1973, in New Philadelphia, Ohio, holds a master of music degree from The Juilliard School and a bachelor of fine arts degree from the Cleveland Institute of Music, where he studied with John Corigliano and Donald Erb, respectively. Mackey particularly enjoys writing music for dance and for symphonic winds, and has focused on those mediums for the past few years.

His works have been performed at the Sydney Opera House, Brooklyn Academy of Music, Carnegie Hall, Kennedy Center, Weill Recital Hall, Jacob's Pillow Dance Festival, Italy's Spoleto Festival, Alice Tully Hall, Joyce Theater, Dance Theater Workshop, and throughout Italy, Chile, Japan, Colombia, Austria, Brazil, Germany, England, Australia, New Zealand, and the United States.

Mackey has received numerous commissions from the Parsons Dance Company as well as commissions from the Cleveland Orchestra Youth Orchestra, New York City Ballet's Choreographic Institute, Dallas Theater Center, Alvin Ailey Dance Company, New York Youth Symphony, Ailey 2, Concert Artists Guild, Peridance Ensemble, and Jeanne Ruddy Dance, among many others. Recent commissions include works for the concert bands of the SEC Athletic Conference, the American Bandmasters Association, and the Dallas Wind Symphony.

As a frequent collaborator, Mackey has worked with a diverse range of artists, from Doug Varone to David Parsons, Robert Battle, and the United States Olympic Synchronized Swim Team, which won a bronze medal performing to his music in the 2004 Athens Olympics. He has been recognized with numerous grants and awards from organizations, including the American Society of Composers, Authors, and Publishers (Concert Music Awards, 1999–2007; Morton Gould Young Composer Award, 2002–2003), American Music Center (Margaret Jory Fairbanks Copying Assistance Grant, 2000 and 2002), and the Mary Flagler Cary Charitable Trust (Live Music for Dance commissioning grants, 1998–2000 and 2005), and an NEA grant in 2007. He was a CalArts/Alpert Award nominee in 2000.

In February 2003, the Brooklyn Philharmonic premiered Mackey's work *Redline Tango* at the BAM Opera House, with Kristjan Jarvi conducting. The Dallas Symphony, under Andrew Litton, performed the piece in both Dallas and Vail in 2004. Litton performed the work again in 2005 with the Minnesota Orchestra, and in 2006 with the Bergen Philharmonic of Norway. Marin Alsop performed the work at the Cabrillo Festival of Contemporary Music in the summer of 2005. Mackey made a new version of the work for wind ensemble in 2004—Mackey's first work for wind band—and that version has since received over 100 performances worldwide. The wind version won the 2004 Walter Beeler Memorial Composition Prize, and in 2005, the ABA/Ostwald Award from the American Bandmasters Association, making Mackey the youngest composer to receive the honor.

Mackey served as a Meet-the-Composer/American Symphony Orchestra League "Music Alive!" composer-in-residence with the Greater Twin Cities Youth Symphony in 2002–2003, and with the Seattle Youth Symphony Orchestra in 2004–2005. He was composer-in-residence at the Vail Valley Music Festival in Vail, Colorado in the summer of 2004 and at the Cabrillo Festival of Contemporary Music in August 2005. He has held college residencies at Florida State, University of Michigan, Ohio State, Arizona State, University of Southern California, University of Texas, and many others. Mackey served as music director of the Parsons Dance Company from 1999–2003.

Unit 2: Composition

Strange Humors was commissioned by the American Bandmasters Association and premiered in 2006 by the Baylor University Wind Ensemble, conducted by Richard Floyd, to whom the work is dedicated. The piece was originally written for string quartet and djembe in 1998 and was subsequently choreographed for dance performances by Robert Battle, with whom the composer has shared a lengthy collaboration. The piece has also been arranged, as of 2008, for saxophone quartet and djembe. The piece itself is a swirl of cultural influence, as the thoroughly Western ensemble performs music based simultaneously on elements of African hand-drumming and middle-Eastern melody. *Strange Humors* is 184 measures, approximately five minutes and thirty seconds in length and published by Osti Music.

Unit 3: Historical Perspective

Though the wind version of *Strange Humors* was composed in 2006, it owes its creation to its prior incarnation as a work for string quartet and djembe in 1998. Consequently, the musical material represents an earlier stylistic period for Mackey, predating all but two of his listed catalogue works (*Elegy and Fantasie* for violin and piano and the orchestral *Do Not Go Gentle into That Good Night*). Mackey has arranged several of his works for larger ensemble. *Breakdown Tango* eventually became *Redline Tango*, and a collection of several movements from different works have subsequently formed the musical material for *Kingfishers Catch Fire* and *Clocking*.

Unit 4: Technical Considerations

Strange Humors is scored for piccolo, two flutes, oboe, English horn, two bassoons, contrabassoon, E-flat clarinet, two B-flat clarinets, bass clarinet, B-flat contrabass clarinet, soprano saxophone, alto saxophone, tenor saxophone, baritone saxophone, four B-flat trumpets, four French horns, three trombones (bass trombone preferred for trombone 3), euphonium, tuba, contrabass, and percussion (five players). Mackey prefers that the instrumentation be limited to one player per part, but has written the work with the understanding that frequently this situation will not be plausible. Cues have also been provided for many of the exposed and soloistic sections in the event that certain instruments are unavailable or strengths and weaknesses within different ensembles might benefit from rescoring. The opening English horn solo, for instance, is cued in both bassoon and alto saxophone parts. This provides the conductor a great deal of latitude when assigning parts.

This being said, there is a fairly substantial amount of exposed playing required of performers. Excluding cued parts, there are solos for piccolo, flute 1, oboe, English horn, bassoon 1, bass clarinet, soprano saxophone, alto saxophone, baritone saxophone, trumpet 1, trombone 1, euphonium, and djembe. This precludes the ensemble having enough quality performers to handle the majority of these parts before even considering the myriad of other exposed and integral effects that occur in the remainder of the parts.

Ostensibly, the most important part within the piece is for djembe, which plays for nearly the entirety of the piece and should always be at least audibly present if not the primary rhythmic voice. Mackey suggests placing the soloist in a visibly prominent position to assist in projection as well as for dramatic effect. The rhythms for djembe are recurrent from measure to measure, although some time and care will need to be taken by the soloist to properly execute and differentiate the five different stroke types requested in the score.

The opening section also presents aleatoric notation in some parts (e.g., horn and percussion). In this section, the marimba has quick, dry articulations of an open fifth between G and D in random rhythms, while the other free voices vary rates of crescendo and decrescendo while sustaining either a drone on the same harmony or a roll (in the case of djembe and bass drum).

Ranges are generally manageable. Piccolo and flute extend, on rare occasion, up to high B-flat. E-flat clarinet has several instances of a written altissimo F. Trumpet has a written C above the staff several times, and trombone is as high as A-flat in the treble staff.

Unit 5: Stylistic Considerations

Like several of Mackey's works, *Strange Humors* relies heavily on the mixture of cultural elements. *Strange Humors* uses two distinct non-Western musical styles within its context: African hand-drumming and middle-Eastern melodies. Several possibilities exist for students to engage in cross-cultural projects to investigate techniques and traits of both African and middle-Eastern musical styles.

The djembe, as the centerpiece of the ensemble, has its own stylistic function within the piece. Though it is among the most frequently seen African drums outside of Africa, many ensemble and audience members will likely be unfamiliar with its design and proper performance practice. The drum itself has a bowl-shaped upper portion with a cylindrical flare to an open end on the bottom. The drum head is pulled very tight with a rope mechanism.

There are three basic strokes within djembe technique: the bass, the lowest of the three, is achieved by a resonant stroke to the center of the head; the tone, a midrange sonority formed by firm finger strokes close to the rim; and the slap, the highest and loudest of the three, created by striking the drum slightly closer to the center of the head with relaxed wrists and fingers (creating a hollow space under the palm).

Mackey's notation asks for two different tone sonorities (one higher and one lower), as well as a deadstroke, which is notated like a slap but with less ringing resonance and more of the sharp articulation.

Conductors should strongly consider presenting or providing access to video and audio recordings of the original version and dance production of *Strange Humors* (both available on the composer's website—see Unit 9). Performers can be assisted with some of the stylistic nuances that may be troublesome when the piece is heard in its original string medium.

Unit 6: Musical Elements

MELODY:
The melodies of *Strange Humors* are not particularly difficult within themselves. With the exception of the second phrase of the introduction (which features a leap of a seventh at its conclusion), all melodic phrases are

contained within a single octave. The melodic content of *Strange Humors* alternates between variations on G minor, most frequently the Phrygian mode. Some performers may not be familiar with these scale alterations. Familiarizing players with the differences between these modes—particularly the active tones, such as the flat supertonic in the Phrygian scale—will help them to become comfortable with both the dissonance and the melodic direction of phrases.

HARMONY:
The harmonies apparent in *Strange Humors* are influenced partly by the modal content created by its scales. Though the language is somewhat contemporary, the general aesthetic is one of functional tonality. Some of the chords, however, are altered because of the Phrygian mode. For instance, frequently at cadence points, a D diminished triad replaces the expected D major dominant sonority.

In addition to this, Mackey frequently makes use of increasing dissonance near cadential points to provide appropriate tension and release. Where certain elements are meant to project, dense cluster harmonies will often appear (e.g., the syncopated horn clusters in mm. 81–84).

RHYTHM:
At first glance, the most difficult element of *Strange Humors* is certainly the rhythmic complexity it presents. The djembe soloist has arguably the most daunting task—maintaining clarity and consistency of the detailed rhythms while providing a steady metric pulse (along with the bass drum) on which the florid melodies and accompaniments can be placed. The rhythms are recurrent, however, so once the patterns are mastered, they can be combined with a greater degree of ease.

Rhythms can also be difficult within the wind parts. Theme 2 tends to be particularly difficult (m. 53 onward) for some players. Breaking up and simplifying the rhythms—such as temporarily eliminating the "turn" figure, or ignoring the opening syncopation—as a pedagogical method can prove effective. Careful attention should also be paid to the accents in this pattern. Thisa can help performers feel how the rhythm and melody drives to the next arrival point. In all cases, providing students a model for how each rhythm should sound is beneficial. Frequently the notation makes the execution of the figures more difficult than it sounds.

TIMBRE:
As a work originally conceived for chamber ensemble, expanding the piece for full band provides challenges, both toward achieving the overall aesthetic of the work as well as balancing within the ensemble to create an ideally matched sound. Mackey provides a great deal of detailed notation to assist the

conductor and performers in achieving his effects. Matching his ideal instrumentation is a good start, and any holes or doublings that are unavoidable can be identified immediately as balance priorities.

The alternation of chamber music and tutti sections requires a different approach from performers. In the more sparse moments, performers should approach their playing more soloistically (even if passages are not explicitly marked solo), while in full sections care should be taken to balance all relevant elements.

The traditionally ideal tone for an instrument may not be the best aesthetic choice for producing some of the effects in *Strange Humors*. At times the timbre might best be described as raucous, biting, sneering, or nasal. Keeping in mind that these are only momentary effects, the extent to which players are permitted to use improper tone is left to the conductor's discretion.

Unit 7: Form and Structure

SECTION	MEASURE	EVENT AND SCORING
Introduction	1–9	English horn solo; mm = c. 76, very free; monophonic presentation of theme 1; G Phrygian
	10–18	English horn and alto saxophone duet; aleatoric accompanimental figures in horns and percussion
A	19–26	Djembe solo; mm = 120–128, strictly in time
	27–40	Theme 1 in solo alto saxophone over bassoon drone and djembe ostinato; G Phrygian
	41–52	Restatement of theme 1 in soprano and alto saxophones; woodwind chordal accompaniment with continuing djembe ostinato and bowed percussion effects
B	53–60	Theme 2 in bass clarinet, outlined by figures in trombone 1-2; djembe ostinato
	61–68	Theme 3 in oboe with syncopated woodwind and percussion accompaniment; djembe ostinato
	69–76	Theme 2 in oboe, English horn and soprano saxophone; syncopated woodwind and contrabass accompaniment; djembe ostinato
	77–84	Theme 3 in flute and trumpet 1; countermelody in euphonium; chordal brass accompaniment; horns add syncopated figure at m. 81

SECTION	MEASURE	EVENT AND SCORING
C	85–94	Shift to 5/8 meter; return of djembe ostinato with trombone and contrabass pedal; accented interjections from saxophones, bassoon, horns, and percussion
	95–102	Chromatic melody in bass clarinet and baritone saxophone based on syncopated theme 2 accompaniment pattern; eighth-note ostinato in soprano, alto, and tenor saxophones
	103–111	Variation on theme 2 in oboe, English horn, and trumpet 1; pattern from previous phrase continued, augmented by bassoon, contrabassoon, contrabass clarinet, trumpets, and horns; djembe ostinato
	112–123	Shout section: theme 1 reappears in piccolo, E-flat clarinet, and soprano saxophone; remainder of ensemble plays *fff* cluster chords; trombone section glissando effect at m. 122 leads into return of previous sections
B	124–131	Theme 2 in English horn, bass clarinet, and tenor saxophone outlined by clarinet 2; oboe, soprano saxophone, and alto saxophone augment melody at m. 128 with addition of bassoon and trombones to the outlining figure; djembe ostinato
	132–139	Theme 3 in oboe, English horn, and euphonium; syncopated woodwind and percussion accompaniment; djembe ostinato
	140–147	Theme 2 in piccolo, oboe, English horn, E-flat clarinet, and soprano saxophone; syncopated woodwind, trombone, and contrabass accompaniment; djembe ostinato
	148–155	Theme 3 in flute and trumpet 1; countermelody in euphonium; chordal brass accompaniment; syncopated figure appears in bassoon, alto and tenor saxophone, horns, vibraphone, and marimba at m. 152

SECTION	MEASURE	EVENT AND SCORING
C	156–164	5/8 meter; monophonic presentation of chromatic melody based on theme 2; accompaniment in trombone 1 followed by tutti restatement of same material with hemiola effect in djembe, snare drum, and contrabass
	165–171	Shout section; theme 2 in flute, oboe, English horn, soprano saxophone, and alto saxophone; syncopated accompaniment in remainder of ensemble
Coda	172–179	Elements of themes 2–3 juxtaposed building from reduced instrumentation to full ensemble *ff*
	180–184	Fragmentation of theme 2 and its accompaniment in full ensemble building from *p* to *fff*

Unit 8: Suggested Listening

Bernstein, Leonard. *Prelude, Fugue, and Riffs*.
Daugherty, Michael. *Desi*.
Mackey, John:
    Clocking
    Kingfishers Catch Fire
    Redline Tango
    Sasparilla
    Strange Humors (original version)
Milhaud, Darius. *La creation du monde*.
Tredici, David Del. *In Wartime*.

Unit 9: Additional References and Resources

Websites:
    Djembe online resource guide. http://www.djembe.org/
    Osti Music: The Website of John Mackey. http://www.ostimusic.com/

Contributed by:

Jacob Wallace
Doctoral Conducting Associate
The University of Georgia
Athens, Georgia

Teacher Resource Guide

Traffic
Symphony No. 3, Movement 2

Ned Rorem
(b. 1932)

transcribed by Daron Hagen
(b. 1961)

Unit 1: Composer

Words and music are inextricably linked for Ned Rorem. *Time Magazine* has called him "the world's best composer of art songs," yet his musical and literary ventures extend far beyond this specialized field. Rorem has composed three symphonies, four piano concertos, and an array of other orchestral works, music for numerous combinations of chamber forces, ten operas, choral works of every description, ballets and other music for the theater, and literally hundreds of songs and cycles. He is the author of sixteen books, including five volumes of diaries and collections of lectures and criticism.

Rorem was born in Richmond, Indiana on October 23, 1923. As a child he moved to Chicago with his family; by the age of ten his piano teacher had introduced him to the music of Debussy and Ravel, an experience which "changed my life forever," according to the composer. At seventeen he entered the music school of Northwestern University, two years later receiving a scholarship to the Curtis Institute in Philadelphia. He studied composition under Bernard Wagenaar at Juilliard, taking his bachelor of arts in 1946 and his master of arts degree (along with the $1,000 George Gershwin Memorial Prize in composition) in 1948. In New York he worked as Virgil Thomson's copyist in return for twenty dollars a week and orchestration lessons. He studied on fellowship at the Berkshire Music Center in

Tanglewood in the summers of 1946–47; in 1948 his song "The Lordly Hudson" was voted the best published song of that year by the Music Library Association. He currently lives in New York City.

Rorem is one of America's most honored composers. In addition to a Pulitzer Prize, awarded in 1976 for his orchestral suite *Air Music*, Rorem has been the recipient of a Fulbright Fellowship (1951), a Guggenheim Fellowship (1957), and an award from the National Institute of Arts and Letters (1968). He received the ASCAP-Deems Taylor Award in 1971 for his book *Critical Affairs: A Composer's Journal*, in 1975 for *The Final Diary*, and in 1992 for an article on American opera in *Opera News*. In 1998 he was chosen Composer of the Year by Musical America. From 2000 to 2003 he served as President of the American Academy of Arts and Letters. In 2003 he received ASCAP's Lifetime Achievement Award, in 2004 the French government named him Chevalier of the Order of Arts and Letters, and in May 2008 the American Music Center awarded him the "Letter of Distinction" for his significant contribution to contemporary American music.

Among his many commissions for new works are those from the Ford Foundation (for *Poems of Love and the Rain*, 1962), the Lincoln Center Foundation (for *Sun*, 1965), the Koussevitzky Foundation (for *Letters from Paris*, 1966), the Atlanta Symphony (for the *String Symphony*, 1985), the Chicago Symphony (for *Goodbye My Fancy*, 1990), Carnegie Hall (for *Spring Music*, 1991), and the New York Philharmonic (for the *Concerto for English Horn and Orchestra*, 1993). Among the distinguished conductors who have performed his music are Leonard Bernstein, Kurt Masur, Zubin Mehta, Dmitri Mitropoulos, Eugene Ormandy, Andre Previn, Fritz Reiner, Leonard Slatkin, William Steinberg, and Leopold Stokowski.[1]

Unit 2: Composition

Traffic is a transcription of movement 2 from Rorem's *Symphony No. 3* for orchestra. The original symphony is dedicated to Robert Holton, who at the time of composition served as director of serious music at Boosey & Hawkes, the eventual publishers of the work. Rorem began composing the piece in Hyères, France in July 1957 and finished it on April 4, 1958 in New York City. *Symphony No. 3* was premiered on April 18, 1959 in Carnegie Hall by the New York Philharmonic, Leonard Bernstein, conductor.

Movement 2 of the symphony, *Allegro molto vivace*, is itself a transcription of Rorem's earlier *Suite for Two Pianos*, written in 1949 for Robert Fizdale and Arthur Gold. Perhaps because the piano version was never performed, Rorem decided to repurpose the material for inclusion in *Symphony No. 3*. Daron Hagen, one of Rorem's first composition students at the Curtis Institute, transcribed movement 2 for wind band in honor of the composer's eightieth birthday in 2003.

Published by Boosey & Hawkes as part of the Windependence series, *Traffic* is included in the Artist Level category, equivalent to a Grade 5 on a Grade-6 scale. Ninety-six measures in length, the work is approximately two and a half minutes in duration.

Unit 3: Historical Perspective

Rorem is most often recognized as a master of the modern art song, and his catalog contains more than 500 works in this genre. However, Rorem has composed music in nearly every classical genre, including two pieces for wind ensembles. The earliest such work is his *Overture for G. I.'s*, an unpublished and unperformed band piece written near the end of World War II for the Army Music School Band, William Strickland, conductor. The second piece, *Sinfonia for Fifteen Wind Instruments and Optional Percussion*, was commissioned through the Howard Heinz Endowment in 1956. Completed the following year, the *Sinfonia* is scored for an expanded wind octet with optional percussion parts (including piano), and was premiered by the American Wind Symphony Orchestra, Robert Austin Boudreau, conductor.

Aside from these two works for wind ensemble, Rorem has composed numerous pieces for instrumental ensembles. As mentioned earlier, *Traffic* is a transcription of movement 2 of *Symphony No. 3*, the final such work of Rorem's with the framework and title of "symphony." All three of the symphonies were written while Rorem was living in France, from 1949 to 1958. This period of the composer's life was spent "among the leading figures of the artistic and social milieu of post-war Europe" and "are absorbingly portrayed in *The Paris Diary and The New York Diary, 1951–1961*."[2]

Though he has ceased to use the title of "symphony" for his works, Rorem has composed many large-scale orchestral pieces since *Symphony No. 3*. These include *Design* (1953), *Eagles* (1958), *Ideas* (1961), *Lions (A Dream)* (1963), *Water Music* (1966), *Air Music* (1974), *Assembly and Fall* (1975), *Sunday Morning* (1977), and *A Quaker Reader* (1988). One of many pieces commissioned from the composer in honor of the bicentennial of the United States of America, *Air Music* earned Rorem the Pulitzer Prize. Large pieces for combined instrumental ensemble and chorus include *Lift Up Your Heads* (1963) for mixed chorus and wind ensemble, *Laudamus Tempus Actum* (1964), *An American Oratorio* (1984), *Goodbye My Fancy* (1988), and *Present Laughter* (1995) for men's chorus and band. His latest works include two operas: *Our Town* (2006), based on Thornton Wilder's play, and *Little Nemo* (2009), inspired by Windsor McCay's early twentieth-century surreal comic strip *Little Nemo in Slumberland*.

The title *Traffic* evokes a picture of the hustle and bustle of city life, and the music certainly portrays this with its elements of jazz-like syncopation, extreme dynamics, and frantic scoring changes. Many composers have used urban settings as inspiration or even programmatic themes for works written for wind band. A small sampling includes *Urban Requiem* (1995) by Michael Colgrass, *Vox Populi* (1998) and *Voice of the City* (2005) by Richard Danielpour, *Metropolis* (1992), *Awayday* (1996) and *Adrenaline City* (2006) by Adam Gorb, *Urban Myth* (2003) by Murray Gross, *Three City Blocks* (1991) by John Harbison, and *George Washington Bridge* (1950) by William Schuman.

Unit 4: Technical Considerations

Though shorter in duration than most Grade 5 pieces, *Traffic* presents many challenges congruent to pieces labeled moderately difficult to difficult. The piece is centered on F major, though never for long (for more discussion of the tonal center, please see Unit 6, Harmony). Players must be comfortable playing in any key throughout the range of their instrument.

The fast but steady tempo, quarter note = 168, presents issues of precision and control. Note durations are rooted primarily in quarter and eighth notes, although there are rare occurrences of sixteenth-note passages. While the notes themselves are not fast, the execution of the syncopated rhythmic aspects can prove to be problematic if individual players are not secure in their application of internal subdivision. The *allegro molto vivace* tempo also creates difficulty with clarity of articulation. Each player must strive for a unified concept of length and stress when encountering any articulation indication.

Special mention should be made of the extended technique of slap-tonguing, notated for alto and tenor saxophones in mm. 76–77. This once-unusual and uncommon effect is now known by a large number of saxophonists and is becoming a standard technique in the repertoire. Slap-tonguing is accomplished by creating suction on the reed with the tongue and then quickly releasing it while producing a tone with the air stream. Though there are other versions of this technique that produce non-pitched sound, it appears that Rorem (Hagen) is looking for a pitched effect due to the specified notation.

Range considerations are appropriate for a Grade 5 work (the following pitches are as written, with C4 equaling middle C): E-flat clarinet, F-sharp 6; clarinet, F6; alto saxophone, G-flat 6; tenor saxophone, F6; trumpet, B5; and horn, A5 with occasional notation in bass clef. Each instrument indicated in the score is crucial to the desired tone color and is rarely cross-cued, including piccolo, E-flat soprano clarinet, and string bass.

Unit 5: Stylistic Considerations

One of the primary stylistic features of *Traffic* is the use of articulation. The subtle variances in articulation are crucial in expressing the slight nuances in Rorem's presentation of thematic material. Besides the obvious contrast of legato to *staccato* and marcato indications, small differences in the placement of slurring and tonguing create intriguing variations on repeated themes.

Other interest is generated by the simultaneity of voices with unison pitch structure but different durational values. There are numerous examples where the thematic idea is presented in both quarter-note and eighth-note/eighth-rest duration, causing the pitches to begin together, but release at different times. Players may need to be informed of those passages where their articulation differs from other voices in order that they effectively produce the desired sound resulting from the juxtaposition of contrasting notation.

Rorem plays with phrasing throughout the work, often negating the organization of the barline in order to fuel syncopation. From the opening statement of the theme there is an absence of the predictable stability generated by 4/4 time. The combination of ever-present syncopation, uneven phrasing, obliteration of the barline, and evolving articulation lend a vibrant and ebullient joy to the mood of the work.

Unit 6: Musical Elements

MELODY:

Much of the melodic material of *Traffic* is generated from theme 1, first introduced in mm. 5–11. As figure 1 illustrates, this playful melody is highly syncopated and tripartite. Each of the three sections, labeled 1a, 1b, and 1c, is presented by three different voices or instrumental combinations each time the theme appears in its entirety. Of the three parts of the theme, 1a appears most often throughout the piece, many times as an isolated figure. Statements of the full theme 1 occur only three times; the remaining material is either a derivation or variation on the original theme.

FIGURE 1. *Traffic*, theme 1

It may also be helpful to keep in mind that despite the accented, syncopated, and loud nature of the work, Rorem always approaches music from a vocal viewpoint. When writing about his Pulitzer Prize-winning orchestral suite *Air Music*, he stated that he "conceived [it] as I conceive all my music, vocally. Whatever my music is written for—tuba, tambourine, tubular bells—

it always is the singer within me crying to get out."[3] Remembering this important aspect of Rorem's concept of sound may assist in maintaining
the integrity of phrases in a more lyrical and horizontal manner while still
observing notated articulations and dynamics.

HARMONY:
Rorem's music is not strictly tonal in a traditional sense. There is a sense of
tonal center, and therefore hints at progression and cadence to much of the
piece, which suggests a key of F major. However, the tonal center of the piece
shifts quickly, and therefore players need to possess mastery over all major and
minor scales to be able to maintain consistent quality and characteristic tone
no matter the key. Rorem is one of a few American composers in the middle
twentieth century who did not embrace the dodecaphonicism of the second
Viennese school, but rather projected a sort of neo-Romantic language,
harmony, and sensibility. In this respect, the music might be considered more
immediately accessible to a wider audience.

RHYTHM:
Syncopation is a key component to the thematic material, as evident from the
very first measure of theme 1. The rhythmic content of theme 1a begins with
a full measure of offbeats, which in the next measure is followed by similar
material placed on the beats. Each subsequent use of the theme and its derivations features syncopation. Players playing off the beat must be secure with
their internal concept of pulse, especially when coming from a passage which
is downbeat-oriented.

With the exception of three separate 2/4 bars of silence, the piece is notated
in 4/4. However, it is not uncommon for the phrasing to conflict with the set
time signature, often breaking the barline. In a few instances eighth-note
rhythms are beamed across a barline. Related to the syncopated nature of the
theme is the frequent use of *hemiola* that spins out of the syncopation. Precision
is crucial to bring out counterpoint between melodic and accompaniment
material which is regularly offset from the melody by an eighth note.

TIMBRE:
There are very few occasions where the entire ensemble plays simultaneously.
Much of the piece is scored in thin textures, with several passages scored for
solo instruments or sections. There is solo work for piccolo, flute, E-flat soprano clarinet, clarinet 1, alto and tenor saxophone, trumpet 1, trumpet 2,
trumpet 3, horn 1, and percussion. This creates a wonderful opportunity for
individual players to express themselves and develop confidence in handling
solos within the framework of a large ensemble. As with ensemble playing,
solo players must be aware of those instances when they are continuing or
echoing a passage to establish or maintain stylistic cohesion. The abundance

of thinly-scored passages make those rare moments of tutti scoring highly effective and dramatic.

Caution must be taken when interpreting loud dynamics in *Traffic*. Players may benefit from gentle guidance regarding Rorem's connection to the voice and art song, remembering to maintain the vocal or singing nature of his music despite the dynamic and articulation. This may help to prevent overbearing and uncharacteristic sound when encountering extreme dynamics, especially in those cases where *fortississimo* is indicated.

Unit 7: Form and Structure

Most of the musical material of *Traffic* is built on the characteristics of the theme that first appears beginning in m. 5. The theme fully returns only twice after the initial statement; however, much of the subsequent material is derived from aspects of the theme. It may therefore be appropriate to consider the structure as a continuously-spinning variation form. The following description of form and structure is merely one approach to organization and may be helpful to the conductor in study and rehearsal.

SECTION	MEASURE	EVENT AND SCORING
Introduction	1–4	Quarter note = 168; snare drum and timpani *crescendo* into syncopated thematic foreshadowing by horns, trombones, and saxophones followed by tutti *sforzando* chords outlining tonic (F) and dominant (C) and a 2/4 bar of silence
Section 1	5–12	Non-legato presentation of theme 1a (see Unit 6) by oboe soli, solo alto and tenor saxophone, horn, and tenor drum; theme 1b in clarinets; horn 3–4 accompanied by bassoons, baritone saxophone, string bass, and tenor drum; theme 1c fully in trombones and partially in horn 1–2
	13–19	Theme is repeated in its entirety; theme 1a in saxophones, trumpets, horns, and trombone 1–2; theme 1b in piccolo, flutes, oboes, clarinets, and xylophone; theme 1c in saxophones, trumpet 1–2, and trombone 1–2
	20–27	Variation on theme 1a in clarinets followed by variation on theme 1b in legato solo flute with accompaniment hemiola figures in clarinets; theme 1a variation returns in solo horn and leads to trumpet solo with hemiola in alto and tenor saxophones

SECTION	MEASURE	EVENT AND SCORING
	28–31	Brief allusion to introductory material with tutti *sforzando* chords outlining tonic-to-dominant followed by a 2/4 bar of silence
	32–39	Return of complete theme in accented tutti outburst except for sustained chords in saxophones, euphonium, and tuba; accompaniment in bass clarinet, bassoons, string bass, and timpani
Section 2	40–48	Theme 2, a variation on theme 1, in clarinet 1, piccolo, flutes, and oboes with sustained chords in horns; trumpets answer with repetition of theme 2 continued by upper woodwinds
	49–53	Hemiola outburst in woodwinds, trumpets, trombones, string bass, timpani, and percussion
	54–60	Return of theme 1a in *fortissimo* tutti woodwinds and brass followed by *fortississimo*, syncopated, jazz-like passage in flutes, oboes, clarinets, alto and tenor saxophones, trumpets, horns, and euphonium
	61–73	Thinly-scored staccato presentation of theme 1a in piccolo, flutes in octaves, and xylophone accompanied by horns; repeated in alto saxophone 1–2 in octaves accompanied by trumpets, tambourine, and wood block; thematic derivation leads to *fortississimo* tremolo and rapid descending and ascending patterns in woodwinds
Section 3	74–80	Theme 1a returns in staccato oboes, cup-muted trumpets, and trombone 1–2; slap-tongued alto and tenor saxophones repeat it with angular accompaniment in flutes
	81–90	Legato variation on theme 1 in clarinets with sustained horns joined by piccolo, flutes, and oboes; theme 2 returns in solo trumpet 2 accompanied rhythmically by solo trumpet 3 and tenor drum while saxophones sustain underneath; solo trumpet 1 leads to return of a 2/4 bar of silence

SECTION	MEASURE	EVENT AND SCORING
Coda	91–96	Final return of theme 1a with tutti *fortississimo* statement ending with three *sforzando* chordal cadential exclamations

Unit 8: Suggested Listening

Colgrass, Michael. *Urban Requiem*. *Urban Requiem: New Works for Winds and Percussion*. University of Miami Wind Ensemble. Gary Green, conductor. Albany Troy 212. 1995.

Danielpour, Richard. Transcribed by Jack Stamp. *Vox Populi*. *Ride*. Indiana University of Pennsylvania Wind Ensemble. Jack Stamp, conductor. Klavier K 11141. 2004.

Gorb, Adam. *Awayday*. *Deja View*. North Texas Wind Symphony. Eugene Migliaro Corporon, conductor. Klavier K 11091. 1998.

Gross, Murray. *Urban Myth*. *Urban Dreams*. North Texas Wind Symphony. Eugene Migliaro Corporon, conductor. GIA CD-743. 2008.

Harbison, John. *Three City Blocks*. *Paradigm*. Cincinnati College-Conservatory of Music Wind Symphony. Eugene Migliaro Corporon, conductor. Klavier K 11059. 1994.

Rorem, Ned:

> *Air Music and Eagles*. *Music of Ned Rorem*. Louisville Orchestra. Peter Leonard and Gerhardt Zimmermann, conductors. Albany Troy 047. 1991.

> *Sunday Morning*. *Ned Rorem Orchestral Works*. Atlanta Symphony Orchestra. Louis Lane, conductor. New World Records NW 353–2.

> *Symphony No. 3*. *Rorem: Three Symphonies*. Bournemouth Symphony Orchestra. José Serebrier, conductor. Naxos 8.559149. 2003.

Schuman, William. *George Washington Bridge*. *American Dreams*. Cincinnati College-Conservatory of Music Wind Symphony. Eugene Migliaro Corporon, conductor. Klavier K 11048. 1993.

Unit 9: Additional References and Resources

Easton, Jay C. *Writing for Saxophones: A Guide to the Tonal Palette of the Saxophone Family for Composers, Arrangers, and Performers*. Camas, WA: Baxter Music Publishing, 2007.

Johnson, Bret. "Still Sings the Voice: A Portrait of Ned Rorem." *Tempo, New Series* 153 (1985): 7–12.

McDonald, Arlys. *Ned Rorem: A Bio-Bibliography*. Westport, CT: Greenwood Press, 1989.

Rorem, Ned. *An Absolute Gift: A New Diary*. New York: Simon and Schuster, 1978.

_____. *Symphony No. 3*. New York: Boosey & Hawkes, 1960.

_____. *The Paris and New York Diaries of Ned Rorem: 1951–1961*. San Francisco: North Point Press, 1983.

Rorem, Ned. Daron Hagen, trans. *Traffic*. New York: Boosey & Hawkes, 2003.

Tommasini, Anthony. "Ned Rorem." In *Grove Music Online*. L. Macy, ed. http://www.grovemusic.com

For more information, go to http://www.nedrorem.com

Contributed by:

Andrew Trachsel
Interim Director of Bands
Ohio University
Athens, Ohio

---

1 Ned Rorem, "About Ned," The Ned Rorem Website, http://www.nedrorem.com
2 Ibid.
3 Ned Rorem, An Absolute Gift: A New Diary (New York: Simon and Schuster, 1978), 54.

Teacher Resource Guide

Vanity Fair

Percy E. Fletcher
(1879–1932)

edited by Brant Karrick
(b. 1960)

Unit 1: Composer

Percy Eastman Fletcher was born in Derby, England, and like a number of his composer contemporaries, made his living as a musical director in the London theatre world. He fulfilled this position successively at the Prince of Wales, Savoy, Daly's, Drury Lane, and from 1915 until his death, His Majesty's Theatre. Having received lessons on violin, piano, and organ, his creative activity was by no means confined to the theatre. In addition to producing light music for the theatre, Fletcher composed ballads, part-songs, choral works, orchestral suites, piano music, marches, works for organ, and works for military band.

In one respect Fletcher was an innovator. Before 1913, brass band contest pieces were customarily operatic selections and transcriptions, but in that year Fletcher was commissioned by the British National Championships to compose the tone poem *Labour and Love*, which is considered to be the first original piece for brass band. This paved the way for other significant composers to contribute test pieces for brass band contests, including Gustav Holst, Edvard Elgar, Gordon Jacob, and Ralph Vaughan Williams. Because of the success of his earlier work, Fletcher was again invited to provide a piece for the National Championships of 1926 and composed *An Epic Symphony*, also used as a test piece for the National Championships of 1938, 1951, and as recently as 1976. The three-movement work is highly reminiscent of Elgar, and could possibly be described as Fletcher's most serious work in any medium. Today, brass bands occasionally play *Labour and Love* and An *Epic Symphony*, much to the delight of their audiences, but sadly, most of Fletcher's music is rarely performed.

Unit 2: Composition

In the original 1924 publication of *Vanity Fair,* Fletcher included the subtitles, "A Comedy Overture" and "In Which Several Characters From Thackeray's Novel are Portrayed." The now-classic novel is a social satire set in early nineteenth-century England and Europe, and was first published in 1847. The story is somewhat cynical and is intended to depict social hypocrisy and fraud. Nine principal characters are woven within, their interaction being similar to a modern television soap opera. Thackeray's main point was that, in a world of social injustices, all people must sin in order to survive.

The themes of Fletcher's rather straightforward Romantic overture are pleasant, symmetric, light, and tonal, but do not particularly reflect the darker behaviors of the novel's main characters. Perhaps Fletcher personally related to the story, enjoyed the energy of the characters, or just needed some inspiration and a title. Whatever the case, the Grade 5 overture is six minutes in length and consists of four main themes.

Unit 3: Historical Perspective

Originally published in 1924 by Hawkes and Son, *Vanity Fair* was composed during the early development of repertoire for the wind or military band. As the majority of works for band at the time were transcriptions, Gustav Holst and Ralph Vaughan Williams seem to have taken the lead in composing serious and high-quality works for band. Perhaps their example sparked Fletcher's interest in the medium, or maybe he became attracted to the ensemble from his prior success with his brass band pieces. Regardless, Fletcher's melodies and harmonies are more romantic and his scoring more lush and less in the mold of the famous British military band suites. The 2006 edition keeps true to Fletcher's original scoring, but adds missing instruments for the modern symphonic band including oboe 2, cornet 3, B-flat bass clarinet, contrabass clarinet, and mallet percussion.

Unit 4: Technical Considerations

The woodwind parts, particularly flute, clarinet, and alto saxophone, contain many sixteenth-note passages and are considerably harder than the brass parts. Although these more technical parts are comprised mostly of scales and scale patterns, the tempo of quarter note = 144 and the number of notes in a grouping can prove challenging.

Proficiency in the keys of B-flat, F, and D-flat major is a must. The fast outer sections are in B-flat and F, while the lyrical and lush middle section is in D-flat. The solo and first clarinet parts go above high C on many occasions and are often rhythmically independent. The solo clarinet part ascends to high G and is the most challenging part of the entire ensemble.

Prominent solos include clarinet, cornet, and euphonium, while shorter solos are required of flute and oboe. While the E-flat clarinet part could be omitted, it adds a strong upper octave to the clarinet choir. However, it is similar in difficulty to clarinet 1. It is interesting to note that Fletcher originally scored for two E-flat clarinets as did Holst in his *First Suite in E-flat.*

The opening section could certainly work well at a tempo a little slower than as marked, and the closing tempo of quarter note = 152 can be downright treacherous! Conductors are encouraged to find the right tempi, even if a little slower, that fit the ensemble's musical and technical ability.

Finally, brass and percussion can easily overpower the woodwinds. Those sections should generally play at least one dynamic less than indicated, and woodwinds, especially when carrying the melodic line, should play a little louder.

Unit 5: Stylistic Considerations

All players are called on to use a myriad of articulations throughout the work. Included is a light staccato, a broad marcato, and the singing style legato with many slurred phrases. While flute and brass players can be encouraged to use a double-tongue with sixteenth notes during the fast sections, reed players will need to develop a clean, fast, and light single tongue.

While the opening theme is to be played "with gay vivacity" dynamic contrast, especially on the softer side, is decidedly important to the effective performance of this piece. This is especially true for the highly romantic middle section which showcases a beautiful melody to be played "with sentimental expression." There is tremendous potential for rubato and expression within this section that is needed to more fully contrast the quick and steady pulse of the outer sections. Percussion scoring is similar to other band pieces of this vintage and perhaps should be felt more than heard.

Unit 6: Musical Elements

MELODY:

All four main themes are diatonic. They are given in figures 1–4.

FIGURE 1. Theme 1

FIGURE 2. Theme 2

FIGURE 3. Theme 3

FIGURE 4. Theme 4

HARMONY:
The harmonic language of *Vanity Fair* is primarily triadic and traditional. Some major seventh and dominant seventh chords are used. Including chorales and homophonic chordal warm-ups into the daily warm up can help prepare a band for the necessary tuning and blend requirements.

RHYTHM:
The main melodic rhythm is mostly eighth and sixteenth notes. The rhythm of the third theme alternates a triple-duple feel with triplet eighth notes and eighth notes. Often players will try to compress the duple eighth notes that follow a triplet (see figure 3). Woodwinds will need to have strong technique and be able to play scales and scale patterns quickly. Many technique and fundamentals method books include appropriate patterns in most keys which could be included in daily drill and training.

TIMBRE:
Woodwinds have the melody for the majority of the piece. Brass introduces the third main theme. The scoring is dense and tutti much of the time. The slow middle section begins and ends with woodwind choir.

Unit 7: Form and Structure

SECTION	MEASURE	EVENT AND SCORING
A	1–22	Theme 1; melody in soprano voices; homophonic tutti scoring; B-flat major
	23–52	Theme 2; melody in flutes and clarinets; F major
	53–68	Theme 3; brass ensemble then tutti; F major
	69–86	Theme 3 continued; sequence; tutti scoring; more polyphonic; F major

SECTION	MEASURE	EVENT AND SCORING
	87–99	Codetta; scoring thins; includes traces of themes 1 and 3;
	100–106	Transition; horns and woodwinds; modulation to D-flat major
B	107–115	Theme 4; woodwind choir; D-flat major
	116–127	Developmental; cornet and euphonium duet; F major with shifting keys to F-flat and A-flat major
	128–146	Theme 4 restated; polyphonic tutti scoring becoming sparse; D-flat major
	147–166	Re-transition; includes themes 1 and 3 in counterpoint; F major
A	167–182	Return of theme 1; melody in soprano voices; tutti scoring; B-flat major
	183–194	Extension; includes themes 1 and 3 in counterpoint followed by theme 2
	195–228	Theme 3 continued; sequence; tutti scoring; similar to mm. 69–86 but now centered on the tonic, B-flat major
	229–251	Closing section; theme 1 variant; woodwind melody, brass accompaniment; tempo increases; theme 3 added in brass; scoring thickens; B-flat major
	252–263	Closing section continues; theme 4 restated in augmentation in brass; B-flat major
Coda	264-end	Theme 3 motive; brass fanfare; B-flat major

Unit 8: Suggested Listening

Elgar, Edward. *Enigma Variations*.
Fletcher, Percy. *An Epic Symphony*.
Holst, Gustav. *A Moorside Suite*.
Jacob, Gordon. *Prelude to Revelry*.
Walton, William. *Crown Imperial*.
Wood, Haydn:
    Mannin Veen
    A Manx Overture

Unit 9: Additional References and Resources

Scowcroft, Philip. *British Light Music: A Personal Gallery of 20th Century Composers*. London: Thames, 1997.

Thackery, William Makepeace. *Vanity Fair*. New York, NY: Barnes and Noble Classics, 2003.

Websites:

http://www.hatii.arts.gla.ac.uk/MultimediaStudentProjects/0001/ 9805164r/brassbands/brassbandstoday.htm

http://www.musicweb-international.com/garlands/fletcher.htm

Contributed by:

Brant Karrick
Director of Bands
Associate Professor of Music
Northern Kentucky University
Highland Heights, Kentucky

Teacher Resource Guide

Vranjanka

Kenneth Hesketh
(b. 1968)

Unit 1: Composer

Kenneth Hesketh, born in Liverpool on July 20, 1968, has composed works in numerous genres, including symphonic and brass band, opera, orchestra, chamber, vocal, and solo. His works for symphonic band are performed around the world and have been recorded by British, Japanese, American, and Canadian ensembles.

Hesketh began composing while a chorister at the Liverpool Anglican Cathedral. From 1987 to 1992 he pursued studies at the Royal College of Music in London with Edwin Roxburgh, Joseph Horovitz, and Simon Bainbridge; he completed his first formal commission, a work for the Royal Liverpool Philharmonic Orchestra under Sir Charles Groves in 1987.

After receiving his bachelor and postgraduate degrees, Hesketh worked in commercial music and completed additional commissions. He attended the Tanglewood Music Center in 1995 as a Leonard Bernstein Fellow, where he was a student of French composer Henri Dutilleux. In 1996 he began a master of music degree in composition at the University of Michigan. Ensuing awards have included a Shakespeare Prize scholarship from the Toepfer Foundation in Hamburg (1996), an award from the Liverpool Foundation for Sport and the Arts (1999), and the Constant and Kit Lambert Fellowship at the Royal College of Music in London (1999). Since 2003 he has served at the Royal College of Music as a professor of composition and orchestration.

Hesketh was a New Music Fellow at Kettle's Yard and Corpus Christi College, Cambridge from 2003–2005, where he curated a series of new music chamber concerts. Hesketh has received numerous commissions which include the Fromm Foundation at Harvard University, the Continuum Ensemble, a Faber Millennium Commission for Birmingham Contemporary Music Group premiered under Sir Simon Rattle, the BBC Philharmonic conducted by Vasilly Sinaisky, Hans Werner Henze and the Endymion, the Munich Biennale, the Michael Vyner Trust for the London Sinfonietta, and The Opera Group.

In 2007 Hesketh began a two-year tenure as Composer in the House with the Royal Liverpool Philharmonic Orchestra.

Unit 2: Composition

The Guildhall School of Music and Drama Wind Orchestra at the Royal Northern College of Music performed the world premiere of *Vranjanka* on November 6, 2005. The work was composed on commission from Timothy and Hilary Reynish in memory of their son, William. Since leaving the Royal Northern College of Music in 2002, Reynish has commissioned over twenty works in memory of his third son, who died in the Pyrenees in 2001. Hesketh's *The Cloud of Unknowing* (2004), published by Schott, is also included in "The William Reynish Commissioning Project."

The composer provides the following program note on the publisher's website:

> *Vranjanka* (the title means "From Vranje," a town in southern Serbia, pronounced VRAHN-yahn-kah) is loosely based on the traditional folksong "Šano Dušo." The melody exists in two versions, one in 7/8 and one in 3/4. I have chosen the version in 7/8 and in doing so, have extended the melodic ideas of the original with new material.[1]

Following a four-measure introduction, *Vranjanka* consists of two sections. The slow section includes extended and sustained lines as the composer presents characteristics of the theme using irregular phrase lengths; soloistic woodwind writing is featured. The second section realizes the folksong as a set of variations that includes characteristics of the melody as well as newly-composed material. The entire work is approximately eight and a half minutes in length.

Unit 3: Historical Perspective

The history of music in southeastern Europe can be categorized into religious, court, and folk music. Complex rhythmic patterns and structures are a significant characteristic of traditional music in Serbia and throughout the Balkan region. Traditional folk instruments include various kinds of bagpipes (gaida), flutes, diple, tamburitza, and gusle. "Šano Dušo." is derived from the 1930s opera *Kostana*, which dramatized the life of a Romantic artist. Songs from the opera became popularized and accepted in the folk repertoire of Vranje.

There is a growing body of repertoire for symphonic band based on the folksongs and dances of cultures from around the world. The inclusion of these works in the symphonic band repertoire gives ensemble musicians access to additional melodic, harmonic, rhythmic, and timbral vocabulary as well as an additional cultural perspective.

Unit 4: Technical Considerations

Vranjanka includes some difficult writing for solo instruments, especially woodwind (flute, oboe, and E-flat and B-flat clarinet), horn, and trumpet. Saxophones are used to provide countermelodies while low reeds and low brass primarily provide rhythmic and harmonic interest. Percussion parts have both melodic and harmonic functions throughout the first and second sections. Percussion parts include timpani, snare drum, bass drum, vibraphone, glockenspiel, xylophone, chimes, tam-tam, triangle, tom-toms, suspended cymbal, finger cymbals, and crash cymbals. There are significant piano and harp parts; piano is essential to a successful performance of the work.

The work includes unison melodic lines that are challenging from both a rhythmic and intonation perspective. Unison writing in upper brass ranges requires a great deal of skill in the section, particularly for cornet and trumpet. Figure 1 illustrates trumpet 1– in a passage that also includes horn 1–4 and cornets 1–3 in a chromatic and dissonant harmonic passage.

FIGURE 1. Mm. 44–47, trumpet 1–2

The work is composed without a key signature, so there are extensive accidentals in both score and parts. There are a significant number of irregular subdivisions in the opening section that require careful counting and performance accuracy, especially since the tempo is established at quarter note = 66. Rhythmic division of the beat in the first section includes division by two, three, four, five, and six. In addition, the work includes a large number of syncopated rhythmic passages.

Throughout *Vranjanka* specific attention must be paid to articulation, as accents, staccatos, and slurring of rhythm patterns contribute to the rhythmic energy of the work. The tempo marking in the 7/8 section of the work is quarter note = 158, and this fast tempo poses challenges for clear articulation of slurs, staccatos, and accents, especially when combined with the written dynamic markings.

Unit 5: Stylistic Considerations

The work is in the style and character of a dance; it is theatre music with role development. The work does not present itself as a melody with accompaniment, but more as leading melodic characters and supporting actors. In order to achieve this, Hesketh's detailed stylistic, dynamic, articulation, and tempo markings must be adhered to with a great deal of attention. It is the contrast of these details that creates the style of the work. Articulations are especially significant in section 2, *ritmico*, where the lilting irregular subdivision is accentuated through deliberate articulation choices. The original melodic ideas maintain the character of the traditional folksong, but the contrasting phrase lengths, melodic construction, and scoring contribute to the unique character of the work.

Unit 6: Musical Elements

MELODY:
The melody of this Serbian love song is traditionally performed by female voice with accompaniment by traditional instruments. The basic form of the melody is aabba'a' with distinct four-measure phrases. The folk melody is presented in mm. 52–75 and shown in figure 2.

A well-prepared performance of the work will include attention to the placement of grace notes, slurs, staccatos, and accents articulated by the composer. The composer indicates that the text for *Vranjanka* has only influenced the composition at an unconscious level, but it is included here for reference.

Sana, my soul, opens the door to me
Open the door to me and I will give you coins.
My heart is burning for you, Sana.
Your fair face, Sana, is snow from the mountains,
Your forehead, Sana, is like moonlight.
That mouth of yours, Sana, like a deep red sunset,
That eye, my darling, makes me burn.
When night comes, marvelous Sana, I twist in sadness,
Your beauty, Sana, will not let me sleep.

Section 1 of Hesketh's composition consists of dramatic melodic gestures in the woodwinds. In section 2 the principal melody's modal melodic construction is repetitive, but the altered ornamentation and rhythmic subdivision create melodic interest.

FIGURE 2. Mm. 52–75, oboe 1–2

HARMONY:

The work begins with a tonal center on C. Chromaticism and dissonance are prevalent throughout the work, and there is significant emphasis on the interval of a perfect fifth (particularly C–G and G–D in the low brass and low reeds). Mm. 20–21 provide an example of a simple cadential pattern from G to C, and mm. 88–89 provide an example of a cadential pattern from D to G. There are numerous examples of pedal tone passages centered on C, B-flat, and G. In addition, there is a great deal of use of minor and major seconds and sevenths.

RHYTHM:

The rhythmic flexibility of Hesketh's style gives this work's melodies an improvisatory character. An example of this characteristic can be found in oboe 1 in section 1 of the work.

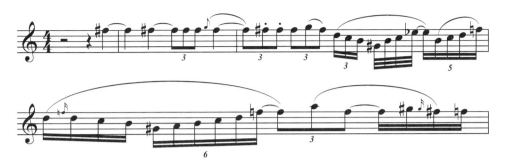

FIGURE 3. Mm. 28–31, oboe

This rhythmic writing creates a strong effect, but makes precision difficult from mm. 7 to 34.

The original folk dance appears in 7/8, but the work also employs the key signatures of 4/4, 5/4, and 6/8. The contrast between duple and triple subdivision is first established in mm. 1–5 of the timpani part.

FIGURE 4. Mm. 1–5, timpani

This rhythmic contrast is especially significant in section 2, written primarily in 7/8 and 4/4.

The work provides both passages with rhythmic unison ensemble writing (e.g., mm. 35–36 and 153–155) and parts with complete rhythmically independent voices (e.g., mm. 25–34 and 114–125). Figure 5 illustrates the ensemble unison employed in section 1.

FIGURE 5. Mm. 35–36, oboe

TIMBRE:

The composer's appreciation of Franco-Russian music of the nineteenth and twentieth centuries has influenced the colorful orchestration of his compositions. Hesketh favors complex textures, but the transparency of his writing ensures that even complex rhythmic countermelodies are heard.

The work includes significant textural contrasts. M. 186 is an example of full ensemble writing. Chamber writing is seen in mm. 7–11 and 114–121. Chimes play a significant rhythmic and melodic line in mm. 206–218.

There are a large number of dynamics given, and significant dynamic contrasts are provided (e.g., the *con tutta forza fortissimo* introduction in m. 1 diminishes to a *pianissimo* staccato in m. 4).

Unit 7: Form and Structure

The musical form of the piece includes a fairly slow introductory section in which only hints of the them are heard. A faster second section includes a set of variations on the folksong *Vranjanka*. These are not variations in the traditional sense with clearly marked beginnings and endings, but rather developments of the folksong's melodic material with additional contrasting and complementary original material.

SECTION	MEASURE	EVENT AND SCORING
Introduction	1–4	Opening timpani solo; ensemble begins at *fortissimo* and decreases to *pianissimo* in m. 4; establishes key center of C
Section 1	5–47	Full ensemble writing; *con tutta forza* (quarter note = 66)
Section 2	48–205	*Ritmico* (quarter note = 158); developmental variation technique
Coda	206–227	Pedal tones in low brass and low reeds; short melodic phrases with allusion to sections 1 and 2

Unit 8: Suggested Listening

Chobanian, Loris. *Armenian Dances*.
Gorb, Adam. *Dances from Crete*.
Hesketh, Kenneth:
    The Gilded Theatre
    Masque
Reed, Alfred. *Armenian Dances* (parts 1 and 2).
?ano Du?o. A recording of a traditional performance is accessible at:
    http://www.dunav.org.il/dances/serbia/vranjanka.html
Sparke, Philip. *Dance Movements*.
Wilson, Dana. *Dance of the New World*.

Unit 9: Additional References and Resources

Kenneth Hesketh. http://www.schott-music.com/shop/persons/featured/38082/index.html

The William Reynish Commissioning Project. http://www.timothyreynish.com

Information on *Šano Dušo* and *Vranjanka*. http://www.dunav.org.il/dances/serbia/vranjanka.html

Description of the dance movements. http://www.phantomranch.net/folk-danc/dances/vranjank.htm

Contributed by:

Wendy McCallum
Instrumental Music Education Specialist
Brandon University
Brandon, Manitoba, Canada

---

1 http://www.schott-music.com/shop/persons/featured/38082/index.html

2 http://www.dunav.org.il/dances/serbia/vranjanka.html

3 http://www.schott-music.com/shop/persons/featured/38082/index.html

Teacher Resource Guide

Wild Nights!

Frank Ticheli
(b. 1958)

Unit 1: Composer

Frank Ticheli joined the faculty of the Thornton School of Music at the University of Southern California in 1991, where he is professor of composition. From 1991 to 1998, Ticheli was composer-in-residence of the Pacific Symphony, and he still enjoys a close working relationship with that orchestra and their music director, Carl St. Clair.

Ticheli's orchestral works have received considerable recognition in the United States and Europe. Orchestral performances have come from the Philadelphia Orchestra, Atlanta Symphony, Detroit Symphony, Dallas Symphony, American Composers Orchestra, the radio orchestras of Stuttgart, Frankfurt, Saarbruecken, and Austria, and the orchestras of Austin, Bridgeport, Charlotte, Colorado, Haddonfield, Harrisburg, Hong Kong, Jacksonville, Lansing, Long Island, Louisville, Lubbock, Memphis, Nashville, Omaha, Phoenix, Portland, Richmond, San Antonio, San Jose, and others.

Ticheli's music has been described as being "optimistic and thoughtful" (Los Angeles Times), "lean and muscular" (New York Times), "brilliantly effective" (Miami Herald) and "powerful, deeply felt crafted with impressive flair and an ear for striking instrumental colors" (South Florida Sun-Sentinel).

Ticheli is well known for his works for concert band, many of which have become standards in the repertoire. In addition to composing, he has appeared as guest conductor of his music at Carnegie Hall, at many American universities and music festivals, and in cities throughout the world. Frank Ticheli is the winner of the 2006 NBA/William D. Revelli Memorial Band Composition

Contest for his *Symphony No. 2*. Other awards for his music include the Charles Ives and the Goddard Lieberson Awards, both from the American Academy of Arts and Letters, the Walter Beeler Memorial Prize, and First Prize awards in the Texas Sesquicentennial Orchestral Composition Competition, Britten-on-the-Bay Choral Composition Contest, and Virginia CBDNA Symposium for New Band Music.

Frank Ticheli received his doctoral and masters degrees in composition from The University of Michigan, where he studied with William Albright, George Wilson, Leslie Bassett, and William Bolcom.[1]

Unit 2: Composition

Wild Nights! was commissioned by the California Band Directors Association in celebration of their fiftieth anniversary. The work was premiered at the Saroyan Theater on February 18, 2007 with Timothy Salzman conducting the California All-State Symphonic Honor Band in Fresno, California.

About this work, the composer states:

WILD NIGHTS! is a joyous, colorful seven-minute musical journey inspired by Emily Dickenson's poem:

> Wild Nights! Wild Nights!
> Were I with thee,
> Wild Nights should be
> Our luxury!
>
> Futile the winds
> To a heart in port,–
> Done with the compass,
> Done with the chart.
>
> Rowing in Eden!
> Ah! the sea!
> Might I but moot
> To-night in Thee!

Numerous composers have set the words of WILD NIGHTS! to music (Lee Hoiby's song setting and John Adams' *Harmonium* come immediately to mind). However, to my knowledge, no one has used this wonderfully sensuous poem as the basis for a purely instrumental tone poem. This is my aim, and in so doing I focused most heavily on the lines "Done with the compass/Done with the chart" and "Rowing in Eden/Ah! the sea!" These words suggested the sense of freedom and ecstatic joy that I tried to express in my work.

Throughout the piece, even during its darker middle section, the music is mercurial, impetuous, optimistic. A jazzy rhythmic motive permeates the journey. Unexpected events come and go, lending spontaneity and a sense of freedom. The work is composed in five distinct sections, but contained within each section are numerous surprises and a devil-may-care swagger. Surprises are found at every turn, and continue right through to the final cadence.[2]

Unit 3: Historical Perspective

Ticheli's compositions cover a wide spectrum of performance mediums and reflect a wide interest in compositional style. Ticheli has received notoriety for his interest in writing quality music that is accessible both technically and aesthetically to wide range of performers. While he feels strongly about the wind band's emergence as one of the premiere performing mediums in the twenty-first century, he also sees himself as clearly interested in a wide variety of performance mediums.

> I don't like the idea of writing for one medium. I would just get sick of writing for band all the time. I don't like the idea of someone calling himself or herself a "band" composer, or "choral" composer, or "orchestra" composer. For me I think it's really important to keep changing things—it keeps things interesting and I think it keeps my music fresh.[3]

Ticheli understands the long compositional heritage of western music and feels comfortable in using many traditional techniques with a new twist in his music. In discussing composers that he admires, Ticheli states,

> I tend to lean toward composers whom I love, people like Britten, Mahler, Bach, Stravinsky, Barber, and Copland. I actually like Alban Berg a lot, too. And I enjoy the music of Carl Nielson, John Adams and Bernstein—just a whole array.[4]

The composer acknowledges that his writing was most influenced by Bach, Beethoven, and Stravinsky.

> I am in awe of Bach. It's not just the counterpoint that impresses me. His melodic gifts rival those of just about anyone else for sheer grace and beauty. [With Beethoven,] it has a lot to do with the burning sense of urgency that drives the music right to the very end. No other composer can move my soul with such directness and power. Every composer has had to come to grips with the music of Igor Stravinsky, and not just for his rhythmic innovations. There is much more, including the harmonic boldness in works such as *The Rite of Spring*,

the spirituality in works such as *Symphony of Psalms*, and the extraordinary use of color in works such as *Agon*. No other twentieth-century composer's music has changed me more deeply at every level.[5]

Craig T. Pare best summarizes Ticheli's approach to composition:

While the twentieth-century music was an eclectic, broad range of compositional styles where sounds, effects, textures, and esoteric formulas were favored, composers in the last fifteen to twenty years have returned to more familiar and understandable compositional means hoping to pique the interest of, and communicate with, listeners immediately. A prominent feature of Ticheli's style is his use of melodies and themes that form the foundation of the growth and development of a work's progress. Whether they are familiar tunes (*Amazing Grace, Shenandoah,* or *Cajun Folk Songs*) or original melodies or motives (*Postcard*), the composer's reliance on these understandable musical elements allows the listener to follow their progress of transformation and development through the course of the piece.[6]

Unit 4: Technical Considerations

On the rhythmic level, technical considerations in this work include maintaining a precise rhythmic pulse, accurately placing sixteenth-note motives into the moving texture, and maintaining the rhythmic drive of the music. Care must be taken to highlight accents and accurately deliver staccato and marcato articulations. Attention must be given to accurate dynamics, including abrupt contrasts and kaleidoscopic shifts in dynamics as well as color and timbre. The conductor must ensure an accurate balance between long, lyric lines and rapid motivic development. Soloistic writing is presented in alto saxophone, trumpets and marimba. Octave glissandi appear in unison horns on concert D-flat.

Unit 5: Stylistic Considerations

In reflecting on Ticheli's compositional style, Linda Moorhouse states:

His music illustrates compositional techniques such as polytonality, modal mixture, counterpoint, canons, augmentation, fragmentation, plaindrone, sequences, ostinatos, walking bass lines, and motive repetition for unity purposes, among many others... His lyrical writing is among the most attractive and sensitive in our current wind band repertoire, and his spirited compositions have a drive to them that is inherently "Ticheli"...[7]

In discussing his compositional style, Ticheli writes:

Since everything that I do has been done before (polymeter, polytonality, modal mixture, added note chords, old forms, etc.) it would make no sense to ignore past masters, because their music holds the keys to all our problems. Of course the real challenge is to make a borrowed technique work in a new context, with new musical ideas. The technique has to be absorbed, and it must serve the greater soul in life of the new piece. There is always a degree of something old in something new. Every new idea has to be rooted in some tradition, and every traditional technique is given a new life.

Like so many composers these days, I am drawn to a dizzying array of influences. For example, in my work for soprano and orchestra, *An American Dream*, I mix a whole gumbo of musical influences—classicism, modernist techniques, Americana, New Orleans jazz, even gospel. You can also hear echoes of Mahler, Copland and Britten... Chromatic mediant modulation is a really important modulation in much of my music. And there's really nothing original about that. Beethoven did it a lot.[8]

Concerning the importance of texture and orchestration is his music, Ticheli states:

Tutti scoring is, of course, most effective when used sparingly... I've certainly developed my own sense of orchestral thumbprints over time. I love reinforcing accents by doubling the attack point with a string bass pizzicato or a muted trumpet bite, the removing the doubling during the sustained portion of the note. This keeps the texture translucent and light, while zinging life into the accents. I also love exploring how an instrument's personality can change with its register—the sensuality of the flute in lower octave... I sometimes enjoy superimposing several layers of activity to make a complex texture. The trick is to strive for maximum activity without sacrificing transparency. If things get too complex, the individual layers combine to form one amalgam, and then I've defeated my purpose... The secret, for me, is to keep air space within and between the individual layers. I use rests within each layer so that a brief window is opened for another layer to come through. Also, I tend to assign each layer its own register and rhythmic identity to maintain its individuality.[9]

Unit 6: Musical Elements

MELODY:

About his melodic writing, Ticheli states:

> When composing, I usually need to think small at first, I can't think "large"... At some point I will have what Joan Tower calls a "package," what others call a section. And so I'll have this package, and it will tell me a lot of what the piece is about—sort of reveal some of the DNA of the piece. And then I'll sit down and try to compose another package... My musical ideas come from many small things that eventually suggest something larger.[10]

With this in mind, conductors must carefully identify motives and recognize motivic development, fragmentation, and augmentation as an essential component in Ticheli's music. The layering of short melodic fragments contrasted against longer, sweeping lyric material should always be clarified in musical preparation.

HARMONY:

Note the frequent use of polytonality presented during sections of *Wild Nights!* The composer frequently alters traditional scalar material with octatonic throughout the composition. Ticheli's use of parallel chords, major chords descending by thirds, and pedals should be noted.

RHYTHM:

Rhythmic drive and high energy are hallmarks of Ticheli's music. He states, "I want energy behind the notes!"[11] Performers will find repeated rhythmic motion reminiscent of the sea contrasted by short, punctuated rhythmic motives. The use of syncopation and heavily accented material frequently obscures the traditional musical pulse.

TIMBRE:

Ticheli is highly sensitive to timbre and the pairing or contrasting of specific instrumental sonorities. He frequently assigns various color instruments (e.g., bass clarinet and English horn) with an assigned register or rhythmic identity in his music. There is a highly contrapuntal aspect in his use of orchestral timbres, and he tends to avoid thick, heavily doubled orchestrations.

Unit 7: Form and Structure

The full score to *Wild Nights!* contains a detailed discussion by the composer. Ticheli breaks his work into five sections:

SECTION	MEASURES
A	1–65
B	66–151
A[1]	152–194
C	195–239
Coda	240–252[12]

Section A opens boldly in F major with a descending line in trumpets and trombones. During this opening section, Ticheli presents a large number of rhythmic motives which are vigorously tossed throughout the band. The section develops these motives in a highly syncopated manner. Broken rhythmic patterns and shifting meters lead to the section's chordal climax in m. 54.

Section B introduces a more cohesive, forward-moving line built on an ostinato in the woodwinds. Above this material, the composer continues to develop small motivic fragments. M. 66 introduces the primary B theme in alto saxophone. This long, lyrical line is continued, with flute, oboe, and trumpet joining the melodic statement. In m. 96, the section continues to develop both contrapuntally and harmonically, leading to a dance-like figure introduced in the low brass and bassoon in m. 118. A softer closing section in m. 138 leads to a return of the A material in m. 157.

The work's third section (mm. 152–194) presents a modified recapitulation of the earlier A material. The section concludes with strong contrapuntal statements leading to a dramatic climax prior to the unexpected arrival of Section C in m. 195.

The fourth section (mm. 195–239) presents chiming chords in woodwinds and percussion. After a brief slowing of the feverish rhythmic drive of earlier sections, the rhythmic momentum is re-established in m. 200. New melodic and textural material is introduced in m. 206, contrasting short rhythmic outbursts in woodwinds set against a four-mallet marimba ostinato pattern. Strong rhythmic development of the sixteenth-note motive introduced in woodwinds leads to the work's powerful chorale-like climax in mm. 229–239.

The work concludes with a twelve-measure coda (m. 240–252). Against a rhythmic wall of woodwind triplets, Ticheli sets an octatonic scalar passage in the brass over an F-sharp pedal in the tuba. In the last five measures, the composer returns to material from the B section to powerfully propel the composition to close in G-flat.

Unit 8: Suggested Listening

Ticheli, Frank. *Blue Shades*. *Deja View*. North Texas Wind Symphony. Eugene Migliaro Corporon, conductor. Klavier Records KCD 11091.

Postcard. The Cincinnati Wind Symphony. Eugene Migliaro Corporon, conductor. Klavier Records KCD 11071.

Symphony No. 2. Allegories. North Texas Wind Symphony. Eugene Migliaro Corporon, conductor. Klavier Records K1114.

Vesuvius. 1999 WASBE. North Texas Wind Symphony. Eugene Migliaro Corporon, conductor. Mark Records MCD 3144.

Unit 9: Additional References and Resources

Camphouse, Mark, ed. *Composers on Composing for Band*. Chicago: GIA Publications, Inc., 2002.

Salzman, Timothy. *A Composer's Insight, Volume 3*. Galesville, MD: Meredith Music Publications, 2006.

Ticheli, Frank. *WILD NIGHTS!* Brooklyn, NY: Manhattan Beach Music, 2007.

Websites:
  Frank Ticheli. www.frankticheli.com
  Manhattan Beach Music. www.manhattanbeachmusic.com

Contributed by:

Edward C. Harris
Director of Bands
San Jose State University
San Jose, California

---

1 "Frank Ticheli," http://www.manhattanbeachmusiconline.com/frank_ticheli/bio.html/

2 Frank Ticheli, *Wild Nights!* (Brooklyn, NY: Manhattan Beach Music, 2007).

3 Linda R. Moorhouse, "Frank Ticheli," *A Composer's Insight*, Timothy Salzman, ed. (Gainesville, MD: Meredith Music Publications, 2006), 209.

4 Ibid, 207.

5 Ibid.

6 Ibid, 210.

7 Ibid, 207.

8 Ibid, 208.

9 Ibid.

10 Ibid, 206.

11 Ibid, 207.

12 Frank Ticheli, *Wild Nights!* (Brooklyn, NY: Manhattan Beach Music, 2007).

Grade Six

Teacher Resource Guide

Anahita

Roshanne Etezady
(b. 1973)

Unit 1: Composer

As a young musician, Roshanne Etezady studied piano and flute, and developed an interest in many different styles of music. One fateful evening in 1986, she saw Philip Glass and his ensemble perform as the musical guests on *Saturday Night Live*. This event marked the beginning of her interest in contemporary classical music and composing.

Previously a fellow at the Aspen Music Festival, Norfolk Chamber Music Festival, and Atlantic Center for the Arts, Roshanne Etezady earned recognition from the American Academy of Arts and Letters, Korean Society of 21st Century Music, Jacob K. Javits Foundation, Meet the Composer, and ASCAP. She has received commissions from the Albany Symphony, Dartmouth Symphony, eighth blackbird, Music at the Anthology, and PRISM Saxophone Quartet. Performers and ensembles including Rêlache, Amadinda Percussion Ensemble, Ensemble De Ereprijs, and Dogs of Desire have performed Etezady's music throughout the United States and Europe.

As one of the founding members of the Minimum Security Composers Collective, Etezady has helped expand the audience for new music. Through collaborative projects with performing ensembles as well as creative outreach programs, MSCC creates an open dialogue between composers, performers, and audiences.

As an active teacher, Etezady taught at the University of Arizona, Interlochen Arts Camp, Yale University, Saint Mary's College, and Crane School of Music at SUNY, Potsdam. She has given masterclasses at MIT, Holy Cross College, The Juilliard School, and Norfolk Chamber Music Festival.

Etezady holds a bachelor of music degree from Northwestern University and a master of music degree from Yale University. She has worked intensively with numerous composers, including William Bolcom, Martin Bresnick, Michael Daugherty, and Ned Rorem. In 2005, she completed her doctorate at the University of Michigan, and currently resides in Tucson, Arizona.

Unit 2: Composition

Written in 2005, *Anahita* was premiered by the University of Michigan Symphony Band, conducted by Michael Haithcock. This three-movement work contains 289 measures and is approximately fourteen minutes in length. The title refers to the Zoroastrian goddess of the night, Anahita. The goddess served as an inspiration to many in the arts. Etezady found inspiration for this composition from photographs of a mural painted by William Morris Hunt, titled *The Flight of Night*. In her notes in the score, Etezady describes the picture of the mural.

> This mural depicts the Persian deity, Anahita, goddess of the night and the moon, as she drives her chariot, pulled by three enormous, spirited horses, across the sky, fleeing the rising sun as a new day begins. At her feet, two figures sleep peacefully in each other's arms, despite the fury of the horses pulling the chariot.

William Morris Hunt, a painter from New England, was inspired to create this mural after reading a Persian poem about Anahita. Hunt received this poem from his brother in 1846 and immediately began to incorporate it into his art. Much of his sketches and work centered around this concept, and in 1878 he was commissioned to paint two murals in the Assembly Chamber of the State Capital Building in Albany, New York. His mural of Anahita, *The Flight of Night*, was the result of that commission. At a size of nearly eighteen feet, the mural was considered to be one of his finest pieces. Two years after the completion of the work, the ceiling of the Assembly Chamber began to leak, damaging the mural. In 1888, the ceiling was condemned and a false ceiling was installed, covering all but the very bottom of the mural. Only the horse's hooves in the mural remain to be seen today.

Unit 3: Historical Perspective

The following is the English translation of the Persian poem that inspired William Morris Hunt to create his mural of Anahita, *The Flight of Night*:

> Enthroned upon her car of light, the moon
> Is circling down the lofty heights of Heaven;
> Her well-trained courses wedge the blindest depths
> With fearful plunge, yet heed the steady hand

That guides their lonely way. So swift her course,
So bright her smile, she seems on silver wings.
O'er-reaching space, to glide the airy main;
Behind, far-flowing, spreads her deep blue veil,
Inwrought with stars that shimmer in its wave.
Before the car, an owl, gloom sighted, flaps
His weary way; with melancholy hoot
Dispelling spectral shades that flee
With bat-like rush, affrighted, back
Within the blackest nooks of caverned Night.
Still Hours of darkness wend around the car,
By raven tresses half concealed; but one,
With fairer locks, seems lingering back for Day.
Yet all with even measured footsteps mark
Her onward course. And floating in her train
Repose lies nestled on the breast of Sleep,
While soft Desires enclasp the waist of Dreams,
And light-winged Fanices flit around in troops.[1]

Etezady titled the movements of her piece based on the mural and the text of the poem. She describes the three movements in her program notes:

The first movement, "The Flight of Night," is characterized by dramatic, aggressive gestures that are meant to evoke the terrifying beauty of the goddess herself. Movement two, "Night Mares," is a scherzo-like movement that refers to the three monstrous horses that pull the chariot across the sky. In the final movement, "Sleep and Repose/The Coming of Light," we hear the gentler side of the night, with a tender lullaby that ends with distant trumpets heralding the dawn.

Unit 4: Technical Considerations

Anahita is scored for full concert band, including piccolo, flute 1–2, oboe 1–2, English horn, clarinet 1–3, bass clarinet, bassoon 1–2, contrabassoon, alto saxophone 1–2, tenor saxophone, baritone saxophone, trumpet/antiphonal trumpet 1–4, horn 1–4, trombone 1–3, euphonium 1–2, tuba 1–2, harp, and percussion. The harp is very important, as it has an extended solo in movement 3. Trumpets will need the following mutes: cup, harmon, plunger, straight, and straight metal. Trombones require both straight metal and cup mutes.

Required percussion instruments include timpani, bass drum, snare drum, tom-toms (high and medium), glockenspiel, vibraphone, marimba, brake drum, suspended cymbal, triangle, cabasa, rainstick, crotales, tam-tam, tambourine, and vibraslap. A minimum of four percussionists are needed to perform this piece. It may be necessary to have two rainsticks available for movement 3 because the rainstick writing is too extended in length for one instrument to play smoothly and continuously throughout the line without a break in sound.

Anahita was written for a mature ensemble. One of the biggest challenges is balance. The piece alternates between thick scoring and highly exposed writing for individual instruments. Throughout the thickly-scored areas it will be necessary to carefully balance all lines, especially within some of the heavier brass and percussion writing. Solo lines for piccolo, flute, oboe, trombone, euphonium, and harp, and cadenza sections for English horn, bassoon, and alto saxophone require strong and confident players.

Abrupt tempo changes are common throughout the piece and will require practice for the conductor and ensemble to find the correct new tempo when moving away from the previous tempo. In movement 1, the tempo at letter D is marked quarter note = 144, yet Etezady indicated in a phone interview[2] that the marked tempo is too fast and should be slightly slower to produce the correct style and atmosphere for the section.

Unit 5: Stylistic Considerations

This piece uses a variety of styles, from bold and strong to delicate and chorale-like writing. Players will need to be prepared for sudden changes in style, tempo, and meter which create exciting and contrasting moments throughout the piece. Etezady often juxtaposes long lyrical lines against agitated staccato or bold accented accompaniment parts. Accurate note length and balance between parts will be most important to bring out all of the lines. Much of the brass writing is very accented, and brass players should avoid the tendency to clip notes too short.

Unit 6: Musical Elements

MELODY:

Marked regal and brazen, movement 1 opens with a horn fanfare. The movement centers on this fanfare as it evolves. It appears in several rhythmic forms, passing through numerous instrumental lines, inverting, and is incorporated within the developed melodic lines.

Movement 2, "Night Mares," begins with a chorale in the clarinets and various woodwind solos accompanied by harp. The relaxed style does not last long and the music becomes more urgent and rhythmic. A variation of the chorale returns in this new section in a darker and more forceful manner. Etezady describes this movement as "part scherzo, part march, and part dance."

Movement 3 is marked *Peaceful*, and opens with harp playing an arpeggiated ostinato to accompany various woodwind solos. The melody develops into a lullaby ending with antiphonal trumpets reintroducing the fanfare from movement 1.

HARMONY:

The piece easily shifts in and out of various tonal centers in every movement and explores the use of seventh chords and open fifths. Students should be familiar with the major keys of C, D-flat, D, E-flat, E, G, A, B-flat, and B, and the minor keys of E-flat, F, and A-flat. Scalar passages are prevalent in the woodwind lines, often following chromatic tendencies.

RHYTHM:

All three movements go through various meter changes. Movement 1 rotates between 3/4, 4/4, and 5/4. The opening slow section of movement 2 contin-ues to switch between 3/4 and 4/4. The fast section becomes much more active in meter changes, switching between 6/8, 9/8, 12/8, 3/4, 3/4, and 5/4. The final movement explores 2/4, 3/4, 4/4, 5/4, 6/4, and 7/4.

Movement 1 provides the greatest rhythmic challenge, presenting three similar rhythms occurring simultaneously. The horn fanfare opens with a six-teenth-and-dotted-eighth-note rhythm. The fanfare then branches into two variations (see figure 1). Care should be taken that the sixteenth note of the original fanfare is played deliberately and not played too fast. In the two rhythmic variations of the fanfare, strive to make a difference in the length of the thirty-second and grace notes.

FIGURE 1. Movement 1, opening fanfare rhythm and variations

TIMBRE:

Etezady uses a combination of strong and bold statements and delicate lyrical lines. The scoring often alternates between brass and woodwind choirs, with battery percussion rounding out the brass and mallet percussion supple-menting woodwinds. Brass should perform with a full, rich tone but avoid overpowering the rest of the ensemble. Woodwind lines can easily be lost without careful balance of timbre and dynamics. While the woodwind writing is often delicate in nature, players should still perform with full tone and confidence for adequate projection and presence.

Unit 7: Form and Structure

SECTION	MEASURE	EVENT AND SCORING
Movement 1: "The Flight of Night"		
A	1–16	Fanfare in horns; answering fanfare in trumpet, piccolo, and flute
	17–22	Expansion of fanfare into melodic material in piccolo and saxophones; fanfare in remaining woodwinds and low brass
	23–40	Full ensemble; scalar passages in woodwinds; fanfare alternates with woodwind interjections
B	41–65	Tempo and style change; percussion break followed by melodic line in low brass and percussive accompaniment in woodwinds
C	66–79	Solos in euphonium, trombone, and piccolo; ostinato in clarinet, alto saxophone, trumpet, and harp
	80–93	Reemergence of fanfare; call-and-response fanfare between alto saxophone and trumpet
	94–96	Percussion transition
Coda	97–101	Full ensemble; scalar passages in woodwinds; fanfare in horn and euphonium
Movement 2: "Night Mares"		
A	1–10	Chorale in clarinet, flute, and English horn; solos in oboe, English horn, and bassoon
B	11–27	Tone clusters in saxophone and brass; rhythmic ostinato in timpani; sweeping scalar gestures in upper woodwinds; chromatic descending lines in low brass
C	28–42	Style change; lyrical melodic line in oboe and clarinet; piccolo, flute, and clarinet accompaniment; new percussion ostinato
B'	43–50	Expansion of chromatic descending lines in brass and woodwinds; return of timpani ostinato
C'	51–58	Expansion of lyrical melodic line in woodwinds; ostinato switches to tom-toms
	59–64	Expansion of lyrical melodic line in brass; staccato countermelody in piccolo and flute; ostinato switches to snare drum

Section	Measure	Event and Scoring
B'	65–67	Transition; expansion and augmentation of descending chromatic lines
A'	68–73	Chorale variation in bassoon, trumpet, and euphonium; horn states variation of fanfare from movement 1
Transition	74–75	New tempo; melody in English horn and alto saxophone; no percussion
A'	76–81	Chorale in woodwinds; trumpet solo
C'	82–88	Lyrical melodic line in diminution in upper woodwinds; new ostinato in snare drum
	89–98	Lyrical melodic line in diminution in trumpet; descending chromatic line from section B in augmentation and inversion; new ostinato in snare drum
Coda	99–105	Canonic entrances of melodic line; timpani ostinato joins snare drum ostinato
	106–108	Descending chromatic line in diminution, augmentation, and inversion

Movement 3: "Sleep and Repose/The Coming of Light"

A	1–9	Solo section 1: harp, clarinet, and oboe
	10–20	Solo section 2: harp, alto saxophone, and saxophone quartet
	21–27	Solo section 3: harp, trombone, and English horn
B	28–33	Melodic material in trumpet
	34–46	Melodic line travels from saxophones to clarinets, English horn, and bassoon
	47–56	Sparse instrumentation; flute and oboe solos; saxophone cadenza
	57–66	Solo melodic line passes through piccolo, flute, vibraphone, oboe, and English horn; trumpet and trombone choral accompaniment
C	67–77	Antiphonal trumpets introduce return of fanfare material from movement 1; solo melodic line in alto and tenor saxophone
	78–83	Second statement of fanfare material in antiphonal trumpet; solo melodic line in flute
	84–89	Third statement of fanfare material in antiphonal trumpets with harmon mutes

Unit 8: Suggested Listening

Etezady, Roshanne:
   Cereus
   In (Harmony)
   Start it Up
Hesketh, Kenneth. *Vranjanka.*

Unit 9: Additional References and Resources

Etezady, Roshanne S. "Anahita." DMA diss., University of Michigan, 2005.
   Abstract in *Dissertations and Theses: A and I*, publ. nr. AAT 3187709.
   http://libproxy.library.unt.edu:2053/
_____. Email correspondence with composer. November, 2007.
_____. Telephone interview of composer. November, 2007.
Gardner, Albert Ten. "A Rebel in Patagonia." *The Metropolitan Museum of Art Bulletin*, n.s., 3, no. 9, (1945): 224–227.
Webster, Sally. *William Morris Hunt*. New York: Cambridge University Press, 1991.

Website:
   Roshanne Etezady. http://www.roshanne.com

Contributed by:

Jennifer Kitelinger
Doctoral Conducting Associate
University of North Texas
Denton, Texas

---

1 Sally Webster, *William Morris Hunt* (New York: Cambridge University Press, 1991).
2 Telephone call with composer, November 29, 2007.

Teacher Resource Guide

As the Sun Rises
Scenery Poetry—Idyll for Wind Orchestra

Chang Su Koh
(b. 1970)

Unit 1: Composer

Originally from Osaka, Japan, Chang Su Koh graduated with a degree in composition from the Osaka College of Music and continued his study at the Musikakademie der Stadt Basel in Switzerland. His composition teachers include Kunihiko Tanaka and Rodolf Kelterborn. He has received numerous awards for his compositions, including second prize at the Fifth Suita Music Competition, first prize from the Twelfth Asahi Composition Competition, and the Yve Leroux Award at the First Comines-Warneton International Composition Competition.

Presently, Koh teaches at the Osaka College of Music and ESA Conservatory of Music and Wind Instrument Repair Academy. A member of the Kansai Modern Music Association, he is commissioned on a regular basis, composing music for bands, orchestras, and chamber ensembles. Works for band include: *As the Sun Rises, Carnival Day, Home, Sweet Home Variations, Korean Dances, Lament, Pansoric Rhapsody,* and *Polkischer Marsch.* In addition, Koh is active as a conductor with amateur bands and orchestras.

Unit 2: Composition

Scenery Poetry—Idyll for Wind Orchestra: As the Sun Rises is the result of a number of separate commissions Koh accepted in 2002. Movement 3, "Inori (a Prayer)," was the first composed, the result of a commission from the Kansai University Symphonic Band. Next was movement 4, "Yoko (Sunshine)," commissioned by the Takarazuka Wind Orchestra. Upon completion of

"Inori" and "Yoko" as separate works, Koh decided to expand both into a symphonic suite. Movements 1 ("Shodo [Impulse]") and 2 ("Jyocho [Emotion]") were commissioned by the Ichigo-Ichie Wind Ensemble and the Soka Gakkai Kansai Wind Orchestra. Although the movements were written independently, each is connected by similar musical material Koh used to create a cyclic connection throughout the work.

The duration of the entire composition is thirty minutes. Movements 1, 3, and 4 are approximately eight minutes in length, while movement 2 is five and a half minutes of music. As the Sun Rises is scored for standard concert band instrumentation, including parts for soprano saxophone (movement 2), string bass, piano (movement 2), and harp (movements 3 and 4). Percussion scoring is also standard, and will require five percussionists (movements 2 and 3 can be covered by three players). Score and parts are available from the CAFUA Rental Library.[1]

Unit 3: Historical Perspective

As this work is reminiscent of music written during the Romantic period of Western music (1820–1900), time spent studying the characteristics of large-scale symphonic compositions from this era would be quite beneficial to conductors and ensembles planning to perform As the Sun Rises. Richard Miles, in his treatise "Teaching Music from a Historical Perspective, lists many of the musical characteristics that apply to this work: "lyricism, chromatic themes, long sequences, chromatic harmony, harmonic color, and new instrumental color" (51. See Unit 9). Indeed, the variety of contrasts often associated with music from this period read as if they were specifically listed for Koh's composition: "loud/soft volume, heavy/light articulation, thick/thin texture, dark/light sonority, intense/relaxed expression, complex/simple color, and programmatic/absolute development (54)."

Also typical of this period was the attempt by composers to describe specific feelings or stories through their writing, often referred to as program music. Koh's use of descriptive titles for the work (Scenery Poetry—Idyll for Wind Orchestra: As the Sun Rises), as well as each movement ("Impulse," "Emotion," "A Prayer," and "Sunshine"), is obviously intended to impact the preparation and performance of this composition.

In addition to studying the symphonic orchestral works of Romantic era composers, becoming familiar with original wind ensemble compositions written with many of these same characteristics would also assist in the preparation of this work for performance. Compositions by Cesarini, Fauchet, Hindemith, Kozhevnikov, Miaskovsky, and Schmitt are especially relevant (see Unit 8).

Unit 4: Technical Considerations

As the Sun Rises is written for a mature ensemble with solid technical abilities. Woodwinds are often required to execute rapid passages of sixteenth notes with chromatic alterations throughout the instruments' range. Saxophones and brass perform many highly articulate fanfare-like figures, and horns are required to play some passages in unison over a two-octave range. With multiple solos for flute and clarinet, there are many chamber ensemble solo moments for piccolo, oboe, E-flat clarinet, bass clarinet, alto saxophone, baritone saxophone, horn, euphonium, and tuba as well.

While there are more stylistic indications included than actual tempo markings, those provided range from quarter note = 40 to dotted quarter note = 130. Primarily written with a quarter-note pulse, the work does include some passages in 3/2 and 12/8, with frequent use of hemiola.

Unit 5: Stylistic Considerations

As discussed in Unit 3, *As the Sun Rises* is clearly reminiscent of the large-scale symphonic works written during the Romantic period of music history. Thus, it is imperative that musicians performing this work be aware of the stylistic considerations of this era. From the sweeping lyrical melodies in "Shodo," the humorous character of "Jyocho," the somber theme in "Inori," to the rhythmic development of "Yoko," this work exploits the Romantic symphonic form in exemplary fashion.

As would be expected in a multi-movement work of this length, musicians are required to perform a variety of styles ranging from smooth, connected, legato playing to very articulate, precise, and rhythmic execution of certain passages. Each movement contains multiple style and tempo markings, such as *Pesante*, *Lento espressivo*, *Andante cantabile*, and *Allegro vivace* to assist musicians in this endeavor.

Careful attention to articulations is crucial for creating clarity. Dynamic range is extensive and must be exploited to assist in presenting the proper mood and texture of each section and movement. The music, while at various times intense, reflective, and serious, also includes moments of a lighter character.

Unit 6: Musical Elements

While this work is intended for mature ensembles with strong technical facility, extended effort on this piece should provide multiple opportunities for growth. Each movement of the work is very clear in its structure, employing a variety of styles and exploiting the symphonic characteristics most often associated with music from the Romantic era.

Here are a few of the specific musical elements explored in *As the Sun Rises*.

MELODY:

The melodic material of this work, although very traditional in character, is unique for each movement and/or segment. Movement 1 is quite angular, featuring fanfares and fugues as well as reflective solo moments. Movement 2, *Scherzando*, captures this particular style of composition quite effectively, with agitated moments of hemiola contrasted with long, legato melodic lines. The reflective movement 3 includes rather lengthy and solemn melodies, often requiring performers to function as a chamber ensemble. After a slow and soloistic introduction, the majority of movement 4 is very energetic, often in 12/8 with a style marking of *Allegro vivace*.

HARMONY:

While there is much chromaticism used throughout this work, the overall sense is very tonal. The scoring is quite consistent with symphonic music written during the late nineteenth century. The use of dissonance contributes to the more dramatic elements of the composition, and assists in creating moments of tension and release so vital to all good music.

RHYTHM:

Every member of the ensemble must possess a strong sense of internal pulse as well as independent performance skills for this piece to be performed effectively. The quarter-note or dotted-quarter pulse is predominant. Rhythmic interplay within and between the various choirs of the ensemble is an important component of this composition.

TIMBRE:

While the majority of the solo passages and chamber ensemble moments are found in the woodwind section, this work generally showcases the full ensemble. With percussion in a supporting role, woodwind and brass sections are often scored in contrast to each other. The use of piano in movement 2 and harp in movements 3 and 4 add unique color contrasts to the work and lend support for creating the overall symphonic texture of the music.

Unit 7: Form and Structure

SECTION	MEASURE	EVENT AND SCORING
Movement 1: "Shodo (Impulse)"		
	1–9	*Pesante*; dramatic fanfare opening by brass with woodwind sextuplets
	10–16	*Lento espressivo*; clarinet solo presents main theme
	17–28	Woodwinds elongate introduction of main theme with quiet, reflective interlude building to a climax in m. 28

SECTION	MEASURE	EVENT AND SCORING
	29–48	*Moderato con moto*; fugal-like development of motives from main theme, beginning with contrabass clarinet, tuba, and string bass; chromatic sixteenth-note activity in woodwinds leads back to brass fanfare
	49–83	*Andante cantabile*; flute solo followed by continued development of motives from main theme, including solos in echo from piccolo, flute, E-flat clarinet, and oboe
	84–98	*Più mosso*; brass chromatic quarter-note triplets move toward fanfare-like figures from introduction
	99–112	*Largamente ma con moto*; interlude with augmentation of theme and layering of textures
	113–130	*Moderato con moto*; restatement of fugal-like passage from m. 30, ending with restatement of material from introduction

Movement 2: "Jyocho (Emotion)"

	MEASURE	EVENT AND SCORING
	1–32	*Scherzando* (dotted quarter note = 108); piano and timpani rhythmic interplay
	33–56	Clarinet 1 introduces theme A with bassoon accompaniment; woodwinds and low brass build toward a tutti ensemble presentation of the theme
	57–71	Rhythmic, chromatic interlude with shifting pulse
	72–81	Low woodwinds and brass play theme A with interlude material layered on top
	82–113	Theme B introduced in soprano, alto, and tenor saxophones with pedal tone quarter-note accompaniment in low woodwinds, brass, and timpani, as well as sixteenth-note rhythmic bursts in the upper woodwinds
	114–124	Tutti ensemble rhythmic interlude
	125–130	Theme A returns in horns and trumpets with tutti ensemble accompaniment
	131–138	Chordal brass interlude

SECTION	MEASURE	EVENT AND SCORING
	139–154	Oboe solo presents theme C with clarinet accompaniment; theme C expanded by flute, oboe, clarinets, and glockenspiel, accompanied by horns
	155–175	Theme D variation played in echo by solo euphonium, clarinets, solo horn, and solo trumpet, with theme C interludes by solo tuba
	176–201	Woodwinds, with trumpet and euphonium, combine themes C and D; two measures of silence in mm. 194–195 and 200–201
	202–215	Return of opening rhythmic interplay, this time by baritone saxophone and bass drum
	216–239	Return of theme A with similar scoring
	240–254	Return of rhythmic, chromatic interlude
	255–265	Return of material and scoring from m. 72
	266–281	Return of theme B from m. 82
	282–290	Return of ensemble rhythmic interlude
	291–296	Return of material and scoring from m. 125
	297–307	Ending passage featuring augmentation of theme B in low woodwinds, brass, and string bass, with chromatic eighth-note pattern in upper woodwinds, piano, and timpani

Movement 3: "Inori (a Prayer)"

	1–22	*Andante sostenuto* (quarter note = 64); brass chorale opening followed by woodwind chorale with development
	23–42	*Lento* (quarter note = 52); thematic material introduced by clarinets, as well as flutes and saxophones
	43–52	*Lento*; climatic conclusion of opening by tutti ensemble
	53–63	*Andante sostenuto*; flute, oboe, clarinet, and bassoon quartet
	64–68	*Sostenuto*; woodwind chorale interlude
	69–84	*Andantino* (quarter note = 70); development of theme with woodwind and harp rhythmic accompaniment
	85–102	Theme development in woodwinds and euphonium, with counterline in alto saxophones, tenor saxophones, and horns

SECTION	MEASURE	EVENT AND SCORING
	103–107	*Andante sostenuto;* tutti ensemble chorale
	108–126	*Con moto;* multiple melodies and counter-melodies with rhythmic triplet accompaniment building to climatic chord
	127–137	Woodwind chorale leading to chamber ensemble of solo flute, oboe, clarinet, horn, and harp

Movement 4: "Yoko (Sunshine)"

	1–16	*Lento espressivo* (quarter note = 40); flute and alto saxophone solos with woodwind, vibraphone, and harp accompaniment stating motives from movement 1 theme
	17–26	Restatement of movement 1 theme in echo, beginning with brass
	27–47	*Andante cantabile* (quarter note = 68); woodwind chorale with brass accompaniment interlude leading to main section of movement
	48–79	*Allegro vivace* (dotted quarter note = 130); development of thematic material from entire work in 12/8
	80–95	Flute and oboe solo interludes with light, rhythmic accompaniment
	96–124	Continuation of thematic development begun in m. 48
	125–133	*Lento espressivo;* flute and oboe solos with return of material from m. 1
	134–139	Return of material from m. 17
	140–157	*Allegro vivace;* return of material from m. 48
	158–178	*Andante maestoso* (quarter note = 68); ending passage with brass chorale and chromatic triplet accompaniment in woodwinds;
	179–182	*Pesante;* final tutti statement of main theme

Unit 8: Suggested Listening

Koh, Chang Su:
>As the Sun Rises. Chronicles. North Texas Wind Symphony. Eugene
>Migliaro Corporon, conductor. GIA CD-774. 2008.
>As the Sun Rises. Kanagawa University Symphonic Band. Toshiro Ozawa,
>conductor. Cafua 0086. 2006.
>As the Sun Rises. Kyo-En IX: A Prosperous Future for Band into the 21st
>Century. Bravo BOCD-7476/77. 2007.

Related listening:
>Cesarini, Franco. Poema Alpestre. 1999.
>Fauchet, Paul. Symphony in B-flat. 1926.
>Hindemith, Paul. Symphony in B-flat. 1951.
>Kozhevnikov, Boris. Symphony No. 3: "Slavanskaya." 1958.
>Miaskovsky, Nikolai. Symphony No. 19 in E-flat, Op. 46. 1939.
>Schmitt, Florent. Dionysiaques, Op. 62. 1913.

Unit 9: Additional References and Resources

Miles, Richard. "Teaching Music from a Historical Perspective." In *Teaching
Music through Performance in Band, Volume 2*. Richard Miles, ed.
Chicago: GIA Publications, 1998. 37–68.

Websites:
>Bravo Music. www.bravomusicinc.com (Note: A majority of the band
>and chamber wind music composed by Chang Su Koh available in
>the United States is published by Bravo Music.)
>Cafua Records. www.cafua.com (Note: *As the Sun Rises* is available from
>the CAFUA Rental Library.)

Contributed by:

James Popejoy
Director of Bands
University of North Dakota
Grand Forks, North Dakota

---

1 http://www.cafua.com/rental/index.php (Please note that the site is in Japanese.)

824

Teacher Resource Guide

Cheetah

Karel Husa
(b. 1921)

Unit 1: Composer

A year and a half before the completion of *Cheetah*[1], Karel Husa commented on the intense quality of energy that is required of a composer. His statement, not unlike his music, distilled the expression to its essence as he explained that, "composing, is a force."[2] Husa, through his composition, conducting, and teaching, has been and remains a force who has inspired and elevated musical expression through an authentic musical voice that is as challenging as it is rewarding to performers and audiences alike.

Though Husa's work demonstrates an enviable breadth that includes chamber, choral, orchestral, and wind band music, no medium has enjoyed more expansion and artistic benefit from his creativity than that of the wind band. Whether considering *Music for Prague 1968*, *Apotheosis of this Earth*, *Les Couleurs Fauves*, the *Concerto for Wind Ensemble*, *Al Fresco*, or any of his other works for band, the repertoire has been significantly enriched by the addition of any one of them. These along with his other works for winds, now expanded by the addition of *Cheetah*, argues for Husa's place as the most enduring and significant composer for band in the past forty years.

Karel Husa was born in Prague, Czechoslovakia in 1921. As he grew up he evidenced a notable inclination for the arts, expressing himself through poetry, painting, and music. Nonetheless, for some time his formal training was directed not toward the arts, but rather toward a future in engineering (a potential career that found favor from his parents' perspective). In 1941, unusual circumstances surrounding the Nazi invasion of Czechoslovakia paved the way for Husa's entry into the Prague Conservatory and later, the École normale de musique in Paris, and the Paris Conservatory.[3]

While beginning to establish his career in Europe, he was invited to teach at Cornell University in Ithaca, New York. Accepting this invitation, Husa immigrated to the United States and enjoyed a distinguished teaching career at Cornell from 1954 through his retirement in 1992. Husa's work has received much international recognition. Some of his most significant awards include the Grawemeyer Award in Music Composition, the Pulitzer Prize, and the State Medal of Merit, First Class, from the Czech Republic.

Unit 2: Composition

Rich instrumental hues, motivic intrigue, and intense lyricism join forces in Husa's powerful and poetic *Cheetah* for wind ensemble. The musical metaphor suggested by the composer is evoked by the portrait of this "magnificent wild animal, now an endangered species—its colors, movements, power, speed."[4]

The energy unfolds from small, quiet flickers of rhythm and expanding interval gesture in horns and percussion, along with gentle, rising cascades of woodwind lines that act as musical premonitions cast against a distant fanfare motive in trombones. These statements expand bit by bit through an additive process to create a brooding sense of dramatic possibility.

Emerging to shape the lyrical section of the piece is a strong, extended melodic *soli* from the saxophones. It is both affective and muscular, with a passionate vocal quality that grows in strength through the continuation of widening intervals and ranges. Throughout, this lyrical statement is provoked by a motor-like pattern in the woodwinds that pulsates as a reminder of the undercurrent of rhythmic energy at the music's core. Together these elements unfold as the staging of a climactic section, identified by energetic fanfares by trumpets and horns combined with rhythmic counterpoint from the percussion. Here the music regathers its rhythmic impulse to create rich, invigorated textures throughout the ensemble.

At the same time, the trombone fanfares first heard near the beginning return to be reshaped, extended, and amplified through the entire brass section, propelling toward the arrival of the culminating *fortissimo* of the work. Echoing out from this visceral release, Husa orchestrates a beautiful *dénouement*, dissolving the musical energy with subtle reminiscence, and suggesting a sublime quality even in the "exhaustion after an unsuccessful chase."[5]

In the *Sequenza21* review of the work's premiere at Carnegie Hall, the writer unified an analysis of both Husa's contributions to the medium and the vigor of work itself in the statement, "considered by many to be one of the greatest composers for the wind ensemble genre, Karel Husa's *Cheetah* lives up to its creator's reputation."[6] This single-movement work of approximately six minutes in duration adds a concise, intensely poetic statement to the already diverse and significant legacy of the Husa catalogue.

Unit 3: Historical Perspective

Cheetah was commissioned by the University of Louisville, Division of Music Theory and Composition for the University of Louisville Wind Ensemble, Frederick Speck, director. This represents the second work commissioned from Husa by the University of Louisville, the first being the ballet *The Trojan Women*, composed in 1980 to commemorate the opening of the School of Music facility at the university's Belknap Campus. Husa's relationship to the musical community of Louisville has been long and rich, with numerous visits over the last several decades in association with both the School of Music (as a guest composer and the 1993 Grawemeyer Award winner) and the Louisville Orchestra for both performances and recording projects.

Cheetah was given its world premiere by the University of Louisville Wind Ensemble at Carnegie Hall on March 8, 2007 as part of a concert celebrating the music of numerous Grawemeyer Award-winning composers. On July 7, 2007, the same ensemble performed the European premiere of the work at the World Association for Symphonic Bands and Ensembles Conference in Killarney, Ireland.

Unit 4: Technical Considerations

The general scoring is for wind ensemble or symphonic band, with such inclusions as E-flat soprano clarinet, alto clarinet, contrabass clarinet, four C trumpets, four trombones, euphonium with occasional divisi, tuba with occasional divisi, and double bass.

Pianissimo dynamic levels in the upper registers coupled with the demands of light, repetitive, tongued articulation in flutes and clarinets bring challenges, as do quiet entry statements from oboes in the low register. The quiet, opening fanfare figures in trombones (with harmon mutes, stem in) require special attention to tuning.

Beyond this, overall balance is critical, making sure that the principal line is not obscured by ornaments or surface rhythms. In sections in which rapid rhythmic figures are exchanged between choirs of instruments, players are challenged to perform their segments in the flow of the prevailing pulse with well-matched articulation.

Unit 5: Stylistic Considerations

Cheetah is a work that demands clarity in the execution of musical detail in order to illuminate the compositional idea. As is common to many of Husa's works, *Cheetah* evokes a romantic expressivity while adhering to a classical core in terms of architecture. Regardless of the romantic allure of its aesthetic, care must be exercised to create the transparency essential for a cogent representation of the music.

Four passages are particularly challenging in this regard. First, the repetitive staccato figures in mm. 14–38 must display a lightness of articulation that is sympathetic with the composer's direction of *leggiero*, as these gestures must stand in stylistic contrast to the growing muscularity of the low brass melody. Later, the long, rising, scale passage of the tuba, double bass, timpani, and euphonium (which begins as a counterline at m. 77 but is transformed into melody by m. 84) must be heard as prominent material, demanding excellent balance from the other instruments performing sustained tones.

In mm. 97–100, the saxophone quartet, with contrabass clarinet and euphonium, expresses a very compressed, agitated reminder of the long, lyrical melody of the preceding section. This stunning passage can only be heard if the trills performed in the other woodwinds are quiet long enough for listeners to grasp the melody. Finally, the colossal fanfare passage of mm. 110–120 must be defined by the two-note sequential fanfares heard in trumpets, horns, and trombones. Again, careful handling of the dynamics of other sustained *fortissimo* tones is critical.

Unit 6: Musical Elements

MELODY:

Husa creates melodic contrast in the work through what are, in simplest form, fanfares and arias. The initial dotted eighth, sixteenth, half-note figure (long, short, long) of the trombone choir (heard in m. 4) provides a melodic/rhythmic motif that is developed within the context of both music of increasing lyricism (e.g., the low brass passage of mm. 21–39 and the saxophone soli of mm. 43–68), as well as in the more overt trumpeting figures that define the *Più vivo* section of the work beginning at m. 88, and the climactic saturation of fanfares heard in mm. 110–125.

Husa's affection for the saxophone section regarding its ability to portray the *vox humana* of the wind ensemble is evident, as the most prominent and extended lyrical role of the work is scored for these instruments as a soli that extends for thirty-nine measures in the heart of the composition. The reminiscence of a similar role for the saxophone section in the *Aria* movement of *Music for Prague 1968*, and to a less-direct extent, the use of the saxophone quartet as the lyrical foil in the final movement of *Concerto for Wind Ensemble* is unmistakable.

Beyond these large-scale thematic elements, there is also melodic content that exists at a small, but potent gestural level. This is heard at the beginning of the work in the three-note interval figure created by the semitone expansion of D, pulling upward to E-flat and downward to C-sharp. This expressive expansion is organic to the work, palpable in both its smallest form and through its effect on the large, sonic architecture of the music.

In terms of the general pitch schematic, a study of the rising woodwind gestures in mm. 1–12 reveals an additive technique that ultimately results in an eleven-note collection which provides the basis for inversionally-related pitch-class set manipulation.[7]

HARMONY:

Localized harmony appears to be oriented toward creating color fields rather than typical tonal harmonic function. Vertical sonorities often feature stacked thirds or even whole-tone structures. In isolation, these chords may be some-what neutral, but when the succession features dissonant links from chord to chord, musical tension is heightened.

There are passages, however, wherein relationships are developed through the suggestion of triadic harmony and tonal function. A prominent example is found beginning at m. 21 in the low brass melody, harmonized to suggest the chord succession A major–D major–D minor–C major–C-sharp major. In the voice leading of these harmonies, nearly every chord is hinged to the next by a semitone. This process continues through three more harmonized melodic statements in a manner suggesting harmonic sequence which produces both unity and direction.

Near the climax, some traditional harmonic tools are used to create the sense of motion and impending arrival. In m. 110, trumpet fanfares coalesce into the fully-diminished seventh chord (C-sharp–E–G–B-flat) which points to the open perfect fifth (D–A) in the chimes. This is followed a measure later with another fanfare that creates the fully-diminished chord B–D–F–A-flat. This diminished seventh chord reaches its target in mm. 114–115 as the harmony moves through an A major triad with a raised fourth.

Following in m. 116, there is a transformation of the voicing to cast the fifth of the chord in the bass. The presence of the E in the bass creates a strong sensation of dominant harmony in the same manner that is typically heard with a cadential six-four chord. Together, this generates momentum through a harmonic succession and bass-line motion drawn from the descending perfect fifths D, A, and E. This harmonic blueprint is particularly significant, as it is the precursor for mm. 122–126 which combine E major and B major sonorities over a B in the bass, providing the dominant for the monumental E minor chord (with an added second) that galvanizes the work.

On an even broader architectural level, the relationships created by pitch strata can be strongly heard in the music. The pillars of D and A predominate until the climactic arrival at E, after which there is a long release of energy that dies away through the descent through E-flat and final arrival on D to create symmetry and resolution.

RHYTHM:

The rhythmic motion of *Cheetah* is drawn from the development of the brief, dotted-note fanfare figures first stated by trombones in m. 4, streams of scale-passage sixteenth notes which are also heard in the beginning, motor-like rhythms and the metric undertow created by contrasting metric expressions layered on one another. In a simple, but powerful way, listeners are led to hear the motion of successive additions to the line of motion created by figures of one, then two, three, four, and five-note groups, and so on (1...1, 2...1, 2, 3...1, 2, 3, 4..., etc.). Throughout the work, there is a temporal drama created through contrasts between surface motion and core metric expression.

A particular example of such metric tension is created in m. 41 and following, as the cyclical and additive figure in temple blocks recurs in five-beat phases against the stubborn, motor-like figure of the upper winds defined by harmonic change heard in three-beat units. Combined, these rhythmic elements provoke an undercurrent of brooding tension against the strongly lyrical argument of the saxophone quartet. It is important to note that as the melody reaches an important structural/aural moment in the saxophone section at mm. 61–62 (with C-sharp leading to D), the temple block cyclical figure expands from five to six beats long.

During a transitional passage later in the work that links the initial fanfares of the *Più vivo* to their magnified transformation at m. 110 through the climax, Husa enhances the sense of forward motion with a feeling of compound meter (using a dotted eighth-note pulse) in measures of common time. As this hypermeter is manipulated, the result is the sensation of a composed accelerando against a steady pulse, ultimately spilling into a stretto at m. 107 that creates tension by seeming to both speed up (trumpet section material) and slow down (upper woodwinds) at the same time!

TIMBRE:

As is generally typical in Husa's music, timbral intensity is germane to musical expression. Brass color, in particular, is altered by means of harmon and straight mutes, as well as the instruction to change the sound by becoming progressively brassy over the course of the phrase.

In other cases, unusual orchestration creates unique color hybrids. An example is the mallet doubling with the saxophone quartet soli at mm. 54–68. Though the marimba doubling is not in itself unusual, the xylophone doubling adds remarkable upper octave intensity to the combined sound. In the case of this line, great care must be taken to choose mallets that allow the line to sing without allowing the articulation of the rolls to become a distraction from the saxophone color.

Unit 7: Form and Structure

It is likely that the work will be heard in five main parts: introduction (mm. 1–13), theme 1 (mm. 14–40), theme 2 (mm. 41–87), development/transition/climax (mm. 88–127), and coda (mm. 128–135). Though these sections have surface characteristics that allow simple aural delineation, they are drawn together by organic intervallic, motivic, and temporal organization into a unified, large-scale, tensional arch.

Along with the notable implication of classical design, *Cheetah* also evidences a fascinating internal structural relationship to the Fibonacci series. The name of the series is attributed to mathematician Leonardo Fibonacci, considered to be perhaps the greatest mathematician of the middle ages. On an absolute level, this is not a series that was invented, but rather one that was observed in the phenomenal organizational characteristics of nature itself. Since its observation it has been applied as a structural and organizational principal in the disciplines of art, architecture, music, and more recently, even in stock trading. In a work with a title that evokes the image of one of nature's most powerful creatures, it is somehow not surprising that a relationship to such a structural paradigm would exist.

Simply stated, beginning with 0 and 1, a series is extended by summing the two numbers before it (e.g., 0, 1, 1, 2, 3, 5, etc.). Linking this application to the organizational blueprint of the work reveals a potent structural dynamism in Husa's writing.

SECTION	MEASURE	EVENT AND SCORING
F 0	0–1*	D4 activated through the trill to E-flat while D3 is sustained via a timpani roll
F 0 + 1 = 1	1–2	Interval expansion to E-flat–C-sharp
F 1 + 1 = 2	2–3	Incipient scale development leading to a culminating punctuation on D4 in bassoons and the first unified phrase
F 1 + 2 = 3	4–5	Introduction of fanfare motive in trombones centered on A4, reinforced by the additional articulation of A2 in timpani
F 2 + 3 = 5	6–8	Second statement of fanfare motive with the descending interval in trombone 1 widened from minor to major third, with additive elements of rhythm figuration in horns and additional scale members in woodwinds

*Measure count reflects measures added in sequence, including the content of 0–1.

SECTION		MEASURE	EVENT AND SCORING
F	3 + 5 = 8	9–13	Third statement of fanfare motive with the descending interval in trombone 1 widened from major third to perfect fourth and the upper interval expanded by semitone, creating a tensional wedge; continued addition of pitches to the rising woodwind line to become an eleven-tone chromatic scale (only G-sharp is absent)
F	5 + 8 = 13	14–21	Development of articulated expansion interval material first presented in horns in m. 2 staged as transition to the upcoming lyrical theme
F	8 + 13 = 21	22–34	Extended thematic statement combining fanfare elements with sustained tones is presented in low brass
F	13 + 21 = 34	35–55	The conclusive low brass theme statement is made, immediately transitioning to the cantabile theme of the saxophone quartet
F	21 + 34 = 55	56–89	The body of the lyrical theme is presented in this section, though at its very end, trumpets announce the return of fanfare material which will provide the emblematic feature of the next section
F	34 + 55 = 89	90–135*	Return of fanfare material, transition, Climax and coda

Another intriguing attribute of the Fibonacci series may be observed by resetting m. 35 as 0 in the series, then observing significant structural consequences related to the extended melody of the saxophone quartet. Note particularly the organization of the melody in groups of five, eight, and then thirteen measures. This is followed by a final phrase statement that merges into the transition to the next section, which is, of course, twenty-one measures in length, matching perfectly with the final return of fanfare material in the trumpets.

---

* Though the raw measure count is only 46, observe that the tempo reduction to quarter note = 60 from m. 125 to the end, coupled with the *rallentando* that precedes it, accounts proportionally for the duration necessary to equal the otherwise expected measure count of 55.

Unit 8: Suggested Listening

Husa, Karel:

Cheetah. The University of Louisville Wind Ensemble at Comstock Hall. Frederick Speck, conductor. http://louisville.edu/music/ensembles/bands.html

Cheetah. WASBE 2007 Killarney, Ireland. The University of Louisville Wind Ensemble. Frederick Speck, conductor. Mark Records 7214 MCD. 2007.

Concerto for Percussion and Wind Ensemble. A Tale of Two Cities. The Moscow Philharmonic Winds and Percussion. Dimitri Kitayenko, conductor. Sheffield Lab SLS-506. 1988.

Concerto for Wind Ensemble. Prevailing Winds. Cincinnati Wind Symphony. Mallory Thompson, conductor. Summit DCD 192. 1997.

Les Couleurs Fauves. New England Conservatory Wind Ensemble. Frank L. Battisti, conductor. Albany Troy 340. 1999.

Music for Prague 1968. Eastman Wind Ensemble. Donald Hunsberger, conductor. CBS MK 44916. 1989.

Unit 9: Additional References and Resources

Acklin, Amy. "Analysis: Cheetah by Karel Husa." Manuscript, 2008.

Camphouse, Mark, ed. *Composers of Composing for Band.* Chicago: GIA Publications, 2002.

Gilliam, Daniel. "Grawemeyer Concert at Carnegie Hall." http://www.sequenza21.com

Hegvik, Arthur. "Karel Husa Talks About His Life and Work." *Instrumentalist*, May, 1975: 32–36.

Husa, Karel. *Cheetah.* New York: G. Schirmer, 2007.

Nelson, Judy Ruppel. "Echoing Mankind Through Music Karel Husa." *Instrumentalist*, October, 1987: 13–15.

Posamentier, Alfred S., and Ingmar Lehman. *The Fabulous Fibonacci Numbers.* Amherst, NY: Prometheus Books, 2007.

Radice, Mark A., ed. *Karel Husa—A Composer's Life in Essays and Documents.* Lewiston, NY: Edwin Mellen Press, 2002.

Contributed by:

Frederick Speck
Director of Bands
Head, Division of Conducting and Ensembles
University of Louisville
Louisville, Kentucky

1 Karel Husa, Cheetah, New York: G. Schirmer, 2007.

2 Telephone conversation with Karel Husa, September 29, 2006.

3 Judy Ruppel Nelson, "Karel Husa: Echoing Mankind through Music,"
  The Instrumentalist, (October, 1987):13–15.

4 Program note, faxed from Karel Husa, September 29, 2006.

5 Ibid.

6 Daniel Gilliam, "Grawemeyer Concert at Carnegie Hall,"
  http://www.sequenza21.com, (March 10, 2007).

7 Amy Acklin, "Analysis: Cheetah by Karel Husa," Manuscript, (April, 2008): 5–6.

Teacher Resource Guide

Day Dreams

Dana Wilson
(b. 1946)

Unit 1: Composer

Along with being an accomplished composer, Dana Wilson has a background as a jazz pianist. He has a doctorate from the Eastman School of Music. Currently Wilson serves as Charles A. Dana Professor of Music in the School of Music at Ithaca College in Ithaca, New York.

Wilson brings the influences of jazz and, to some degree, rock, to much of his music. This can be found in his harmonies, complex rhythms, and angular melodies. The influences of current music have made his music extremely popular with performers and audiences alike.

The works of Dana Wilson have been commissioned and performed by such diverse ensembles as the Chicago Chamber Musicians, Detroit Chamber Winds and Strings, Buffalo Philharmonic, Memphis Symphony, Washington military bands, Netherlands Wind Ensemble, Syracuse Symphony, and Tokyo Kosei Wind Orchestra.

He has become very popular and has written many works for concert band and wind ensemble since winning the ABA/Ostwald Prize (1988) and the Sudler International Wind Band Composition Prize (1987) for his work *Piece of Mind (1987)*. Among his many works for wind band are *Shortcut Home* (1998), *Shakata: Singing the World into Existence* (1989), *Sang!* (1994), *Vortex* (1999), *and Dance of the New World* (1992). More information is available at the composer's website, http://www.ithaca.edu/wilson/

Unit 2: Composition

Day Dreams was commissioned by former members of the Ithaca High School (New York) bands, wishing to honor their director, Frank Battisti, who developed one of the country's great high school band programs there between 1954–67. The four movements of the work are entitled I. "Sunrise: an infinite expectation," II. "Morning: all intelligences awake," III. "Afternoon: hopes shot upward, ever so bright," and IV. "Sunset: having lived the life imagined."

In the program notes, Wilson writes,

> *Day Dreams* traces a metaphorical day. (The movement titles all come from Thoreau's *Walden*—a place very close to where Frank spent a good part of his life.) The work begins with a dramatic sunrise. The second movement represents morning (or youth), and juxtaposes two extremely contrasting and seemingly irreconcilable types of material typical of that stage of life. The third movement explores the afternoon (adulthood), a period of sophisticated balancing of life's many forces. The final movement is a sunset, with each player saying goodbye....

Day Dreams is published by Alfred Publishing Company.

Unit 3: Historical Perspective

Composers have always reflected the times in which they live through their music. In past centuries popular music and art music were closely related in many ways. As art music and pop music have evolved, especially through the end of the twentieth century, they have moved farther and farther away from each other. Dana Wilson is one of several current composers whose music is reflective of the times and boldly references popular music. It is very idiomatic of both jazz and funk styles. Current compositional trends implicit in Wilson's music also tend to explore a wider variety of colors, often pairing uncommon groups of instruments, writing in lighter textures, making use of the piano as a vital component, and using many uncommon percussion instruments.

Unit 4: Technical Considerations

Day Dreams is playable by a very good high school band, though it provides significant challenges. Many rhythms are fast-moving and syncopated, though also often repetitive. As is often the case in Wilson's music, a particular melody or accompaniment is presented in a pointillistic fashion with the material passed quickly between sections or players. Additionally, the work calls for significant independence of all parts. Many fast-moving melodies chase each other in close canon with only an eighth note separating them.

There is some beautiful slow music, particularly in the last movement, often with extended or dissonant harmonies. Players will find challenge in tuning, balancing, and sustaining these slow sections. Additional tuning trials are found in the large number of melodies played in unison and octaves, often scored in very interesting but transparent ways. As is often the case with Wilson's music, a good pianist is essential.

Unit 5: Stylistic Considerations

The biggest performance challenge of this work is capturing the large variety of styles. Many portions of the piece are to be played freely or even in a blurred fashion. Wilson is always concerned that his performances have the right feel, so, particularly in the freer outside movements, mood is more important than metronomic meticulousness. In the contrasting faster sections, a solid funk style is essential. Many of the rhythms used in the quicker sections will not read well, but will become easier as the licks become more familiar. Nonetheless, getting a concert band to play funky is the true challenge. Lots of singing should help.

Composer suggestions like "warm, intimate," "on the edge," and "funk" are helpful.

Unit 6: Musical Elements

MELODY:
The musical motive used throughout all movements of the piece was derived from the dedicatee's name, **FrAnk BA**ttisti. Thus the motive: F–A–B–A. The melodies throughout the work seem to flit between the whole step pitches and then move to the tritone. After hearing the piece the motive becomes easily recognizable, even in its many different adaptations. This piece would be a superb way to teach students how to find the motive in its countless hidden forms and many transpositions. Such a treasure hunt would result in a much deeper understanding of the construction of this work.

HARMONY:
The work is tonal, even in its furthest-reaching sections. While harmonies are basically tertian, most chords include extended harmonies, and often a fair amount of dissonance. Often chords will move in parallel motion, but to unexpected places with interesting and most often unpredictable results. Typical of the composer, he often sets up certain harmonic expectations, only to resolve the harmonies to a completely different place, if they are resolved at all. Students would benefit from discussion of how musical expectations are constructed in the piece, and how, when, and why they are treated as they are.

RHYTHM:
As stated earlier, the rhythms in *Day Dreams* provide most of the challenge in the work. While there are a fairly large number of meter changes, they present little challenge and do not provide the major rhythmic interest. This interest comes from frequent syncopation, accenting and grouping of fast notes, (e.g., groups of many sixteenth notes slurred into uneven groups with accents) and the need to enter with a complex figure on a weak beat (e.g., one sixteenth note before a beat.)

Sometimes it is necessary to set up a groove (jazz or funk) under several other rhythmic elements. Furthermore, Wilson often makes use of rhythmic canons at very close intervals. Students can benefit from discovering these canons and rehearsing them together before perfecting them as written. As mentioned earlier, the last rhythmic issue is one of appropriate style. The ensemble should sing the rhythmic figures regularly in order to perfect these styles.

TIMBRE:
While harmonic structure is advanced, textures are often very transparent, with constant color changes. Sometimes the composer presents fast woodwind figures intended to be played not together. He often wants a blending of sound, allowing the listener to recognize just for a second bits and pieces of material as it moves quickly through many instruments. The ethereal effects are stunning. Even when large numbers of performers are playing, the work can usually be drawn down to three to four different strata which are fairly easily discernable.

Unit 7: Form and Structure

SECTION	MEASURE	EVENT AND SCORING
Movement 1: "Sunrise: an infinite expectation"		
Introduction— slow	1–9	Low pedal tones and percussion strikes under free flute solo
Introduction— fast	10–38	Running sixteen notes in drums, pedal tones and chords built on top of each other—building anticipation; short canonic episodes in flutes and saxophones
Main motive/ theme	38–60	Melody using main motive presented for the first time in trumpet and trombone (over six measures); sharp brass chords answer, along with fast sixteenth-note punctuations; woodwinds answer with slower-moving canonic episode using four-note theme

SECTION	MEASURE	EVENT AND SCORING
Closing material	61–70	Sixteenth notes continue running in drums; one final woodwind canonic episode using first two notes of theme; movement ends, fading away with bass clarinet and bassoon pedal tones over waning drums

Movement 2: "Morning: all intelligences awake"

SECTION	MEASURE	EVENT AND SCORING
Introduction	1–9	Very fast gestural patterns with same patterns of notes overlapping each other (clarinets and flutes) to produce ethereal effect; piano strumming up and down strings in middle range
Main theme— funk!	10–26	Eight-measure theme presented in unison by saxophones with rock accompaniment in percussion, with sparse interplay from bassoon and trombone; trombones present melody second time with accompaniment becoming busier and thicker
Interlude	26–29	Ethereal fast passages return in clarinets and flutes to interrupt funk material—like a "change of channels."
Main theme returns	30–37	Rich, full saxophone section with a new version of the funk section; piano and bass instruments interjecting, then brass join saxophones for second phrase
Section 2	38–62	Very active piano interlude with other instruments interrupting, followed by soft block chords overlapping each other in horns, then clarinets, then flute, then trumpets; piano vamp using syncopated octaves drives the rhythm; return to more ethereal sounds from fast-moving, overlapping woodwind gestures, like the introduction, but this time building energy

SECTION	MEASURE	EVENT AND SCORING
Main theme returns	63–72	Trumpet and trombone funk melody with fast woodwind sections (beginning) intermixed
Closing	73–80	Fast, ethereal motive returns in trumpets, but *forte* this time, creating a climax; a quick diminuendo is followed by receding octave figure in piano again

Movement 3: "Afternoon: hopes shot upward, ever so bright"

Theme 1	1–13	The jazz-influenced melody has a distinct Lydian flavor taken from the work's motive; melody occurs first in unison trombones, then trumpets, with short, crisp accompanimental "pops."
Theme 2	14–23	Theme 2—quick-moving and short—is presented in upper woodwinds over two measures; followed by a return of theme 1
Theme 1 spun out	23–38	Theme 1 motive is expanded and developed as it passes through the saxophone section soloistically; very busy, fast, eighth-note accompaniment/vamp in piano, double bass, and percussion
Transition	39–44	Short return of theme 1 similar to opening
Middle section (development)	45–61	Main theme developed in new ways, with less energy, pseudo half-time feel with aug-mented melody lyrical and sustained over easy-feeling syncopated accompaniment, suggesting 6/8 against the established 4/4 meter
Return of themes 1 and 2	62–95	All material presented so far returns, switching quickly between themes as if interrupting each other; tension builds
Closing	96–117	Preceded by a two-measure drum break, the closing section begins softly, then builds quickly to a loud, abrupt, and exciting end

Section	Measure	Event and Scoring

Movement 4: "Sunset: having lived the life imagined"

Section	Measure	Event and Scoring
Introduction	1–5	Slow introduction by piano and chimes
Main theme	6–23	Slow, lyrical theme using main motive appears in horn; repeated quarter-note chords (changing to a different major or minor chord every few measures) with sustained low chords in clarinets; first nine-measure phrase in horn is answered with five-measure melody in alto saxophone
Main theme spun out	24–38	Theme appears in trumpet as eight-measure melody with oboe countermelody; continued long-note accompaniment with constant piano quarter notes; seven-measure euphonium melody (same material) follows with solo flute countermelody
Main theme material—change of textures	39–53	Melody appears in clarinets and oboes (unison octaves) with countermelody building in horns; energy builds with busier sextuplets in piano; first climax occurs at m. 51 with melody in all upper woodwinds; energy level quickly subsides
Transition	54–58	New melodic material (short and fleeting) passes between oboe, flute, and trumpet solos with very sparse trombone chords beneath
Middle section	59–73	Arpeggios at various speeds in piano, celeste, and vibraphone accompany two-measure chordal figures passed between various sections; texture remains very light and ethereal, but building; at m. 67, large climax begins with repeated quarter-note chords from virtually the entire ensemble; all *fortissimo* sounds release to only a soft piccolo

SECTION	MEASURE	EVENT AND SCORING
Main theme returns	74–93	Major triad quarter notes (repeated) return in the piano; main theme returns in short episodes passed between solo bassoon, euphonium, oboe, and alto saxophone
Coda	94–119	Flute countermelody dies away over the repeated four-note motive in horns; this is accompanied by piano quarter notes, and soft, blurred, fast undulations in clarinet; mm. 105–108 brings one last fierce interruption to the tranquility of the coda with loud, tutti, dissonant half notes from the entire ensemble; this is followed by one soft chord, tied over nine measures in clarinets, repeated quarter notes, dying away in the chimes, and one last motivic call by horn

Unit 8: Suggested Listening

Wilson, Dana:

> *Dance of the New World.* University of North Texas. Corporon conducting. Klavier Records.
>
> *Dance of the New World.* Ithaca College. Peterson conducting. Mark Records.
>
> *Piece of Mind.* Kosei Wind Orchestra. Fennell conducting. Kosei.
>
> *Piece of Mind.* Cincinnati College-Conservatory of Music. Corporon conducting. Mark Records.
>
> *Shakata: Singing the World into Existence.* Ithaca College. Peterson conducting. Mark Records.
>
> *Winds on the Steppes.* American Chamber Winds. Mark Records.
>
> *Vortex.* University of North Texas. Fisher conducting. Klavier Records.
>
> *Vortex.* University of Florida. Waybright conducting. Mark Records.
>
> *Vortex.* Ithaca College. Peterson conducting. Mark Records.

Unit 9: Additional References and Resources

Battisti, Frank L. *The Winds of Change*. Galesville, MD: Meredith Music, 2002.

Camphouse, Mark, ed.: *Composers on Composing for Band, Volume 2*. Chicago: GIA Publications, 2004.

Emge, Jeffrey. "Third-Stream Music for Band: An Examination of Jazz Influences in Five Selected Compositions for Winds and Percussion." Doctoral diss., University of Cincinnati College-Conservatory of Music, 2000.

Ferrari Lois. "Two Symphonic Wind Ensemble Compositions of Dana Wilson: *Piece of Mind* and *Shakata: Singing the World into Existence*." Doctoral diss., Eastman School of Music, 1995.

Reynish, Tim. "The Wind Music of Dana Wilson." http://www.timreynish.com/wilson.htm, 2006

Salzman, Timothy. *Composer's Insight: Thoughts, Analysis and Commentary on Contemporary Masterpieces for Wind Band, Volume 4*. Galesville, MD: Meredith/Hal Leonard, 2008.

Taylor, Robert. "The Vernacular Made Artful: An Analysis of Dana Wilson's *Vortex* and *Dance of the New World*." Doctoral diss., Northwestern University, 2005.

Contributed by:

Stephen Peterson
Director of Bands
Ithaca College
Ithaca, New York

Teacher Resource Guide

Finish Line

Cindy McTee
(b. 1953)

Unit 1: Composer

Cindy McTee is a Regents Professor of Composition at the University of North Texas. A student of Penderecki, Robbins, Clark, Druckman, Hervig, Stachowski, and Moszumanska-Nazar, McTee has a musical voice and language that is unique. She has received countless awards and recognitions for her music, including a Creative Connections Award from Meet the Composer, two awards from the American Academy of Arts and Letters, a Guggenheim Fellowship, a Composers Fellowship from the National Endowment for the Arts, and a Fulbright Fellowship. McTee was also selected to participate with the National Symphony Orchestra in "Music Alive," a residency program sponsored by Meet the Composer and the American Symphony Orchestra League.[1]

McTee has been commissioned to compose works by many of the premier symphony orchestras and wind groups in the United States. Her most recent commissions include requests from the Houston Symphony Orchestra (*Solstice for Trombone and Orchestra*), a consortium of wind groups (*Finish Line*), Amarillo Symphony Orchestra (*Finish Line*), Dallas Symphony Orchestra (*Einstein's Dream* and *Timepiece*), Bands of America (*Ballet for Band*), National Symphony Orchestra (*Symphony No. 1: Ballet for Orchestra*), and another consortium of wind groups (*Timepiece*).[2] In addition to these commissions, her music has been performed by leading orchestras, bands, and chamber ensembles in Japan, South America, Europe, Australia, and the United States.[3]

Unit 2: Composition

Finish Line, premiered on March 24, 2006, was commissioned by the Amarillo Symphony Orchestra and James Setapen, music director, to celebrate the seventy-fifth anniversary of the Amarillo Orchestra Guild. The version for winds was created after a consortium of university bands contacted McTee. The wind version was then premiered on May 20, 2006.

McTee, an avid racing enthusiast, took the painting, *Abstract Speed + Sound*, by Giacomo Balla, as a strong influence as non-musical source material. Throughout *Finish Line* there are numerous driving and racing inferences. In fact, the composer describes several sections of the piece in racing terms. McTee writes the following about the piece.

In *Finish Line*, the use of repeated fragments (ostinatos), a steady pulse, and a spirited tempo attempts to portray the swirling gestures and mechanized agitation of Balla's painting. Multiple points of view are represented by the simultaneous presentation of two tempos at the beginning and end of the work, and also by tempo transformation using a seamless process analogous to gear-shifting, where the tempo, or RPM, of the engine modulates smoothly to a new frequency.

The form of this seven-minute work is ABA. Within this structure, the piece can be divided into seven distinct sections. *Finish Line* is published by Rondure Music.

Unit 3: Historical Perspective

McTee uses Futurism, the early twentieth-century art movement, as a major source of influence. In the score, she writes the following about Futurism:

Centered in Italy at the beginning of the 20th century, the artistic movement known as *Futurism* embraced an aesthetic that glorified the speed and power of machines, especially automobiles. The *Futurist Manifesto* of 1909 by F. T. Marinetti proclaimed that "a racing automobile...is more beautiful than the *Victory of Samothrace*." Is it any wonder, then, that Italy has led the pack in producing finely crafted racing machines noted for their style and grace?

I decided to use the work of futurist artist, Giacomo Balla, as a point of departure for the creation of *Finish Line* and chose several paintings suggesting the transformation of landscape by the passage of a speeding automobile. The title of one work in particular, *Abstract Speed + Sound*, suggests that Balla sought to render on canvas the whirling noise of the automobile itself.

Italian *Futurists* were, of course, not the only artists affected by the dawn of the machine age. Russian composer, Igor Stravinsky, is actually the composer credited with having produced the first important piece of "machine music," the *Rite of Spring*, its rhythmic pulsations depicting not just prehistoric, ritualistic dance, but also the nervous energy of a modern, mechanized city. There are references to this famous work at the beginning and end of *Finish Line*.

Unit 4: Technical Considerations

The wind scoring for *Finish Line* includes: piccolo 1–2, flute 1–2, oboe, English horn, E-flat clarinet, B-flat soprano clarinet 1–3, bass clarinet, E-flat contra-alto clarinet (optional), B-flat contrabass clarinet, bassoon 1–2, contrabassoon, E-flat alto saxophone 1–2, B-flat tenor saxophone, E-flat baritone saxophone, horn 1–4, B-flat trumpet 1–3, trombone 1–3, euphonium, and tuba. The work also includes a part for string bass.

The percussion music is divided into four parts by the composer. Percussion 1 includes the following instruments: four brake drums or metal plates, suspended cymbal, guiro, vibraphone, and shaker. Percussion 2 includes orchestra bells, triangle, castanets, ratchet, and large suspended cymbal. Percussion 3 requires vibraslap, tambourine, medium woodblock, bass drum, and tam-tam. Percussion 4 requires only a marimba. In addition to the four percussion parts, there are parts for timpani and piano.

Finish Line creates typical Grade 6 challenges for the performers. There are extended ranges in many parts, and the instrumentation calls for more than the standard timbres—especially the use of the contrabassoon, contrabass clarinet, and string bass.

The work is written mostly in traditional meters, including 2/4, 3/4, 4/4, and 5/4. *Finish Line* is notated using both traditional and modern notation, including the use of extender boxes. Rhythmic demands are consistent with a piece of this grade level, as are dynamic, stylistic, and articulation demands.

Unit 5: Stylistic Considerations

Finish Line will require performers and the conductor to understand contemporary performance practices, implied musical gestures, and have the ability to perform various musical styles. Versatility in style and communication of emotion is necessary.

In this piece, McTee does not often use musical terminology to describe stylistic characteristics; instead she meticulously paints the parts and score with high-level articulation markings and gestures. Paralleling the diverse use of articulation is the varied markings of dynamics, including all shades between the expected *pianissimo* through *fortissimo*, with other special effects including the repeated uses of *sforzandos* and a non-traditional sound effect for horn intended to recreate a Doppler effect.

Unit 6: Musical Elements

MELODY:

The melodic input for *Finish Line* is mostly motivic quotes and manipulations. Like much of McTee's music, the derivations and variations of small motives are the backbone to what might be considered the melodic content.

The pitch content for the piece is derived from both octatonic structure (an eight-note scale based on alternating half and whole steps)as well as twelve-tone structure.

HARMONY:

McTee's harmonic language is a combination of tonal and non-tonal elements. The skillful use of octatonic structure allows the use of expected vertical structures which might imply tonality; however the changes of vertical structures (harmony) does not follow traditional harmonic rules and expectations.

The jazz idiom has also had a significant influence on the composer. This influence can also be found easily throughout *Finish Line*. McTee's harmonic language does create an easily identifiable voice, one that is often referred to as an American style.

RHYTHM:

Finish Line, like most Grade 5 and 6 works, exposes the player, conductor, and listener to rhythmic demands from somewhat simple to very complex ideas. The work has several instances of three-against-four and similar uneven divisions of the beat. Rhythmic clarity has to be a high priority in the rehearsal and performance of the work.

TIMBRE:

McTee writes some of the most quiet and intimate moments as well as some of the most full and energetic orchestrations. Attention to detail will be necessary in order to balance the smaller chamber music sections as well as the *fortissimo* tutti sections.

Unit 7: Form and Structure

Finish Line is a work in ABA form, with seven distinct sections. The following shows the basic formal structure.

SECTION	MEASURE		EVENT AND SCORING
	1	1	Introduction
A			
	2	26	Ostinato texture 1
	3	66	Ostinato texture 2

Section		Measure	Event and Scoring	
B				
	4		101	Twelve-tone texture 1
	5		177	Twelve-tone texture 2
A				
	6		269	Recapitulation of most of section 3
	7		303	Ending with return of material in the introduction

Section	Measure	Event and Scoring
1	1	"Fasten your seatbelts" (composer's description); based on octatonic scale 1 (In this case, ahalf- and whole-step alternation beginning with C–D-flat)
	6	"Start your engines"; piccolo, flutes, and glockenspiel "starter music"; emphasizes "A" for Amarillo; E–D-sharp adds dissonance to the open A–E sonority
	9	"Double clutch"; metric modulation to pit "engine music" against tempo of "Stravinsky music" and to make "Stravinsky music" easier to play
	25	A–B-flat trill prolongs the A–B-flat tension
2	26	"Pedal to the metal"; ostinato texture 1; the A-major triad within this scale is emphasized in contrabass instruments; ostinatos change slightly from time to time; parts are added gradually to create movement
	31	Horn quarter-note triplets suggest another tempo and foreshadow trumpet tune at m. 70
	42	Transposition up a half step for two bars
	46	"Starter music" spliced in
	48	Ostinato texture 1 spliced in
	50	"Car horn" music spliced in
	51	Ostinato texture 1 spliced in
	53	"Drifting music 1" interrupts forward progress
	55–56	Brief return of ostinato texture 1; various octatonic transpositions are used to create motion and tension

SECTION	MEASURE	EVENT AND SCORING
3	66	Ostinato texture 2
	70	Trumpet tune uses same octatonic scale as the accompanying texture with the exception of the final note of the phrase
	91	"Engine music" sneaks in as part of transition to next section
4	101	First occurrence of tutti twelve-note chord; serial bass line begins
	107–109	Flutes introduce material which is slightly augmented by clarinets at m. 125
	158	Familiar "engine music" returns using the same octatonic scale
	173–177	Repetition of mm. 97–101 provides transition to section 5 and ends on second occurrence of tutti twelve-note chord
5	177	"Upshift"; music based on same series in section 4; bass line starts with first note of serial bass line and plays every other note
	233	Triplets introduced briefly to create a hint of trouble
	239	Trouble takes hold
	247	"Grinding halt"
	253	Exact recapitulation of transition material bars 50 and following
	256	"Yellow flag"; "drifting music 1" again
6	269	Exact recapitulation of section 3 through m. 299
	300	Material from m. 280 in the winds combined with a hint of the "Stravinsky music"
7	303	"Downshift"; metric modulation reversing m. 9; repetition of "Stravinsky music"
	310	Modulation back to m. 152 in order to use previous music—a third, extended version of the music that points to the tutti twelve-note chord at m. 318
	329	"Out of gas"

Unit 8: Suggested Listening

McTee, Cindy. *Finish Line*. *Composers Collection: Cindy McTee*. North Texas
  Wind Symphony. Eugene Migliaro Corporon, conductor. GIA
  Publications CD-746.

Unit 9: Additional References and Resources

www.cindymctee.com
http://www.guggenheimcollection.org/site/movement_work_md_Futurism_11
_1.html

Contributed by:

Nicholas Enrico Williams
Assistant Director of Wind Studies
University of North Texas
Denton, Texas

---

1 Cindy McTee, http://www.cindymctee.com/awards.html
2 Ibid.
3 Ibid.

Teacher Resource Guide

Four Factories

Carter Pann
(b. 1972)

Unit 1: Composer

Carter Pann began piano lessons at an early age, and by the age of fifteen was a student of Emilio Del Rosario at the North Shore School of Music in Winnetka, Illinois. In 1994, Pann received his bachelor of music in composition from the Eastman School of Music, where his teachers included Samuel Adler, Joseph Schwantner, Warren Benson, and David Liptak. Following graduation, he pursued his master of music in composition at the University of Michigan, studying with William Bolcom, William Albright, and Bright Sheng.

Pann is the recipient of numerous awards and honors for his compositions, including the K. Serocki Competition for his *Piano Concerto*, first prizes in the Zoltan Kodaly and François d'Albert Concours Internationales de Composition, a Charles Ives Scholarship from the Academy of Arts and Letters, and five ASCAP composer awards, including the Leo Kaplan award. In addition, his *Piano Concerto* was nominated for a Grammy Award as "Best Classical Composition of the Year."

His works have been performed by the London Symphony, City of Birmingham Symphony, Seattle Symphony, Budapest Symphony, Irish National Symphony, New York and Chicago Youth Symphonies, National Repertory Orchestra, and the Radio Symphonies of Berlin, Stockholm, and Finland. Pann currently serves on the composition faculty at the University of Colorado in Boulder.

Unit 2: Composition

Four Factories is a four-movement work that represents Pann's most ambitious writing to date for winds. The composer provides the following in the score regarding the origin of the work:

> The idea to write a piece evoking the sense of factories or large generators came a while back when I was reading *The Fountainhead* by Ayn Rand. Coincidentally, I was reading a biography of George Antheil (composer of *Ballet Méchanique*) at the same time. It occurred to me that it might be a rewarding experience to write a symphonic work called *Man's Greatest Achievement* (or some such grandiose title) depicting three or four of the world's highest skyscrapers (a nod to the architect-hero Howard Roark from Rand's novel). At that time however, I turned to writing a single-movement orchestral scherzo about downhill skiing called SLALOM (which itself became a work for wind symphony later on).

Four Factories is approximately sixteen minutes in length. Though the work is programmatic, no dramatic program is developed between movements. The piece is published and available for performance through the composer. For information, go to http://www.carterpann.com/

Unit 3: Historical Perspective

Four Factories was written for the University of North Carolina at Greensboro Wind Ensemble, John R. Locke and Kevin M. Geraldi, conductors. The piece was premiered under the direction of Kevin M. Geraldi on February 16, 2007.

The work represents a culmination in the composer's scoring practice for winds. All instruments play an integral role within the ensemble. He uses thick textures and multiple layers to create an orchestration that is distinctive to his style. Thinner textures, such as the "heralding clarinets" in movement 3, come at opportune moments and provide a brilliant contrast to the previously lush material.

The piece is characterized by a blending of multiple genres. Pann draws on classical influences and juxtaposes them with jazz, big band, and pop, as well as Baroque styles. Each movement provokes a vivid imagery of the material, while not confining itself within the boundaries of programmatic music.

Pann's other compositions for winds include: *Slalom* (2002), *American Child* (2003), and *The Wrangler* (2006).

Unit 4: Technical Considerations

Instrumentation

Four Factories calls for standard wind ensemble orchestration with E-flat clarinet, English horn, contrabassoon, soprano saxophone, piano (with tam-tam), and contrabass. Many sections have extended instrumentation: there are six parts for flute (with flute 1–2 doubling piccolo), clarinet, and trumpet, and two for euphonium and tuba.

The percussion writing is extensive and calls for four players. More players are advisable to help facilitate an easier set-up within the section. The wide array of percussion sounds allows for a distinctive color that is motivic as well as accompanimental. Using three woodblocks with distinctly different pitches at the beginning will help create clarity in the opening motive, which returns throughout the movement as well as recapitulating in movement 4. The timpani hairpin dynamics in the beginning are also important and play an important motivic role throughout movement 1 and in the final recapitulation of the piece.

The use of piano in the piece, as well as in many of Pann's other works, is essential to ensure a representative performance. Pann states in the score that the piano part is "Muscular and should be approached as one of the most important colors in the work. It cannot be faked or regarded with timidity."

Technical Demands

There are many technical demands in the work and virtuosic playing is required for all musicians in the ensemble. Though the parts are technically challenging, Pann did not intend for them to be impractical. All demands are secondary to the music, and are a result of the overall aesthetic created by the composition.

Rhythmic accuracy is required throughout the work to ensure that the "motors" of each movement are precise. The clarinet section provides the motor material through most of movement 3 and is written in six independent parts. This material is canonic, and players should be aware of how their part fits within the context of the section. A canon at the eighth note occurs in m. 50 of movement 3 between flute, piano, and mallet percussion. Clarity of articulation is crucial to ensure that this section moves forward at the new tempo until the return of the opening motive in m. 62. Isolating these sections during rehearsal, along with all other "motor" materials throughout the piece, will help to stabilize pulse within the ensemble.

Further rhythmic considerations include frequent changes between simple and compound meters, double-tonguing in brass parts, and rapid scalar movement in multiple keys and modes. The entire ensemble should have a full awareness of the eighth-note pulse in movement 4 from the beginning to m. 60 to ensure rhythmic precision. Isolating subsections of the work and

playing them with a metronome or percussionist on steady eighth notes will help players to maintain the pulse.

Brass ranges are wide, particularly for trumpets, and requires endurance to sustain the demands of the part.

Unit 5: Stylistic Considerations

The composer's articulation markings are sufficient, and careful observation of these will help to achieve the proper style. Pann has provided colorful notes in individual parts which will help players understand the character of the piece. Orchestral effects are used extensively to express the program of the work. The brutish brass and low woodwind chords at m. 19 in movement 1 depict the engine's sputtering attempt to start until it finally turns over in m. 29 and is fully running by m. 34. Light, crisp articulations should be used at m. 34 throughout the ensemble to ensure clarity and keep the motion moving forward.

Four Factories is an overtly twentieth-century work. Pann's American influences are apparent, and he incorporates many popular idioms into his composition. A particularly striking twist is taken in movement, 2 "Gothic," which Pann states in the score is "set staunchly in a very Baroque B-minor." Suddenly, in m. 20, a pop-influenced jam session is led by the cowbell player, who is instructed to "Hold [the instrument] and whack above head, real glam!"

Unit 6: Musical Elements

MELODY:
Pann uses a variety of melodic writing styles to convey his motivic material. Movement 1 is minimal, and is motivically driven by rhythmic activity depicting grinding motors. Brief melodic themes, such as the brass entrances in mm. 88–95 and 211–218, are quickly interrupted by the return of the pulsating machine. Melodies in movements 2 and 3 are more extended, staying primarily within their tonal contexts. The lush melodies of movement 3 are layered over top of the pulsating motor. The long chords that start movement 3 are harmonically driven and provide a stark contrast to the rhythmically-driven melodies of movement 2.

HARMONY:
Key signatures are stated throughout the work, although the composer often manipulates tonal centers through the use of accidentals. Players will need to be proficient these keys: F, B-flat, G, and A-flat major as well as B minor. Pann uses keys based on their colors in order to achieve a brilliance and economy of color.

RHYTHM:

Changing meters, uneven meters, and nonmeters are present throughout the work. The meter changes at the beginning of movement 4 happen rapidly, and the ensemble should focus on consistency of the eighth-note pulse. Rehearsing this section with a metronome or percussionist tapping out the eighth note will help players to internalize the subdivision and develop rhythmic independence.

Establishing clean articulations will help players with rhythmic precision. It is important to keep the slur-two/tongue-two pattern in m. 34 of movement 1 together as it is passed around the ensemble. Be sure to not let the low woodwinds and piano bury the moving sixteenth notes in this section.

Rhythmic drive is an essential element of *Four Factories* and is used to create forward motion and maintain the energy of the composition. Though the tempo is specifically marked in all movements, choosing a tempo which allows the ensemble play passages cleanly is more important to ensuring a strong performance.

TIMBRE:

The movements of *Four Factories* are all an exploration in "motorized" color-palettes. Pann states in the score: "Each movement is like its own canvas or grid in which sound-color is painted." He orchestrates sections of the ensemble to depict these sound-colors. Percussion is used in a rhythmically precise way throughout movement 1. Non-pitched percussion is the driving force of this movement, with woodblocks continuously restating their mechanical theme throughout. The movement ends with percussion sputtering to a stop through a written-out ritardando.

Unit 7: Form and Structure

SECTION	MEASURE	EVENT AND SCORING
I. "Locomotive"		
Introduction	1–33	Staggered entrances in winds alternate with the woodblock "machine" motive; low brass state the "starting up" theme in m. 14
A	34–61	Clarinets, low woodwinds, and piano establish F major tonal center on passing sixteenth-note passages; bass clarinet has melody in m. 51
Transition	62–67	Trumpet and percussion provide another mechanical theme as they establish four-against-five rhythmic motive

Section	Measure	Event and Scoring
A	68–95	Passing sixteenth-note passage returns in upper woodwinds; trumpet melody m. 88 at *mp*, answered by low brass at *subito f*
B	96–121	Legato melodies introduced first in low reeds in m. 98, then with low brass in hocket in m. 106; legato melody agogically peaks at m. 117 and descends down C
	122–174	Brief transitional material; introduction gestures return in percussion and winds; "starting up" theme returns in m. 149 in low brass
A	175–198	F major; sixteenth-note theme returns with added soprano and alto saxophone duet
A	199–218	Horn melody in m.199–210 precedes return of trumpet melody from m. 88 which is answered by the entire brass section in m. 215
B	219–249	Legato melodies return in winds; m. 237 is an extended version of m. 113, transitioning to the coda
Coda	250–275	Percussion plays a written-out ritardando as the machine slowly grinds to a halt
II. "Gothic" Introduction	1–3	Brief establishment of B minor in winds and timpani
A	4–19	Motor in bassoon, tenor sax, and piano with sand block accompaniment; flute, clarinet, saxophone, and trumpet play theme 1 sequentially; *subito mp* section at m. 12 sets up return of theme 1 in m. 17
B	20–27	Pop-influenced jam led by an explosive cowbell; trumpet and soprano saxophone play new theme
A	28–46	Shortened recap of section A material
Transition	47–50	Ascending and descending chromatic passages softens to silence in flute, trombone, and percussion
Coda	51–63	Piano returns with "motor" motive; piano and percussion drive to the end before a last shrill gasp from trombone

SECTION	MEASURE	EVENT AND SCORING
III. "At Peace"		
A	1–24	Clarinet "motor"; brass melodic chords in B-flat major
B	25–37	Theme 1 stated in flute, oboe, and soprano saxophone; trumpets join clarinet on "motor"
C	38–49	Ensemble statement of theme 1; brief clarinet transition; woodwinds and vibes play cascading transition into tempo of new section
D	50–58	*Più mosso*; half-beat canon in flute and mallet percussion; big moment of anthem-like heroism in mm. 57–58
A	59–82	Recapitulation of clarinet "motor"; brass, saxophone,a nd bassoon reestablish B-flat major with melodic chords
B	83–88	Theme 1 stated in upper woodwinds
Coda	89–101	Seven heralding clarinets break away from the "motor" motive briefly before movement ends in moment of repose

IV. "Mercurial, with Great Precision"		
A	1–60	Tempo established in sand blocks and snare drum; brief motives based on later melodic materials; brass in m. 54 set up swing feel of next section
B	61–81	Big-band swing; saxophone melody echoed by woodwinds
C	82–103	Heroic statement in winds dies away; reminiscent of movement 1
A	104–125	Return of section A
	126–146	Transitional motives first in trumpet, then upper woodwinds drive toward the coda
Coda	147–189	*Scherzo brilliante*; both primary motives from the movement return
Recapitulation	190–219	Return of material from movement 1; timpani and winds alternate pulsating crescendos and decrescendos

Unit 8: Suggested Listening

Antheil, George. *Ballet Mécanique*.
Grainger, Percy Aldridge. *The Warriors*.
Mackey, John. *Redline Tango*.
McTee, Cindy. *Finish Line*.
Pann, Carter:
    American Child
    SLALOM
    The Wrangler
Stravinsky, Igor. *Les noces (The Wedding)*.

Unit 9: Additional References and Resources

Sadie, Stanley, ed. *The New Grove Dictionary of Music and Musicians*. Second
    ed. New York: Macmillan Publishers Limited, 2001.
Lynch, John P., "SLALOM." In *Teaching Music through Performance in Band,
    Volume 6*. Richard Miles, ed. Chicago: GIA Publications, 2007.
Whitesitt, Linda, Charles Amirkhanian, and Susan C. Cook. "George
    Antheil." In *Grove Music Online*. L. Macy, ed.
    http://www.grovemusic.com

Website:
    Carter Pann. http://www.carterpann.com/

Contributed by:

Shannon Kitelinger
Doctoral Conducting Associate
University of North Texas
Denton, Texas

Teacher Resource Guide

Give Us This Day
Short Symphony for Wind Ensemble

David Maslanka
(b. 1943)

Unit 1: Composer

David Maslanka was born in New Bedford, Massachusetts in 1943. He attended the Oberlin College Conservatory, where he studied composition with Joseph Wood. After earning his bachelor of music education degree, he spent a year at the Mozarteum in Salzburg, Austria. Maslanka completed his graduate work at Michigan State University, where his primary teacher was H. Owen Reed. He holds both a master of music and doctor of philosophy in music theory and composition.

Maslanka's nearly forty works for winds and percussion have become especially well known to wind conductors and musicians worldwide. These works include, among others, *A Child's Garden of Dreams*, *Concerto for Piano, Winds and Percussion*, the *Second, Third, Fourth, Fifth, Seventh* and *Eighth Symphonies*, *Mass* for soloists, chorus, boys' chorus, wind orchestra and organ, and the two *Wind Quintets*. His percussion works include *Variations of "Lost Love"* and *My Lady White* for solo marimba, and three ensemble works: *Arcadia II: Concerto for Marimba and Percussion Ensemble*, *Crown of Thorns*, and *Montana Music: Three Dances for Percussion*. In addition, he has written a wide variety of chamber, orchestral, and choral pieces.

David Maslanka's compositions are published by Carl Fischer, Inc., Neil A. Kjos Music Company, Marimba Productions, Inc., the North American Saxophone Alliance, and OU Percussion Press, and have been recorded on Albany, Cambria, CRI, Mark, Novisse, and Klavier labels. He has served on the faculties of the State University of New York at Geneseo, Sarah Lawrence College, New York University, and Kingsborough College of the City

University of New York. He now lives in Missoula, Montana. David Maslanka is a member of ASCAP.

Unit 2: Composition

Give Us This Day was commissioned by a consortium headed by Eric Weirather of Rancho Buena Vista High School in Oceanside, California. The premiere took place at Rancho Buena Vista High School in February 2006, performed by the Rancho Buena Vista Wind Ensemble, Eric Weirather, conductor. The piece is in two movements; the subtitle "Short Symphony" alludes to the use of a symphonic model for this work. The piece lasts approximately seventeen minutes and is scored for wind ensemble, augmented by E-flat contra-alto clarinet, piano, and extensive percussion.

Maslanka offers the following program notes in the score:

> The words "Give us this day" are, of course, from the Lord's Prayer, but the inspiration for this music is Buddhist. I have recently read a book by the Vietnamese Buddhist monk Thich Nhat Hanh (pronounced "Tick Not Hahn") entitled *For a Future to be Possible*. His premise is that a future for the planet is only possible if individuals become deeply mindful of themselves, deeply connected to who they really are. While this is not a new idea, and something that is an ongoing struggle for everyone, in my estimation it is the issue for world peace. For me, writing music, and working with people to perform music, are two of those points of deep mindfulness.

> Music makes the connection to reality, and by reality I mean a true awakeness and awareness. *Give Us This Day* gives us this very moment of awakeness and awareness so that we can build a future in the face of a most dangerous and difficult time.

> I chose the subtitle "Short Symphony for Wind Ensemble" because the music isn't programmatic in nature. It has a full-blown symphonic character, even though there are only two movements. The music of the slower first movement is deeply searching, while that of the highly energized second movement is at times both joyful and sternly sober. The piece ends with a modal setting of the choral melody *Vater Unser in Himmelreich* (Our Father in Heaven), no. 110 from the 371 Four-part chorales by Johann Sebastian Bach.

Unit 3: Historical Perspective

David Maslanka's prolific contribution to the wind band canon is significant because he has developed a distinctive and unique compositional voice that stands out within the genre. His works are an exceptional demonstration of the many scoring and sonorous possibilities available from the wind ensemble, and offer a new model for future generations of wind composers. *Give Us This Day* is yet another example of Maslanka's ability to create a Modern work in a traditional framework. Maslanka has been continually inspired by the music of Johann Sebastian Bach, and has included settings of Bach's work in many of his compositions. The use of the chorale melody "Vater Unser in Himmelreich" contributes a melodic style to the work, as well as an extra-musical association from which Maslanka describes the inspiration for the music. It is interesting to note that this borrowed chorale melody was not original to Bach, either—the Lutheran church leader Martin Luther discovered the melody and transformed it into a congregational hymn to accompany the text of the Lord's Prayer.

Unit 4: Technical Considerations

Give Us This Day is a very approachable work for advanced amateur players. Maslanka has written a work with a great deal of variety in color and timbre without the use of extensive ranges for any of the instruments. There are significant solo parts for flute, oboe, clarinet, and alto saxophone. The piano part includes solo material, and while the part is not technically demanding, it requires the use of extended techniques, including plucking and strumming inside the instrument. Percussion parts require two strong mallet players as well as confidence on a wide range of instruments on each part.

The tempo marking of movement 2 is quarter note = 184; however, the fastest rhythmic markings found at that tempo are repeated eighth-note triplets. The repetitive nature of this section creates a motored pulse that drives the movement's momentum. There are some meter changes throughout both movements of the work, but they are mostly used to extend or augment musical phrases, and therefore do not create technical challenges.

Unit 5: Stylistic Considerations

Dynamic markings in *Give Us This Day* are very specific and require individual care and attention by every player to achieve optimum ensemble balance. In particular, movement 1 of the work opens with a very atmospheric and ethereal style, and later develops into a powerful chorale. To achieve this, Maslanka uses a wide range of dynamics, from *ppp* to *ff*, ranging from soloist with quiet accompanying chords to full ensemble tutti. Articulations are clearly identified and must be uniform across the ensemble, especially in accompanying ostinato voices.

Unit 6: Musical Elements

MELODY:
Movement 1

There are two melodic ideas in movement 1. The first is stated at the very beginning of the piece by solo clarinet, moving in slow, stepwise tones and semitones within the interval of the open fifth which accompanies it. This chant-like melody is characterized by the use of modal mixture created by the use of a flat sixth scale degree relative to the accompanying open fifth. This ambiguous melody is restated and expanded, adding further voice parts, becoming more agitated, and eventually developing into a full ensemble fanfare figure before fading back into its original incarnation.

The second melodic figure is much more hopeful in character, settling into a definitive tonal centre (G major). This moving eighth-note line is consistently harmonized in a hymn-like style, supported by moving parallel thirds and fourths. The melody moves throughout the ensemble in a call-and-response style, and like the first section of the movement, it expands on itself, intensifying in rhythmic activity and dynamic growth, developing into a full and powerful ensemble statement. The movement ends with a return to a fragmented reprise of the original melodic material.

Movement 2

Several themes appear in movement 2. Section A has three distinct melodic ideas, while section B has one primary theme that is spun out into an expanded and fantasy-like motive passed throughout the ensemble. The coda of the movement is a setting based on Bach's chorale melody "Vater unser in Himmelreich." All of the melodic material in the movement is developed from a strong tonal background rooted in triadic harmony.

Aside from the modal quality of the final chorale hymn, Maslanka writes in a scalar fashion that modulates comfortably from major to minor keys, occasionally using chromatic motion that continues the ambiguity of the modal mixture of major and minor. Maslanka uses the technique of augmentation in the recapitulation of the first theme.

HARMONY:
Movement 1

The use of harmony in movement 1 incorporates several interesting ideas. Maslanka emphasizes the perception of modal mixture by the use of repeated accompanying figures, whether it is the ambiguous open fifth of the opening (E-flat–B-flat), or the pervasive chord progression of vi–V–I in E-flat major. As the melodic material develops in the first section of the movement, the harmony offers a sense of stability despite its non-committal tonality.

In the second section, Maslanka uses a constant pedal bass line underneath the hymn-like harmonization of the melody, offering an even stronger tonal center. He shifts between three pedal tones which create three main key areas for this section: G major, E major (via an open fifth C-G), and finally ending in C major. The movement then returns to a quiet reiteration of the vi–V–I progression, again in E-flat major, underneath the fragmented melodic line. He ends the movement with a secondary dominant chord—V of vi, which leads immediately into movement 2.

Movement 2

The triadic harmony of movement 1 is also prevalent in this movement. Maslanka again fluctuates between major and minor tonality, presenting both the first and fourth themes in a major and minor context. Accompaniment lines are permeated by a great deal of chromaticism, further complicating the central tonality at any given moment.

For example, the movement begins in a very resolute and aggressive C minor tonality, but the heroic quality of the melodic line easily translates into C major. It is this melodic line that the composer later uses in augmentation with a very gentle and peaceful C major triadic accompaniment.

The fourth theme is also tonally ambiguous, having a somewhat pentatonic feel and sound. This becomes harmonized in fourths as the movement progresses, never truly settling in a definitive major or minor tonality. There are several shifts of tonality throughout the movement, yet none of these tonal shifts ever feels abrupt or even unexpected.

The final section of the movement is Maslanka's setting of the chorale melody "Vater unser in Himmelreich," in which he chooses a modal harmonic style, full of open fourths and fifths in the accompanying harmony. This modality, followed by a definitive ending in C major, creates a very surprising yet powerful ending to the work.

Rhythm:
Movement 1

In the opening of this movement, Maslanka creates a very improvisatory feeling with slow-moving rhythms against a still accompaniment. The rhythm of this free-sounding chant is quite irregular, and Maslanka uses changing meters as well as several ritardandos and fermatas to add further space and breadth to this concept.

Throughout the first section of the movement, as voices are added and the music intensifies, there are only two rhythmic ideas taking place at any given moment—the recitative style of the melodic line and the slower bass line progression, thus maintaining focus on the melodic material. The challenge to the conductor and players is the unification of the ensemble so as to sound as one improvised line, especially with the more complex dotted rhythms that appear. A mutual understanding of where to lift and breathe will allow for better ensemble.

The second section of the movement uses a repeated rhythmic figure that travels between voices of the ensemble. Again, there is little or no counterpoint to the rhythm in this section; the melodic rhythm is supported only by the pedal bass line, which remains arrhythmic for the majority of the section, intensifying only when it leads into the climactic arrival in E major. At this point in the movement, a third rhythmic line appears, but offers more harmonically than rhythmically. The movement ends as it began, with a soft and slow chant moving against a still accompaniment.

Movement 2

In great contrast to movement 1, there is a constant, driving, rhythmic feel to movement 2. Maslanka moves between duple and triplet eighth notes, both of which create a constant ostinato that help to maintain the triumphant melodic lines. The only departure from this driving feel appears in the few moments where meter changes, often right before the start of a new section, creating an unpredictability to challenge what the listener expects to hear.

TIMBRE:

Movement 1

Maslanka masterfully demonstrates a variety of tone colors and timbres in this movement. He combines several uncommon groupings of instruments to generate the ethereal chant sound: clarinet with trumpet using Harmon mute, punctuated by plucked piano strings; bassoon, horn and euphonium; oboe, alto and tenor saxophones, and trombones, accentuated by xylophone. These combinations serve to stimulate and challenge the listener as they create new opportunities for color and texture that are unexpected yet beautiful. The rich, harmonic sound of the second section allows the ensemble to demonstrate a warm, blended tone as the hymn-like melody is passed between sections.

Movement 2

A great deal of this movement is very densely scored, creating a thick and heavy texture. Maslanka achieves great power by augmenting the melodic lines in several voices, complementing this with strong, accompanying ostinato lines. These two roles are shared equally between sections of the ensemble, and tend to shift based on the tonal quality of major or minor. In minor keys low voices are combined to create a dark timbre, while in major keys the melodic material shifts to the higher tessitura.

The middle section of the movement is a dramatic departure from this overriding style, with piano and mallets accompanying the gentle melodic line in a chamber-like style. They quietly maintain the ever-present ostinato, though very unobtrusively. This adds a delicacy that is somewhat of a reprieve to the listener, while maintaining a link to the outer sections of the movement.

Unit 7: Form and Structure

SECTION	MEASURE	EVENT AND SCORING

Movement 1: ABA form

A	1–8	Chant; solo clarinet
	9–19	Expanded chant; add solo muted trumpet
	20–32	Chord progression vi–V–I; trio of bassoon, horn, and euphonium further expand chant
	33–44	Chant in oboe, clarinet, and trumpet develops into upper tessitura; expands outside of octave for the first time; full ensemble joins and then fades
	45–54	Chant in upper woodwinds, fading
B	55–79	Second melodic idea (G major) passed throughout sections of the ensemble in call-and-response, building in intensity
	80–97	Arrival of E major tonality; full ensemble tutti; chant is reintroduced; modulates into C major; builds again to climax at m. 97
A1	98–109	Reprise of chant in solo voices (flute and clarinet with vibraphone accent); vi–V–I progression returns; slow fade to end of movement

Movement 2: Arch form (A-B-A1-B-A-Coda)

A	1–4	Introduction; duple ostinato established
	5–18	Theme 1; C minor; low woodwinds and low brass
	19–32	Theme 1; C major; alto sax, horn, and euphonium
	33–40	Transition; triplet ostinato; chromatic bass line
	41–58	Theme 2; upper woodwinds and brass
	59–67	Theme 3; rising sequential pattern
	68–71	Transition; quarter-note ostinato
B	72–87	Theme 4; clarinet and bassoon; light triplets; dance-like
	88–96	Theme 4 with counter-theme; duple
	97–109	Theme 4 expanded, staggered, and legato
	110–118	Theme 4; D minor accompaniment; aggressive, building
	119	Grand Pause
	120–121	Transition

Section	Measure	Event and Scoring
A1	122–145	Theme 1 in augmentation; chamber accompaniment
		Theme 1 variation and development; slowing
	186–190	Transition
B	191–199	Theme 4; D minor; staggered and expanded
	200–201	Transition; duple ostinato
A	202–217	Recapitulation; theme 1; theme 3 incorporated into accompaniment
	218–234	Theme 1; C major; theme 4 incorporated into accompaniment
	235–241	Transition
	242–248	Theme 2 in augmentation
	249–251	Transition; theme 4
	252–260	Theme 3; rising sequential sequence expanded
Coda	261–278	Chorale tune setting; full ensemble tutti

Unit 8: Suggested Listening

Bach, Johann Sebastian. 371 Chorales
Maslanka, David:
>   Symphonies 2, 3, 4, and 5
>   A Child's Garden of Dreams
>   Tears
>   Mass

Unit 9: Additional References and Resources

Wubbenhorst, Thomas Martin. "A Child's Garden of Dreams: Conversations with David Maslanka. Doctoral diss., University of Missouri-Columbia, 1991.

Booth, David Martin. "An Analytical Study of David Maslanka's A Child's Garden of Dreams." Doctoral diss., University of Oklahoma, 1994.

Varner, Michael. "The Marimba Concertos of David Maslanka: An Analytical Study." Doctoral diss., University of North Texas, 2000.

Ambrose, Robert Joseph. "An Analytical Study of David Maslanka's Symphony No.2." Doctoral diss., Northwestern University, 2001.

Bolstad, Steven. "An Analytical Study of David Maslanka's Symphony No.4." Doctoral diss., University of Texas-Austin, 2002.

Blackwell, Leslie. "An Analytical Study of David Maslanka's A Litany for Courage and the Seasons for SATB Chorus, Clarinet, and Vibraphone." Doctoral diss., University of Kentucky-Lexington.

Composer's website:
   www.davidmaslanka.com

Contributed by:

Angela Schroeder
Director of Bands
University of Alberta
Edmonton, Alberta, Canada

Teacher Resource Guide

Homages
Michael Djupstrom
(b. 1980)

Unit 1: Composer

Michael Djupstrom was born in St. Paul, Minnesota in 1980 and began music studies at the piano at the age of eight. He continued his training at the University of Michigan with Lynne Bartholomew, Sergio de los Cobos, and Katherine Collier, and began formal composition study with composers Bright Sheng, Susan Botti, William Bolcom, and Karen Tanaka. As a composition fellow at the Tanglewood Music Center in 2002–03, Djupstrom worked with composers Michael Gandolfi, Augusta Read Thomas, Osvaldo Golijov, and George Benjamin, and at the 2005 Aspen Music Festival and School, his teachers were Robert Beaser and Christopher Rouse. Djupstrom received his BM and MA in music composition from the University of Michigan, followed by studies in composition and analysis in Paris as a student of Betsy Jolas. Djupstrom currently lives in Philadelphia, where he teaches piano at Settlement Music School and courses in orchestration and music theory for Boston University's online graduate programs in music.

Djupstrom's work has been recognized through honors and awards from institutions such as the American Academy of Arts and Letters, American Composers Forum, ASCAP Foundation, BMI Foundation, Chinese Fine Arts Society, Académie musicale de Villecroze, and the Sigurd and Jarmila Rislov Foundation. The Music Teachers National Association named him the 2005 MTNA-Shepherd Distinguished Composer of the Year for his work *Walimai*, an alto saxophone and piano duo that is quickly becoming part of the American classical saxophone repertoire. He has been commissioned by the

Tanglewood Music Center in collaboration with Boston University Tanglewood Institute, New York Youth Symphony, Lotte Lehmann Foundation, Michigan Music Teachers Association, and St. John in the Wilderness Episcopal Church (White Bear Lake, Minnesota), among others. As part of a team of eight composers, Djupstrom also provided music for a 2003 production of *King Lear* at Shakespeare and Company of Lenox, Massachusetts.

As a pianist, Djupstrom has performed throughout the United States in traditional venues, including Philadelphia's Kimmel Center and the Tanglewood Music Center, as well as abroad at the Foundation des Etats-Unis in Paris and the Académie musicale de Villecroze (France). He has also presented many concerts in communities throughout the northeastern United States as a member of the Phoenix Trio, an ensemble that seeks to promote classical music beyond its conventional performance spaces and typical audiences. In August 2006, Djupstrom was invited to Yichao Music Training Center in Shenzhen, China, for a series of master classes and duo performances with pianist Wenli Zhou, a guest lecture, and to serve on the judging panel of the 2006 "Yipei" Cup Piano Duet Competition.

Unit 2: Composition

Homages, Djupstrom's first composition for wind ensemble, was written for Frank Battisti and the Boston University Tanglewood Institute Young Artists Wind Ensemble. It was premiered by that group on August 3, 2002, in Seiji Ozawa Hall, Tanglewood, Massachusetts. The work was commissioned as part of a fellowship to attend the Tanglewood Music Center that summer. *Homages* was awarded the Walter Beeler Memorial Composition Prize from Ithaca College and the first Frederick Fennell Prize from ASCAP and the College Band Directors Association.

Michael Djupstrom writes in the score:

> I was excited to have an opportunity to write a piece for winds, after having played in bands for years—from elementary school through college. I felt that the concert band was a medium I understood and one to which I could contribute something. Due to the time constraints of the project, I did not decide on any kind of program before the composition of the piece, nor, in the beginning, even a general plan for the work; rather, I just began to write. What came out may have owed more to tradition than other recent projects, for I did not set out to expand my technical vocabulary, explore any particular compositional device or idea. Writing this piece helped me to realize that I am deeply connected to the compositional tradition, and deeply indebted to it. In the end, I was not surprised to discover that certain characteristics of my piece resemble the work of other long-dead composers. These three

movements do not aim to pay homage in the usual sense; they are not tributes to anyone in particular. In naming the work, I simply wanted to acknowledge my debt to my compositional predecessors, and in doing so, seek my place in the lineage.

According to Djupstrom, *Homages* was a very important piece for his compositional development, as it freed him from the restrictions that he had been placing on himself as a student composer. Because he had very little time between the actual commission and his arrival at Tanglewood in 2002, Djupstrom didn't have the opportunity to do much planning for the composition, and thus stopped "running from the music he loved," which he had been doing with previous pieces. As a result of this, the music came out "quite differently." Djupstrom admits in the score:

> Many early 20th Century composers whose music I adored exercised their influence, powerfully and a bit suddenly: Debussy, Bartók, Ravel, Hindemith, and Stravinsky, of course.

Homages is composed in three movements and is approximately twelve minutes in length. It is written for standard wind ensemble instrumentation: piccolo, flute 1–2, oboe 1–2, English horn, bassoon 1–2, contrabassoon, B-flat soprano clarinet 1–3, B-flat bass clarinet, alto saxophone 1–2, tenor saxophone, baritone saxophone, B-flat trumpet 1–3, horn 1–4, trombone 1–3, euphonium 1–2, tuba 1–2, string bass, timpani, and percussion 1–4 (including bass drum, brake drum, Chinese Cymbal, crotales, crash cymbals, suspended cymbals, gong, marimba, snare drum, triangle, tubular bells, vibraslap, whip/slapstick, woodblocks, and xylophone).

Unit 3: Historical Perspective

An "homage" is a show of respect to someone to whom one feels indebted. In the sense of musical composition, a reference within a creative work to someone who greatly influenced the artist would be considered an homage.

As Djupstrom states in his program note to *Homages*, the three movements do not pay homage to any specific composers or influences. He uses the title to acknowledge a debt to his compositional predecessors. Dupstrom explains:

> The first movement of "Homages" was well under way when I realized there was no way it could escape comparison to Stravinsky (and I had certainly heard his "Symphonies of Wind Instruments" before), but because of the time constraints, I wasn't about to scrap an entire movement. I simply kept on going, when midway throughout the scherzo movement, I became aware that this piece was going to be a turning point for me. Though I hadn't made a conscious attempt to evoke

specific composers anywhere in the piece (even the Stravinsky "pastiche" was not deliberate), writing this piece made me quite aware of the intimate connection I felt with my compositional predecessors, and naming the work "Homages" seemed very natural to me.

Musical compositions that include the word "homage" in their titles abound throughout all musical genres, particularly in contemporary music. More commonly, compositions tend to be an homage in character or intent. This usual type of homage is often a tribute to an event, a specific person, or to a people.

In the band repertoire, there are many examples of homages, both in title and character:

COMPOSER	COMPOSTION	HOMAGE TO
Camphouse, Mark	*A Movement for Rosa*	Rosa Parks
Ewazen, Eric	*A Hymn for the Lost and the Living*	Sept. 11, 2001
Gillingham, David	*Heroes, Lost and Fallen*	Vietnam veterans
Goto, Yo	*Lachrymae*	Sept. 11, 2001
Hutcheson, Jere	*Caricatures*	various artists and celebrities
Lo Presti, Ronald	*Elegy for a Young American*	John F. Kennedy, Jr.
Nelson, Ron	*Medieval Suite*	Medieval composers Leonin, Machaut, and Perotin
Nelson, Ron	*Passacaglia (Homage on B-A-C-H)*	Johann Sebastian Bach
Rudin, Rolf	*Bis Ins Unendiche*	Vincent Van Gogh
Ticheli, Frank	*American Elegy*	Columbine High School tragedy
Turrin, Joseph	*Hemispheres*	Sept. 11, 2001
Van der Roost, Jan	*Homage*	Jan de Haan
Wagner, Richard	*Huldigungsmarsch (Homage March)*	Ludwig II, King of Bavaria

Unit 4: Technical Considerations

Homages is a wonderful, yet very difficult work. The majority of the difficulty lies in the transparent and individual nature of the orchestration. Complex metric and rhythmic demands are placed on many individuals and small sections. In short, there is not much place to hide. Extensive solo passages are required for oboe, trumpet, and bass clarinet. There are also short, but virtuosic solo passages for flute and bass clarinet. Each section of the wind ensemble must perform independently.

Movement 2 is written for clarinet in A, which is a bit unusual for a wind ensemble work. Multiple tonguing is required in movement 2, which is particularly low for trumpets (G3). The contrabassoon part is very soloistic, and most definitely required. There are extremes in range for trumpet 1 and the entire horn section.

All woodwinds are required to perform running technical passages in movement 2, and a great deal of ornamentation can be found throughout the entire work.

Unit 5: Stylistic Considerations

The key to performing *Homages* is to understand its compositional influences, particularly the compositional styles of Igor Stravinsky. Every performer must maximize the stylistic and expressive intent of the myriad of distinct motives that comprise the work.

Unit 6: Musical Elements

MELODY:

Homages is motivic in nature, and not necessarily melodic or obviously thematic. Each movement contains two or three short motivic devices, often quite rhythmic in character. Stravinsky's concept of juxtaposing two or more distinctly opposing "musics," (with different characters, motives, orchestrations) and moving back and forth between them (without interaction) is a hallmark of the composition. Very few of these motives are long enough to be perceived as distinct melodies. The one possible exception is the opening gesture of movement 1.

This thematic idea is seven measures long, yet only consists of four pitches (see figure 1).

FIGURE 1. Movement 1, thematic idea, mm. 1–7

The second motivic gesture used throughout movement 1 is a type of rhythmic variation on a set of similar pitches. While the opening motive is used consistently throughout the movement, this motivic device is always slightly varied in contour and length (see movement 1, m. 8–11, 14–21, and 30 -37).

Movement 2 of *Homages* functions much in the same way. An opening bass clarinet "theme" is presented many times, each time with an increasing orchestration, and with little development of the material. Eventually, when this "theme" cannot get any bigger, it simply stops, as happens several times in Stravinsky's *The Rite of Spring* (see movement 2, m. 1–6).

The larger sections of movement 2 are in 6/8 and consist of two very short and distinct motives (see movement 2. m. 33 and mm. 42–43).

The second 6/8 motive is the basis for the most tuneful section of the movement. A playful oboe duet breaks the intensity of the preceding sections. Even though this duet feels more melodic, it is basically a repetition of this motive (see movement 2, mm. 61–69).

Djupstrom briefly brings back the opening bass clarinet thematic idea, but again as a tool for textural expansion and marking a transition through abruptly stopping (see movement 2, mm. 122–126).

Movement 3 is the most strictly motivic, with one motive making up the majority of the movement. While this descending four-note motive appears at several pitch levels, it is most often heard in its original key, where the sequence of pitches is E-flat–D-flat–C-flat–B-flat (see movement 3, mm. 4–5).

The final section (*Lento assai*) again uses the technique of juxtaposing two different musical cells, the first of which is a transformation of the movement's original motive. This alternation leads to the final restatement of the main motive of movement (see movement 3, mm. 57–60, 60–61, and 66–69).

HARMONY:

The harmonization of the thematic motives in movement 1 of *Homages* remains consistently separate. Just as the motives themselves remain distinct and do not really interact, their harmonizations are also unique in defining their character.

The opening motive is always chordally harmonized as a static E-flat major seventh chord with an added A-flat (eleventh). While the melodic contour of the motive changes (slightly), the harmony remains the same.

The second motive of movement 1 is more open in its harmonization, consisting of mostly fifths, fourths, and sevenths.

While the contour of the opening section of movement 2 is strictly chromatic, its harmonization is strictly whole-tone. Overlaying chromatic lines harmonized at major second intervals interplay between clarinets, bassoons, and flutes, with whole-tone chord clusters in the horns punctuating their cadences. Open intervals of a perfect fourth and fifth mark the climactic moments that abruptly stop.

The larger sections of 6/8 meter in movement 2 are marked by a continuous G pedal over which this section's motives are nicely harmonized in simple third patterns.

The final movement is the most harmonically rich, and possesses the strongest sense of harmonic movement. The opening D minor harmony is the perfect juxtaposition for the descending E-flat minor motive. As the motive and accompanying harmony slightly modulate after the first sixteen bars, its harmonic destination is clear—the arrival of G major in the final chord.

RHYTHM:

The most obvious feature of *Homages* is the way in which rhythmic motives interact with meters and tempos. The character of the rhythmic motives in movement 1 are transformed by the alternation of 5/4, 4/4, 3/4, and 2/4 meters in alternating tempos (at the half-note pulse). Short, syncopated back-beat patterns are interjected between motivic areas. As the movement expands, the alternating motivic sections become more and more rhythmically complex, with the triplet often used to create more rhythmic density and forward motion.

The use of compound meter and rhythm defines the rhythmic character of movement 2. The large 6/8 sections are marked by an unrelenting sixteenth-note ostinato of the G pedal. This ostinato provides a driving foundation for the alternating 6/8 motivic rhythms.

These compound rhythms are foreshadowed earlier in the movement in the variety of sixteenth-note triplet fanfare motives that punctuate the climactic and abrupt "stopping" moments. An interesting rhythmic device can be found in these moments. Djupstrom uses quintuplets, sixteenth notes, and triplets simultaneously in different instruments on the same melodic line—perhaps for pitch reasons (the chromatic destination of the line).

The opening section of movement 3 is the least dense rhythmically. The chorale writing of the movement favors its melodic and harmonic sensibility. The strong rhythm of the movement's main motive (see figure 1) is the defining rhythmic feature.

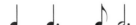

FIGURE 2. Movement 3, rhythm of main motive

In the finale section (*Lento assai*), Djupstrom returns to the structure of alternating meters and tempos found in movement 1. He creates a wonderful polyrhythmic character to this final section (and the triumphant ending) by using the triplet as a juxtaposed rhythmic motive.

TIMBRE:

Djupstrom was very familiar with much of the standard band literature, having played in bands from elementary school through college. He knew how to make a classic, blended band sound. This is most notably found in the first half of movement 3 and the climax of movement 1. However, Djupstrom always felt uneasy with pieces that were heavily orchestrated throughout. He thought it would be a shame not to be able to experience the individual colors of the different instruments in a band because, according to Djupstrom, it is such a "heterogeneous bunch." So, in *Homages*, Djupstrom deliberately tried to write music that allows the listener to hear the plethora of colors that a band can produce.

Djupstrom succeeds quite well. Every instrument and every section is featured in very transparent textures. In this sense, *Homages* could be considered a mini-concerto for wind ensemble. He uses very distinct and colorful orchestration to mark the distinct motivic gestures of the work. Solos, duets, and chamber-like sections abound.

Djupstrom uses an interesting timbral device which he calls a "contour line." The semi-improvisatory "wavy" line is found in movement 2 and allows players to choose their own pitches for fast-running passages. These contour lines produce a wonderful effect of both color and blazing technique.

Djupstrom's use of timbral color is fresh and unique. For this reason alone, *Homages* can be considered a very important contribution to wind ensemble repertoire.

Unit 7: Form and Structure

SECTION	MEASURE	EVENT AND SCORING
Movement 1		
A (characterized by short alternations of two distinct motives)		
a	1–7	Tempo 1; opening motivic fanfare in trumpets and trombones
b	8–11	*Poco più mosso*; dancing motive in double reed choir
a (c)*	12–13	Tempo 1; very short interjection characterized by explosive syncopation
b	14–22	*Più mosso*; double reed choir returns in an extended passage
a	23–29	Tempo 1; clarinet choir in true statement of the opening motive, accompanied by the previous explosive syncopation gesture
b	30–37	*Più mosso*; dance motive continues in clarinets
a (c)*	38–39	Tempo 1; very short interjection characterized by explosive syncopation
b	40–44	*Più mosso*; dance motive continues in clarinets
Codetta	45–46	Short closing to the first half of the movement

* The short "C" motives can be considered to be related to the "A" motives because of their pitch content and tempo.

SECTION	MEASURE	EVENT AND SCORING

B (characterized by larger extrapolations of the two motives)

a	47–53	Tempo 1; oboe solo; pointillistic trombone accompaniment
	54–61	Motive expands to woodwind trio
	67–70	Motivic section concludes with trumpet solo
b	71–77	*Più mosso*; trumpet and horn present a slight variation on the Tempo 1 motive
	78–84	Saxophone choir continues, mutating the varied Tempo 1 motive into the *più mosso* motive
a	85–94	Tempo 1; full ensemble expansion of the *più mosso* motive; interjecting explosive syncopation motive returns
Coda	95–101	Opening motive returns, restored and fully orchestrated

Movement 2

A	1–5	Begins slowly; first statement of bass clarinet solo
	6–9	Second statement of bass clarinet solo
	10–16	Third statement of bass clarinet solo; scoring expands and tempo increases
	17–27	Final statement of opening motive; fully expanded, continually accelerating, accompanied by contour lines, and ending abruptly
B	28–32	6/8 frantic introduction
	33–42	6/8 motive 1
	43–54	6/8 motive 2
	55–60	Climax of 6/8 section and transition
C	61–69	*Meno mosso*; playful oboe duo
	70–75	English horn and alto saxophone duet
	76–83	Oboe duo returns
	84–89	Horn duet with virtuosic flourishes in flute and bass clarinet
	90–99	Transition to return of frantic 6/8 introduction material
B	100–110	6/8 motive 1; more dense accompaniment
	111–121	6/8 motive 2 begins but is not constant; the original motive is developed instead

SECTION	MEASURE	EVENT AND SCORING
A	122–130	Material from the beginning of the movement briefly returns at the faster frantic tempo
D	131 –137	Trumpet cadenza
B	138–141	Intro to final frantic 6/8 section
	142–148	6/8 motive 1
	149–158	6/8 motive 2
	159–169	Final statement of 6/8 motive 1; ends abruptly

Movement 3

A	1–56	Large chorale-like section; develops descending motive
	57–76	Return of alternating meters and tempos juxtaposing two motives
	77–82	Final statement of descending motive

Unit 8: Suggested Listening

Igor, Stravinsky:
  Symphonies of Wind Instruments
  Octet

Unit 9: Additional References and Resources

All quotations come from email correspondence with the composer.

Contributed by:

Ryan T. Nelson
Northwestern University
Evanston, Illinois

Teacher Resource Guide

Kokopelli's Dance

Nathan Tanouye
(b. 1974)

Unit 1: Composer

Nathan Tanouye was born in Platteville, Wisconsin and later moved to Hawaii, where he attended high school and began college at the University of Hawaii, Manoa. While at university, Tanouye studied trombone with members of the Honolulu Symphony, including Jim Decker and Mike Becker. After receiving a performance scholarship to the University of Nevada, Las Vegas, he moved to Las Vegas and completed his degree in both classical and jazz performance.

As a freelance trombonist, he has performed with artists such as Natalie Cole, Johnny Mathis, Tony Bennett, The Temptations, Luciano Pavarotti, and Andrea Bocelli. In addition, Tanouye has been the principal trombonist in the Las Vegas Philharmonic since 1998.

As a composer, he has written works for many different ensembles, ranging from jazz trio to wind symphony. In February of 2004, the UNLV Wind Orchestra premiered *Three Steps Forward*, a piece written by Tanouye to feature Eric Marienthal, Will Kennedy, Jimmy Haslip, and Russell Ferrante, later recorded and released on the Klavier label. Tanouye has also done extensive work as an arranger, including arrangements for a diverse range of ensembles, including jazz groups and flute and harp duo.

Unit 2: Composition

Predominantly a jazz composer, *Kokopelli's Dance* is one of Tanouye's first classical compositions. Tanouye writes the following in the score regarding the work:

The piece begins with Kokopelli's theme played by a solo flute, the instrument that Kokopelli himself played. The theme is then passed through the ensemble in a fugue-like fashion. This style of writing emits the feelings of happiness and joy that Kokopelli was the ancient Indian symbol for. As different sections of the piece progress, the atmosphere of Kokopelli's theme changes, just as the atmosphere of a dance changes with the entrance of each new person. A light-hearted, spirited composition, Kokopelli's Dance is a delightful illustration of an old Indian Legend.

Kokopelli's Dance is approximately eight minutes in length. The piece is published and available for performance through the composer. For information, go to http:// www.nntmusic.com/

Unit 3: Historical Perspective

Kokopelli's Dance was commissioned by the University of Nevada, Las Vegas Wind Orchestra, Thomas G. Leslie, conductor. Tanouye was inspired by the ancient character, Kokopelli, a fertility deity who is typically depicted as a hunchbacked, dancing flute player. Although the figure's origins are a mystery, Kokopelli's oldest manifestations can be found on prehistoric American rock carvings and in many Native American stories from the Southwestern United States, being especially prominent in the Anasazi culture of the Four Corners area. Although his symbols often appear in the context of rain, fertility, and prosperity, he is also commonly known as a trickster god and represents the spirit of music.

Tanouye's other compositions for winds include *Three Steps Forward* and *Four Flew Over the Hornet's Nest*.

Unit 4: Technical Considerations

Tanouye states in the score that the piece is "perfect for professional, university, or even advanced high school wind ensembles." Soloistic playing is required for many sections within the ensemble, including flute, clarinet, bassoon, alto saxophone, trumpet, tuba, and timpani.

The piece calls for standard wind ensemble orchestration with English horn, E-flat contra-alto clarinet, B-flat contrabass clarinet, contrabassoon, harp, piano, cello, and contrabass. The cello and contrabass parts are doubled throughout the work by winds and piano. From mm. 86–127, the accompaniment uses the pizzicato timbre of the cello and contrabass. Although much of this section is doubled by bassoon and low reeds, there are a few measures that will require rescoring if cello and contrabass are not available. Although the left hand of the piano also doubles all notes in the cello and contrabass, the doubling will help to project the line.

Rapid scalar passages are present in the upper woodwinds and players will need to be familiar with the tonal centers listed in Unit 6: Harmony. Additionally, many of these passages proceed upwards diatonically but descend chromatically.

Instrument ranges are moderate and should be within the capability of most college ensembles and advanced high school groups.

Unit 5: Stylistic Considerations

The primary stylistic challenge in this piece is to differentiate the stylistic atmospheres of each section. A clean, lifted articulation is needed at the opening to ensure the dance-like character of the opening theme. Players should match articulation throughout the opening, particularly during contrapuntal statements.

The flute statement of theme 2 in m. 61 should be smooth and connected, with special care to play the triplet rhythm accurately. All subsequent statements of this theme should match style with the flute and maintain the same rhythmic precision. Beginning in m. 90, the return of the primary motive should be appropriate to the waltz-like style of this section. The notes should be slightly elongated while still maintaining the original character of the theme. Players should listen down to the pizzicato basses as a guide for the length of notes in this section.

Unit 6: Musical Elements

MELODY:
The melodies in *Kokopelli's Dance* are primarily tonal. The primary theme presented by flute at the opening is brought back throughout the work, typically fragmented or augmented, but with little alteration to the intervallic relationships. The primary theme is augmented in mm. 128–140 (the timpani and tuba duet). The secondary theme, stated first in m. 61, provides a flowing contrast to the rhythmically precise theme 1.

Although the piece does not follow a specific program, Tanouye does incorporate programmatic gestures such as the "laughing" motive in m. 162. Stated in open fifths, the gesture is passed throughout the ensemble in conjunction with the return of the primary motive of the piece.

HARMONY:
The piece is primarily tonal and key signatures are used to indicate tonal centers for each section. Tanouye often creates harmonies through the use of counterpoint. Countersubjects are stated a fifth above the original idea and create consonant harmonies throughout the counterpoint.

In mm. 42–58, the main motive is presented imitatively, proceeding through the circle of fifths. The next section, beginning in m. 59, modulates to F minor. The use of the D-natural in this section provides a good opportunity to teach students about Dorian mode, the minor mode with a raised sixth scale degree.

Players will need to be proficient in the following keys: C, G, and A major, and F, G, and A minor.

RHYTHM:

The work is primarily in 4/4 and 3/4 meters, with a few changing and uneven meters present. Beginning in m. 29, the meter changes between simple and compound. The 5/8 and 7/8 bars act as an elongation of the phrase and should be played evenly to ensure proper phrasing. Rehearsing this section with a metronome or percussionist tapping out the eighth note will help players to internalize the subdivision and develop rhythmic independence.

The rhythms throughout the work are active but not complex. Most rhythmic passages are recognizable within a duple subdivision. Although the rhythmic demands are moderate, players, particularly woodwinds, will need to have good technical facility to play at the marked tempos. Establishing clean articulations will help players with rhythmic precision and clarity.

TIMBRE:

Contrapuntal textures created by the counterpoint will require players to listen throughout the ensemble and balance appropriately. Melodies are easily recognizable in each section, and players should be aware of their role within the texture. One way to help players with balance is to isolate melodic lines for the rest of the ensemble to hear, then put the melodic lines back into the context of the ensemble.

The unique texture of the pizzicato cello and contrabass in mm. 86–126 is helpful in creating the waltz-like quality of this section. If cello is not available, the section can easily be transposed for two contrabasses. Rewriting the section for bassoons or low reeds is another solution if strings and piano are not available.

Unit 7: Form and Structure

Kokopelli's Dance is in compound ternary form. The large tripartite ABA' structure is outlined by tempo changes, and each of the three larger sections is constructed in a binary or ternary design.

SECTION	MEASURE	EVENT AND SCORING
A (*Allegro*)		
a	1–12	Flute introduces the primary theme of the piece with imitative counterpoint at the fifth; clarinet, oboe, alto saxophone, and xylophone continue counterpoint; opening tonality is C major, with harmonies created through counterpoint

Section	Measure	Event and Scoring
Fanfare motive	13–20	Trumpet, horn, oboe, English horn, and alto saxophone state fanfare motives, followed by flourishes in upper woodwinds outlining C major
b	21–41	Descending minor thirds are harmonized in brass, clarinet, and xylophone; timpani transition briefly on the dominant to next section; clarinets state theme 2, which is repeated by upper woodwinds; A-flat pedal point is introduced in m. 29 by low voices
a'	42–58	The primary theme is passed through the ensemble, beginning in G major and moving through the circle of fifths on each statement; brief return to C major in m. 58 before horns and upper woodwinds sustain a D-flat in m. 58; cadence into F minor in m. 59
B (*Moderato*)		
a	59–85	Secondary theme is stated and passed through the ensemble; following each statement of this theme, low winds outline new tonality of F minor; oboe, flute, and clarinet state fragmented version of primary theme
b	86–127	Primary and secondary themes are passed through the ensemble over a G minor, waltz-like accompaniment in the basses; descending, chromatic gestures in woodwinds follow each statement of secondary theme
Transition	128–140	Tuba and timpani duet state the primary theme in augmentation
A' (*Allegro*)		
Fanfare	141–160	Horn and trumpet fanfare based on primary theme are stated and followed by woodwind flourishes and dominant-tonic punctuations in the rest of the ensemble; syncopated transition beginning in m. 157 cadences in the new key of A minor at m. 161

Section	Measure	Event and Scoring
a	161–191	New "laughing" motive is presented first in alto and tenor saxophone, then passed throughout the ensemble; primary theme returns after each statement of the "laughing" motive; a mode change to A major in m. 191 transitions to next section
b	192–216	Secondary theme is stated three times in augmentation by mid-range voices
a'	217–230	Primary theme returns in key of A major
Coda	231–249	Fanfare motive returns in m. 244 over a dominant pedal before cadences in A major

Unit 8: Suggested Listening

Bernstein, Leonard:

> Overture to *Candide*. *American Dreams*. Cincinnati Wind Symphony. Eugene Migliaro Corporon, conductor. Klavier K11048. 1992.
> *Symphonic Dances from West Side Story*. *Bernstein*. The New York Philharmonic. Leonard Bernstein, conductor. Sony Masterworks Expanded Edition SK92728. 2004.

Grantham, Donald:

> *Baron Cimetiére's Mambo*. *Altered States*. North Texas Wind Symphony. Eugene Migliaro Corporon, conductor. GIA Publications CD-685. 2006.
> *Baron Samedi's Sarabande (and Soft Shoe)*. *Altered States*. North Texas Wind Symphony. Eugene Migliaro Corporon, conductor. GIA Publications CD-685. 2006.

Mackey, John. *Redline Tango*. University of Kansas Wind Ensemble. John P. Lynch, conductor. Naxos 8.570074. 2005.

Unit 9: Additional References and Resources

Alpert, Joyce M. "Kokopelli: A New Look at the Humpback Flute Player in Anasazi Rock Art." *American Indian Art Magazine* 17, no. 1 (winter 1991): 48–57.

Berry, Wallace. *Form in Music*. Englewood Cliffs, NJ: Prentice-Hall, Inc., 1966.

Sadie, Stanley, ed. *The New Grove Dictionary of Music and Musicians*. Second ed. New York: Macmillan Publishers Limited, 2001.

Website:

> Nathan Tanouye. http://www.nntmusic.com/

Contributed by:

Shannon Kitelinger
Doctoral Conducting Associate
University of North Texas
Denton, Texas

Teacher Resource Guide

Millennium Canons

Kevin Puts
(b. 1972)

transcribed for band by Mark Spede
(b. 1962)

Unit 1: Composer

Kevin Puts (earlier spelled "Putz") was born in Michigan and raised in St. Louis, Missouri. He earned his BM from the Eastman School of Music (in piano and composition), studying with Samuel Adler and Joseph Schwantner. His master's in composition is from Yale, where he studied with Jacob Druckman, Martin Bresnick, and David Lang. As a Tanglewood fellow he studied with Bernard Rands and William Bolcom. Puts returned to Eastman for a doctor of musical arts degree, studying composition with Christopher Rouse and piano with Nelita True. He served on the composition faculty at the University of Texas at Austin (1997–2005), and now teaches at the Peabody Institute of Johns Hopkins University.

Kevin Puts has composed music for a variety of ensembles, including four symphonies, other large orchestral works, chamber music, concerti, and solo works. Among his awards are the Benjamin H. Danks Award for Excellence in Orchestral Composition of the American Academy of Arts and Letters, a John Simon Guggenheim Memorial Foundation Fellowship, a Rome Prize from the American Academy in Rome, and the Barlow International Prize for Orchestral Music. His music has been performed by the New York Philharmonic, Houston Symphony, Tonhalle Orchestra (Zurich), Minnesota Orchestra, Pacific Symphony, Utah Symphony, Atlanta Symphony, Baltimore Symphony, Cincinnati Symphony and the St. Louis Symphony, among others. Puts has been composer-in-residence with the California Symphony, Fort Worth (Texas) Symphony, and the Mobile Symphony. His only original work for wind ensemble is *Chorus of Light*, premiered in 2003 by Jerry Junkin for the University of Texas Wind Ensemble.

Unit 2: Composition

The composer states in the program notes: "I wrote *Millennium Canons* to usher in a new millennium with fanfare, celebration and lyricism. Its rising textures and melodic counterpoint are almost always created through use of the canon, which also provides rhythmic propulsion at times." Funding was provided by the Institute for American Music of the Eastman School of Music of the University of Rochester. The premiere took place in June 2001 at Symphony Hall, Boston, with the Boston Pops Orchestra under the direction of Keith Lockhart.

Mark Spede transcribed *Millennium Canons* from the orchestral score with the composer's approval in late 2001. The University of Texas Wind Ensemble, Jerry Junkin, conductor, premiered the band version on December 5, 2001 in Austin, Texas.

The nine-minute single-movement work is written in a very tonal neo-Romantic style, although it does contain some unusual modulations and contemporary suspensions (mostly fourths and seconds—in fact the last suspension sequence is 4–2–3 (A-flat–F–G) over E-flat and B-flat). It is a very accessible work for the listener, as it was written for an orchestral pops concert. It does however, have musical depth, and is orchestrated utilizing the full color palette of the contemporary orchestra/wind ensemble including piano, harp, and melodic percussion. The band version is scored for piccolo flute 1–2, flute 1–2, oboe 1–3, bassoon 1–2, contrabassoon, E-flat clarinet, clarinet 1–3, B-flat bass clarinet, E-flat contrabass clarinet, soprano saxophone, alto saxophone 1–2, tenor saxophone, baritone saxophone, trumpets 1–4 in C (trumpet 1 has an assistant), horn 1–4, trombone 1–2, bass trombone, euphonium 1–2, tuba, contrabass, timpani, percussion 1–4 (suspended cymbal, bass drum, 3 tam-tams—large, medium and small—tubular bells, vibraphone, glockenspiel, crotales, marimba, cymbals, xylophone, triangle, high and low woodblocks, and high and low temple blocks), harp, and piano.

A word of caution: the alto saxophone players (and to a lesser extent the soprano saxophonist) must be comfortable moving into the altissimo register, and as noted above, there are five distinct saxophone parts. In addition, the arranger has split trumpet 1 into an A and B player due to upper register endurance issues. This is not a transcription for the inexperienced ensemble, but worth the time investment of the conductor and ensemble.

In his program notes for *Chorus of Light* (2003), his only work written specifically for wind ensemble, Puts states:

> Almost all of my recent projects involve the transformation of a theme or melody by placing it in a variety of what could be called "expressive contexts." In other words, I write a melody and say to myself "what if it were played in a really bold, declamatory way?" or "what if it were played sweetly and serenely?" I try to imagine it within different textures, with different accompaniments, and played by different groups of instruments. Then I try to tell a musical story by placing these ideas within the context of a continuous musical narrative. After a while I begin to imagine the original theme as the "main character" of the story. I imagine this character exploring and being affected by different worlds and environments.

These words well apply to *Millennium Canons*. The fairly simple diatonic canon theme is first presented at the eighth note, and many times in eight or more voices, creating a very complex texture. First stated in the brass, it quickly takes on the flavor of a bold fanfare, then just as quickly evaporates and starts again quietly in low woodwinds. The canon is sometimes presented in augmentation, sometimes in diminution, and sometimes as a melody with shimmering colors and harmony. It all leads to an impressive climax that leaves the listener quite sated.

Unit 3: Historical Perspective

Kevin Puts was in his late twenties when *Millennium Canons* was composed in 2001. By the turn of the millennium, younger composers were more influenced by the neo-Romantic movement (return to tonality) than by the academic style so prevalent at the academy for most of the twentieth century. Puts's orchestration is colorful and idiomatic, and he uses the percussion section, piano, and harp to great effect. His music is generally built on the transformation and variation of relatively simple material. His music is accessible to performers and audiences alike, and may be influenced by film music in addition to his many famous composition teachers.

One may deduce from the bright, colorful, and upbeat mood of *Millennium Canons* that the composer found the turn of the century an upbeat and hopeful time; the horrific events of 9/11 did not seem in the realm of possibility. Just three months later this work might have turned out much differently.

Unit 4: Technical Considerations

The opening of *Millennium Canons* is in 2/2 and marked "Elegantly ascending, half-note = 60." Aside from an occasional 3/2 measure, the piece is in 2/2 throughout, although the conductor and ensemble may feel more comfortable feeling it in 4/4 and 6/4.

The arranger kept the original key of the orchestral version, and the transfer of some high string parts to wind and percussion instruments will present challenging intonation issues. Specifically, alto saxophone goes to a written A one octave higher than the first line above the staff. Two distinct piccolo parts were also employed to keep melodic material in the original register. These instruments (and others) must tune to melodic percussion, piano, and harp in similar registers. The transcription makes use of many of the "color" woodwinds to enhance the extreme upper and lower tessitura, although the conductor should probably feel free to omit some of the rarer instruments if necessary.

Rhythmically the work presents a challenge in the way the opening canon is presented: there are eight separate entrances in the first two measures, and the four trumpets enter only an eighth note apart, creating an echo effect. Each player must have the confidence and maturity to play the line independently while those around seem to be playing the same material in the wrong place. Brass players will need to double and triple tongue, and woodwind parts contain some passages with rapid arpeggios and wide-interval tremolos.

The four percussionists must move between a variety of instruments, and all play melodic instruments at some point. The timpani part is standard.

Millennium Canons is firmly rooted in the key of E-flat and is very diatonic. Puts keeps melodic and harmonic variety by moving through key centers often, with forays into the keys of F and A minor as well as C, G, A-flat, B, and B-flat major before resolving in E-flat.

Unit 5: Stylistic Considerations

A variety of articulations are marked, as well as short-duration crescendos from soft to loud. Some quarter notes are marked *sffp* with a crescendo to *ff* or *fff*. Many of these passages are fanfare-type figures, so an aggressive articulation should be considered. Other sections are very flowing and lyrical, requiring a mature legato approach.

Many of the phrases begin softly, build to a loud moment, and recede to start the process again. Puts employs some specific verbiage in the score which may give the conductor some interpretive insight: "steadily emerging," "with nobility, "with sincerity," "...a sudden flourish," "majestic," "impassioned," "risoluto," affetuoso," and at the end, "with tremendous energy and excitement."

An understanding of how the composer employs the canon material at any given moment is essential to creating the correct style, whether it be fanfare, lyrical, rhythmically driving, etc. Each section of the work has its own mood which should be communicated to the audience. The correct attention to the many dynamics and pacing of the final climax are essential to a meaningful and satisfying performance.

Unit 6: Musical Elements

MELODY:

Puts eloquently uses the relatively simple and diatonic canon material in a variety of ways. The opening measures played at a slower tempo will not only help align entrances, but help players understand some of the later sections in the piece. The diatonic quality of the material is offset by frequent modulations to remote and sometimes unrelated (and unprepared) keys.

HARMONY:

The basic harmonic structure employed in *Millennium Canons* is the diatonic triad. Some passing suspensions add momentary spice as they enter and resolve. Occasionally there will be a dissonant bass note (such as the C-flat pedal under an E-flat major triad one bar before letter P) or a harmonic sequence above a prolonged pedal point that adds interest and drama.

RHYTHM:

The basic meter of 2/2 (and occasional 3/2) is fairly incessant. The tempo shifts slightly, depending on the mood and style of a particular section, but there are no extremely slow or fast tempos in the piece. The rhythmic difficulties lie in the canon entrances, the double- and triple-tongue passages, and occasional odd note groupings.

TIMBRE:

Millennium Canons is an optimistic piece, filled with bright, shimmering colors. Many instruments are taken to the edge of their ranges and have to play long, flowing lines there. The percussion section, along with piano and harp, add to the brightness on metallic instruments such as glockenspiel, tubular bells, vibraphone, and crotales. The bright color palette is offset by a number of low-register instruments, creating a very wide range of timbres.

Unit 7: Form and Structure

The rehearsal letters are placed at structural points in the work, helping the conductor navigate the architecture of the form. Essentially the form is a through-composed, sectionalized hybrid of variation and rondo form. A canon is presented and varied, then a lyrical theme based on the canon material appears. This canon and theme are varied and alternated throughout the work, mainly through the use of modulation and scoring.

MEASURE	KEY	EVENT AND SCORING
1	E-flat	Canon and fanfare in brass
A	C	Canon in low woodwinds
C	G	Canon in full orchestration
D	A minor	Lyrical theme with canon underneath
E	A-flat	Lyrical theme builds with canon variation
F	E-flat	Climax and transition
G	B	Quiet canon variation in alto sax duet
H	G/B-flat	Transition flourishes and build
I	A-flat	Canon variation in woodwinds and low brass
J	F/A minor	Bright variation on lyrical theme
K	E-flat	Sustained canon with woodwind and percussion flourishes over B-flat pedal
L	E-flat	Lyrical theme variation over B-flat pedal
M	E-flat	Canon restarts in woodwinds
N	A-flat	Opening canon in A-flat (down a fifth)
O	E-flat	Fanfare and build moving from V to I
P	E-flat	Coda: canon with fourth and second suspensions and build to final climax

Unit 8: Suggested Listening

Lang, David. *Are You Experienced?* For narrator, electric tuba, and ensemble.
Puts, Kevin:
   Canyon. For solo marimba.
   Dark Vigil. For string quartet.
   Inspiring Beethoven. For orchestra.
   Ritual Protocol. For marimba and piano.
   Simaku. For string quartet.
Rouse, Christopher:
   Karolju. For chorus and orchestra.
   Rapture. For orchestra.

Unit 9: Additional References and Resources

Puts, Kevin. *Millennium Canons.* The University of Texas Wind Ensemble.
   Jerry Junkin, conductor. Mark Custom Recording Service B0013A1IHU.
www.kevinputs.com

Contributed by:

Mark Spede
Clemson University
Clemson, South Carolina

Teacher Resource Guide

New Morning for the World
Daybreak of Freedom

Joseph Schwantner
(b. 1943)

transcribed for winds by Nikk Pilato
(b. 1972)

Unit 1: Composer

Joseph Schwantner was born in Chicago, Illinois, on March 22, 1943. He holds degrees from the American Conservatory (in Chicago) and Northwestern University, where he studied with Bernard Diester, Alan Stout, and Anthony Donato. He has held teaching positions at Pacific Lutheran University, Ball State University, the Eastman School of Music, The Juilliard School, and Yale University.

Schwantner is the recipient of numerous awards and prizes, including three BMI Student Composition Awards, the Bearns Prize, the first Charles Ives Scholarship, four NEA grants, a Guggenheim Foundation Fellowship, and the 1979 Pulitzer Prize in Music for his orchestral composition, *Aftertones of Infinity*. At the invitation of Leonard Slatkin, Schwantner served as the Composer-in-Residence for the Saint Louis Symphony Orchestra from 1982 to 1985. Slatkin and the SLSO would later record two of Schwantner's works, *Magabunda: Four Poems of Agueda Pizzaro* (1985), and *A Sudden Rainbow* (1987), both of which were nominated for Best New Classical Composition Grammy awards.

In 2007 the American Symphony Orchestra League and the Meet the Composer foundation announced that Schwantner was selected as a Ford Made in America composer. The foundation gives orchestras with small budgets representing all fifty states in the U. S. an opportunity to commission American composers of international reputation. The new work, *Chasing Light*, will receive its premiere with the Reno Chamber Orchestra in September of 2008. It will subsequently be performed by orchestras in each of the fifty states.

Unit 2: Composition

New Morning for the World: Daybreak of Freedom for narrator and orchestra was commissioned by the American Telephone and Telegraph Company for the Eastman Philharmonia, David Effron, conductor. It was premiered on January 15, 1983, at the Kennedy Center for the Performing Arts in Washington DC, with Pittsburgh Pirates baseball star Willie Stargell narrating. The wind transcription was premiered by the Florida State University Wind Orchestra on April 20, 2007, Nikk Pilato, conductor, and David Eccles, narrator. Both versions of the work are published by Schott-Helicon Music, Inc.

Over the years, *New Morning for the World* has become one of Schwantner's most popular works. It has received numerous performances worldwide, in part due to its political subject matter as well as a host of past narrators that include Danny Glover, Robert Guillaume, James Earl Jones, Vernon Jordan, Coretta Scott King, Yolanda King, Sidney Poitier, William Warfield, and Alfre Woodard, among others.

The twenty-five-minute work calls for flute 1–2 (3–4 double piccolo), oboe 1–2 , English horn, bassoon 1–3 , E-flat soprano clarinet, B-flat soprano clarinet 1–3, B-flat bass clarinet, B-flat contrabass clarinet, soprano saxophone, alto saxophone 1–2, tenor saxophone, baritone saxophone, trumpet 1–3 in C, horn 1–4, trombone 1–4, euphonium 1–2, tuba, string bass, amplified piano, amplified celesta, harp, and percussion 1–6 requiring a total of thirty instruments which include bass drum 1–2, crotales, glockenspiel, marimba 1-2, a small button gong, suspended cymbals 1–2, tam-tams 1–3, timbales 1–2, timpani, tom-toms 1–2 (three in each set), triangle 1–2, tubular bells, vibraphone 1-2, and xylophone 1–2.

Unit 3: Historical Perspective

Schwantner has composed four works specifically for winds: *...and the mountains rising nowhere* (1977), *From a Dark Millennium* (1981), *In evening's stillness...* (1996), and *Recoil* (2004). In addition to this transcription of *New Morning*, two other transcriptions for winds of Schwantner's orchestral works exist: *Concerto for Percussion* (1994, by Andrew Boysen, Jr.) and *Beyond Autumn* (2006, by Timothy Miles).

The composition of *New Morning for the World* was suggested to Schwantner by Robert Freeman, former director of the Eastman School of Music. It was Freeman's wish to initiate a project honoring the memory of

Martin Luther King, Jr. The texts are selected from a variety of King's speeches, addresses, and writings, encompassing a period of more than a decade of his life. Schwantner states in the score: "These words, eloquently expressed by the thrust of his oratory, bear witness to the power and nobility of Martin Luther King Jr.'s ideas, principles, and beliefs."

Unit 4: Technical Considerations

The technical challenges of *New Morning* are myriad, ranging from difficult rhythmic considerations to the sheer stamina required to perform this lengthy work. Most immediately vexing to conductors unfamiliar with Schwantner's compositions is his use of open or French scoring (sometimes also referred to as "cut-out" scoring). This is a type of score layout in which staves of instruments that rest do not appear at all in the score until they are called for again. This means that staves can also appear mid-page for a few measures and vanish again (see figure 1). This type of scoring tends to create large, open gaps throughout pages of the score that can be a distraction to those not familiar with this technique.

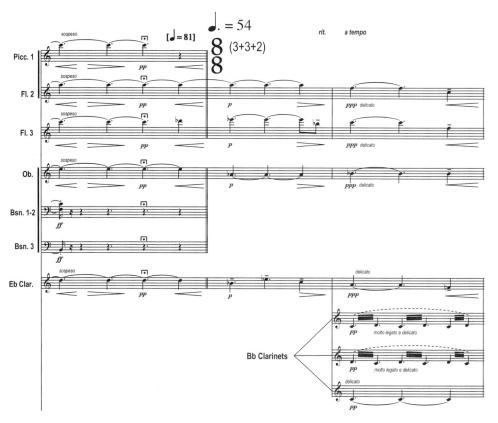

FIGURE 1. Open scoring

The meter changes often, with frequent use of unusual meter signatures such as 6/16, 11/16, 12/16, 11/8, and 7/2. In addition, the pulse breakdowns do not always remain the same; for example, the 11/8 meter is found broken down as 3 + 3 + 3 + 2 and 2 + 2 + 2 + 2 + 3; the 9/8 is broken down as 2 + 2 + 3 + 2 and 3 + 3 + 3, etc. Subdivisions at the thirty-second and or sixty-fourth note are employed as well. *New Morning for the World* does not use a key signature, making a large number of accidentals necessary. There is no use of modes or of tonic-dominant function; the melodic and harmonic materials are derived from pitch sets encountered during the introduction.

Percussion demands are numerous, including the sheer number of instruments required and the complicated patterns that must be performed. The transcription calls for six percussionists, five of which must possess advanced mallet skills; the sixth is the timpanist. In addition, the work calls for an amplified piano, an amplified celesta (this part cannot be covered by the pianist), and a harp (which is not optional, but integral).

The conductor also faces the challenge of balancing the large forces required for this work with the narration. The relationship between orchestra and narrator is for the most part kept simple, with alternating sections that allow the speaker to be heard clearly. When the narrator and the orchestra are used concurrently, the orchestration is thin and the dynamic level must be balanced to the narrator.

Last but not least, the work requires a narrator with a powerful voice and an ability to convey the emotions represented by King's words. Although the work is in one continuous movement, the text itself is presented in three different sections: the oppression of the past, the present and continuing struggle for equality, and the desired future outcome of King's "dream." The narrator must understand and express the different tenor each of these sections requires.

Unit 5: Stylistic Considerations

As in many of Schwantner's compositions, attention has been paid to the role of percussion, keeping it on an equal footing with winds (and strings in the original). This transcription strives to keep the composer's sentiment in mind: although an additional percussion part was necessary, none of the intent of the percussion writing is fundamentally changed. It is therefore important to treat the percussion as an equal to the brass and woodwinds.

Precise attention must be paid to articulations and dynamic contrasts, particularly in the mallet percussion parts. Melodies are often initiated by mallet percussion because of the clear attacks these instruments can produce. This technique makes timing and precision of the utmost importance: wind instruments attacking an entrance incorrectly might not stand out as would melodic percussion with hard mallets.

Schwantner is able to achieve startling sonorities in part due to the creative orchestration he employs. His use of unusual instrumental combinations, coupled with his creative percussive writing, tends to give the impression of rich orchestral color. Samuel Adler once said of Schwantner: "His main concern is the beauty of sound and progression that will make sense to the listener."[1]

Unit 6: Musical Elements

MELODY:

Schwantner frequently uses a technique he refers to as "shared monody," in which the melodic idea is shared by doublings among several different instruments. This concept entails several players entering and then sustaining a different pitch of the melody. In turn, these notes become a single line (shared by several instruments), as opposed to one instrument performing one solo musical line (see figure 2).

FIGURE 2. Shared monody

Note that piccolo and flute trade off between having the melodic ostinato in full and sharing the line. In the first measure, piccolo 2 and flute 2 would in tandem yield the piccolo 1 and flute 1 melody, but with a hint of sustain.

New Morning for the World represents one of the more melodically-driven works in Schwantner's compositional output. Most of the musical material in the work is derived from one of seven musical motives. Motive 1 (figure 3) is introduced in percussion, but also figures prominently in the winds in various transformations throughout the composition. This motive is extended during each repetition (figure 4), and often signals the beginning of a new section of music.

FIGURE 3. Motive 1

FIGURE 4. Motive 1 extension sequence

Motive 2 (figure 5) consists of a series of triplets presented in the harp, keyboard instruments, and metallophones. Motive 2 is used several times, most often in its original form, but twice in transposed forms (m. 153 and 286), and at the end in rhythmic augmentation.

FIGURE 5. Motive 2

Motive 3 (figure 6) is first presented in the horns at m. 3, with bassoons and trombones (and sometimes tuba) adding parallel perfect fifths underneath. Motive 3 is usually expanded throughout each of its appearances in the score in the same manner as motive 1. (See figure 7 for the full expansion of motive 3.) The three preceding motives present the majority of the source material throughout the work.

FIGURE 6. Motive 3

FIGURE 7. Motive 3 extension sequence

Motive 4 (figure 8) is an ostinato first appearing in the piano, celesta, harp, and vibes at m. 57. The ostinato is based on an artificial seven-note scale: B-flat–C–D-flat–E-flat–F–G–A. Throughout the work this ostinato will appear in different rhythmic and harmonic transformations, such as the 11/16 measures beginning at m. 115.

FIGURE 8. Motive 4

Motive 5 (figure 9) is a slow, mournful melody that serves as the beginning of segment B at m. 203. Each iteration of the melody ends with a suspension leading into a fermata.

FIGURE 9. Motive 5

Motive 6 (figure 10) is the bright triplet gesture that will later be paired with King's powerful words: "I have a dream." The motive first appears at m. 218.

FIGURE 10. Motive 6

The final motive (motive 7, figure 11) is a development of motive 5, constructed from a synthetic scale: F–G-flat–A-flat–B-flat–C-flat–D-flat–E-flat. It is first introduced at m. 254. Every other measure (during the 3/2 bars) the theme ends in a suspension, by which Schwantner affirms the tonality for each two-measure phrase. The tonality travels upwards from F Major (mm. 254–255) to C major (m. 256–257) to G major (m. 258–263), before arriving at A-flat minor at m. 264.

FIGURE 11. Motive 7

HARMONY:
For Schwantner, tonal centers are highlighted by pitch emphasis, not keys or cadential progressions. The main thematic elements of his works can often be found in the first few bars of the composition, as is the case with the sustained

pitches of the glass crystals in *…and the mountains*, the opening sixteen pitches in the piano part of *From a Dark Millennium*, and the opening piano and horn chords from *In evening's stillness*. The thematic elements are often drawn from sepatatonic or octatonic scales.

Schwantner also employs what he calls "static pillars" of harmonies, in which blocks of sound may be held unchanging for a length of time. This idea is a reflection of the composer's experiences with the guitar and its sustaining capabilities. Over these pillars of sound Schwantner often writes other instrumental parts engaged in the "shared monody" concept described above.

RHYTHM:

Recurring rhythmic motives are found in abundance in Schwantner's writing, and *New Morning* is no different. Rhythmic motive A (figure 12) first appears in m. 3 in the trumpets.

FIGURE 12. Rhythmic motive A

The second rhythmic motive (figure 13) appears frequently in conjunction with motive 1. It makes its first appearance at m. 73 in the upper woodwinds and xylophone, and also appears in an altered form (as in m. 87).

FIGURE 13. Rhythmic motive B

Rhythmic motive C (figure 14) is first presented by bassoons, clarinet 3, saxophones, and low brass at m. 288:

FIGURE 14. Rhythmic motive C

TIMBRE:

Timbre and color are important considerations in all of Schwantner's compositions, but especially in those for winds. Many of his creative solutions to issues of balance and orchestral color are evident as trademarks in his music. Jeffrey Briggs (1984) states that "orchestration is a controlling element in Schwantner's compositional technique. Most sections of his music seem to have been designed to exploit his coloristic imagination."[2]

Unit 7: Form and Structure

SECTION	MEASURE	EVENT AND SCORING
A	1–202	
Introduction	1–17	Most of the musical material in *New Morning* is derived from motives 1–3 and rhythmic motive A, presented in this introductory section
	18–35	Transitory section; woodwinds have the melody, percussion and keyboards reiterate motive 2
Narration 1	36–49	Motive 1 is presented via expansion in brass and woodwinds
	50–56	Transitional material
	57–64	Motive 4 (ostinato) introduced
	65–71	Example of shared monody in woodwinds, horns, and vibes (this figure is a variation on the motive 4 ostinato); trumpet and trombone fanfare

SECTION	MEASURE	EVENT AND SCORING
	72–86	Transitory section; variation on motive 1 presented by brass; introduction of Rhythmic motive B
	87–97	Rhythmic variation on motive 4 ostinato in conjunction with Rhythmic motive B; transition
Narration 2	98–109	Motive 4 ostinato in original form presented in keyboards and mallet percussion
	110–123	Variants of motive 4 presented in woodwinds and harp
	124–151	Transitory section, fantasia
Narration 3	152–163	Motives 2 and 3
	164–185	Transitory section; fragments of motive 4 variant
	186–202	Variant of motive 1 presented by trumpets, horns, and woodwinds
B	203–285	
Narration 4	203–217	Motive 5; saxophone choir with low reeds and string bass; focus of narration shifts from past to present
	218–227	Introduction of motive 6
	228–244	Motive 5; saxophone choir with low reeds and string bass
	245–253	Solo horn presentation of motive 1; "church bells"
Narration 5	254–285	Introduction of motive 7; woodwinds and horn
A1	286–381	
	286–292	Variants on motive 4; rhythmic motive C in saxes, low reeds, and brass
	293–299	Rhythmic motive A in tandem with motives 1, 3, and 4
	300–327	Shared monody in woodwinds, horns, and vibes; variant on motive 4; trumpet and trombone fanfare
	328–345	Motive 7 presented with rhythmic motive C to heighten rhythmic and harmonic tension
Narration 6	346–361	Narration focus shifts to the future; motive 5

SECTION	MEASURE	EVENT AND SCORING
	362–371	Motive 6; "I have a Dream"
	372–381	Motive 5
Coda	382–406	
Narration 7	382–396	Light, delicate scoring; emphasis on percussive and amplified keyboard texture
	397–406	Triplet quarter notes in mallets and keyboards; variant of Motive 2; wind vocalizations

Unit 8: Suggested Listening

Schwantner, Joseph:
>*Aftertones of Infinity*. The Juilliard Orchestra. Leonard Slatkin, conductor. New World Records.
>*...and the mountains rising nowhere*. The North Texas Wind Symphony. Eugene Corporon, conductor: Klavier.
>*From a Dark Millennium*. The North Texas Wind Symphony. Eugene Corporon, conductor. Klavier.
>*In evening's stillness...*. The North Texas Wind Symphony. Eugene Corporon, conductor. Klavier.
>*Music of Amber*. The Holst Sinfonietta. Klaus Simon, conductor. Naxos.
>*New Music for the World* (orchestral version). The National Symphony Orchestra. Leonard Slatkin, conductor. Vernon Jordan, narrator. RCA.
>*Recoil*. The North Texas Wind Symphony. Eugene Corporon, conductor. Klavier.

Unit 9: Additional References and Resources

Briggs, Jeffery L. "The Recent Music of Joseph Schwantner: Unique and Essential Elements." Doctoral diss., University of Illinois, 1984. UMI#8502083.

Chute, James E. "The Reemergence of Tonality in Contemporary Music as Shown in the Works of David Del Tredeci, Joseph Schwantner, and John Adams." Doctoral diss., University of Cincinnati, 1991. UMI#9302359.

Folio, Cynthia J. "An Analysis and Comparison of Four Compositions by Joseph Schwantner." Doctoral diss., University of Rochester, Eastman School of Music, 1985. UMI# 8508803.

Higbee, Scott. "Joseph Schwantner: A Composer's Insight." Salzman, ed. Galesville, MD: Meredith Music Publications, 2003.

Montgomery, Ronald. "The Use of Voice in Five Selected Works for Band." Doctoral diss., University of Arizona, 2005. UMI# 3205465.

Pilato, Nikk. "A Conductor's Guide to Wind Music of Joseph Schwantner."
    Doctoral diss., Florida State University, 2007.
Renshaw, Jeffrey. " Schwantner on Composition." *Instrumentalist*, 45, no. 10
    (1991): 14–17.
Schwantner, Joseph. Interview with the composer by the author. March 25,
    2007.

Contributed by:

Nikk Pilato
Assistant Director of Bands
University of Georgia
Athens, Georgia

---

1 David Stearns, "Joseph Schwantner," Musical America, 29: 25–34, 1979.
2 Jeffery L. Briggs, "The recent music of Joseph Schwantner: Unique and essential
   elements, Doctoral diss., University of Illinois, 1984, UMI no. 8502083.

Teacher Resource Guide

Nine Greek Dances

Nikos Skalkottas
(1904–1949)

edited by Gunther Schuller
(b. 1925)

Unit 1: Composer

Nikos Skalkottas was born in Halkis, Greece in 1904 and spent most of his youth in Athens, Greece. Raised in a musical family, Nikos began violin lessons at the age of five when his teachers were his father and uncle. By the age of ten he was enrolled in the Athens Conservatory. Upon gradating at the age of sixteen from the Conservatory, he won several scholarships, which led him to the Berlin Hochschule für Musik. There he studied violin with Willy Hess and composition with Juon and Robert Kahn.

In his early years, Skalkottas earned his living as a violinist in the café and cinema orchestras in Berlin. In 1923 he gave up his career as a violinist to pursue composition full time. His most notable composition teachers include Kurt Weill, Phillipp Jarnach, and Arnold Schoenberg. Skalkottas took much effort in blending the influences of his teachers into his own unique style. During his time in Berlin many of his chamber and symphonic works were performed publicly.

Financial burdens and the rise of Nazism led to little support in Berlin in the early 1930s. Skalkottas returned to Athens in 1933, where his atonal and serial music was not widely accepted. He intended to return to Berlin, however his passport was seized by Greek authorities as tensions escalated leading up to World War II.

During the last decade of his life he isolated himself, refusing to talk about music except to a few close friends. He composed diligently until his

unexpected death in 1949. Despite his remarkable output of atonal and twelve-tone pieces, many regard Skallkottas as the Bartók of Greece. Although much of his music remained unknown, unpublished, and unplayed during his lifetime, during his twenty-five year career he composed over 170 works, many with remarkable erudition and complexity. Only in recent years has Skalkottas's work been recognized for its ingenuity.

Unit 2: Composition

Nine Greek Dances was originally composed for string orchestra and was derived from a series of thirty-six Greek dances that Skalkottas wrote between 1934–36. Skalkottas drew on melodies and folk tunes found in the Merlier archive recordings, published collections, and popular songs. These dances were arranged for various ensembles, including orchestra, string quartet, violin, and piano. Approximately two-thirds of the thirty-six dances are based on actual folksongs from different parts of the Greek mainland and islands, while the other third are original to Skalkottas's folksong style. Unlike most of his works, many of the dances were performed publicly during his lifetime. Dated between 1940–42, this arrangement of nine dances for military band existed only in manuscript form.

This work is nine movements and approximately twenty minutes in length. Each movement has a unique character, specific scoring, and technical demands. The editor, Gunther Schuller, has indicated suggestions in the score for two separate suites each approximately ten minutes in length.

Unit 3: Historical Perspective

Dance has a long-standing tradition in the Greek culture traced back to before the time of Plato and Aristotle. There are over 4,000 traditional dances that developed from all regions of Greece. Traditional Greek dance is an expression of feeling and everyday life. Dance was used in war preparation, to ensure fertility, and is still used today for religious ceremonies and festivals. Dances vary between different regions and are often named after the village where they originated. There are two categories of traditional Greek dance: a leaping or jumping dance, and a dragging dance known as the *syrtos*. The *syrtos* is the oldest form of Greek dance.

The most popular dance, the *kalamatianos*, originated in the town of Kalamata in southern Greece. Danced in an open circle, participants on either end hold scarves and perform variations of the dance, leaps, and spins. This dance consists of a 7/8 meter and is usually moderate in tempo.

Unit 4: Technical Considerations

Nine Greek Dances demands enormous technical prowess from the entire ensemble. There are a numerous virtuosic solo sections in movements 2 and 7. Woodwinds, especially oboe, E-flat clarinet, English horn, and B-flat clarinet have many demanding scalar passages throughout the entire work. Ranges are also extended in much of the brass writing. Trombones are written to third space C in the treble clef. The alto horn parts, particularly in movements 4–7, are primarily above the staff. This could present a problem if these parts are played on modern horns.

Another element to consider is scoring. *Nine Dances* was composed for European military band. This type of scoring includes A clarinet, E-flat alto horn, C trumpet, E-flat trumpet and F tuba. The euphonium part is often written in treble clef, similar to the scoring of a brass band.

Unit 5: Stylistic Considerations

Melody, rhythm, articulation, and tempo are particularly important when recreating dance music. The conductor must strive to make the melody heard at all times. Balance is often difficult due to the scoring in many of the movements. Frequently, only one or two voices have the melody while many have the rhythmic background.

Accurate articulation is crucial in conveying the correct style of the dance. Dancers of this music would often move against strong beats, therefore accents on weak beats and syncopations are very important. The music must remain light and consistent throughout. Solo sections are representative of the improvisatory nature of Greek dance. They should be free and unbridled.

When conveying the appropriate style of a dance it is important to consider tempo. The tempo of each of dance is specific and often taken too fast. The conductor should be mindful of the most challenging sections of the movement when setting the tempo.

Unit 6: Musical Elements

There are a variety of melodies in each of the movements of *Nine Greek Dances*. Each has a different character, yet has similar musical features. The melodic material is often chromatic and melismatic in nature. Even though most of the melodic lines are unison, it is the clever timbre pairings that give each melody its character.

Skalkottas brings unique scoring choices to his work. He often pairs specific voices to create a single timbre. It is crucial that each timbre combination is audible through what are often thick textures. Muted sonorities also add a unique flair to the work. Muted brass is frequently scored in extreme registers. The use of the European military band instrumentation, specifically alto horn, F tuba, and E-flat trumpet, also lend to the overall timbre of the piece.

Even though Skalkottas was a student of Schoenberg and a master of atonal music, he was very insistent that modern techniques not be used with folk music. The majority of the movements are in minor mode with colorful dissonances scored throughout.

Rhythms found in the melodic lines are quite demanding, mostly in the woodwinds. Complex melodic lines superimposed on each other make many of the rhythms in the woodwinds difficult to unify. With the 7/8 meter of movement 2, there are many dotted and sixteenth-note patterns involving several accidentals. It is important that, however difficult these rhythmic passages, the tempo and style remain consistent.

Unit 7: Form and Structure

SECTION	MEASURE	EVENT AND SCORING
Movement 1: "Epirotikos (Dance from Epirus)"		
	1–25	Theme A; dialogue between clarinet/alto sax and horn/trombone
	25–35	Transitional section; motive (sixteenth and dotted eighth)
	36–53	Theme A' in horn, alto horn, and alto sax with sixteenth-note counterline in E-flat clarinet, clarinet, oboe, and flute
	54–55	Transition to theme B
	56–63	Theme B introduced by double reeds and clarinets
	63–66	Piccolo, flute, C trumpet and trombone introduce counterline
	67–71	Piccolo and flute join theme B; brass continues counterline; horn and euphonium bring back motive from m. 25
	72–78	Coda; tempo change to quarter note = 126; melody in English horn and clarinets reinforced by piccolo and flute; trombone, saxes, and bassoon have supporting line
Movement 2: "Peloponnisiakos (Dance Peloponnesos)"		
Section 1	1–8	Theme A; low clarinet, saxes, and brass
	9–16	Theme A repeated with reduced scoring; upper woodwinds
	17–24	Transitional section; sixteenth and eighth-note motive; fragmented entrances in woodwinds; triplet in clarinet foreshadows theme C; ends with horn call in mm. 24–25

Section	Measure	Event and Scoring
	25–32	Theme B introduced by brass in one-measure cannon; statement of theme B ends with same horn call as mm. 24–25
	33–40	Theme B repeated
Section 2	41–47	Theme C; develops out of triplet motives begun in low reeds
	48–53	Syncopation in low brass builds to the end of the section with a tutti entrance at m. 54
	54–66	Transition to the new section reminiscent of beginning; clarinet echoes tutti statement in mm. 58; bass clarinet and bassoon echo motive from m. 17; ending on a fermata in the brass on a major third
	67–75	Theme C'; slower; beginning with oboe, then passed to brass; falling half steps in accompaniment; ends on a fermata on A major
	76–86	Theme C''; solo version of theme C; cadenza-like solos in clarinets and trombone; final statement of theme C in woodwinds and horn ending on an A minor chord
Section 1		D. S. repeats mm. 1–40

Movement 3: "Kalamatianos (Dance from Kalamata)"

	Measure	Event and Scoring
	1–4	Introduction
	5–8	First melodic phrase in upper woodwinds
	9–10	Melodic phrase echoed by cornets and trumpets
	11–15	Melodic lines intertwine over the 7/8 ostinato established by low voices
	16–19	Melody in trumpet and trombone with flourishes in clarinet
	20–27	Second melodic phrase introduced in oboe and E-flat clarinet, first **mf,** then repeated **mp**; horns; syncopated rhythm drives against the 7/8 ostinato in low brass and low reeds; counterline in clarinet and alto sax
	28–40	Timpani solo on downbeat of m. 28 followed by a tutti entrance; pairs of voices take turns with the main melodic idea

SECTION	MEASURE	EVENT AND SCORING
	41–43	M. 41 same as m. 28, this time without timpani solo; last melodic statement in woodwinds
	44–47	Timpani solo under sustain in winds

Movement 4: "Mariori Mou (My Mariori)"

	1–6	Quarter note = 63; theme A in English horn and alto sax with pulsation accompaniment; B-flat trumpet adds to accompaniment in m. 9
	17–20	New tempo: half note = 84; meter change to 5/4; theme B in alto horn, cornet, and trombone
	21–24	Theme B answered by clarinet
	25–41	Tempo change to quarter = 63; theme A varied; pulsating accompaniment in woodwinds at m. 25, then brass at m. 33
	50–55	Theme B extension
	56–67	Theme A varied
	68–75	Theme B returns; alto horn and euphonium added to melody; thicker texture; pulsating accompaniment in all voices except the melody
	76–80	Ending; descending and ascending quarter notes

Movement 5: "Pediake pios to petaxe (Children, who threw it?)"

	1–11	Theme A; melody in trombone
	12–16	Theme A answered by horn and woodwinds
	17–21	Theme B; muted trombone accompanied by muted horns and euphonium
	22–33	Theme C; sixteenth-note passages in woodwinds.
	34–40	Melody in woodwinds reminiscent of theme B
	41–50	Melody in flute and oboe derived from theme A

Movement 6: "Kritikos (Dance from Crete)"

	1–18	Theme A in flute and oboe, accompanied by grace notes and staccato eighth notes

Section	Measure	Event and Scoring
	18–26	Theme B introduced by B-flat cornet and finished with a tutti entrance
	26–34	Theme C introduced by solo clarinet and continued by woodwinds
	26–34	Pairs of voices in two-measure phrases with simple eighth-note accompaniment
	43–52	Transition; call-and-response section between woodwinds and brass
	53–60	Theme D in upper woodwinds and upper brass
	61–68	Pairs of voices in one-measure phrases with accented half-note accompaniment
	68–76	Theme C returns in B-flat cornet

Movement 7: "Sifneikos"

Section	Measure	Event and Scoring
	1–10	Melody in horns and C trumpet; accompanied by two sixteenth-eighth note
	11–17	New sixteenth-note melodic pattern introduced in woodwinds
	18–21	Transition; thirty-second notes in bassoon and alto horn and half-step motion in quarter notes
	22–29	Melody in woodwinds, taken over by brass; m. 26 syncopated concert E-naturals in horn and euphonium drive to end of phrase
	30–34	E-flat clarinet and English horn soli, supported by *fp* in accompaniment
	35–40	Transition; scalar passages lead to final tutti
	41–44	Tutti; melodic passage with similar accompaniment from mm. 1–10
	45–50	Coda; reduced scoring

Movement 8: "Makedonikos (Dance from Macedonia)"

Section	Measure	Event and Scoring
Section 1	1–26	Melody in clarinet; syncopated accompaniment figures; mm. 1–10 in low clarinets, mm. 11–18 in horns, and mm. 19–26 in bass clarinet and bassoon
	27–44	Melody in flute and horn; tutti from m. 39 to the end of the section
Section 2		Recitative solo section
	45–55	Oboe solo; interjected with melismatic runs in woodwinds

SECTION	MEASURE	EVENT AND SCORING
	56	Clarinet solo interjection
	57–64	C trumpet and B-flat cornet solo, then duet
	65–66	Clarinet and bass clarinet duet supported by unison rhythm in A major
	67–69	Horn solo supported by unison rhythm in brass
	70	Trombone solo interjection
Section 3	71–78	Transition back to music from section 1
	79–88	Melody in horn similar to m. 19 with similar syncopated accompaniment

Movement 9: "Enas Aitos (An Eagle)"

	1–8	Statement 1; melody in oboe; quarter- and eighth-note supporting line in woodwinds
	9–16	Statement 2; melody in cornets; supporting line in B-flat trumpet and trombone have similar rhythmic pattern as the melody but in contrary motion
	17–20	Transition; *Meno Mosso*, quarter= 108
	21–36	Statement 3; slower; reduced scoring; slurred phrases
	37–57	Statement 4; faster; quarter note = 120; brass and woodwinds trade off main melodic statements; tutti at m.48 in a waltz style
	58–59	Transition; slower; melody in clarinet
	60–65	Statement 5; thinnest texture of all statements
	66–65	Transition to last statement; accelerando into m. 74
	74–81	Last statement; suddenly broader; quarter note = 112; melody in flute, oboe, tenor sax, cornet, and trombone

Unit 8: Suggested Listening

Cesarini, Franko. *Greek Folksong Suite*.
Gorb, Adam. *Dances from Crete*.
Skalkottas, Nikos:
    Five Greek Dances for Stings
    Nine Greek Dances for String Quartet
    Thirty-six Greek Dances

Unit 9: Additional References and Resources

The Official Site of the Friends of Nikos Skalkottas Music Society.
http://www.skalkottas.de

Leonidou, Anne. "Portrait of Greek Dance." Nostos: Hellenic Information
Society. http://www.nostos.com/dance

Skalkottas, Nikos. *Nine Greek Dances*. New York: G. Schirmer, Inc., 1933.

Thornley, John. "Nikos Skalkottas." In *Groves Music Online* L. Macy, ed.
http://www.grovemusic.com

Websites:
http://www.helleniccomserve.com
http://www.nostos.com/dance
http://www.skalkottas.de

Contributed by:

Gina M. Lenox
Masters Conducting Associate
University of North Texas
Denton, Texas

Teacher Resource Guide

Savannah River Holiday

Ron Nelson
(b. 1929)

Unit 1: Composer

Ron Nelson is a native of Joliet, Illinois, and received all his degrees (bachelor of music, master of music, and doctor of musical arts) from the Eastman School of Music, where he studied with Howard Hanson and Bernard Rogers. Under a Fulbright grant, he also studied at the École Normale de Musique and the Paris Conservatory. After completing his education in 1955, he began teaching at Brown University, where he remained until his retirement in 1993. In that same year, his *Passacaglia (Homage on B-A-C-H)* received awards from all three major band composition contests: the National Band Association, the American Band Association Ostwald Award, and the Sudler International Prize. The following year he received the Medal of Honor from the John Philip Sousa Foundation. Over the course of his career he has received commissions and awards from numerous colleges and universities.

His rich and varied music training provided him with a background and context to compose for a wide variety of media, including orchestral, choral, film, and chamber, in addition to his works for band. His works for band and wind ensemble are for a wide variety of difficulty levels and styles, and encompass everything from short fanfares to major works of significant length and difficulty.

Unit 2: Composition

Savannah River Holiday was originally composed for orchestra. It received its premiere over NBC radio on March 16, 1953 and its first public performance at the Founders Day Concert of the 23rd American Music Festival in Rochester, New York. The work was recorded by the Eastman-Rochester Symphony Orchestra on the album *Hanson Conducts Fiesta in Hi-Fi* (reissued on CD [Mercury 434324]). The piece was transcribed for band by the composer in 1973. The score's program notes indicate that it is a "tour de force" for wind ensemble which can be equally effective for full band, though the composer has more recently indicated that "minimum to no doubling" would be preferable.

The working title of the piece was originally *Savannah River Payday*, after a short story by Erskine Caldwell, but the composer changed the title to *Savannah River Holiday* to avoid potential copyright infringements. The short story depicts the violent and quixotic exploits of two young men, and the music may be described as capturing the energy and frivolity of their day.

The piece is approximately nine minutes long and possesses significant technical and musical challenges appropriate for an advanced high school or college/university ensemble. The bright colors, energetic rhythmic figures, and expansive lyricism typify a style that Nelson was to use in several other pieces, including *Rocky Point Holiday*, *Aspen Jubilee*, and *Sonoran Desert Holiday*.

Unit 3: Historical Perspective

The overture form has a history and usage well documented in this series and other sources. Suffice it to say that overtures may be placed in two categories: those originally written as introductions to larger (frequently theatrical) works; or those written as independent, one-movement pieces often used to open or sometimes conclude a concert. Terms such as "overture," "symphony," "suite," and "prelude" were used interchangeably until the early nineteenth century, when they started to assume more specific definitions.

The prevalence of the overture form, particularly in school band usage, may be so familiar to conductors that inaccurate or inappropriate assumptions may sometimes be made that are not sensitive to each composer's individual tastes and decisions. Specifically, the common characterization of ABA as a description of overture form is often overly simplistic, and is only helpful at the broadest and most general levels of description. Care should be taken to examine and interpret the manner in which each composer manipulates the materials, forms, and proportions of a given work.

Conductors should study and listen to other operatic and dramatic overtures such as Mozart's *Marriage of Figaro*, Beethoven's *Egmont*, and others (see Unit 8). Countless interpretations are easily accessible and should be used to enrich the breadth and depth of interpretation. It may be very helpful to play a recording of a Classical overture, particularly an operatic overture by Mozart, to give students an idea of how an overture manipulates contrasting musical ideas and depicts dramatic action.

Unit 4: Technical Considerations

One of the first concerns facing the conductor of this work is its function as a transcription. The piece in its original orchestral version makes extensive use of winds so, technical demands are for the most part quite idiomatic. A few exceptions occur where woodwinds have to cover extended runs of sixteenth notes originally written for high strings (mm. 68–69 and 223–226) or low winds and brass have to simulate cello and bass accompaniment lines (mm. 6–21, 103–108, and 161–176).

Low winds and brass frequently have fast ostinato passages that must be performed staccato and lightly. Instruments such as bass clarinet, baritone saxophone, euphonium, and tuba must be able to execute fairly long eighth-note passages at the indicated tempo of quarter note = 176–184 without slowing down or getting too heavy.

Unit 5: Stylistic Considerations

As mentioned above, one of the primary stylistic priorities of performing this piece will be maintenance of a light articulation in all instruments. The need to maintain the tempo of quarter note = 176–184 in the *allegro vivace* sections mandates that all players execute the various running eighth- and dotted-note rhythmic passages with energy, facility, and lightness. Buoyant, floating, dancing, spinning, propelling, and playing on tip-toe are all possible ways of describing the playing style needed.

The middle *sostenuto* section provides many opportunities for expression, with melodic parts for oboe, clarinet (all parts), bass clarinet, horn, euphonium, and several others. The writing in this section is quite active, even in the accompanimental parts, and divided among various instrument groups. The possibilities for teaching expressive and lyrical playing are rich and varied for every member of the ensemble.

Unit 6: Musical Elements

MELODY:

Theme 1 of the piece has an overall span of an octave but a narrower focus of a fourth centering on E-flat (see figure 1).

FIGURE 1.

The limited range of this melody makes it imperative that players keep the musical line moving forward and avoid letting the dotted eighths get too heavy. Some interesting interpretive choices can be made here as to the focal point of the phrasing: should the line go to the final note or peak at beginning of the third measure, pulling back after the accented sixteenth? Either way can be defended, but the importance of making a decision is paramount, and as one of countless interpretive decisions afforded in this piece, it provides the conductor a wide array of opportunities for music making.

Theme 2 is in complete contrast to theme 1 in both length and range, beginning with the motive shown in figure 2.

FIGURE 2.

Where theme 1 needs attention to quick, repeated notes, here the emphasis is on spanning a ninth in a very angular fashion, all the while playing cantabile. The other important factor here is how this short motive is traded among instruments every two measures. Each occurrence must be carefully played both on its own and in context; players must be aware of what precedes or follows their statement of the melody and make sure that a consistent sense of phrasing towards the whole note is followed. Making each of these building blocks work toward the longer phrase is imperative in interpretation.

In general, the melodic materials of *Savannah River Holiday* consist of short motivic cells that must receive full attention both individually and in the larger context.

HARMONY:
The four chords in the opening measure (shown in figure 3) form an important basis for the entire piece.

FIGURE 3.

Each pair of ninth chords descends by thirds, and the overall descent by a fourth provides a strong harmonic propulsion which moves the music forward. The attention to ninth chords, this short progression, and its variants are important building blocks for the piece and its execution.

No key signatures are used, so accidentals indicate the numerous harmonic shifts. These frequent changes make attention to vertical sonorities particularly critical, and players of bass instruments must be aware of their role in clarifying the harmonic rhythm.

RHYTHM:
With few exceptions, issues of meter are not a major difficulty in this piece. The first decision facing the conductor will be whether to conduct in four or two, and the score gives justification for either choice. The tempo indication is *Allegro vivace* (quarter note = 176–184), but the meter is cut time; the conductor may want to conduct in four during the reading and early rehearsal portions of preparation and change to two in order to achieve a lighter and more fluid feel as the technical aspects of the piece come under control.

The ability to spontaneously go back and forth between the two patterns may be the ideal solution, both musically and pedagogically. The meter does not change in the opening fast section and only changes to 3/4 for six measures toward the end of the final *allegro vivace*.

Manipulation of the rallentandos and ritards that precede the *adagio* and *sostenuto* will need to be carefully planned, especially since the euphonium and bass clarinet have sixteenth-note ostinatos in lower registers that could easily slow down earlier than indicated in the score. The middle *sostenuto* has some meter changes between 3/4 and 4/4, but otherwise the meter challenges of this piece are not as daunting as the technical ones.

The main rhythmic challenges in the piece involve execution of the three patterns shown in figure 4.

FIGURE 4.

All of these could easily be incorporated into an ensemble scale warm-up. Particularly important is the differentiation between patterns A and B, the latter occurring in the recapitulation of the *allegro vivace* in limited use, but may still be a helpful rhythm and articulation exercise in contrast to the more common A pattern.

The rhythmic challenges in this piece are quite closely tied to articulation, and if focus is placed on clear, resonant, and appropriately-spaced notes, the rhythmic drive and excitement will emerge. Consistent, slow practice, both individually and as an ensemble, will likely be important during the rehearsal process.

TIMBRE:

Instrumentation demands of this piece are extensive but not exotic. Examples include a fourth clarinet part, three cornet and three trumpet parts in addition to English horn, contrabass clarinet and string bass. Harp, celeste, and piano parts are also included, which provide important timbral reinforcement. Percussion demands are standard by contemporary wind band standards, with important parts for mallet instruments being particularly important in the *sostenuto* section and ostinato parts in the *allegro vivace* for the marimba.

There are solo parts for piccolo, flute, clarinet, and oboe. As stated elsewhere, important melodic and motivic parts exist for other instruments as well, but in combinations of two or three instrument groups. Much of the piece features scoring that includes at least half to two-thirds of the ensemble, so weight of orchestration can be an issue to monitor very closely. Traditional doublings occur, with groupings of high woodwinds, and middle and low voices found together. The horn section often has independent parts from either woodwinds or brass and needs to be able to project. While cornet and trumpet are scored in a traditional fashion, with cornets having more melodic material and the trumpets having more aggressive and brassy material, it should be noted that cornets are used much less than trumpets, even being tacet the first seventy-seven measures.

Unit 7: Form and Structure

SECTION	MEASURE	EVENT AND SCORING
Introduction	1	*Allegro vivace*
Theme 1	8	Scored for clarinet, flute, oboe, and piccolo
Theme 2	42	Upper woodwinds and cornet
	99	Transition
Theme 3	119	*Sostenuto*
	148	*Allegro vivace* returns
Theme 1	163	Recapitulation in upper woodwinds, tenor and baritone saxophone, and euphonium
Theme 2	197	A recapitulation in upper woodwinds and cornet
	243	Coda

Unit 8: Suggested Listening

Nelson, Ron:

> *Savannah River Holiday. Holidays and Epiphanies.* Dallas Wind Symphony. Jerry Junkin,   conductor. Reference Recordings RR 76CD. A great recording to hear a broad sampling of Nelson's wind band music.

> *Savannah River Holiday. Hanson Conducts Fiesta in Hi-Fi.* Eastman-Rochester Orchestra. Howard Hanson, conductor. Mercury 434 324–2.

> *Savannah River Holiday. Music for Winds and Percussion, Volume 3.* Northern Illinois University. Stephen E. Squires, conductor. Music Educator DR HSB 003.

Other Ron Nelson works written in a similar style:

> *Aspen Jubilee*
> *Rocky Point Holiday*
> *Sonoran Desert Holiday*

Other overtures for reference:

> Beethoven, Ludwig van. *Egmont.*
> Bernstein, Leonard. *Candide.*
> Brahms, Johannes. *Academic Festival.*
> Mozart, Wolfgang Amadeus. *The Marriage of Figaro.*

Unit 9: Additional References and Resources

http:www.ronnelson.info

Byrne, Frank. Program notes for *Holidays and Epiphanies: the Music of Ron Nelson.*

Miles, Richard, ed. *Teaching Music through Performance in Band, Volumes 1, 3–4.* Chicago: GIA Publications, 1997, 2000, and 2002.

Peterson, Stephen. "Profile of Composer Ron Nelson." *The Instrumentalist,* June 1994: 49.

Email correspondence with the composer. May 17, 2008.

Contributed by:

Andrew Mast
Director of Bands
Lawrence University Conservatory of Music
Appleton, Wisconsin

Teacher Resource Guide

Shadow Dance

David Dzubay
(b. 1964)

Unit 1: Composer

David Dzubay was born in 1964 in Minneapolis, Minnesota and grew up in Portland, Oregon. He earned the DM in composition at Indiana University, and undertook additional study as a Koussevitzky Fellow in composition at the Tanglewood Music Center and at the June in Buffalo Festival. His principal teachers were Donald Erb, Frederick Fox, Eugene O'Brien, Lukas Foss, Oliver Knussen, Allan Dean, and Bernard Adelstein. David Dzubay's music has been performed in the United States, Europe, Canada, Mexico, and Asia. He has been honored with a 2007 Guggenheim Fellowship, 2007 Djerassi Artist Residency, 2006–07 MacDowell Colony Fellowships, 2004 William Revelli Memorial Prize from the National Band Association, 2003 Commission from the Metropolitan Wind Symphony, 2001 Walter Beeler Memorial Prize, and grants from the Aaron Copland Fund for Music. David Dzubay is currently professor of music, chair of the composition department, and director of the New Music Ensemble at the Jacobs School of Music at Indiana University in Bloomington. From 1995 to 1998 he served as composer-consultant to the Minnesota Orchestra, and during 2005–2006 he was composer-in-residence with the Green Bay Symphony Orchestra.

Unit 2: Composition

Shadow Dance was commissioned by the University of North Carolina Greensboro Wind Ensemble, and received its premiere on March 4, 2007 at the Music Center at Strathmore in North Bethesda, Maryland, under the baton of John R. Locke. The work is a re-composition of the composer's 1999 work for the Minnesota Orchestra by the same title. In a single nine-minute work that the composer considers a "dance for the new millennium," Dzubay explores a Medieval organum by Perotin on the chant "Viderunt omnes." The title comes from the composer's perspective that Perotin's organum is a lengthened "shadowing" of the original chant melody. *Shadow Dance* is a further shadowing of the chant, taking *Viderunt Omnes* as a base and adding newly-composed music above, below, and between phrases of the Perotin. At the work's midpoint, the rhythm of the dance changes and the Perotin recedes into the background before all the various elements are combined at the conclusion of the piece. In his program note, Dzubay writes, "Like the age in which we live, the character of this dance is unstable: by turns ominous, peaceful, celebratory, reflective, frantic, joyful, raucous, anxious, hopeful."

Shadow Dance is orchestrated for large wind ensemble, including important parts for English horn, three bassoons, contrabass clarinet, harp, piano, and an extensive percussion section. The third bassoon part is often cued in other instruments, but for timbral and orchestrational purposes, a third bassoon is preferable.

Unit 3: Historical Perspective

Shadow Dance is based on "Viderunt omnes," an organum composed by Perotin in approximately 1199. Near the end of the twelfth century, two musicians at the cathedral of Notre Dame in Paris began writing what are now some of the earliest examples of polyphonic music. The elder of these musicians, Leonin, assembled the *Magnus liber organi*, a collection of original two-voice settings of solo portions of Gregorian chants normally used for major festivals.

One of the major achievements at this time was the application of determinate rhythmic relationships to melodic lines. Musicians made use of the metrical feet common in poetry in establishing rhythmic modes that led to improved coordination between voice parts.

In Leonin's *Magnus liber*, the syllabic portions of the chant were set using long, unmeasured notes in the tenor, while a second voice (the *duplum*) elaborated in fairly strict modal rhythm. When the chant became melismatic, the tenor was forced to speed up rhythmically, creating a clausula during which both voices moved according to the rhythmic modes.

The rhythmic quality of these Medieval modes best lends itself in transcription to modern in 6/8 meter, the primary meter of *Shadow Dance*. Though Perotin did not compose dance music, the lilting feel created by the rhythmic modes lends itself to interpretation in dance style. Dzubay takes this characteristic as the point of departure in this work.

Perotin, one of Leonin's successors at Notre Dame, is credited with expanding Leonin's innovative two-voice textures into works for three or four parts. In Perotin's music, the tenor continued to present the chant tune in long note values while the three or four upper voices moved in similar modal rhythm. These upper voices often crossed and exchanged parts so that they functioned as equal partners in the texture.

Several terms related to music of the Medieval period require definition for understanding Dzubay's application of the principles in *Shadow Dance*:

Organum	Medieval polyphony on a cantus firmus; initially the chant melody was doubled at a consonant interval, but became increasingly independent.
Clausula	Passage of a polyphonic work during a melismatic fragment of the original chant, in which the speed of the tenor (singing the cantus firmus) becomes more rhythmically active.
Trope	Newly-composed words and or music to an official liturgical chant, but usually blended stylistically with the chant itself.

The text of "Viderunt omnes":

Viderunt omnes fines terrae salutare Dei nostri	*All the ends of the earth have seen the salvation of our God.*
Jubilate Deo omnis terra	*Rejoice in the Lord, the whole earth.*
Notum fecit Dominus salutare suum	*The Lord has made known his salvation;*
Ante conspectum gentium revelavit justitiam suam	*He has shown His righteousness in the sight of the people.*

Unit 4: Technical Considerations

The work is extremely challenging for all players in the ensemble in all aspects of ensemble performance. Rhythmically, a group must be able to navigate rapidly-changing asymmetrical meters, including 6/8, 9/8, 7/8, 5/8, and 3/2, with various subdivisions and eighth-note groupings. There is a lengthy polyrhythmic passage, during which some members of the ensemble play in 7/8 and others in 6/8.

Woodwinds must have dexterity to perform extremely rapid technical passagework. An ensemble must be capable of playing with great musical maturity in order to navigate the many slight adjustments of tempo, the extremely fast speed of many sections of the work, and the transparent orchestration with confidence.

The orchestration often employs the Medieval/Renaissance principle of consorts of instruments: families of like instruments playing together. The resulting textures are often thinly scored as consorts are placed in opposition to one another. Cup, straight, and harmon mutes are required for brass to provide additional color. Members of the ensemble must sing portions of the chant at the beginning and end of the composition.

Unit 5: Stylistic Considerations

Stylistically, *Shadow Dance* provides a unique juxtaposition of elements of music from the Medieval period and the twentieth century. The manner in which Dzubay orchestrates Perotin's organum (originally composed for voices) for consorts of instruments requires players to perform these portions of the work with a light, gentle, singing quality.

Articulations should not be too aggressive, and there should be a clear sense of decay in each motivic fragment. Dzubay clearly uses paired crescendo/diminuendo markings to clarify this interpretive point. In contrast, the Dzubay's original textural layers often call for a greater degree of accentuation, intensity, and aggressiveness.

The overall style of the work must highlight a progression from graceful and light Medieval music to chaotic and extroverted twentieth-century dance music. In the passages that require the ensemble to sing, Dzubay carefully provides phonetic pronunciation guides, but it would be helpful to have a choral conductor visit rehearsal to help with diction and sound production. Additionally, a successful interpretation depends on the conductor's careful pacing of subtle fluctuations in tempo, with a global view on the pacing of dynamics and intensity throughout the work.

Unit 6: Musical Elements

MELODY:

Shadow Dance is comprised of three primary melodic ideas: a fragment of the chant "Viderunt omnes," Perotin's organum on that chant, and Dzubay's original "1999" rhythmic idea.

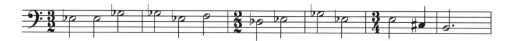

FIGURE 1a. Fragment of "Viderunt omnes"

The melodic idea in figure 1a is used to begin and end the work. The initial presentation is in the lowest tessitura of the ensemble, while the closing statement is sung to the text "justitiam suam." It is important that ensemble members understand the connection between these two seemingly disparate ideas. Singing the chant fragment at the end of the work will help clarify how the piece begins.

FIGURE 1b. Fragment of "Viderunt omnes"

Dzubay makes use of only a small portion of this section of the chant. During the first main formal section (mm. 26–99), members of the ensemble sing "Viderunt" to the F–F–A melodic pattern of the original. At the point of the first clausula, beginning in m. 138, the melismatic presentation of "omnes" is set in the dotted half-note motion in the horns: C–D–C–A–C–C, etc. Having the entire ensemble sing these portions of the chant with the appropriate text, and then isolating them in the context of the work, will help develop understanding of how the chant unfolds.

FIGURE 2. Perotin's organum on "Viderunt omnes"

Perotin's three-voice organum pervades virtually all of *Shadow Dance*. In these repetitive yet spellbinding two-measure groups, it is important to note the occurrences of voice crossing, and where dissonant and perfect intervals are placed. Dzubay is often extremely careful to note the crescendo/diminuendo dynamic contour within each two-measure passage. Carefully adhering to this instruction will create the lilting rhythmic style, mimic the Medieval sense of decay through the phrase, and allow for balance throughout the ensemble. Ensemble members must be aware of when the organum is present in the texture and must allow it to be heard.

FIGURE 3a. "1999"

When Dzubay was commissioned by the Minnesota Orchestra in 1999 to compose the original version of *Shadow Dance*, he attempted to capture the turning of the millennium in a rhythmic motive that mimics the syllabic construction "Nine-teen-Nine-ty-Nine."

FIGURE 3b. "1999" set with six-note melodic pattern

The rhythmic device of "1999" receives melodic treatment throughout the work utilizing a six-note melodic pattern that plays against the five-note rhythmic motive. The rhythm and melody cycle against one another, creating a chaotic sense of discontinuity. Having ensemble members chant the rhythm of the "1999" motive, and in the case of figure 3b, clapping on the first note of the melodic pattern, will highlight the connections between these ideas.

HARMONY:
Harmonically, *Shadow Dance* juxtaposes Medieval modal harmonies with twentieth-century chromaticism and dissonance. The piece begins ambiguously in the tonal center of C-flat, but moves to a centricity of F for the exploration of "Viderunt omnes" at both the beginning and end of the work. The central section, based on Dzubay's "1999" idea, uses a pedal point of D-flat with stacked fifths, often in parallel half steps. The texture throughout is polyphonic.

RHYTHM:
As the harmonic and melodic content of the piece is constructed to contrast Perotin and Dzubay, the rhythmic content provides similar variety. The sections that can clearly be ascribed to Perotin's influence flow in a regular 6/8 meter, with original layers by Dzubay that contain irregular accents and syncopation. The sections that contain predominantly Dzubay's "1999" material use a wide range of changing asymmetrical meters. A great degree of rhythmic independence is required of all players throughout the piece.

TIMBRE:

Dzubay's masterful orchestration is one of the creative highlights of *Shadow Dance*. The transparent scoring and the use of instruments in consorts during the sections elaborating on "Viderunt omnes" achieve vivid colors. Generally, tenor-range instruments provide much of the primary melodic material, with higher-tessitura instruments providing ornamentation, elaboration, and intricate counterpoint. In the "1999" section, the full ensemble is employed to create greater intensity and less heterogeneous tone colors. Percussion, piano, and harp provide coloristic support to the wind voices. The pianist is asked to pluck strings, the harpist to create pedal buzzes, and the mallet percussionists to play with the handles of their mallets on the bars of the marimba. It is important for the conductor to have a clear image of the colors that should be heard at any given moment in the piece, and that the ensemble listen attentively to create as vivid a sonority as possible.

Unit 7: Form and Structure

SECTION	MEASURE	EVENT AND SCORING
Introduction	1–25	Beginning in C-flat, chant fragment and "1999" rhythm are introduced as texture builds and tessitura ascends; harmony moves to F
A	26–204	Elaboration on Perotin
"Vi-"	26–54	Organum introduced by bassoons and trombones; ensemble members sing "Vi" as cantus firmus; light interjections by upper woodwinds; F pitch center
Link	55–62	Trombones continue organum with bassoons and saxophones; intensity of layering increases as dynamics build to *forte*
"de-"	62–70	Organum continues with changing consorts; "de" sung by ensemble; new hocket line introduced (vibraphone plays entire idea); F pitch center with pulsing eighth notes
Trope	71–86	New trumpet descant introduced over material similar in content to organum; pulsing eighth notes continue and build
"runt"	87–99	Cantus firmus returns, now pitched on A; organum in saxophones and oboes; new ornamented ideas in upper woodwinds more rhythmically active

Section		Measure	Event and Scoring
		100–137	Melisma on "runt" (not sung but in horn pedal point) moves pitch center to C; organum in imitation one beat apart; "1999" alluded to in m. 137
	Clausula	138–146	Cantus firmus moves more rapidly through melismatic section on "omnes"; ascending lines in saxophones from introduction; rapid flourishes in upper woodwinds
	Link	147–154	Connects clausula to contrasting section by rhythmically altering organum and accenting beat 2 with handclapping
	Trope	155–194	Organum returns, first in bassoons then in imitation between horns and trombones; intensity of contrasting layers increases
	Transition	195–204	Oblique motion in trumpet announces change in section; "1999" rhythmic motive emerges
B		205–337	Departure from Perotin
	a	205–229	"1999" in full ensemble with perfect fifths stacked in half-steps, alternating with "1999" set with six-note melodic motive
	Link	230	Connects to contrasting section
	b	231–244	Displaces downbeat in bass instruments
	c	245–271	Modified organum returns in flutes with shadowy accompaniment in duple meter by clarinets, muted brass, and percussion
	Clausula	272–305	Cantus firmus returns in trumpet 4; accompaniment layers become increasingly unsettled and intense with *fp*, *sfz*, and dramatic dynamic contrasts
	a	304–334	"1999" returns in full ensemble with intrusive outbursts in 3/2 meter, leading to chaotic 4/4 interjection that connects to six-note motive
	Link	335–337	Thinly scored reference to organum
A + B		338–382	Combines Dzubay and Perotin ideas
	Clausula	338–368	Recapitulation of organum in 6/8 meter set against asymmetrical 7/8 accompaniment and melismatic cantus firmus in horns
	Chant	369–382	Climactic return of chant melody

SECTION	MEASURE	EVENT AND SCORING
Coda	383–414	Organum returns and disintegrates, layered with motives from mm. 71 and 181; fades into ensemble singing of "justitiam suam"

Unit 8: Suggested Listening

Dzubay, David:
  Myaku
  Ra!
  Shadow Dance (orchestral version)
Perotin, *Viderunt omnes*.

Unit 9: Additional References and Resources

Jenny, Herbert J. "Perotin's Viderunt omnes." *Bulletin of the American Musicological Society* 6 (August 1942): 20–21.
La Trobe University medieval music database.
  http://www.lib.latrobe.edu.au/MMDB/index.htm
Perotin. *Viderunt omnes*. The Hilliard Ensemble. Paul Hillier, conductor. ECM Records B000025ZXO.
Yudkin, Jeremy. *Music in Medieval Europe*. Englewood Cliffs, NJ: Prentice Hall, 1989.

Contributed by:

Kevin M. Geraldi
Associate Director of Bands
The University of North Carolina at Greensboro
Greensboro, North Carolina

Teacher Resource Guide

Starry Crown

Donald Grantham
(b. 1947)

Unit 1: Composer

Donald Grantham was born on November 9, 1947 and was raised with his two younger brothers in Duncan, Oklahoma. Along with studies on piano and trumpet, Grantham's early interest in composing was encouraged by his high school band and church choir director, who programmed performances of his works. Following high school, he completed his bachelor of music degree at the University of Oklahoma (1970), and later earned both his master of music (1974) and doctor of musical arts (1980) in composition from the University of Southern California. Grantham spent two summers in the early 1970s studying at the American Conservatory in Fontainebleau, France, where he was a scholarship student of Nadia Boulanger. His principal teachers have also included Halsey Stevens, Robert Linn, and Ramiro Cortés.

Grantham is a versatile composer who has fulfilled commissions in media from solo instruments to opera. He is the recipient of numerous honors and awards in composition, including the Prix Lili Boulanger, the Nissim/ASCAP Orchestral Composition Prize, First Prize in the Concordia Chamber Symphony's Awards to American Composers, a Guggenheim Fellowship, three grants from the National Endowment for the Arts, three First Prizes in the NBA/William Revelli Competition, two First Prizes in the ABA/Ostwald Competition, and First Prize in the National Opera Association's Biennial Composition Competition. His music has been praised for its "elegance, sensitivity, lucidity of thought, clarity of expression and fine lyricism" in a citation awarded by the American Academy and Institute of Arts and Letters. In recent years, the Cleveland, Dallas, Atlanta, and American Composers

Orchestras, among many others, have performed his works. To date, Grantham has composed over twenty works for wind ensemble, many of which are counted among the wind band's core repertoire.

Grantham is professor of composition at the University of Texas at Austin, where he has served on the faculty since 1975. With Kent Kennan, he is coauthor of *The Techniques of Orchestration*, the most widely-used orchestration text in English, now in its sixth edition.

Unit 2: Composition

Starry Crown was commissioned by a consortium of ensembles and associations led by Kevin Sedatole, director of bands, Michigan State University, and was completed in February 2007. It is dedicated to John Whitwell, director of bands emeritus at Michigan State University "for his career-long service to music education."[1] Grantham provides the following description about the ten-minute work in the score's preface:

> *Starry Crown* is based on gospel music of the 1920s and 30s from the Deep South—a style sometimes referred to as "gutbucket" gospel because of its raw, earthy and primitive character. Three authentic tunes are used in the work: "Some of These Days," "Oh Rocks, Don't Fall on Me!" and "When I Went Down in the Valley." The title of the work was derived from a textual reference in the latter song:
>
> > "When I went down in the valley to pray,
> > Studyin' about that good ol' way,
> > And who will wear the starry crown,
> > Good Lord, show me the way."
>
> These songs are used at the beginning and end of the piece. The middle of the work recreates the atmosphere and shape of the call-and-response sermons typical of the period. The preacher (represented by three trombones, then the rest of the brass section) makes declamatory statements that the congregation (represented by the remainder of the ensemble) responds to. The exchanges become quicker and quicker until finally all join together in a very fast and exuberant chorus.

The instrumentation of *Starry Crown* follows Grantham's predilection in scoring for full wind band: the woodwind choir is enhanced by a third flute part, English horn, contrabassoon, and contrabass clarinet; the saxophone quartet employs soprano saxophone rather than two alto saxophones; and the piece requires string bass, piano/celesta, and six percussionists (including timpanist). Score and parts are available for rental from the composer's publishing company, Piquant Press (www.piquantpress.com/).

Unit 3: Historical Perspective

Gospel music is a distinctly American genre. Evolving from a backdrop of political and social unrest, it was cultivated in African-American churches, which grew to provide a sanctuary where culture and music could thrive.

Late in the nineteenth century, there began to emerge a new type of African-American sacred music—the gospel hymn—in which sophisticated, spiritual-like texts, incorporating simile and colorful imagery, were set to music in the white hymn tradition represented by Lowell Mason and later composers, but transformed by African-American styles of rhythm (syncopation and re-accentuation), pitch (flexible inflection and blue notes), harmonization (quartal and quintal harmony), and performance (e.g. call-and-response delivery).[2]

Pentecostal churches rose dramatically at the start of the twentieth century, and fostered an increase in gospel hymnody among black congregations.[3] Unlike the blues, another musical form that evolved from tragic social and economic conditions, gospel songs expressed a message of hope and eternal salvation.

Evolving from the popular, nightly revival meetings led by Reverend William Seymour that took place on Azusa Street in Los Angeles between 1906–09, Pentecostal churches bred a worship style that was uninhibited and highly demonstrative.

Congregants sang and danced exuberantly to the accompaniment of instruments shunned by the established denominations, such as piano, guitar, banjo, trumpet, trombone, and percussion. Revival preachers elevated their message in sermons that moved people to uncontrollable states of ecstasy through mesmerizing, high-energy delivery.

Choirs often featured the upper extreme of the female vocal range in antiphonal counterpoint with the preacher's sermon. This form of call-and-response manifests itself in gospel songs when either the choir or a soloist repeats and/or answers the lyric that has just been sung by the other, with the soloist improvising embellishments of the melody for greater emphasis.

During the Great Depression of the 1930s, gospel music spread quickly through concerts, recordings, sheet music publication, and radio and television broadcasts of religious services. Its gradual merge with popular music directed spiritual intensity into more secular areas and inspired the emergence of both soul music and rhythm-and-blues.

Unit 4: Technical Considerations

This high-energy romp demands a drum set player with an exceptional sense of time, an imaginative approach, and a familiarity with jazz idiom to play the dedicated part.

The trombone section is featured during a large extent of the work and serves a vital role as "preacher." Its bluesy, recitative-style introduction to the "sermon" must be powerfully delivered in unison, and requires facility to span the two-and-a-half octave range it encompasses. Added issues of ensemble precision in the sermon's opening are created by the rubato tempo indications and suspension of pulse.

Rapid scalar passages for woodwinds exist but are limited in scope and demand relative to Grantham's oeuvre. Exposed lines are written for each member of the saxophone section, including an extended improvisatory-like solo for alto saxophone. Predominate and integral parts for piano, string bass, and drum set are consistent with this work's genre.

Unit 5: Stylistic Considerations

Performance of jazz-styled phrasings, articulations, and rhythms is demanded of each member of the ensemble. The singing nature of the melodic lines should prevail, and will be enhanced by knowledge of the text and thematic intent of the three tunes on which the work is based. Additionally, consideration should be given to the important role silence plays in achieving rhythmic cohesion and impact.

Starry Crown's overall effectiveness is contingent on a successful realization of the lengthy accelerando that occurs during the "sermon" in the middle of the work (mm. 122–213). Intended to simulate the heightened intensity of a Pentecostal preacher's delivery, a well-paced gradual accelerando should occur organically throughout this section, propelling the music seamlessly forward. Target tempo markings indicated in the score are intended merely to assist the conductor in gauging the accelerando from tempo of half note = 56 to 126.

The architecture and pacing of this musical sermon was modeled on actual field recordings of religious sermons delivered in the southern United States during the 1920s and 30s.[4]

Gospel music of this type was performed with unrestrained emotion and often physicality in order to express the spiritual ecstasy the music attempts to evoke. From gritty soulfulness to exuberance, the celebratory nature of the music must be evident in its performance. This can be further achieved through energized articulations, attention to proper balances, and uniformity of style as the ensemble strives to emulate the performance practice of the early gospel experience.

Unit 6: Musical Elements

Often in Grantham's music, material is presented in its most simple form, and is then subjected to elaboration and further development. This technique of intensification is particularly evident in his treatment of melody, harmony, texture, and form in this work.

MELODY:

The authentic hymn tunes on which *Starry Crown* is based are inherently sim-plistic in their construction and lend themselves to manipulation and transformation. Two of the original tunes that first appear at the beginning of the piece, "Some of These Days" (m. 12), and "Oh Rocks, Don't Fall on Me" (m. 46), were selected by the composer due to their complementary nature ("Some of These Days" is also referred to by the first line of its verse, "I'm Gonna Cross the River of Jordan").[5] Presentation of the final authentic hymn tune, "When I Went Down in the Valley," is reserved for the pinnacle of the work (m. 371). These gospel tunes serve merely as a point of departure for Grantham, whose own distinctive voice can be heard throughout *Starry Crown*, not only in the treatment of these tunes, but in the abundant, origi-nal thematic material surrounding them.

As was customary in gospel tradition, diatonic melodies are subjected to grace-note embellishments and infused with blues notes (the flatted third and fifth scale degrees). The antecedent/consequent phrase structure and call-and-response nature of the hymns are preserved. However, phrase extensions of varying lengths add an element of surprise to the sense of symmetry intrinsic in the tunes. Techniques of fragmentation, imitation, and melismatic treat-ment of the melodic line are also evident.

HARMONY:

Modified blues scales and extended harmonies (added sevenths, ninths, and thirteenths) enrich the traditional, strong tonic-dominant relationship presented by the hymns. Tonal centers of B-flat and D-flat major are primary, with E-flat major assuming a secondary role. The alteration of key areas with each thematic presentation generates harmonic motion and tension, providing momentum and drama to the piece. This harmonic conflict is not resolved until m. 371, when the homophonic chorale-style presentation of "When I went Down in the Valley" in D-flat prevails. The purity of its texture, cadence, and resolution of tonal centers, and freshness of the tune serve as a triumphant culmination to the work.

An understanding of twelve-bar blues form, shout chorus, and walking bass line will facilitate the performance of the music surrounding Grantham's original gospel-style tune at mm. 213–281.

RHYTHM:

Starry Crown is a fast, energetic piece written almost entirely in *alla breve* meter. In one segment of the piece, intermittent bars of 3/4 and 3/2 meter are interjected occasionally to maintain a fluid, linear sense of vocal line. The tempo of the majority of the music functions on two main tiers: the first section remains at a metronome marking of half note = 96, while excitement is heightened at the end of the piece when the tempo increases to half note = 126+. The middle of the work (m. 103, *ff*), which includes a lengthy accelerando, presents a stark contrast in the use of rhythm and tempo. Here, the suspension of pulse and subsequent quickening of pace recreates the fervent declamations of a religious preacher, advancing the dramatic quality of the music.

As expected from a work in this idiom, syncopation is prevalent. Occurrences of cross-rhythms, counterpoint, and the use of triplet and quintuplet groupings are also notable.

TIMBRE:

Grantham alternates thin, transparent textures with full vertical sonorities that heighten impact and add variety. His colorful orchestration relies on differentiated writing with a keen regard for registral spacing, which he masterfully manipulates to achieve contrast and influence overall shape of the music.

Interplay between woodwind and brass choirs is more apparent here than in the composer's previous works, replicating a vocal quality in keeping with the nature of the thematic material.

Tremolos and glissandos performed by the "rhythm section" to accompany the "sermon" (m.122, *ff*) are atypical of Grantham's writing, yet included as authentic representations of the performance practice.

Unit 7: Form and Structure

Starry Crown is constructed in a modified ternary form (ABA'). The music signifying the preacher's sermon and the congregation's ensuing jubilant chorus clearly delineate the middle or B section of the work. Introductory material reappears throughout the work, punctuating the form and serving as a thematic link. The reprise of section A is extended with the presentation of a new theme that functions as the closing.

SECTION	MEASURE	EVENT AND SCORING
A		
Introduction	1–11	Raucous *fortissimo* opening marked *Bright and crisp*, half note = 96; quickly subsides into trombone vamp
Theme 1	12–39	"Some of These Days" presented by flute trio and celesta in B-flat; consequent phrase by solo saxophones in improvisatory fashion
	40–45	Return of opening material; dramatic change in texture and dynamic
Theme 2	46–81	"Oh, Rocks Don't Fall on Me" introduced by brass chorale in D-flat; sentence structure [2 + 2 + 4]; repeated by woodwind choir, then by solo alto saxophone in call-and-response with clarinet choir

SECTION	MEASURE	EVENT AND SCORING
Transition	82–102	
B		
"Sermon"		
Part I	103–121	Trombone section recitative in B-flat blues, punctuated with short exclamations from the ensemble; slow, free-time feel
	122–200	Trombones, supported by rhythm section, begin relaxed, lazy narrative at half note = 56; gradual accelerando begins; restated in E-flat by trumpets in counterpoint to trombones and piano; then in D-flat by solo alto saxophone in improvisatory manner, akin to preacher going off on a tangent
Transition	201–212	
Part 2		
Theme 3	213–280	*Accelerando* peaks at half note = 126+ to begin rhythmically active jubilant theme in E-flat; modified blues form; initially presented by brass and answered by hocketed woodwinds; restatement intensified by fuller texture, walking bass line, and tutti shout chorus
A'		
Introduction	281–284	Opening material returns in B-flat at tempo I
Themes 1 and 2	285–318	Recollection of "Some of These Days" and "O Rocks, Don't Fall on Me" with varied orchestration; call-and-response treatment among woodwind choirs
Transition	319–337	
Theme 3	338–370	Full statement of jubilant theme returns in E-flat with fanatical activity; added layer of sustained countermelody in woodwinds
Closing		
Theme 4	371–405	Climactic arrival of "When I went Down in the Valley"; full chorale presentation of two choruses in D-flat
Tag	406–421	Return of opening material leads to dramatic, big band-style ending

Unit 8: Suggested Listening

Grantham, Donald:
 Bum's Rush. 1994.
 Fayetteville Bop. 2002.
 J'ai été au bal. 1999.
 Southern Harmony. 1998.
Larsen, Libby. *Holy Roller.*
Various artists. *American Primitive, Volume 1: Raw, Pre-War Gospel (1926–36).* Revenant CD-206. 1997.
Various artists. *O Brother, Where Art Thou?* Soundtrack from the original motion picture. Mercury Records. 2000.

Unit 9: Additional References and Resources

Camphouse, Mark, ed. *Composers on Composing for Band, Volume 2.* Chicago: GIA Publications, 2004.
Composer's Collection: Donald Grantham. North Texas Wind Symphony. Eugene Migliaro Corporon, conductor. GIA Publications, Inc. CD-682. 2006.
Goff, James R. *Close HARMONY: a History of Southern Gospel.* Chapel Hill, NC: University of North Carolina Press, 2002.
Havlice, Patricia Pate. *Popular Song Index.* Metuchen, NJ: Scarecrow Press, 1975.
Kernfeld, Barry, ed. *The New Grove Dictionary of Jazz.* Second ed. London: MacMillan Publishers, 2002.
Miles, Richard, ed. "Teacher Resource Guide: J. S. Dances." In *Teaching Music through Performance in Band, Volume 6.* Chicago: GIA Publications, 2007.
Miles, Richard, ed. "Teacher Resource Guide: Baron Cimitiere's Mambo." In *Teaching Music through Performance in Band, Volume 6.* Chicago: GIA Publications, 2007.
Miles, Richard, ed. "Teacher Resource Guide: Court Music." In *Teaching Music through Performance in Band, Volume 6.* Chicago: GIA Publications, 2007.

Website:
 Donald Grantham. www.piquantpress.com

Contributed by:

Mary K. Schneider
Director of Bands
Eastern Michigan University
Ypsilanti, Michigan

1 Donald Grantham, *Starry Crown* (Austin, TX: Piquant Press, 2007).

2 H. C. Boyer, Howard Rye, and Barry Kernfeld, "Gospel," Grove Music Online,
  L. Macy, ed., http://www.grovemusic.com

3 Ibid.

4 Grantham, telephone interview by author, May 27, 2008.

5 Ibid.

Teacher Resource Guide

Symphonic Dances from "West Side Story"

Leonard Bernstein
(1918–1990)

orchestrated by Sid Ramin
(b. 1924)

transcribed by Paul Lavender
(b. 1951)

Unit 1: Composer

Leonard Bernstein was born in Lawrence, Massachusetts in 1918. He was an American-educated and -trained composer, conductor, pianist, author, and music lecturer. His work, which included tenures with the New York Philharmonic and Israel Philharmonic, creation of the "Omnibus" program, the "Young People's Concerts with the New York Philharmonic," a rejuvenation of Mahler, and hundreds of recordings, made him an international inspiration. Additionally, his teaching contributions included several books, articles, lectures, music festivals, mentoring of young conductors, advocacy of Modern composers, and educational television programs. As a result, Leonard Bernstein is considered one of the most influential icons in the history American music.

As a composer, Bernstein was most active writing symphonic music and music for the Broadway stage. In 1942 (one year before he was appointed Assistant Conductor of the New York Philharmonic), he completed

Symphon'y No. 1: "Jeremiah," his first large-scale work. Over the course of twenty years, two more symphonies emerged, *Symphony No. 2:* "The Age of Anxiety" (1949) and *Symphony No. 3:* "Kaddish" (1963). His most frequently performed concert works include (chronologically) *Three Dance Episodes from "On the Town"* (1945), *Prelude, Fugue and Riffs* for solo clarinet and jazz ensemble (1949), *Overture to "Candide"* (1956), *Symphonic Dances from "West Side Story"* (1960), *Symphonic Suite from "On the Waterfront"* (1964), *Chichester Psalms* for chorus, boy soprano, and orchestra (1965), *Two Meditations for Orchestra from "Mass"* (1971), *Slava!* (1977), *Divertimento for Orchestra* (1980), and *Orchestral Suite from "A Quiet Place"* (1991).

Bernstein's achievements were numerous and varied. He was awarded countless prizes, honors, and distinctions for his musical and educational contributions. His career as composer and conductor helped build a new relationship between classical and popular music that continues today.

ORCHESTRATOR:
Sid Ramin was born in Boston, Massachusetts in 1924. He is most well known as an American composer and orchestrator for Broadway and Hollywood musicals, movies, and television shows from the 1950s and 60s. His orchestrations won him acclaim and many awards, the two most notable from his work with *West Side Story* (a Grammy for the soundtrack and an Academy Award for the movie score). Ramin studied at the New England Conservatory of Music and at Boston University.

After his studies, he moved to New York City and worked as the staff composer and arranger for *The Milton Berle Show* and RCA Studios. Ramin and Bernstein met in 1932 and were good friends throughout their lives. Ramin assisted Bernstein with the orchestrations of *Wonderful Town, West Side Story, Mass,* and *A Quiet Place*. Bernstein expressed his gratitude for Ramin's "invaluable assistance in executing the orchestration" of *Symphonic Dances from "West Side Story"* by the following dedication on the score: "To Sid Ramin, in friendship."

TRANSCRIBER:
Paul Lavender was born in Hancock, Michigan in 1951. He is a prolific American composer and arranger with a catalogue of over one thousand works. Lavender did his undergraduate and graduate work in music theory and composition at Central Michigan University. After his studies, he led a career as a freelance arranger. In 1980, Lavender joined a team of writers for Jenson Publications, who, in 1989 became part of Hal Leonard Corporation. Currently, Lavender serves as vice president of Instrumental Publications for Hal Leonard.

Lavender's transcription of *Symphonic Dances from "West Side Story"* came from a request from Colonel Michael J. Colburn, Director of "The President's

Own" United States Marine Band, in 2006. The transcription was published in 2008. Lavender states in the score:

The continuing popularity of the Symphonic Dances has distinguished it as one of our American music treasures. It's been a privilege to adapt it for band, and particularly so, for such a prestigious and artistic ensemble, the United States Marine Band.

UNIT 2: COMPOSITION

West Side Story (1957) can be best classified as a hybrid of American opera and musical theater. For the stage production, Bernstein closely collaborated with three other up-and-coming artists of the time: Jerome Robbins (director and choreographer), Arthur Laurents (author), and Stephen Sondheim (lyricist). In John Mauceri's article "Crossing Broadway, West Side Story's landmark opening and enduring legacy" (2007), he states:

> While one might give the nod to Jerome Robbins as "the boss," it was clearly a group effort. As Bernstein wrote in his log on August 20, 1957, "I guess what made it come out right is that we really collaborated; we were all writing the same show. Even the producers were after the same goals we had in mind."

The premiere was on August 19, 1957, at the National Theater in Washington, and it opened on Broadway that same year. *West Side Story* stands as a significant chapter in the history of American opera and musical theater: the gripping story of young love set against choreographed gang warfare has found a place in American popular and artistic culture.

Symphonic Dances from "West Side Story" was crafted in 1960. According to Mauceri, the orchestral suite was created for a fundraising gala for the New York Philharmonic's pension fund the evening before Valentine's Day, February 13, 1961.

> The occasion–perfectly timed to celebrate Bernstein's ongoing relationship with the orchestra, just cemented by a new seven-year contract—cried out for a new work. So [with the assistance of Sid Ramin and Irwin Kostal who had just completed the orchestration for film], Bernstein extracted nine sections from *West Side Story*, reordering them [the suite order is different from the order in the musical] according to strictly musical principles; the result, *Symphonic Dances*, became one of the most popular and frequently performed of Bernstein's works for orchestra.

The premiere of the suite was at Carnegie Hall with the New York Philharmonic conducted by Lukas Foss. The first performance conducted by

Bernstein was February 7, 1963, at Philharmonic Hall (now Avery Fisher Hall), Lincoln Center with the New York Philharmonic.

Unit 3: Historical Perspective

The Program Note and Synopsis from the 1993 Revised Edition orchestral score of *Symphonic Dances from "West Side Story"* by Jack Gottlieb (composer and Bernstein's assistant at the New York Philharmonic from 1958–1966) reads:

> The four shows *On The Town, Wonderful Town, Candide, and West Side Story* show a progressive line of stylistic integration in Bernstein's compositional development [*Candide* and *West Side Story* were composed in tandem]. An ever-advancing economy of musical means and tightening of structure proceeds from one show to the next. It was almost predictable from this trend that when *West Side Story* hit Broadway like a bombshell, in September, 1957, it would be hailed as a landmark in American theater. It was indeed recognized as a major leap toward an original kind of theatrical conception. Bernstein had speculated much earlier that a genuine, indigenous form of American musical theater would eventually arise out of what has been known as musical comedy. Many people think that, in *West Side Story*, this theory began to be implemented. Elements from the European and American musical stage traditions were fused into an original art form that is neither opera nor musical comedy.
>
> From the European tradition came complicated vocal ensembles, the use of music to project the story line, and the dramatic devise of leitmotifs. In addition, from Europe came the deductive-inductive species of developing materials, by basing much of the score on transformations of the tritone interval, or by immediately developing the opening statement of any given song with melodic or rhythmic variation.
>
> From the American tradition came idiomatic jazz and Latin timbres and figurations (most of the dance music), a fluid and constant change from word to music and scene to scene, and a kinetic approach to the stage—communication through choreographic music—delineated, in concentrated form, in these *Symphonic Dances*.

Unit 4: Technical Considerations

The band transcription of *Symphonic Dances from "West Side Story"* is an exact replica of the orchestral suite. It is set in the same key (often in sharp keys) and is written as one large movement with transitions between the sections/dances. Although it is preferable to play the entire piece, sections/ dances can be performed alone or as a mini-suite. In its entirety, *Symphonic Dances* is twenty-three minutes in length.

The technical demands are considerable, especially for percussion, principal trumpet, and upper woodwinds. Additionally, all wind players must demonstrate comfort in several extended techniques and stylistic shifts.

Extended techniques in woodwind and brass include:
- flutter-tonguing
- slides and glissandos
- shakes
- wide-intervallic grace note embellishments
- double accidentals and enharmonic spellings

Additional technical considerations:
- physical endurance: twenty-three minutes in length
- rhythmic complexity in simple and compound meters
- articulation variety
- extended ranges and dynamics
- intonation (especially in the "Finale")

The transcription features the same instrumentation as the orchestral suite (including piano/celesta and harp) with common large band inclusions (expanded clarinets, alto clarinet, saxophone quartet, and baritone/euphonium). Percussion is slightly expanded from the orchestral suite to five parts and timpani:

Part 1:   Bass drum, drum set, bongos, ride cymbal, timbales, woodblock, conga, two tom-toms, cowbell, and tenor drum

Part 2:   Bongos, choke cymbal, cowbells, congas, suspended cymbal, tam-tam, crash cymbal, triangle, finger cymbals, tambourine, and snare drum

Part 3:   Tenor drum, bongos, four pitched drums, timbales, woodblock, maracas, snare drum, xylophone, tom-toms, and marimba

Part 4:   Xylophone, marimba, four pitched drums, gourd, chimes, glockenspiel, vibraphone, bongos, tom-toms, and guiro

Part 5:   Marimba, vibraphone, police whistle, xylophone, glockenspiel, and timbales

Unit 5: Stylistic Considerations

The stylistic goal for each section/dance of *Symphonic Dances from "West Side Story"* is to achieve the appropriate musical character in relation to the action.

"Prologue," *Allegro moderato*
The growing rivalry between two teenage gangs, the Jets and the Sharks, is set in two styles: a finger-snapping compound duple meter with a laid-back jazzy feel and an energetic march with drive and persistence.

"Somewhere," *Adagio*
In a dream ballet, the two gangs are united in friendship, modestly expressed in a lyrical and nostalgic setting.

"Scherzo," *Vivace e leggiero*
In the same dream, the gangs break away from the city walls and suddenly find themselves in a playful world of space, air, and sun. The music is whimsical and seductive.

"Mambo," *Meno presto*
In the real world again, a competitive dance between the gangs at the gym is aggressively evoked with wild Latin grooves, irresistible drive, and big-band-style splashes.

"Cha-Cha," *Andantino con grazia*
The star-crossed lovers Tony and Maria see each other for the first time; they dance together to calm, steady, and delicate gestures.

"Meeting Scene," *Meno mosso*
Wistful and slowly-layered transitional material accompanies the lovers' first words spoken to one another.

"Cool Fugue," *Allegretto*
An elaborate dance sequence, in which Riff (the Jets' leader) leads his gang in harnessing their impulsive hostility (figuratively "cooling their jets") is set to third-stream, be-bop-like riffs.

"Rumble," *Molto allegro*
Climactic gang battle. The two gang leaders, Riff and Bernardo, are killed. This section is set in a compound duple meter with explosive rhythmic gestures, angular fragments, and an insistent drive.

"Finale," *Adagio*
Maria's "I Have a Love" develops into a procession, which recalls the vision of "Somewhere." As a patient repose, the musical affect is both tragic and optimistic.

Unit 6: Musical Elements

The four standard musical elements for each section/dance of *Symphonic Dances from "West Side Story"* are described below:

"Prologue"

MELODY: Short jazz-derived fragments and bursts of motivic interruptions

HARMONY: Parallel chord motion (non-conventional) with dissonant chord sweeps and hits

RHYTHM: Two subsections: 6/8 meter with jazz syncopations and 2/4 meter with percussive drive and angular rhythmic bursts

TIMBRE: Alternations of sectional, tutti unison-and-octave doublings as well as occasional solo and soli interruptions

"Somewhere"

MELODY: Memorable monophonic tune in small, two-bar phrases within a larger phrase

HARMONY: Tonal and mostly conventional

RHYTHM: 4/8 meter and contrapuntal

TIMBRE: Transparent with solo lines throughout

"Scherzo"

MELODY: Fragmentary linear motives

HARMONY: Tonal and contrapuntal

RHYTHM: Combined meters, compound and simple jazzy inflections and straight, simple driving motives, similar to the two characters in the "Prologue"

TIMBRE: Mostly tutti with chamber music areas

"Mambo"

MELODY: Memorable motivic tune with exciting energy

HARMONY: Primarily static parallel chord motion with dissonance (ninths, sevenths, and altered chord members)

RHYTHM: 2/4 meter with fast, repetitive, and consistently driving rhythms

TIMBRE: Mostly sectional (woodwind, brass, percussion, and combined families within) or tutti

"Cha-Cha"

MELODY: Memorable, simple tune passed around various solo voices and soli sections

HARMONY: Fragmented and arpeggiated implied chords with parallel motion to the melodic lines, and stacked quintal intervals

RHYTHM: Common time with simple, classical rhythms

TIMBRE: Sparse and transparent

"Meeting Scene"

MELODY: Brief, recollection of material from the "Prologue," this time lyrical and slow

HARMONY: Layered building of slightly dissonant chords which feel static and unresolved

RHYTHM: Simple eighths in moderate common time

TIMBRE: Very sparse and transparent; woodwinds replace strings from original suite

"Cool Fugue"

MELODY: Two-measure, memorable motivic riffs

HARMONY: Both contrapuntal and quartal harmonies with moments of motives and rhythm dominating texture

RHYTHM: Common time with swing feel (written out as a dotted-eighth-and-sixteenth-note pattern) throughout

TIMBRE: Transparent, then tutti with interruptions

"Rumble"

MELODY: Angular and short motivic material

HARMONY: Sometimes dense and dissonant, sometimes conventional stacked chords

RHYTHM: 6/8 meter with steady eighth notes until the chordal hits on irregular beats

TIMBRE: Tutti; dense throughout

"Finale"

MELODY: Monophonic with memorable tune passed through various solo voices; also motives from previous material presented

HARMONY: Static; accompanimental and tonal with moments of unexpected dissonant harmonies

RHYTHM: 4/8 meter with very simple rhythms

TIMBRE: Soloistic, transparent, and extremely delicate

Unit 7: Form and Structure

The complete piece is a composition of dance movements and strophic songs. Each contains its own unique formal outline, often through-composed and gestural to enhance stage action and dialogue. The divisions are suggestive formal guidelines. See Unit 6 for musical content, and see the score for orchestration decisions.

SECTION	MEASURE	EVENT AND SCORING
"Prologue"	1–275	Introduction (m. 1)
	17	Section 1
	133	Transition, similar to Introduction
Section 2 with six subsections	141	Subsection 1
	179	Subsection 2
	195	Subsection 3
	209	Subsection 4
	225	Subsection 5
	243	Subsection 6
	264	Section 1 returns
	276	Brief Transition to "Somewhere"
"Somewhere"	278–346	[A A' B A" B' A and B]
	278	A—eight-measure English horn solo
	286	A'—eight-measure horn solo
	294	B—eight-measure bridge
	302	A"—eight-measure soli in canon
	310	B—five- and seven-measure bridge material
	322	Short motivic fragments of A and B material
	335	Transition to "Scherzo"
"Scherzo"	347–399	[A A (repeated) A' A"]
	347	A—fourteen measures with a motivic interruption (m. 356)
	361	A'—seven and thirteen measures with a motivic interruption (m. 376)
	381	A"—ten and four measures; predominantly motivic material

SECTION	MEASURE	EVENT AND SCORING
	396	Brief Transition to "Mambo"
"Mambo"	400–544	Introduction (m. 400)
	410	Theme 1
	438	Theme 2
	466	Theme 3
	508	Theme 4
	524	Theme 1 returns
Cha-Cha	545–568	[A (two mini-themes) A' B]
	545	A—mini-theme 1
	549	A—mini-theme 2
	555	A'—mini-theme 1
	557	A'—mini-theme 2
	563	B
	567	Brief Transition to "Meeting Scene"
"Meeting Scene"	569–680	Brief, twelve-measure interlude
"Cool Fugue"	581–729	[A A' B C D A"]
	581	A—motivic material established (mm. 581 and 585)
	589	A'—construction of motivic materials stated building to m. 666
	607	B—fugue (ride cymbal)
	666	C—culmination; tutti unison jazz break with elements of A and B
	685	D—shout chorus; also with elements of A and B
	705	A"—with motivic C and D interruptions
"Rumble"	730–812	[A A' B C]
	730	A (with B vamp material)
	740	A'
	746	B vamp with gestural material from "Prologue"
	763	A"
	776	C motivic development
	807	A'" with gestural material from "Prologue"—the last gesture like the opening of entire suite; brief flute cadenza to "Finale"
"Finale"	813-end	[A B A' B' A" Coda]
	813	A—six measures
	819	B—four measures
	823	A'—led by solo horn; eight measures

SECTION	MEASURE	EVENT AND SCORING
	831	B'—six measures
	837	A"—seven measures
	844	"Somewhere" quote; five measures
	849	Coda

Unit 8: Suggested Listening

Symphonic Dances from *West Side Story* has been recorded by many orchestras over the past fifty years. The recordings below are of the composer conducting and the first band transcription recording.

> The New York Philharmonic. Leonard Bernstein, conductor. Columbia Records CD CBS MK 42263. Sony CD SMK 46701, SM3K 47154, SMK 47529.

> The Los Angeles Philharmonic Orchestra. Leonard Bernstein, conductor. Deutsche Grammophon CD 410 025–2, 429 366–2, 427 806–2.

> *Symphonic Dances.* "The President's Own" United States Marine Band. Colonel Michael J. Colburn, director.

Unit 9: Additional References and Resources

Garebian, Keith. *The Making of "West Side Story."* Toronto: ECW Press, 1995.

Gottlieb, Jack, compiler. *Leonard Bernstein: A Complete Catalogue of His Works/Celebrating His 60th Birthday, August 25, 1978.* New York: Amberson Enterprises, Inc.

Guernsey, Otis L, Jr. Broadway Song and Story: Playwrights/Lyricists/Composers Discuss Their Hits. New York: Dodd, Mead, and Company, 1985.

The Library of Congress, Music Division. The James Madison Building. 101 Independence Avenue, S. E. Washington, DC 20540. Mark Eden Horowitz, Archivist.

Mauceri, John: "Crossing Broadway: West Side Story's Landmark Opening and Enduring Legacy." Symphony Magazine, September-October, 2007.

Schiff, David. "Bernstein, Leonard." In *Grove Music Online*. L. Macy, ed. www.grovemusic.com (An extensive bibliography is provided on site.)

Websites:
> www.leonardbernstein.com
> www.westsidestory.com
> www.spaceagepop.com/ramin.htm
> www.jackgottlieb.com
> www.nysbda.org/Symposium2007/lavender.html

Contributed by:

Emily Threinen
Director of Bands
Shenandoah Conservatory
Winchester, Virginia

Teacher Resource Guide

Symphony for William
Op. 212

Derek Bourgeois
(b. 1941)

Unit 1: Composer

Derek Bourgeois was born in Kingston on Thames on October 16, 1941. He attended Cambridge University (1959–63) and graduated with a first-class honors degree in music and a subsequent doctorate. He spent two years at the Royal College of Music (1963–65), where he studied composition with Herbert Howells and conducting with Sir Adrian Boult. While he was a student at Cambridge, the premiere of his *Symphony No. 1* (1960) gained him recognition in the music community and was nearly selected for a performance as part of the BBC Proms.

He has composed thirty-five symphonies, seventeen concertos, several other extended orchestral works, seven major works for chorus and orchestra, two operas and a musical. As well as a considerable quantity of chamber, vocal, and instrumental music, he has composed twelve extended works for brass band and six symphonies for wind band. He has also written a considerable amount of music for television productions.

He began an academic teaching career as an assistant director of music at Cranleigh School, and from 1970 to 1984 he was a lecturer in music at Bristol University. He was the conductor of the Sun Life Band from 1980 until 1983, and during the same period was Chairman of the Composers' Guild of Great Britain and a member of the Music Advisory Panel of the Arts Council. His work with Sun Life Band led to his significant contributions to the brass band repertoire.

In September 1984 he gave up his university post to become the musical director of the National Youth Orchestra of Great Britain, a position he held until 1993. In 1988 he founded the National Youth Chamber Orchestra of Great Britain which held its first course in the Summer of 1989. In 1990 he was appointed artistic director of the Bristol Philharmonic Orchestra.

He left the National Youth Orchestra in August 1993 to become the director of music of St Paul's Girls' School in London, a position previously held by Gustav Holst. His compositional style has been described as being akin to composers such as Shostakovich, Strauss, Walton, and Britten. His compositional style reflects a largely accessible language with effective use of dissonance and chromaticism. Bourgeois has described his language as "essentially tuneful, but with a bitter sweet tonal language." He retired to Mallorca in July 2002 where he now lives as a full-time composer.

Unit 2: Composition

Symphony for William was composed on a commission from Timothy and Hilary Reynish in memory of their son, William Reynish, who died in a tragic 2001 accident in the Pyrenees. The William Reynish Commissioning Project was instituted in 2002 and as of 2008 has resulted in over twenty commissioned works for wind ensemble. Other commissioned composers include Judith Bingham, Adam Gorb, Kenneth Hesketh, Christopher Marshall, Stephen McNeff, and Marco Pütz.

Symphony for William was written during a six-day period in July of 2004 and was premiered on October 13, 2004 by the Tennessee Tech Wind Orchestra, conducted by Timothy Reynish. Regarding the commission, Reynish stated:

> In June, 2004, my wife and I spent a week with Derek on Mallorca, nursing his wife Jean who had motor neurone disease, and listening to a huge range of music including many of his seventeen symphonies. He agreed to write a new work in memory of our third son, and the *Symphony for William* arrived in daily segments by email over the following six days."

The work is divided into three movements with the name of each movement paying homage to the name William. Bourgeois states, "For the titles of the movements I looked for phrases that used the word Will, the name by which he was known to his family and friends, and that would reflect the varying character of his nature."

Symphony for Wiliam is scored for full band including string bass and is approximately twenty minutes in length.

Unit 3: Historical Perspective

Symphony for William falls within the lineage of large-scale symphonies written for band during the twentieth century. This includes the works of Hindemith, Persichetti, Miaskovsky, and others. Similar to many twentieth- and twenty-first-century symphonies, the work deviates from the Classical four-movement model into an extended three-movement form. In performing this work, it essential to understand the composers' background in brass band writing. This style of scoring and melodic writing is often reflected within the symphony.

Unit 4: Technical Considerations

Symphony for William has numerous technical concerns and requires a mature ensemble. The primary technical concern in movement 1 deals with rhythmic and metric demands. There is an extended use of hemiola, and all metric changes must be performed with a constant sixteenth-note relationship.

In movement 2 there is an extended horn solo that requires extreme control and musicianship. The range of this solo extends to B-flat above the staff. In addition, there are oboe and euphonium solos within this movement. During certain transparent transitions, the conductor may choose to have one player per part, which will help to achieve the appropriate timbre.

Unit 5: Stylistic Considerations

The piece requires a wide variety of stylistic challenges for the ensemble. Movement 1 takes on a scherzo character, and the ensemble should strive for an articulation length that maintains a playful quality. Toward the close of movement 1, the extreme dynamic and scoring can distract from the scherzo.

In contrast to the scherzo, movement 2 challenges the ensemble to play in a cantabile style. Within this texture, the ensemble must maintain a continuity of musical line and phrase. The final movement requires a contrast of fanfare versus lyrical playing.

Unit 6: Musical Elements

MELODY:
Throughout the entire symphony the melodic construction is largely tonal with a frequent use of chromaticism. The melodic material is often scored for upper brass or woodwind voices, and there is a large use of doublings throughout the work. These two factors should be taken into consideration when dealing with tonal balance and timbre. The most lyrical part of the work arrives during movement 2 with an extended horn solo. The solo material encompasses a large tessitura and is constructed in large phrases.

HARMONY:

The harmony is largely derived from tertian structures and often includes "wrong-note" dissonance. This style of harmonic language can create difficulty in tuning and timbre. Players should be encouraged to locate the pitches that create dissonance within the harmony and perform them with energy. The majority of the harmonic material is scored for low brass and lower woodwinds. Bourgeois is not afraid to move the ensemble through some difficult harmonic areas, and great care must be taken to achieve the appropriate timbre and quality.

RHYTHM:

The rhythmic language is largely straightforward. In movement 1 there is an extended use of hemiola. Additionally, there are several transitions from 3/8 to 6/16 and 3/4 to 13/16 which require integrity to the sixteenth note. Toward the end of movement 1 the dotted eighth note should equal the quarter in m. 319. Attention to this modulation will accomplish the *l'istesso* tempo.

In movement 3 the ensemble should be encouraged to listen for composite rhythms. This occurs in figures such as m. 438, where trumpets play opposite woodwinds. This composite rhythm is important to accomplish the transition in m. 489, where a triplet eighth note equals the new quarter note. In m. 490, the conductor may choose to conduct in four to accomplish appropriate ensemble, however the overall feeling of four-measure phrases should not be negated.

TIMBRE:

Symphony for William is scored in a manner such that instruments often have the same role within the ensemble. For example, lower brasses often carry accompaniment figures while upper woodwinds and brasses carry melodic material. The conductor should keep this in mind when considering tone color and timbre. In addition there is an extensive use of doubling, particularly at climactic moments. Percussion is used sparingly throughout the score.

Unit 7: Form and Structure

SECTION	MEASURE	EVENT AND SCORING
Movement 1		
Introduction	1–24	Opening scherzo in upper woodwinds with standard triadic harmonies in lower brasses; a chromatic passage leads to B-flat major at m. 23; this establishes a relationship for the following phrase that centers around E-flat major
Exposition	25–42	A series of four-measure phrases with the primary melodic material for flute 1 and clarinet 1

SECTION	MEASURE	EVENT AND SCORING
	43–50	Beginning on C major, clarinets have a passage of parallel harmonies which is punctuated by triadic harmonies in lower brass and woodwinds
	51–62	The phrasing moves toward three-measure sequences with the first appearance of hemiola
	63–73	A return to four-measure phrases with a restatement of the previous phrase scored for brasses; harmonies are polychordal in nature
	74–85	Similar to m. 25, the primary material returns in a transparent texture and is passed between trumpet 1 and horn 1
Development	86–97	A change to 6/16 meter with the sixteenth note constant; the phrase structure remains in four-measure segments
	98–105	Four-measure phrases scored for alto saxophone, piccolo, and horn; once again, accompaniment figures are triadic in nature but are rhythmically complex
	106–113	A return to 3/8 meter with a continued use of four-measure phrasing; the phrase finishes with a hemiola figure and the woodwind statement is an inversion of the original
	114–134	6/16 meter returns; texture is more transparent; the music gains momentum to an octave C-sharp arrival at m. 133
	135–162	The previous C-sharp becomes a pedal point; horns and trumpets carry the melodic material
	163–181	The melodic material is carried by upper woodwinds with added counterpoint in lower woodwinds and euphonium; phrase structure continues in four-measure segments
	182–197	An arrival point on E-flat^{m7} which abruptly changes to a woodwind melody of transparent texture

Section	Measure	Event and Scoring
Transition	198–210	A pedal of G and D is used to introduce new melodic material in horn
Recapitulation	211–235	A return to the introductory material which arrives on B-flat major in m. 234
	236–254	Woodwinds have a sequence of scalar patterns while low reeds carry the melodic material; there is a repetition of this material in m. 248
	255–272	Horn repeats the previous material at a *pianissimo* dynamic level; in m. 265, flute carries an inverted version of this material
	273–282	An ostinato which uses contrary motion is introduced in upper woodwinds and xylophone; tenor saxophone introduces the melodic material, which is an augmentation of the primary material from m. 25
	283–300	The ostinato continues in upper woodwinds, forming composite sixteenth notes; horn 1–3 have the augmented version of the primary material; the music continues to gain momentum through an accelerando in 13/16 meter
	301–318	A series of four-measure phrases; most of the material is repeated in two-measure segments while woodwinds spin the melodic material
	319–330	An arrival on G and D recalls the previous transition into the recapitulation; brass and saxophone sates the two-part melody
Movement 2		
A	330–362	The movement begins with an extended horn solo with accompanying harmonies scored for low brass; harmony begins firmly in E-flat major and moves toward B-flat^7 in m. 337; second phrase of the horn solo reaches an apex in m. 341; during this apex of the phrase, great care must be taken to achieve an appropriate balance, particularly between trombone 1–2

SECTION	MEASURE	EVENT AND SCORING
	346–355	Horn restates the opening of the first phrase with continued harmonies in low brass
Closing	356–362	Harmony resolves to A-flat major in second inversion; this harmony pyramids from trombones into trumpets, expanding the harmony to G^{maj7} in second inversion; the music then recedes through trumpet 2 and horn 1; harmony moves to C minor before resolving into major; timbre is transferred to clarinet
Transition	363–366	Clarinet enters at *pianissimo* with an Am^7 harmony; this creates a large contrast in texture from the previous brass statement; harmony continues to move in a parallel fashion before resolving in m. 366 to A-flat^7
B	367–376	Oboe introduces theme B with accompanying harmonies in clarinet; conductor and oboist will need to decide on phrasing and appropriate breathing locations to create an eight-measure phrase structure
Transition	377–384	Fragmented transition with melodic material leading from flute 1, alto saxophone 1, and horn 1–3; great care should be taken to achieve a seamless quality between melodic voices; harmony resolves to B-flat minor in m. 384 and serves as a dominant to the following section
A	385–410	Similar to the opening measures, the harmony begins in E-flat major with a restatement of the A material by woodwinds; scoring is four-part writing and melodic material is scored for flute 1–2, E-flat clarinet, and clarinet 1; to achieve a unity of timbre, the conductor should raise players' awareness to their individual role within the four-part texture

Section	Measure	Event and Scoring
Apex	411–417	A sudden brass entrance; during the first four measures, a major chord is transformed into a minor sonority by woodwinds (C-flat major, A minor, G-flat major, D minor); harmony moves to B-flat major before resting on C–F–G in m. 417
B	418–429	Texture changes abruptly to alto saxophone with E and G-sharp played at *pianissimo*; euphonium restates the B material with a simpler harmonic structure; again, conductor and player will need to decide on appropriate breathing locations, particularly as the range descends in m. 428
Codetta	430–434	Muted trombone has a C-minor harmony while glockenspiel introduces the beginning of theme A; harmony resolves to B major in the penultimate measure

Movement 3

Fanfare	435–447	Style changes to an abrupt fanfare, ushered in by bass drum and timpani; woodwinds answer with an inversion followed by an intricate rhythmic passage which forms a composite sextuplet between lower brass/woodwinds and trombone; this rhythmic idea is repeated by woodwinds and trumpet; the alignment of this rhythmic passage will become crucial during a later transition; a new intensity is added in m. 439, where there is a unison octave statement by trumpet and horn which uses an extended range; this is followed by a series of parallel harmonies which finishes on C major; this harmonic passage is repeated by woodwinds at a new dynamic level, creating a seamless transition
Transition	448–453	Against the sustaining C major harmony, low brass enters with a G-flat major harmony; alto saxophone carries the melodic material while low brass has triadic harmonies with added dissonances; harmony in m. 453 recalls C major against G-flat major

SECTION	MEASURE	EVENT AND SCORING
Fugato	454–462	The final measure of alto saxophone melody is used to develop a brief fugato which begins at three-measure statements and condenses to two-measure statements
Extension	463–474	Saxophone section enters with a 5/8 rhythmic passage derived from the previous fugato section; tuba and euphonium take over this motive, accompanied by triadic harmonies in woodwinds; harmony becomes declamatory in m. 473–474 with B-flat^{maj7}
Re-transition	475–485	Using the final two measures of the euphonium passage, low brass and trombone ushers in a declamatory statement by horn; this leads the harmony into C major
Truncated	486–489	Opening fanfare returns in identical fanfare form; composite rhythm of m. 489 is crucial to an effective transition; one triplet eighth note should equal the new quarter note; thus the displacement of the rhythm should remain equal from m. 489 into m. 490
	490–517	An extended scherzo which consists of a series of four-measure phrases; harmony remains stagnant during each four-measure sequence; extended technical demands are required of woodwinds and upper brasses
Fanfare	518–531	Second part of the opening fanfare is presented in an augmented form; woodwinds provide chromatic scales which connect the fanfare statements; in m. 522, the fanfare moves from unison to triadic harmonies which lead to a G-flat^{maj7} harmony; note the range demands required of horns; woodwinds provide a chromatic transition into m. 532
	532–551	Previous texture returns in lower woodwinds; euphonium and tenor saxophone provide important melodic material derived from the previous section; woodwinds provide an inverted version of motives from the previous section

Section	Measure	Event and Scoring
	552–559	A brief tutti arrival which uses extended chromaticism and parallel harmonies from upper brass and woodwinds; harmonic motion moves chromatically
Aug. Fanfare	560–569	Opening fanfare is presented in augmentation with horns, saxophones, and clarinet 2–3 providing counterpoint; bass line outlines a chromatic scale, evident in timpani
Re-transition	570–597	Transition from m. 449 returns in augmentation with the original pitch structure; accompanying harmonies rely on polychordal structures; this is evident in m. 594, where the harmony resolves to B-flat^7 against C major
Coda	598–605	The thematic material from movement 2 returns in the original tonal center of E-flat major; accompanying harmonies move through a series of dominant seventh chords which descend chromatically; these leads to a harmonic resolution into G major

Unit 8: Suggested Listening

Bourgeois, Derek:
    Concerto Grosso, Op. 61
    Serenade, Op. 22c
    Trombone Concerto, Op. 114b
    William and Mary, Op. 106
Elgar, Edward:
    Symphony No. 1
    Symphony No. 2
Hindemith, Paul. *Symphony in B-flat*. For Concert Band.

Unit 9: Additional References and Resources

Bourgeois, Derek. *Concerto for Trombone*. *Fandango*. University of New Mexico Wind Symphony. Eric Rombach-Kendall, conductor. Summit Records DCD 271. 2000.

_____. *Concerto for Trombone*. *Windpower*. Kosei Wind Orchestra. Chikara Imamura, conductor. Bis 848. 1997.

_____. *Symphony for William*. *Winanga-il*. The Royal Symphonic Band of the Belgian Guides. Derek Bourgeois, conductor. HaFaBra Music ES 47.480. 2006.

_____. *William and Mary*, Op. 106. *Black Castles*. Brass Partout. Hermann Bäumer, conductor. Bis 1354. 2007.

Norton, Doug. "*Serenade, Op. 22c* by Derek Bourgeois." In *Teaching Music through Performance in Band, Volume 4*. Richard Miles, ed. Chicago: GIA Publications, 2002. 375–379.

Sutherland, C. Scott. "The Six Symphonies of Derek Bourgeois." *British Music Society Newsletter* (1998): 78–79.

Contributed by:

Donald J. McKinney
Doctoral Graduate Student Instructor
University of Michigan School of Music
Ann Arbor, Michigan

---

1 Derek Bourgois, email correspondence with the author, May 3, 2008.

2 Timothy Reynish, email correspondence with the author, May 15, 2008.

3 Liner notes for Winanga-il, (HaFaBra Music, ES 47.480).

Teacher Resource Guide

Symphony No. 1
"In Memoriam David Diamond"

Jack Stamp
(b. 1954)

Unit 1: Composer

Jack Stamp was born in Washington, DC, in 1954 and grew up in the nearby Maryland suburbs. He received a BS degree in music education from Indiana University of Pennsylvania in 1976, a MM degree in percussion performance from East Carolina University in 1978, and a DMA degree in wind conducting from Michigan State University in 1988, where he studied with Eugene Corporon. His primary composition teachers have included Robert Washburn and Fisher Tull. He has most recently studied with noted American composers David Diamond, Joan Tower, and Richard Danielpour.

Stamp, currently professor of music and director of bands at Indiana University of Pennsylvania, conducts the university Wind Ensemble and Symphony Band and teaches courses in undergraduate and graduate conducting. He is a member of the American Bandmasters Association and founder and musical director of the Keystone Wind Ensemble, a professional recording group dedicated to the advancement of American concert band music.

Unit 2: Composition

Symphony No. 1: "In Memoriam David Diamond" was commissioned by Steven K. Steele, director of bands at Illinois State University, on behalf of a consortium of twenty-five universities and colleges. During the summer of 2005, Stamp, serving as a composer-mentor at a weeklong forum for the National Band Association, expressed to fellow composers and colleagues his interest in writing longer works. He also shared his grief over the recent death of his friend and mentor, David Diamond, and mentioned that he was compelled to write a work in memory of him. At the end of the week, Steele approached Stamp with the offer to commission his first symphony. The Illinois State University Wind Symphony premiered the work on November 16, 2006, with Steele conducting.

Symphony No. 1 is a four-movement work written to honor the composer David Diamond, who in Stamp's opinion was "probably the greatest American symphonic composer." In this composition, Stamp used motives from Diamond's third and fourth symphonies and from the *String Quartet in F* by Diamond's favorite composer, Maurice Ravel. The piece illustrates Stamp's varying compositional styles, from lyrical to highly contrapuntal, with syncopation, changing meters, modal and extended harmonies, and colorful use of percussion—characteristics found in his works at all ability levels.

Unit 3: Historical Perspective

David Diamond (1915–2005) studied composition at the Cleveland Institute of Music and with Bernard Rogers, Paul Boepple, and Roger Sessions in New York. In 1928, he met Maurice Ravel, the composer he revered above all others. At Ravel's suggestion, Diamond went to Paris in 1937 and studied with Nadia Boulanger. The composer received numerous awards and commissions throughout the 1940s, including a commission by the Koussevitzky Foundation for his *Symphony No. 4*. After becoming professor of composition at The Juilliard School in 1973, he taught well into the 1990s. Renewed interest in Diamond's music, beginning in the 1980s, came with several awards of the highest honor, culminating in the National Medal of Arts, which he received at the White House in 1995.

Symphony No. 1 has the typical four-movement structure of a Classical symphony. Movement 1: "Elegy" is the longest of the four and has elements of sonata form. The "Scherzo" is the lightest, shortest and fastest movement of the symphony while movement 3: "Romanza" is slow and lyrical. The "Finale" is uplifting and quick in tempo, and incorporates the themes from the previous three movements in the recapitulation.

Unit 4: Technical Considerations

Movement 1: "Elegy"

This movement is highly modal, so there are no key signatures, which is true for the other movements as well. The use of polychords and extended harmonies create a lot of accidentals in the music. A full complement of keyboard percussion is used (crotales, chimes, bells, vibraphone, and marimba) as well as timpani and accessory instruments and requires at least nine players. The piano and double bass are also essential. Woodwinds are featured throughout, with solos in flute, oboe, English horn, bassoon, and clarinet. Brass ranges are not extreme, although trumpet 1 has a couple of sustained notes on C-sharp and D. While the movement is not technically difficult, the slow tempo and mixed meter require good breath control and confident counting and subdivision.

Movement 2: "Scherzo—Dance of the Hippos"

Stamp's characteristic trademarks are his rhythmic language and use of counterpoint, both of which are emphasized in this movement. The low reed, euphonium, and tuba parts are particularly demanding in these sections. The music is rhythmically challenging. It is highly syncopated, written primarily in 3/4 with accents that give it a 6/8 feel, and also includes a lot of mixed meter, hemiola, and rhythms that displace the barline. Harmonically, this movement also uses polychords and emphasizes the interval of a major second throughout.

Movement 3: "Romanza—with a nod to Aaron Copland"

This movement is unique in that it features a mezzo-soprano soloist. The vocalist must have a range from B-flat below the staff to the C above. The composer's program notes include directions for the entrance and stage movement of the soloist. To contrast the voice, Stamp scored the movement as darkly as possible, using alto flute and flugelhorn. A saxophone quartet with soprano saxophone is featured, and there are several solos.

The third movement is a contrasting example of Stamp's "gentler" harmony. Using the major keys of E-flat, B-flat, D-flat, G-flat, and G minor, he presents the chords in inversions, creating a vertical sound that is more like a collection of intervals than a chord.

Movement 4: "Finale"

The "Finale" features techniques already used in previous movements: counterpoint, polychords, modal and extended harmonies, syncopation, mixed meter, hemiola, and displaced barlines. In this movement Stamp employs a favorite technique: simultaneous recapitulation, or superimposing melody over melody. The themes from each of the previous movements return and are superimposed over the melody of movement 4.

Unit 5: Stylistic Considerations

Movement 1: "Elegy"

Written in memory of David Diamond, this movement is the only one of the four that includes the expression marking *With respect and anguish*. This suggests that solo players should use expression in their phrasing, and the conductor can employ tempo rubato throughout. Articulations are specifically marked and should be enforced (i.e., an accent with a tenuto should be accented and connected, not separated as most accents tend to be performed). Dynamics are contrasting throughout, with the full ensemble encouraged to play true *fortissimo* at climactic sections. Solo players are reminded to play their dynamics stronger than when playing with the full ensemble.

Movement 2: "Scherzo—Dance of the Hippos"

Due to the highly contrapuntal nature of this movement, it is very important for the ensemble to think linearly and play with forward motion. Individuals should strive for clarity in articulation in order to bring out all lines of the fugal sections. With a tempo marking of quarter note = 180–185, the movement should not sound hectic or rushed.

Movement 3: "Romanza—with a nod to Aaron Copland"

The composer suggests tempo markings throughout this movement ranging from quarter note = 48–62, creating an impression of rubato. Soloists are encouraged to play phrases with great expression. There is an obvious concern of balance between the voice and the full ensemble at the climax of the movement, but the dark scoring and the range of the vocal solo help with this.

Movement 4: "Finale"

Again, careful attention to articulation markings is important. The contrast between short and long notes characterizes the main melody of this movement. There should also be contrast between the accented, separated sections and the smoother, chorale-like episodes.

Unit 6: Musical Elements

MELODY:

Stamp pays tribute to David Diamond by basing the primary motive of movement 1 on the theme from movement 1 of Diamond's *Symphony No. 4*. This motive is first introduced in partial form in m. 5, and then the full motive is stated at the climax in m. 71. In playing this melody, performers should allow dynamics to follow the contour of the line, bringing out both the high and low points of the motive.

FIGURE 1. Movement 1, mm. 5–7, partial motive

FIGURE 2. Movement 1, mm. 71–72, full motive

The entire movement is derived from the notes of the motive, creating organic unity in the piece. Stamp presents the theme in different ways, including octave displacement, where the notes of the melody occur in different octaves throughout the instrumentation. Each note must be emphasized for the melody to be heard.

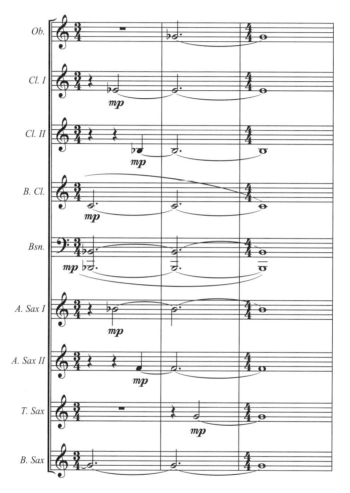

FIGURE 3. Movement 1, mm. 33–35, octave displacement

The initial motive of the "Scherzo" is based on the initial motive of Ravel's *String Quartet in F* and is immediately stated in the first two measures by the low reeds. As the movement progresses, Stamp divides this first theme into two smaller motives, 1A (measure 1 of the theme) and 1B (measure 2).

The movement features several variations of this motive through techniques such as augmentation, octave displacement, and fugue. The ensemble should strive to bring out each motive statement as it occurs. In the fugal sections, bring out each entrance of the subject and balance accordingly. Consecutive entrances should match the style of the first.

A second motive stated in m. 10 begins with the voices on the notes A and B, the interval of a major second, and moves in a contrasting contour. Encourage players to be confident in playing the dissonance and balance the contrasting lines.

FIGURE 4. Movement 2, mm. 1–3, initial motive

FIGURE 5. Movement 2, mm. 10–12, motive 2

The melody of the "Finale" begins in m. 9 and incorporates much syncopation. Work for clarity of articulation and emphasize note length.

FIGURE 6. Movement 4, mm. 9–12, melody

An example of Stamp's trademark contrapuntal writing occurs in m. 78 with a four-voice fugue that becomes a four-voice canon in m. 95 and then a two-voice canon in octaves in m. 102. Emphasize the pickup notes to the canons to bring out this change.

FIGURE 7. Movement 4, mm. 95–96, four-voice canon

FIGURE 8. Movement 4, mm. 102–103, two-voice canon

The final statement of the work features one of Stamp's favorite techniques: simultaneous recapitulation, or superimposing melody over melody. All the themes from the previous three movements return in the "Finale," superimposed with the motive of that movement. The ensemble should work for balance of the two motives.

FIGURE 9. Movement 4, mm. 181–184, "Elegy" and "Finale" motives

FIGURE 10. Movement 4, mm. 194–197, "Scherzo" and "Finale" motives

FIGURE 11. Movement 4, mm. 213–220, "Romanza" (in trumpet) and "Finale" motives

HARMONY:

Polychords (two triads sounding simultaneously) are signatures of Stamp's harmonic language, and he uses them to begin the entire work. These polychords are based on major triads (i.e., E-flat/C, D-flat/F-sharp, etc.). In rehearsal, have the ensemble play and balance the triads separately, listening for the chord quality, then play the triads together and work for overall balance.

FIGURE 12. Movement 1, mm. 20–26, polychords

Much of Stamp's music has what he calls "Lydian implications," or use of the Lydian mode. The "Elegy" chorale in m. 127 uses the Lydian mode. This same raised fourth also appears at the end of the "Romanza." The chorale-like episodes in the "Finale" also incorporate modal harmony.

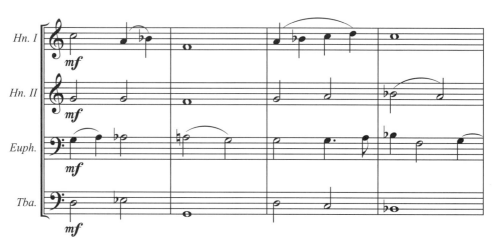

FIGURE 13. Movement 1, mm. 127–132, ending chorale

RHYTHM:
Syncopation, mixed meter, hemiola, and displacement of the barline are all characteristics of Stamp's rhythmic language. Using a metronome set on the eighth-note subdivision will help the ensemble with steady pulse.

FIGURE 14. Movement 4, mm. 46–53, syncopation and displacement of barline

A hemiola statement of the "Scherzo" motive occurs several times in the 3/4 meter, creating a feeling of 2/4. Isolate this rhythm and explain the subdivision in two. In some instances this rhythm can be conducted in two.

FIGURE 15. Movement 2, mm. 32–33, hemiola

TIMBRE:

Stamp spent a lot of time developing the tone colors in this piece in order to create variety. There is a lot of alternation between brass and woodwind choirs of varying instrumentation (i.e., flute, double reeds, and clarinet; clarinet and sax; horn, euphonium, and tuba). The release of one choir should dissolve into the entrance of the next.

Stamp loves the timbre of the English horn, and uses it as a solo voice throughout. He also likes to use E-flat clarinet to strengthen the sound of soprano voices.

The percussion choir of keyboard instruments, including crotales, should be played with hard mallets to produce the metallic sound preferred by the composer. Keyboard instruments are used several times to enhance upper woodwinds in important melodic areas.

Unit 7: Form and Structure

SECTION	MEASURE	EVENT AND SCORING
Movement 1		
Introduction	1–20	"Grief" chords in percussion; melodic motive introduced in euphonium
A	20–33	Polychords in brass choir
Transition	33–42	Motive in octave displacement
B	42–64	Contrapuntal statements of motive in woodwind solos
Climax	64–74	Polychords combined with motive, full ensemble
Development	74–127	Alternating choirs with variations of motive statements
Coda	127–142	Brass choir (Lydian chorale); final statement in octave displacement
Movement 2		
Introduction	1–24	Initial statements of melodic and rhythmic motives
Variation	25–54	Fragmented theme in low winds; rhythmic motive in brass; motive 2 in woodwinds

Section	Measure	Event and Scoring
Arrival point	55–74	Rhythmic motive with interjections of initial motive; full ensemble
Variation	75–94	Augmented theme in two-voice canon (euphonium/oboe and clarinet/saxophone) over ostinato; motive 2 in low winds
Variation	95–124	Three-voice fugue of initial motive starting in low winds; motive 2, then rhythmic motive in mid and low winds
Variation	125–144	Three-voice fugue of initial motive starting in low winds; rhythmic motive; full ensemble
Variation	145–153	Octave displacement statement of theme; second motive in woodwinds and low brass
Variation	154–172	Theme in hemiola in brass choir answered by motive statements in woodwinds and percussion; motive 2 in woodwinds and low brass
Coda	173–193	Rhythmic motive in upper woodwinds, horns, and percussion with "Elegy" theme in mid range
Movement 3		
Introduction	1–8	Open fifths in keyboard percussion; melody fragments in voice
A	9–15	Duet with melody in voice and counterpoint in bassoon
B	16–23	Alto flute and clarinet duet, adding oboe and euphonium
C	24–31	Saxophone choir; variation of B melody
B	32–39	Voice and English horn duet, adding full woodwind choir
A	40–46	Climax: melody in alto flute and horn, then flugelhorn with vocal obbligato and accompaniment in clarinets and low winds
Coda	47–55	Duet with flugelhorn and horn, another with euphonium and tuba; return of open fifths in keyboard percussion and voice
Movement 4		
Introduction/A	1–19	Melody in upper woodwinds; chords in saxophones and horns; syncopated counterpoint in basses

Section	Measure	Event and Scoring
B	20–27	Chorale-like episode in woodwind choir
Transition	28–45	Quartal chords and polychords in brass with motivic statements in upper woodwinds and bells
Variation	46–67	Fugal ostinato in woodwinds and percussion; augmented theme low brass
B'	68–77	Chorale-like episode in woodwind choir
Development/ variation	78–109	Woodwinds and percussion: four-voice fugue becomes four-voice canon, then two-voice canon
Transition	109–128	As before, chords in brass and motivic statements in woodwinds
Variation	129–146	Fugal ostinato in woodwinds and percussion; augmented theme from "Elegy" in saxophones and low winds
Variation	147–155	Duet: solo trumpet plays theme with solo euphonium in inversion
Variation	156–164	Polychords from "Elegy" as heavy accents in brass accompany a timpani solo that has melodic motives
Variation/ transition	165–180	Woodwind choir with theme and inversion, joined by brass in canon; sequence of motive outlined in chords
Simultaneous recapitulation	131–224	"Elegy" theme with "Finale" motive (saxophone choir with flute, oboe, and bassoon); "Scherzo" theme with "Finale" motive (bassoon and oboe); motive 2 of "Scherzo" builds to "Romanza" theme with "Finale" motive (full ensemble)
Coda	225–240	Full ensemble; rapid alternation of themes; "Finale: theme in bass voices accompanied by heavily accented and syncopated polychords in full ensemble

Unit 8: Suggested Listening

Diamond, David:
> *Heart's Music*
> *Tantivy*
> *Symphonies No. 3* and *4* (orchestral)

Persichetti, Vincent. *Symphony No. 6.*

Schumann, William. *George Washington Bridge.*

Stamp, Jack:
> *Divertimento in F*
> *Escapade*
> *Four Maryland Songs*
> *Pastime*

Tower, Joan. *Fascinating Ribbons.*

Unit 9: Additional References and Resources

Dvorak, Thomas L., Robert Grechesky, and Gary M. Ciepluch. *Best Music for High School Band.* Bob Margolis, ed. Brooklyn, NY: Manhattan Beach Music, 1993.

McCrann, James P. "An Analysis of Stamp's *Pastime* with Comments by the Composer." *The Instrumentalist* 56 (March, 2002): 20–22+.

Perry, Dawn A. "Jack Stamp: A Biographical Sketch and Analysis of *Symphony No. 1—"In Memoriam David Diamond."* DMA diss., The University of Southern Mississippi, 2008.

Schmidt, Daniel L. "An Examination of Four Song Cycles for Solo Voice and Wind Ensemble by Twentieth-century Composers Bernard Gilmore, William Penn, John Heins, and John Stamp." DMA. diss., University of Cincinnati, 2000.

Stamp, Jack. "Composing Music that Educates." In *Teaching Music through Performance in Band, Volume 2.* Richard Miles, ed. Chicago: GIA Publications, 1998. 92–102.

_____. Interview by author. June 6–7, 2007. Digital recording. Indiana, PA.

_____. "Jack Stamp." In *Composers on Composing for Band.* Mark Camphouse, ed. Chicago: GIA Publications, 2002. 323–348.

Contributed by:

Dawn A. Perry
Director of Bands
Wingate University
Wingate, North Carolina

Teacher Resource Guide

Turbine

John Mackey
(b. 1973)

Unit 1: Composer

John Mackey was born in New Philadelphia, Ohio, October 1, 1973. Many in his family were musicians, but, prior to college, he received almost no musical training. At a young age he enjoyed using an early music notation computer program, given to him by his grandfather, to play back musical scores that he input. After experimenting with composition for several years during middle and high school, Mackey was accepted to study composition with Donald Erb at the Cleveland Institute of Music, where he graduated with a bachelor of fine arts degree in 1995. He continued his studies with Pulitzer Prize-winning composer John Corigliano at The Julliard School and graduated with a master of music degree in 1997.

While attending Julliard, Mackey participated for three consecutive years in a Composers and Choreographers Workshop. This type of collaboration yielded several new compositions for instrumental chamber ensembles and led to the format for much of Mackey's work over the next several years: music to accompany dance. This included pieces that paired Mackey with prominent choreographers such as Robert Battle.

His work with wind ensemble began with a transcription he undertook of his own *Redline Tango* in 2004 and his first original composition for wind ensemble, *Sasparilla*, in 2005. Since then, several new original works and transcriptions of earlier chamber ensemble and orchestral pieces have been completed. His complete list of compositions for wind ensemble as of 2008 includes *Kingfishers Catch Fire, Undertow, Concerto for Soprano Sax and Wind Ensemble, Strange Humors, Redline Tango, Turning, Sasparilla, Turbine*, and *Clocking*.

Mackey is a two-time winner of the Morton Gould Young Composer Award, nine-time winner of the ASCAP Concert Music Award, recipient of grants from the American Music Center, the Mary Flagler Cary Charitable Trust, and the NEA, and has received several composer-in-residence appointments. His *Redline Tango* won the Walter Beeler Memorial Composition Prize in 2004 and the ABA/Ostwald Award from the American Bandmasters Association in 2005. He currently resides in Los Angeles, California where he composes full-time and runs his ASCAP publishing company, Osti Music, Incorporated.

Unit 2: Composition

Turbine is a single-movement original work featuring a constant tempo of quarter note = 184 (although Mackey prefers 190) and is both multimetric and polymetric in design. In this contemporary piece, the composer uses both harmonic and metric dissonance (metric dissonance occurs when musical factors [in this case polymeter and conflicting syncopated accent patterns] combine to create a passage that is metrically ambiguous). The harmony employs atonality, modality, and shifting tonal centers. Melody, in the traditional sense, is often absent and is replaced by alternating ostinatos and motivic development through which the composer explores the myriad of tone colors afforded him within the wind and percussion sections.

Mackey writes of the work:

> I'm afraid of flying. This piece was my way of dealing with that. The first three minutes are rough, grinding, and tense, as the jet engine builds up speed (through texture, not tempo), and eventually goes racing down the runway. Once the jet takes off, though, the music changes, and we realize that flying really isn't so bad. In fact, it can be beautiful once the plane is airborne. But in the back of my mind, I'm always aware that we're up quite high—and our lives (and that beauty) depend on these massive pieces of machinery. If that machinery (in this case, the percussion) should fail, we'd all be in serious trouble, so I keep my knuckles gripped to the armrest, look out at the clouds, think pretty thoughts, and hope that the pulse of that engine never lets up.

Unit 3: Historical Perspective

The Southeastern Conference Band Directors Association commissioned *Turbine*, Mackey's second original work for wind ensemble, and the piece is dedicated by the composer to Frank B. Wickes, director of bands at the Louisiana State University. The piece was commissioned to be performed at the Southern Division Convention of the College Band Directors National

Association at Vanderbilt University in Nashville, Tennessee and was premiered by the University of Kentucky Wind Ensemble, John Cody Birdwell, conductor, on February 24, 2006. *Turbine* continues to be performed throughout the United States and other countries, and has been performed at numerous regional and national conferences. *Turbine* has been also been professionally recorded by several outstanding college and university wind ensembles.

Unit 4: Technical Considerations

Turbine is an advanced work, and the demand on each player, particularly in terms of rhythm and energy, are extremely high. Extended dynamic ranges from *niente* to ***ffff*** can be found within the piece, and having players on all instruments able to produce these levels with controlled tone and intensity is crucial. A constant eighth-note pulse can be heard throughout the majority of the work, and this pulse is unaffected by the frequent meter changes. An irregular meter of 5/8 + 2/4 is used often to create an effect of a 9/8 measure with an irregular grouping of eighth notes (2 + 3 + 2 + 2). The piece is a fast-paced and aggressive exploration of the many textures and timbres of the ensemble. Performers must exhibit confidence and independence in order to effectively communicate each shifting nuance of color as voices are removed or brought in amidst the layered and rhythmic ostinatos.

Much of the demand in the woodwind voices is created through the presence of triplet, sixteenth-note, quintuplet, and sextuplet runs that are usually chromatic and often occur with several rhythms combined in the same line. Solo lines appear for most woodwind instruments. Scoring includes prominent parts for E-flat clarinet, contrabass clarinet, and contrabassoon. There are two parts for piccolo, oboe, bass clarinet, and bassoon, and four parts for flute and clarinet. Ranges are extended in most woodwind voices (C4 for piccolo and flute and G3 for B-flat clarinet).

For brass, effects such as flutter-tonguing and glissandos are common, and many of these effects occur at extreme dynamic levels and at higher or lower extents of range. Clear articulation on frequent eighth-note ostinatos is necessary, and the ability to sustain and control both gradual and *subito* dynamic figures with quality tone and attention to ensemble balance is a must. There are four parts for trumpet, horn, and trombone, and range issues are minimal (C-sharp 3 in trumpet 1, B2 in trombone 1, and CCC-sharp in the tuba).

The piano part is fundamental to this composition and is featured prominently as a solo melodic instrument as well as an integral part of the percussion section. The use of non-traditional percussion instruments and techniques, such as four varying brake drums or metal sheets, muted and randomly tuned timpani, trash can lids, and an assortment of cymbal and tam-tam scrapes are featured. Players are encouraged to discover the strangest and most grotesque sound possible in many instances. Percussionists can expect a highly physical performance, where constant energy and intensity are expected. Of particular note is that the work calls for two five-octave marimbas. In his online blog, Mackey credits James Campbell, professor of percussion at the University of Kentucky, with a great deal of refinement of the percussion elements of *Turbine*.

Unit 5: Stylistic Considerations

Mackey's *Turbine* forces players to control a broad range of expressive tools. Dynamics reach extremes, and producing a controlled tone at all levels is critical. Additionally, in areas of sustained and gradual dynamic movement, performers must have a clear understanding of the ultimate goal of each segment and must execute crescendo or decrescendo effects evenly. Maintaining balance in the ensemble is of paramount importance, as important motives or melodic fragments can easily be lost among the layered ostinatos. It is important to ensure that elements such as the individual notes of the frequent tone clusters or chromatic runs (often in intervals of a second or third among voices) are in appropriate proportion to one another.

Precision and clarity of articulations in *Turbine* will require constant focus by performers and a clear conveyance of expectations from the conductor. Performers must have a uniform view of how to produce each articulation in terms of attack, sustain, and release. With regard to percussion, attacks and releases must be executed precisely and care must be taken to avoid lengthy decay unless written or appropriate.

The tempo of the work, whether set at quarter note = 184 or faster, should be considered inflexible, and the conductor must move forward with unyielding drive. The guide for tempo choice must come from the conductor's understanding of the ensemble's ability to perform the more technical aspects of the piece. Once tempo is determined, all must agree to remain steadfast. Drive and intensity are inherently required of both the conductor and performers. In lighter sections there is always a sense of restrained energy and the need for aggressive focus by performers.

Unit 6: Musical Elements

MELODY:

Within *Turbine*, melody is secondary to rhythm, as melody appears sparsely and in varying forms. There is a primary melody, a secondary melody, a countermelody, and four melodic/harmonic motives. Of all of the melodic elements, only two appear before m. 111. All other melodic elements occur during Part B of the work (see Unit 7). The primary melody appears in its entirety only four times throughout the composition, as well as in fragments (mm. 155–156, 206, and 208). The secondary melody appears once (mm.

128–138), centered in F, and the Lydian countermelody appears. The four thematic motives are varied and of simple construction.

HARMONY:

Mackey's harmonic language in *Turbine* features the use of modes, most prominently Lydian, and an abundance of atonality, tone clusters, and simple tertian harmonies. Often within the work, harmonic progressions are created simply by the direction in which tone clusters move.

RHYTHM:

Without question, rhythm is of primary importance in *Turbine*. Central to this is the feeling of constant energy, drive, and forward motion that must be sustained by rhythm. This is mainly achieved through Mackey's creative use of four principal ostinatos. They are presented in a variety of formats, including non-pitched percussion presentations, single pitches in tonal voices, harmonic rhythms in piano or other combinations of instruments, and as both melodic/harmonic rhythms when motives are incorporated.

Meter may or may not play an important role on these ostinatos, as some work within the confines of barlines while others do not. Syncopated accent patterns coupled with layering of ostinatos create and maintain a frequent sense of metric ambiguity (dissonance). Interest is maintained by incorporation of these rhythmic complexities and mixed meters.

TIMBRE:

An array of tone colors within the contemporary wind ensemble is used by Mackey to create an ever-shifting pallet of sounds and textures. From subdued, fragmented motives and single-instrument ostinatos to forceful tutti sections that push the dynamic limits of the ensemble, Mackey explores them all. Special care must be taken by the conductor and performers to ensure an appropriate balance of these colors. The use of non-traditional percussion instruments and techniques leads to many unexpected and often surprising timbres. Percussionists are encouraged to think big and experiment with items like drill bits, scuba tanks, and steel pipes in order to create the sounds called for. As this piece is meant to depict flying on a jet, Mackey considers the percussion to be the "engine" in this composition.

Unit 7: Form and Structure

Turbine is essentially a work in two parts (A-B) with sections governed by shifting tonal centers, orchestration, and varying rhythmic/melodic material.

SECTION	MEASURE	EVENT AND SCORING
Part A (mm. 1–110)		
Introduction	1–18	Presentation of ostinato 1 (mm. 1–4) in percussion and ostinato 2 in bass drum (mm. 5–6); very loud, energetic initial introduction; sustained woodwind dynamic effects and trombone glissandos; ostinatos in bassoon and percussion
Section 1	19–45	Ostinatos 1 and 2 continue; motive 1 in bass clarinet and piano (mm. 21–23); metric dissonance created by conflicting ostinatos and hemiola; chromatic flourishes in woodwind voices; brass alternate between ostinato figures and sustained dynamic effects
Section 2	46–66	Ostinatos 1 and 2, motive 1; metric dissonance continues; thinner texture than earlier sections; increase in density as m. 66 approaches; trombone glissandos; conflicting ostinatos in woodwinds and percussion; climactic two-measure tutti at mm. 65–66
Section 3	67–78	Metric dissonance continues; trombone glissandos; multiple chromatic woodwind flourishes with a variety of beat divisions; ostinatos continue; sustained tone clusters in brass voices
Section 4	79–88	Ostinatos 1 and 2, motive 1; chromatic woodwind flourishes; brass glissandos and sustained tone clusters; metric dissonance continues; very loud, intense ending to this section with the entire ensemble from mm. 84–88
Transition	89–110	Ostinatos 1 and 2, motive 2 presented by bassoons in mm. 105–106; becomes thinner in texture following m. 88; piano and marimba are the primary vehicle of the ostinato; motive fragments and runs in woodwinds; brass has subdued dynamic effects

SECTION	MEASURE	EVENT AND SCORING
Part B	111–303	
Section 1	111–139	Ostinatos 1 and 2, secondary melody, motive 2; marimba duet; secondary melody in solo woodwind voices; isolated, important fragment in the piano
Section 2	140–148	Primary melody in bass clarinet, motive 2; ostinato continues in percussion; sustained left hand octaves in piano; fragments and dynamic effects in other voices
Section 3	149–184	Ostinato 2; fragments of primary melody appear in several voices; motive 2; motive 3 in bass clarinet mm. 180–181; subito *piano* effect and return of ostinato in marimbas; flute and piccolo runs; *forte-piano* sustained tones in trumpet
Section 4	185–192	Primary melody in woodwinds voices; ostinatos continue; sustained dynamic effects; dynamic push and chromatic runs in woodwinds ends the section
Section 5	193–213	Multiple layers of alternating motives and ostinatos; motive 2 becomes an ostinato in marimbas; motive 4 in bass clarinet mm. 199–202; ostinato 3 in flute, oboe, and marimba m. 203; motive 3 reappears m. 209
Section 6	214–221	Primary melody in oboe, alto saxophone, and trumpet; countermelody in tenor saxophone, trombone, and euphonium; more flourishes in woodwinds; trombone glissandos
Section 7	222–241	Alternating extremes of dynamics and orchestration; measures of loud ensemble tutti alternate with lighter statements of ostinatos, motive 2, and chromatic woodwind flourishes
Section 8	242–276	Layering of ostinatos and motives; texture becomes more dense; number of layers increases; energy and dynamic intensity builds; extensive woodwind runs with varied beat divisions

SECTION	MEASURE	EVENT AND SCORING
Section 9	277–284	Primary melody first in piccolo, tenor sax, trumpet, and upper horns. then E-flat and soprano clarinets; and saxophones join; countermelody appears in several of the low brass and winds; piano is the primary vehicle of the ostinato eighth-note pulse
Coda	285–303	Ostinatos 1 and 2; ending with components of previous themes, motives, and ostinatos; tone clusters; woodwind runs (including extended chromatic runs) and trombone glissandos; the work concludes on a unison concert D

Unit 8: Suggested Listening

John Mackey:
>   *Clocking*
>   *Kingfishers Catch Fire*
>   *Redline Tango*
>   *Turning*

John Adams:
>   *Harmonielehre*
>   *Short Ride in a Fast Machine*
>   *Slonimsky's Earbox*
>   *Lateralus*. By the rock band *Tool*.
>   *Turbine*. *Distilled in Kentucky*. University of Kentucky Wind Ensemble. John Cody Birdwell, conductor. Mark Records MCD 6739.
>   *Turbine*. *Stravinsky and Friends*. University of Florida Wind Symphony. David A. Waybright, conductor. Mark Records MCD 6565.

Unit 9: Additional References and Resources

Phillips, Rebecca L. "John Mackey: The Composer, His Compositional Style and a Conductor's Analysis of *Redline Tango* and *Turbine*." Monograph. Louisiana State University, 2007.

Websites:
>   Battleworks Dance Company. www.battleworksdance.com (Robert Battle, choreographer, runs the Battleworks Dance Company in New York City. Info and some video clips of performances of works by Battle and John Mackey can be found here.)
>   John Mackey's personal weblog. http://ostimusic.com/blog/2006/02/ (Has an account of the premier of *Turbine*.)

Osti Music, Incorporated. http://www.ostimusic.com (The online home of John Mackey's ASCAP publishing company.)

Contributed by:

DuWayne Dale
Director of Bands and Orchestra
Grant County Schools
Dry Ridge, Kentucky

Teacher Resource Guide

Wolf Rounds

Christopher Rouse
(b. 1949)

Unit 1: Composer

Christopher Rouse is one of America's most prominent composers of orchestral music. His works have won a Pulitzer Prize (for his *Trombone Concerto*) and a Grammy Award (for *Concert de Gaudí*), as well as election to the prestigious American Academy of Arts and Letters. Rouse has created a body of work perhaps unequalled in its emotional intensity. The New York Times has called it "some of the most anguished, most memorable music around." The Baltimore Sun has written: "When the music history of the late 20th century is written, I suspect the explosive and passionate music of Rouse will loom large."

Rouse developed an early interest in both classical and popular music. He graduated from Oberlin Conservatory and Cornell University, numbering among his principal teachers George Crumb and Karel Husa. Rouse maintained a steady interest in popular music (e.g., at the Eastman School of Music, where he was professor of composition until 2002, he taught a course in the history of rock for many years). Rouse is currently a member of the composition faculty at The Juilliard School.

While the Rouse catalog includes a number of acclaimed chamber and ensemble works, he is best known for his mastery of orchestral writing. His music has been played by every major orchestra in the United States and numerous ensembles overseas, including the Berlin Philharmonic, City of Birmingham Symphony Orchestra, Sydney and Melbourne Symphonies, London Symphony, Philharmonia Orchestra, Royal Concertgebouw Orchestra, Stockholm Philharmonic, Zurich Tonhalle Orchestra, Orchestre de Paris, Gulbenkian Orchestra of Lisbon, Toronto Symphony, Vienna

Symphony, Orchestre National de France, Moscow Symphony, Royal Scottish National Orchestra, Bamberg Symphony, Bournemouth Symphony, and the Orchestre Symphonique du Montreal, as well as the BBC Symphony Orchestra and the radio orchestras of Helsinki, Frankfurt, Hamburg, Leipzig, Tokyo, Austria, and Berlin.

Unit 2: Composition

Wolf Rounds was commissioned by the Frost School of Music at the University of Miami for their wind ensemble. The piece is dedicated to the group's music director, Gary Green.

The composer's concept of the work was to introduce a series of circular musical ideas that would repeat over and over until metamorphosing to a new idea that would then also be repeated in the same fashion until becoming yet another. These musics would be of different lengths so that their repeated overlaps would produce a constantly changing sonic landscape. Sometimes these ideas would repeat verbatim; at other times there would be gradual but constant development within each repetition. Some instruments would introduce new musics while others would continue to repeat material for a longer period of time before moving on to a new idea.

Rouse's first impulse was to entitle the work *Loops*, as it seemed to him that this was an accurate description of the processes involved in composing the piece. However, this title seemed a bit prosaic. The word *loops*, though, led him to think of the Latin word *lupus*, which means "wolf." He was put in mind of the way in which wolves circle their prey, and these predatory rounds, of course, reminded him of the circular nature of his musical presentation. Thus the final title: *Wolf Rounds*.

It is scored for piccolo, flute 1–2, oboe 1–3, clarinet 1–2, bass clarinet, bassoon 1–2, contrabassoon, baritone saxophone, bass saxophone, horn 1–4, trumpet 1–3, trombone 1–3, tuba, timpani, percussion 1–5, and amplified string bass.

Wolf Rounds was completed in Baltimore, Maryland on October 16, 2006, and lasts approximately seventeen minutes in performance.

Unit 3: Historical Perspective

With this composition, Christopher Rouse joins a growing list of established, internationally recognized composers who are composing for wind band for the first time. Many of these composers, including Rouse, have won major composition prizes, including the Pulitzer Prize in Composition.

Wolf Rounds is actually Rouse's second work for wind medium. He composed *Thor* in 1981, but has since withdrawn the work.

This new cache of composers who are writing for wind band for the first time come from a background heavily influenced by the symphony orchestra and/or chamber music. Their background and experience, often unencumbered by the traditional timbres and instrumentation of the band, result in sonorities and expressions that are atypical to the medium. This is certainly the case with *Wolf Rounds*.

Unit 4: Technical Considerations

This work is technically extremely challenging. Scored for thirty-two instrumental voices, each part is often rhythmically independent. Occasionally voices are scored in an extreme tessitura, as is the case with horn 4 and tuba. Creating a unified musical form is also challenging for both conductor and ensemble.

Unit 5: Stylistic Considerations

In this work, Rouse is heavily influenced by rock and pop music. The effect that the composer has achieved is one of a strong funk feel throughout. This is often achieved through careful adherence to articulation and accents.

Unit 6: Musical Elements

MELODY:

    [Note: All examples are at the tempo of half note = 100.]

    Melodic material is mostly motivic fragments that are constantly moving, evolving, added, subtracted, and repeated. An example of this cyclic development is the motive in m. 1 and the continuous transformation of the material over several bars.

FIGURE 1.

HARMONY:
Rouse's harmonic approach is very eclectic. The fundamental material is based on a minor third motion as shown in material from Sections A and B (see in figure 2).

FIGURE 2.

The composer also expands the harmonic material in a consonant manor similar to two of his favorite composers: Wagner and Strauss. Contrasting sections become extremely dissonant and chromatic.

RHYTHM:
A major trait in all of Rouse's music is his fascination with rhythmic interplay and interaction. In *Wolf Rounds*, rhythmic juxtaposition is a major compositional method. It varies from combining individual lines into a separate "whole" unit, as in the earlier examples shown in figure 1, to individual rhythmic layers, such as the "box notation" in figure 3, and finally, complete fugal independence as shown in figure 4.

FIGURE 3.

FIGURE 4.

TIMBRE:

Rouse has said that it is unfortunate when composers become typecast in certain styles and genres. Having stated that, he has a propensity for large ensembles and especially the resources of the symphony orchestra.

Color and gesture have important roles in *Wolf Rounds*. By way of example, Rouse's use of baritone and bass saxophones (note that he does not score for soprano, alto or tenor saxophones) and amplified double bass (with enough amplification to simulate a rock band sound) creates an unusual and aurally identifiable funky, gritty timbral unit. This base palate is then expanded and evolved into numerous other instrumental combinations.

Unit 7: Form and Structure

As stated earlier, *Wolf Rounds* is based on continually evolving motivic devices. A detailed outline of form would be extremely involved and prohibitively complex. The basic form is A-B-A, and awareness of the macro sections will help organize study of the work. Note that not all rehearsal numbers in the score indicate formal structures or thematic divisions.

SECTION	MEASURE	EVENT AND SCORING
A	1–249	Motivic material based on short, rhythmic fragments
B	250–450	Motivic material based on legato motivic lines
A"	451–717	Combining material from sections A and B
Coda	718–733	Unison rhythmic punch

Unit 8: Suggested Listening

Rouse, Christopher:
- *Flute Concerto*
- *Iscariot*
- *Phantasmata*
- *Rapture*
- *Symphony No. 2*

Unit 9: Additional References and Resources

Composer's website. www.christopherrouse.com

Contributed by:

Jeffrey Renshaw
Conductor
University of Connecticut
Storrs, Connecticut

Appendix A

A Chronological Survey of Nineteenth, Twentieth, and Twenty-first Century Wind Repertoire with Orchestral Literature and Prize Winner Reference Guide

Eugene Migliaro Corporon
Director of Wind Studies
University of North Texas

Appendix

Wind	Orch.	Composer	Title
1810		Paer, Ferdinand	*Four Grand Military Marches*
	1812	Beethoven, Ludwig van	*Symphony No. 8*
1813		Beethoven, Ludwig van	*Siegesinfonie*
1813		Maschek, Vincenz	*The Battle of Leipzig*
1815		Bochsa, Charles	*Requiem*
1815		Reicha, Anton	*Commemoration Symphony*
1816		Weber, Carl Maria von	*March*
1820		Spohr, Louis	*Notturno*
	1822	Schubert, Franz	*Symphony No. 8, "Unfinished"*
	1824	Beethoven, Ludwig van	*Symphony No. 9*
1824		Mendelssohn, Felix	*Ouverture für Harmoniemusik* (E. Boyd)
1825		Krommer, Franz	*Partita for Band*
	1830	Berlioz, Hector	*Symphonie Fantastique*
	1833	Mendelssohn, Felix	*Symphony No. 4, "Italian"*
	1838	Berlioz, Hector	*Benvenuto Cellini Overture*
1840		Berlioz, Hector	*Grande Symphonie Funébre et Triomphale*
1840c		Donizetti, Gaetano Rossini, Gioacchino	*Two Marches for the Sultan Abdul Medjid*
1844		Wagner, Richard	*Trauermusik WWV 73* (E. 1994/Votta/Boyd)
1846		Meyerbeer, Giacomo	*Dance No. 1* (S. Lake)
	1853	Verdi, Giuseppe	*La Traviata*
	1859	Wagner, Richard	*Tristan und Isolde*
1864		Wagner, Richard	*Huldingungsmarsch* (Homage March)
1865		Bruckner, Anton	*Apollo March*

WIND	ORCH.	COMPOSER	TITLE
1865		Fucik, Julius	*Florentiner*, Op. 214
1865		Strauss, Johann	*Radetsky March*
	1867	Mussorgsky, Modest	*Night on Bald Mountain*
1869		Saint-Saëns, Camille	*Orient et Occident*, Op. 25 (E. 1995/Reynish and Parry)
	1876	Brahms, Johannes	*Symphony No. 1*
1877		Rimsky-Korsakov, Nicolai	*Concerto for Trombone*
1878		Rimsky-Korsakov, Nicolai	*Variations for Oboe*
1878		Rimsky-Korsakov, Nicolai	*Concerto for Clarinet*
1878		Reeves, David Wallis	*Yankee Doodle-Fantasie Humoresque*
1878		Dvorak, Antonin	*Serenade* Op. 44
	1878	Tchaikovsky, Peter	*Symphony No. 4*
1884		Tchaikovsky, Peter	*Dance of the Jesters* (S. 1997/Cramer)
	1885	Massenet, Jules	*Le Cid* (S. 1985/Reynolds)
	1888	Rimsky-Korsakov, Nicholai	*Schéhérazade*
	1891	Ives, Charles	*Variations on America* (S. 1949/Schuman & S. 1967/Rhodes)
1892		Ives, Charles	*March Intercollegiate*
1892		Tchaikovsky, Peter	*Military March in F*
	1894	Bruckner, Anton	*Symphony No. 9*
	1894	Debussy, Claude	*Prelude to the Afternoon of a Faun*
1896c		Grieg, Edward	*Funeral March*
1896		Joplin, Scott	*Combination March*
	1896	Mahler, Gustav	*Symphony No. 3*
	1896	Strauss, Richard	*Also Sprach Zarathustra*
	1899	Debussy, Claude	*Nocturnes*
	1899	Schoenberg, Arnold	*Verklärte Nacht*, Op. 4
1901		Grainger, Percy	*Ye Banks and Braes O' Bonnie Doon*
1901		Mahler, Gustav	*Um Mitternacht*
1902		Grainger, Percy	*Hill Song No. 1*
	1903	Ives, Charles	*Country Band March* (S. 1978/Sinclair)

WIND	ORCH.	COMPOSER	TITLE
	1904	Ives, Charles	*Overture and March 1776* (S. 1978/Sinclair)
	1904	Webern, Anton	*Im Sommerwind*, Op. 16
	1905	Debussy, Claude	*La Mer*
	1905	Grainger, Percy	*Lads of Wamphray* (S. 1938/Grainger)
1905		Novacek, Ottokar	*Sinfonietta*, Op. 48
1906		Enesco, Georges	*Dixtuor*, Op. 14
1906		Ives, Charles	*Scherzo "Over the Pavements"*
	1906	Schoenberg, Arnold	*Kammersymphonie No. 1*, Op. 9
1907		Ives, Charles	*Calcium Light Night*
1907		Grainger, Percy	*Hill Song No. 2*
	1907	Holst, Gustav	*A Somerset Rhapsody* (S. 1980/Grundman)
1907		Stravinsky, Igor	*Pastorale*
	1908	Mahler, Gustav	*Das Lied von der Erde*
	1908	Webern, Anton	*Passacaglia*, Op. 1
1909		Hahn, Reynaldo	*La Bal de Béatrice d'Este*
1909		Holst, Gustav	*First Suite in E-flat*
	1909	Schoenberg, Arnold	*Five Pieces for Orchestra*
	1909	Webern, Anton	*Six Pieces for Orchestra*, Op. 6
	1909	Ravel, Maurice	*Daphnis et Chloé*
	1909	Vaughan Williams, Ralph	*Symphony No. 1: A Sea Symphony*
	1910	Grainger, Percy	*Shepherds Hey* (S.1918/Grainger)
1910		Schmitt, Florent	*Lied et Scherzo*, Op. 54
	1910	Stravinsky, Igor	*The Firebird*
	1910	Vaughan Williams, Ralph	*Fantasia on a Theme of Thomas Tallis*
1911		Holst, Gustav	*Second Suite in F*
	1912	Berg, Alban	*Altenberglieder*, Op. 4
	1912	Ives, Charles	*Decoration Day* (S. 1984/Elkus)
	1912	Nielson, Carl	*Paraphrase on "Nearer My God to Thee"*
	1912	Schoenberg, Arnold	*Pierrot Lunaire*

Wind	Orch.	Composer	Title
1913		Ives, Charles	*The See'r*
	1913	Stravinsky, Igor	*Le Sacre du Printemps*
	1913	Turina, Joaquin	*La Procession del Rocio*, Op. 9 (V. 1962/Reed)
	1913	Webern, Anton	*Five Pieces for Orchestra*, Op. 10
	1914	Dohnanyi, Erno	*Variations on a Nursery Theme*, Op. 26 (S. Paynter)
	1914	Grainger, Percy	*Colonial Song* (S. 1997/Rogers)
1914		Schmitt, Florent	*Dionysiaques*, Op. 62
	1915	Berg, Alban	*Three Pieces for Orchestra*, Op. 6
	1916	Grainger, Percy	*The Warriors* (S. 1999/Pappajohn)
	1916	Holst, Gustav	*The Planets* (S. 1998/Patterson)
	1916	Ives, Charles	*Symphony No. 4*
	1916	Prokofiev, Serge	*Symphony No. 1 (Classical)*, Op. 25
	1917	Ives, Charles	*Three Places in New England*
1917		Stravinsky, Igor	*Ragtime for Eleven Instruments*
1917		Stravinsky, Igor	*Tango*
	1918	De Falla, Manuel	*Three Cornered Hat*
1918		Grainger, Percy	*Colonial Song*
1918		Hanson, Howard	*Triumphal Ode*
1918		Grainger, Percy	*Irish Tune from County Derry*
1918		Stravinsky, Igor	*L'Histoire du Soldat*
1919		Grainger, Percy	*Children's March "Over the Hills and Far Away"* (S. 1971/Erickson & S. 1995/Rogers)
1920		Grainger, Percy	*Molly on the Shore*
1920		O'Donnell, B. Walton	*Theme and Variations*, Op. 26
	1920	Ravel, Maurice	*La Valse*
1920		Stravinsky, Igor	*Symphonies of Wind Instruments* (Revised 1947)
1921		Faure, Gabriel	*Chant Funéraire*, Op. 117
1921		Honegger, Arthur	*King David* (original version)

WIND	ORCH.	COMPOSER	TITLE
1921		Ives, Charles	*Anne Street*
	1922	Berg, Alban	*Wozzeck*
1922		Jacob, Gordon	*William Byrd Suite*
1922		Milhaud, Darius	*Dixtuor* "Little Symphony No. 5
	1922	Stravinsky, Igor	*Mavra: Comic Opera*
1922		Varèse, Edgard	*Offrandes*
1923		Milhaud, Darius	*La Création du Monde*
1923		Stravinsky, Igor	*Octet* (Revised 1952)
1923		Varèse, Edgard	*Hyperprism*
1923		Varèse, Edgard	*Octandre*
1923		Vaughan Williams, Ralph	*Folk Song Suite*
1923		Walton, William	*Façade*
	1924	Copland, Aaron	*Symphony No. 1*
1924		Fletcher, Percy	*Vanity Fair* (E. 2006/Karrick)
1924		Gershwin, George	*Rhapsody in Blue*
1924		Krenek, Ernst	*Symphony No. 4*, Op. 34
	1924	Respighi, Ottorino	*Pines of Rome* (S. 1974/Duker)
1924		Strauss, Richard	*Wiener Philharmoniker Fanfare*
1924		Stravinsky, Igor	*Concerto for Piano* (Revised 1950)
1924		Vaughan Williams, Ralph	*Sea Songs*
1924		Vaughan Williams, Ralph	*Toccata Marziale*
1924		Weill, Kurt	*Concerto for Violin*, Op. 12
1925		Antheil, George	*A Jazz Symphony*
1925		Antheil, George	*Ballet Mécanique* (Revised 1953)
1925		Berg, Alban	*Chamber Concerto for Violin, Piano, and Thirteen Wind Instruments*, Op. 8
	1925	Honegger, Arthur	*Concertino for Piano and Orchestra*
1925		Martinu, Bohuslav	*Concertino for Cello and Winds*
1925		Varèse, Edgard	*Integrales*
1926		Casadesus, Francis	*London Sketches*
1926		Fauchet, Paul	*Symphony in B-flat*

WIND	ORCH.	COMPOSER	TITLE
1926		Hindemith, Paul	*Konzertmusik*, Op. 41 (Donaueschingen)
1926		Ibert, Jacques	*Concerto for Cello*
1926		Janacek, Leos	*Capriccio for Piano Left Hand*
1926		Krenek, Ernst	*Three Merry Marches*, Op. 44 (Donaueschingen)
1926		Pepping, Ernst	*Kleine Serenade* (Donaueschingen)
	1926	Prokofiev, Serge	*Overture*, Op. 42
1926		Toch, Ernst	*Spiel*, Op. 39 (Donaueschingen)
1927		Hindemith, Paul	*Concerto for Organ and Wind Instruments, Kammermusik , no. 7 Op. 46, No. 2*
	1927	Krenek, Ernst	*Jonny Spielt Auf*
1927		Weill, Kurt	*Mahagonny Songspiel*
1927		Weill, Kurt	*Vom Tod im Wald*, Op. 16
1928		Holst, Gustav	*Bach's Fugue a la Gigue*
1928		Jacob, Gordon	*An Original Suite*
1928		Krenek, Ernst	*Kleine Blasmusik*, Op. 70a
1928		McPhee, Colin	*Concerto for Piano and Wind Octet*
	1928	Ravel, Maurice	*Bolero*
	1928	Sessions, Roger	*The Blackmaskers*
	1928	Thomson, Virgil	*Symphony on a Hymn Tune*
	1928	Webern, Anton	*Symphony*, Op. 21
1928		Weill, Kurt	*Berlin Requiem*
1928		Weill, Kurt	*Little Threepenny Music*
1929		Persichetti, Vincent	*Serenade No. 1*, Op. 1
1929		Poulenc, Francis	*Aubade for Piano and Eighteen Instruments*
1929		Weill, Kurt	*Happy End*
	1930	Hanson, Howard	*Symphony No. 2* (Romantic)
1930		Holst, Gustav	*Hammersmith*, Op. 52
1930		Hindemith, Paul	*Konzertmusik*, Op. 49 (Piano, Harp, and Brass)

WIND	ORCH.	COMPOSER	TITLE
1930		Stravinsky, Igor	*Symphony of Psalms* (Revised 1948)
1930		Strens, Jules	*Danse Funambulesque*, Op. 12
1931		Krenek, Ernst	*Music for Wind Orchestra*
1931		Serly, Tibor	*Symphony No. 1*
1931		Varèse, Edgard	*Ionisation*
1932		Auric, Georges	*Le Palais Royale*
1932		Brant, Henry	*Angels and Devils for Solo Flute and Flute Orchestra* (Revised 1947)
1932		Holst, Gustav	*Jazz Band Piece*
1932		Ireland, John	*A Downland Suite*
1932		Respighi, Ottorino	*Huntingtower Ballad*
	1932	Tailleferre, Germaine	*Overture* (S. 1960/Paynter)
	1932	Thompson, Randall	*Symphony No. 2*
1932		Toch, Ernst	*Miniature Overture*
	1933	Rogers, Bernard	*Three Japanese Dances* (V. 1953/Rogers)
1933		Ruggles, Carl	*Sun Treader*
	1933	Wood, Haydn	*Mannin Veen* (V. 1933)
1934		Grainger, Percy	*The Immovable Do*
1934		Shostakovich, Dmitri	*Jazz Suite No. 1*
1934		Shostakovich, Dmitri	*The Story of the Priest and His Helper Balda Op. 36*
	1935	Berg, Alban	*Lulu*
1935		Harris, Roy	*When Johnny Comes Marching Home*
	1935	Ibert, Jacques	*Concertino da Camera for Alto Saxophone* (S. Paynter)
	1935	Hindemith, Paul	*Mathis der Maler*
1935		Koechlin, Charles	*Quelques Chorals pour des fêtes Populaire*
1935		Poulenc, Francis	*Suite Française*
	1935	Vaughan Williams, Ralph	*Symphony No. 4*
	1936	Barber, Samuel	*Adagio for Strings*

WIND	ORCH.	COMPOSER	TITLE
	1936	Bartók, Béla	*Music for Strings, Percussion, and Celeste*
	1936	Copland, Aaron	*El Salón México* (S. 1972/Hindsley)
	1936	Kennan, Kent	*Soliloquy for Flute* (V. 1966/Kennan)
	1936	Prokofiev, Serge	*Romeo and Juliet*, Op. 64
	1936	Prokofiev, Serge	*Peter and the Wolf*
1936		Roussel, Albert	*Prelude to Act II, "The 14th of July"*
	1936	Skalkottas, Nikos	*Nine Greek Dances* (V. 1942) (E. 1984/Schuller)
	1936	Thomson, Virgil	*The Plow that Broke the Plains*
1937		Grainger, Percy	*Lincolnshire Posy*
	1937	Harris, Roy	*Symphony No. 3*
1937		Honegger, Arthur	*The March on the Bastille*
	1937	Orff, Carl	*Carmina Burana Suite* (S. 1967/Krance & S. 2002/Mas Quiles)
1937		Prokofiev, Serge	*Athletic Festival March*
	1938	Copland, Aaron	*Billy the Kid*
	1938	Martinu, Bohuslav	*Double Concerto for Two String Orchestras, Piano and Timpani*
	1938	Piston, Walter	*The Incredible Flutist*
	1939	Cage, John	*First Construction in Metal for Percussion*
	1939	Copland, Aaron	*An Outdoor Overture* (V. 1942/Copland)
1939		Cowell, Henry	*Shoonthree*
1939		Miaskovsky, Nikolai	*Symphony No. 19*, Op. 46
1939		Martinu, Bohuslav	*Messe Militaire*
1939		Schuman, William	*Newsreel*
1940		Creston, Paul	*Concerto for Marimba*, Op. 43
1940		Donovan, Richard	*Fantasy on American Folk Ballads*
	1940	Webern, Anton	*Variations*, Op, 30
1940		Gould, Morton	*Jericho Rhapsody*

WIND	ORCH.	COMPOSER	TITLE
1941		Harris, Roy	*Cimarron Overture*
1941		Sowerby, Leo	*Spring Overture*
	1941	Schuman, William	*Symphony No. 3*
	1942	Barber, Samuel	*Essay No. 2*
1942		Bekerath, Alfred von	*Sinfonia für Blasorchester*
	1942	Britten, Benjamin	*A Ceremony of Carols*
1942		Copland, Aaron	*Fanfare for the Common Man*
	1942	Copland, Aaron	*Lincoln Portrait* (S. 1951/Beeler)
	1942	Copland, Aaron	*Rodeo*
1942		Cowell, Henry	*Festive Occasion*
1942		Cowell, Henry	*Little Concerto for Piano*
1942		Creston, Paul	*Legend*
1942		Harris, Roy	*Concerto for Piano and Band*
1942		James, Philip	*Festal March*
1942		Riegger, Wallingford	*Passacaglia and Fugue*, Op. 34
1942		Shepherd, Arthur	*Hilaritas*
1942		Stravinsky, Igor	*Circus Polka* (S. Raksin)
1943		Barber, Samuel	*Commando March*
1943		Cowell, Henry	*Hymn and Fuguing Tune No. 1*
	1943	Bartók, Béla	*Concerto for Orchestra*
	1943	Carter, Elliott	*Symphony No. 1*
	1943	Hindemith, Paul	*Symphonic Metamorphosis* (S. 1962/Wilson)
1943		Khachaturian, Aram	*Armenian Dances*
	1943	Piston, Walter	*Symphony No. 2*
1943		Prokofiev, Serge	*March*, Op. 99
1943		Schoenberg, Arnold	*Theme and Variations*, Op. 43a
	1943p	Schuman, William	*Secular Cantata No. 2, "A Free Song"* (Pulitzer) (S. DeRusha)
1943		Strauss, Richard	*Sonatina in F* (Invalid's Workshop) A.V. 135
1943		Strauss, Richard	*Fanfare der Stadt Wien* "Festmusik"

Wind	Orch.	Composer	Title
	1943	Webern, Anton	*Cantata No. 2*
	1944	Bernstein, Leonard	"Profanation" from *Jeremiah Symphony* (S. 1995/Bencriscutto)
1944		Creston, Paul	*Zanoni*
	1944p	Hanson, Howard	*Symphony No. 4*, Op. 34 (Pulitzer)
	1944	Prokofiev, Serge	*Symphony No. 5*, Op. 100
1944		Strauss, Richard	*Sonatina in Eb* (Happy Workshop) A.V. 143
1944		Van Otterloo, Willem	*Serenade for Twelve Brass, Harp, Piano, Celeste, and Percussion*
	1945p	Copland, Aaron	*Appalachian Spring* (Pulitzer)
1945		Milhaud, Darius	*Suite Française*
1945		Prokofiev, Serge	*Ode to the End of the War*, Op. 105
1945		Stravinsky, Igor	*Ebony Concerto*
	1946	Copland, Aaron	*Symphony No. 3*
1946		Françaix, Jean	*Rhapsodie pour Alto Saxophone et Petite Orchestra*
1946		Françaix, Jean	*Rhapsodie for Solo Viola and Wind Instruments*
1946		Gould, Morton	*Ballad for Band*
1946		Hindemith, Paul	"Geschwindmarsch" from *Sinfonia Serena*
	1946p	Sowerby, Leo	*The Canticle of the Sun* (Pulitzer)
	1947	Barber, Samuel	*Knoxville Summer of 1915*
1947		Henze, Hans Werner	*Concertino for Piano and Wind Ensemble*
1947		Hindemith, Paul	*Apparebit Repentina Dies*
	1947p	Ives, Charles	*Symphony No. 3* (Pulitzer)
1947		Pascal, Claude	*Octuor*
	1948	Diamond, David	*Symphony No. 4*
1948		Hindemith, Paul	*Septet*
	1948	Messiaen, Olivier	*Turangalîla Symphonie*
	1948p	Piston, Walter	*Symphony No. 3* (Pulitzer)
1948		Stravinsky, Igor	*Mass*

WIND	ORCH.	COMPOSER	TITLE
1948		Van Otterloo, Willem	*Symphonietta*
1949		Arnell, Richard	*Serenade*, Op. 57
1949		Bennett, Robert Russell	*Suite of Old American Dances*
	1949	Berio, Luciano	*Magnificat*
1949		Bernstein, Leonard	*Prelude, Fugue and Riffs*
1949		Dahl, Ingolf	*Concerto for Alto Saxophone and Wind Orchestra*
1949		Khachaturian, Aram	*The Battle of Stalingrad*
1949		Reed, H. Owen	*La Fiesta Mexicana*
1949		Riegger, Wallingford	*Music for Brass and Percussion*, Op.45
1949		Thomson, Virgil	*A Solemn Music*
	1949p	Thomson, Virgil	*Louisiana Story* (Pulitzer)
	1950	Mennin, Peter	*Symphony No. 5*
	1950p	Menotti, Gian-Carlo	*The Consul* (Pulitzer)
1950		Persichetti, Vincent	*Divertimento*
1950		Piston, Walter	*Tunbridge Fair*
	1950	Rogers, Bernard	*Tale of Pinnochio*
1950		Schuller, Gunther	*Symphony for Brass and Percussion*, Op. 16
1950		Schuman, William	*George Washington Bridge*
	1951	Arnold, Malcolm	*English Dances* (S. 1965/Johnstone and Cole)
	1951	Dello Joio, Norman	*Triumph of St. Joan*
1951		Gulyás, Laszlo	*Music from Szek*
1951		Hindemith, Paul	*Symphony in B-flat*
1951		Jacob, Gordon	*Music for a Festival*
1951		Mennin, Peter	*Canzona*
	1951p	Moore, Douglas	*Giants in the Earth* (Pulitzer)
1951		Riegger, Wallingford	*Dance Rhythms*
1952		Cushing, Charles	*Angel Camp* (West Point)
1952		Dvorak, Robert	*West Point Symphony*, Op. 311 (West Point)

WIND	ORCH.	COMPOSER	TITLE
1952		Gould, Morton	*Symphony No. 4* (West Point)
1952		Harris, Roy	*West Point Symphony* (West Point)
	1952p	Kubik, Gail	*Symphony Concertante* (Pulitzer)
1952		Milhaud, Darius	*West Point Suite* (West Point)
1952		Persichetti, Vincent	*Psalm*
1952		Stravinsky, Igor	*Concertino for Twelve Instruments*
	1952	Stockhausen, Karlheinz	*Spiel* (Revised 1973)
	1952	Thomson, Virgil	*Three Pictures for Orchestra*
	1953p		No Pulitzer
1953		Benson, Warren	*Transylvania Fanfare March*
	1953	Bergsma, William	*Carol on a Twelfth Night*
	1953	Britten, Benjamin	"The Courtly Dances, " from *Gloriana* Op. 53a (S. 1995/Bach)
1953		Grainger, Percy	*The Power of Rome and the Christian Heart*
1953		Hartmann, Karl Amadeus	*Konzert für Klavier, Bläser, und Schlagzeug*
1953		Jacob, Gordon	*Flag of Stars*
1954		Benson, Warren	*Concertino for Alto Saxophone*
1954		Blackwood, Easley	*Chamber Symphony, No. 2 for Fourteen Wind Instruments*
1954		Hanson, Howard	*Chorale and Alleluia*
1954		Jolivet, André	*Concerto No. 2 for Trumpet*
	1954p	Porter, Quincy	*Concerto for Two Pianos and Orchestra* (Pulitzer)
	1954	Shostakovich, Dmitri	*Festive Overture*, Op. 96 (S. 1963/Hunsberger)
1954		Varèse, Edgard	*Déserts*
	1955	Carter, Elliott	*Variations for Orchestra*
1955		Creston, Paul	*Celebration Overture*
1955		Erickson, Frank	*Toccata*
	1955p	Menotti, Gian-Carlo	*The Saint of Bleecker Street* (Pulitzer)
1955		Persichetti, Vincent	*Pageant*

WIND	ORCH.	COMPOSER	TITLE
	1956	Bernstein, Leonard	*Overture to Candide* (S. 1960/Beeler & 1992/Grundman)
1956		Bottje, Will Gay	*Symphony No. 4*
1956		Gould, Morton	*Santa Fe Saga*
1956		Messiaen, Olivier	*Oiseaux exotiques*
1956		Persichetti, Vincent	*Symphony No. 6, Op. 69*
	1956	Schuman, William	*New England Triptych* (V. 1975/Schuman)
	1956p	Toch, Ernst	*Symphony No. 3* (Pulitzer)
1956		Vaughan Williams, Ralph	"Scherzo Alla Marcia" from *Symphony No. 8*
1956		Williams, J. Clifton	*Fanfare and Allegro* (ABA/Ostwald)
	1957	Arnold, Malcolm	*Four Scottish Dances* (S. Paynter)
1957		Babbitt, Milton	*All Set*
	1957	Barber, Samuel	"Intermezzo" from *Vanessa* (S. 1962/Beeler)
1957		Bergsma, William	*March with Trumpets*
	1957p	Dello Joio, Norman	*Meditations on Ecclesiastes* (Pulitzer)
1957		Hartley, Walter	*Concerto for 23 Winds*
1957		Kurka, Robert	*The Good Soldier Schweik Suite*, Op. 22
1957		Latham, William	*Three Chorale Preludes*
1957		Rorem, Ned	*Sinfonia* (American Wind Symphony)
	1957	Stockhausen, Karlheinz	*Gruppen*
1957		Vaughan Williams, Ralph	*Variations for Wind Band* (S. 1997/Hunsberger)
1957		Williams, J. Clifton	*Symphonic Suite* (ABA/Ostwald)
	1958p	Barber, Samuel	*Vanessa* (Pulitzer)
1958		Bennett, Robert Russell	*Concerto Grosso for Woodwind Quintet* (American Wind Symphony)
1958		Bennett, Robert Russell	*Symphonic Songs*
1958		Bonsel, Adrian	*Folkloristische Suite*
1958		Bottje, Will Gay	*Theme and Variations*
1958		Copland, Aaron	*Variations on a Shaker Melody*

WIND	ORCH.	COMPOSER	TITLE
1958		Giannini, Vittorio	*Preludium and Allegro*
1958		Hovhaness, Alan	*Symphony No. 4, Op. 165 (American Wind Symphony)*
1958		Kechley, Gerald	*Antiphony for Winds*
1958		Quinn, Mark J.	*Portrait of the Land* (ABA/Ostwald)
	1958	Rorem, Ned	*Eagles*
1958		Villa-Lobos, Hector	*Fantasy in Three Movements in Form of a Choros*
1959		Castérède, Jacques	*Concertino for Trumpet and Trombone* (S. Cramer)
1959		Creston, Paul	*Prelude and Dance*
1959		Davies, Peter Maxwell	*St. Michael Sonata*
1959		Giannini, Vittorio	*Symphony No. 3*
1959		Gould, Morton	*St. Lawrence Suite*
1959		Hartmann, Karl	*Concerto for Viola and Piano*
1959		Hovhaness, Alan	*Symphony No. 7, Op. 175 "Nanga Parnat"*
1959		Jenkins, Joseph Wilcox	*American Overture*
	1959p	LaMontaine, John	*Concerto for Piano and Orchestra* (Pulitzer)
1959		Lendvay, Kamillo	*Concertino for Piano, Winds, Percussion and Harp*
1959		Moore, Douglas	*The Peoples' Choice*
1959		Porter, Quincy	*Concerto*
1959		Surinach, Carlos	*Paens and Dances of Heathen Iberia (American Wind Symphony)*
1959		Weed, Maurice	*Introduction and Scherzo* (ABA/Ostwald)
	1960p	Carter, Elliott	*Second String Quartet* (Pulitzer)
1960		Hartley, Walter	*Rondo for Winds and Percussion*
1960		Hemel, Oscar van	*Concerto for Wind Instruments*
1960		Jacob, Gordon	*Old Wine in New Bottles*
1960		Kirchner, Leon	*Concerto for Violin, Cello, Ten Winds and Percussion*

WIND	ORCH.	COMPOSER	TITLE
1960		McPhee, Colin	Concerto for Wind Orchestra (American Wind Symphony)
1960		Mueller, Florian	Overture in G (ABA/Ostwald)
1960		Nixon, Roger	Fiesta del Pacifico
	1960	Pendericki, Krzysztof	Threnody to the Victims of Hiroshima
1960		Reed, H. Owen	Renascence
1961		Beglarian, Grant	Sinfonia
1961		Benson, Warren	Helix for Tuba
1961		Benson, Warren	Polyphonies for Percussion
	1961	Carter, Elliott	Double Concerto for Harpsichord and Piano
1961		Chance, John Barnes	Symphony No. 2 (completed 1972/McBeth)
1961		Chou, Wen-chung	Metaphors for Wind Orchestra
1961		Dahl, Ingolf	Sinfonietta (CBDNA)
1961		Gould, Morton	Prisms
1961		Jenkins, Joseph W.	Cumberland Gap Overture (ABA/Ostwald)
	1961	Ligeti, György	Atmosphères
	1961	Lutoslawski, Witold	Venetian Games
1961		Lutyens, Elizabeth	Symphonies for Solo Piano, Winds, Harp and Percussion, Op. 46
1961		Mayuzumi, Toshiro	Concerto for Percussion (American Wind Symphony)
	1961p	Piston, Walter	Symphony No. 7 (Pulitzer)
1961		Rövenstrunck, Bernhard	Kammersinfonie für 15 Bläser und Kontrabass
	1961	Schmidt-Wunstorf, Rudolf	Ardennen Symphony
1961		Schuller, Gunther	Double Woodwind and Brass Quintet
1962		Adler, Samuel	Southwestern Sketches
1962		Benson, Warren	Remembrance
	1962	Boulez, Pierre	Pli Selon Pli
1962		Brant, Henry	Verticals Ascending

Wind	Orch.	Composer	Title
	1962	Britten, Benjamin	*War Requiem*
1962		Crosse, Gordon	*Concerto da Camera*, Op. 6
1962		Erb, Donald	*Space Music*
1962		Etler, Alvin	*Concerto for Clarinet*
1962		Grainger, Percy	*Handel in the Strand* (S. Goldman)
1962		Linn, Robert	*Concerto Grosso for Brass Trio and Wind Ensemble*
1962		Murray, Lynn	*Ronald Searle Suite* (S. Steiner)
1962		Persichetti, Vincent	*Bagatelles for Band*
1962		Persichetti, Vincent	*Chorale Prelude: "So Pure the Star"*
1962		Russell, Armand	*Theme and Fantasia*
1962		Stout, Alan	*Pulsar*
1962		Velke, Fritz	*Concertino for Band* (ABA/Ostwald)
	1962p	Ward, Robert	*The Crucible* (Pulitzer)
1962		Wimberger, Gerhard	*Stories*
1962		Zimmermann, Bernard	*Rheinische Kirmestänze*
1963		Ashe, Frederic H.	*Concert Suite* (ABA/Ostwald)
1963		Badings, Henk	*Concerto for Flute* (American Wind Symphony)
	1963p	Barber, Samuel	*Piano Concerto No. 1* (Pulitzer)
1963		Benson, Warren	*The Leaves are Falling*
1963		Benson, Warren	*Symphony for Drums and Wind Orchestra* (American Wind Symphony)
1963		Bottje, Will Gay	*Symphony No. 6*
	1963	Creston, Paul	*Corinthians XIII*
1963		Dello Joio, Norman	*Variants on a Medieval Tune*
1963		Leeuw, Ton de	*Symphonies of Winds*
1963		Hemel, Oscar van	*Three Contrasts*
1963		Lopatnikoff, Nikolai	*Concerto for Wind Orchestra*, Op. 41 (American Wind Symphony)
1963		Lutoslawski, Witold	*Trois poèmes d'Henri Michaux*

WIND	ORCH.	COMPOSER	TITLE
1963		Messiaen, Olivier	*Colors of the Celestial City*
1963		Schuller, Gunther	*Meditation*
1963		Schuller, Gunther	*Study in Textures* (S. Hunsberger)
1963		Tippett, Michael	*Mosaics* (Concerto for Orchestra, Mvt. I)
1963		Tischenko, Boris	*Concerto for Cello, Seventeen Winds and Percussion*
	1964p		No Pulitzer
1964		Arnold, Malcolm	*Water Music*, Op. 82
	1964	Babitt, Milton	*Philomel* (Tape)
1964		Bozza, Eugène	*Children's Overture* (American Wind Symphony)
1964		Cable, Howard	*Stratford Suite*
1964		Chance, John Barnes	*Incantation and Dance*
1964		Copland, Aaron	*Emblems* (CBDNA)
1964		Delden, Lex van	*Sinfonia VII*, Op. 83
1964		Dello Joio, Norman	*Scenes from the Louvre*
1964		Giannini, Vittorio	*Variations and Fugue*
1964		Jager, Robert	*Symphony for Band* (ABA/Ostwald)
1964		Linn, Robert	*Elevations*
1964		Lo Presti, Ronald	*Elegy for a Young American*
1964		Meyerowitz, Jan	*Three Comments on War* (CBDNA)
1964		Nelhybel, Vaclav	*Trittico*
1964		Nelhybel, Vaclav	*Prelude and Fugue*
1964		Pyle, Francis	*Concerto for Horn and Wind Ensemble*
1964		Rochberg, George	*Apocalyptica*
	1964	Riley, Terry	*In C*
1964		Schuller, Gunther	*Diptych for Brass Quintet and Band*
	1965p		No Pulitzer
	1965	Bernstein, Leonard	*Chichester Psalms*
1965		Benson, Warren	*Recuerdo for Oboe/English Horn*

WIND	ORCH.	COMPOSER	TITLE
1965		Benson, Warren	*Star Edge*
1965		Beyer, Frederick	*Overture for Band* (ABA/Ostwald)
1965		Casterède, Jacques	*Divertissement d'Eté* (American Wind Symphony)
1965		Chance, John Barnes	*Variations on a Korean Folk Song* (ABA/Ostwald)
1965		Childs, Barney	*Six Events for Fifty-six Players*
1965		Dello Joio, Norman	*From Every Horizon*
1965		Gensemen, Paul	*Sinfonia*
1965		George, Thom Ritter	*Proclamations*
1965		Gilmore, Bernard	*Five Folksongs for Soprano and Band*
1965		Grainger, Percy	*The Sussex Mummer's Christmas Carol* (S. Goldman)
1965		Hartley, Walter	*Sinfonia No. 4*
1965		Jager, Robert	*Second Suite*
1965		Ketting, Otto	*Interieur: Balletmusik*
1965		Ketting, Otto	*Time Machine*
1965		Klebe, Giselher	*Missa "Miserere Nobis" for 18 Wind Instruments*
1965		Messiaen, Olivier	*Et Exspecto Ressurrectionem Mortuorum*
1965		Michalsky, Donal	*Fanfare after Seventeenth Century Dances*
	1965	Perle, George	*Three Movements*
1965		Persichetti, Vincent	*Masquerade*, Op. 102
1965		Pyle, Francis	*Concerto for Trumpet*
1965		Rochberg, George	*Black Sounds*
1965		Russell, Armand	*Theme and Fantasia*
1965		Stoelzel, Gottfried	*Concerto Grosso a Quattro Cori* (c 1650) (S. Rogers) (American Wind Symphony)
1965		Washburn, Robert	*Concertino*
1965		Xenakis, Iannis	*Akrata*
1966		Auric, Georges	*Divertimento* (American Wind Symphony)

WIND	ORCH.	COMPOSER	TITLE
1966		Bassett, Leslie	*Designs, Images and Textures*
	1966p	Bassett, Leslie	*Variations for Orchestra* (Pulitzer)
1966		Blackwood, Easley	*Un Voyage à Cytherei, Op. 20*
1966		Bottje, Will Jay	*Sinfonia Concertante*
1966		Chance, John Barnes	*Introduction and Capriccio for Piano*
1966		Foss, Lukas	*For 24 Winds*
1966		Hennagin, Michael	*Jubilee Overture*
1966		Kelterborn, Rudolf	*Miroirs*
	1966	Kraft, William	*Concerto for Four Percussion (S. 1995/Kraft)*
1966		Maconchy, Elizabeth	*Music for Brass and Woodwinds*
1966		Persichetti, Vincent	*Celebrations for Chorus and Wind Ensemble* (Cantata No. 32)
1966		Persichetti, Vincent	*Chorale Prelude: Turn not thy Face, Op. 105*
1966		Rodrigo, Joaquin	*Adagio* (American Wind Symphony)
1966		Rosenberg, Hilding	*Symphonie fur Bläser und Schlagzeug*
	1966	Schuller, Gunther	*Concerto for Orchestra No. 1, "Gala Music"*
1967		Adler, Samuel	*Music for Eleven*
1967		Amram, David	*Concerto for Horn* (American Wind Symphony)
1967		Amram, David	*King Lear Variations* (American Wind Symphony)
1967		Barber, Samuel	*Mutations from Bach*
1967		Beyer, Frederick	*Symphony for Band*
1967		Bielewa, Herbert	*Spectrum* (Tape)
1967		Borden, David	*All American Teenage Lovesongs*
1967		Creston, Paul	*Anatolia*
1967		Dello Joio, Norman	*Fantasies on a Theme by Haydn*
1967		Erb, Donald	*Stargazing* (Tape)
	1967	Foss, Lukas	*Baroque Variations*
1967		Husa, Karel	*Concerto for Alto Saxophone and Concert Band*

WIND	ORCH.	COMPOSER	TITLE
1967		Jager, Robert	Diamond Variations (ABA/Ostwald)
1967		Kaneda, Bin	Divertimento for Band
	1967p	Kirchner, Leon	Quartet No. 3 (Pulitzer)
1967		Mailman, Martin	Liturgical Music
1967		Nelhybel, Vaclav	Symphonic Movement
1967		Nelson, Ron	Rocky Point Holiday
1967		Penderecki, Krzysztof	Pittsburgh Overture (American Wind Symphony)
	1967	Persichetti, Vincent	Symphony No. 8
1967		Rhodes, Phillip	Three Pieces for Band
1967		Washburn, Robert	Symphony
1967		Weiner, Lawrence	Daedalic Variations (ABA/Ostwald)
1968		Badings, Henk	Armageddon (Tape/Soprano) (American Wind Symphony)
1968		Benson, Warren	The Mask of Night
	1968	Berio, Luciano	Sinfonia
1968		Bielewa, Herbert	Concert Fanfare
	1968p	Crumb, George	Echoes of Time and the River (Pulitzer)
1968		Franchetti, Arnold	The Birds
1968		Genzmer, Harald	Divertimento für Sinfonisches Blas Orchester
1968		Hovhaness, Alan	Hymn to Yerevan
1968		Hovhaness, Alan	Suite for Band
1968		Hovhaness, Alan	Tapor No. 1
1968		Husa, Karel	Music for Prague 1968
1968		Morawetz, Oscar	Elegy for Martin Luther King, Jr.
1968		Nixon, Roger	Elegy and Fanfare March
1968		Reed, Alfred	Russian Christmas Music
1968		Schuman, William	Dedication Fanfare
	1968	Sessions, Roger	Symphony No. 8
1968		Southers, Leroy W.	Concerto for Four Horns, Euphonium and Wind Orchestra

Wind	Orch.	Composer	Title
1968		Tubb, Monte	*Concert Piece*
1969		Benson, Warren	*The Solitary Dancer*
1969		Bielewa, Herbert	*Ricochet for Band and Tape*
1969		Bush, Alan	*Scherzo, Op. 68*
	1969	Carter, Elliott	*Concerto for Orchestra*
1969		Dello Joio, Norman	*Songs of Abelard*
	1969p	Husa, Karel	*String Quartet No. 3 (Pulitzer)*
1969		Jacob, Gordon	*Concerto for Band*
1969		Jager, Robert	*Variations on a Theme by Robert Schumann*
1969		Kushide, Tetsunoko	*Asuka*
	1969	Partch, Harry	*Delusions of the Fury*
1969		Pennington, John	*Apollo*
1969		Willis, Richard	*Aria and Toccata (ABA/Ostwald)*
	1970	Copland, Aaron	*The Red Pony (S. Copland)*
	1970	Crumb, George	*Ancient Voices of Children*
1970		Duckworth, William	*The Sleepy Hollow Elementary School Band*
1970		Frederickson, L. Thomas	*Wind Music One*
1970		Hartley, Walter	*Symphony for Wind Orchestra*
1970		Jolas, Betsy	*Lassus Ricercare*
1970		Karlins, William	*Passacaglia & Rounds*
1970		Nixon, Roger	*Reflections*
1970		Reed, H. Owen	*The Touch of the Earth*
1970		Tull, Fisher	*Toccata (ABA/Ostwald)*
	1970	Wuorinen, Charles	*Grand Bamboula*
	1970p	Wuorinen, Charles	*Time's Encomium (Pulitzer)*
1970		Zappa, Frank	*The Dog Breath Variations*
1971		Balassa, Sandro	*Lupercalia*
	1971	Bernstein, Leonard	*Mass*
1971		Bottje, Will Gay	*Metaphors*

WIND	ORCH.	COMPOSER	TITLE
1971		Chance, John Barnes	*Blue Lake Overture*
1971		Childs, Barney	*Supposes: Imago Mundi*
	1971p	Davidovsky, Mario	*Synchronisms No. 6 for Piano and Electronic Sound* (Pulitzer)
1971		Finney, Ross Lee	*Summer in Valley City*
1971		Fiser, Lubos	*Report* (American Wind Symphony)
1971		Husa, Karel	*Apotheosis of this Earth*
1971		Husa, Karel	*Concerto for Percussion and Wind Ensemble*
1971		Kaneda, Bin	*Passacaglia*
1971		Kroeger, Karl	*Divertimento for Concert Band* (ABA/Ostwald)
	1971	Ligeti, György	*Melodien*
1971		McBeth, W. Francis	*The Seventh Seal*
1971		Penderecki, Krzysztof	*Preludium*
	1971	Penderecki, Krzysztof	*Ultrenia*
1971		Persichetti, Vincent	*O Cool is the Valley*
1971		Reed, H. Owen	*For the Unfortunate*
1971		Reynolds, Verne	*Scenes*
1971		Sclater, James	*Prelude & Variations on "Gone is my Mistress"*
	1971	Shostakovich, Dmitri	*Symphony No. 15*
1971		Tull, Fisher	*Sketches on a Tudor Psalm*
1971		Williams, John T.	*Sinfonietta*
1972		Beall, John	*Concerto for Piano and Winds*
	1972	Birtwistle, Harrison	*The Triumph of Time*
1972		Bilik, Jerry	*Symphony for Band*
1972		Bozza, Eugène	*Octanphonie*
1972		Brant, Henry	*An American Requiem*
1972		Broege, Timothy	*Sinfonia III*
1972		Cage, John	*Cheap Imitation* (24-player version)
1972		Chance, John Barnes	*Elegy*

Wind	Orch.	Composer	Title
1972		Dollarhide, Theodore	Music for the Food King
	1972p	Druckman, Jacob	Windows (Pulitzer)
1972		Erb, Donald	The Purple Roofed Ethical Suicide Parlor
1972		Françaix, Jean	Sept Danses
1972		Hanson, Howard	Dies Natalis
1972		Hutcheson, Jere	Sensations
1972		Jager, Robert	Sinfonietta (ABA/Ostwald)
1972		Karlins, M. William	Reflux: Concerto for Double Bass Solo and Wind Ensemble
1972		Knussen, Oliver	Choral
1972		Linn, Robert	Propagula
1972		Nelhybel, Vaclav	Toccata for Harpsichord and Thirteen Wind Instruments
1972		Persichetti, Vincent	Parable IX, Op. 121
1972		Pyle, Francis	Symphony No. 1
1972		Strange, Alan	Rocky Top Screamers and Further Scapes
1972		Zdechlick, John	Chorale and Shaker Dance
	1973	Adams, John	Christian Zeal and Activity
1973		Albright, William	Foils
1973		Bach, Jan	The Eve of St. Agnes (Theater)
1973		Badings, Henk	Transitions (CBDNA)
1973		Binkerd, Gordon	Noble Numbers
1973		Broege, Timothy	Sinfonia V
	1973p	Carter, Elliott	String Quartet No. 3 (Pulitzer)
1973		Eberhard, Dennis	Morphos
1973		Françaix, Jean	Nine Characteristic Pieces
1973		Hartley, Walter	In Memoriam
1973		Husa, Karel	Concerto for Trumpet
1973		Kessner, Daniel	Wind Sculptures (CBDNA)
1973		Nixon, Roger	Elegy and Fanfare March (ABA/Ostwald)
1973		Reed, Alfred	Armenian Dances, Part 1

WIND	ORCH.	COMPOSER	TITLE
1973		Yurko, Bruce	Concerto for Winds and Percussion
1974		Bennett, Robert Russell	Four Preludes for Band
1974		Benson, Warren	The Beaded Leaf
1974		Benson, Warren	The Passing Bell
1974		Berio, Luciano	Points on a Curve to Find
1974		Brant, Henry	Sixty
1974		Broege, Timothy	Three Pieces for American Band
1974		Finney, Ross Lee	Concerto for Alto Saxophone
1974		Ives, Charles	Old Home Days (S. Elkus)
1974		Kaneda, Bin	Symphonic Movement
1974		Keulen, Geert Van	Chords
1974		Lees, Benjamin	Labyrinths
	1974p	Martino, Donald	Notturno (Pulitzer)
1974		McBeth, W. Francis	To Be Fed by Ravens
1974		Sclater, James S.	Visions (ABA/Ostwald)
1974		Yun, Isang	Harmonia für Blasinstrumente, Harfe und Schlagzeug
	1975p	Argento, Dominick	Diary of Virginia Woolf (Pulitzer)
	1975	Bassett, Leslie	Echoes from an Invisible World
1975		Borden, David	Variations on America (Tape)
	1975	Boulez, Pierre	Rituel
1975		Broege, Timothy	Sinfonia VII
1975		Chobanian, Loris	The Id
1975		Hanson, Howard	Laude (CBDNA)
1975		Hodkinson, Sydney	Cortege: Dirge Canons
1975		Hodkinson, Sydney	Stone Images
1975		Husa, Karel	Al Fresco (Beeler Commission)
1975		Latham, William	Revolution
1975		Loudova, Ivana	Chorale (American Wind Symphony)
1975		Loudova, Ivana	Hymnos (American Wind Symphony)
1975		Panerio, Robert	Jubiloso (ABA/Ostwald)

WIND	ORCH.	COMPOSER	TITLE
1975		Paulson, Jon	*Epinicion*
1975		Peck, Russell	*American Epic*
1975		Ricker, Ramon	*Variations on Sweelinck's "My Young Life has Ended"*
	1975	Rochberg, George	*Violin Concerto*
1975		Selig, Robert	*Pometacomet 1676*
1975		Stokes, Eric	*The Continental Harp and Band Report*
1975		Tubb, Monte	*Intermezzo*
1975		Yurko, Bruce	*Concerto for Horn and Wind Ensemble*
1976		Creston, Paul	*Liberty Song '76* (Beeler Commission)
	1976	Davies, Peter Maxwell	*Symphony No. 1*
	1976	Del Tredici, David	*Final Alice*
1976		Dollarhide, Theodore	*Jungles*
	1976	Glass, Philip	*Einstein on the Beach*
1976		Gubaidulina, Sofia	*Hour of the Soul* (soprano)
1976		Hodkinson, Sydney	*Tower*
1976		Husa, Karel	*An American Te Deum* (chorus/soloists)
1976		Jankowski, Lorette	*Todesband* (ABA/Ostwald)
1976		Latham, William	*Fusion*
1976		Rautavaara, Einojuhani	*Annunciations* (organ)
1976		Reed, Alfred	*Armenian Dances*, Part II
	1976	Reich, Steve	*Music for Eighteen Musicians*
1976		Reynolds, Verne	*Scenes Revisited*
	1976p	Rorem, Ned	*Air Music* (Pulitzer)
1976		Ward-Steinman, David	*Scorpio* (CBDNA)
1976		Wilder, Alec	*Fantasy for Piano*
1976		Yurko, Bruce	*Chant and Toccata*
1977		Bassett, Leslie	*Sounds, Shapes and Symbols*
	1977	Bernstein, Leonard	*Songfest* (E. 1995/Amis)
1977		Brant, Henry	*American Debate*

WIND	ORCH.	COMPOSER	TITLE
	1977	Carter, Elliott	*Symphony for Three Orchestras*
1977		Chobanian, Loris	*Armenian Dances*
	1977	Corigliano, John	*Clarinet Concerto*
1977		Finney, Ross Lee	*Skating on the Sheyenne*
1977		Hill, William H.	*Dances Sacred and Profane* (ABA/Ostwald)
1977		Hodkinson, Sydney	*Bach Variations*
1977		Hodkinson, Sydney	*Cortege*
1977		Krenek, Ernst	*Dream Sequence*, Op. 224 (CBDNA)
1977		Martino, Donald	*Triple Concerto* (for clarinet, bass clarinet, contra clarinet, and sixteen instruments)
1977		Maslanka, David	*Concerto for Piano*
1977		Morris, Robert	*In Different Voices*
	1977	Pärt, Arvo	*Fratres* (Version C)
1977		Russell, Armand	*Myth for Winds and Percussion* (Beeler)
1977		Schwantner, Joseph	*. . . and the mountains rising nowhere*
1977		Sorczek, David	*Variations for Band* (NBA/Revelli)
	1977p	Wernick, Richard	*Visions of Terror and Wonder* (Pulitzer)
1977		Wilder, Alec	*Five Vocalises for Soprano*
1978		Barnes, James	*Symphony*, Op. 35 (ABA/Ostwald)
1978		Clayton, Laura	*Cree Songs to the New Born*
	1978p	Colgrass, Michael	*Dèjá Vu for Percussion and Orchestra* (Pulitzer) (V. 1987/Colgrass)
1978		Corigliano, John	*Gazebo Dances* (V. Corigliano)
1978		Dollarhide, Theodore	*Faces at the Blue Front*
1978		Hodkinson, Sydney	*Bach Variations* (S. 1987/Colgrass)
1978		Hutcheson, Jere	*Chromophonic Images*
1978		Lukàs, Zdenek	*Musica Boema*
1978		Peck, Russell	*Cave*
1978		Reed, Alfred	*Othello* (Beeler Commission)
	1978	Schwantner, Joseph	*Sparrows* for Soprano

Wind	Orch.	Composer	Title
	1978	Wuorinen, Charles	*A Reliquary for Igor Stravinsky*
1978		Yurko, Bruce	*Danza*
1979		Bulow, Harry	*Textures* (NBA/Revelli)
	1979	Druckman, Jacob	*Aureole*
1979		Erb, Donald	*Cenotaph*
1979		Gregson, Edward	*Metamorphoses*
1979		Láng, István	*Concerto for Violin and Wind Ensemble*
1979		Millner, Anthony	*Concerto for Symphonic Wind Band* (Beeler Commission)
1979		Noon, David	*Three Sweelinck Variations*
1979		Perle, George	*Concertino* for Piano, Winds and Timpani
1979		Pinkham, Daniel	*Serenades* for Trumpet and Wind Ensemble
1979		Reich, Steve	*Octet*
	1979p	Schwantner, Joseph	*Aftertones of Infinity* (Pulitzer)
1979		Shostakovich, Dmitri	*Folk Dances* (S. Reynolds)
1979		Wilder, Alec	*Serenade for Winds*
1980		Adler, Samuel	*Symphony No. 3 "Dyptych"*
1980		Broege, Timothy	*Streets and Inroads*
1980		Curnow, James E.	*Mutanza* (ABA/Ostwald)
1980		Davidovsky, Mario	*Consorts* (CBDNA)
	1980p	Del Tredici, David	*In Memory of a Summer Day* (Pulitzer)
	1980	Druckman, Jacob	*Prism*
1980		Kraft, William	*Dialogues and Entertainments* (Theater)
1980		Margolis, Bob	*Terpsichore*
	1980	Penderecki, Krzyzstof	*Symphony No. 2*
1980		Reynolds, Verne	*Concerto for Band*
1980		Schuller, Gunther	*Eine Kleine Posaunenmusik*
1980		Schuman, William	*American Hymn*
1980		Schwantner, Joseph	*From a Dark Millennium*
1980		Tate, Byron	*Between Worlds* (NBA/Revelli)

WIND	ORCH.	COMPOSER	TITLE
1980		Tcherepnin, Ivan	*Concerto for Oboe* (American Wind Symphony)
1980		Tull, Fisher	*Concerto Grosso for Brass Quintet and Band* (Beeler Commission)
	1980	Ward, Robert	*Sonic Structure*
1980		Yurko, Bruce	*Divertimento*
	1981p		No Pulitzer
1981		Amram, David	*Ode to Lord Buckley for Saxophone*
1981		Barnes, James E.	*Visions Macabre* (ABA/Ostwald)
1981		Bolcom, William	*Broadside for Band*
1981		Françaix, Jean	*Mozart New-Look*
1981		Gillingham, David	*Concerto for Bass Trombone* (NBA/Revelli)
1981		Iannaccone, Anthony	*After a Gentle Rain*
1981		Jager, Robert	*Concerto for Band* (Beeler Commission)
1981		Krenek, Ernst	*Dream Sequence*, Op. 224
1981		Lang, Philip	*Tribute* (Beeler Commission)
1981		Maslanka, David	*A Child's Garden of Dreams*
1981		Reale, Paul	*Dies Irae* for Violin, Cello and Piano
1981		Reale, Paul	*Screamers*
1981		Schuller, Gunther	*Symphony No. 3* "In Praise of Winds"
1981		Thorne, Nicholas	*Adagio Music*
1981		Van Keulen, Geert	*Wals*
1981		Zappa, Frank	*Envelopes*
1982		Adams, John	*Grand Pianola Music*
1982		Bedford, David	*Sun Paints Rainbows Over the Vast Waves*
1982		Benson, Warren	*Symphony II - Lost Songs*
1982		Boda, John	*Concertpiece* for Viola and Wind Ensemble
1982		Françaix, Jean	*Onze Variations sur un thème de Haydn*
1982		Henze, Hans Werner	*Ragtimes and Habaneras*

WIND	ORCH.	COMPOSER	TITLE
1982		Holsinger, David R.	*Armies of the Omnipresent Otserf* (ABA/Ostwald)
1982		Husa, Karel	*Concerto for Wind Ensemble* (Sudler)
1982		Nelson, Ron	*Medieval Suite*
	1982p	Sessions, Roger	*Concerto for Orchestra* (Pulitzer)
1983		Balentine, J.S.	*Good Night to the Old Gods* (CBDNA)
1983		Bassett, Leslie	*Concerto Grosso for Brass Quintet and Winds*
1983		King, Jeffrey	*"Denouément" Symphonic Variations*
1983		Lunde, Ivar	*Cobidinaas* (CBDNA)
	1983	Lutoslawski, Witold	*Symphony No. 3*
1983		Mahr, Timothy	*Fantasia in G*
1983		Mailman, Martin	*Exaltations* (ABA/Ostwald)
1983		Nixon, Roger	*San Joaquin Sketches* (Beeler Commission)
1983		Reale, Paul	*Moonrise, A Polonaise, Early Light* (Revised 1985) (Beeler Prize)
1983		Rogers, Rodney	*Prevailing Winds*
1983		Ross, Walter	*Suite No. 1*
1983		Snow, David	*Sinfonia Concertante* (CBDNA)
1983		Stockhausen, Karlheinz	*Luzifer's Tanz* (Theater)
1983		Sweelinck, Jan	*Ballo del Granduca* (S. Walters)
1983		Wilby, Philip	*Firestar*
1983		Woolfenden, Guy	*Gallimaufry*
1983		Youtz, Gregory	*Scherzo on a Bitter Moon* (NBA/Revelli)
	1983p	Zwilich, Ellen Taaffe	*Symphony No. 1* (Pulitzer)
1984		Amram, David	*Andante and Variations on a Theme for MacBeth* (Beeler Commission)
1984		Andriessen, Jurriaan	*Sinfonia "Il Fiume"*
1984		Bassett, Leslie	*Colors and Contours* (CBDNA)
	1984	Bennett, Richard	*Sinfonietta*
1984		Benson, Warren	*Wings*

WIND	ORCH.	COMPOSER	TITLE
1984		Braunlich, Helmut	*Concerto for Cello and Wind Ensemble*
1984		Curnow, James E.	*Symphonic Variants for Euphonium and Band* (ABA/Ostwald)
	1984	Danielpour, Richard	*Symphony No. 1*
	1984	Glass, Phillip	*Akhnaten*
1984		Gottschalk, Arthur	*Concerto for Wind and Percussion Orchestra* (NBA/Revelli)
1984		Gregson, Edward	*Concerto for Tuba*
1984		Husa, Karel	*Concerto for Piano*
1984		Husa, Karel	*Smetana Fanfare*
1984		Israel, Brian	*Concerto for Clarinet*
1984		Liptak, David	*Soundings*
1984		Nelson, Ron	*Aspen Jubilee*
1984		Perera, Ronald	*Chamber Concerto for Brass Quintet, Nine Winds, Piano, and Percussion*
	1984p	Rands, Bernard	*Canti del Sole for Tenor and Orchestra* (Pulitzer)
1984		Rodriguez, Robert	*The Seven Deadly Sins*
1984		Sapp, Allen	*The Four Winds*
1984		Schmidt, William	*Tuba Mirum for Tuba*
	1984	Schuller, Gunther	*Jubilee Music*
1984		Stucky, Steven	*Voyages* (Cello and Wind Ensemble)
	1984	Thorne, Nicholas	*Symphony No. 2*
1984		Welcher, Dan	*Arches*
1984		Yurko, Bruce	*Incantations*
	1985	Adams, John	*Nixon in China*
	1985	Adler, Samuel	*Symphony No. 6*
	1985p	Albert, Stephen	*River Run* (Pulitzer)
1985		Bassett, Leslie	*Lullaby for Kirsten*
1985		Bukvich, Daniel	*Surprise, Pattern, Illusion*
1985		Colgrass, Michael	*Winds of Nagual* (Sudler and NBA/Revelli)

WIND	ORCH.	COMPOSER	TITLE
1985		Downing, Joseph H.	*Symphony for Winds and Percussion* (ABA/Ostwald)
1985		Gregson, Edward	*Festivo*
1985		Maslanka, David	*Symphony No. 2*
1985		Persichetti, Vincent	*Chorale Prelude: "O God Unseen"*
1985		Tcherepnin, Ivan	*Statue* (American Wind Symphony)
	1986	Adams, John	*Short Ride in a Fast Machine* (S. 1991/Odom)
1986		Bennett, Richard Rodney	*Morning Music*
1986		Bukvich, Daniel	*Voodoo!*
1986		David, Thomas Christian	*Sinfonia Concertante* for Violin, Clarinet, and Piano
1986		Druckman, Jacob	*Paean*
1986		Freund, Don	*Jug Blues and Fat Pickin'*
	1986	Gubaidulina, Sofia	*Stimmen. . . Ver Stummen. . .*
1986		Harbison, John	*Music for Eighteen Winds*
1986		Holsinger, David R.	*In the Spring, at the Time When the Kings Go Off to War* (ABA/Ostwald)
1986		Kallman, Daniel	*Metamorphosis (On an Original Cakewalk)*
	1986p	Perle, George	*Wind Quintet No. 4* (Pulitzer)
	1986	Ung, Chinary	*Inner Voices*
1986		Woolfenden, Guy	*Illyrian Dances*
1987		Adler, Samuel	*Double Visions*
1987		Ball, Michael	*Omaggio*
1987		Bassett, Leslie	*Fantasy for Clarinet*
1987		Benson, Warren	*Dawn's Early Light*
1987		Broege, Timothy	*No Sun, No Shadow* (Elegy for Charles Mingus)
1987		Camphouse, Mark	*Elegy*
1987		Cooper, Paul	*Antiphons*
1987		Druckman, Jacob	*"Engram" from Prism* (V. Druckman)

Wind	Orch.	Composer	Title
1987		Druckman, Jacob	*In Memoriam Vincent Persichetti*
1987		Finney, Ross Lee	*Small Town Music*
1987		Fox, Frederick	*Polarities*
	1987p	Harbison, John	*Cantata: The Flight Into Egypt* (Pulitzer)
1987		Iannaccone, Anthony	*Apparitions* (NBA/Revelli)
1987		Reed, H. Owen	*Of Lothlorien*
	1987	Reich, Steve	*The Four Sections*
	1987	Rochberg, George	*Symphony No. 6*
1987		Roseman, Arnold	*Double Quintet*
1987		Sartor, David	*Synergistic Parable* (ABA/Ostwald)
1987		Slothouwer, Jocham	*Concert Variations for Piano and Band*
1987		Vaughan, Roger	*Suite No. 2*
1987		Wilson, Dana	*Piece of Mind* (ABA/Ostwald and Sudler)
	1988p	Bolcom, William	*Twelve New Etudes for Piano* (Pulitzer)
1988		Brouwer, Leo	*Cancion de Gesta*
1988		de Meij, Johan	*Symphony No. 1: Lord of the Rings* (Sudler)
1988		Diamond, David	*Tantivy*
1988		Keuris, Tristan	*Catena*
1988		Mailman, Martin	*For Precious Friends Hid in Death's Dateless Night* (ABA/Ostwald and NBA/Revelli)
1988		McKinley, William Thomas	*Symphony of Winds*
1988		Mobberly, James	*Ascension*
1988		Nelson, Ron	*Te Deum Laudamus* (Choir)
1988		Reed, Alfred	*Symphony No. 3*
1988		Saylor, Maurice	*Duo Concertante in G*
1988		Thomas, Augusta Reed	*Wheatfield with Lark* (Violin and Viola)
	1989	Corigliano, John	*Symphony No. 1*
	1989	Davies, Peter Maxwell	*Symphony No. 4*

Wind	Orch.	Composer	Title
1989		Diamond, David	*Hearts Music*
1989		Gregson, Edward	*The Sword and the Crown*
1989		Jones, Stephen	*Penumbral Tapestries*
	1989	Kraft, William	*Veils and Variations*
1989		Larson, Libby	*Grand Rondo: Napoleon Dances The Can-can with Italy, Hungary, and Poland*
	1989p	Reynolds, Roger	*Whispers out of Time* (Pulitzer)
1989		Ring, Gordon	*Concert for Piano, Winds and Percussion* (NBA/Revelli)
1989		Schuller, Gunther	*On Winged Flight:* A Divertimento
1989		Ticheli, Frank	*Music for Winds and Percussion* (Beeler Prize)
1989		Turok, Paul	*Canzone Concertante No. 5*
1989		Weinstein, Michael	*Concerto for Wind Ensemble*
1989		Welcher, Dan	*The Yellowstone Fires*
1989		Wilson, Dana	*Shakata: Singing the World into Existence*
1989		Zwilich, Ellen Taaffe	*Ceremonies*
1990		Benson, Warren	*Meditation* on "I am for Peace"
1990		Colgrass, Michael	*Arctic Dreams*
1990		Epstein, Paul	*The Adventures of Matinee Concerto, as Broadcast Live from the Late Twentieth Century, With Notes* (NBA/Revelli)
1990		Galbraith, Nancy	*with brightness round about it*
1990		Gillingham, David	*Heroes Lost and Fallen*
1990		Gillingham, David	*Serenade "Songs of the Night"*
1990		Ito, Yasuhide	*Gloriosa*
1990		Larson, Libby	*Sun Song*
1990		MacMillan, James	*Sowetan Spring*
1990		Maslanka, David	*Concerto for Marimba*
1990		Maw, Nicholas	*American Games* (Sudler)
1990		McTee, Cindy	*Circuits*

WIND	ORCH.	COMPOSER	TITLE
	1990p	Powell, Mel	*Duplicates*: A Concerto for Two Pianos and Orchestra (Pulitzer)
1990		Schuller, Gunther	*Song and Dance*
1990		Stanhope, David	*Folksongs for Band—Suite No. 3*
	1990	Tilson-Thomas, Michael	*From the Diary of Anne Frank*
1990		Toensing, Richard	*Concerto for Flutes*
1990		Wilson, Dana	*Time Cries Hoping Otherwise*
1990		Youtz, Gregory	*Fire Works* (ABA/Ostwald)
1991		Bennett, Richard Rodney	*The Four Seasons*
1991		Benson, Warren	*Danzon*
1991		Camphouse, Mark	*To Build a Fire* (NBA/Revelli)
1991		Daugherty, Michael	*Desi*
1991		Dove, Jonathan	*Figures in the Garden*
1991		Gregson, Edward	*Celebration*
1991		Harvey, Jonathan	*Serenade in Homage to Mozart*
1991		Heiden, Bernhard	*Voyage* (CBDNA)
1991		Holloway, Robin	*Entrance: Carousing: Embarcation*
1991		Mahr, Timothy	*The Soaring Hawk* (ABA/Ostwald)
1991		Maslanka, David	*Symphony No. 3*
1991		McCabe, John	*Canyons*
1991		Oliver, Stephan	*Character Pieces for Wind Octet*
1991		Osborne, Nioel	*Albanian Nights* (Wind Octet)
1991		Penn, William	*A Cornfield in July - The River*
	1991p	Ran, Shalumit	*Symphony* (Pulitzer)
1991		Saxton, Robert	*Paraphrase on Mozart's "Idomeneo"*
1991		Wilson, Dana	*Winds on the Steps*
1992		Bazelon, Irwin	*Midnight Music*
1992		Benson, Warren	*Adagietto* (Beeler Prize)
1992		Benson, Warren	*Shadow Wood*
1992		Cage, John	*Fifty-Eight*
1992		Camphouse, Mark	*A Movement for Rosa*

WIND	ORCH.	COMPOSER	TITLE
1992		Delinger, Larry	*Elegies for Flute, Winds and Percussion*
1992		Harbison, John	*Three City Blocks*
1992		Hartley, Walter	*Sinfonia IX*
1992		Mahr, Timothy	*Endurance* (Ostwald Commission)
1992		Maslanka, David	*Symphony No. 3*
1992		Nelson, Ron	*Passacaglia: Homage on B-A-C-H* (ABA/Ostwald, Sudler, and NBA/Revelli)
	1992p	Peterson, Wayne	*The Face of the Night, the Heart of the Dark* (Pulitzer)
1992		Rands, Bernard	*Ceremonial*
1992		Schuller, Gunther	*Festive Music*
1992		Sparke, Philip	*Sinfonietta No. 2*
1992		Stucky, Steven	*Funeral Music for Queen Mary (after Purcell)*
1992		Ticheli, Frank	*A Postcard to Meadville*
1992		Tippett, Michael	*Triumph*
1992		Wilson, Dana	*Dance of the New World*
1993		Bennett, Richard Rodney	*Concerto for Trumpet*
	1993	Daugherty, Michael	*Red Cape Tango* (S. 1997/Spede)
1993		Gibson, John	*Sweet Melusine*
1993		Gillingham, David	*Prophecy of the Earth*
1993		Hart, Paul	*Cartoon*
1993		Hearshen, Ira	*Symphony on Themes by John Philip Sousa*
1993		Hodkinson, Sydney	*Symphony No. 7*
1993		Jager, Robert	*The Wall*
1993		McTee, Cindy	*California Counterpoint*
1993		Reller, Paul	*Tre Moderne for Piano and Chamber Orchestra* (CBDNA)
	1993p	Rouse, Christopher	*Trombone Concerto* (Pulitzer)
1993		Stamp, Jack	*Divertimento in F*

WIND	ORCH.	COMPOSER	TITLE
1993		Syler, James	*The Hound of Heaven* (NBA/Revelli)
1994		Barnes, James	*Third Symphony*
1994		Binney, Malcolm	*Visions of Light*
1994		Cichy, Roger	*Divertimento*
1994		Daugherty, Michael	*Bizarro*
1994		Daugherty, Michael	*Motown Metal*
1994		Ellerby, Martin	*Paris Sketches*
1994		Gorb, Adam	*Metropolis* (Beeler Prize)
1994		Grantham, Donald	*Bum's Rush* (NBA/Revelli)
1994		Hass, Jeffrey	*Lost in the Funhouse* (NBA/Revelli and Beeler Prize)
1994		Hodkinson, Sidney	*Duae Cantatae Breves* (CBDNA)
1994		Holsinger, David	*Easter Symphony*
	1994	Kernis, Aaron	*Colored Field*
1994		Maslanka, David	*Symphony No. 4*
1994		Maslanka, David	*Tears* (CBDNA)
1994		McBeth, Francis	*Through Countless Halls of Air*
1994		Nelson, Ron	*Chaconne -In Memoriam* (Ostwald Commission)
1994		Nelson, Ron	*Epiphany*
1994		Rudin, Rolf	*The Dream of Oenghus*
	1994p	Schuller, Gunther	*Of Reminiscences and Reflections* (Pulitzer)
	1994	Schwantner, Joseph	*Concerto for Percussion* (V. 1997/Boysen)
1994		Syler, James	*Fields*
1994		Syler, James	*Minton's Playhouse*
1994		Thomas, Augusta Reed	*Danse*
1994		Ticheli, Frank	*Amazing Grace*
1994		Ticheli, Frank	*Pacific Fanfare*
1994		Welcher, Dan	*Zion* (ABA/Ostwald)
1994		Whitacre, Eric	*Ghost Train Tryptich*

WIND	ORCH.	COMPOSER	TITLE
1994		Wuorinen, Charles	*Windfall*
1995		Adams, John	*Lollapalooza* (V. 2006/Spinnazola)
1995		Arnold, Malcolm	*The Sound Barrier*
1995		Bremer, Carolyn	*Early Light*
1995		Camphouse, Mark	*Watchman Tell Us of the Night*
	1995p	Gould, Morton	*Stringmusic* (Pulitzer)
1995		Hart, Paul	*Circus Ring*
1995		Iannaccone, Anthony	*Sea Drift* (ABA/Ostwald)
1995		Jacob, Gordon	*Symphony A.D. 78* (CBDNA)
1995		Larson, Libby	*Short Symphony*
1995		Maslanka, David	*A Tuning Piece*
1995		McTee, Cindy	*Soundings*
1995		Nelson, Ron	*Courtly Airs and Dances*
1995		Stamp, Jack	*Four Maryland Songs*
	1995	Thomas, Augusta Read	*Words of the Sea*
1995		Yurko, Bruce	*In Memoriam*
1996		Abe, Keiko	*Prism Rhapsody II*
1996		Bedford, David	*Canons and Cadenzas*
1996		Forte, Aldo R.	*Van Gogh Portraits*
1996		Godfrey, Daniel	*Jig*
1996		Gorb, Adam	*Awayday*
1996		Harbison, John	*Olympic Dances* (CBDNA)
1996		Iannaccone, Anthony	*Psalms for a Great Country* (Ostwald Commission)
1996		Mays, Walter	*Dreamcatcher* (NBA/Revelli)
	1996	Salonen, Esa-Pekka	*LA Variations*
1996		Schwantner, Joseph	*In Evening's Stillness* (CBDNA)
1996		Sierra, Roberto	*Diferencias* (CBDNA)
1996		Sparke, Philip	*Dance Movements*
1996		Ticheli, Frank	*Blue Shades*
1996		Ticheli, Frank	*Gaian Visions*

WIND	ORCH.	COMPOSER	TITLE
	1996p	Walker, George	*Lilacs* (Pulitzer)
1996		Whitacre, Eric	*Gawd$illa Eats Las Vegas*
1997		Benson, Warren	*The Drums of Summer* (NBA/Revelli)
1997		Cichy, Roger	*Galilean Moons*
1997		Daugherty, Michael	*Niagara Falls*
1997		Galbraith, Nancy	*Danza de los Duendes*
1997		Gillingham, David	*Concertino for Percussion and Winds*
1997		Grantham, Donald	*Fantasy Variations* (NBA/Revelli) (ABA/Ostwald)
1997		Gryc, Stephen	*Masquerade Variations*
1997		Hutcheson, Jere	*Caricatures*
1997		Kessner, Daniel	*Symphonic Mobile No. 2* (CBDNA)
1997		Kraft, William	*Quintessence Revisited*
	1997p	Marsalis, Wynton	*Blood on the Fields* (Pulitzer)
1997		Rudin, Rolf	*Baccanale*
1997		Sallinen, Aulis	*Palace Rhapsody* (CBDNA)
1997		Schuller, Gunther	*Blue Dawn into White Heat*
1998		Chambers, Evan	*Polka Nation* (Beeler Prize)
	1998	Danielpour, Richard	*Vox Populi* (S. 2003/Stamp)
1998		Frantzen, John	*Poem*
1998		Grantham, Donald	*Fantasy on Mr. Hydes's Song*
1998		Hagen, Daron	*Overture and Dance Suite* ("The Bandana")
1998		Hearshen, Ira	*Divertimento*
	1998p	Kernis, Aaron Jay	*String Quartet No. 2* (Pulitzer)
1998		Patterson, Robert	*Stomp Igor*
1998		Welcher, Dan	*Symphony No. 3 "Shaker Life"* (Ostwald Commission)
1998		Woolfenden, Guy	*French Impressions*
1998		Young, Charles	*Tempered Steel*
1999		Cesarini, Franco	*Poema Alpestre*
1999		Dzubay, David	*Myaku* (Beeler Prize)

Wind	Orch.	Composer	Title
1999		Grantham, Donald	*J'ai ete au bal*
1999		Grantham, Donald	*Southern Harmony* (ABA/Ostwald and NBA/Revelli)
1999		Hagen, Daron	*Bandanna* (CBDNA) (opera)
1999		Hartley, Walter	*Angel Band*
1999		Hesketh, Kenneth	*Danseries*
	1999	Musgrave, Thea	*Aurora*
	1999p	Wagner, Melinda	*Concerto for Flute, Strings, and Percussion* (Pulitzer)
1999		Wilson, Dana	*Vortex*
1999		Yurko, Bruce	*Sinfonietta for Wind Ensemble*
1999		Zaninelli, Luigi	*Lagan Love*
2000		Alkema, Henk	*Sunset Jericho* (8 solo trombones)
2000		Broege, Timothy	*Sinfonia XXI*
2000		Daugherty, Michael	*UFO*
2000		Gillingham, David	*Be Thou My Vision*
2000		Gillingham, David	*Cantus Laetus*
2000		Hesketh, Kenneth	*Masque*
2000		Kechley, David	*Restless Birds Before the Dark Moon* (NBA/Revelli)
2000		Maslanka, David	*Symphony #5*
2000		Patterson, Robert	*Symphonic Excursions*
2000		Ramage, Greg	*The Last Days of Summer*
	2000	Sierra, Roberto	*Fandangos* (V. 2003/Scatterday)
	2000p	Spratlan, Lewis	*Life is a Dream* (Pulitzer)
2000		Ticheli, Frank	*An American Elegy*
2000		Torke, Michael	*Grand Central Station*
2000		Tower, Joan	*Fascinating Ribbons*
2000		Walker, George	*Canvas* (CBDNA)
2000		Welcher, Dan	*Songs Without Words*
2000		Whitacre, Eric	*October*
2000		Yurko, Bruce	*Concerto for Bassoon*

WIND	ORCH.	COMPOSER	TITLE
2001		Bolcom, William	*Song*
	2001	Carter, Elliott	*Cello Concerto*
	2001p	Corigliano, John	*Symphony No. 2 for Strings* (Pulitzer)
2001		Daugherty, Michael	*Rosa Parks Boulevard*
2001		Godfrey, Daniel	*Shindig* (horn solo)
2001		Gorb, Adam	*Downtown Diversions for Trombone*
2001		Graham, Peter	*Harrison's Dream* (ABA/Ostwald)
2001		Grantham, Donald	*Variations on an American Cavalry Song*
2001		Hokoyama, Wataru	*Beyond*
2001		Lindroth, Scott	*Spin Cycle*
2001		McCarthy, Daniel	*Chamber Symphony No. 2*
2001		McTee, Cindy	*Timepiece*
2001		Pann, Carter	*Slalom* (V. 2003/Pann)
2001		Prior, Richard	*earthrise*
	2001	Puts, Kevin	*Millennium Canons* (V. 2003/Spede)
2001		Spaniola, Joseph	*Escapade* (NBA/Revelli)
2001		Sparke, Philip	*Sunrise at Angel's Gate*
2001		Stamp, Jack	*Escapade*
	2002p	Bryant, Henry	*Ice Field* (Pulitzer)
2002		Daugherty, Michael	*Bells for Stokowski*
2002		Djupstromm, Michael	*Homages* (Beeler Prize)
2002		Dzubay, David	*Ra!* (NBA/Revelli)
2002		Gillingham, David	*Concerto for Piano and Percussion* (V. 2004/Fisher)
2002		Grantham, Donald	*J.S. Dances*
2002		Roush, Dean	*Illuminations* (NBA/Revelli)
2002		Turrin, Joseph	*Hemispheres*
	2003p	Adams, John	*On the Transmigration of Souls* (Pulitzer)
2003		Bryant, Steven	*Stampede*
	2003	Daugherty, Michael	*Raise the Roof* (V. 2007/Daugherty) (ABA/Ostwald) (timpani solo)

Wind	Orch.	Composer	Title
2003		Del Tredici, David	*In Wartime*
2003		Gross, Murray	*Urban Myth*
	2003	Hartke, Stephen	*Symphony No. 3*
2003		Hesketh, Kenneth	*Diaghilev Dances*
2003		Lauridsen, Morten	*O Magnum Mysterium* (S. Reynolds)
2003		Lindberg, Christian	*Concerto for Wind Ensemble*
2003		McTee, Cindy	*Ballet for Band*
2003		Ticheli, Frank	*Symphony No. 2* (NBA/Revelli)
2003		Torke, Michael	*Bliss: Variations on an Unchanging Rhythm*
2003		Yurko, Bruce	*Danza No. 2 for Wind Ensemble*
2004		Alarcón, Luis Serrano	*Concertango*
2004		Bourgeois, Derek	*Symphony for William*
2004		Gandolfi, Michael	*Vientos y Tangos*
2004		Graham, Peter	*The Red Machine*
2004		Gross, Murray	*Urban Myth*
	2004	Hailstork, Adolphus	*Violin Concerto*
2004		Mackey, John	*Redline Tango* (Beeler Prize and ABA/Ostwald)
	2004p	Moravec, Paul	*Tempest Fantasy* (Pulitzer)
	2004	Rims, Wolfgang	*Two Other Movements*
2004		Schwantner, Joseph	*Recoil*
	2004	Tower, Joan	*Made in America*
2004		Turrin, Joseph	*Illuminations for Solo Trombone* (NBA/Revelli)
	2005	Adams, John	*Doctor Atomic Symphony*
2005		Botti, Susan	*Cosmosis* (Soprano and Women's Voices) (Theater)
2005		Colgrass, Michael	*Bali*
2005		Corigliano, John	*Symphony No. 3: "Circus Maximus"* (Theater)
2005		Danielpour, Richard	*Voice of the City*

WIND	ORCH.	COMPOSER	TITLE
2005		Etezady, Roshanne	*Anahita*
2005		Grantham, Donald	*Court Music*
2005		Grantham, Donald	*The Barons*
2005		Maslanka, David	*Give Us This Day*
2005		Maslanka, David	*Symphony No. 7*
	2005	McTee, Cindy	*Finish Line* (V. 2006/McTee)
2005		Sparke, Philip	*Music of the Spheres* (NBA/Revelli)
	2005p	Stucky, Steven	*Second Concerto for Orchestra* (Pulitzer)
2005		Tanouye, Nathan	*Kokopelli's Dance*
2005		Ticheli, Frank	*Sanctuary*
	2005	Welcher, Dan	*Jackpot*
2005		Welcher, Dan	*Symphony No. 4 "American Visionary"*
2006		Bryant, Steven	*Radiant Joy* (NBA/Revelli)
2006		Dzubay, David	*Shadow Dance*
2006		Koh, Chang Su	*As the Sun Rises*
2006		Pann, Carter	*Four Factories*
2006		Rouse, Christopher	*Wolf Rounds*
2006		Wilson, Dana	*Day Dreams*
	2006p	Wyner, Yehudi	*"Chiavi in Mano" Piano Concerto* (Pulitzer)
2007		Bryant, Steven	*Parody Suite* (completed)
2007		Grantham, Donald	*Starry Crown*
2007		Husa, Karel	*Cheetah*
2007		Mackey, John	*Kingfishers Catch Fire*
2007		McAllister, Scott	*Krump*
	2007p	Ornette, Coleman	*Sound Grammar* (recording)
2007		Ticheli, Frank	*Wild Nights!*
2007		Yurko, Bruce	*Dialogues and Fanfares for Wind Ensemble*
2008		Gillingham, David	*Symphony No. 2, "Genesis"*
	2008p	Lang, David	*The Little Match Girl Passion* (Pulitzer)

WIND	ORCH.	COMPOSER	TITLE
	2008	Rands, Bernard	*Chains Like the Sea*
	2008	Stucky, Steven	*August 4, 1964*
2008		Ticheli, Frank	*Angels in the Architecture*
2008		Wagner, Melinda	*Scamp*

Key to Special Designation:

A = Arranged
S = Scored
V = Wind Version
E = Edited
P = Pulitzer

ABA/Ostwald = American Bandmasters Association Ostwald Award
Beeler Prize/Commission = Walter Beeler Memorial Composition Prize, Ithaca College
CBDNA = College Band Directors National Association Commission
Donaueschingen = Donaueschingen Music Festival 1926
NBA/Revelli = National Band Association William D. Revelli Memorial Composition
    Contest
Pulitzer = Pulitzer Prize in Music (note that pieces are listed by award year)
Sudler = Sudler Prize for Wind Band Composition
Theater = Work incorporating theatrical aspects
West Point = United States Military Academy Band Sesquicentennial Celebration
    Commissions, 1952

Edited by: Erin Bodnar, Master's Conducting Associate, University of North Texas

Appendix B

Historical Repertoire by Grade Level and Year of the Recommended Curriculum Sequence

Richard Miles

Grade 2, Year 1 • Medieval, Renaissance, and Baroque Literature

RECOMMENDED WORKS FROM THE *TEACHING MUSIC THROUGH PERFORMANCE* SERIES WITH TEACHER RESOURCE GUIDES

TITLE	COMPOSER/ARRANGER/TRANSCRIBER	PUBLISHER	VOLUME	PAGE
Air and March	Henry Purcell/Philip Gordon	Bourne	5	116
Aria	Georg Philipp Telemann/Larry Daehn	Daehn	6	176
The Battle Pavane	After Tielman Susato/Bob Margolis	Manhattan Beach	1	77
Cathedral Music: Two Renaissance Choral Masterpieces	Thomas Tallis and Jacob Handl/Kenneth Singleton	Grand Mesa	6	181
Fanfare Ode and Festival	After Claude Gervaise/Bob Margolis	Manhattan Beach	12	128
Fitzwilliam Suite	Arranged by Philip Gordon	Masters Music	5	151
No Shade So Rare	George Frederick Handel/Leland Forsblad	Grand Mesa	6	205
Renaissance Festival and Dances	Arranged by Bruce Person	Neil A. Kjos	3	185
Soldier's Procession and Sword Dance	After Tielman Susato/Bob Margolis	Manhattan Beach	1	148

OTHER WORKS TO CONSIDER

TITLE	COMPOSER/ARRANGER/TRANSCRIBER	PUBLISHER
Arioso	George Frederick Handel/John Kinyon	Pro Art/Alfred
Christ Lay In The Bonds Of Death	J. S. Bach/D. Mairs	Bourne
Dances from Terpsichore	Michael Praetorius/Kathryn Fenske	Daehn
Grand Finale	J. S. Bach/ Philip Gordon	Bourne
Largo And Bourrée	George Frederick Handel/Albert Lynd	Barnhouse
Prelude and Fughetta	George Frederick Handel/Eric Osterling	Ludwig/Masters
A Renaissance Festival	Claude Gervaise/Kenneth Singleton	Grand Mesa
Telemann Suite	Georg Philipp Telemann/Don Schaeffer	Barnhouse
Three Bach Chorales	J. S. Bach/Eugene Mitchell	Barnhouse
Triumphant Festival	George Frederick Handel/John Kinyon	Alfred
Two 17th-Century Italian Songs	Claudio Monteverdi and Domenico Scarlatti/Thomas Tyra	Branhouse

Grade 2, Year 2 • Classical and Romantic

TITLE	COMPOSER/ARRANGER/TRANSCRIBER	PUBLISHER
Air And Alleluia	Wolfgang Amadeus Mozart/John Kinyon	Alfred
Austrian Hymn	Franz Joseph Haydn/Leland Forsblad	Carl Fischer
Ave Verum Corpus	Wolfgang Amadeus Mozart/Barbara Buehlman	Ludwig/Masters
The Barber of Seville	Gioacchino Rossini/Mitchell S. Bender	Carl Fischer
Don Giovanni: "Minuet"	Wolfgang Amadeus Mozart/Don Schaeffer	Pro Art/Alfred
Pavane	Gabriel Fauré/Larry Clark	Carl Fischer
Poet And Peasant Overture	Franz von Suppé/Mark Williams	Alfred
Prelude and Fugato	Cesar Franck/John Cacavas	Presser/Carl Fischer

Grade 2, Years 3 and 4 • Contemporary Literature, Part I

RECOMMENDED WORKS FROM THE *TEACHING MUSIC THROUGH PERFORMANCE* SERIES WITH TEACHER RESOURCE GUIDES

TITLE	COMPOSER/ARRANGER/TRANSCRIBER	PUBLISHER	VOLUME	PAGE
Ancient Voices	Michael Sweeney	Hal Leonard	1	70
Chant Rituals	Elliot Del Borgo	Alfred	3	133
Dinosaurs	Daniel Bukvich	Phoebus	3	146
Down a Country Lane	Aaron Copland/Merlin Patterson	Boosey & Hawkes/Hal Leonard	1	88
Four Sketches	Bela Bartok/William E Schaefer	TRN	5	166
The Headless Horseman	Timothy Broege	Manhattan Beach	1	96
In the Bleak Midwinter	Gustav Holst/Robert Smith	Alfred	2	132
Joy	Frank Ticheli	Manhattan Beach/BandQuest	6	201
Kachina: Chant and Sprit Dance	Anne McGinty	Queenwood/Neil A. Kjos	4	169
Kentucky 1800	Clare Grundman	Boosey & Hawkes/Hal Leonard	1	100

TITLE	COMPOSER/ARRANGER/TRANSCRIBER	PUBLISHER	VOLUME	PAGE
Mini Suite	Morton Gould	G. Schirmer/Associated/Hal Leonard	1	122
New Wade 'N' Water	Adolphus Hailstor	American Composers Forum/Hal Leonard	5	187
Old Churches	Michael Colgrass	American Composers Forum/Hal Leonard	4	180
Rites of Tamburo	Robert Smith	Alfred	5	203
Sinfonia VI: "The Four Elements"	Timothy Broege	Manhattan Beach	3	189
Snakes!	Thomas Duffy	Ludwig/Masters	1	144
Three Pieces for American Band, Set No. 2	Timothy Broege	Bourne	2	184
Tricycle	Andrew Boysen, Jr.	Neil A. Kjos	4	233

OTHER WORKS TO CONSIDER

TITLE	COMPOSER/ARRANGER/TRANSCRIBER	PUBLISHER
Canto	Francis McBeth	Southern
In A Quiet Mood	Béla Bartók/Stanley Applebaum	Chappell/Leonard
The Lowlands of Scotland	Ralph Vaughan Williams/LarryDaehn	Daehn
Rythmos	Robert W. Smith	Belwin/Alfred
Two Songs and A Dance	Béla Bartók/Ross Hastings	Wynn RBC Music

Grade 3, Year 1 • Medieval, Renaissance, and Baroque Literature

RECOMMENDED WORKS FROM THE *TEACHING MUSIC THROUGH PERFORMANCE* SERIES WITH TEACHER RESOURCE GUIDES

TITLE	COMPOSER/ARRANGER/TRANSCRIBER	PUBLISHER	VOLUME	PAGE
The Battell	William Byrd/Gordon Jacob	Boosey & Hawkes/Hal Leonard	6	423

TITLE	COMPOSER/ARRANGER/TRANSCRIBER	PUBLISHER	VOLUME	PAGE
Belle Qui Tien Ma Vie	After Thoinot Arbeau/Bob Margolis	Manhattan Beach/Belwin/Alfred	1	160
Courtly Airs and Dances	After Claude Gervaise and others/Ron Nelson	Ludwig/Masters	3	213
If Thou Be Near Bist Du Bei Mir	J. S. Bach/Alfred Reed	Barnhouse	4	324
Komm', Süsser Tod (Come, Sweet Death)	J. S. Bach/Alfred Reed	Barnhouse	1	173
My Jesus! Oh What Anguish	J. S. Bach/Alfred Reed	Barnhouse	5	290
O Mensch, bewein' dein' Sünde gross	J. S. Bach/Percy Grainger	G&M Brand/C. Alan	5	314
Prelude in the Dorian Mode	Antonio de Cabezon/Percy Grainger, edited by Brion and Brand	RSmith/G&M Brand/C. Alan	4	365
Renaissance Suite	Tielman Susato/James Curnow/Hal Leonard	Hal Leonard	2	259

OTHER WORKS TO CONSIDER

TITLE	COMPOSER/ARRANGER/TRANSCRIBER	PUBLISHER
Baroque Suite	Johann Phillipp Kirnberger/Eric Osterling	Ludwig/Masters
Baroque Suite	Georg Philipp Telemann/William Hill	TRN
Come, Sweet Death	J. S. Bach/Mark Hindsley	Hindsley
Fervent Is My Longing and Fugue in G Minor	J. S. Bach/Lucien Cailliet	Southern
Forget Me Not, O Dearest Lord	J. S. Bach/Alfred Reed	Barnhouse
Fugue in D Minor	J. S. Bach/James Barnes	Tempo
Jesu, Joy Of Man's Desiring	J. S. Bach/Mark Hindsley	Hindsley
Jesu, Joy Of Man's Desiring	J. S. Bach/Eric Leidzen	Carl Fischer
Jesu, Joy Of Man's Desiring	J. S. Bach/Alfred Reed	Barnhouse
An Occasional Suite	George Frederick Handel/Eric Osterling	Ludwig/Masters
Prelude and Fugue in D Minor	J. S. Bach/R. L. Moehlmann	FitzSimmons/Alfred
Prelude and Fugue in F Minor	J. S. Bach/R. L. Moehlmann	FitzSimmons/Alfred
Prelude No. 4	J. S. Bach/Alfred Reed	Barnhouse
Renaissance Fair	Bob Margolis	Manhattan Beach

TITLE	COMPOSER/ARRANGER/TRANSCRIBER	PUBLISHER
Rondeau from "Abdelazer"	Henry Purcell/David Farnon	G&M Brand/C. Alan
Royal Coronation Dances	Claude Gervaise/Bob Margolis	Manhattan Beach
Sarabande and Bourrée	George Frederick Handel/Eric Osterling	Ludwig/Masters
Spring from The Seasons (Autumn is still available)	Antonio Vivaldi/John Cacavas	Presser POP
Who Puts His Trust in God Most Just	J. S. Bach/James Croft	Shawnee

Grade 3, Year 2 • Classical and Romantic

TITLE	COMPOSER/ARRANGER/TRANSCRIBER	PUBLISHER
Air and Alleluia	Wolfgang Amadeus Mozart/John Kinyon	Alfred
Alleluia	Wolfgang Amadeus Mozart/John Boyd	Ludwig/Masters
Ave Maria	Franz Schubert/Frank Ticheli	Manhattan Beach
Blessed Are They	Johannes Brahms/Barbara Buehlman	Ludwig/Masters
From a Schumann Album	Robert Schumann/Jared Spears	Barnhouse
Il Re Pastore Overture	Wolfgang Amadeus Mozart/Albert Davis	Ludwig/Masters
Impresario Overture	Wolfgang Amadeus Mozart/Clifford Barnes	Ludwig/Masters
Laude Alla Vergina Maria	Giuseppi Verdi/Barbara Buehlman	Barnhouse Archive Edition
Open Wide the Heavens	Johannes Brahms/Kenneth Singleton	Grand Mesa
Prelude	Cesar Franck/Earl Slocum	TRN
La Traviata: "Prelude to Act I"	Giuseppi Verdi/Leonard Falcone	Niel A. Kjos
Trauermusik	Wolfgang Amadeus Mozart/Eric Osterling	Ludwig/Masters
Viennese Sonatina	Wolfgang Amadeus Mozart/Walter Beeler	Ludwig/Masters

Grade 3, Years 3 and 4 • Contemporary Literature, Part I

RECOMMENDED WORKS FROM THE *TEACHING MUSIC THROUGH PERFORMANCE* SERIES WITH TEACHER RESOURCE GUIDES

TITLE	COMPOSER/ARRANGER/TRANSCRIBER	PUBLISHER	VOLUME	PAGE
Acrostic Song	David Del Tredici	Boosey & Hawkes/ Hal Leonard	6	289
Alligator Alley	Michael Daugherty	BandQuest/Hal Leonard	5	241
Cajun Folk Songs	Frank Ticheli	Manhattan Beach	1	166
Candide Suite	Leonard Bernstein/Clare Grundman	Boosey & Hawkes/ Hal Leonard	4	281
Chant and Jubilo	Francis W. McBeth	Southern	1	170
Crystals	Thomas Duffy	Ludwig/Masters	4	301
The Fire of Eternal Glory	Demitri Shostakovich/Timothy Rhea	TRN	5	357
Flourish for Wind Band	Ralph Vaughan Williams	Oxford	1	179
Fortress	Frank Ticheli	Manhattan Beach	5	255
Ginger Marmalade	Warren Benson	Carl Fischer, LLC	1	182
In Memorian: Kristina "In Praise of Winds"	Bruce Yurko	Ludwig/Masters	2	246
Mazama	Jay Chattaway	William Allen	3	253
Mysterian Landscapes	Timothy Broege	Boosey & Hawkes/ Hal Leonard	5	295
Rhosymedre	Ralph Vaughan Williams	Galaxy/ECS	2	267
Rollo Takes A Walk	David Maslanka	Neil A. Kjos	5	339
Sun Dance	Frank Ticheli	Manhattan Beach	3	285

Grade 4, Year 1 • Medieval, Renaissance, and Baroque Literature

OTHER WORKS TO CONSIDER

TITLE	COMPOSER/ARRANGER/TRANSCRIBER	PUBLISHER
The Girl with the Flaxen Hair	Debussy Akey	Queenwood/Kjos
Past The Equinox	Jack Stamp	Neil A. Kjos
Sang!	Dana Wilson	Ludwig/Masters
Stargazing (with tape)	Donald Erb	Theodore Presser Merion

RECOMMENDED WORKS FROM THE *TEACHING MUSIC THROUGH PERFORMANCE* SERIES WITH TEACHER RESOURCE GUIDES

TITLE	COMPOSER/ARRANGER/TRANSCRIBER	PUBLISHER	VOLUME	PAGE
Fantasia in G Major	J. S. Bach/Richard Franko Goldman and Robert L. Leist	Mercury/TP	1	247
Fugue in G Minor	J. S. Bach/Yoshihiro Kimura	DeHaske/Leonard	2	313
Medieval Suite	Ron Nelson	Boosey & Hawkes/ Hal Leonard	3	383
1. Homage to Loenin				
2. Homage to Perotin				
3. Homage to Machaut				
Toccata	Girolamo Frescobaldi; Gaspar Cassado, Hans Kindler/Earl Slocum	Alfred	2	370

OTHER WORKS TO CONSIDER

TITLE	COMPOSER/ARRANGER/TRANSCRIBER	PUBLISHER
Adagio	J. S. Bach/Clark McAlister	Masters
Fantasia in G	J. S. Bach/Robert Leist and Edwin Franko Goldman	Mercury TP
Little Prelude and Fugue	J. S. Bach/Donald Stauffer	Barnhouse
O Mensch, Bewein Dein Sunde Gross	J. S. Bach/Percy Grainger	G&M Brand
Prelude in the Dorian Mode	Antonio De Cabezon/Percy Grainger	RSmith/G&M Brand
Sheep May Safely Graze	J. S. Bach/Alfred Reed	Barnhouse

TITLE	COMPOSER/ARRANGER/TRANSCRIBER	PUBLISHER
Sleepers Awake	J. S. Bach/Alfred Reed	Barnhouse
St. Anne's Fugue	J. S. Bach/William E. Rhoads	Southern Rental
Thus Do You Fare, My Jesus	J. S. Bach/Alfred Reed	Barnhouse

Grade 4, Year 2 • Classical and Romantic

RECOMMENDED WORKS FROM THE *TEACHING MUSIC THROUGH PERFORMANCE* SERIES WITH TEACHER RESOURCE GUIDES

TITLE	COMPOSER/ARRANGER/TRANSCRIBER	PUBLISHER	VOLUME	PAGE
Chant funéraire	Gabriel Faure/Myron Moss	Hal Leonard	6	468
Elsa's Procession to the Cathedral	Richard Wagner/Glenn Lucien Cailliet	Alfred	4	462
Three Choral Preludes, Op. 122	Johannes Brahms/John Boyd/Frederick Fennell	Ludwig/Masters	5	523

OTHER WORKS TO CONSIDER

TITLE	COMPOSER/ARRANGER/TRANSCRIBER	PUBLISHER
Classic Overture In C	Francois Joseph Gossec/Robert Leist	Mercury Rental
Coronation Scene from Boris Godunov	Modeste Mussorgsky/John Cacavas	Ludwig/Masters
Egmont Overture	Ludwig/Masters van Beethoven/Mark Hindsley	Hindsley
Finlandia (only score available)	Jean Sibelius/Lucien Cailliet	Carl Fischer
Grant Them Rest (print on demand)	Gabriel Fauré/Barbara Buehlman	Shawnee
Huldigungsmarch	Richard Wagner/William Schaefer	Shawnee
Light Cavalry Overture	Franz von Suppé/Henry Filmore	Carl Fischer
Magic Flute Overture	Wolfgang Amadeus Mozart/James Barnes	Tempo
A Musical Toast	Leonard Bernstein/Claire Grundman	Boosey & Hawkes
Slavonic Dance No. 1, Op. 46	Antonin Dvorak/Robert Longfield	Barnhouse
St. Anthony Divertimento	Franz Joseph Haydn/Wilcox	G. Schirmer
Tancredi	Gioacchino Rossini/Leonard Falcone	Neil A. Kjos

Grade 4, Years 3 and 4 • Contemporary Literature, Part I

RECOMMENDED WORKS FROM THE *TEACHING MUSIC THROUGH PERFORMANCE* SERIES WITH TEACHER RESOURCE GUIDES

TITLE	COMPOSER/ARRANGER/TRANSCRIBER	PUBLISHER	VOLUME	PAGE
Bagatelles, Op. 87	Vincent Persichetti	Masters	5	393
Blue Lake Overture	John Barnes Chance	Boosey & Hawkes/ Hal Leonard	4	455
Color	Bob Margolis	Manhattan Beach	2	293
Colors and Contours	Leslie Bassett	C. F. Peters Rental	3	310
English Folk Song Suite	Ralph Vaughan Williams	Boosey & Hawkes/ Hal Leonard	1	241
Epinicion	John Paulson	Neil A. Kjos	4	470
The Final Covenant	Fisher Tull	Boosey & Hawkes/ Hal Leonard	4	704
First Suite in E-flat	Gustav Holst/Colin Matthews	Boosey & Hawkes/ Hal Leonard	1	251
Hymn of St. James	Reber Clark	C. Alan	2	317
Kaddish	Francis W. McBeth	Southern	2	325
Laude	Howard Hanson	Carl Fischer, LLC	3	357
Night Dances	Bruce Yurko	Ludwig/Masters	1	263
Old Home Days	Charles Ives/Elkus	Peer/Theodore Presser	1	267
Pageant, Op. 59	Vincent Persichetti	Carl Fischer, LLC	1	271
Sanctuary	Frank Ticheli	Manhattan Beach	6	549
Satiric Dances	Norman Dello Joio	Associated/GS/Hal Leonard	2	344
Scenes from The Louvre	Norman Dello Joio	Marks/Hal Leonard	1	282
Sinfonia V: Symphonia Sacra et Profana	Timothy Broege	Manhattan Beach	1	300
Symphonic Songs for Band	Robert Russell Bennett	Hal Leonard	3	427

OTHER WORKS TO CONSIDER

TITLE	COMPOSER/ARRANGER/TRANSCRIBER	PUBLISHER
Bagatelles for Band	Vincent Persichetti	Masters
Chorale and Shaker Dance	John Zdechlik	Neil A. Kjos
Cloudburst	Eric Whitacre	Hal Leonard
The Golden Light	David Maslanka	Carl Fischer Rental
O Cool is the Valley	Vincent Persichetti	Theodore Presser/Elkan Vogel/CFN
Psalm	Vincent Persichetti	Elkan-Vogel/Presser/CFN
Psalm 46	John Zdechlik	Schmitt/Alfred
Serenade for Band	Vincent Persichetti	Elkan-Vogel/Presser/CFN
Symphony No. 1 for Winds, Brass, and Percussion: "In Memoriam, Dresden 1945"	Daniel J. Bukvich	Wingert Jones

Grade 5, Year 1 • Medieval, Renaissance, and Baroque Literature

RECOMMENDED WORKS FROM THE *TEACHING MUSIC THROUGH PERFORMANCE* SERIES WITH TEACHER RESOURCE GUIDES

TITLE	COMPOSER/ARRANGER/TRANSCRIBER	PUBLISHER	VOLUME	PAGE
Ricercare a 6	J. S. Bach/McAlister/Fennell	Ludwig/Masters	2	492
Selections from the Danserye	Tielman Susato/Patrick Dunnigan	Monroe Music	6	684
Toccata and Fugue in D Minor	J. S. Bach/Erik Leidzen	Carl Fischer	1	369
William Byrd Suite	William Byrd/Gordon Jacob	Boosey & Hawkes/Hal Leonard	1	385

OTHER WORKS TO CONSIDER

TITLE	COMPOSER/ARRANGER/TRANSCRIBER	PUBLISHER
Allegro from Brandenburg Concerto No. 3	J. S. Bach/Larry Daehn	Bourne
Chaconne	J. S. Bach/Larry Daehn	Daehn

TITLE	COMPOSER/ARRANGER/TRANSCRIBER	PUBLISHER
Fantasia and Fugue in G minor	J. S. Bach/John Boyd	Ludwig/Masters
Fugue à la Gigue	J. S. Bach/Gustav Holst	Boosey & Hawkes/Hal Leonard
Passacaglia and Fugue in C Minor	J. S. Bach/Leonard Falcone	Southern
Passacaglia and Fugue in C Minor	J. S. Bach/Donald Hunsberger	G. Schirmer
Music for the Royal Fireworks	George Frederick Handel/Baines	Oxford Rental
Music for the Royal Fireworks	George Frederick Handel/Mark Hindsley	Hindsley
Toccata and Fugue in D Minor	J. S. Bach/Mark Hindsley	Hindsley
Toccata and Fugue in D Minor	J. S. Bach/Donald Hunsberger	Warner

Grade 5, Year 2 • Classical and Romantic

RECOMMENDED WORKS FROM THE *TEACHING MUSIC THROUGH PERFORMANCE* SERIES WITH TEACHER RESOURCE GUIDES

TITLE	COMPOSER/ARRANGER/TRANSCRIBER	PUBLISHER	VOLUME	PAGE
Dance of the Jesters	Peter Ilyich Tchaikovsky/Ray Cramer	Curnow/Hal Leonard	2	437
Grand Symphonie Funebre et Triomphale	Hector Berlioz	Barenreiter Rental	3	492
Overture for Winds, Op. 24	Felix Mendelssohn/John Boyd	Ludwig/Masters	1	337
Overture in C	Charles Simon Catel/Richard Franko Goldman/Roger Smith	Theodore Presser	1	334
Trauermusik, WWV 73 Trauersinfonie	Richard Wagner/Michael Votta/John Boyd	Ludwig/Masters	1	372

OTHER WORKS TO CONSIDER

TITLE	COMPOSER/ARRANGER/TRANSCRIBER	PUBLISHER
1812 Overture	Peter Ilyich Tchaikovsky/Mayhew Lake	Carl Fischer
Beatrice and Benedict Overture	Hector Berlioz/Henning	Carl Fischer
Capriccio Espagnol	Nicolas Rimsky-Korsakov/Mark Hindsley	Hindsley

TITLE	COMPOSER/ARRANGER/TRANSCRIBER	PUBLISHER
Capriccio Espagnol	Nicolas Rimsky-Korsakov/Frank Winterbottom	Boosey & Hawkes/Hal Leonard
Introduction to Act III from Lohengrin	Richard Wagner/Mark Hindsley	Hindsley
Italian in Algiers Overture	Gioacchino Rossini/Lucien Cailliet	Fox
La Forza Del Destino	Guiseppi Verdi/Franco Cesarini	Mitropa/DeHaske/Hal Leonard
La Forza Del Destino	Guiseppi Verdi/Mayhew Lake/H.R. Kent	Carl Fischer
La Forza Del Destino	Guiseppi Verdi/Mark Rogers	Southern
Les Preludes	Franz Liszt/Mark Hindsley	Hindsley
Liebestod	Richard Wagner/Glenn Bainum	Neil A. Kjos Print on Demand
March Slav	Peter Ilyich Tchaikovsky/Laurendeau	Carl Fischer
Marriage of Figaro	Wolfgang Amadeus Mozart/James Duthoit	Boosey & Hawkes
Marriage of Figaro	Wolfgang Amadeus Mozart/Earl Slocum	Belwin
Morning, Noon and Night in Vienna	Franz von Suppé/Henry Fillmore/Robert Foster	Carl Fischer
Nabucco	Guiseppi Verdi/Franco Cesarini	Mitropa/DeHaske/Leon
New World Symphony, Finale	Antonin Dvorak/Mark Hindsley	Hindsley
Night on Bald Mountain (Night on the Bare Bald Mountain)	Modeste Moussorgsky/Mark Hindsley	Hindsley
Night on Bald Mountain	Modeste Moussorgsky/William Schaefer	Schaefer
Overture 1812	Peter Ilyich Tchaikovsky/Mark Hindsley	Hindsley
Overture to the Flying Dutchman	Richard Wagner/Mark Hindsley	Hindsley
Pictures at an Exhibition, Nos. 2 and 3	Modeste Moussorgsky/Erik Leidzen	Carl Fischer
Poet and Peasant Overture	Franz von Suppé/Henry Fillmore	Carl Fischer
Prelude and Love Death from Tristan	Richard Wagner/Mark Hindsley	Hindsley
Procession of the Nobles	Nicolas Rimsky-Korsakov/Erik Leidzen	Carl Fischer
Prometheus	Ludwig/Masters van Beethoven/Earl Slocum	TRN
Romeo and Juliet Fantasy Overture	Peter Ilyich Tchaikovsky/Mark Hindsley	Hindsley
Rosamunde Overture	Franz Schubert/Mark Hindsley	Frank
Russlan and Ludmilla Overture	Mikhail Glinka/Mark Hindsley	Hindsley
Semiramide	Gioacchino Rossini/V.F. Safranek	Carl Fischer
Slavonic Dances	Antonin Dvorak/James Curnow/Hal Leonard	Jenson
Swan Lake	Peter Ilyich Tchaikovsky/Mayhew Lake	Ludwig/Masters

TITLE	COMPOSER/ARRANGER/TRANSCRIBER	PUBLISHER
Symphony No. 4: "Finale"	Peter Ilyich Tchaikovsky/Mark Hindsley	Hindsley
Symphony No. 4: "Finale" (score only available)	Peter Ilyich Tchaikovsky/V. F. Safranek/Van Ragsdale	Carl Fischer
Symphony No. 5: "Allegro con Brio"	Ludwig/Masters van Beethoven/Joseph Kreines	Boosey & Hawkes
Symphony No. 5: "Finale"	Antonin Dvorak/Erik Leidzen	Carl Fischer
Tannhauser Overture	Richard Wagner/Mark Hindsley	Hindsley
The Tsar's Farewell	Nicolas Rimsky-Korsakov/Alfred Reed	Southern Rental
Variations on a Theme by Haydn	Johannes Brahms/Mark Hindsley	Hindsley
William Tell	Gioacchino Rossini/Erik Leidzen	Carl Fischer

Grade 5, Years 3 and 4 • Contemporary Literature, Part I

RECOMMENDED WORKS FROM THE *TEACHING MUSIC THROUGH PERFORMANCE* SERIES WITH TEACHER RESOURCE GUIDES

TITLE	COMPOSER/ARRANGER/TRANSCRIBER	PUBLISHER	VOLUME	PAGE
Aegean Festival Overture	Andreas Makris	Galaxy/E.C. Schirmer	4	575
Al Fresco	Karel Husa	Associated/Hal Leonard	2	386
An Outdoor Overture	Aaron Copland	Boosey & Hawkes/Hal Leonard	2	408
Canzona	Peter Mennin	Carl Fischer, LLC	1	309
Celebration Overture, Op. 61	Paul Creston	Shawnee	5	561
Commando March	Samuel Barber	G. Schirmer/Associated/Hal Leonard	5	572
Country Band March	Charles Ives/James Sinclair	Theodore Presser	3	451
Danceries	Kenneth Hesketh	Faber	4	603
Die Natalis (rental only)	Howard Hanson	Carl Fischer, LLC	4	623
Divertimento	Karel Husa/John Boyd	Ludwig/Masters	5	581
Galactic Empires	David Gillingham	C. Alan	3	487

TITLE	COMPOSER/ARRANGER/TRANSCRIBER	PUBLISHER	VOLUME	PAGE
In Evening's Stillness…	Joseph Schwantner	Helicon/European American	3	506
Overture to "Candide"	Leonard Bernstein	Boosey & Hawkes/Hal Leonard	1	341
Sea Drift	Anthony Iannaccone	Ludwig/Masters	3	529
Short Ride in a Fast Machine	John Adams/Lawrence T. Odom	Boosey & Hawkes/Hal Leonard	3	537
Sketches on a Tudor Psalm	Fisher Tull	Boosey & Hawkes/Hal Leonard	1	345
The Solitary Dancer	Warren Benson	Carl Fischer, LLC	2	502
Suite Francaise	Darius Milhaud	Alfred	1	349
Symphony No. 2	John Barnes Chance	Boosey & Hawkes	6	703
Symphony No. 3	Mittorio Giannini	Alfred	1	365
Symphony No. 6	Vincent Persichetti	Theodore Presser	1	361
The Red Pony: Film Suite	Aaron Copland	Boosey & Hawkes/Hal Leonard	4	711
Toccata Marziale	Ralph Vaughan Williams	Boosey & Hawkes/Hal Leonard	2	522
Variations on "America"	Charles Ives/William Schuman/William Rhoads	Theodore Presser	1	382

OTHER WORKS TO CONSIDER

TITLE	COMPOSER/ARRANGER/TRANSCRIBER	PUBLISHER
Children's Corner	Claude Debussy/Frank Winterbottom	Boosey & Hawkes
Danse Tarantelle Styrienne	Claude Debussy/John Boyd	Ludwig/Masters
The Engulfed Cathedral	Claude Debussy/Merin Patterson	Manhattan Beach
In Memoriam	David Maslanka	Carl Fischer
La Vallée Des Cloches	Maurice Ravel/Donald Hunsberger	Ludwig/Masters
Marche Ecossaise	Caude Debussy/William Schaefer	Shawnee
Morning Star	David Maslanka	Carl Fischer
Petite Suite	Claude Debussy/Frank Winterbottom	Boosey & Hawkes
Phedre	Jules Massenet/Lucien Cailliet	Fox

TITLE	COMPOSER/ARRANGER/TRANSCRIBER	PUBLISHER
Profanation	Leonard Bernstein/Frank Bencriscutto	Boosey & Hawkes
Selections from West Side Story	Leonard Bernstein/James Duthoit	Boosey & Hawkes/Leon
Slava!	Leonard Bernstein/Clare Grundman	Boosey & Hawkes
Symphonic Dance Music from West Side Story (Four Dances from West Side Story)	Leonard Bernstein/Ian Polster	Boosey & Hawkes/Leon
Tears	David Maslanka	Carl Fischer Rental
A Tuning Piece (rental only)	David Maslanka	Carl Fischer
Vortex	Dana Wilson	Boosey & Hawkes/Leon

Grade 6, Year 1 • Medieval, Renaissance, and Baroque Literature

RECOMMENDED WORKS FROM THE *TEACHING MUSIC THROUGH PERFORMANCE* SERIES WITH TEACHER RESOURCE GUIDES

TITLE	COMPOSER/ARRANGER/TRANSCRIBER	PUBLISHER	VOLUME	PAGE
Passacaglia and Fugue in C Minor	J. S. Bach/Donald Hunsberger	G. Schirmer/Associated	1	429
Terpsichore	After Michael Praetorius/Bob Margolis	Manhattan Beach	1	476

OTHER WORKS TO CONSIDER

TITLE	COMPOSER/ARRANGER/TRANSCRIBER	PUBLISHER
Fantasia and Fugue in C, BWV 537	J. S. Bach/Donald Hunsberger	Warner
Sicilian Vespers	Guiseppi Verdi/John Bourgeois	Wingert Jones
And those from the Grade 5 Listing		

Grade 6, Year 2 • Classical and Romantic

TITLE	COMPOSER/ARRANGER/TRANSCRIBER	PUBLISHER
Academic Festival Overture	Johannes Brahms/Mark Hindsley	Hindsley
Carnival Overture	Antonin Dvorak.Steiger	Neil A. Kjos
Der Freischutz	Carl Maria von Weber	Masters
Die Meistersinger Overture	Richard Wagner/Mark Hindsley	Hindsley
Don Juan	Strauss/Mark Hindsley	Hindsley
Dream of a Witches Sabbath	Hector Berlioz/Mark Rogers	Southern
Ein Heldenleben	Strauss/A. A. Harding	Neil A. Kjos
Ein Heldenleben	Strauss/Mark Hindsley	Hindsley
Euryanthe Overture	Carl Maria von Weber/Mark Hindsley	Hindsley
March to the Scaffold	Hector Berlioz/Mark Rogers	Southern
Nutcracker Suite	Peter Ilyich Tchaikovsky/Mark Hindsley	Hindsley
Oberon Overture	Carl Maria von Weber/Mark Hindsley	Hindsley
Pictures at an Exhibition	Modeste Moussorgsky/John Boyd	Ludwig/Masters
Pictures at an Exhibition	Modeste Moussorgsky/Mark Hindsley	Hindsley
Rienzi	Richard Wagner/Mark Hindsley	Hindsley
Salome's Dance	Strauss/Mark Hindsley	Hindsley
Scheherazade	Rimsky-Korsakov/Mark Hindsley	Hindsley
(four separate movements)		
Symphony No. 3, Movement 1	Gustav Mahler/William Schaefer	TRN
Thus Spake Zarathustra	Strauss/Mark Hindsley	Hindsley
And those from the Grade 5 Listing		

Grade 6, Years 3 and 4 • Contemporary Literature, Part I

RECOMMENDED WORKS FROM THE *TEACHING MUSIC THROUGH PERFORMANCE* SERIES WITH TEACHER RESOURCE GUIDES

TITLE	COMPOSER/ARRANGER/TRANSCRIBER	PUBLISHER	VOLUME	PAGE
...and the mountains rising nowhere	Joseph Schwantner	Helicon/European American Music	2	529
Apotheosis of This Earth	Karel Husa	Associated Music Pub/ Hal Leonard	3	612
Blue Shades	Frank Ticheli	Manhattan Beach Music	2	547
A Child's Garden of Dreams (rental only)	David Maslanka	Carl Fischer, LLC	3	592
Circus Polka	Igor Stravinsky	Schott Musik/European American	2	555
Concerto for Percussion and Wind Ensemble	Karel Husa	Associated Music/ Hal Leonard	5	722
Concerto for Twenty-Three Winds	Walter Hartley	Accura Music	2	559
Dance of the New World	Dana Wilson	Ludwig	2	577
Designs, Images and Textures	Leslie Bassett	C. F. Peters	5	732
Dionysiaques, Op. 62 (rental only)	Florent Schmitt/Guy Duker	Theodore Presser	3	652
Divertimento in "F"	Jack Stamp	Neil A. Kjos	2	584
El Salon Mexico	Aaron Copland	Boosey & Hawkes/ Hal Leonard	3	659
Emblems	Aaron Copland	Boosey & Hawkes/ Hal Leonard	1	400
Et exspecto resurrectionem	Olivier Messiaen	Alphonse Leduc/ Theodore Presser	4	781
From a Dark Millennium	Joseph Schwantner	Helicon/European American	3	682
In Wartime	David Del Tredici	Boosey & Hawkes/ Hal Leonard	5	775

TITLE	COMPOSER/ARRANGER/TRANSCRIBER	PUBLISHER	VOLUME	PAGE
The Leaves Are Falling	Warren Benson	Edward B. Marks/Hal Leonard	2	615
Masquerade for Band, Op. 102	Vincent Persichetti	Theodore Presser	1	415
Music for Prague 1968	Karel Husa	Associated Music/Hal Leonard	1	420
Parable IX, Op. 121	Vincent Persichetti	Theodore Presser	3	722
Passacaglia Homage on B-A-C-H	Ron Nelson	Ludwig	1	435
The Passing Bell	Warren Benson	ECS Publishing	1	441
Piece of Mind	Dana Wilson	Ludwig	1	444
Recoil	Joseph Schwantner	Atherton Hill	6	852
Sinfonia No. 4	Walter Hartley	Wingert-Jones	1	456
Sinfonietta	Ingolf Dahl	Tetra/Continuo Music Group	1	461
Skating on the Sheyenne (rental only)	Ross Lee Finney	C. F. Peters	3	735
Spin Cycle	Scott Lindroth	Boosey & Hawkes/Hal Leonard	5	810
Symphonies of Wind Instruments (rental only)	Igor Stravinsky	Masters Music/Boosey & Hawkes/Hal Leonard (1947 version)	3	754
Symphony in B-flat, Op. 51	Paul Hindemith	Schott Musik/European American	1	465
Symphony No. 1: "Profanation from Jeremiah"	Leonard Bernstein/Frank Bencriscutto	Boosey & Hawkes/Hal Leonard	2	620
Symphony No. 2	Frank Ticheli	Manhattan Beach	5	824
Symphony No. 4 (rental only)	David Maslanka	Carl Fischer, LLC	4	887
Symphony No. 4: "West Point"	Morton Gould	G. Schirmer/ Associated/Hal Leonard	1	469
Theme and Variations, Op. 43a	Arnold Schoenberg	Belmont Music	1	482
Three City Blocks (rental only)	John Harbison	G. Schirmer/Associated/Hal Leonard	4	924
Timepiece (rental only)	Cindy McTee	MMB Music	4	935

TITLE	COMPOSER/ARRANGER/TRANSCRIBER	PUBLISHER	VOLUME	PAGE
Tunbridge Fair	Walter Piston	Boosey & Hawkes/Hal Leonard	2	639
Urban Requiem (rental only)	Michael Colgrass	Carl Fischer, LLC	4	943

OTHER WORKS TO CONSIDER

TITLE	COMPOSER/ARRANGER/TRANSCRIBER	PUBLISHER
Bells for Stokowski	Michael Daugherty	Peer Rental
Epiphanies	Ron Nelson	Ludwig/Masters
Gazebo Dances	John Corigliano	Carl Fischer Rental
Overture to the School for Scandal	Samuel Barber/Hudson	G. Schirmer
Symphony No. 1 (rental only)	Samuel Barber/Guy Duker	G. Schirmer
Symphony No. 3: "Circus Maximus" (rental only)	John Corigliano	Carl Fischer

RESEARCH ASSISTANCE BY THE FOLLOWING IS GRATEFULLY ACKNOWLEDGED:
Stanton's Sheet Music, Columbus, Ohio
Ben Huntoon
Kris Lehman

Index by Title for Teaching Music through Performance in Band: Volumes 1–7

TITLE	COMPOSER	VOL.	GRADE	PAGE
Festivo	Gregson, Edward	2	5	447
Fiesta Del Pacifico	Nixon, Roger	2	6	592
Fifth Symphony "Phoenix"	Barnes, James	6	5	632
The Final Covenant	Tull, Fisher	4	5	704
Finish Line	McTee, Cindy	7	6	844
The Fire of Eternal Glory	Shostakovich, Dmitri/Rhea	5	3	357
First Suite in E-flat, Op. 28 No. 1	Holst, Gustav/Matthews	1	4	251
First Suite in F	George, Thom Ritter	3	4	344
Fitzwilliam Suite	Gordon, Philip	5	2	151
Five Miniatures	Turina, Joaquin/Krance	4	4	474
Five Variants of Dives and Lazarus	Vaughan Williams/Gregson	6	4	486
Flag of Stars	Jacob, Gordon	7	5	667
Fleisher Pass	Bolin, Greg	6	6	824
Flourish for Wind Band	Vaughan Williams, Ralph	1	3	179
Flurry for Winds and Percussion	Kinyon, John	4	2	159
Folk Dances	Shostakovich, Dmitri/ Vakhutinskii/Reynolds	4	4	482
For precious friends hid in death's dateless night, Op. 80	Mailman, Martin	3	6	671
For the New Day Arisen	Barton, Steven	5	2	161
Fortress	Ticheli, Frank	5	3	255
Four Breton Dances	Broege, Timothy	7	2	214
Four Factories	Pann, Carter	7	6	851
Four French Songs	Hanson, Robert	2	4	308
Four Scottish Dances	Arnold, Malcolm/Paynter	2	5	452
The Four Seasons	Bennett, Richard Rodney	5	6	845
Four Sketches	Bartok, Bela/Schaefer	5	2	166
French Impressions	Woolfenden, Guy	4	5	644
From a Dark Millennium	Schwantner, Joseph	3	6	682
From Every Horizon (A Tone Poem to New York)	Dello Joio, Norman	6	4	491
Fugue in C	Ives, Charles/Sinclair	5	4	424
Fugue in G minor	Bach, J. S./Kimura	2	4	313
Funeral Music for Queen Mary	Stucky, Steven	5	6	750
Galactic Empires	Gillingham, David	3	5	487
Gazebo Dances for Band	Corigliano, John	2	6	598
Geometric Dances	Cichy, Roger	7	5	673
George Washington Bridge	Schuman, William	1	5	326
Ghost Train Triptych	Whitacre, Eric	5	5	616
Ghosts	McNeff, Stephen	6	5	641
Giles Farnaby Suite	Jacob, Gordon	4	3	316
Ginger Marmalade	Benson, Warren	1	3	182
Give Us This Day (Short Symphony for Wind Ensemble)	Maslanka, David	7	6	859
Gloriosa	Ito, Yasuhide	4	5	656
God of Our Fathers	Smith, Claude T.	5	4	432
Gran Duo	Lindberg, Magnus	6	6	830
Grande Symphonie Funèbre et Triomphale	Berlioz, Hector	3	5	492
Grant County Celebration	Williams, Mark	3	2	159
Greek Folk Song Suite	Cesarini, Franco	5	3	260
Green Passacaglia	Broege, Timothy	6	2	195
Greenwillow Portrait	Williams, Mark	1	2	92
The "Gumsuckers" March	Grainger, Percy /Rogers	3	4	352

Index by Title and Publisher
Teaching Music through Performance in Band:
Volumes 1–7

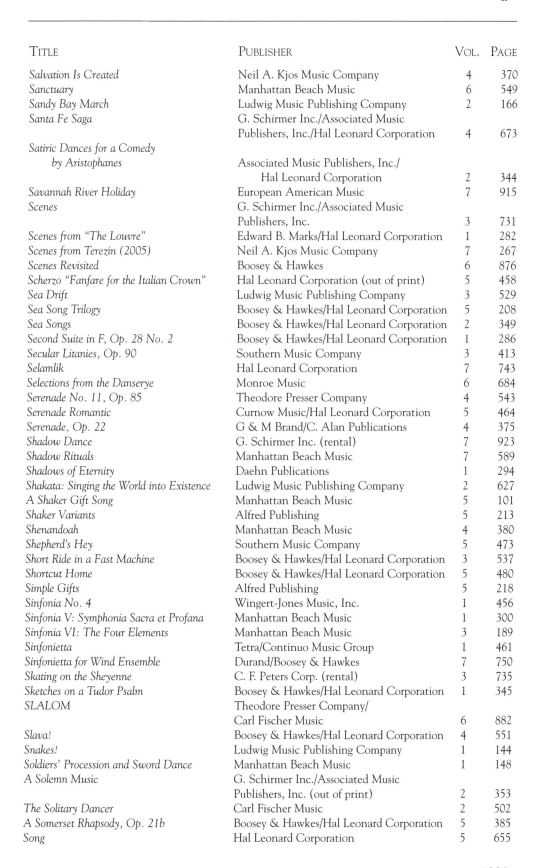

Index by Composer, Arranger, and Transcriber
Teaching Music through Performance in Band:
Volume 7

Index by Title
Teaching Music through
Performance in Band:
Volume 7